D1130620

THE CAMBRIDGE HISTORY OF AFRICA

General Editors: J. D. FAGE and ROLAND OLIVER

Volume 2

from *c.* 500 BC to AD 1050

THE CAMBRIDGE HISTORY OF AFRICA

1 From the Earliest Times to *c*. 500 BC
edited by J. Desmond Clark

2 From *c*. 500 BC to AD 1050
edited by J. D. Fage

3 From *c*. 1050 to *c*. 1600
edited by Roland Oliver

4 From *c*. 1600 to *c*. 1790
edited by Richard Gray

5 From *c*. 1790 to *c*. 1870
edited by John Flint

6 From *c*. 1870 to *c*. 1905
edited by G. N. Sanderson

7 From *c*. 1905 to *c*. 1940
edited by A. D. Roberts

8 From *c*. 1940 to the 1970s
edited by Michael Crowder

THE CAMBRIDGE HISTORY OF AFRICA

Volume 2

from *c.* 500 BC to AD 1050

edited by

J. D. FAGE

CAMBRIDGE UNIVERSITY PRESS

CAMBRIDGE

LONDON · NEW YORK · MELBOURNE

Published by the Syndics of the Cambridge University Press
The Pitt Building, Trumpington Street, Cambridge CB2 1RP
Bentley House, 200 Euston Road, London NW1 2DB
32 East 57th Street, New York, NY 10022, USA
296 Beaconsfield Parade, Middle Park, Melbourne 3206, Australia

First published 1978

Printed in Great Britain by
W & J Mackay Limited, Chatham

Library of Congress Cataloguing in Publication Data (Revised)
Main entry under title:
The Cambridge history of Africa
Bibliography: v. 2, v. 3, v. 4, v. 5
Includes index.
CONTENTS:
v. 2. From *c.* 500 BC to AD 1050, edited by J. D. Fage.
v. 3. From *c.* 1050 to *c.* 1600, edited by R. Oliver.
v. 4. From *c.* 1600 to *c.* 1790, edited by R. Gray.
v. 5. From *c.* 1790 to *c.* 1870, edited by J. Flint.
1. Africa – History – Collected works. I. Fage, J. D.
II. Oliver, Roland Anthony. III. Gray, Richard. IV. Flint, John.
DT20.C28 960 76-2261
ISBN 0 521 21592 7 (v. 2)

CONTENTS

FIGURES

PLATES

PREFACE

In the English-speaking world, the Cambridge histories have since the beginning of the century set the pattern for multi-volume works of history, with chapters written by experts on a particular topic, and unified by the guiding hand of volume editors of senior standing. *The Cambridge Modern History*, planned by Lord Acton, appeared in sixteen volumes between 1902 and 1912. It was followed by *The Cambridge Ancient History, The Cambridge Medieval History, The Cambridge History of English Literature,* and Cambridge Histories of India, of Poland, and of the British Empire. The original *Modern History* has now been replaced by *The New Cambridge Modern History* in twelve volumes, and *The Cambridge Economic History of Europe* is now being completed. Other Cambridge Histories recently completed include a history of Islam and of the Bible treated as a central document of and influence on Western civilization; Histories in progress include a history of Arabic Literature, China, Inner Asia, Iran and Judaism.

It was during the later 1950s that the Syndics of the Cambridge University Press first began to explore the possibility of embarking on a Cambridge History of Africa. But they were then advised that the time was not yet ripe. The serious appraisal of the past of Africa by historians and archaeologists had hardly been undertaken before 1948, the year when universities first began to appear in increasing numbers in the vast reach of the African continent south of the Sahara and north of the Limpopo, and the time too when universities outside Africa first began to take some notice of its history. It was impressed upon the Syndics that the most urgent need of such a young, but also very rapidly advancing, branch of historical studies, was a journal of international standing through which the results of ongoing research might be disseminated. In 1960, therefore, the Cambridge University Press launched *The Journal of African History*, which gradually demonstrated the amount of work being undertaken to establish the past of Africa as an integrated whole rather than – as it had usually been viewed before – as the story of a series of incursions into the continent by peoples coming from outside, from the Mediterranean basin, the Near

East or western Europe. This movement will of course continue and develop further, but the increasing facilities available for its publication soon began to demonstrate a need to assess both what had been done, and what still needed to be done, in the light of some general historical perspective for the continent.

The Syndics therefore returned to their original charge, and in 1966 the founding editors of *The Journal of African History* accepted a commission to become the general editors of a *Cambridge History of Africa*. They found it a daunting task to draw up a plan for a co-operative work covering a history which was in active process of exploration by scholars of many nations, scattered over a fair part of the globe, and of many disciplines – linguists, anthropologists, geographers and botanists, for example, as well as historians and archaeologists.

It was thought that the greatest problems were likely to arise with the earliest and latest periods: the earliest, because so much would depend on the results of long-term archaeological investigation, and the latest, because of the rapid changes in historical perspective that were occurring as a consequence of the ending of colonial rule in Africa. Initially, therefore, only five volumes were planned, of which the first, Africa before *c.* 500 BC, based entirely upon archaeological sources (and edited by an archaeologist), would be the last to appear, while of the others – dealing with the periods of approximately 500 BC to AD 1050, 1050–1600, 1600–1790, and 1790–1870 – it was thought that the first to be published would probably be the last. (In the event, it has turned out to be Professor Richard Gray's volume 4, though Professor John E. Flint's volume 5 and Professor Roland Oliver's volume 3 followed next in order.) Only after these volumes were well under way would an attempt be made to plan for the period after *c.* 1870. Eleven years later, it can be said that three further volumes have been planned and editors appointed, and that it is hoped that these will appear at regular intervals following the publication of volume 1.

When they started their work, the general editors quickly came to the conclusion that the most practicable plan for getting out the first five volumes within a reasonable period of time was likely to be the simplest and most straightforward. The direction of each volume was therefore entrusted to a volume editor who, in addition to having made a substantial contribution to the understanding of the period in question, was someone with whom the general editors were in close touch. Within a volume, the aim was to keep the number of contributors to a minimum. Each of them was asked to essay a broad survey of a particular area or theme with which he was familiar for the whole of the period covered by the volume. In this survey, his purpose should be to take account not only of all relevant research done, or still in progress, but also of the gaps in knowledge. These he should try to fill by new thinking of his own, whether based on new work on the available sources or on interpolations from congruent research.

It should be remembered that the plan for these first five volumes was drawn up over a decade ago, when little or no research had been done on many important topics, and before many of today's younger scholars – not least those who now fill posts in the departments of history and archaeology in the universities and research institutes in Africa itself – had made their own deep penetrations into such areas of ignorance. Two things follow from this. If the general editors had drawn up their plan in the 1970s rather than the 1960s, the shape might well have been very different, perhaps with a larger number of more specialized, shorter chapters, each centred on a smaller area, period or theme, to the understanding of which the contributor would have made his own individual contribution. Indeed, the last three volumes seem likely to be composed more on such lines. Secondly, the sheer volume of new research that has been published since the contributors for the first five volumes accepted their commissions has often led them to undertake very substantial revisions in their work as it progressed from draft to draft, thus protracting the length of time originally envisaged for the preparation of these volumes.

But histories are meant to be read, and not simply to be continually rewritten and modified by their authors and editors. Volume 2 of *The Cambridge History of Africa* is therefore now launched for public use and appraisal, together with a promise that four further volumes should follow it at more or less regular intervals.

J. D. FAGE
ROLAND OLIVER

February 1977

ACKNOWLEDGEMENTS

The editor gratefully acknowledges the work of Mrs Marion Johnson in compiling the index and collating the bibliography, of Mr Reginald Piggot in preparing the maps and line drawings, and of the staff of the Cambridge University Press.

INTRODUCTION

As is remarked in the Introduction to the third volume of the *Cambridge History of Africa*, there are obvious pitfalls in marking out periods of African history which are equally valid for all parts of the continent. Africa is a vast land mass, and also the only one to be centred in the tropics. It has presented quite as many and as varied difficulties for its human inhabitants to master as it has resources to be exploited. Thus until the general world-wide acceleration of processes of change brought about by the rise and spread of modern scientific technology, there could be extremely wide variations in the degrees of social and material development to be found among African peoples. During the very long period of history covered by this volume, these differences seem to have been accentuated by the fact that the more temperate lands north of the Sahara (and to some extent the eastern littoral also) were in much closer touch with developments in other parts of the world than were the great tropical heartlands of the continent or its southerly temperate zone.

A by-product of this fact that historians cannot escape is an imbalance of historical source materials for the period. Some of the implications of this are are more fully discussed later in this Introduction. Here no more need be said than that this imbalance makes it possible to consider the course and the significance of events in northern Africa in greater detail and with less recourse to hypothesis or speculation than is the case for the other three-quarters of the continent. In form, therefore, though not – it is suggested below – in substance, it is difficult for some parts of the volume to avoid the appearance of stressing the activities and the achievements of outsiders at the expense of those of truly indigenous Africans. But in reality there is much more unity to this volume, and an African-centred unity, than may at first sight appear. The problem may be that this unity is so vast, of so continental a scale, that it is neither easily appreciated nor expressed. Perhaps the simplest way to put it is to say that the period covered in this volume, from about the middle of the first millenium BC to about the beginning of the second millenium AD, is one which sees a beginning to history in almost every part of Africa.

Only two extreme corners of the continent totally escape this generalization. One is Egypt, in the north-east, long a participant in an older tradition of history, while the other is the arid and very thinly peopled lands of the remotest south-west, which had hardly entered history even in the nineteenth century.

What constitutes 'a beginning to history' is less easily defined in historical substance than it is in terms of historiographical methodology. But the use of iron to make weapons and tools is a useful marker, and the period of this volume almost entirely embraces its introduction and spread throughout the African continent. Iron-working would seem to have become established in Egypt and in North-West Africa following the Assyrian conquest of the former and Phoenician colonization in the latter. It had very soon crossed the Sahara into West Africa, where it was known at Nok by about the fifth century BC, and it was then quickly spread over almost all the rest of sub-Saharan Africa by the expansion of the Bantu-speaking peoples. Perhaps iron-working was not quite as momentous a step forward from the Stone Age into history as was the invention of agriculture, and there have been many who have seen history beginning only when men have taken to writing. Egypt certainly had some millennia of history without iron while, of course, possessing both agriculture and writing. But the possession and use of iron tools and weapons was nevertheless an important factor helping to consolidate earlier socio-economic achievements and providing a platform from which further, wider and ever-accelerating advances might be made. In Africa, the adoption of iron-working could well have been more significant than it was in some other parts of the world. South of the Sahara – as may be seen from Chapter 5 – men seem to have gone straight from the Stone Age to the use of iron as their first metal, without any intermediary bronze or copper age. Secondly, as is explained in the following chapter, over the larger part of sub-Saharan Africa the introduction of iron-working seems to have been due to the same agency – the expanding Bantu-speaking Africans – as the introduction of agriculture. Compared with many other parts of the world – Egypt, for example – there was a minimal time gap between the two great innovations. It might be supposed, therefore, that in much of Africa the growth and expansion of agriculture may have been associated more with iron-working, for example for the clearing of heavy vegetation, than may have been usual elsewhere.

But if this is a volume dealing with the beginning of history in Africa, it will not have escaped notice that it is not the first volume of this

History of Africa. This is because it is preceded by a volume of prehistory. Volume 1 is an account of the remotest past of Africa put together from prehistorians' – archaeologists' – knowledge of and interpretation of the random artefacts left behind from the activities of societies which for the most part did not succeed in recording and transmitting for posterity their own accounts of their achievements. Volume 3, on the other hand, is written by historians, in the faith that it is feasible to put together an account and interpretation of the course of events in Africa from the eleventh to the sixteenth centuries very much in the same way, and with much the same validity, as other historians have reconstructed processes of change in medieval Europe. The present volume may thus seem to be definable methodologically, as a work of what has come to be known as 'protohistory'.

This is certainly true in that it deals with a period in which archaeological evidence is still of major importance, but for which there are also increasing amounts of historical information, even it if is very unevenly spread (so that the authors of some chapters write primarily as archaeologists, and of others primarily as historians). However, Volume 2 is not unique in this, for with reference to Africa the concept of protohistory has considerable elasticity. Some historical evidence is available even for the period of Volume 1, for both pharaonic Egypt and the kingdom of Kush left some conscious memorials of their history, even if they happen to be more accessible and comprehensible to archaeologists than they are to historians. On the other hand, there is precious little unequivocally historical evidence available for the period covered by Volume 3 for substantial parts of Africa south of the Sahara. Despite the increasing survival of the oral traditions of historically conscious peoples, substantial gaps in the historical record still remain even for the period of Volume 4.

Nevertheless, the nature of the evidence that is available for reconstructing and evaluating the past is important for proper understanding of both the structure and the significance of the present volume. It is about the middle of the first millennium BC – one might say from the time of Herodotus, the Greek historian who was writing about 430 BC – that historical evidence begins to become available not only for Egypt and the adjacent part of the Nile Valley, but for the whole of the continent north of the Sahara. And it is about the beginning of the second millennium AD that historical evidence first begins to have some significance for lands south of the desert, specifically and first for the whole width of the Sudan and for much of the east coast. It follows that for the whole of the period covered by this volume, the northern third of Africa is squarely – albeit sometimes rather dimly – in the light of history, while for the southern two-thirds there is some historical evidence, even if precious little of it. Sometimes there is not much archaeological evidence either, for the greatest incentive for archaeologists to work in sub-Saharan Africa has lain in its remotest prehistory, when it was the cradle of mankind, the nursery in which modern man, *Homo sapiens*, emerged and took his first footsteps. It is only very recently that later periods of its prehistory have begun to attract much attention (and it has therefore seemed sensible to invite the editor of Volume I to provide, in the first chapter of the present volume, some essential first fruits of these enquiries).

For the period covered in this volume, the relative scarcity of evidence, of any kind, from the larger part of the continent lying south of the Sahara, means – as has already been indicated – that less attention can be given to it than can be given to North Africa, the Nile Valley and Ethiopia. Indeed, of the specifically regional chapters, only two are devoted directly and wholly to sub-Saharan Africa. One of them, chapter 5, looks at what evidence there is for West Africa from the fifth century BC to the eleventh century AD, but perforce does this from a perspective grounded in the much better-known history of North Africa and, even, of the Sahara desert that joins West Africa to northern Africa. This leaves chapter 6 as the sole one dealing with the whole southern half of the continent, Africa south of the Equator. This chapter is based firmly on the available archaeological evidence. But, as its authors know very well, this evidence is very unevenly spread, is often slight in the sense that only a handful of sites may have been excavated in any one particular area, and is constantly in need of revaluation in the light of new discoveries. It is thus not surprising that Professor Oliver and Professor Fagan's interpretation of the archaeological picture needs to be coloured by the historical inferences that may be drawn from modern cultural evidence, that of language in particular.

The scarcity of evidence relating to the past of sub-Saharan Africa for the period of this volume is not due to any perversity on the part of archaeologists. Perhaps little more needs to be said but that archaeology, an expensive science, has naturally flourished first and most in the richer and more developed countries of the world. So much of Africa is underdeveloped that it need surprise no one that its archaeology also tends to be underdeveloped. But it is also true that once tropical Africa had given birth to modern man, his major advances tended to be made in more temperate lands further to the north. Perhaps these posed greater challenges to his ingenuity, particularly perhaps, as their climates became drier and as his populations increased, in the sphere of food production. The spectacular nature of these advances, from the food-producing revolution onwards, necessarily became a major focus for investigation by archaeologists and, after the invention of writing (one of the most significant of these advances), also by historians. Although other areas were of equal or greater interest to those concerned with the past of eastern or southern Asia, the key area for those concerned with the history alike of Africa and of Europe became that which Europeans came to know as 'the Near East'. So far as Europe and its historians are concerned, this is an appropriate term. But it is somewhat misleading when it is borrowed – as perhaps it must be – for the writing of African history. For some parts of Africa are part of this 'Near East'. This is certainly the case with Egypt and the Nile Valley, for this is the western end of the Fertile Crescent, which is regarded as central in the emergence of civilization in the Near East. Their adjacent deserts might also be included, in so far as these are relevant to this theme, and a good case can certainly be made for including Ethiopia and the Horn of Africa (as it certainly was included in the equivalent thinking of medieval Europe), for this part of Africa has much history in common with nearby Arabia.

The historical reality behind the uneven geographical distribution of the regional chapters in this volume is that, for the whole of the period covered by it, Africa north of the Sahara participated (together with southern Europe) in the rise of a general world civilization which first emerged in the Near East (and thus partly in Africa), and which found in the Mediterranean a natural axis for expansion. The Red Sea was another such axis, albeit its significance appears to be somewhat less (or perhaps simply less studied and less understood), so that much of the whole of north-east Africa also shared in this civilization.

At first sight, much of the initiative in introducing African peoples to this civilization appears to come from outside Africa. Thus chapters 2 and 3 refer to North Africa 'in the period of Phoenician and Greek colonization' and 'in the Hellenistic and Roman periods', while chapter 8 bears the title 'The Arab conquest and the expansion of Islam in North Africa'. This need not surprise us, because for most of the period the great power-house of innovation remained in nearer Asia, and only the western end of the Near East and of the Fertile Crescent are African. The three great monotheistic religions – Judaism, Christianity and

Islam – which were carried into Africa (and into Europe) during this period were conceived among the Semitic-speaking peoples of nearer Asia. Their earlier invention of the alphabet had brought the art of writing to perfection, and thus greatly facilitated both the growth of civilization generally and the expansion of the particular idea that all mankind should be subject to one Supreme Creator. The same stock had also produced the first colonists of North Africa (the Phoenicians) and of Eritrea and Ethiopia (see chapter 4). In some respects, too, southern European peoples, most notably the Greeks and the Romans, appear as more active and positive proponents of the common civilization than do African peoples. But perhaps this is less a matter of history than of the perspectives in which history has been written. For the most part the perspective that is current today is that of historians in a European cultural tradition which can be traced back to ancient Greece and Rome. Such historians have not unnaturally tended to stress the European development of the original inheritance from the Near East, and they have given relatively little attention to what was achieved by Africans on the basis of the same inheritance, which they had received often more directly. It is therefore easy to overlook how much of the common world civilization during the period covered in this volume was in fact developed in Africa.

Thus the Phoenicians, a Semitic people from what is now called the Lebanon, achieved their greatest power when some of them had based themselves in Africa and become Carthaginians. The Roman empire was far from being exclusively European. At its peak it probably encompassed as many African and Asian subjects and citizens as it did European inhabitants. It certainly treated many peoples who are now regarded as quintessentially European as tribal barbarians who must be forcefully excluded from its civilized world lest they destroy it. Of the four greatest cities of this empire, two – Alexandria and Carthage – were in Africa. More importantly, perhaps, Alexandria was the greatest of all Greek cities; and this not simply in terms of its population, but as the major intellectual centre of the whole *oikoumene*, where Greek philosophy and science were being developed and brought together with the Near Eastern inheritance to reach their final achievements. Classical astronomy, mathematics and geography reached their peak in the figure of the second century Graeco-Egyptian scholar, Claudius Ptolemy. In all these fields, the work of Ptolemy and the Alexandrian school set standards which were to prevail for the next thousand years. His concept of African geography, to give a minor example of some importance to this *History*, was not to be improved upon until the great voyages of discovery of the fifteenth century. It was also, as much as anywhere else, in Alexandria, with its substantial number of Jews as well as Greeks, that an aberrant Judaic sect began to develop into the new religion of Christianity with its claim on a universal allegiance. It should be remembered too that Christianity was firmly established throughout North Africa long before it made significant headway in western Europe. Chapter 7 bears witness to the fact that many of the most notable protagonists in the formulation of the new religion were Africans: for example, Arius and Athanasius in the east, based on Alexandria, and in the west, centred on Carthage, Tertullian and Cyprian and the greatest of all the early Christian fathers, Augustine. It was out of the controversies in which they played such leading roles that there eventually emerged the major branches of the Christian Church that remain to this day. One of these branches, the Monophysites, took firm root in Africa, penetrating deep into the interior of the continent long before any Christian missionary from Europe had touched its shores, and producing the first specifically African churches, the Coptic (i.e. Egyptian) Church and the Ethiopian Church.

The idea that Christianity is more a religion of Europeans than of Africans would in fact have been totally impossible prior to the rise of Islam, the other great world religion derived from the Semitic peoples' attachment to monotheism. The manner in which Islam was introduced into Africa by conquerors from Arabia and Syria, with the consequent extirpation of the Christianity of northern Africa except as the religion of a minority of Egyptians and – in its most African guise – in the highlands of Ethiopia, seems again to suggest that the role of Africans was to be one of passive recipients of alien innovation rather than one of active participants in new development. But yet again this may be less a matter of history than of historical perspective. Until the last two hundred years – when western scholars also began to turn to its study – the chroniclers and philosophers of Islam were all themselves Muslims. Almost from the beginning, certainly from the time of the ʿAbbasīd Caliphate which was instituted in AD 750, the prime centre for this scholarship lay in eastern Islam, specifically in Iraq (chapter 8). The result has been to stress influences from the east, including those from Persia and from conquered Asian provinces of the Byzantine empire, in the process by which this Semitic religion developed into an all-embracing cultural tradition. There is perhaps only one major Muslim historian who stands aside from this approach. This is the fourteenth century Tunisian-born scholar Ibn Khaldun, who had pursued an active career in politics throughout North Africa. Ibn Khaldun was well aware of the extent to which Islamic society and culture had benefited in the west by being able to take over foundations laid by the earlier Mediterranean civilizations. He was also aware of the extent to which western, African Muslims were able to develop particular aspects of the new world religion to suit their own interests.

The major and the enduring advances of Islam in the west were in Africa. Although the contributions of Iberian Muslims must not be forgotten, it was essentially in Africa that Islamic culture received its legacies from earlier Greek, Roman and Christian civilizations. It was also Africans who were most adept in converting aspects of the newly proclaimed universal faith to their own particularist purposes. The role of the ancient cities was again a crucial one. It was principally through Alexandria that the new culture acquired a vital grounding in Greek philosophy and science. But where circumstances elsewhere were also favourable to civilization, as they were for example in the Tunisian plains around Carthage, there was quite a substantial wider influence to be absorbed from the earlier Phoenician, Judaic, Roman and Christian traditions. There was also, of course, a general Hellenistic influence to be assimilated throughout the former Byzantine province of Egypt – despite this country's openness to eastern influences and the growing arabization of its people.

West of Egypt, however, in the real Muslim West, the Maghrib, there was no large-scale arabization before the incursions of beduin that began in the eleventh century. The same century also saw the conquest of most of the Maghrib by the Almoravids, recent and rigid converts to Islam from among the Berber nomads of the Sahara. As Professor Levtzion remarks (p. 683), the conjunction of these two events marks a turning point in North African history, and therefore a suitable point at which to conclude its treatment in this volume. The coming of the beduin made possible a general arabization of the Berbers, while the victory of the Almoravids did much to ensure the triumph of orthodoxy in North African Islam. Some of the greatest Berber achievements, notably the empire of the Almohads, were to be achieved under the banner of this orthodoxy. But it is notable how Berber peoples had earlier seized upon doctrinal divergencies within Islam to serve as catalysts or inspirations releasing their energies for their own purposes and advantage. A collective title for much of the contents of chapters 8, 10 and 11 might almost be 'The great period of *African* Islam'. This period begins when Berber warriors joined with the Arabs in carrying Islam across the Straits of Gibraltar into Europe. It was one in which independent Ibadite Muslim Berber communities arose right across the North African steppes and the northern oases of the Sahara, thus providing bases for a substantial development of trans-Saharan trade and for the first introduction of Islam to the Africans of the western and central Sudan. It was also one in which many other less widely influential adoptions of more or less heterodox Islam launched other Berber initiatives as varied as the Barghawāṭa, the Idrisid kingdom of Morocco, or the Ṣanhāja states of the eastern Maghrib. Its culmination came when the Fatimids from Tunisia virtually reversed the original Arab conquest, established a caliphate of their own in Cairo, and laid claim to the Muslim heartlands of Syria and the Hejaz.

While North Africans were participating in the great civilizations derived from the Near Eastern tradition and its Mediterranean and Red Sea offshoots, it is not to be supposed that their fellow Africans south of the Sahara lay sleeping in barbaric torpor. They were not in fact altogether cut off from the momentous developments in world civilization to the north and north-east. The Sahara was not wholly desert before about 2000 BC, and – as may be seen from chapter 5 – even afterwards the desert acted more as a filter for, than a barrier to, the dissemination of ideas. There was also some contact across the Red Sea and the Indian Ocean. The main reason why sub-Saharan Africans could not immediately share in the culminating advances of human social evolution – in which initially they had been among the pioneers – was a technical one. These culminating advances were all founded on the food-producing revolution, in particular on agriculture. But, as has been seen, the concept of plant cultivation was first developed in temperate climates. The first staple crops – among which the most significant were the cereals, wheat and barley – were developed from the wild plants of temperate lands. As such, they could not be successfully cultivated in the tropics, where there were no lengthening spring and summer days and no gentle transitions between the seasons, but equal hours of light and dark and harsh alternations of wet and dry.

The Africans who were forced south into the Sudan by the emergence of the Sahara desert seem to have been as familiar with cultivation as those who concentrated in the Nile Valley or in North Africa. But if they were themselves to cultivate south of the Sahara, and so to achieve the security for the future, the growth of population, and the possibilities of occupational specialization and technological advance which hunting–gathering economies could never support, they had to discover tropical plants suitable for domestication and for development as cultivars. This they did: the outstanding cereals being the sorghums and millets, and the outstanding rootcrop being the African yams. But a slow, painstaking process of trial and error was needed to achieve this. The details of this effort are generally obscure to us, and its exact chronology is also uncertain. Its beginnings would certainly seem to lie much more within the period of Volume 1 of this *History* than within the scope of the present volume. But the evidence currently available suggests that it was around the time with which this volume opens that this great enterprise began to reach its triumphant conclusion. Sub-Saharan Africans had found and developed from their own soils the seeds and roots on which agriculture might be based, and with this agriculture and, shortly, with iron technology, they could begin to develop an African civilization to parallel that which had been earlier pioneered in the Near East. The first results were the significant advances in the Sudan and in West Africa which are glimpsed by Professor Mauny in the concluding pages of chapter 5. From these came the momentous outpouring of people, energy and ideas that is outlined by Professors Oliver and Fagan in the following chapter, 'The emergence of Bantu Africa'. Within the space of a few centuries only, hardy pioneers had burst out to establish the new civilization throughout the southern half of Africa save in those parts, mainly in the remote south-west, where conditions were too arid to permit of agriculture. Once again, much of the detail and chronology are far from being determined; they remain the subject of argument and speculation. The present state of knowledge is not sufficiently detailed and secure to allow of more than a single chapter sketching the broad outline of what was achieved.

Nevertheless it may certainly be claimed that the independent development by sub-Saharan Africans of their own foundations for civilization, followed by their rapid distribution of these foundations throughout the world's largest tropical land mass, an environment particularly hostile to the growth of civilization, should rank among the major achievements of human history.

CHAPTER 1

THE LEGACY OF PREHISTORY: AN ESSAY ON THE BACKGROUND TO THE INDIVIDUALITY OF AFRICAN CULTURES

SETTING THE STAGE

The ethnographer or economist – as, indeed, most social scientists – begins with the advantage that he is studying living people. His conclusions are based upon his own direct observations of human behaviour and of the structural organizations that man has developed to enable him to adjust to the changing patterns of his society. The historian also possesses this advantage, though usually at second hand, through the personalities and personal records of the past preserved in the written word. The archaeologist – or rather the palaeo-anthropologist, which would be a more accurate description of him – has no such advantage. No identifiable personalities project themselves from the stage on which his nameless actors play their part and he has no script from which to discover their characteristics; thus most things about them – their abilities, emotions, aspirations and limitations – are likely never to be known. Fortunately, however, not all understanding need be lost, for an increasing amount of information is becoming available through knowledge of the context in which the changing pattern of human behaviour took place. Although, as one scene follows another, and the scenario and props of the earlier ones become dispersed, lost or disarranged, interpretation is rendered more difficult or ambiguous, yet the closer in time to the present, the more complete are the sets and the more recognizably are the players related to some of those who still walk the stage today, so that the more reliable will be the reconstruction possible from a study of their habits and behaviour. When all this information is gathered together and correlated, palaeo-anthropologists have a basis for interpreting the more distant past and so for reconstructing the life and ways of the actors.

It goes without saying that behaviour is intimately related to the context in which it is performed. Different situations require different ways of dealing with them and so different sets of activities are devised to meet the particular needs encountered by a community. As contextual and biological changes succeeded each other in the past, as technology advanced and man learned to make better use of his material resources, and as social and economic organization became more complex, leading to the formation of the political state, so man became more adapted to the environment in which he lived. In addition he became able to use more varied environments and eventually to change them, as he acquired more freedom to choose the methods for exploiting his resources, until finally more stable and regular basic food supplies gave societies a wider opportunity for intellectual development. Thus the ways in which the indigenous African peoples have become differentiated, and express themselves in their organizational, ethical and artistic behaviour, are the outcome of many millennia of involvement, adjustment and improvement within the varied eco-systems in which they played an increasingly more important role until, for better or worse, they – like all men – came to dominate the ecological system in which they had evolved.

Palaeo-anthropology is the means whereby the developmental stages in man's intellectual and cultural evolution are investigated and interpreted and, on the evidence as it exists today, it would appear that man the tool-maker was a product of the African tropical savannas. The data on which this and the other statements that follow are based are the outcome of the combined research of physical and natural scientists, palaeo-anthropologists and social scientists.[1] The close association and teamwork that this collaboration implies has introduced into archaeology something of the precision and discipline of the natural sciences while at the same time enabling it to draw with increasing relevance from the social sciences for interpretation of the evidence within its context. It is, however, as well to remember that it is only too easy to be misled by interpretations and inferences based on the second without a proper understanding or use of the first.

The most important requirement of the palaeo-anthropologist is a sound chronological framework into which the evidence can be fitted so that reliable comparisons become possible. This is now available in the form of various radiometric and isometric dating methods, the most reliable of which are the Potassium Argon (K/Ar) method in conjunction with Palaeo-Magnetic Reversal Chronology for periods prior to

[1] For the sources of this evidence the reader is referred to the works cited in the bibliographical essays at the end of Vol. 1 of this *History*; these have been summarized in the Bibliographical Essay for the present chapter, pp. 685–91.

c. 200,000 BP[1] and Radiocarbon (C-14) for later Pleistocene and Recent times. The new chronology has revolutionized concepts of the length of time covered by human and cultural evolution. This has meant that, whereas only thirty years ago it could be suggested that the beginning of the Pleistocene – the geological period during which it was believed that man evolved – was no older than half a million years, now the radiometric chronology shows the beginnings of tool-making to go back two to two and a half million years, and the first unquestionable hominids are found in sediments now known to be twice as old as that. Today, this radiometric time-scale supersedes all others – such as, for example, the 'pluvial/interpluvial' chronology based upon believed correlations with high-latitude glacials and interglacials or dating by presumed cultural correlations with Eurasia.[2]

Faunal assemblages preserved in dated sedimentary sequences are another means of estimating *relative* associations in space and time; the more prolific speciation of some forms, such as elephants and pigs, during the later Cainozoic, can be a valuable indication of age.[3] Of course, a great deal more than this can be learned from faunal assemblages, in particular those associated with human activities, which provide inferences as to the nature of the habitat, seasonality, man's scavenging or hunting ability and methods, food preferences, butchery techniques, distribution of meat and so on.[4]

Similarly, with improved methods of extracting and identifying pollen from ancient sediments, information is now becoming available about vegetation patterns at sites that range in time from the Plio-Pleistocene up to the recent past. These studies provide evidence of temperature and humidity, of the way in which the different plant communities within an eco-system interacted and the changes that occurred through time. Significantly, it becomes apparent that, under the pressure of climatic change, some communities expanded while others contracted but that, with some exceptions, there was surprisingly little change in the African environments as a whole. For example, the Plio-Pleistocene environment of *c.* 2.5–2.0 million years (m.y.) ago in the lower basin of the Omo river, while reflecting a change to drier

[1] BP = 'Before the Present' for which the conventional date is 1950, the year of the invention by W. F. Libby of the radiocarbon method of dating.

[2] See C. E. P. Brooks, *Climate through the ages* (London, 1949).

[3] See H. B. S. Cooke and V. J. Maglio, 'Plio-Pleistocene stratigraphy in relation to Proboscidean and Suid evolution', in W. W. Bishop and J. A. Miller, eds., *Calibration of hominoid evolution* (Edinburgh, 1972,) 303–29.

[4] G. L. Isaac, 'The diet of early man: aspects of archaeological evidence from Lower and Middle Pleistocene sites in Africa', *World Archaeology*, 1971, **2**, 278–98.

conditions, was similar to the dry savanna and gallery forest existing there today; the grasslands that predominated on the South African highveld when the Australopithecines were living there were similar, though somewhat more lush, than the present sourveld; in highland Ethiopia, Acheulian man exploited the same open savanna and montane forest fringe that can be seen there today; and the deciduous woodlands of northern Zambia are not significantly different from what they were 20,000 years ago.[1]

Knowledge of the biome provided by faunal remains and palynology is basic to the reconstruction of past human behaviour, since the origins of man's genetic and cultural variability lie in the ecological variability of the African continent, and there is reason to believe that the palaeogeography of Africa since the Plio-Pleistocene was not greatly different from that of today; in fact, it was essentially the same. A look at a map of the ecological zones of Africa (fig. 1) shows complementary regions north and south of the Equator – equatorial forest forming a belt on either side of the Equator, replaced by savanna woodlands and wet and dry grasslands with desert in the higher latitudes, as the effects of the summer rainfall regimen of the tropics become less influential. Only the extreme northern and southern ends of the continent fall within the temperate belts and enjoy winter rainfall and a more equable climate. This pattern is interrupted, in particular down the centre and the eastern side, by altitudinal changes. There elevated ranges and plateaux up to 3,000 metres and more enjoy cooler temperatures and support montane grasslands and evergreen forest. This zonal patterning, determined by the polar fronts and the wind systems they control, was modified to some extent on several occasions in the past by glacial advances and retreats. At the end of the Middle Pleistocene, for example, much of the Congo basin and the Guinea Coast was subjected to a semi-arid climate, with the redistribution of the sands of Kalahari type from the Cape to Gabon, and this clearly influenced population movement.[2]

[1] (a) R. Bonnefille, 'Palynological evidence for an important change in the vegetation of the Omo Basin between 2.5 and 2 million years', in Y. Coppens, F. C. Howell, G. L. Isaac and R. E. F. Leakey, eds., *Earliest man and environments in the Lake Rudolf basin* (Chicago, 1976), 421–31. (b) E. S. Vrba, 'Chronological and ecological implications of the fossil Bovidae at Sterkfontein Australopithecine site', *Nature*, 1974, **250**, 19–23. (c) R. Bonnefille, 'Associations polliniques actuelles et quaternaires en Ethiopie (vallées de l'Awash et de l'Omo)', unpublished Ph.D. thesis (University of Paris, 1972); see pt III, 260–431. (d) D. Livingstone, 'Late Quaternary climatic change in Africa', *Annual Review of Ecology and Systematics*, 1975, **6**, 249–80.

[2] E. M. van Zinderen Bakker, 'Upper Pleistocene and Holocene stratigraphy and ecology on the basis of vegetation changes in sub-Saharan Africa', in W. W. Bishop and J. D. Clark, eds., *Background to evolution in Africa* (Chicago, 1967), 125–47.

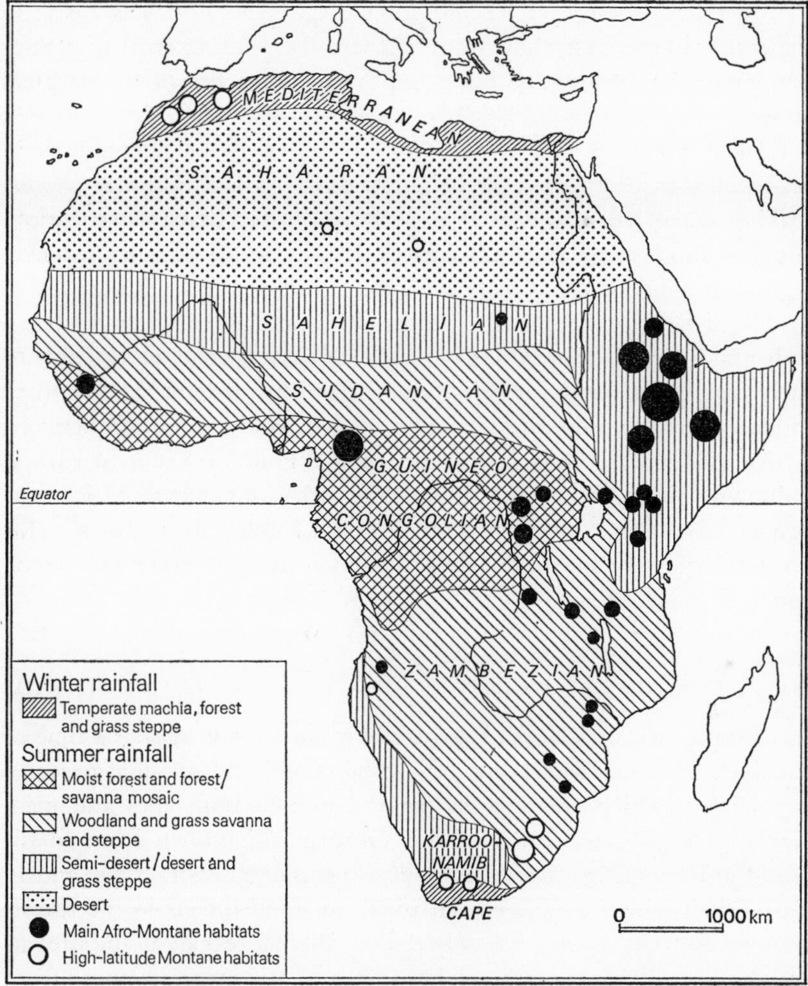

1 The main phyto-geographic regions of Africa.
(After F. White, *The evergreen forests of Malawi*, 1970, p. 53.)

Also, the rapid withdrawal of the Arctic front about 12,000 BP resulted in the expansion into the Sahara of the tropical monsoonal rain belt and a well-watered savanna (Sahelian and Sudanic patterns), thus transforming the desert of the preceding 10,000 years into one of the most favourable habitats in the continent and permitting its rapid reoccupation.[1] Similar phenomena were probably responsible for earlier occupation of the Sahara during the Lower and Middle

[1] M. Van Campo, 'Pollen analyses in the Sahara', in F. Wendorf and A. E. Marks, eds., *Problems in prehistory: North Africa and the Levant* (Dallas, 1975), 45–64.

Pleistocene. Although such ecological changes were not so extensive in the east as in the west, they occurred there also; but, in areas of greater precipitation, changes are not so apparent as in the drier, marginal zones.

Glacial advances and retreats also brought about fluctuations in sea-level, sometimes, as at the height of the last Glaciation *c.* 20,000 BP, making extensive new coastal areas available for human occupation, (e.g. the south coast of South Africa). It is doubtful whether sea-level fluctuations during the Pleistocene were of sufficient magnitude to have produced land bridges at the Straits of Gibraltar, between Southern Italy and Tunisia, or at Bab el Mandeb.[1] If these were ever available to early man it was only for brief periods, and for at least the last three million years the only certain and permanent land connection between Africa and Eurasia was that north of the Gulf of Suez. In earlier, Cainozoic times, however, there were occasions when Africa was connected quite extensively with Eurasia, which is important for understanding the spread of man's prehuman ancestors some 18–20 m.y. ago.[2]

MAN'S PREHUMAN ANCESTORS AND THE EARLIEST HOMINIDS

In Europe, Asia and North-East Africa some 20 m.y. ago, at a time of equable climate and forest dispersal, certain hominoid, ape-like creatures were living which are regarded as ancestral to both apes and man. Named *Dryopithecus*, forms of this creature are known from fossils found in Egypt (*Aegyptopithecus zeuxis*, an earlier, ancestral type) and in East Africa where they lived on fruits, nuts and insects in the forest/savanna ecotone, making use of both the gallery forest along the streams and the open savanna on the higher slopes. A still more advanced form (*Ramapithecus*), dating to some 10–14 m.y. ago, is known from north-west India, East Africa and, more recently, from Hungary, though it cannot yet be established unequivocally whether it is advanced enough to be considered as a hominid.[3]

[1] M. H. Alimen, 'Les "Isthmes" Hispano-Marocain et Siculo-Tunisien aux temps acheuléens', *L'Anthropologie*, 1975, **79**, 399–436.

[2] See the relevant pages of ch. 1, Vol. 1 of this *History*.

[3] (a) G. C. Conroy and D. Pilbeam, '*Ramapithecus*: a review of its hominid status', in R. L. H. Tuttle, ed., *Palaeoanthropology: morphology and ecology* (The Hague, 1975), 59–86. (b) M. Kretzoi, 'New ramapithecines and *Pliopithecus* from the Lower Pliocene of Rudabanya in north-eastern Hungary', *Nature*, 1975, **257**, 578–81. (c) P. Andrews and A. Walker, 'The primate and other fauna from Fort Ternan, Kenya', in G. L. Isaac and E. R. McCown, eds., *Human origins: Louis Leakey and the East African evidence* (Menlo Park, Calif., 1976), 279–303.

About 12 m.y. ago a major climatic change occurred and confined these hominoids to the tropical zones.[1] Some 5.5 m.y. ago, when the Mediterranean began to fill again after the late Miocene desiccation and after the land bridge at the lower end of the Red Sea was breached, the Arabian peninsula was permanently separated from Africa except at the Isthmus of Suez.[2] It would, therefore, seem that after *c.* 5.0 m.y. ago, gene pools in Eurasia and Africa must have evolved largely independently of each other. The many fossil hominid remains of Australopithecines found in South and East Africa, and the abundant and early appearance there of tool-making, strongly suggest that it was in the African tropics that man the tool-maker evolved. This evidence has been uniquely preserved in old cave sediments in the interior plateau of southern Africa[3] and within the Rift Valley in eastern Africa.[4] In the latter, rich assemblages of fossils and artefacts have survived with little or no natural disturbance since they were accumulated, and studies of the micro-stratigraphy and associated fauna show that the habitat was one of open, fairly dry savanna with plenty of available surface water and an abundance of the gregarious and large Ethiopian fauna. Although the circumstances of preservation have favoured East Africa, there is good reason to suppose that some 3 m.y. ago the hominids were spread throughout those parts of the African tropical savanna where their favoured habitats were to be found.

The significance of this becomes apparent when the size of the African continent is taken into account. The savanna zones stretch some 12,000 kilometres from the Senegal to the Cape, and the opportunities within the savanna/forest ecotone for interaction among early hominids becoming adapted to savanna living must have been very considerable. Not only is the African savanna one of the richest biomes

[1] For a review of the stratigraphic evidence relating to inferred but incorrectly interpreted aridity, see W. W. Bishop, 'Pliocene problems relating to human evolution', in Isaac and McCown, eds., *Human origins*, 139–53. There is also evidence, based on deep-sea cores, for a world cooling during the late Miocene/early Pliocene, in N. Shackleton and J. P. Kennett, 'Late Cenozoic oxygen and carbon isotopic changes at DSDP Site 284: implications for glacial history of the northern hemisphere and Antarctica', in J. P. Kennett, R. E. Houtz and others, eds., *Initial reports of the Deep Sea Drilling Project*, **39** (Washington, 1975).

[2] (a) K. J. Hsü, W. B. F. Ryan and M. B. Cita, 'Late Miocene desiccation of the Mediterranean', *Nature*, 1973, **242**, 240–4. (b) R. W. Gurdler and P. Styles, 'Two stage Red Sea floor spreading', *Nature*, 1974, **247**, 7–11.

[3] (a) C. K. Brain, *The Transvaal ape-man-bearing cave deposits, Transvaal Museum Memoirs*, **11** (Pretoria, 1958), 1–131. (b) C. G. Sampson, *The Stone Age archaeology of southern Africa* (New York and London, 1974), 16–101.

[4] G. L. Isaac, 'East Africa as a source of fossil evidence for human evolution', in Isaac and McCown, eds., *Human origins*, 121–37.

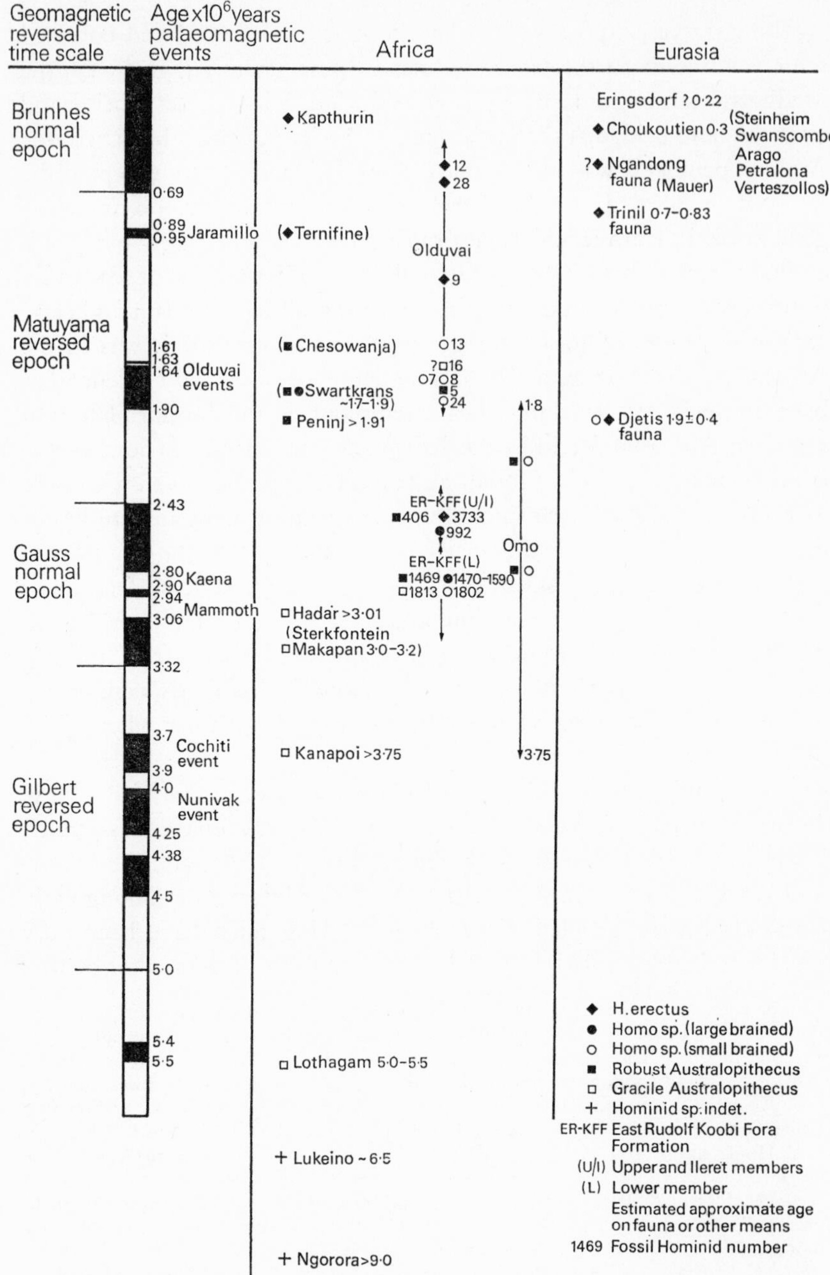

2 Radiometric and palaeo-magnetic chronology for fossil hominids in the Plio-Pleistocene time-range in Africa and Eurasia.

Only the more significant fossils found up to 1975 are shown. Note the

in the world, but the variety of vegetable and animal life that can be found there, and the challenge of the long dry season, must have provided incentive for experiment with new sources of food and new life styles.

Whether, as has been postulated, the human ancestor passed through a knuckle-walking stage (that gives speed and steadiness to principally ground-dwelling primates),[1] or whether the ancestral form in the later Miocene was already bipedal, cannot be determined without further fossil evidence to bridge the gap between *Ramapithecus* and the Australopithecines – but, clearly, the late Miocene/Pliocene was a most crucial time for hominid evolution. It was during this time that the locomotor pattern became fully bipedal (though not the striding gait of modern man) and the forelimbs were adapted to the manipulation of objects, the collection of food and the use of simple tools. These last must have begun to assume much greater significance in the life of the groups by reason of the possibilities their use provides – in particular in regard to meat-eating – for a creature unendowed by nature with either serviceable claws or extra-large teeth.

The very close biological relationship between the African apes and ourselves is unquestionable, as Huxley showed in the last century, and recent work in molecular biology has shown that the differences between apes and man are minimal compared to those between apes and monkeys. Using the immunological distances, it has been demonstrated that African apes and monkeys are likely to have separated some 24 m.y. ago and man and ape some 5.0–10 m.y. ago.[2] Clearly, therefore, the studies carried out over the past fifteen years by primatologists are highly relevant to attempts to understand hominid behaviour. On account of the more evolved biology of the hominids, however, their behaviour can be expected to have been more complex than that of forest-dwelling chimpanzees, though nearer to that than to the behaviour of modern hunter-gatherers. Relative to their body weight, the brains of Australopithecines were large (450–550 cc compared to 350–650 cc for the heavier gorilla and 1,250–1,550 cc for modern man)

[1] S. L. Washburn, 'Behaviour and the origin of man', *Proceedings of the Royal Anthropological Institute, 1967,* 1968, 21–7.

[2] V. M. Sarich, 'A molecular approach to the question of human origins', in P. C. Dolhinow and V. M. Sarich, eds., *Background for man* (New York, 1972), 60–91.

alternative dating now available for the KBS tuff, i.e. 1.6–1.8 m.y., and so the possible younger age of the East Rudolf fossils from the lower member of the Koobi Fora Formation.

(After J. D. Clark, 'Africa in prehistory: peripheral or permanent?', *Man*, N.S., 1975, 10, fig. 1.)

but, when compared to the size of the face, were contained in a still ape-like skull. However, the Australopithecines were clearly hominids when one takes into account the various modifications that had taken place in the skull and in the post-cranial skeleton with its evidence for bipedal locomotion and for a hand dexterous enough to make simple stone tools.[1]

3 The distribution of early hominid and Lower and Middle Palaeolithic sites referred to in the text.

[1] S. L. Washburn and R. Moore, *Ape into man: a study of human evolution* (Boston, 1974).

Most of the Australopithecine fossils date between *c.* 3.0 and 1.5 m.y. BP, though the earliest yet found (at Lothagam in the Lake Rudolf basin) would appear to be *c.* 5.0 m.y. old (fig. 2). We already have several hundred of these fossils from localities in northern Kenya and Ethiopia and from brecciated old cave sediments in the Transvaal and northern Cape of South Africa, as well as an enigmatic fossil from the Lake Chad basin. Their distribution (fig. 3) suggests that they were living throughout the range of the African dry savanna, adapted to an open country habitat, whereas the absence of fossils from the forested regions, not due entirely to circumstances of preservation, suggests that the inexhaustible supply of plant foods there offered no incentive to the ancestral chimpanzees and gorillas to modify the development of their brachiating and other particular characteristics.

Among the fossil population of hominids that has been found in sediments dating between *c.* 3.0 and 3.5 m.y. at Hadar in the Afar Rift, Ethiopia, there is present a gracile Australopithecine form as well as a number of fossil species that approximate to *Homo*.[1] Since they are found together in the same sediments, such an association might mean that there were two distinct contemporaneous lineages which, presumably, would have used different resources to avoid competition. Alternatively, only one lineage is represented, any biological differences being explained by sexual dimorphism. Selection for heavier build and other features might be explained for males with responsibilities for group protection, hunting and scavenging by driving carnivores from their kills. If two species were present, the implication would be that the *Homo* lineage was already separated from the Australopithecines more than 3.0 m.y. ago and that the latter cannot, therefore, be directly ancestral to man. Only one species would suggest that the ancestral form was a gracile Australopithecine. It can be expected that the recent find of a large part of the skeleton of a gracile individual from Hadar, and of the new mandibular fossils from Laetolil discovered in 1974 by Dr Mary Leakey and dating to *c.* 3.75 m.y. ago, will help to clarify some of these issues.[2]

Most authors recognize two species of Australopithecines – a gracile and a robust form – within a single genus. The gracile was first found in

[1] (a) M. Taieb, D. C. Johanson, Y. Coppens and J. L. Aronson, 'Geological and palaeontological background of Hadar hominid sites, Afar, Ethiopia', *Nature*, 1976, **260**, 289–93. (b) D. C. Johanson and M. Taieb, 'Plio-Pleistocene hominid discoveries in Hadar, Ethiopia', *Nature*, 1976, **260**, 293–7.

[2] (a) D. C. Johanson and M. Taieb, 'Plio-Pleistocene hominid discoveries in Hadar, Ethiopia', *Nature*, 1976, **260**, 293–7. (b) M. D. Leakey, R. L. Hay, G. H. Curtis, R. E. Drake and M. K. Jackes, 'Fossil hominids from the Laetolil Beds, *Nature*, 1976, **262**, 460–6.

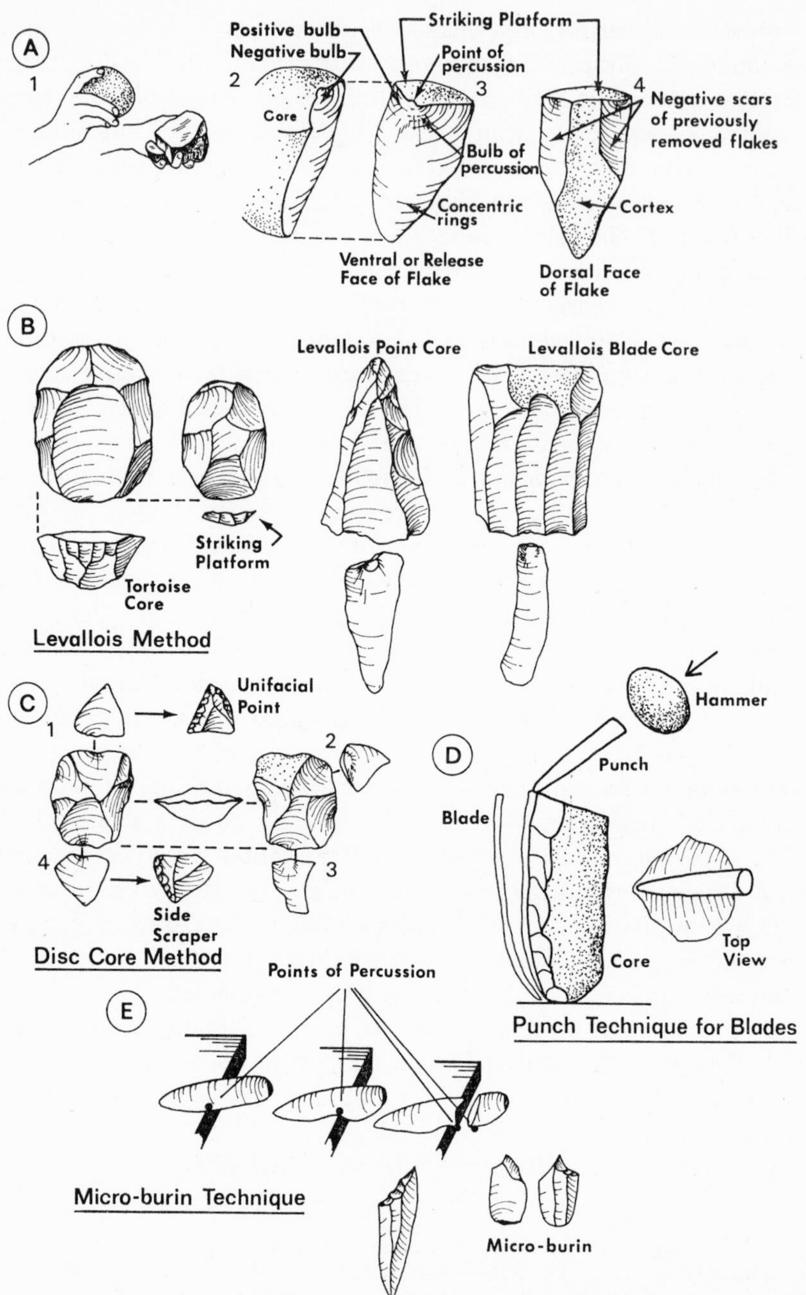

4 Attributes of human flaking and some of the basic techniques in stone-tool manufacture. (*For explanation, see opposite.*)

the older South African cave breccias, where it is known as *Australopithecus africanus* and, on faunal evidence, dates to some 3.0 or more m.y. ago. It is also present in the Omo stratigraphic succession in East Africa, where it – or a comparable form – dates to between 3.0 and 2.0 m.y. ago. The robust Australopithecine (*A. robustus*) is also present at Omo in a sub-specific form – *Australopithecus boisei* – where it is dated between just over 2.0 and 1.0 m.y. ago, and at the Olduvai Gorge the time-range of the robust form is from some 1.75 to 1.0 m.y. ago. From Bed I and the lower part of Bed II at Olduvai comes a small-brained but advanced form that is ascribed to the genus *Homo* and referred to as *H. habilis*. At Omo, a similar form is present at about 1.85 m.y. ago, and by *c.* 1.0 m.y. ago or earlier, this is generally considered to have developed into *H. erectus*, the large-brained form of man that was widespread in the Old World during the Middle Pleistocene.[1] In the East Rudolf sequence, the robust Australopithecine is represented by a number of cranial and post-cranial fossils, contemporary with which is a large-brained *Homo*.[2] Of crucial importance for the interpretation of the long, rich, fossil record from East Rudolf is the age of the specimens; this question hinges largely on that of the KBS tuff that seals the Lower Member of the Koobi Fora Formation in which these fossils first occur.[3] The East Rudolf evidence now shows con-

[1] F. C. Howell and Y. Coppens, 'An overview of Hominidae from the Omo succession, Ethiopia', in Coppens *et al.*, eds., *Earliest man and environments*, 522–32.

[2] This *Homo* form is best represented by the KNM-ER 1470 and KNM-ER 1590 crania. Another nearly complete cranium, KNM-ER 1813, represents a more gracile and small-brained hominid, which has been variously referred to both *A. africanus* and *H. habilis*. See R. E. F. Leakey, 'Further evidence of Lower Pleistocene hominids from East Rudolf, North Kenya, 1973', *Nature*, 1974, **248**, 653–6.

[3] The KBS tuff was originally assigned an age of *c.* 2.6 m.y., but later K/Ar results indicate that it may be younger, with an age of *c.* 1.6–1.8 m.y. The associated fossil faunal assemblages appear to favour the later date – see G. H. Curtis, T. Drake, T. E. Cerling, B. L. Cerling and J. H. Hempel, 'Age of KBS tuff in Koobi Fora Formation, East Rudolf, Kenya', *Nature*, 1975, **258**, 395–8. Robust Australopithecine fossils occur also in the

A Main attributes of human flaking shown by percussion-flaked stone
B Levallois method of core preparation and flake production, showing some of the commoner core and flake forms
C Disc core method and resulting flake forms
D Blade production using a punch
E Micro-burin method of obtaining short sections of blades for making microliths

(A after K. P. Oakley, *Man the tool-maker*, 1976; B, C after J. D. Clark, *The prehistory of Africa*, 1970; D after F. Bordes, 'Considérations sur la typologie et les techniques dans le Paléolithique', *Quartar*, 1967, **18**, 25–55; E after J. Tixier, *Typologie de l'Épipaléolithique du Maghreb*, Mémoire du C.R.A.P.E. no. 2, 1963.)

clusively that two distinct hominids – *A. boisei* and *H. erectus* – were existing contemporaneously in the time-range of 1–1.5 m.y. ago. Thus this opens the possibility that several sympatric hominid lineages occupied the African savanna during the Pliocene and earliest Pleistocene.[1] For this writer, therefore, the evidence is perhaps best expressed by the hypothesis of two Australopithecine species – a gracile and a robust, the latter divided into the regionally distinct sub-specific forms *A. robustus* and *A. boisei* – that derived from a gracile ancestor probably during the earliest Pliocene. The *Homo* lineage that resulted from further speciation among the gracile population may have been present as early as 3 m.y. ago, and it appears probable that all these hominid lineages existed together for a time before first the gracile Australopithecine and later the robust form finally succumbed to competition from *Homo erectus* some 1 m.y. ago.[2] Many of these fossils are associated with cultural evidence, and from that at present available from East and South Africa, where *Homo* fossils seem to be more usually associated with stone artefacts, it is likely that the regular exploitation of this discovery was more specifically the prerogative of this form. There is also reason to suppose that the accelerated biological changes attendant upon improved tool manufacture may have produced not a little genetic variability in these semi-isolated populations.

BEHAVIOUR PATTERNING OF THE PLIO-PLEISTOCENE TOOL-MAKERS

Attempts to understand the behaviour of the first tool-makers have to

Upper Member above the KBS tuff with ages between *c.* 1.5 and 1.1 m.y., and there is now indisputable evidence that *H. erectus* was present in East Rudolf by *c.* 1.5 m.y. ago, represented in particular by the almost complete cranium with face, known as KNM-ER 3733. See R. E. F. Leakey, 'New Hominid fossils from the Koobi Fora Formation in northern Kenya', *Nature*, 1976, **261**, 574–6.

[1] R. E. F. Leakey and A. C. Walker, '*Australopithecus, Homo erectus* and the single species hypothesis', *Nature*, 1976, **261**, 572–4.

[2] For a recent summary of early hominid taxonomy and the problems involved, see pp. 400–9 of P. V. Tobias, 'African hominids: dating and phylogeny', in Isaac and McCown, eds., *Human origins*, 377–422. Most authors recognize that two genera, *Australopithecus* and *Homo*, are present from the late Pliocene, the Australopithecines being sub-divided into two species – *A. robustus*, with sub-species *A. robustus* and *A. boisei*, and *A. africanus* (see B. G. Campbell, *Human evolution*, 2nd edn [Chicago, 1972], and D. Pilbeam, *The ascent of Man: an introduction to human evolution* [New York, 1972]). The gracile species is seen more generally as being ancestral to the robust species and to *H. habilis*. Other writers (e.g. M. H. Wolpoff, 'Competitive exclusion among Lower Pleistocene hominids: the single species hypothesis', *Man*, 1971, **6**, 4, 601–14) group the Australopithecines and *H. habilis* into a single genus on the evidence of dental morphology, while still others (e.g. C. E. Oxnard, 'The place of the Australopithecines in human evolution: grounds for doubt?', *Nature*, 1975, **258**, 389–95) consider the Australopithecines as lying outside the direct line of human evolution. For a complete review see ch. 2 (by F. C. Howell) in Vol. 1 of this *History*.

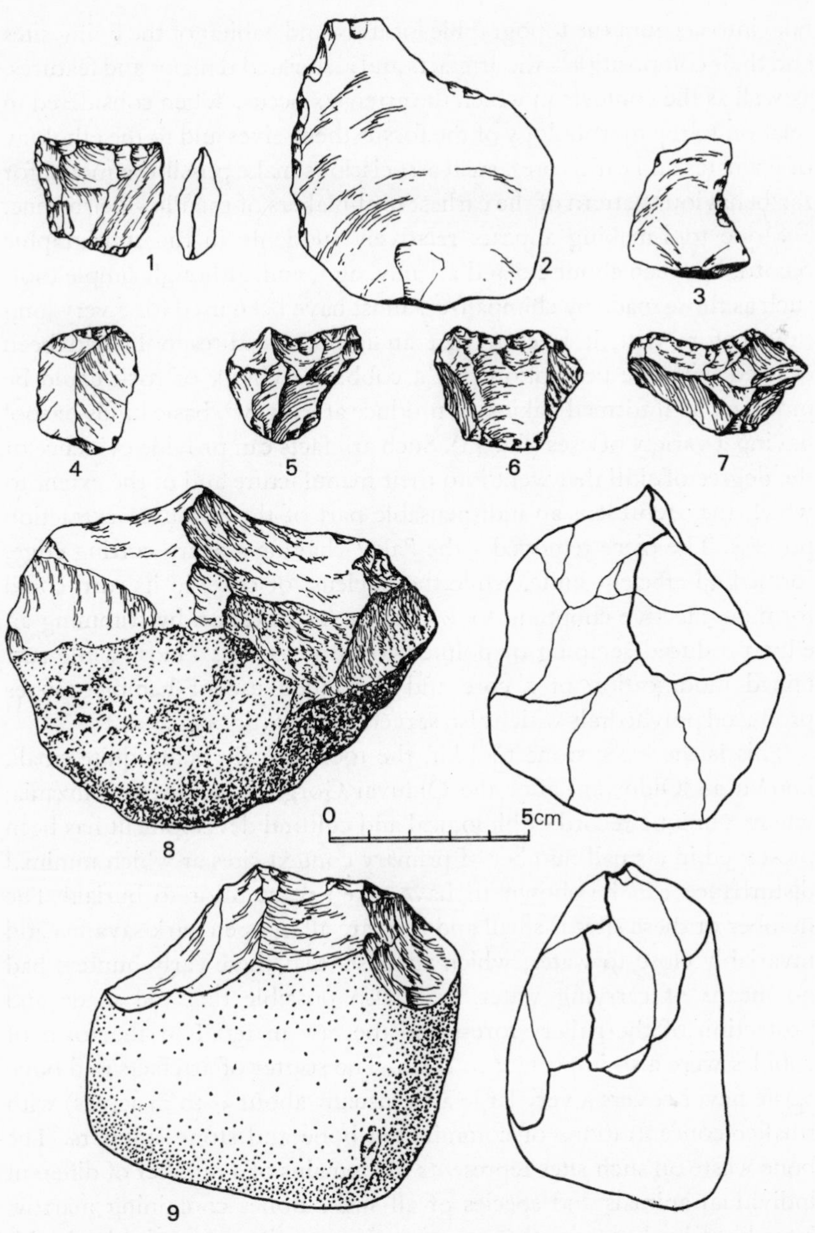

5 Tools of the Oldowan Industrial Complex from Bed I, Olduvai Gorge, Tanzania.
1 Knife-like tool 2, 3 Utilized flakes 4 End-scraper
5–7 Concave scrapers (no. 7 with *bec*) 8, 9 Side choppers
(After M. D. Leakey, *Olduvai Gorge*, III, 1971, pp. 27, 35, 38.)

take into account the topographic location and habitat of the living sites and their composition – the artefacts and associated remains and features, as well as the contexts in which the artefacts occur. When considered in relation to the morphology of the fossils themselves and to the ethology of primates and carnivores, such associations make possible a model for the behaviour pattern of the earliest tool-makers of the Plio-Pleistocene.

Stone tool-making appears relatively suddenly in the stratigraphic record, between about 2.0 and 2.5 m.y. ago, and, although simple tools such as those made by chimpanzees must have been used for a very long time before that, it is clear that an important threshhold had been crossed with the perception that a cobble or chunk of rock could be modified by informed flaking to produce at least two basic kinds of tool having a variety of uses (fig. 4A). Such artefacts can provide evidence of the degree of skill that went into their manufacture and of the extent to which they represent an indispensable part of the resource extraction process. The piece removed – the flake – having a sharp cutting edge, formed an efficient knife, while the nucleus, or core, in its turn could form an effective chopping tool. Further modification by trimming an edge produced scraping or pointed tools of various kinds, while sustained modification of a core and continued use of hammer-stones produced polyhedrals which also served as tools (fig. 5).

This is the basic stone tool-kit, the tools usually being quite small, known as 'Oldowan' after the Olduvai Gorge in northern Tanzania, where a unique record of biological and cultural development has been preserved in a small number of primary context sites at which minimal disturbance can be shown to have taken place prior to burial.[1] The number of these sites is small and they are all in open park savanna and invariably close to water, which suggests that these early hunters had no means of carrying water. It is also possible that the shade and protection of the gallery forest and the raw material in the form of cobbles were also important to them. The scatter of artefacts and bone waste never covers a very large area (usually about 3–10 m across) with smaller concentrations of comminuted bone and stone splinters. The bone waste on such sites represents the remains of a number of different individual animals and species of all sizes. Bones containing marrow have been broken, and the stone artefacts used are found mixed with the pieces of bone. Sometimes the bones of a single, large animal – a

[1] (a) M. D. Leakey, *Olduvai Gorge*, Vol. III, *Excavations in Beds I and II, 1960–1963* (Cambridge, 1971), 1–299. (b) R. L. Hay, *Geology of the Olduvai Gorge* (Berkeley, 1976), 1–198, esp. 180–6 and Appendix B.

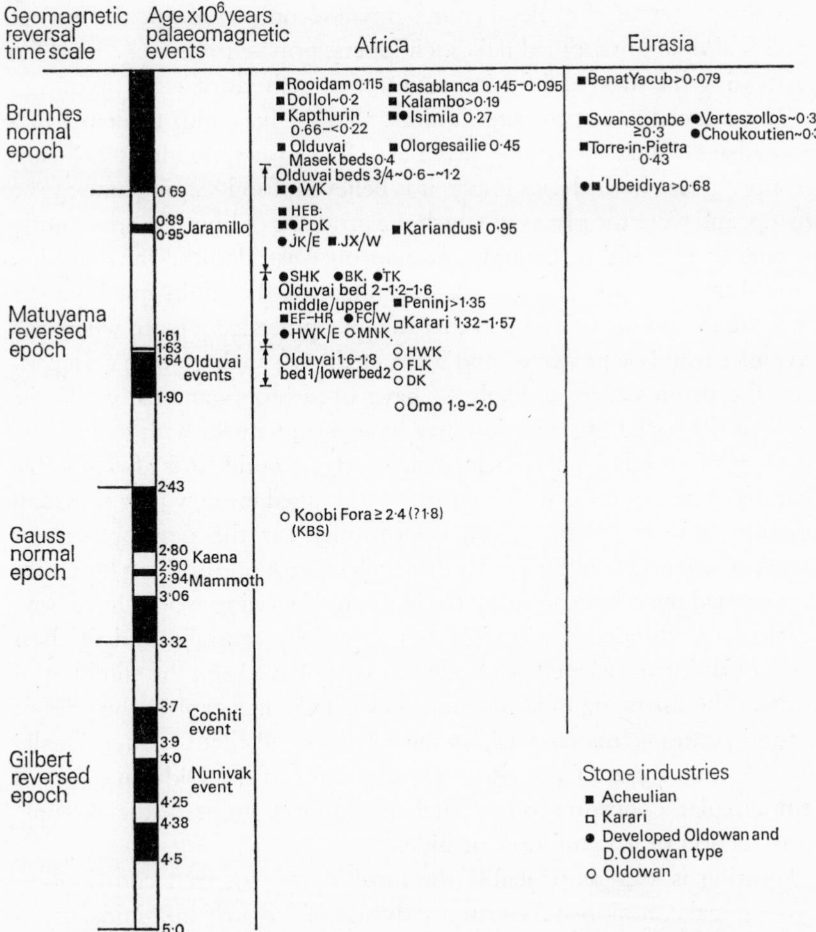

6 Radiometric and palaeo-magnetic chronology for stone industries in the late Pliocene/earlier Pleistocene time-range in Africa and Eurasia up to 1975.
Only the main Olduvai Gorge assemblages have been shown. Note that due to the possible younger age of the KBS tuff at Koobi Fora the contained archaeological occurrences may date to *c.* 1.6–1.8 m.y. The archaeological occurrence excavated from Member C (Shungura Formation) from Omo, i.e. Omo 84, has an age of *c.* 2.5 m.y.
(After Clark, 'Africa in prehistory', fig. 2.)

hippopotamus at Koobi Fora or a *Deinotherium* or an early form of elephant (*Elephas reckii*) at Olduvai – are found together with the same basic tool-kit, in circumstances strongly suggesting that the implements were used in dismembering it. Man is not naturally equipped to deal with the procuring of meat, and the benefits derived from making meat a regular part of the diet became possible only through the use of tools – simple unmodified flakes, choppers, polyhedrons etc. – used for processing the meat and for improving the methods of securing it.

The associations at the sites indicate that the hominids made use of a home base which, no doubt, acted as a focus for individuals and sub-groups. These home bases imply, it is believed, food-sharing among the group, and were the places to which the products of hunting, scavenging or collecting could be brought. Studies on Australopithecine dentition have shown that the young were dependent on the adults much longer than are the young of apes, so that the group needed a place where the juveniles could be protected and instructed.[1] On analogy with chimpanzees the groups were unlikely to have been monogamous, while the basis of the social organization may have been females with young, the mother/infant relationship being the strongest bond. It is also possible that the males, again as with chimpanzees, ranged more widely at certain seasons; this may have given opportunity for the development of hunting organization. Relatively defenceless, ground-dwelling hominids that carried meat back to camp for communal sharing would have been particularly vulnerable to carnivores, especially at night, and the best form of defence – as well as of offence – may have been the climbing of trees or the throwing of stones and rocks. This may explain the piles of natural stones – 'manuports', as the Leakeys call them – intentionally carried onto some of the sites.[2] On site DKI in the Olduvai Gorge a semi-circular concentration of such manuports suggests the possible construction of a windbreak or hide.

Hunting is seen as probably the most significant trait contributing to the social cohesion and cultural activities of the early hominids. Small creatures – frogs, lizards, tortoises, rodents etc., all of which occur on the Olduvai living floors in Bed I – could be obtained by individual foraging, but the securing of larger, swifter and more dangerous game would have been possible only through communal effort. The kind of success suggested by the density of the bone refuse on the living-sites shows that the makers of the Oldowan Industry were already organized to a level of efficiency that required some form of adequate communication and exchange of information which, though most unlikely to have been anything like language as we know it, nevertheless, by making

[1] A. E. Mann, *Some palaeodemographic aspects of the South African Australopithecines*, Pennsylvania University Publications in Anthropology, 1, *The Palaeodemography of Australopithecus* (Philadelphia, 1975).

[2] Manuports are natural stones that show no artificial modification but which appear to have been carried into occupation sites by human agency; see Leakey, *Olduvai Gorge*, III, 8.

possible some skilful organization and strategy, compensated for the hominids' lack of the speed possessed by the larger carnivores. In particular, communal hunting is seen primarily as a male activity, while females and young can be expected to have concentrated more on the collecting of plant foods. However, due to their perishable nature, very little evidence of plants is preserved in the archaeological record, although the identification of *Typha* roots at one of the Bed I sites at Olduvai, and of fig leaves at East Rudolf, gives some indication of the plant foods available. If plant foods were brought back to the home base and not consumed as snacks while on the move, then some form of simple container would have been needed, such as a tortoise-shell or a section of tree bark. There is no means of knowing the relative importance of meat and vegetable foods, but, by analogy with present-day hunter-gatherers in the tropics, plant foods can be expected to have constituted perhaps 75% of the diet. While, therefore, the hominids could probably have got along without meat, the hunting organization was, for some of these populations, the catalyst that led to more structured organization and improved tool manufacture. Scavenging as a means of acquiring meat has been given less attention than has hunting, and we have now no means of knowing whether the butchered hippos and elephants were killed or found dead by the hominids. But at this early period the latter seems more probable, and it is clear that scavenging *could* have provided a regular, if not abundant, supply of meat.[1]

The early hominids responsible for the Oldowan tool-kit were, therefore, occupants of the dry savanna on the eastern side of the continent where, on faunal evidence, they can be seen to have been exploiting several different micro-environments. The terrestrial range of these early hominid groups is not known but, based on the distance that raw material for the stone tools found on some of their sites must have been carried, this most probably did not exceed a few kilometres, about forty at the most. The hominids were probably organized into smaller rather than larger groups for communal activities, with their basis in food-sharing. Some had adopted an omnivorous diet and a simple but efficient stone tool-kit. It is unlikely that these populations were ever very numerous and the great distances separating hominids in the West African savanna from those in South Africa must have

[1] For a general review of earlier hominid occupation sites and associated finds see p. 13, n. 4 and also G. L. Isaac, 'The activities of Early African hominids: a review of archaeological evidence from the time span two and a half to one million years ago', in Isaac and McCown, eds., *Human origins*, 483–514.

afforded plenty of opportunity for experiment and local divergence among such semi-isolated populations. The Oldowan Industry underwent minimal change for close on 1.5 m.y., and, during this time, stone tool technology and the hominids that possessed it appear to have been confined to Africa. It is just possible, however, that man may have penetrated to southern Europe during the Lower Pleistocene, but the evidence on which this claim is based is not unambiguous.[1]

HOMO ERECTUS AND THE ACHEULIAN INDUSTRIAL COMPLEX

Approximately 1.5 m.y. ago, perhaps a little less, new tool forms and technology make their appearance in Africa. These are known as the 'Acheulian Industrial Complex' after the site of St Acheul in northern France where the characteristic tools – the handaxes – were first found (fig. 7). These tools are often made from large flakes which bear witness to the skill and strength needed to remove them from large boulder cores. The earliest Acheulian – from the Olduvai Gorge – dates to *c.* 1.5 m.y. ago, and assemblages are known from several other sites in East Africa dating variously from 1.32 to 1.57 m.y. ago. Other early, but undated, assemblages come from North and South Africa.[2] Assemblages which, on stratigraphic and faunal grounds, can be shown to belong to a Lower Acheulian are not common, but their distribution shows that the makers of this Complex were able to adapt to living in a wide range of habitats that included probably all the continent had to offer except for the moist evergreen forests. This adaptability is even more apparent with the later or Upper Acheulian in the Middle Pleistocene, and sites of this period are relatively numerous and no longer confined solely to Africa. Around 1.0 m.y. ago it would seem that a spread of tool-making hominids erupted into Eurasia. This has been dated from various localities in the Near East (e.g. 'Ubedeiya in Israel,

[1] Only very few of the southern European artefact sites claimed as being of Plio-Pleistocene age call for serious consideration, since acceptable dating evidence is lacking. The site of La Vallonet near Menton is the most important. Here a small number of simple artefacts – flakes and flaked pebbles – appear to be associated with a late Lower Pleistocene (lower Biharian) fauna. Other finds come from high-level terrace gravels in the Somme, Rousillon, Rhone and Garonne valleys and are dated on geomorphological evidence; see H. de Lumley, 'Cultural evolution in France in its palaeoecological setting', in K. W. Butzer and G. L. Isaac, eds., *After the Australopithecines: stratigraphy, ecology and culture change in the Middle Pleistocene* (The Hague, 1975), 745–808, esp. 747–55.

[2] General reviews of the Middle Pleistocene cultural and palaeo-environmental evidence will be found in ch. 3 (by G. L. Isaac) of Vol. 1 of this *History* and also in: (a) J. D. Clark, 'A comparison of the Late Acheulian Industries of Africa and the Middle East', in Butzer and Isaac, eds., *After the Australopithecines*, 605–59; and (b) G. L. Isaac, 'Stratigraphy and cultural patterns in East Africa during the middle ranges of Pleistocene time', ibid. 495–542.

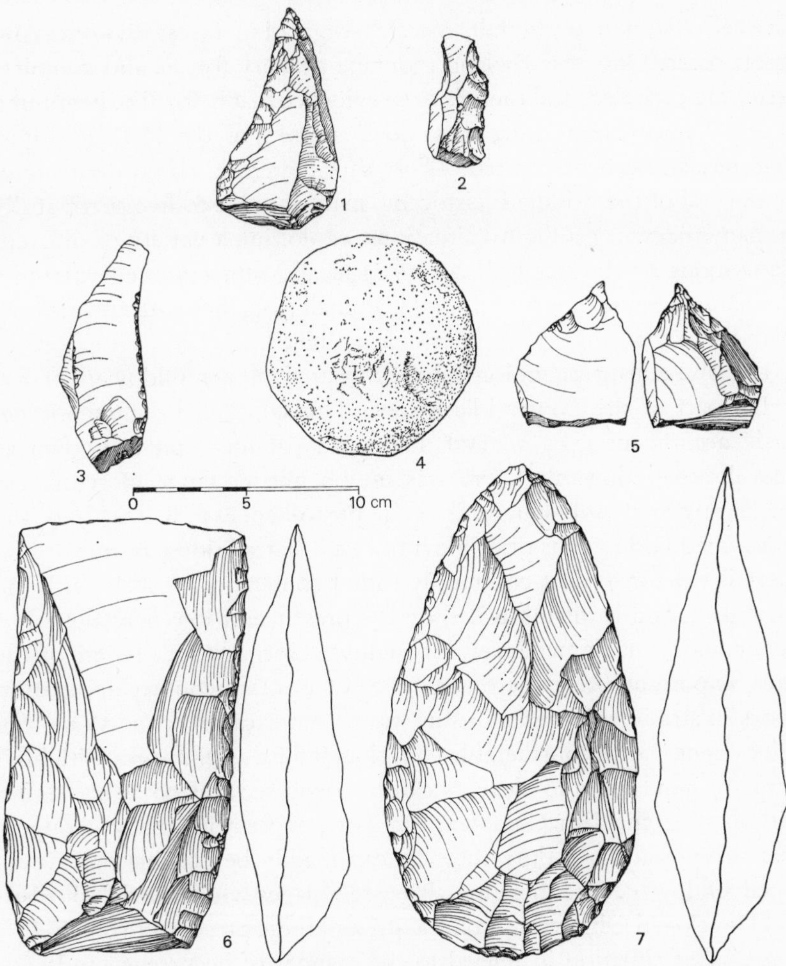

7 Tools of the Upper Acheulian Industrial Complex from the Kalambo Falls.

1 Concave side-scraper
2 Denticulated side-scraper
3 Utilized flake knife
4 Spheroid
5 Awl and *bec*
6 Cleaver
7 Handaxe

(After Clark, *Prehistory of Africa*, fig. 19.)

0.68 m.y.), the Far East (Choukoutien, 0.3 m.y.) and in Europe (e.g. Swanscombe in England, *c.* 0.3 m.y.). Now, besides the traditional dry savanna with good supplies of surface water, sites are found at all elevations from sea-level to about 2,700 m and cover most eco-systems between the winter rainfall, macchia-vegetation forest ecotones and desert oases. Only the lowland montane primary forests and complete desert are excluded, and there is even evidence that before the beginning of the Upper Pleistocene, *c.* 125,000 years ago, the lowland forest ecotone had been penetrated. There can, therefore, be no doubt that, by the end of the Middle Pleistocene, man was able to live successfully in many different ecological situations, exploiting a variety of different plant foods of the tropical, sub-tropical and temperate regions and a comparable range of large and small animals (together with fish at some inland sites but not, apparently, marine life).

The Acheulian technology did not supplant the Oldowan of the earlier part of the Lower Pleistocene. This continued contemporaneously accompanied by several new forms of tool and is known as 'Developed Oldowan'. There was now a greater range of retouched small scrapers, sub-spheroids and proto-handaxe forms, and the Developed Oldowan is divisible into two sub-traditions, A and B. The latter is the form most commonly found contemporaneously with the Acheulian, and is distinguished by the presence of low percentages of rather poorly made handaxes. At Olduvai Gorge, which is one of the most important sites where a number of primary context occupation floors in stratigraphic relationship have been excavated, the stone-tool component shows considerable variation. Those assemblages with high ratios of handaxes and cleavers can be easily recognized as belonging within the Acheulian Complex. Similarly, those with many choppers and heavy- and light-duty scrapers can readily be classified as Developed Oldowan. But there are also assemblages with mixed Acheulian and Developed Oldowan components, and these present a problem.[1]

A similar situation in regard to the manner of occurrence and contemporaneity of Acheulian and Oldowan tool traditions appears to pertain also fairly generally in Eurasia during the Middle Pleistocene, except that there are here very few multiple context sites. There still remains uncertainty as to the meaning of these two contemporaneous and evolving stone-tool traditions. The present writer views them as being related primarily to activity differences, the different classes of tool comprising the Developed Oldowan and Acheulian tool-kits being designed to carry out the functions these activities required in the most expeditious manner possible given the technological ability of their makers.

Since *Australopithecus robustus* was still present as late, perhaps, as

[1] M. D. Leakey, 'Cultural patterns in the Olduvai Sequence,' in Butzer and Isaac, eds., *After the Australopithecines*, 447–93.

1.0 m.y. ago when competition with *Homo* brought about its extinction, it might have been possible that two hominid taxa were involved. However, for most of the time that the Acheulian tradition was practised, there is evidence for only one taxon. This is *Homo erectus*, a relatively large-brained, efficiently bipedal tool-maker whose remains are known from localities in South, East and North Africa and also from Eurasia. Indeed, there is now clear evidence for a rapid spread out of Africa throughout the more temperate and tropical parts of Eurasia by 1 m.y. ago, if not earlier.

From the distribution and configuration of Acheulian and related assemblages, some significant differences from the Oldowan living sites become apparent (although many sites are still located close to water), and this may well imply a different use of resources or the need for different sizes of raw material. At some sites, a succession of occupation horizons shows that these were reoccupied over a span of time, and the succeeding assemblages of artefacts show much variation. One way of interpreting this kind of variation is that, over the years, the activity pattern changed with the replacement, in the site catchment area, of one set of resources by another, and so of the artefacts used to process them. Archaeologists are, however, still a very long way from being able to determine function from stone-tool typology, and the uses of the Acheulian handaxes and cleavers still remain a mystery. These tools show improved technical ability on the part of the makers, and a clear conception of preference in design that leads to standardization and sometimes, in some of the bifaces, to a degree of regularity and symmetry which appears to exceed any purely utilitarian value of the specimen, and thus is thought to show a sense of aesthetic appreciation.

Many of the Acheulian occupation sites cover much larger areas than did the Oldowan (sometimes more than 100 × 100 m). There is a greater range of tool forms on some of them, suggesting that a number of activities were carried out there, while other smaller and more diffuse scatters with a more restricted range of tool forms imply single-activity areas. The larger concentrations are often in, or on the bank of, a seasonally dry, shallow stream and usually have sharply defined limits, perhaps determined by the area of shade available.

Large animal butchery sites become more frequent and, as with the Oldowan, the tool-kit associated is usually, though not always, one of small tools. There is some indication that small herds of often quite large animals were now successfully hunted and killed. In the upper part of Bed II at the Olduvai Gorge, at site BK II, are the remains of twenty-four extinct bovids (*Pelorovis*) which would appear to have been driven into a stream and butchered; at another Olduvai site (SHK) are the remains of a small herd of springbok. Again, this time at Olorgesailie (DE/89, Horizon B), there are the remains of a minimum of sixty-three adults and juveniles of the giant baboon, *Simopithecus oswaldi*, strongly suggesting that these animals were the victims of a successful hunt by Acheulian man who, in this instance, left some five hundred bifaces at the site.

Of great significance is the evidence for the use of fire, in particular from sites in Eurasia but present also with the Upper Acheulian at some African sites, e.g. Kalambo Falls in Zambia, the Jos Plateau and Nyabusora. Controlled use of fire and the ability to manufacture it made fundamental changes possible in behaviour, in social groupings and in technology. Fire was used to facilitate the shaping of weapons and digging tools – for example the wooden spear found with a dismembered *Elephas antiquus* kill at Lehringen in West Germany or the digging sticks at Kalambo Falls. Hearths and burnt bones at some Eurasian sites bear witness to the use of fire for warmth, protection and cooking. It may also have been from this time that fire began to be used in hunting, man taking advantage, just as do predatory animals and birds, of the creatures fleeing before an advancing bush fire.

The Acheulian Industrial Complex lasted more than a million years, during which it underwent some modification and refinement. But this is of so gradual a nature that it still has to be precisely documented, though, at the end, a general diminution in the size of the bifacial elements is easy to recognize. Although changes in style are unpredictable and no consistent pattern has so far emerged, variability within the Acheulian centres around the opportunity for differentiation made possible by the interplay between the biface and chopper/chopping tool traditions. And, while the resources exploited must have differed greatly from one eco-system to another, the equipment that these exploitation patterns made use of seems to have remained basically (though not quantitatively) the same. The implication is thus that there was a general pattern of behaviour and economy that maintained the same level of efficiency and did not differ significantly from one end of the Acheulian world to the other.

If, however, technology shows no very clear regional differentiation by the end of the Middle Pleistocene, there is more definite evidence for biological variation as between North-West, eastern and southern Africa by this time. The great distances and geographical barriers separating isolated populations in environments as different as these allowed selective processes to develop adaptive patterns of behaviour that manifest themselves also in the regional gene pools. Thus, in the Maghrib, human fossils dating to the later part of the Middle Pleistocene (for example those from the Moroccan coastal sites at Casablanca and Rabat, and the Sale plateau) are described as showing features that link them with the *Homo erectus* fossils, first called *Atlanthropus*, from Ternifine on the Algerian plateau, though they also have affinities with Neanderthal man and at least one (Temara) has recently been re-described as Neanderthal.[1] From late Middle or early Upper Pleistocene beds in the Omo basin (Kibish Formation), dating, it is thought, to *c.* 100,000 years ago, come two fossil crania that already show a range of variation between a form retaining *H. erectus*-like features and one more specifically *H. sapiens*.[2] In central and South Africa the evidence suggests that a robust 'rhodesioid' population was present by the end of the Middle Pleistocene, represented by the fossils from Kabwe (Broken Hill), now believed to date to *c.* 100,000 years ago, and the one from Elandsfontein associated with an Acheulian industry. Indeed, attention has also been drawn to the resemblance between the *H. rhodesensis*-type cranium and some of the features shown by the earlier *H. erectus* calvarium from the middle of Bed II (LLK) at Olduvai and the fragmentary fossil from the VEK site in Bed IV, thus giving a long ancestry to the 'rhodesioid' physical type. On the evidence of a fossil from Lake Eyasi in northern Tanzania, this appears to have persisted into the later Pleistocene and to be associated with artefacts described as belonging to the Middle Stone Age.[3]

THE MIDDLE PALAEOLITHIC/MIDDLE STONE AGE

The later Pleistocene is considered to have begun *c.* 125,000 years ago with the onset of the Last Interglacial and the resultant rise in sea-level of about eight metres. By this time, the Acheulian tool-kit had either been superseded or significantly modified. Although bifaces are still occasionally found (e.g. with evolved Acheulian [Stage 8] at Sidi Abderrahman, with the earlier Aterian in North Africa, or the pan

[1] (a) F. C. Howell, 'European and North-West African Middle Pleistocene hominids', *Current Anthropology*, 1960, 1, 195–232. (b) J. J. Jaeger, 'The mammalian faunas and hominid fossils of the Middle Pleistocene of the Maghreb', in Butzer and Isaac, eds., *After the Australopithecines*, 399–418.

[2] M. H. Day, 'Omo human skeletal remains', *Nature*, 1969, **222**, 1135–8.

[3] G. P. Rightmire, 'Relationships of Middle and Upper Pleistocene hominids from sub-Saharan Africa', *Nature*, 1976, **260**, 238–40.

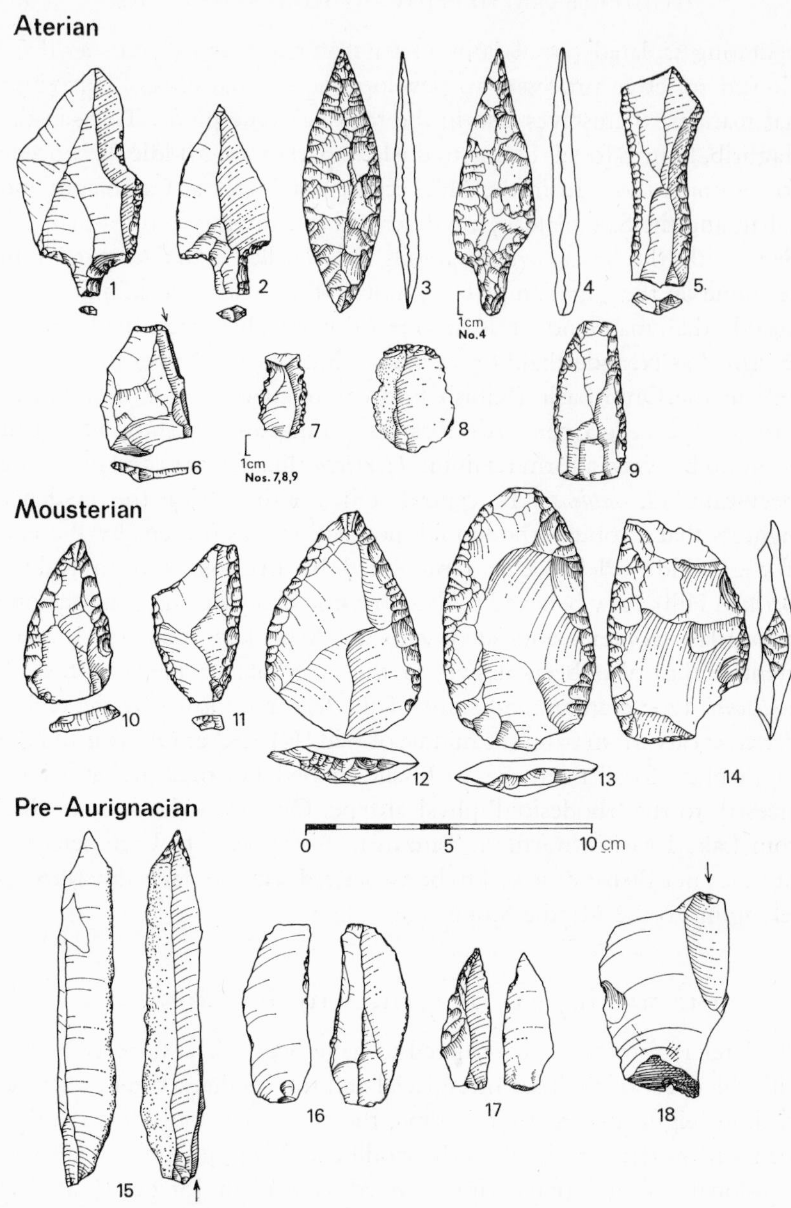

8 Middle Palaeolithic tools from northern Africa.
Aterian
1 Tanged Levallois flake
2 Tanged point
3 Bifacially retouched point
4 Bifacially retouched and tanged point

deposits at Rooidam in the northern Cape), they are now often diminutive, and it is the light equipment that becomes dominant. This is made on flakes and blocks struck from specially prepared cores, often by the Levallois and disc core methods,[1] and these techniques provided a range of light, thin flake and blade forms that could be trimmed into a variety of knives, points, scrapers or awls. In North Africa and as far south as Nubia, these tool-kits exhibit patterns comparable to the Mousterian tradition recognized in Eurasia and collectively known as 'Middle Palaeolithic' (fig. 8). In sub-Saharan Africa the equivalent cultural expressions are loosely referred to as belonging to the 'Middle Stone Age', which radiocarbon dates now show to correlate, not, as previously thought, with the Upper Palaeolithic in Eurasia, but with the Middle Palaeolithic, as, indeed, the technology itself suggests (figs. 9, 10).

In North Africa, the earliest Middle Palaeolithic/Middle Stone Age assemblages date within the period of the Last Interglacial high sea-level. They are found within or immediately overlying the ±8m beach, on the Moroccan coast dated to ±80,000 BP, with fully evolved assemblages dating to 50,000–40,000 BP. In southern Africa also the Middle Stone Age is of similar antiquity, so that the Middle Palaeolithic/Middle Stone Age in Africa spans the period of warmer climate and higher sea-level of the Last Interglacial and the earlier part of the Last

[1] The *Levallois* method involves the preparation of special cores for the removal of, generally, a single large and relatively thin flake or blade of predetermined form. Repreparation of the flaking surface is usually necessary before a further flake/blade is removed. *Disc cores* are radially prepared for the removal from one or both faces, round the circumference, of several usable flakes that can be further modified by retouch. See fig. 4, B & C.

---

5 Double concave side-scraper
6 Burin on truncation
7 Denticulated scraper
8, 9 End-scrapers

Mousterian
10 Mousterian point
11 Double side-scraper
12 Mousterian point
13, 14 Side-scrapers

Libyan Pre-Aurignacian
15 Awl-burin
16, 17 Utilized and backed blades
18 Proto-burin

(Nos. 4 after J. D. Clark *et al.*, 1975, p. 268; 7–9 after C. R. Ferring, 'The Aterian in North African prehistory', in F. Wendorf and A. E. Marks, eds., *Problems in prehistory*, 1975, p. 118; remainder after Clark, *Prehistory of Africa*, pp. 115, 126.)

Glaciation.[1] During this time, while much of the Sahara probably enjoyed a Mediterranean and Sahelian environment, the Congo basin experienced a significant retreat of the humid rain-forest. This was replaced over much of the southern and western part of the basin by deciduous woodland savanna with grassland on the Kalahari sands that form the plateau surface between the main rivers. Thus, in northern and western Africa, large, hitherto unpopulated areas became available for occupation, or others, previously favourable, again became so. The number of archaeological sites now found in the Congo basin and much of the maritime region of West Africa indicates that these were now favoured localities. Population movement into these hitherto 'empty areas' was made possible by the extension of the deciduous woodland and by the development of technologies adapted to exploiting the resources of a more closed habitat.

The number of different tool-kits, some of them regionally distinct, developed by the hunting-gathering populations of Africa by the beginning of the Last Glaciation some 70,000 years ago, can be seen as reflecting increasing involvement with experimenting in the use of local resources. The new methods of core preparation, for instance, permitted a more economical use of raw material – important if preferred rocks had to be carried any distance. Also some rocks can easily be used for the production of blades – quartzite, obsidian or flint, for example – while others, such as quartz, are less tractable. In the more open country the stone equipment is now essentially 'light duty' and a number of standardized 'types' make their appearance. In regions of heavier rainfall and thicker vegetation, heavier-duty forms are more common and it is now possible to detect varying degrees of geographical specialization. However, although the amount of specialization is appreciably in advance of anything manifested by the Acheulian Complex, it is on a much more general basis than that which comes after. In part this may be due to the limitations imposed by the technology and the intellectual ability but it may also be caused by the still relative sparseness of the human population. The great increase of Middle Stone Age over Early Stone Age sites in Africa, implying an overall population increase, was in part in regions with little or no evidence of previous occupation, so that competition for resources would still, it is suggested, have remained minimal.

[1] For bibliographical references and a discussion on the dating of the Middle Palaeolithic/Middle Stone Age in Africa see J. D. Clark, 'Africa in prehistory: peripheral or paramount?', *Man*, N.S., 1975, **10**, 175–98, and also ch. 4 (by J. D. Clark) in Vol. 1 of this *History*.

The climatic changes of this period and their effects on the vegetation communities can be seen reflected in the bone refuse of the occupation sites. For example, at Klassies River Cave in South Africa the fauna of the earliest Middle Stone Age is of forest/grassland and macchia species, similar to today. The second stage shows an increase in tragelaphine antelopes (bushbuck and kudu), implying a relative increase in forest/bush, while in the third stage the open country again predominates with a return of the alcelaphines (wildebeeste/hartebeeste) and quagga.[1] These changes are reflected in the tool-kits, which, through time, tend to form geographical traditions, assemblages from one region generally having more in common than those of any one time level from different regions. Although archaeologists have sought to explain changes in stone-tool assemblages (e.g. the replacement of the Acheulian by the Middle Palaeolithic) by population movement and replacement, there is increasing reason to believe that anything other than small-scale movements are a product of later agricultural and urban communities – unless they are into 'empty areas' or as the result of severe climatic deterioration. The replacement of one technology by another is now coming to be regarded as being more likely the result of technical innovation and stimulus diffusion.

The physical populations of the Middle Palaeolithic/Middle Stone Age are inadequately known.[2] Everywhere these industries are associated with *Homo sapiens*, though in northern Africa the sub-specific form *H. sapiens neanderthalensis* is represented by fossils from Jebel Irhoud in Morocco, Haua Fteah Cave in Cyrenaica, and perhaps from Dire Dawa (Porc Epic Cave) in Ethiopia, and other sites in North Africa. None of the African neanderthaloid fossils is of the extreme, classic type found in western Europe; these fossils resemble more the populations from Mount Carmel and other Middle East caves. Recent reports of new fossil cranial material from two Aterian contexts in Morocco may provide the first clear evidence of the physical affinities of the makers of this industrial complex, which has its origins in the Middle Palaeolithic tradition.[3] Sometime towards the close of Aterian

1 R. G. Klein, 'Environment and subsistence of prehistoric man in the southern Cape Province, South Africa', *World Archaeology*, 1974, **5**, 249–84.

2 See ch. 2 of Vol. 1 of this *History* for a review of the latest finds and interpretations.

3 (a) For cranial and mandibular remains of two or more robust individuals from a lower Aterian horizon, see A. Debénath, 'Découverte de restes humains probablement atériens à Dar es Soltan (Maroc)', *C.R. Académie des Sciences* (Paris), 1975, **281**, 875–6. (b) For occipital bone associated with an upper Aterian industry see J. Roche and J.-P. Texier, 'Découvertes de restes humains dans un niveau atérien supérieur de la Grotte des Contrebandiers à Temara (Maroc)', ibid. 1976, **282**, 45–7.

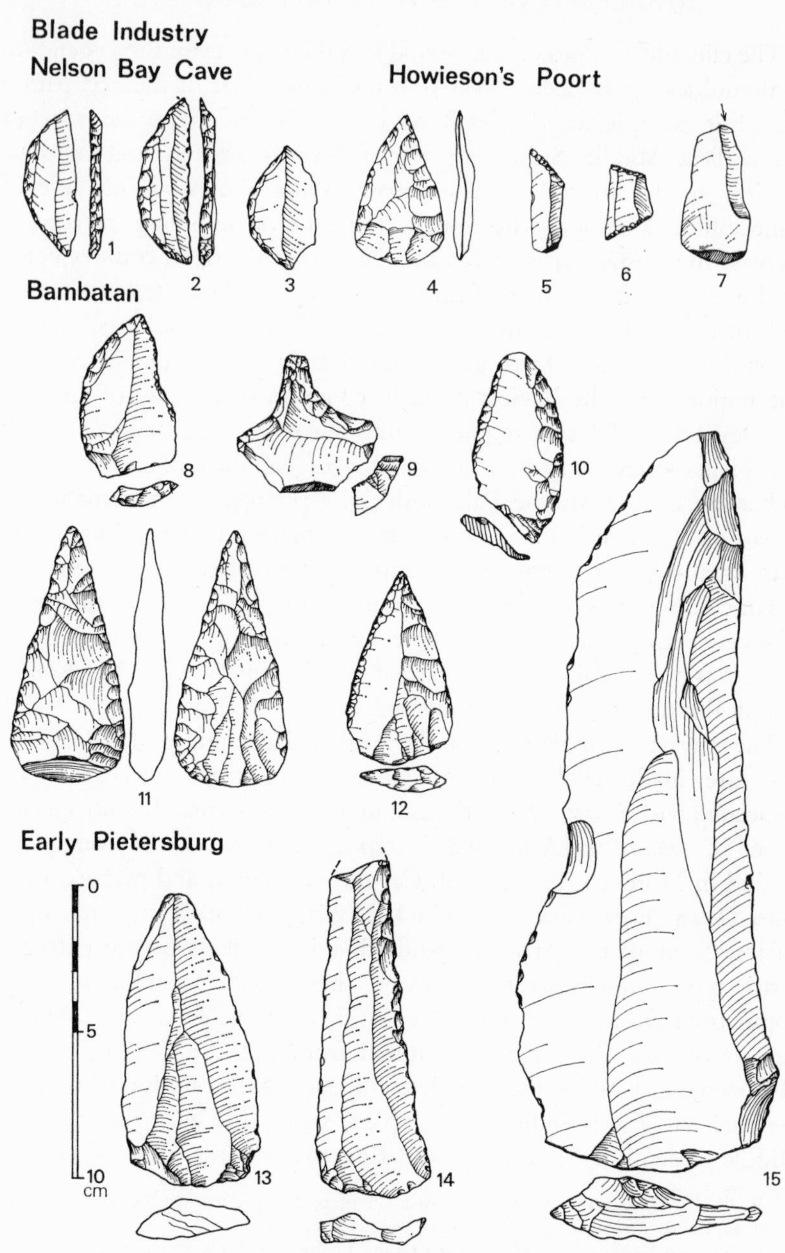

9 Middle Stone Age tools from sub-Saharan Africa.
Blade Industry (? = Howieson's Poort) from Nelson Bay Cave, South Africa
1–3 Large backed segments
Howieson's Poort tools from the type-site
4 Unfaced point

times (? *c.* 30,000 BP) the Neanderthal stock in northern Africa was replaced by modern man just as central and southern Africa also saw the replacement of residual 'rhodesioid' stock by modern man. Thus the Lake Eyasi fossil with artefacts made by the Levallois method presumably represents an early stage of development, while the only early dated fossil from this time (more than 45,000 years ago) in South Africa, *H. helmei* from Florisbad in the Orange Free State, belongs with modern man – albeit an archaic form with some 'rhodesioid' characteristics. It was clearly, therefore, within this time range – 100,000–40,000 years ago – that modern man made his appearance in Africa, at the same time, in fact, as he did in the Middle East.

In Africa it is the East African region that has produced the earliest evidence as yet of *H. sapiens* (Omo 1 and 2 from the Kibish Formation) and, if the dates can be relied on, it can be seen to have taken something less than 60,000 years for modern man to make his appearance and cover the whole continent, replacing all other more archaic forms. Whether the secret of modern man that made him so far in advance of all other forms was in his superior intellectual ability, adaptability and technology, or a combination of these and other traits, it was, as has been previously suggested, his ability to communicate by means of a fully developed language system and exchange abstract and precise information that was chiefly responsible for giving him his unique advantage.

The extent of Middle Palaeolithic/Middle Stone Age variability will serve to demonstrate the degree of environmental adaptation that had been achieved by the early *H. sapiens* populations (figs 8, 9 & 11). Along the Mediterranean littoral and on the plateau north of the Sahara are

---

5 Truncated blade
6 Trapeze
7 Burin

Bambata Industry tools from the type-site

8 Backed flake
9 Borer
10 Side-scraper
11 Bifacial point
12 Unifacial point

Early Pietersburg Industry tools from Bed 4, Cave of Hearths

13–15 Triangular flake and blades with discontinuous utilization and retouch

(Nos. 1–3 after R. G. Klein, 1972; remainder after Clark, *Prehistory of Africa*, figs. 35, 50.)

found Mousterian industries resembling the 'typical Mousterian' of south-west France, with retouched points and scrapers of various kinds. The Levallois element is even more significant in Cyrenaica in the cave of Haua Fteah and at other sites, where it is known as *Levallois-Mousterian* and is characterized by many thin-sectioned tools on Levallois flakes. It began more than 45,000 years ago and ended *c.* 38,000 years ago, and its age and attributes link it with the equivalent tradition in Palestine. Similarly, the association is with Neanderthal stock. The only evidence from North Africa as to the stone-tool tradition that directly preceded the Levallois-Mousterian also comes from the Haua Fteah Cave. The only other sites where it is known are on the coast in Palestine and in a cave in Syria – which last makes it unlikely that it was developed for the exploitation of marine resources, for which also some of the earliest evidence in the world comes from Haua Fteah. Surprisingly, this is a blade industry,[1] termed 'Libyan Pre-Aurignacian', which thus anticipates the Upper Palaeolithic blade tradition, though separated from it by the Levallois-Mousterian and a time difference of 30,000 years (fig. 8).

Experimental innovation and/or adaptive patterning may lie behind this early blade tradition and it appears to be a phenomenon associated with the south-eastern Mediterranean.

It is in North-West Africa that the first clear evidence for the hafting of stone tools is found. This is the development of the tang. Tanged flakes retouched into points, scrapers and various other forms of tool are recognized as belonging to the Aterian tradition and are characteristic of artefact assemblages in the Maghrib and almost the whole of the Sahara north of the 16° parallel, including the oases of the Western Desert but not the Nile itself. In the Sahara also, bifacial lanceolate forms are often a feature of this tradition. Apart from the tanged forms, the Aterian resembles the Mousterian and it was at one time thought to have evolved from it. Recently, however, dating of the Aterian has shown it to be of an age generally similar to the Mousterian, though it probably lasted longer, so that it must now be regarded as a regional form of Middle Palaeolithic rather than as a North African equivalent of the Upper Palaeolithic, and the presence or absence of tanged forms may have been determined by local needs and traditional usage (fig. 8).[2]

[1] Blade technology employs cores with a parallel, sometimes convergent scar pattern on the release face(s), and they may have one or more striking platforms. Blades can be struck either by direct percussion or by using a punch. This technique makes maximum use of the raw material. See fig. 4 D, and also C. B. M. McBurney, *The Haua Fteah (Cyrenaica) and the Stone Age of the south-east Mediterranean* (Cambridge, 1967), 75–104.

[2] C. R. Ferring, 'The Aterian in North African prehistory', in Wendorf and Marks, eds., *Problems in prehistory*, 113–26.

The Aterian has been described as a desert-oriented tradition and it is particularly common on the Saharan side of the Atlas in the Maghrib and in the desert itself. The home bases were often centred on caves, springs and shallow lakes. The people appear to have been competent hunters of larger antelopes and equids, and some sites (e.g. the caves of Dar es Soltan and Taforalt) were regularly made use of over a lengthy period of time, while others, such as Hajj Creiem near Derna, were hunting camps only.

The Middle Palaeolithic in North Africa and the Sudan seems to have ended about the time of the onset of the main Würm Glaciation (*c.* 30,000 years ago), for there is a stratigraphic and temporal hiatus between the Aterian and the succeeding epi-Palaeolithic blade industry in the Maghrib. At sites in the Sahara, there is clearer evidence for desertification between more than 22,000 and 12,000 years ago, and it has been suggested that the onset of the main Würm Glaciation and the desiccation may have caused large areas of North-West Africa and the Sahara to become depopulated.[1]

In the Nile Valley the evolved Acheulian was replaced by local Mousterian industries with a variable Levallois element and, in particular, many tools with denticulate retouch; it begins to look as if denticulation in North Africa is in some way related to an arid environment.

In the Upper Nile also there is evidence for some kind of hiatus after the Mousterian, but no such gap is seen in Ethiopia, where abundant obsidian sources were used to produce a Middle Stone Age tradition that made use of the Levallois method for flakes and blades to trim into points, scrapers and other forms. Two K/Ar dates from a site in the Galla Lakes area suggest a very considerable antiquity (*c.* 180,000 years ago) for the earlier part of the Ethiopian Middle Stone Age, though additional results from other localities are needed to confirm this.[2] Little is known of the pattern in the northern savanna region, but characteristic Middle Stone Age assemblages have been found in Nigeria (the Jos Plateau), East Africa and the Horn, where they are largely still undated and evolutionary development remains to be stratigraphically demonstrated.

[1] For detailed summary of the Saharan evidence for climatic fluctuations see M. Servant, 'Séquences continentales et variations climatiques: évolution du bassin du Tchad au Cénozoique supérieur', unpublished Ph.D. thesis (University of Paris, 1973). A general review of evidence for late Quaternary lake-level fluctuations throughout the continent is found in F. A. Street and A. T. Grove, 'Environmental and climatic implications of late Quaternary lake-level fluctuations in Africa', *Nature*, 1976, **261**, 385–90.

[2] F. Wendorf and others, 'Dates for the Middle Stone Age of East Africa', *Science*, 1974, **187**, 740–2.

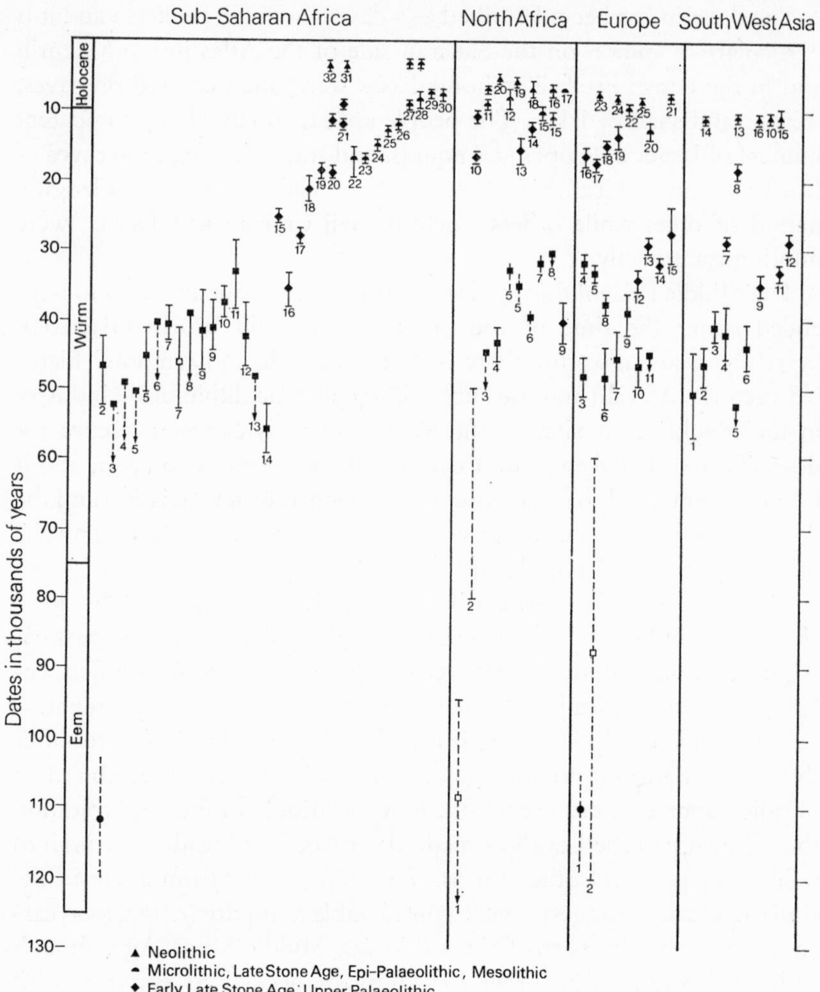

10 Radiometric dates for comparable later Quaternary techno-complexes in Africa and Eurasia.

Assemblages selected to show the first appearance and general time-range of each complex. The sites and dates selected are listed below.

Site lists, dates and Industrial Associations

A. Sub-Saharan Africa

Acheulian

1 Rooidam, Cape. 115,000±10,000 BP

'Middle Stone Age'

2 Hout Bay, Cape. 47,100, +2,800, −2,100 BP

3 Bushman's Rock Shelter, Transvaal. >53,000 BP (Pietersburg)

4 Florisbad, O.F.S. >48,900 BP (Hagenstad)
5 Montagu Cave, Cape. 45,900±2,100; >50,800 BP (Howieson's Poort)
6 Mufo, Angola. >40,000 BP (2 samples) (Lupemban)
7 Kalambo Falls, Zambia. 46,100, +3,500, −2,400 (Lupemban)
8 Klassies River Mouth, Cape. >38,000 (?Mossel Bay)
9 Red Cliff, Rhodesia. 41,800±3,000; 40,780±1,800 (Bambata)
10 Zombepata, Rhodesia. 37,290±1,140 (Bambata)
11 Witkrans, Cape. 33,150±2,500 (?Pietersburg)
12 Pomongwe, Rhodesia. 42,200±2,300 (Bambata)
13 Border Cave, Ingwavuma, Natal. >48,250 (Pietersburg)
14 Ndutu Beds, Olduvai Gorge, Tanzania. 56,000±3,500

Early 'Later Stone Age'

15 Heuningsneskrans Shelter, Natal. 24,640±300
16 Border Cave, Ingwavuma, Natal. 35,700±1,100
17 Rose Cottage Cave, Ladybrand, O.F.S. 29,430±520 ('Pre-Wilton')
18 Leopard's Hill Cave, Zambia. 21,550±950 ('Proto-Later Stone Age')
19 Sahonghong, Lesotho. 20,900±270 ('Howieson's Poort')
20 Nelson Bay Cave, Cape. 18,660±110 (Robberg Ind.)
21 Nelson Bay Cave, Cape. 11,950±150 (Albany Ind.)

Late Stone Age (microlithic)

22 Naisiusiu Beds, Olduvai Gorge, Tanzania. 17,550±1,000 ('Kenya Capsian')
23 Leopard's Hill Cave, Zambia. 16,715±95 (Nachikufu I)
24 Zombepata Cave, Rhodesia. 15,120±170 ('Wilton')
25 Kamasongolwa, Zambia. 13,300±250 ('Wilton')
26 Lake Nakuru, Kenya; transgressive phase to ~60m. 12,140±206 (Blade Ind.)
27 Nelson Bay Cave, Cape. 9,080±180; 2,660±150 (Wilton)
28 Wilton Rock Shelter, Cape. 8,260±720 (Wilton)
29 Melkhoutboom, Cape. 7,300±80 (Wilton)
30 Matjes River Rock Shelter, Cape. 7,750±300 (Wilton)

Neolithic

31 Kintampo (K6), Ghana. 3,400±74
32 Narosura, Kenya. 2,760±115

All the above are radiocarbon dates except (14), which is an amino-acid racemisation age (Bada & Protsch, 1973).

B. North Africa and the Sahara

Acheulian and 'Pre-Mousterian'

1 Harounian beach, Casablanca, Morocco. ~145,000–~125,000 (Moroccan Acheulian, Stage 8)
2 Haua Fteah, Cyrenaica. ~80,000–~50,000 (extrapolation dates) '(Pre-Aurignacian')

Middle Palaeolithic (Mousterian/Aterian)

3 Bir Sahara, Egypt. >44,680 (Aterian)
4 Haua Fteah, Cyrenaica, Libya. 43,400±1,300 (Levalloiso-Mousterian)
5 Taforalt, Morocco. ±34,550
±32,350 (Mousterian/Aterian)
6 Bou Hadid, Algeria. ±39,900 (Aterian)
7 Berard, Algeria. ±31,800 (Aterian)
8 Dar-es-Soltan, Morocco. >30,000 (Aterian)

Upper Palaeolithic: epi-Palaeolithic

9 Hagfet ed Dabba, Cyrenaica, Libya. 40,500±1,600 (Dabban)
10 Haua Fteah, Cyrenaica, Libya. 16,070±100; 10,600±300 (Eastern Oranian)
11 Haua Fteah, Cyrenaica, Libya. 8,400±150; 7,000±110 (Libyco-Capsian)
12 El Mekta, Tunisia. 8,400±400 (Capsian)
13 Gebel Silsila, Egypt. 15,200±700; 16,000±800 (Sebekian)
14 Wadi Halfa, Sudan. 14,000±280 (Ballanan)
15 Taforalt, Morocco. 12,070±400; 10,800±400 (Ibero-Maurusian)
16 Khanguet el Mouhaad, Tunisia. 7,200±120 (Upper Capsian)
17 Columnata, Algeria. 7,750±300 (Capsian)

Neolithic

18 Khanguet Si Mohamed Tahar. 7,800±250; 5,400±140
19 Haua Fteah (VI), Cyrenaica. 6,810±97
20 Fayum A, Egypt. 6,391±180

All the above are radiocarbon dates except no. (1), which is an Th^{230}/U^{234} age.

C. *Europe*

Acheulian

1 Grotte du Lazaret, France. 110,000±10,000

Middle Palaeolithic

2 Weimer-Ehringsdorf, Germany. 60,000–120,000 (Mousterian)
3 Gorham's Cave, Gibraltar. 47,700±1,500 (Mousterian)
4 Calombo Cave, Italy. 32,000±680 (Mousterian)
5 Velika Pécina, Yugoslavia. 33,850±520 (Mousterian)
6 Grotte aux Ours, France. 48,300±230 (Mousterian)
7 Regourdoux, France. 45,500±1,800 (Mousterian)
8 Les Cottes, France. 37,600±700 (Mousterian/Lower Perigordian)
9 Combe Grenal, France. 39,000±1,500 (Mousterian)
10 Broion Cave, Italy. 46,400±1,500 (Mousterian)
11 Moldova, Ukraine, USSR. >44,000 (Mousterian)

Upper Palaeolithic

12 Abri Pataud, France. 33,300±760; 34,250±675 (Basal Aurignacian)
13 Abri Pataud, France. 29,300±450; 32,800±450 (Aurignacian)
14 Willendorf, Austria. 32,060±250 (Aurignacian)
15 Abri Facteur, Dordogne, France. 27,890±2,000 (Aurignacian)
16 Puits de l'Homme, Lascaux Cave, France. 16,100±500 (?Magdelenian)
17 Arka, Hungary. 17,050±350 (Eastern Gravettian)
18 Angles sur l'Anglin, France. 14,160±80 (Magdelenian)
19 Cueva Reclau, Spain. 13,200±600 (Solutrean)

Mesolithic

20 Grotte di Ortucchio, Italy. 12,619±410
21 Shippea Hill. 7,610±150 (Tardenoisian)
22 Starr Carr. 9,557±210 (Maglemosian)

Neolithic

23 Nea Nicomediea, Greece. 7,780±270; 7,280±112
24 Franchthi Cave, Greece. 7,794±140
25 Knossos, Crete. 8,050±180

All the above are radiocarbon dates except (1), dated by Th^{230}/U^{234}, and (2), dated by $Th^{230}/U.$ and Pa^{231}

D. South-West Asia
Middle Palaeolithic
1 Shanidar Cave, Iraq. 50,600±3,000 (Mousterian)
2 Shanidar Cave, Iraq. 46,900±1,500 (Mousterian)
3 Tabun Cave, Mt. Carmel, Israel. 40,900±1,000 (Mousterian)
4 Geulah Cave, Mt. Carmel, Israel. 42,000±1,700 (Mousterian)
5 Ras el Kelb, Lebanon. >52,000 (Mousterian)
6 Ksar Akil, Lebanon. 43,750±1,500 (Mousterian)
Upper Palaeolithic
7 Ksar Akil, Lebanon. 28,840±380 (Aurignacian)
8 Ein Ager, Negev. 17,510±290 (Final Upper Palaeolithic)
9 Rasaket. ±34,600 (Aurignacian)
11 Shanidar, Iraq. 33,300±1,000 (Baradostian)
12 Shanidar, Iraq. 28,700±700 (Zarzian)
Mesolithic/early Neolithic
10 Zawi Chenu, Shanidar, Iraq. 10,800±300 (Pre-Pottery Neolithic)
13 Shanidar, Iraq. 10,600±300 (Mesolithic)
14 Jericho, Israel. 11,116±107 (Natufian)
15 Jericho, Israel. 10,300±500 (Pre-Pottery Neolithic)
16 Ganj-i-Darch, Iran. 10,400±150 (early Neolithic)

In the southern savanna lands there is a repetition of the pattern of light- rather than heavy-duty equipment, and two main techno-complexes are recognized (fig. 9).[1] One, sometimes called the 'Pietersburg Complex', with three geographically distributed industries, is found on the south coast and interior plateau mainly south of the Limpopo and makes varying use of the Levallois, disc core and blade core techniques, the products of which were used generally with a minimum of secondary retouch. It is believed to date to more than 40,000 BP and probably belongs mostly within the Last Interglacial, *c.* 100,000–75,000 years ago.

The second techno-complex – the 'Bambata Complex' – is differentiated from the first by the amount of retouch present on the tools. It is confined more to the northern parts of the interior plateau from the Zambezi to the Orange river and Natal, and four regionally distributed industries are recognized. While its earliest stages may be contemporary with the Pietersburg Complex, the later stages appear to be as recent as 30,000 years ago and so would overlap in time with the early Upper Palaeolithic in Eurasia.

Another complex or tradition which combines the prepared and blade core techniques is known from a number of scattered sites from East Africa to the Cape and in Equatoria, where geographical identification is even more pronounced. The prepared core products show

[1] See Sampson, *Stone Age archaeology*, 151–257.

marked refinement and the small punched blade element, from which various backed and otherwise trimmed tools are made, is evidence of the introduction of the 'composite tool' made from more than one element – wood, mastic, sinew, bone etc. – in which the stone components, which usually formed the working parts, could be greatly reduced in size and weight. This meant that the finest cryptocrystalline material (agates, jaspers, chalcedonies etc.), which often occur only as small inclusions or pebbles, could now be brought into use. Together with this small blade element – precursor of the Later Stone Age – are two new forms in the equatorial forests: the tanged point and the trapeze or *tranchet*.

The dates associated with the assemblages composing this industrial unit (formerly defined as being of 'Magosian' or Howieson's Poort type) range from more than 50,000 to *c.* 9,000 years ago, though more precise study will undoubtedly cause these dates and so the range to be revised. Younger ages – between *c.* 30,000 and *c.* 13,000 – have been obtained for some assemblages, particularly in Rhodesia, which indicate contemporaneity with, for instance, the Upper Palaeolithic in Cyrenaica. However, there is at least one site (Montagu Cave at the Cape) with a date of more than 50,000 years, and several more which suggest some overlap, perhaps appreciable, between this 'evolved' tradition and the other two Middle Stone Age complexes. This 'overlap' could be interpreted in several possible ways but, on the existing incomplete and inconsistent evidence, the Middle Stone Age of sub-Saharan Africa can best perhaps be seen as a technological continuum beginning with flake and blade forms that were minimally retouched, but supplemented by other and later traditions in which retouched tools predominate and the production of small blade forms becomes important. These overlapping traditions or complexes of the savanna, like the more specialized Lupemban and derived forms in the Congo basin, are of course the surviving parts of the equipment with which geographically adapted populations selectively exploited the resources of their environment up to the limits of their technological capability. Some temporal changes are stratigraphically demonstrated within the complexes. But the way in which they interacted cuts across ecological zones, and may be related to climatically induced changes in the resource base and the need to make compensating technological adjustments, as well as to the spread of more efficient extractive processes and the technology associated with them.

In the deciduous woodlands and forest-savanna mosaic of central and western Africa, the Middle Stone Age takes on a more specifically regional appearance with an emphasis on heavier equipment, though the small, lighter tools are still present (fig. 11). The earliest are *c.* 50,000 years old and the characteristic forms are heavy-duty picks, bifacial core-axes and core-scrapers, first described as forming an archaeological entity known as the Sangoan. This kind of tool-kit can perhaps best be regarded as one that will be manifest wherever and whenever heavy-duty equipment is needed, though the end-products in each particular time period will be characteristic of that time. For example, the earlier Karari Industry from Lake Rudolf might perhaps be explained in this way, as also can the later 'axe' forms with the Neolithic in Equatoria and West Africa.

These crude Sangoan forms, best thought of as special-activity tools associated with working wood, give way to more evolved, shapely forms in the Congo basin (Lupemban Industrial Complex) with working ends suggesting use for cutting, adzing and gouging. With these there occur long, finely made lanceolate points worked bifacially, which are some of the finest examples of the skill of the Palaeolithic craftsman in the Old World.[1] They may have served as matchets and/or the blades of stabbing spears, just as do the metal blades of the forest Negroes and Pygmies today. Unfortunately, practically no faunal remains have been found with any of the archaeological sites in the equatorial forest, so that we have little precise information on the economic base of this industrial complex.

In the West African forest zone, although the situation is less well known, there would appear to be an increase in the number of sites, and occupation was continuous from this time onwards. 'Sangoan' forms of heavy-duty implements are recognized in both Nigeria and Ghana, though with less standardization of tool-types. Pollen evidence from north-eastern Angola and Katanga shows, however, that the climate during the time this Lupemban Industrial Complex was in vogue was cooler by about 6°C, and also drier than today, with little evidence of the humid rain-forest. Extrapolating from ethnographic evidence and faunal distributions, it appears likely that these populations exploited several micro-environments – gallery forest along the rivers, deciduous woodland on the slopes, and grassland on the tops of the interfluves. It is suggested that the groups may have concentrated on hunting the large numbers of elephant and hippopotamus in the Congo system,

[1] J. D. Clark, *Prehistoric cultures of north-east Angola and their significance in tropical Africa*, 2 vols. (Lisbon, Companhia de Diamantes de Angola, 1963).

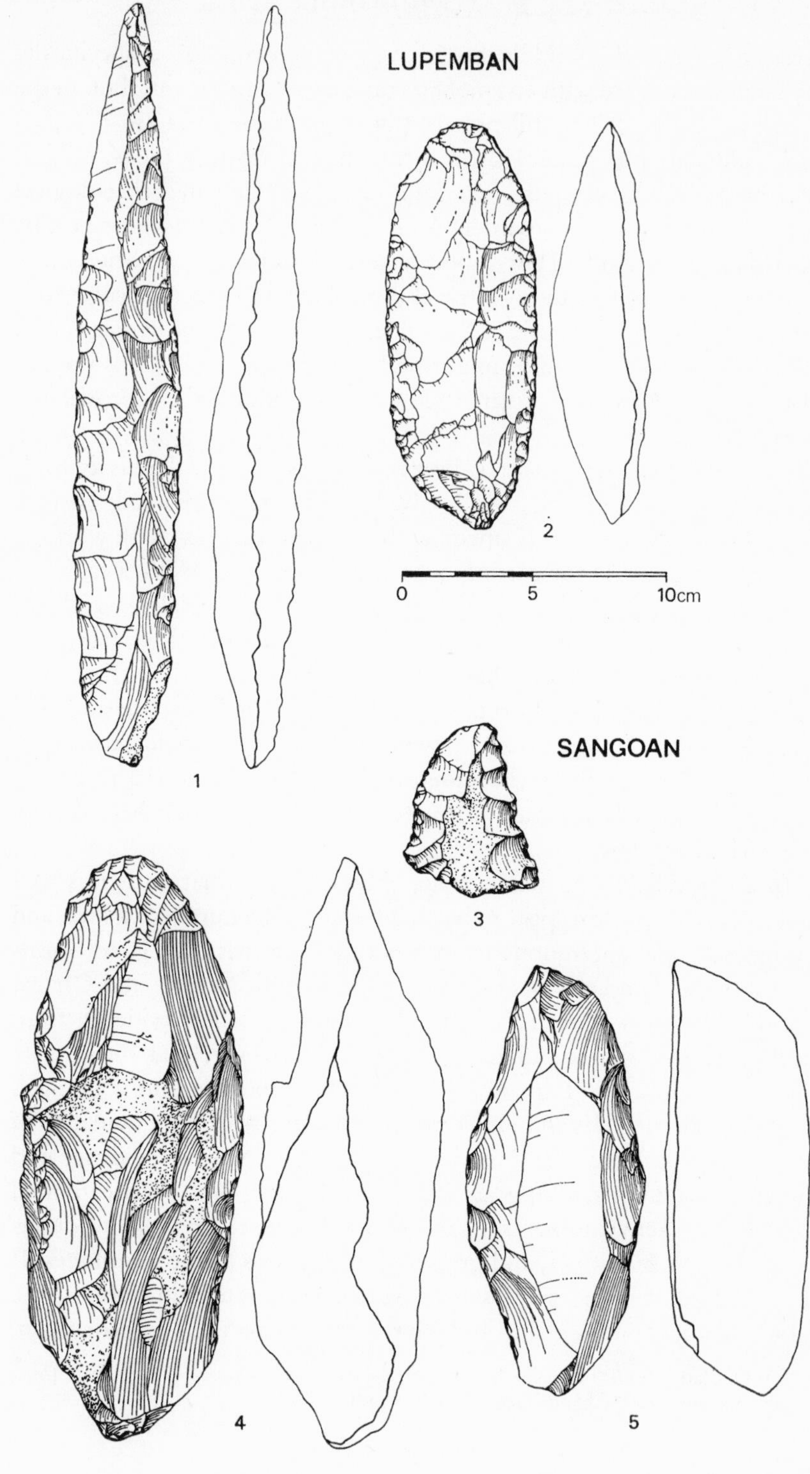
LUPEMBAN
1
2
0
5
10cm
SANGOAN
3
4
5

using traps and the other methods described by ethnographers and the classical authors.

Adequate knowledge of the economy of the Middle Stone Age depends on studies of site location and faunal content of which, as yet, there are very few. It is, however, probable that in Equatoria, as has been suggested, the very large animals were preferred for hunting, and that in the grasslands the grazing antelopes were the predominant forms, while the range of environments in between would have induced different kinds of choice and adjustment. One important difference between the Lower and Middle Palaeolithic, however, is the regular use, or reuse, of one site over a much longer period of time, as is manifested in the thickness of accumulated occupation sediments in caves. This suggests that, instead of a group's moving from one temporary camp to another in the course of the seasonal round through its territory, it was now able to make use of one or two more permanent camps, occupied over a longer period of the year by reason of the more intensive pattern of resource use and the improved technology. From these base camps several micro-environments within a range of *c.* 10 km radius could be exploited and, at another time, temporary camps, e.g. for hunting, would be set up for the recovery of more distant and specifically seasonal resources. The multiplicity of activities at the base camp can be seen in the wide range of artefacts present, those on the special-purpose camps being much more limited. For example, the hunting camp at Porc Epic Cave, Dire Dawa, has a preponderance of unifacial points and knives but not many other kinds of tool.[1] Flake knives and scrapers (for working skins) predominate at the Mousterian butchery site of Hajj Creiem, where the animals brought back reflect the several micro-habitats exploited – coastal plain (zebra [3–4] and

[1] J. D. Clark, M. A. J. Williams and K. R. Williamson, *Further excavations (1974) in the Porc Epic Cave, Dire Dawa, Ethiopia* (forthcoming).

---

11 (*opposite*) Tools of the earlier (Sangoan facies) and later stages of the Lupemban Industrial Complex from the Congo and Zambezi basins.

Upper Lupemban, from Kalina Point, Zaïre

1 Lanceolate point
2 Core-axe

Lower Lupemban, from Livingstone, Zambia

3 Denticulate scraper
4 Sangoan core-axe
5 Pick

(Nos. 1–2 after Clark, *Prehistory of Africa*, fig. 39; 3–5 after Clark, *The Stone Age cultures of Northern Rhodesia*, 1950, pl. 12, nos. 2, 8, and pl. 14, no. 12.)

gazelle [1]), forested slopes (buffalo [2–3]) and rocky slopes (Barbary sheep [5–10]). These animals would have provided between 2,800–4,075 kg of useable meat.[1] Here an estimate of the camp area of 190 m^2 suggests, on analogy with San (Bushman) space requirements, that there may have been thirteen individuals in the group. Again from the small cave of Witkrans in the escarpment overlooking the Harts valley in the northern Cape, hunters were able to exploit the permanent population of antelopes occupying the thicket bush local to the site, or to take their toll of the gregarious animals migrating seasonally between the valley and the eastern Kalahari. At these temporary camps bones were sometimes piled; there is evidence for this even in Acheulian times from the Munro site in the Transvaal. At Kalkbank in the northern Transvaal, the bones of thirty-eight bushveld animals representing thirteen different specimens were stacked. In the spring deposits at El Guettar, a pile of stone spheroids was found with the Mousterian, and a similar concentration was recovered with Middle Stone Age artefacts from another spring deposit at Windhoek. While the significance of such piles is unknown, it is more likely to have been utilitarian than magical in purpose, as has been suggested for El Guettar. Other features are the regular occurrence of well-delineated hearths of ash and charcoal at several sites. On the Orange river in the van der Kloof dam area, seven arcs and semicircles of stones represent the footings of single-family windbreaks on a camp site of the Orangia Industry of the Pietersburg Complex, and another site, Zeekoegat 27, gives evidence of a larger but somewhat later semi-circular structure, delineated by stones, such as could have been used to keep a thorn fence in position, for occupation by a number of individuals engaged in some group activity.

Middle Palaeolithic/Middle Stone Age living-site components and artefact assemblages suggest that social cohesion and organization was now sufficiently well developed for the populations to be able to become more ecologically selective and adapted. There is also evidence for concern with conceptual expression and symbolism, especially in regard to the utilitarian and ritual uses of pigment found in the form of

[1] See C. B. M. McBurney and R. W. Hey, *Prehistory and Pleistocene geology in Cyrenaican Libya* (Cambridge, 1955), 141–56. Estimates of meat weights were calculated by using the F.A.O. *Food composition table for use in Africa* (Maryland and Rome, 1968). See also K. V. Flannery, 'Origins and ecological effects of early domestication in Iran and the Near East', in P. J. Ucko and G. W. Dimbleby, eds., *The domestication and exploitation of plants and animals* (London, 1969), 50–79, and T. White, 'A method of calculating the dietary percentage of various food animals butchered by aboriginal peoples', *American Antiquity*, 1953, 18, 396–8.

crayons and the intentional burial of the dead in sites such as Mumbwa Caves, Fishhoek Cave, the Border Cave and Nswatugi, which reflect the more complete evidence from Eurasia at this time. The characteristics of self-awareness and geographical identity are, therefore, now discernible, albeit in embryonic form, though they may have been sufficient to have brought some groups into conflict with others, especially in times of scarce resources or other stress. Besides wooden spears and stone-headed projectile weapons, the equipment of the hunter included throwing-sticks and clubs with wooden and perhaps stone heads, the latter enclosed in sleeves of greenhide. Such weapons could, on occasion, be turned to account in inter-group feuding, as the depressed fractures and holes in some of the fossil crania suggest, though never on the scale that appears after domestication.

Study of the faunal assemblages associated with the Middle Stone Age industries at two caves in the southern Cape (Die Kelders Cave 1 and Klassies River Mouth Cave 1) provides important evidence of selective hunting preferences as determined in part by environmental differences. The abundance of muskrats and hares at Die Kelders, with a minimal number of foot bones, suggest that these animals were hunted for their pelts as well as for food;[1] while medium to large antelopes are the commonest forms at Klassies River. There are, however, indications that the Middle Stone Age populations were not such efficient hunters as were those of the Later Stone Age. The number of large and dangerous game is not so great – the eland, a relatively docile animal, is the predominant large mammal at both sites, while pigs are considerably under-represented. On the other hand there are the remains of the giant buffalo – presumably dangerous – but these consist of a preponderance of very young, with some fully adult, animals, thus suggesting that the hunters may have concentrated on females in advanced pregnancy or giving birth, and so perhaps contributed to the extinction of this species. The Klassies River evidence is the best and oldest anywhere in the world for the regular exploitation of coastal resources; besides abundant shellfish are found remains of seals and penguins, but remains of fish and flying birds are almost completely absent. The same is also the case at Die Kelders, contrasting markedly with the Later Stone Age, and suggesting that the Middle Stone Age

[1] R. G. Klein, 'Ecology of Stone Age man at the southern tip of Africa', *Archaeology*, 1975, **28**, 238–47. Since foot bones are generally removed with the pelts of animals that were used for clothing, blankets and containers, a significant reduction in the number of these bones in relation to the other body parts of the species hunted and killed for these purposes may be expected in the food assemblages at the base camps.

population did not yet possess the technology for efficient fishing and fowling.

UPPER PALAEOLITHIC AND EPI-PALAEOLITHIC TRADITIONS IN NORTHERN AFRICA AND LATER STONE AGE COMPLEXES SOUTH OF THE SAHARA

It is significant that clear evidence of a stratigraphic break of long duration (e.g. between *c.* 10,000 and more than 25,500 years at three sites in the Cape winter rainfall area) between the Middle Stone Age and later occupation levels is evidenced from a number of excavated sites in Africa (fig. 12). In North Africa, in only a few instances do we have knowledge of the industrial stages immediately succeeding the Middle Palaeolithic/Middle Stone Age. One such site is Haua Fteah Cave in Cyrenaica, where an Upper Palaeolithic blade industry (the Dabban; fig. 13) makes its appearance at *c.* 38,000 BC and is found stratigraphically overlying the Levallois-Mousterian. This industry lasted for some 25,000 years but is known as yet from only one other Cyrenaican site. This limited distribution is surprising if, as used to be thought, Upper Palaeolithic technology, the product of modern man, was so much in advance of any other.

Only in the Nile Valley, mostly north of Aswan, is there evidence for blade assemblages of anywhere near comparable antiquity (e.g. from Dishna, with a probable age of 20,000 years and combining Middle and Upper Palaeolithic technology). Although these show no close comparison with the Cyrenaican industry, they do suggest that they may both have been the outcome of infiltration along the Mediterranean littoral and up the Nile of small groups coming from south-west Asia and practising an Upper Palaeolithic blade technology. However, for the most part the earlier blade industries of Upper Egypt date to between *c.* 16,000 and 15,000 BP, and both macrolithic (Idfuan) and fully microlithic (Fakurian) forms are found. The combination in the early stages of prepared core and blade components is reminiscent of the Middle Stone Age Howieson's Poort and comparable assemblages from southern Africa, and the dating overlaps. In Nubia, the continuation of the Middle Stone Age prepared core tradition is attested after *c.* 34,000 BC by local facies using ferruginised sandstone (Khormusan) and Nile pebbles of chert (Halfan). By *c.* 15,000 BC the artefacts had become diminutive, and a significant blade element is present and replaces the specialized forms of minute Levallois flakes and cores (Halfan).

12 Upper Palaeolithic, epi-Palaeolithic, Later Stone Age and Neolithic (with domestication) sites referred to in the text.

Between 16,000 and 10,000 BC there is evidence for much local variation in the forms of the stone industries in Nubia and Upper Egypt. These variations and the differences in the size of the assemblages and the food waste show that a range of seasonal activities was being pursued. Many sites, both large and small, show a preponderance of large mammal remains, in particular wild cattle, hartebeeste and hippopotamus.

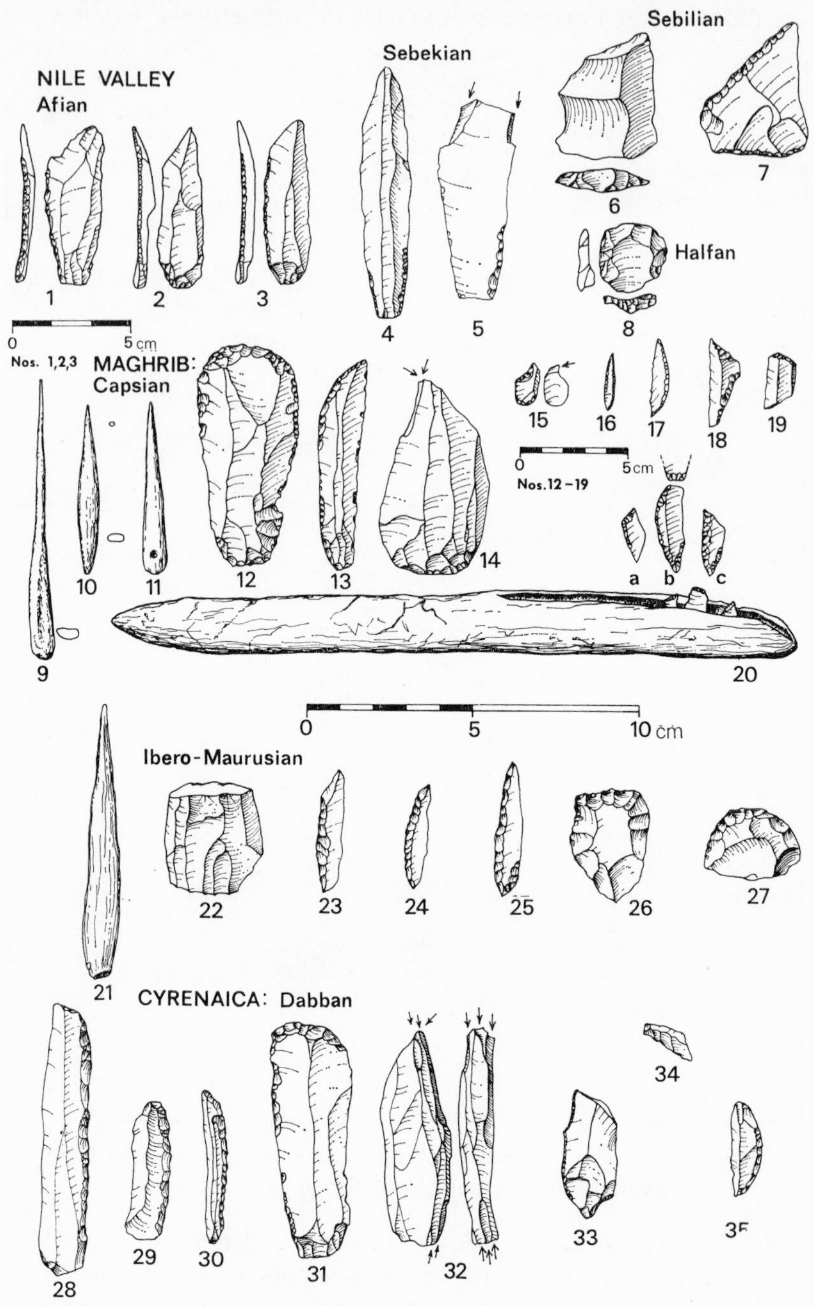

13 Tools from Upper Palaeolithic and epi-Palaeolithic sites from North Africa. (*For explanation, see opposite.*)

Others again show much fish bone, and at such sites fireplaces with a quantity of burned rock may be evidence of smoking fish; fresh-water oysters were also collected. At one site dating to *c.* 13,000 BC, the fauna shows evidence of possible year-round occupation where the group made use of large mammals, the fish and molluscs of the Nile, and of wild-fowl. In addition, at this and other sites (Qadan and Afian in particular) numerous examples of grinding equipment are present, showing that wild grasses were now an important and regular part of the seasonal diet, and sickle gloss is found on a proportion of the

---

Nile Valley
1–3 Upper Palaeolithic tools of the Afian Industry from Esna; marginally retouched and backed flake and bladelets
4, 5 Proximally retouched blade and burin of the Sebekian Industry from Jebel Silsileh
6, 7 Flake with basal retouch and tranchet of the Sebilian Industry from Kom Ombo
8 Diminutive Levallois flake of the Halfan Industry from Wadi Halfa
Maghrib
Tools of the Capsian Industrial Complex
9–11 Bone awl, point and needle
12 End-scraper
13 Backed blade
14 Burin
15 Micro-burin
16–19 Various forms of microlith
20 Slotted bone 'sickle' handle and (a–c) microlithic insets
Tools of the Ibero-Maurusian Industrial Complex
21 Bone point
22 Opposed platform core for micro-blades
23–5 Microliths
26–7 Short end- and convex scrapers
Cyrenaica
Tools of the Upper Palaeolithic Dabban Industry from Haua Fteah
28–30 Backed blades and bladelets
31 End-scraper
32 Double-ended burin
33 Chamfered blade
34 Resharpening spall from chamfered blade
35 Lunate

(Nos. 1–3 after drawings by L. Addington in F. Wendorf and R. Schild, 'The Palaeolithic of the Lower Nile Valley', in Wendorf and Marks, *Problems in prehistory*, p. 152; remainder after Clark, *Prehistory of Africa*, pp. 127–8, 156, 159, 161, 170.)

bladelets. By 10,000 BC, therefore, there is mounting evidence for a broadened resource base and considerable variability in locality, camp size, equipment and the resources being exploited, these now including those of the rivers and lakes as well as of the grassland, desert and gallery forest. Furthermore, the frequency with which wild cattle are represented in the food waste, and the fact that they could well have been dangerous game to hunt by conventional methods, suggest that they may have been secured by heavy fall traps in which the trapeze was used as the cutting implement. There are now signs that populations were becoming more territory conscious; this is borne out by cemeteries in Nubia dating to ±12,000 BC, where a high proportion of the individuals – a robust form of modern man resembling the Mechta-Afalou race from the Maghrib – appear to have met a violent death.[1]

In Cyrenaica and the Maghrib the situation was similar, and after 14,000 BC is found an industry (the Ibero-Maurusian) with many backed forms, chisels and scrapers made on small blades. Variations of this tradition occur on the coast and on the plateau and lasted until *c.* 6000 BC. Grinding equipment is rare, but simple bone tools (projectile points and awls) make their appearance and a variety of resources were exploited, mostly large mammals such as zebra and hartebeeste, small mammals, and, sporadically, at both coastal and inland sites, fish and shellfish. Giant deer are also present in the bone refuse and may have been brought to the point of extinction by these populations, much as was the giant buffalo in southern Africa (fig. 13).[2]

Habitation sites were often on sandy ground with the floors of the dwellings a little below ground level and thickly strewn with artefacts and charcoal. Floor areas were about 6 m², and the houses may have been made of reeds. These hunting and collecting groups must have have been well organized and semi-sedentary, with a permanent base camp, or camps, and smaller, temporary camps from which more peripheral or special resources were seasonally exploited. Moreover, the pathology of some of the skeletal remains indicates that the group cared for its physically handicapped members. The number of small rodent remains on the sites suggests that they were hunted for their skins – for clothing or utensils; pendants and beads are found, of

[1] The main text for the Nubian section of the Nile is F. Wendorf, ed., *The prehistory of Nubia*, 2 vols. (Dallas, 1968), particularly Vol. II. See also the review of the North African Upper Palaeolithic in A. E. Marks, 'The current status of Upper Palaeolithic studies from the Maghrib to the north-west Levant', in Wendorf and Marks, eds., *Problems in prehistory*, 439–58.

[2] See ch. 8 (by G. Camps) in Vol. I of this *History*.

mollusc shell and occasionally of bone or ostrich eggshell. Here also at this time large cemeteries are recorded in which more than a hundred individuals are buried, the physical type being described as a robustly built African race (Mechta-Afalou) of Cromagnon stock. Its origins are still a matter of conjecture but an autochthonous development from the North African Neanderthaloid stock cannot be ruled out and, for this author, has the most to commend it; the recently discovered remains in Aterien contexts are now said to exhibit characteristics of the Mechta-Afalou race.[1] It is also possible that the Ibero-Maurusian is similarly an autochthonous cultural development following stimulus diffusion from the east.

Around 6500 BC a new technology and tool-kit appear in southern Tunisia and eastern Algeria, spreading later westwards along the eastern part of the Atlas and northwards to the Tunisian coast. This is the Capsian, represented by two, in part contemporary, facies (*Capsien typique* and *Capsien supérieur*), making use of large blades that were either retouched into scrapers, backed blades or burins (chisels), or else first broken down by the micro-burin technique into smaller sections from which geometric microliths were made to be mounted in seriation in mastic as knife blades, or hafted as the cutting parts and barbs of projectile weapons, spears or arrows. The bow and arrow may well have been an African invention in view of the Aterian tang, and sixteenth-millennium BC dates for fully microlithic industries from Central Africa suggest that it was most probably present in the continent before the close of the Pleistocene (figs. 4E, 13).

The Capsian lasted some 3,000 years, until *c.* 4300 BC, and several regional and developmental facies are recognized. It is associated with skeletal remains that are more slender than the robust Mechta-Afalou populations and are described as proto-Mediterranean, though the former race still continued in the north and east. This raises the question of Capsian origins and, so far, either North-East or East Africa appears to have the best claim. The closest typological resemblances are probably with those industries using obsidian in the East African Rift system and named the 'Kenya Capsian Complex'. Recent research has shown this blade tradition to be more than 14,000 years old in the Ethiopian Rift, with beginnings going back appreciably further, perhaps as much as 20,000 years, and an ultimate derivation in the local Middle Stone Age.

[1] (a) D. Ferenbach, 'Les restes humains de la Grotte de Dar-es-Soltane 2 (Maroc), Campagne 1975', *Bull. et Mem. de la Soc. d'Anthrop. de Paris,* 1976, **3**, Series XIII, 183–93. (b) D. Ferembach, 'Les restes humains atériens de Temara (Campagne 1975)', *Bull. et Mem. de la Soc. d'Anthrop. de Paris*, **3**, Series XIII, 1976, 175–80.

The distribution of the Capsian in the Maghrib is focused on the eastern plateau, while the earlier Ibero-Maurusian is mainly a coastal phenomenon. It could thus be a demonstration of some general population movement from the coast up to the plateau *c.* 7000 BC, as the coastal plain became more restricted following the return of the sea to its present position from the low levels that persisted during much of the Last Glaciation. The later facies of the Ibero-Maurusian (e.g. the Columnatan) would thus represent the tool-kits of the period of re-adjustment. Technological differences might in part be due to different raw materials in the two areas, and changes in the physical stock could have resulted from differences in nutrition following the use of new food sources made possible by new techniques and exploitive behaviour.[1]

In particular the Capsian is associated with shell-mounds (*Helix* being the commonest mollusc). These are sometimes extensive (7,000 m^2 and up to 5 m deep) and reoccupied – most likely seasonally – over many centuries by small rather than large groups. Capsian sites are situated generally, though not always, by water or on a hill, in country that was wooded with Mediterranean species at higher elevations, covered by grassland or drier steppe to the south. Besides collecting the *Helix*, which was probably cooked in water in baskets or skin containers, heated by dropping in hot stones, the people spent much time in hunting, and the remains of wildebeeste, wild cattle and, particularly, giant buffalo, small horses (comparable to the quagga) and Barbary sheep are found in quantity at their sites. Grinding equipment testifies to the importance of various wild plant foods and grasses such as *Panicum* and barley, which were collected with 'sickles' having microlithic teeth set obliquely in a slotted bone handle (fig. 13).

The Capsian also has a well-developed bone industry and art, and it is clearly the beginning of the artistic tradition in North-West Africa. Ritual and symbolism are also seen in the burial of the dead and the so-called 'trophy skulls' and other modified human bones. Besides the frequent use of red ochre, small anthropomorphic and zoomorphic sculptures occur, and much use was made of ostrich eggshells, often engraved, as containers for liquids or broken up for making into beads.

The late Palaeolithic and epi-Palaeolithic populations of North Africa and the Nile Valley during the close of the Pleistocene and the early Holocene were, thus, still living by an essentially hunting and collecting economy, with, however, a broader base and a greater

[1] See ch. 5 (by P. E. L. Smith) in Vol. 1 of this *History*.

dependence than previously on the regular use of a few selected resources. Should one of these fail, the routine of life would not have been significantly disrupted, since its place could have been taken by the others. Although evidence of any kind of domestic animal or plant is absent, it is now quite likely that experimentation and selective manipulation of local resources over a large part of the continent had preconditioned some of these populations towards domestication.

From the Sahara the earliest epi-Palaeolithic assemblages of which we have record are similar and apparently date no earlier than the eighth millennium. They suggest a repopulation following the desiccation that drew to a close *c.* 12,000 years ago and was replaced by a comparatively well-watered habitat, highly favourable for both man and animals. Although the archaeological evidence still awaits interpretation, it seems probable that the repopulation of the central Sahara came from the north, since the affinities of the artefact assemblages are with the North African epi-Palaeolithic, and those of this period from the southern parts of the desert remain quite unknown. In the Western Desert, these epi-Palaeolithic sites are mostly small concentrations associated probably with portable dwelling structures and small lined hearth areas. Grindstones show the importance of collecting grain, which may also be in some way connected with the significant number of notched and denticulate tools in the stone industries. Repopulation must have been as rapid as the climatic amelioration, which caused lakes to begin to rise *c.* 10,000 BC, reaching the maximum high *c.* 6000 BC, by which time 'neolithic' traits are already present.

South of the Sahara, as in North Africa, a similar long hiatus is often present between the Middle and Later Stone Age deposits, and the traditions that followed immediately after the Middle Stone Age are inadequately known here also. The reason for this break remains unknown; in some parts the hiatus was partially filled by the 'intermediate complex' using evolved Levallois/disc and blade technologies, which in places (e.g. the upper Zambezi) may have lasted until the end of the Pleistocene. But it appears to have been more generally replaced, between 20,000 and 12,000 years ago, either by fully microlithic traditions or by macrolithic 'informal' industries making less use than previously of standardized types of tool. In any case, it is now apparent that small blade industries make their appearance in this part of the continent much earlier than was previously thought (fig. 14).[1]

[1] For general reviews of the Later Stone Age see Sampson, *Stone Age archaeology*, 258–435, and ch. 6 (by D. W. Phillipson) in Vol. 1 of this *History*.

14 Tools from various Later Stone Age Industries and Industrial Complexes from sub-Saharan Africa. (*For explanation, see opposite.*)

Some of the best-documented economic evidence comes from the south coast. Here, between 18,500 and 12,000 years ago, post-Middle Stone Age industries, characterized by small carinate scrapers or bladelet cores (Robberg Industry) were being made by a population exploiting grassland resources from a coastal plain then *c.* 80 km wide. They used practically no marine food sources and concentrated on hunting the gregarious grazing animals. This is the latest occurrence of the giant buffalo and hartebeeste in the southern Cape and it seems possible that man may have hastened their extinction.

The Robberg Industry is, as yet, known only in the southern Cape, but that which followed (known variously as Smithfield, 'Pre-Wilton', Albany Industry and Oakhurst Complex) is recorded from a number of sites from the central plateau to the southern escarpment and the winter rainfall belt south of the mountains. Apart from various scraper forms

---

Tshitolian Industrial Complex tools from Zaïre and Angola
1 Bifacial, tanged point
2 Bifacial, leaf-shaped point
3, 4 Trapeze
5 Core-axe
Nachikufan II Industry tools from the type-site, northern Zambia
6 Edge-ground axe
7 Strangulated scraper
8–10 Microlithic broad crescent, triangle and trapeze
11 Drill
Nachikufan I Industry tools from the type-site, northern Zambia
12–15 Retouched and backed micro-blades
16 Bored stone
17 Core scraper
Pomongwan Industry tools from the type-site, Rhodesia
18, 19 Large circular and end-scrapers
Matopan Industry tools from the Matopo Hills, Rhodesia
20–4 Microliths and bone point
Wilton Industrial Complex tools from the type-site, Cape Province, South Africa
25–8 Short end- and convex scrapers
29–33 Microliths
Lockshoek Industry tools from the Orange Free State, South Africa
34, 35 Side- and core scrapers
Oakhurst Industry tools from Cape Province, South Africa
36, 37 Side- and end-scrapers
(Nos. 1–17, 20–4 after Clark, *Prehistory of Africa*, figs. 54ff.; 18–19, 34–7 after C. G. Sampson, *The Stone Age archaeology of southern Africa*, 1974, figs. 99–101, 25–33 after J. Deacon, 1972.

it is characterized by few standardized tools, together with utilized and modified flakes from unprepared 'informal' cores. Radiocarbon dates range from 12,500–9000 BP in southern Africa, and the eco-systems varied from wooded grassland in Rhodesia, to steppe/grassland in the Karroo and northern Cape, to thicker bushveld and grassland south of the mountains.

On the coast, the Albany Industry belongs in the time of the end of the Pleistocene/early Holocene rise in sea-level, and this is reflected in the economy by quantities of shellfish and the bones of sea birds, fish and seal. The preponderance of grassland species in the large game animals suggests a rather more open environment than the present one.

Much less is known of the economy on the plateau due to lack of adequate faunal assemblages, but again grassland and bushveld species are important at some sites in the north, so that it would seem that at the inland, more tropical, sites there are indications of more varied use now being made of different resources, just as in the Maghrib, with the consequent reduction of dependence on mobility for securing an adequate diet.

Also in this time-range belongs the Smithfield A Industry (now renamed the 'Lockshoek Industry of the Oakhurst Complex'), with core-scrapers and many end- and side-scrapers on flakes but no microlithic blade elements. Presumably some of the tools were used to make others out of materials that have since perished – perhaps traps and snares, for instance, judging by the number of small animal bones in a related industry from Rhodesia (the Pomongwan). It seems possible, from the evidence of recorded sites, that the population was lower between 9500 and 4600 BP on the southern parts of the plateau, perhaps due to drier conditions, than in the coastal and escarpment zones. Certainly in the latter regions there is greater continuity in the occupation of sites until, with the appearance of the microlithic Wilton Complex *c.* 8000 BP, some of these caves (e.g. Oakhurst, Maatjes river) must have been almost permanently occupied. However, on the west coast there is also evidence for seasonal movement over some 120 km or more in the spring and summer for small game, and back to the coast in the winter, when shellfish and sealing became important. The Wilton Complex included, in addition to varying scraper forms, small segments and other backed tools and a much more elaborate bone industry. But in the coastal regions, where the makers concentrated more exclusively on the use of seafoods, the later in time the less, usually, the number of formal tools found.

The microlithic tradition epitomized in southern Africa by the Wilton Complex makes its appearance appreciably earlier in the tropics, and fully microlithic blade assemblages with segments and other backed forms are first found in East and Central Africa almost 20,000 years ago.

A number of regional facies of these microlithic industries are recognized: those in the more open grass and park savanna, where forms more comparable to the Wilton industries from South Africa are found (e.g. 'Kenya Wilton', 'Zambia Wilton' or 'Matopan' in Rhodesia), and other forms in the northern *Brachystegia* woodlands of Zambia (Nachikufan) and Malawi, where, however, scraping equipment, ground axes and bored stones together with much grinding equipment point to significant exploitation of both animal and plant foods (especially fruits and nuts) from a single base. For the first time, sites began to become more common in the forest itself, and particularly in the ecotone with the grassland. The tool-kits (Tshitolian) of these groups show both chronological and geographic variation. Two main sets of equipment have been distinguished – one in the valleys, with high percentages of trapezes and tranchets, and another on the hills or plateau, with various kinds of leaf-shaped and tanged arrowheads, with both of which are found numbers of refined axe and adze forms in the Lupemban tradition. This division suggests the possibility that the trapping of large game (hippopotamus and elephant) was important in the gallery forest, where the camps were also larger, and that seasonal hunting of antelope was carried out on the plateau. The earliest of these Tshitolian industries date from about 12,000 BC in Angola, and some of the latest yet dated are *c*. 3,000 years old.

Nothing is known of the origins of the Later Stone Age in West Africa. Non-ceramic industries are found there mostly, but not always, in the savanna or forest ecotone and come chiefly from rock-shelters. The raw material was generally quartz, but fine-grained materials were preferred if available, and at Iwo Eleru were carried in from *c*. 50 km away. Most of the lithic material must have been used with only minimal modification. Retouched tools include segments for chisel-ended arrows, forms with single and double truncation, and also many 'splintered' pieces (*outils esquillés*), many or all of which originated as bipolar cores but which may also have been used as adze-blades or wedges, for example for splitting wood. This stone tool-kit appears in the West African savanna and forest ecotone from Sierra Leone to Nigeria and, in the more closed habitats, with high rainfall, percussion-flaked axe forms became an increasingly important part of the equipment.

In those parts with few external or other pressures, the hunting-collecting way of life was able to continue perhaps as late as the beginning of the present era (e.g. Rop Rock Shelter on the Jos Plateau in Nigeria). Elsewhere, however, the readjustment towards domestication was already manifest by the third millennium BC and perhaps before. That it was able to come about comparatively rapidly was clearly the result of a long prior period of experimentation, of more intensive use of territorial resources and the intentional spreading of the wild staples that formed the economic base during the period of relative equilibrium following the end of the Pleistocene. The significant increase in the number of Later Stone Age sites with pottery and ground stone tools ('neolithic') must imply that populations had been able to increase during the period prior to the third millennium BC sufficiently for ethnic identities to become established and territories to become more rigidly defined during the Neolithic.

These Later Stone Age hunting-gathering populations continued using stone equipment of this general kind up to recent times in some parts of the continent, particularly in South Africa, where they can be identified with the San (or Bushmen) and Khoi (Hottentots), or in Central and eastern Africa with various small negroid, pygmoid and Khoisan populations. Some of them there had already developed the art of painting and perhaps engraving on rocks 12,000 years ago. Certainly the origins of the justly famous rock art of southern Africa were firmly established in the Later Stone Age, the oldest examples dating to *c.* 28,000 years ago,[1] even if much of that still extant may not be more than two or three thousand years old. It should, perhaps, be emphasized here that whatever can be learned from this art about the characteristics of the artists probably applies equally well, in view of the well-known conservatism of hunter-gatherers, to antecedent populations several millennia before.

Data from ethnography, excavated sites and rock art suggest that the Later Stone Age peoples in the interior plateau in southern Africa lived either in small bands with from eight to twelve members or in larger bands with between twenty and twenty-five individuals. Larger temporary groupings (sixty individuals and over) represent the coming together of several bands for special purposes such as communal hunting, trading, ceremonial dancing etc., mostly during the rainy season.[2]

[1] W. E. Wendt, *Die ältesten datierten Kunstwerke Afrikas*, special issue, *Felskunst* (Stuttgart), Bild der Wissenschaft, 1975, 44–50.

[2] T. M. O'C. Maggs, 'Some observations on the size of human groups during the Late

Since the vegetation patterns of tropical and southern Africa during the Holocene were not very different from the present, except where modified by human interference, it is possible, using ethno-botanical and ethno-zoological data, to construct a model of the changing resource base and probable movement patterns for a group with one regular 'core area' and base camp. Thus, for example, a number of plant and animal resources identified in the Kalambo Falls locality can be expected to have been available to groups living there during the third millennium BC, and to have been used in a way similar to that in which the present-day rural population traditionally use them. Hunter-gatherers (e.g. the Kalahari San) have been observed to make extensive use of only a few of the wide range of resources of which they have knowledge, and this is a product of deliberate selection and a planned pattern of seasonal movement. Where the selected resources are less abundant and become exhausted more quickly, the mobility of the group is of necessity greater, or where staples exist (e.g. *mungongu* or shea-butter nuts, fish and shellfish) that can be collected for most or all of the year, mobility is less.

Hunters and collectors in the rich environment of the African tropical savanna developed specialist practices to deal with the large herds of grazing and browsing animals. On the Kenya plains by *c.* 13,000 BC (Lukenya Hill), larger grazing animals were hunted in preference to medium or small ones. At Gwisho Hot Springs in Zambia, successful hunting of a wide range of animals from the grassland Kafue flats, the *Brachystegia* woodland and the thicket bush, dates to *c.* 2800–1700 BC. The quarry was probably secured with bows and poisoned arrows – strongly suggested by the numbers of backed stone segments among the bone refuse in the archaeological deposits of the site, and collected *Swartzia* pods. The scarcity or absence of fish, small animals, hippopotamus and swamp antelope may, perhaps, be a product of the habitat. But, more probably, these were the preferred resources of dry-season camps closer to the main river and its tributaries. The number of grindstones and the range of nuts and seeds point also to the importance of fruits that became available towards the end of the rainy season.

AFRICAN PHYSICAL POPULATIONS AND THE ORIGIN OF 'RACES'

The Later Stone Age physical population of southern and Central

Stone Age', in M. Schoonraad, ed., *Rock paintings of southern Africa*, Special Publication 2, *South African Journal of Science* (Johannesburg), 1971, 49–53.

Africa is known as yet only from the drier parts of the continent, no skeletal remains having been recovered from the forest zones. These remains essentially represent individuals of what is sometimes called the 'large Khoisan' stock as opposed to the 'small Khoisan', or small-statured historic San (Bushman) of South and South-West Africa. Claims that skeletal remains exhibiting Khoisan affinities ('Bushman' or 'Boskopoid') have been found far to the north of their present distribution have, on more recent assessments, been discounted, the crania in question (e.g. from Inyanga and Gwisho) being considered to resemble negroid crania as much as they do those of Bushmen.[1]

In South Africa the antiquity of the Khoisan stock is not in doubt – for example the Fishhoek cranium dates either to more than 35,000 BP, if contemporary with the layer in which it was found, or to *c.* 18,500 BP if buried *into* the layer. An origin in the Middle Stone Age is also attested by other fossils, usually exhibiting greater robustness with age. The affinities of the 'large' Khoisan, exemplified in the Cape by the historic Hottentot, and of the 'small' San stock are clearly seen in skeletal remains from Later Stone Age contexts reaching back some 11,000 years.

The origin of the African Negro is less well known, probably because the high rainfall areas generally preserve little or no fossil material and an antiquity equal to that of the Khoisan stock cannot yet be demonstrated, even though it may be suspected. It is, however, claimed that the partial cranium from Lukenya Hill in Kenya, associated with a microlithic industry and dating to 17,600 years ago, though it shows some primitive features, also displays others that suggest negroid affiliations. Negroid affiliations have also been claimed (Iwo Elero, Nigeria) or demonstrated (Asselar, Mali) from various sites dating from the fifth to the seventh millennia BC. And on the Upper Nile, negroid affinities have been demonstrated for the robust population of Early Khartoum dating probably to the sixth or seventh millennium BC. Even more robust are the populations from the Wadi Halfa cemeteries dating to *c.* 12,000 BC and resembling, so it is claimed, the Mechta-Afalou race of the Maghrib. Detailed comparisons yet remain to be made between the Wadi Halfa late Palaeolithic peoples, 'Early Khartoum', and the late Neolithic/Early Iron Age populations at Jebel Moya. Predictably these populations could demonstrate the emergence of the Sudanese Negro, the origin of which must have an antiquity on the Upper Nile equal to that of the Khoisan stock in the south.

[1] G. P. Rightmire, 'Problems in the study of Later Pleistocene man in Africa', *American Anthropologist*, 1975, 77, 28–52, esp. 43–4.

Skeletal remains from the Kenya Rift previously considered as 'Afro-Mediterranean' or 'Caucasoid' have now been shown to group with African Negro samples. They date within the first millennium BC and, on physical characteristics, it is suggested they may be of proto-Nilotic stock. But it is necessary also to make comparisons with Cushitic speakers, since burials found recently in association with a Kenya Capsian-like industry from Lake Besaka in the Ethiopian Rift, dating probably to *c.* 5000 BC, also show negroid features, and linguistic evidence indicates a long history for Cushitic in Ethiopia. However, until adequate samples become available from each of the main eco-systems, it is impossible to arrange the fossil material into any coherent picture. If modern man could have evolved out of the regional Neanderthaloid/early *Homo sapiens* populations between 100,000 and 50,000 years ago, through social selection and an enlarged gene pool brought about as a result of a fully developed language communication system, then it is not necessary to look outside the continent for the origin of the modern African races. The basic stock was perhaps as variable as are the Kibish crania from Omo in East Africa, and became differentiated during the 40–50,000 years' duration of the later Pleistocene, in the same way that culture became differentiated – coincidently with the genetic changes that followed increasing identification of the populations with specific geographical regions and eco-systems.

Thus the influence of environment is of paramount importance in bringing about biological diversity, and the effects of climatic fluctuations in causing changes in these environments had equally significant results. The ways in which populations adapt to their environment may cause movement and changes in density patterns, and affect growth rates and physique, social and sexual selection, nutritional levels and resistance to disease. The effect of these various selective pressures operating on semi-isolated populations during the later Pleistocene cannot as yet be documented stage by stage, due to the paucity and unsatisfactory nature of the existing fossil data. The final effect, however, is certainly observable by the end of the Pleistocene, in the emergence of several 'races' for which ethnic affinities can be suggested. One late Pleistocene stage of differentiation is represented by the early Khoisan stock in southern Africa and Mechta-Afalou related forms in the more northern parts of the continent. Later still, after 10,000 years ago, the large and small Khoisan stocks became differentiated as did also the robust and gracile Negro forms, and possibly also the 'proto-Mediterranean' type from Mechta-Afalou stock in the Maghrib. Such genetic changes are surely within the range of what can be expected to have been brought about by those selective pressures previously referred to. Whether future work confirms or rejects this kind of model, there can be no doubt at all that the indigenous African races have a very long history, and an equally long relationship with the geographical regions that are their traditional home.

The extent to which the African gene pool was enriched by elements from outside the continent in and prior to the earlier Holocene is unknown. It is to be expected, however, that some infiltration occurred at times across the Isthmus of Suez, perhaps twice – towards the beginning and near the end of the later Pleistocene. But there is as yet little convincing evidence in support of such movements, other than inference following from technological innovation and replacement, and the problem involving the appearance of modern man. At the lower end of the Red Sea, the dissimilarity of cultural forms between the Horn and the Arabian Peninsula until the Neolithic would argue that there was little or no communication across the Straits of Bab-el-Mandeb during the later Pleistocene; the exotic contributions to the biological characteristics of the populations of the Horn and Ethiopia are probably no older than the mid-Holocene at the earliest. Suggested connections across the Mediterranean between southern Europe and Tunisia have little to substantiate them before the Neolithic. In the absence of adequate skeletal samples of prehistoric populations, serological studies probably hold out the best hope of determining degrees of exotic admixture in indigenous African populations; these suggest that, apart from among North Africans and the Cushitic-speaking peoples of the Horn, such contributions from outside the continent before late prehistoric and historic times were small and fairly quickly absorbed.[1]

THE AFRICAN NEOLITHIC AND THE ORIGINS OF DOMESTICATION

For some archaeologists the term 'neolithic' has a technological meaning related to the presence of pottery and various kinds of ground stone tool. For others, including this author, the term carries with it also the implication of cultivation and/or herding of stock – in other

[1] Origins and development of modern African races are examined in J. Hiernaux, *The people of Africa* (London, 1974).

words of a food-producing and not a food-collecting economy. Until, therefore, a satisfactory substitute is proposed, the term 'neolithic' when used here in inverted commas signifies that some form of food production was either not the economic base or is unproven (figs. 15, 16)[1].

Outside the Nile Valley in Egypt little *direct* evidence for the presence of domestication from remains of the plants and animals themselves is preserved in the earlier archaeological record in Africa. The abundant remains of emmer wheat and barley in the silos of the Fayum A peasant Neolithic, dating from the latter part of the fifth millennium BC, are still the oldest and best evidence for cultivation in Africa. In the Sahara, discounting ambiguous pollen grains, the oldest convincing evidence for domestic grain (impressions in pottery) comes from Dar Tichit in south-central Mauritania, where a rapid change *c.* 1100 BC from the use of several wild grasses to the almost exclusive use of one species, *Pennisetum*, carries a strong implication that bulrush millet was being cultivated there at that time.

South of the desert, carbonized grains of *Sorghum bicolor* race bicolor are identified from one site on the Upper Nile (Jebel Tomat) and two in Nubia dating from *c.* 80 BC to AD 350. *Sorghum bicolor* is recorded again from another late site in Guinea (AD 860) and caudatum sorghum occurs in a ninth to tenth-century AD context at Daima in the Chad basin. Barley, chick-peas and legumes of south-west Asian origin are present by *c.* 520 BC in northern Ethiopia (Lalibela Cave, Begemder). Further south in East and southern Africa, the earliest cultivated plant remains belong with an Early Iron Age technology in the earlier part of the first millennium AD. Of course, these dates give no real indication of when these plants were first brought under cultivation, and certain indirect evidence from archaeological cultural contexts, the genetic composition and distributions of the plants themselves, and from lexico-statistical studies suggest an appreciably greater antiquity for the origin of these and other African cultigens. For example, though the cowpeas (*Vigna* species) and oil-palm husks (*Elaeis guineensis*) at the Kintampo sites in Ghana (dated *c.* 1400 BC) cannot be identified for certain as domestic forms, the cultural context strongly suggests they were

[1] Archaeological evidence for domestication is listed in C. T. Shaw, 'Early agriculture in Africa', *Journal of the Historical Society of Nigeria*, 1972, **6**, 143–91. A general review of the spread of herding and indigenous African plant domesticates in the continent will be found in J. D. Clark, 'The domestication process in sub-Saharan Africa with special reference to Ethiopia', *IXe Congrès de l'Union International des Sciences Préhistoriques et Protohistoriques* (*Nice, Sept. 1976*), preprint vol., Colloque xx, *Origine de l'élevage et de la domestication*, 56–115.

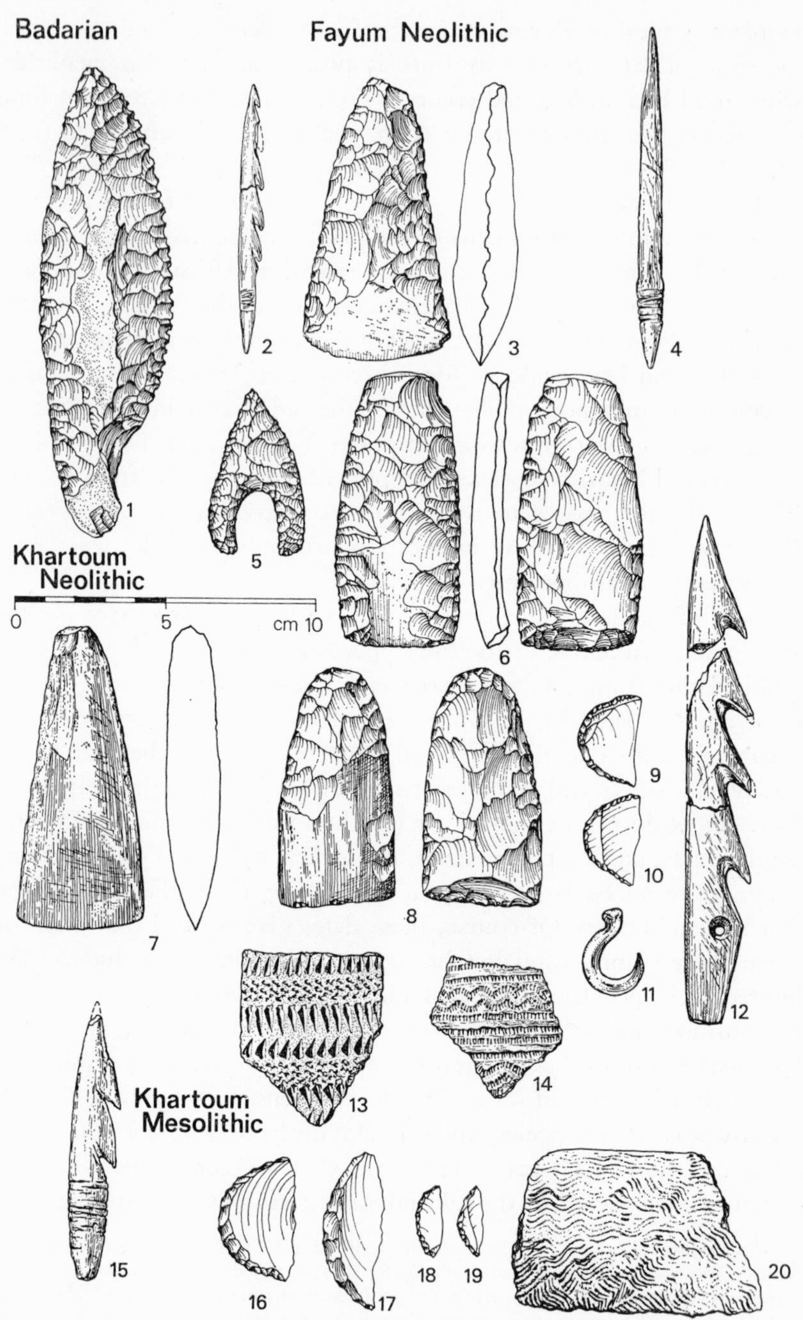

15 Tools from 'Mesolithic' and Neolithic Industries from Egypt and the Sudan. (*For explanation, see opposite.*)

being cultivated there by that time. In the same way the decorated gourd (*Lagenaria* species) from a site (Njoro River Cave) on the Kenya Rift escarpment may indicate that calabashes were being intentionally grown there by the pastoral populations at the beginning of the first millennium BC.

There is rather better *direct* evidence for domestic stock, but while a wide range of indigenous domestic plants can be seen to have been brought under cultivation or under controlled cropping in tropical Africa, the domestic food-animals that were adopted there are either of south-west Asian (sheep/goat, cattle, pig) or of northern African origin (cattle, ?pig). Aside from the cattle, sheep/goats and pigs with the Fayum A and other Egyptian Neolithic settlements, sheep/goats are present in Cyrenaica (Haua Fteah Cave) at the beginning of the fifth millennium BC, and cattle as well as sheep/goats are now known to be present in the Algerian plateau from the middle of the fifth millennium.[1] For domestic animals in the Sahara, the earliest direct evidence dates to the end of the fifth and beginning of the fourth millennia and comes from the Fezzan and Adrar Bous, north-east of Aïr; the animals are

[1] At the Capeletti Cave (Khanguet si Mohamed Tahar), the greater part of the food waste throughout the occupation consists of sheep/goat bones, but remains of cattle, believed domesticated, are also present (C. Roubet and P. L. Carter, personal communication).

Badarian tool
1 Bifacial and serrated knife
Fayum A Peasant Neolithic tools
2 Barbed bone point
3 Polished axe
4 Bone point with distal bevel
5 Hollow-based arrowhead
6 Gouge
Khartoum Neolithic tools from Esh Shaheinab, Sudan
7 Bone celt
8 Gouge
9, 10 Deep crescents
11 Shell fish-hook
12 Harpoon
13 Sherd with punctate decoration
14 Sherd with burnished dotted wavy line decoration
Khartoum 'Mesolithic' tools from Early Khartoum, Sudan
15 Barbed bone point
16, 17 Large crescents
18, 19 Microlithic crescents
20 Sherd with wavy line decoration
(After A. J. Arkell, *The prehistory of the Nile Valley*, 1975, figs. 3–8, 14.)

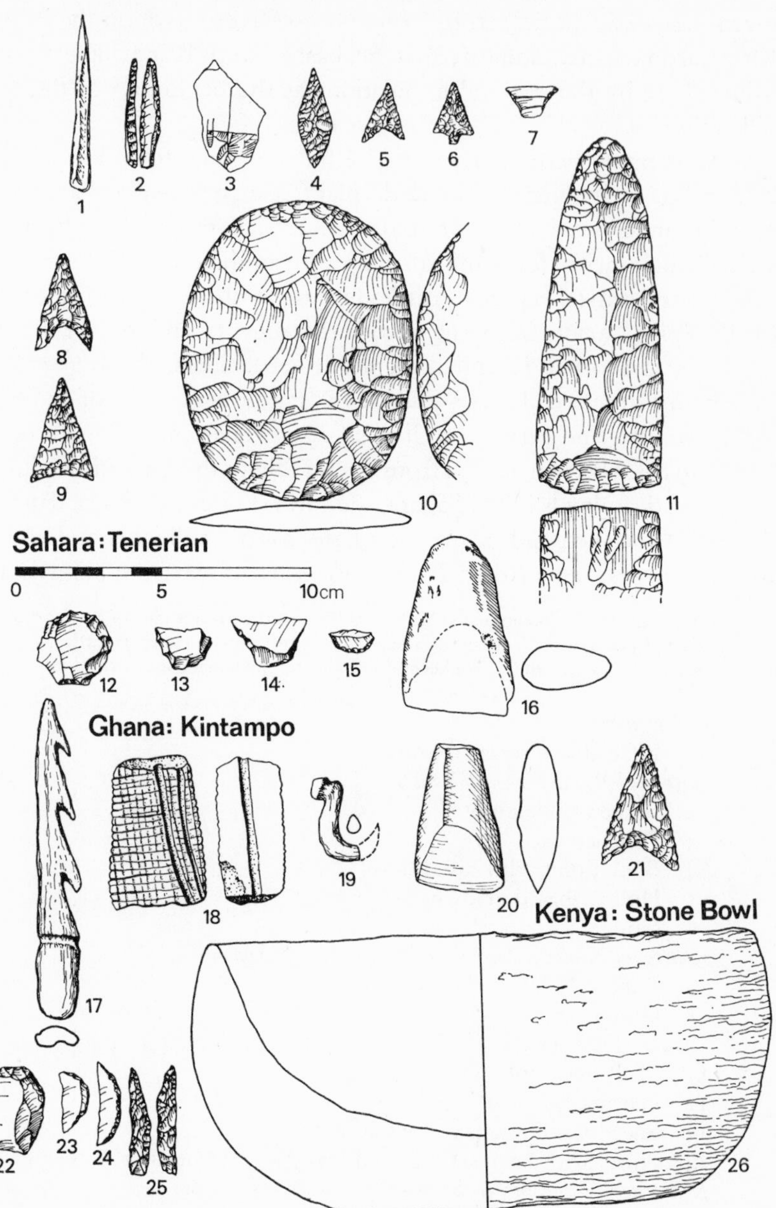

16 Tools of 'Neolithic' Industries and Complexes from northern, West and East Africa. (*For explanation, see opposite.*)

short-horned cattle. However, claims have been made for domesticated *Bos* bones in the Fezzan as early as the seventh millennium. The earliest period of the rock art (Hunter, *c.* 6000–4000 BC) suggests that during this time wild cattle and other animals were captured and, perhaps, tamed, since domestic cattle are already present as stated above in the eastern Atlas in the fifth millennium. It is, therefore, apparent that there were already domestic cattle in the Sahara by the beginning of the fourth millennium and later part of the fifth millennium BC, which is as early as or, perhaps, even earlier than, they appear in the Nile Valley. This provides good reason to argue that the North African wild cattle (*Bos primigenius* and *Bos ibericus*) were independently domesticated by central Saharan peoples during the fifth millennium or even earlier, and that by the fourth millennium cattle and small stock were spread widely in the northern parts of the desert and perhaps the Maghrib. Other groups, however, in particular those occupying the northern parts of the desert and the Maghrib highlands (e.g. Neolithic of Capsian

---

Neolithic of Capsian Tradition, from the Maghrib
1 Bone awl
2 Drill
3 Engraved ostrich eggshell
4–6 Bifacial arrowheads
7 Transverse arrowhead
Tenerian Neolithic, from the Tenere Desert, Niger
8, 9 Concave-based arrowheads
10 Bifacial disc knife
11 Shaheinab-type gouge
Kintampo-related Bosumpra Industry, from Ghana
12 Convex scraper
13–15 Lunates and trapeze
16 Ground stone celt
Kintampo Industry, from Ghana
17 Barbed bone point
18 Fragment of a terracotta/stone 'grater'
19 Bone fish-hook
20 Stone celt
21 Hollow-based arrowhead
Stone Bowl Complex from the Kenya Rift
22 Short end-scraper
23, 24 Lunates
25 Borer
26 Stone bowl

(After Clark, *Prehistory of Africa*, Nos. 12–16, after Shaw, 'Bosumpra', p. 5.)

tradition), acquired 'neolithic' traits rather later and appear to have continued the hunting-gathering way of life rather longer.

It has generally been assumed that nomadic pastoralism is a secondary development out of mixed farming whereby marginal areas can be used more efficiently. However, in northern Africa, apart from the valley of the Nile and the maritime parts of the Mediterranean, the evidence appears more in favour of an independent development of stock-herding in the desert, followed there only appreciably later by crop cultivation in the oases. Again, south of the desert it would seem that cultivation is intimately connected with stock-keeping and, indeed, the eruption of pastoralists into the tropical savanna lands could have been the catalyst producing the disequilibrium to which readjustment was made by the adoption of cultivation. Normally, increases in population at the hunter-gatherer level of subsistence can be expected to have been absorbed by the richness of the tropical biome and the opportunity for freedom of movement within the savanna zone.

The following synthesis of the origins of agriculture in Africa should, therefore, be considered only as a model, because it is based on very inadequate direct evidence, with the addition of indirect evidence from cultural associations and the contributions of ethnography and linguistics that cannot be precisely assessed until founded on a firm radiometric chronology. In particular, caution needs to be exercised in respect of the situation in the Nile Valley, where systematic investigation of earlier Holocene sites still remains to be carried out; until this has been done, any conclusions as to the origins of agriculture there must remain at best highly tentative.

Until recently there was little or no evidence to challenge the conventional view that agriculture was introduced into the Egyptian section of the Nile Valley in the fifth millennium BC from south-west Asia. Indirect evidence from predynastic and early dynastic pictorial representations strongly suggests that the degree of experimentation with potential local domesticates, in particular the preoccupation with wild cattle and antelope species, was extensive and had a long history. Recent thermoluminescence dates for the Badarian settlement at Hemmemiya, for example, suggest that the neolithic economy was already a well-established phenomenon in Upper Egypt by 5000 BC. It would not, therefore, be too surprising if future discoveries were to show that the domestication process had almost as great an antiquity in North-East Africa as in south-west Asia. In North Africa, the evidence shows that the changes in the traditional economy of the established communities were the outcome of the diffusion process and not of movement into the area by a new population. On the Upper Nile in the Sudan, hunting-fishing-collecting communities had been living since the seventh millennium BC, occupying large base camps overlooking the river and making regular use of selected seasonal resources from large and medium game animals to fish, birds and molluscs. They had a developed stone and specialized bone tool technology, and they also made pottery, though whether the latter was a product of stimulus diffusion or independent invention remains to be seen. The characteristic wares ('Wavy Line' tradition) appear at much the same time as does pottery in Cyrenaica, but the two are quite unrelated stylistically. Dates for this predomestication phase (Early Khartoum Mesolithic) lie between 6000 and *c.* 4500 BC (e.g. from Tagra and Shabona), but, although the Khartoum tradition is found spread very widely in the Sahara and as far as Lake Rudolf, there is no indication that the Nile was necessarily the nucleus for this westward and southward expansion.

The kind of model suggested by the settlement patterning of this time is one of regular transhumance, when the population occupied, perhaps, a single base camp by the water, splitting seasonally into several smaller exploitation camps at times when more distant and temporary resources became available and falling back again on the base camp when these had been exhausted. Such a pattern can be seen to be spread across much of the central and all of the southern Sahara, where it forms the earlier or older 'neolithic' phase of what has variously been called the 'Neolithic of Sudanese tradition' or the 'Saharan-Sudanese Neolithic'.

Some overall assessment of the growing complexity of social organization and behaviour can be arrived at by reconstructing economic levels. The following model is proposed, taking into account the results of previous research and bearing in mind that, until more work has been done, no claim can be made for anything more than a very general validity. Only more precise recovery and recording methods and further teamwork in field and laboratory will show how accurately this model portrays the sequence of events in northern Africa that led up to domestication.

By about 15,000 BC, if not before, more intensive use was being made in the Nile Valley of the main sources of food – game animals, fish, wild grains and, a little later, wild-fowl. On the sea coasts, shellfish had been important since the beginning of the later Pleistocene and land and freshwater molluscs had begun to be used extensively by some inland communities by 6000 BC. The terminal Pleistocene/earlier Holocene climatic amelioration produced many water sources in the Sahara – in particular, lakes – with a high fish yield, as well as hippopotamus, crocodile, turtle and other aquatic foods. In addition the vegetation became Sahelian on the plains, with dry Mediterranean macchia vegetation on the massifs with much grass and many trees for grazing and browsing animals. The Ethiopian fauna spread throughout the desert, and hunting-gathering communities began to repopulate the Sahara about 10,000 years ago, probably by convergence from the periphery and expansion from the montane refuges in the interior.

Greater reliance on aquatic foods made possible near permanent settlements in the more favourable localities, and the need for seasonal movement was reduced by devising means of storing food and by developing processing methods such as smoking and drying techniques, which enabled it to be kept longer. On the Upper Nile and in the Sahara, pottery can be seen as a direct answer to the need for more efficient use of fish and molluscs, which could now form a reserve to be used during the 'famine months' to reduce or eliminate the need to move. As a result of improved nutrition, birth periods could be more closely spaced and an overall increase in population density would result. The extent to which the surplus population could be absorbed would depend on the carrying capacity of a group's territory but, well before the limit was reached, some of the surplus can be expected to have moved away and probably to have placed greater reliance on territorial animals and grasses and, so, on mobility. From 4000 BC onwards the increasing tempo of desiccation in the desert, which began in the north and spread southwards, was probably the most significant factor in reducing or redistributing the game population and causing some of these mobile communities to acquire small stock (sheep/goats) and later to domesticate the wild cattle. By so doing they were able not only to continue to use their traditional territories, but the greater security of this ever-available resource meant a more regularized pattern of seasonal mobility and at least a stabilization, if not an increase, of population levels.

There is as yet no evidence that stock-herding in the Sahara was accompanied by the cultivation of the south-west Asian cereals, and more probably all the grasses used were local wild species. If, however, wheat and barley were grown in some of the oases and the wild ancestral forms of *Pennisetum*, sorghum and other Sudanic species occurred as weeds in the field plots, they *could* have been brought into use by manipulation in a similar manner as that in which, for example, *Paspalum* has become a pseudo-crop among some of the rice growers of Guinea.[1]

After 3000 BC, with the growing impetus of desertification, lakes and swamps began to dwindle and disappear and with them the aquatic resources, so that more and more of the communities dependent upon these resources acquired stock – in particular, cattle – and perhaps from this time also the milking trait began to spread in the northern part of the desert.

Around 2000 BC natural and man-made destruction of the fragile Sahelian habitat in the Sahara had become acute for cattle pastoralists and triggered a process of widespread movement that gained momentum during the two succeeding millennia, farther into the desert massifs on the one hand, and outside the desert on the other, into the Mediterranean coastal lands in the north, into the Sahel and savanna of West Africa in the south and into the Nile Valley in the east. Similar movements can also be projected within the Horn, from the Ethiopian Rift and Somalia onto the plateau and both northwards into the Sudan and south to East Africa.

Some populations living in the Sahel/Sudan zones, which climatic oscillation had relocated several degrees to the north of their present latitudes, had now not only to find a substitute for the vanished aquatic foods, but also had to adjust to the increased population pressure resulting from the movement into their territory of nomadic pastoralists from the north. The solution found by some of these groups, probably sometime after 2000 BC, was more intensive use and protection of wild grasses and a heavier concentration on one or more species, which, in time, led to intentional sowing of seed and retention of seed grown for next year's crop. The depressions and stream courses also provided the most favourable localities for experimentation. Intentional cultivation thus not only restored the food resource for man and beast and made it possible for these neolithic communities to continue the sedentary or semi-sedentary way of life, but also established them in their traditional territories and enabled them to compete successfully with the influx of nomadic, milk-using cattle-keepers with whom they were now regularly juxtaposed. The symbiotic relationship between herder and cultivator that is traditional in West Africa and the Horn must have been early

[1] See R. Portères, 'Le Millet coracan, ou finger millet (*Eleusine coracana gaertner*)', in J. R. Harlan, J. M. J. de Wet and A. Stemler, eds., *Origins of plant domestication in Africa* (The Hague, 1976), 45–52.

established. In some cases after *c.* 1000 BC, Libyan-Berbers with metal weapons were able to eliminate or make subservient some of these desert communities. But naked force was unable to prevail as, in the richer southern grasslands, exchange and barter provided each group with the kind of commodities that are still exchanged today – grain, chiefly, for the nomads and livestock, field manuring, milk products and some 'luxury' goods for the agriculturalists. In favourable localities such as the Middle Niger, Lake Chad and the Upper Nile basin, other communities were able to continue their hunting-fishing and collecting ways of life, and became specialized fishermen whose products were successfully exchanged with pastoralists and husbandmen.

The development of cereal cultivation, perhaps of agriculture in general, south of the Sahara is considered, therefore, by this author, as a direct effect of climatic deterioration and the failure of the aquatic sources: in other words of the desiccation, partly natural, partly man made, in the desert, for which we have abundant documentation and which initiated a sequence of events leading to the use of small stock and the domestication of cattle and, finally, to the cultivation of the Sudanic food-plants. Similarly, the population movements that follow from disequilibrium between a community and its ecology brought into juxtaposition, south of the desert 'Mediterranean', Cushitic and Negro peoples, and so began the symbiotic relationship between pastoralists, fishers, mixed farmers and cultivators that can be observed today from Senegal through to East Africa and which comes into clearer focus only in historic times.

The southward spread of domestic animals and plants into the subcontinent belongs more to proto-history than to prehistory, but the movements in the northern savanna zone triggered by the mid-Holocene desiccation are likely also to have been a major factor in causing pastoral peoples with cattle and sheep/goats to spread into the Lake Victoria basin and the eastern Rift from the Nile/Congo watershed area and Ethiopia after *c.* 1000 BC. However, the extent to which any or all of these people were cultivators as well as herders can be determined only by indisputable evidence from archaeological excavation. Similarly, vegetation changes and rapid valley-filling recorded from the Jos Plateau, the Lake Victoria basin, Angola and northern Zambia *c.* 3,000 years ago may perhaps be evidence for some kind of agriculture, but might equally well be due to systematic burning associated with more efficient group hunting methods.

The range of indigenous wild grasses, root, bean and pea crops brought under cultivation in the Sahel/Sudan zone, and the different centres of origin proposed for these, shows that the domestication process did not spread throughout sub-Saharan Africa from a single nuclear area.[1] Rather can it be seen as a series of reactions by a number of populations who had little or no direct communication with each other so that each tended to develop its own selected staple cereals – a range of different millets and dry rice in West Africa, sorghum further east in Chad and the Sudan, *teff* in Ethiopia and perhaps finger millet on the Upper Nile. If the pressures bringing about the economic revolution came from the north as the evidence suggests, this is the kind of situation that might be expected. In the forest/savanna ecotone the emphasis was on various plant-crops – yams and other root-crops, oil-plants, beans etc. in West Africa, and the false banana (*Ensete*) on the more southern parts of the Ethiopian plateau. When these became cultivated staples is unknown; presumably they were made regular use of in the wild form for a very long time before they were brought under cultivation. If the makers of the Nok Culture with its fluted pumpkins cultivated these and other crops, then there were already populations of farmers in central Nigeria by the middle of the first millennium BC, and the occupants of the mound settlements in the firki lands of eastern Chad, which date back to *c.* 2000 BC, may have cultivated sorghum. Although the oldest archaeological sorghum dates only to the last century BC, the mound settlements in the Sudan where this is located, in association with a late neolithic culture, are as old as the middle of the third millennium. In Ethiopia, *teff, ensete, nug* and the other local domesticates are likely to have been brought under cultivation before the introduction of the south-west Asian cereals, which was most probably after 500 BC by the pre-Aksumite settlers from southern Arabia. On the evidence available today, therefore, the most likely time when plant resources began to be cultivated south of the Sahara was some time in the second millennium BC. However, when more evidence becomes available, it would not be at all surprising to find that cultigens were already present in the third millennium, though less likely before that.

Whether cultivation in the forest ecotone was independent of the events further north is at present unknown. Intensive use there of wild plants such as yams or oil-palm could have made possible larger

[1] For a list of African domesticates and the regions where these may have originated see J. R. Harlan, *Crops and man* (Madison, 1975), ch. 9, 'Indigenous African agriculture', 191–206.

groupings from an early date. Any resulting population increase could have been absorbed by a process of hiving-off and continuing the same way of life, namely one of restricted transhumance, in which movements of game animals and the seasonal harvesting of wild plant-crops were the controlling factors. Such data as exist suggest that the appearance of pottery and ground stone axes in the forest ecotone and the forest itself occurred at much the same time (after 3000 BC) as it did in the savanna, being similarly related to stock-keeping and, in the wetter savanna, where not precluded by tsetse fly, adequate grazing for stock meant that permanent village settlements could be established. The old vegecultural way of life developed into intentional planting of hitherto wild staples and, with the resulting increase in population density, inroads began to be made in clearing and occupation of the forest.

CONCLUSIONS

The truth of the suggestions made by Charles Darwin and Thomas Huxley that the African tropics may have been the place where man originated and that he shares very close affinities with the African apes, has been fully borne out today by palaeo-anthropological studies which are confirmed by the molecular biological evidence. Man most probably evolved in the African tropical savanna, and his developmental history over the past five million years or more has been one, first, of expanding horizons in which ever more varied eco-systems were occupied and brought under control. Secondly, his development has been towards increasingly more structured social and economic organization, made possible by the feedback relationship existing between biological and cultural evolution. Mental ability and technology evolved together, and with them the control that human societies were able to exercise over their environment. This control depended, however, upon the fluidity of the social unit and the degree to which it was able to avail itself of the opportunities for more efficient ecological adaptation and readjustment whenever external or internal pressures dictated. The observation that well-adapted human societies remain stable until pressured by factors inducing disequilibrium with their surroundings, and so bringing about the necessity for readjustment, is thus wholly applicable to the African situation.

From the time of the first stone tools it has taken the human race some two to two and a half million years to work up to the complex technological civilization of the present day. The first stage in this record is evident only in Africa. It lasted for more than a million years and, during this time, although technologically the tool-kits show very little change indeed, natural and social selection were operating to produce ever more efficient biological forms through *Homo habilis* to small- and large-brained *H. erectus*, who had appeared by 1.4 m.y. ago, and with them major additions to the technology. Whereas, in the beginning, the communities appear to have occupied only the more open savanna, the makers of the Acheulian Complex industries not only successfully occupied all parts of the continent except the rain-forest, but also spread into Eurasia and became adapted to an even wider range of environments. While he was able to take advantage of considerable ecological diversity, however, *H. erectus* may be seen as an unspecialized food-gatherer, and, although the resources of which he availed himself were very varied, the extent to which he made use of them suggests a shallow or generalized rather than an intensive level of exploitation.

It is not until the beginning of the Upper Pleistocene, rather more than 100,000 years ago, that any close identification with geographical areas becomes apparent and is reflected in the regional tool technologies. This time also marked the prelude to the appearance of modern man in the continent, and from then onwards intellectual ability, improved technology, and a nearly fully evolved language system enabled the still relatively unspecialized African populations to become ever more closely geographically adapted. They also became more selective in the resources they made use of, and more skilful in their methods, with the result that more intensive exploitation was possible. By the end of the Pleistocene some 10,000 years ago, the effects of these adaptations were becoming apparent in the fossil evidence from which we are beginning to identify ancestral Berbers, Negroes, 'elongated Africans' and 'Mediterraneans' within those diverse regions that are their traditional homelands, and which over the many millennia have contributed to making them and their culture what they are today.

Population movements in the more remote prehistoric times are most likely to have been associated with climatic and topographic changes and their effects on the habitats. Where such changes produced 'empty areas' favourable for occupation and also the means of moving into them, man was not slow to avail himself of this opportunity – as happened during the late Middle and early Upper Pleistocene. Movement *into* the continent also seems likely, if not certain, on at least two occasions during the later Pleistocene. These movements affected more specifically North Africa and the Egyptian Nile, but the geographically distinctive technologies the immigrants are credited with having introduced suggest that the populations that brought them became rapidly identified as essentially African.

Thus, the results of research in archaeology and collaborating disciplines are beginning to provide a picture of the emergence of man and of his biological and cultural evolution in Africa. To be sure, it is as yet broad, generalized and, in places, admittedly tenuous. But, to date, it is the best available and, as such, indispensable to an informal appreciation of the history and proto-history of the present-day peoples of Africa. Without doubt, future work will throw fresh light on this remote past and so contribute still further to our understanding of the complexities of modern Africa. To summarize, therefore, this background picture may be divided into five broad periods:

(1) *Late Pliocene/Lower Pleistocene* – 2.5 *to c.* 1.5 *m.y.* BP (*Australopithecus/Homo habilis*)

Group organization must have been very open, with groups varying seasonally considerably in size and individual composition – which, in fact, is still a feature of hunter-gatherers in Africa today. The focus for the home base was probably females with their young, and it seems unlikely that the communities were monogamous. Groups were small – probably fewer than twenty-five individuals – and the pattern of movement was one of circulating round small camps, which were never occupied for long and rarely revisited. The extraction process demanded only a limited amount of planning. Energy output may have been considerable, as also were the distances travelled.

(2) *Later Lower and Middle Pleistocene* – *c.* 1.5 *to c.* 0.2 *m.y.* BP (*Homo erectus*)

Organization had become more complex, with a likely pattern of male domination and possible beginning of pair bonding. Communities were larger with a more structured system of strategic camping-places reoccupied at irregular intervals. At favourable seasons and for special activities, such as communal hunting, groups of well over twenty-five individuals can be projected. Larger groupings and longer occupation of camps were associated with a less superficial but still general level of resource use on a plaaned, seasonal basis.

(3) *Upper Pleistocene – c.* 200,000 *to c.* 12,000 BP (*Homo sapiens*)

Community identity was now established through family groupings, and the economic base was now broadened. Resource consumption was geared more specifically to the regional ecology, and more intensive use began of a few selected staples for which more specialized techniques and technologies were developed As such resources became seasonally available, they were exploited from one or two base camps, each with its satellite extraction camps. Geographical or other restrictions on expansion produced more closely structured and larger groupings. By the end of the Pleistocene, delimitation of territories had begun so that unauthorized use might now be liable to cause group warfare.

(4) *Terminal Pleistocene/Early Holocene – to about* 10,000 BP

In most favourable localities, a single large base camp, often with permanent structures, was established, supplemented by the use of several regular exploitation camps. Intensive consumption and manipulation of selected staples enabled specialized hunter-gatherers to remain in permanent occupation of the base while, at the same time, a reserve or surplus was possibly built up at the base camp through feedback from the more distant satellite camps. A similar pattern is projected for early farming societies, comparable to that of many present-day Nilotes: the drier the terrain and the greater the importance of stock, the more significant became the exploitation camps, whereas cultivators on good lands and with minimal stock may have been able to dispense entirely with temporary satellite settlements.

(5) *Mid-Holocene – to about* 3000 BC

Urban civilization in the Nile Valley, where the urban centre was fed from the satellite village communities and the input of resources, labour etc. from the rural areas into the town, formed the basis of the economic pattern. In return, the rural centres received protection under a political system based upon a judicial code and social hierarchy of specialists and peasants held together by common religious beliefs and ritual.

Finally, it may be asked, what effect did the dynastic civilization of the Nile Valley have on the inhabitants of 'inner' Africa? This is a difficult question to answer. Some predynastic Egyptian artefacts (e.g.

bifacial knife forms) are found in Siwa Oasis and in the Tenere desert, and dynastic Egyptians settled some of the more easterly oases in the Western Desert, penetrating south of the Nile to beyond the Second Cataract and down to Eritrea on the Red Sea coast. The eastward movements of Libyans and C-Group people into Egypt and the Sudan show the attraction of Egyptian civilization for pastoral nomads driven eastwards to seek pasture for their herds. Mostly it seems to have been a one-way process of absorption into the valley with not very much output from it. In times of strong rulers in Egypt, the Saharan pastoralists had little chance to enter, but, when rule was ineffective, some of them were able to settle in the valley and became absorbed.

The main source of the metal weapons and chariots that began to be adopted by the northern pastoralists after 1500 BC, but especially in the first half of the first millennium, was most probably Egypt (though Phoenician and Greek colonies must also have contributed). Possession of this equipment enabled these northern nomads to occupy large parts of the central and southern desert at the expense of the late neolithic negroid population. The major contribution of dynastic Egypt, however, was to the Nubian civilization on the Upper Nile and, though this remains, as yet, not much more than speculation, in Ethiopia also. Here the spread of cattle-herding about 1500 BC,[1] and the presence of pressures similar to those operating in the Sahara, caused experiment with local wild plant sources that were well established by the time pre-Aksumites from southern Arabia began to occupy the Eritrean coast and plateau after 500 BC.

[1] On evidence of bones of believed domestic *Bos* from the painted rock-shelter site of Laga Oda, south-eastern Ethiopia: faunal identification by P. L. Carter, Cambridge, and dates by R. Gillespie, Sydney, New South Wales (personal communication).

CHAPTER 2

NORTH AFRICA IN THE PERIOD OF PHOENICIAN AND GREEK COLONIZATION, *c.* 800 to 323 BC

Before the first millennium BC, the only part of Africa for whose history there survive written records is the Nile Valley. The remainder even of North Africa had remained beyond the limits of the activities and knowledge of the literate civilizations of the eastern Mediterranean. But from around 800 BC there took place an extension of the sphere of the literate civilizations which brought the North African littoral west of Egypt for the first time within the bounds of recoverable history. This came about through the maritime expansion of two eastern Mediterranean peoples, the Greeks and the Phoenicians.[1] These two peoples were not in origin related, though there was much commerce and reciprocal cultural influence between them, and they were always in competition and often in open conflict. The Greeks, whose language belonged to the Indo-European family, had spread from mainland Greece to occupy Crete and the islands of the Aegean and the western coast of Asia Minor. The Phoenicians, who spoke a Semitic language closely related to Hebrew, inhabited Canaan, the coastal area of what is now the Republic of the Lebanon. Neither people, though both were conscious of a distinct nationality, constituted an integrated political entity. Both comprised numerous self-contained 'city-states'. The maritime expansion of the Greeks and Phoenicians had two aspects: the development of trade, especially the search for new sources of foodstuffs and metals; and the removal by colonization of the excess population of the homelands. The principal direction of Greek expansion was westwards to Sicily and Italy, but they also penetrated south-eastwards into Levantine waters: around the middle of the seventh century BC some of them began to trade with and settle in Egypt, and a little later others began to colonize the coast of Cyrenaica to the west of Egypt. The Phoenicians had long traded with Egypt, but during this period they extended their activities into the western

[1] These names are not those by which these peoples referred to themselves. 'Greeks' we derive from the Latin *Graeci*: the people called themselves (as they still do) *Hellenes*. 'Phoenicians' we derive from the Greek *Phoinikes* (Latinized as *Phoenices*): the people called themselves *Kinanu*, or 'Canaanites'.

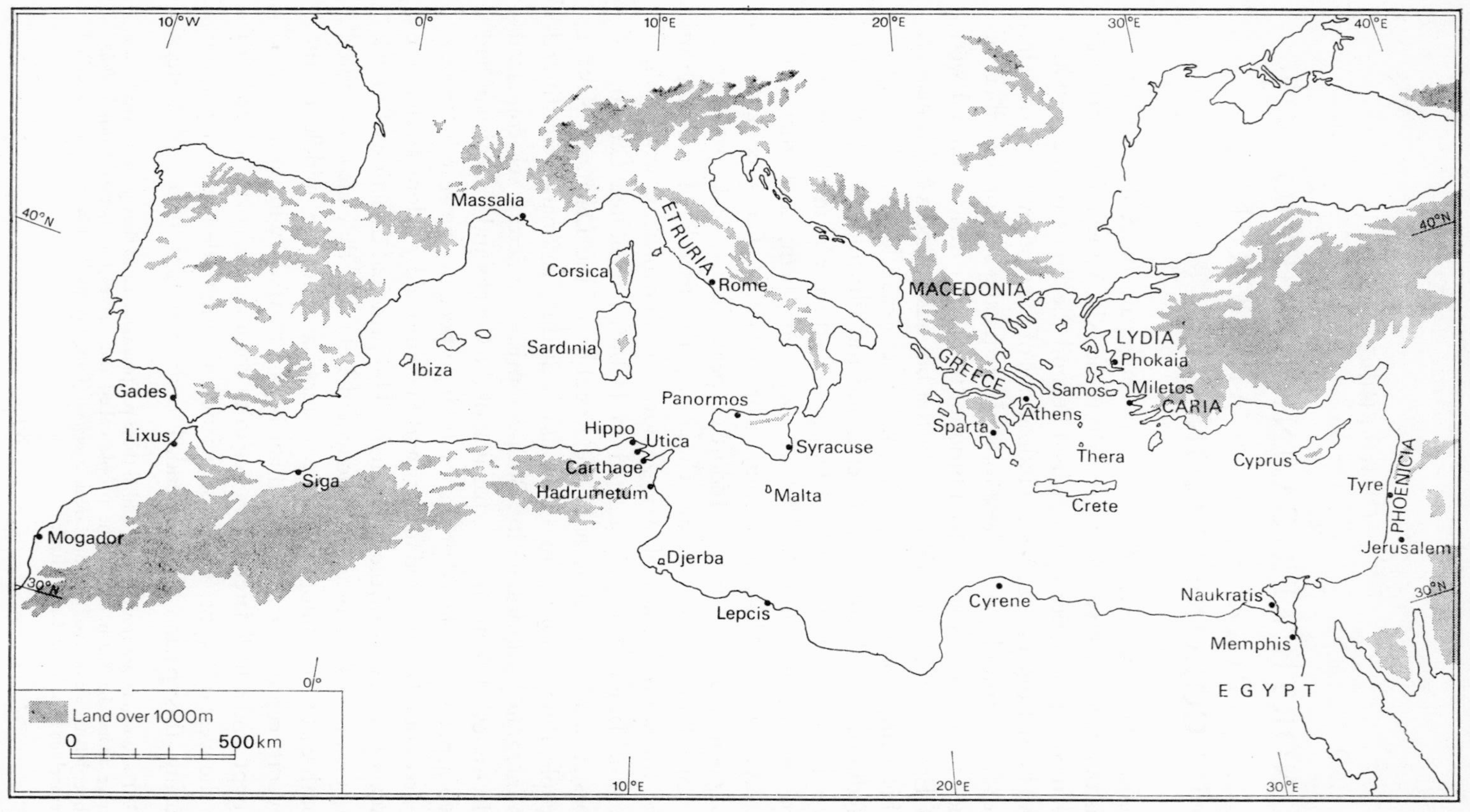

17 The Mediterranean in the era of Phoenician and Greek colonization.

Mediterranean, as far as Spain, and planted colonies along the North African coast west of Cyrenaica.

It should be stressed that Greek and Phoenician colonization had a different character from that of the European nations in recent times. It was unusual for a colony to remain subject to the state which planted it. Any permanent settlement was normally organized from the first as an independent city-state, though it would usually maintain strong sentimental ties with its mother-city. It should also be pointed out that while the immigration and settlement of aliens provide to some extent a common theme in the history of Egypt and of the rest of North Africa in this period, the colonizers in Egypt and those further west had quite different experiences. In Egypt they found a concentrated population organized in a sophisticated state, which was able to impose conditions on the newcomers. Along the North African littoral west of Egypt, which was inhabited by peoples to whom the Greeks applied the general name 'Libyans',[1] there were no such concentrations of population or strong states, and the Greeks and Phoenicians were able to displace or subjugate the natives and establish their own self-contained and independent communities.

THE SAITE DYNASTY IN EGYPT, 663 TO 525 BC

By the eighth century BC Egypt had greatly declined, both in external strength and in internal cohesion, since the days of its glory under the New Kingdom. Egyptian control over Syria and over Kush to the south had been lost. In Syria the dominant power was now the empire of Assyria, while in Kush there had arisen an independent kingdom with its capital at Napata. Internally, the central power of the Pharaoh had effectively collapsed. Upper Egypt was ruled as a virtually independent principality by the High Priest of the god Amun-Reʿ at Thebes,[2] while in Lower Egypt there were rival dynasties of Pharaohs, and effective power passed increasingly to the hereditary governors of the individual 'nomes' (administrative divisions) of the Delta. The later Pharaohs of the New Kingdom had adopted the practice of granting allotments of land to the foreign (especially Libyan) soldiers whom they employed in

[1] On the name 'Libyans', see p. 141.

[2] Amun-Reʿ had become, with the rise of Thebes to political dominance in Egypt, the most powerful, and the most richly endowed, of the Egyptian gods. Every Pharaoh was officially a son of Amun-Reʿ. With the decline of pharaonic power after the New Kingdom, the High Priest of Amun-Reʿ increasingly arrogated to himself effective power in the south of Egypt.

their armies. The descendants of these soldiers now formed a distinct class, called by Greek writers the *machimoi* or 'warriors', enjoying hereditary possession of their allotments in return for military service. Their primary allegiance, it would seem, was not to the Pharaoh, but to the governor of the nome in which they held their land. With this support, the nome-chiefs were able to defy the authority of the titular Pharaohs, and became increasingly absorbed in a power struggle among themselves.

The integrity of the kingdom was briefly restored, not by the Egyptians, but by their erstwhile subjects of Kush. The kings of Napata established control first over Thebes and then over the petty chiefs of the Delta during the latter half of the eighth century BC. But they failed in their attempts to reassert Egyptian power in Syria, running up against the might of Assyria, and their ineffectual aggressions brought down upon Egypt the Assyrian army. Egypt thus became, from the 670s, a battleground between the forces of Assyria and Kush. In 671 the Assyrians drove the Kushite king Taharqa from the Delta and forced the submission of the nome-chiefs, among the more important of whom was Necho, chief of Sais. But there remained much support for Taharqa in the Delta, and the nome-chiefs periodically intrigued for his return. In 669 Taharqa was able to march north and occupy Lower Egypt, but the Assyrians expelled him again in 666. In 664 Taharqa's successor at Napata, Tanwetamani, marched north in his turn and penetrated into the Delta, where he apparently killed Necho of Sais. But the Assyrians drove him back, and this time pushed into Upper Egypt and subjected Thebes to a ruinous sack (663). The continual superiority of the Assyrians over the Kushites and Egyptians in these wars was probably in part due to their possession of an iron weaponry, while Egypt and Kush were still using bronze.

From this unpromising situation, a son of Necho of Sais, called Psamtek (whose name the Greeks rendered as 'Psammetichos'), emerged as the ruler of a reunited and independent Egypt, establishing the dynasty conventionally enumerated as the XXVIth. Precisely how this happened is unclear. For official purposes Psamtek reckoned the beginning of his reign from the death of Taharqa. One possibility is that he was appointed as viceroy of Egypt, perhaps with the nominal status of Pharaoh, by the Assyrians after the repulse of Tanwetamani. However, Egyptian traditions reported by the Greek historian Herodotus, which patriotically fail to recall the circumstance of conquest by the Assyrians, assert that Egypt was divided between twelve 'kings', among whom was Psamtek, and that Psamtek by force overthrew the other eleven and seized sole power for himself. However fanciful the details, this story no doubt preserves an authentic tradition of fighting against the rival nome-chiefs of the Delta. Psamtek also had to vindicate his claim to rule Egypt against Assyria and Kush. He profited by the decline of Assyrian power after the 660s, but apparently some fighting against the Assyrians was necessary: an Assyrian inscription refers to the sending of military forces by Gyges, King of Lydia in Asia Minor (who died in 652), to aid the rebellion of the King of Egypt. In the south Tanwetamani still controlled the resources of Kush, and claimed to be the rightful king of Egypt. During Psamtek's early years, Thebes continued to acknowledge Tanwetamani as Pharaoh. A Greek story of a campaign by Psamtek against an 'Ethiopian' king called 'Tementhes' (Tanwetamani?) perhaps recalls fighting at this time. In 654 Psamtek was able to secure recognition at Thebes, by arranging the adoption of one of his daughters as heir to the 'God's Wife' of Amun-Reʿ. (This office had replaced that of high priest as the most important in the Theban priesthood, and was at this time held by a sister of Taharqa.) A garrison was placed at Elephantine to guard the southern frontier against Kush. Other garrisons at Marea and Daphnae protected Egypt against the Libyans in the west and against attack from Syria in the east.

It appears that Psamtek and his successors of the Saite Dynsaty were anxious to claim that they had restored the glories of Old Egypt. This at least is a plausible explanation of the conscious archaism which characterized Egyptian civilization during the Saite period. There was a great vogue for art in an archaizing style, especially in the paintings and relief sculptures of funerary monuments, which were often copied exactly from ancient models. This style, it is true, can already be traced at Memphis under the Kushite Dynasty, but it certainly attained its fullest expression and its greatest popularity under the Saite kings. The archaizing style in fact outlived the Saite Dynasty, and persisted into the third century BC. An interesting feature is that the models for Saite art were usually taken from the remote IV–VI Dynasties of the Old Kingdom, the great pyramid-builders of Memphis, ignoring the more recent period of imperial greatness under the New Kingdom Dynasties (XVIII–XIX) of Thebes. This was perhaps an expression of local partisanship by a dynasty of northern origin, against the cultural dominance of the now overshadowed southern capital of Thebes. Saite archaism was not restricted to art. The period also saw the revival of cults, priesthoods and titles of the Old Kingdom which had long been neglected or defunct.

Yet there was a crucial difference between the Saite period and the past glories whose memory it cultivated. The Saite achievement did not rest upon native effort alone. The independence, military power and material prosperity of Saite Egypt depended to a large extent on foreigners. Most important of these were the Greeks, who first came to Egypt in large numbers under Psamtek. Apart from its significance for the actual course of Egyptian history, this involvement of Greeks in the affairs of Egypt marks an important historiographical development, since from the reign of Psamtek a considerable amount of information on Egyptian history can be derived from the written records of the Greeks. The main strength of Psamtek's army was a force of mercenaries from Greece and Caria (in Asia Minor). Under a later king, this force is said to have numbered 30,000. According to the tradition recorded by Herodotus, the first of these mercenaries were pirates who had landed in the Delta on a plundering expedition, and were taken into the service of Psamtek and used by him to defeat his rivals in Egypt. It is also likely that the forces sent to Psamtek's aid by Gyges of Lydia would have consisted of such mercenaries. The activities of such soldiers of fortune illustrate a less formal process than that of organized colonization by which the excess population of Greece might find its way into foreign lands. Psamtek established his mercenaries in two settlements astride the Pelusian branch of the Nile below Bubastis, which the Greeks called the *Stratopeda* or 'camps', whose site has not been precisely located. Archaeological evidence attests the presence of Greeks among the garrison of Daphnae also, while an Egyptian inscription refers to Greeks among the garrison of Elephantine. There were also apparently Phoenician mercenaries, since we hear of a 'Camp of the Tyrians' at Memphis, and, later, Jews were recruited. It was the Carians who defeated 'Tementhes' for Psamtek, and the mercenaries were regularly employed in the foreign wars of the Saite kings.

The Saite kings also developed Egypt's foreign trade. Psamtek is said to have adopted a deliberate policy of encouraging Phoenician and Greek merchants to come to Egypt. The Greek traders established their own settlement at Naukratis, on the Canopic branch of the Nile. One tradition asserts that the first settlement at Naukratis was made by some Greeks of Miletos (a city in Asia Minor) who were engaged in naval operations in the Delta – whether in the service of Psamtek or as freelance adventurers is not clear. However that may be, there is no

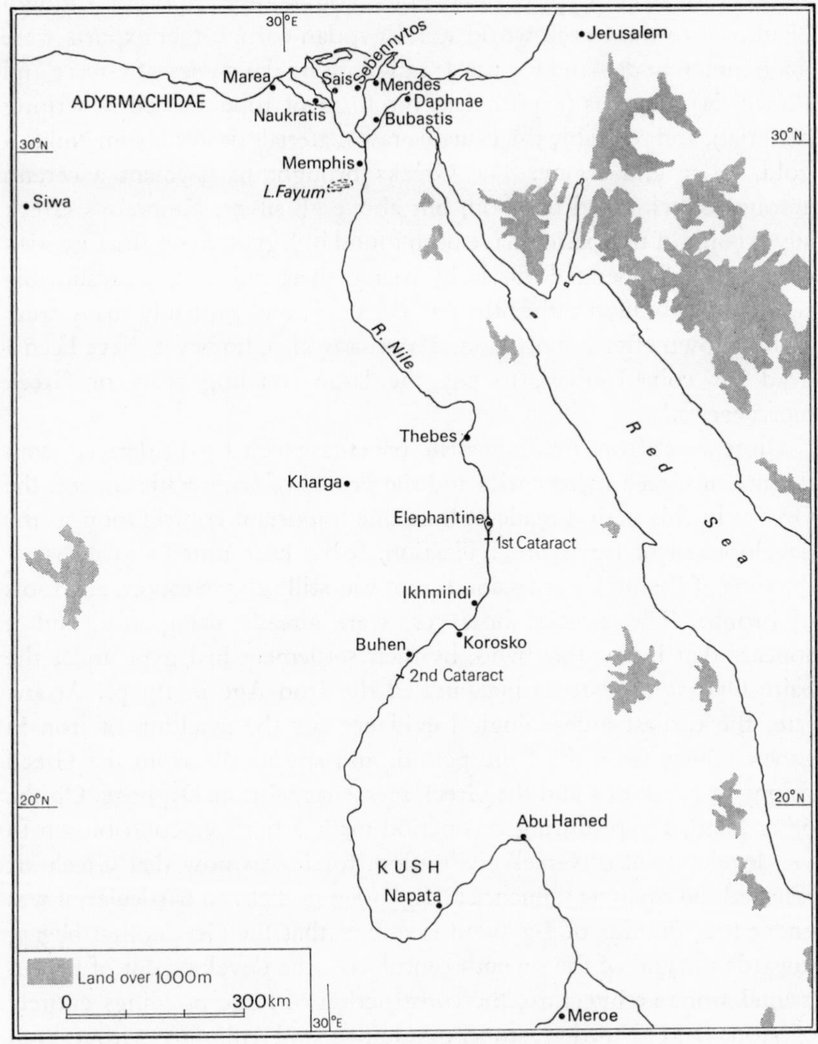

18 Egypt, 663–323 BC.

doubt about the commercial character of the city later on. Archaeological evidence indicates that the site was occupied by *c.* 620 BC at the latest. Naukratis was unlike most Greek colonies, which were founded as self-contained city-states by a single mother-city. It developed purely as a settlement of traders, and at first probably had few permanent settlers and little organized civic life. It was also cosmopolitan, attracting settlers from numerous Greek cities in the Aegean and Asia Minor, as well as from Cyprus. The chief commodity exported through Naukratis to the Greek world was Egyptian corn. Other exports were linen (much in demand for use as sail-cloth by the navies of Greece and Phoenicia), papyrus (exported in the form of rope as well as writing material), and probably the valuable raw materials derived from Nubia – gold, ivory and ebony. The Greeks brought in payment a certain amount of wine and olive-oil, but above all silver. Numerous Greek silver coins of this period have been found in Egypt. Since the Egyptian economy still operated purely by barter, these coins were presumably regarded as bullion rather than as currency, and probably many were melted down after importation. There may also, however, have been a need for coined silver, to pay the large standing army of Greek mercenaries.

Quite apart from the immediate benefits which Egypt derived from the use of Greek mercenaries and the profits of trade with Greece, the Greeks in this period made at least one important contribution to the development of Egyptian civilization. It has been noted above that at the time of Psamtek's accession Egypt was still using weapons and tools of bronze. The Greeks, however, were already using iron, and it appears that it was they who, by their settlement in Egypt under the Saite Dynasty, belatedly inaugurated the Iron Age in Egypt. At any rate, the earliest archaeological evidence for the smelting of iron in Egypt comes from the Saite period, and specifically from the Greek colony at Naukratis and the Greek mercenary fort at Daphnae. On the other hand, Egypt during this period made a decisive contribution to the development of Greek civilization, for it was now that Greek art received the catalytic influence of Egyptian models. In particular, it was under the stimulus of Egyptian examples that the Greeks first began, towards the end of the seventh century BC, the development of monumental stone architecture, the construction of large buildings entirely of stone and featuring stone mouldings and columns with carved capitals and bases, and of monumental stone sculpture, the carving of life-size and larger human figures in stone.[1]

Though able to defend the independence and integrity of Egypt, the Saite kings were less successful in asserting Egyptian power abroad. Psamtek, during his long reign (663–610 BC), seems prudently to have eschewed any extravagant projects. Towards the end of his reign, however, he sent forces into Syria. The empire of Assyria was now

[1] On this, see further J. Boardman, *The Greeks overseas: the archaeology of their early colonies and trade*, 2nd edn (London, 1973), 139–51.

threatened by a powerful coalition of Babylon and the Medes, and the interests of the balance of power aligned the Egyptians with their former Assyrian conquerors. In 616 Psamtek's forces operated in support of Assyria, but this aid could not prevent the capture and destruction of the Assyrian capital, Nineveh, in 612. Psamtek's son and successor, another Necho (who is the Necho of the Old Testament), who reigned from 610 until 595, campaigned personally in Syria with more substantial forces, at first in support of the claimant to the defunct throne of Assyria, and later on his own account. He had some successes, and for a short while controlled Judah and Phoenicia, but in 605 was decisively defeated at Carchemish by Nebuchadnezzar of Babylon. The Syrian conquests were lost, though Necho was able to beat off a Babylonian attack on Egypt in 601. Necho also built up Egypt as a naval power, and maintained warships in both the Mediterranean and Red seas. As with the army, Egypt was here dependent upon foreigners, for many of Necho's ships seem to have been manned by Phoenicians and Greeks. Necho's maritime interests were directed especially towards the Red Sea. He undertook, and possibly completed, the cutting of a canal between the Nile and the Red Sea, following the line of the Wadi Tumilat.[1] He also attempted to open up a sea-route between the Mediterranean and Red seas. Some Phoenicians in his service were ordered to sail around Africa from the Red Sea and return to Egypt through the Mediterranean. They are said to have achieved this, taking over two years, though many modern scholars have doubted whether they can in fact have done so. In any case, even if this feat was achieved, the sea-route was evidently judged too long or too difficult for the establishment of regular communications by it to be worth while, for there was no immediate attempt to follow up the voyage.

Necho's son and successor, Psamtek II (595–589 BC), became involved, in uncertain circumstances, in a war in Kush. In 593 Psamtek's army, including Greek and Carian mercenaries, invaded Kush and seems to have sacked the capital at Napata. Egyptian control was perhaps extended south to the Second Cataract, for there is some evidence for the presence of garrisons of Carians at Ikhmindi and Buhen. Egypt thus secured control of the gold-mines of the Wadi ʿAllaqi, in the desert east of the Nile between the First and Second

[1] The sources assert that Necho abandoned the canal before it was complete. However, it appears that the canal required periodic recutting, so that it is possible that the notion that Necho failed to complete it is a false inference from the fact that it had later to be cut again by the Persian King Darius (521–486 BC): see p. 100.

Cataracts, the main gold-producing area of Nubia. There was no attempt at a permanent occupation of Kush itself, but the Kushite kingdom now ceased to present a threat to Egypt. In fact, during the sixth century BC, perhaps as a direct result of Psamtek II's invasion, the centre of the kingdom was shifted south, and Meroe replaced Napata as the capital. (See chapter 4, pp. 217–18.)

Psamtek II's son and successor, Waḥibreʿ, who took the throne-name Ḥaʿaʿibreʿ (whence the 'Hophra' of the Old Testament and the 'Apries' of the Greeks), rashly resumed the offensive in Syria, and raised Judah and Phoenicia in revolt against Babylon. However, the Egyptian forces appear to have played little effective role, and to have soon been withdrawn, leaving the Babylonians to reduce Jerusalem (586) and Tyre (573). Some remnants of the defeated Jews after the fall of Jerusalem were received into Egypt and settled, according to the Old Testament, at 'Tahpanhes', probably the fort of Daphnae. The Jewish colony at Elephantine, whose existence is first attested in 494 BC, probably had its origin in the same circumstance. Under Waḥibreʿ, the Egyptian king's dependence on foreign mercenaries was shown to be doubly dangerous. In the first place, the loyalty of these foreigners was doubtful. At some point during the reign of Waḥibreʿ, the Greek and other foreign troops in the Elephantine garrison mutinied and threatened to migrate into Nubia, but were pacified by the commander of the garrison, Nesḥor, who recorded the incident in an extant inscription. Even more serious was the resentment aroused among the Egyptians by the presence of the foreigners. The Greek settlers in Egypt were extremely unpopular. Resentment was strongest among the warrior-class, the *machimoi*, who felt particularly slighted by the privileged position of the Greek mercenaries. These tensions came to a head when, in *c.* 570, Waḥibreʿ sent aid to the Libyans of Cyrenaica, who were involved in a war with the Greek colonists of Cyrene. For this campaign he did not use his Greek mercenaries, possibly because he doubted their loyalty against fellow-Greeks, but an army of Egyptians. The Egyptian army made the long desert march westwards, only to be overwhelmingly defeated by the Cyrenaeans. To the Egyptian soldiers, this defeat by Greeks could only be due to treachery. They mutinied, declaring that Waḥibreʿ had deliberately sent them to destruction. ʿAḥmose, a high-ranking palace official sent to appease the rebels, instead put himself at their head. Waḥibreʿ was apparently forced to accept the installation of ʿAḥmose as co-king (569). Three years later he raised his Greek and Carian mercenaries, 30,000 strong, in an attempt to recover power. The Egyptians rallied to ʿAḥmose, and the mercenaries, heavily outnumbered, were defeated. Waḥibreʿ was captured and executed.

ʿAḥmose (called by the Greeks 'Amasis'), who thus became sole king (566 BC), was a native of Sais, and is conventionally counted among the kings of the XXVI Dynasty, though he does not appear to have been related to the earlier Saite kings. He endeavoured to placate the Egyptian xenophobic feelings which had brought him to the throne by placing limitations on the movements of Greeks in Egypt, and rigorously restricting Greek traders to the single port of Naukratis. But he did not attempt to close Egypt to Greek traders. Their trade was too profitable. In fact, the archaeological evidence seems to indicate that under ʿAḥmose the volume of trade with Greece increased. He did not even disband the hated Greek mercenaries. They also were too valuable. In fact, ʿAḥmose was to end up as hated as Waḥibreʿ had been for his dependence on the Greeks. The Greeks remembered him as a 'friend of the Greeks' (*philhellen*), and recalled his numerous gifts to Greek temples. The attitude of his Egyptian subjects may be judged from the fact that he found it necessary to move the Greek and Carian mercenaries from the Stratopeda to the capital at Memphis to protect himself against them. The internal unrest persisted. If, later, Egyptians were disposed to look back upon the reign of ʿAḥmose as a time of unparalleled good fortune and prosperity, when 'the river was generous to the land, and the land to the people',[1] this was no doubt primarily by contrast with the period of subjection to foreign rule which followed his death.

In his foreign policy, ʿAḥmose fared little better than his predecessors. While still co-king with Waḥibreʿ (*c.* 568 BC), he appears to have sent a force of Greek mercenaries into Syria, but when this was defeated by the Babylonians he made no further attempts to interfere in this area. He also attempted to redeem the failure of Waḥibreʿ at Cyrene, and we find him exploiting the internal dissensions of that city in an attempt to establish his control there. However, when his candidate for the Cyrenaean throne was murdered, he was induced to accept the succession of his rival, and he subsequently signified his reconciliation to Cyrene by marrying a Cyrenaean woman and dedicating gifts in Cyrenaean temples. The one solid achievement of ʿAḥmose was to use the fleet created by Necho to reduce Cyprus and exact tribute from the island. The main factor in foreign affairs at this time was the rise of

[1] Herodotus, *Histories*, II, 177.1.

Persia under its king Cyrus II, who in 550 had overthrown and incorporated the empire of the Medes. The other powers, Egypt along with Babylon, Lydia and Sparta, the most powerful state in Greece, gravitated together in an alliance to resist the Persian advance. Their resistance was uncoordinated and ineffectual, and Cyrus was able to conquer Lydia in 545 and Babylon in 538. ʿAḥmose, isolated, then attempted to strengthen his position by an alliance with the Greek island state of Samos, then, under its 'tyrant' Polykrates,[1] the leading naval power. It was probably his military dependence on the Greeks, both the mercenaries in Egypt and allies outside, in the face of the Persian threat, which motivated the 'philhellenism' of ʿAḥmose in the later years of his reign. The son and successor of Cyrus, Cambyses II (529–522), was already preparing the invasion of Egypt when ʿAḥmose died in 525. The son of ʿAḥmose, a third Psamtek, succeeded to the Egyptian throne, but occupied it only for six months. He was able to put up little effective resistance when the Persian army moved in (525). Polykrates and the Cyprians deserted Psamtek, and supplied forces for Cambyses. One of the commanders of Psamtek's Greek mercenaries also defected to the Persians. Psamtek was quickly defeated and captured. He was at first spared, but, on being detected plotting rebellion, was executed.

PERSIAN RULE IN EGYPT, 525 TO 404 BC

Egypt secured, Cambyses seems to have conceived a grandiose scheme of conquests in Africa. On the fall of Egypt, the Libyans bordering Egypt on the west (the Adyrmachidai) and the Greek cities of Cyrenaica, Cyrene and Barce (Barca), sent gifts to Cambyses in token of submission. Cambyses wished to send his fleet to reduce Carthage, the principal Phoenician colony in North Africa, but the Phoenicians, who formed the main strength of his fleet, refused to attack their own colonists. He did, however, launch attacks by land against the Ammonii, the inhabitants of the Oasis of Siwa in the desert to the west of Egypt, and against Kush to the south. An expedition was sent against Siwa from Thebes, and reached the Oasis of Kharga, but was lost in the desert between Kharga and Siwa. The Ammonii thus escaped, though Kharga was subjected to Persian rule. The expedition against Kush, led by Cambyses himself, also encountered trouble when it ran out of pro-

[1] The Greek term *tyrannos* was applied to rulers who held absolute power unconstitutionally, and did not originally imply 'tyrannical' rule in the modern sense.

visions in the desert, having probably taken the route from Korosko to Abu Hamed in order to cut out the great westerly bend of the Nile, and was forced to turn back. Cambyses did not reach Napata or Meroe, but he did reduce the 'Ethiopians' of Lower Nubia above the First Cataract, thus securing for Persia control of the ʿAllaqi gold-mines. After Cambyses's departure from Egypt, Aryandes, the first Persian *satrap* or governor of Egypt, used the internal dissensions of the Greek cities of Cyrenaica as an excuse to send a large Persian force westwards, which captured Barce and penetrated as far west as Euhesperides (Benghazi). A second expedition repeated the capture of Barce in *c.* 483. Later in the fifth century BC, Cyrene and Barce recovered their independence, but the Adyrmachidai seem to have remained subject to Persia.

The Persian kings attempted initially to conciliate Egyptian national feeling by representing themselves as a new dynasty of Pharaohs. Cambyses had himself formally invested with the titulary of a Pharaoh at a ceremony in the Temple of Neith at Sais, taking the Egyptian throne-name Mesutireʿ. His example was followed by his successor Darius (521–486), who took the name Stitureʿ. The Persian kings could not, however, reside permanently in Egypt, and the day-to-day administration of the country was in the hands of the *satrap*, who resided at Memphis, and who was always a Persian of royal or noble birth. With the resources of Egypt under his control, the *satrap* was in a strong position to defy the central authority of the Persian king, but this is only recorded to have occurred once, with the first *satrap*, Aryandes, who was executed by Darius.[1] Initially some Egyptians retained important posts under the *satrap*, but ultimately all but the lowest levels of the administration were staffed by Persians, and Aramaic replaced Egyptian as the language of the bureaucracy. The native priesthood, however, was maintained. A large garrison was established in the White Fort, the citadel of Memphis, and others at the Saite forts of Daphnae and Elephantine. These garrisons were always commanded by Persians, and were largely Persian in composition, though later, at any rate, the Elephantine garrison also included locally resident Jews and some Egyptians. The Greek and Carian mercenaries of the Saite period now disappeared. The *satrapy* or province of Egypt paid under Darius, according to Herodotus, a tribute of 700 *talents* of silver annually,[2]

1 Aryandes's offence is said to have been the striking of silver coins (which might imply a claim to independence). But this story raises difficulties, since coinage was certainly not used in Egypt at this time.

2 The *talent* was a unit of weight and currency, variously calculated, but here representing approximately 37 kg.

besides revenues traditionally due to the Pharaoh, such as the profits of the fisheries of the Fayum, and the burden of supplying corn for the garrison of the White Fort. Egypt also had to supply troops for the Persian army and ships for the Persian fleet. The Adyrmachidai and the Greek cities of Cyrenaica seem originally to have formed a separate province, called by the Persians 'Putaya', but later Darius incorporated them into the Egyptian *satrapy*. They were obliged to pay tribute and to provide troops, but do not appear to have suffered the imposition of a Persian administration. Probably the Persians were content to ensure that dependable men served as their kings. The 'Ethiopians' of Lower Nubia conquered by Cambyses also formed a separate province, called Kushiya. They were obliged to provide troops, and to pay a regular tribute of gold, ivory, ebony and slaves.

Though Egypt was subjected once more to foreign rule, the Persian conquest was far from being an unmixed evil. The burden of the tribute was probably not crippling, especially as the Persians were able to maintain the prosperity of Saite times. The trade with Greece, indeed, seems, from archaeological evidence, to have been interrupted for a few years after the conquest in 525 BC, but by *c.* 500 it had revived again. In another direction, the Persian occupation proved a stimulus to Egypt's foreign contacts, for the Persians resumed Necho's work in developing Egyptian interests in the Red Sea. Their main concern was probably to establish communications between the various provinces of their extensive empire, of which Egypt was one of the more remote, but their activities no doubt stimulated trade also. Under Darius, a Carian in the service of Persia, Skylax, undertook a voyage of exploration in which he sailed in thirty months from the river Indus along the coasts to Egypt, thus demonstrating for the first time the possibility of seaborne contacts between Egypt and India. Darius also completed or renovated Necho's canal between the Nile and the Red Sea, and used it to establish regular seaborne communications between Egypt and Persia. His son and successor, Xerxes (486–465), attempted to emulate Necho's alleged circumnavigation of Africa. A Persian nobleman, Sataspes, was ordered to sail around Africa from west to east. He picked up a ship in Egypt and set off down the Atlantic coast of Morocco, but lost heart and turned back, to be executed for his failure. In other respects also Egypt benefited from the efficient administration of the early Persian kings. Darius, for example, carried out a codification of the laws of Egypt, and was remembered in one tradition as one of the great lawgivers of Egypt.

Nevertheless, Persian rule was unpopular in Egypt. The justification for this which the Egyptians offered in retrospect was the lack of respect allegedly shown by the Persians towards the traditional institutions of Egypt. Herodotus reports allegations that Cambyses violated the mummified body of ʿAḥmose, and even that he killed the bull-god Apis.[1] These stories have been doubted, but it does appear that Cambyses made severe cuts in the revenues of the Egyptian temples. This policy seems hardly consistent with his having himself formally proclaimed as Pharaoh at Sais, and it seems likely that his measures against the temples were provoked by the political intrigues of the priests. Moreover, Darius took care to advertise his respect for the gods of Egypt. In 518, on a visit to Egypt, he granted money for the burial of the Apis bull, and later he undertook building works in the service of the gods, notably a temple for Amun-Reʿ in the Oasis of Kharga. It would appear probable, in fact, that Persian hostility to Egyptian institutions was rather a result than a cause of Egyptian resistance to Persian rule. The truth is probably that the articulate classes of Egyptian society, and especially the priests, had a developed national consciousness which precluded any whole-hearted acceptance of alien rule. The Egyptians certainly took every opportunity offered by Persian internal dissensions or military weakness to revolt.

The first such revolt occurred in 487 BC, the Egyptians being no doubt encouraged by the defeat of the Persians in an invasion of Greece at the battle of Marathon (490). Darius died (486) before he could deal with the revolt, but Xerxes suppressed it with great severity in 484. He appointed his brother Achaemenes as *satrap*, and, according to Herodotus, Egypt 'was reduced to a much worse state of slavery than under Darius'.[2] The Persian kings abandoned their attempt to conciliate Egyptian national feeling. Xerxes did not, like Cambyses and Darius, take the Egyptian royal titles, and there was little building in honour of the gods of Egypt. After Xerxes, indeed, no Persian king even visited Egypt.

The death of Xerxes and the ensuing civil war in Persia (465) were the signal for a second revolt. The leader of this revolt, whose name was rendered by the Greeks as 'Inaros', was king of the vassal Libyans west of Egypt, the Adyrmachidai, but his name is Egyptian (Ienheru) and, as his father's name is given as 'Psammetichos', possibly he was a

[1] The god Apis was supposedly incarnated in a succession of actual bulls, which were kept in the Temple of Apis at Memphis.

[2] Herodotus, *Histories*, VII.7.

descendant of the Saite kings. Inaros succeeded in raising most of Lower Egypt in revolt, but the *satrap* Achaemenes retained control of Memphis. In *c.* 460 a Greek fleet of the anti-Persian alliance led by Athens appeared at Cyprus, and Inaros persuaded its commanders to send him aid. The Greeks sailed up the Nile, joined forces with Inaros and defeated and killed Achaemenes. The remnants of the Persian army, together with some 'loyal' Egyptians, were then besieged in the White Fort at Memphis. The White Fort, however, survived a protracted blockade, and in 456 the Persians were able to send an army into Egypt, defeat the besiegers and relieve Memphis. Inaros and the Greeks were then besieged in turn on the island of Prosopitis, which was finally taken by storm in 454. The remnants of the Greek force escaped overland to Cyrene. Inaros surrendered on a promise of his life, but after being kept prisoner for five years was crucified. His son Thannyras, however, was allowed to succeed him as King of the Adyrmachidai. This was not quite the end of the revolt. A leader called by the Greeks 'Amyrtaios' (Amonortais) held out in the marshes of the Delta. In *c.* 451 an Athenian fleet again appeared at Cyprus, and forces were detached to aid Amyrtaios in Egypt. But after some fighting in Cyprus the Greeks withdrew, and soon after (*c.* 449) Athens appears to have made peace with Persia, abandoning her Egyptian allies to their fate. The end of Amyrtaios is not recorded, but the revolt evidently died out or was suppressed soon after. In 445/4 we find a 'Psammetichos, King of Libya', probably a successor of Thannyras, or perhaps Thannyras himself, tempting Athens with a large gift of corn, but Athens was no longer interested. That the Egyptian revolt could only be sustained as a serious threat to Persia as long as it enjoyed Greek support is a striking illustration of how one essential feature of the Saite period, military dependence on the Greeks, persisted into the fifth century – though now it was a question of allies rather than of mercenaries.

The suppression of the revolts opened a brief period of peace and relative prosperity. The chief interest of this period is the visit to Egypt of the Greek historian and geographer Herodotus, probably in the 440s BC. Herodotus recorded a fascinating, if not always wholly accurate, account of the Egyptian society which he observed. Trade with Greece, interrupted during the wars, had revived. The Greek traders were no longer restricted to Naukratis, and might be met in any Egyptian market. They were no more popular for that. Herodotus found the Egyptians, secure in the pride of their ancient culture, as xenophobic as ever. 'They refuse', he observes, 'to adopt Greek customs, or indeed the customs of anyone else at all.'[1] Greeks in particular they regarded as unclean, because they did not observe the Egyptian prohibition on the meat of cows (sacred to the goddess Isis), so that

> No Egyptian man or woman will kiss a Greek on the mouth, or use a knife or skewers or a cauldron belonging to a Greek, or taste meat cut up with a Greek knife.[2]

Not the least valuable section of Herodotus's account of Egypt is that recording the traditions about Egypt's past which he was able to collect, from both Egyptians and locally resident Greeks, upon which any account of the Saite and Persian periods must lean heavily. Interestingly, the memories of his Egyptian informants exhibited the same selectivity as had directed Egyptian tastes in art since Saite times. They had a great deal to say about the Memphite pyramid-builders of the Old Kingdom, and next to nothing about the Theban kings of the New Kingdom.

THE LAST NATIVE DYNASTIES AND THE ESTABLISHMENT OF GREEK RULE IN EGYPT, 404 TO 323 BC

Despite the apparent calm of Egypt during Herodotus's visit, the Egyptians were far from being reconciled to Persian rule. The decline of Persian power during the latter half of the fifth century BC held out the prospect of a more successful revolt, and, in 404, on the death of King Darius II, with Persia riven by civil wars, the Egyptians seized their opportunity and revolted a third time. Thereafter Egypt maintained a precarious independence for some sixty years. The gods of Egypt at least benefited thereby. They recovered the revenues of which they had been deprived under the Persians, and temple-building was resumed. But this period, the last – until modern times – in which Egypt was ruled by Egyptians, was not one of strength or internal cohesion. Egypt hardly counted any longer as a major power. In the west, control over the Adyrmachidai seems to have been maintained, but the Greeks of Cyrenaica, and in the south the kingdom of Meroe, were never threatened by Egyptian might, while attempts to reassert Egyptian power in Syria proved wholly abortive. Internally, the period was characterized by chronic political instability, and punctuated by rebellions and coups d'état. Eight kings (grouped conventionally in

[1] Ibid. II. 91.1. [2] Ibid. II. 41.3.

three dynasties) ruled in sixty-one years. In effect, Egypt returned to the conditions which had existed before 663, when the petty chiefs of the Delta nomes had competed for power among themselves. And there was the same military dependence upon the Greeks as had characterized the Saite Dynasty and the revolts of the fifth century. We still hear of the indigenous warrior class, the *machimoi*, but the Egyptian kings increasingly relied upon the services of Greek mercenaries. Indeed, one important development of this period was that the Greeks, through their long involvement on the Egyptian side against Persia, at last began to be accepted by Egyptians with a measure of tolerance and even of friendship. The relative success of the revolt of 404 was due, not to Egyptian strength, but to Persian weakness. Distracted by wars with the Greeks, revolts in other provinces of their empire, and civil wars of their own, the Persians were unable to concentrate their resources on the reduction of Egypt.

The first king of the newly independent Egypt was a chief of Sais, a second Amyrtaios, who is conventionally counted as the sole king of the XXVIII Dynasty.[1] From his name, one might conjecture that he was a descendant of the rebel leader of the 450s. One Greek source appears to refer to him as 'Psammetichos, a descendant of the famous Psammetichos', which, taken with his origin from Sais, suggests that he was also descended from the earlier Saite Pharaohs. When Amyrtaios died in 399 BC, power was seized by the chief of Mendes, Nef'aurud (called by the Greeks 'Nepherites'), who thus became the founder of the XXIX Dynasty. On his death in 393, his son was pushed aside and the throne usurped by a certain Pshenmut, who reigned for only one year before being deposed in his turn by Hakor. Hakor sent aid to the Greeks of Cyprus, who were also in revolt against Persia, and in 385–383 beat off a Persian attack on Egypt. He was deposed in 380, and succeeded by a second Nef'aurud, who was murdered after a reign of only four months. Power was then seized by the chief of Sebennytos, Nekhtnebef (called by the Greeks 'Nektanebes'), who founded the last native dynasty of Egypt (the XXXth). Under this dynasty, as its numerous monuments attest, Egypt enjoyed considerable prosperity, but there were still troubles enough. Nekhtnebef survived a second Persian attempt to recover control of Egypt in 373 BC. His son and successor, Djeḥo, who succeeded in 362, planned to exploit the weakness of Persia, then apparently on the verge of disintegration, by invading Syria. For this purpose, he built up a large army of Greek mercenaries,

[1] The Persian kings from Cambyses to Darius II are counted as the XXVII Dynasty.

and called in Agesilaos, King of Sparta, an old enemy of Persia, to command it. To pay for this army, Djeḥo had recourse to a policy of systematic extortions from the temples of Egypt.[1] These exactions aroused widespread unrest in Egypt, and eventually rebellion. When Djeḥo invaded Syria, accompanied by Agesilaos and his own nephew Nekhtḥareḥbe, who commanded the Egyptian troops, Egypt was left in the charge of his brother, the father of Nekhtḥareḥbe, whose name is not recorded. This man led a revolt, and proclaimed his son Nekhtḥareḥbe as Pharaoh in place of Djeḥo. Agesilaos also declared for Nekhtḥareḥbe, and Djeḥo was compelled to flee for refuge into Persia. Nekhtḥareḥbe (called by the Greeks, somewhat confusingly, 'Nektanebos') thus became the last king of the dynasty (360). He was at once faced by a revolt in Egypt, led by a chief of Mendes. The new king was evidently too compromised in the policies of his uncle for his elevation to assuage the popular resentment at the latter's exactions. The Syrian project was abandoned, and Agesilaos and the Greek mercenaries were employed instead in suppressing the revolt inside Egypt. Meanwhile, Persia had recovered somewhat her strength under King Artaxerxes III, who had succeeded in 358. In 351 BC Artaxerxes led a third Persian attempt on Egypt, but the Egyptians, reinforced by Greek mercenaries, repulsed the Persians again. Then in 344 Nekhtḥareḥbe rashly took the offensive, supporting a revolt in Phoenicia. He sent a force of Greek mercenaries into Syria, where it deserted to Artaxerxes. Artaxerxes then augmented his army with more Greeks, and invaded Egypt. The Egyptian army, which also included Greek mercenaries, was defeated, and Egypt fell a second time to Persia (343). Nekhtḥareḥbe escaped into Kush. Resistance to the Persians continued. On the death of Artaxerxes (338), a certain Khabbash appears to have set himself up as Pharaoh, being acknowledged at both Memphis and Thebes, and ruled for two years. Having been presumably expelled from Egypt by the Persians, he appears (from an inscription of the Meroitic King Nastasen) to have turned south to invade Kush, only to be defeated there also (cf. chapter 4, p. 225).

Persian rule in Egypt was not to survive long, but its overthrow was not the work of the Egyptians. In 336 BC a Greek army, led by Alexander III (Alexander the Great), King of Macedonia, invaded the Persian empire. The Persian *satrap* of Egypt, summoned to fight against the

[1] Some silver coins bearing the name of Djeḥo in Greek and Demotic were probably struck to pay the Greek mercenaries recruited at this time. They are of interest as the earliest coins known to have been struck in Egypt (but cf. above, p. 99, n. 1).

invader, fell in battle in Syria. Control of Egypt was then briefly usurped by a commander of the Greek mercenaries on the Persian side, Amyntas, who represented himself as the newly appointed *satrap*, but he alienated the Egyptians by plundering the country and was killed in a local uprising. In 332 BC Alexander himself arrived in Egypt from Syria, and the Persian authorities surrendered to him without a fight. The Egyptians looked upon Alexander as a liberator, and he was enthusiastically welcomed at Memphis, where, to point the contrast with the Persian Cambyses, he sacrificed ostentatiously to the bull-god Apis. He also visited the Temple of Amun-Reʿ in the Oasis of Siwa west of Egypt, where the priests formally greeted him as Pharaoh and son of Amun-Reʿ. Early in 331 he left Egypt, and spent the rest of his life campaigning in the east. By his death in 323, he had completely conquered the old Persian empire.

During his brief visit to Egypt, Alexander ordered the foundation of a new Greek city at the western tip of the Delta, which still bears his name – Alexandria. In his arrangements for the administration of the country he made some attempt to conciliate Egyptian national feeling. Two Egyptians, Peteesis and Doloaspis,[1] were appointed as governors of Upper and Lower Egypt: before long, Peteesis relinquished his post, and Doloaspis became viceroy of all Egypt. But effective power lay rather with the army commanders, who were Macedonians, and more particularly with Kleomenes, a Greek from Naukratis, who was appointed to administer the finances of Egypt. The system was, in any case, short-lived. On Alexander's death in 323 BC, his generals divided up his empire among themselves, and the *satrapy* of Egypt was allotted to Ptolemaios (Ptolemy). Ptolemy quickly established his control within Egypt by executing Kleomenes, maintained his position against the rival generals, and finally (in 305 BC) assumed the title of king, establishing a dynasty which was to rule Egypt for almost three centuries.

It would be easy to see in this, the formal establishment of Greek rule in Egypt, the logical culmination of three centuries of Greek influence and patronage. But, except in so far as the earlier involvement of Greeks in Egyptian affairs prepared the Egyptians psychologically to accept Greek rule, such a view would be misleading. Alexander's conquest of Egypt was a by-product of his conquest of the Persian empire, and in no way grew out of the earlier, maritime, contacts of the

[1] The sources assert that both men were Egyptians, but the name of Doloaspis is not Egyptian, and perhaps he was an Asian.

Greeks with Egypt. Alexander, indeed, as a great territorial ruler who entered Egypt from Syria, was rather in the tradition of the Assyrians and the Persians. The establishment of the dynasty of the Ptolemies thus represents in a sense a real break in the continuity of Egyptian history. It can certainly be taken as a convenient point at which to end our consideration of Egypt.

THE GREEK COLONIZATION OF CYRENAICA; THE BATTIADAI (*c.* 639 TO *c.* 439 BC) AND THE REPUBLIC (*c.* 439 TO 322 BC)

While, as has been seen, one important theme in Egyptian history from the seventh century BC onwards was the establishment of Greek influence over the country, a parallel process was taking place further west, with the colonization of the North African coast by the Greeks and Phoenicians. In Egypt the Greeks had to come to terms with an organized and strong indigenous society, and were consequently obliged to serve or exploit, and ultimately to take over, the indigenous state structure. But the Libyans, less populous, less organized and less advanced, were more easily pushed aside by the colonists, who estabished their own state systems. While, therefore, the history of Egypt during the 'period of colonization' was still the history of the Egyptian state, that of the rest of North Africa has to be treated as the history of the new states established by the Greek and Phoenician immigrants.

The Greek colonists occupied the area subsequently known, from the name of their principal city Cyrene, as Cyrenaica. This was in a sense a natural extension of the Greek occupation of the Aegean islands and of Crete. Geographically, Cyrenaica belonged as much to the Greek Aegean world as to North Africa. The plateau of the Jebel Akhdar secures sufficient rainfall to make Cyrenaica cultivable, but on all sides – in the east, towards Egypt, and in the west, as well as to the south – it is surrounded by arid desert. Cyrenaica was thus more easily approachable by sea than by land; and it is, in fact, nearer to Crete than to Egypt.

The first move was in *c.* 639 BC, when the island state of Thera, after suffering a prolonged drought, sent out a small number of colonists (they sailed in only two ships) to establish a settlement in North Africa. They were guided by a Cretan purple-fisher who had some acquaintance with the coast, and settled first on the off-shore island of Platea (Bomba?). After only two years there, they moved to Aziris (unidentified) on the mainland opposite. After six years at Aziris, they were persuaded by the local Libyan tribe, the Giligamai, to move to a better site further west. This was not mere helpfulness on the part of the Giligamai. They took care to conceal from the Greeks the best site in the area, their own ceremonial centre at Irasa (Erasem?), and in fact led them to a site within the territory of a neighbouring tribe, the Asbystai. At any rate here – in 631 BC, according to the most probable account – the Theraeans founded a city which they called 'Cyrene'.[1]

The other successful Greek colonies in North Africa seem all to have been offshoots of Cyrene. Three settlements appear, on archaeological evidence, to have been established soon after Cyrene itself: Apollonia (Marsa Susa), which served as the port of Cyrene, and two settlements on the coast further west, one at a site whose original name is not recorded, which was later known as Ptolemais (Tolmeta), and one at Taucheira (Tocra). The city of Barce (El Merj), in the hinterland of Ptolemais, is said to have been founded by dissidents from Cyrene around the middle of the sixth century BC. Ptolemais and Taucheira

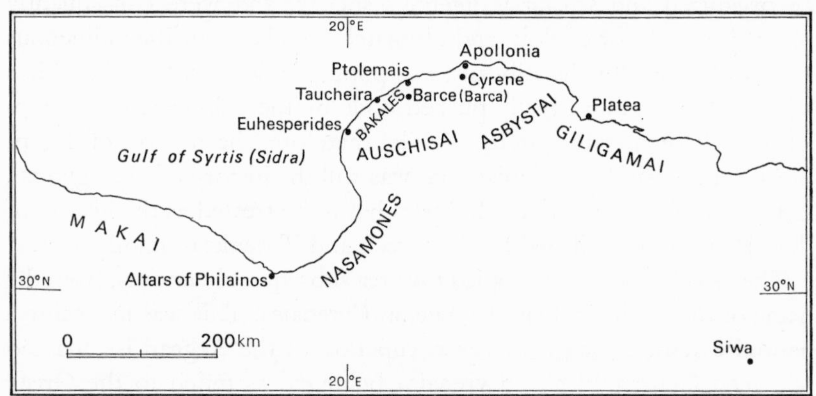

19 Cyrenaica.

became dependencies of Barce, the former serving as its port. A third independent city was founded further along the coast at Euhesperides (Benghazi), on archaeological evidence probably in the early sixth century. In later times, Cyrenaica was sometimes referred to as the 'Pentapolis', the 'Five Cities', the five being Cyrene, Apollonia, Ptolemais (which ultimately overshadowed Barce), Taucheira and Euhesperides. The Greeks thus colonized the western portion of the cultivable littoral of Cyrenaica. There were aspirations to colonize

[1] Actually, in the Doric dialect of Greek which the colonists spoke, *Kyrana*: in the more familiar Attic dialect, *Kyrene*, which was Latinized as *Cyrene*.

further west, but these were frustrated by the opposition of the Phoenicians, who were already established in the area. About 515 BC Dorieus, from Sparta, founded a city on the river Kinyps (Wadi Tareglat?) in Tripolitania, just east of the Phoenician settlement of Lepcis. He employed guides from Thera, and appears to have put in at Cyrene to pick up followers, but there is no indication that the Cyrenaean government officially supported the expedition. However, after only two years Dorieus was expelled by an alliance of the local Libyan tribe, the Makai, and the Phoenicians of Carthage. Greek ambitions in this area are also reflected in unfulfilled oracles quoted by Herodotus, predicting the establishment of a Spartan colony on the island of Phla (Djerba?) and the foundation of Greek cities on the shores of 'Lake Tritonis' (the Gulf of Gabes?). But the Carthaginians were able to secure Phoenician control over these areas and, at a date which is uncertain, some time during the fifth or early fourth centuries BC, after fighting between the Carthaginians and the Greeks of Barce, the boundary between the Phoenician and Greek spheres was set away to the east at the Gulf of Syrtis (Sidra), and formally marked by two tumuli known in antiquity as the 'Altars of Philainos'.

The pattern of these enterprises illustrates the fact that in this part of Africa Greek interests were primarily agricultural, and not commercial. Unlike the founders of Naukratis in Egypt, the Greek colonists in Cyrenaica and further west were interested not in trade with the natives, but in acquiring good agricultural land for settlement colonies. Theraean tradition connects the foundation of Cyrene with a prolonged drought, and it is likely that the main purpose of the enterprise was to unload the surplus population of the island. The non-commercial character of the Greek colonization is also indicated by the location of the two principal cities, Cyrene and Barce, some way inland, and not on the coast. The land of Cyrenaica was celebrated in antiquity for its fertility. Herodotus, who probably visited Cyrene, describes with wonder its three annual harvests, crops ripening successively on the three terraces of the plateau, and also speaks enthusiastically of the fertility of the Euhesperides area. Both cereals and tree-crops were grown, and the Greeks also raised herds of cattle, sheep and horses. The Kinyps area, the scene of Dorieus's venture, was likewise an island of relative fertility in the desert of the Tripolitanian littoral, enjoying a higher rainfall because of the relief of the Jebel Nefusa. Herodotus, who had not been there, describes it with some exaggeration as the best agricultural land in Africa.

Nevertheless, the Greek cities of Cyrenaica soon developed a considerable external trade. Archaeological evidence from Cyrene shows that from very early times the city maintained commercial contacts both with Greece and with Naukratis in Egypt. In the first place, the fertility of Cyrenaica was such that it yielded agricultural produce far in excess of the requirements of the Greek colonists, who were therefore able to supply quantities of corn to the Greek world. Wool and ox-hides were also exported. In the second place, trade with the Libyans of the interior developed to an unpremeditated importance. This was due to the discovery of the mysterious plant called in antiquity *silphion*, whose root served a variety of culinary and medicinal purposes. The plant grew only in Cyrenaica, and there it disappeared during Roman times, so that it cannot be botanically identified. It grew in the desert margins to the south of Greek territory, and the roots were collected by the Libyans, who brought them to the Greek cities. The kings of Cyrene endeavoured to exercise a monopoly of the trade in *silphion*, but a certain amount was smuggled out to the Carthaginians further west along the coast, and Carthage was also to some extent a supplier of *silphion* to the Mediterranean world. The profits derived by the Greeks from the trade in *silphion* were considerable, in token whereof the *silphion* plant became a favourite device on the coins of Cyrene, Barce and Euhesperides.

Thera, backward among Greek states, was still ruled by a king in the seventh century BC, and her political institutions were replicated in her colony at Cyrene. The founder and first King of Cyrene was Aristoteles, who after arriving in Africa assumed the title or surname 'Battos', which Herodotus explains as the Libyan word for 'king', and which his descendants adopted as a personal name. Aristoteles Battos is said to have reigned for forty years, reckoning probably from the first settlement on the island of Platea *c.* 639, so that he would have died *c.* 599. He was succeeded by his son Arkesilas, who reigned for sixteen years, presumably from *c.* 599 to *c.* 583. The house of Battos, the Battiadai, ruled Cyrene for eight generations, the kings being called alternately Battos and Arkesilas.

For half a century after its foundation, Cyrene remained a small settlement, but a great expansion took place under the third king, Battos II, surnamed 'Eudaimon' ('The Prosperous'), who succeeded probably *c.* 583. Battos invited new settlers from Greece, promising them allotments of land. There was a flood of immigrants from Crete and the Aegean islands, and from the Peloponnese on the Greek mainland. This development raised two problems. First, there was the difficulty of integrating the newcomers with the descendants of the original Theraean settlers. Second, land had to be taken from the local Libyans, the Asbystai, to provide for the new settlers. The Libyans, under their King Adikran, resisted and, as has been seen above, appealed for aid to the Egyptian King Waḥibreʿ, who sent an army west to fight the Greeks. The Cyrenaeans marched eastwards to meet the Egyptians as they emerged from their long desert march, and completely defeated them at Irasa (*c.* 570). Cyrenaean rule was extended over a considerable area of the interior, and the security of the Greek estates protected by the construction of fortified farmhouses, called in Greek *pyrgoi* ('towers'), around which small villages developed.

Battos II was succeeded by his son Arkesilas II, whose reign was beset by troubles, the Libyan problem inherited from his father, and now also internal divisions at Cyrene. Tradition alleges a deterioration in the character of the ruling family, the first Battos being a good and paternal ruler, but his successors avaricious and tyrannical. This certainly seems true of Arkesilas II, whose cruelty earned him the surname 'Chalepos' ('the Harsh'). He quarrelled with his brothers, four of whom left Cyrene and founded their own city away to the west at Barce. Moreover, the dissidents at Barce incited the discontented Libyans to revolt again against Cyrene. Arkesilas marched against the rebel Libyans, but they withdrew eastwards, drawing the Cyrenaeans into the desert, and defeated them with great slaughter at Leukon (unidentified). Arkesilas was then murdered by another brother, Laarchos. Laarchos seized power in Cyrene, nominally as regent for Arkesilas's young son Battos, and obtained a force of Egyptian soldiers from King ʿAḥmose to support himself in power. He proposed to consolidate his position by marrying Arkesilas's widow Eryxo and adopting the young Battos as his own son, but he was himself murdered by Eryxo and her brother Polyarchos. ʿAḥmose planned action against Cyrene, but he was pacified by a visit of Eryxo and Polyarchos to Egypt, and induced to acquiesce in the succession of Battos. Subsequently ʿAḥmose, as has been noted, maintained friendly relations with Cyrene, even taking to wife a Cyrenaean woman, probably a member of the royal family.

Under Battos III, constitutional reforms were effected at Cyrene in an attempt to prevent a repetition of these troubles. The royal house had forfeited its popularity by its excesses, and the king was now reduced to purely religious functions. No details of the new arrangements are recorded, but it can be presumed that, in accordance with the usual Greek pattern, effective power now passed to a council and elected magistrates drawn from the richer citizens. At the same time, the descendants of the non-Theraean settlers who had come to Cyrene under Battos II were brought into the citizen body on the same terms as the Theraeans. But this settlement was not to endure. Battos's son, Arkesilas III, supported by his formidable mother Pheretime, repudiated the reforms and claimed the ancient royal powers. Driven out of Cyrene, Arkesilas gathered an army of adventurers from Greece by promising grants of land. With this force he recovered power in Cyrene, and carried out a purge of his political opponents. He also gained control of, or an alliance with, Barce, for we find that city subsequently ruled by a certain Alazeir, who was the father-in-law of Arkesilas. Arkesilas was on the throne when in 525 BC Cambyses conquered Egypt, and he and Alazeir sent gifts to the Persian king to signify their submission. The Greek cities of Cyrenaica thus became tributary to Persia. Subsequently, alarmed by an oracle which appeared to forebode divine retribution for a massacre of his enemies, Arkesilas retired to the protection of Alazeir at Barce, leaving Cyrene under his mother Pheretime. But at Barce both Arkesilas and Alazeir were assassinated (*c*. 515?). Pheretime then appealed for aid to Aryandes, the Persian *satrap* of Egypt, who took the opportunity to strengthen Persian influence in Cyrenaica and provided her with an army. The Persians besieged and captured Barce. Pheretime crucified those implicated in her son's murder, and a large part of the population of Barce was carried off into slavery by the Persians. On this expedition, Persian forces penetrated as far west as Euhesperides. There was more trouble with Barce *c*. 483, when she refused to supply forces for the Persian invasion of Greece, and the city was a second time besieged and captured. The Greeks of Cyrenaica probably recovered their independence soon after the defeat of the Persians in Greece in 479. At any rate, Cyrene was presumably free again by 454, when it served as a refuge for the remnants of the Greek force defeated by the Persians in Egypt.

Pheretime died soon after the first Persian capture of Barce. The kingdom passed to a fourth Battos, surnamed 'Kalos' ('The Handsome'), of whom little is known, and then to a fourth Arkesilas, the last of the Battiad Dynasty. Arkesilas IV is chiefly renowned for having, in 462 BC, commissioned the poet Pindar to write two odes (*Pythian Odes*, IV and V), which are extant, in celebration of his victory in the chariot-race of the Pythian Games in Greece. Arkesilas had to suppress a popular rising in Cyrene, and killed or exiled many of his opponents. He also recruited mercenaries in Greece, and sent them as colonists to Euhesperides, apparently preparing a refuge for himself in case of trouble at Cyrene. In the event, however, he was assassinated at Cyrene. His son, yet another Battos, apparently escaped to Euhesperides, only to be murdered there. One source asserts that the Battiadai ruled Cyrene in all for 200 years. While this is clearly only an approximation, a date of *c.* 439 for the death of Arkesilas IV is consistent with what little other evidence we possess, and it can be accepted as approximately correct.

Much less is known of the history of Cyrenaica after the fall of the Battiad monarchy. Our relatively full knowledge of the early history of Cyrene is due principally to the chance fact that Herodotus visited the city and recorded its traditions. There is no comparable source for the later period. Cyrene was not an important Mediterranean power, and its affairs therefore attracted little attention from historians of the Greek world. It is known that after the assassination of Arkesilas IV, constitutional reforms of a democratic character were effected at Cyrene, but few details are recorded. The reforms did not, however, establish a stable political regime in Cyrene, which continued to suffer periodically from bitter internal dissensions. In 401 BC a popular leader named Ariston seized control of the city, and executed or expelled many of the more prominent citizens. The exiles procured an army of adventurers from Greece and attacked Cyrene but, after considerable bloodshed, a peaceful settlement was arranged and the exiles were readmitted to the city. There is also evidence of continued clashes between the Greeks and the local Libyans. In 413 Euhesperides was besieged by Libyans, but was relieved through the chance arrival of a Greek fleet blown off course on the way to Sicily. An inscription from Cyrene, of the fourth or third century BC, refers to a successful campaign against the Nasamones and Makai, Libyan tribes inhabiting the coast to the west of Euhesperides. Egypt during this period was hardly strong enough to interfere in Cyrenaica, but it is recorded that the Egyptian King Hakor (392–380) made a treaty with Barce. No details are given, however, of the content or context of this treaty.

The relative isolation of Cyrenaica was ended when the Greek army under Alexander occupied Egypt in 332 BC. Cyrene sent envoys to offer alliance, which Alexander accepted. Cyrene did not become subject to

Alexander. Alexander claimed to be leading a Greek national crusade against Persia, and could hardly claim to rule over Greeks. Ptolemy, who became *satrap* of Egypt on Alexander's death in 323, had less concern for such scruples. He found an excuse for intervention, as had ʿAḥmose and Aryandes before him, in the internal dissensions of Cyrene. About 325 a large force of Greek mercenaries, commanded by a Spartan adventurer called Thibron, arrived in Cyrenaica with the encouragement of some Cyrenaean exiles, seized Apollonia, the port of Cyrene, and began extorting money and armaments from the Greek cities, on the pretext of mounting a campaign against the local Libyans. The Cyrenaeans at first submitted, but later, encouraged by the defection to them of one of Thibron's subordinates, resisted. Thibron secured the alliance of Barce and Euhesperides and laid siege to Cyrene, while the Cyrenaeans summoned assistance from the local Libyans and from Carthage. Protracted fighting followed, and the situation was further complicated when a civil war broke out in Cyrene, which ended in a victory for the democratic party and the expulsion of the richer citizens. Some of these exiles appealed for aid to Ptolemy in Egypt, and Ptolemy sent his general Ophellas with a large army into Cyrenaica (322 BC). The democrats of Cyrene now made common cause with Thibron against Ophellas, but Ophellas defeated them, captured and executed Thibron, and gained possession of Cyrene and the other cities. Ptolemy thus secured control over Cyrenaica. The Greek cities were left nominally autonomous, but their freedom was a pretence. The loyalty of Cyrene to Ptolemy was guaranteed by the imposition of a large garrison, and the general Ophellas remained in the city as the effective ruler.

GREEKS AND LIBYANS

It has been seen above how the extension of Greek settlement in Cyrenaica provoked wars with the local Libyans, and how clashes with the Libyans recurred throughout the period. But Greeks and Libyans did not always meet as enemies. Libyans are on occasions found in alliance with the Greeks, as with Cyrene against Thibron in the 320s. It is also probable that the contingents of war-chariots which served with the armies of Cyrene and Barce in the fifth and fourth centuries were provided by Libyan allies. There was also a considerable absorption of Libyan elements into the population of the Greek states. It is not clear whether the Libyans were expelled from the lands taken by the Greek settlers or retained as subjects. It can, however, be assumed that the slaves employed by the Greeks on the land and in the cities would have been predominantly Libyans. What is more remarkable is the assimilation of Libyans into the free population. It is possible that the Greek colonists brought few women of their own. At any rate, it apparently became quite normal for Greek men to take Libyan wives. A poem written by Pindar for a citizen of Cyrene in the time of Arkesilas IV (*Pythian Ode*, IX) relates how one of the early settlers at Cyrene (an ancestor of Pindar's client) competed successfully in an athletic competition at Irasa, in the territory of the Libyan tribe of the Giligamai, to win the hand of a Libyan woman. That such marriages were common is proved by the constitutional regulations imposed on Cyrene by Ptolemy after 322 BC, which are preserved in an inscription, and which include the provision that the children of Cyrenaean men by Libyan wives should have citizen status.

This Libyan element in the population of the Greek cities evidently had some impact on their culture. A few Greeks adopted Libyan names. It has already been noted that the royal name Battos was, according to Herodotus, of Libyan origin. Alazeir, the name of the ruler of Barce in the time of Arkesilas III, is also Libyan. Libyan influence on the Greeks was most evident in the sphere of religion. Herodotus observes that the women of Cyrene celebrated the festivals of the Egyptian goddess Isis, and observed the prohibition on the meat of cows (which were sacred to Isis), while the women of Barce also observed the Egyptian prohibition on the eating of pork, and states that these Egyptian customs came to the Greeks through the Libyans. It is significant that Herodotus speaks here of the *women* only, confirming the suggestion that the Libyan element was strongest among the women of the cities. It is also interesting that Libyan influence was apparently stronger at Barce than at Cyrene. Another cult which the Greeks adopted from the Libyans was that of a god whom the Greeks called 'Ammon', a version of the Egyptian god Amun-Reʿ, in origin a fusion of the sun-god Reʿ with the ram-god Amun, who was often represented as a ram-headed man. The principal centre of the cult of Ammon was his temple in the Oasis of Siwa, famous for its oracle, and the cult was widespread among the Libyan tribes further west. The oracle at Siwa was frequently consulted by Greeks from Cyrenaica and even from further afield, as by Alexander in 332 BC. The Greeks identified Ammon with their own principal god Zeus, and worshipped him in their own cities as 'Zeus Ammon', who was usually represented as a man with a ram's horns. Representations of

Zeus Ammon were a favourite device on the coins of Cyrene, Barce and Euhesperides. From the Greek cities of Cyrenaica the cult of Zeus Ammon spread to the rest of the Greek world. This was, however, only a very superficial form of assimilation. The Greeks worshipped Zeus Ammon as a Greek god, borrowing only the name Ammon and the device of the ram's horns, without adopting any Libyan or Egyptian forms of ritual. Among other borrowings, the Cyrenaean passion for chariot-racing was certainly influenced by the local Libyans, among whom the horse-drawn war-chariot was still in normal use, whereas it had long ago been abandoned in Greece. Herodotus, indeed, claims that the Greeks learned from the Libyans the technique of using teams of four horses for chariots.

That the Greek colonists in turn influenced the culture of the Libyans is highly probable, but difficult to establish in detail. Herodotus states of the Asbystai, in the hinterland of Cyrene, that 'for the most part they copy the customs of the Cyrenaeans', and observes that the same was true of the Auschisai and the Bakales, neighbours of Barce and Euhesperides.[1] But he does not go into any details. Greek influence possibly explains the practice of extended burial which Herodotus notes among the Libyans, since the Nasamones to the west of Cyrenaica buried their dead in a sitting posture. Beyond this, it can only be hoped that clearer evidence of Greek influence on the Libyans will be obtained when archaeology succeeds in recovering the material remains of the Libyan tribes.

PHOENICIAN COLONIZATION IN NORTH AFRICA; CARTHAGE AND ITS EMPIRE

The Phoenicians colonized a much greater area of North Africa than the Greeks, and their influence on Africa was probably more profound as well as being more widespread. But in many respects Phoenician activies in Africa are less well documented than those of the Greeks. Though they were literate, few of their records have survived, and we are usually dependent for their history upon the writings of Greek and Roman historians. This is especially unfortunate for a historian of Africa, since the Greek and Roman historians were naturally mainly concerned with the dealings of the Phoenicians with their own peoples – that is, with their operations in the Mediterranean rather than with their activities in Africa.

[1] Herodotus, *Histories*, IV, 170–1.

The Phoenicians were established on the coast of North Africa considerably earlier than the Greeks. They colonized along the coast to the west of the Greek sphere in Cyrenaica. The principal colonizer among the Phoenician cities was Tyre. Unlike the Greeks in Cyrenaica, the Phoenicians were not, at least initially, interested in the establishment of substantial settlement colonies. Their only interest was in trade. Their colonies, being essentially trading-posts or victualling stations for their ships, tended to be sited on off-shore islands and peninsulas which provided easy access from the sea, but were readily defensible against interference from the land. Indeed, the Phoenicians at first were not really interested in Africa at all. The interest which drew them into the western Mediterranean was trade with southern Spain, with the Spanish kingdom called by the Greeks 'Tartessos', which is probably to be identified with the 'Tarshish' of the Old Testament. The chief commodities traded by the Tartessians were metals – silver, from the mines of southern Spain, and tin, which they imported by sea from Brittany and Britain. The first Phoenician colonies in the west were sited with a view to this trade with Tartessos. The earliest was Gades (Cadiz), on what was then an island off the Atlantic coast of Spain close to Tartessos. The colonies founded along the North African coast, the first of which, Utica in Northern Tunisia, is said to have been founded soon after Gades, were intended to safeguard and provide stopping-places along the coasting route from Phoenicia to Gades and Tartessos. Besides Spain and North Africa, the Phoenicians also planted colonies on Sardinia, in western Sicily – Motya (Mozia), Panormus (Palermo), and Soloeis (Soli) – and on Malta.

There is some doubt as to when Phoenician colonization in the western Mediterranean began. Ancient writers claim that Gades was founded *c.* 1110 BC and Utica *c.* 1100, and some modern scholars have accepted these dates as substantially accurate. However, the evidence of archaeology casts some doubt on these early dates. Little excavation has been possible at Gades, but extensive excavations have been undertaken at Utica, and have yielded nothing earlier than the eighth century BC. It is always dangerous to argue from this sort of negative evidence in archaeology, but in this case the lack of material earlier than the eighth century is remarkably consistent throughout the excavated Phoenician sites in the west. Altogether, it is difficult to claim with any confidence that Phoenician trade and colonization in Spain and North Africa go back appreciably before *c.* 800 BC.

Besides Utica, the North African cities which are said to have been founded from Tyre are Lepcis in Tripolitania, Hadrumetum (Sousse) on the eastern coast of Tunisia, Carthage to the south and Hippo (Bizerta) to the west of Utica in northern Tunisia, and Lixus on the Atlantic coast of Morocco. Another Tyrian colony in North Africa referred to by ancient historians, Auza, evidently did not survive, and cannot be located. Little in the way of dates can be established for these foundations. The date usually quoted for the foundation of Carthage, 813 BC, is in fact only one, though the most popular, of several calculations made by ancient Greek chronologists.[1] Excavations at Carthage have yielded nothing earlier than *c.* 750 BC, and it is possible that the conventional date is too early. Lixus actually claimed to have been founded before Gades, but excavation at the site has not carried the occupation further back than the seventh century. Archaeological evidence also indicates a foundation from Phoenicia before the end of the seventh century for Siga (Rachgoun) on the Algerian coast and for a colony, not mentioned by ancient authors, on the island of Mogador off the Atlantic coast of Morocco. The Mogador settlement, however, seems to have been abandoned at the end of the sixth century.

By far the most important of the Tyrian colonies in North Africa was Carthage, or, to give it its Phoenician name (of which 'Carthago' is a Latin transcription), 'Qart Hadasht' ('New City'), which was planted in the bay to the west of the Cape Bon peninsula, to the south of Utica. Carthage ultimately came to exercise a hegemony over all the western Phoenicians. In fact, it had from the start a somewhat different character from the other colonies. Its foundation was not motivated solely by trade, for it is said to have been established by a group of political dissidents from Tyre. According to the legend of its foundation recorded by Greek writers, the founder of Carthage was Elissa (also called Dido), the sister of Pygmalion, King of Tyre. Elissa fled from Tyre, accompanied by many of the Tyrian nobles, after Pygmalion had murdered her husband. She went first to Cyprus, where she picked up more followers, and then to North Africa. There she purchased land from the local Libyans, on which the citadel of Carthage, the *Byrsa*, was built. As the colony expanded in size, the other sections of the city were built on further land leased from the Libyans in return for the payment of an annual tribute. Elissa is said ultimately to have committed suicide,

[1] Other dates range from 1234 BC (Appian, *Punic wars*, 1) to 751 BC (Apion, quoted by Josephus, *Against Apion*, II. 17).

to avoid marrying a local Libyan chief. If there is any truth in this story, the foundation of Carthage was the result of a considerable migration from among the ruling class of Tyre. But despite the circumstances of its foundation, Carthage always retained sentimental and religious ties with Tyre. For many years the Carthaginians sent a tithe of their revenues annually for dedication in the temple of the god Melqart at Tyre. Later the scale of these offerings was reduced, but they continued to be sent into the second century BC, and probably down to the destruction of Carthage in 146 BC.

It is likely that Elissa founded a line of kings at Carthage, but it is problematical whether this monarchy still survived at the time when history first records anything of the city's affairs, in the sixth century BC. We then hear of a general called apparently (in a corrupt text) 'Malchus', who, after suffering a military defeat, was condemned to exile by the Carthaginian Senate. 'Malchus' then used his army to besiege and capture Carthage, and executed some of the senators. Later, however, he was himself brought to trial and executed. It has been suggested that 'Malchus' is in reality not a personal name, but a transcription of the Phoenician title *melek* ('king'). If this is so (and it is extremely speculative), perhaps the Carthaginian monarchy ended with the death of 'Malchus'. Greek writers, it is true, frequently apply the title of 'king' (*basileus*) to Carthaginian leaders during the fifth and fourth centuries, and some modern scholars believe that this also translated the Phoenician term *melek*, and that some form of kingship persisted at Carthage until some time in the fourth century. But it seems more probable that the Greeks used the term *basileus* imprecisely to refer to the chief civil magistrates of Carthage, who had the Phoenician title of *sufet* ('judge'). By the third century BC, but perhaps not originally, there were two *sufets*, who were elected annually. Real power in the Carthaginian Republic lay with the Senate or Council, recruited probably from ex-magistrates. An Assembly of adult male citizens also existed, but had little effective power. Command of the army was not a regularly filled post, generals being chosen ad hoc, perhaps originally elected by the Assembly. In the early years of the Republic, the generals were often the rivals of the Senate for power.

It is sometimes suggested that Carthage was founded from the first to replace Tyre as the political capital of the western Phoenicians, this being the significance of its name, 'New City'. But there is no evidence that Carthage exercised any form of hegemony over the western Phoenicians before the sixth century BC. The leadership of Carthage arose as a reaction to the Greek threat to the Phoenician position in the western Mediterranean. The Greeks, having colonized southern Italy and eastern Sicily, began to intrude into the Phoenician sphere in Spain. About 638 BC a Greek trader accidentally found his way to Tartessos, and broke the Phoenician monopoly of trade there. Trade with Tartessos was developed especially by the Greeks of Phokaia (in Asia Minor), who in *c*. 600 founded a colony at Massalia (Marseilles) to protect the coasting route to Spain along the southern coast of France, and were soon colonizing along the eastern coast of Spain itself. About the same time, the Greeks began to encroach upon the Phoenician sphere in western Sicily, while the colonization of Cyrenaica raised the threat of a Greek challenge to the Phoenician position in North Africa. The western Phoenicians could no longer look to Tyre for leadership or aid: the mother-city was at this time engaged in a struggle against the overlordship of Babylon, which culminated in a protracted Babylonian siege of Tyre in 586–573. For reasons which are lost to us, it was Carthage (rather than, say, Gades or Utica) among the Phoenician cities of the west which took the lead in resisting Greek expansion. The earliest attested Carthaginian venture overseas was the foundation of a colony on the island of Ebesos (Ibiza) off the coast of Spain. This is said to have taken place 160 years after the foundation of Carthage. This would be *c*. 653 BC if the conventional date for the latter event is accepted, but it seems more likely that the colony was founded rather later, in response to the Greek intrusion into the Phoenician sphere in Spain after *c*. 638. The Carthaginians are also said to have resisted the foundation of Massalia by the Phokaians in *c*. 600. A little later 'Malchus' conducted campaigns for Carthage in Sicily and Sardinia. After his execution, command of the army was given to a certain Mago, whom tradition represents as the true founder of the Carthaginian empire: he was

> the first man who, by regulating military discipline, laid the foundations of the Punic empire, and strengthened the power of the state no less by his skill in warfare than by his courage.[1]

Mago and his descendants, by monopolizing military appointments, established themselves as the effective rulers of Carthage during the next hundred years. Fighting in Sardinia continued under Mago and his son Hasdrubal (who was killed there) and Hasdrubal's brother or nephew Hamilcar, and the coastal plains of the island were conquered

[1] Justin, *Epitoma historiarum Philippicarum Pompeii Trogi*, XIX. I. I.

and colonized. In about 540 the Carthaginians, in alliance with the Etruscans of Italy, who were also threatened by Greek expansion, fought against the Phokaians in a naval battle off Corsica, and forced them to abandon their settlement on the island. Carthage and the Etruscans remained in close alliance for many years afterwards. The Greek threat in the western Mediterranean was eliminated. Gades was brought under Carthaginian protection, while Tartessos disappears from history and was probably destroyed. About 515 the Carthaginians inflicted a further reverse on the Greeks when they expelled Dorieus from his colony in Tripolitania. As has been seen, the eastern boundary of the Phoenician sphere in North Africa was ultimately set at the Altars of Philainos on the Gulf of Syrtis.

This run of Carthaginian successes ended when in 480 BC Hamilcar led an attack on the Greeks of Sicily. Greek resistance was led by the largest of the Greek colonies in Sicily, Syracuse, and Hamilcar was defeated and killed at the battle of Himera. The terms imposed by the Syracusans after this victory were mild: Carthage paid a large indemnity, but lost no territory. Nevertheless, the reverse at Himera seems to have had a profound impact on the development of Carthage. Expansion in the Mediterranean was abandoned for seventy years. Even peaceful contacts with the Mediterranean world declined: after 480 the importation into Carthage of commodities from the Greek world, and even from friendly countries such as Etruria and the Persian empire in the east, practically ceased. Presumably this came about through the deliberate policy of the Carthaginian government, which may have sought to conserve its supplies of precious metals and prevent their drain to potential enemies. At the same time, Carthage took steps to develop the resources which she still monopolized in Africa and the far west. Under the sons of Hasdrubal and Hamilcar, who ruled Carthage in the generation after 480, Carthage defeated the local Libyans, ending the payment of tribute to them, and began the acquisition of an extensive territory in the interior. Other wars were fought against the Numidians and Mauri, the tribes inhabiting the coastal plains west of the Carthaginian territory, these wars being probably in connection with colonization along the coast. Two of Hamilcar's sons undertook voyages of exploration in the Atlantic, presumably in an attempt to tighten the grip of Carthage on the trade of the area: Himilco sailed along the Atlantic coast of Spain and across the Bay of Biscay at least as far as Brittany, and probably intended to explore the old Tartessian tin-trade; Hanno sailed south, founding several colonies along the

Atlantic coast of Morocco, and exploring perhaps to beyond the Sahara, establishing or confirming Carthaginian access to supplies of West African gold. (On Hanno's voyage, see further on pp. 128, 134–7.)

Despite these successes, Mago's family did not retain its position of power in Carthage. The tension between the generals and the Senate was resolved in favour of the Senate. Hanno and other members of the family were brought to trial and exiled, and a board of 104 members of the Senate, who held office for life, was set up to supervise the activities of the generals and punish delinquents. A close control was thus established over the generals, and military failure was frequently punished by execution. Mago's descendants remained important at Carthage, and continued to monopolize military appointments into the fourth century BC, their final fall from power being perhaps due to the suicide of Hanno's son Himilco after a disastrous defeat in Sicily in 396. Thus was established the oligarchic regime under which Carthage was governed until the democratic reforms of Hannibal in 196 BC. The Senate, acting in harmony with the *sufets*, was all-powerful. If the *sufets* and the Senate were agreed on a measure, it did not need to come before the Assembly. The Senate seems even to have appointed the generals in this period. Carthage was praised by conservative Greek writers, such as Aristotle, for its political stability and the docility of its masses. Aristotle attributed this to the wealth derived from the Carthaginian empire, which was used to buy off popular discontent. We hear, in fact, of two attempts by aspiring 'tyrants' to seize power in Carthage under the Republic, but neither attracted popular support. In *c.* 360 BC the leading politician of the day, another Hanno, having failed in a plot to assassinate the entire Senate by poison, fled from the city and attempted to raise an army of slaves and Libyans, but was captured and executed. In 308 a general, Bomilcar, used his troops in an attempted coup d'état, but the citizens rose against him. Surrendering on a promise of his life, he too was executed. The admiring Greeks, however, criticized the importance of wealth (as opposed to birth or 'merit') in the acquisition of political power at Carthage. The governing class of Carthage was simply the rich, without distinction of origin, and even (another fault in the eyes of the gentleman-philosophers of Greece) without distinguishing between landed and commercial wealth.

Carthage ended her isolation in 409 BC by again attacking the Greeks in Sicily. This resumption of military expansion in the Mediterranean was accompanied by a revival of commercial contacts with the Greek world. Indeed, paradoxically, this period of renewed military conflict with the Greeks was also one in which Carthaginian civilization became deeply influenced by Greece, as seen most dramatically in the official institution at Carthage of a cult of the Greek goddesses Demeter and Kore in 396 BC. Throughout the fourth century, Carthage fought a series of wars in Sicily against Syracuse and the other Greek cities, without either side gaining a decisive victory. The most interesting episode from an African point of view occurred in 310, when Agathokles, the 'tyrant' of Syracuse, faced by a Carthaginian siege of Syracuse, attempted to draw off the besieging forces by himself invading North Africa. Agathokles won some spectacular successes, capturing Tunis and Hadrumetum, and inciting revolts among the Libyan subjects and Numidian allies of Carthage. In 308 he won the alliance of Ophellas, whom Ptolemy had left in control of Cyrene, for a joint assault on Carthage, after which Ophellas should rule Africa, and Agathokles Sicily. Ophellas, with a strong army and a vast body of prospective Greek colonists, made the long desert march along the coast of Tripolitania to join Agathokles. At this point the situation of Carthage was rendered even more desperate by the abortive coup d'état of the general Bomilcar to which reference has been made above. But dissension broke out on the Greek side also, and Ophellas was murdered by Agathokles. Though Agathokles went on to capture Utica and Hippo, and his forces overran much of the interior, the Carthaginians still controlled the sea and could supply the city by ship, so that Agathokles never really came close to a decisive victory. The Libyans and Numidians increasingly held aloof from the conflict, awaiting the outcome before they would commit themselves to either side, and Agathokles was finally (307 BC) forced to abandon his army in Africa and retire to Sicily. The last war fought by Carthage against the Greeks of Sicily was that in which the Greeks were led by Pyrrhos, King of Epeiros (276–275 BC). By 270 the Romans had completed their conquest of southern Italy, and Carthage found her position in Sicily threatened from a new quarter. Previously relations between Carthage and Rome had been friendly. There had been treaties recognizing spheres of influence, and even a measure of common policy against Pyrrhos. But now there was a confrontation which led (in 264 BC) to open war, and ultimately (in 146) to the destruction of Carthage by the Romans.

The Carthaginian empire was commercial rather than territorial, centred on the Mediterranean rather than on North Africa. The empire comprised the North African coast from the Altars of Philainos in the east to the Atlantic coast of Morocco in the west, Gades and other coastal cities in southern Spain, western Sicily and the western Mediterranean islands – Malta, Sardinia, and Ibiza and the Balearic islands. Effective rule was everywhere limited to the coast: even in Sardinia, the Carthaginians never occupied the mountains of the interior. Only in the immediate hinterland of Carthage itself was a large area of territory controlled. The subject Phoenician cities paid to Carthage customs duties, but not normally tribute, and were required to supply forces for the Punic army. Internally they were virtually autonomous. The city of Utica had a special position as a (nominally) free and equal ally. Carthage also on occasion exacted tribute from some of the Greek cities in Sicily. The main concern of the Carthaginians was to maintain their empire as a trade monopoly. This policy is illustrated by the treaties made between Carthage and Rome in 509 and 348 BC. In the first, in return for the recognition by Carthage of Roman interests in central Italy, the Romans undertook not to sail along the coast of Africa west of Carthage unless forced to do so by weather or enemy action, and, if so forced, not to trade, but to leave within five days. Romans could trade in the rest of North Africa and in Sardinia only in the presence of an official, and had equal rights of trade with Carthaginian citizens only in Carthage itself and in the Carthaginian province in Sicily. The treaty of 348 BC further restricted the Romans, forbidding them to sail south of a point on the Spanish coast, and barring them completely from Sardinia and North Africa, allowing them to trade only in Carthage and Sicily. Similar treaties appear to have been made with the Etruscans. Non-friendly peoples, such as the Greeks, were dealt with more summarily: any Greek ship venturing into Carthaginian waters was sunk. By these means Carthage maintained a monopoly of the supply of the commodities of the west – Sardinian and North African corn, Spanish silver, British tin and West African gold – to the Mediterranean world. It seems that Carthaginian manufactures were in general inferior to those of Greece, and would never have survived in an open market. Carthage secured by her military power a situation in which, free from competition, her traders could purchase precious metals with goods of little value – wine, olive-oil, perfume, cloth and trinkets. These precious metals could then be used to pay for the commodities which Carthage desired to import from the Greeks, who were not interested in Carthaginian manufactures (with the exception of some textiles). One puzzle about Carthaginian commerce is that, despite her extensive involvement in trade, Carthage did not begin to issue coins until relatively late. This is perhaps to be explained in terms of the odd structure of her commerce: her main trade was with the primitive peoples of Spain and Africa, and operated by barter, while to the Greeks she paid silver in bullion rather than coin form. The first Carthaginian coins were struck only at the end of the fifth century BC, a century and a half after the earliest coins of Greece, and then only for the payment of Greek mercenaries employed in Sicily. Carthage established a regular metropolitan coinage only in the third century BC, a development which is probably to be connected with an intensification of trade with Egypt under the dynasty of the Ptolemies.

The commercial monopoly of Carthage rested ultimately on her military power, on her ability to deny to others by force access to the resources of the west. Carthage had the strongest navy in the western Mediterranean. Her galleys were probably manned mainly by Phoenicians, though in emergencies at any rate slaves might be employed. Probably Carthage alone of the western Phoenician cities possessed warships. The Carthaginian army was quite different in character. Carthaginians formed a very small proportion of the troops, and indeed, after the fourth century BC no substantial citizen forces ever served outside Africa. This was a considered policy on the part of Carthage, to avoid crippling losses from among the citizen body. The army was recruited partly from the subject Phoenician cities, but mainly from non-Phoenicians subject or allied to Carthage or engaged as mercenaries. The generals, however, were normally Carthaginians, and it was rare even for non-Carthaginian Phoenicians to hold a high command. The main strength of the Punic army was the heavy infantry, armed with swords and thrusting-spears, drawn principally from the subject Libyans, though considerable use was also made of Greek, Italian and Gallic mercenaries. The best light infantry troops were javelin-throwers recruited from the Numidians and Mauri, and slingers from the Balearic islands. Cavalry was supplied by the Phoenicians, and in the third century BC also by Numidian allies. During the fifth and fourth centuries, Punic armies frequently made use of horse-drawn war-chariots, which were probably also supplied by the Numidians, and which made a massed charge at the beginning of the action to disorder the enemy's ranks. Later the tactical role of the war-chariot was taken over by the war-elephant, which Alexander had discovered in use in India and adopted, and which Pyrrhos introduced into the western Mediterranean in the 270s BC. The Carthaginians began to train North African elephants for use in war, sending expeditions into the Numidian interior to capture them. The practice of employing foreign, mainly mercenary, troops may have been successful in conserving citizen manpower, but it had the disadvantage of expense. A protracted land war was a ruinous financial drain for Carthage. At the end of her first war with Rome (241 BC), Carthage was unable to pay her mercenaries, who mutinied and fought a vicious war against Carthage for three years before being suppressed. Carthaginian power thus rested upon her financial rather than upon her human resources. Control of the silver of Spain was necessary for the military power of Carthage, just as her military power was necessary for the maintenance of that control.

CARTHAGE AND NORTH AFRICA

While it is true that, as has been observed above, Carthage was essentially a Mediterranean rather than an African power, nevertheless her dominion and influence extended over a considerable area of North Africa, and the specifically African aspects of her history require special consideration in a history of Africa. Carthage itself was, after all, situated in North Africa, as were the majority of the Phoenician cities subject to her. It is difficult to estimate the scale of Phoenician settlement in North Africa. Carthage itself was a great city, with a population estimated by one ancient writer somewhat improbably as 700,000, more conservatively by modern scholars as perhaps up to 400,000. Of the other North African colonies, some of the older Phoenician foundations, such as Utica and Lixus, were considerable cities, but most were mere trading-stations, or, to use the Greek term for them, *emporia*. These settlements served as victualling stations along the coasting routes to Spain and Egypt, but they also had an economic significance of their own as centres for fishing and as posts for trade with the peoples of the interior.

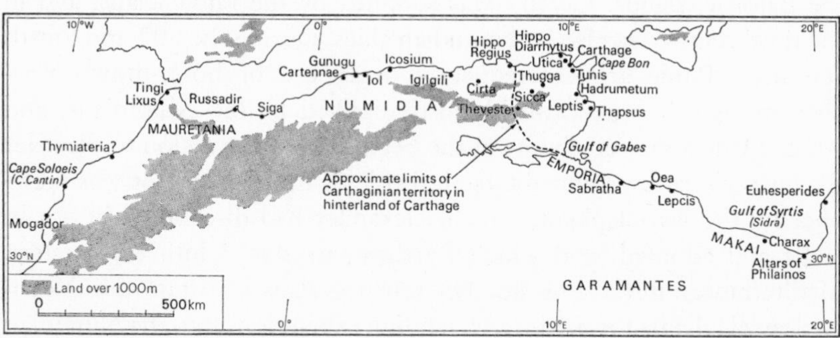

20 The Carthaginian sphere in North-West Africa.

In the east, as has been seen, the boundary of Phoenician control of the coast was set at the Altars of Philainos on the Gulf of Syrtis. On the coast of Tripolitania, the most important city was the old Tyrian foundation of Lepcis. Lepcis, with its western neighbours Oea (on the site of modern Tripoli) and Sabratha, formed the 'Tripolis', or 'three Cities', from which the name of Tripolitania is derived. The hinterland of Lepcis, the Kinyps area, produced corn, flax and probably (as it certainly did later, in Roman times) olive-oil. Another important agricultural area was the Gulf of Gabes littoral to the west, which was called by the Greeks (probably translating a Punic term) the 'Emporia', or 'Trading-Stations'. The term *emporia* is sometimes extended to include Lepcis, and it has been suggested that Lepcis functioned as the administrative headquarters of the whole coast from the Gulf of Gabes to the Altars of Philainos. Lepcis paid to Carthage, perhaps on behalf of the whole province, customs dues amounting to no less than one *talent* of silver per day. Besides agriculture, the coastal settlements of Tripolitania were also important for fishing, including the collection of 'purples', the molluscs from which the Phoenicians extracted dye for their textiles, and for trade with the interior. In the east, the Carthaginians traded wine at Charax for *silphion* smuggled out of Cyrenaica, and precious stones were obtained from the Nasamones, the Libyan tribe inhabiting the shores of the Gulf of Syrtis. Lepcis and the other cities of the Tripolis appear to have functioned as the *termini* of trade-routes extending across the Sahara to the oases of the Fezzan, which were inhabited by the Libyan tribe of the Garamantes. From the Garamantes the Carthaginians imported the precious stones known in antiquity as *carbuncles* (not certainly identified), which were re-exported, at great profit, to the Mediterranean world, and perhaps a few slaves, which the Garamantes could obtain by raiding among the negroid peoples to their south. There is, however, no evidence in Punic times for any trans-Saharan trade in ivory, such as seems to have existed later in Roman times: at this period, a plentiful supply of ivory could still be derived from the elephants of North-West Africa. Nor is there any evidence that the Carthaginians imported West African gold across the Sahara. The operation of the trans-Saharan caravans was normally left to the Garamantes, but Carthaginian merchants may occasionally have travelled to the Fezzan. A tall tale of a Carthaginian called Mago who 'crossed the desert three times, eating dry barley and not drinking',[1] is possibly an echo of such journeys (but see chapter 5, p. 284).

[1] Athenaios, *Deipnosophistai*, II. 44e.

The densest Phoenician settlement in North Africa was to be found on the coasts of what is now Tunisia. Here were several cities of some size. On the eastern coast the principal cities were Thapsus, Leptis[1] and Hadrumetum. In the north were Tunis, Carthage itself, Utica and Hippo.[2] Further west, there were numerous small Punic *emporia*, which provided access to the commodities of the interior of Numidia and Mauretania, principally ivory, hides and cedar wood. Siga, as has been seen, was an early Phoenician colony. Igilgili (Djidjelli), Icosium (Algiers), Iol (Cherchel), Gunugu (Gouraya), Cartennae (Tenes), where there was an important copper-mine, and Rusaddir (Melilla) were all occupied in Punic times. Tingi (Tangier) was possibly in origin a Libyan town, but it came under Carthaginian control and acquired a Phoenician character. On the Atlantic coast of North Africa the most important city was the Tyrian colony of Lixus. Further south, the Phoenician settlement on Mogador island had been abandoned by the end of the sixth century BC, but was reoccupied in the third century. In the generation after 480 Hanno colonized along the coast, founding Thymiateria (Mehedia?) and five other cities south of Cape Soloeis (Cape Cantin) whose sites have not been located. A final (but abortive) colony was established by Hanno on the island of Cerne, unidentified, but apparently off the Saharan coast. The Atlantic coast was chiefly important for fishing, including fishing for purples. Cerne also served as a base for trade with the native peoples, from whom the Carthaginians purchased hides, ivory and, apparently, West African gold. (On Hanno's voyage and the trade of Cerne, see further on pp. 134–9.)

Through most of North Africa Carthaginian rule was restricted to the coastal cities, but in the immediate hinterland of Carthage itself the Carthaginians also came to rule over a considerable territory in the interior. This extension of Carthaginian rule inland did not begin until many years after the foundation of Carthage. Initially, as has been seen, the Carthaginians paid to the local Libyans an annual tribute in return for possession of the land on which the city was built. 'Malchus', in the sixth century BC, is said to have campaigned successfully against the Libyans, and perhaps as a result of his campaigns the payment of the

[1] Leptis was known in Roman times as Leptis Minor ('Lesser Leptis'), to distinguish it from Lepcis in Tripolitania, whose name was often mis-spelt as Leptis, and which was called Leptis Magna ('Great Leptis').

[2] Hippo was later known as Hippo Diarrhytus ('Flowed-through Hippo', meaning that it was situated on a river), to distinguish it from another, much less important, Hippo which was situated near Bone. The second Hippo became known as Hippo Regius ('Royal Hippo') when it was included in the independent kingdom of Numidia in the second century BC.

tribute lapsed. But in the generation before 480, in the time of Hasdrubal and Hamilcar, the Libyans defeated the Carthaginians and again exacted payment, with arrears. It was only in the generation after 480 that Hanno, son of Hamilcar, with his brothers and cousins, finally defeated the Libyans and ended the tribute. Hanno's victory, which was quickly followed by the extension of Carthaginian rule into the interior, marks the beginning of the development of Carthage as a truly African power. As one Greek writer put it, with some rhetorical exaggeration: 'Hanno transformed the Carthaginians from Tyrians into Africans – thanks to him, they lived in Africa rather than in Phoenicia.'[1] The precise stages by which Carthaginian rule was extended over the interior are not recorded. Our sources refer vaguely to wars with the Libyans, but give few details. Our earliest evidence for the extent of Carthaginian rule in the interior comes from a Greek account of the campaigns of Agathokles against Carthage in 307 BC, from which it appears that the town of Thugga (Dougga), about 120 km south-west of Carthage, was by then already subject to Carthage.[2] On the other hand, the town of Theveste (Tebessa), some 140 km beyond Thugga, is recorded to have been captured by the Carthaginians in the 240s BC. The ultimate boundaries of Carthaginian rule are equally obscure. At some point the Carthaginians are said to have demarcated their territory with earthworks known as the 'Phoenician Trenches'. The course of these earthworks is unknown, but in any case by the end of the third century BC the Carthaginians had conquered and garrisoned towns beyond the 'Phoenician Trenches'. Greek writers sometimes use the term 'Libyans' (*Libyes*) in a restricted sense to refer to the native subjects of Carthage, as opposed to the independent tribes of the Numidians and Mauri to the west. Latin writers, presumably transcribing some Punic or Libyan name, call the same people *Afri*. The name *Africa* ('Land of the Afri') was originally applied to the Roman province created out of the conquered Carthaginian territory in 146 BC.

The land acquired by the Carthaginians was treated in two different ways. In the Cape Bon peninsula east of Carthage, the Libyan occupants were evicted, and the land passed into private Carthaginian ownership. Here the wealthy Carthaginians developed large estates, using slave labour, on which they practised mixed farming – cereal culture, arboriculture (olives, figs, pomegranates), herding (cattle, sheep, horses) and

[1] Dio Chrysostom, *Discourses*, xxv. 7.

[2] Diodorus Siculus, *Library of history*, xx. 57.4: for the interpretation of this passage, see S. Gsell, *Histoire ancienne de l'Afrique du Nord*, II (Paris, 1921), 95.

bee-keeping. Punic farming was technically advanced: there was a famous farming manual written by a Carthaginian called Mago, which was translated into Latin, and from which a few quotations survive. In the interior there was no such colonization. The only exception is the town of Sicca (Le Kef), which is said to have been a settlement of the Elymoi, a native people of western Sicily who were subjects of Carthage. Elsewhere the Libyans were left in possession of their land, but subjected to heavy taxation. In these areas, farming was apparently confined to cereal culture. During the first war of Carthage against Rome (264–241 BC), the rural Afri paid to Carthage no less than one-half of the produce of their lands: since at the same time the taxes imposed on the native towns had been doubled to finance the war, the normal tax at this period was presumably 25%. The cereals paid in taxes by the Afri served not only to feed the enormous population of Carthage, but also to supply the Punic armies abroad, and probably quantities were also exported to other Mediterranean countries. It is her control of the interior and its corn which explains the continued prosperity of Carthage even after 201 BC, when, by her defeat in the second war against Rome, she had lost control of Spain and its silver. In the fifth and fourth centuries BC the Afri were also liable to conscription for service in the Punic army. In the third century, however, the Afri were recruited on a voluntary basis as mercenaries: most of the mercenaries involved in the great mutiny of 241–238 BC were Libyans. By thus professionalizing the army the Carthaginians no doubt secured better soldiers. The change was probably accompanied by an increase in the scale of taxation of the Afri. The Afri, equipped in Carthaginian fashion as heavy infantry, formed the main fighting strength of the Punic armies. Little is known of how the administration of the subject area was organized. On the probable assumption that the Romans and the Numidian kings who partitioned the Carthaginian territory after 146 BC took over the Punic system of administration, it can be inferred that the territory was divided into several, probably six, administrative districts, called in Punic *'rst* (in Latin, *pagi*), but the precise boundaries and functions of these districts are unclear. Carthage secured the loyalty of the Afri by placing garrisons in the towns and taking hostages from suspect communities.

Our sources leave little doubt that Carthaginian rule was harsh and unpopular. Polybius, writing with specific reference to the war of 264–241 BC, observes:

The Carthaginians admired and honoured among their generals not those who treated the [Libyan] people mildly and kindly, but those who secured for them the greatest revenues for civil and military purposes, and who treated the people in the countryside most harshly.[1]

Polybius is a hostile witness, but his judgement on Carthaginian rule is supported by the frequency of revolts among the Afri. The first recorded revolt occurred in 396 BC, when the Afri were encouraged by a disastrous plague which had weakened Carthage, and infuriated by the action of a Carthaginian general in abandoning a large force of Libyan troops in Sicily. The rebels, who were joined by many slaves from the Carthaginian farms, captured Tunis and besieged Carthage, but the city could be supplied by sea, and dissensions and treachery within the rebel leadership led to their speedy defeat. A second revolt is recorded in 379. No details are reported, but the revolt seems to have lasted for several years. In *c.* 360 BC Hanno attempted to raise the Afri in support of his coup d'état, but it is not recorded whether they responded. Many of the Afri joined Agathokles against Carthage in 310–307, and supported the mercenaries in 241–238. After 238 BC, however, no further serious revolts are recorded. Perhaps the Carthaginians had learned the advantages to be gained, in the long run, by a more conciliatory treatment of their subjects.

Besides the area which they controlled directly, the Carthaginians included many of the coastal Libyans to the west in a system of alliances which bound them to supply troops for the Punic army. Most important of these were the various tribes of the Numidians, situated between the Carthaginian territory and the river Moulouya, but the Mauri, to the west of the Moulouya, also provided troops on occasions. The earliest evidence for these alliances is from a campaign of 406 BC. Numidians and Mauri were also recruited individually as mercenaries. During the third century, Carthage was especially dependent upon her Numidian allies for the excellent light cavalry which they provided. The Numidians were as liable as the Afri to prove false in times of Carthaginian weakness. Many of the Numidians allied with Agathokles in 310–307 BC. Another war with the Numidians is recorded in 255, and some Numidians joined the mercenaries in 241–238. During the second war of Carthage with Rome (218–201), the Numidian kings intrigued with both sides, and ultimately the defection to Rome of a Numidian chief, Masinissa, was crucial in causing the defeat of the Punic army in North Africa in 202 BC.

It is natural to suppose that during their long residence in North

[1] Polybius, *Histories*, I. 72.3.

Africa the Phoenicians, like the Greeks in Cyrenaica, absorbed Libyan elements into their population and culture. But Libyan influence is more difficult to document in the case of the Phoenicians. As with the Greeks, it can be assumed that the slave population of the Phoenician cities was predominantly Libyan, though the Phoenicians also made considerable use of prisoners of war taken from other Mediterranean nations. Intermarriage may be suspected, but is difficult to document. As in Cyrenaica, Libyan influence on the culture of the colonists is perhaps to be found in the sphere of religion. In certain respects, the religion of the Phoenicians in North Africa was extremely conservative. They retained, for example, the custom of human sacrifice, particularly of infants, after it had fallen into disuse in the Phoenician homeland. But in other respects there was a startling transformation. In their homeland, the principal deities of the Phoenicians had been the god Melqart and the goddess Astarte. In North Africa, Melqart remains important, but Astarte almost disappears. The most venerated deities in Carthage were the paired sun and moon deities, the god Baal Hammon and the goddess Tanit Pene Baal ('Tanit, Face of Baal'), with the latter, though nominally inferior, the more regarded. Both these deities probably owe something to the Libyans. Baal Hammon is often represented as a man with a ram's horns, and was evidently identified with the Libyan sun-god called by the Greeks Ammon, whose influence in Cyrenaica has been mentioned. It is tempting to see Baal Hammon as a simple fusion of a Phoenician Baal with the Libyan Ammon, but modern scholars incline to the view that the name *Baal Hammon* is a genuine Phoenician title, meaning probably 'Lord of the Incense Altars'. The identification with Ammon is, however, incontestable as a secondary development, no doubt facilitated by the similarity of names. The case of Tanit is more mysterious, since she is virtually unknown in the Phoenician homeland, and even her name seems not to be Phoenician. It is at least possible that she was a Libyan goddess adopted by the Phoenician colonists.[1]

The Phoenicians in turn influenced the culture of the Libyans. Their influence was naturally strongest in the area conquered and directly controlled by Carthage. The Afri learned new military techniques while serving as heavy infantry in the Punic army, and suffered the imposition of a Carthaginian administration. Knowledge of the Punic language and Punic culture became widely disseminated in the area. We

[1] For a recent statement of the case for ascribing an African origin to Tanit, see V. Giustolisi, *Le Origine della Dea Tanit e dei suoi simboli* (Palermo, 1970).

later find the Afri practising Punic religion and adopting Punic municipal institutions. The town of Sicca became an important cult centre, frequented by the surrounding Libyans, for a goddess (perhaps Astarte) identified by the Romans with Venus, in which the Oriental custom of temple prostitution was practised. There is archaeological evidence that the people of Thugga practised the Phoenician rite of infant sacrifice. Thugga and other Libyan towns also had constitutions of Phoenician type, in which the chief magistrates had the title of *sufet*. Phoenician influence also became strong among the Numidians outside the Carthaginian territory, but this development is unlikely to have become important before the third century BC, and Carthaginian influence became strongest, paradoxically, after Carthage had lost her political dominance over the Numidians in 201 BC, so that it falls outside the chronological scope of this chapter. However, the Carthaginians were probably responsible for the introduction of certain technical innovations which may have been widely adopted by the peoples of the Maghrib at an early date, notably the practice of arboriculture and the technique of iron-smelting. That the Libyans owed their knowledge of iron to the Phoenicians seems, on purely presumptive grounds, probable, and is perhaps directly attested by the apparent derivation of the Berber word for iron, *barzel*, from the Punic *azzel* (though this derivation has been disputed). But it is as yet unclear how soon the Libyans learned the technique of smelting iron. On this point, as on others connected with the question of Phoenician influence in North Africa, it is to be hoped that the progress of archaeological research will provide some hard evidence.

CARTHAGE AND SUB-SAHARAN AFRICA

The main importance of Carthage in African history lies in her activities in and influence upon North Africa. But perhaps an equal interest, if not an equal importance, attaches to the question of her possible relations with sub-Saharan Africa. By this is meant not her trans-Saharan contacts, which, if they existed, were indirect, passing through the agency of the Garamantes or other peoples of the desert, but the direct contacts which she appears to have established by sea. The sources which refer to these contacts raise, without answering, important questions for the early history of West Africa. (See also chapter 5, pp. 292–300.)

Maritime enterprise along the West African coast was not exclusively

Carthaginian. Euthymenes, a Greek from Massalia (Marseilles), at an uncertain date sailed down the coast as far as a large river in which he observed crocodiles and hippopotamuses – conceivably the Senegal. The Persian Sataspes, as has been noted above, was sent by King Xerxes (486–465 BC) on an abortive attempt to circumnavigate Africa from the west. He returned claiming that his ship had stuck fast and refused to go forwards; presumably it had run into adverse currents. At his furthest point, he reported seeing 'small men' who lived in towns and kept cattle. It is unfortunate that there is no way of telling how far south Sataspes had reached – quite possibly not even to beyond the Sahara. But despite occasional intrusions by such outsiders, the Atlantic was normally a Carthaginian preserve. The Carthaginians had secured control over the old Phoenician cities of Gades and Lixus, probably towards the end of the sixth century BC, and founded colonies of their own further along the Atlantic coast of Morocco. Fishing operations, in which ships of Gades were especially active, carried the Phoenician colonists beyond the limits of their permanent settlements. In this way, the Gaditans appear to have discovered, but not colonized, the island of Madeira. But the exploration of the coast along and beyond the Sahara was due not to local initiative, but to the action of the Carthaginian government.

The achievement of first reaching sub-Saharan Africa by sea from the west probably belongs to a certain Hanno, who was commissioned by the Carthaginians to establish colonies along the Atlantic coast of Morocco, and explored a good deal further. The date of Hanno's voyage is uncertain. Modern scholars are agreed that it is to be placed in the fifth century BC, but a more precise dating is difficult. The view adopted above, which identifies this Hanno with the Hanno son of Hamilcar known to have been prominent at Carthage in the generation after 480, is perhaps the most attractive, but it is by no means beyond dispute. Hanno inscribed an account of his voyage in the Temple of Baal Hammon at Carthage, and we possess what purports to be a Greek translation of his account. Briefly, Hanno relates that he established six colonies along the Moroccan coast, and sailed on to a river Lixus, where he picked up interpreters from the local nomads. He then sailed for three days along a desert coast before founding a final colony on the island of Cerne. From Cerne, two further voyages were undertaken. On the first, Hanno explored a river Chretes, apparently in the immediate vicinity of Cerne. On the second, he explored further along the coast, which beyond Cerne was inhabited by people described as 'Ethiopians'.

Twelve days' sail brought Hanno to a wooded headland. Passing this headland, he explored the coast for some distance beyond it, noting in particular a large mountain with fire issuing from it (presumably a volcano) called the 'Platform (or Chariot) of the Gods'. He finally turned back when his provisions gave out.

The identification of the places described by Hanno is disputed. No scholar has yet succeeded in producing an entirely satisfactory interpretation of the text. This is perhaps not altogether surprising. It is unlikely that the text has altogether escaped mutilation in the process of translation from Punic to Greek and in its subsequent transmission. There may also have been some interpolation of additional material, though the view that the whole text, or at least the latter portion of it which appears to refer to exploration beyond the Sahara, is a literary forgery,[1] lacks plausibility. A further difficulty in the identification of the places mentioned is the possibility of substantial changes in the configuration of the coastline since Hanno's time. It is a measure of the obscurity of the problem that while some commentators have argued that Hanno reached the Gabon area, others have taken him no further than southern Morocco. Among the latter group, special consideration needs to be given to Professor Mauny (cf. chapter 5, pp. 292–300), who argues on general grounds that neither Hanno nor any other ancient navigator could have passed Cape Juby.[2] Along this section of the coast, the prevailing winds and currents facilitate a voyage from north to south, but make the return journey northwards extremely difficult. Mauny argues that the return journey from beyond Cape Juby became feasible only with the introduction of the 'lateen' sail, which enabled ships to sail close to the wind, in the Islamic period, and that it would have been altogether impossible for the square-rigged ships used in the Mediterranean during classical times. He concedes that the voyage might have been possible for galleys, powered by oars rather than sails, such as Hanno is explicitly said to have used, but argues that galleys could not have carried sufficient supplies of water for their large crews of rowers for the long journey along the dry Saharan coast. But not all scholars would accept Mauny's general argument, and it is difficult to see how, in the absence of practical tests, it could be established with any certainty.

A study of Hanno's text itself seems to indicate that he got much

[1] For this view, see G. Germain, 'Qu'est-ce que le Périple d'Hannon? Document, amplification littéraire, ou faux intégral?', *Hespéris*, 1957, **44**, 205–48.

[2] See especially R. Mauny, 'La navigation sur les côtes du Sahara pendant l'antiquité', *Revue des Études Anciennes*, 1955, **57**, 92–101.

further along the coast. Most commentators, indeed, have held that Hanno's river Lixus is the Wadi Darʿa, having nothing to do with the city of Lixus further north, and that the wooded headland twelve days' sail south of Cerne is Cape Verde. Beyond this, the 'Platform of the Gods' has been alternatively identified with Mount Kakulima in the Republic of Guinea and with Mount Cameroun. This last question is difficult to resolve, and, however fascinating, it is of little importance to fix the furthest limit of Hanno's explorations, since there is no question that the Carthaginians ever established regular contacts so far along the coast. The crucial question is the location of Cerne, Hanno's furthest colony, which later served as a base for Carthaginian trade in the area. Hanno places it three days' sail south of the river Lixus, and twelve days north of the wooded headland identified with Cape Verde

21 Carthaginian exploration along the Atlantic coast.

(supposing these figures to be correctly transmitted in the text), and also states vaguely that it was about the same distance from the Straits of Gibraltar as Carthage. He also implies that it was near to a river called Chretes. An independent description of Cerne, in a Greek commercial guide of *c.* 340 BC wrongly attributed in antiquity to Skylax, places it twelve days' sail from the Straits, and confirms that it was close to a river, which the writer however names as Xion. No satisfactory identification for Cerne has been found. The islands of Herne and Arguin have been frequently suggested, but there is no appropriate river by either place. Numerous other guesses have been made, some seeking to place Cerne as far south as the Senegal estuary. The question cannot be settled by a study of the texts, and its resolution must await a thorough archaeological examination of the suggested sites. To date, the most southerly site on the coast to have yielded archaeological evidence of Phoenician occupation is the island of Mogador. Mauny, indeed, would identify Cerne with Mogador, but this is difficult to accept, as the Phoenician settlement there seems to have been established during the seventh century BC and abandoned at the end of the sixth century, some time before the probable date of Hanno's voyage.

The importance of Cerne lies in its use as a base for Carthaginian trade down the west coast of Africa. This trade is described in any detail in only two passages of ancient literature. Neither account is first-hand, both being written by Greeks from information given by Carthaginians. The first account is from Herodotus (*c.* 430 BC):

> The Carthaginians say that there is a part of Africa with people living in it outside the Straits of Gibraltar. When the Carthaginians arrive there, they take out their wares, set them in a row along the shore, and raise smoke; when the natives see the smoke, they come to the shore, set down gold in payment for the goods, and withdraw; the Carthaginians disembark and examine the gold, and if they think it equals the value of the goods they pick it up and depart, but if not they go back into their ships and wait, and the natives approach and add more gold until they persuade them; neither party is dishonest – the Carthaginians do not touch the gold until it equals the value of the goods, and the natives do not touch the goods until they take the gold.[1]

Close parallels to this system of silent barter can be found in later accounts of the gold-trade in the interior of West Africa. The second account of the west coast trade comes from 'Pseudo-Skylax', the writer of *c.* 340 BC referred to above:

[1] Herodotus, *Histories*, IV. 196.

Beyond Cape Soloeis [Cape Cantin] is a river called Xion, around which dwell Ethiopians . . . Here there is an island called Cerne . . . The voyage from Soloeis to Cerne takes seven days, and the whole voyage from the Straits of Gibraltar to the island of Cerne takes twelve days. It is not possible to sail beyond Cerne because of the shallowness of the sea, mud, and weeds. The merchants are Phoenicians. When they arrive at the island of Cerne they moor their ships, setting up tents for themselves on Cerne. They unload their wares and take them across in small boats to the mainland. There are Ethiopians on the mainland, and it is these with whom they trade. They trade for hides of deer, lions, leopards, hides and teeth of elephants, and hides of domestic cattle. The Ethiopians use ornaments and cups of ivory; their women use anklets of ivory; they even use ivory ornaments for their horses. These Ethiopians are the tallest of all men that we know, over four cubits: some of them are even five cubits. They have beards and long hair, and are the handsomest of men, and whoever is tallest is their king. They employ chariots, javelins, and bows and arrows, using missiles hardened by fire. The Phoenicians import for them perfume, Egyptian stone [probably glass], Attic pottery and jars . . . These Ethiopians drink milk and eat meat, and make much wine from vines. The Phoenicians take away the wine also. They have a large city, to which the Phoenicians sail.[1]

The reference here to the pitching of tents on Cerne suggests that Hanno's attempt to establish a permanent settlement on the island had been abandoned. The description of the 'Ethiopians' is of considerable interest in itself. Its authenticity may be suspected, since the writer appears to have incorporated details from Herodotus's account of the quite different 'Ethiopians' of the Upper Nile, in particular the description of them as tall and handsome, their method of selecting kings, and their diet of milk and meat (though this last is a cliché applied generally to pastoral peoples). But the other details are very probably genuine. It is to be noted that if they had prominent beards and long hair, these 'Ethiopians' are unlikely to have been Negroes. It is also of interest that they appear to have had no knowledge of metals.

There is an odd contradiction between the accounts of Herodotus and Pseudo-Skylax. Herodotus describes a trade by silent barter for gold, Pseudo-Skylax a trade for ivory, hides and wine, with a 'large city' whose inhabitants he is able to describe in some detail. The latter's omission of gold is perhaps no great difficulty, explicable on the supposition that his Phoenician informants did not wish to reveal too much about the most profitable aspects of their trade. That Cerne in the fourth century BC *was* a base for trade in gold seems to be attested by Palaiphatos, a rationalizer of myths, who locates the legend of

[1] Pseudo-Skylax, *Periplus*, 112.

Perseus and the Gorgons on Cerne, which he describes as 'very rich in gold'.[1] The contradiction over the circumstances of the trade is more serious. One solution would be to suppose that the conditions of trade had changed between *c.* 430 and *c.* 340 BC, Herodotus possibly reporting the practice before Hanno's colonization of Cerne. A more attractive solution, however, is to refer the two descriptions to different places on the coast. The silent trade for gold perhaps took place south of Cerne, possibly in the Senegal area. The informants of Pseudo-Skylax will then have been strictly accurate in their account of the commodities traded for at Cerne, but suppressed the fact that the Carthaginians also sailed beyond Cerne to trade for gold.

Wherever Cerne was, and wherever the silent trade for gold took place, the ultimate source of the gold is presumably to be found in the alluvial goldfields of Galam and Bambuk, around the upper Niger and upper Senegal – the same goldfields which later formed the basis of the prosperity and power of Ghana and later states of the western Sudan. It is unprofitable to speculate, on the basis of the written evidence, about the possible impact of the trade on West Africa. It can only be hoped that archaeology will ultimately throw some light on the question. It might, for example, show how far and by what routes the Greek pottery and other commodities imported by the Carthaginians penetrated into the interior.

The west coast trade of the Carthaginians does not seem to have lasted long, for the Romans, who should have gained access to it when they conquered Gades in 206 BC, have little to say about it. The last possible allusion to it is from Caelius Antipater (*c.* 120 BC), who records that he met a man who claimed to have sailed for trade from Spain (no doubt from Gades) to 'Ethiopia', meaning probably the land of the Ethiopians opposite Cerne.[2] By the end of the second century BC, though Gaditan ships continued to fish along the coast, the normal limit of their voyages was the river Lixus (Wadi Darʿa). There were occasional later voyages by non-Phoenicians. In about 147 BC, the Greek historian Polybius took a Roman fleet some way down the coast, and reached an island which he thought was Cerne. Another Greek, Eudoxos, made two voyages along the coast in *c.* 105 BC in an attempt to open up a sea-route around Africa to India, but failed to return from the second. But these later voyages did not lead to any regular contacts. It is not clear why the trade thus came to an end. One source refers to the destruction by the Pharusii and Nigritae, peoples of

[1] Palaiphatos, περὶ ἀπίστων, 31.

[2] Quoted by Pliny, *Naturalis historia*, II. 169.

the western Sahara, of 'cities of the Tyrians' on the west coast of Africa.[1] It is not certain when this disaster occurred, or even which were the cities involved in it. If the reference to 'cities of the Tyrians' is to be taken literally, they may have been colonies founded direct from Tyre in the days before Carthaginian hegemony, and destroyed possibly even before Hanno's voyage (such as Mogador, perhaps). But the reference may be to Hanno's colonies, destroyed at some time after *c.* 340 BC. This question might be settled by archaeological investigation. It is at least a possibility that one factor in the decline of Carthaginian trade with West Africa was the destruction of the Phoenician cities along the Moroccan coast.

This is all rather speculative and nebulous. Hardly a single statement of importance is established with any certainty. Altogether, it is difficult to establish the geographical scope, and still more the historical significance for West Africa, of Punic enterprise along the West African coast by a study of the available written evidence. Indeed, it is possible, as Mauny argues, that the Carthaginians never reached sub-Saharan Africa at all. The written sources merely raise a number of tantalizing possibilities, which can be proved or disproved, if at all, only by the provision of more substantial data by the progress of archaeology.

THE LIBYANS

In this final section, some attempt is made to present an account of the indigenous peoples of North Africa during the period of Phoenician and Greek colonization. It is clearly unsatisfactory thus to relegate the Libyans, as it were, to an appendix, but the state of the evidence makes this procedure unavoidable. The historian of North Africa during this period is faced, perhaps to an even greater degree, with problems similar to those involved in the reconstruction of the history of tropical Africa during the period of European colonization. The Libyans were not at this time literate, and all our written sources come from the colonizing peoples. Hence it is difficult not to concentrate attention upon the activities of the colonists, to the neglect of the indigenous peoples. It is unfortunate also that there is as yet no considerable body of archaeological evidence which might compensate for the lack of written information about the Libyans. A certain amount has been recorded above of those of the Libyans who were most directly involved with the colonists. But the greater part of the Libyans were never

[1] Strabo, *Geography*, XVII. 3.3.

brought under Greek or Phoenician rule, and their history cannot conveniently be considered with that of the immigrant states. Here, therefore, is offered an account, fragmentary and often speculative, of the culture of the Libyans.

In the first place, some comment is needed on the use of the name 'Libyans' as a general term for the inhabitants of North Africa. The North Africans themselves certainly did not call themselves 'Libyans'. It is, indeed, unlikely that they had any common name for themselves, or any feeling of community. The name 'Libyans' (*Libyes*) was apparently derived by the Greeks from *Libu*, the name by which the Egyptians referred to *one* of the tribes on their western border, and the Greeks gave it a general application for which there was no real justification. The name seems to have had for the Greeks an essentially racial significance. They divided the indigenous inhabitants of Africa, outside Egypt, into the 'Libyans' of the north and the 'Ethiopians' of the south. The former were light-skinned, the latter dark-skinned: the word 'Ethiopian' (*Aithiops*) appears to mean 'burnt-faced'. It is easy to slip into supposing that the distinction between Libyans and Ethiopians corresponds with that between Caucasoids and Negroids, but this equation is demonstrably unsound. The term 'Ethiopian', which was in any case not always used with consistency or precision, is often applied to Saharan peoples who must have been Caucasoid, though darker-skinned than the peoples of the Mediterranean seaboard. The presumption is strong, though there is a lack of direct evidence, that the Libyans spoke languages ancestral to the modern Berber dialects of North Africa, which are remotely related both to the Semitic languages and to Ancient Egyptian. The few 'Libyan' words cited by ancient writers are not demonstrably Berber, and the inscriptions left by the Libyans from the second century BC onwards have not yet been successfully deciphered. But various place names and personal names mentioned by classical writers do show that Berber was spoken in North Africa in this period, and it seems likely, though it cannot be proved, that all the Libyans spoke Berber.

The Libyans comprised numerous distinct tribes. The first detailed account of the various Libyan tribes was given by the Greek geographer Hekataios (*c.* 500 BC), but only a few fragments of his work survive. The earliest writer on the Libyans whose account is preserved in full is Herodotus (*c.* 430 BC). Little purpose would be served by giving a comprehensive catalogue of all the Libyan tribes mentioned by these and later writers, especially as the nomenclature applied to the tribes, and very possibly in some cases the distribution and composition of the tribes themselves, were unstable, but the more important tribes will be listed. In the east, bordering upon Egypt, were the Adyrmachidai, who, as has been seen above, were at times subject to Egypt. They were also Egyptianized culturally – Herodotus says of them: 'For the most part they adopt Egyptian customs, though they wear the same sort of clothes as the other Libyans.'[1] Further west, the hinterland of Cyrenaica was occupied in Herodotus's time by four tribes, from east to

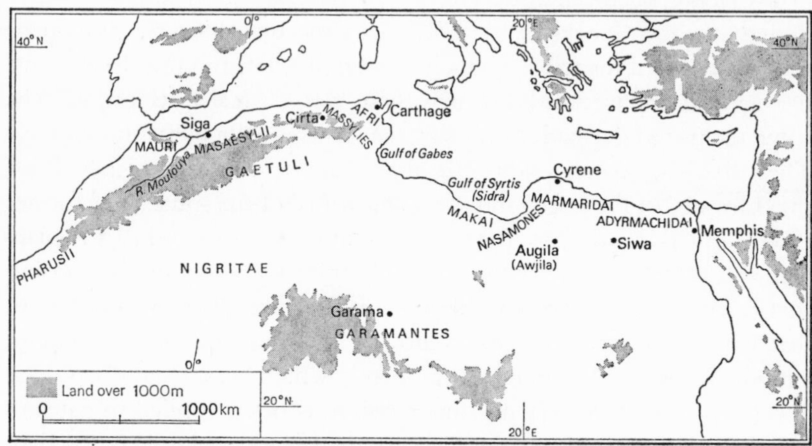

22 Major Libyan peoples.

west, the Giligamai, the Asbystai, the Auschisai and the Bakales. Later writers, however, apply to the Libyans of Cyrenaica the general name Marmaridai. This may represent primarily a change in nomenclature only, but probably there was also some redistribution and reorganization of the tribes, for some of the later writers refer to the Asbystai as living on the coast of Tripolitania away to the west. To the south-west of Cyrenaica, the shores of the Gulf of Syrtis were occupied during several centuries by the populous tribe of the Nasamones. In Hekataios's time, the western portion of the shore of the gulf had been occupied by a tribe called the Psylloi, but by the time that Herodotus gathered his information, the Psylloi had been dispossessed by their eastern neighbours, the Nasamones, and apparently driven into the interior, where they are noted by later writers. To the west of the Gulf of Syrtis, the eastern section of the coast of Tripolitania was inhabited by the Makai. Western Tripolitania was occupied by a bewildering succession of small

[1] Herodotus, *Histories*, IV. 168.1.

tribes. In North-West Africa, inhabiting the littoral plain to the west of Carthaginian territory as far as the river Moulouya, were the Numidians (Latin *Numidae*, Greek *Nomades*). Before the second century BC, the Numidians comprised several distinct tribes, the most powerful of which were the Massylies in the east and the Masaesylii in the west. Further west again, beyond the Moulouya, were the Mauri or 'Moors' (Greek *Maurousioi*).[1] To the south of the Numidians and Mauri, in the highlands of the Atlas mountains and their eastward extensions and in the northern margins of the Sahara, were the Gaetuli. This was a name applied to several distinct tribes. One writer of Roman times asserts that the Gaetuli were divided into three tribes,[2] and probably the real situation was still more complex. In the western Sahara we hear of the Pharusii, living on the Atlantic shore, and of the Nigritae, inhabiting the valley of a river Nigris or Nigeir,[3] which is probably to be identified with the Wadi Saoura. In the central Sahara, the oases of the Fezzan were inhabited by the Garamantes, who had their capital at Garama (Djerma). To the south of these desert peoples, in the southern Sahara and the Sudan, were the 'Ethiopians'.

The culture of the Libyans differed widely from area to area of North Africa. A principal distinction was between those whose economy was based upon agriculture and those who lived by pastoralism. Herodotus states that the Libyans to the east of 'Lake Tritonis' (the Gulf of Gabes) were nomadic pastoralists, while those of the Maghrib were sedentary agriculturalists. This generalization contains a considerable element of truth, in that agriculture was much more commonly practised in the Maghrib than in the east, but it is a gross oversimplification. In the east, it is unclear whether the Libyan tribes of Cyrenaica ever cultivated crops, but in Tripolitania it was presumably the Libyan Makai rather than the Phoenician colonists who farmed the land around the river Kinyps which was so much admired by Herodotus. Moreover, agriculture was certainly practised in the oases of the desert, and Herodotus himself describes the agricultural methods of the Garamantes. In North-West Africa, while it seems clear that the Libyans were practising agriculture before the arrival of the Phoenician colonists, after the fifth

[1] The land of the Mauri was known as *Mauretania*: the modern use of this name is one of the more egregious misnomers of African geography.

[2] Pliny, *Naturalis historia*, v. 17: the three Gaetulian tribes were the Autololes in the west, the Baniurae in the east, and the Nesimi in the desert to the south of the Atlas range.

[3] The river Nigris was to become, through a series of textual corruptions and geographical confusions, the origin of the application of the name *Niger* to the great river of West Africa. The name *Nigris* is, in fact, merely a transcription of the Berber word *n'gher*, meaning 'river'.

century BC most of the cultivated area was brought under Carthaginian control. Outside Carthaginian territory, the Numidians are said to have remained basically nomadic and pastoral for many centuries, and only to have adopted agriculture and urbanism on any scale during the reign of their King Masinissa (201–148 BC), though there were some large towns, notably Masinissa's own capital Cirta (Constantine), even before this time. The Mauri, to the west of the Numidians, retained an essentially nomadic way of life even longer, into Roman times.

Libyan agriculture consisted principally of cereal culture. It seems probable that the techniques of arboriculture were only disseminated in North Africa by the Phoenician colonists. The Libyans did, however, collect the fruits of wild trees: Herodotus describes how the Nasamones used to make seasonal expeditions to the Oasis of Augila (Awjila) in the interior to harvest the dates there. The pastoral economy was based upon oxen, and to a lesser extent on sheep and goats. Pigs were not reared, an omission which Herodotus explains as due to the influence of Egypt, where pigs were regarded as unclean. Also important was the horse, which was the main transport animal during this period not only along the North African littoral but even in the Sahara. Horses were originally employed to draw carts or chariots. The horse-drawn war-chariot was introduced into Egypt from Asia, probably by the Hyksos invaders of the seventeenth century BC, and was presumably adopted by the Libyans from the Egyptians. Such chariots are frequently depicted in the rock art of North Africa, and their use by the Libyans is described by Herodotus and later writers. Subsequently chariots were replaced for military purposes by cavalry. In North-West Africa this development can be dated to the early third century BC, since the last recorded instance of the operation of chariots there concerns the Libyan allies of Agathokles in 307 BC, and the earliest of the use of cavalry relates to Numidian allies of Carthage fighting against the Romans in Sicily in 262. In the Sahara, the use of chariots may have persisted until much later, for Strabo in the first century BC mentions their use by the Pharusii and Nigritae. The replacement of chariotry by cavalry among the allies of Carthage seems to be related to the adoption by Carthage of the war-elephant, which took over the military role of the war-chariot. But the techniques of horse-riding were not introduced to the Libyans by the Carthaginians. North Africa had an indigenous tradition of cavalry fighting, distinguished by the fact that the horses were ridden without saddle or reins, being directed by a stick. The camel, which ultimately replaced the horse as the principal transport animal of North Africa and the Sahara, appears to have been unknown at this time: the earliest evidence for its use in the Maghrib is only of the second century BC (see chapter 5, p. 288). The usual weapon of the Libyans, employed by their infantry as well as by their chariotry and cavalry, was the javelin. The desert peoples, the Pharusii and Nigritae, and the 'Ethiopians', practised archery as well as the use of the javelin.

It appears that the Libyans whom the first Phoenician and Greek colonists encountered were basically Neolithic in culture. There is little evidence of their using metals before the period of colonization. In the east, the Libyans might have learned the techniques of bronze-smelting and, after the seventh century BC, of iron-smelting from Egypt, but the evidence does not suggest that they did so. It is significant that Herodotus describes a Libyan contingent in the army of Persia in 480 BC, recruited probably from the Adyrmachidai, as using wooden spears with points hardened by fire. However, some metal objects, if not the actual technique of smelting, evidently found their way westwards, since Herodotus elsewhere refers to the wearing of bronze anklets by the women of the Adyrmachidai. In the west, there is some archaeological evidence suggesting that the peoples of what is now Morocco and Mauritania derived a knowledge of copper (but not, to any great extent, of bronze) from the Chalcolithic cultures of Spain (see chapter 5, p. 319). But the scarcity of local supplies of copper no doubt limited the impact of this innovation. It seems probable that the knowledge of iron did not spread among the Libyans until the arrival of the Phoenicians in North-West Africa in the eighth century BC and of the Greeks in Cyrenaica in the seventh century, but it is quite uncertain how quickly the Libyans adopted the use of the metal from the colonists. It is to be noted that, as appears from the description of Pseudo-Skylax quoted above, the Ethiopians on the Atlantic coast opposite Cerne did not profit in this respect from their contacts with the Phoenicians, since in *c.* 340 BC they were still using wooden spears and arrows with points hardened by fire.

When we turn our attention from the material culture of the Libyans to their beliefs and customs, we find the evidence even more fragmentary. The religion of the Libyans, like that of the Egyptians, seems to have been characterized by a preference for zoomorphic deities. Herodotus states that in general the Libyans worshipped only the Sun and the Moon. The most popular form of the sun deity, and the principal deity of the Libyans, was the ram-headed god Ammon, whose adoption by the Greeks of Cyrenaica and by the Phoenicians of Carthage has been mentioned. The main centre of the Ammon cult was his temple in the Oasis of Siwa in the east, but he was worshipped by Libyans throughout North Africa, and rock engravings depicting rams bearing the Egyptian sun disc between their horns have been found as far west as the Oran province of Algeria. According to Herodotus, the Siwa temple was an offshoot of the Temple of Amun-Reʿ at Thebes in Egypt, and it seems clear that the Libyan Ammon was basically a borrowing of the Egyptian god Amun-Reʿ, though probably his cult became fused with those of sun-gods and ram-gods of purely Libyan origin. Of the Libyan moon deity, nothing can be said beyond what Herodotus himself states, unless the Carthaginian moon-goddess Tanit is, as has been suggested, a borrowing from the Libyans. Herodotus also states that the eastern Libyans venerated the Egyptian cow-goddess Isis, and observed the Egyptian prohibition on the meat of cows. Other Egyptian deities adopted by the Libyans were perhaps the gods Osiris and Bes, who seem to be depicted in rock engravings of the Fezzan. The Libyans also practised a cult of the dead. Herodotus, for example, states that the Nasamones

> swear oaths by men who are said to have been especially just and good, laying their hands on their tombs, and for divination they go to the graves of their ancestors and, after praying, lie down to sleep upon them, and make use of whatever dreams come to them.[1]

The social and political institutions of the Libyans are even more elusive than their religion. As regards their social structure, there are several references to polygamy, an institution which Greek and Roman writers often misinterpreted or misrepresented as promiscuity. Polygamy was evidently widespread, if not universal, among the Libyans. There is also evidence that succession among the Numidians originally passed not from father to son but, probably, to the eldest surviving member of the family.[2] Somewhat surprisingly, there is no evidence in the classical period for matrilineal succession, which is known to have been practised in more recent times by at least some of the Berber tribes.

Not much more is known of the political institutions of the Libyans. It is even difficult to identify political units among them. It must often be in doubt whether the application by ancient writers of a single name to the Libyans occupying a particular area can be taken to imply that they formed in a political sense a single tribe, or even a confederation of

[1] Herodotus, *Histories*, IV. 172.3.

[2] Livy, *Ab urbe condita*, XXIX. 29.6, records that on the death of Gaia, King of the Massylies, *c.* 208 BC, the throne passed not to his son but to his brother, and observes, *ita mos apud Numidas est* ('This is the custom among the Numidians').

tribes. This was certainly not true, for example, of the Gaetuli or of the Numidians before the second century BC, and probably not of the Marmaridai. There are occasional references to 'kings' of various Libyan tribes in this period. The indigenous title so translated in our sources was, among the eastern Libyans, according to Herodotus, *battos* – which title, it will be recalled, was adopted as a personal name by the Greek kings of Cyrene. The title *battos* cannot be connected with any word known in any of the languages of North Africa: the suggestion that it is to be related to *bity*, the Egyptian title of the King of Lower Egypt, is most improbable. The kings of Numidia, at least in the second century BC, used the title *gld*, which perhaps represents *aguellid*, a Berber word for 'king'. In the east, one might suspect a derivation of political forms from Egypt. The kings of the Adyrmachidai, who played a prominent role in the Egyptian revolts against Persia in the fifth century BC, were, it will be recalled, Egyptians, and possibly appointed from Egypt. However, the only custom described by Herodotus in connection with kingship among the Adyrmachidai, that of the deflowering of prospective brides by the king, was evidently of indigenous inspiration, though Herodotus notes that it was practised only by the Adyrmachidai among the Libyans. Further west we occasionally hear of kings of other Libyan tribes, such as Adikran, who led the Asbystai against the Greeks of Cyrene *c.* 570 BC, but no details are recorded of the organization of their rule. In North-West Africa, the existence of 'kings' among the Numidians and Mauri is first directly attested at the end of the fifth century BC, but here again we know nothing of the extent or nature of their rule. By the end of the third century BC, kingdoms of considerable extent and power had emerged among the Mauri, the Masaesylii (with their capital at Siga), and the Massylies (with their capital at Cirta), but their history falls outside the chronological scope of this chapter.

CHAPTER 3

NORTH AFRICA IN THE HELLENISTIC AND ROMAN PERIODS, 323 BC to AD 305

By the end of the fourth century BC, the two colonizing nations, Greeks and Phoenicians, appeared to be securely established in control of the Mediterranean, and northern Africa was effectively divided between a Greek and a Phoenician state. In the east, the conquests of Alexander had extended Greek colonization and political control over vast new areas, substantially accelerating the process of 'hellenism', the adoption of Greek culture by non-Greek peoples, from which the name conventionally applied to the post-Alexandrine period, the 'Hellenistic' era, is derived. When, on Alexander's death in 323 BC, his empire broke up into several rival kingdoms, control of Egypt was secured by the Macedonian house of Ptolemy, to whose realm the older, more westerly Greek settlements in Cyrenaica were also annexed. In the west, the Phoenician state of Carthage, having survived the invasion of its North African territories by the Greek leader Agathokles in 310–307 BC, had re-established its control over North-West Africa and throughout the western Mediterranean. But these states were quickly to find themselves overshadowed and eventually subjugated by the rising power of Rome. Rome had risen from the position of a minor Italian city-state to the control, by the 270s BC, of all southern Italy. The Romans defeated Carthage in two wars (264–241 and 218–201 BC), after which the Phoenician city was reduced to the status of a client of Rome and ultimately (146 BC) destroyed. They also began to interfere in the east, between the warring Greek states, and imposed their dominance and finally their direct rule. Egypt, from being a friend and ally of Rome in the third century, sank to being its client in the second century, and was finally annexed in 30 BC. By that time, the Romans effectively controlled the entire North African littoral, though their formal rule was not consolidated over the whole area until the annexation of Mauretania (the western Maghrib) in AD 40.

EGYPT UNDER THE PTOLEMAIC DYNASTY, 323 TO 30 BC

On the premature death of Alexander in 323 BC, his feeble-minded brother Philip III Arrhidaios and his posthumous son Alexander IV were set up as joint kings of his empire, with a regent to rule in their name. Alexander's principal generals were appointed *satraps* (governors) of the various provinces of his empire, Ptolemy (Ptolemaios) securing appointment as *satrap* of Egypt. At once civil war broke out, as the successive regents and the *satraps* struggled for effective power. The nominal kings were murdered, Philip in 316 and Alexander in 310 BC. One of the generals, Antigonos, seemed for a while to come near to establishing his authority throughout the empire, and proclaimed himself king in 306, but his defeat and death in 301 ended any prospect that the unity of the empire might be maintained. Instead, three principal kingdoms emerged: Egypt, ruled by Ptolemy; Syria (which initially included most of the Asian provinces of Alexander's empire), under Seleukos; and Macedonia, which eventually fell to the descendants of Antigonos.

In the wars which followed Alexander's death, Ptolemy's control of Egypt was seriously threatened only once, when Antigonos attempted an invasion in 306/5, and he ruled until his death in 283. He was succeeded by his son, a second Ptolemy, usually distinguished by the surname Philadelphos (283–247 BC), and he in turn by his son, Ptolemy III Euergetes (247–221 BC). The house of Ptolemy ruled Egypt for almost three centuries, until the Roman annexation in 30 BC, the fourteen kings of the dynasty all bearing the name of Ptolemy.

The realm of the early Ptolemies included a considerable empire outside Egypt. To the west, the Greek cities of Cyrenaica had been annexed by Ptolemy I in 322 BC. To the north-east, across the peninsula of Sinai, the Ptolemies normally controlled the southern portion of Syria, including Palestine and Phoenicia. Control of this area was disputed by the kings of the house of Seleukos, with whom a series of wars were fought during the third century BC. In one of these wars, in 246 BC, Ptolemy III Euergetes invaded the Seleukid kingdom and briefly occupied its capital, Seleukeia on the river Tigris, but effective Ptolemaic control was never established beyond the Lebanon. Egypt was also, under the early Ptolemies, the principal naval power in the eastern Mediterranean, controlling Cyprus, the southern coast of Asia Minor, the Cyclades and other islands in the Aegean, and several towns in the area of the Dardanelles. Ptolemaic naval power in the Aegean was, however, successfully challenged during the third century by Macedonia, at whose hands the Egyptian fleet suffered a crushing defeat off the island of Andros in 245 BC. Control of the Cyclades was thereby lost, though the Ptolemies still retained their possessions in Asia Minor and the Dardanelles area.

Ptolemy I ruled Egypt originally as *satrap*, but in 305 BC, following the example of Antigonos, he assumed the title of king, and for official purposes numbered his regnal years from the death of Alexander in 323. The Ptolemies in Egypt, in common with the Seleukid kings of Syria and some other Hellenistic rulers, adopted and elaborated notions of divine kingship which had been originally conceived in the entourage of Alexander. When Alexander visited Egypt in 332 BC, he had been greeted by the local priesthood as a son of the Egyptian god Amun-Reʿ, whom the Greeks identified with their own supreme god Zeus. This was, of course, a normal part of the titulary of an Egyptian Pharaoh, but Alexander was deeply impressed, and seems to have become increasingly convinced of his divine paternity. In posthumous portraits on the coins of his successors, Alexander is always represented with the ram's horns of Amun-Reʿ. Ptolemy I had every interest in encouraging belief in the divinity of Alexander, since he represented himself as the successor to Alexander's kingship. Moreover, in 322 BC Ptolemy had secured possession of Alexander's body, and brought it for burial to Memphis, whence his son Ptolemy II Philadelphos later transferred it to the famous *Sema* (tomb) at Alexandria. At some point, perhaps when he assumed the royal title in 305 BC, Ptolemy I instituted an official cult of Alexander as a god at Alexandria. On Ptolemy's own death in 283, he and his wife Berenice were in turn deified, as the *Theoi Soteres* ('Saviour Gods'). The second Ptolemy and his wife (who was also his sister) Arsinoe went further, proclaiming themselves divine as the *Theoi Adelphoi* ('Brother-and-Sister Gods') during their own lifetime. Thereafter, all the rulers of the Ptolemaic dynasty in turn became gods while still alive. The surnames by which the various Ptolemies are customarily distinguished – Euergetes ('Benefactor'), Philopator ('Father-loving'), etc. – are the cult-names under which they were worshipped. The marriage of the king with his sister, first practised by Ptolemy Philadelphos, also became normal under the later Ptolemies. (Whether this was an imitation of the brother-sister marriages of the earlier native Pharaohs is not clear.)

The official cult of Alexander and the Ptolemies at Alexandria was designed to legitimize the dynasty in the eyes of its Greek subjects. The Hellenistic institution of divine kingship, though in part inspired by the Egyptian example, meant nothing to the native Egyptians. For them, the Ptolemies had to be presented as a new dynasty of Pharaohs. They are represented on their monuments as wearing the traditional pharaonic regalia, and given the traditional pharaonic titulary in vernacular inscriptions. The Ptolemies also patronized the indigenous religion, making substantial gifts to existing temples and building new temples for the Egyptian gods. The indigenous priesthood was maintained, but its political subservience was secured by royal control of the administration of the temple lands, the king transmitting the revenues from these lands to the temples rather than allowing the priests to exploit them directly. The early Ptolemies, however, do not seem to have felt any pressing need to secure the loyalty of their Egyptian subjects by a systematic exploitation of indigenous political and religious forms.

Outside the priesthood, the Ptolemies abandoned the policy of Alexander of retaining Egyptians in positions of authority (see chapter 2, p. 106). The upper levels of the Egyptian administration under the early Ptolemies were filled entirely by Greeks, and Greek replaced Egyptian as the official language of the Egyptian bureaucracy. At the head of the central bureaucracy, and the most powerful man in Egypt after the king, was an official called the *dioiketes* (manager), always a Greek, who had a general responsibility for the collection and disbursement of the state revenues. At local level, the native *nomarchs*, the hereditary governors of the nomes or provinces of Egypt, who had survived under Persian rule, were now displaced, authority over each nome passing to a Greek official with the title *strategos* (general). The *nomarch* became a minor financial official subordinate to the *strategos*, and seems also to have been normally a Greek. Egyptian officials were probably to be found, certainly in any numbers, only at the lowest level of the administration, in the villages.

The Ptolemaic military system also depended upon Greeks rather than upon Egyptians. The early Ptolemies recruited large numbers of soldiers from Greece and Macedonia. These were granted allotments (*kleroi*) of land, which they cultivated in return for their military service. Tenure of a *kleros* and the obligation of military service which it involved were hereditary. Besides this regular army of hereditary *klerouchoi* (holders of *kleroi*), the Ptolemies commonly hired additional forces of Greek mercenaries on an ad hoc basis. The indigenous military class, the *machimoi* (warriors), who were also hereditary allotment-holders, continued to exist, but were not, under the early Ptolemies, normally employed in actual combat, being restricted to transport and, inside Egypt, police functions. (For the *machimoi*, cf. chapter 2, pp. 89–90.)

To supply the manpower needed for the Ptolemaic system of administration and military organization, a large number of Greeks and Macedonians came to settle in Egypt. This settlement, it should be stressed, had a very different character from that of earlier Greek colonization in Egypt and elsewhere. Traditionally, Greeks had settled in autonomous city-states. In Egypt, this pattern of settlement was represented only by the old city of Naukratis, by Alexander's colony of Alexandria, and by Ptolemais, in Upper Egypt, which was founded by Ptolemy I. The bulk of the Greek settlers in Ptolemaic Egypt, including the military *kleroucboi*, lived dispersed over the country and enjoyed no institutions of civic self-government. They did, however, commonly seek to preserve their national identity, by forming voluntary associations called *politeumata* (literally, 'governments') to regulate their own affairs. An official legal distinction was also maintained between Greek settlers and native Egyptians, the two communities having their own separate systems of civil law and their own judges. It should not be supposed, however, that the Greeks held themselves racially separate from the Egyptians. Intermarriage, or at least the taking of Egyptian wives by Greek men, was common, and ultimately the distinction between Greeks and Egyptians came to be more a matter of language and culture than of descent.

Besides Greeks and Macedonians, foreigners of many other nationalities came to Egypt under the Ptolemies – Thracians and Illyrians from the Balkans, Cilicians and Carians from Asia Minor, and above all, perhaps, Jews. Such foreigners were often recruited, alongside the Greeks and Macedonians, into the Ptolemaic army. They often were, or became through residence in Egypt, Greek-speaking and culturally 'hellenized', but in at least some instances they formed their own national *politeumata* separate from those of the Greeks. The Jews were especially numerous in Alexandria, where they occupied a distinct quarter of the city and formed a partly self-governing community. The Alexandrian Jews came to speak Greek rather than Hebrew, and it was in Ptolemaic Alexandria that the Old Testament was translated into Greek.

Under the Ptolemies Egypt, or rather Alexandria, became a leading centre of Greek culture. The Museum, or Temple of the Muses, established at Alexandria by Ptolemy I, functioned as an association of learned men maintained at royal expense, and attracted philosophers, scientists and poets from all over the Greek world. The Library of Alexandria, also founded by Ptolemy I, built up the largest collection of Greek books (in the form of papyrus rolls) in the world. Besides

Greeks of culture, Alexandria could boast an occasional Egyptian who had acquired a Greek education and won acceptance in the Greek literary world. The only such of whom anything is known was Manetho, a priest of Heliopolis and a religious adviser to Ptolemy I, who wrote in Greek a compendious history of Egypt, which unfortunately survives only in fragments and inaccurate summaries. It is to Manetho that we owe the conventional division of the kings of Egypt up to the time of Alexander into thirty dynasties.

Despite the position of Alexandria as an international centre of Greek learning and culture, the progress of 'hellenism' among the indigenous population of Ptolemaic Egypt appears to have been minimal. There were, no doubt, many others besides the historian Manetho among the Egyptian priests – the only section of the indigenous élite to survive

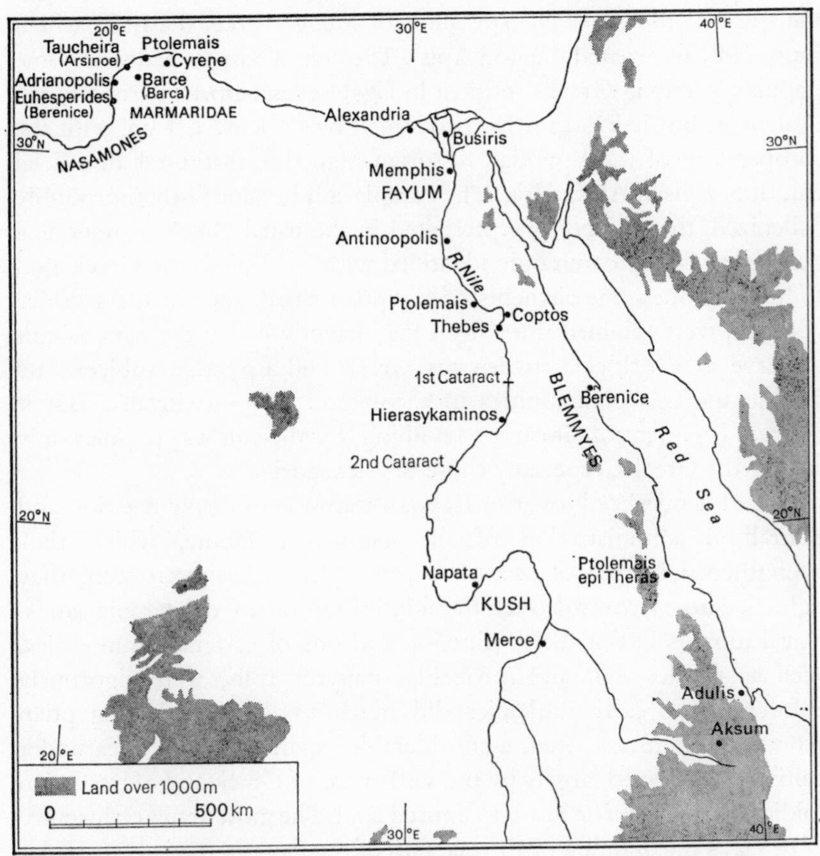

23 North-eastern Africa in the Hellenistic and Roman periods.

under the Ptolemies – who acquired a knowledge of the Greek language and culture. And at a lower level, many Egyptians outside the priesthood sought advancement by learning Greek, and in some instances by adopting Greek names and becoming, to all intents and purposes, Greeks. But there was no attempt to assimilate culturally the mass of the Egyptian people. The Ptolemies were not, in this context, cultural missionaries, and were content to leave the Egyptians largely to themselves, provided only that they paid their taxes. Indeed, the Greeks in Egypt, far from imposing their culture on the indigenous people, to some extent themselves adopted Egyptian culture. Such assimilation is evident, at least, in the sphere of religion. Many Greeks adopted elements of Egyptian religion, either by assimilating Greek to Egyptian gods or by actually joining local cults. In this connection, a special interest attaches to the cult of Sarapis, in origin apparently Osiris-Apis, the spirit of the deceased Apis-bulls of Memphis (i.e. the bulls which supposedly incarnated the god Apis). The cult of Sarapis had won some popularity among Greeks resident in Egypt even before the time of the Ptolemies, but it was greatly encouraged by Ptolemy I, who, with the co-operation of the Egyptian historian Manetho, instituted an official cult of Sarapis at Alexandria. The Sarapis cult became fairly thoroughly hellenized, the god being represented in the usual Greek manner as a bearded man and commonly identified with Asklepios, the Greek god of healing, but some elements of Egyptian ritual, such as the sacrifice of geese, were retained. Ptolemy I may have intended the Sarapis cult to serve as a bridge between his Greek and Egyptian subjects, by uniting the two communities in a common religious loyalty. But if this was his intention, it came to nothing, for the cult was popular only among the Greeks, especially those of Alexandria.

The Ptolemies took over in Egypt a tradition of heavy taxation and centralized administration of the national economy, which they strengthened in various ways. For example, as has been seen, they tightened royal control over the administration of the temple lands. Royal monopolies of the production and sale of certain commodities, such as textiles, salt and (probably) papyrus rolls, were rigorously enforced. The early Ptolemies did much to develop the Egyptian economy. There was, first, a considerable expansion of the area under cultivation, effected largely by the settlement of Greek and Macedonian soldiers as *kleroucboi* on hitherto unused land. The most dramatic instance of this was the draining of the marshes of the Fayum, carried out under Ptolemy Philadelphos. Settled principally by Greek and Macedonian *kleroucboi*, the Fayum area became the 'Arsinoite nome', named in honour of Arsinoe, the wife and sister of Philadelphos. Second, the Ptolemies developed or encouraged the cultivation of new or hitherto unimportant crops. Most notable was the production of wine and vegetable oils (the latter an important royal monopoly), both of which were developed in response to the demand of the vastly increased Greek population in Egypt for the articles to which they had been accustomed in the Greek homeland. Third, existing industries were improved. For example, sheep from Asia Minor were introduced to improve the wool-bearing qualities of the local breed. Transport was improved through the use of camels, which seem to have first become numerous under the early Ptolemies, probably through state initiative. An innovation of the later Ptolemaic period was the use for irrigation of a 'screw' turned in a wooden shaft, said to have been an invention of the Sicilian Greek mathematician Archimedes. Fourth, the Ptolemies effected the belated monetization of the Egyptian economy, a regular coinage in gold, silver and copper being instituted by Ptolemy I. A sophisticated system of banking (also a royal monopoly) was developed.

The early Ptolemies also revived and developed Egypt's traditional commercial contacts with the Red Sea area and with Nubia. Exploration of the Red Sea began under Ptolemy I, one of whose admirals discovered the island of Zebirget, an important source of the precious stone known as chrysolites. Ptolemy Philadelphos sent expeditions to explore both the African and Arabian coasts of the Red Sea. He also recut the old canal between the Nile and the Gulf of Suez,[1] and established an over-land route (using camels) between Coptos in Upper Egypt and the port of Berenice on the Red Sea coast. An Egyptian fleet was maintained permanently in the Red Sea to suppress piracy. Philadelphos was principally interested in securing supplies of elephants for military purposes. The use of war-elephants had been introduced from India into the Greek world as a result of Alexander's eastern campaigns, and Philadelphos, finding himself cut off by the rival Seleukid kingdom of Syria from supplies of Indian elephants, determined instead to use African elephants. That the African elephant (*Loxodonta africana*) was by temperament very much less docile than the Indian elephant (*Elephas maximus*) was not, at first, appreciated. Bases for the hunting of elephants were established along the African coast of the Red Sea, the principal early centre being Ptolemais epi Theras ('Ptolemais at the Hunting-Ground'), near Suakin, which was founded under Philadelphos.

[1] Last renovated by the Persian King Darius (521–486 BC): cf. ch. 2, p. 100.

By the reign of the third Ptolemy, Euergetes, elephant-hunting operations had been extended along the coast as far as the port of Adulis, near Massawa, and before the end of the third century BC Ptolemaic elephant-hunters were active outside the straits of the Bab el-Mandeb, on the coast of what is now Somalia. Besides elephants (and, no doubt, ivory), the Ptolemies also imported frankincense, from southern Arabia, and cinnamon, which came ultimately from southern Asia but could be obtained from Arab traders on the Arabian or Somali coasts. Egyptian traders did not, under the early Ptolemies, themselves penetrate as far as India. Philadelphos is reported to have sent an ambassador to India, presumably by sea, but it is clear that no regular commercial contacts were established. Probably the Sabaean kingdom of south-western Arabia was strong enough to enforce its monopoly of the supply of Indian products to Egypt.

To the south of Egypt, the Nubian kingdom of Kush, with its capital at Meroe, was still powerful. Philadelphos is recorded to have undertaken an expedition into 'Ethiopia', probably of a commercial rather than a military character. War-elephants were obtained from Ethiopia as well as from the Red Sea coast, and there was probably also trade for Nubian gold and ivory. Certainly, friendly relations were established between the early Ptolemies and the kings of Meroe. Formal Egyptian rule seems not to have been extended above the First Cataract, Lower Nubia being under Meroitic control (see chapter 4, p. 228).

The first three Ptolemies seem all to have been able rulers, but a decline in the quality of the dynasty became evident with the son and successor of Euergetes, Ptolemy IV Philopator (221–205 BC). Philopator was indolent and debauched, and effective power during his reign was exercised by his unscrupulous minister Sosibios, who held, or at least had earlier held, the post of *dioiketes*. The contemporary king of the Seleukid Dynasty, Antiochos III, sought to exploit the opportunity presented by Philopator's inadequacy by making war upon Egypt. He drove the Ptolemaic forces from southern Syria, and threatened to invade Egypt itself. Sosibios, however, gained time by affecting to negotiate with Antiochos, and laboured to build up an army strong enough to resist him. A substantial army was raised, including – an unprecedented move – some 20,000 native Egyptians armed in Greek fashion. A large force of African elephants was also assembled. When fighting again broke out, Antiochos was decisively defeated at the battle of Raphia, in southern Syria (217 BC). The African elephants of the Ptolemaic army proved useless, fleeing in panic at the approach of the Indian elephants of Antiochos, but victory was secured by the Ptolemaic infantry, the native Egyptians as well as the Greeks fighting bravely. Antiochos was obliged to sue for peace, and Ptolemaic control over southern Syria was restored.

Despite its contribution to the defeat of Antiochos, the use of Egyptian troops at Raphia had unfortunate consequences for the Ptolemies. It stimulated a revival of Egyptian nationalism, since, as a Greek historian observed, the Egyptians,

> priding themselves on their victory at Raphia, were no longer disposed to obey orders, but began to look for a leader and figure-head, thinking themselves quite capable of looking after their own interests.[1]

An Egyptian revolt broke out soon after the battle of Raphia. It appears to have been confined at first to the Delta, where the rebels for several years held the city of Lycopolis, but subsequently it spread also to Upper Egypt, where two leaders called Harmachis and Anchmachis, possibly Nubians, successively set themselves up as Pharaohs. A vernacular nationalist literature grew up, predicting the arrival of a liberator from the south and the destruction of the Greek city of Alexandria. Revolts by native Egyptians were henceforth a recurrent problem throughout the Ptolemaic period.

In the face of this nationalist opposition, the later Ptolemies set out systematically to conciliate Egyptian national feeling. The influence of the Egyptian priesthood increased, as the Ptolemies ostentatiously increased their patronage of the indigenous religion. In 197 BC, Philopator's son and successor, Ptolemy V Epiphanes, was crowned in a traditional pharaonic ceremony at Memphis, the indigenous capital of Egypt, and his example was followed by all the later Ptolemies. Native Egyptians also began to be employed on a substantial scale in the Ptolemaic armed forces. This, no doubt, was motivated as much by the proof given at Raphia of the worth of Egyptian soldiers as by the need to secure the loyalty of the Egyptian population. The indigenous warrior-class, the *machimoi*, was revived, and many Egyptians were also granted military allotments as *klerouchoi*. The terms *machimoi* and *klerouchoi* ceased to refer to a distinction of nationality, and designated merely soldiers with smaller and larger allotments. Greek and Macedonian allotment-holders came to be called *katoikoi* (settlers), to distinguish them from the new native *klerouchoi*. By the 160s BC, we even begin to

[1] Polybius, *Histories*, V.107.2–3.

find native Egyptians holding senior military posts, and serving as the *strategoi* of nomes. It would not be inaccurate to speak of the progressive 'Egyptianization' of the Ptolemaic state, but the extent of this process should not be exaggerated. There is, for example, no evidence that any ruler of the Ptolemaic Dynasty before the last, the famous queen Cleopatra (51–30 BC), even spoke the Egyptian language.

When Ptolemy Philopator died in 205 BC, his son Ptolemy V Epiphanes was still only a child, and there followed a period of political confusion, as successive regents and their principal generals and ministers struggled for power. The Greek populace of Alexandria took a hand in these disturbances, on more than one occasion lynching unpopular ministers. The struggle for power persisted even after the premature coronation of Ptolemy Epiphanes, at the age of only twelve, in 197 BC. But despite this political instability at the capital, the ministers of Epiphanes were able to stamp out the native Egyptian revolt which had broken out under Philopator. Lycopolis, the principal rebel stronghold in the Delta, was taken in 197 BC, though the rebellion in Lower Egypt was not finally crushed until 184/3. In Upper Egypt, Ptolemaic control was restored by 187/6. As part of an administrative reorganization following the end of the rebellion, the *strategos* of the nome of Thebes was made *epistrategos* (over-general) or viceroy of the whole of Upper Egypt. The friendly relations which the earlier Ptolemies had maintained with the kings of Meroe were now broken, perhaps because the Meroitic kings had supported the revolt in Upper Egypt, and Ptolemaic troops appear to have occupied lower Nubia as far as the Second Cataract. The Ptolemies thereby secured control of the gold-mines of Lower Nubia, which they worked under a system of immense cruelty, using the labour of prisoners of war.

Though order was thus eventually restored inside Egypt, the reign of Ptolemy Epiphanes brought disaster in external affairs. In 202 BC Antiochos III of Syria and Philip V of Macedonia, taking advantage of the confusion inside Egypt which followed the accession of Epiphanes, formed an alliance to attack the Ptolemaic possessions outside Egypt. Antiochos proceeded to overrun southern Syria, while Philip attacked and conquered the Ptolemaic dependencies in the Dardanelles area and on the coast of Asia Minor. In this extremity, the government of Epiphanes sought to invoke the support of the rising power of Rome. The Greek world had first been forced to take account of Roman power when Rome emerged victorious from its war with the Greek king, Pyrrhos of Epeiros, in 280–274 BC. The then King of Egypt, Ptolemy Philadelphos, saw the significance of this event, and is said to have negotiated a commercial treaty with Rome in 273 BC. Subsequently, during the second war between Carthage and Rome, in 218–201 BC, while Philip V of Macedonia took the side of Carthage, Ptolemy Philopator of Egypt supplied corn to the Romans. It was therefore with some confidence in Roman goodwill that the ministers of Epiphanes, in 200 BC, appealed to Rome for protection against Syrian and Macedonian aggression. The Romans did, in fact, in response to this and other appeals, proceed to intervene in the east, and fought victorious wars against Philip V of Macedonia in 200–196 and against Antiochos III of Syria in 192–188. But Egypt derived no benefit from this, since its rulers had been unwise enough to come to terms with Antiochos prematurely, probably in 196 BC. Under the settlement, the loss of southern Syria to the Seleukid kingdom was recognized. The Ptolemaic kingdom thus lost all its foreign possessions, except Cyprus and Cyrenaica.

Ptolemy Epiphanes died prematurely in 181 or 180 BC, leaving the kingdom once more to a minor, his son Ptolemy VI Philometor. Effective power was again exercised by a succession of regents. In 170 BC, Philometor's ministers foolishly declared war on the Seleukid kingdom, in an attempt to recover possession of southern Syria. The Seleukid king, Antiochos IV, routed the Ptolemaic forces in southern Syria, and in 169 BC invaded Egypt itself, where he gained control of Memphis and captured Philometor. Alexandria, however, defied Antiochos, and set up Philometor's younger brother, Ptolemy VII Euergetes II, as king in his place. Antiochos withdrew from Egypt, after installing Philometor as king at Memphis in opposition to Euergetes, presumably hoping that rivalry between the two brothers would keep Egypt distracted and weak. But in his absence Philometor and his brother were reconciled, and the two were installed as joint kings at Alexandria. In 168 BC Antiochos returned to Egypt, and this time had himself crowned as King of Egypt in a pharaonic ceremony at Memphis. Antiochos seemed likely to make good his claim to rule Egypt, but the Ptolemaic dynasty was preserved through the intervention of Rome. The Romans, evidently fearing that the threatened union of Egypt and Syria would create a power strong enough to defy them, sent an embassy to order Antiochos to withdraw from Egypt, and Antiochos felt obliged to comply.

The joint rule of Philometor and Euergetes II after 168 BC was disturbed by a recrudesence of native Egyptian revolts, and by continued rivalry between the two kings. Euergetes at first enjoyed greater support, and in 163 he was able to expel Philometor from Alexandria. Philometor then appealed to Rome, and the Romans, seeing an opportunity to weaken further Ptolemaic power, decided that the kingdom should be divided, assigning Egypt and Cyprus to Philometor and Cyrenaica to Euergetes. During the later years of Philometor's reign, however, the Ptolemaic kingdom for the last time presented the appearance of a great power. The Seleukid kingdom was disintegrating in civil war, and Philometor was able to interfere in its troubles, allying in turn with various claimants to the Seleukid throne. In 145 BC, in the course of these campaigns, he entered Antioch, the western capital of the Seleukid kingdom, and was offered the Seleukid throne by its inhabitants. But he declined the offer, possibly fearing the disapproval of Rome, and contented himself with a promise of the retrocession of southern Syria to Egypt. However, though he was victorious in battle, Philometor was fatally wounded. With his death (145 BC), his army dissolved, and the Ptolemaic claim to southern Syria was again forgotten.

On the death of Philometor, his brother Ptolemy VII Euergetes II was able to return from Cyrenaica to assume the Egyptian throne. Euergetes, more commonly known by the nickname 'Physcon' ('Pot-Belly'), is unanimously represented in the sources as a monster of cruelty, whose reign was stained by many crimes. He was hated by the Greeks of Alexandria, who frequently clashed with his soldiers, and especially by the learned men of the Museum, many of whom he persecuted and drove out of Egypt. While it is clear that Euergetes was ruthless and unscrupulous, the received picture of him is certainly overdrawn. It is likely that his unpopularity with the Greeks of Egypt was at least in part due to his deliberate policy of favouring the native Egyptians. He seems to have been especially active in building and adorning temples for the indigenous gods of Egypt, and even appointed a native Egyptian, Paos by name, to be *epistrategos* of Upper Egypt.

However this may be, the reign of Euergetes II was catastrophic for Egypt, since it brought a protracted period of civil war. During the 130s BC, Euergetes quarrelled with his wife and sister Cleopatra (II), and several years of fierce fighting between their supporters ensued. Although Euergetes and Cleopatra were eventually reconciled in 124, this did not put an end to the disorders, since the breakdown of central authority during the civil wars had encouraged independent banditry in many areas. A decree of Euergetes in 118 BC, intended to restore the situation, vividly illustrates this breakdown of order: it provides for an amnesty for offenders, the remission of arrears of taxes and the confirmation of the tenures of those who had irregularly come into possession of allotments of land, and enacted measures to check extortion by tax-collectors and to protect the native Egyptian system of civil law against encroachment by Greek officials. How far this decree was effective in curing the abuses to which it refers is uncertain.

The death of Euergetes II in 116 BC brought a further diminution of the territorial extent of the Ptolemaic kingdom. By his will, he bequeathed Cyrenaica to his illegitimate son, Ptolemy Apion. Under Apion, Cyrenaica became effectively independent of Egypt, and after his death in 96 BC it was brought under Roman rule. In Egypt, Euergetes was succeeded by one of his legitimate sons, Ptolemy VIII Soter II (better known by his nickname, 'Lathyros' or 'Chick-Pea'). Dynastic troubles continued to plague the kingdom, and in 108/7 BC Soter II was overthrown in favour of his younger brother, who became king as Ptolemy IX Alexander. Soter II, however, escaped from Egypt, and seized control of Cyprus, the only remaining Ptolemaic dependency outside Egypt. Ptolemy Alexander in turn was overthrown and killed in a rising of the populace of Alexandria in 88 BC. Ptolemy Soter II was then able to return from Cyprus to recover the Egyptian throne. His second reign was marked by another serious native revolt in Upper Egypt, which centred upon Thebes. This revolt was brought to an end, with a destructive sack of Thebes, in 85 BC.

Ptolemy Soter II died without legitimate male issue in 80 BC. A son of Ptolemy Alexander, having secured the backing of Rome, arrived in Egypt to claim the throne, becoming king as Ptolemy Alexander II. But the new king reigned only for three weeks before he was lynched by the Alexandrian mob. With him ended the legitimate line of the Ptolemaic dynasty. There were, however, two illegitimate sons of Soter II, one of whom was made king as Ptolemy XI Philopator II (more commonly known by his nickname, 'Auletes' or 'The Flute-Player'), while the other became ruler of Cyprus.

The reign of Ptolemy XI was dominated by the threat of a Roman annexation of Egypt. The succession crisis of 80 BC had put in question the formal independence of Egypt, since Ptolemy Alexander II had allegedly left a will by which he bequeathed Egypt to Rome. The authenticity of this document was questionable, but this would not deter the Romans from basing a claim to authority over Egypt upon it. There was, in fact, an abortive proposal at Rome to annex Egypt in 65 BC. Ptolemy XI was therefore concerned above all to win the recognition and support of Rome. When the Romans annexed the rump of the Seleukid kingdom in Syria in 63 BC, Ptolemy sent forces to their assistance, an action which was very unpopular with the Greeks of Alexandria. Finally, by lavish bribes to Roman politicians, Ptolemy secured formal recognition as the legitimate king of Egypt in 59 BC. To pay for these bribes, however, he was obliged to impose additional taxation in Egypt, which made him still more unpopular. Popular resentment at Alexandria was further exacerbated when the Romans annexed Cyprus, the last Ptolemaic dependency outside Egypt, in 58 BC. Ptolemy sought safety in flight, and made his way to Rome, where he borrowed large sums of money with which to offer further bribes in return for Roman support. He was ultimately reinstated in Egypt by the Roman governor of Syria, who left a substantial force of Roman soldiers in the country in 55 BC to secure him in power. In order to repay the debts which he had contracted while in exile, Ptolemy had recourse to further financial exactions, and appointed a certain Rabirius, a Roman financier who was his principal creditor, as *dioiketes* to administer the collection of the taxes. Rabirius, however, was soon driven out of Alexandria by a popular rising.

When Ptolemy XI died in 51 BC, his daughter, Cleopatra VII, the famous Cleopatra, succeeded to the throne, with the elder of her two younger brothers (Ptolemy XII) as co-ruler. However, war soon broke out between Cleopatra and her brother, and there were apparently also risings among the native Egyptians. At this point, Egypt became implicated in the Roman civil war, between the partisans of Caesar and Pompey, which broke out in 49 BC. The ministers of Ptolemy XII at first supported Pompey, to whom they sent forces, but after Caesar's defeat of Pompey in Greece, when Pompey sought refuge in Egypt, they attempted to retrieve this error of judgement by murdering him. Caesar, arriving in Egypt in pursuit of Pompey, was not gratified by this service, and proceeded to provoke a popular rising in Alexandria by his arrogant conduct. During the winter of 48/7 BC, he was besieged in the royal palace at Alexandria. Ptolemy XII eventually associated himself with the besieging forces, while Cleopatra made her way to the palace to join Caesar, and indeed became his mistress. The arrival of reinforcements in 47 BC enabled Caesar to crush the rising, and to reinstate Cleopatra as the ruler of Egypt. Ptolemy XII having been killed in the fighting, her other brother (Ptolemy XIII) was associated with her on the throne. Caesar appears also to have restored possession of Cyprus to Cleopatra.

After the assassination of Caesar at Rome in 44 BC, Cleopatra secured her position inside Egypt by murdering her brother, and taking as co-ruler in his place her own son (so she claimed) by Caesar, Ptolemy XIV Caesarion. Her position was further strengthened when she became the mistress of the principal successor to Caesar's power, Mark Antony, in 41 BC. From Antony, Cleopatra demanded and obtained additional territorial concessions, being ultimately promised Cyrenaica, Cilicia in Asia Minor, Syria and other territories (as yet unconquered by Rome) further east. It might have appeared that the greatness of the Ptolemaic kingdom had been restored. But all this came to nothing when Antony was defeated by his rival, Caesar's adoptive son Caesar Octavian (the later Augustus), in Greece in 31 BC. Antony and Cleopatra retreated to Egypt, where they both committed suicide. Cleopatra's son and co-ruler, Ptolemy Caesarion, was put to death by Octavian, and Egypt finally became a province of the Roman empire (30 BC).

The decline of Egypt under the later Ptolemies was measured not only by the loss of its external dependencies, and ultimately of its own independence: the period also brought an economic decline. During the second and first centuries BC, there was considerable economic distress among Egyptian cultivators. The rural population declined, and Ptolemaic officials had difficulty in maintaining land under cultivation. This was no doubt due in part to the frequent civil wars and other disturbances of the period. Apart from the physical destruction and loss of life which these involved, the collapse of effective central authority led to the neglect and decay of essential irrigation works. But it appears that the unrest, and the fall in population, in the rural areas was also due to increasing poverty, the result of high rates of taxation, which were maintained inflexibly even during years of poor harvests, and exaggerated by the irregular extortions of dishonest officials. Rural distress was exacerbated by the difficulties of operating the Ptolemaic trimetallic currency. In the second century BC, owing to a shortage of silver, the ratio at which copper coins were exchanged for silver coins deteriorated substantially: for the poorer classes, who normally used only the copper coins, this amounted to a catastrophic inflation. These economic troubles no doubt contributed to the recurrent nationalist uprisings.

There was, however, at least one area in which the rule of the later Ptolemies was a period not of decline, but of development – namely, the Red Sea trade of Egypt (see also chapter 4, pp. 244–5). The failure of the African elephants in the Ptolemaic army at Raphia in 217 BC (cf. pp. 156–7) did not immediately lead the Ptolemies to despair of the military capabilities of these animals, and elephants continued to be sought along the African coast of the Red Sea for many years. As late as 145 BC, the army with which Ptolemy Philometor invaded Syria is said to have included an elephant contingent. Thereafter, however, the Ptolemies appear to have abandoned their interest in war-elephants. The Red Sea did not thereby decline in importance, for the former elephant-hunting stations on the African coast of the Red Sea, especially Adulis, continued to be important as bases for trade in ivory, rhinoceros horns and tortoise-shells. The trade with Arabia and India in incense and spices also became increasingly important, and Greeks for the first time began to trade directly with India. The discovery, or rediscovery, of the sea-route to India is attributed to a certain Eudoxos, who was sent out for this purpose towards the end of the reign of Ptolemy Euergetes II (died 116 BC). Eudoxos made two voyages to India, and subsequently, having quarrelled with his Ptolemaic employers, perished in an unsuccessful attempt to open up an alternative sea-route to India, free of Ptolemaic control, by sailing around Africa.[1] The establishment of direct contacts between Egypt and India was probably made possible by a weakening of Arab power at this period, for the Sabaean kingdom of south-western Arabia collapsed and was replaced by the Himyarite kingdom around 115 BC. Imports into Egypt of cinnamon and other eastern spices, such as pepper, increased substantially, though the Indian Ocean trade remained for the moment on quite a small scale, no more than twenty Egyptian ships venturing outside the Red Sea each year. On his second expedition, Eudoxos, blown off course on the return voyage from India, also discovered the East African coast to the south of Cape Guardafui, but it is not clear how soon Egyptian Greeks developed a regular trade with this area.

CYRENAICA UNDER PTOLEMAIC RULE

The Greek settlements in Cyrenaica – Cyrene, Barce (Barca), Euhesperides, and their dependencies – were subject to the Ptolemies throughout almost the whole period of their rule in Egypt. It has been seen in the preceding chapter how in 322 BC Ptolemy I intervened in the internal disputes of the cities of Cyrenaica and established his control over them (see chapter 2, p. 114). An extant inscription from Cyrene appears to record the arrangements made by Ptolemy for the govern-

[1] For the attempted circumnavigation of Africa by Eudoxos, see ch. 2, p. 139.

ment of that city on this occasion. The Cyrenaean exiles who had called in Ptolemy's assistance were restored, and an ostensibly republican regime established. But Ptolemy was not prepared to allow Cyrene more than a pretence of internal autonomy, and the detailed constitutional regulations include provisions for the nomination of the Cyrenaean senate by Ptolemy and for the appointment of Ptolemy as one of the five generals (*strategoi*) of the Cyrenaean army. The inscription makes no reference to the garrison of troops which Ptolemy is known to have left in Cyrene, nor to Ptolemy's general Ophellas, who remained in the city in some capacity, presumably as commander of this garrison, and in fact became the real ruler. The Cyrenaeans were not easily reconciled to the loss of their real independence. In 312 BC there was a rising at Cyrene, and Ptolemy's garrison was besieged in the citadel of the town, but Ptolemy sent reinforcements to suppress the revolt. Shortly after this, Ophellas appears to have joined forces with the Cyrenaean nationalists, and declared himself independent of Ptolemy. However, the rule of Ophellas at Cyrene came to an end when in 308 BC he marched west to join Agathokles of Syracuse in his attack on Carthage, only to be treacherously murdered by Agathokles (cf. chapter 2, p. 123). Ptolemy was then able to reassert his control over Cyrene, appointing his own stepson Magas as its governor.

Magas ruled Cyrene as a Ptolemaic vassal for over thirty years, but in 274 BC, following the example of Ophellas, he took advantage of the embroilment of Ptolemy II Philadelphos in a war with Syria to declare himself an independent king. Magas even set out to invade Egypt, but had to turn back to Cyrene when the local Libyans, the Marmaridai, rose in revolt in his rear. Despite the failure of his offensive ambitions, however, Magas remained independent at Cyrene, which he ruled until his death in 259/8 BC. Before his death, he became reconciled to Ptolemy Philadelphos, and arranged for the eventual reunion of Cyrene to Egypt by betrothing his daughter Berenice to Ptolemy's son, the later Ptolemy III Euergetes. There was opposition to this policy in Cyrene, and the death of Magas was followed by a further period of internal strife. Berenice was apparently driven out of Cyrene, and a republican regime again established, under the guidance of two revolutionary agitators from mainland Greece, Ekdemos and Megalophanes, students of the Platonic Academy at Athens. But the republic was quickly suppressed, probably before the death of Ptolemy Philadelphos (247 BC), and Ptolemy Euergetes and Berenice seem to have maintained their control over Cyrenaica without difficulty. It was probably on the occasion of this reconquest that, in token of their subjection to the Ptolemies, the lesser cities of Cyrenaica were renamed after members of the Egyptian royal family. The port of Barce, whose original name is not known, and which had by now become more important than Barce itself, was renamed Ptolemais (whence its modern name, Tolmeta), Euhesperides became Berenice (whence Benghazi), and Taucheira became Arsinoe.

Cyrenaica was now firmly attached to the Ptolemaic realm, and was governed by a viceroy, entitled the *Libyarches* (Governor of Libya), sent out from Egypt. Cyrenaean Greeks were prominent in Egypt, providing some noted members of the Museum of Alexandria, and Cyrenaean forces (Greek and Libyan) served with the Ptolemaic army. Cyrenaica was again separated from Egypt by the decision of the Romans, who, as related above, resolved the dispute between Ptolemy VI Philometor and his brother Ptolemy VII Euergetes II in 163 BC by granting the latter an independent realm in Cyrenaica. The Cyrenaeans themselves, however, were reluctant to accept this decision, fearing the cruelty and tyrannical character of Euergetes. In 162 BC, when Euergetes went on a mission to Rome, leaving Cyrene under the control of an Egyptian general, Ptolemy Sympetesis, the Cyrenaeans rose in revolt, and were joined not only by the local Libyans but also by Sympetesis himself. However, Euergetes returned and was able, with great difficulty, to restore his control over Cyrene. He continued to rule there until the death of his brother Philometor in 145 BC, when he returned to Egypt to take the throne, thus reuniting Cyrenaica once again to Egypt.

The final separation of Cyrenaica from Egypt came, as has been seen, with the death of Euergetes II in 116 BC. By his will, Euergetes bequeathed Cyrenaica to his illegitimate son Ptolemy Apion. Apion ruled Cyrenaica for twenty years, and died without heirs in 96 BC, leaving a will by which he bequeathed his kingdom to the people of Rome. The Romans, however, had no desire to undertake responsibility for the administration of Cyrenaica, and contented themselves with sending agents to take over ownership of the royal estates there, restoring self-government to the Greek cities. Left to themselves, the Greeks of Cyrenaica displayed their usual capacity for misgovernment and civil strife. A leader called Nikokrates seized power in Cyrene, which he ruled tyrannically until assassinated by his own brother, Leandros, whose rule was no improvement. The political opponents of Leandros brought about his downfall by stirring up a war of the local Libyans against him, and then treacherously delivering him up to the chief of the Libyans. In 87 BC a Roman general, arriving to seek military assistance for a war in Greece, restored order, and, at the request of the Cyrenaeans, enacted constitutional reforms. Whether this put an end to the disturbances is not recorded. The Romans finally decided to annex Cyrenaica, probably to prevent its use as a base by pirates, in 74 BC.

THE FALL OF CARTHAGE, 264 TO 146 BC

In North-West Africa, the Phoenician city of Carthage had, by the early third century BC, survived more than a century of warfare with the Greeks of Sicily without lasting loss to its power or to the territorial extent of its empire. Carthage had been most seriously threatened during its war with Agathokles of Syracuse, who in 310–307 BC had invaded the North African territory of Carthage, raising a revolt of its Libyan subjects and securing assistance from the independent Numidians to the west. But after the defeat and withdrawal of Agathokles, Carthaginian authority was re-established in the hinterland. In 276–275 BC the Carthaginians faced a final war with the Sicilian Greeks, who called in Pyrrhos of Epeiros, then campaigning against the Romans in southern Italy, to their aid. Pyrrhos won some initial successes, and contemplated emulating Agathokles by invading North-West Africa, but he failed to win a decisive victory and soon withdrew again to Italy, whence he was finally expelled by the Romans in 274 BC. The Carthaginians not only survived the war against Pyrrhos, but benefited from it, learning from him innovations in the military art which considerably strengthened the effectiveness of their armies. Pyrrhos had brought with him from Greece some Indian war-elephants, which he used to great effect in Italy and Sicily. The Carthaginians were impressed, and set about creating their own force of war-elephants, using, like the Ptolemies in Egypt, the locally available African elephants. The Carthaginians probably also owed to the example of Pyrrhos their more intelligent and systematic use of cavalry, employing local Numidian auxiliaries, in the later third century BC.

However, the defeat of Pyrrhos had other consequences which threatened the security of the Carthaginian empire. It allowed the Romans to consolidate their control over southern Italy, a process completed with their capture of the city of Tarentum (Taranto) in 272 BC. The Carthaginians in Sicily now found that they had to take account not only of the independent Greek cities of the island, but also of the expansionist power of Rome across the straits of Messina. In earlier times, relations between Carthage and Rome seem always to have been friendly, and the two states had co-operated against their common enemy Pyrrhos. But now the Romans sought to extend their influence into Sicily, threatening Carthaginian interests. In 264 BC rivalry between the two states for control of the strategic city of Messana (Messina) led to open war.

The first war between Carthage and Rome lasted for twenty-three years (264–241 BC), and ended in the total defeat of Carthage. The war was principally a contest for the control of Sicily, which the Romans progressively wrested from the Carthaginians. Messana, the object of the original dispute, was quickly secured by the Romans. The two principal Greek cities in Sicily, Syracuse and Akragas, began the war as allies of Carthage, but Syracuse defected to the Roman side in 263 BC and Akragas was taken by the Romans in 262. The Carthaginian forces were gradually restricted to the western portion of Sicily, the part of the island originally colonized by the Phoenicians.

The Romans also resolved to challenge Carthaginian domination of the sea, and in 261 BC began the construction of a large war fleet. Somewhat surprisingly, in view of the much greater experience and expertise of the Carthaginians in naval warfare, the Roman fleet was quickly successful. A naval victory in 256 BC enabled the Romans to repeat the venture of Agathokles, by sending a large army, commanded by a general called Regulus, to invade North-West Africa. Regulus landed on the Cape Bon peninsula, where he plundered the estates of the rich citizens of Carthage, and proceeded to defeat a Carthaginian army in battle and seize control of the town of Tunis, from which he could blockade Carthage by land. The Carthaginians were sufficiently alarmed to offer peace, but Regulus threw away this opportunity by insisting upon excessively harsh terms. Negotiation having failed, the Carthaginians turned again to war, and in 255 BC, giving battle in open terrain where their war-elephants and cavalry could be used to the greatest effect, they inflicted a decisive defeat on the Romans, taking Regulus captive. The threat to the Carthaginian capital was thus for the moment ended.

Despite the failure of this invasion of North Africa, the Romans continued to drive back the Carthaginians in Sicily, and in 250 BC succeeded in capturing the Phoenician city of Panormus (Palermo). But the city of Lilybaeum, at the extreme western end of Sicily, was held by the Carthaginians despite a prolonged Roman siege. The defence of Lilybaeum was conducted, after 247 BC, by Hamilcar Barca, a brilliant general whose family was to dominate Carthaginian politics for the rest of the third century BC.

In addition to these operations in Sicily, Carthage was involved at this time in difficulties in her African territories. It is recorded that in 256/5 BC, during the campaign of Regulus in Africa, Carthaginian territory was also under attack by the Numidians, the Libyan peoples to the west who were normally allied to Carthage. Later, probably around 247 BC, a large Carthaginian army, commanded by a general called Hanno, operated in the interior, and captured the town of Theveste (Tebessa), about 260 km south-west of Carthage. It is surprising that the Carthaginians should have been prepared to commit substantial forces so far inland at the same time as they were engaged with the Romans in Sicily. Unfortunately, the circumstances leading to Hanno's operations are not recorded. But Hanno is known to have been a personal enemy of Hamilcar Barca, the Carthaginian commander in Sicily, and it is possible that internal political differences were involved. Hanno may have advocated that Carthage should concentrate upon the extension of its territorial empire in Africa, while Hamilcar Barca perhaps stood for maritime expansion in the Mediterranean. The suggestion that Hanno's policy was that of the 'great landowners' of Carthage, while Hamilcar Barca represented the commercial interests, is very much more speculative.[1]

By the late 240s BC, Carthage appeared to have fought the Romans to a stalemate in Sicily, but the fundamental strength of the empire was being progressively eroded. Since Carthage depended primarily upon mercenary troops, who had to be paid regular and substantial wages, the protracted war was a ruinous drain upon its financial resources. The position cannot have been helped by the simultaneous commitment of large forces for Hanno's campaigns in Africa. To meet the costs of the war, the Carthaginians doubled the level of taxation imposed upon their subjects in Africa; but even so the revenues were inadequate. In the late 240s the Carthaginians appear, as a measure of economy, to have laid up their fleet. In 242 BC the Romans exploited the opportunity thus presented to them by putting to sea a large naval force. A hastily mustered Carthaginian fleet was defeated off Sicily, and the Carthagin-

[1] For this view, see T. Frank, 'Rome and Carthage: the first Punic War', in S. A. Cook, F. E. Adcock and M. P. Charlesworth, eds., *Cambridge ancient history*, VII (Cambridge, 1928), 665–6, 689.

ians, faced with the prospect of a second Roman invasion of North-West Africa, felt obliged to sue for peace. Under the terms eventually agreed in 241 BC, Carthage evacuated its forces from Sicily and undertook to pay a large indemnity to Rome in annual instalments over twenty years.

The loss of Sicily was followed by a crisis in Africa. Following the peace, the Carthaginian authorities attempted to disband the large army of mercenaries which had been employed in Sicily. This consisted mainly of Libyans from the territory subject to Carthage, but also included many Greeks, Italians and other nationalities. Substantial arrears of wages were due to the soldiers, and it was not clear that money was available to meet their demands. Mustered at Sicca in the interior to await payment, the soldiers mutinied, led by a Libyan called Mathos and an Italian called Spendios. This was followed by a general revolt of the Libyan subjects of Carthage, resentful at the heavy taxation which had been imposed upon them during the war. The Numidians to the west of Carthaginian territory also joined the revolt, and the rebel forces laid siege to the Phoenician cities of Hippo (Bizerta) and Utica. Hanno and Hamilcar Barca, laying aside their personal and political differences, laboured to bring the revolt under control, and were greatly assisted by the defection to the Carthaginian side of a Numidian chief called Naravas, who brought with him essential cavalry forces. The Carthaginians suffered a serious setback in 239 BC, when the cities of Hippo and Utica joined the revolt and massacred their Carthaginian garrisons. But by 237 BC, after a war of appalling atrocities on both sides, the revolt had been completely crushed.

Though successful in restoring their control in North-West Africa, the Carthaginians suffered a further territorial loss outside Africa. Under the terms of the peace of 241 BC, Carthage had retained possession of the island of Sardinia. But during the revolt in Africa which followed the peace, the mercenary forces forming the Carthaginian garrison in Sardinia also mutinied, and the Carthaginians lost control of the island. When it became clear that the revolt in Africa had failed, the rebels in Sardinia appealed for protection to Rome, and the Romans, after some hesitations, sent forces to annex the island (238 BC). Carthaginian protests were met with a threat of war, and the Carthaginians were obliged to acquiesce.

The Roman annexation of Sardinia ended any prospect of a lasting reconciliation between Carthage and Rome. When the revolt in Africa had been suppressed, Hanno, who had shared the command with

Hamilcar Barca, was ousted from office, leaving Hamilcar in power (237 BC). This is represented in the sources as a victory for the popular and democratic forces in Carthage against the wealthier citizens, though it does not appear that it was accompanied by any specific reforms to the constitution. The victory of Hamilcar Barca over Hanno also reflected the determination of Carthaginians to build up their power in preparation for a second war with Rome, for Hanno was an advocate of friendship with Rome and an opponent of Carthaginian expansion outside Africa.

After the loss of Sicily and Sardinia, the only remnant of the Carthaginian empire outside Africa was in Spain, where the Carthaginians still controlled, or at least claimed, Gades and the other Phoenician colonies along the southern coast. Here the Carthaginians determined to win a new overseas empire. Hamilcar Barca was sent to Spain in 237 BC, and campaigned there until his death in battle in 229 BC. The command in Spain then passed to Hamilcar Barca's son-in-law Hasdrubal, and, after Hasdrubal's death in 221 BC, to Hamilcar's son Hannibal. These three extended Carthaginian control for the first time beyond the coastal area, annexing a large territory in the Spanish hinterland. They thereby won for Carthage considerable resources of manpower from subject and allied Spanish tribes for service in the Carthaginian army, and control of the extremely valuable Spanish silver-mines. A new capital for this Spanish empire, New Carthage (Cartagena), was built by Hasdrubal.

There was also some consolidation and extension of the Carthaginian empire inside North-West Africa, but this process is poorly documented and impossible to trace in detail. Before departing to Spain, Hamilcar Barca is said to have campaigned against the Numidians, probably in response to the assistance which they had afforded to the recent Libyan revolt, and to have extended the boundaries of Carthaginian territory. Subsequently, at some point before the death of Hamilcar in 229 BC, there was further trouble with the Numidians, and Hamilcar's son-in-law Hasdrubal fought successfully against them, further expanding the area tributary to Carthage.

The Romans viewed the recovery of Carthaginian power with apprehension, and in 226 BC sought and obtained from Hasdrubal an undertaking that Carthaginian forces would not operate beyond the river Ebro in northern Spain. Subsequently, however, the Romans violated the spirit, if not the letter, of this agreement by themselves forming an alliance with the town of Saguntum to the south of the

Ebro. When he felt that he was ready, Hannibal provoked a Roman declaration of war by attacking and destroying Saguntum (218 BC). Carthaginian strategy in this second war with Rome sought victory by a direct attack on Rome's position inside Italy. There was no attempt to revive Carthaginian naval power and recover the command of the sea lost to Rome in the previous war. Leaving Spain under the command of his brother Hasdrubal, Hannibal marched overland through southern France and across the Alps to invade Italy from the north. In Italy, he won a series of victories, culminating in the crushing defeat of the Romans at Cannae (216 BC). But Rome refused to consider surrender, and Hannibal's expectations of defections among Rome's allies and subjects in Italy were only partially fulfilled. Hannibal's failure became clear beyond doubt when, in 207 BC, his brother Hasdrubal brought reinforcements from Spain but was defeated and killed at the river Metaurus in northern Italy before he could join forces with Hannibal. Though undefeated in any major battle, Hannibal found that his effective power steadily declined, and he was compelled to withdraw into the southernmost portion of Italy.

Meanwhile, the Romans had, as early as 218 BC, sent forces to challenge the Carthaginian position in Spain. For several years they achieved no decisive success, though their presence prevented the departure of forces from Spain to reinforce Hannibal in Italy. But after 210 BC, under the brilliant generalship of Scipio, the Romans rapidly swept away Carthaginian power in Spain, taking New Carthage in 209 BC and Gades in 206 BC. A Carthaginian attempt to recover control of Sicily in 214–211 BC, though it had the support of many of the Greeks in the island, also ended in failure.

During the second war with Rome, as in the first, the Carthaginian war effort was hampered by difficulties inside Africa. In 215 BC war broke out with Syphax, the powerful ruler of the Masaesylii, a western Numidian tribe. The Roman commanders in Spain sent military advisers to assist Syphax, and the Carthaginians had to recall Hasdrubal from Spain to undertake the command against him. Although the Carthaginians were assisted by the Massylies, a rival Numidian tribe, they were unable to inflict a decisive defeat upon Syphax, and a peace negotiated in 212 BC left him in possession of his territory. Subsequently Syphax intrigued with both Rome and Carthage, but was eventually won over to a firm alliance with Carthage.

In 204 BC Scipio, the conqueror of the Carthaginians in Spain, landed with a large Roman army in North Africa. Syphax brought forces to the assistance of Carthage, but Scipio secured the alliance of Masinissa, the rival ruler of the Massylies, and was able to defeat the Carthaginians in two major battles (203 BC). Roman forces then invaded Numidia, in co-operation with Masinissa, and defeated and captured Syphax, thus depriving Carthage of the support of any substantial body of Numidian cavalry. The Carthaginians recalled Hannibal from Italy to take command against Scipio, and a final battle was fought at Naraggara, near Zama, in 202 BC. Owing principally to his weakness in cavalry, Hannibal was decisively defeated. In a similar situation a century before, during the invasion of Agathokles, Carthage had been able to survive defeat in Africa, since the city could be supplied with provisions by sea. But now the sea also was controlled by the enemy, and the Carthaginians had no alternative to surrender.

By the terms of peace imposed in 201 BC, Carthage not only lost her second empire, but was reduced, in effect, to the status of a Roman dependency. The Carthaginians gave up all claim to Spain, and also lost extensive territories inside Africa. They were compelled to evacuate all the areas which they held in Africa outside the 'Phoenician Trenches', the system of earthworks constructed to delimit Carthaginian territory at an earlier period (cf. chapter 2, p. 129), and undertook to restore to Rome's ally Masinissa all the lands which had at any time belonged to him or his ancestors, even if these lay within the 'Trenches'. Carthage was disarmed, being compelled to surrender its entire force of war-elephants and forbidden to train elephants in the future, and having the size of its war fleet restricted to ten ships. Moreover, Carthage was forbidden to wage war outside Africa, or inside Africa except with the permission of Rome, and was obliged to supply whatever assistance Rome demanded in its own wars. A large indemnity was imposed, to be paid in annual instalments over fifty years.

The catastrophic defeat of Carthage in its second war with Rome was followed by a political and financial crisis. The political opponents of Hannibal seized the opportunity to drive him from power at Carthage. In 200 BC, following pressure from Rome, Hannibal was dismissed from command of the Carthaginian army in Africa, and brought to trial for peculation. However, the court acquitted him. At the same time, the Carthaginian authorities had great difficulty in paying the annual indemnity due to Rome under the peace of 201 BC, and a proposal was put forward to impose direct taxation on Carthaginian citizens in addition to the customary indirect taxes. This aroused great resentment, since it was known that much of the revenue from the existing taxes was lost to the state through the corruption of its financial officials. In 196 BC Hannibal was elected one of the two *sufets*, the annually elected chief civil magistrates of Carthage, and introduced reforms to prevent embezzlement of state revenues. Finding himself obstructed by the political establishment, Hannibal proposed and carried constitutional reforms also, destroying the power of the Council of 104 Judges (cf. chapter 2, p. 122), by providing that its members should no longer hold office for life but should be elected annually by the people. Though his reforms appear to have been effective, Hannibal himself was destroyed politically by his success. In 195 BC his opponents laid false information against him at Rome, asserting that he was negotiating with Antiochos III of Syria with a view to making war upon Rome. A Roman mission was sent to Carthage to investigate the accusation, and Hannibal, to avoid being handed over to the Romans, fled from Carthage. He made his way to the east, where he served for some time as a general of Antiochos III in his war against Rome, and finally committed suicide to avoid capture by the Romans in 183 BC.

The financial reforms of Hannibal quickly restored the Carthaginian state to solvency. In 191 BC, indeed, Carthage was even able to offer to pay all the outstanding instalments of the indemnity due to Rome (the last of which was not due until 151 BC). The Romans, not wishing to surrender their hold over Carthage, declined the offer. Despite the loss of all its overseas dependencies, Carthage still controlled an extensive territory of good agricultural land in the interior of North Africa, which yielded a substantial surplus of corn for export. The enforced reduction of military expenditure under the terms of the treaty with Rome must also have facilitated the process of economic recovery.

The Carthaginians appear to have pursued a sincere policy of accommodation with Rome after 201 BC. On several occasions they supplied large quantities of corn for the provision of Roman armies operating in Greece and Asia. But Roman suspicions and fears of Carthage were not assuaged. The Romans looked to their ally Masinissa, now ruler of a united Numidia, to hold Carthage in check, and encouraged him to encroach upon Carthaginian territory in the interior of Africa. The vague terms of the treaty of 201 BC, granting to Masinissa all the lands ever held by him or his ancestors, made it easy for Masinissa to put forward plausible claims to further cessions of Carthaginian territory, while the Carthaginians were restrained from offering military resistance to Masinissa by the provision of the same treaty which prohibited them from waging war in Africa without Roman permission. Masinissa appears to have begun encroaching upon Carthaginian territory already by 195 BC, and there followed a series of frontier disputes between him and Carthage, regularly referred to the arbitration of Rome, which as regularly upheld Masinissa's claims or, what amounted in practice to the same thing, evaded passing judgement on the issue. The precise stages by which Masinissa extended his kingdom at Carthaginian expense cannot be reconstructed, but he is recorded to have seized control of the Emporia, i.e. the coastal area of Tripolitania in the east, in 162 BC, and of the two Carthaginian provinces of the 'Great Plains' (around Vaga) and 'Tusca' (apparently the Mactar area) in the west in about 153 BC.

During the 150s the Carthaginians, exasperated by Masinissa's aggressions and the failure of Rome to check them, began to rearm, building up their military forces for a war with Masinissa. The final outbreak of open war between Carthage and Masinissa in 150 BC, which could be represented as a breach of the provision of the treaty of 201 BC forbidding Carthage to go to war without Roman permission, provided the Romans with both a specious justification for their fears of a Carthaginian revival and a pretext for intervention. After the refusal of a demand that Carthage should be evacuated and its people settled elsewhere, Rome declared war in 149 BC. Several Phoenician cities, including Utica, Hadrumetum and Leptis Minor, went over to the Romans, who also received assistance from Masinissa's successors in Numidia. But the Carthaginians appear to have retained the loyalty of most of their Libyan subjects and were also aided by some of the Mauri who lived to the west of Numidia. Carthage endured a long siege, but eventually, after the command of the Roman army had been conferred upon Scipio Aemilianus, the adoptive son of Hannibal's conqueror, the city was taken by storm in 146 BC. It was then razed to the ground, and those of its inhabitants who had not been killed were enslaved. The greater part of the remaining Carthaginian territory was annexed to Rome as the province of 'Africa'.

It should be stressed that the destruction of Carthage was by no means the end of Phoenician influence in North Africa. The other Phoenician cities which had deserted to Rome in good time survived, Utica becoming the capital of the Roman province of Africa. In these cities, and among the Libyans formerly subject to Carthage in the interior, the Phoenician language, institutions and religion persisted for several centuries after the fall of Carthage. Even the Numidians, who had grown strong at the expense of Carthage, absorbed much of its culture, and in the century following its destruction diffused Phoenician culture over large areas of the interior which Carthage had never effectively ruled.

THE BERBER KINGDOMS OF NORTH AFRICA, *c.* 250 BC TO AD 40

With the decline and ultimate destruction of Carthage, and the initial unwillingness of Rome to extend its control over large areas of North Africa, effective power in North-West Africa passed for a century and a half to the states which had arisen among the indigenous peoples

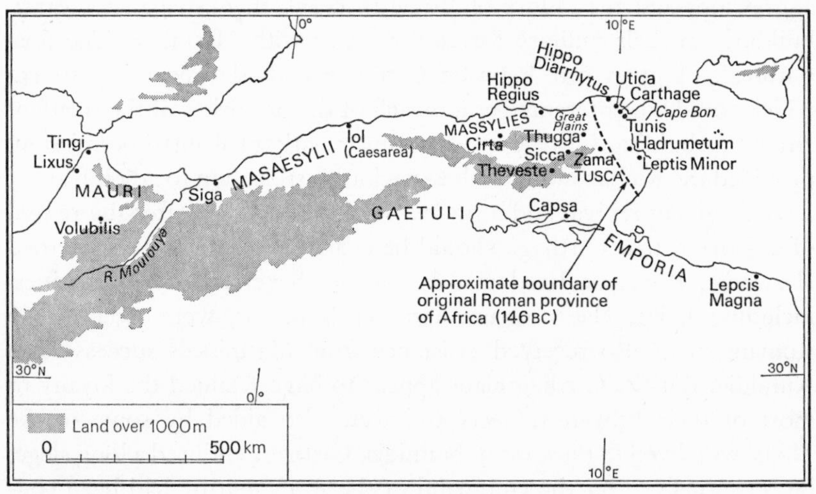

24 North-West Africa, third to first centuries BC.

inhabiting the littoral plain to the west of Carthaginian territory, the 'Numidians' (Latin *Numidae*; Greek *Nomades*), whose country extended west as far as the river Moulouya, and the Mauri (Greek *Maurousioi*), who occupied the land beyond this river. Of the culture of these peoples, some account has been given in the preceding chapter (see chapter 2, pp. 140–7). A more detailed consideration is offered here of what is known of the origins and development of their state-systems.

The states of Numidia and Mauretania were ruled by people to whom our sources give the title 'king' (Greek *basileus*; Latin *rex*), or occasionally 'chief' (Greek *dynastes*). The indigenous title, as we know from a

Numidian inscription of the second century BC, was *gld*, presumably a cognate of the modern Berber title *aguellid*. The native rulers also applied to themselves the Phoenician royal title, *melek*. Of the character of their 'kingship' we know little. Eligibility for the kingship seems regularly to have been restricted to a royal family or lineage, succession passing – at least originally – not from father to son, but from brother to brother, or perhaps to the eldest surviving member of the royal family (see chapter 2, p. 146). It also appears that kings were commonly deified after their death. At least, it is clear that such posthumous deification was practised by the Mauri during the Christian era, and there is rather more ambivalent evidence for it in Numidia in the second and first centuries BC. This practice may have owed something to the example of Hellenistic (and, later, Roman) divine kingship, but it might equally have arisen out of the indigenous cult of the dead, which was noticed by the earliest Greek writers on North Africa (see chapter 2, p. 146).

We first hear of 'kings' among the Numidians and Mauri in 406 BC, when they appear among the allies providing forces for the Carthaginian army.[1] But there is no indication in our source of how many of these kings there were, or how large were their kingdoms. The occasional references to kings during the next century and a half are similarly vague. By the time of the second war between Carthage and Rome (218–201 BC), there is evidence for kingdoms of considerable extent and power among both the Numidians and the Mauri. But this date probably marks a stage in the development of our knowledge of North African conditions rather than in the political development of the North African peoples. It remains unclear precisely when kingdoms of any size emerged in North-West Africa.

We possess an account of the origins of the kingdoms of Numidia and Mauretania given by a Numidian king of the first century BC, Hiempsal II, in a historical work written in Punic (Phoenician), though unfortunately it survives only in an abbreviated quotation by a Roman writer.[2] Hiempsal traced the emergence of organized government and kingship in North-West Africa to the death of the hero Hercules in Spain and the dispersal of his army, which consisted of contingents of Asian peoples. The Medes in his army crossed the Straits of Gibraltar and settled on the North African coast, where they intermarried with the local people to become the Mauri. The Mauri maintained contact

[1] Diodorus Siculus, *Library of history*, XIII.80.3.
[2] Sallust, *Bellum Jugurthae*, 16–18.

with Spain across the Straits, and the stimulus of this trade quickly led them to become urbanized. The Persian contingent in the army pushed further into the interior of Africa and settled in the desert, among the Gaetuli, with whom they intermarried to become the Pharusii. These desert-dwellers, unlike the Mauri, remained nomadic, but eventually a section of them broke away and moved north, where they overran the littoral between Mauretania and the Carthaginian sphere and became the Numidians. Clearly, it would be wrong to take all this very seriously. It is too obviously the result of the sort of speculative comparison of names dear to ancient scholars, seeking to derive *Mauri* – improbable as this may seem – from *Medi*, and *Pharusii* from *Persae*. Added to this is a desire to establish a connection with Carthaginian legend, since 'Hercules' here probably represents not the Graeco-Roman hero, but the Phoenician god Melqart with whom he was regularly identified. The connection with Hercules also appears in another story, according to which the first king of the Mauri was a certain Syphax, a son of Hercules by Tinga, the eponym of the town of Tingi (Tangier).[1] But there may also be some genuine traditions incorporated in Hiempsal's fantasy. The early connection of Mauretania with Spain at least has some archaeological support (cf. chapter 2, p. 145). And it is a noteworthy, and possibly authentic, detail that Hiempsal attributes the foundation of the kingdoms of Numidia, but not of Mauretania, to immigrants from the Sahara, from among the Pharusii.

It is possible that the origins of state-formation among the Numidians and Mauri should be sought, at least in part, in the stimulus of contact with the Phoenician settlers in North-West Africa. There were Phoenician settlements all along their coasts, which presumably traded with the interior, seeking ivory, hides and precious stones. Individual Numidians and Mauri served in the armies of Carthage as mercenaries, and the Numidians, and less consistently the Mauri, also provided troops for Carthage under treaties of alliance. Possibly the creation of monarchical states was a response to the problems raised by the organization of trade and recruitment for service in the Carthaginian army. But this suggestion is purely speculative, and unsupported by any direct evidence. Phoenician influence of a different kind is suggested by a Numidian inscription of the second century BC, which gives to Zilalsan, the ancestor of the royal dynasty of the eastern Numidian tribe of the Massylies, who flourished in about 250 BC, the title of *sufet*, which is the usual title of the chief civil magistracy in a Phoenician city.

[1] Plutarch, *Sertorius*, 9.4.

The precise significance of this is unclear, but it seems likely that Zilalsan was the principal authority in some Numidian municipality organized on Phoenician lines. Possibly the elevation of his descendants to kingly status was deliberately encouraged by the Carthaginians in order to facilitate the administration of a dependent area.

An alternative, or additional, factor which may have contributed to the creation of extensive kingdoms in North-West Africa owed nothing to Phoenician influence. This was the abandonment of the use of war-chariots in favour of cavalry, which appears to have taken place early in the third century BC (see chapter 2, p. 144). The adoption of cavalry would have greatly increased the mobility of military forces, and facilitated the extension of a chief's authority over wider areas.

The first Numidian chief about whom there is any detailed information is the Naravas who, during the Libyan revolt against Carthage after its first war with Rome (241–237 BC), defected to the Carthaginian side and employed his cavalry to great effect in assisting in the suppression of the revolt (cf. p. 170). For this he was rewarded by marriage to a daughter of the Carthaginian general Hamilcar Barca. But we do not know where Naravas ruled, or whether he was the ancestor of any of the Numidian dynasties which were later important. The size of the contingent which he brought over to the Carthaginians, only 2,000 in number, does not suggest that his territory was very extensive.

A fairly detailed picture can be reconstructed of political conditions in Numidia during the second war of Carthage with Rome (218–201 BC). The country was then divided among several chieftaincies. The most powerful of these was that of the Masaesylii in the west, with its capital at the coastal city of Siga, which had earlier, during the fourth century BC, been under Carthaginian control. Syphax, the King of the Masaesylii, may have had some formal position of hegemony among the Numidian chiefs. This at least seems to be implied in the words of the Greek historian Appian:

> There were many separate chieftains of the Numidians in Africa, but Syphax occupied the highest place of all, and was held in great honour by all the others.[1]

Syphax was certainly the most powerful chief, and was also the only one of this period to issue coins of his own. A few of these, struck in bronze and bearing the bearded portrait of Syphax and the legend 'Syphax the

[1] Appian, *Punic wars*, 10.

King' in Punic, are extant. Of the lesser chieftains, the most considerable was Gaia, the son of the *sufet* Zilalsan mentioned above, who was King of the Massylies in the east, bordering Carthaginian territory, and had his capital probably at Cirta. Syphax and Gaia were enemies, disputing possession of border territories. Gaia had also clashed at some time with the Carthaginians, and had annexed territory claimed by them. But at this period he had close links with Carthage. His son Masinissa (born *c.* 238 BC) had been educated at Carthage, and his brother Oezalces had among his wives a niece of the Carthaginian general Hannibal.[1]

Mention has already been made (p. 172) of the war which Syphax fought against the Carthaginians and the Massylies in 215–212 BC. The commander of the Massylian forces in this war was Gaia's son Masinissa, who was rewarded by betrothal to the daughter of another leading Carthaginian general, Hasdrubal, son of Gisgo. After 212 BC Masinissa commanded a force of Massylian cavalry which fought with the Carthaginians against the Romans in Spain. Syphax meanwhile continued to intrigue with the Romans, but was eventually (*c.* 205 BC) won over to the Carthaginian side through the diplomacy of Hasdrubal, son of Gisgo. Hasdrubal's daughter, earlier promised to Masinissa, was then married instead to Syphax.

While Masinissa was in Spain, the kingdom of the Massylies became involved in a serious internal crisis. Gaia, the King of the Massylies, died *c.* 208 BC, and was succeeded by his brother Oezalces. Oezalces dying soon after his accession, the kingship passed to the elder of his two sons, Capussa. Now, however, a rebellion was led by a member of a rival segment of the royal lineage, called Mazaetullus, who defeated and killed Capussa and set himself up as regent for Lacumazes, Capussa's younger brother. Fearing that Masinissa would challenge his position, Mazaetullus made an alliance with Syphax and sought to secure the favour of Carthage by marrying the Carthaginian widow (Hannibal's niece) left by Oezalces. Masinissa, hearing of these events, made a secret alliance with Scipio, the Roman commander in Spain, and crossed back to Africa (206 BC). Having applied unsuccessfully for aid to the King of the Mauri, he made his way back to the country of the Massylies, where he quickly defeated Lacumazes and Mazaetullus and persuaded them to acknowledge his own right to the kingship. How-

[1] A daughter of a sister of Hannibal (Livy, *Ab urbe condita*, XXIX.29.12): possibly a daughter of the earlier Numidian chief Naravas by his Carthaginian wife, who was a daughter of Hamilcar Barca and thus a sister of Hannibal (cf. p. 179).

ever, Syphax, with the encouragement of Carthage, proceeded to invade the land of the Massylies and, after fierce and protracted fighting, expelled Masinissa and annexed his kingdom, apparently transferring his own capital from Siga to Cirta. Masinissa fled eastwards, and maintained himself for a while in the desert hinterland of Tripolitania.

When the Roman army under Scipio landed in Africa in 204 BC, Masinissa joined him with the small cavalry force which he still retained. Syphax marched to the support of Carthage, whose forces were commanded by his father-in-law Hasdrubal, bringing no less than 50,000 infantry and 10,000 cavalry. After Scipio's victories in 203 BC, Syphax retreated westwards into Numidia, pursued by Masinissa and a portion of the Roman army, by whom he was defeated and captured. He was taken by the Romans to Italy, where he died in captivity not long after. Masinissa was able to occupy Cirta and recover possession of the kingdom of the Massylies, though princes of the line of Syphax continued to control the old kingdom of the Masaesylii to the west. In the decisive battle of Zama in 202 BC. Masinissa brought to the aid of Scipio a force of 6,000 cavalry and 4,000 infantry, which played a crucial role in securing Scipio's victory. Hannibal, the Carthaginian commander, had to be content with the support of lesser Numidian chiefs. A son of Syphax called Vermina brought substantial forces to assist Hannibal, but these arrived too late for the battle, and were caught and destroyed by the Romans when they did arrive.

By his good fortune or good judgement in choosing the winning side in 202 BC, Masinissa had taken the decisive step which was to carry him to possession of a kingdom embracing the whole of Numidia. His achievement was not, however, due solely to the favour and support of Rome. He was himself a redoubtable figure, a man of great vigour who remained active, even commanding his troops in person, up to his death at the age of ninety, and who fathered no less than forty-four sons, the last of them at the age of eighty-six. The peace settlement of 201 BC brought him immediate territorial gains at the expense of Carthage (cf. p. 173). He also received some of the war-elephants confiscated from Carthage, and developed the use of elephants as a normal arm of Numidian warfare. More important, he had won the lasting gratitude of Rome, which he reinforced throughout his long reign by supplying provisions and forces, especially cavalry and elephants, for Rome's wars in Spain, Greece and Asia. By the favour of Rome he was able, as has been seen earlier, to encroach steadily upon the territory remaining to Carthage after 201 BC, until his aggressions precipitated the third and final war between Carthage and Rome in 149 BC.

While Masinissa's relations with Carthage and Rome are reasonably well documented, little is known of his dealings with the rival chiefs of Numidia. Yet by the end of his reign Masinissa had apparently suppressed or subjected the independent chiefs and united all the Numidians under his rule. The most considerable of his opponents must have been the successors of Syphax in the kingdom of the Masaesylii, still maintaining themselves in western Numidia. Vermina, the son of Syphax, survived the defeat of 203 BC, and in 200 BC we find him negotiating with Rome and apparently securing a formal treaty of peace and recognition of his position. He was at any rate well enough established to issue coins, in silver, bearing his own portrait and name in Punic. How and when Masinissa was able to overcome the Masaesylii is not recorded. But by the 150s BC the last of the Masaesylian princes, a grandson of Syphax called Arcobarzanes, was a fugitive in Carthaginian territory. The unification of Numidia was effected, but the state created by Masinissa was a fragile structure. There were frequent revolts by minor Numidian chieftains, and apparently also disaffection among the agricultural population of the areas in the east annexed from Carthage.

Besides imposing political unity on the Numidians, Masinissa undertook a transformation of their economy and way of life. He encouraged the development of agriculture, creating vast estates for all of his many sons. Numidia became a considerable exporter of corn to the Mediterranean world, and some progress was made in developing arboriculture as well as cereal-culture. According to a contemporary witness, the Greek historian Polybius,

> Before his time, the whole of Numidia was barren, and considered naturally incapable of bearing cultivated crops. He first and he alone demonstrated that it could bear all kinds of cultivated crops.[1]

This tribute is echoed by a later writer, who declares that Masinissa 'turned the Numidians into town-dwellers and farmers'.[2] This is certainly a gross exaggeration. There had been agriculture in Numidia, and some large towns, such as Cirta, even before Masinissa, and Masinissa's own activities appear to have affected principally the eastern areas of Numidia (already developed to some extent under Carthaginian influence) and to have had little impact upon western Numidia. However, it is unquestionable that Masinissa's reign brought a great advance in this respect. Masinissa also effected the monetization of the Numidian

[1] Polybius, *Histories*, XXXVI.3.7. [2] Strabo, *Geography*, XVII.3.15.

economy. Coins had been struck earlier by Syphax and Vermina, but apparently not in great numbers, and perhaps rather for prestige and as a token of their kingly status than for economic purposes. The coins of Masinissa, however, struck in bronze and lead and bearing his bearded portrait and initials in the Punic script, are very numerous, and evidently served as a circulating currency among the Numidians, or at least among the eastern Numidians.

Masinissa died, at the age of ninety, in 148 BC, not long after the outbreak of the third war between Carthage and Rome. He was survived by three legitimate sons, Micipsa, Gulussa and Mastanabal, as well as seven illegitimate sons. Influenced, no doubt, by the disastrous crisis which followed the death of his father in *c.* 208 BC, Masinissa was anxious to avoid a disputed succession at his own death, and sought to solve the problem by designating his eldest son, Micipsa, as substantive king, and requesting a Roman friend, Scipio Aemilianus, to arrange the precise division of his inheritance between him and his brothers. It is to be noted that on this occasion and later, in contrast to earlier Numidian practice, there was no question of the kingship passing to anyone but the king's sons. Presumably we see here the supersession of the indigenous principle of succession by one derived from Phoenician (or perhaps even Roman) practice. Scipio confirmed Micipsa in possession of the palace at Cirta and of the royal treasury, while appointing Gulussa as commander of the Numidian army and Mastanabal as chief judicial authority in the kingdom. The illegitimate brothers were installed as subordinate chiefs of territorial divisions of the kingdom. A more unstable arrangement is difficult to imagine. But we hear of no troubles, and the potential weakness was quickly removed when the deaths of Gulussa and Mastanabal left Micipsa as the sole ruler.

Gulussa took forces to assist the Romans against Carthage in 148–146 BC, and the territorial settlement which followed the fall of Carthage in 146 BC brought Numidia further gains. An earthwork, the *fossa regia* ('Royal Ditch'), was constructed to demarcate the boundary between the Numidian kingdom and the Roman province of Africa. The Numidian kingdom was by now an immense state. Micipsa ruled over the whole of the coastal plain from the river Moulouya in the west to the Roman province in the east, including the Phoenician cities along the coast such as Hippo Regius (Bone).[1] To the east of the Roman province, Lepcis Magna and the other cities of the Tripolitanian coast were

[1] 'Royal Hippo' or 'Hippo in the Kingdom', so called to distinguish it from the more important Hippo (Bizerta) which was included in the Roman province of Africa. The latter was sometimes called Hippo Diarrhytus.

subject, having been conquered by Masinissa in 162 BC. In the interior, Micipsa's realm included the town of Capsa (Gafsa) and a section of the Gaetuli. From these territories, Micipsa could raise a powerful army of infantry and cavalry, and a considerable force of war-elephants. There was even a small Numidian fleet, originally created by Masinissa.

The culture of the Numidian kingdom was to a considerable degree Phoenician. The Numidians had, of course, long been subject to Phoenician influence, through trade and service in the Carthaginian army and through marriage alliances between Numidian rulers and prominent Carthaginian families. Masinissa himself, it will be recalled, had been educated at Carthage. Phoenician influence became still stronger after 201 BC, even though the political domination of Carthage had ended. This process was no doubt assisted by the absorption into the Numidian kingdom of Phoenician towns on the coast, such as Hippo Regius and Lepcis Magna, and of towns in the interior which had been under Carthaginian rule, such as Thugga and Sicca. But Phoenician influence penetrated also into purely Numidian areas. The towns of Cirta and Capsa, for example, had municipal institutions modelled on those of the Phoenicians, their chief magistrates bearing the Phoenician title *sufet*. The Numidian court also adopted elements of Phoenician religion: for example, the occurrence in the Numidian royal family of the names Adherbal (a purely Phoenician name) and Mastanabal (a hybrid form, combining Numidian and Phoenician components) advertises its devotion to the Phoenician god Baal. Punic was employed as the official language of the Numidian kingdom, as is shown by monumental inscriptions and coin legends. Numidia even became something of a centre of Punic literary culture. In 146 BC the Romans presented to Micipsa the captured library of Carthage, and in the following century, as has been seen, a Numidian king (Hiempsal II) wrote a history of his country in Punic.

The defeat of Carthage also opened up Numidia to other foreign influences besides that of the Phoenicians. Roman influence came with the service of Numidians as auxiliaries in the Roman army, and with the penetration of Italian traders into Numidia in quest of corn and other commodities. By the end of the first century BC there was a substantial colony of Italian merchants resident at Cirta. Numidia also developed commercial and diplomatic relations with the Greek world. Masinissa's son Mastanabal is recorded to have been literate in Greek, while Micipsa took an active interest in Greek philosophy, encouraging learned Greeks to come to settle at Cirta.

It would be wrong, however, to see the development of Numidian civilization during this period solely in terms of the absorption of foreign influences. The vitality of the indigenous culture is demonstrated, for example, by the creation of an alphabetic script for the writing of the Numidian language. This script is apparently ancestral to the *tifinagh* script employed by the Berbers of the Sahara in recent times: at any rate, several characters are common to both scripts. The precise date at which the script was developed is unknown, but the earliest dateable text in it is an inscription of the tenth year of Micipsa (i.e. 139 BC) at Thugga. The idea of an alphabetic script was presumably borrowed from the Phoenicians, though of the actual characters employed only some five out of twenty-three are obviously derived from the Phoenician alphabet.[1]

The destruction of Carthage in 146 BC removed the basis of the long friendship between Rome and Numidia. Their common enemy was removed, and the Numidian kingdom now had as its neighbour a Roman province. Masinissa is reported to have been aggrieved that the Romans had forestalled his own ambition to conquer Carthage, and after his death in 148 BC his sons were initially reluctant to supply forces to assist the Roman army besieging Carthage. But after these early difficulties, the implications of the new situation were slow to work themselves out. Friendship between Rome and Numidia was maintained throughout the reign of Micipsa, and the clash finally arose from a disputed succession which followed Micipsa's death in 118 BC. Micipsa left two sons, Adherbal and Hiempsal, as well as the older and abler Jugurtha, an illegitimate son of Mastanabal, whom he had adopted. Solicitous as his father about the succession, he apparently left a written will naming all three as his heirs, probably envisaging a triumvirate such as had been established in 148 BC, with Jugurtha in the position of Micipsa as substantive king. But in the event, Adherbal and Hiempsal were too jealous to work with Jugurtha, and it was decided instead to divide the Numidian kingdom into three separate chieftaincies. Jugurtha, however, murdered Hiempsal and attacked and expelled Adherbal, and seized sole power for himself. Adherbal then made his way to Rome and appealed for support. A Roman mission was sent to Numidia to arrange a new division of the kingdom, and assigned the eastern portion of the kingdom, including the capital Cirta, to Adherbal, and the western portion to Jugurtha. Jugurtha, however, remained

[1] For the Numidian, or 'Libyan', alphabet, including a comparison with the *tifinagh* and Phoenician scripts, see O. Bates, *The eastern Libyans* (London, 1914), 84–90.

unsatisfied, and proceeded to encroach upon Adherbal's lands. Finally, in 112 BC he defeated Adherbal in battle and besieged him in Cirta. Despite protests from Rome, he forced the surrender of the town, and put to death not only Adherbal, but also the Italian traders resident in the town, who had assisted in the defence. This so antagonized Roman popular opinion that war was declared against Jugurtha in 111 BC.

The Romans quickly secured control of Cirta and other principal towns of Numidia, and forced Jugurtha to take refuge among the Gaetuli (108 BC). However, there Jugurtha gathered a new army, and also secured aid from his son-in-law Bocchus, the king of the Mauri, with which he was able to renew the war. In 106 BC the Roman general Marius penetrated along the whole length of Numidia to reach the river Moulouya. Jugurtha again invoked the aid of Bocchus, though he now had to pay for it by ceding to him the western portion of his kingdom, and attacked Marius on his march back to Cirta. However, these attacks having failed, Bocchus opened negotiations with Marius, and after many hesitations agreed to arrest Jugurtha and surrender him to the Romans (105 BC). Jugurtha was taken captive to Italy and ultimately put to death. The kingdom of Masinissa and Micipsa was now dismembered. In the east, Lepcis Magna in Tripolitania had defected to the Roman side during the war, and remained independent after it. In the west, Bocchus kept the territory which Jugurtha had promised him in 106 BC. In the interior, Marius granted independence to several chieftains of the Gaetuli who had come over to Rome in good season. The rump of the Numidian kingdom was divided into two. Over the eastern half was placed Gauda, a son of Mastanabal and half-brother of Jugurtha. The capital of this kingdom was established at Zama. The west, including the traditional capital Cirta, was apparently constituted a separate kingdom.

Our knowledge of the history of these two Numidian states, now reduced to the status of Roman client-kingdoms, is very fragmentary. By 88 BC Gauda had been succeeded by his son Hiempsal II, the author of the historical work cited above. Numidia now became involved in the Roman civil wars between the partisans of Marius and Sulla. In 81 BC the province of Africa was held by the Marians, who enjoyed the alliance of a Numidian king called Hiarbas. Who Hiarbas was is obscure: perhaps he had usurped the throne of Hiempsal, or perhaps he was the ruler of the western Numidian kingdom centred on Cirta. Sulla's general Pompey defeated the Marians, and Hiarbas fled westwards, but found his escape blocked by Bogud, a Mauretanian king, and was captured and put to death by Pompey. Pompey reinstated or confirmed Hiempsal in his kingdom, and enlarged his dominions by subjecting to him the Gaetuli to whom Marius had granted independence in 105 BC.

Hiempsal survived at least until 62 BC, and was succeeded by his son Juba. The increasing importance of Roman influence upon Numidia by this period is illustrated by the fact that the coins of Juba bear legends in Latin as well as in Punic. To Juba possibly belongs the credit of introducing the use of camels into North-West Africa: one of the earliest records of the existence of camels in this area relates to animals in his possession.[1] It is clear, however, that camels did not become common in North-West Africa until much later (cf. p. 204). Early in his reign, Juba sent forces to raid the city of Lepcis Magna, which obtained restitution by an appeal to Rome. It was presumably this which provoked an abortive proposal at Rome to annex Juba's kingdom in 50 BC. After 49 BC, Numidia again became implicated in the civil wars of the Romans, now between the parties of Caesar and Pompey. The Roman province of Africa was held by the Pompeians, who won the support both of Juba and of the ruler of the western Numidian kingdom centred on Cirta, who bore the great name of Masinissa. When Caesar invaded Africa in 46 BC, both Juba and Masinissa II assisted his opponents. Caesar, however, was able to divert some of the Numidian forces by arranging an invasion of Numidia from the west by Bocchus II, a Mauretanian king, and Publius Sittius, an Italian renegade commander of mercenaries in the service of Bocchus, who occupied Cirta. Caesar was eventually victorious, and Juba committed suicide. Juba's kingdom was annexed to Rome, becoming the province of Africa Nova ('New Africa'). The kingdom of Masinissa II was broken up, the western part being ceded to Bocchus of Mauretania, while the east, including Cirta, was granted to Sittius as an independent principality.

This was not, however, quite the end of the native Numidian kingdoms. A son of Masinissa II called Arabio escaped the defeat of 46 BC, and joined the Pompeian forces still fighting in Spain. In 44 BC he returned to Africa, murdered Sittius, and recovered his father's kingdom. For a brief while he maintained his position, and played a role in the civil wars which followed Caesar's death, interfering in fighting between rival governors of the two Roman provinces. But in

[1] In 46 BC Caesar captured twenty-two camels belonging to Juba: Pseudo-Caesar, *De Bello Africo*, 68.4. See also ch. 5, pp. 288–9.

40 BC Arabio was expelled from his kingdom and then murdered. Cirta also was now incorporated into the Roman empire.

The history of Mauretania is even more obscure and fragmentary than that of the Numidian kingdoms to the east. The geographical remoteness of the Mauri from Carthage and, later, from the Roman province of Africa ensured that they attracted only occasionally the attention of the Greek and Roman historians who are our principal sources of information. It does appear, however, that by the time of the war of 218–201 BC a powerful kingdom existed among the Mauri as among the Masaesylii and Massylies of Numidia. It was to the King of the Mauri, named Baga, that Masinissa appealed for aid in his attempt to seize the throne of the Massylies in 206 BC. Baga refused to become involved, but did give Masinissa an escort of 4,000 troops to see him safely to the borders of his father's kingdom. After Baga's fleeting appearance in recorded history, the kingdom of the Mauri is lost in almost total obscurity for nearly a century. It must be supposed, however, that it was during the period following the defeat of Carthage by Rome in 201 BC that the Mauri gained control of the Phoenician cities established on their coasts, the most important of which were Tingi and Lixus. It is also recorded that some of the Mauri aided Carthage in its final war against Rome (149–146 BC), but it is not clear whether the central Mauretanian kingdom was involved.

We again hear something of the kingdom of the Mauri through the involvement of King Bocchus in the war of Rome with Jugurtha of Numidia (111–105 BC). Bocchus had married a daughter of Jugurtha, but at the beginning of the war he sent envoys to Rome offering his alliance. His approach was, however, rebuffed, and, as has been seen, on two occasions (108 and 106 BC) Bocchus marched east to aid Jugurtha against the Romans, on the second occasion exacting as the price for his assistance the cession of the western portion of Numidia. By betraying Jugurtha and making peace with Rome in 105 BC, Bocchus secured unchallenged possession of this territory. He also became an ally of Rome, and from this date we find Mauretanian as well as Numidian auxiliaries serving with Rome's armies.

Bocchus lived at least until 91 BC, but apparently died soon after. On his death, his kingdom seems to have been divided, one king ruling over the original Mauretanian territory to the west of the river Moulouya and another over the new territory in the east annexed in 105 BC. Like the Numidian kings, the successors of Bocchus became involved in the

Roman civil wars of the 80s BC. The Bogud who in 81 BC aided Pompey against Hiarbas (cf. p. 187), and who is described as a son of Bocchus, was presumably ruler of the eastern kingdom. About the same time (*c.* 81 BC), we find another king in the west: Askalis, son of Iphtha. Under Askalis, a rebellion broke out in western Mauretania. The Marian general Sertorius, expelled from Spain by Sulla's forces, joined forces with the rebels, and besieged Askalis in Tingi. A Roman army sent by Sulla to assist Askalis was defeated, and Sertorius forced the surrender of Tingi. What followed is unfortunately not recorded.

The kings of Mauretania sponsored the same sort of development as had Masinissa and his successors in Numidia, but the rate of progress in the west was much slower. A large part of the population was still essentially nomadic and pastoral at the end of the first century BC, and the principal urban centres in the west were the old Phoenician cities on the coast, especially Tingi and Lixus, though some purely indigenous towns did develop in the interior, notably Volubilis. It is also noteworthy that the Mauretanian kings did not issue any coins until the second half of the first century BC. However, during the first century BC, the country was opened up by Italian traders, seeking ivory, cedar-wood and animals for the Roman Games. It is also recorded that the Mauri of the first century BC habitually wore gold ornaments, but it is not known whether this gold was obtained from Spain or from the Sudan across the Sahara.

Little is known of the history of Mauretania for thirty years after 81 BC, except for the remarkable career of the Italian renegade Sittius. This man traded in Mauretania for many years, and in 64 BC, being in fear of prosecution at Rome, came to reside there permanently, setting himself up as the commander of a force of mercenaries which he hired out to the warring rulers of North-West Africa. In 49 BC, we again find two kings in Mauretania, a second Bogud in the west and a second Bocchus in the east. These kings were the first rulers of Mauretania to strike coins: those of Bocchus bear legends in Punic, while those of Bogud bear legends in Latin. Caesar sought the alliance of Bogud and Bocchus as a counter to the Numidian kings who supported the Pompeians, and both rendered him good service. Bogud took forces to aid the Caesarians in Spain in 47 BC, and Bocchus, as has been seen, together with Sittius invaded Numidia in support of Caesar in 46 BC. Later, however, the two kings became jealous of one another, and took opposite sides in Rome's civil wars. In 45 BC, when Bogud again fought on Caesar's side in Spain, Bocchus sent his sons to fight for the

Pompeians. In the civil wars which followed Caesar's death, Bogud took the part of Antony while Bocchus supported Caesar Octavian. In 38 BC Bogud invaded Spain in the interest of Antony, but in his absence the town of Tingi revolted, and Bocchus marched west in support of the rebels. Bogud found himself unable to re-enter his kingdom, and went east to join Antony, for whom he died fighting in 31 BC. Bocchus meanwhile annexed his kingdom and ruled over a reunited Mauretania.

Bocchus died in 33 BC, apparently without heirs, and his kingdom was annexed to Rome by Caesar Octavian. Several colonies of demobilized Roman soldiers were established in the towns of Mauretania. Octavian decided, however, that Mauretania did not warrant the trouble and expense of administering and defending permanently, and in 25 BC re-established it as a client-kingdom. He set upon the throne a son of Juba of Numidia, also called Juba, who had been captured as a child in 46 BC and brought up in Octavian's household. Juba established his capital at the old Phoenician city of Iol, which he renamed Caesarea (whence the modern name, Cherchel) in honour of his patron. He received as his consort Cleopatra Selene, a daughter of Cleopatra VII of Egypt by Antony, who had fallen into Roman hands at the fall of Egypt in 30 BC. It is difficult to believe that this Romanized Numidian and his Greek wife could really command the loyalty of the Mauri, but not much is known of the internal situation in Mauretania during Juba's reign. In AD 6, however, when the Gaetuli in his kingdom revolted and even raided Roman territory, Juba had to call in Roman assistance to suppress them.

Juba has a special interest to the historian as the author of a compendious work, in Greek, on the geography of Africa and Asia, which unfortunately survives only in fragmentary quotations. In pursuance of his researches in this field, Juba organized explorations in Africa, sending men into the interior to explore the northern margins of the Sahara and a naval expedition down the Atlantic coast of Mauretania. The latter reached at least as far as the island of Mogador, where Juba established a factory for the extraction of purple dye, and from there explored, but did not colonize, the Canaries.

Juba died after a long reign in AD 23/4, leaving the kingdom to his son by Cleopatra Selene, who bore in honour of his maternal ancestry the name of Ptolemy. The change of ruler encouraged a revolt among the Mauri, but this was apparently soon suppressed. In AD 40, however, Ptolemy was summoned to Rome by the Emperor Caius Caligula and murdered, and Mauretania was a second time, and finally, annexed to

Rome. Roman authority was established only after a serious rising among the Mauri, but whether this was due to the popularity of Ptolemy or simply to fear of the Romans must remain uncertain.

THE ROMAN EMPIRE IN AFRICA

The annexation of Mauretania in AD 40 completed the process, begun with the establishment of the Roman province of 'Africa' in 146 BC, whereby the entire coastal area of northern Africa was brought under Roman rule. Thereafter, Roman authority was maintained more or less effectively over northern Africa until the collapse of Roman power in the early fifth century AD.

Before considering the history of northern Africa under Roman rule, it is necessary to give some general account of Roman administrative and military practices. During the earliest stages of its imperial expansion, Rome was governed by a republican regime. Executive authority was exercised by popularly elected annual magistrates, headed by the two *consuls*, and legislative authority rested with the general assembly of Roman citizens. Effective power, however, lay rather with the Senate, a council of ex-magistrates. Wealthy citizens who were not members of the Senate were called, from their obligation of military service as cavalrymen, *equites* ('knights'), and these provided the merchants and financiers who exploited the opportunities afforded by Rome's imperial expansion. During the first century BC, owing in part to the effects of the new sources of wealth derived from the expansion of the empire, the Roman republic disintegrated in a series of civil wars. The ultimate outcome was military dictatorship, and the seizure of sole and absolute power by the victor in the last of the civil wars, Caesar Octavian (Augustus). In 27 BC, Augustus ostensibly 'restored the republic', resigning power once more to the Senate and contenting himself with the position of a republican magistrate. In fact, he established a quasi-hereditary monarchy, and he and the successors to his position are customarily accounted emperors of Rome. The Roman emperors even adopted some of the trappings of Hellenistic divine kingship, being regularly deified posthumously at Rome and often worshipped even during their lifetime in the provinces.

Under the republic, the provinces of the Roman empire were administered by ex-magistrates who held office for short periods with the title of *proconsul* or *propraetor*. In 27 BC Augustus divided the administration of the empire with the Senate. The provinces assigned to the Senate were administered according to republican practice, while Augustus governed the others through deputies of senatorial rank, called *legati*, or in some instances through an official of equestrian rank, with the title *praefectus* or *procurator*. Subsequently, Augustus acquired overriding powers which enabled him to interfere in the administration of the senatorial provinces also. In Africa, the provinces of Africa Proconsularis (incorporating both the original 'Africa' annexed in 146 BC and the 'New Africa' annexed in 46 BC) and Cyrenaica were assigned to the Senate, while Egypt was governed by an equestrian *praefectus* and Mauretania was usually divided into two provinces, each of which was governed by an equestrian *procurator*. The province of Numidia, carved out of Africa Proconsularis in *c*. AD 40, was assigned to the emperor and administered by a *legatus* of senatorial rank.

The basic component unit of the Roman army was the legion (*legio*), a force of heavy infantry nominally 6,000 strong. Legions were originally recruited ad hoc and disbanded at the conclusion of each war, but after 27 BC Augustus turned them into permanent garrison forces for the provinces of the empire, and these were increasingly recruited from the areas in which they were stationed. At the death of Augustus (AD 14), the total military establishment of the empire comprised twenty-five legions. Only three of these were stationed in Africa, two in Egypt and one in Africa Proconsularis (after *c*. AD 40, in Numidia). In principle, only Roman citizens could serve in the legions. Non-citizen subjects and allies served in auxiliary formations (*auxilia*). Under the empire, these also tended to become permanently localized garrison forces (not necessarily, or even usually, in their country of origin) and to be recruited locally.

The legal distinction between the inhabitants of the metropolitan country and those of the provinces was progressively obscured under the empire, both by the settlement of Roman citizens in the provinces and by the granting of Roman citizenship to subject peoples and individuals. This process was consummated in AD 212, when citizenship was granted to nearly all freeborn inhabitants of the Roman empire. By that time, there had already been many emperors of non-Italian origin, and the current dynasty, the Severi (AD 193–235), hailed from northern Africa.

The North African territories of the Roman empire were never administered as a single unit. Even under Roman rule, the old distinction persisted between the Greek sphere in the east, in Egypt and

Cyrenaica, and the Phoenician sphere in the west; these two areas will be treated separately.

EGYPT AND CYRENAICA UNDER ROMAN RULE

After the suicide of Cleopatra VII, the last ruler of the Ptolemaic Dynasty, in 30 BC, the Romans were able to establish their authority throughout Egypt without great difficulty. There was a rising in the Thebaid, in Upper Egypt, but this was quickly suppressed. The only

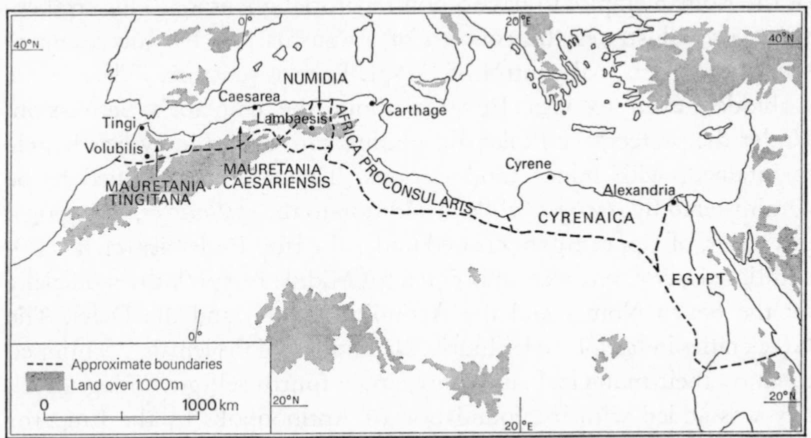

25 Roman provinces in Africa, early third century AD.

serious threat to the Roman position in Egypt was provided by the kingdom of Meroe to the south. Under the later Ptolemies, control of Lower Nubia above the First Cataract appears to have passed again from Egypt to Meroe. In 29 BC, after suppressing the revolt in the Thebaid, the Romans negotiated with the king of Meroe, who had possibly supported the revolt, and it was agreed that an independent buffer state with its own king should be created in the frontier zone between the First and Second Cataracts, while the Meroitic king himself accepted Roman protection. This arrangement, however, soon broke down, and war broke out with Meroe in 25 BC. Meroitic forces raided Upper Egypt, and a Roman army carried out a retaliatory invasion of Nubia, in which they sacked the town of Napata. (See chapter 4, pp. 245–50.) Peace was finally made in 21 BC, leaving the Meroitic kingdom still independent. The Lower Nubian buffer state disappeared, and the southern boundary of Roman authority was set at Hierasykaminos (Maharraqa), between the First and Second Cataracts.

Thereafter, friendly relations were maintained between Rome and Meroe, and Egypt was threatened only by occasional raids by the Blemmyes, the people who inhabited the desert east of the Upper Nile. The large Roman garrison in Egypt – originally three legions, later reduced to two – was not justified by any foreign threat to the country, and was probably intended primarily to secure Egypt against any Roman challenger to the emperor's power.

Egypt was administered by a prefect (*praefectus*) of equestrian rank appointed by the emperor, and was by far the most important province of the Roman empire to have a non-senatorial governor. This arrangement also illustrates the concern of Augustus and his successors to secure their personal control of Egypt. Roman senators, indeed, were forbidden even to visit Egypt without the emperor's permission. Under the prefect, the Ptolemaic administrative machinery was largely maintained, with minor modifications. The nomes continued to be administered by *strategoi*, while in addition to the *epistrategos*, or regional governor, of Upper Egypt created under the later Ptolemies (cf. p. 158), additional *epistrategoi* were appointed for Middle Egypt (known officially as 'the Seven Nomes and the Arsinoite Nome') and the Delta. The Greek cities in Egypt – Alexandria, Naukratis and Ptolemais – continued to enjoy their municipal autonomy, and a fourth self-governing Greek city was added with the foundation of Antinoopolis by the Emperor Hadrian in AD 130. Alexandria, however, had ceased to be truly self-governing: it had apparently lost its governing 'senate' (*gerousia*) under the later Ptolemies, and the Romans rejected petitions for its restoration.

Roman rule did not involve any considerable degree of 'Romanization' for Egypt. Only the most senior officials – the prefect, the *epistrategoi*, and a few others – were Romans. The bulk of the bureaucracy continued to be recruited from Greeks and Hellenized Egyptians, and Greek remained the principal language of the Egyptian administration. Alexandria continued to be an important centre of Greek literature and learning, and with the spread of Christianity among the Egyptian Greeks it became also a principal intellectual centre for the Greek-speaking section of the Christian Church. The indigenous Egyptian culture also persisted. The Roman emperors, despite their claim to be merely the principal magistrates of a republic, found it necessary in Egypt to appeal to traditional loyalties by presenting themselves as Pharaohs, and were accorded the customary pharaonic titles and represented as wearing pharaonic regalia in their Egyptian monuments. The indigenous Egyptian priesthood was maintained, though it was subjected to even greater central control than under the Ptolemies, being placed under a Roman official entitled the 'High Priest of Alexandria and all Egypt'. Loyalty to the traditional gods of Egypt faded only when Christianity began to spread on a large scale among the native Egyptians during the third century AD. Even then, the educated Egyptian élite continued the tradition of literacy in their native language, though this had by now begun to be written in Greek characters more often than in the indigenous scripts.

The Romans were principally interested in Egypt for the revenues which they could derive from it. They largely took over and elaborated the existing Ptolemaic system of taxation. After the traditional tax on agricultural produce, the most important source of revenue was a poll-tax imposed on adult male native Egyptians. The Egyptians continued to be liable to this poll-tax even when, by the decree of AD 212, they had become Roman citizens. The Romans took over control of the royal lands in Egypt, but abandoned the Ptolemaic system of royal monopolies of the production and sale of certain commodities in favour of the sale of licences to private producers. They also sought to reduce the expense of administering Egypt by progressively running down the salaried bureaucracy which they inherited from the Ptolemies, and instead making service in administrative posts a civic obligation (or 'liturgy') for the wealthier inhabitants. The overall level of taxation was certainly higher than under the Ptolemies, and the strain on the Egyptian economy was increased by the fact that much of the revenue collected was taken out of the country without bringing any return. The most onerous burden was the obligation to supply annually, without payment, a large fixed amount of corn to Rome.

Despite the heavy taxation imposed by the Romans, it is clear that initially the establishment of Roman rule brought a period of increased prosperity to Egypt. The restoration of an effective central authority checked brigandage and other disruptive local disorders, and the Romans carried out a renovation of the irrigation canals. At the same time, though probably not as the result of official initiative, irrigation techniques were improved by the introduction into Egypt from Mesopotamia of the ox-powered irrigation wheel (nowadays called the *saqia*). The work of the later Ptolemies in developing the Red Sea trade of Egypt was also continued. Already under Augustus, as many as 120 ships sailed annually from Egypt to trade beyond the straits of the Bab el-Mandeb. Trade with India was greatly facilitated when, at an uncertain date, probably in the early years of Roman rule, a Greek merchant called Hippalos discovered the regularity of the monsoon winds, which enabled ships to sail direct across the Indian Ocean rather than keeping close to the coast. The flourishing state of the Red Sea and Indian Ocean trade is vividly illustrated by the anonymous *Periplus of the Erythrean Sea*, a Greek commercial guide probably of the later first or early second century AD. The *Periplus* shows that, besides sailing to India, Greek merchants from Egypt were still trading for ivory along the north-eastern coast of Africa, where the Ptolemaic port of Adulis now afforded access to the rising kingdom of Aksum, and had also begun trading down the East African coast beyond Cape Guardafui, an area earlier monopolized by Arab traders. At the time of the *Periplus*, Greek merchants traded regularly as far south as the Zanzibar area, and during the second century AD they appear to have reached as far as Cape Delgado.

The principal internal problem of Egypt during the early years of Roman rule was the deterioration of relations between the Greek and Jewish communities in Alexandria. The substantial Jewish population in Alexandria had its origins in the Ptolemaic period (cf. p. 152), but Greek jealousy of the Jews does not appear to have been significant until the Roman period, when the Alexandrian Jews collaborated with the Roman conquerors and received various privileges from them. Disputes over the status of Jews vis-à-vis the Greek citizens of Alexandria first led to serious disturbances in AD 38, when Greek mobs attacked the Jewish quarter in Alexandria and killed many Jews. Further communal riots occurred at Alexandria in AD 53 and 66. Subsequently, the hostility between Greeks and Jews was complicated by the rise of Jewish nationalist opposition to Roman rule. The troubles culminated in the great Jewish revolt of AD 115, the immediate causes of which are obscure. This revolt began in Cyrenaica, where the local Jews seized control and massacred the Greek population. Greek refugees from Cyrenaica fled to Egypt, where they instigated a retaliatory massacre of the Jews of Alexandria. The Jews of Cyrenaica then invaded Egypt and besieged Alexandria, and the Jews of Cyprus and Mesopotamia, though not of the Jewish homeland, also revolted. The revolt was suppressed with great bloodshed, and thereafter, though a Jewish community survived at Alexandria, it was apparently so reduced in size that the Egyptian 'Jewish problem' ceased to be of any importance.

By the second century AD, however, Egypt had other equally serious internal problems, as the pernicious effects of the Roman system of taxation became apparent. The heavy demands of Roman taxation, though they could be met without difficulty in years of good harvest, were a severe burden when the harvest was poor, and the Romans showed little readiness to moderate their demands in difficult years. This resulted in the progressive impoverishment of the Egyptian population. Already in the first century AD there is evidence of rural depopulation, as farmers unable to pay their taxes abandoned their farms and took to brigandage in the marshes of the Delta. The Roman response to this problem was to hold each village collectively responsible for the cultivation of the land belonging to such fugitives and for the payment of the taxes due upon it, thus increasing the burden on the farmers who remained. During the second century AD, the economic situation of the rural population of Egypt continued to deteriorate, and rural discontent was expressed in two serious risings among the native Egyptians, in AD 152–4 and 172.

An attempt to remedy the problems of Egypt was made by the Emperor Septimius Severus during a visit to the country in AD 199–201. Besides various short-term palliatives, including an amnesty for fugitive farmers, Severus undertook a substantial reorganization of the Egyptian administrative system. Severus conceded the long-standing demand of Alexandria (cf. p. 194) for the restoration of its municipal senate, and at the same time established senates in the capitals of each of the Egyptian nomes. Though the senates of the nomes were subordinate to the *strategoi*, the change could be represented as a grant of a measure of municipal self-government. Its primary significance, however, was financial, since the members of each senate were made collectively responsible for the collection of imperial taxation in its nome. The ultimate effect of this was to complete the financial ruin of the wealthier classes in Egypt. The grant of Roman citizenship to all freeborn inhabitants of the empire in AD 212 further increased the burden of taxation in Egypt, since Egyptians now became liable to certain taxes levied on citizens (principally a 5% tax on inheritances) while remaining subject to the Egyptian poll-tax. During the third century AD, however, the poll-tax appears to have declined in importance, being replaced by a tax on landed wealth and by communal levies of corn. What is clear is that the economic decline of Egypt continued and accelerated throughout the third century.

Cyrenaica, annexed by the Romans in 74 BC, was always administered separately from Egypt. After the Roman annexation of Crete in 67 BC, Crete and Cyrenaica were usually combined together to form a single province. The Greek cities of Cyrenaica, like those of Egypt, retained their municipal autonomy under the Romans, and Cyrenaica remained Greek in language and culture. The Greek cities benefited from effective Roman action against the local tribes of nomadic Libyans, successful wars being fought against the Marmaridai in (?) AD 2 and against the Nasamones *c.* AD 86. Apart from these campaigns, Cyrenaica seems to have presented few military problems to the Romans, and the province was normally garrisoned only by a small force of non-Roman auxiliary troops.

As has been seen, Cyrenaica as well as Egypt suffered during the early Roman period from tensions between its Greek and Jewish populations. The Jewish community in Cyrenaica appears, like that of Alexandria, to have originated during the Ptolemaic period, but much less is known of its early history. Though there is evidence of Greek resentment at Jewish privileges in Cyrenaica, we do not hear of any attacks by Greek mobs on the Jews similar to those in Egypt. However, an abortive Jewish nationalist-messianic rising in Cyrenaica had to be suppressed by the Roman authorities in AD 73. In the great revolt of AD 115, the Jews in Cyrenaica were initially successful, and carried out a massacre of the Greek population, in which some 220,000 Greeks are alleged to have perished. This figure is doubtless grossly exaggerated, but extensive material destruction in the cities of Cyrenaica on this occasion is attested by archaeological evidence. The Roman Emperor Hadrian, after suppressing the Jewish revolt, had to undertake a substantial programme of rebuilding to make good the damage. He also effected the repopulation of the province by bringing in new settlers, and founded a new city named (after himself) Adrianopolis on the coast between Berenice and Ptolemais.

Economically, Cyrenaica presumably benefited from the restoration of order after the misgovernment of the last years of independence before 74 BC. But a principal source of Cyrenaean wealth, the export of the medicinal plant *silphion* (cf. chapter 2, p. 110), was lost during the first century of Roman rule, when this plant became extinct. It is alleged that the Libyans of the interior maliciously destroyed the *silphion* roots. The Cyrenaean economy became principally dependent upon stock-breeding: besides cattle and sheep, camels (introduced from Egypt) appear to have become numerous during the early Roman period. An economic decline is suggested by the fact that, even with the official rebuilding efforts of Hadrian, some of the buildings destroyed in the revolt of AD 115 were not restored for seventy or eighty years.

TRIPOLITANIA AND NORTH-WEST AFRICA UNDER ROMAN RULE

In the west, it will be recalled, the establishment of Roman rule began with the annexation of the remaining territory of Carthage, as the province of 'Africa', in 146 BC. A second Roman province, 'Africa Nova' or 'New Africa', was added with the annexation of the eastern Numidian kingdom of Juba I in 46 BC. Western Numidia, including Cirta, was presumably absorbed into the province of Africa Nova after the death of its last independent king, Arabio, in 40 BC. Subsequently, the Emperor Augustus united the two provinces, together with the previously independent coastal cities of Tripolitania, to form a single province, 'Africa Proconsularis' or 'Proconsular Africa', so called because it was a senatorial province governed by a *proconsul*. In *c.* AD 40 the western portion of Africa Proconsularis, including its legionary garrison, was placed under an imperial *legatus*, and in effect became the separate province of Numidia, though the *legatus* of Numidia remained nominally subordinate to the *proconsul* of Africa until AD 203. Mauretania, annexed in AD 40, was normally administered as two separate provinces under equestrian *procuratores*: Mauretania Caesariensis, administered from Caesarea, in the east, and Mauretania Tingitana, which was named after the town of Tingi but seems usually to have had its governor resident at Volubilis, in the west.

Africa Proconsularis probably originally had a garrison of two or even three legions, but by the end of the reign of Augustus it had been reduced to a single legion, the Third Augustan Legion (*Legio III Augusta*). After *c.* AD 40, this legion was under the command of the *legatus* of Numidia. It was stationed originally at Ammaedara (Haidra), but in the latter half of the first century AD it was moved, first south-west to Theveste, and then west to Lambaesis. The garrison of Mauretania after AD 40 normally consisted only of non-Roman (including Spanish, Gallic and Asian) auxiliary troops. Tripolitania and North-West Africa continued to present military problems to the Romans throughout the period of their rule, as they sought to protect the areas which they held against the incursions of the largely nomadic peoples of the interior. Several campaigns were fought by governors of Africa Proconsularis in the early years of Augustus, but no details are recorded except in the case of two punitive raids deep into the interior undertaken in *c.* 20 BC, against Vescera (Biskra) and other native settlements beyond the Aures mountains to the south of Numidia, and against Cydamus

(Ghadames) and Garama (Djerma), the capital of the Garamantes of the Fezzan, in the hinterland of Tripolitania. In AD 6 Roman forces had to intervene in Mauretania (then an independent kingdom), to suppress a revolt of the Gaetuli, who had raided Roman territory and won the support of the Musulamii, a Numidian tribe inhabiting the area to the east of Theveste. There was a more serious revolt of the Musulamii in AD 17–24, led by Tacfarinas, a local man who had served as an auxiliary in the Roman army, which was supported by the Garamantes of the Fezzan and by some of the Mauri. The annexation of Mauretania in AD 40 brought further trouble, provoking a revolt among the Mauri which again infected the tribes of southern Numidia. Thereafter, apart from a raid on Lepcis Magna by the Garamantes in AD 69, serious trouble seems to have been largely restricted to Mauretania, where there were major risings in AD 118–22 and AD 144–52.

It was apparently only in Numidia that the Romans established a

26 Numidia and Africa Proconsularis.

permanent military occupation of extensive areas in the interior. Under the Emperor Trajan (AD 98–117), a line of Roman forts was constructed in the plain to the south of the Aures mountains, from Ad Maiores (Besseriani) in the east to Vescera (Biskra) in the west, though the Aures massif itself, which separated Vescera from the legionary headquarters at Lambaesis, does not seem to have been penetrated by Roman troops until the 140s. The territory won in southern Numidia was protected by an elaborate *limes* ('frontier'), a defensive system of forts organized in depth, the principal feature of which was an earthen wall and ditch (*fossatum*). Beyond the *limes* proper, advanced outposts were established at Gemellae (Mlili), on the Wadi Djedi south-west of Vescera, in AD 126, and at Castellum Dimmidi (Messad), on the upper Djedi to the south of the Saharan Atlas, in AD 198. The territorial extent and frontier organization of the Roman provinces in Mauretania are much more obscure, but it is clear that Roman authority was never established over the highlands of the Rif and the Atlas and remained restricted to the coastal plains. In Tripolitania, the extension of permanent military occupation into the interior was undertaken only under the Emperor Septimius Severus (AD 193–211). The *limes* in this area (known as the *Limes Tripolitanus* or 'Tripolitanian Limes') does not appear to have included a linear earthwork as in Numidia. Numerous small forts were established in the immediate hinterland, and three isolated outposts deep in the interior, at Cydamus (Ghadames), Gheria el-Garbia and Bu Njem, which guarded the approaches to Tripolitania from the Fezzan.

In contrast to the situation in Egypt and Cyrenaica, the Roman provinces in the west received a substantial number of Roman colonists. Roman colonization in North-West Africa began in 122 BC, when it was proposed to settle landless Roman citizens from Italy at the deserted site of Carthage. Though this project was eventually abandoned, some of the settlers arrived and were allowed to retain their allotments of land in the Carthage area. Subsequent Roman colonization involved principally the settlement of demobilized soldiers from the Roman army. Some of the soldiers who fought in the war against Jugurtha of Numidia (111–105 BC) were granted land in the province of Africa, one colony being established on the island of Djerba in the Gulf of Gabes. After 46 BC, Caesar made further settlements of military veterans in Africa, while his ally Sittius settled his soldiers at Cirta and elsewhere in Numidia. Caesar also projected the foundation of a Roman colony on the site of Carthage, but this was carried out only after his assassination in 44 BC. The new Carthage grew to be the largest city in North-West Africa, and became the capital of the province of Africa Proconsularis. Later, Augustus founded numerous settlements of demobilized soldiers in North-West Africa, including several colonies established in Mauretania during the brief period of Roman rule there in 33–25 BC, and further military colonies were founded in Mauretania after its annexation in AD 40. Roman colonization in North-West Africa normally took the form of the settlement of Romans in existing Phoenician or native townships rather than the establishment of completely new communities.

The romanization of the western provinces was effected as much through the assimilation of the existing population as through the introduction of Roman colonists. Roman citizenship was granted to many of Phoenician or native African origin even before the decree of AD 212 extended the privilege to all free provincials. Citizenship was granted to individual Africans as a reward for particular services to Rome probably from the earliest period of Roman rule, and the practice later developed of conferring upon African townships (usually townships whose population already included a substantial proportion of Roman citizens) a communal grant either of full citizenship or of the inferior 'Latin status',[1] under which the senior magistrates of the township became Roman citizens ex officio. The latter process began with the granting of Latin status to the town of Utica in 59 BC, and grants of this sort were made extensively in Africa by Augustus and the later emperors. Many Africans not only attained Roman citizenship, but rose to occupy positions of importance in the Roman empire, the most dramatic instance being that of Septimius Severus, of the Phoenician city of Lepcis Magna, who became Emperor of Rome in AD 193.[2]

Under the impact of Roman colonization and assimilation, the civilization of North-West Africa lost the Phoenician character which it had acquired under Carthaginian domination. Latin gradually replaced Punic as the language of the urban centres, though the population of the rural areas continued to speak principally Libyan (Berber). The North African townships adopted municipal constitutions of Roman type, and were reconstructed in Roman style with public baths, amphitheatres for gladiatorial shows, and aqueducts to supply fresh

[1] So called because it was modelled on the status originally granted by Rome to the neighbouring cities of Latium.

[2] In addition to Septimius Severus and his descendants, two of the ephemeral emperors of the third century were of African origin, viz. Macrinus (AD 217–18), a Mauretanian, and Aemilianus (AD 253), a native of the island of Djerba.

drinking water. North Africa even produced several of the leading figures of the Latin literary world, notably Apuleius of Madauros, author of the romance *The golden ass* (*c.* AD 170). African dominance was still more marked in the literature of the Latin-speaking branch of the Christian church, beginning with Tertullian of Carthage in the early third century AD (see chapter 7, pp. 455ff.). The Phoenician culture of North-West Africa, however, for some time showed considerable tenacity. Punic remained the official language of several North African towns well into the first century AD, and unofficial Punic inscriptions survive from even later, including some of the fourth century AD in the Latin alphabet.[1] Phoenician institutions such as the magistracy of the *sufets* can also be traced during the first century AD, not only in Phoenician towns such as Lepcis Magna, but also in indigenous towns such as Thugga in Numidia and Volubilis in Mauretania. Phoenician influence proved most durable in the sphere of religion. The Carthaginian supreme deities Baal Hammon and Tanit (cf. chapter 2, p. 132) retained their popularity in North Africa, only thinly disguised under Latin names as Saturnus and Caelestis, until the mass conversion of the indigenous population to Christianity in the latter half of the third century AD. If we can believe contemporary Christian propaganda, even the Phoenician rite of infant sacrifice, though technically illegal, persisted into the third century AD.

North-West Africa, like Egypt, was principally important to the Roman empire as a source of corn. In the first century AD, it could be said that Egypt supplied the corn requirements of the city of Rome for four months, and Africa for eight months of each year.[2] The principal corn-producing areas were, as in pre-Roman times, the northern areas of the provinces of Africa Proconsularis and Numidia. The Roman period also saw a considerable growth in the production of olive-oil in North Africa. Besides the hinterland of Tripolitania, an important source of oil even in pre-Roman times, extensive areas were turned over to olive cultivation in the southern parts of Proconsularis and Numidia. By the systematic construction of wells and irrigation canals, the

[1] See F. Millar, 'Local cultures in the Roman Empire: Libyan, Punic and Latin in Roman Africa', *Journal of Roman Studies*, 1968, **58**, 126–34. It is disputed whether the later references of Augustine (late fourth–early fifth century) and Procopius (sixth century) to the use of the 'Punic' or 'Phoenician' language in the rural areas of North-West Africa should be understood to refer to Punic or to Berber. See, in addition to Millar, W. H. C. Frend, 'Note on the Berber background in the life of Augustine', *Journal of Theological Studies*, 1942, **43**, 188–91; C. Courtois, 'Saint Augustin et le problème de la survivance du Punique', *Revue Africaine*, 1950, **94**, 259–82; E.-F. Gautier, *Le Passé de l'Afrique du Nord: les siècles obscurs* (Paris, 1952), 118–44.

[2] Josephus, *The Jewish war*, II.383,386.

Romans effected a substantial expansion of the area under cultivation, principally in Numidia and Africa Proconsularis but also on a smaller scale in Mauretania and Tripolitania. The achievement is reflected in the impressions of the North African writer Tertullian:

> Famous marshes have been blotted out by fair estates, forests have been conquered by ploughed fields, wild beasts have been put to flight by flocks of sheep, the sands are sown, the rocks planted, the marshes drained, there are more towns than there used to be huts . . . everywhere there are houses, people, organised government, life.[1]

It was apparently also under Roman rule, probably during the third century AD, that the use of camels as beasts of burden for the first time became common in Tripolitania and North-West Africa. It is sometimes suggested that the Roman authorities were responsible for the introduction of the camel in the west, but there is no direct evidence for this, and it may have been due rather to the nomadic tribes of the northern Sahara outside Roman territory.[2]

The Romans also developed trade with the areas outside their formal control in the interior. From the hinterland of Mauretania they obtained principally cedar-wood and wild animals of various kinds for slaughter in the 'Games'. Initially, Mauretania was also an important source of ivory, but ivory-hunting to supply Roman demands rapidly diminished the elephant population of North-West Africa: supplies of ivory from Mauretania were already dwindling in the first century AD, and by the fourth century the North African elephant was believed to be extinct. In Tripolitania, Lepcis Magna and the other coastal cities developed a lucrative trade across the desert with the Garamantes of the Fezzan. They imported from the Garamantes principally the precious stones (of uncertain provenance) known as 'carbuncles', and probably also (after the failure of ivory supplies from Mauretania) ivory from the Sudan.

There can be no doubt that initially, and for many years, the imposition of Roman rule was enormously beneficial to North Africa. In contrast to their treatment of Egypt, the Romans did not impose taxation at a level which jeopardized North African prosperity. Rather, they did much to enrich and civilize North Africa, continuing the work

[1] Tertullian, *De Anima*, xxx.3. This passage does not refer specifically to Africa, but to the world in general. However, it seems reasonable to suppose that it reflects primarily conditions in Tertullian's homeland.

[2] Both the date and the circumstances of the introduction of the camel into Tripolitania and North-West Africa are controversial: see e.g. O. Brogan, 'The camel in Roman Tripolitania', *Papers of the British School at Rome*, 1954, **22**, 126–31; E. W. Bovill, 'The camel and the Garamantes', *Antiquity*, 1956, **30**, 19–21; Gautier, *Le Passé de l'Afrique du Nord*, 177–96. See also ch. 5, pp. 288–90.

begun by the Carthaginians and the indigenous kings of Numidia and Mauretania of encouraging the development of agriculture, urbanization and literacy among the North African peoples. The most flourishing period of Roman urban civilization in North Africa was that of the rule of the Severi (AD 193–235), the dynasty of African origin, whose rulers took an active interest in the development of their homeland. But the prosperity of North Africa came to an end during the third century AD. At the risk of some oversimplification, the beginning of the decline can be dated from the year AD 238, in which there were serious disturbances inside the province of Africa Proconsularis. These began with a rising at the town of Thysdrus (El Djem) against excessive exactions by the imperial tax-collectors. This rising quickly broadened into a rebellion against the then emperor, Maximinus, and the *proconsul* of Africa, Gordianus, was proclaimed emperor by the insurgents. This initiated a general rebellion against Maximinus throughout the empire, and Maximinus was eventually overthrown. In North Africa, however, the *legatus* of Numidia, who controlled the only legionary force (*Legio III Augusta*) in the area, remained loyal to Maximinus, and intervened in Africa Proconsularis to crush the revolt of Gordianus. The legionary troops then proceeded to sack and plunder several of the towns of the province. The fragility of the economic basis of the urbanization which the Romans had stimulated in Africa Proconsularis is indicated by the fact that its towns never fully recovered from the material destruction inflicted upon them on this occasion.

DECLINE AND REORGANIZATION OF THE ROMAN EMPIRE IN THE THIRD CENTURY AD

During the third century AD the Roman empire suffered a prolonged period of political and economic crisis. The overthrow of the Emperor Maximinus in AD 238 was followed by a half a century of instability and civil war as rival claimants fought for the position of emperor. These internal disorders were exploited by hostile neighbours of the empire, who seized the opportunity to raid or even to annex its frontier provinces. The economic dislocation caused by these disturbances was exacerbated by an uncontrolled inflation, due to the progressive debasement of the imperial coinage. Order was eventually restored, and a systematic reorganization of the empire undertaken, by the Emperor Diocletian (AD 284–305). The abdication of Diocletian was followed by a further brief period of disorder, until the supreme power passed to Constantine (AD 307–37), who is best known for having established Christianity as the official religion of the Roman empire and for having (in AD 330) transferred the imperial capital to Byzantium (Constantinople). The power of the empire was, however, permanently impaired.

In Egypt, the impoverishment of the population by excessive taxation and compulsory 'liturgies' was exacerbated rather than checked by the administrative reforms of Septimius Severus in AD 199–201 (cf. p. 197), and the economic decline continued throughout the third century. A second attempt at a systematic reorganization of the Egyptian administration under the Emperor Philip 'the Arabian' (AD 244–9) was equally ineffective. During the latter half of the third century, Egypt suffered also from the raids of the Blemmyes of the Eastern Desert, who overran Upper Egypt in AD 249 and on several subsequent occasions. In AD 269 Egypt was briefly lost to the Roman empire, when it was occupied by the forces of Zenobia, queen of the Arab state of Palmyra. The Palmyrenes enjoyed considerable local support in Egypt, but were expelled by the Romans in AD 272. Two years later, in AD 274, there was a serious rising at Alexandria, and there were further revolts at Coptos and Busiris in Upper Egypt in AD 291 and at Alexandria in AD 296–7. The condition of Cyrenaica during this period is more obscure, but it appears that a campaign against the local Libyan tribe, the Marmaridai, was necessary *c.* AD 268.

In North-West Africa, the sole legion in the Roman garrison, *Legio III Augusta*, was dissolved after the fall of Maximinus as a punishment for its role in the defeat of Gordianus in AD 238. The defence of the Roman provinces in North-West Africa was then left entirely to auxiliary forces, until the legion was reconstituted in AD 253. During this period, the area under Roman occupation was reduced, as advanced outposts such as Castellum Dimmidi in Numidia and the forts at Ghadames, Gheria el-Garbia and Bu Njem in the hinterland of Tripolitania were abandoned. In the latter half of the third century AD, there was a recrudescence of trouble with the tribes of the interior. In AD 253–62 a major war was necessary against three hitherto unrecorded peoples, the Quinquegentiani (i.e. the 'People of the Five Tribes'), the Bavares and the Fraxinenses, who had broken into the provinces of Mauretania Caesariensis and Numidia. A second war was fought against the Quinquegentiani and the Bavares in AD 289–97. Trouble of a different character, but equally ruinous to the prosperity of North-West Africa, was represented by a revolt of the Roman governor of Africa in AD 305, in suppressing which the imperial forces sacked the towns of Carthage and Cirta.

The reforms of Diocletian sought to prevent a recurrence of the troubles of the third century by increased centralization. The pretence, maintained to some degree since Augustus, that the emperor shared authority with the Senate was abandoned, and an overt autocracy was established. In the sphere of provincial administration, the distinction between senatorial and imperial provinces (cf. pp. 191–2) disappeared, and all the provinces were brought under the emperor's control. To reduce the danger of revolts by provincial governors, the provinces were reduced in size by subdivision, and military and civil authority in the provinces was separated. A few of the new provinces were still administered by ex-consuls with the title *proconsul*, others by senators of lower rank with the title *corrector* or by officials of equestrian rank with the title *praeses*. Adjacent provinces were grouped together to form twelve regional divisions of the empire called 'dioceses' (*dioeceses*), each of which was placed under the immediate authority of an equestrian 'vicar' (*vicarius*) responsible to the emperor. The senior military commanders, who were by now always recruited from men of equestrian rank only, bore the title of 'duke' (*dux*) or 'count' (*comes*). Diocletian also reorganized the imperial system of taxation, extending to the whole empire the practice originally developed in Egypt (cf. p. 197) of replacing money-taxes by a tax on agricultural produce levied in kind (the *annona*).

Under Diocletian's reorganization of the provinces, Egypt and Cyrenaica were grouped with the provinces of Syria to form the

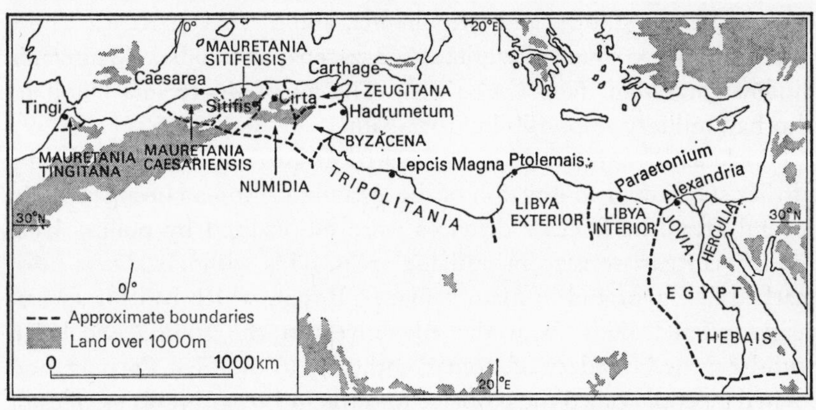

27 Roman provinces in Africa, early fourth century AD.

'diocese' of the East (*Oriens*). Egypt was subdivided to form three new provinces – the Thebais, Aegyptus Jovia (the western Delta, including Alexandria) and Aegyptus Herculia (the eastern Delta) – though the governor of Aegyptus Jovia retained the title of *praefectus* of Egypt and authority over the *praesides* of the other two provinces. Cyrenaica was divided into two: Libya Exterior (Outer Libya) in the west, administered from Ptolemais, and Libya Interior (Inner Libya) in the east, administered from Paraetonium. The former provinces of Africa Proconsularis, Numidia and Mauretania Caesariensis were combined to form the 'diocese' of Africa. Africa Proconsularis was divided into three new provinces: the northern portion, including the capital Carthage, became the province of Zeugitana (also called Proconsularis, since it was still governed by a *proconsul*); the southern portion became the province of Byzacena, administered from Hadrumetum; and Tripolitania became a separate province, with its capital at Lepcis Magna. Mauretania Caesariensis was divided into two, the eastern portion becoming the separate province of Mauretania Sitifensis, administered from Sitifis (Setif). Numidia was also divided by Diocletian, the north becoming the province of Numidia Cirtensis, with its capital at Cirta, while the south (the Aures area) became Numidia Militiana ('Military Numidia'), administered from the legionary headquarters at Lambaesis. Subsequently, however, the Emperor Constantine reunited the two Numidian provinces under Cirta, which at the same time received its modern name, Constantine, in his honour. In the far west, Mauretania Tingitana, which was not divided, was attached to the 'diocese' of Spain. The military commands in Africa did not altogether correspond to the new groupings of provinces and 'dioceses'. There were separate *duces* for Egypt, the two Libyas and Tripolitania, and a *comes* of Africa whose responsibility covered Zeugitana, Byzacena, Numidia, Mauretania Sitifensis and Mauretania Caesariensis. The *dux* of Mauretania Tingitana also had military responsibility for Spain.

Diocletian's reorganization of the African provinces also involved a further substantial contraction of the area under Roman occupation. In several areas the frontier defences were rationalized by pulling back the Roman garrisons from outlying areas. This withdrawal was most marked in Egypt and in Mauretania. In Egypt, which had for several years suffered raids from the Blemmyes to the south, Diocletian withdrew the boundary of Roman authority to the First Cataract, and invited a people called the Nobatae to settle in Lower Nubia as allies of Rome in order to defend Upper Egypt against the Blemmyes. At the same time, he agreed to pay an annual subsidy to both the Nobatae and the Blemmyes (see also chapter 4, pp. 269–70). In North-West Africa, much of the hinterland of Mauretania Tingitana and the westernmost portion of Mauretania Caesariensis appear to have been evacuated. The two provinces were separated by a considerable tract of independent country, and Mauretania Tingitana was reduced to a small coastal area, even the former administrative headquarters at Volubilis being abandoned.

Though the reforms of Diocletian thus represented a contraction as well as a reorganization of the Roman empire in Africa, the Romans were able to maintain their position in North-West Africa until the Vandal conquest of AD 429 and in Egypt until the Arab conquest of AD 639. However, Diocletian's reforms, together with the action of Constantine in granting official recognition to the Christian Church, so transformed the character of the Roman empire that it has become conventional to regard the reign of Constantine as marking the beginning of a distinct historical period, and this is treated separately in chapter 7.

CHAPTER 4

THE NILOTIC SUDAN AND ETHIOPIA, *c.* 660 BC to *c.* AD 600

THE ORIGINS OF MEROITIC CIVILIZATION

The ancient Egyptians had entered what is now the northern Sudan, known to them as Kush (perhaps the native name), in about 1500 BC and had rapidly occupied it as far upstream as Kurgus, near to the modern Abu Hamed. During the five hundred or so years of their rule, they had effected a transformation in the life of the country by forming an effective structure of Egyptian administration and by the building of towns and temples. What influence this had on indigenous village life is not certain, since archaeological investigation has as yet thrown no light on this interesting question; but there seems little doubt that chiefly families were much influenced, and it is likely that numbers of richer Kushites had moved into the towns and adopted many Egyptian customs and ways of life.

The nature of the end of Egyptian rule in Kush is extremely obscure, but by the latter part of Dynasty XX Egyptian troops and administrators were gone, and by *c.* 750 BC the beginnings of an independent Kushite state can be seen. The evidence for this and for the subsequent invasion of Egypt by Piankhy (or Piy as he should perhaps be called) and Taharqa, who, with their successors, are known in Egyptian history as Dynasty XXV, as well as some indication of Kushite influence in Egypt and the origins of the royal family, is given in Volume 1, chapter 12 of this *History* and need not be repeated here. The period of Kushite rule in Egypt ended when in 654 BC King Tanwetamani withdrew from Egypt, in face of military invasion by the Assyrians, and returned to his own country, from which he and his successors never again emerged.

It has usually been assumed that these first independent Kushite rulers lived at Napata, near to the temples built beside the conspicuous sandstone hill known today as Jebel Barkal. Originally an Egyptian foundation, Napata and its temples became the religious and, perhaps, the political centre of an important indigenous state which, owing much of its culture to Egypt, developed on its own independently of Egypt, and, with its centre either at Napata or at Meroe, lasted for a thousand years or more. Evidence for the first Kushite rulers and for the culture of their people is scanty, but royal burials at Kurru and Nuri provide some information and enable a king-list to be compiled. Those buried at Kurru, with their dates and place of burial, are:

1 Kashta	Ku. 8	*c.* 760–751 BC
2 Piankhy	Ku. 17	751–716 BC
3 Shabako	Ku. 15	716–701 BC
4 Shebitku	Ku. 18	701–690 BC
5 Taharqa	Nu. 1	690–664 BC
6 Tanwetamani	Ku. 16	664–653 BC

(NOTE: The royal Kushite tombs are numbered and designated as Ku. (Kurru), Nu. (Nuri), Bar. (Barkal) and Beg. for Begarawiya (Meroe). This numbering, now universally used, was designed by Reisner.)

Excavations of temples and of a large non-royal cemetery at Sanam, consisting of over 1,500 graves, provide further material. The sites of the town of Napata, where those buried in the cemetery presumably lived, and of the royal residence have not been identified. They may be under the present-day town of Merowe, or on the opposite side of the river close to the temples of Jebel Barkal and the modern town of Karima. Although the royal burials are good evidence for at least the religious significance of Napata, it is not certain that it was an administrative centre or that the kings lived there, and it may be that Meroe was the centre from which the royal family of Piankhy and his successors emerged. There is plenty of evidence for royal activity at Meroe from the middle of the seventh century BC, and that town may have been the royal residence from considerably earlier. On the other hand, the use of royal cemeteries at Kurru and Nuri, close to Napata, for some 450 years suggests some very close identification of royalty with that area. In spite of the similarity in name, unlikely to be coincidence, modern Merowe should not be confused with ancient Meroe; the latter lay considerably further south and will be described later.

Failure to find Napata or to identify any other contemporary dwelling-site north of Meroe causes a serious gap in our knowledge of the culture of the time, and this knowledge is almost entirely restricted to grave goods and temple ruins. Study of the material objects show them to be in no significant way different from Egyptian material of the same period, and indicates how profoundly Egyptian techniques and taste had permeated the country. That there was still an indigenous element is shown only by the finding of a few pots of non-Egyptian style in the Sanam cemetery. These pots, of black fabric with impressed decoration, though few in number, show the persistence of a pottery tradition which stretches as far back as 2000 BC and forward to Meroitic times in the first few centuries AD.

The withdrawal of Tanwetamani from Egypt was decisive for the history of Kush, for from this date the resources of the royal and religious power were concentrated in their own country, and it is possible to see, though dimly, a line of development which became increasingly indigenous as separation from Egypt was prolonged. But Egyptian cultural influence remained important for several hundred years until the end of Meroitic times and, even when pharaonic canons of art and religious observances decayed, the subsequent Coptic and Byzantine elements in Egypt were reflected in the south. In spite of the strong Egyptian influence which can be seen in Kush at this time, there are also indications of a quite different, and presumably indigenous, element, particularly in social matters. The invitation by Taharqa to his mother to come from Kush to visit him in Egypt, and the quite

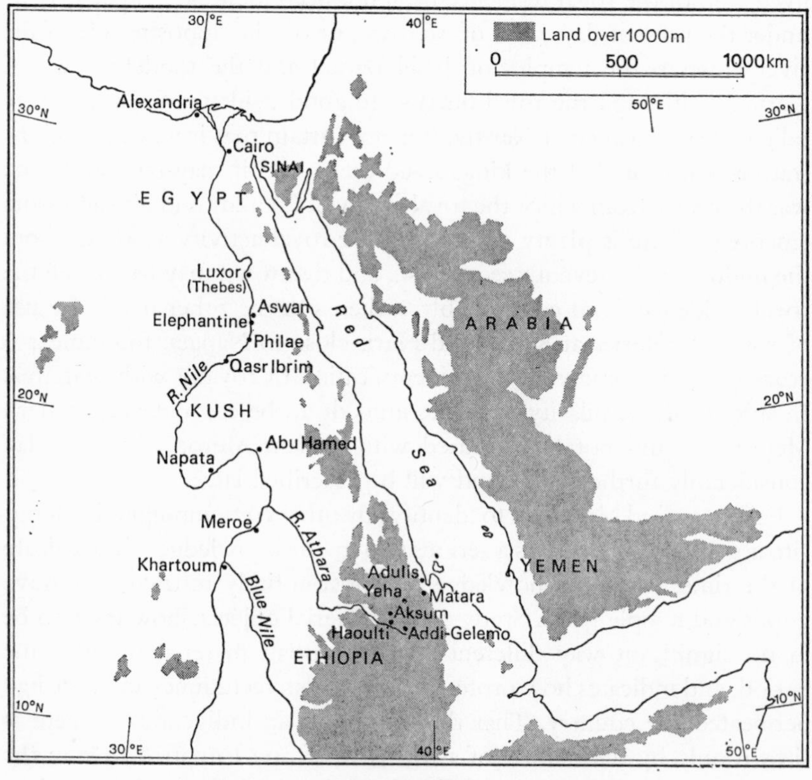

28 Nubia in relation to Egypt and Ethiopia.

un-Egyptian succession system, in which the crown passed not, as in Egypt, from father to son, but to brothers of the late ruler, are good examples of this, and even more striking is the indication that maternal descent was important to claimants to the throne.

Tanwetamani was the last of the kings of Kush to be buried in the ancestral cemetery at Kurru. Already his predecessor Taharqa had had a pyramid tomb, perhaps the first Kushite royal pyramid, erected at Nuri, on the left bank of the Nile and upstream of Jebel Barkal. There is some mystery about Taharqa's tomb; the pyramid (Nu. 1) seems to have been built in two stages, an original comparatively small one having been subsequently encased in another much larger, as though the king had decided that the first attempt was not sufficiently grandiose for one whose reputation, from the evidence of the large number of occurrences of his name from buildings stretching from Karnak to Sanam, must have been great. A further complication has been the finding of his name on the door jamb of a modest brick pyramid much further north, at Sadenga, where in recent years a cemetery of such pyramids has been investigated. First examination of this tomb suggested that perhaps Taharqa had been buried there, and that the Nuri pyramid was a cenotaph: this view was strengthened by the absence of any body in the burial-chamber at Nuri, though this may well be the result of later robbing, since all the Nuri pyramids had been ransacked, largely in medieval times. But it seems most probable that the Sadenga block with Taharqa's name on it had been removed from an otherwise unknown temple in the vicinity. From the reign of Tanwetamani's successor, Atlanersa, twenty rulers were buried at the Nuri cemetery, covering the period from *c.* 640 BC to *c.* 300 BC. During this period of nearly 350 years, we have the names of the kings, and know with reasonable certainty under which pyramids they were buried, and from a study of the grave-goods and of architectural features of the pyramids and burial-chambers dug into the rock beneath them, it seems likely that the conventional order for these rulers is correct.

The kings known from this cemetery, together with their suggested dates and burial-places, are as follows:

5	Taharqa	Nu. 1	690–664 BC
6	Tanwetzmani	Ku. 16	664–653 BC
7	Atlanersa	Nu. 20	653–643 BC
8	Senkamanisken	Nu. 3	643–623 BC
9	Anlamani	Nu. 6	623–593 BC

10 Aspelta	Nu. 8	593–568 BC
11 Amtalqa	Nu. 9	568–555 BC
12 Malenaqen	Nu. 5	555–542 BC
13 Analmaye	Nu. 18	542–538 BC
14 Amani-nataki-lebte	Nu. 10	538–519 BC
15 Karkamani	Nu. 7	519–510 BC
16 Amaniastabarqa	Nu. 2	510–487 BC
17 Siaspiqa	Nu. 4	487–468 BC
18 Nasakhma	Nu. 19	468–463 BC
19 Malewiebamani	Nu. 11	463–435 BC
20 Talakhamani	Nu. 16	435–431 BC
21 Amani-nete-yerike	Nu. 12	431–405 BC
22 Baskakeren	Nu. 17	405–404 BC
23 Harsiotef	Nu. 13	404–369 BC
24 Unknown?	Ku. 1	369–350 BC
25 Akhratan	Nu. 14	350–335 BC
26 Nastasen	Nu. 15	335–310 BC
27 Amanibakhi?	Nu.?	310–295 BC

The dates given are those of F. Hintze,[1] and it should be appreciated that these are not to be taken as firm dates but rather as approximations to give a relative chronology. Dates for the early kings, those buried at Kurru, can be established from the knowledge that we have of the dating of events in Egypt, and there are sufficient written documents to make these dates accurate within narrow limits. Later rulers have been put in order as indicated, but the dates are calculated by taking an assumed average length of reign and making adjustments according to the size of the pyramid and the richness of the grave contents. There are a few fixed dates in the whole period up to the end of the Meroitic state and they will be referred to in their proper places. But for this early period, Aspelta's reign must be fairly accurately dated, since it seems that he was reigning at the time of Psamtek II's invasion of Napata, which we know took place in 593 BC.

Our knowledge of the history of the time is scanty. Senkamanisken built a temple at Napata, and his name is also known at Meroe. He is the first king who is known for certain to have built there, though it is possible that the reference in an inscription of Tanwetamani to his having come 'from the place where he had been' may indicate that he too had a residence in the southern city. Anlamani is known from his

[1] F. Hintze, *Studien zur Meroitischen Chronologie und zu den Opfertafeln aus den Pyramiden von Meroe* (Berlin, 1959), 23–4.

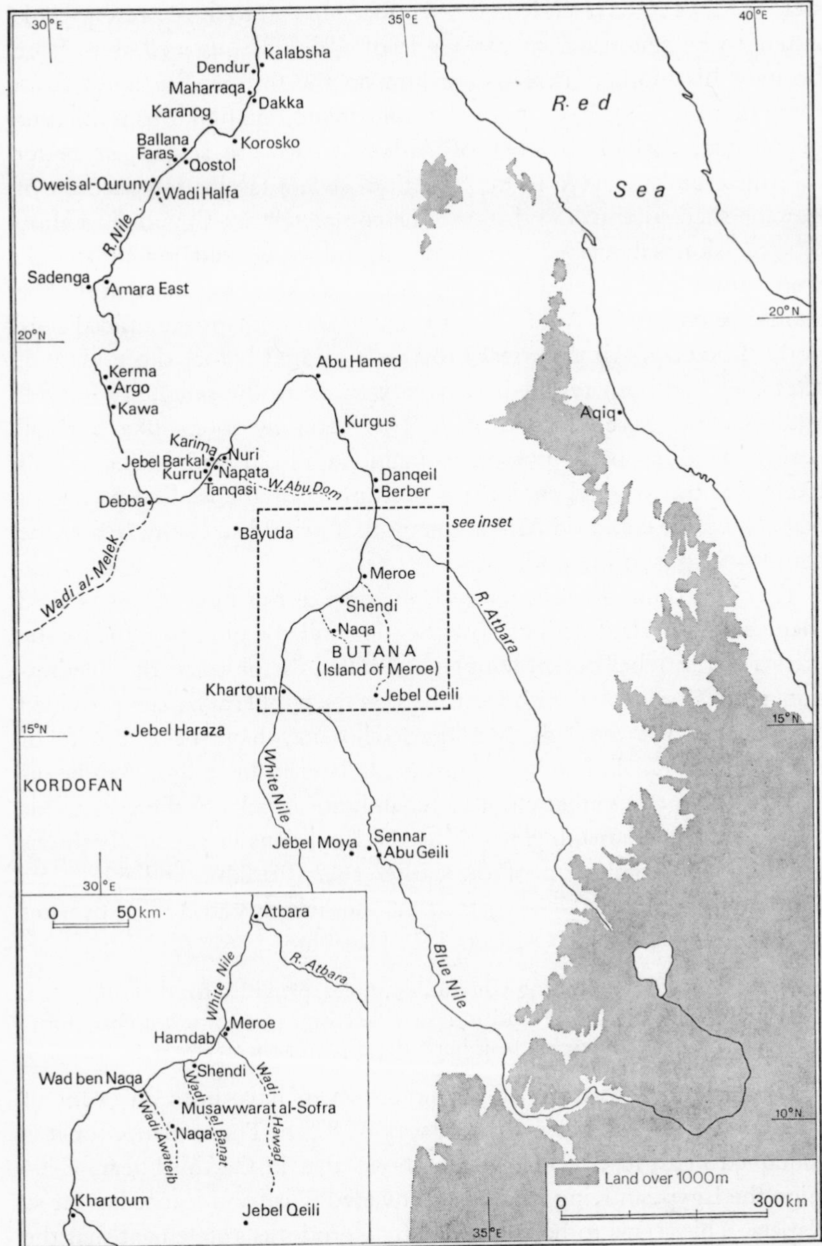

29 Nubia in Meroitic times.

stele at Kawa to have endowed a prophetship and to have presented his sisters to be priestesses in various leading temples, as well as to have brought his mother there to see him on the throne. But apart from these ritual acts, we have no further information on him. From the time of Aspelta, perhaps brother of Anlamani, we are somewhat better informed, and we have in his 'Election' stele a fascinating account of how he succeeded to the throne. The completely un-Egyptian method of succession is described in some detail, and we are told how the people were summoned to Jebel Barkal to elect their king, but decided that he should be chosen by Amun-Reʿ, the chief, and perhaps the official state god, of Napata. All the royal brothers appeared before the god, and, after they had been rejected, Aspelta went in to the sanctuary himself and the god gave his approval. This certainly looks like a ritual performance, probably put on to maintain an old tradition, and it is likely that the original choice had been made by the leading people of Napata, by the common African method of prior discussion, before the matter was put to the god.

There are other documents from the time of this king. The so-called 'Banishment' stele describes how the king foiled a plot, perhaps by the priests of the Jebel Barkal temple, and killed the plotters; the 'Dedication' stele is concerned with ensuring that the temple at Sanam provided maintenance for the lady Madiqen, who may have been a wife of Aspelta. The Khaliut stele perhaps made later in his reign, may be, as Haycock suggests,[1] an attempt to rehabilitate Aspelta in the eyes of his people after the damaging attack by the Egyptians in 593 BC. It shows Khaliut, who was a son of the earlier ruler Piankhy, and who thus must surely have been dead by the time the stele was erected, as praying for Aspelta to the gods Osiris and Re-Harakhte

> as a worthy and religious king who built temples, provided for their offerings, and cared for the cult of the dead and provided tombs for those who had none, and respected priestly rights to inherit the posts of their fathers.

The Egyptian invasion of 593 BC seems to have been an event of considerable importance for the history of Kush. The evidence for it is contained in an inscription, which shows that in the third year of his reign the Egyptian King Psamtek II invaded Kush and reached as far as Napata. This seems to be confirmed by Herodotus's statement that the Egyptians attacked Ethiopia at this time; while soldiers of the Egyptian army, including foreign mercenaries from Greece and Caria, left graffiti

[1] B. G. Haycock, 'Towards a better understanding of the kingdom of Cush (Napata-Meroe)', *Sudan Notes and Records*, 1968, **49**, 14.

at Abu Simbel and Buhen. The principal graffito, at Abu Simbel, gives the names of two leaders of the expedition: Potasimto, who led the foreigners, and Amasis, who led the Egyptians, and adds that they went as far as Kerkis. This place cannot be identified with certainty, but if, as has been suggested,[1] it is the same as modern Kurgus, upstream from Abu Hamed, then a deep penetration of the Kushite homeland had been made. Possible evidence for a sack of Napata is to be seen in the number of fragments of statues of Napatan rulers found in the Jebel Barkal temples. Of these fragments, it is probably not without significance that the latest in date is that of Aspelta.

This is perhaps the place to discuss the apparent shift in importance from Napata to Meroe as centres of Kushite administration and culture. This has been much argued, and a number of different dates have been suggested for the transfer of the royal residence from Napata to the southern centre. It has also been argued that no such transfer took place, and that Meroe was both the residence of royalty and the centre of administration from the very beginning of the dynasty. There is little to support this view as yet, though there certainly seems to have been a town at Meroe before about 700 BC, and some burials in the west cemetery there may well be of this early date. Wherever the earlier kings were living, there is no doubt that they were buried at Kurru and Nuri, but from about 300 BC the royal cemetery was established at Meroe, at first under the group of pyramids known as the south cemetery and later in the north cemetery. What is uncertain is whether or not Meroe had become the main royal residence at an earlier period.

There is no doubt that there were buildings, temples and perhaps a palace at Meroe from early Napatan times. As already mentioned, the name of Sekamanisken has been found there, as have also those of Aspelta, Malenaqen and Analmaye. In the west cemetery, some of the graves seem from their contents to date back to the time of Piankhy, and one object bearing the name of Kashta has been found there. Specifically, the evidence of the pottery found in recent excavations by the present writer strongly suggests domestic occupation as early as the seventh century BC if not earlier. None of this, though, would suffice to prove a move of the royal residence, and royal burials at Nuri continued to at least the reign of Nastasen at the end of the fourth century.

It seems probable that the move was not as sudden and dramatic as previous writers have suggested, and there may be some truth in the

[1] S. Sauneron and J. Yoyotte, 'La campagne nubienne de Psammetique II et sa signification historique', *Bulletin de l'Institut Français de L'Archéologie Orientale*, 1952, 50, 189.

view expressed years ago by Reisner that in the time of Piankhy a branch of the royal family had gone south to hold southern Kush. However this may be, we know, as has already been said, that a number of early kings built temples at least at Meroe, and Tanwetamani may have been living there. Firm evidence for royal residence at Meroe can be seen in the inscription of Amani-nete-yerike from Kawa, in which he says he was living at Meroe and that his predecessor, Talakhamani, died (*c.* 430 BC) there. This is the first mention of the town by the name for which it is now famous. Although Talakhamani died at Meroe, he was certainly buried at Nuri, in Nu. 16, so burial at Nuri does not exclude the possibility of residence at Meroe. It may well be that for a while the kings used both towns as a residence, though it seems highly likely that Meroe came to dominate at least by the time of Harsiotef, for in the thirty-fifth year of his reign the palace at Napata is described as being sanded up, and it was therefore presumably not suitable for occupation. It is worth noting that Herodotus, writing in about 430 BC, refers to Meroe, and gives some details, but does not mention Napata.

If we are to look for a time at which there was a major switch of emphasis from one centre to another, the reign of Aspelta would seem to be likely. Such a suggestion seems to fit the evidence so far as it goes, but, failing discovery of a royal residence at Napata, there can be no certainty. The military success of the Egyptian invasion would certainly be a compelling reason for shifting the main centre of the state to somewhere further south.

Whatever the date of the change, it had very important results for the development of Kushite civilization, and it was only after the move to Meroe – and some time after the initial move, if the date of around 590 BC suggested here is correct – that indigenous elements in the culture begin to emerge, so that one can begin to speak of a specifically Meroitic civilization. In this chapter, the term 'Meroitic' is used to describe the period from Aspelta onwards.

The site of Meroe was well chosen and had many advantages over Napata in addition to military security. Whatever it may have been that led to the foundation of a town on the sandy ridge between two small wadis, the founders had a good eye for a strategic position. Excavation suggests that there was a village of huts at this place before the establishment of a town, and the new elements that are seen in Meroitic culture in later centuries may reflect the influence of people different from those of the Napata region (even perhaps with a different language) – the inhabitants of the area between the Nile and the Atbara, which is now called Butana, but which the ancient writers knew as 'the Island of Meroe'.

Meroe lies far enough south of Napata to fall within an area that today gets summer rainfall nearly every year and, if the present writer's view that rainfall was slightly heavier and its furthest limit further north in the first millennium BC is correct, the region of Meroe would have been markedly more fertile than that of Napata. Today the contrast between the two areas is very clear: downstream from the bend of the river below the Fourth Cataract, the country is mainly desert away from the irrigated areas along the river banks, and it is only in this narrow strip that, with considerable effort, water can be raised to irrigate the land for cultivation. There are small areas, known today as *seluka* land, where, as soon as the annual Nile flood has subsided, it is possible to plant grain and other crops, since the necessary moisture is contained in the freshly deposited and fertile river silt. It is likely that ancient cultivation was the same as that of today, in which, with the special *seluka* stick from which the soil takes its name, a series of holes is made in the mud and the seeds dropped into the holes. For the higher land, it is essential to raise water from the river to pour onto the soil and to water the crops, and until some time after 300 BC this could only be done by the simple and effective, but laborious, method of the *shaduf*, a large pivoted pole with counter-weight at one end and a bucket at the other. Even if kept working day and night by relays of men, the area that could be irrigated by this means was severely limited. Even after the introduction from Ptolemaic Egypt of the ox-driven water-wheel, the *saqia* (which, as will be seen later, had very important results in the populating of Lower Nubia), there were still severe restrictions on the amount of foodstuffs that could be grown, and it is known from recent experience that the oxen required to drive the wheel themselves constitute a heavy drain on the food resources of the land. All this meant considerable restraint on population expansion in the north, especially since Napata, backed up against the Fourth Cataract, was not in a good position to act as a trading centre and so to attract foodstuffs in exchange for other products. It had virtually no products of its own other than the limited food resources already mentioned, and though it stood at the river end of several large wadis running south and west – the Wadi Abu Dom, leading into the Bayuda, and the Wadi el-Melik, serving as a route to the west – all goods directed towards Egypt, which must always have been the main customer for the luxury products of the south, would have had to go by the river route northwards, with all the problems involved in getting past the cataracts, particularly the difficult transit of the Second Cataract.

A word should be said about these products; though most of our information about them comes from earlier times, it seems highly probable that the goods valued by the Egyptians of the Middle and New Kingdoms and known from many tomb-paintings were still the main items of commerce. These were ivory, skins (especially of the leopard), ostrich feathers, ebony and, above all, gold. This range of goods suggest that sources of supply were tapped lying a considerable distance south of the main areas of Egyptian or even Napatan influence, though, except perhaps for ebony, they are likely all to have been available close to Meroe, where there is good evidence for the presence of the elephant. Lions were to be found there only 150 years ago, so the presence of the leopard is not improbable, and the author himself has seen ostriches within 100 km of Meroe within the last twenty years. Gold is rather a different matter, and though the main sources of supply are known to have been in the Red Sea Hills, it was worked anciently at several places along the Nile, particularly near the Second Cataract.

Meroe was also well placed both for trading activities and for agriculture. So far as trade is concerned, it controlled routes eastwards towards the Red Sea and northwards to Egypt. The routes that led east to the Red Sea became increasingly important after the development of Ptolemaic trade by sea and of the equally important land routes that led up the Arabian side of the Red Sea to the merchant centres of Syria, of which Palmyra was the most important. The route northwards to Egypt ran along the river to the bend by the modern town of Abu Hamed, and from there ran north again through the desert to come to the river once more near Korosko. As a result of this desert route, which remained in use well into the nineteenth century, Meroe, though further away from Egyptian markets, was in fact in easier contact with them than Napata had been, at least after the introduction of the camel.

From the point of view of agriculture, Meroe's superiority was even more marked. In addition to the riverain land, both *seluka* and *saqia*, there were, as there are today, wide areas in the beds of wadis such as the Hawad and the Awateib which could grow large quantities of grain, mostly sorghum, during the rains. After the flash floods caused by rain have subsided, these wadi beds absorb sufficient moisture to make possible the growing of grain, and in them there was sufficient agricultural land to support such towns as Meroe, and the towns that are assumed to have been at Naqa and Wad ben Naqa. In addition to the grain-growing possibilities of the wadi beds, there was also, after the rains, plenty of pasture for the cattle. There are sufficient representations of cattle in Meroitic art, particularly in the reliefs on the walls of pyramid chapels, to make it clear that they played a large part in Meroitic life, and the present writer's discovery that a large percentage of the animal bones from domestic refuse in the town at Meroe were of cattle confirms their importance in Meroitic life and diet. Analogy with many of the modern peoples of the Sudan suggests that cattle may have been one of the main sources of power and wealth, and, if this was so, the possibility of maintaining large herds in the Island of Meroe would certainly have recommended such a region to rulers who may already have been the owners of herds before permanently moving their place of residence.

The immediate successors of Aspelta left no details of the events of their reigns, and it is not until the time of Amani-nete-yerike in the latter part of the fifth century BC that there is any information from written sources. There are four inscriptions of this king on the walls of Taharqa's temple at Kawa, and they provide much interesting detail. The language in which they are written, though Ancient Egyptian (as were all Kushite texts for many centuries), shows a loss of knowledge of that language, and the influence of an indigenous language causes an erratic use of it. There is some difference in the knowledge of Egyptian shown in different texts, presumably a reflection of varying scholarship by different scribes. This suggests that Egyptian was no longer in ordinary colloquial use, even if it had been in earlier times. The main inscription of this king, known as Kawa IX, is of particular importance since, as noted above, it gives the first mention of Meroe and also the information that the king was living there. It also shows that Talakhamani was Amani-nete-yerike's predecessor, thus confirming Reisner's deductions made on purely archaeological evidence before the inscription was known, and therefore strengthening reliance on his ordering of the kings buried at Nuri. Malewiebamani is also mentioned, though his relationship to Amani-nete-yerike is not clear; he may have been either father or brother.

The details of activities by the king as described in this inscription are of much interest since they show that, though now dwelling at Meroe, the king still needed to go to Napata to be accepted by the god Amun-Reʿ in the Jebel Barkal temple in the same way as Aspelta had been. The inscription, after saying that he was forty-one years old and dwelling at Meroe, tells how, after the death of Talakhamani at Meroe, the new ruler first put down a revolt by a people called the *Rehrehs*, probably near to the confluence of the Nile and the Atbara. After that he went overland, across the Bayuda to Napata, taking nine days for the journey. Did he perhaps take the body of Talakhamani with him in mummified form for burial below Nuri pyramid 16? At Napata he went through various ceremonies both in the palace and in the Temple of Amun-Reʿ, where the god spoke to him and gave him the kingdom. After this traditional acceptance as king, he went on what must be considered an inspection tour, perhaps required of all kings, to some of the most sacred places in the kingdom. But first he fought an action downstream from Napata against a people called the *Meded* and described as desert-dwellers; the site of this battle was *Krtn*, which it has not been possible to identify. After this, visits were made to the important temples at Kawa and at Argo (*Pnubs*); at Argo a donation of land was made to the temple, and at Kawa the approach to Taharqa's temple, apparently sanded up for forty-two years, was cleared and building repairs were undertaken. While at Kawa, the king also received a visit from the queen mother and this, like Taharqa's earlier invitation to his mother, shows that such events were of sufficient importance to be entered in official records, and thus emphasizes the role of women in the royal family. One of the other Kawa inscriptions gives a regnal year of twenty-five for Amani-nete-yerike, so he must have reigned for at least that number of years.

The earliest foreign description of Meroe, that of the Greek writer Herodotus, dates from this time. Herodotus was in Egypt in about 450 BC, and therefore perhaps during the reign of Malewiebamani. He did not go further south than Elephantine (Aswan), but he presumably met Meroites there and gathered his information from them. His descriptions are rather diffuse, and some of the geographical information cannot easily be reconciled with the facts, but there is no doubt that he had some first-hand informants, and it is of importance that he knew of Meroe, and that it lay upstream of the Fourth Cataract, whilst Napata is not mentioned. He knew of Psamtek's campaign, and describes how some of the Egyptian troops had deserted and had settled south of Meroe. It is not clear how much credence can be given to this story, which may be entirely fanciful, but it has been suggested by Wainwright that it is substantially correct, and that the deserters sailed up the White Nile and settled in southern Kordofan.[1] There is no archaeo-

[1] G. A. Wainwright, 'Some ancient records of Kordofan', *Sudan Notes and Records*, 1947, **28**, 11–24.

logical evidence for such a settlement, but the region is virtually unexamined.

Herodotus also described activities by the Persian King Cambyses, who, he says, attempted an invasion in about 525 BC, a period for which native documents are lacking, but which was possibly during the time of Amani-nataki-lebte. The Persian campaign came to grief in the desert, but prior to that Cambyses had sent spies to Meroe to see, according to Herodotus, if the 'Table of the Sun' was in the land of Ethiopia.[1] This 'Table' was said to be in a meadow near the city of the Ethiopians (presumably Meroe), and it was filled with meat by the priests every night so that all who came might eat. The spies were shown the 'Table' and other wonders and then returned. If the story is true, then the aim of the spies would have been to advise Cambyses on the feasibility of his projected invasion. It is difficult to relate these, perhaps mythological, stories to known facts, but it has been suggested that a temple which was excavated by Garstang in 1910 and which lies less than 2 km east of Meroe town should be identified with the 'Table',[2] and it is now normally, though without warrant, known as the Sun Temple; it is more likely to be a temple to the lion-god, Apedemek. Apart from this, Herodotus's information is of little value; he says that the spies took presents to the King of Meroe, who countered by giving them a bow which he suggested Cambyses would not be able to draw; they were shown various wonders and returned home. Cambyses's abortive invasion is said to have followed their return. There is little to be got from this for the history of Meroe, though the reference to the bow may be authentic in view of the long-standing association of Kush, known originally to the Egyptians as the 'Nine Bows', with archery. There are many examples of arrowheads; in temple and chapel reliefs there are a number of representations of kings and gods holding bows of considerable length; and stone thumb-rings, very probably used in archery, are common.

Of the last few kings to be buried at Nuri, we have inscriptions of Harsiotef and Nastasen. That of Harsiotef is very similar in subject matter to that of Amani-nete-yerike; it describes the king's journey to Napata to get the god's approval, as well as military campaigns against the *Meded* and the *Rehrehs*. It also records the king's many gifts to temples, and is particularly full of gratitude to the gods for the help

[1] The ancient writers normally use 'Ethiopia' to indicate the region of the Nile south of Egypt. It was so used also by Reisner to cover what we now call Kush (Napata/Meroe), but since Abyssinia took over the name as its official designation, it is no longer appropriate.

[2] A. H. Sayce in J. Garstang, *Meroe – the city of the Ethiopians* (Oxford, 1911), 27.

they had given him; before one of his campaigns Harsiotef asked Amun of Napata for his opinion and guidance before going into the field. The inscription is particularly interesting in showing, as Haycock says,[1] that Napata 'was a town full of aged buildings crumbling into ruin', and the imminent transfer, perhaps three generations later, of the royal burial-place from Nuri to Meroe shows that the glory of Napata had largely departed, even though the king still required the formal support of Amun-Reʿ, an authority no doubt controlled by the priesthood.

Harsiotef's burial under Nuri pyramid no. 13 is the first one in which the model tools which are normally buried with a king, are made of iron rather than bronze. Though this is not the first appearance of iron, some having been found in the tomb of Taharqa, it is the first time that this metal is found in any quantity, and this is presumably an indication of its increasing commonness. In the same tomb were found fragments of a human skull, a rather rare event, since in the robbing of these tombs all the skeletons had been very badly damaged. This skull was sufficiently complete, and has been claimed to be that of a man in his middle twenties. If this is so, it cannot be of Harsiotef, since his inscription states clearly that it was written in the thirty-fifth year of his reign.

The inscription of Nastasen, the last king to be buried at Nuri, was written in the eighth year of his reign, but describes events happening some years earlier. It is concerned mainly with the ceremonies of his coronation. He describes how he was living at Meroe when he was summoned north, ostensibly by the god Amun of Napata, to undertake the traditional ceremonies which were necessary for accession to the kingship. He does not refer to his predecessor, but it is made quite clear that the journey to the north was made for the purpose of being formally accepted by Amun in the Temple at Jebel Barkal. Haycock has argued interestingly that the choice of successor was by this time being made at Meroe, and that the northern visit was merely to give notification of a fait accompli.[2] The words of the inscription are:

He [Nastasen] says 'While I was the good young man in Meroe, my good father Amun of Napata called to me saying "Go and summon the king's brothers who are in Meroe". I told them saying "Come let us go and enquire together about our [future] Lord", but they said "We will not come with you – it is you he wants for the good young man [i.e. the new king] because Amun of Napata your good father loves you."'

[1] Haycock, 'Towards a better understanding', 15.

[2] B. G. Haycock, 'The kingship of Kush in the Sudan', *Comparative Studies in Society and History*, 1965, 7, 472.

This certainly strongly suggests that Nastasen had been chosen by a consensus. The journey to Napata is described, and this is followed by a description of the very elaborate ceremonial in which the new king had to participate, which included sacrifices and dances, and was followed by visits to other major religious centres in the region as far north as Kawa. On his way back for the final ceremonies at Napata, Nastasen stopped at Argo (where recently a large Meroitic temple has been found), and at each of these places was given ceremonial gifts. After returning to Napata, he stayed there five days, and then went to *Tore* (still not identified; Haycock suggests Sanam Abu Dom).[1] Ten days later Nastasen was once more at Napata, where the god gave him 'all the heaven, all peace, all the river and all men, and I went up and sat on the throne'. In return the king gave the god a number of gifts: four gardens with thirty-six men to maintain them, as well as many vessels of silver and copper, gold statues and cattle.

The remainder of the text is concerned with military affairs, written in the normal bombastic style. It is not clear whether the campaigns came some time after the coronation ceremonies, though this surely must have been so. The places where the military victories were gained cannot be identified; most of the enemies appear to have been desert tribes, and one of them is reported to have sacked temples at Kawa and Tore and to have stolen gold vessels originally presented by Aspelta and which were replaced by Nastasen.

More important, because of its chronological implications, is the account of a campaign against an enemy with boats. This enemy, whose name perhaps should be read as *Kambasuten* or something similar, was at one time taken to be Cambyses. But his invasion, if it took place, would have been *c.* 525 BC, far too early for Nastasen, unless the whole chronology of the kings has gone seriously astray. Hintze's reasonable suggestion that the name represents a variation of Khabbash, known from Egyptian sources to have been a local ruler of the region to the north of the Second Cataract *c.* 338–336 BC who campaigned against the Persians in Egypt, makes more sense, and if right gives a valuable check on the assumed date for Nastasen.[2]

The name of Amanibakhi is normally inserted in the king-list at this point, though there is no tomb which can be identified as his. The evidence for him is the existence of a stele and of an offering-table bearing his name, both found in the ruins of a church which was built in medieval times amongst the pyramids at Nuri as part of a Christian

[1] Haycock, 'The kingship of Kush', 473. [2] Hintze, *Studien*, 17–20.

community which lived in and amongst the royal graves, and was responsible for much of the grave-robbing. On stylistic grounds the two pieces belong here, but Amanibakhi could as well have come before Nastasen as after him. In any case Nastasen's death would seem to have been about 300 BC.

MEROE FROM *c.* 300 BC TO THE ROMAN INVASION

The death of Nastasen marks the end of royal burials at Nuri, and though there is no way of knowing what was happening at this time, there may have been events of considerable importance for the royal line. There are various elements of confusion: the first king to be buried at Meroe seems to have been Arakakamani, in the south cemetery under Beg. S. 6., but there is also a group of pyramids at Jebel Barkal which stylistically belong to the end of the fourth century. There has been much discussion as to the significance of this group and as to those who are buried there.

In his original historic scheme, Reisner assumed that these pyramids represented an independent line of rulers who had re-established the importance of Napata free from Meroe. When a group of royal names, of about this date, was found at Kawa, it was suggested that these might be some of those in the Barkal tombs. These names were:

Aryamani
Piankh-yerike-qa
Sabrakamani
Arnekhamani

These inscriptions, particularly that of Aryamani, are almost unintelligible. They are written in a form of Egyptian, presumably by scribes whose own language was Meroitic and who knew very little Egyptian. So far as they can be read, they seem to deal with records of gifts to temples and of festivals held in them. Arnekhamani's name was also found on a bronze head from the same site.

The identification of these kings with the Jebel Barkal pyramids, and the suggestion of a separate kingdom, had to be reconsidered when the name of Arnekhamani was found with good-quality Egyptian inscriptions on the walls of the Lion Temple at Musawwarat es-Sofra, which is further south even than Meroe, thus making it clear that Arnekhamani controlled that area and was likely to have been living at Meroe. Whatever the truth may be, and whatever the significance of the pyramids at Barkal, the shift of the main royal cemetery from Nuri to Meroe seems to have taken place at a date not far removed from 300 BC. It may be of significance that this is close to the date of Alexander's conquest of Egypt in 332 BC, though no direct causal effect of that event can be seen. Further doubt about the existence of an independent line of rulers at Barkal comes from the writing of the name of Amanislo, perhaps the successor of Arakakamani, on two granite lions – the Prudhoe lions, found at Barkal. These lions, which were originally made in the reign of the Egyptian Pharaoh Amenophis III (1405–1370 BC), were at some time moved to Barkal, where Amanislo had his name carved on them. Since he was buried at Meroe (Pyramid S. 5), it again seems likely that rulers living at Meroe were controlling the north. It has however been suggested again recently that there was a brief period after the death of Nastasen before royal burials started at Meroe, and Wenig has suggested that the three, otherwise unknown, kings whose names were found at Kawa were buried at Barkal before burials started at Meroe.[1] His reconstruction of the succession and chronology of this period is as follows:

Aryamani	Bar. 11	315–290 BC
Piankh-yerike-qa	Bar. 14	298–280 BC
Sabrakamani	Bar. 15	280–270 BC

It is from about this time that elements of Meroitic art which are quite distinct from Egyptian art begin to appear, and the style of chapel reliefs in many cases takes on an increasingly indigenous appearance. (This was not always so: the reliefs and inscriptions on the walls of the Lion Temple at Musawwarat have a very close resemblance to those current at this time in Ptolemaic Egypt.) Hintze has used this stylistic evidence, together with the titles used in the royal titulary, to suggest that Arnekhamani, the builder of the temple, was in part a contemporary of Ptolemy IV (211–205 BC).[2] However, Haycock has criticized this view, suggesting that the king and the temple be dated somewhat earlier, perhaps *c.* 250 BC, in the reign of Ptolemy II.[3] All attempts at establishing a precise chronology for Meroitic rulers are highly hypothetical, but some help is given by the Greek writer Diodorus Siculus, who tells us that Ergamanes, King of Meroe, was a contemporary of

[1] S. Wenig, 'Bemerkungen zur Chronologie des Reiches von Meroe', *Mitteilungen des Instituts für Orientforschung der Deutschen Akademie der Wissenschaften zu Berlin*, 1967, 13, 9–14.

[2] F. Hintze, 'Preliminary report on the excavations at Musawwarat es Sufra, 1960–1', *Kush*, 1962, 10, 177–8.

[3] B. G. Haycock, 'Towards a date for King Ergamenes', *Kush*, 1965, 13, 264–6.

both Ptolemy II and Ptolemy IV. Ergamenes is usually taken to be the Meroitic Arqamani, who is known from inscriptions to have had a hand in temple-building in the far north at Philae and at Dakka. Parts of these same buildings bear the name of Ptolemy IV, so the equation of Ergamanes with Arqamani seems not implausible. On the other hand, it is not impossible that names as similar as Arakakamani, Arnekhamani and Arqamani may all have been rendered 'Ergamanes' by the Greeks. It certainly seems both that at this time there was closer contact with Egypt than at any other period of Meroitic history and that Arqamani's temple-building in Lower Nubia was an unusual event. Since the name of another Meroitic king, Adikhalamani, is also found on the temple at Dabod, there may have been some Meroitic occupation of the area, though no dwelling-sites or cemeteries of the period have been found. This was a time of rebellion against the Ptolemies in Upper Egypt, which persisted from *c.* 207 to *c.* 186 BC, and it is possible that the Meroites may have given aid to the Egyptian rebels. At some time after 180 BC, Ptolemy VI (180/1–145 BC) enlarged the Dabod temple, so Ptolemaic control must have been re-established by then, but perhaps not until after the Seleukid invasion of Egypt in 169 BC. There is no certainty that the king at Meroe had political control of this northern region, and evidence of Meroitic domestic occupation on any scale only appears considerably later.

The close contact with Ptolemaic Egypt was probably the reason for the very Egyptian style of the reliefs on the walls of Arqamani's pyramid chapel and on the walls of the Lion Temple at Musawwarat. On the other hand, there are also some very non-Egyptian representations in this temple, such as those of elephants and cattle, the regalia of the king, and of the god, Apedemek, to whom the temple is dedicated.

It seems unwise to press the evidence too far in an attempt to get precise dates, and it is safer to say that Arakakamani was buried at Meroe in about 300 BC and that amongst his immediate successors were Arnekhamani and Arqamani. These spanned the period from about 250 to 200 BC, during which the Musawwarat Lion Temple was built. Though Diodorus may have conflated several rulers in his description of Ergamanes, his account is extremely interesting in what it tells us about the choice of the king. This closely parallels the account given in the inscriptions of Nastasen and others, and therefore suggests that his other information may well be accurate. The best-known section of his account is that in which he describes Ergamanes's ending of the tradition by which the kings committed suicide on the instructions of the priests. Since this account has been used many times in recent histories, it may be useful to give a translation of the whole passage:

Of all their customs the most astonishing is that which obtains in connection with the death of their kings. For the priests at Meroe who spend their time in the worship of the gods and the rites which do them honour, being the greatest and most powerful order, whenever the idea comes to them, despatch a messenger to the king with orders that he die. For the gods, they add, have revealed this to them, and it must be that the command of the immortals should in no wise be disregarded by one of mortal frame. And this order they accompany with other arguments, such as are accepted by a simple-minded nature, which has been bred in a custom that is both ancient and difficult to eradicate and which knows no argument that can be set in opposition to commands enforced by no compulsion. Now in former times the kings would obey the priests, having been overcome, not by arms nor by force, but because their reasoning powers had been put under a constraint by their very superstition; but during the reign of the second Ptolemy, the king of the Ethiopians, Ergamenes, who had had a Greek education and had studied philosophy, was the first to have the courage to disdain the command. For, assuming a spirit which became the position of a king, he entered with his soldiers into the unapproachable place where stood, as it turned out, the golden shrine of the Ethiopians, put the priests to the sword, and after abolishing this custom thereafter ordered affairs after his own will.

As for the custom touching the friends of the king, strange as it is, it persists, they said, down to our own time. For the Ethiopians have the custom, they say, that if their king has been maimed in some part of his body through any cause whatever, all his companions suffer the same loss of their own choice; because they consider that it would be a disgraceful thing if, when the king had been maimed in his leg, his friends should be sound of limb, and if in their goings forth from the palace they should not all follow the king limping as he did; for it would be strange that steadfast friendship should share sorrow and grief and bear equally all other things both good and evil, but should have no part in the suffering of the body. They say also that it is customary for the comrades of the kings even to die with them of their own accord, and that such a death is an honourable one and a proof of true friendship. And it is for this reason, they add, that a conspiracy against the king is not easily raised among the Ethiopians, all his friends being equally concerned both for his safety and their own. These, then, are the customs which prevail among the Ethiopians who dwell in their capital and those who inhabit both the island of Meroe and the land adjoining Egypt.

It may be useful at this point to list the rulers and their tombs at Meroe together with the dates which Hintze allocates to them. It will be seen that many of the identifications are uncertain, and that the list contains many more guesses than does that of the earlier rulers buried at Kurru and Nuri; this makes the dates as given even more uncertain, and they must be used with the greatest caution. This is not the place to give detailed arguments for the ordering of these rulers or for their allocation to individual tombs; the reader who wishes to pursue this matter should refer to Hintze's book. Detailed arguments concerning the list will continue for a long time – for example, Wenig has proposed a considerable number of changes, as can be seen by the list of rulers which he gives from Nastasen on.[1]

List of kings buried at Begarawiya (Meroe), with tombs and dates according to Hintze:

28	Arakakamani	Beg. S. 6	295–275 BC
29	Amanislo	Beg. S. 5	275–260
30	Queen Bartare	Beg. S. 10	260–250
31	Amani . . . tekha ?[a]	Beg. N. 4	250–235
32	(Arnekhamani)[b]	Beg. N. 53	235–218
33	Arqamani	Beg. N. 7	218–200
34	Tabirqa ?	Beg. N. 9	200–185
35	. . . iwal ?	Beg. N. 8	185–170
36	Queen Shanakdakhete	Beg. N. 11	170–160
37	Unknown king	Beg. N. 12	160–145
38	(Naqrinsan) ? ?[c]	Beg. N. 13	145–120
39	((Tanyidamani))[d]	Beg. N. 20	120–100
40	((. . . Khale))	Beg. N. 21	100–80
41	((. . . amani)) ? ?	Beg. N. 14	80–65
42	(Amanikhabale)	Beg. N. 2	65–41
43	Queen Amanishakhete	Beg. N. 6	41–12
44	Netekamani	Beg. N. 22	12 BC – AD 12
45	Queen Amanitare	Beg. N. 1	12 BC – AD 12
46	(Sherkarer)	Beg. N. 10	AD 12–17
47	((Pisakar))	Beg. N. 15	17–35
48	Amanitaraqide	Beg. N. 16	35–45
49	Amanitenmemide	Beg. N. 17	45–62
50	Queen Amanikhatashan	Beg. N. 18	62–85
51	Tarekeniwal	Beg. N. 19	85–103
52	((Amanikhalika))	Beg. N. 32	103–108
53	(Aritenyesbekhe)	Beg. N. 34	108–132
54	((Aqrakamani))	Beg. N. 40	132–137
55	((Adeqetali))	Beg. N. 41	137–146
56	Takideamani	Beg. N. 29	146–165
57	((. . . reqerem)) ?	Beg. N. 30	165–184

[1] Hintze, *Studien, passim*; Wenig, 'Bemerkungen zur Chronologie', 42–4.

58 ...	Beg. N. 37	187–194
59 ((Teritedakhatey))	Beg. N. 38	194–209
60 Aryesbekhe	Beg. N. 36	209–228
61 Teritnide	Beg. N. 51	228–246
62 Aretnide	Beg. N. 35	246
63 Teqerideamani	Beg. N. 28	246–266
64 ((Tamelerdeamani))?	Beg. N. 27	266–283
65 ((Yesbekheamani))?	Beg. N. 24	283–300
66 ((Lakhideamani))??	Beg. N. 26	300–308
67 ((Maleqerebar))?	Beg. N. 25	308–320

[a, b] ? and ?? mean reading of name uncertain
[c] ( ) means identification with a tomb uncertain but probable
[d] (( )) means identification with a tomb is only a guess

The listing of the rulers, their burial-places and approximate dates as given by Hintze does not imply that this list has greater authority than those of other scholars, but it is convenient and uncomplicated and gives some notion of order and date. The arguments given by Wenig in support of his alterations are substantial.

The change in the place of royal burials from Nuri to Meroe suggests some political events of which we know nothing, and it presumably also indicates a loss of influence by the priesthood of Napata. Perhaps the important religious role of the god Amun at Napata was now transferred to Meroe and exercised from the Amun Temple at that place. This date, of around 300 BC, also sees the beginning of a change in the culture, and it is from this time on that objects in the style usually described as Meroitic are found. The changes go much further than just reflecting changes in Egyptian styles brought about by Ptolemaic influence, and the most noticeable aspect is the increasingly indigenous style which is now found. Material for description is not plentiful but there are sufficient monuments, other than the pyramids, to allow a general assessment to be made.

By far the most important, as well as the most plentiful, information is to be found in the royal burials, and, as already indicated, it is this series of burials, first excavated and studied by Reisner some fifty years ago, that has provided the evidence on which a chronological and historical framework has been based. From the beginning of the use of the cemetery at Nuri, all the rulers of Kush appear to have been buried under pyramids, thus marking a radical change from the practice in the earlier cemetery at Kurru. At Kurru the earliest graves were surmounted

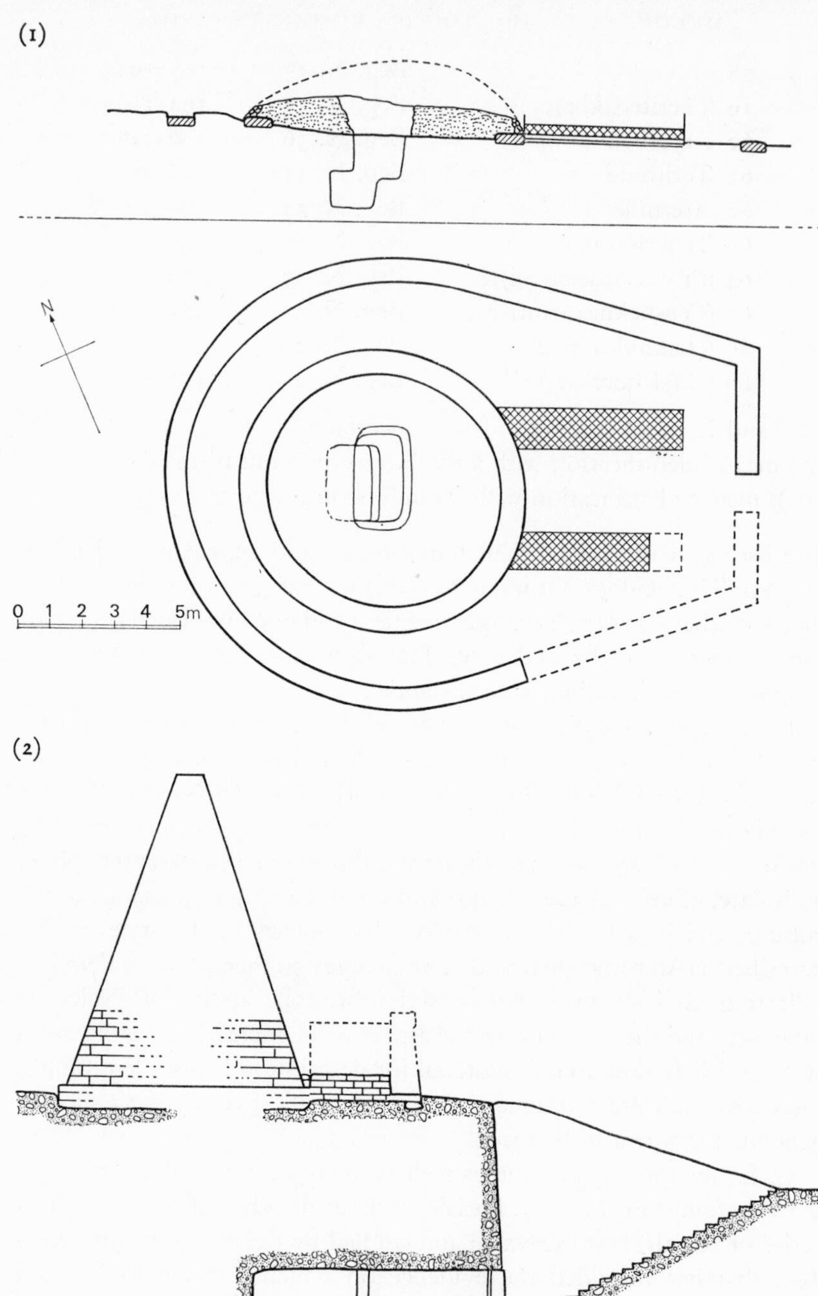

30 Meroitic royal burials: (1) Tumulus at Kurru; (2) Section through a typical pyramid and burial-chamber.
(No. 1 after D. Dunham, *El Kurru*, 1950, p. 21; no. 2 after Shinnie, *Meroe*, 1967, fig. 17.)

by mounds or tumuli, and the later ones probably by the truncated pyramidal structures known in Egyptian archaeology as 'mastabas'. It has been suggested that the tomb of Piankhy at Kurru, at least, was covered by a pyramid, but such of the superstructure as remains suggests that its interpretation as a mastaba is more likely.

What cultural influences, or changes in local fashion, led to the introduction of the pyramid for Taharka's burial cannot now be known. It may be that the idea of pyramid-burial was derived from Egypt, where, although use of pyramids for royal burials had long ceased, private individuals had been buried in or under pyramids to at least a little before 1000 BC. These late Egyptian burials, as at Deir el-Medina, though separated in time by 300 years from the appearance of the first Meroitic (Kushite) ones, resemble them by their pointed shape, which differs considerably from the Egyptian royal ones of earlier times. At least one private pyramid-burial is known from the Sudan: that of Amenemhat, a local chief, at Oweis el Quruny, a little north of where Wadi Halfa once stood. The style of chapel associated with the Egyptian burials is different from those at Nuri and Barkal, and in Kush this feature, at least, may be indigenous. The first appearance, in a rather simple form, of what was to become the normal Meroitic funerary chapel is at Kurru, where Tumulus no. 6 has a small chapel consisting of two parallel mud brick walls built on to the east side of the mound. From that time on it became normal to build such chapels against the east side of the tomb superstructure, whether tumulus or pyramid, progressing from the undecorated walls of Kurru and Nuri to the elaborately sculptured ones at Meroe.

Apart from the royal burials, our information was until very recently confined to the large non-royal cemetery at Sanam Abu Dom, across the river from the temples of Jebel Barkal and a few kilometres downstream from Nuri, and the non-royal burials (the great majority) in the South Cemetery at Meroe and those in the West Cemetery at the same place. In all these cemeteries there are burials dating certainly from the eighth century BC and, in the case of the Meroe West Cemetery, continuing in use for many centuries.

These cemeteries show a variety of burial customs, and the interpretation of the significance of the variations has been the subject of much discussion. At Meroe two types are observable, one consisting of a rectangular grave in which the body was laid on a bed, a burial method known from Kurru and certainly indigenous, and the other much closer to Egyptian custom, in which the bodies, in this case mummified, were placed in wooden coffins and frequently covered with a bead net in a manner similar to contemporary burials in Egypt. Whether this difference in burial customs reflects the presence of two communities, or possibly social classes, living contemporaneously, or whether it reflects a chronological difference, is not clear. At Sanam Abu Dom the burials show some variation from this, and several different types of grave have been found, the two main types being, first, a rectangular chamber either dug into the rock or built up of brick within a pit, and secondly, simple rectangular or oval pits. In the more elaborate graves, the bodies were usually mummified, but there were also a number of simpler burials in which the bodies were either laid on their backs in an extended attitude, or were contracted with the knees tightly bent. This cemetery was dated by the excavator from *c.* 750 to 425 BC.[1]

It is again not clear what the real significance of these differences is, although we are certainly in the presence of two separate cultural traditions, one Egyptian, representing perhaps a section of the native population influenced by Egyptian ideas rather than actual Egyptians, and the other maintaining a burial custom which was entirely indigenous. The material from the graves is much of it of Egyptian style: it consists in the main of pottery, beads, faience amulets in considerable variety, and a small number of metal objects both of copper and iron. Amongst the pottery however are a certain number of vessels of non-Egyptian type. These, unlike the wheel-made pottery of Egyptian style, are made by hand and are in a very old Sudanese tradition of pottery, with incised decoration going back to 'C-Group' times of about 2000 BC, and which became once more rather popular after about 300 BC. This, together with the non-Egyptian style of burial, is our only information for the persistence of a native tradition, which presumably continued to affect a large proportion, perhaps the majority, of the population away from the main centres where Egyptian cultural influence was at its strongest. Further evidence for this indigenous culture will probably only be obtained when dwelling-sites, and particularly non-urban ones, in the region of Napata have been identified and investigated.

The only place where information is now available about the living rather than the dead at this time is from the recent excavations by the present writer at Meroe. Here it seems that there was occupation from some time well before 500 BC, perhaps going back earlier than *c.* 750 BC.

[1] F. Ll. Griffith, 'Oxford excavations in Nubia', *Liverpool Annals of Archaeology and Anthropology*, 1923, 10, 73.

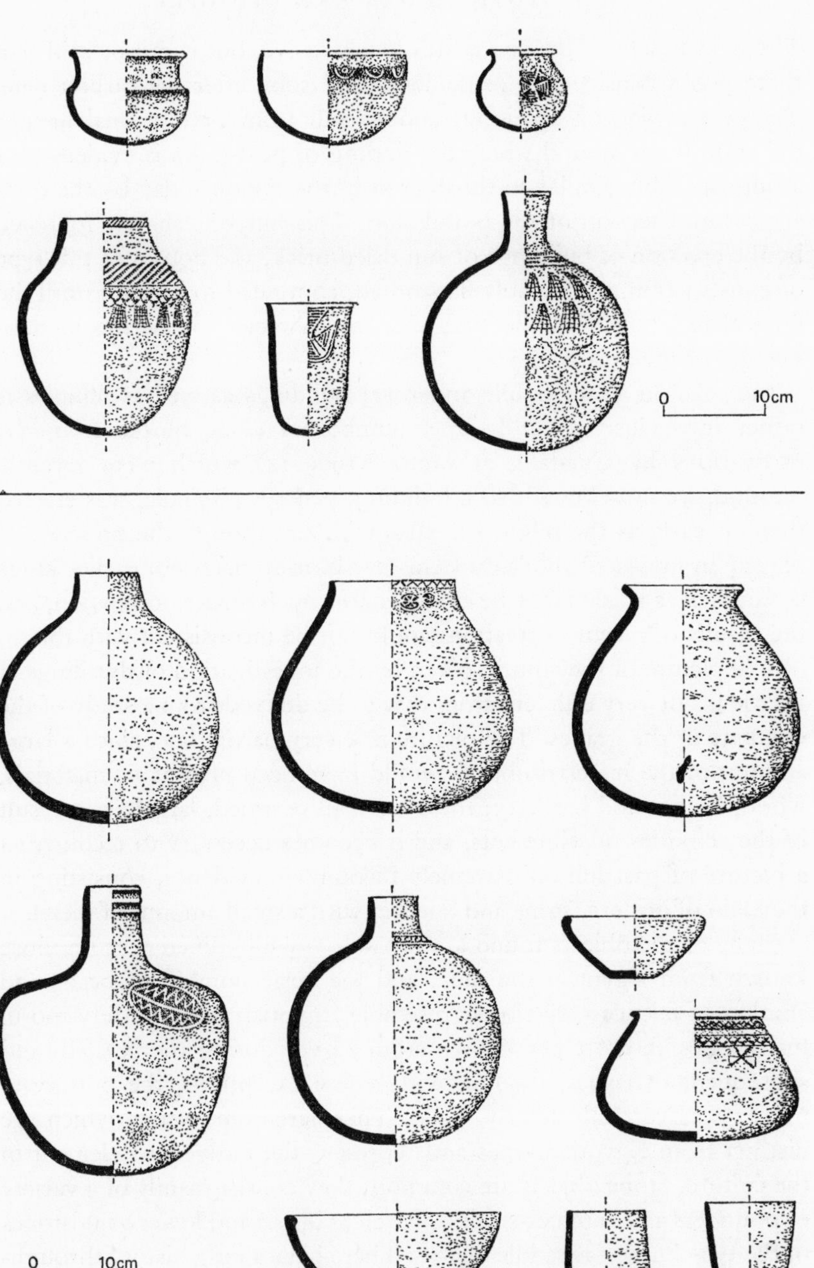

31 Meroitic domestic pottery of non-Egyptian styles.
(After Shinnie, *Meroe*, fig. 41, and plates 56–9, the latter courtesy The Ashmolean Museum, Oxford.)

The evidence from the site is still inconclusive, but it can be said that there was a considerable settlement from soon after the earliest date. The very earliest occupation is known only from a rather small area of the main town mound where the finding of post-holes is evidence for a hut, probably similar to those used in the region today by the non-agricultural section of the population. This hut was shortly followed by the erection of buildings of sun-dried brick, and houses of this type of construction, presumably flat-roofed, continued to be built until the final abandonment of the site, and are characteristic of the modern villages of the area.

Information about public and royal buildings as well as temples is rather inconclusive, but from a number of stone blocks from the excavations by Garstang at Meroe (1909–14) which were recently refound, we now know that a building, perhaps a temple, was erected there as early as the reign of Senkamanisken, though the presence of objects in graves of the West Cemetery bearing names of earlier kings as far back as Kashta may be evidence for much earlier occupation, and the results of recent excavation would not be inconsistent with this.

The picture of the culture given by the investigation of dwellings at Meroe is not very different from that to be derived from a study of the contents of the graves. The picture is a very partial one, since a large amount of the material objects would have been of organic materials, wood, leather and basketry; these have all perished, largely as a result of the activities of white ants, and it becomes necessary to reconstruct a picture of past life on extremely incomplete evidence, consisting in the main of pottery, stone and faience, with a small amount of metal.

Many of the objects found are not substantially different from those known from Egypt at the time, and the large number of beads and amulets of faience very closely resemble Egyptian ones. Pottery too in many cases shows types known from Egypt during the XXVth and subsequent dynasties, though, with a few exceptions, the pottery at Meroe was certainly locally made. There are some wares which are distinct from Egyptian types and represent the indigenous element in the culture. Stone objects are common; they consist mainly of a variety of pounders and hammer-stones, as well as upper and lower grindstones of the type known as saddle querns. These have a long history throughout the world and are still in use today, including in the region round Meroe, for grinding grain as well as other substances such as spices, cosmetics and various types of incense.

The picture we get of the culture of the time is that of an organized state with a ruling house, which in the tradition of ancient Oriental monarchies may have had considerable powers, but whose claim to the throne appears to have been based on choice by a consensus of opinion, rather than by direct right of succession. Succession, where we have evidence for it from inscriptions – and this means only from early times – was from brother to brother, and the mother of the king, to be known in later times as Candace, was of considerable importance. Of the nature of Meroitic administration we know little, but to maintain rule over such a long stretch of river valley must have called for some form of organization able to carry the king's instructions through the country. Temple priesthoods certainly played an important part, even in the selection of the ruler, and, if the story about Ergamenes is correct, they had the power to remove the king, at least until about the middle of the third century BC. Much of the wealth of the country was probably in their hands.

Most of the population was probably living in villages in huts of wood and straw which have left virtually no trace, and many of the inhabitants away from the river are likely to have been nomads, or at least semi-nomads, practising transhumance like many of the dwellers in the Butana today. These people, who during the dry season dwell close to the river, move away from it as soon as the rain begins to fall in June or July, and travel eastwards along a number of large wadis in whose beds they plant sorghum as soon as sufficient rain has fallen. They also take herds of cattle up to the grazing grounds, and the same may well have been the practice in Meroitic times.

The urban population lived in buildings of sun-dried brick as already described, and it seems likely that there were a number of large towns in existence before 500 BC. Evidence from Meroe, where blocks from a Temple of Malenaqen (*c*. 550 BC) have been found, makes it certain that there was a town of considerable size there by that date; there may have been one at Napata, even if it has not been found, and it is highly likely that the large mound at Kawa, only superficially examined so far, covers another town beginning far back in early Napatan times. We know of other towns – Danqeil, north of Berber, and Wad ben Naqa, south of Meroe – while several large mounds which probably cover other towns lie close to the river between Meroe and Wad ben Naqa. There may also have been a town associated with the several temples at Naqa, though until that site has been investigated we cannot say how early was the first occupation there. A date of 500 BC is conservative, and it may well be that there were flourishing towns as early as the time of Taharqa. The remarkable and unique complex of temples at Musawwarat es-Sofra appears to go back at least to the fifth century BC, and there may have been buildings even earlier. Since several of these towns lie upstream of Napata, the view that Kushite civilization began at Napata, as a provincial copy of Egyptian culture of the time, and spread south only at some time in the fourth century, requires revision: the southern province of Kush was certainly of importance by 500 BC.

The discovery that there was a considerable urban settlement at Meroe well before 500 BC, and perhaps as early as the eighth or ninth centuries, may therefore be an indication that Meroe was of equal importance to, perhaps of even greater importance than, Napata in the first centuries of Kush. Such a view would help to explain some of the indigenous elements in the life of the country. It is not, however, an essential prerequisite for explaining non-Egyptian elements, since there had been a long-standing independent tradition certainly since the time, *c.* 2000 BC, when Sudanese chiefs had ruled at Kerma and traded with Egypt.

The only certain fact about a transfer of authority from Napata to Meroe, if such ever happened, is that by about 300 BC the place of royal burial had been moved from Nuri to Meroe, where the cemetery was to remain for as long as there was an organized Meroitic kingdom. Since, as has been seen, the royal residence had been at Meroe for a century or more before this, the assumption is that this marked some important change in the religious centre. Napata, whether or not it had been a royal residence and administrative centre, was certainly of great religious importance, and the implication of the ceremonies that kings underwent there is that the Temple of Amun at Barkal enshrined the centre of the royal cult. The later history of this temple is somewhat obscure, but though it was not abandoned, and some restoration and even new building was carried out there in the first century BC and early first century AD, its importance had probably considerably decreased.

There are pyramids at Barkal which on stylistic grounds should date from the first century BC, so the area had not lost all its former importance, and Reisner suggested that during this time there was an independent state centred at Napata.[1] In assessing the significance of Napata, it is perhaps noteworthy that although Herodotus mentions Meroe as the metropolis, Strabo, writing in about 7 BC, clearly thought that Napata was the royal residence and says so in the unambiguous words: 'Napata,

[1] G. A. Reisner, 'The Meroitic Kingdom of Ethiopia', *Journal of Egyptian Archaeology*, 1923, **9**, 59–62.

Plate I Iron-smelting furnace at Meroe. [ch. 4]
(Photo: P. L. Shinnie.)

Plate 2 Scenes on the Sun Temple at Meroe. [ch. 4]
(Photo: J. Garstang; courtesy School of Archaeology and Oriental Studies, University of Liverpool.)

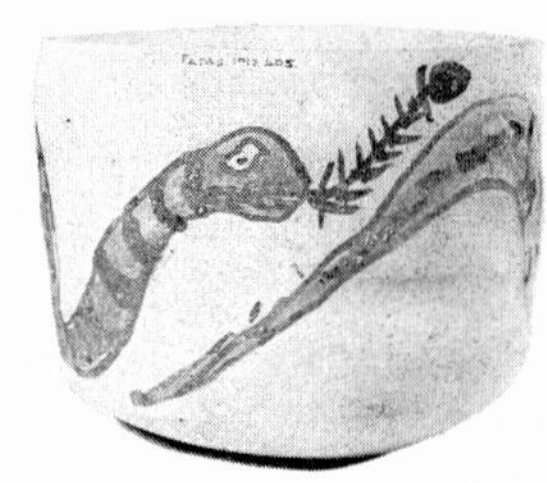

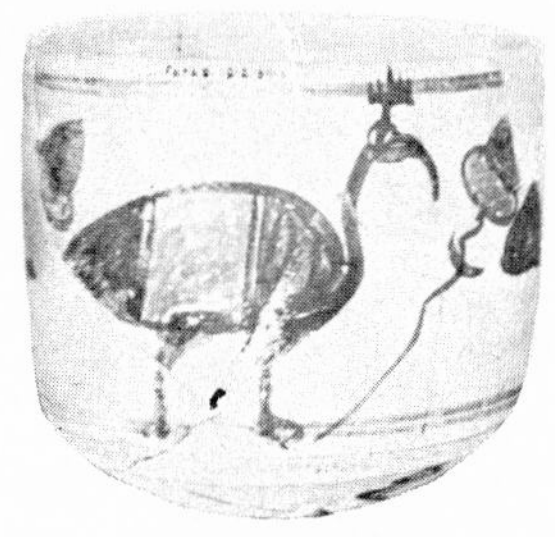

Plate 3 Meroitic pottery.
Actual sizes, from top left: 8.7 cm, 7.4 cm, 6.8 cm, 7.5 cm, 7.6 cm, 9.0 cm, 15.0 cm. [ch. 4]
(Photos courtesy Ashmolean Museum, Oxford.)

Plate 4 The Kiosk at Naqa. [ch. 4]
(Photo: P. L. Shinnie.)

Plate 5 Aksum: standing stelae. [ch. 4]
(Photo courtesy British Institute
in Eastern Africa [B.I.E.A.].)

Plate 6 Aksum: fallen stele. [ch. 4]
(Photo: B.I.E.A.)

Plate 7 Aksum, Stele Park: detail on main stele. [ch. 4] (Photo: B.I.E.A.)

Plate 8 Aksum: 'Tomb of the False Door'. [ch. 4] (Photo: B.I.E.A.)

Plate 9 Aksum: entrance to the Mausoleum. [ch. 4]
(Photo: B.I.E.A.)

Plate 10 Aksum: 'Tomb of the Brick Arches'
(entrance archway, showing brickwork). [ch. 4]
(Photo: B.I.E.A.)

this was the royal residence of Candace', having already stated a little earlier that Candace was ruler of the Ethiopians. Although the Amun Temple at Meroe in the form now known does not seem to be earlier than the first century BC, no investigation has been carried out to see if there was an earlier building there. But this is extremely likely, and it may be, as already suggested, that this temple took the place of that at Barkal and became the centre of the Amun cult. Perhaps it was here, rather than, as is usually supposed, at Napata, that Ergamenes carried out his coup against the Amun priesthood.

Whatever the reality may be, from about 300 BC Meroe became both royal residence and royal cemetery and the site of a large temple dedicated to Amun, who maintained the position of official state god, a notion originally derived from Egypt, although from this time onwards several local deities begin to be known and have temples built for their worship.

Fortunately, unlike Napata, the town of Meroe is known and identified, and many facets of Meroitic life and funeral customs can be studied here. Descriptions of the site can be found elsewhere, and all that need be said here is that the town, standing about 500 m from the present east river bank, consists of a large complex containing both a walled area – conventionally, and probably rightly, known as the Royal City – containing large public buildings – some perhaps being the royal residence – together with a very remarkable bath and several small temples, the large Temple of Amun outside the wall to the east, and two large mounds which cover the buildings of the non-royal town, one of which has been investigated during the last few years (fig. 32). Small temples discovered during 1974–6 suggest a ceremonial way running east from the Amun Temple towards the Sun Temple. The town complex is bounded on the east by a number of mounds of slag, the debris from iron-working activities (pl. 1). Within this area are the remains of several small shrines, two of which are built on top of an artificially made mound constructed of iron slag. Further east lies another temple, that conventionally known as the 'Sun Temple' (pl. 2), close beside an artificially made reservoir, and the cemeteries. These cemeteries fall into several groups. Nearest to the town are a large number of simple mound graves, investigated by Garstang and grouped by him into three: South (graves 1–99), Middle (300–99), and North (500–99); these cemeteries are all rather late in the history of the town, do not appear to be earlier than the first century BC, and continued in use until AD 300 or later. Beyond them to the east lie the better-known three groups of pyramids which contain the royal burials. Of these

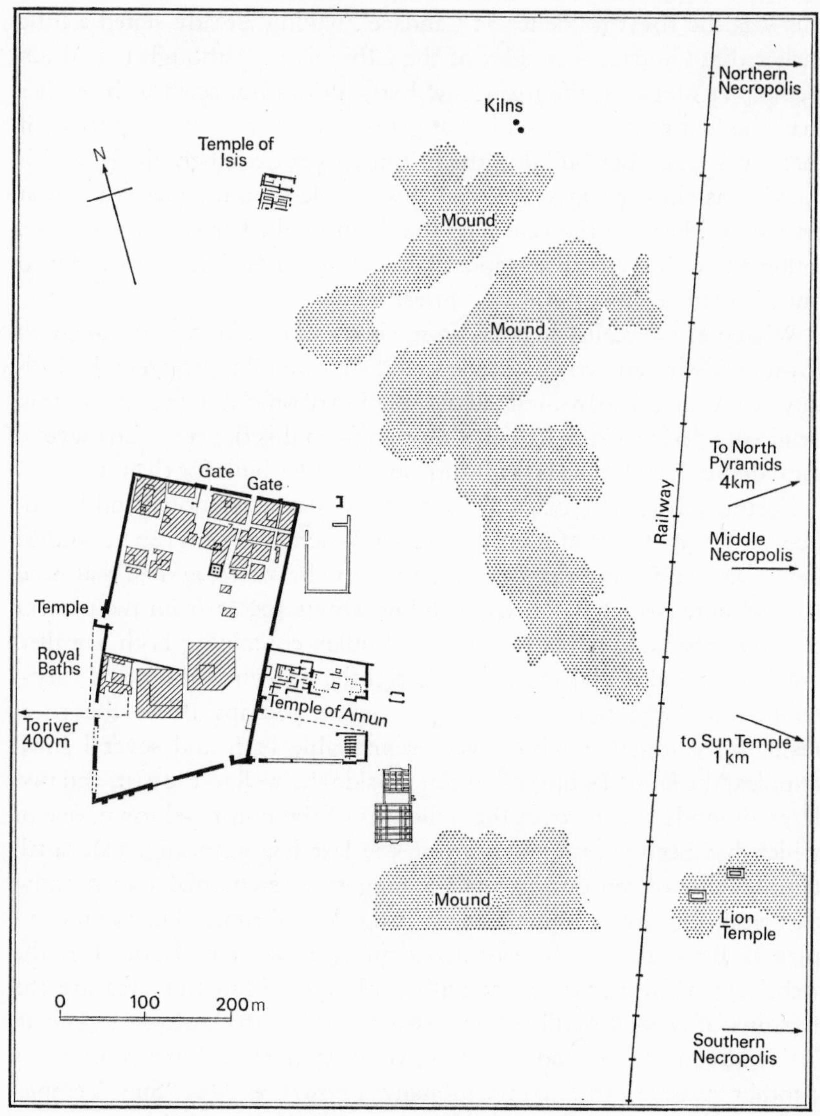

32 Plan of the town of Meroe.
(After Shinnie, *Meroe*, fig. 19.)

three cemeteries, the south one appears to be the oldest, with graves going back well into the eighth century BC. It was only towards the end of the use of this cemetery that rulers were buried in it, and the pyramid of Arakakamani, the first ruler to be buried at Meroe, is here. Only two other rulers' burial-places are known from this cemetery: those of

Amanislo, already mentioned as moving the Prudhoe lions, and of Queen Bartare, both assumed to be direct successors of Arakakamani (though Wenig would remove Bartare's name from the list of rulers, together with several other queens usually so listed, on the grounds that though they have the title Candace, they do not carry the title *qere* which seems normal for rulers).[1] After this the cemetery was abandoned, presumably because there was no convenient space left, and all later rulers seem to have been buried under pyramids erected along the ridge a short way further north. The third group of burials, the West Cemetery, lies between those two and the town, and, although it contains a number of pyramids, it does not appear that any rulers were buried there. This cemetery covers a long time-span, and it is usually assumed that many of those buried there were related to the royal family.

Since there are no detailed inscriptions in Egyptian, other than ones of a purely religious nature, it is impossible to give any account of events during the time of the first rulers to be buried at Meroe. Even the restoration of the list of rulers and identification of their burial-places is fraught with difficulty. For example, no pyramid can certainly be identified with Arnekhamani, though he is well known from his inscription at Musawwarat es-Sofra. Pyramid N. 53 is attributed to him, but this is only a guess, since no name has been found on the pyramid itself. The argument for the attribution is that, from its location, this pyramid should belong in the later third century BC, and that the burial-chamber is the only three-roomed one, that is of the type associated with kings, in the period immediately before Arqamani.

There seems little doubt that Arakakamani was the first to be buried at Meroe in the South Cemetery, and that pyramid N. 4 was the first to be erected on the north ridge. The name of the ruler buried there is damaged in the chapel inscription, but what is left can be read as 'Amani . . . tekha'. Arqamani, presumably to be identified with Ergamenes, came soon after, perhaps succeeding Arnekhamani. The problems concerning his identification and date have already been discussed, as have his temple-building activities in Lower Nubia (p. 228), which perhaps suggest a Meroitic invasion and occupation of the region during his reign. This, implying closer contact with Egypt, whether friendly or hostile, may account for the good Egyptian style of his chapel reliefs.

There is a great deal of uncertainty about the names of the next few rulers. A Queen Shanakdakhete is known from an inscription in a

[1] Wenig, 'Bemerkungen zur Chronologie', 3–4. See also p. 248.

temple at Naqa – it is the first in Meroitic hieroglyphs to be approximately dated, the conventional date for this queen being 170–160 BC. She may have been buried under Beg. N. 11. The chronological order of the pyramids is entirely dependent on a study, originally made by Reisner, of the architectural styles and the tomb contents, and though later study may change it in detail, the over-all arrangement is likely to be right. Another ruler from about this time is Tanyidamani, whose name occurs twice at Barkal, once on a stele, and on a votive tablet from the Lion Temple at Meroe as well as in a graffito at Musawwarat. It is guessed that he was buried under pyramid Beg. N. 20, which is of a style which marks something of a change from what went before: it is smaller than earlier ones, and the burial-chamber consists of only two rooms instead of the three which were previously used.

Since there are pyramids at Barkal which, architecturally, seem to belong to this time, Reisner assumed that there had been another independent line of rulers at that place. But the finding of Tanyidamani's name at Meroe, and the wide geographical distribution of the names of some of his successors, make this unlikely. The list of rulers drawn up by Hintze also allows for a separate group, whom he assumes to have been buried at Barkal and therefore to have ruled from there; this includes Akinidad, Teriteqas and a Queen Amanirenas, whose names have been found in the north, at Dakka and at Kawa, but are also known from Meroe. Since there is a large inscription from the temple at Hamdab, close to Meroe, bearing the name of Akinidad, it seems most improbable that he was ruling from Napata.

This period, at the end of the first century BC and the beginning of the first century AD, is of considerable complexity and importance. It marks a flowering of Meroitic culture and is the time when most of the artistic attributes normally described as Meroitic were developed. There are more buildings and inscriptions known from this period than from any other, and the reliefs on pyramid chapels, which comprise the greater part of Meroitic art, mainly date from this time, as do most of the pieces of sculpture in the round. The pyramid chapel reliefs are perhaps the most important for the study of artistic change and development, since some attempt can be made to date them. These reliefs, which span nearly six hundred years, provide a mass of valuable information for the study of Meroitic art, iconography and religious ideas, and show a development from the Hellenistic Egyptian style of such chapels as that of Arqamani at the very end of the third century, to those like Beg. N. 11, perhaps of Queen Shanakdakhete, where more distinctive Meroitic elements are seen in a procession of small figures, representing priests bearing palm branches (a scene which was to persist in these depictions down to the end of the Meroitic state; the last one is at pyramid Beg. N. 26 of about AD 300), as well as in the completely non-Egyptian style of representation of royalty. The chapel of Queen Amanishakhete (Beg. N. 6) of the very end of the first century BC is a good example of this; the depiction of the queen as a very plump woman, with neck wrinkles and face scars is distinctively Meroitic. So also are the details of clothing and personal adornment, the fringed garment worn over the right shoulder, the tassels hanging from the shoulders and the large beads.

In the art of this period we see a distinctive Meroitic culture – certainly owing much to Egypt, but also with a marked flavour and character of its own. It can be assumed that this art developed first at Meroe, and that the main centre of artistic activity was there close to the royal court. Certainly the chapel reliefs are there, and probably more examples of the art have been found at Meroe than anywhere else. There may have been other influences from outside in some aspects of Meroitic art, and there are hints of eastern and Syrian elements but, however this may have been, native genius was the most important element in creating a distinctive art style which continued in being for several hundred years and contributed something to succeeding civilizations. Perhaps the most distinctive Meroitic contribution was in its pottery (pl. 3). Indeed, pottery, by virtue of the quantity in which it has been found as well as by the high artistic quality of some of it, is the best known of all the products of Meroitic culture. The fine painted wares, such as the famous 'egg-shell' pottery with its range of painted decoration, have been much admired, and so too has much of the rather larger and thicker wares grouped by Adams into his group II, 'Meroitic Utility', where the larger surface areas allowed the artist to develop more elaborate anthropomorphic and zoomorphic designs. The smaller and finer pots tend to have more conventional designs, in many cases of Egyptian origin, such as the *ankh*, the lotus and the Uraeus, but they also at times carry zoomorphic designs which are surely based on local observation, as in one sherd recently found at Meroe showing a guinea-fowl, giraffes etc. This particular pottery style and ware does not have a very long time-range – it may not go back earlier than the beginning of the first century AD and it lasted perhaps for two hundred years. But its importance as a fresh, new artistic form of considerable merit cannot be overestimated.

This was also the period of Meroe's closest contact with the world of the Mediterranean, when it was best known to that world, and could be regarded as an extension of it. Certainly some travellers, perhaps merchants and scholars, from the classical world visited Meroe, and the names of several are given by Pliny, amongst them Simonides, who is said to have resided at Meroe for five years. A little later, in the third century AD, Meroe was the setting for the literary work, the *Aethiopica* of Heliodorus, in which the heroine was daughter of the King of Meroe. This shows that the town and kingdom were well known at that time. It is presumably to an event in the first century AD that the story in the Acts of the Apostles about the eunuch of Candace who was baptized by Philip refers.

A number of objects of Mediterranean origin, both Hellenistic and Roman, have been found in the royal burials and amongst the ruins of the town of Meroe. One of these pieces is an Attic rhyton, a pottery vessel for the pouring of libations, bearing the signature of the well-known Athenian potter Sotades (*c*. 400 BC). This remarkable object was found in tomb Beg. S. 24, and is good evidence for dating the tomb later than the beginning of the fourth century BC, though no greater precision can be given on the evidence of the rhyton alone, since there is no way of knowing how long such a piece might have been kept – perhaps as an heirloom – before being placed in a burial. Beg. S. 24 is regarded as being dated approximately to 350 BC. Apart from this, a fine gilded silver goblet of Roman work dating from the first century AD was discovered amongst the fallen blocks of Beg. N. 2, and other pieces of artistic merit have been found.

The finding of these pieces suggests that trade between the eastern Mediterranean, principally Alexandria, and Meroe was considerable. It can be presumed that the goods sent in exchange were the precious natural products of the country which had been exchanged for manufactured objects since early pharaonic times (see p. 220). Although a scattering of Ptolemaic and Roman coins has been found at Meroe and other places, the Meroites themselves never developed a coinage.

We know very little about the routes by which Meroitic trade was carried on, but it seems likely that two main lines of traffic were in use. It is improbable that the river carried much trade, and such trade as went directly north to Egypt from Meroe is more likely to have left the river at Abu Hamed and gone across the desert to Korosko, from where goods could have been loaded on boats for Egypt with only the First Cataract to negotiate. Certainly after the introduction of the camel, this desert route, which continued in use until recent times, would have presented no great difficulty. The other route, which may have been the most important, would have gone eastwards across the Butana (Island of Meroe) to the Red Sea, and then either northwards to one of the Egyptian Red Sea ports, such as Berenice, or across to Arabia and then northwards to Syria. This route had been in use for centuries, as is shown by the famous voyage to Punt in the reign of Hatshepsut (*c.* 1500 BC), since whatever the precise location of Punt, it was certainly at the southern end of the Red Sea. No trace of routes across the Butana to the sea have yet been found, but since these would have been mere caravan trails they would have left little trace. However, we know that the Ptolemys, and after them the Romans, were trading along the coast, and after the Roman trade to India began in the second century AD, there must have been watering-stations at the very least. There is good information for the time of the Ptolemies, and it is known that in the search for war-elephants, with which to oppose the Indian elephants of their Seleukid rivals, many expeditions were sent to the east coast of Africa and the harbour of Ptolemais Theron was established. Strabo, though writing somewhat after the event, describes the establishment of what was a trading post rather than a formal harbour by Eumedes, who had been sent by Ptolemy II. It continued in use into the first century AD (or, if new ideas on the dating of the *Periplus* are right, somewhat later), when it was described by the writer of *The Periplus of the Erythrean Sea* as a small trading town without harbour installations. The trade in elephants had ceased by then, the African elephant having been found inferior to the Indian one for war purposes, but the *Periplus* says that ivory was obtained. The site of Ptolemais has not been identified with certainty, but Crowfoot, basing himself on the rather tenuous topographical indications given by classical writers and on the finding of one stone block with Hellenistic-style mouldings, proposed that it was at the site of the modern settlement of Aqiq.[1]

MEROE AND THE ROMAN EMPIRE

Meroe came fully into the classical world with the invasion of its northern region by the Roman governor of Egypt, Publius Petronius, in the year 23 BC. This campaign was the first serious Roman incursion into Meroitic territory, though an inscription at Philae of Gaius

[1] J. W. Crowfoot, 'Some Red Sea ports in the Anglo-Egyptian Sudan', *Geographical Journal*, 1911, 37, 530–4.

Cornelius Gallus, the first Roman prefect of Egypt, describes his taking an army south of the First Cataract, where he received envoys from the King of Meroe, perhaps Amanikhabale, and took him into Roman protection in 29 BC. We have no other evidence for this event and it may in part be Roman boasting. If the date is right, then Hintze's date for Amanikhabale needs adjusting, since he has Queen Amanishakhete reigning at this time.

By the time of Petronius, who became governor in 28 BC, there had been considerable contact between Roman Egypt and the Meroites, mostly at Philae, where an annual pilgrimage to the Temple of Isis was an important event in the life of Lower Nubia until it was prohibited by Justinian in the sixth century AD. The frontier seems at this time to have been just south of Syene (modern Aswan) and relations were in the main friendly, but, apparently taking advantage of the absence of part of the Roman garrison in Egypt, the Meroites attacked Syene, Philae and Elephantine; the account by Strabo implies that Dakka (Pselchis) lay within the area of Meroitic rule. The military events were recorded by Strabo, Pliny and Dio Cassius. Strabo's account (Bk XVII, Pt 1, Secs. 53, 54) is the fullest and says:

Now Egypt was generally inclined to peace from the outset, because of the self-sufficiency of the country, and of the difficulty of invasion by outsiders, being protected on the north by a harbourless coast, and by the Egyptian sea, and on the east and west by the desert mountains of Libya and Arabia, as I have said; and the remaining parts, those towards the south, are inhabited by Troglodytes, Blemmyes, Nubae, and Megabari, those Ethiopians who live above Syene. These are nomads, and not numerous, or warlike either, though they were thought to be so by the ancients, because often, like brigands, they would attack defenceless persons. As for those Ethiopians who extend towards the south of Meroe, they are not numerous either, nor do they collect in one mass, inasmuch as they inhabit a long, narrow and winding stretch of river-land, such as I have described before; neither are they well equipped for warfare or for any other kind of life. And now, too, the whole of the country is similarly disposed to peace. And the following is a sign of the fact; the country is sufficiently guarded by the Romans with only three cohorts, and even these are not complete, and when the Ethiopians dared to make an attack upon them, they imperilled their own country. The remaining Roman forces in Egypt are hardly as large as these . . .

But the Ethiopians, emboldened by the fact that a part of the Roman force in Egypt had been drawn away with Aelius Gallus when he was carrying on war against the Arabians, attacked the Thebais and the garrison of the three cohorts at Syene and by an unexpected onset took Syene and Elephantine and Philae, and enslaved the inhabitants, and also pulled down the statues of Caesar. But Petronius, setting out with less than 10,000 infantry and 800 cavalry against 30,000 men, first forced them to flee back to Pselchis, an Ethiopian city, and sent ambassadors to demand what they had taken, as also to ask the reasons whey they had begun war; and when they said that they had been wronged by the Monarchs, he replied that these were not rulers of the country but Caesar; and when they had requested three days for deliberation, but did nothing they should have done, he made an attack and forced them to come forth to battle; and he quickly turned them to flight. since they were badly marshalled and badly armed; for they had large shields, and those too made of raw oxhide, and as weapons some had only axes, others pikes, and others swords. Now some were driven together into the city, others fled into the desert, and others found refuge on a neighbouring island, having waded into the channel, for on account of the current the crocodiles were not numerous there. Among these fugitives were the generals of Queen Candace, who was a ruler of the Ethiopians in my time – a masculine sort of woman, and blind in one eye. These, one and all, he captured alive, having sailed after them in both rafts and ships, and he sent them forthwith down to Alexandria; and he also attacked Pselchis and captured it; and if the multitude of those who fell in the battle be added to the number of the captives, those who escaped must have been altogether few in number. From Pselchis he went to Premnis, a fortified city, after passing through the sand-dunes, where the army of Cambyses was overwhelmed when a wind-storm struck them; and having made an attack, he took the fortress at the first onset. After this he set out for Napata. This was the royal residence of Candace; and her son was there, and she herself was residing at a place near by. But though she sent ambassadors to treat for friendship and offered to give back the captives and the statues brought from Syene, Petronius attacked and captured Napata too, from which her son had fled, and razed it to the ground; and having enslaved its inhabitants, he turned back again with the booty, having decided that the regions farther on would be hard to traverse. But he fortified Premnis better, threw in a garrison and food for four hundred men for two years, and set out for Alexandria. As for the captives, he sold some of them as booty, and sent one thousand to Caesar, who had recently returned from Cantabria; and the others died of diseases. Meantime Candace marched against the garrison with many thousands of men, but Petronius set out to its assistance and arrived at the fortress first; and when he had made the place thoroughly secure by sundry devices, ambassadors came, but he bade them to go to Caesar; and when they asserted that they did not know who Caesar was or where they should have to go to find him, he gave them escorts; and they went to Samos, since Caesar was there and intended to proceed to Syria from there, after despatching Tiberius to Armenia. And when the ambassadors had obtained everything they pled for, he even remitted the tributes which he had imposed.

From this account it is clear that the Meroitic attack is to be considered as a raid for booty rather than as an invasion, and the famous bronze head of the Emperor Augustus, now in the British Museum, which was found during the earlier excavations at Meroe (1909–14), may have been part of such booty and was perhaps from one of the statues which Strabo says were pulled down. It should be noted that Strabo, as well as the other classical writers, claims that the capital of the Meroites was at Napata, and that this was the residence of Queen Candace. This has been used as an argument to support the view that at this time there was an independent line of rulers at Napata who were buried at Barkal. In view of the discovery of the head of the statue of Augustus at Meroe, and of the occurrence of the names of approximately contemporary Meroitic rulers both at Meroe and in the north, it seems more likely that Strabo and Pliny were misinformed, though the persistence of a tradition that Napata was a royal residence suggests that it was still of importance, and there is no reason why royalty should not have resided there from time to time. Many African rulers, both ancient and modern, have been peripatetic, and even if Meroe were the main centre, the rulers may well have had other centres where they stayed on occasion. If a large military force with the ruler in command had been formed to oppose the Romans, it is only reasonable to suppose that the commander would not have stayed back at Meroe.

The mention of Candace (*Kandake*) by both Strabo and Dio Cassius is interesting, as is also the mention of her in the Acts of the Apostles, even though Strabo misunderstood what we now know to be a title as a personal name. The title is known from a number of examples, of which the earliest is that of Bartare, buried under pyramid Beg. S. 10 in *c.* 250 BC, and although the exact significance is not clear, it is likely to be a high title meaning 'queen', 'queen mother' or something very similar. Recently it has been suggested (cf. p. 241) that the title does not mean that the bearer of it was a ruler, the Meroitic word for which was *qere*, but that it designated some important female royal or administrative function in Meroitic society; unless the title *qere* is also given, the Candace was not a ruler. If this is correct, 'queen mother' may be the best translation.

There are four Meroitic royal personages known from about this time. The names are found in widely scattered places and in various arrangements and associations. The names are of two women, Amanirenas and Amanishakhete, both of whom bear the title *qere* as well as Candace, and were therefore presumably ruling queens, and two men, Akinidad and Teriteqas. The burial-place of only one of these four is known – that of Amanishakhete, who was buried under pyramid Beg. N. 6, the pyramid in which, it is alleged, was found the magnificent find of jewellery taken away by an Italian adventurer, Ferlini, in 1834.

No certain burial-place is known for the others, but close contemporaneity is shown by the occurrence of Amanishakhete's name with that of Akinidad on a stele recently found at Qasr Ibrim, whilst Akinidad is associated with Teriteqas and Amanirenas in an inscription on the temple at Dakka, and also at Meroe.

Occurrences of the names of these rulers are widely enough scattered for it to be assumed that they controlled the whole area of Meroitic culture. The following list shows where they appear:

Teriteqas:	Dakka, Meroe
Amanirenas:	Dakka, Meroe, Hamdab, Kawa
Akinidad:	Qasr Ibrim, Dakka, Kawa, Meroe, Hamdab
Amanishakhete:	Qasr Ibrim, Meroe, Kawa

It is not possible with any certainty to determine their relationships and to know which of them opposed the Romans, but an examination of how the names are grouped may help.

(1) Teriteqas as king, Amanirenas (his consort?), and Akinidad occur together at Dakka; Teriteqas also occurs on a small stele from the Isis Temple at Meroe, with the name of Amanirenas associated.

(2) Amanirenas, in addition to the two occurrences already mentioned, also has her name coupled with that of Akinidad at Kawa and at Hamdab, a suburb of Meroe.

(3) Akinidad is known additionally to the above from a separate inscription at Dakka, on a block from Kawa, and in association with Amanishakhete at Qasr Ibrim.

(4) Amanishakhete is known from her pyramid (Beg. N. 6.), on a block from Kawa which is stylistically very similar to that of Akinidad, on an obelisk in the Amun temple at Meroe, and at Qasr Ibrim.

So Teriteqas, Amanirenas and Akinidad are associated in different arrangements, all three together, Teriteqas and Amanirenas, and Akinidad and Amanirenas. The situation is further complicated by the Qasr Ibrim stele which bears the names of Akinidad and Amanishakhete, a combination not previously known.

The two large stelae from the Hamdab temple have been assumed to contain a record of the campaign against the Romans, and it has usually been considered that Amanirenas was Strabo's Candace. A neat scheme was suggested by Hintze,[1] in which the Dakka inscription of three royalties is taken to mean that all three went there at the beginning of the campaign, that Teriteqas died and was succeeded by Akinidad (his son?)

[1] Hintze, *Studien*, 24–9.

who, together with his mother Amanirenas, continued the war, attacking Philae and Syene, and carrying off the bronze statue of the emperor. Perhaps the Hamdab stele was set up to celebrate the victory, short-lived though it was. The Roman counter-attack was quickly successful against a Meroitic army led, according to Strabo, by the son of Candace (Akinidad?), and the Romans then withdrew, leaving a garrison at Premnis (Qasr Ibrim). The Meroites failed in an attack on this fortress, and then agreed to peace terms and sent their ambassadors to the emperor, who was at Samos. If Amanishakhete were not mentioned until later, she could be assumed to have been a successor of Akinidad, but the finding of the two names in one inscription at Qasr Ibrim which, on the conventional view, must have been in Roman hands, throws doubt on the whole reconstruction, since she and Akinidad must have been associated in some way before the Romans advanced to Napata. Until the large inscriptions of Hamdab and Qasr Ibrim and the obelisk of Amanishakhete at Meroe can be translated, it is unlikely that our knowledge of the history of the period can advance very much.

But there can be no doubt that there was a serious clash between Meroites and Romans in which the Romans were ultimately victorious, and the official Roman inscription, the *Monumentum Ancyranum*, at Ankara, makes it certain that Roman troops reached Napata. The early Meroitic victory and the capture of the statue at Syene may be commemorated by the small temple, known as no. 292, at Meroe. The bronze head of Augustus was found, by Garstang in 1912, just in front of the temple, and the curious nature of the rebuilding on top of an earlier shrine of an identically sized building with a large pedestal of reused blocks in the centre may mean that this was erected as a base for a statue of which the head is all that is now known. The unusual painted scenes, which can be seen on the mud brick wall of the temple in one of Garstang's photographs, show prisoners beneath the king's feet, and nearby a human skull can be seen to have been placed in the wall. This appearance of a skull, unique in Meroitic buildings, together with the picture of prisoners, strongly suggests that the temple may have been put up, or rebuilt, to celebrate the victory and accommodate a statue of Augustus.

Shortly after this time we have evidence of considerable building activity by King Netekamani. More buildings are known bearing his name than that of any other Meroitic ruler, and they are also more widespread. His name has been found on the now destroyed temple at Amara East, well to the north; at Jebel Barkal; several times at Meroe, where also his pyramid is firmly identified; on two temples at Naqa; and at Wad ben Naqa. In most cases his name is given in association with a lady named Amanitare, and she has normally been assumed to have been his consort. This is nowhere stated in unambiguous terms, and it is possible that she was in fact the queen mother. She carried the title of Candace, but not of *qere*.

The depiction of these two personalities together, as in the pylons of the Lion Temple at Naqa, where they face each other on opposite sides of the doorway, is unique in Meroitic art, and whatever the relationship between the two it was certainly one that impressed their contemporaries. Another unusual feature is that on several occasions a younger figure, who can be termed a prince, is shown with them. There are three of these young men, and they are likely to be either children of Netekamani and Amanitare or, if the couple were not consorts, perhaps younger brothers of Netekamani. The three young men include Arikankharer, who is shown with Netekamani and Amanitare at the Lion Temple at Naqa, in the Amun temple at Meroe, and by himself in a remarkable stone plaque from Meroe (where he is shown in garments

33 King Sherkarer smiting his enemies.
Based on a rock-carving from Jebel Qeili.
(Shinnie, *Meroe*, fig. 7; by permission of Thames and Hudson.)

which suggest he was king and with his name written in a cartouche), and also on his pyramid, Beg. N. 5. Sherkarer is shown associated with his parents (?) at Amara East and by himself at Jebel Qeili, in what is the most southerly Meroitic royal representation. Finally, Arikakhatani is shown on the Amun Temple at Naqa with Netekamani and Amanitare. Of these, only Sherkarer is given in the conventional king-lists, and the Jebel Qeili carving where his name is shown in cartouches makes it certain that he should be so included. This carving is of exceptional interest since it shows the king standing with captured prisoners, before a depiction of the sun-god, who is unusually shown full face and with the sun's disk with rays behind his head, and holding in his hand what appear to be several heads of sorghum (fig. 33). This king's burial-place has not been found with certainty, but pyramid Beg. N. 10 is tentatively associated with him since, on stylistic grounds, it appears to follow immediately after that of Netekamani.

The Meroe plaque also strongly suggests that Arikankharer was king, but whether before or after Sherkarer it is not possible to say. His tomb, Beg. N. 5, is identified with certainty. It contained a number of unusual objects, one of which, a small bronze figure of a kneeling camel, is the only evidence for the existence of this animal in the Sudan at this time. Two human heads in bronze of Hellenistic style, presumably originally from statuettes, were also found here; unfortunately they are not of much help in dating, as pieces of this type have a wide time-span – from the fourth century BC to the middle of the first century AD.

THE LATER CULTURE OF MEROE

Although we lack historical detail for the period immediately following the Roman campaign, Meroitic power seems to have maintained itself, and it was a time of considerable cultural achievement. The building activities of Netekamani are good evidence for this, and the group of temples at Naqa is perhaps the clearest expression of the Meroitic achievement that we have. At this place, on the north side of the Wadi Awateib and some 30 km east of the Nile, there lay a town of considerable size. No excavation has yet been carried out there, so nothing can be said of the nature of the domestic occupation or of the large number of mounds, which seem to be of temples or public buildings. Three temples, however, still stand in a remarkable state of preservation and show different aspects of Meroitic culture and religious belief.

These three are commonly known as the Lion Temple, the Kiosk, and the Amun temple. All are different in style. The Lion Temple, dedicated to the indigenous lion-god Apedemek, is of a type that we know as distinctively Meroitic and of which several other examples exist, though none of them is as well preserved. The reconstruction of the Lion Temple of Arnekhamani at Musawwarat es-Sofra now provides another example of a still standing temple of this type. The building at Naqa consists of a simple rectangle with pylons on either side of an east-facing doorway, bearing sculptured reliefs showing Netekamani and Amanitare defeating their enemies, in a scene derived from Egyptian prototypes. The walls of the temple carry scenes of king and queen (or queen mother) together with Arikankharer worshipping a variety of gods, most of whom are from the Egyptian pantheon and who, together with the royalties, are shown in the conventional style, derived from Egypt, which shows their faces in profile. On an inside wall one god, perhaps Jupiter Sarapis, is shown full face and with a heavy beard in Roman style.

The sculptures on the outside of the back wall are perhaps the best known of all Meroitic temple reliefs and show a three-headed and four-armed Apedemek standing in the middle with Netekamani and Arikankharer on one side of him, and Amanitare and the prince once more on the other. The multi-headed and armed depiction of the lion-god has been used to argue Indian influence, but this is unlikely, since such representations in India are not known before *c.* AD 500.

Close to the Lion Temple, with its unambiguous Meroitic style, stands the small building known as the Kiosk (pl. 4), in a quite different tradition. This temple has usually been assumed to be contemporary with the Lion Temple, but there are no real grounds for this. The axes of the two buildings are not the same, and it is improbable that the Kiosk was built to form part of the Lion Temple complex, or that it was used as part of a processional way. A recent study shows that it is probably somewhat later in date, and the third century AD has been suggested.[1] It resembles a number of kiosks known from Egypt, of which the most famous is that at Philae built in the reign of Trajan (AD 98–117); it shows very strong Alexandrine influence in many of its architectural features, and may even have been designed by an Alexandrian architect, though some elements suggest indigenous influence.

The third major building at Naqa was certainly, like the Lion Temple, built in the time of Netekamani. It was a temple dedicated to the god Amun and, like the temple of the same god at Meroe, its layout is

[1] T. Kraus, 'Der Kiosk von Naga', *Archäologische Anzeiger*, 1964, 834–68.

essentially of Egyptian style, approached along an avenue lined with stone rams. The entrance, flanked by pylons, leads into a pillared court, and there then follow a series of rooms leading to the shrine where originally stood the statue of the god. Although of Egyptian plan, the temple is covered with scenes of distinctively Meroitic style showing Netekamani, Amanitare, and this time the third young man, Arikakhatani, and with inscriptions in Meroitic hieroglyphs. Thus Naqa provides architectural examples of the main strands of Meroitic culture, and shows how the Meroites borrowed from Egypt and the Mediterranean to produce a distinctive artistic tradition of a new kind which, though drawing on models from outside, turned them into something quite different. Evidence for earlier buildings at Naqa is to be seen in another temple, which bears the name of Queen Shanakdakhete of early in the second century BC.

Since it was the discovery (at the site of Wad ben Naqa, at the mouth of the Wadi Awateib on the Nile) of the names of Netekamani and Amanitare written in both Egyptian and Meroitic hieroglyphs that made possible the decipherment of the Meroitic writing, this is perhaps an appropriate place to discuss the problem of the Meroitic language and inscriptions. All known inscriptions up to the early second century BC are in the ancient Egyptian language. Though they show widely different levels of understanding of that language, it is probable that Egyptian was the official language. Many of them, in particular those of the earlier kings from Piankhy to Aspelta, show complete control of the language and are linguistically no different from equivalent documents from Egypt itself. But as time went on knowledge of Egyptian decreased, and some of the later documents, such as those of Harsiotef and Nastasen in the fourth century BC, show extremely little knowledge of standard Egyptian grammar. The local language, which we can call Meroitic, seems to have influenced the writing, and the inscriptions strongly suggest that they had been translated into Egyptian by scribes whose knowledge of that language was limited. There were still to be some periods in which correct Egyptian was written, and the Lion Temple of Arnekhamani at Musawwarat es-Sofra contains such inscriptions; even as late as the time of Netekamani, writing in Egyptian is found. So the development of a system for writing the indigenous language does not necessarily mean that it was so developed only because Egyptian was no longer known, and it may well be that the development of a feeling of cultural independence, which one can assume to have increased from the time of the first royal burials at Meroe, caused the Meroites to wish to write in their own language. Whatever the reason, by the early part of the second century BC a writing system had been developed, and it is first known from the inscription of Queen Shanakdakhete (*c.* 170–160 BC) in temple F at Naqa, already referred to.

Although Meroitic used Egyptian signs, or modifications of them, for its writing, it made a fundamental change in the way in which they were used by selecting only twenty-three of them and using them as an alphabet or a simple syllabary. Two separate systems were developed, one using Egyptian hieroglyphs (it is with these signs that Shankdakhete's inscription is written), and another, usually rather unsuitably known as 'cursive', in which much-abbreviated equivalents are used. There is an exact correlation between the two systems and many, if not all, the 'cursive' signs seem to be based on the late Egyptian writing known as hieratic. It is not possible to be sure when the 'cursive' writing was introduced, though it was presumably also in the second century BC. The two systems continued to be used concurrently, though hieroglyphs were used only for more formal inscriptions and became rare after the first century AD.

The finding of a stone base for a sacred boat at Wad ben Naqa with the names of Netekamani and Amanitare written on them in both Egyptian and Merotic hieroglyphs made it possible to obtain phonetic values for eight signs, and subsequently the British scholar Griffith was able to establish such values for all twenty-three signs in both writing systems.[1] Understanding of the phonetic values made possible the reading of names, and showed that a previously unknown language was in use by the Meroites. Although a considerable number of texts are now known, the great majority of them funerary monuments, very little progress has been made in understanding the meaning of these documents, and the language itself still remains something of a mystery. Attempts have been made to suggest that the Meroitic language is related to either Beja or Nubian, the two main non-Arabic languages spoken in the northern Sudan today, but none of these has been very convincing and certainly none has helped in the translation of the texts. There are some hints that Meroitic might be related, though not very closely, to Nubian, and that it may belong to the very large family of Eastern Sudanic languages. But if so, it is still linguistically too far

[1] The first account of the determination of the phonetic values is by F. Ll. Griffith in D. Randall MacIver and C. L. Woolley, *Areika* (Oxford, 1909), 43–54.

apart from any of those that have been studied to enable translations to be made.[1]

The Meroitic language, whatever its relationship to other tongues of the area, was in use for several centuries and over a considerable territory. It was certainly the official language of the state from at least the beginning of the second century BC, and the latest inscriptions we have in it date from the fifth century AD. How it arose and how it came to an end we do not know, but we can assume that it was the spoken language of part, at least, of the Meroitic state from long before it was first written until it was replaced by Nubian, after the fifth or sixth centuries AD. (The problem of its replacement by Nubian will be further discussed below.) It is possible that in origin Meroitic was the language of the Island of Meroe, and that its importance grew at the expense of Egyptian as a result of the domination of that southern region from the fourth century BC onwards.

After the time of Netekamani, we have very little information other than the names of a number of rulers, some of whose burial-places are identified. The town of Meroe continued to flourish, and though no buildings at Musawwarat es-Sofra can be shown to be later than Netekamani, the place seems to have continued in use as a religious centre and perhaps as a place of pilgrimage. Contacts with Rome were maintained, and Pliny and Seneca describe Roman exploration as far as Meroe and perhaps beyond in the reign of Nero and about AD 61. Whether the two accounts refer to the same expedition or to different ones is not certain. They have been regarded by most scholars as different versions of the same story, but there are sufficient variations to suggest that they may record two independent military groups that penetrated up the Nile at about the same time. The version given by Seneca says that the aim of the expedition was to find the source of the Nile, and that with the aid of the king of Meroe the explorers penetrated far to the south until they came to an area of marshes and thick vegetation in the river.

The third century AD work of fiction, the *Aethiopica* of Heliodorus, though rather weak on local colour, is also evidence for knowledge of Meroe in the classical world, while finds of Roman objects in the

[1] The main proponent of the Beja theory is E. Zyhlarz. His views are to be found in E. Zyhlarz, 'Das Meroitische Sprachproblem', *Anthropos*, 1930, **25**, 409–63. This has been strongly criticized by Hintze, *Die Sprachliche Stellung des Meroitischen* (Berlin, 1955). Many scholars have tried to see a link between Meroitic and Nubian; this question is best summed up in B. Trigger, 'The languages of the northern Sudan: an historical perspective', *Journal of African History*, 1966, **7**, 19–25.

cemeteries, and of coins and sherds of *terra sigillata* at the town of Meroe, show that contact with Roman Egypt was considerable. The objects found imply that a trading connection continued, though perhaps with breaks, from Ptolemaic times. Written evidence for this contact is not to be found in the south, except for one mysterious inscription in Latin from Musawwarat es-Sofra, but in the north graffiti in the Dodecaschoenus provide records of Meroitic embassies to Rome, or at least to Roman Egypt. One of these at Philae, written in Egyptian demotic, describes the journey of Abratoi, an ambassador of the king of Meroe to the Romans. It contains the name of the Meroitic King Teqerideamani, whose burial-place (Beg. N. 28) is known and whose name is on a statue base from the Lion Temple at Meroe, and gives the date of the graffito as being in the third year of the Roman Emperor Trebonianus Gallus. This is equivalent to AD 253 and it thus provides one of the few fixed dates for a Meroitic ruler. The only other Meroitic ruler whose name occurs both in Lower Nubia and at Meroe is Yesbekheamani, who is known from a graffito at Philae, a stone lion recently found at Qasr Ibrim, and from an inscription from the Lion Temple at Meroe. The inscription on the Qasr Ibrim lion is of special interest since it is written in hieroglyphs, and thus considerably extends the time-range for this writing, of which it is the latest approximately dated example.

Material from the north is comparatively plentiful during the first few centuries AD, and the marked contrast of considerable Meroitic occupation of Lower Nubia after the early first century BC compared with sparse material for earlier periods suggests that there was a move by Meroitic settlers into territory that had previously been almost uninhabited since the end of the Egyptian New Kingdom. The existence of pyramids at Sedenga (Meroitic *Ateye*) of the third century BC implies a settlement of some size and importance at that place, but with the exception of a few small villages, Lower Nubia further north seems to have been uninhabited.

The occupation of Lower Nubia by people of Meroitic culture and whose written language, at least, was Meroitic, seems to have started in the first century BC. One of the factors that made this possible was the introduction of the *saqia*, the ox-driven water-wheel, which, coming from the Near East, had already in Ptolemaic times transformed much of Egyptian agriculture. Its manifest advantage over hand methods of raising water for irrigation, such as the *shaduf*, caused it to be very rapidly adopted, and evidence for its use can be found in the special type of pottery vessel, the *qadus*, which was tied to the wheel and in which the water was raised. Although body fragments of these pots would not necessarily be recognizable, the characteristic knobs on the bottom to which the rope by which they were tied to the wheel was fixed are unmistakable – and from the first century BC onwards they are found in large numbers in all settlements. They are not found at Meroe or in any other southern site, and this suggests that here only *seluka* and wadi bed areas were used for growing crops, flood and rainfall making irrigation unnecessary.

By the end of the first century BC the Meroites had settled in numbers throughout Lower Nubia, and many sites are known. The battles with the Romans, already described, may well have been due to conflicts over the area known as the Triakontaschoenus, stretching for thirty *schoeni*[1] south of the First Cataract.

The agreement made between the two sides at the termination of the campaign may have led to some withdrawal by the Romans, or at least to abandonment of claims to sovereignty, and the frontier was established at Maharraqa (Hierasykaminos) at the southern end of the smaller area known as the Dodecaschoenus. It is noteworthy that the temples built in the time of Augustus, such as those at Kalabsha and Dendur, lie within it. There are some reasons even for thinking that the Dodecaschoenus was subject to joint rule and was not a purely Roman dependency.[2] (See also chapter 3, pp. 193–4.) Some of the inscriptions and graffiti at Philae and other parts of the Dodecaschoenus refer to 'kings', as for example one at Dendur of about 10 BC, where an important official of the area speaks of remission of dues to the temple at Philae for the sake of the 'kings'; other documents make it clear that even if the Romans had military forces there, many important people were Meroites and owed allegiance to their own king. It has been suggested that the Meroitic settlement of this area precedes that of southern Lower Nubia, and that it was an isolated enclave at the end of desert caravan routes and not a northern extension of the settlement that we know from places like Faras and Karanog, which only began in the first century BC and only became considerable later.

South of the Dodecaschoenus, Meroitic authority was firmly established; it is likely that power was exercised through local governors, and names and titles of some of these are known from the large number

[1] The *schoenus*, from the Greek word for rope, was a measure of length of varying size. Here it must have been equivalent to about 10.5 km.

[2] Arguments for this view are presented by N. B. Millett in his unpublished 1968 doctoral thesis for Yale University, 'Meroitic Nubia'.

of grave inscriptions that have been found. The region became thickly populated by the third and fourth centuries AD, and the population would seem to have been prosperous and able to afford a considerable number of luxury goods imported from Egypt and other parts of the eastern Mediterranean. Evidence from both cemeteries and villages indicates a marked increase in population and there are all the signs of a well-developed agricultural village life, not markedly different from that of contemporary rural communities in other parts of the ancient world.

We have virtually no information about political events in any part of the area in which Meroitic culture was spread. It reached from immediately south of the First Cataract to Sennar on the Blue Nile, where the nearby village of Abu Geili has produced typical material. Other sites along the Blue Nile have not been found, but they can be assumed, and the strange assemblage from Jebel Moya suggests that there were people there with a separate culture but closely influenced by Meroitic traditions. The situation on the White Nile is not known and, until the many mounds which lie along it have been investigated, nothing can be said of the spread of Meroitic civilization into this region. Whether the whole region from Aswan to Sennar was subject to the central authority of the king at Meroe cannot be known at present, but the existence close to the First Cataract of graffiti containing royal names as well as references to Meroe town implies that there was control of at least this northern area.

Relations between Meroe and other neighbouring peoples are unknown, but the persistent theme in Meroitic art of the captured prisoner, shown either being smitten by the king or in friezes of prisoners with their arms tied at the elbows, together with the remarkable sculptured relief scene on the Sun Temple at Meroe (where on the south wall it seems that the victorious Meroitic soldiers are massacring their prisoners, whilst the north-wall frieze shows captured women, children and cattle), suggest a constant state of war with other peoples (pl. 2). The Sun Temple, which also bears the names of captured towns on the east wall, may well have been put up to celebrate some major victory under the auspices of the war-god, Apedemek. But as yet there is no evidence of a material sort for whatever military activities may have been carried on.

THE RISE OF AKSUM

The final end of the Meroitic state is still a matter of considerable discussion. The royal burials seem to finish at some time in the early part of the fourth century AD, though this does not mean the end of occupation of Meroe town. The archaeological evidence from there is very difficult to interpret owing to the surface erosion that has taken place, but it seems likely that occupation continued very much later – even if the centralized administration associated with royalty may have come to an end. The conventional view has been that the Meroitic state was dealt its final blow by an expedition of King Ezana (Aezanes in Greek) of Aksum at some time close to AD 350. The evidence for this expedition is to be found in an inscription at Aksum written in Geʿez, which describes an Aksumite campaign in the Island of Meroe, though there are a number of varying interpretations as to the nature of the campaign and the situation at Meroe at the time.

The text itself begins with the protocol normal in Aksumite inscriptions of this period. Ezana states the countries over which he claimed to rule, including some in South Arabia, such as Himyar and Saba, and some in the neighbourhood of Aksum, such as Bega and Kasa (presumably Kush or Meroe), thus implying that he already controlled it. The inscription then describes the campaign and says that Ezana 'took the field against the Noba, when the people of the Noba revolted', and 'when they boasted, "he will not cross the Takazze"', and when they made attacks on unidentified neighbouring peoples – the Mangurto, Hana and Barya – and plundered envoys sent by Ezana. The Takazze is the river Atbara, and the text certainly implies that the Noba were a people previously subject to Aksumite rule and that the campaign was a punitive one. The text goes on to describe how he defeated the Noba at the crossing of the Atbara, burnt their towns and seized much material including stocks of cotton, and killed many of his enemy, among whom were several chiefs whose names are given. Two of these are described as riding on camels, and a priest from whom a silver crown and a gold ring were taken was also killed. The troops of Ezana then attacked both up and down the Nile from a point near the junction of the Nile and the Atbara, and at this junction Ezana erected a throne, presumably similar to stone platforms known from the neighbourhood of Aksum.[1]

If this document is to be taken at face value, always a difficult matter with boastful royal inscriptions of this type, we must assume that Aksum had established an authority over Meroe sufficient to warrant a campaign to maintain its authority. Possible evidence for earlier

[1] For an English version of this text, see L. P. Kirwan, 'The decline and fall of Meroe', *Kush*, 1960, 8, 163–5.

Aksumite activity at Meroe may be seen in a fragmentary inscription in Greek, certainly of Aksumite origin and, from its mention of Ares, a pagan god, probably to be dated prior to the Christianization of Ezana in about AD 350. Unfortunately the exact conditions of discovery of this inscription are not known, but Sayce, who published the piece, says it was brought to him at Meroe, and it probably came from there.[1] The only other Aksumite object from Meroe is one copper coin found in the excavations of 1969–70; this coin, though it does not bear the name of Ezana, is of about his time and, since it bears the symbol of a cross, cannot be earlier than *c.* AD 350. Since there were two levels of building above the spot at which the coin was found, it provides some evidence for occupation into at least the later fourth century. There is also a graffito on the wall of the chapel of pyramid N. 2 at Meroe which is thought to be in Geʿez, the language of Aksum, but no satisfactory translation has ever been established; it has been suggested that it is evidence for the presence of one of Ezana's soldiers.

There has been considerable discussion as to the interpretation of the Ezana text and its relevance as evidence for the end of the Meroitic kingdom. There is no reference to Meroitic royalty in it, an implication that the area was already in some way subject to Aksum, and a clear statement that it was the Noba who were the main enemy. This suggests that the Meroitic royal house and the administration associated with it had already disappeared, and it is tempting to see the Noba as the agents of final Meroitic collapse. The problem of the identity of the Noba and

34 Aksumite coin found at Meroe.

[1] A. H. Sayce, 'A Greek inscription of a king (?) of Axum found at Meroe', *Proceedings of the Society for Biblical Archaeology*, 1909, **31**, 189–203.

the archaeological material that perhaps can be identified with them will be discussed further below, but it is now necessary to look to the Ethiopian highlands and to say something of the origins and history of the kingdom which so suddenly and dramatically irrupted into the Nile Valley.

The origins of the Aksumite kingdom go back well into the first millennium BC, when settlers from South Arabia and the Yemen introduced Semitic languages, building in stone, and literacy. They may also have been the first to introduce agriculture into the area, though the small amount of investigation carried out so far makes this a hazardous hypothesis – the only dates known to the present writer for cultivated grain from northern Ethiopia are of the sixth century AD, from the caves in Begemder province investigated by Dombrowski.[1] The period from the fifth century BC, which is about as early a date as can be established with confidence, to the end of Aksumite times in the tenth century AD can conveniently be divided into three, the evidence for which is primarily archaeological, since inscriptions are few and it is not yet possible to write a connected history. The first period, which can be called 'South Arabian', dates from the fifth century BC or perhaps somewhat earlier. The material remains as shown by sites at Yeha, Haoulti and Matara show very clearly their South Arabian origin. The impressive architecture of the temples at Yeha, and of the newly discovered one near by at Grat-Beal-Guebri, which employed, in typical South Arabian style, both wood and stone in their construction, are good evidence for this, and for the introduction of South Arabian religious practices. Grat-Beal-Guebri appears to be built above the massive foundations of an earlier building, going back perhaps to the time of the first settlers. There is little information on domestic dwellings, but they seem mostly to have been rectangular in shape and built of stone with mud mortar.

The second period, lasting from about the beginning of the third century BC to the first century AD, shows the earlier South Arabian cultural influences being assimilated to local conditions and the development of the first distinctively Ethiopian styles. The writing system was modified, and changes are to be seen in the pottery and metal work. No historical events or personages can be identified with either of these first two periods, and inscriptions are all of a religious or funerary nature. However, the archaeological material makes it possible to see the material base on which the later Aksumite culture was developed.

[1] J. Dombrowski, *Excavations in Ethiopia: Lalibela and Natchebiet Caves, Begemeder Province,* unpublished doctoral thesis (Boston University, 1971).

By the first century AD the development of the town of Aksum begins the third period, known as 'Aksumite', which continued until the tenth century. The evidence suggests that many of the earlier sites were abandoned and new towns founded. Of these, Aksum, perhaps by reason of its sheltered situation, plentiful water supply and adequacy of agricultural land, became the most important, and the seat of a long line of rulers. This Aksumite period is marked by a number of important changes in the styles of architecture, as well as of pottery and other manufactured articles. A coinage was developed by the third century AD, and from the representations of royalty, often with their names, on the coins, a list of kings can be established. There was certainly an increase in prosperity, largely as a result of trading activities. Many more sites are known than from pre-Aksumite times, and there is a greater richness in the material culture, together with a considerable import of objects from the eastern Mediterranean.

During this period Aksum became a town of some size and contained numerous temples and palaces, as well as the large monolithic stelae for which it is best known (pls. 5–7). The purpose and exact dating of these stelae is not certain and they carry no inscriptions, but they were presumably to commemorate people or events, and the recent excavations of H. N. Chittick may enable us to date them with greater precision. A considerable part of ancient Aksum is under the moderate town, but some idea of the nature of the richer, perhaps royal, buildings can be got from the large 'chateau' (as the excavator has described it) of Dongour on the western outskirts of the town.[1] This complex building is an irregular rectangle with each side about 57 m long. Some walls still stand to a height of 5 m, and it contains over forty rooms ranged round a central pavillion reached by a monumental stone staircase. It is a massive and splendid construction bearing witness to the wealth and technical competence of the Aksumite kingdom. Dating – as of all Aksumite buildings at present – is difficult, but the pottery and the coins found suggest it belongs late in Aksumite history, perhaps to the seventh century AD.

The town of Adulis, on the coast, became the port through which trade flowed. It seems to predate Aksum, and may have been in existence as early as the time of Ptolemy III (246–221 BC), perhaps replacing Ptolemais Theron as the main emporium for Ptolemaic trade. By the date at which *The Periplus of the Erythrean Sea* was written, perhaps about AD 100, it was certainly the main port on the south-western coast of the

[1] F. Anfray, 'L'Archéologie d'Axoum en 1972', *Paideuma*, 1972, 18, 69–70.

Red Sea, and was an important centre for the trade in ivory from the interior.

Our main source of information for this period comes from the *Periplus*, which mentions Aksum as lying eight days' journey inland from the coast and as being ruled by a king whose name in Greek was Zoscales, who is thus the first Aksumite ruler whose name is known. Zoscales is said by the unknown author of the *Periplus*, in a phrase which has a ring of that used by Diodorus Siculus for Ergamenes, to have had some Greek education. Certainly contacts with Hellenistic Egypt were close and Greek influence was of significance. This can be seen in the number of Aksumite inscriptions which were written in Greek, and it is probable that it was Hellenistic Greek influence that led to the development of a coinage. The use of coins would have given Aksum an advantage over Meroe, which never adopted this commercial convenience.

Another important document for the period comes from Cosmas Indicopleustes, a mid-sixth-century AD merchant from Alexandria, who recounts how, when on a voyage that took him to Adulis, he copied two Greek inscriptions from that place; one dealt with events in the time of Ptolemy III, and the other with the military exploits of a king who campaigned widely on both sides of the Red Sea. Unfortunately neither the date nor the name of this king is given, but the inscription has been assumed to be of the third century AD and of a king of Aksum, and it is possible that the king referred to is Aphilas, who is known from coins of about this period. A recent paper suggests that the geographical details indicate that the royal author of the inscription was ruling from south-west Arabia and not from Aksum.[1] If this is correct, there must have been an Arabian conquest leading to a new dynasty at Aksum, and this may have been the cause of the resurgence in the fortunes of that place. Cosmas also visited Aksum, and though his description of the town is brief, he refers to a palace with four towers.

By the middle of the fourth century, Aksum had become a considerable power and the court of the king had been Christianized. The main bringer of Christianity was Frumentius, who, according to the account by the Roman historian Rufinus, was captured on the coast by agents of the king of Aksum. By reason of his ability and education, Frumentius rose to a position of importance at the court of King Ella Amida, and on that king's death became virtual ruler of the country during the

[1] L. P. Kirwan, 'The *Christian Topography* and the Kingdom of Axum', *Geographical Journal*, 1972, 138, 166–77.

minority of Ezana, son of Ella Amida. This power enabled Frumentius to strengthen the position of Christianity. After a visit to Alexandria, he returned to Aksum with the title of bishop, and was successful in spreading his religion widely and in winning the king for the new faith.

The inscriptions from the reign of Ezana make it clear that he adopted Christianity during the course of his reign, since earlier ones show him as a worshipper of the traditional gods, of whom Ares, presumably an indigenous deity identified with the Greek god, is perhaps the main one. Later inscriptions, including the famous one describing the campaign on the Nile, while dropping the names of pagan gods, are not unambiguously Christian. However coins of this king's reign carry the cross, and there can be little doubt that Christianity had become the court religion by about AD 350, and it is from this time that there began the close connection between Christianity and what was to become the Ethiopian nation.

The inscriptions of Ezana, both in Greek and Geʿez, the indigenous language and the forerunner of Amharic and Tigrinya, the main Semitic tongues of modern Ethiopia, are the main sources for knowledge of contact between Aksum and Meroe. The few Aksumite objects from Meroe have been mentioned; Meroitic objects in Ethiopia are equally few. Two bronze bowls, certainly of Meroitic manufacture, have been found at Addi-Gelemo in the eastern part of Tigre, and two faience figures, one of the Egyptian god Bes and one of a human figure with a sun disk, were found at Haoulti in a level dated to the fifth or sixth century BC. This is very scanty evidence on which to base any suggestion of contact between the two cultures, but it seems unlikely that these well-developed states could have remained in close proximity for several centuries without such contact.

THE END OF MEROE

It has usually been assumed that there was a decline in the power and wealth of Meroe after the first century AD. Pyramids certainly became smaller and funeral furniture poorer, and though this may reflect changed attitudes rather than poverty, it is noteworthy that no monumental buildings later than the reign of Netekamani can be identified. On the other hand the fine painted pottery, which suggests prosperity and some sophistication, belongs to this period. At Meroe town, buildings are not noticeably poorer except in the very topmost level, where roughly made walls patched together with reused material have been found. No date can yet be given to this latest building, other than that it appears to be considerably later than the coin of Ezana whose discovery has already been referred to. If there were an absolute impoverishment of the Meroitic kingdom, an important part may have been played by declining Meroitic participation in the Red Sea trade. The use of the port of Adulis during the early centuries AD may have drawn trade away from further north and have helped to enrich Aksum at the expense of Meroe.

Although it is clear enough that the royal line, at least as revealed by their burials, came to an end at some time in the fourth century AD, perhaps as a result of Aksumite pressure, information on the date of the end of Meroitic culture as a whole and the reasons for it is much more difficult to determine, and the archaeological evidence difficult to interpret. In the far north, close to Egypt, cultural changes after the fourth century AD can be identified, and a sequence running through to at least the fourteenth century AD can be discerned. At Meroe itself, and in the surrounding country, this cannot be done: with the end of a distinctive Meroitic culture, whenever that may have been, there is a gap in the archaeological record until virtually modern times.

A large number of mound graves of about the fourth and fifth centuries AD are known on both sides of the Nile, stretching from south of the confluence of the Blue and White Niles to at least as far north as the junction with the river Atbara and across the Bayuda desert to Tanqasi, where a cemetery of such mounds has been excavated. These mounds represent a change in burial custom, and from those that have been excavated, at Meroe, Ushara and Tanqasi, material of a new and distinctive type has been recovered. Most of it is pottery, in the main large vessels of the shape usually described as 'beer pots'. These vessels, which have a large bulbous body and a long narrow neck, were not made on the wheel, as was most Meroitic pottery, and they are frequently characterized by markings on the lower part of the body conveying the impress of the mat on which the pot was rolled. They are sufficiently distinctive to be easily identified and, though common in the cemeteries, do not appear in the ruins of the town, although it is possible that some of the featureless hand-made sherds found there come from vessels of this type.

The dating of these graves is far from certain and nothing can be said of their earliest occurrence, though it is unlikely to be before *c.* AD 300. The very large number may suggest that they were in use for a considerable period of time. The only objects from the graves which are datable are foreign imports, but in fact there are only two such pieces, which, as it happens, cannot be dated with any precision. These are, from grave 300 at Meroe, a glass vessel of Alexandrian type which dates between AD 200 and AD 400, and, from grave 361 at the same site, an amphora which should date to the fifth or sixth century AD. All that can be said, then, is that it would not be unreasonable to assume that the new burial custom which these mounds illustrate was introduced at some time not too distant from Ezana's campaign and the supposed end of Meroe.

In view of Ezana's reference to the Noba as being the people in occupation of the Island of Meroe, it is tempting to see in them the introducers of mound burial as well as of a new pottery type. But whether this is to be interpreted as the influx of a new people, or of the resurgence of social groups whose culture had been swamped by that of the Meroitic aristocracy, is impossible to determine. Some aspects of the burials, such as the laying of the bodies on beds, hark back to much earlier practices along the Sudanese Nile. Evidence for the end of Meroitic culture in this area is far from clear; there is no gradual change of the material remains under outside influences as in the north, and such information as there is points to a rather sudden collapse. Whether this was due to attacks by enemy peoples such as the Noba, or to internal decay, or to a combination of the two, cannot at present be known.

A further problem, which may be related to the question of the end of Meroe, is that of a change in the language of the country. Meroitic was the written language of the whole stretch of river over which the Meroitic kings ruled from at least as early as 200 BC until the fourth century AD. After that there is a span of over 300 years from which there is no written material in an indigenous language. When writing once more appears, it is in Old Nubian and written with a modified Greek alphabet.

There are two ways of explaining this situation, firstly that Meroitic was the spoken as well as the written language throughout Meroitic territory, and that it was supplanted by Nubian in about the fifth century; this has until recently been the standard view of the linguistic history. An alternative possibility is that Meroitic, whilst being the written and official language, was only used colloquially in the Island of Meroe, the part of the country where power resided, and that Nubian was already present in the Nile Valley and was being spoken along the northern stretch of the river between the First and Fourth Cataracts.

The occurrence of such written materials as ostraca and funerary monuments in Meroitic in this area does not necessarily disprove the hypothesis, since a similar situation exists today in those parts where Nubian is still spoken but Arabic always used for written purposes.

If Nubian came to the Nile Valley only in the fifth century, the question of its original home is of some importance, and the present distribution of Nubian languages may provide a clue. At the present day Nubian is spoken – or was until the disruption caused by resettlement as a result of the building of the new Aswan dam and the resultant flooding of much of Nubia – along the Nile from a little north of Aswan to Debba, and there is good evidence from place names for its further extension upriver, perhaps to the neighbourhood of Khartoum, in medieval times. Related languages are spoken in the Nuba hills to the south-west, where a group of dialects usually known as 'Hill Nubian' are spoken by a people very different physically and culturally from the speakers of 'River Nubian'. A little north of this group, at Jebel Haraza, evidence for a closely related language has recently come to light, and, in northern Darfur, Meidob and Birged are also related.

This distribution suggests that in the past there may have been a wide area of the northern Sudan over which Nubian was spoken, and that it was one of the main language groups of the ancient Sudan. The modern distribution of related languages suggests that the original home of the ancestral language lay to the west, and that it spread from there to the Nile Valley. It is therefore tempting to identify the people buried in the mound graves at Meroe and elsewhere in the area with the Noba of Ezana and with the bringers of Nubian language to the Nile. The name Noba, and the subsequent use of this or a very similar name by medieval Arab writers for the inhabitants of the northern Sudan, from which the modern use of the word Nubian is derived, is unlikely to be coincidence.

While these obscure events concerned with the collapse of the Meroitic state were going on in the Island of Meroe, a somewhat different situation can be seen in the north, and it is not easy to see if any correlations existed between historical developments in the two areas.

As already suggested, the northern regions of the Meroitic state enjoyed a period of reasonable prosperity in the first few centuries of the Christian era, and, far from Aksum, did not suffer either from trade rivalry nor from military attack from that region, although raids by the Blemmyes, presumed to be the ancestors of the Beja of the Red Sea hills, are recorded from as early as the middle of the third century AD. Although the effect of the Blemmye raids is not discernible in the archaeological material, they were a cause of considerable anxiety to the Roman rulers of Egypt, and the aid they gave to the Egyptian rebel Firmus at the time of the Palmyrene invasion of AD 272, together with other raids, must have contributed to Diocletian's decision in AD 297 to withdraw Roman garrisons, to abandon Lower Nubia, and to establish the southern frontier of the Roman Empire at the First Cataract (cf. chapter 2, pp. 206–9).

This withdrawal of Roman troops from the Dodecaschoenus did not have any immediate effect on the Meroitic settlements. These lay somewhat further south and they certainly flourished through much of the fourth century until the appearance of new elements at the very end of that century or early in the next. This new culture element in the area is that commonly known until recently as the X-Group, a term coined by Reisner when carrying out the first archaeological survey of Nubia, which began in 1907 as a consequence of the building of the first Aswan dam. Faced with the discovery of a great deal of new archaeological material whose identity could not be accommodated by the traditional divisions of Ancient Egyptian history, Reisner gave designations by letters of the alphabet, thus giving rise to the well-known archaeological entities, the A-Group and the C-Group. Finding material of much later date, he used the term X-Group to identify an immediately post-Meroitic culture. The increase of knowledge in recent years has made the need for this anonymous type of terminology superfluous, and here the term 'Ballana' culture, as proposed by Trigger,[1] will be used. It has the advantage that it follows normal archaeological tradition by naming the culture after the most spectacular of the sites where it has been found.

This new element in the history of Lower Nubia, which lasted at most from *c.* AD 400 to 600, is attested by the finding of archaeological material which, though showing resemblances, also has some marked differences from that of late Meroitic times. This Ballana culture, which is sufficiently distinctive to be readily identified, is known from cemeteries and villages stretching from the First Cataract to Sesibi, a short way north of the Third Cataract. It has not yet been found further south. There is no sudden break with Meroitic tradition, but the pottery, the best-known material because of its vast quantity, shows new shapes, in the main derived from the north, and a considerable simplification in painted design. No monumental buildings are known, except perhaps at Faras, where the rulers of the time may have had their residence, and the

[1] B. G. Trigger, *History and settlement in Lower Nubia* (New Haven, 1965), 132.

evidence on the whole suggests that village life was somewhat poorer than in Meroitic times. But the spectacular remains of the period found in the large burial-mounds of Ballana and Qostol, with their rich funeral furnishings, show that this was a period of wealth and power, at least for the rulers. These burials, surely of powerful chiefs, contain a surprising number of luxury objects imported from the eastern Mediterranean, including silver vessels and jewellery, a wide range of bronze objects, and wooden boxes inlaid with ivory, as well as a range of locally made weapons and other war-like equipment. These were powerful and rich princes, and many scholars have assumed that there must have been an incursion of a new people into the river valley at this time.

Since two exotic groups are known from classical writers to have been in the area at the appropriate time, the Nobatae and the Blemmyes, there has been much argument as to which of these two peoples was responsible for the changes, and which of them is represented not only in the rich burials of Ballana and in the rather less elaborate ones at Qasr Ibrim, Gemai and Firka (perhaps the burial places of local chiefly families), but also in the large number of commoners' graves throughout Lower Nubia. The Blemmyes seem to have been firmly identified as ancestors of the Beja; the origin of the Nobatae is less clear. Procopius, writing in the sixth century AD, says that they came from the western oases, and were invited by Diocletian to fill the gap left by his withdrawal of the Roman garrison and to act as a buffer between the Blemmyes and the frontier of Egypt.

The great deal of extra information from skeletal analysis now available makes it certain that there was no large-scale movement by a people of different physical type.[1] Whether the same is true of their rulers it is not possible to say, since the skeletal remains were not well preserved nor studied in detail. Today the majority view is that there was no massive immigration, and not only the skeletons but also cultural material argue strongly in favour of such a view. It is possible that small, well-armed horse and camel-riding military groups from outside established leadership over the indigenous population. If this were so, then these are presumably the Nobatae, and Procopius's story could well imply that this was the nature of the Nobataean immigration.

[1] O. V. Nielson, *Human remains*, Scandinavian Joint Expedition to Sudanese Nubia, 9 (Stockholm, 1970), and D. L. Greene and G. Armelagos, *The Wadi Halfa Mesolithic population*, Research Report No. 11, Department of Anthropology, University of Massachusetts (Amherst, 1972), are the two main reports so far published. A number of preliminary reports have appeared.

The name and its close resemblance to the name Noba may suggest that they were speakers of 'river Nubian', and the later medieval kingdom of Nobatia continued to use the name. There is the striking apparent coincidence of similarity with the name of the old royal and religious centre Napata, and it could also be reasonably argued that the Nubian speakers, and hence the Nobatae, were the indigenous Nubian riverain population who had been subjected to Meroitic rule and acquired the characteristic Meroitic culture. Even if the Nubian language had already been spoken along the Nile for a long period, it does not mean that the warriors of the Ballana tombs were not a new people from elsewhere. If, as is suggested above, they were a small military group, perhaps brought in as an unofficial garrison, they may have come without women, and would have taken wives from the local population; in that case, as many other examples from Africa show, their children would have adopted the local language.

With the disappearance of Meroitic as a written language towards the end of the fourth century AD, we are left with no written documents in an indigenous language, though Roman writers continue to tell of Nobatae and Blemmyes. Such writing as there was appears to have been in Greek, and letters by Blemmye chiefs in that language which have been found in Egypt attest to deep penetration into Upper Egypt. They were presumably written for illiterate masters by Egyptian secretaries with some knowledge of Greek. The scanty written evidence suggests conflicts between Nobatae and Blemmyes continuing into the sixth century, when the Greek inscription on the temple at Kalabsha of Silko, who calls himself 'kinglet' (*basiliskos*) of the Nobatae, describes a major defeat of the Blemmyes. It has been suggested that Silko, whose inscription says 'God gave me the victory', was a Christian, but the representation of him that accompanies the inscription shows him riding a horse and wearing a crown with the emblems of various Egyptian gods. The use of the word 'god' is no greater evidence of Silko's attachment to Christianity, completely belied by the details of his dress, than are the lamps and pots bearing Christian emblems from the chiefs' graves at Ballana and Qostol. But this is the last stage of the long story of the kingdom of Kush from its beginnings before 700 BC to the last pagan kings still retaining some elements of Kushite culture into the sixth century AD. The culture of Nubia was about to change again under the impact of Eastern Christianity, which, coming from Egypt, was to influence it for the next 800 years.

CHAPTER 5

TRANS-SAHARAN CONTACTS AND THE IRON AGE IN WEST AFRICA*

THE CLIMATIC BACKGROUND: THE DESICCATION OF THE SAHARA

Today all authorities agree that the Sahara had a humid climate during the six to eight millennia prior to about 2000 BC. Great lakes like the modern Lake Chad covered much of the southern Sahara. These have left evidence of their presence in the form of deposits of diatoms (which can provide radiocarbon dates); the skeletons of reptiles, mammals and fish; and waterside human habitation sites possessed of rich Stone Age industries. The largest of these lakes, 'Mega-Chad', then extended over 330,000 sq. km to the 325 m contour, whereas the modern lake has an area of only 25,000 sq. km, and is bounded by the 282-metre contour. The latter, it should be noted, is not at the lowest point of the Chad basin, which in Djourab is only 165 m above sea level.

In these favourable conditions, a wide variety of fauna were able to live in areas which are today wholly desert, such as Tenere, Tanezrouft and Majabet al-Koubra. Innumerable neolithic sites have been found and, moreover, most of those rocks which are suitable are covered with pictures of the large 'Ethiopian' fauna which could then live in the Sahara, including elephants, rhinoceroses, giraffes, antelopes and hippopotamuses. Saharan man was then a hunter-gatherer and sometimes also a fisherman.

From about 5000 BC, the Sahara began slowly to change into desert, a development which is probably connected with the general increase in temperatures in the northern hemisphere which led to the melting of the glaciers of northern Europe. The final stage of the Neolithic[1] on the shores of Lake Chad is found only below about the 250 m contour (there is a 1210 BC date for the shell-mounds at Bochianga, near Koro Toro in the Republic of Tchad), and Early Iron Age sites are found only below 240 m (Kerki, Mortcha, Moji, Daima). But despite the desiccation, the climate then was still much more humid than it is today. A

* Translated from the French by J. D. Fage.

[1] The term 'Neolithic' is used in this chapter instead of 'Late Stone Age' because – as will be seen – of the presence in the Sahara of agriculture and of stock-raising.

mixed woodland and grassland savanna provided abundant pasture for wild animals, and also for numerous herds of *Bovidae* and *Capridae*, which are represented on some hundreds of ancient Saharan rock sites.

However if, as has just been said, the principal cause of dessication was

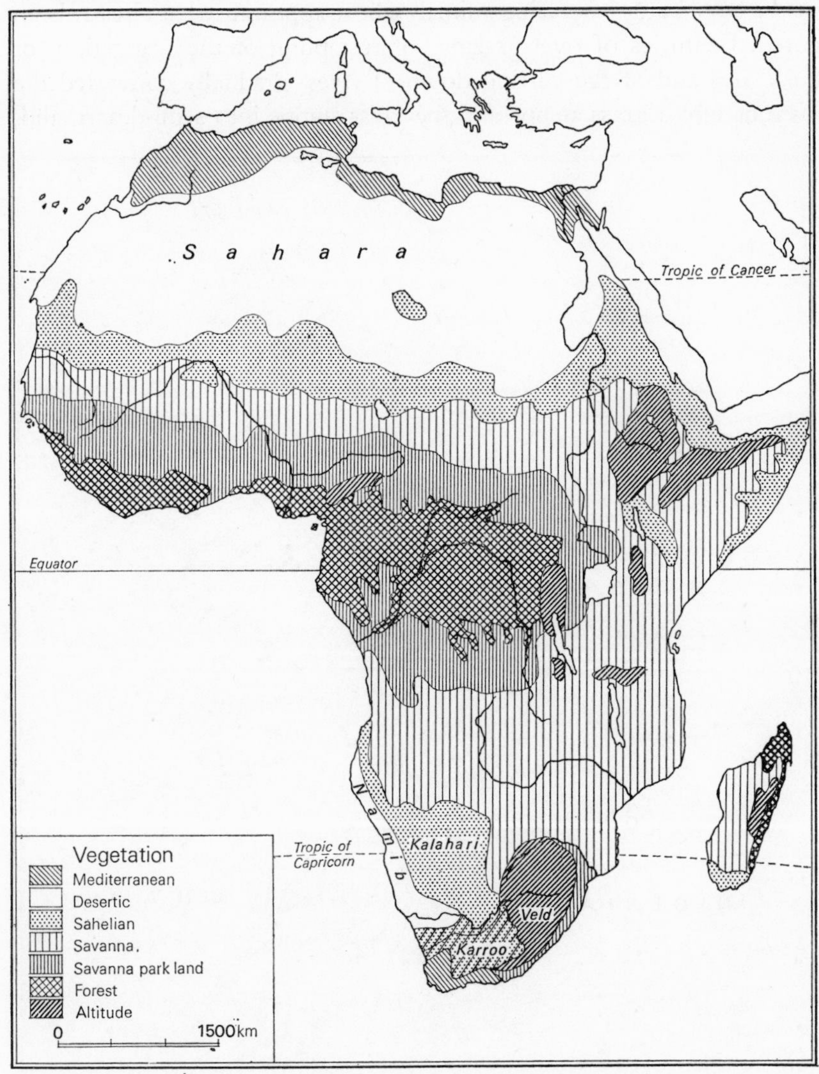

35 The vegetation of Africa in modern times.
At the end of the Late Stone Age, about the beginning of the Christian era, the Sahelian climate extended much further northwards into the Sahara.

climatic – the decreasing amounts of rainfall, and therefore the conversion into desert of the less well-watered regions and a general lowering of the water-table – other factors were also at work. One of the most important of these was that, at the same time the ecological balance of the vegetation was being degraded, it was being ruthlessly exploited by the large herds of grazing animals whose appearance has already been noted. Centuries of over-grazing, of trampling of the vegetation, of bush fires and of the cutting down of trees, gradually converted the savanna into a grass steppe and the grass steppe into semi-desert, and,

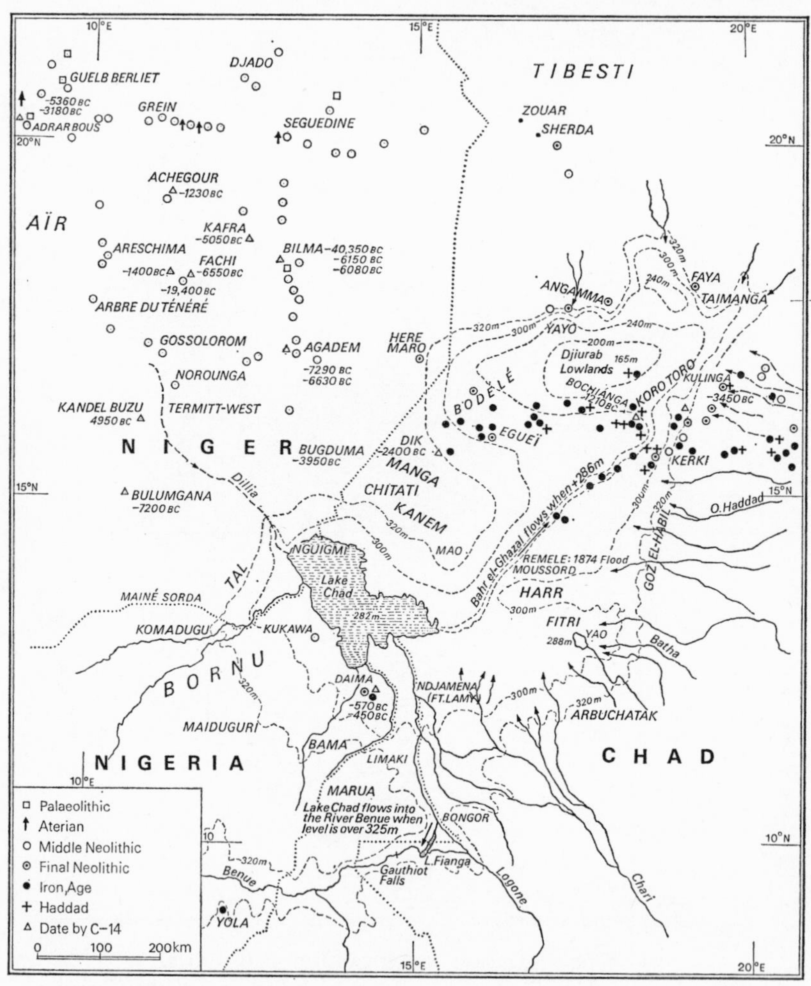

36 Mega-Lake Chad, dessicated only at the end of the Neolithic. Note: sites under 320m are all Final Neolithic or Iron Age.

as the Saharan pastures became exhausted, this misuse of the environment was extended ever further to the south. All that is needed to imagine what was going on in the Sahara during the last millennia BC is to transpose to it the activities practised by the Fulani in the Sudanese savannas during modern times.

The Saharan pastoralists, Libyan-Berbers in the north and ancestors of the Zaghāwa, Teda and Fulani towards the south, were thus led to drive their flocks and herds southwards, to trespass onto lands occupied by sedentary Negroes who were already passing from vegeculture to agriculture. The pressures being exerted on sedentary Sudanese peoples by the nomadic pastoralists at the end of the Neolithic are particularly evident in Mauritania. Here, all along the Tichit-Walata escarpment, are to be seen the remains of some dozens of villages, for the most part fortified, which are built on naturally defensive sites close by sources of water. These walled villages – some of which extend over more than a square kilometre – indicate that men had passed beyond hunting and gathering to become settled cultivators and herders, and also that they were threatened by external dangers, most probably the slaving raids of Libyan-Berber warrior nomads from the Sahara. Excavations have been carried out in these villages by the American archaeologist, Patrick Munson, who has secured radiocarbon dates from them of 1400 to 380 BC. It is worth noting that in this region today the annual rainfall is less than 100 mm, and that agriculture is no longer feasible. Here therefore processes of desiccation have continued into the Christian era.

From about 3000 BC onwards, the Sahara began to exert a constraining influence on the freedom of human movement. Hitherto traversable virtually anywhere, it now began to be broken up into a number of different regions. We may note first the areas of complete desert, such as the Libyan Desert, Edeyen, Tenere, Tanezrouft and Majabet, from which people had virtually withdrawn, and where only with metal tools was it possible to dig wells. Such regions became the exclusive preserves of hunters of the addax and the oryx, who were based on peripheral wells and water-holes. Secondly, there were the dry zones – the great southern plains, the medium altitude plateaux, the edges of the desert proper – which man could inhabit during the rainy seasons, pasturing herds of goats and even cultivating in the depressions on the plains of the piedmont which could hold temporary moisture. Thirdly, there were the semi-arid zones, where there was some seasonal rainfall, sufficient to maintain a permanent vegetation cover and to feed surface water-holes or shallow wells dug in the beds of wadis. These were the mountain massifs and their piedmont plains which were watered by the floods coming down the wadis from the mountains – Tibesti, Tassili, Ahaggar (Hoggar), Aïr, Adrar of the Iforas, the Mauritanian Adrar. Here nomad life was possible, and even sedentary life, for fields of millet and groves of palms were cultivated by people who were tributary to the nomads.

Human movement in and across the Sahara, though much less easy than it was before 3000 BC, was still possible if the areas of complete desert were avoided, and if movement were planned to take place during the most favourable season, the winter, when some rain fell in the north, when the coolness of the air made longer and easier stages possible, and when the southern water-holes still held some of the rain which had fallen during the summer. Before the introduction of the camel, which reached Egypt about 1600 BC, and subsequently slowly spread into Libya, the Maghrib and the Sahara, movement in the desert must have been essentially on foot, with the help of some pack-animals, such as donkeys and oxen. There is in fact practically no information relating to Saharan travel in this period, but it seems reasonable to take as an example the journey undertaken further to the east about 2250 BC from Egypt towards the land of Yam (?Darfur) by Harkhuf. Similar journeys, with caravans of donkeys, could have been made towards the central Sahara following the establishment of organized governments on the southern shore of the western Mediterranean – by the Phoenicians after 1100 BC, by the Carthaginians after 800 BC, and by the Greeks of Cyrenaica after 600 BC. But it should be noted that by the latter part of this period, horse-drawn chariots had come into use; more will be said about these below.

Before the first millennium BC, moreover, there can have been no question of trans-Saharan links being forged with commercial motives such as those which had already elsewhere inspired trade-routes in amber, tin, incense, ivory and obsidian. The most that can have been established would have been interregional and intertribal links based on subsistence economies of the most primitive kind, for the Sahara was one of the poorest regions of the world, in which man could subsist only through the exploitation of the most meagre food resources. No real trade could be expected with tribes like the Teda, who even today have to make do for their daily sustenance with a few dates, wild grains and occasional *Acrididae* or reptiles. Those who were best off were those who lived in symbiotic relationship with a herd or flock on which they depended wholly for their subsistence. Their journeyings were a continuing transhumance between the pastures that sprang up following the occasional rains, to the seasonal salt-cure for their herds at some southerly water-point; their only trade of any importance was when at the beginning of the dry season they might barter desert salt for the millet produced by southern farmers. The greatest travellers were hunters, who would leave the tribe in search of game, itself dependent on the rains. But there must also have been many other motives for human migration; men might often be away from their homes for many years.[1]

It should be appreciated that at this time confrontations between individuals or tribes were apparently not of major significance. There were disputes over the use of pastures and over watering rights at wells, and there were sentimental quarrels, but these did not lead to troubles above the level of the family or tribal group. Because man possessed no better weapons than those of stone and, above all, because he did not possess fast-moving riding animals, it was rare for him to engage in the long-distance raids to capture booty to take back into the desert which became characteristic after the introduction of the horse and the camel. However, the gradual extension of the desert necessarily caused important movements of its population towards better-watered regions further to the south, with the result that major confrontations did occur between the desert peoples and the tribes onto whose land they had moved.

Thus, before the first millennium BC, although from time to time there were a very few fleeting contacts with the outside world, limited in scope and with no importance other than that they led to the reciprocal borrowing of a few innovations – in weaponry, in wood and leather-working etc. – from or to the worlds of the Mediterranean and the Nile Valley, and their adaptation to local technology, the peoples of West Africa and the Sahara did not take any part in the developing networks of world trade.

TRANS-SAHARAN CONTACTS: HORSES, CHARIOTS AND THE INTRODUCTION OF THE CAMEL

It is difficult to know for certain when the horse first enters into African history. However, *Equus mauritanicus*, fossils of which have been found at some prehistoric sites in the Maghrib, may now be ruled out of the

[1] J. Chapelle, *Nomades noirs du Sahara* (Paris, 1957), 172–6.

reckoning. It was extinct before man began to domesticate animals. Moreover it was not a horse, but a zebra similar to the quagga,[1] and there is no rock-drawing of a horse which goes back as far as the period of the hunters or of that of the first cattle-herders.[2] It is also relevant to remark that the horse was not known in western Asia in neolithic times. On the other hand, the Nubian donkey is represented there in seventeen different levels of the excavations at Mureybit, in Syria on the left bank of the Euphrates, where no signs have been found of any of the wild Asian donkeys.[3]

It has long been argued that the horse was introduced to Egypt by the Hyksos, a nomadic Asian people. However, when in the eighteenth century BC the Hyksos invaded the Delta, it seems that – like the Egyptians themselves – they fought on foot. It is tolerably certain in fact that it was the Aryans that introduced the horse and the war-chariot throughout the Near East from the seventeenth century onwards. The people of the Nile Valley adopted both about 1600 BC, at the end of the period of Hyksos domination.

Initially horses were not ridden, but harnessed – usually in pairs – to a light chariot in which two men could ride. The horse and the war-chariot were adopted by the Libyans from the thirteenth century onwards, and by the Nubians from the beginning of the first millennium.[4]

But what genus of horse was thus spread into Africa from Asia? This question has long been the subject of study and experiment by Spruytte, who moreover is well acquainted with the Sahara and the problem of its 'chariot tracks'. Basing his work on the numerous surviving contemporary representations of Egyptian chariots, and also the model found in Tutankhamun's tomb and now in the Cairo Museum, Spruytte succeeded experimentally in reconstructing one of these chariots. Made entirely of wood and leather, with some ornamentation in copper, this

[1] L. Balout, in W. W. Bishop and J. D. Clark, eds., *Background to evolution in Africa* (Chicago, 1967), 598.

[2] H. Lhote, 'Le cheval et le chameau dans les peintures et gravures rupestres du Sahara', *Bulletin de l'IFAN*, 1953, 15, 3 (sér. B.), 1140.

[3] P. Ducos, 'The Oriental Institute excavation at Mureybit, Syria: preliminary report on the 1965 campaign; Part IV, Les Restes d'équidés', *Journal of Near Eastern Studies*, 1970, **29**. The author owes this information to M. J. Spruytte, who has made a special study of ancient chariots, and who has speculated whether the animals harnessed to Egyptian war-chariots, which are neither horses nor donkeys, may not be crosses between ponies (small horses?) and Nubian donkeys.

[4] J. Yoyotte, in G. Posener, ed., *Dictionnaire de la civilisation Égyptienne* (Paris, 1959), 51. But the horse should have been known in Nubia much earlier than this if the *Equida* found at Buhen and dated to *c.* 1675 BC is really a horse (cf. *Illustrated London News*, 12 Sept. 1959, 232–3, 249, 251).

chariot weighs only 34 kg. The wheels have leather tyres, and the rubbing of the wooden spindles on the wooden naves does not cause excessive wear provided the surfaces are highly polished and are kept greased with mutton fat. The harness is the original one. On an earth road, with a driver weighing 75 kg, over short distances this chariot can achieve 38 k.p.h.

The horses used were two Shetland ponies, each standing 1.15 m. Ponies were used, and not full-sized horses, because Spruytte noted that the animals depicted in XVIII Dynasty (*c.* 1450 BC) representations were always very small. The height of the Shetlands chosen by Spruytte was assessed in the light of the size of the animals in the paintings when compared with the size of the chariots and their drivers. Such horses were so small that it is rather unlikely that they can ever have been used as saddle-horses. At this period, cavalry was unknown in Egypt, and the rare representations of horses being ridden show the rider mounted well back, almost on the rump. There can be no doubt that this means that the mounts were not useful for load-carrying; hence the use of the animals to draw light chariots rather than to carry men. It was only later, following the development of systematic breeding (and also the improvement of materials and techniques) that, through selective breeding, man succeeded in getting taller, longer and heavier horses.[1]

From the thirteenth century BC, the Libyan allies of the 'People of the Sea' were equipped with horses pulling chariots, and it was through Cyrenaica and Libya that the horse entered the Saharan world of the Libyan-Berbers. From 1100 BC onwards, Phoenician settlement at a number of points on the southern Mediterranean coast brought the horse as far west as the Straits of Gibraltar. Although the Phoenicians themselves did not penetrate the interior to any appreciable extent, it is highly probable that it was they who introduced horses and chariots to their Libyan-Berber neighbours and clients west of the Gulf of Syrtis (Sidra). It is thus from about 1000 BC onwards that it seems best to place the diffusion of the horse and the chariot to the lands adjacent to Libya, such as Tassili n-Ajjer, where the chariot horses are depicted in a 'flying gallop', a style peculiar to this region. However there are innumerable other representations of horse-drawn chariots farther to the west and south which are less artistically and more schematically drawn. These must be supposed to be later, contemporary with a period

[1] J. Spruytte, 'Le cheval et le char de l'Égypte ancienne', *Plaisirs Équestres*, 1971, 51, 171–6.

of rock art which is decadent by comparison with that of the cattle-herders. These later rock-drawings may be notionally dated to the second half of the first millennium. The chariots were finally to disappear from the Sahara following the introduction of the camel about the first century BC. Conceivably the change occurred earlier than this, when better breeds of horses became available and chariotry gave place cavalry, thus freeing the Saharan peoples from all the inconveniences of maintaining chariots in a hostile environment. It cannot have been easy to repair a broken wheel or shaft in the middle of the desert, far from watering-places, sources of timber and places of human habitation.

It is now appropriate to consider the 'chariot tracks', to use the term developed by Henri Lhote and the present author – and, for want of a better, still in use – to denote those regions of the Sahara where the use of chariots seems to have been particularly well established.

Of the thousand or so known sites of rock-drawings in the Sahara and its approaches, from the Nile to the Atlantic and from the Atlas to the southern savannas, only about fifty have engraved or painted representations of chariots. Althogether, about five hundred drawings of chariots are known to exist, though the total increases every year. These drawings of chariots are not distributed indiscriminately over the whole range of sites but, with a few exceptions, they are grouped along two relatively narrow bands across the desert. One of these runs from the Fezzan towards Gao on the Niger bend, passing through Tassili n-Ajjer, Ahaggar and Adrar of the Iforas, with two recently recognized flanking lines, one towards Tibesti and Djado, and the other towards Aïr. The other runs from southern Orania and southern Morocco towards Goundam, just north-west of the Niger bend, and passes through Zemmour and the Mauritanian Adrar and along the Tichit-Walata escarpment.

Obviously these are not roads in any modern sense, in which specific places are linked together with metalled surfaces along specific lines. They are more or less parallel tracks running from one well or water-hole to the next, avoiding rock outcrops and areas of sand-dunes, using specific cols to cross mountain ranges, and running through those lands which afforded the best going for wheeled vehicles and which were furnished with the best pastures. Nor is it necessary to suppose that the same chariots served for a whole trans-Saharan journey. Despite anything which their drivers might do, the chariots were clearly too fragile to last for more than a few hundred kilometres of driving over difficult terrain.

The 'tracks' then were rather areas of country, no doubt linked together, through which the concept of the chariot and the techniques necessary to make chariots had become established. Individual Libyan-

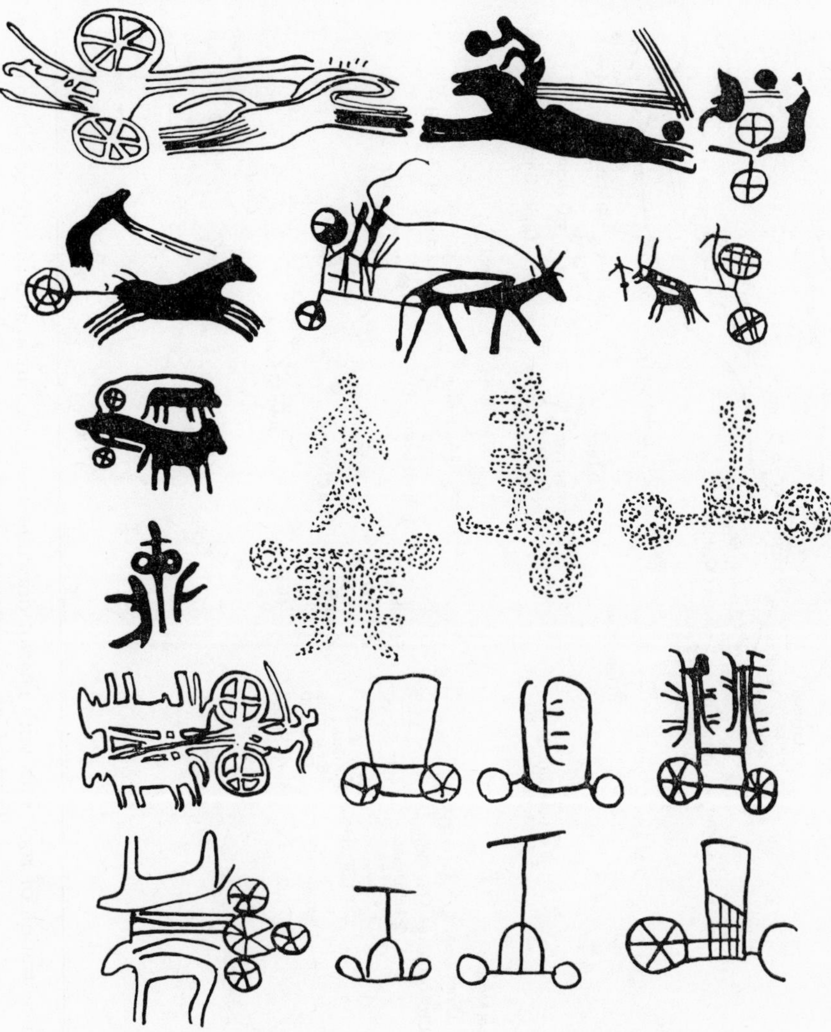

37 Saharan rock-painted or engraved chariots. They are either 'flying gallop' in the Aegean tradition, or more schematic. The former are to be found chiefly in the Tassili n-Ajjer, and the latter are more and more schematic the further south they are.

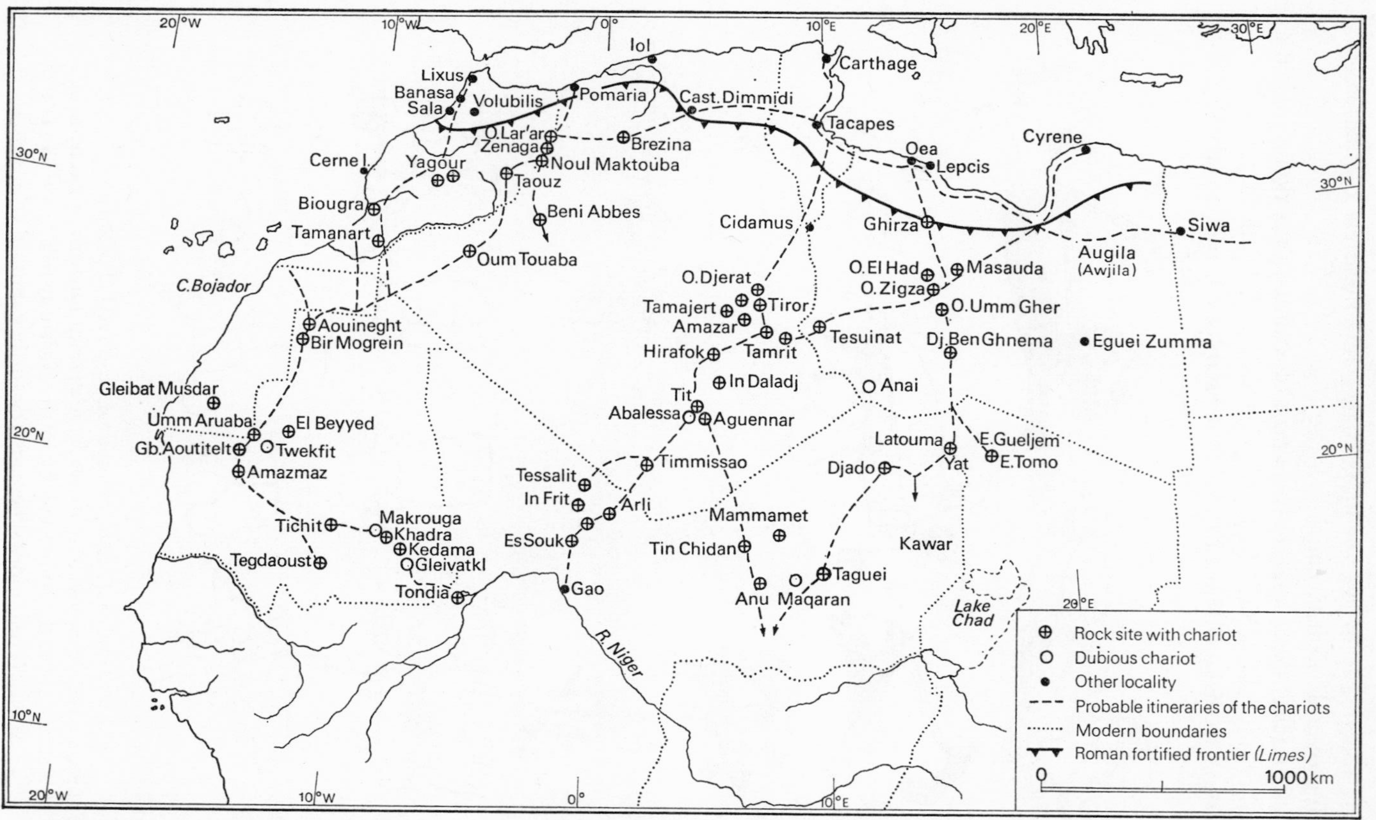

38 The concentration of rock sites with chariot drawings along two main axes: Morocco-Niger in the west; in the east, Tripoli-Gao via Ahaggar, and lesser ones to Tibesti and Aïr.

Berbers or small groups of them, who knew how to make and maintain chariots, could have circulated through these areas with horses, making chariots when the need arose or when they were asked to do so, either on their own behalf or on that of local chiefs with whom they had dealings.

This leads to the question of why chariots were introduced to the Sahara; whether they were for warfare, pleasure or trade. Doubtless it was for all three purposes. We learn from Herodotus (Bk. IV.183) that the Garamantes of the Fezzan went to fight the troglodyte Ethiopians (of Tibesti?) in chariots drawn by four horses: presumably these were slave-raids. In the same latitudes further to the west, Strabo says (XVII.3.7) the purpose of chariots was to carry archers and to spread panic in the ranks of the enemy. But except in perfectly flat and unobstructed country, chariots cannot have been a very effective weapon, and their horses must have been a very vulnerable target for enemy arrows.

Chariots could have been used for purposes of pleasure in two interrelated ways – sport and hunting. As with Near Eastern and European peoples, chariot-racing could have been one of the sports of those Libyan-Berbers who were well enough off to possess horses: this is the best interpretation, for example, of the Tassili n-Ajjer pictures of chariots drawn by horses in a 'flying gallop'. As for hunting, there is for the southern Sahara a typical picture from Tegdaoust which shows a hunter in a chariot chasing a giraffe.[1] To this it must be added that, because of the difficulties that must have been experienced in securing and maintaining horses in the desert, and also because of the prestige attached to them, the possession of horses must have been an attribute of chieftaincy.

It does not seem likely that horses served to promote or facilitate the carriage across the Sahara, on the chariots drawn by them, of trade goods. In Saharan conditions, the animals were too prestigious, too scarce and also too dear for them to have been used for such a purpose. Such fragile vehicles as the chariots were could only have carried a very small useful load, and it is difficult to see what they could have transported. The most that can be envisaged is that caravans of donkeys or oxen could have been accompanied by chiefs or rich traders travelling in their chariots to do business on behalf of Carthaginian or Roman merchants. It is possible to suppose that the young Nasamonians

[1] R. Mauny, in D. and S. Robert, eds., *Tegdaoust I: recherches sur Aoudaghost* (Paris, 1970), 74.

mentioned by Herodotus (II.32) crossed the Sahara with the help of chariots. These are not specifically mentioned, but the most logical itinerary by which the Nasamonians could have reached a great river on the borders of Negroland, which had crocodiles in it and which flowed from west to east (perhaps the Niger bend between Bourem and Timbuktu), would be the central Saharan 'chariot track'. But the aim of the Nasamonians' journey was discovery, not trade. Moreover it cannot be too strongly stressed that trans-Saharan trade must have been of inconsiderable volume before the coming of the Arabs in the seventh century AD, and virtually nonexistent before the introduction of the camel.

The horse continued to be of importance in the Sahara up to the first century BC. Strabo tells us that the Garamantes were then raising as many as 100,000 colts a year, and that the Pharusii and Nigritae travelled through their territories with waterskins tied underneath the bellies of their mounts. But this was in the northern Sahara, and it is unlikely that local resources would have allowed the raising of horses on this scale in the middle of the desert. Conditions could have become better again to the south of the Sahara, where local agriculture would have provided the grain required for fodder.

The few accounts that have survived of journeys in the northern Sahara, like that of the Nasamonians already mentioned, suggest that these were made with the help of horses. According to Athenaios, on the authority of Aristotle, a Carthaginian named Mago crossed the waterless desert three times, eating dry flour and without drinking. What is involved here must have been a short trip, perhaps between two oases not too far from the Mediterranean, in southern Tunisia, Tripolitania or the Fezzan, and not a crossing of the whole desert. This would have been impossible without water, even in a chariot. A man needs an absolute minimum of a litre of water a day in the Sahara, and this is with severe rationing and assuming the most favourable circumstances. The normal average consumption is 4.5 litres a day.[1] It is not surprising that the journeys attributed to Mago have aroused the scepticism of many modern authorities.

Cornelius Balbus's campaign of 19 BC (Pliny, *Natural history*, v.5) took place, according to J. Desanges, in the south of the Department

[1] On the consumption of water in the Sahara, see T. Monod, *Majabat al-Koubra, contribution à l'étude de l'empty quarter ouest saharien*, *Mémoires de l'IFAN* (Dakar, 1958), **52**, 296–302; on Mago, J. Leclant, 'Témoinage des sources antiques sur les pistes menant à l'Oasis d'Ammon', *Bulletin de l'Institut Français d'Archéologie Orientale*, 1950, **49**, 208.

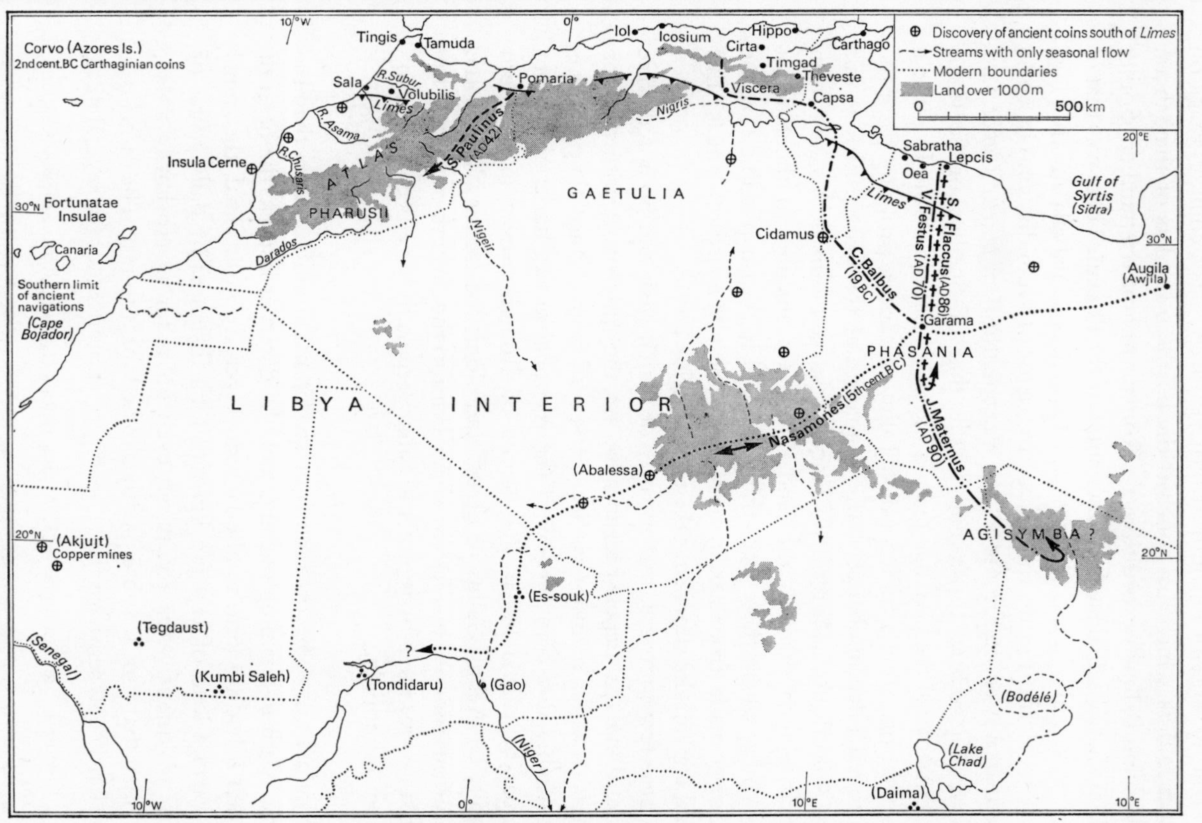

39 The Ancient World's knowledge of the Sahara.
It is uncertain whether the Nasamones actually reached the Niger.

of Constantine, in Ghadames and the Fezzan.[1] Suetonius Paulinus's expedition in AD 42 from Pomaria (the modern Tlemcen) to the river Ger (the Wadi Guir in south-eastern Morocco) was a counter-attack on desert raiders which just touched the northern borders of the Sahara. Following Balbus's expedition, the Romans mounted a number of other military actions against the Garamantes of the Fezzan. There was that of the Proconsuls Junius Blaesus and Cornelius Dolabella in AD 21–4; that of Valerius Festus, the legate proprietor of Numidia, who in AD 69 discovered a shorter route to the Fezzan, the *Iter praeter Caput Saxi* (Pliny, *Nat. Hist.,* v.38); and finally that of Suellius or Septimus Flaccus against the Garamantes and the Ethiopians in AD 86. In AD 90 a traveller, probably a trader, called Julius Maternus, profiting from the improved relations between the Romans and the Garamantes at this time – no doubt as a result of Flaccus's success – made his way from Lepcis Magna through the land of the Garamantes to the land of Agisymba, where there were rhinoceroses.[2] It is also possible that the journeys made from AD 69 onwards made some use of camels; this could explain the short-cut taken by Valerius Festus.

These few journeys, the majority of which it should be noted were made along the Lepcis-Fezzan axis, are the only penetrations of the Sahara of which memory has been preserved from classical times. This is remarkably few compared with the reconnaissances undertaken over comparable distances at the height of Roman power in southern Arabia, by Aelius Gallus in 25 BC, and along the Upper Nile, by the centurions sent out by Nero in AD 66. Prior to the seventh century of the Christian era, the crossing of the Sahara seems to have been a Libyan-Berber monopoly.

The camel was to become much more important in the Sahara than the horse. With the coming of the camel, the desert at last had the beast of burden it had hitherto totally lacked. A very robust animal, the camel can carry a load of 125–150 kg over long distances by daily stages of 25 to 30 km; if necessary, it can even go as far as 150 km in a day, provided that time is subsequently allowed for it to rest. The camel is at once hardy and sensitive; it is able to go without water for several days,

[1] J. Desanges, 'Le Triomphe de Cornelius Balbus (19 BC)', *Revue Africaine* (Algiers), 1957, **101**, 5–43.

[2] On the general subject of these journeys to the lands of Garamantes, see J. Desanges, 'Note sur la datation de l'expédition de Julius Maternus au pays d'Agysymba', *Latomus: Revue d'Études Latines*, 1964, **23**, 4, 713–25. The information concerning Blaesus and Dolabella is based on Tacitus, *Histories*, IV.50, and Pliny, *Natural History*, V.38; and that for Flaccus and Maternus on Zonaras, XI.19, and for Marinus of Tyre on Ptolemy, I.8.

though it drinks considerable quantities, even of brackish water, once it has reached a water-point, and it knows how to survive on the poor vegetation that the desert affords provided that it can get it in adequate amounts.

When considering the question of when the camel was introduced into Africa, it should first of all be noted that remains of a camelid animal, *Camelus thomazi*, occur in Early and Middle Stone Age sites, but very rarely at sites of the Late Stone Age or at neolithic sites. There are some who think that camels have been continuously present in Africa, but one of the best authorities on this subject, Henri Lhote, has observed that, so far as the Sahara is concerned, there is not a single representation of a camel among the thousands of known rock-drawings surviving from the time of the early hunters and herders in the desert.[1] There is therefore a definite break between the disappearance of *Camelus thomazi* and the introduction of *Camelus dromedarius*. It is symptomatic that very careful excavation of the Haua Fteah Cave in Cyrenaica revealed not a single camelid bone (whereas a fragment of the pelvis of *Equus mauritanicus* was found in the Early Stone Age levels).[2]

In the Nile Valley also, the camel makes no appearance at all in the large corpus of Egyptian paintings; it is represented only by a few rare objects – the theriomorphic vase from Abusir el-Meleq, which is probably predynastic, i.e. earlier than about 3400 BC, and on another proto-dynastic vase which, though found at Byblos, is undoubtedly of Egyptian provenance; by camel-hair cords from Dynasties III and IV (after 2778 BC); and by some other objects and in some rock-drawings whose dating is uncertain.[3] In view of the very early caravan links between Arabia and the Nile Valley, it would be very surprising if the camel had not reached Egypt before the first millennium BC; doubtless there were religious reasons for the lack of representations of the animal earlier than this.

Camels could have been first introduced to Egypt from 1680 BC by the invading Hyksos, but it is not until the end of the second millennium that references to them begin to be found: there is a pottery figure of a camel bearing a load from the time of the XIV Dynasty, and there are references in Genesis (37:26) and Exodus (9:3) which indicate that

[1] H. Lhote, 'Le cheval et le chameau', 1213.

[2] C. B. M. McBurney, *The Hana Fteah (Cyrenaica) and the Stone Age of the south-east Mediterranean* (Cambridge, 1967).

[3] G. Caton-Thompson, 'The camel in dynastic Egypt', *Man*, 1934, 21; V. G. Childe, *New light on the most ancient East* (London, 1954), 65; A. L. Robinson, 'The camel in antiquity', *Sudan Notes and Records*, 1936, 47–69; F. E. Zeuner, *A history of domesticated animals* (London, 1963), 349–58.

Arabs (Ishmaelites) had brought camels to Egypt with loads of spices, balm and myrrh. The Assyrian conquerors of the seventh century BC, with their Arab auxiliaries, brought with them a contingent of camels,[1] and in effect it is from the time of the Saite Dynasty that these animals begin to be depicted on Egyptian monuments. When Cambyses conquered Egypt in 525 BC, he too made use of cameleers, and it would be very surprising if the Sabaeans on their part did not bring camels across the Red Sea when they established themselves in the Ethiopian coastlands.

According to Herodotus (VII.69–70, 125, 184–5), 10,000 camels were used by Xerxes's army on its European expedition; it would therefore seem reasonable that he brought them to Egypt when he reoccupied the country in 484 BC. Alexander must have done the same for his expedition to the Siwa Oasis in 332 BC, even if there is no evidence for this before the late references in Quintus Curtius (*Hist. Alex.* IV.7.30). Antigonos had a large contingent of camelry in his army when he tried to occupy Egypt in 306 BC, and in 283 BC the animal took part in the ceremonies attending the installation of Ptolemy.

It was probably during the Ptolemaic period, when Cyrenaica was an Egyptian province, that the camel spread to the west of the Nile and also towards Eritrea – as is testified by an inscription at Adulis. There is mention of a camel-driver in an inscription on the sanctuary of Masinissa at Dougga in Tunisia in *c.* 150 BC, and this is followed by the well-known reference by Caesar (*Bell. Afr.*, LXVIII.4) to the twenty-two camels captured from Juba by the Romans on the occasion of the battle of Thapsus in 46 BC. Camel bones found in a pyramid at Meroe (20 BC) belong to approximately this period.

Camels became common in the Roman provinces of Africa and then spread into the Sahara only after the beginning of the Christian era, and doubtless this was a slow process. The *Notitia Dignitatum*, of the fourth century AD, demonstrates that there were camelry squadrons in Egypt at Maximianopolis, Psinaula and Prectis, and the Syrian troops stationed on the Numidian *limes* certainly included some camel units. But there are few references to camels in the western provinces: according to Ammianus Marcellinus (XXVIII.6.5), Romanus, *comes Africae*, required the inhabitants of Lepcis in AD 363–4 to provide him with 4,000 camels (Charles Courtois thinks that this figure should read 400); there is a passage in Vegesus (*Epit. rei mill.*, III.23) referring to the Berbers' use of

[1] A. J. Arkell, *A history of the Sudan to AD 1821* (London, 1955), 128: King Esarhaddon's campaign in 671 'crossing the desert of Sinai with the help of a camel train'.

the camel in warfare; two passages in Procopius (*Bell. Vand.*, I.8, 25ff; II.11, 1759) describe the engagements between the Vandals and the Byzantine forces in southern Tunisia; some fifteen references in Corippus's *Johannis* relate to the end of the Vandal and the beginning of the Byzantine period.[1]

This is little enough for the first five centuries of the Christian era, and for a region for which the archaeological data and the literary sources are relatively good. Charles Courtois has thus seen fit to question E. F. Gautier's conclusions concerning the introduction of the camel to Africa at the end of the Roman empire, which he says was 'a major development' with 'incalculable consequences', 'an economic revolution planned and effected by the Roman administration'. In similar fashion he takes a stand against the rigid acceptance of Stéphane Gsell's thesis that it was at this time and thanks to the camel that the Berbers conquered the northern Sahara. He points out that the Berbers were already in the northern desert, and that the Ethiopians noticed in these regions by the classical authors were 'burned faces', i.e. Libyan-Berbers.[2] More recently, E. W. Bovill in his turn sought to prove that the introduction of the camel into Libya by the Romans was of major significance.[3] He argues that the resultant shortening of the roads to the Fezzan must have brought the Romans and the Garamantes closer together. Thanks to camel transport, the latter's territory became more easily accessible, thus making possible the southerly expeditions of V. Festus (*c.* AD 69), S. Flaccus (*c.* AD 86) and J. Maternus (*c.* AD 90), and leading, through the increase of trans-Saharan trade, to the economic growth of Tripolitania under the Severus family.

In the last resort, it is impossible to say that any of the authorities is wrong; in the absence of more explicit written sources and in the present state of the archaeological evidence, the best that can be done is to venture a balanced assessment. Gautier was right in thinking that in the long term the introduction of the camel meant an economic revolution, a major development with incalculable consequences. But the coming of the Arabs and the establishment of organized and lasting commercial relationships based on profitable exchanges were necessary before this revolution could be manifest, and these things did

[1] C. Courtois, *Les Vandales et l'Afrique* (Algiers–Paris, 1955), 100–4.

[2] Courtois, *Les Vandales*, 101, with reference to E.-F. Gautier, *Le Passé de l'Afrique du Nord: les siècles obscurs* (Paris, 1952), 208–9; S. Gsell, 'La Tripolitaine et le Sahara au IIIe siècle de notre ère', *Mémoires de l'Académie d'Inscriptions et Belles Lettres*, 1926, **43**, 149–66; see also Desanges, 'Note sur la datation'.

[3] E. W. Bovill, *The golden trade of the Moors*, 2nd edn (Oxford, 1968), 36–44.

not happen until the seventh century AD. It is by no means proven that the Romans had any inkling of the importance of the introduction of the camel into Africa, and Courtois is right to mistrust the large figure given for the number of camels in Tripolitania in the third century. It would seem more reasonable to suppose that the prosperity of this province from this time was due rather to the attention given to it by members of the Severus family. By bringing peace to the province and defending its frontiers, on the one hand they encouraged its agriculture (olives and grain), and on the other they encouraged the growth of its towns – through the garrisons they stationed in the province and also through the public and prestigious works they caused to be erected (eloquently demonstrated by the ruins of Lepcis).

As for Bovill's thesis concerning the closer relations which developed between the Romans and the Garamantes in the second half of the first century AD, it is by no means impossible that Rome's use of camel-eers drawn from the ranks of their Syrian legions helped them to bring the Garamantes to heel, enabling the Romans to take them by surprise by making use of routes which horses could not take for lack of water. And there is no reason why the Garamantes should not have shown their goodwill by allowing a Roman such as Maternus to take part in one of their expeditions (including camelry) against the southern 'Ethiopians' (in all probability the people of Teda and Tibesti and their neighbourhood). But it should be noted that there is no mention whatsoever of camels in the all too brief narrative given by Ptolemy (I.8). There is nothing to justify a belief in an increase in trans-Saharan trade in the time of the Severi. It is not until the seventh and, above all, the ninth and tenth centuries of the Christian era that one can see the inception of a regular trade of major significance – the slave-trade – along the route from the Mediterranean to Lake Chad via the Fezzan. The most that can be seen for this route for the period from the first to the fourth centuries is the trade in circus animals (such as the two-horned desert rhinoceros which is depicted on Roman coins of Domitian's reign – exactly the time when, *c.* AD 90, Maternus undertook his famous expedition), and in ivory, hides and a few slaves.

The most serious consequence for the Roman colony in Tripolitania was obviously that henceforward the Saharan Berbers were possessed of camels. This meant that later, when, after Diocletian, the African *limes* were pulled back, the Berbers were able to regain control of lands which the Romans had originally colonized, and to threaten the Roman towns. But this development, of some importance in the Mediterranean coastlands, is the principal reason for the growth of Berber power in the Sahara as a whole. Henceforward the Berbers possessed a beast ideally suited to the terrain, giving them not only the means to subsist in the desert, but also military strength and the ability to control the trans-Saharan roads. In the seventh and eighth centuries AD, the Arabs were faced with a desert inhabited by tribes of cameleers, and in the tenth century one account has Tin Beroutan sending 15,000 camels against his enemies, while another has him putting 100,000 camelry into the field on his own account and another 50,000 at the disposition of his ally, Tarin. It is possible to believe that the Saharan Berbers possessed comparable numbers of camels well before the seventh century AD.

The paucity of written sources and of archaeological evidence makes it impossible to date this growth of the camel resources of the Sahara more exactly. Lhote justly observes that the camel can be viewed as 'progressively replacing the horse with no sudden change, as though this newly arrived animal was seen by a horse-owning society to meet its needs better than horses ever could'[1] – to which one must add, 'its needs *in the desert*'.

The introduction of the camel to the Ennedi massif between the Nile and Lake Chad took place as late as it did in the northern Sahara because, as Bailloud has pointed out, 'The camel's appearance in the rock-drawings suggest that this took place after the beginning of the Christian era.'[2]

The main victims of the introduction of the camel to the Sahara were its southern peoples, the black tribesmen of the Sahel. To enable them to push home their slaving-raids, the Saharan nomads now possessed a riding and pack-animal ideally suited to the country, 'the perfect instrument for the raider; the mount of the brigand and not of the soldier', as Lhote has somewhat severely commented.[3] It should, however, be noted that the conquering warrior (as opposed, that is, to Lhote's raiding brigand), even if he preferred the horse, nevertheless did not entirely neglect the camel. If it was a useful auxiliary in the Maghrib, it was indispensable in the desert: ʿUqba b. Nāfiʿ undertook his expedition from Wadan to Kawar in AD 666 with 'a force of 400 light cavalry, 400 camels and 800 waterskins'.[4] And, as was pointed out

1 H. Lhote, 'Le cheval et le chameau', 1216.

2 G. Bailloud, 'Dans les tiroirs du Tchad', *Le Nouvel Observateur* (Paris), 1965, 14, 1.

3 H. Lhote, 'Le cheval et le chameau', 1224.

4 Ibn ʿAbd al-Ḥakam, *Conquête de l'Afrique du Nord et de l'Espagne*, ed. and trans. [of the part dealing with the Maghrib of *Kitāb futūḥ Miṣr wa'l-Maghrib wa-akhbārihā*] by A. Gateau (Algiers, 1942), 57.

earlier, the Romans were already using squadrons of camelry in Upper Egypt in the fourth century.

The Sahara has thus been traversable at all times since the beginning of the neolithic period. First of all, it was crossed on foot – and this even into modern times – by isolated individuals or by pastoralists driving their flocks or herds, the most formidable enemy being man rather than the climate or the lack of water. Then, throughout the first millennium BC, it was traversed by horses pulling light chariots, and finally it was crossed with the aid of camels, these being the transport animals best suited to survive in and to journey across the desert, and, above all, to carry goods across it. The vital factors were to have good knowledge of the routes that were best supplied with water, to avoid brigands, and to travel in the most favourable season, namely the winter. In short, successful crossing was essentially a matter of good organization, and this was most efficaciously developed by the caravans which, after the coming of the Arabs, were developed to meet the need to establish regular commercial relations between the Maghrib and the Sudan.

THE FAILURE TO MAKE MARITIME CONTACT WITH WEST AFRICA

In view of the great difficulty involved in crossing the Sahara and the inadequacy of the means of transport available before the coming of the camel, it would be logical to ask why men did not think of outflanking the desert by sea. The distance between the mouths of the Wadi Darʿa and the river Senegal, which respectively mark the northern and southern limits of the Sahara, is only about 1,800 km. From about 1100 BC, the Phoenicians had been established astride the Straits of Gibraltar, at Ceuta, Tangier and Cadiz. A little later, the Carthaginians founded settlements at Lixus (Larache), and subsequently at Sala (Chella, near Rabat) and, further to the south, to as far as the island of Soueira (Mogador), the *Cerne contra Atlantem* of Polybius, where pottery, coins, glassware, bronze-work and other antiquities have been found dating from the seventh century BC to the fifth century AD. It is also known from writers such as Pliny and Ptolemy that the Carthaginians had discovered the Canary Islands, as well as Cape Juby, opposite them on the mainland. The question thus arises as to why they did not proceed further to the south. The trade winds blow throughout the year from the

Canaries to Cape Blanco in Mauritania, and in the winter to as far as Cape Verde, beyond the mouth of the Senegal. It would thus seem that in principle the ships of classical times would have experienced no major problem in voyaging from Morocco to Senegal other than that of carrying adequate supplies of food and water.

In the parallel case of seas with regular monsoon winds, such as the Indian Ocean, it is known from Pliny (*Nat. Hist.*, VI) that sailors could cover the 3,800 km from southern Arabia to southern India in forty days, implying a mean daily run of some 100 km. Thus eighteen days should have been enough for a voyage from the Wadi Darʿa to the Senegal. Yet – although a considerable number of historians have argued the contrary – it would seem that the sailors of classical times never went further south than the Canaries – nor, for that matter, further west (despite Thor Heyerdahl's spectacular voyage in 1970). Essentially the explanation is that the *return voyage to the north was impossible*; off these western coasts, the prevailing wind is always from the north, providing a head wind which would effectively prevent the northwards advance even of ships which could use oars for propulsion.

It should be remembered that the sailors of classical times possessed two types of sea-going vessel. One type, with a square sail and a steering oar, was broad and fat (with a length-to-beam ratio of about 2:1), and could be managed by a small crew. The other was a galley, propelled by oarsmen. The number of oarsmen needed, even if it rarely exceeded fifty, meant that only national navies and very rich individuals could afford such ships. The galleys, of course, used a sail when the wind was favourable to save the strength of their rowers. But neither type of vessel could make progress against contrary winds of even moderate force, and this was the situation which faced anyone wanting to go from south to north along the Saharan coastline.

In support of this thesis it must be noted that no substantial authentic finds from classical times have been found by archaeologists to the south of Soueira/Mogador. The islands of Herne (in the gulf of Rio de Oro), Arguin, Tidra and Goree – which had they been further north would certainly have attracted the attention of the Phoenicians, Carthaginians and Romans, and which would consequently have revealed evidence of pottery, coins and other classical remains – have been surveyed and excavated without any result whatsoever. Such few finds as have been made – Roman coins at Goree and a cameo at Conakry – have been practical jokes played on local archaeologists by

40 Square-sailed and rudderless Roman ship.
Such ships could not tack, and even galleys with oars could not advance against the steady trade winds. Thus they could not return northwards to the Canary Islands, which were joined to the Mediterranean by a zone of variable winds.

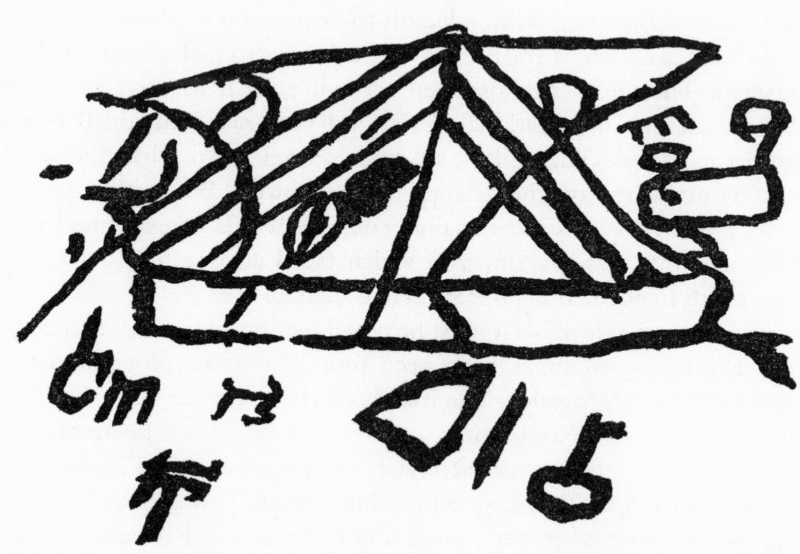

41 Ancient or medieval ship engraved at Azru Aklan, Dar'a, southern Morocco.
(After photo: Institut Fondamental d'Afrique Noire [IFAN], Dakar.)

their friends.[1] The *akori* beads of the lands bordering the Gulf of Guinea, which until very recently were thought to go back to classical times, are now known to have a history of no more than a few centuries. The chevron beads, once thought to be evidence of contact with Ancient Egypt, have been manufactured continuously down to modern times. The mysterious cylindrical blue *cori* beads referred to by sixteenth-century Portuguese travellers and writers are still a subject for discussion, but no one now supposes a classical origin for them.[2] There is no doubt that two 'bronze' lamps found at Attabubu in Ghana resemble those of sixth- and seventh-century Coptic Egypt,[3] but they could quite simply be copies of authentic prototypes taken across the desert by Arab merchants when the gold-trade of the Niger was opened up in the eighth and ninth centuries, no doubt as part of an assortment of out-of-date objects which could be passed off as trade goods.

Some explanation is still needed for the discovery of a few isolated finds of classical coins, such as those at Buea in Cameroun and at Matadi in Zaïre, though it is not impossible that these are the results of practical jokes such as those known to have been practised at Goree and Conakry. Clearly the utmost caution is necessary, such as that displayed by Schofield when, in reference to similar finds on the East African coast, he talked of 'the ancient coin myth'.[4] In any case, however, it is certain – from the evidence of Ptolemy and of *The Periplus of the Erythrean Sea* – that the sailors of classical times did sail as far as southern Tanzania. On the east coast the seasonal reversal of the monsoon winds made it easy to sail to the south during the winter, and no less easy to sail back towards the Gulf of Aden in the summer.

There is the further question of what traders might hope to find on the coast of the Sahara desert, and, beyond this, on the shores of the Gulf of Guinea. Skins and hides, animals for the circus, ivory, perhaps a little gold (if it may be supposed that Sudanese peoples were already exploiting their deposits of the metal), and some slaves would hardly have made such a long journey profitable. The only merchandise of sufficiently high value in relation to its bulk and weight would have

[1] R. Mauny, *Les siècles obscurs de l'Afrique noire, histoire et archéologie* (Paris, 1970), 79–81.

[2] R. Mauny, *Tableau géographique de l'ouest africain au moyen âge* (Dakar, 1961), 273–4; M. Kalous, 'A contribution to the problem of Akori beads', *Journal of African History*, 1966, 7, 1, 61–6; and Kalous, 'Akori beads', *Bässler Archiv.*, 1968, **16**, 1, 89–97.

[3] A. J. Arkell, 'Gold Coast copies of Vth–VIIIth century bronze lamps', *Antiquity*, March 1950, 38–40.

[4] Bovill, *The golden trade*, 36; O. de Bouveignes, 'Note sur quelques monnaies trouvées au Congo belge', *Brousse* (Leopoldville), 1946, **1–2**, 25; J. F. Schofield, 'L'Âge des peintures rupestres du sud de l'Afrique', *L'Anthropologie* (Paris), 1949, 20–32.

been gold. On the assumption that gold-mining had already begun in the Sudan – and this is far from having been proved – it is not impossible to believe that Carthaginians engaging in silent barter for gold on the African coast beyond the Straits of Gibraltar mentioned by Herodotus (IV.196; text quoted in chapter 2, p. 137) should have gone to seek for the precious metal from the Sudan on the coasts between the Atlas and the Wadi Darʿa, i.e. to as far south as the winds would permit their return northwards.

The literary sources dealing with the voyages of classical times along the west coast beyond the Wadi Darʿa are neither numerous nor very informative. The subject has been fully discussed by the author elsewhere,[1] and the discussion here will eschew detail and concentrate on the major issues (see also chapter 2, pp. 133–40).

The earliest surviving account is of a voyage undertaken about 600 BC, on the initiative of the Pharaoh Necho II, by Phoenician sailors starting from the Red Sea. Their instructions were to sail round Africa and to return to Egypt through the Mediterranean. According to Herodotus, the sole source for the story, they took three years on the journey, landing at each seed-time and continuing after each harvest. 'These men made a statement which I do not myself believe, though others may, to the effect that as they sailed on a westerly course round the southern end of Libya, they had the sun on their right.' (IV.43) For us, this is *the* evidence, but not for Herodutus's contemporaries; for they supposed that the African coast ran directly west from Cape Guardafui to the Atlantic and the Straits of Gibraltar, i.e. that the southern limit of Africa was well north of the Equator. Opinions are evenly divided as to whether this voyage of Necho's Phoenician sailors did actually occur; Herodotus's own reservation seems to suggest that it is certainly possible that it did. The only possible explanation for the Phoenician's success in going from the Senegal to Morocco against the prevailing winds would be that they abandoned their boats and made this part of the journey overland by the western 'chariot track', only taking to the sea again in southern Morocco, where they could borrow boats from the Carthaginians, who, as has been seen, traded on its coast.

Second, there is the story of the voyage of Sataspes, a Persian who was condemned to death by Xerxes (485–465 BC), only to have his sentence commuted for one thought to be even more severe, namely to oblige him to circumnavigate Africa by sea, this time starting out to the west. According to the account given by Sataspes on his return, as

[1] Mauny, *Les siècles obscurs*, 91–107.

recorded by Herodotus (IV.43), he proceeded southwards for several months until he reached a country inhabited by small men wearing clothes made from palm leaves, who fled into the hills when he landed. He went no further, since at this point his vessel could make no headway. Xerxes, thinking that Sataspes was lying as well as having failed in the task assigned to him, had him impaled. In point of fact, Sataspes must have been lying: he cannot have gone further than southern Morocco, and must have tarried there in some isolated anchorage for Xerxes's anger to cool. His crew, doubtless Phoenicians, would have had no difficulty in convincing him that he could not venture further south. In any case, even if Sataspes's ship had got as far as the Gulf of Guinea, it would not have been able to proceed further in the teeth of the contrary winds which prevail from Gabon to the Cape of Good Hope and from the Cape to the mouth of the Zambezi (where he would have been able to pick up the summer monsoon).

Next there comes a voyage said to have been made before the fourth century BC, by Euthymenes of Marseilles, to a river in which it appears that there were 'animals similar to those of the Nile'. Indeed, he apparently thought he was dealing with a branch of that river. Little can be made of the short passages which refer to this voyage, which are the work of writers who lived much later: Seneca (first century AD), Aelius Aristides (second century) and Marcium of Heracles (fourth century). No doubt this story is based on the tales of sailors returning from southern Morocco, where *Varanus niloticus* is found, a species of large lizard which could well be transformed into a crocodile in the imaginations of sailors swapping stories in quayside taverns.

The well-known text called the *Periplus of Hanno* raises quite other problems, and there is a very considerable literature on this subject. Most commentators have accepted the authenticity and the truth of the *Periplus* – including, for a long time, the present writer.

The Carthaginians, a nation of shopkeepers, wrote little, and the capture of Carthage by the Romans in 146 BC led to the destruction of most of what they did write. But this quite long text, eighteen paragraphs in all, has survived from this all but complete darkness into the light of the present. It gives details of an expedition which was made at the height of Carthage's power in the fifth century BC, with the intention of settling the Atlantic coasts of Morocco and of exploring the coastline further afield. For the various stages of Hanno's expedition, for interpretations of its various adventures, and for identifications of the furthest point reached, reference may be made to a number of authorities.[1] Cary and Warmington think that the high and fiery mountain which Hanno called the 'Chariot of the Gods' must be Mt Kakulima in the Republic of Guinea, and that his 'Horn of the South' is Sherbro Sound in Sierra Leone. But many other commentators think that the fiery Chariot of the Gods can only be Mt Cameroun, the only active volcano on the West African coast, and that the Horn of the South must be the Gulf of Gabon.

Only a few authorities have attacked the authenticity of the text of the *Periplus* itself; most take this for granted. However in a little-known article published as long ago as 1882,[2] Henri Tauxier demonstrated that the text is a Hellenistic forgery, dating from the first century BC (the first reference to the *Periplus* is in Pliny), which borrows from Homer, Herodotus, Pseudo-Scylax, Polybius and other authors. He concluded that it was nothing but a 'tissue of lies' and 'absurd errors'. More recently, Gabriel Germain, though more subtle in his emphases and less categorical in his opinions, comes to more or less the same conclusions: the *Periplus* is 'for three-quarters of its length at least the work of a mediocre *littérateur*', and its style betrays its relatively recent date. In his opinion, serious discussion of the significance of this literary concoction is permanently invalidated.[3] The present writer is now wholly of the same opinion.

If it is difficult to believe that the Carthaginians could have overcome the problem of returning to the north against the trade-winds, it is even more difficult to recognize West African reality in the tangled description given in the *Periplus*. The text does not ring true after the first seven paragraphs, which relate to northern Morocco. This, of course, was well known to the Ancient World to as far as the colony of Sala (Chella, near Rabat), where the Roman *limes* reached the Atlantic, and even beyond, to as far as the island of Soueira (Mogador), where have been found remains of Getulian purple ware and numerous other objects – the evidence, that has already been discussed, that it was long frequented by the sailors and merchants of classical antiquity.

Carthaginian activity on the coasts of southern Morocco is also evident from the *Periplus* written by an unknown Greek author of the fourth century BC who is commonly referred to as 'Pseudo-Scylax'.

[1] See in particular M. Cary and E. H. Warmington, *The ancient explorers*, revised edn (London, 1963), 63–8.

[2] H. Tauxier, 'Les deux rédactions de Périple d'Hannon', *Revue Africaine* (Algiers), 1882, 15–37.

[3] G. Germain, 'Qu'est-ce que le Périple d'Hannon? Document, amplification littéraire, ou faux intégral?', *Hespéris*, 1957, **44**, 205–48.

This describes the coast from the Straits of Gibraltar to as far as an island called Cerne (see quotation in chapter 2, p. 138), near which the Phoenicians traded with 'Ethiopians' (i.e. 'people with burnt faces' – not necessarily Negroes) who were very tall and good-looking, were good horsemen, and who cultivated grapes and made wine – which indicates that the travellers were still in a Mediterranean and not in a tropical climate. Subsequently, the Greek historian Polybius himself travelled along the Atlantic coast of Morocco as part of an 'armistice commission' sent out at the time of the fall of Carthage in 146 BC. His job was to reconnoitre the Punic settlements along the length of this coastline and especially at the river mouths. Polybius thus mentions Lixus (the modern Loukkos), Subur (Sebou), Sala (the river at Sala, Chella), Anatis (Oum er-Rbia), Quosenus (the river of Couz, Tensift), the island of *Cerne contra Atlantem* (Mogador), Salsus (Sous), Masatat (Massa), Bambotus (Noun) and Darados (Darʿa). Here, then, from an authoritative source, is a list of the principal ports on the Atlantic coast of Morocco, places with recognizable names which have changed very little over two thousand years. This is all the more reason for rejecting the *Periplus of Hanno*, with its very fluid toponymy, of a few centuries earlier.

According to Posidonius and Strabo, a Greek called Eudoxos of Cyzica also travelled in the same regions in the second century BC. Sailing from Gades (Cadiz), he was apparently shipwrecked in southern Morocco in a land 'adjacent to the kingdom of Bocchus'. During the course of this voyage, he landed on an island which was well watered and wooded (doubtless Madeira). He took to the sea again with one sailing vessel and a fifty-oar galley, but he did not return from this second expedition. At the beginning of the first century BC, the Canary Islands were discovered by sailors from Cadiz. The successful mariners are named by Pliny (VI.31–2) as Statius Sebosus and, subsequently, Juba, King of Mauretania. The islands which he mentions and very briefly describes were Ombrion, the two Junonias, Capraria and Ninguria.

All this information is recapitulated in Ptolemy's *Geography*, composed about the middle of the second century AD, and which represents the *Summum* of the classical world's knowledge of Africa beyond the Roman *limes*. It is obviously of very varied value. Ptolemy has much to say about the Mediterranean countries which formed part of the Roman empire, and here his information may commonly be taken at face value. But as soon as he begins to deal with the northern Sahara immediately beyond the *limes*, caution becomes necessary. Further south, and to as far as his Equator, Ptolemy gives us a series of mountains, rivers and lakes, and tribal names, very few of which can be identified except to the east of the Nile, for here, of course, the Graeco-Romans did have a first-hand acquaintance with the coast to as far as Zanzibar and beyond.[1]

To the west of the Nile, it seems clear that Ptolemy expanded the meagre data that he possessed for the northern Sahara and, on the coast, for southern Morocco and the Canaries, almost indefinitely far to the south. Thus he sometimes used the name of a single Moroccan river two or even three times. The Wadi Sebou appears twice, as *Soubour* and *Soubos*; there are three *Sala* or *Salathos*; the Wadi Tensift-Couz occurs as *Cousa* and as *Chousaris*; the Wadi Noun occurs twice, as *Nouios* and *Nias*; the Wadi Massa twice as *Massa* and *Masitholos* – even if there is only one Wadi Darʿa, *Darados*. It should be noted that his *Theon Ochema*, the 'Chariot of the Gods', is given as the source of the Masitholos; it must therefore be identified with the Anti-Atlas. Finally, Ptolemy's Canary Islands (*Makaron nesoi*) are stretched southwards almost to 16°N, whereas in fact their southernmost point lies in about 28°N. Ptolemy's map, drawn at the height of the Roman empire, is the best possible illustration of the classical world's lack of knowledge of the Atlantic coast of Africa south of Cape Juby.

There was certainly no maritime contact in the west between the Maghrib and tropical Africa, and contact by land across the Sahara was minimal. The lure of exploring the unknown territory to the south could lead a handful of adventurous young Nasamonians of Libyan-Berber stock to reconnoitre to the Niger in the fifth century BC but, as has been seen, no one seems to have repeated this exploit. The most the Romans did at the height of their imperial power was to mount a few counter-raids against the peoples living immediately south of the *limes*; only Julius Maternus's expedition of about AD 90, which either saw or heard tell of rhinoceroses in the land of Agisymba, seems to have reached further to the south, conceivably to the western borders of Tibesti.

There was nothing in West Africa to parallel the direct and continuing contact which the Romans had with India from the first century BC, or the sea-voyages made by their agents in the second century AD to China and Indonesia and to the coasts of modern Tanzania, many

[1] J. Desanges, 'Catalogue des tribus africaines de l'antiquité classique à l'ouest du Nil', *Publications de la Section d'Histoire de la Faculté des Lettres de Dakar*, 1962, 4, 297f.; R. Mauny, 'L'Ouest africain chez Ptolemée (vers + 141 AD)', *IIe Conference Internacional dos Africanistas Ocidentais (Bissau, 1947)* (Lisbon, 1950), I, 241–93.

thousands of kilometres beyond their own Mediterranean sea. Even at the height of their empire, Roman traders did not think it worth their while to cross the Sahara to lands which could provide them – and then only at great expense – with no more than the occasional animals for their circuses, the little ivory, and the few precious stones and rare medicines, which were brought to their frontier posts in the Fezzan.[1] Possibly things would have been different had they known of the existence of gold on the upper Niger and of tin on the Bauchi plateau. But the lands beyond their *limes* had no merchants of their own, whether Negro or Libyan-Berber, who could have acted as intermediaries in or providers of trade, to compare with the Parthian, Chinese, Scythian and Arab traders. At the beginning of the Christian era, West Africa had hardly emerged from the Neolithic, and its primitive economy was still at the stage of tribal barter.

There is only one Libyan-Berber site at any distance beyond the *limes* on the route to the Niger which has revealed any evidence of the culture of the classical Mediterranean world. This is the ruins of the residence or funeral monument near the Oasis of Abalessa, west of Ahaggar, which is traditionally associated with a Berber woman called Tin Hinan. Excavations here in 1929 by Khun de Prorok and, again, in 1933 by M. Reygasse produced glass and stone beads, fourth-century Roman lamps, and coins of Constantine's reign. Thus between Roman North Africa and at least the Ahaggar there were relations of some kind in the fourth century AD, but it is impossible to say more than this. By sea, after the exploratory voyages of the first century BC and of the early years of the Christian era, even contact with the Canary Islands seems to have lapsed. No writer after Ptolemy offers any new information and, as has already been made plain, despite the research which has been undertaken on the islets along the coast from southern Morocco to Cape Verde, archaeology has revealed no trace of any contact between the classical Mediterranean world and West Africa.

EARLY FOOD PRODUCTION IN THE SAHARA AND THE WESTERN SUDAN

The object of this section is less to consider the problem of the origins and the development of agriculture and animal husbandry in Africa south of the Tropic of Cancer, than to try and establish the situation

[1] R. Mauny, 'Le Périple de la mer Erythrée et le problème du commerce romain en Afrique au sud de limes', *Journal de la Société des Africanistes*, 1968, **38**, 1, 30–3.

relating to food production in the Sahara and in the sub-Saharan western Sudan towards the beginning of the Christian era. Despite important recent work[1] and current research, for example by Patrick Munson and Thurstan Shaw, the question of the origins of sub-Saharan African agriculture is far from being solved. There was certainly a proto-agricultural stage in which certain wild food-plants – such as *Digitaria*, *Pennisetum*, *Sorghum*, *Oryza glaberrima*, *Dioscorea*, to name only a few – were specifically selected for gathering. A principal issue is whether there was an independent invention of agriculture by the Negroes of West Africa, as is supposed by G. P. Murdock,[2] or whether they adapted to their own conditions the agriculture that they could see being practised in the Nile Valley upstream of Aswan. This was itself inspired from Egypt, which in this respect cannot be distinguished from the Near East, which – on the basis of the present evidence – seems to have been the part of the world in which agriculture was first developed from vegeculture.

It would seem that Murdock's hypothesis cannot be accepted in so far as it envisages the upper Niger as the birthplace of an agriculture which was then diffused towards the Nile; such a suggestion is in no way supported by the archaeological evidence. It would have been the only example known to history in which a people passed from a food-gathering to a food-producing economy without having given birth to a high culture as expressed by the improvement of their stone- and bone-working techniques, by pottery, and by the development of towns, even of modest dimensions. The Niger above Mopti affords no evidence whatsoever of this sort. On the contrary, the excavations at Kourounkoro-Kale, upstream from Bamako, and the reconnaissances made of numerous other sites in this region, show that it had one of the least-developed stone industries (in quartz and dolerite) of all West Africa. It is true that, for lack of adequate support, the search and excavations undertaken by prehistorians and archaeologists in West

[1] See the special number of *Journal of African History*, 1962, 3, 195–267, with articles by R. Portères, J. D. Clark, H. G. Baker, W. B. Morgan, P. A. Allison, W. R. Stanton and W. Kirk. Also, T. Monod, 'The late Tertiary and the Pleistocene in the Sahara', in F. C. Howell and F. Bourlière, eds., *African ecology and human evolution* (Chicago, 1963), 117–229; J. D. Clark, 'The problem of neolithic culture in sub-Saharan Africa', in Bishop and Clark, eds., *Background to evolution*, 601–27; O. Davies, H. J. Hugot and D. Seddon, 'Origins of African agriculture', *Current Anthropology*, 1968, **9**, 5, 478–509; P. Huard, 'Contribution à l'étude des premiers travaux agraires au Sahara tchadien', *Bulletin de la Société Préhistorique Française, Études et Travaux*, 1970, **67**, 2, 539–58; J. D. Clark, *The prehistory of Africa* (London and New York, 1970), 187–223.

[2] G. P. Murdock, *Africa: its peoples and their culture history* (New York, 1959), 33–148; see the criticisms of J. D. Fage in *Journal of African History*, 1961, **2**, 299–309, and of H. G. Baker in ibid. 1962, **3**, 2, 229–33.

Africa are far from being as advanced as those in Europe, western Asia and Central America; nevertheless, survey work has proceeded far enough to enable it to be said that the upper Niger valley cannot be accorded primacy in the evolution of tropical agriculture.

In the present state of knowledge concerning the dating of the beginnings of agriculture in the Near East, where agriculture has existed since the eighth millennium BC, and in West Africa and in the Sahara, where the evidence is later,[1] it seems that the conclusions of Professor J. Desmond Clark may be accepted:

> Knowledge of cultivation of cereal crops was, on the existing available evidence, transmitted across the Sahara from South-West Asia via the Nile and perhaps the Maghrib, and with this agricultural knowledge must have come domestic stock, long- and short-horned cattle, sheep and goats. The sedentary hunters and fishers, as also the 'vegeculturalists' of the savannah dambos and forest fringes, were not slow to develop by experiment and adaptation their own domesticates, and to occupy territory which formerly had permitted only temporary settlement.[2]

The position concerning knowledge of agriculture in West Africa during the first millennium BC on the eve of the introduction of metal-using technologies seems likely to have been that everywhere where rainfall was sufficient to permit of agriculture without resort to irrigation, there were small-scale societies which, without having abandoned the collection of wild crops and fruits, were engaged in agriculture. Food-gathering is still important even today, especially in the difficult period before the first crops of the rainy season in the Sudanic zone, and still more in the Sahel and Sahara, where man can hardly subsist without it.[3] It is therefore logical to suppose that food-gathering was even more necessary two or three thousand years ago.

Evidence for the existence of agriculture in West Africa in the first millennium BC should be considered in the light of the framework established by Seddon,[4] namely:

(i) Direct archaeological evidence – the remains of domesticated plants (in the form of pollen, seeds or macroscopic remains) in context;

[1] The earliest evidence is the pollen grains of cultivated *Pennisetum* at Amekni (6100 BC?). See G. Camps, *Amekni: Néolithique ancien du Hoggar*, Centre de Recherches Anthropologiques, Préhistoriques et Ethnographiques, Mémoire **10**, Algiers, 1968, 188.

[2] 'The spread of food production in sub-Saharan Africa', *Journal of African History*, 1962, 3, 2, 227. This is also the view taken by H. J. Hugot, in *Current Anthropology*, 1968, **9**, 5, 488.

[3] J. M. Dalziel, *The useful plants of west tropical Africa* (London, 1937); H. Lhote, *Les Touaregs du Hoggar*, 2nd edn (Paris, 1955), 262–5; J. Chapelle, *Nomades noirs du Sahara* (Paris, 1957), 191–5; and, above all, M. Gast, *Alimentation des populations de l'Ahaggar, étude ethnographique* (Algiers, 1968), 199–246.

[4] *Current Anthropology*, 1968, **9**, 5, 489.

(ii) indirect evidence – all other material discovered in an archaeological context that, by its nature, suggests the presence of agriculture and a food-producing community;

(iii) evidence provided by botanical, ethnographic and linguistic studies.

The direct archaeological evidence for the presence of agriculture in West Africa at the relevant period is not very great, and comes principally from the work done by Patrick Munson, of the University of Illinois, in a campaign of excavations along the Tichit-Walata escarpment in southern Mauritania.[1] Here a large number of neolithic villages had long been known, but they had not before been properly surveyed or excavated. Some of these villages are remarkably well preserved, because they had been built of stone and lie in an area which is today entirely desert. Walls still often stand 2 m high; the doorways are clearly defined; and in a number of villages there are still unexplained subsidiary constructions. The villages are in general sited on cliff-tops, protected by the sheerness of the cliffs, and sometimes also by perimeter walls. The importance of these villages may be judged from air photographs. Some of them encompass areas of up to a square kilometre; there is thus a strong suggestion that they depended on a food-producing and not merely a food-gathering economy. On the other hand, some villages are on open sites on the shores of the lakes which once existed along the northern border of Awkar at the foot of the escarpment, and seem to represent the habitations of vegeculturalists, herdsmen and fisherfolk.

Although Munson did not discover cultivated grains, he was nevertheless able to establish that cultivation was already taking place in this region by the end of the neolithic period. He was able to secure a whole series of radiocarbon dates. The lakeside sites relate to between about 1500 and 1100 BC. The large fortified villages on the cliff-tops, easily identifiable from air photographs, gave dates running from about 1150 to 850 BC, while small unfortified cliff sites dated from around 700 BC, and some very small fortified sites, which were well concealed within the rocky terrain, marked a period of decline from about 650 to 380 BC. All the pottery fragments recovered from these villages have been examined. About a thousand have grain impressions

[1] No full account of this important work has yet been published. However, Munson's Ph.D. thesis, 'The Tichitt tradition: a late prehistoric occupation of the southwestern Sahara', is available in microform from University Microfilms, Ann Arbor, Michigan. See also P. J. Munson, 'Archaeological data on the origins of cultivation in the south-western Sahara and their implications for West Africa', in J. R. Harlan, J. M. J. de Wet and A. B. L. Stemler, eds., *Origins of African plant domestication* (The Hague and Paris, 1976), 187–209.

on them, made in the wet paste before firing, and some 600 of these impressions have been identified by the botanist H. Jacques-Félix. In the earliest phases, numbers two to four, which are dated to about 1420 BC (Khimiya, Goungou, Nkhal), sixty-seven out of sixty-eight impressions are of *Cenchrus biflorus* (kram-kram), a wild grass which is still gathered and used as a food by Saharan peoples today, and which is highly esteemed in the preparation of couscous.[1] The sixty-eighth was a variety of *Pennisetum* which could have been either wild or cultivated. If these results are confirmed by other similar finds, it would seem then that this region still had a wholly pre-agricultural, gathering economy in the middle of the second millennium BC.

In the fifth, or Naghez, phase, two new wild species occur, *Brachiaria deflexa* and *Panicum lactum* (a kind of wild *Digitaria*), and *Pennisetum* provides only 3% of the impressions. Thus, on the basis of this evidence (and there are as yet no other comparable finds), this was still a food-gathering economy. It is towards the end of this phase that the large stone villages began to be built. It is only in the sixth, or Chebka, phase, for which the radiocarbon dates are between 1150±105 BC and 830±140 BC, that *Pennisetum* provides the majority (60%) of the impressions. This is the phase to which belong the large fortified villages on the cliff-tops. In the last two phases, dated approximately to 700–800 BC, the proportion of *Pennisetum* impressions rises to more than 80% of the total, *Panicum turgidum* coming a very poor second. This, it should be recalled, is the period of decline, with very small fortified sites hidden among rocks on the cliffs.

This very important work by Munson gives some idea of the progressive replacement of food-gathering by agriculture in the south-western Sahara. It would seem as if the people of the Tichit-Walata escarpment, having experimented with various indigenous plants, finally recognized that *Pennisetum* gave the best results. It would thus practically displace other grains as the staple food for organized villages, the others becoming neglected and left for the nomadic peoples of less favoured areas. However it should not be forgotten that *Cenchrus biflorus* has such an unpleasant sting that 'the presence of this accursed grass in a pasture is sufficient to keep out anyone who is neither mounted nor wearing shoes',[2] and for this reason alone pottery-makers would

[1] Lhote, *Les Touaregs*, 264; J. Chapelle, *Nomades noirs*. *Cenchrus biflorus* today grows only towards the extreme south of the cliff, near Walata (Wadi Initi), and in the south of Awkar, in the Rkiz.

[2] R. Capot-Rey, *Le Sahara français* (Paris, 1953), 28–9. This geographer marks the southern limit of the desert by the appearance of *Cenchrus biflorus* (p. 30).

not use it for their fires if other types of straw, such as that from *Pennisetum*, were available.

However it must not be thought that the question of the transition from food-gathering to agriculture in West Africa is finally solved. There is some evidence that *Pennisetum* was being cultivated in the Ahaggar region of the Sahara as early as about 6000 BC.[1] If this is confirmed by other, comparable discoveries, it would seem difficult to suppose that agriculture would have taken 5,000 years to cover the 1600 km from Ahaggar to Tichit. It has to be admitted that here, as with many other questions of debate in African prehistory, the area of ignorance is greater than the area of certain knowledge. In the opinion of the present writer, 6000 BC seems on the early side for the presence of agriculture in Ahaggar, while 1150 seems rather late for its arrival at Tichit.

Far away to the south, Oliver Davies has drawn attention to another isolated example of grain impressions on pottery: 'What are almost certainly impressions of *Pennisetum* cobs have been recognised on sherds from Ntereso.' This is a site in northern Ghana which Davies dates to late in the second millennium BC, but Thurstan Shaw has suggested caution on the dating of this site and on the association of the material found at it.[2] When the tomb of Tin Hinan at Abalessa in Ahaggar was excavated, baskets were found containing date-stones and grain; unfortunately the latter seems neither to have been identified nor preserved. Unfortunately, too, Desmond Clark's expedition to the Aïr mountains in 1970 provided no certain evidence for the presence or absence of cultivated plants at the Adrar Bous site during the Tenerian period (*c*. 4000–2000 BC).

In conclusion, it should be noted that over much of West Africa, in the forest zone where roots provide the best foodstuffs, there is little prospect of finding either grains or pollen; these are unlikely to survive for long in its wet, acid soils. However it may be noted that carbonized cowpeas and oil-palm-nut shells were found by Colin Flight at Kintampo in Ghana, and have been dated to the second half of the second millennium BC.

Indirect evidence. A key question here is when one can be sure that Stone Age tools do provide evidence for the existence of cultivation in a

[1] Camps, *Amekni*, 188. The level (1.4 m) from which came the sample that furnished two grains of the pollen of *Pennisetum* 'is largely earlier than 4850 BC (0.8 m) and probably contemporaneous with the burial of child 2, dated to 6100 BC'.

[2] O. Davies, H. J. Hugot and D. Seddon, 'Origins of African agriculture', *Current Anthropology*, 1968, **9**, 5, 481; C. T. Shaw in ibid. 1969, **10**, 2–3, 228.

given area. It was long thought that the presence of hoes, mortars and pounding-tools, stone-weights for digging-sticks, sickles and pottery was sufficient to prove the existence of agriculture, but this is now not so certain.

According to Raymond Vaufrey and Henri Hugot,[1] hoes – i.e. stone tools with a more or less straight blade – are found in many Saharan neolithic industries, such as that of Tenere. But it should be noted that in the opinion of Tixier, the typologist who has studied the tools from the type-site of this industry, Adrar Bous III, objects of this kind are not hoes; he classifies them as 'adzes', and considers that they were wood-working tools. Moreover pre-agricultural societies could have used a kind of hoe as a digging-stick to collect edible roots, and indeed for other kinds of digging in light soil – for example for the construction of shallow wells or the capture of burrowing animals.

The presence of sickles, which were made from bone or from a piece of curved wood armed with cutting-teeth before they were made of metal, is equally no proof of the presence of agriculture, since sickles might well have been used to harvest uncultivated grasses or reeds. But there seems to be only one known case of a sickle in the West African Neolithic, namely the 'part of a sickle' mentioned in Tixier's catalogue of the stone tools found at Adrar Bous. At Haua Fteah, the absence of sickles has been remarked, though they are recorded in the neolithic period in North Africa.[2]

Grindstones and mullers are today no longer considered as attributes only of agricultural societies. They were much earlier used to pound up pigments, and they are still used in this way today in the Sahara whether or not they are also used for grinding cultivated grains. Grindstones are commonly found in neolithic sites in the Sahara and Sudan; they are collected by the desert nomads, who take them for use in their camps, and by passing tourists. When suitable stone was available, it could become the basis for the manufacture of grindstones on a considerable scale; thus the people of Tenere must have gone long distances to provide themselves with grindstones from Grein.[3]

[1] R. Vaufrey, 'Le Néolithique para-Toumbien: une civilisation agricole primitive du Soudan', *Revue Scientifique*, 1967, 3267, 205–32; his hoes rather seem to be adzes. J. D. Clark, *Journal of African History*, 1962, **3**, 2, 215, sees in these 'hoe-like celts' the 'working-ends of digging-sticks'; H. J. Hugot, ed., *Missions Berliet Tenére-Tchad, Documents Scientifiques*, (Paris, 1962), 149–78; Hugot, in *Current Anthropology*, 1968, **9**, 5, 484; and Hugot, *Le Sahara avant le désert* (Paris, 1974), 230ff.

[2] Hugot, ed., *Missions Berliet*, 344; McBurney, *The Haua Fteah*, 298; Hugot, in *Current Anthropology*, 1968, **9**, 5, 484.

[3] Hugot, ed., *Missions Berliet*, 176.

Pottery also is no longer thought to provide conclusive evidence for agriculture, but only of a human group's becoming sedentary (because of its fragility, pottery is rarely thought useful by nomadic peoples). While all African agricultural societies possess pottery, it should be noted that it is equally used by elements of nomadic societies that have become sedentary. However, it is important not to be hypercritical here. When pottery is present in large quantities, it is reasonable to assume that it was made by societies of cultivators, or by those which had at least reached the stage of vegeculture (pl. 13).

There is unfortunately no West African example of grains of cultivated cereals being found in neolithic pots, though at Ehi Dohar in Tenere (Niger) grains of *Celtis*[1] have been found. On the other hand, it has already been noted that numerous impressions of *Pennisetum* have been identified on the pottery of the sites on the Tichit-Walata escarpment excavated by Munson.

In a number of places on the Rkiz massif near Tegdaoust in Mauritania, Claude Richir has found 'shielded subterranean granaries', with their entrances carefully concealed among rocks, and containing numerous silos made of dried clay, bracketed together, and 120–30 cm high. These silos were used to store grain, but none of it remained: rodent-droppings showed why this was so. In Dr Richir's opinion, the existence of such silos presupposes an annual rainfall of 350 to 400 mm, compared with the 250 mm of the present day, and a population of some 50–100 persons living in a locality which is now practically total desert. Unfortunately no radiocarbon dates were secured for these granaries, but they probably date from the first millennium AD, contemporary with the numerous pre-Islamic tombs of the area.[2]

The very existence of the large neolithic villages along the Tichit-Walata escarpment, built from cereal-gathering times onwards, and in all probability flourishing around 1000 BC, must certainly be held to afford clear proof of the presence of agriculture. So much building in so small a space (the villages are sometimes only 2 km or even less

[1] Ibid. 175; T. Monod in Howell and Bourlière, *African ecology and human evolution*, 194. This pottery, discovered by the photographer Montengerand on 27 November 1960, was excavated by H. J. Hugot and the present writer in the presence of P. Quezel, the expedition's botanist. It was while he was cleaning it out that the present writer recognized the grains of *Celtis*. Both the pottery and the grains unfortunately disappeared as a result of the serious troubles in Algeria following the expedition's arrival at Ouargla. Much of the material collected by the Berliet-Chad expedition was lost. The grains were therefore not exactly identified as *C. Australis* or C. *integrifolia*.

[2] See C. Richir's third cycle doctoral thesis, 'Constructions et vestiges protohistoriques du massif du Rkiz. Essai de paléoethnoécologie' (Paris I University, 1974).

apart, suggesting a population density comparable to that of the best agricultural lands in the Sudan today) can only be explained if their inhabitants were farmers (pl. 12). Their principal crop seems to have been *Pennisetum*, which requires a minimum of 275 mm of annual rainfall, but which can also be cultivated in areas of less rainfall in damp hollows or in depressions at the outflows of wadis running down from mountain massifs.

Similar conclusions may be reached for other village sites, such as those of Karkarichinkat in the Tilemsi valley, radiocarbon dated to 1360±110 BC, and the village on the Algeria-Mali frontier in 21°07′N, 1°10′E, which has been dated to 2800±80 BC. There are certainly many other sites which should be put into the category of 'neolithic villages', but which were built in open country and not, as with these two examples, in a clearly defined area, on an island surrounded by swamp in the first case, and within an encircling wall in the second.

Further south, where the annual rainfall is greater than 600 mm, the grain cultivated today is not *Pennisetum*, but *Sorghum*, but so far as is known, neither grains of sorghum nor pottery impressions of it have been found in archaeological contexts. However it is permissible to suppose that Negro societies which were cultivating *Pennisetum* in the Sahel would further south have cultivated instead various species of sorghum. The map showing the distribution of *Sorghum bicolor* in *The atlas of African foodcrops* suggests that the West African Sudan has been cultivating this crop since 3000/2500 BC, and that the forest zone further south has been cultivating it since 1000/500 BC, while Desmond Clark thinks that incipient cultivation and vegeculture were practised in the same Sudanic zone since about 2000 BC.[1] Here again the truth cannot be more precisely established until the results of current research become available. But in the opinion of the present writer, there is no doubt that the sedentary societies of the West African Sahel and Sudan were all acquainted with agriculture by about 1000 BC. But these were societies belonging to what Roland Portères has defined as the *complexe agricole séminal*.[2] These specifically inhabited open and unforested country, which they were able to extend by clearing adjacent forested zones. Such societies were essentially cultivators of cereals, and it is with these that Portères associates his primary cradles of agriculture in

[1] Clark, in *Journal of African History*, 1962, 3, 2, 215.

[2] R. Portères, 'Berceaux agricoles primaires sur le continent africain', *Journal of African History*, 1962, 3, 2, 208.

West Africa and Ethiopia. He distinguishes them from a *complexe agricole végétal*, which was specific to the forested regions; here smaller cradles of agriculture developed the cultivation of root-crops and tubers, which were planted not in fields, but in gardens close by the people's dwellings. There is little information available relevant to the birth and development of this second complex, which is much more difficult than the first for the archaeologist to discern.[1]

The evidence from botany, ethnography and language. Botanists like N. I. Vavilov have spoken of the world's 'cradles of agriculture'; in Africa in particular Vavilov recognized Mediterranean and Abyssinian centres. The first of these is of relatively little importance to the theme of this chapter, except in that it could have provided an example which would have stimulated peoples in contact with it, especially via Egypt and the Nile Valley, to look among the wild cereals which they gathered for food for those which were worth selecting, sowing and protecting from wild or domestic animals. It should not be forgotten, however, that Mediterranean cereals are cultivated as far as the southern Sahara, in irrigated plots during the winter.

Auguste Chevalier thought that the Sahara could have been one of the centres of origin for African cultigens, while Snowden demonstrated beyond any doubt that the sorghum millets originated in Africa.[2] G. P. Murdock came to the conclusion 'that agriculture was probably invented independently on the upper Niger before it had diffused from Asia to the lower Nile, though doubtless later than its earliest development in the Near East'.[3] Doggett, taking account of the numerous varieties of sorghum, wild as well as cultivated, to be found in the Nilotic Sudan to the north of latitude 10° (in and to the east of Kordofan), thought that this plant must have been domesticated there, and that it spread thence throughout the tropical zone further to the west.[4]

Using the material supplied by Snowden, Portères advanced the view that

> the African cereal sorghums had an independent botanico-geographical origin, that their birth was both in many places and in many species, that there were different regions in which they were developed from a wild

[1] W. B. Morgan, 'The forest and agriculture in West Africa', ibid. 235–9; Portères, 'Berceaux agricoles', 206.

[2] A. Chevalier, 'Le Sahara, centre d'origine de plantes cultivées . . .', *Mémoires de la Société de Biogéographie de Paris*, 1938, **6**, 307–22; J. D. Snowden, *The cultivated races of sorghum* (London, 1936).

[3] Murdock, *Africa*, 68.

[4] H. Doggett, 'The development of the cultivated sorghums', in Sir J. Hutchinson, ed., *Essays in crop plant evolution* (London, 1965), 50–69.

species, and that the resultant varieties were still cultivated in the area in which each of these species originated.

Early West African peoples alone derived cultivable varieties from *Sorghum arundinacum*, a wild species to be found throughout the wet tropical and equatorial zones from Cape Verde all the way to the Indian Ocean. Another wild species, *S. verticilliflorum*, which was localized in East Africa, Eritrea and south-east Africa, was the parent of the 'kaffir' varieties (*S. caffrorum* etc.); and yet a third, *S. aethiopicum*, native to Eritrea and Ethiopia, provided the stock from which a number of locally cultivated varieties, such as *S. durra*, were derived, for example throughout the Near East from Turkey to India. According to Portères, therefore, there were three independent centres in which the cultivated varieties of sorghum were evolved and diversified: one in West Africa; a Nilo-Ethiopian one; and one in East Africa, with rebounds from India.[1]

Portères also regards the pennisetum millets (bulrush millet, pearl millet) as being African creations. He sees centres of domestication for these millets as follows: a West African centre (*P. pychnostachyum*, *P. nigritanum*, *P. leonis*, *P. gambiense* and *P. cinerum*); a centre in the Chad region (*P. ancylochaete*, *P. gibbosum* and *P. maiwa*); a Nilotic centre (*P. orthochaete*, *P. perspeciosum*, *P. vulpinum*, *P. niloticum*); and an East African centre (*P. echinurus*, *P. malachochaete*, *P. albicanda*, *P. typhoides*). In respect of the West African centre, it has already been said that pennisetum impressions are known from pottery dated to the second millennium BC found in the villages excavated on the Tichit-Walata escarpment. Pennisetums are cultivated today in West Africa, where they are a major food-crop for the peoples of the Sahel where the annual rainfall lies between 275 and 300 mm; where the rainfall is greater than this, they give way to sorghum. Two species of finger millet (*Digitaria*) are found in West Africa: *D. iburua*, which is very little cultivated except in particular areas in Dahomey and on the Bauchi plateau; and *D. exilis*, known in West Africa as *fonio*. The latter is an important food-crop for the whole region from Cape Verde to Lake Chad, though the greatest number of forms are found in modern Mali, where it has an important role in the mythology of the Dogon. According to Portères, these two varieties derive respectively from *D. ternata* and *D. longiflora*.

[1] R. Portères, 'Berceaux agricoles', the quotation coming at p. 201. It should be noted that there is late evidence for sorghum in a first century AD. Meroitic engraving at Jebel Qeili (see above, chapter 4, pp. 251–2). At a slightly earlier date, Strabo (XVII.2) says that the staple food of the Ethiopians was millet, and this is probably sorghum.

Portères has also considered the case of the African rices, *Oryza barthii* and *O. breviligulata*, which are species which are gathered and collected in West Africa, and the cultivated species, *O. glaberrima*, which is probably from *O. breviligulata*, which is grown in the Sudan and the Sahel from the Atlantic to Ubangui-Chari. The primary centre of varietal diversification of the latter was the middle Niger delta; secondary centres of variation have been recognized in Senegambia and on the mountain backbone of the Republic of Guinea. On the other hand, *O. sativa*, the cultivation of which is well established today, is an introduction from Asia. In his study of rice, Portères has made interesting use of linguistic data. He has shown that the names used for rice in the West African cradle of rice cultivation – *malo*, *maro*, *mano* and their derived forms – are indigenous words. But in parts of Africa where rice was not known before the introduction of *O. sativa*, the names are derivations from 'eruz', 'arroz', 'riz', 'rice' etc. Portères associates the Senegambian megaliths with the early cultivators of African rice. Though there may well be some connection, especially in the *bolons* or *arroyos* of this region, the megaliths are not as old as he supposed. They date not from the period 1500–800 BC, but from the end of the first millennium and the beginning of the second millennium AD.[1]

A critical examination of the list of cultivars which Murdock thought to have been domesticated by the 'nuclear Mande' led the botanist H. G. Baker to remark that it was by no means proven 'that they were only brought into cultivation at the western end of the Sudan zone'.[2] Indeed examination of the work of Portères and other botanists has demonstrated beyond any doubt that Murdock's concept of a 'nuclear Mande' zone must be enlarged into a West African cradle of agriculture which was responsible for the domestication of many cultivated plants. Among the more important of those mentioned by Baker are *Sorghum vulgare*, *Pennisetum typhoideum*, *Coleus dazo* and *Coleus dysentericus* (Kaffir potatoes), *Vigna sinensis* (cowpea), *Voandzeia subterranea* (earth pea), *Citrullus vulgaris* (water-melon), and *Hibiscus esculentus* (okra), and, in the Guinea zone further to the south, the *Dioscorea* species of African yams, *Elaeis guineensis* (the oil-palm), *Cola acuminata* and *Cola nitida* (kola nuts), and *Blighia sapida* (the Aku apple). There are also some West African

[1] R. Portères, 'Berceaux agricoles', 199; on the date of the Senegambian megaliths, see Mauny, *Tableau géographique*, 171, and C. A. Diop, *Le Laboratoire de Radiocarbone de l'IFAN* (Dakar, 1968), 27, who gives a date of AD 750±110 for the stone circle at Wassu in the Gambia.

[2] H. G. Baker, 'Comments on the thesis that there was a centre of plant domestication near the headwaters of the River Niger', *Journal of African History*, 1962, 3, 2, 231.

plants which are both wild and cultivated, thus providing evidence of the process which was passed through by the domesticates which have already been mentioned. These include *Digitaria exilis*, which is very close to *D. longiflora*; *Telfairia occidentalis*, the fluted pumpkin (which is shown on two terracottas of the Nok Culture); and *Kerstingiella geocarpa*, a kind of ground-nut, the only representative of its group and certainly native to West Africa. Finally, *Butyrospermum parkii*, the shea-butter tree, which is found to as far as the Nile in the east, is no more than a wild tree which is protected by man – as is also the case (in the opinion of the present, non-botanical author) with the two peppers, *Aframomum melegueta* (malagueta) and *Piper guineense*.

The question still remains as to when these West African domesticates began to be cultivated. The historical evidence that is available for some of them does not go further back than the period of the Arabic writers. Here there is space to mention only the principal authorities.[1]

Some early information has already been given for the northern Sahara. Date palms, and the irrigated gardens shaded by them, in the Fezzan, in Tassili n-Ajjer and, probably, in the whole of modern southern Algeria, go back to at least the first millennium BC. The paintings of date palms being climbed by man, which have been found at a site on the banks of the Wadi Oua Molin, are contemporary with the representations of the Garamantian chariots, and the cultivation of dates in the Fezzan is reported by Herodotus. It should also be remembered that date-stones were found in the fourth century AD tomb of Tin Hinan at Abalessa. In the ninth century, al-Yaʿqūbī called Awdaghust an oasis, implying agriculture there, and elsewhere he mentions *dhura* (*durra*) – probably sorghum – at Zawila in the Fezzan and at Sijilmasa in Tafilelt. Ibn al-Faqīh reported in the tenth century that the inhabitants of Ghana were fed on *dhura* and that *dukhn* was their name for millet.

Al-Bakrī (1068) says that Awdaghust had gardens where date palms, irrigated wheat, small fig trees, vines, henna and gourds were all grown, and which contained orchards, while for Silla in Takrur he mentions sorghum and cotton. Although he refers to vegetable gardens surrounding the capital of Ghana, he does not specify what was grown in them. However he does tell us that Tadmekka (Es-Souk in Adrar of the Iforas) imported sorghum and all its other cereals from Negroland.

[1] For further details, see R. Mauny, 'Notes historiques autour des principales plantes cultivées d'Afrique Occidentale', *Bulletin de l'IFAN*, 1953, **16**, 684–730, and Mauny, *Tableau géographique*, 235–54; also T. Lewicki, *West African food in the Middle Ages according to the Arabic sources* (Cambridge, 1974).

Al-Idrīsī (1154) gives us a little information. The inhabitants of Takrur had sorghum as their staple. Most people in the Sudan practised agriculture, cultivating onions, gourds and water-melons, and having hardly any cereals other than millet, which they used to make beer. At Madasa, rice and sorghum were cultivated, and at Kawar, the date palm.

Al-ʿUmarī (1337) lists the principal foodstuffs of Mali as rice, *fonio* (*Digitaria exilis*), wheat (which was scarce), sorghum, yams (*al-qāṭī*), kidney beans (*Vigna sinensis*), gourds, onions, garlic, aubergines, cabbage and shea-butter among others. The 'bitter and disagreeable' fruit he mentions must be *Cola nitida*. Ibn Baṭṭūṭa (1353) also provides some information, the more valuable since he actually visited the Sudan. At Walata, water-melons were planted in the shade of date palms. He also mentions shea-butter (*garti*), calabashes, pennisetum (*anilī*), 'pulped lotus flour', rice, *fonio*, flour made from kidney beans, and yams. He also says that rice and melons (*inani*) were among the local produce of Gao.

There can indeed be no doubt that by the tenth and eleventh centuries AD, the Arabic sources afford evidence for the existence throughout West Africa of a flourishing agriculture which had been established for many centuries. In the Sudan, the principal food-crops were pennisetum, sorghum, *fonio* and rice, while in the forest zone there were yams, the oil-palm and kola, together with the cocoyam (*Colocasia esculentum*) – brought from Asia no doubt as the result of Arab seafaring in the Indian Ocean. However there is no literary evidence for this last before the fifteenth century, or, for that matter, for other plants introduced from Asia as a result of the involvement of the East African coast in Indian Ocean trade, until the accounts left by European visitors to the west coast in the fifteenth and sixteenth centuries. Both cocoyam and plantain (*Musa sapientum*, var. *paradisica*) are mentioned about 1506 by Valentim Fernandes, the first by the name of *herva coco* in Mandingo territory, and the latter under the name of *avalaneyra* in the island of São Tomé. It seems odd that such a delicious and easily diffusable plant as the mango (*Mangifera indica*), of Indian origin, but observed at Mogadishu by Ibn Baṭṭūṭa in the fourteenth century, does not seem at this stage to have followed them to the west coast.

When studies of African languages are further advanced, linguistics will no doubt make a great contribution to the study of African history in general and that of its cultivated plants in particular. As things stand at present, however, little more has been done except that a number of writers have made use of linguistics to bolster their hypotheses as to the diffusion of certain plants. While the work of Malcolm Guthrie on the Bantu languages and of David Dalby and some others indicates what history may eventually gain from linguistic research,[1] one interesting experiment that has been made is R. G. Armstrong's comparison of the Idoma and Yoruba languages in Nigeria.[2] If glottochronology can be relied upon, these two languages must have separated some 6,000 years ago; it is therefore interesting to note that they share common words for beans, yams and palm-wine, and also for cotton (though this may not have been spun at this period). In general, however, linguistic evidence needs to be used with circumspection, because botanical popularization carries with it snares which are difficult to appreciate when there is no corroborative data from other sources. Thus the recent exchanges between M. D. W. Jeffreys and other specialists on the question of the introduction of maize into Africa show how easy it is to arrive at diametrically opposite conclusions by the use – or perhaps the abuse – of linguistic evidence in attempts to prove the presence of maize in the continent before the time of Colombus.[3]

Animal husbandry. The origins and development of animal husbandry do not present a problem comparable with that involved in research into the history of agriculture. There is no doubt that the three principal domestic animals providing West African Iron Age peoples with meat and other products, such as milk, were all introductions. Cattle, sheep and goats are not of West African origin. Nor, for that matter, did Africans derive their domestic pigs from the wild hogs to be found south of the Tropic of Cancer; the pigs which are today to be seen on some parts of the coast, small black animals, seem pretty certainly to have been introduced by the Portuguese, and therefore to date from the fifteenth century or later.[4] The horse and the camel have already been considered earlier in this chapter, in their role as beasts of burden.

As far as cattle, sheep and goats are concerned in West Africa south of the Sahara, the only question at issue is the manner of their diffusion.

[1] M. Guthrie, *Comparative Bantu*, 4 vols. (Farnborough, 1967), and Guthrie, 'Some developments in the prehistory of the Bantu languages', *Journal of African History*, 1962, **3**, 2, 275–82, and D. Dalby (ed.), *Language and history in Africa* (London, 1970).

[2] R. G. Armstrong, 'The use of linguistic and ethnographic data in the study of Idoma and Yoruba history', in J. Vansina, R. Mauny and L. V. Thomas, eds., *The historian in tropical Africa* (Oxford, 1964), 127–44.

[3] M. D. W. Jeffreys, 'Maize and the Mande myth', *Current Anthropology*, 1971, **12**, 3, 291–320; Jeffreys's views have occasioned a great deal of controversy, but it may be said that they are completely rejected by the majority of historians of Africa.

[4] See V. Fernandes, *Description de la côte occidentale d'Afrique* [1506–10], tr. by P. de Cenival and T. Monod, ed. by T. Monod, A. Teixeira da Mota and R. Mauny (Bissau, 1951), 123. Fernandes remarks that, *c.* 1506, 'many pigs brought from Portugal were being raised', whereas he does not mention the presence of pigs at all on the coasts of Senegal.

Black Africa did not domesticate the buffalo, the elephant, the zebra or the wild hogs, and all its herds and flocks come from north of the tropics. Even today, among Negro populations herding is essentially an occupation reserved for pastoralists from the Sudan and, above all, for the Fulani.

The breeds of cattle to be found in West Africa today are the result of crosses between African species, such as *Bos taurus*, and the Asian zebu, *Bos indicus*. *Bos taurus* itself would seem to descend from the now extinct *Bos africanus* of large stature and with lyre-shaped horns (Stewart's 'Hamitic longhorn'), which is the Egyptian Apis bull, and was domesticated very early. It is depicted both in innumerable rock-drawings in the Sahara and in ancient Egyptian paintings. Its direct descendants today are the *ndama* of Futa Jalon and the Chad breed with very large, bowl-shaped horns (pl. 14). The origin of *Bos brachyceros* (Stewart's 'shorthorn'), or *Bos ibericus*, is not clear, although it belongs to the same major family as *Bos taurus*, which, being resistant to the trypanosomiases, today inhabits the West African forest and its fringes in which *Bos indicus* cannot live. The latter is without question of Indian origin. But it could have been introduced into Egypt at a relatively early period, since it is often depicted in paintings of the second millennium BC. It is not known whether it reached Egypt via Mesopotamia and Sinai, via the Hadhramaut, from Arabia via the Horn of Africa, or directly from India along the sea lanes.

There are innumerable Late Stone Age representations of *Bos taurus* which demonstrate beyond question the importance of cattle-herding in the Sahara in the fourth and third millennia BC, especially in Tassili n-Ajjer, Tibesti, Adrar of the Iforas, the Mauritanian Adrar, Ahaggar and Aïr. Indeed this abundance of drawings of cattle has led to the recognition of a 'cattle-herder period' of Saharan prehistory, for which there are radiocarbon dates of 3550±200 BC from Jabbaren and 3070±300 BC from Sefar. Direct proof of the presence of cattle in the West African Neolithic is provided by finds of their bones. Remains of *Bos taurus* occur in all but the first stages of the village sites on the Tichit-Walata escarpment; site VIII at Uan Muhuggiag, dated to 4000 BC, afforded evidence of cattle bones, especially of *Bos brachyceros*; while a complete skeleton of a domesticated *Bos* was found at Adrar Bous, which has been dated to 3810±500 BC.[1] Large quantities of

[1] P. J. Munson, 'Corrections and additional comments concerning the "Tichitt tradition"', *West African Archaeological Newsletter*, 1970, **10**, 47; Camps, *Amekni*, 207; J. D. Clark, in *British expedition to Aïr*, 1970 (n.p., n.d. [1971?]), 10.

cattle bones were also found in Graham Connah's excavation of the settlement mound at Daima in north-eastern Nigeria, dated between 450±95 BC and AD 980±90, and in Colin Flight's at Karkarichinkat, north of Gao, dated between 1670 and 2010 BC.

It would be tedious to recapitulate the references to cattle in West Africa in the Arabic sources,[1] but it must be pointed out that these make no distinction between the smaller breeds, such as *Bos taurus*, and the zebu cattle. Thus it is still not possible to say when the latter reached West Africa, and whether they came from the north, across the Sahara, or from the east, through the savanna from the Nile to Lake Chad. Cattle-farming has thus been practised by West African peoples in the Sahara, the Sahel and the Sudan throughout the Iron Age. As the Sahara and Sahel became drier, so the tsetse zone retreated further to the south, thus opening up new areas for the cattle farmers.

The only sheep represented in the West African Iron Age were *Ovis longipes*, a hairy breed which has two varieties, one large and one of smaller stature. These sheep were once known in North Africa, and may have first been domesticated in the Nile Valley. They are related to East African breeds which are susceptible to the trypanosomiases, which suggests that they are not authochthonous. They are represented in rock-drawings of the Saharan Neolithic,[2] while ancient Egyptian sheep (*O. platycera* and *O. egyptiaca*), of which a large number have been mummified and are thus perfectly preserved, are also represented on river-bank sites in south-western Algeria. It is not known when sheep crossed the Sahara, but it was probably during the 'cattle-herder period', because sheep are often seen together with cattle on the Tassili n-Ajjer drawings. But today sheep are considered to be less 'noble' than cattle, and it was doubtless for this reason that they figure less often in the rock-drawings. In the eleventh century, al-Bakrī mentioned the presence south of the Sahara of sheep which had hair like a goat instead of wool, and later authors – al-ʿUmarī, Ibn Baṭṭūṭa, al-Maqrīzī, Valentim Fernandes and Leo Africanus – say the same.

It would seem that goats have always been widespread in the Sahara and in West Africa since neolithic times. The goats of the Sahara and the Sahel are related to *Hircus mambrinus*, perhaps of Asian origin, while those of the Sudan and Guinea, of the Nile Valley and Ethiopia, which are smaller and resistant to the trypanosomiases, are similar to *H.*

[1] The relevant references may be found in Mauny, *Tableau géographique*, 276–9.

[2] At Haua Fteah, C. B. M. McBurney dates the presence of domestic sheep and goats to as far back as *c.* 4800 BC; they were known in the Fayum from the somewhat later date of *c.* 4300 BC (*The Haua Fteah*, 317).

thebaïcus and *H. reversus*. The goats of dynastic Egypt and those on the rock-drawings of Tassili and the Fezzan are *H. mambrinus*, as also is the specimen engraved at Amguid. In the tenth century, Ibn Ḥawqal noted the presence of goats in the Sahara, while later on al-Bakrī and al-Idrīsī report them on the borders of Senegal and al-ʿUmarī in Mali. Portuguese and other explorers of the fifteenth century met with them on the Senegal and Guinea coastlands. In neolithic sites, in the absence of complete skeletons, it is difficult to distinguish between the bones of goats (*Capra* species) and sheep (*Ovis*), and confusion is also possible with the bones of wild members of the *Caprinae* family to which both belong, for example the mouflon.

It is clear that stock-raising was fully developed in the period covered in this chapter. It made by no means a negligible contribution to the support of sedentary peoples, while the nomads depended on it for the greater part of their food, in the form of meat and milk, for hides, skins and waterskins, and for the carriage of men and goods (for which oxen and asses were employed as well as horses and camels).

TECHNOLOGY: THE TRANSITION FROM THE LATE STONE AGE TO THE IRON AGE IN WEST AFRICA

The Iron Age is by definition the epoch during which this metal was used to meet man's main requirements in the manufacture of tools and weapons. There have been marked differences between societies in the dates of their transition from the use of stone implements to those made of iron. Some passed directly from the use of one to the other, and this seems to have been the case for the greater part of tropical Africa. But others passed through intermediary stages in which first copper and then bronze provided a transition from the Stone Age to the Iron Age. Copper was known in western Asia from about the sixth millennium. By the fifth millennium, it was known in Egypt (in the form of the beads excavated from the cemeteries at Badari); by the fourth millennium in Persia and India, in the third millennium in western Europe, and at the end of the second millennium in North-West Africa. But it must not be supposed that the use of stone was immediately abandoned; it has continued to be used for many purposes even into modern times. Moreover some societies, like those of pre-Columban America, never knew iron and continued to work with copper and bronze, while others, like those of the Canary Islands and Oceania, had no knowledge of metals prior to the opening up of contact by Europeans in the fourteenth and eighteenth centuries respectively. Since ordinary wood fires can hardly exceed a temperature of 600 or 700 °C., and copper does not melt until about 1,085 °C., it is thought that the discovery of copper-smelting must have been an accidental one during the preparation of the copper frit or glaze which began to be used quite early on in the history of pottery: 'in any event, it would appear that the potter's kiln is the origin of the smelter's furnace'.[1]

Copper metallurgy reached Egypt from Asia at the time of Dynasties I and II, i.e. *c.* 3200–*c.* 2780 BC. Warriors of the Old and Middle Kingdoms employed copper weapons, but the metal was rare during these periods (*c.* 2686–*c.* 1786 BC). The mines in the Sinai peninsula and the Arabian desert were not rich, and Egypt was in practice dependent on imports of the metal from Cyprus and Asia. Bronze came by the same route during the second millennium and, always conservative, Egypt continued to make use of bronze even after the beginnings of the Iron Age. By the time of the New Kingdom, from 1570 BC onwards, detailed information is available. Thus an inscription of the Pharaoh Meneptah (1236–1223 BC) at Karnak records that he captured bronze vases and 9,111 bronze weapons from Libyans who had invaded the Nile Delta. The Libyans must have obtained these things from the Peoples of the Sea, who in their turn must have brought them from Europe and the Near East. Thanks to the work of Camps and Souville, it has recently been established that there was a Bronze Age in North-West Africa – both the raw metal and bell-shaped bronze vases have been found there. This is hardly surprising, since the Phoenicians had been established on the North-West African coasts from the twelfth or eleventh centuries BC. Indeed, Malhomme suggested as early as 1951 that Morocco must have had a Bronze Age. He based his opinion on the presence in Oukaimeden of rock-drawings in which there are depicted daggers and axes of similar types to those known to have been made in bronze in the Iberian peninsula, and especially in the Al-Argar culture of 1700–1200 BC.[2]

Curiously enough, the most important material evidence for a North-West African Bronze Age has begun to come to light far to the south

[1] J. Hawkes and Sir L. Woolley, *Prehistory and the beginnings of civilization* (UNESCO and London, 1963), 551.

[2] G. Camps, 'Les traces d'un âge du bronze en Afrique du Nord', *Revue Africaine*, 1960, 462–3, 1e–2e trim., 31–55; G. Souville, 'Recherches sur l'existence d'un âge du bronze au Maroc', *Atti del VIe Congresso Internazionale delle Scienze Prehistoriche e Protohistoriche* (Rome, 1965), II, 419–24; J. Malhomme, 'Les gravures préhistoriques du Grand Atlas de Marrakech', *7e Congrès AFAS* (Tunis, 1951), 1953, 3, 149–53, and Malhomme, 'Représentations de haches du bronze (Grand Atlas)', *Bulletin de la Société Préhistorique du Maroc*, 1953, 105–9.

of Morocco, in Mauritania. The first finds, a hatchet and a very thin arrowhead, were reported as early as 1912 by Mme Crova. Since then the finds have multiplied to the extent that the handful published by the present author in 1952 had increased to 45 by 1955 and to 139 by 1971. This last figure represented 87 weapons (arrows, socketed lance-heads, daggers), 27 tools (axes, pins, little rods, burins, hooks), 13 pieces of jewellery (rings, bracelets, earrings, pendants), and 12 copper ingots or fragments. It should be noted that the typical daggers and halberds of the High Atlas rock-drawings have not been found: the Mauritanian assemblage would appear to date from a later period than that of the Al-Argar culture. All the objects found are made of pure copper or of a bronze which has little more than a trace of tin. This most interesting picture has been rounded off and given even more substance by the results of Nicole Lambert's excavations in the 'Cave of the Bats' at Guelb-Moghrein near Akjoujt. This 'cave' was in fact a gallery dug by miners to follow a particularly rich vein of copper ore. From it Mlle Lambert obtained two sets of radiocarbon dates, one of which covered the fifth century BC, while the other gave one date in the sixth century and one in the ninth, the last of which would seem to be too early. Mme Lambert has also excavated another site near Akjoujt, that at Lemdena, which is today in desert country, where she has found evidence both for the mining and the smelting of copper ore, including

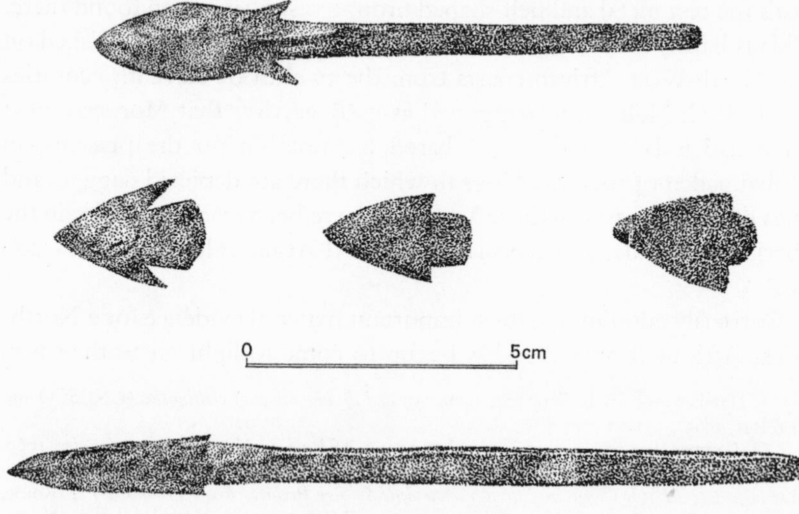

42 First-millennium copper arrowheads from western Mauritania. (After photo: IFAN, Dakar.)

fragments of a furnace equipped with tuyères and, nearby, pieces of copper slag.

There seems to be a good chance that some of the copper-mines known in Morocco[1] may be broadly contemporary with the Mauritanian mines, and that it was from Morocco that miners and smelters went out to prospect and to exploit the copper ores of Mauritania. However, there will be no positive evidence for this until the Moroccan mines have been excavated as those at Akjoujt have been. But the two copper-mining areas are in effect at either end of the western 'chariot track' of the first millennium BC which has already been discussed (pp. 280–3). The Moroccan mines were of course nearer to the ancient metallurgical centre of Betica in southern Spain, and more accessible to Carthaginian prospectors, who, from their coastal trading-posts at Mogador and elsewhere, would hardly have neglected to penetrate inland looking for suitable sites to mine. It therefore seems likely that the mines in Morocco would have been known and worked before the remoter and less accessible mines in Mauritania. Attention should be given, moreover, to the very great concentration of finds of objects of copper in the western Sahara, and especially in western Mauritania, where the richest concentration is around Medinet Sbat, close by the Akjoujt copper-mines. Another area where a considerable number of copper artefacts has been found is the Tichit-Walata escarpment, with its multitude of neolithic villages and along which many rock-drawings of chariots have been discovered. It is evident that this was on a line of penetration from southern Morocco which reached the Niger in the Niafunke-Goundam area. Doubtless it is no coincidence that it was here that there arose and prospered the pre-Islamic civilization that produced the great tumuli and megaliths, as yet undated, at Tondidarou.[2]

But a very interesting find has been made far outside the western Sahara, some 120 km to the south-west of Agades in the modern Niger Republic; this was of an unusually thin copper arrowhead of the kind used in the Mediterranean basin in the second and first millennia BC. The question therefore arises as to whether this region, like that of Akjoujt, was an early centre of copper-working. This was certainly the case in more recent times, because the copper-mine at Takedda which

[1] N. Lambert, 'Les industries sur cuivre dans l'ouest saharien', *West African Journal of Archaeology* (Ibadan), 1971, 1, 9–21; B. Rosenberger, 'Les vieilles exploitations minières et les anciens centres métallurgiques du Maroc', *Revue de Géographie du Maroc* 1970, 17–18, 71–102.

[2] Mauny, *Tableau géographique*, 92–111, 129–36. The great tumulus at Kouga has been radiocarbon dated to AD 1000 ± 150.

was visited by Ibn Baṭṭūṭa in 1354 can in all probability, if not with complete certainty, be identified with the modern Azelik, 130 km west-north-west of Agades, where there is evidence for the presence of copper ore throughout the area to the west and south-west of the town, and where, moreover, at Marendet, there is evidence that it was once smelted. The likeliest hypothesis that this might be an early copper-working area is in fact heightened by the very recent discovery that there are chariot drawings both to the west and the east of Aïr between latitudes 18° and 19°N.[1] Thus here, as at Akjoujt, there is a conjunction of the three factors – copper-mining, finds of copper weapons and rock-drawings of chariots – that indicate hitherto unsuspected trans-Saharan contacts, indeed that suggest active exploration from the north. The territory around Marendet and the Teguiddas, not to mention that around Azelik, clearly calls for specific archaeological exploration and excavation, the more so as this Sahelian region leads directly to the savanna lands of the Nok Culture and of the Bauchi tin-mines, hardly more than 1,000 km away.

Little information is available for the territory further to the east. Few ancient copper or bronze objects have come to light in the northern parts of the Chad Republic – no more than one pendant, one bracelet and some odd pieces in the grave of a weaver. The copper and bronze ornaments excavated by Lebeuf from his 'Sao' (So) sites have not been dated, and his finds did not include any copper or bronze weapons. There is no information at all from the south-western area of the Sudan Republic in which lay the copper-mines of Hofrat en-Nahas, which could well provide future archaeologists with some surprises.

The present position is then that there was at least one important centre of copper-working in the southern Sahara, in Mauritania, during the first millennium BC, and it seems almost certain that the future will show that it was developed by a technology imported from the Mediterranean by Libyan-Berbers, no doubt as a result of Phoenician and Carthaginian initiatives in looking for new mines to exploit in southern Morocco. It would seem too that the same process may have been at work in the central Sahara, leading from Carthage or Lepcis Magna towards the Niger bend near Gao on the one hand, and on the other to Aïr and the copper-mines to its south-west. Although there is as yet no evidence to confirm it, it would seem not wholly absurd to put forward the hypothesis that the Nok Culture, which perhaps had access to the

[1] H. Lhote, 'Découverte de chars de guerre en Air', *Notes Africaines* (Dakar), 1970, **127**, 83–5; J. P. Roset, 'Art rupestre en Air', *Archeologia* (Paris), 1971, **39**, 24–31.

tin of the Bauchi plateau, could have gained in its formative stages from Mediterranean influences of some kind, which may then have reached even further to the south, to Ife. The so-called 'Atlantic' influences which Leo Frobenius thought to have influenced West Africa must have come *overland* and not by sea because, as has already been explained, it would have been impossible for the ships of ancient times to return to the Straits of Gibraltar along the coast from the Gulf of Benin.

It now remains to tackle the important question of the appearance of iron in Africa, and in particular the question of whether iron-working was borrowed from outside the continent, or whether it was independently invented within it. Before considering this problem – and others posed by iron-working in Africa – it is important to be clear on two other questions: the actual nature of the metal itself, and when it is possible to refer to 'iron-working'. There are in fact a number of kinds of iron, and these must be distinguished if one is to avoid the error into which some authors have fallen in talking of the presence of iron-working in Africa from the times for which the earliest finds of the metal have been made.[1]

First of all, there is *meteoritic iron*. This has reached the earth from outside its atmosphere, and it always contains a substantial proportion of nickel. It was known in Egypt from predynastic times, in the fourth millennium BC, when small tubular beads were made from it. Those found at Ermant (tomb 1494) and at El-Gerzeh (tombs 63 and 113) contain up to 7.5% nickel. To make such objects, nothing more than hammering was necessary. Secondly, there is *soft iron*, which is simply a by-product of the manufacture of other metals, such as gold and copper. The gold-bearing gravels of ancient Nubia, for example, were 65% iron, and when these were panned for gold, a high concentration of magnetite was left with it. The mixture was then smelted in a crucible, as a result of which the gold, being heavier, went to the bottom, and molten slag rich in iron floated to the top, while in between there appeared an iron paste which could easily be forged.[2] Heating the copper ore of Akjoujt, which also contains a considerable amount of iron, would have given a similar result. This unintentionally obtained soft iron could be used to

[1] L.-M. Diop, 'Métallurgie traditionelle de l'Age du Fer en Afrique', *Bulletin de l'IFAN*, 1968, **30**, 1 (ser. B), 10–38; C.-A. Diop, 'La métallurgie du fer sous l'ancien empire Égyptien', ibid. 1973, **35**, 3, 532–47.

[2] A. Lucas and J. R. Harris (*Ancient Egyptian materials and industries*, 4th edn [London 1962], 242–3), however, point out that this theory of iron production requires experimental verification before it can be accepted. See objection in Diop, 'La Métallurgie du fer'.

make amulets and jewellery, but it was not suitable for making weapons or working-tools, which in Egypt continued to be made of bronze during the whole period up to about the seventh century BC. Soft iron, therefore, was never made deliberately; it was always the by-product of the manufacture of other metals, and it had no real, practical value. Finally, there is *hard iron*, which is produced after smelting (usually from iron oxides, which do not look in the least like a metal) by a complex technique of alternately heating with a forced draught and hammering, with the object of fusing the metal together in contact with charcoal, the carbon in the charcoal being essential to harden the iron. Moreover, further complex operations are necessary if the raw iron so made is to be turned into useful wrought-iron objects. It is only from the time that these operations came into use – and obviously their inventors would seek to keep them secret for as long as they could – that it is possible to speak of iron-working in any meaningful sense.

This most important invention is generally attributed to the Chalybeans of Asia Minor, a people related to the Hittites, and archaeologists date it to *c.* 1500 BC. But mastery of the necessary techniques spread slowly. Societies as advanced as those of pre-Columban America never knew them, and at the end of the fifteenth century AD, iron-working was unknown east of Japan. This may seem surprising, since temperatures no higher than 800 or 900 °C. are needed to produce malleable iron from iron ore, appreciably lower than the 1,085 °C. needed to smelt copper, and iron ores are much more widely spread than sources of copper. As has been seen in the case of Akjoujt, copper ores can contain much more iron than they contain copper. The metal-workers there, as also the gold-workers in ancient Nubia, did not know how to get rid of the soft iron they made, which to them was a useless by-product of their activities. The reason for the late discovery and diffusion of iron-working is simply the difficulty, already referred to, of incorporating carbon in the smelting process. To this must be added the subsequent need to forge the metal to make useful objects, in which iron is unlike copper and bronze, which only require to be cast in moulds. It is not difficult to imagine the centuries of trial and error, of gradual improvements, which would be needed to make weapons and tools which could gradually supersede those made of bronze.

The first objects of hard iron known in Africa were exported by the Hittites to Egypt, where they were greatly valued. All the iron objects which have been found in Egypt which date to earlier than the New Kingdom, which began in 1580 BC, were made of meteoritic iron or of accidentally produced soft iron. Professor Leclant has compiled a detailed inventory of the earliest finds of hard iron: a few weapons, military equipment and bracelets, many of them from the tomb of Tutankhamun (*c.* 1340 BC), a sword from the reign of Seti I (1318–1298 BC), and a halberd which was found in the foundations of the temple of Ramses III (1198–1166 BC) at Abdyos.[1] It was only much later that objects of iron began to appear in appreciable numbers. As Leclant says,

There is general agreement that the diffusion of iron to Egypt took place during the period, in the first half of the seventh century BC, when it had close relations with Assyria. The first really important assemblage of iron implements has been found at Thebes in association with an Assyrian helmet, and has been dated to Ashurbanipal's expedition of 663 BC. Conversely, the booty taken back from Egypt by this conqueror does not include anything made of iron. A little later, when he sent Necho I back to Egypt as his vassal, Ashurbanipal invested him with an iron sword.

During the Saite, or XXVI Dynasty (663–525 BC), the presence of iron in Egypt is attested by many finds. Its diffusion has been attributed to Greek mercenaries, Carians and Ionians, but it would seem that these would rather have been equipped with bronze weapons . . . Iron is often mentioned in the papyri of the Ptolemaic period, and it is at this time that there are the first references to the local working of iron ore.

In view of this evidence, the once widespread hypothesis that iron-working began in the continent of Africa and reached Egypt, from which it was subsequently diffused, from the south, must be abandoned. The advance of iron-working in Africa proceeded in the reverse direction, from Asia to Egypt, and from Egypt into the rest of the continent.[2]

This opinion is shared by other Egyptologists:

Egypt displayed a precocious mastery of many things. But it was relatively mediocre in the field of metal-working. Here ancient Egypt was backward in comparison with western Asia. The tentative beginnings of copper-working appear at the end of the prehistoric period, and Egypt did not begin to use bronze until about 2000 BC, a thousand years later than the Near East. As for iron, it entered Pharaonic industry haltingly between 1000 and 600 BC . . . Egypt was never a great innovator in the field of metal-working.[3]

Nubia became acquainted with iron contemporaneously with Egypt, at the time of the Assyrian invasion of the seventh century BC. G. A. Wainwright mentions only eighteen iron objects found at Napata of a

[1] J. Leclant, 'Le fer dans l'Égypte ancienne, le Soudan et l'Afrique', *Annales de l'Est* (Nancy), 1956, Mém. **16**, 83–91; see also B. G. Trigger, 'The myth of Meroe and the African Iron Age', *African Historical Studies*, 1969, **2**, 1, 23–50, and Mauny, *Les siècles obscurs*, 69–71.

[2] Leclant, 'Le fer dans l'Égypte ancienne', 86–7.

[3] Posener, ed., *Dictionnaire de la civilisation égyptienne*, 171–2; also Lucas and Harris, *Ancient Egyptian materials*, 235–43.

date earlier that 400 BC, of which eleven are later than Amtalqa (*c.* 560 BC) and only seven earlier than his reign. These he dates to the time of Shabako and Tarharqa, members of the Nubian royal family who provided Egypt with its XXV Dynasty (*c.* 716–664 BC), the second of whom was Pharaoh at the time of the Assyrian invasion.[1] A radiocarbon sample taken from a trench which was dug at Meroe by Professor Shinnie during his 1967–8 excavations, which contained Napatan pottery and fragments of iron and iron slag, has been dated to 514±73 BC. If this date is confirmed by other radiocarbon dates, then iron-working at Meroe is rather earlier than has hitherto been supposed. It would seem probable that it was the Greek and Carian mercenaries of Psamtek II (*c.* 595–589 BC) who first brought iron weapons to Napata, but this is not the same thing as the introduction of iron-working. Nevertheless it should be remembered that Herodotus indicates that the Ethiopian soldiers in Xerxes's army (480 BC) were the only ones who still had stone rather than iron arrowheads. Indeed it was only in the time of Harsiotef, *c.* 400 BC, that stone, bronze and copper were finally supplanted at Kush by iron. B. C. Trigger notes that

> no iron whatever was found in any of the well-dated tombs that were constructed at Nuri after reign 7 or before reign 13 (*c.* 538–520 BC), and there are only a few isolated occurrences of iron in [Kush] prior to reign 23 (Harsiotef) ... Iron working was not established yet in the Sudan.[2]

After reign 40 (*c.* 116–99 BC), iron becomes more and more common, but the date of the enormous heaps of iron slag at Meroe, which stand up to 4 m high, is not yet known. On the evidence of a stele with an ancient Meroitic inscription that was found in a temple built on one of the slag-heaps at Meroe, Wainwright suggested a date in the first century BC. However, Shinnie suggests that this Lion Temple at Meroe belongs to the reign of King Teqerideamani (*c.* AD 246–66), whose name was found on the base of a stone statue in the temple.[3]

The question arises as to whether iron-working was diffused from Meroe westwards through the savanna belt towards Lake Chad. It is obvious that the only impediments to such diffusion would be the distances involved and, possibly, hostility from the peoples en route. Although no objects of Meroitic origin have been found beyond Kordofan and Darfur, Huard thinks that this was the route along which

[1] G. A. Wainwright, 'Iron in the Napatan and Meroitic ages', *Sudan Notes and Records*, 1945, **26**, 5–36.

[2] Trigger, 'The myth of Meroe', 42.

[3] For discussion of the dating of the rulers of Kush, see ch. 4, pp. 213–31. For Teqerideamani, see p. 247.

knowledge of iron-working was transmitted to the Chad region. In a number of very important articles,[1] he has reviewed all the relevant evidence – literary, military and paleo-ethnographic as well as technological, and has taken account of the archaeological finds from graves and other sources, and also the very large number of rock-drawings in the area, many of which have been published as a result of his efforts. Huard's conclusion is that iron-working arrived from Meroe during the first centuries of the Christian era. The prime evidence for this is found in Ennedi, where there are traces of the mining and working of iron, pottery of Nilotic origin, and evidence for the presence of warriors each equipped with a single broad-bladed lance who were associated first with horses, then with camels bearing pack-saddles which enclosed their humps in the Meroitic manner.

The question whether iron-working was diffused westwards from Meroe will only finally be settled by archaeology. Recent work providing some clues includes that by G. Bailloud, Y. Coppens and J. Courtin. These archaeologists have made a major contribution to the question by showing the distribution of various categories of late Neolithic and Early Iron Age sites that can be distinguished by the manner in which their pottery is decorated, whether by stamping, channelling, painting, piercing or appliqué work. The sites in question are related to the successive shorelines of Lake Chad as it gradually dried up. Unfortunately, however, there are as yet no absolute dates for these sites. Consequently it is not yet possible to establish a satisfactory chronological order for them. In particular, there is no positive date for the beginning of the Haddadian period, which involves the arrival, at some time during the first millennium AD, of a considerable number of immigrant blacksmiths. These people established sizeable villages, with considerable accumulations of iron slag, and in the Koro Toro region they replaced an earlier population of fishermen who made channelled pottery and bone harpoons and fish-hooks. In Arkell's opinion, Haddadian pottery is certainly related to that of Christian Nubia (*c.* AD 800–1200).[2]

[1] P. Huard: 'Contribution à l'étude du cheval, du fer, et du chameau au Sahara occidental', *Bulletin de l'IFAN*, 1960, **22** (sér. B), 134–78; 'Nouvelle contribution à l'étude du fer au Sahara et au Tchad', ibid. 1964, **26**, 297–396; and 'Introduction et diffusion du fer au Tchad', *Journal of African History*, 1966, **7**, 3, 377–404.

[2] G. Bailloud, 'L'Évolution des styles céramiques en Ennedi', *Actes du Première Colloque International d'Archéologie Africaine* (Fort-Lamy, 1966), 1969, 31–45; Y. Coppens, 'Les Cultures protohistoriques et historiques du Djourab', *ibid.* 129–46; J. Courtin, 'Le Néolithique du Borkou', ibid. 147–59; Y. Coppens, 'L'Époque haddadienne: une page de la protohistoire du Tchad', Publicações da Faculdade de Letras, Lisbon, *In memoriam do Abade H. Breuil*, 1965, **1**, 207–16.

In the absence of radiocarbon dates for the channelled pottery sites and for the Haddadians, only two things can be said. First, even if one takes the earliest date of AD 800, the arrival of these people would be very late for the introduction into the area of iron-working techniques which were established in Nubia in the pre-Christian era. Secondly, on the other hand, this is the extreme westernmost limit of influence from Christian Nubia. To the best of the author's knowledge, no glazed and painted pottery of the distinctive Christian Nubian type has been found west of Koro Toro, and, had there been any, examples would have been found in the numerous excavations which have been undertaken in the 'Sao' (So) country. However it is not impossible that, before the Haddadian period, with its spectacular slag-heap evidence, there could have been an earlier and less archaeologically obvious introduction of iron-working, about the beginning of the Christian era. This remains to be demonstrated, but it is something that archaeologists should look out for between Borku and Koro Toro, for this is an area which migrants proceeding from the Nile Valley to Chad and beyond would certainly have had to cross.

Despite excavations over a period of more than thirty years, and an important series of publications,[1] the picture in the region around Lake Chad itself remains a confused one. The classification of the hundreds of known sites is peculiar in that it is based first and foremost not, as would be logical, on established archaeological criteria, but on distinctions between the present outward appearance of the surviving habitation mounds. Thus, for J.-P. Lebeuf, 'Sao I' mounds are those which have no walls, while 'Sao II' are old mounds with walls and 'Sao III' are newer sites without walls.[2] Thus it is hardly surprising to find mounds which are morphologically 'Sao I' providing dates from 120 BC to AD 40 (Amkoumjdo), AD 970 (Messo) and AD 1700 and 1705 (Maguira), while 'Sao II' mounds are dated from AD 1090 to 1800 (Gawi) and from 425 BC to the present at Mdaga. The mere statement of such results is enough for such an illogical system of classification to be condemned outright. If these 'Sao' sites are to be fitted into their proper chronological place in African archaeology, further excavations

[1] See the bibliography in J.-P. Lebeuf, *Carte archéologique des abords du lac Tchad*, 2 vols. (Paris, 1969).

[2] Thus in *Current Anthropology*, 1969, **10**, 2–3, Thurstan Shaw could write on this subject in these terms: 'Until more stratigraphical details associated with these dates are published, it is difficult to know how to assess them. Sao I, II and III are all "Iron Age" cultures, but the divisions do not seem to be satisfactorily defined in terms of stratigraphy and cultural material. If the date of 425 BC could be demonstrated to be associated with the use of iron, its importance is obvious.'

will have to be undertaken in accordance with modern methods, with the results published level by level, and with the stratigraphy dated by radiocarbon samples (as has been done just across the Cameroun border, at Daima in Nigeria).[1] A scientifically conducted excavation at a site like Amkoumjdo, with its three radiocarbon dates around the beginning of the Christian era, would have revealed more about the culture of the peoples once living around Lake Chad and about the presence or absence of iron than the whole present corpus of publications about the 'Sao'.

Graham Connah's excavation at Daima, an artificial tell more than 10 m high on the *firki*, 60 km to the west of Ndjamena (Fort Lamy), and thus right in the middle of 'Sao country', is in fact an admirable example of modern, scientific archaeology (pl. 15). In the lowest levels, about 10 m from the top of the mound, which provided radiocarbon samples giving dates of 570±110 and 450±95 BC, Connah found neolithic stone and bone implements and pottery figurines. Such artefacts virtually disappeared between 7 and 6 m, levels which gave radiocarbon dates of AD 450±670 and 480±270. The first iron object, a flat-sectioned knife or spear-head, appeared in complete isolation in an intermediate level at about 8 m, with a radiocarbon date of AD 630±190. (It may be noted that this date is later than the previous two, and also that all three have considerable standard errors; problems of this kind, however, are only to be expected when, as in all three cases, the material sent for radiocarbon dating is bone.) The nearest other iron objects, together with more clay figurines, were found at about the 4 m level, which gave radiocarbon dates of AD 810±90 and 980±90. A further date of AD 1060±90 was obtained from the topmost level, less than 1 m deep. It may thus be concluded that the Daima tell was formed between about the sixth century BC and the eleventh century AD. Until more precise dates are available, or further archaeological excavations have been made, the provisional hypothesis must be that the first introduction of iron-ware, possibly of imported objects, occurred about the middle of the first millennium of the Christian era, and that this was followed by the diffusion of iron-working about the end of the same millennium. Such a hypothesis must be consistent with the picture that has already been suggested for the Haddadian period in the Koro Toro area.

Thus in the Chad region, it would seem that iron makes a first

[1] It may be noted that, on a comparative basis, Lebeuf (*Carte archéologique*, 8) classifies this site as 'Sao II', even though, to the knowledge of the present author, it has no encircling wall.

tentative appearance about the beginning of the Christian era, and that its manufacture was not significantly established until the arrival of the Haddadians at the end of the first millennium. About 900 km to the west-south-west, at Taruga in central Nigeria, 60 km south-east of Abuja and 90 km south-west of Nok, iron would seem to have arrived on the scene nearly five centuries earlier than it did in the Chad region and, indeed, to have been actually worked as early as this. At Taruga, following earlier discoveries of figurines in the characteristic Nok style, excavations were undertaken by Bernard Fagg which revealed – besides stone tools – pottery, more Nok-style figurines, iron slag and iron-smelting furnaces. Radiocarbon tests gave very early dates for this site: 440±140 BC, 300±100 BC (from charcoal from inside furnace no. 2), and 280±120 BC. A date which is very close to these has been established from the grey clay beds at Nok itself, namely AD 206±50. Taruga is at the moment the only site south of the Sahara at which it is certain that iron-working was practised from the second half of the first millennium BC. So long as only one Taruga date was available (that of 280±120 BC), it was possible to be sceptical; now that two further confirmatory dates have been established, one of them from charcoal found actually inside a furnace, the evidence must be accepted. What is now needed is the establishment of comparable dates from other metal-using sites which would confirm the antiquity of iron-working in Nigeria and its connections with the Nok Culture.

It must not be forgotten that Taruga is an isolated case. At Daima, there is no evidence for iron before about AD 500, while only 170 km north-east of Taruga, at the Rop rock-shelter, a skeleton found in association with a microlithic industry gave a date as late as 25±120 BC. It is possible, of course, that this was a later burial in a grave dug into a Stone Age level. Alternatively, however, the inhabitants of the Bauchi plateau might have remained at a hunting-gathering stage while 400 years earlier the farmers of the near-by plain were already iron-users. This hypothesis is the more worthy of further investigation in that it would be very interesting to know more about the Nok Culture, which flourished in precisely this area, which produced such famous masterpieces of terracotta sculpture, and which was perhaps the parent of the world-renowned art of Ife and the Yoruba country generally. And yet, until the establishment of the radiocarbon dates for the Taruga excavations, in which Nok Culture terracottas were found, the best that could be done to date this culture was to place it between two dates from Nok itself, one of 925±70 BC, which came from the layer below the figurines, and the other of AD 200±50, from the layer above which they were found.

The relatively early presence of iron in Nigeria is attested by the excavations undertaken at Yelwa, which is on the Niger about 400 km west-north-west of Taruga. Here evidence of iron was found at all levels, and the earliest of these provided radiocarbon dates of AD 100±115 and 200±110. The site was occupied until AD 700 by a small community of farmers, who were also hunters and fishermen. On the other hand it no longer seems possible to continue to accept as evidence for the Iron Age the very early dates obtained by Oliver Davies for Ntereso, near Tamale Port on the lower White Volta in modern Ghaan. Here 'a very little iron was found in the third level', which was that of a very fine neolithic industry giving the dates 1630±130 and 1240±120 BC. The excavator, discarding the earlier date, concluded that 'iron was known in Ghana before 1000 BC'.[1] But this conclusion has been disputed by the other archaeologists who best know the area, Colin Flight and Thurstan Shaw. The former, who conducted important excavations at Kintampo, only 130 km to the south of Ntereso, says that Davies's claim that iron was known at Ntereso before 1000 BC is 'not to be taken seriously'; and the second, who is also well acquainted with the area, also regrets that these dates have been associated with the Iron Age, and concludes that, 'until [the picture] is clarified and we have a coherent picture of the site, it must be held in a "suspense account" and can contribute little'.[2]

In the same article, Shaw also demolishes the hypothesis advanced by Davies, as also by L.-M. Diop,[3] that there was an independent invention of iron-working by West African peoples. The present author equally rejects this hypothesis, on the following grounds: (1) It would be difficult for any people who did not already have experience of working other metals, such as copper, to discover how to work iron. It would not be easy to accept that West African neolithic peoples could make this discovery when the pre-Columban Amerindians, who were technologically much more advanced and knew how to work copper, failed to do so. (2) There is no archaeological evidence for iron-working in West Africa before the fifth century BC. (3) On the other hand, there

[1] O. Davies, comments on 'The Iron Age in sub-Saharan Africa', *Current Anthropology*, 1966, 7, 4, 471; see also the same author's *West Africa before the Europeans* (London, 1967), 238, 277, 282.

[2] C. Flight, 'Kintampo, 1967', *West African Archaeological Newsletter*, 1968, **8**, 17; T. Shaw, 'On radiocarbon chronology', *Current Anthropology*, 1969, **10**, 2–3, 228.

[3] Davies, 'The Iron Age', 471; L.-M. Diop, 'Métallurgie traditionnelle', 1038.

is a good deal of evidence that in West Africa the Late Stone Age continued to the beginning of the Christian era and sometimes, indeed, much later. This was the case at Afikpo Rock Shelter in Nigeria, where the dates are 105±85 BC, 95±95 BC and AD 15±80; at Kamabai in Sierra Leone, where the Guinean Neolithic lasted until about AD 340, and iron did not appear until about AD 700; at another Sierra Leonian site, Yagala, not far from Kamabai, where the Neolithic continued even further, to about AD 1070; and in Fernando Po, where sites which are styled Neolithic have given dates of AD 680, 1020 and even 1230. There is also the evidence of the geographer Al-Zuhrī, who, writing about AD 1137, refers to the animistic peoples in the west who 'are ignorant of iron and who fight with ebony clubs; the people of Ghana can defeat them because they have spears and lances'.[1] This would accord well with the late date for the survival of the Neolithic in Sierra Leone into the eleventh century; Stone Age survivals are mentioned, for that matter, by some nineteenth-century authors.

It seems reasonable in fact to suppose that there were sectors in West Africa to which iron-working had not penetrated even by the beginning of the second millennium of the Christian era, that forests and mountains sometimes served as places where 'paleonigritic' peoples took refuge from the attacks of slave-raiders from the Sudan, and that there were similar survivals in islands like Fernando Po. The situation would thus be similar to that found with the Khoisan peoples in South Africa. Similarly, when the Canary Islands were rediscovered in the fourteenth century, their inhabitants were ignorant of iron and other metals, and were continuing to practise a crude neolithic culture which could not be compared with the excellent tools and weapons with which peoples of the adjacent Saharan coastlands had equipped themselves more than two millennia earlier. But this would be an exceptional situation; the general picture would be that most West African peoples passed directly from the Neolithic to the Iron Age, in the Sahel and the Sudan from the fifth century BC, and in the forest lands after the beginning of the Christian era, with 'paleonigritic' peoples in their mountain or island fastnesses catching up between about the fifth and eleventh centuries AD. The only exception to this general picture would be in Mauritania (and perhaps also in modern Niger), where there was a first millennium BC Copper Age contemporary with the end of the North African Bronze Age.

Having discounted the hypothesis that iron-working spread from

[1] al-Zouhri in Youssouf Kamal, *Monumenta cartographica Africae et Aegypti*, 1952, 3, 3, 801.

Meroe westwards to Lake Chad and beyond, it remains to consider what route could have been used to establish the industry in the West African Sudan, specifically in modern Nigeria, as at Taruga, by the fifth century BC. It would seem necessary to look northwards again, across the Sahara, working on the hypothesis that iron-working arrived in the footsteps of copper-working.

The Phoenicians, who were acquainted with iron, began to settle at points on the Mediterranean coast of Africa from about 1100 BC. Their empire grew after the foundation of Carthage in about 800 BC, but it was not until about the sixth century BC that iron objects appear in their tombs, nor until about the third century that iron finally replaced bronze for articles in general use. It would be surprising if by this date knowledge of iron-working had not already been transmitted to the Libyan-Berbers of the Maghrib and the Sahara. Indeed, lances with broad, leaf-shaped heads, and also with small, arrow-shaped heads, are depicted in the rock-drawings of the chariot period and even more commonly in the Libyan-Berber period. Moreover it has already been shown that metal-working in copper was well established in Mauritania from at least the fifth century BC, and that the copper ore used here contained a high proportion of iron which the local smelters discarded with their slag. These would therefore be ideal conditions for the development of an iron industry out of the earlier copper industry as soon as workers were available who knew the secret of the complex techniques needed to produce hard iron and to forge it into useful objects. Moreover there is no reason to suppose that the Akjoujt metal-workers should not have known how to obtain iron as well as copper, and that they should not have made both metals.

Although in modern times all Saharan peoples, Moors, Tuareg and Teda alike, have blacksmiths who know how to smelt iron if there is the need to do so, there is little evidence of ancient iron-working in the Sahara. This is hardly surprising. The enormous deposits of iron ore, such as those of Gara Djebilet and Kedia d'Idjil, which alone interest modern industrialists, were of no concern to early iron-workers who, in Africa as in Europe or elsewhere, were usually content to work with iron-rich stones picked up from surface deposits. Such small-scale exploitation is unlikely to leave many traces. In the Sahara itself, the fuel needed for smelting (e.g. wood), water and provisions, and men themselves were all scarce, and favourable conditions for iron-working would not occur until the further side of the desert had been reached. In the same way, in the Nile Valley, conditions in respect of the supply of fuel and ore were much better in Nubia than they were in Egypt. Thus no more iron would have been produced in the Sahara than was absolutely necessary to meet the needs of its scanty population; the opportunities and the need would both be much greater once the necessary techniques had reached the lands of the sedentary peoples south of the desert.

Traditions have been collected in modern times which suggest that iron-working may have been transmitted across the Sahara to the Sudan by Jewish blacksmiths.[1] But these could relate to a relatively recent period, perhaps contemporary with the development of trans-Saharan trade in Islamic times. It would seem unlikely that any traditions could have survived from a period as remote as about the fifth century BC. On the archaeological side, the best evidence is provided by the rock-drawings. Graves of the pre-Islamic period have been consistently pillaged, and corrosion would have destroyed most of the iron-work which might have been placed in them. But there has been no real search for Iron Age sites in the Sahara, and discoveries may still be made comparable to those at Taruga and Daima further south. Particular attention should be given to the territory around the 'chariot track' between the Fezzan and Gao. The tomb of Tin Hinan at Abalessa, dated to the fourth century AD, lies in this traversable stretch of the desert, and it was from here that, just before the advent of Islam, Jolouta is said to have fled to Es-Souk in Adrar of the Iforas, taking with him 'all the iron to be found in the Abalessa *casbah*'.[2] In a most important study, Denis Williams has drawn attention to three different types of iron-smelting furnace that are used in sub-Saharan Africa: the Meroitic pattern, confined to the Nile Valley; that of the La Tène Celts (copied by the Romans), which was adopted to as far as the western Sudan; and the Catalan pattern, found mainly in Nupe in Nigeria. He concludes that there were two early influences diffusing iron-working south of the Sahara, one originating in Meroe, and the other stemming from North Africa during classical times. In his opinion, the Catalan pattern of smelter was a late introduction, subsequent to the eighth century AD, and due to Muslim influence.[3]

Until there is further archaeological evidence, no positive conclusion

[1] For the western Sahara, see C. de la Roncière, *La découverte de l'Afrique au moyen âge*, I (Cairo, 1925), 102–8, and O. du Puigaudeau, *La route de l'ouest* (*Maroc-Mauritiaie*) (Paris, 1945), 66; for Tuareg country, see Huard, 'Contribution à l'étude du cheval', 145. In modern times, the blacksmiths in the Sahara are often Negroes.

[2] M. Reygasse, *Monuments funéraires préislamiques d'Afrique du Nord* (Paris, 1950), 97.

[3] D. Williams, *Icon and image* (London, 1974), 51–67.

is really possible. But it does seem reasonable to suppose that knowledge of iron-working was transmitted across the Sahara, probably from the Gulf of Syrtis and from Morocco (where it would be connected with the Akjoujt copper industry), and that it passed through the inhospitable and thinly populated desert both earlier and more quickly than was once thought, until about the fifth century BC it became established among the communities of neolithic Negro farmers living in the southern savannas, fertile and well-peopled lands, adequately provided with the necessary ore (e.g. laterite) and fuel. In the eastern Sudan, iron could also have been diffused westwards from Meroe towards the Chad basin, in two stages: a first tentative stage around the beginning of the Christian era, perhaps one in which only ready-made tools and weapons were transmitted; and a later stage at the end of the first millennium, when iron-working itself was introduced by the Haddadians. But in some isolated areas of West Africa, Stone Age technologies were retained until the beginning of the second millennium.

THE PEOPLES OF WEST AFRICA DURING THE EARLY IRON AGE

The oldest-known skeleton of a West African was found in Nigeria at Iwo Eleru; it is of a negroid man and is dated to 9250±150 BC. But for the period under review in this chapter, the end of the Stone Age and the beginning of the Iron Age, the only evidence available (and it has become available only very recently) to indicate the types of man that were then inhabiting West Africa comes from the Sahara and the Sahel. It has recently been analysed by Marie-Claude Chamla.[1]

For the neolithic period, Mme Chamla was able to examine the remains, sometimes very fragmentary, of fifty-eight individuals found at some thirty sites between latitudes 15° and 21°N. From the nine skulls which alone were sufficiently complete in their frontal parts to provide some information, she was able to distinguish three principal types. Typically negroid characteristics were present in six skulls; three of these (from Ibalaghen, Tin Lalou and Karkarichinkat South) showed features of the classic West African Negro, and three (from Tamaya Mellet and El Guettar 2, and the so-called 'Man of Chad') were of a more robust build. Two skulls (from Yao and Wadi

[1] M.-C. Chamla, *Les populations anciennes du Sahara et des régions limitrophes*, *Mémoires CRAPE*, 1968, 9, esp. pp. 83, 87 and 200–1. See also L. Cabot Briggs, *The living races of the Sahara desert* (Cambridge, Mass., 1958).

Inamoulay) presented mixed or undifferentiated characteristics, and one (El Guettar 1) was not negroid. This evidence for a marked preponderance of negroids is supported by the evidence of the unquestionably negroid fossil skeleton found in 1927 at Asselar, some 400 km north-east of Timbuktu, and now dated to about 4400 BC, and of the equally negroid mummified skeleton of a child found in the rock-shelter at Ouan Muhaggiaj in the Fezzan, and dated to 3446 BC. On the other hand, as Mme Chamla points out, no negroid features are present in the skeletal evidence of the same period in the Maghrib.

Three principal morphological types were discerned by Mme Chamla for the proto-historical period. Twenty-five per cent of the identifiable remains were negroid, and these were rare in the Sahara but preponderant further south. A third were of a 'mixed' type in which both negroid and non-negroid features were found. The remainder were not negroid in their characteristics, and these were predominant in the Sahara but extremely rare further to the south. The same racial mixture was evident in the Fezzan at the same period; here there was a preponderance of Mediterranean characteristics and a smaller proportion of classical negroids. Bearing in mind the limited nature of the evidence available for examination, the physical anthropological work which has been done to date suggests that in this region the negroid element was more strongly represented in neolithic times than it was in the later period.

Physical anthropology has thus provided striking confirmation for the opinion, long held by almost all prehistorians, that the climate was wetter in neolithic times and that the inhabitants of the Sahara were then predominantely negroid, and that this was followed in proto-historic times by a period in which desiccation drove the Negroes towards the south and in which they were replaced in the desert by Libyan-Berbers. Further work in physical anthropology may well help to establish this sequence of events even more clearly, and in particular help to date this population change in the Sahara and to establish the northern limits of its earlier occupation by negroid peoples.

Further south, from the Sahel to the Gulf of Guinea, the issue is simpler, at least in theory. There can be no doubt that the basic population was negroid. But it must equally be stated that south of 15 °N there is practically no skeletal evidence of the kind that made it possible for Mme Chamla to establish her inventory for the Sahara and Sahel. In the catalogue drawn up by the present author in 1961,[1] the only human

[1] R. Mauny, 'Catalogue des restes osseux humains préhistoriques trouvés dans l'Ouest africain', *Bulletin de l'IFAN*, 1961, **16** (sér. B), 388–410.

remains known from prehistoric times in the whole area south of 15 °N were those found at Kourounkoro-Kale and at Segoukoro (neither of which was available for Mme Chamla to study). Skeletal remains must of necessity be rare in this region, because high humidity and acid soils do not provide good conditions for the preservation of bones. Indeed, human skeletons of any antiquity are hardly likely to be found anywhere except in caves and rock-shelters, in artificial shell-mounds, or in deep graves which have been protected by the subsequent development above them of a layer of roots capable of absorbing most of the water seeping down from the surface. Two recent discoveries, the preneolithic skeleton found at Iwo Eleru, already referred to, and the more recent skeleton, dated to 25±120 BC, which was found in the rock-shelter at Rop, also in Nigeria, do in fact demonstrate that it is possible for skeletons to survive for some length of time in favourable conditions in the woodland zone. North of this, a number of skeletons have been found by excavators, but few have been studied by physical anthropologists (though some studies are being prepared for publication), and most of them seem to date from the present millennium if they can be dated at all. Among those for which there is published data may be noted the eleventh- to sixteenth-century skulls excavated by Dutch archaeologists from the Tellem Caves in the Dogon Cliff in Mali; among those on which work is still being done are the skeletons found by Serge Robert in the cemetery at Tegdaoust (to be published in one of the volumes of his excavation report). But both these lie outside the period covered by the present chapter, and only serve to draw attention to the lack of evidence for the Early Iron Age.

Nevertheless there can be no doubt that Early Iron Age West Africa was everywhere inhabited by the ancestors of its present Negro peoples. There may well have been important and numerous population movements subsequently, but the basic population distribution can have changed little since the neolithic period. As has been seen, desiccation tended to drive the Negroes southwards from the Sahara, where to the west of Aïr their place was taken by Libyan-Berbers. Throughout the desert zone north of the Senegal and the Niger bend and in Aïr, the Saharan rock-drawings show that cattle-herders (doubtless the ancestors of the modern Fulani) gave way to Libyan-Berber warriors, often charioteers. On the other hand, the Teda, a negroid people with some Berber admixture, were able to hold their position in the Tibesti massif and the surrounding desert to as far as the borders of the Fezzan in about 25 °N. Further to the south, where sedentary life was possible, a large number of Negro groups evolved, cultivating the soil and sometimes keeping cattle as well. Biologically they were a homogenous people, but they were divided into groups distinguishable one from another by language, customs, material culture, social structure and religion. The multiplicity of different West African languages and dialects – when compared, for example, with the comparative unity of the much more widely spread Bantu languages – is sufficient evidence that the peoples who speak them have remained in situ for many millennia.

The manner of life of these peoples during the Early Iron Age, in the savannas at least, cannot have been very different from that still to be found not so very long ago among the so-called 'paleonigritic' peoples in mountain refuge areas from that inhabited by the Bassari in Senegal to the Nuba in Kordofan: intensive hoe cultivation, building in mud, almost total nudity, a high status for blacksmiths, group totems, ancestral cults, absence of circumcision, and the fissioning of ethnic groups into a number of independent units, each led by the eldest fit male with no idea of a hereditary succession. But elsewhere, in the forests of what is now southern Nigeria, in what Baumann calls his 'East Atlantic Circle',[1] things began to take a different turn. Here a combination of local conditions and, it would seem, some as yet little-understood external influence, led to the development of an indigenous centre of civilization which, long before the slave-seeking warfare of the second millennium, must have begun to expand northwards to the Bauchi plateau. This southern culture, which reached its full flowering first at Ife and then at Benin in the first half of the present millennium, was probably in some way descended from the earlier Nok Culture. Thurstan Shaw's recent excavations at Igbo-Ukwu have shown, if the radiocarbon dates he has secured are correct, that by the end of the first millennium there already existed on the lower Niger a civilization which had developed high arts in copper-casting by the lost-wax process, in ironware and in pottery, and which had wide trade connections. The wealth of the finds revealed by Shaw's excavation of the burial of a high dignitary of this culture demonstrates that it must have had a well-developed social organization, perhaps little inferior to that which little if any later led to the emergence of the priest-kings of Ife.

In the north, in the Sahel, other Negroes, essentially the Sarakole (or Soninke) of the Mande group, who were in close contact with the Libyan-Berbers of the desert, began an evolution of their own. It has

[1] See H. Baumann and D. Westermann, *Les peuples et les civilisations de l'Afrique* (Paris, 1948).

already been seen how the clusters of neolithic villages on the Tichit-Walata escarpment, which were flourishing about 1000 BC, thereafter began to decline and then were altogether abandoned by the beginning of the Christian era. The principal cause of this was the desiccation of the Sahara, but another factor which must not be underestimated was the perpetual threat presented to these Negro communities by the Libyan-Berber nomads, equipped first with horses and chariots and then, after the beginning of the Christian era, with camels. These Negro villages were protected by walls and were sited in good defensive positions on the cliff-tops, and their main foe must have been the desert nomads, raiding the settled farmers to obtain grain and slaves. The latter were needed to provide an adequate labour force to tend the nomads' flocks, to give them adequate supplies of kindling and of water, and to do innumerable domestic jobs around the fires and tents of their masters' encampments. These first slave-raids, to secure domestic slaves, must therefore be distinguished from the later raiding to secure slaves for the trade to North Africa. But we know from Arabic sources that this also had begun by the eighth century AD, that is to say even before desert Berber chieftains had begun to convert to Islam. There must therefore be a strong possibility that this kind of exploitation might also go back to the close of the neolithic period.

In this region close to the desert, therefore, unlike the stateless societies in the south, the communities of agricultural Negroes would have been forced by their need to defend themselves effectively to group themselves together into confederations, and to choose war-leaders who in course of time erected themselves into dynasties of rulers. The herdsmen could provide them with cavalry, and the sedentary farmers with battalions of bowmen. Thus equipped, the Negroes would be able to withstand invasions from the desert, the threat of which would always be great in the cyclical periods of drought when, if the Saharans were to survive, they had no choice but to gain access to the southern supplies of pasture and water. It is therefore no accident that the first great Negro state known to history, ancient Ghana, arose out of the contacts between the Sahara and the northern marches of the Mande Sudan. (See chapter 11, pp. 665–75.) It is not known exactly when the kingdom began; if the *Ta'rīkh al-Fattāsh* is to be believed, it would have been in the sixth or seventh century AD, since this chronicle says that Ghana had some twenty kings before the Muslim *Hijra* (AD 622). This first dynasty is said also to have come to an end during the first century AH, i.e. before AD 718. Virtually nothing is known of this dynasty, except that the authors of both the *Ta'rīkh al-Fattāsh* and of the *Ta'rīkh al-Sūdān* believe that it was not of Negro origin. The seat of its government was called Kumbi, and in 1914 traditions surviving in Walata suggested to A. Bonnel de Mézières that this should be identified with the ruins at Kumbi-Saleh (15°46′N, 8°00′W, just inside the southern boundary of modern Mauritania). Bonnel de Mézières undertook the first excavations at this site in 1914, and there were further excavations in 1949–51 and 1970. Though these were taken to considerable depths, unfortunately no recognizably pre-Islamic levels were reached. The ground floors of the houses that were excavated seem to relate to the traders' quarter of Ghana described by al-Bakrī in 1067; radiocarbon dates of AD 828±115, 963±114 and 1210±120 were obtained. A similar disappointment was experienced at Tegdaoust, 330 km away to the north-west, presumed to be the ruins of the ancient caravan centre of Awdaghust, where excavations were sometimes taken as far down as 8 m without disclosing any evidence for a pre-Islamic occupation. Since this site is adjacent to the Aguentour-Labiod Cave, which contains chariot paintings, there would seem every chance that it was occupied in the pre-Islamic period, yet the earliest radiocarbon date so far produced from it is AD 800±80.

Nothing whatsoever is known about Sahelian architecture in the period immediately before the advent of Islam. Investigation of the neolithic villages on the Tichit-Walata escarpment has shown that stone was used for building before 1000 BC. Kumbi-Saleh, Tegdaoust, Es-Souk and similar sites are all in areas with outcrops of rock, so it would be unreasonable to suppose that men ceased to build in stone. But it would seem that nothing has remained of structures which later generations regarded as primitive, unfashionable and, no doubt, decayed; they must have simply served as quarries to provide stone for new buildings.

What is known is that, around AD 790, when the astronomer al-Fazārī was writing, there was a vast Berber empire, that of the Anbiya, in the western Sahara, and that just to the south of this lay the smaller kingdom of Ghana. This was 'the land of gold', and in this statement lies the explanation of Ghana's subsequent growth; it was situated where the trade-routes from the alluvial gold-washings of Galam and of Bure approached the desert. Unlike many later states in Negro Africa, which remained small kingdoms based on exiguous local resources, Ghana grew in wealth, power and territory because it was situated where islamized Berber merchants carrying Mediterranean goods and Saharan salt met to interact with itinerant Negro traders, the ancestors of the Dyula merchant class, who brought gold from lands in the south. The appearance in the eighth century of islamized Berbers in what is now southern Mauritania meant the end of the isolation of western tropical Africa; it became positively attached to the Islamic Mediterranean world, in religion and culture as well as from the standpoints of trade and technology.

The Early Iron Age was now coming to its close, and West Africa was emerging from proto-history. Henceforward there are written records of its past – far fewer than we would like, but nevertheless adequate enough to throw some light on the subsequent development of its Negro peoples. From the eighth century to the end of the sixteenth, great empires were to flourish in the western Sudan: Ghana, Mali and Songhay. The civilizing influence of these empires would be felt throughout the Sahel and the Sudan, and, sheltered behind their protective screen, countless Negro communities were to continue with their traditional lives, though they were now subject to the enslaving attacks of their islamized northern neighbours and, if close to the Guinea coasts, they were shortly also to experience the further rape of manpower occasioned by the growth of slave-trading by the Europeans who began to appear on the scene in the fifteenth century.

As for the Iron Age period, what is needed is systematic work by archaeologists to uncover sites which will provide the detailed evidence of material and spiritual life which is now so sadly lacking. The information available for the neolithic period is relatively good, but it cannot be too much stressed – as has often been done in the present chapter – how few excavations have been undertaken on sites relating to the Iron Age prior to the advent of Islam. Taruga and Daima are for all practical purposes the only excavations producing the evidence which is so badly needed for an understanding of the appearance and the development of iron-working in West Africa. On the Niger bend, between Timbuktu and Niafunke, there are countless pre-Islamic Iron Age sites – tumuli, former villages, the Tondidarou megaliths – awaiting the spade of the archaeologist. It is precisely in this area that archaeologists investigating the beginning of the West African Iron Age should concentrate, just as it is along the Tichit-Walata escarpment and in the Tilemsi valley that the answers will be found to questions relating to the end of the Neolithic and the beginnings of agriculture.

CHAPTER 6

THE EMERGENCE OF BANTU AFRICA

STONE AGE FOOD PRODUCTION

In Africa south of the Equator the period from 500 BC until AD 1000 was first and foremost the period which saw the change to food production. Before 500 BC there may have been a little deliberate 'vegeculture', or intentional planting of vegetable foods, but most food was either hunted or gathered. After AD 1000, though people still hunted and gathered, most of their food came from agriculture and stock-raising, the emphasis in the economy depending largely on ecological factors. This transition to food production coincided, more or less, with the transition from the Stone to the Iron Age. On present evidence it would seem safe to say that before 500 BC no metal tools were in use, and also that after AD 1000 Stone Age hunters only flourished within limited enclaves in parts of the Congo basin, East Africa and southern Africa, with iron being used elsewhere from the Equator to the Cape of Good Hope. Only somewhat more speculatively, it may be surmised that these 1,500 years saw not only a great increase in the human population of this part of the continent, but also a considerable change in its physical type. Before 500 BC the most widespread type of man had been the Bush physical type, most successfully adapted to hunting in the open savannas and drier woodlands of eastern and southern Africa. After AD 1000 the predominant type of man was the Negro, adapted originally to hunting, gathering and perhaps also to vegeculture, in the wetter woodlands of West and western Central Africa, but which became proficient in agriculture and stock-raising, and spread rapidly over the whole sub-continent except for one small corner in the south-west. The characteristic languages of Bush peoples, wherever they have survived into modern times, are the clicking languages called Khoi and San. The characteristic languages of Negro peoples living to the south of the Equator are those of the Bantu family.

It has already been shown in chapter 5 that, from the point of view of the incipient food-producer, the climate and vegetation of most of Africa between the northern tropic and the Equator was arranged in a comparatively simple system of latitudinal zones. There was the desert zone, suited only to a sparse occupation by transhumant pastoralists.

There was the dry savanna, in which stock-raising could be supplemented by the cultivation of the smaller *Pennisetum* millets, which can survive with as little as 300 to 400 mm of rain a year. There was, next, the very diverse 'Sudanic' region, enjoying 500 to 1,200 mm of rainfall. Much of this country, left to itself, supported light woodland, but food-producers soon turned it into man-made savanna, the prime cereal country of Africa north of the Equator. Here millet was accompanied by the tall sorghums and the dry rice, *Oryza glaberrima*. Here cattle and goats could thrive as well as cereals. Here the conditions for subsistence farming were the best of any. Numerous micro-environments offered a wide range of opportunities for specialization in the quest for food, whether towards fishing, gathering, cultivation or stock-raising. The cultivation of both cereal and root-crops was possible in quite a wide belt to the north of the forest. The fringes of the forest combined savanna woodlands with gallery forest along the river banks. These marginal areas were especially favourable ones for pre-Iron Age peoples to experiment with new economies. South again lay the damp woodlands, merging into the rain-forest of the Guinea coastlands and the Congo basin, where tree shade and cloud cover prevented the growth of cereals, and where malaria, amoebic dysentery and other diseases endangered the life of man. Here cereal agriculture had to be replaced by fruits and root-crops, few of which were native to Africa, and therefore, except where fishing provided an element of protein, the early food-producing population was probably nearly as sparse as in the desert, and much less satisfactorily nourished.[1] While there was some early penetration of the forest regions by food-producers following river lines, much of the primary rain-forest was probably occupied fairly late in the Iron Age. The difficulties of the forest heartlands stand in marked contrast to the opportunities of the forest margins.

In Africa south of the Equator the environmental conditions for incipient food-producers were much more complex. The forest environment was concentrated in the southern half of the Congo basin, while the dry savanna conditions comparable to those existing on the southern edge of the Sahara extended from the low country surrounding the Ethiopian highlands in the north-east of the region, across the central part of East Africa and the Southern part of Central Africa, to the Kalahari and the dry tablelands adjoining it in the south-west. The intermediate country of adequate but not excessive rainfall, corresponding to the light woodland or man-made savanna of the Sudanic zone,

[1] R. Mauny, *Tableau géographique de l'ouest africain au moyen âge* (Dakar, 1961), 193–223.

occurred here in two main areas: first, in a broad arc around the east, south and south-west of the Congo forest, where the forest margin from the Lower Congo to Manyema provided a favourably diverse environment similar to that north of the rain-forest; and secondly in a narrow lowland belt following the Indian Ocean coast from Kenya to the Transkei. These two areas were tenuously connected by the low-lying country between the Rovuma and Zambezi valleys. Otherwise, the conditions suited to dense population by subsistence cultivators occurred only in the foothills of the great mountains, such as Kilimanjaro, Kenya and Elgon, and also in highland areas like the Pares, the Usambaras and the southern highlands of Tanzania, where perennial rainfall provided an environmental contrast to the surrounding dry upland savanna. Doubtless because of the forest clearance involved, the colonization of these mountain valleys seems to have been a late development. For the early stages of food production, the crucial area would seem to have been the first one, comprising the interlacustrine region to the east of the Congo forest, the Katanga and Kasai to the south of it, and the region between the Katanga and the Indian Ocean coast. South of the Equator, this was the region which corresponded ecologically with the Sudanic region to the north – the intermediate, light woodland zone, enjoying 500 to 1,200 mm of annual rainfall. This diverse area extended right up to the margins of the forest, allowing the cultivation of root-crops, as well as millets and sorghums, on carefully selected soils. Cattle and small stock could flourish with game animals on the grasslands wherever tsetse was absent. The gallery forests of river valleys and the fringes of the rain-forest itself allowed both the cultivation of root-crops and the intensive use of the vegetable foods of the dense woodland.

The archaeological evidence for the origins of food production and iron-working in northern Africa, the Sahara and the Sudanic belt have been described in chapter 5, where it is shown how a pattern of intensive exploitation of wild vegetable foods preceded the introduction of cereal agriculture. A widespread pastoral culture flourished in the Sahara between the fifth and the third millennia BC, with Afro-Mediterranean and Negro peoples from north and south of the desert meeting and interacting in the Sahara and adopting the same cultural traits. The southward diffusion of food production was certainly hastened by the gradual desiccation that set in during the second half of the third millennium BC. By the end of the second millennium, if not before, sedentary communities of cereal agriculturalists were beginning

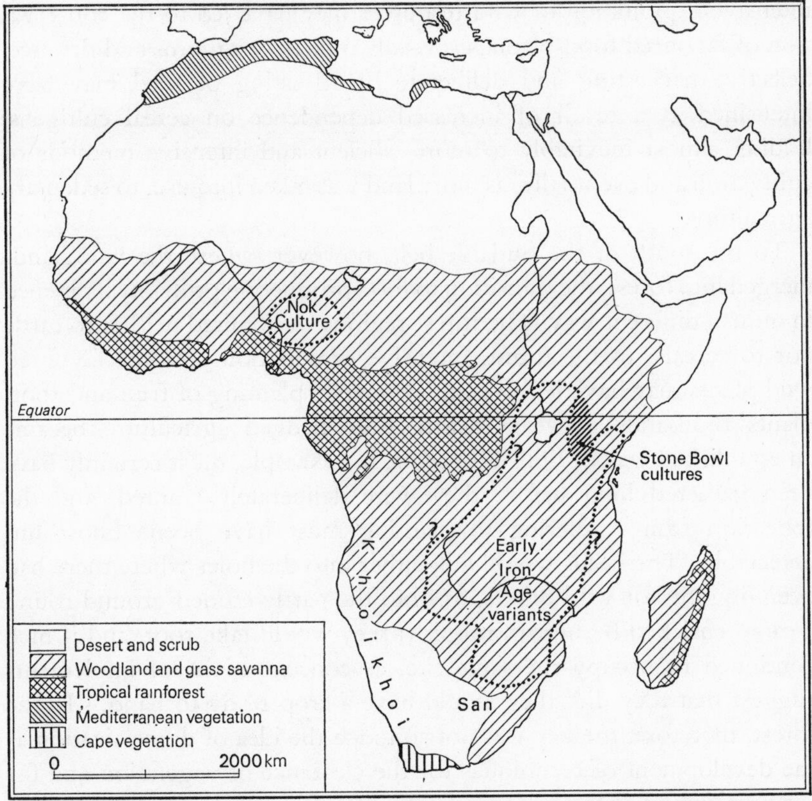

43 Vegetational zones and major archaeological configurations.

to penetrate the Sudanic latitudes north of the equatorial forests, and by the second half of the first millennium some of these communities were beginning to use iron. From the shores of the Mediterranean to the margins of the forest, the pattern of the transition from hunting and gathering to food production seems clear enough, at least in outline. One vital element was the intensified exploitation of game and vegetable foods before the idea of domesticating both animals and cereal food-plants provided the catalyst for a complete transformation of the economy. A specialized tool-kit, which included axes and adzes as well as pottery, accompanied the main innovations. The hunting and gathering populations increased steadily, even before the beginnings of food production, so that the carrying capacity of some areas became inadequate. This may have led to exchange relationships between groups, and so to mutual dependence, and perhaps some competition. The more intensive exploitation of wild resources may have led to the conservation of favoured food-plants, especially millets, sorghums and dry rice. Selective harvesting and deliberate broadcasting of seed may have intensified as a result of increased dependence on cereal cultigens, leading almost inevitably to more efficient and intensive methods of cultivation and eventually, as more land was taken into use, to sedentary agriculture.

To the south of the Sudanic belt, however, where the woodlands merged into forest, the transition to food production probably happened in quite a different way. The forest regions were suited neither to cattle nor to cereals. In the forest, intensive exploitation of some favoured wild plants may have led to some deliberate planting of fruit and root-plants thousands of years before fully fledged agriculture became an established way of life. Wild yams, for example, must certainly have been gathered long before they were deliberately planted, and the transition from gathering to planting must have been almost undetectable. 'The heads would fall, either into the holes where there had been digging for wild tubers, or onto the partly eroded ground round a camp enriched by human rubbish; they would take root, and if men continued to occupy the same site, as concentrations of implements suggest that they did, they would have a crop ready to hand.'[1] In the forest, therefore, the key was not so much the idea of domestication as the development of techniques for the clearance of vegetation and for the preparation of the soil for planting. Clearing tools were most likely much improved by the new techniques of grinding and polishing. Probably, these techniques came only through contact with the new methods of lithic manufacture which accompanied the transition to food production further north. Probably they spread at first along the edges of the forest rather than deep into it.

Food-producers are thought to have lived on the fringes of, and in, the West African rain-forest from about the third millennium BC, but the archaeological evidence for them is scanty. Much of the modern forest is now secondary, but the earliest farmers probably followed river lines, leaving the interfluves unsettled, as is the case with forest people in the Amazon basin. The ringing of trees and the burning of undergrowth is an effective means of forest clearance under these conditions. A scatter of sites and artefacts, mainly hoes and other stone tools, occurs both in the forest and on its margins. Some pottery and stone axes have also been found in the north-western and north-eastern

[1] O. Davies, *West Africa before the Europeans* (London, 1967), 151.

parts of the Congo basin, as if the new techniques spread southwards before the advent of iron, but the evidence is uncertain. The scattered finds do, however, suggest quite substantial settlement of the rain-forest before the coming of iron, and some forest clearance by stone-using farmers.

Some of the best evidence so far available about the transition from gathering to food production on the margins of the equatorial forest comes from the central region of modern Ghana, where a series of rock-shelters near Kintampo show a 'Late Stone Age' culture using microlithic stone tools and pottery underlying a later occupation by Stone Age farmers. The earlier, Punpun, phase is characterized by the gathering of wild fruit, including *Celtis* species, the trapping of small game and the collecting of snails. There are no traces of domestic animals or cultivation in the Punpun horizons, which were abandoned around 1400 BC. An abrupt break in the cultural tradition was followed by the occupation of people practising the 'Kintampo culture', who probably kept domestic cattle and goats, and who certainly cultivated oil-palms and cowpeas. Polished axes, terracotta rasps, bracelets and grooved stones were in common use. Microlithic stone tools were still common. The Kintampo culture people lived in mud huts and occupied permanent settlements. Their sites extend from the Black Volta in the north to the Accra plain in the south. One Kintampo culture site, at Ntereso, has been claimed as a centre of early iron-working, but the evidence is disputed. Dates for the Kintampo culture fall in the late second millennium BC, but it is possible that it continued to flourish until well on in the following millennium, until the arrival of iron-working in West Africa, or even later.

The appearance of the new food-producing economies elsewhere in West Africa is marked by the occurrence of some new types of artefact. No organic finds have been made, the forest environment being generally unfavourable to the preservation of vegetable remains and animal bones. However, flaked and polished axes and hoes occur in many sites, while pottery makes its first appearance. A 'waisted' form of stone axe, characteristic of Saharan food-producers, is frequently found as far south as Ghana, Nigeria and Cameroun. Crude stone objects made from softer rocks are often interpreted as hoes. These were often percussion-flaked and unpolished, although axes were made of harder materials. The new artefacts are found in a wide variety of environments, from the edge of the desert near Bamako on the one hand, to cleared areas within the forest, as in Ghana, on the other. Essentially, however, their distribution shows them to have belonged to a tool-kit of the forest fringes, representing the first widespread attempt at deliberate food production in the moist woodland environment surrounding the Guinea and the Congo forests. It could very well be that the ethnic, cultural and linguistic relationships still existing between these two regions reflect a common process of colonization which took place at this time. Oliver Davies, for example, envisages a 'hoe neolithic' culture, with its centre of dispersion in the modern Congo Republic, whence it would have travelled both westwards along the edge of the Guinea forest and southwards around the forests of the Congo basin.[1] Most archaeologists do not accept the concept of a 'hoe neolithic', arguing that the so-called hoes are stray finds without accurate stratigraphical contexts or absolute dates. While the widespread distribution of these artefacts may reflect a broadly similar technological response to the need for forest clearance and garden cultivation over a wide area where dense undergrowth had to be cleared for agriculture, a similar tool-kit does not necessarily imply either a cultural or a political continuum. Nevertheless, such a development in material culture might well be correlated with the occurrence of Bantu-like features in a number of otherwise unrelated, or very, very remotely related language groups strung out across West Africa in these latitudes. These features have nothing to do with the ultimate classification of West African and Bantu languages as Niger-Congo or Niger-Kordofanian (as described below). They refer to a set of special relationships between the Bantu languages and those formerly called 'Semi-Bantu' – especially the Ekoid languages of Nigeria, the Akan languages of Ghana and the Ivory Coast, and the Mel languages of Liberia and Sierra Leone, Guinea and Senegal. These languages have grammatical as well as lexical affinities with Bantu, and it is significant that these affinities are stronger between the central Bantu languages and the Mel languages of the far west than they are between the central Bantu and the Ekoid languages which are geographically so much nearer. This pattern could well reflect a process of colonization by some originally concentrated population speaking a language akin to Bantu, which in neolithic times became especially skilled in the arts of a waterside existence, and spread both westwards and southwards, following the river lines of the Benue-Niger and of the Chari-Congo. We have to remember that, for most of the width of the continent, the equatorial forest provided an effective barrier to the transmission of cattle and cereals, which had

[1] Ibid. 216.

been the main ingredients of the food-producing economies further north. It is therefore probable that, throughout the humid regions of the Guinea Coast and the Congo basin, the effects of Sudanic food production were expressed mainly in the new developments in stone technology, which enabled an already existing marginal practice of vegeculture to be more widely and deliberately extended.

The only part of Sudanic Africa from which cattle and cereals could easily be transmitted southwards was the eastern sector. Here, so-called 'C-Group' or 'C-horizon' people are thought to have been living in Lower Nubia by the close of the Egyptian Old Kingdom (*c.* 2500 BC), or slightly later. They were sedentary farmers, who kept cattle especially for religious and prestige purposes. Their origins are uncertain, some authorities considering them to be descendants of an earlier indigenous population, others as migrants from the steppe country to the east or west of the Nile who had been driven from their former homelands by the general desiccation of the Saharan latitudes. At all events, the C-Group peoples were probably influential in the diffusion of food-producing economies southwards into the Nilotic Sudan and Ethiopia.[1] There is, of course, good evidence for early contact between Egypt and the Horn of Africa, where the available data indicate that animal and vegetable domesticates were introduced in the third or second millennium BC.[2]

At least by the end of the second millennium, therefore, cattle and cereals must have reached the Sudanic latitudes of north-eastern Africa. In considering how they passed still further to the south, we have to remember that southern Uganda was probably largely forested, at least in a belt from the Ruwenzori to Mount Elgon. It is significant that during the first millennium BC pollens of forest species from Lake Victoria show a sharp drop, with a corresponding rise in grass pollens, and also that *Acalypha*, an early stage pioneer in the regeneration of forests after gardens have been abandoned, shows an increase in

[1] Some ground hoes have been found to the east of the C-Group area, in south-west Ethiopia, which are suggestive of the existence of Stone Age agriculture at a period corresponding to the appearance of similar artefacts in the western forests of Africa. This area is one where *Ensete edule* has a long history and may well have been domesticated before the introduction of cereal crops. J. D. Clark, 'The problem of neolithic culture in sub-Saharan Africa', in W. W. Bishop and J. D. Clark, eds., *Background to evolution in Africa* (Chicago, 1967), 612.

[2] An early date for North-East African cereal crops may also be indicated by the presence of African cereals such as *Eleusine* and *Pennisetum* in southern India at Hallur and Paiyampalli, in contexts dating to *c.* 1800 BC. F. R. Allchin, 'Early cultivated plants in India and Pakistan', in P. J. Ucko and G. W. Dimbleby, eds., *The domestication and exploitation of plants and animals* (London, 1969), 323–9.

frequency from this period on.[1] These pollen diagrams may be indirect evidence for an early date for some kind of Stone Age food production in the interlacustrine region, but direct archaeological evidence for this is so far limited to a few isolated finds of polished stone axes in Uganda, and to a possible Late Stone Age pottery type, known as Kansyore ware, found in the western and southern parts of the Victoria Lake basin. On the whole, therefore, it would seem likely that Stone Age food production to the west of Lake Victoria was limited to the kind of incipient vegeculture characteristic of other sectors of the forest periphery at the same period. East of Lake Victoria, however, the ecological situation was certainly very different. From the southern Sudan and south-western Ethiopia southwards into Kenya and northern Tanzania there ran a wedge of highland savanna country, all of it suited to cattle, and much of it to millet and sorghum. This must certainly have been the main route by which cattle penetrated into sub-equatorial Africa in Late Stone Age times. As to cereals, the evidence is not yet conclusive. It could be that, here as elsewhere, cereals only entered sub-equatorial Africa with the coming of the Iron Age.

Of the introduction of cattle, archaeology in the Rift Valley region of Kenya and northern Tanzania has provided ample evidence. During the first millennium BC, all this area was occupied by the stone-using pastoralists who practised the 'Stone Bowl' culture, characterized by the presence of a large number of stone bowls and platters, as well as by deep clay bowls, some with scored decoration, in the midst of a lithic assemblage consisting of derivatives of the Kenya Capsian of Late Stone Age times (fig. 44).[2] The stone bowls are accompanied by pestles. Flat stones were used for grinding, and at the great burial site at Njoro River Cave it appears that both men and women were interred with a bowl and pestle apiece.[3] The natural supposition would be that these implements were used for grinding grain. But the fact that the human remains had been heavily smeared with ochre, which must have been ground before use, leaves in suspense the question of whether the Stone Bowl people were agriculturalists as well as stock-raisers. No carbonized seed or other direct evidence for agriculture has yet come from Stone Bowl sites. At the same time, faced with the problem of accounting for an early spread of eleusine millet into eastern and southern Africa, it is

[1] R. L. Kendall and D. A. Livingstone, 'Palaeoecological studies on the East African plateau', in H. J. Hugot (ed.), *Actes du VIe Congrès Panafricain du Préhistoire* (Chambéry, 1972), 386.

[2] L. S. B. Leakey, *The Stone Age cultures of Kenya Colony* (Cambridge, 1931).

[3] M. D. Leakey and L. S. B. Leakey, *Excavations at the Njoro River Cave* (Oxford, 1950).

tempting to assume that the Stone Bowl people were responsible, for they are the only Stone Age food-producers as yet firmly identified in eastern Africa. Physically, the Stone Bowl people are comparatively well known from their skeletal remains, which do however need re-evaluation by physical anthropologists. Certainly, these remains have many features in common with the modern highland population. At this rate, they presumably spoke languages of the Cushitic family, which today has its main focus in Ethiopia and Somalia, but has also some outlying remnant members in central Kenya and northern Tanzania. It certainly looks as though the Cushitic languages formerly extended much more deeply into East Africa than they do now, and as though sparse Cushitic-speaking populations of the Late Stone Age have been overlaid and absorbed by Bantu pressing in from the west and south, as well as by Paranilotic and Nilotic speakers arriving more recently from the north (see Volume 3, chapter 9).

One further set of external stimuli for food production in sub-equatorial Africa needs a brief consideration, namely those entering by the Indian Ocean coast. Without any doubt, several food-plants of South-East Asian origin, notably the banana, the Asian yam (*Dioscorea alata* and *D. esculenta*) and the cocoyam (*Colocasia*), have been of very great significance in tropical Africa. The question is when they arrived. Here the crucial consideration seems to be the negative evidence from Madagascar, where the fact that a Malayo-Polynesian language is still spoken argues strongly for an original colonization from South-East

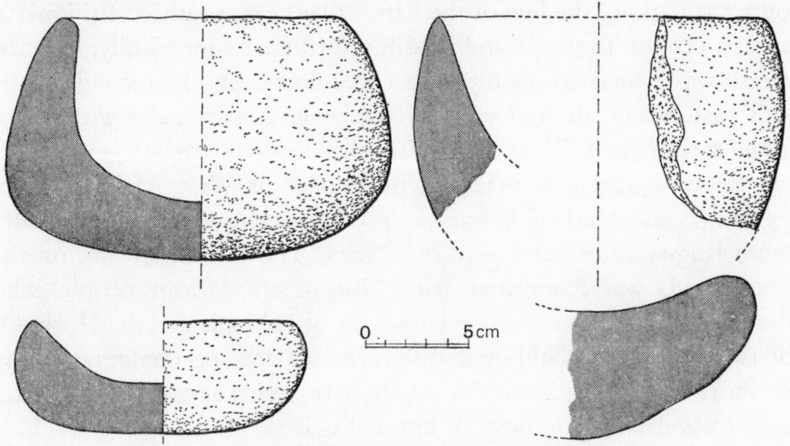

44 Stone bowls from Prospect Farm, Kenya.
(After M. Cohen, 'A reassessment of the Stone Bowl culture of the Rift Valley, Kenya', *Azania*, 1970, **5**, fig. 3.)

Asia. No stone industry having yet been found on Madagascar, the clear implication would seem to be that this migration occurred within the Iron Age. Of course, it is theoretically possible that stone-using South-East Asians reached East Africa before their iron-using descendants discovered Madagascar, but it seems a little unlikely. On the whole, it does not seem at all probable that stimuli from South-East Asia initiated the progress of sub-equatorial Africa towards food production, but rather that they accelerated the process at a later stage. The same is even more probably true of seaborne influences from western Asia, via the Red Sea and the Persian Gulf. Climatically, and therefore botanically, western Asia was hardly comparable to tropical Africa, while technologically it was so much further advanced by the first millennium BC that any significant degree of contacts should have left abundant traces.

The conclusion would seem to be that, before the coming of iron, the vital techniques and new economic patterns involved in food production reached sub-equatorial Africa across its long land frontier with the northern hemisphere, and that these stimuli travelled in two main streams. There was a western stream, associated in material culture with some form of hoe and axe tool-kit, which extended southwards through, or round the margin of, the humid forest of the northern Congo basin to the light woodland and forest/savanna mosaic of the Katanga and the Kasai. And there was an eastern stream, associated in central Kenya with the Stone Bowl people, but perhaps representing a more widely spread, if very tenuous, stream of neolithic influences extending southwards along the line of the Rift Valley from southern Ethiopia at least to central Tanzania and possibly further. Economically, the first stream was associated mainly with vegeculture, and the second mainly with pastoralism, though perhaps also at least marginally with cereal agriculture. Ethnically and linguistically, the western stream was, as will be seen, surely associated with people of West African origin, speaking some kind of Benue-Congo language ancestral to the later Bantu languages of sub-equatorial Africa. The eastern stream, on the other hand, was associated with North-East African people who presumably spoke the Cushitic languages of Ethiopia and the Horn. Of the two streams, it could be that the western one was demographically the more important, since the preliminary archaeological distribution maps of undated sites show an unusually dense concentration of 'Late Stone Age settlement' along the southern and western rim of the Congo basin.[1] Demographically, the eastern stream may have been compara-

[1] J. D. Clark, ed., *Atlas of African prehistory* (Chicago, 1967), 'Later Stone Age' map.

tively insignificant, since a mainly pastoral people living on dry ranching lands is apt to be very thinly spread. Remarkably enough, the populations which do not seem to have been represented in sub-equatorial Africa during the period of Late Stone Age food production were those speaking Central Sudanic, Nilotic and Paranilotic languages, who were to play such a large part in the later history of the region. Recently, one linguistic historian has postulated the existence of Central Sudanic loan-words, including words for cattle and grain-crops, in a number of central and eastern Bantu languages, and has proceeded to argue that both agriculture and pastoralism must have been practised by Central Sudanic-speaking peoples throughout the central part of sub-equatorial Africa during Stone Age times.[1] But such an hypothesis finds no confirmation in the archaeological record.

THE CLASSIFICATION OF BANTU

It is against some such assessment of the likely demographic situation at the end of the Stone Age that the historical implications of recent work on the classification of the Bantu languages have to be considered. All authorities have long been agreed that most of the 300 or so Bantu languages spoken in sub-equatorial Africa today are so closely related, both grammatically and lexically, that they can be thought of as the descendants of a single parent language, which was once spoken in a very much more concentrated area than that now occupied by its descendants. Again, all are agreed that, because of the vast geographical spread of the Bantu languages and the relatively small degree of differentiation that has occurred between them, the expansion of Bantu must have been, by African standards, an exceptionally rapid one. Much skill and ingenuity has been devoted to the search for the nuclear area of this great expansion, and one of the obvious lines of inquiry has been the establishment of the relations of Bantu, as a whole, with other groups of African languages. Here, the conclusions foreshadowed by Westermann in the 1920s and 1930s, and developed by Joseph Greenberg in the 1950s, today command almost universal acceptance. They are that the outside relationships of Bantu lie, not with the language families dominating the region immediately to the north of the Bantu sphere, but rather with the languages of sub-Saharan West Africa, classified by Greenberg in a wider grouping called at first Niger-Congo

[1] C. Ehret, 'Patterns of Bantu and Central Sudanic settlement in Central and southern Africa', *Trans-African Journal of History*, 1974, 4, 1–27.

and later Niger-Kordofanian.[1] As one of six main sub-divisions of this wider grouping, Greenberg postulated one called Benue-Congo, extending south-eastwards from the eastern part of northern Nigeria, of which Bantu, for all its vast extension, was merely one member. While linguists continue to debate the precise degree of validity attaching to Greenberg's methods, and while the sub-divisions of Niger-Kordofanian will doubtless be subject to considerable elaboration, Greenberg's work in fact leaves little doubt that the ultimate origins of Bantu have to be sought in the eastern part of West Africa, in the region between the upper Benue and the northern tributaries of the Congo drainage system.

Taken by itself, however, the evidence about the external relationships of Bantu tells us nothing more than that the oldest Bantu-like languages should have been spoken somewhere in or near the north-western corner of the present Bantu sphere, in the general area of the modern state of Cameroun. This is certainly a precious indication; but for evidence about the subsequent course and pace of the spread of Bantu speech we have to turn to the internal classification of the Bantu languages themselves. Here, the most substantial conspectus of basic evidence is that by Malcolm Guthrie, who identified common items from more than 200 languages and made a detailed comparison of the interrelationships of 28 'test languages', selected partly for their wide geographical distribution across the Bantu sphere and partly for the quality of the information available about them. For the purpose of analysis, Guthrie divided the whole sphere into six regions and fifteen zones, a map of which is reproduced, together with the test languages, in fig. 45. In the identification of 'general' word-roots, which could be assumed to have occurred in the 'proto-language', Guthrie required that reflexes formed according to a regular process of sound-shifts should be found in at least five of his six regions. The most important result of his investigations was the identification of 455 such 'general' roots, and of some 1,800 other 'common series', of which reflexes occur in at least three of the six regions, in most cases with a distribution occurring predominantly either in the three western regions or the three eastern ones. The tendency of the Bantu languages to throw up pairs of synonyms, one with an eastern and one with a western distribution, is very marked.[2]

[1] D. Westermann, 'Die westlichen Sudansprachen und ihre Beziehungen zum Bantu', *Mitteilungen des Seminars für orientalische Sprachen*, 1927, 30; J. H. Greenberg, *Studies in African linguistic classification* (New Haven, Conn., 1955); Greenberg, *The languages of Africa* (The Hague, 1963).

[2] M. Guthrie, *Comparative Bantu, an introduction to the comparative linguistics and prehistory of the Bantu languages*, 4 vols. (Farnborough, 1967–72).

It is now generally recognized that, in the interpretation of his own evidence, Guthrie was unduly influenced by the distribution pattern of the 'general' roots reflected in his test languages. This showed the highest percentages in the languages of his L and M zones in the geographical centre of the Bantu sphere, with progressively falling percentages in the peripheral zones. On this basis Guthrie identified the historical centre of the proto-language with the area of highest retention of 'general' roots and saw the lower percentages of the peripheral zones as the result of a geographical dispersal away from this centre. This interpretation has been challenged by a number of linguists. Greenberg

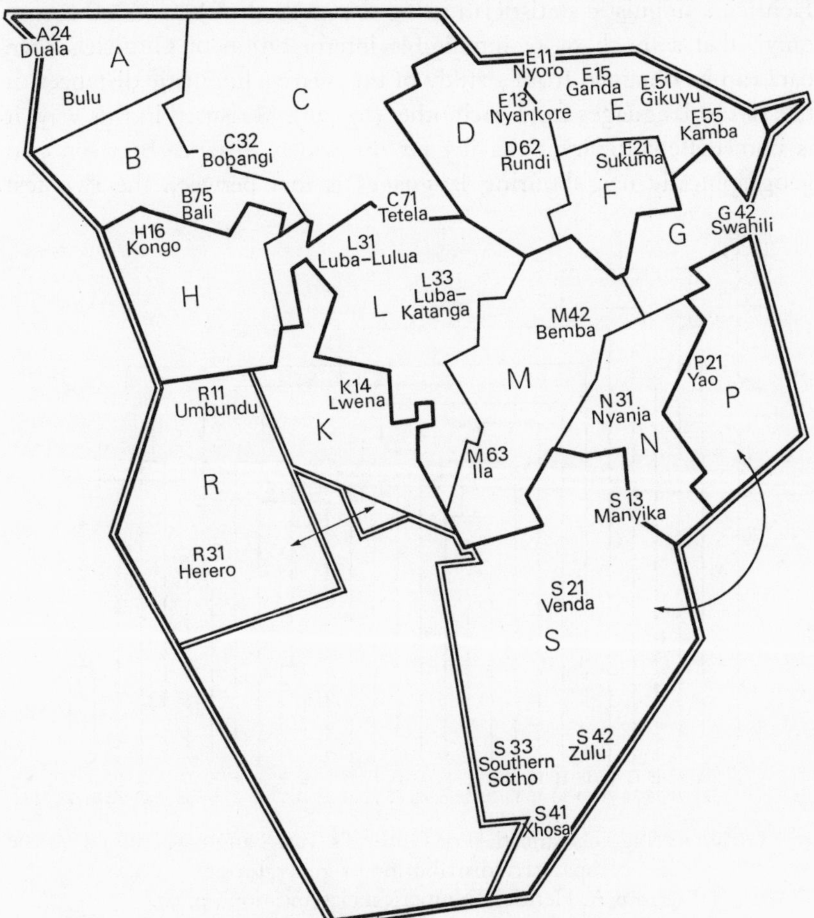

45 Guthrie's Zones and Test Languages.
(From A. Henrici, 'Numerical classification of Bantu languages', *African Language Studies*, 1973, 14, p. 83.)

questioned Guthrie's basic assumption that the greatest retention of original roots would occur at the point of origin, arguing that on the same assumption the cradleland of Germanic would be Iceland and that of the Romance languages Sardinia.[1] Meanwhile, Heine had produced a completely independent classification of Bantu based upon percentages of common vocabulary in 137 languages, using a hundred-word list of basic items. This showed eleven main sub-divisions, of which ten lay in the north-western quadrant of the Bantu sphere, while the eleventh comprised all the languages spoken to the south and east of the Congo forest.[2] Most strikingly, however, it has been demonstrated by Dr Alick Henrici, a linguistic statistician using the method of 'numerical taxonomy', that a much more intelligible interpretation of Guthrie's own data can be obtained from a study of the relative linguistic distances of the 28 test languages from each other (fig. 46). Measured in this way, it is immediately apparent that by far the widest distance between two geographically neighbouring languages is that between the two test

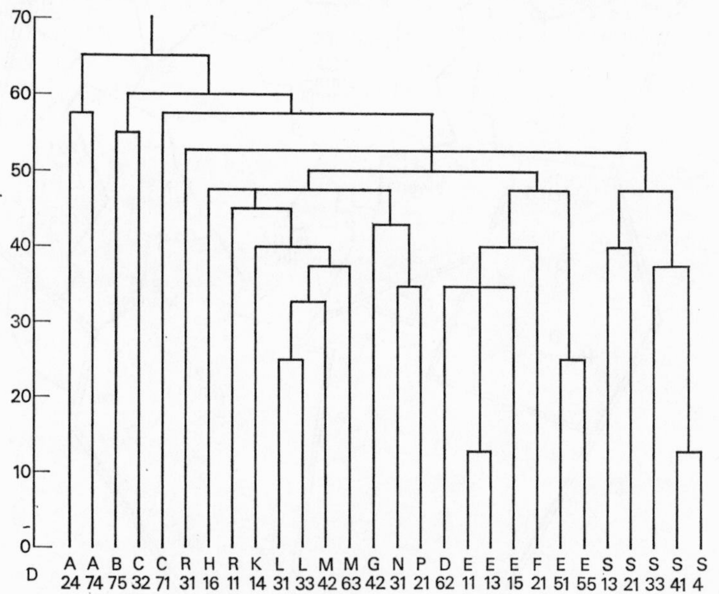

46 Group average classification of Guthrie's Test Languages, based on the comparative distribution of general roots. (From A. Henrici, 'Numerical classification', p. 97.)

[1] J. H. Greenberg, 'Linguistic evidence regarding Bantu origins', *Journal of African History*, 1972, **13**, 2, 193.

[2] B. Heine, 'Zur genetischen Gliederung der Bantu-Sprachen', *Afrika und Übersee*, 1972–3, **56**, 164–85.

languages of Guthrie's Zone A, the north-western zone. Summing up the results of his exercise, Henrici says:

In the first place there is a clear indication of a primary split between the two Zone A languages and the remaining twenty-six. Following this there is also little doubt that the next three languages to split off were the three from Zones B and C, though the relationship between these three is not clearly indicated. This leaves a group of twenty-three languages remaining which I shall refer to as the Central Bantu languages. There is a far greater overall similarity among this group than among the remaining five. Indeed if it were required to divide the complete set of Test Languages into six groups it would seem proper to allocate each of the five Zone A, B and C languages to a group on its own, forming a single group from all the remaining Central Bantu languages.

As Henrici concludes,

In support of the classification arrived at there is the fact that it fits conveniently into a wider framework. The Semi-Bantu languages can take their places naturally as early offshoots from the same stem that later generated the Zone A, B and C offshoots and finally came to its full flowering in the Central Bantu languages. With this picture the vexed question of the whereabouts of the place of origin of the Bantu peoples becomes less important. There is room in the theory for a succession of places of origin depending on how broadly the Bantu group is defined.[1]

The most important historical inference to be drawn from the classification of the Bantu languages is, therefore, that there was a very long period, probably lasting several thousand years, during which Bantu-speaking populations were confined more or less to the north-western of Guthrie's six regions (and for much of it perhaps only to a small part of that region), and that this period was followed by a much shorter one during which Bantu speech was carried into the other five regions. One further conclusion is inescapable. Since the north-western region coincides almost exactly with the equatorial forest, the second period of Bantu history must represent the expansion of a population of the forest, or the forest margins, into the surrounding savannas. Such an expansion at the expense of other languages and cultures can hardly have been based on superior methods of hunting and gathering. It must have been based upon some kind of food production which enabled its practitioners to establish relatively dense and permanent settlements capable of exerting a linguistic and cultural attraction over the sparser and more mobile communities of hunters and

[1] A. Henrici, 'Numerical classification of Bantu languages', *African Language Studies*, 1973, 14, 98, 101.

gatherers. In its origins this food-producing economy was doubtless that associated with the ground and polished stone axes which have been found especially around the forest margins. In its later stages, however, and throughout most of the savanna regions into which it expanded, it must have been associated with an iron technology, since we know that over most of the savanna, food production began only with the Iron Age.

If Henrici's calculation of the distances separating Guthrie's twenty-eight test languages is approximately correct, it should follow that the main parent language of those spoken in Zones D–S would have been geographically situated somewhere on the outer margin of Zone C. It would have included most of Guthrie's 'general' roots – indeed, it is remarkable that 30% of these have no reflexes in the north-western region, and that a very much larger proportion have no reflexes in Zones A and B. Guthrie's analysis of the 'general' roots bearing on the environment and the economy remain, therefore, fully relevant. It shows, for example, well-attested words for 'forest patch' and 'thicket', but none for either 'grassland' or 'unbroken forest'. Words for wild fauna are numerous, but do not include the animals of the open savanna, such as lion, zebra, rhinoceros, or, among birds, the ostrich. Domestic animals include dog, goat, chicken and possibly cattle – there is a 'general' root, but it can also mean 'buffalo' – and there is no special term either for 'cow's milk' or for 'milking'. Words for flora are few, but they include two terms for 'palm tree', which grows both in the forest and the forest margin, and a word for 'fig tree', which occurs in the savanna and the forest margin, but not in the unbroken forest. Cultivated plants include beans, mushrooms, oil, vegetables, possibly some kinds of yam and, surprisingly, bananas (though this root could conceivably be a mutation of a word for beans). These are accompanied by words for 'garden', 'to cultivate' and 'to weed'; but there is no 'general' root for any cereal crop. There is a comprehensive set of terms connected with boats and fishing, but nothing very definite connected with hunting.[1] None of these items taken in isolation would be of significance, but in combination they suggest fairly convincingly an environment of the forest or the forest margin, a land of moist climate and flowing water, a land for planting rather than for sowing, a land situated very definitely in the western half of the Bantu sphere.

On the economic side, therefore, the picture presented by the 'general' word-roots is clearly one in which vegecultural food production was

[1] Guthrie, *Comparative Bantu*, II, paras. 83.13–83.25.

established alongside a well-developed tradition of riverside fishing. Initially, no doubt, these arts were practised with stone tools; and it is a matter of great interest to establish at what stage in the development of the Bantu languages stone tools were superseded by iron. Unfortunately, the linguistic evidence concerning technical innovations is full of pitfalls. A word for 'iron' can descend from a word for 'stone'. A verb 'to forge' can descend from a verb 'to pound'. Knives, hammers, axes, adzes, hoes and spears were all made of stone before they were made of iron, and the same nouns were probably used for the metal artefacts as for their stone predecessors. Thus, although there are 'general' roots for all these items, and although all of them occur in the A–C zones as well as in the D–S zones, it would be rash to conclude, as Guthrie did, that the common ancestors of all the Bantu had an iron technology before their languages diverged.[1] It may be more significant that a few terms more exclusively connected with iron-working, such as 'bellows', 'to blow bellows' and 'wire', though widely distributed in other regions, do not occur in the north-western region. It may well be that the parent language of Zones D–S was in origin that of a stone-using population, which learned the elements of iron technology only on the eve of a period of great geographical expansion, and which learned them from a non-Bantu population living somewhere around the northern periphery of Zone C.

THE SPREAD OF IRON-WORKING

It is hard to be completely definite about the nature of the superiority of a primitive iron technology over a Stone Age technology that included ground and polished axes and adzes. While the working of iron leaves virtually indestructible evidence in the shape of slag and in the remains of furnaces and tuyères, iron objects themselves, being liable to corrosion, in most areas seldom last for more than a few centuries. Often enough, therefore, the presence of a particular class of iron tools has to be inferred from the disappearance of its stone predecessor. Also the practical limitations of early metallurgical techniques need to be borne constantly in mind. Early iron technology is not thought to have been able to produce tempered metal capable of standing up to continuous percussion against parched earth or hard wood. Oliver Davies has speculated that most of the thousands of polished stone axes discovered in the forest regions of modern Ghana

[1] Ibid. para. 83.24.

must have been made during the Iron Age, but firm dates are lacking.[1] Nevertheless, in the few stratified sites in which the coming of iron can be observed against an earlier lithic background, there seems to be no doubt that the coming of iron led rapidly to the disappearance of most of the stone tools comprised in the large microlithic element in neolithic and Late Stone Age assemblages. In domestic life, iron tools must have made a great difference in the building and furnishing of houses, in the preparation of skins for clothing and of bark and other fibres for mats and basketry.

So far as the food supply was concerned, however, it seems clear that the initial impact of the Iron Age must have been felt as much in improved techniques for hunting and fishing as in more efficient agriculture and stock-raising. Iron is almost irrelevant to pastoral activities, except in the shape of weapons for the protection of stock. In agriculture, the iron bush-knife must have marked an important advance in the clearing of soft vegetation, and the iron sickle in reaping. In agriculture, as in pastoralism, weapons are of importance in protecting gardens from the inroads of wild animals. But the main significance of iron weapons was doubtless in converting wild animals into food. Armed with spear-heads and harpoons of iron, men were readier to hunt a full range of game animals, including elephants and hippopotamuses, although Stone Age hunters were fully capable of taking large mammals. With iron tools for wood-working, fishermen could make larger and stronger canoes, and thus could greatly extend their exploitation of rivers, lakes and coastal waters. Therefore, in subequatorial Africa at least, we seem to face the interesting paradox that, to the incipient food-producers of the Late Stone Age, the coming of iron meant, among other things, more intensive hunting and fishing, and the realignment and extension of human settlement according to the opportunities for these pursuits. In these circumstances, even though the lives of individual groups might be becoming more sedentary, the hiving off of younger generations could have resulted in the extensive infiltration of new country, especially by fisherfolk following river lines, lakeshores and ocean coasts.

In the same way, we may be quite sure that the dispersion of cereal agriculturalists during the Early Iron Age was a process of wide and rapid infiltration rather than one of slow and systematic extension of areas under cultivation. Early farming communities knew nothing of population pressure or land shortage. They were therefore able to be

[1] Davies, *West Africa*, 200–1.

highly selective in their choice of land, using only the best soils, such as those on forest margins and along the base of mountain escarpments, and cultivating them only for a few years before abandoning them for good. Pioneer farmers had no need to return to the same land after allowing a period for natural regeneration, and one of the pressures to keep moving on may well have been a desire to locate new gardens adjacent to new hunting-grounds from which iron weapons could bring

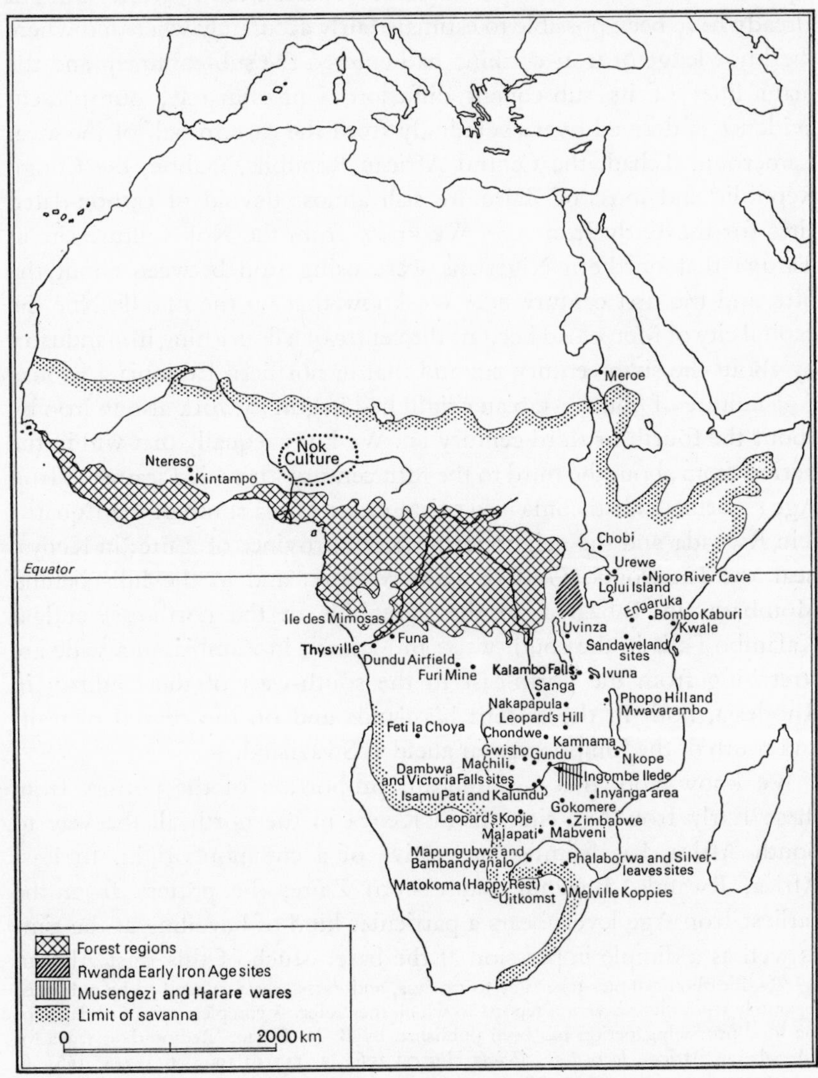

47 Principal archaeological sites mentioned in chapter 6.

a rich addition of protein to the diet. It is thus quite possible to envisage that by developments of this kind the first ethnic and linguistic community to make effective use of iron could have been able in the course of a few generations to infiltrate and absorb its less successful Stone Age neighbours.

If archaeological work had been more evenly spread across sub-equatorial Africa, and if more radiocarbon dates were available, it might already have been possible to estimate fairly accurately when and where the knowledge of iron-working had entered the sub-continent and the main lines of its subsequent diffusion. Unfortunately, our present evidence is derived overwhelmingly from the eastern half of the area. Cameroun, Tchad, the Central African Republic, Gabon, the Congo Republic and most of Zaïre are still almost devoid of carbon-dated sites for the Early Iron Age. We know from the Nok Culture site at Taruga that northern Nigerians were using iron between about the fifth and the first century BC.[1] We know that on the middle Nile the capital city of Meroe had become the centre of a flourishing iron industry by about the sixth century BC, and that in northern Ethiopia a Bronze Age culture of South Arabian origin had begun to work also in iron by about the fourth or third century BC. We know equally that within the period from about the third to the fifth century AD a wide scatter of Iron Age settlements had come into existence in Africa south of the Equator – in Rwanda and the neighbouring Kivu province of Zaïre; in Kenya, near the Kavirondo Gulf of Lake Victoria and in the hills behind Mombasa; in Tanzania, in the Pare hills of the north-east and at Kalambo Falls in the south-west; in Malawi; in Zambia, in a wide arc stretching from the north-east to the south-west of the country; in Rhodesia, both in the eastern highlands and on the central plateau; and south of the Limpopo as far afield as Swaziland.

We know, too, that a significant proportion of the pottery from these Early Iron Age sites, from Kenya in the north all the way to South Africa, has features suggestive of a common origin. In East Africa, Rwanda, Burundi and eastern Zaïre, the pottery from the earliest Iron Age levels bears a particular kind of bevelling at the rims as well as a dimple impression at the base. Much of this East African

[1] Radiocarbon samples take time to process, and dates therefore tend to be published separately from the excavation reports to which they refer. A complete record of dates for the food-producing period has been published by B. M. Fagan, 'Radiocarbon dates for sub-Saharan Africa', *Journal of African History*: 1961, **2**, 137–9; 1963, **4**, 127–8; 1965, **6**, 107–16; 1966, **7**, 495–506; 1967, **8**, 513–27; 1969, **10**, 149–69. Subsequently biennial surveys have appeared by different authors, starting from 1970.

'Dimple-based' pottery is decorated with boldly executed grooving, which follows a limited number of highly stereotyped designs. Some of these designs recur, though without the dimples, on a good deal of the earliest Zambian and Rhodesian pottery, which used to be known as 'Channelled Ware'. Specialists have now begun to discard both these terms, since they are not sufficiently inclusive of all the early wares which now have to be classified. The current preference is for more specific local terms and for looser and vaguer general terms, such as 'Early Iron Age'. However, this increasing sophistication does not deny a basic relationship between the Early Iron Age pottery of eastern and southern Africa, although it does make it a little less direct than it was formerly thought to be. The broad proposition that Early Iron Age pottery and the earliest iron technology entered Bantu Africa side by side and from a single general area of origin remains unimpaired.

Until recently, the main problem in interpreting the spread of the Early Iron Age culture was that the earliest evidence of it in the areas which had been archaeologically explored appeared to be nearly contemporary. Since these areas lay in eastern and southern Africa, and since nothing resembling Early Iron Age pottery was known to occur in north-eastern Africa, the tendency was to look for a north-westerly origin and to postulate a secondary dispersal area somewhere in the unexplored western half of the sub-continent roughly equidistant from the eastern and southern sites. Such a theory seemed to fit not only the archaeological evidence but also Guthrie's theory of the dispersal of the Bantu languages from his L and M zones in the region to the south of the forest.[1] Great potential significance seemed to attach to a few unusually early carbon dates from isolated sites in the western region, and especially to one site at the source of the Funa river near Kinshasa, where pottery sherds buried at a depth of 1.05 m in a layer of humic earth yielded a date around the third century BC. The sherds from the Funa site have still not been published, nor is there firm evidence that they were associated with an Iron Age culture, although it is known that both iron and copper were mined in the neighbourhood during Early Iron Age times.[2] Nevertheless, the strategic situation of Kinshasa, where the waterways leading downstream through the forest from the north meet the edge of the Angolan savanna, needs no emphasis. If the Funa date should be confirmed in an Iron Age context, it would afford

[1] e.g. T. N. Huffman, 'The Early Iron Age and the spread of the Bantu', *South African Archaeological Bulletin*, 1970, **25**, 3–21.

[2] J. D. Clark, *Further palaeo-anthropological studies in northern Lunda* (Lisbon, 1968), 191–2.

precious evidence of an early transit of iron technology through the forest.

Meanwhile, however, somewhat firmer evidence than that from the Funa site has come to light of the appearance of the Iron Age in the region immediately to the east of the Congo forest at a comparable period. This comes on the one hand from Katuruka and other nearby sites in the Bukoba district of north-western Tanzania, and on the other hand from Rutare in north-eastern Rwanda. Though both sets of excavations were unpublished at the time of writing, it would seem likely from the preliminary reports that the Early Iron Age of the interlacustrine region must now be held to have originated some four of five centuries earlier than was previously supposed, and within two or three centuries, at most, of the appearance of iron-working anywhere to the south of the Sahara.[1] In the circumstances it is no longer sensible to look for a dispersal centre of the Early Iron Age culture in the region south of the Congo forest. It seems in every way more likely that the Iron Age reached the interlacustrine region around the north-eastern margins of the forest, and that it spread from there to the regions further to the south and the east. Obviously, this hypothesis gains credibility if, as we have suggested, the parent language of Guthrie's Zones D–S was one spoken around the confines of Zone C rather than around Zones L and M.

The pottery from Katuruka and Rutare is said to resemble clearly the 'Dimple-based' pottery of the interlacustrine region, nowadays known as 'Urewe ware' (fig. 48). On present evidence, this would seem to be by far the most widely distributed of the Early Iron Age pottery types, having been found in some fifty sites spread between the Nyanza province of Kenya and the Kivu province of eastern Zaïre, while isolated finds have been reported from as far afield as Tshikapa (fig. 49) on the upper Kasai, Katoto near Lake Kisale on the Lualaba, Kalambo Falls near the south-east corner of Tanganyika, and Lelesu in the Kondoa district of central Tanzania. Within this larger area, the Katuruka site resembles some of those in Rwanda, Burundi and Kivu, in that the pottery was found in association with large iron-smelting furnaces, built with care and skill, indicating an industry operated by specialists serving what must already have been fairly dense communi-

[1] P. Schmidt, notes in *Tanzania Zamani*, 1970, 7, 4–6, and 1971, 8, 6–7; more detailed publications by Schmidt are still awaited in the shape of three articles in preparation for *Azania*, and a forthcoming book entitled *Historical archaeology in an African culture*. F. L. Van Noten, *Les Tombes du roi Cyirima Rujugiza et de la reinemère Nyizayulu Kanjogera: description archéologique* (Tervuren, 1972).

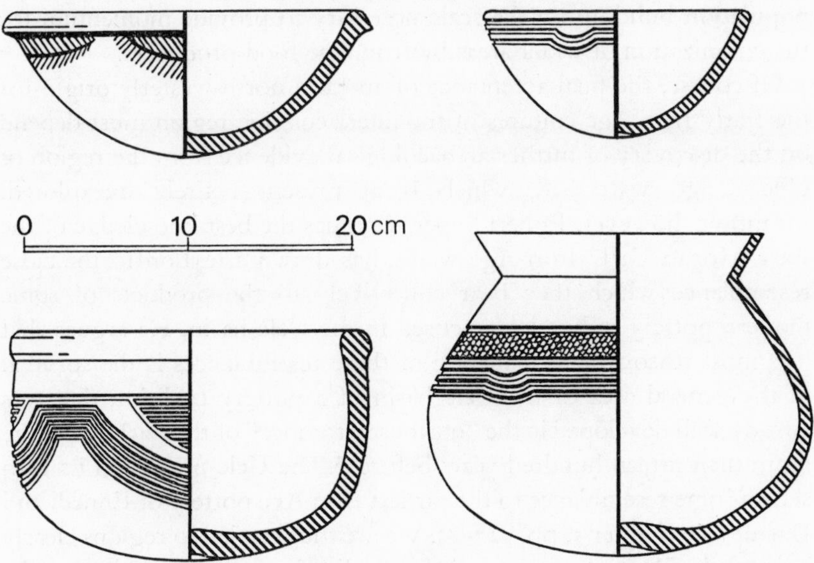

48 Dimple-based ware from Urewe, Kenya, with well-defined dimpled bases. (After B. M. Fagan, *Southern Africa*, 1965, fig. 10.)

ties. The time-depth added to this series by the Katuruka dating is obviously of great significance. It suggests that at the heart of the interlacustrine region, a relatively uniform Iron Age culture was developing without major interruption over a period of more than a thousand years. In this light it is much easier than formerly to envisage

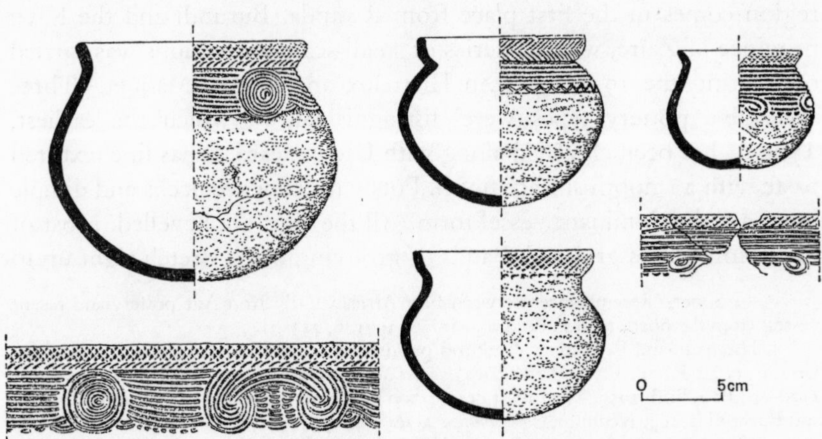

49 Pottery from Tshikapa, Zaïre. (After J. Nenquin, in *Man*, 1959, **242**, fig. 3.)

population build-up on the scale necessary to provide momentum for the colonization of wider areas by Iron Age food-producers.

Of course, the final acceptance of an early north-westerly origin for the Early Iron Age cultures of the interlacustrine region must depend on the discovery of further archaeological evidence from the region of Nile–Congo watershed, which is at present entirely unexplored. Meantime, however, Robert Soper, who has the best knowledge of the East African Early Iron Age wares, has drawn attention to the close resemblance which they bear collectively to the products of some modern pottery industries practised in the Uele basin. He argues that 'the most reasonable explanation of these resemblances is the survival in the general area of the Uele basin of a pottery tradition that was already well developed in the "northern province" of the Early Iron Age more than fifteen hundred years before'.[1] The Uele pottery in its turn shows some resemblance to the earliest Iron Age pottery of Ennedi and Darfur (see chapter 5, pp. 327–8). We are thus carried to regions clearly beyond the Bantu frontier, and the implication is presumably that the norther-most Bantu of the period around the middle of the first millennium BC, who were probably those living around the northern edges of Zone C, were those who acquired the Early Iron Age culture by contact with their neighbours to the north and in due course transmitted it southwards.

THE EARLY IRON AGE IN EAST AFRICA

The more detailed evidence of the Early Iron Age in the interlacustrine region comes in the first place from Rwanda, Burundi and the Kivu province of Zaïre, where a series of small-scale excavations was carried out during the 1950s by Jean Hiernaux and Emma Maquet.[2] Three successive pottery types were distinguished, of which the earliest, Type A, has been classified along with Urewe ware. It has fine textured paste with a smooth surface finish. Pots with concave necks and dimple bases are the dominant vessel form. All the rims are bevelled. Most of the decoration is grooved. Bands of grooving often stretch right up to

[1] R. C. Soper, 'Resemblances between East African Early Iron Age pottery and recent vessels from the north-eastern Congo', *Azania*, 1971, 6, 233–41.

[2] J. Hiernaux and E. Maquet, 'Cultures préhistoriques de l'âge des métaux au Ruanda-Urundi, et au Kivu', Pt 1, *Académie Royale des Sciences Coloniales; Bulletin des Séances*, 1957, 1126–49; Pt 2, ibid. 1959. The fullest description of the pottery taken from sites in Rwanda and Burundi is in J. Nenquin, *Contributions to the study of the prehistoric cultures of Rwanda and Burundi* (Tervuren, 1967), 257–87. Pottery descriptions in this chapter are based on published accounts. We recognize that complex sampling and decorative considerations are involved when describing and comparing different wares.

the lips of the vessels, while elaborate scroll and loop effects are used to enhance the shoulders of pots and bowls. The largest collection of Type A pottery was made at Nyirankuba, a small hill near Kinkanga in southern Rwanda. Nyirankuba is undated, but the stratigraphical position of Type A ware has been established at Mukinanira rock-shelter, where potsherds in association with iron slag overlie a 'Wilton' Stone Age level. Two radiocarbon dates came from Type A levels associated with iron-smelting furnaces at Ndora and Cyamakusa in Rwanda, and were of the third and fourth centuries AD. These furnaces were constructed of wedge-shaped bricks of a type found in association with dimple-based vessels at other sites. Two Kivu sites, at Tshamfu and Bishange, have likewise yielded dimple-based pots, iron slag and brick-built furnaces. The Bishange site is in a sand-pit, some 60 m above the level of Lake Kivu, and it is centred around a tall, cylindrical furnace, some 1.5 m in diameter, built of wedge-shaped clay bricks, some of them decorated with finger impressions or other circular depressions. Similar bricks were also found at Tshamfu, which was also an iron-working site, and clay bricks appear at several other Early Iron Age sites in the area.

The Type A pottery of Rwanda, Burundi and Kivu has clear associations with the Early Iron Age pottery traditions of Uganda and western Kenya, the sites of which are mainly distinguished from the former by the absence of high furnaces. The Nyanza sites were the first to be discovered, and it was here, at Urewe, that 'Dimple-based' pottery was so named.[1] All the Nyanza sites are situated on the sides of valleys, overlooking the courses of streams or rivers. The pottery is concentrated in small associations together with patches of hard, baked clay, occasional iron objects and charcoal. Most of the potsherds are found in the uppermost horizons of a fine, brick-red earth deposit, overlain by bedded hill-wash. Both Urewe deposits are much dissected by erosion, and none of the sites can be described as an occupation area in the strict sense, for no traces of hut-floors or midden accumulation has been found. In all probability a considerable amount of the cultural material has been sorted by water action. The site at Urewe I has yielded three carbon dates ranging from about the third to about the fifth century AD. Finds of pottery in the Urewe-ware tradition have been reported from about ten different sites in Uganda. Unfortunately, the only one of them to have been convincingly dated is that at Chobi on the

[1] M. D. Leakey, W. E. Owen and L. S. B. Leakey, 'Dimple-based pottery from central Kavirondo', *Occasional Papers of the Coryndon Museum*, **2** (Nairobi), 1948.

Victoria Nile, upstream of the Murchison Falls, which has yielded a date around the third or fourth century AD. The most significant common feature of these sites is their distribution, which is confined to the Victoria lakeshore and the river valleys of the Nile and the Kagera. It would seem that the Early Iron Age people of Uganda preferred the moist areas suited to fishing and vegeculture.

In Uganda and western Kenya, as in Rwanda and Burundi, the Early Iron Age sites are succeeded by another series containing markedly different and inferior wares, often poorly fired, and characterized by roulette or cord-impressed decoration. The most outstanding feature of these later Iron Age sites is that they are distributed both in the moister areas preferred by the Early Iron Age people and in the drier areas which may previously have been occupied only by hunters. Some of the best identified of them, notably those of the Bigo-ware group in the dry grasslands of western Uganda, were clearly the settlements of fairly specialized pastoralists. In most areas, however, cattle-keeping was doubtless pursued side by side with a vigorous cereal agriculture. The supersession of the Early Iron Age culture by those of the later Iron Age is discussed in more detail in Volume 3 (chapter 9, pp. 625–30), where it is argued that it would be reasonable to attribute the Early Iron Age culture to Bantu people expanding from the forest margins to the west of the interlacustrine region, and the later Iron Age sites associated with rouletted wares to pastoralists and mixed farmers, who arrived much later in time, and from the north. The newcomers, whether of Central Sudanic, Nilotic or Paranilotic speech, would have established close relations with the Bantu cultivators of the moister lands to the east and west of them, and would thus in time have adopted their languages. The Bigo wares of western Buganda, Ankole and Toro are roulette decorated, and are often found on sites traditionally associated with the Chwezi dynasty, which preceded the present series of hereditary chieftainships in the interlacustrine region. The Type B wares of Rwanda are likewise associated with an earlier series of rulers called Barenge, and this pottery, being quite unlike either Type A or the modern Type C, is particularly likely to have been the result of an outside intrusion into the area. Unfortunately, we still have very little evidence concerning the period at which this important transition from the Early to the later Iron Age took place in the interlacustrine region. Theoretically, it could have been at any time between about the fifth century AD, when the latest of the Urewe sites are securely dated, and about the fifteenth century, when we have radiocarbon dates and also traditional, genealogical evidence for the later Iron Age site at Bigo in western Uganda. It is greatly to be hoped that a stratigraphical sequence may soon be established, perhaps at a site such as that on Lolui Island in the north-eastern corner of Lake Victoria, where a long history of occupation has yielded surface finds of Urewe ware, rouletted pottery and modern Luo wares. According to Posnansky, the earlier Lolui wares are made of clay imported from the lakeshore, and bear small, neat dimples, closely wrought parallel channelling and well-executed decoration. The later pottery, while following this tradition, is cruder, being made from the poor, sandy clays of Lolui itself. The rouletted ware and the modern Luo pottery presumably follow in sequence, and a set of radiocarbon dates from Lolui would therefore be of great value.[1]

Eighty kilometres eastwards from the Kavirondo Gulf of Lake Victoria there rise the western highlands of Kenya, which reach 2,700 m at Mau Summit and are divided from the Nyandarua (Aberdare) range and Mount Kenya by the Rift Valley with its chain of lakes running southwards from Baringo through Nakuru, Naivasha and Natron to Manyara in northern Tanzania. All this western highland region is to this day non-Bantu country, inhabited by peoples of Paranilotic or Cushitic speech. The Rift Valley, as we have seen, is strewn with the relics of the Stone Bowl culture, dating from the first millennium BC, which was the earliest food-producing culture in sub-equatorial Africa. But here, too, the Stone Age apparently lasted longest, with no Iron Age site as yet identified until late in the first millennium AD. When iron at last appeared, the pottery associated with it consisted, significantly, of rouletted wares comparable with those of Uganda and the Type-B wares of Rwanda. In the western highlands of Kenya this is probably to be identified with the entry into the area of Paranilotes ancestral to the modern Kalenjin, who came from the north and settled among Stone Age pastoralists of Cushitic speech.[2] It would seem, therefore, that the Early Iron Age culture associated with the Bantu expansion lapped around the southern edge of this highland region, reaching the hill country of north-eastern Tanzania and the low plateau land behind Mombasa as early as the second or third century AD, and spreading from there to the highlands

[1] M. Posnansky, 'The Early Iron Age in East Africa', in Bishop and Clark, eds., *Background to evolution*, 630–4; G. Jackson, J. S. Gartlan and M. Posnansky, 'Rock gongs and associated rock paintings from Lolui Island, Lake Victoria', *Man*, 1965, **65**, 38–9.

[2] J. E. G. Sutton, *The archaeology of the western highlands of Kenya* (Nairobi, 1973).

east of the Rift Valley in central Kenya, but leaving the valley itself and the highlands to the west of it virtually unaffected.

The Early Iron Age culture of this north-eastern Bantu province is clearly linked through its pottery with the same broad tradition as the 'Dimple-based' wares of the interlacustrine region (fig. 50). The Kwale sites, from which the eastern variety of Early Iron Age wares was first recovered, lie about 30 km south-west of Mombasa, near the once

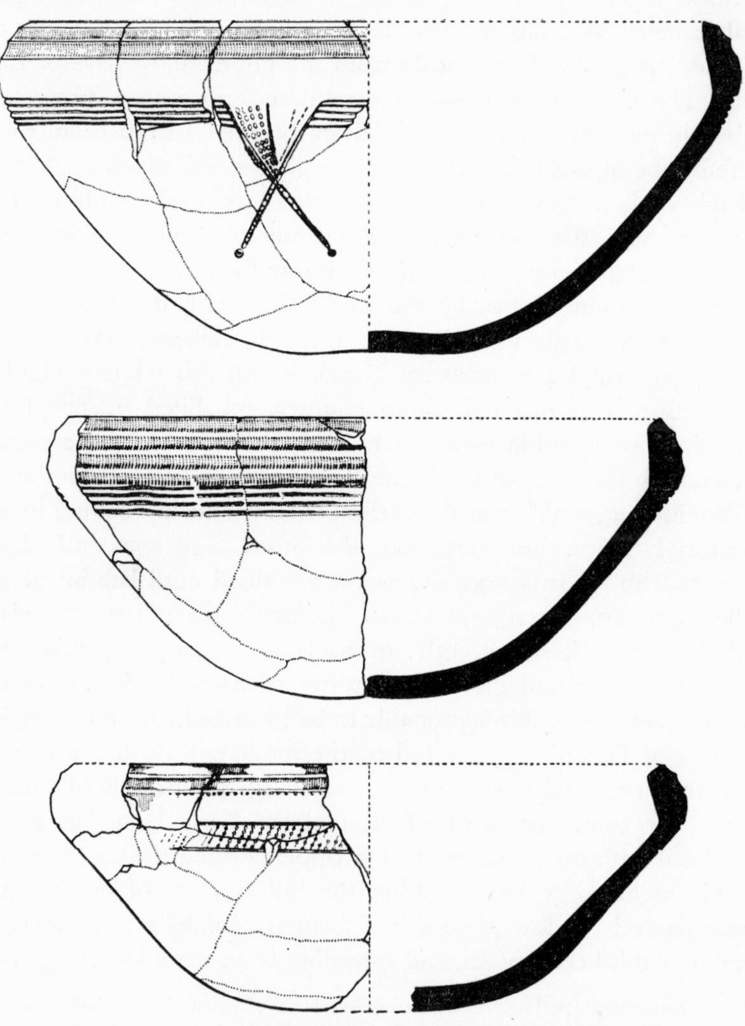

50 Kwale pottery: scale 3:5.
(After R. Soper, 'Kwale: an Early Iron Age site in south-eastern Kenya', *Azania*, 1967, **2**, fig. 4.)

forested crest of a range of low hills rising from the coastal plain. The archaeological material was contained within a level of brown sand overlying sterile reddish sand, and represents a series of single-level occupations. Most of the finds consisted of pottery, but a much corroded arrowhead, some iron slag and a piece of carbonized heartwood were also recovered.[1] Four remarkably consistent radiocarbon dates have come from the occupation levels, all within the second and third centuries AD, indicating that the Early Iron Age inhabitants of Kwale were approximately the contemporaries of those of Ndora and Cyamakusa in Rwanda and also of those of the Urewe sites in western Kenya. Since the excavation at Kwale in 1966, similar collections of pottery have been found at Early Iron Age sites scattered around the lower slopes of the Pare, Usambara and Ngulu mountains in north-eastern Tanzania, and in the foothills of Mount Kenya.[2] The upper slopes of all these ranges were formerly mantled in forest, which has been progressively cleared by man. The distribution of Kwale-ware sites around the foothills suggests a pattern of Early Iron Age occupation which followed the forest margins, clearing and burning the edges of the woodland so as to obtain a fertile and uneroded soil for cultivation. The most important of these sites is at Bombo Kaburi in the South Pare hills, where charcoal associated with Kwale-ware sherds has been dated to around the third century. The pottery at Bombo Kaburi also compares closely with Early Iron Age sherds found many years ago in a surface collection at Lelesu, near Kondoa, on the western edge of the Masai steppe. Both the Kwale wares and those from Lelesu, though possessing the bevelled rims characteristic of all East African Early Iron Age pottery, are conspicuously lacking in the scrolls and complex curvilinear patterns which are so obvious a feature of the contemporary Dimple-based wares from the interlacustrine region, although in some other respects the Lelesu collection shows features closer to Urewe ware than to Kwale ware.[3] The Lelesu collection may thus be regarded as intermediate between the western and eastern variants of the East African Early Iron Age pottery of the first millennium AD, and it will be a matter of the greatest interest, when the pottery from the Katuruka and Rutare sites of the first millennium BC has been published, to determine whether this can be regarded as

[1] R. C. Soper, 'Kwale: an Early Iron Age site in south-eastern Kenya', *Azania*, 1967, **2**, 1–18.

[2] R. C. Soper, 'Iron Age Sites in north-eastern Tanzania', *Azania*, 1967, **2**, 19–38; A. Siiriainen, 'The Iron Age site at Gatung'ang'a, central Kenya', *Azania*, 1971, **6**, 199–232.

[3] G. Smolla, 'Prähistorische Keramik aus Ostafrika', *Tribus*, 1957, **6**, 35–64.

ancestral to both variants.[1] The final solution to this problem will no doubt be found eventually in the archaeology of central Tanzania, which at present is scarcely explored. Meantime, all that can be said about this area is that the Early Iron Age pottery found at Uvinza salt springs in the lower Malagarasi valley, which has been dated by radiocarbon to the fifth or sixth century AD, belongs, as might be expected, to the western rather than the eastern type, while a feature of particular interest is the presence of incised lines and false chevron relief patterns on some sherds, which recall early Zambian pottery techniques.[2]

Neither in Kenya nor in Tanzania is it yet possible to reconstruct even the most rudimentary outline of the progress of the Iron Age from its earlier into its later stages. One later site must however be mentioned, even though necessarily in isolation, which is the extensive complex of stone walls and revetments at Engaruka in northern Tanzania.[3] Here, where a perennial stream drops down the western wall of the Rift Valley, stone-built structures extend over an area of more than 5 sq. km, and include terraces, stone circles, cairns, field systems and stock enclosures. At least two populations have occupied Engaruka, the terraced platforms of the western escarpment predating the stone circles of the valley floor. No stratified sequence of cultures has been obtained, for the occupation tended to fan outwards rather than to reoccupy the older village sites again and again (pls. 16, 17). Two radiocarbon samples from the hillside platforms have yielded dates around the fourth and the eighth centuries AD, while samples from the lower-lying areas belong to around the fifteenth century. The pottery from the hillside is decorated with two bands of incised lines on the neck of a simple pot with a slight shoulder. Some panels of impressed decoration also occur. Potsherds from the valley structures, however, bear broad, parallel incised bands, occasionally repeated in vertical panels. Neither of the Engaruka pottery types has been certainly identified outside the general area of the site, although a possible occurrence of the earlier one has been reported from the Narok area of

[1] It is relevant that Soper, in describing the modern pottery of the Uele basin (as cited on p. 366), adds: 'The fact that some of the relevant characteristics are specific to Kwale ware and some to Urewe, further suggests that the tradition descends from a stage prior to the hypothetical separation of the different variants of this "province", which would put it back to at least the first century AD and probably a good deal earlier.'

[2] J. E. G. Sutton and A. D. Roberts, 'Uvinza and its salt industry', *Azania*, 1968, **3**, 45–86.

[3] H. Sassoon, 'Engaruka: excavations during 1964', *Azania*, 1966, **1**, 79–100; and Sassoon, 'New views on Engaruka, northern Tanzania: excavations carried out for the Tanzania government in 1964 and 1966', *Journal of African History*, 1967, **8**, 201–17.

Kenya. In a more general sense, however, Engaruka is likely to remain unique, since it is almost certain that any other stone-built site of this size would by now have been discovered.

It is against this background of archaeological data that the earliest written evidence about the eastern coast of sub-equatorial Africa has to be considered, although unfortunately it raises more questions than it answers. First and foremost stands the Alexandrian Greek handbook called *The Periplus of the Erythrean Sea*, now generally attributed to the early second century AD. The *Periplus* describes in some detail the markets and staging ports of a well-established maritime trade-route worked by Arab merchants from the Sabaean kingdoms, which reached as far south as a great ivory mart called Rhapta. This was probably situated not far south of the Zanzibar channel, and therefore perhaps in the Rufiji delta, where its remains would long since have been buried deep in the river silts. From places called Serapion and Nikon, which were evidently situated in southern Somalia, as far as Rhapta, the trade was with 'barbarians', who hunted ivory and collected tortoise-shell, using small sea-going boats made with planks sewn together. The ivory and tortoise-shell were purchased with iron weapons – spears and hatchets, swords and awls. This does not necessarily imply that the local people were still without the means to smelt iron for themselves, for we know that the same imports were popular at Aksum, where iron had been worked from the third or fourth century BC. The Arabs also brought wheat and wine to East Africa, not for trade, but to gain the goodwill of the natives, whose language they understood and whose women they married. The single sentence of the *Periplus* which refers to the physical appearance of the coastal people describes them merely as 'men of the tallest stature', who were of piratical habits, and who had set up their own chiefs in each of the trading settlements.[1] There is no mention of the distinction, so apparent to travellers from medieval times onwards, between the fair-skinned peoples of the Somali coast and the dark-skinned people south of the Juba. The implication would seem to be that Negro people had not yet spread to any part of the East African coast north of the Rufiji, or at least not in any numbers. On the whole, 'men of the tallest stature' suggests a Cushitic-speaking population like the Stone Bowl users of the Kenya Rift Valley, and it is

[1] The standard English translation of the *Periplus* is that by W. H. Schoff, *The Periplus of the Erythrean Sea* (London and New York, 1912), which has been described as 'a free translation of an imaginatively edited text'. G. S. P. Freeman-Grenville, *The East African coast* (Oxford, 1962), provides an English translation of the better-edited Greek text by H. Frisk (Göteborg, 1927).

relevant that there is at least one Southern Cushitic remnant language, Dahalo, which is spoken on the Kenya coast, north of Mombasa. This hypothesis receives some confirmation from the *Geography* of Claudius Ptolemy, which in the much edited state in which we have it probably represents the sum of knowledge available in the Byzantine Greek world towards the end of the fourth century. By this time Rhapta was no longer the southern terminus of the trade, and, far beyond it, probably around Cape Delgado, there lived man-eating savages, who are elsewhere described as the 'fish-eating Ethiopians' and distinguished from 'the Ethiopians who make sewn boats' who lived to the north of them. It is not impossible that we have here the earliest reference to Bantu people living on the East African coast as fishermen, although, if so, it is perhaps surprising that they should have been remarked quite so far to the south.

THE EARLY IRON AGE IN ZAMBIA AND MALAWI

In turning from the north-eastern to the southern sector of sub-equatorial Africa, it has to be remembered that the overwhelming proportion of the relevant archaeological evidence comes from Zambia and Rhodesia, and the remainder from southern Zaïre, Malawi, Swaziland and South Africa. The vast areas comprised within modern Mozambique, South-West Africa (Namibia), Botswana and southern Angola are still almost bare of Iron Age archaeological data. In all of these areas to some extent, but particularly in Mozambique, the lack of evidence has to be attributed primarily to a lack of research. In the three western areas, however, a contributory factor has certainly been the comparatively late and sparse penetration of Iron Age cultures. In these areas, and also in the Cape Province of South Africa, Late Stone Age cultures persisted until historical times, and the late survival of stone-using communities speaking languages quite unrelated to Bantu forms one of the most important elements in any consideration of the relationship between the coming of the Iron Age and the spread of the Bantu languages.

Throughout the western areas the predominant languages were those called Khoi, the speakers of which, known to the Cape Dutch settlers as 'Hottentots', were people of medium height and yellowish hue, living some as hunters and gatherers, and some also as herders of long-horned cattle and fat-tailed sheep on the dry lands west and south of the Kalahari desert, where agriculture, even today, is possible only in the immediate vicinity of streams and water-courses. According to one early recorded and often-repeated tradition, Khoi herders were said to preserve the memory of a great migration from the north-east, and in 1930, C. G. Seligman, the foremost ethnologist of his day, wrote:

There is little doubt that the Hottentots are the result of the mixture of Bushmen with early invading Hamites, from whom they received those linguistic and cultural features which distinguish them from Bushmen. It is generally held that the mixed race arose in the north, perhaps in the neighbourhood of the great lakes, and that the Hottentots did not reach South Africa until after the Bushmen, crossing the upper waters of the Zambezi and reaching the west coast, then pressing forward to the south, where they were found by the first Europeans to visit the Cape.[1]

However, the fact that Khoi-speaking groups of hunters and gatherers, practising no form of food production, still survive in widely spread areas of southern Angola and the northern parts of South-West Africa and Botswana, makes it highly probable that Khoi-speakers formed the main Late Stone Age population of all this region, and that legends of long distance migration must refer, at most, to small groups which entered the region comparatively recently. The discovery of pottery and domestic sheep bones dating to about two thousand years ago in cave sites in the southern Cape Province, suggests that some form of herding techniques have been practised by Khoi-speakers in South Africa since Late Stone Age times.[2]

If Khoi were the basic Late Stone Age population of the western half of South Africa, a population which was able to preserve its language and culture owing to its partial adoption of food-producing techniques, it is no less clear that the basic Late Stone Age inhabitants of the eastern half of South Africa were Bushmen speaking the languages called San, which were distinct both from Khoi and from Bantu, though employing a number of clicking sounds similar to those of Khoi. All of the San described by outside observers have been hunters and gatherers, and within the period of European memory in South Africa they occupied all the higher land from the mountains of the western Cape Province to the north-easternmost ranges of the Drakensberg. They also lived in the valleys of the Orange and the Vaal and on the intervening plateau. They were seen in the valleys of the Kei, the Mzimvubu and the Tukela, and along the ocean coast. The presence of San clicks in the Bantu languages of the southern Sotho, Zulu, Swazi

1 C. G. Seligman, *The races of Africa* (London, 1930), 33.

2 J. R. Grindley, E. Speed and T. Maggs, 'The age of the Bonteberg Shelter deposits, Cape Province', *South African Archaeological Bulletin*, 1970, **25**, 24.

and southern Tsonga must indicate that a large number of San were later incorporated into the expanding Bantu population of this region. The most common pattern of absorption was described by an eighteenth-century European traveller in the Orange river valley, who wrote that 'every tribe that owns cattle also has a number of Bushmen under its protection'. Stock-raisers, whether Khoi or Bantu, had a much more reliable source of food than the hunters. Therefore hunting bands took to visiting stock-owning patrons. Some settled permanently, learning, but also influencing, the languages of the patrons. Others confined themselves to periodic exchanges of produce, and retained much more of their own cultural inheritance. A few hunters remained wholly independent of the food-producers by withdrawing into the least hospitable parts of the region. Elsewhere, the more efficient economy slowly drove out the less efficient, and the languages of the patrons prevailed over those of the clients. As Monica Wilson has pointed out, this is logical enough if one remembers that a hunting band usually numbered between thirty and fifty persons, whereas a horde of Khoi herders numbered between two and three thousand. Bantu societies practising agriculture as well as stock-raising were usually organized in even larger communities.[1]

There is thus no serious doubt that in most of southern Africa the expansion of Bantu speech occurred in an area previously dominated by Khoisan peoples, speaking Khoi languages in the west and San in the east. Of the two language families, Khoi was almost certainly the more widely spread. In much of Rhodesia and Zambia it probably extended eastwards, to the north of San, and the fact that the Sandawe language of central Tanzania is confidently classified with Khoi[2] raises the suspicion that at one time, before the eastward expansion of Bantu, Khoi languages may have bordered with Cushitic somewhere in this region. At this rate, Bantu, spreading into East Africa from the west, would have broken the continuity of the Khoi speech area somewhere between central Tanzania and central Zambia, leaving Sandawe as an isolated enclave far to the north-east of its linguistic relatives. It is against the background of some such very broad design as this that the Early Iron Age archaeology of Zambia and Malawi can best be appreciated.

The pioneer finds of Early Iron Age occupation in Zambia were made by Desmond Clark, who in 1950 obtained early pottery from a series of

[1] M. Wilson and L. Thompson, *Oxford history of South Africa*, I (Oxford, 1969), 41, 63–4, 74.

[2] Personal communication from Professor A. N. Tucker.

soil pits at the Machili Forest Station, about 150 km north-west of the Victoria Falls. A demonstrated association of charcoal was subsequently radiocarbon dated to AD 96±212. This date had a very large standard error, because it was one of the first radiocarbon samples ever processed. But it gave an indication that iron-working in southern Central Africa had a much longer history than had previously been suspected. The most complete vessel found at Machili was a globular pot with a band of grooved or channelled decoration on the neck (fig. 51). It was immediately recognized that there was a typological

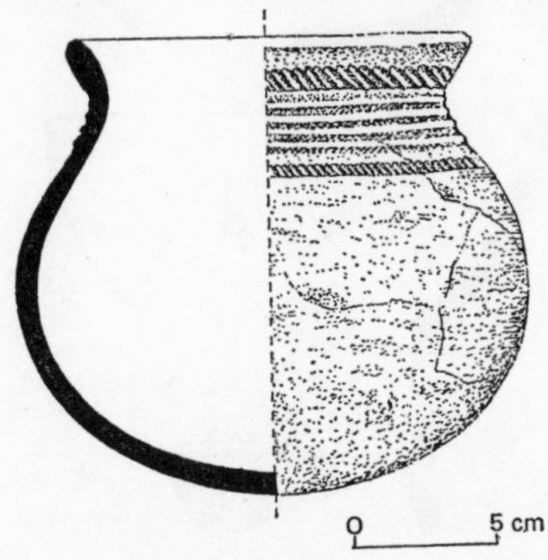

51 Channel-decorated pot from Machili, Zambia.
(After J. D. Clark and B. M. Fagan, 'Charcoals, sands and channel-decorated pottery from northern Rhodesia', *American Anthropologist*, 1965, **67**, p. 358.)

affinity between this decoration and that of the dimple-based pottery of the Nyanza Province of Kenya, which was at that time already known, though not yet dated. The suggestion of a link with the north was reinforced by the discovery in 1951 of the prehistoric site at Kalambo Falls, on the borders of Zambia and Tanzania, near the southern extremity of Lake Tanganyika. Here Clark found thick layers of Iron Age occupation, strewn with numerous potsherds, lumps of iron slag, and the remains of pole and mud huts representing the remains of several villages which had flourished in the Kalambo Lake basin. A series of tests carried on over a period of years dated the occupation from about the fourth till about the eleventh century. The grooved and incised potsherds from the occupation levels included vessels with bevelled rims, while two sherds had dimple bases similar to those found in the East African sites (fig. 52). During the decade which followed these discoveries, while Early Iron Age material was still

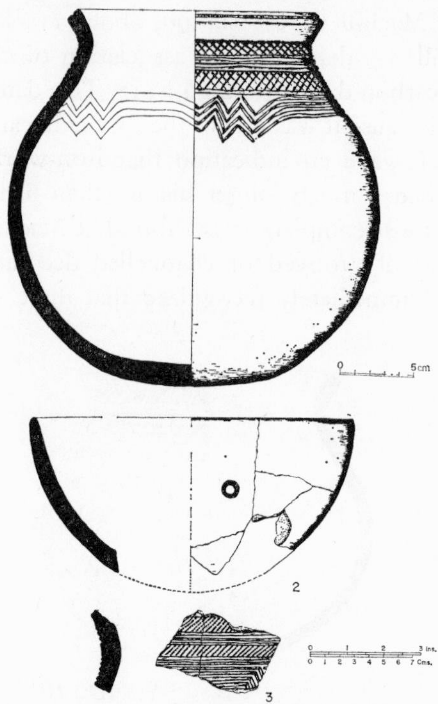

52 Early Iron Age pot from Kalambo Falls, Zambia.
(After Clark, *The Kalambo Falls prehistoric site*, II, 1974, fig. 12.)

sparse, and while the processing of carbon samples from most of the known sites was still being awaited, it was almost inevitable that theories should be formulated postulating a simple, southward spread of iron-working peoples from the interlacustrine region of East Africa through the central plateau lands to Zambia, Rhodesia and South Africa.[1]

In the light of present knowledge such a theory requires considerable elaboration. Just as the Early Iron Age cultures of East Africa are now seen to have divided into a western (Urewe) and an eastern (Kwale) province, so in Zambia and Malawi it is now possible to distinguish a number of regional variants of Early Iron Age culture, based on the analysis of finds from more than fifty sites extending over every major region of Zambia and much of Malawi. Pottery is the most common artefact found at all sites and provides the basis for comparison of the different regional groups discussed briefly here. In general, the earliest Zambian pottery is characterized by necked pots and by numerous bowls with varying profiles. Decoration is based for the most part on the use

[1] e.g. B. M. Fagan, *Southern Africa during the Iron Age* (London, 1965), 50–1.

of grooving and stamping. Undecorated vessels are an important element in many industries. Most pots and bowls have comparatively thick walls; lips are sometimes bevelled; rim-bands are often decorated; and bands of grooved or incised lines form the basis of many decorative motifs. The effect of a 'false relief chevron', achieved by careful placing of triangular or quadrilateral stamps, is an especially persistent feature. Even in this more detailed analysis, however, the general features of Zambian and more southerly Early Iron Age pottery show similarities with the earliest equivalent wares in East Africa. Grooved decoration is common in both, and globular pots and bowls are the dominant forms. But the Central African pottery is less elaborate; dimples are absent, except at Kalambo Falls; and the decoration is less flamboyant. There is a definite connection between the two regions, but there are also important differences.[1]

Within Zambia and Malawi, the northernmost of six regional variants of Early Iron Age culture is found in the woodland area between the Katanga pedicle and the Luangwa river. The principal site is Kalambo Falls, with Early Iron Age occupation dated, as we have seen, from the fourth century AD until about the eleventh. Here there is abundant evidence of iron-working in the villages of the lake basin but, despite the nearness to the Katanga deposits, copper objects are very rare. It would seem that cattle were not kept by the Early Iron Age inhabitants of the site, but the presence of grindstones makes it likely that cereals were cultivated. Scatters of the characteristic Kalambo potsherds have been found at ten other sites in the area, including some open sites by the shores of Lake Tanganyika and on the plateau above, and also at some Late Stone Age cave sites where sherds occur in the upper levels. The most important of these sites is Nakapapula rock-shelter in the Serenje District, where two carbon samples gave readings between about the eighth and about the eleventh centuries. Late Stone Age tools were found at both these levels, and the pottery probably reached the rock-shelter through trade or other sporadic contacts between the cave-dwelling hunters and neighbouring Iron Age farming communities.

The region to the east of the Luangwa is still little known, but a large Early Iron Age village at Kamnama near Chipata has been dated to around the fourth century.[2] The Kamnama pottery is very similar to the earliest Iron Age pottery from Malawi. At Phopo Hill in northern

[1] D. W. Phillipson, 'The Early Iron Age in Zambia – regional variants and some tentative conclusions', *Journal of African History*, 1968, **9**, 191–211.

[2] D. W. Phillipson, 'The prehistoric succession in eastern Zambia: a preliminary report', *Azania*, 1973, **8**, 3–24.

Malawi, Early Iron Age pottery has been found in lenses of midden ash and charcoal dated to the third or fourth century.[1] The Phopo sherds resemble those found by Keith Robinson at Mwavarambo's village on the Rufira river, for which a date is still awaited. It is significant that these Early Iron Age wares of northern Malawi are typologically quite distinct from the second-millennium Rukuru and Mbande Industries of the area, which show trading connections with later pottery traditions from the Tanzanian side of the lake. Robinson has also found Early Iron Age pottery at Nkope Bay at the southern end of Lake Malawi, which has been radiocarbon dated to the period between the third and the ninth centuries. Nkope-type pottery has also been found to the west of Lake Malawi and on the Shire river.[2] The pottery of Kamnama, Phopo and Nkope Bay is closer to East African Early Iron Age wares than to material from west of the Luangwa river, and within East Africa it is closer to Kwale ware than to Urewe ware. In the southerly direction, these wares are also closer to the Early Iron Age pottery types of Rhodesia, called after type-sites at Gokomere and Ziwa. It appears also that these sites differ from those to the west of the Luangwa in that domestic cattle were unknown, although sheep and goats were undoubtedly herded.[3] It seems likely that here there is evidence of a southerly dispersal of the eastern branch of the East African Early Iron Age culture, which may become much clearer when we have some parallel data from the region to the east of Lake Malawi, in southern Tanzania and northern Mozambique.

A more westerly and possibly somewhat later stream of Early Iron Age culture is indicated by the Chondwe, Kapwirimbwe and Kalundu groups of sites to the west of the Luangwa, in central Zambia. The first of these groups is located in the Zambian copperbelt, where Early Iron Age sites have been identified on the edges of clearings in the dense *Brachystegia* woodland. At the Chondwe Farm site near Ndola, iron slag and some quartz flakes were found underlying a horizon of modern wares, and were radiocarbon dated to around the ninth century.[4] Pottery from the Chondwe group of sites shares some characteristics

[1] K. R. Robinson, 'A preliminary report on the recent archaeology of Ngonde, northern Malawi', *Journal of African History*, 1966, 7, 169–88.

[2] K. R. Robinson, 'The Iron Age of the southern lake area of Malawi', *Dept. of Antiquities, Zomba, Publication 8*, 1970, 117–18.

[3] D. W. Phillipson, 'The Early Iron Age in eastern and southern Africa', *Azania*, 1976, 11, 1–25.

[4] D. W. Phillipson, 'Early Iron Age sites on the Zambian Copperbelt', *Azania*, 1972, 7, 93–128. Mr Michael Bisson has also investigated important, and as yet unpublished, Early Iron Age sites in the same area (1973).

with that from the Kalambo group, and others with that from the Kapwirimbwe group to the south of it. Comb-stamping is more common than at Kalambo; false relief chevron stamping is also frequent; but the bevelled rims so characteristic of Kalambo are absent, while the inturned rims of the Kapwirimbwe group are sometimes found. Kapwirimbwe is the most prolific Early Iron Age site in the Lusaka area, and is situated about 13 km to the east of the city (pl. 18). This is a single-level occupation site, where much iron slag was found, together with thirteen iron tools, including a razor, a spear-point and a ring. Cattle bones were found, and three radiocarbon samples gave an average date in the fifth century AD. Ninety per cent of the abundant pottery consisted of necked vessels and hemispherical bowls. Decoration falls into two categories – horizontal bands of grooved or incised hatchings, and bands of opposed impressions of a single, triangular stamp, giving the effect of a false relief chevron. The stratigraphical position of this pottery group has been established from a site at Twickenham Road in Lusaka city, where the upper half metre of a 2 m deposit yielded modern Soli pottery, underlain by 15 cm of sterile clay sealing an Early Iron Age occupation. The Twickenham Road vessels are larger and more elaborately decorated than those from Kapwirimbwe, and the lower level of the site has been dated to around the eleventh century.[1]

The Kalundu group of sites is centred around the Batoka highlands, in the higher part of the southern plateau. Here, an Early Iron Age horizon at the base of the Kalundu mound in the Kalomo district passes imperceptibly into an overlying later occupation, but the grooved pottery of the lowest levels is quite distinct from that of the later occupation. The earlier horizons, dated to around the fourth century, are regarded as representing a separate village. The pottery from the lower levels, much of which was recovered from storage pits, is thicker and coarser than the overlying 'Kalomo type' pottery. Similar wares have been found as far north as Gundu, near Batoka, where they have been dated to around the fifth century. The southern limit of this pottery is presently represented by the Kabondo site, some 25 km north of Livingstone. Bones of cattle and small stock have been found in both the Kalundu and Gundu levels, as well as iron arrowheads, some copper fragments, and three cowrie shells, the last two indicating early contact with long-distance bartering networks.

Another grouping of sites occurs near the Victoria Falls and as far as

[1] Phillipson, 'Early Iron Age sites', 196–7.

Sesheke in the upper Zambezi valley. The settlements are confined to the Kalahari sand country on either bank of the Zambezi, and have yielded a large number of globular vessels with prominent rim-bands bearing incised, grooved or stamped decoration. One typical settlement is that at Dambwa near Livingstone, which has been radiocarbon dated to around the seventh or eighth century. J. O. Vogel has distinguished no less than four stages of the Early Iron Age in this region – the earliest having affinities with the Machili site of the very early first millennium, while the latest phases belong to a period nearly one thousand years later. There is some confusion about the naming of this grouping, which is variously described as the 'Dambwa group' and the 'Shongwe tradition'. The potteries associated with these sites (fig. 53) have some similarities with the wares typified in the lower levels of the Kalundu mound, but their most striking parallels are with lowland sites to the south of the Zambezi and with the Gokomere-type wares of the Rhodesian Plateau – so much so, in fact, that the Dambwa-group sites are held by some to represent a north-westward extension of the eastern stream of Early Iron Age traditions postulated above.[1]

A site which cannot as yet be assigned to any firmly established series is that at the Machili Forest Station, already mentioned as the first site in Zambia to yield Early Iron Age pottery. The pottery itself is inconclusive. The single more or less complete vessel bears a band of broad grooving on the neck, while the remaining sherds are indetermin-

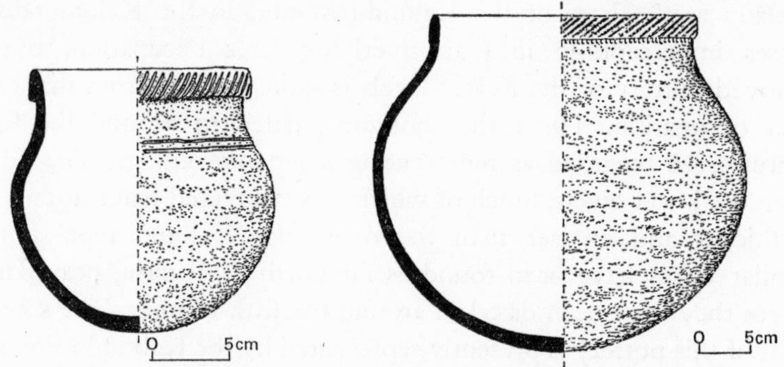

53 A pair of large vessels from Dambwa, Zambia.
(After Fagan, D. W. Phillipson and S. G. H. Daniels, *Iron Age cultures in Zambia*, II, 1969.)

[1] B. M. Fagan, D. W. Phillipson and S. G. H. Daniels, *Iron Age cultures in Zambia*, II (London, 1969), 3–56; J. O. Vogel, 'Some Early Iron Age sites in southern and western Zambia', *Azania*, 1973, **8**, 25–54.

ate. The general characteristics of the grooved vessel are absent from the Dambwa, Kalundu and Kapwirimbwe groups, but do occur in some Chondwe vessels and in the Kalambo group, as well as at Lubusi and Sioma in the west. Isolated finds of Machili-like vessels have been made in southern Zambia, at Gwisho Hot Springs and at Leopard's Hill, as well as south of the Zambezi. These finds all belong in what was formerly known as the 'Channel-decorated' pottery type, but this category has never been adequately defined, for the materials are still too scanty. When further discoveries permit a closer analysis of Machili ware, it will probably be shown to have close connections with the Dambwa pottery, as well as with the Gokomere and Ziwa Industries from south of the Zambezi. The typological development of these wares is now fairly well known, and their later manifestations show development away from the Machili type of vessel. Thus, the Machili site and its associated pottery may represent a very early stage of the Zambian Iron Age sequence, although the single radiocarbon date has a large enough standard margin of error to allow its inclusion within the broad range of dates for the earliest farmers.[1]

Thus, the latest researches indicate that by the middle of the first millennium AD the Iron Age was well established all over Zambia and Malawi. In the belt of country between the Luangwa and Lake Malawi, iron-working food-producers were growing cereal crops and tending sheep and goats by about the third or fourth century AD, while only a century or two later cereal farmers keeping some cattle as well as small stock were established in the area between the Luangwa and the upper Zambezi. The densest settlements appear to have been in the south, where soils are more fertile and where the plateau country is particularly suitable for cattle. It is significant that, whereas in the northern and central regions the occurrence of iron and pottery in numerous Late Stone Age sites shows that hunter-gatherers must have co-existed with neighbouring food-producers over a long period, in the southern region the persistence of Late Stone Age cultures into the Iron Age is attested only at a few sites in the upper and middle Zambezi valley. It is noteworthy that, while the spread of metallurgy and food production appears to have been rapid, reaching all parts of the area within a couple of centuries, the associated pottery displays marked regional variations which are apparent from the very inception of the Iron Age. This typological variation must almost certainly reflect a diversity of origin

[1] Phillipson, 'The Early Iron Age in Zambia', 207; J. O. Vogel, *Kamangoza* (Zambia, 1971); and Vogel, *Kumadzulo* (Zambia, 1972).

among the earliest food-producers, which is indeed only to be expected on the assumption that the coming of the Iron Age to this sector represented a southerly drift of the food-producing populations already established further to the north. The primary distinction appears to be that between a slightly earlier, eastern tradition, lacking cattle, which entered the southern sector through the gap between lakes Tanganyika and Malawi, and a western tradition, equipped with cattle, which crossed the Congo–Zambezi watershed from southern Zaïre.[1]

Today, the main problem of the Early Iron Age in Zambia and Malawi is not so much how it began as how it ended. In northern and central Zambia, as also in Malawi, it is fairly clear that a basic cultural continuity persisted right through the first millennium, and that it was brought to a sudden close around the eleventh century, when the Early Iron Age pottery traditions were superseded by a later Iron Age tradition, named by Phillipson the Luangwa tradition, which is ancestral to that practised by the modern populations of the region – the Chewa, Nsenga, Ngoni, Tumbuka, Soli, Lala, Lamba, Bisa, Bemba, Lungu, Mambwe and eastern Lunda. The only Early Iron Age sites with pottery remotely resembling that of the Luangwa tradition are those of the Chondwe group, from which the conclusion may perhaps be drawn that the pioneers of the Luangwa tradition entered central Zambia from southern Zaïre.[2] It is likely that they represented a strong new population element, which brought not only a new pottery tradition but also improved metallurgical techniques and a strong emphasis on cattle-keeping as an adjunct to cereal agriculture. In southern Zambia, however, we have seen that the Early Iron Age pottery at the base of the Kalundu mound is succeeded by a completely distinct 'Kalomo' pottery type, which is neither grooved nor channelled and lacks the bevelled rims so characteristic of Early Iron Age wares. This pottery is found at a number of other mound sites on the Batoka plateau, and at Isamu Pati it persists through nearly 2.5 m of occupation debris, corresponding to a period from about the seventh to about the eleventh century. Although Kalomo pottery is considered by some archaeologists to be derived from the Dambwa group of the middle Zambezi,[3] it may alternatively represent the intrusion of a new population group

[1] D. W. Phillipson, 'The chronology of the Iron Age in Bantu Africa', *Journal of African History*, 1975, **16**, 321–42.

[2] D. W. Phillipson, 'Iron Age history and archaeology in Zambia', *Journal of African History*, 1974, **15**, 1–25.

[3] J. O. Vogel, 'The Kalomo culture of southern Zambia', *Zambia Museums Journal*, 1971, **1**, 77–8.

practising a later Iron Age culture at a date some three hundred years earlier than the makers of the Luangwa wares.

At all events, it is in the mound sites of the Batoka plateau and at settlement sites of the upper Zambezi valley, both containing Kalomo pottery, that excavations by Fagan and Vogel have produced a wealth of evidence about this later Iron Age way of life, which clearly has application far beyond the boundaries of Zambia, and which, in the absence of comparably detailed evidence for the earliest Iron Age, must be used as a standard of reference for that also. One of the most thoroughly investigated settlements is the Isamu Pati mound, the inhabitants of which are known to have been planting sorghum, and possibly also millet, using iron hoes and perhaps also weighted digging-sticks (pl. 19). The methods of cultivation are uncertain, but may have involved careful selection of land for gardens in the grassland areas with deeper soils and minimum tree cover, for certainly the axes used were of the lightest weight. Iron tools, except for arrowheads and razors, were rare, and one has the impression that metallurgy had not, even by the end of the period, had a full impact on the economy and material culture (fig. 54). Certainly, a wide range of fruit and vegetables was gathered wild, and hunting was practised throughout the occupation, the favoured animals being the smaller antelope such as oribi and duiker. In the lowest level of the site it is the bones of game animals that

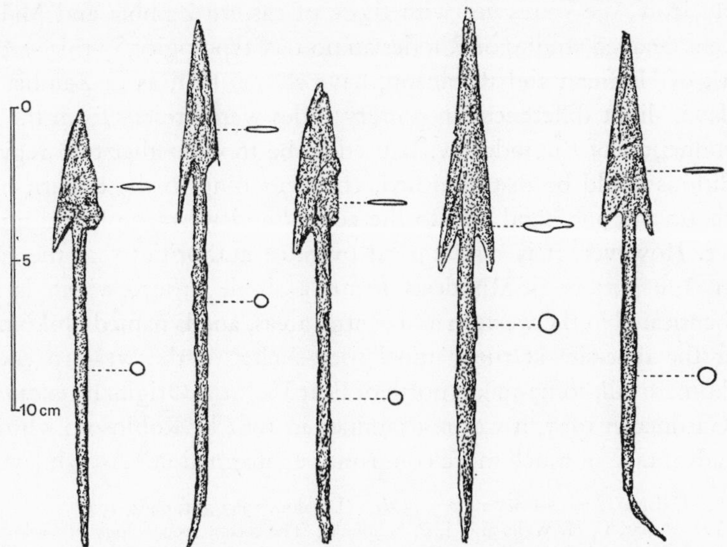

54 Simple Iron Age arrowheads from Isamu Pati, Zambia. (After Fagan, *Iron Age cultures*, I, fig. 26.)

predominate, but domestic species become more and more important in the later stages. Cattle were probably of the Sanga short-horn type. Small stock, dogs and chickens, were also kept. The inhabitants of Isamu Pati lived in pole and mud houses, the stick walls being plastered on the inside, while roofs were of thatch. Grain bins were used, and storage pits were dug into the underlying soil. The layout of the village is imperfectly known, but it was probably built around a central cattle kraal. The burials, deposited in a crouched position and accompanied by a few grave-goods, reveal a predominance of negroid over Bush characteristics.[1]

THE EARLY IRON AGE OF SOUTHERN AFRICA

From this picture of Iron Age development in Zambia and Malawi we turn to Rhodesia, where a long history of archaeological research has resulted in the discovery of many more Iron Age sites than are yet known in any comparable area of sub-equatorial Africa. Here, as further north, food production and metallurgy appear to have been introduced simultaneously, with a resulting standardization of technology and basic economic practices over the whole area. That these innovations came to Rhodesia across the Zambezi is not in doubt, and, as we have seen, the closest external resemblances of the Rhodesian Early Iron Age wares are with those of eastern Zambia and Malawi. Recent detailed studies of Rhodesian pottery typologies, in this case the work of Huffman and Robinson, have shown that, as in Zambia and Malawi, slight differences in pottery styles were present from the first introduction of the industry. It used to be thought that two regional traditions could be distinguished, corresponding to the eastern highlands on the one hand and to the central and western plateau on the other. However, it is now agreed by most authorities that the Early Iron Age pottery of Rhodesia forms a single group, which is best authenticated in the western and central areas, and is named Gokomere, after the type-site at the Tunnel rock-shelter at the western end of Gokomere hill, some 30 km north of Fort Victoria. Originally excavated by Gardner in 1937, it was re-examined in 1962 by Robinson, who had the advantage of much more comparative information.[2] An ash layer of

[1] B. M. Fagan, *Iron Age cultures in Zambia*, 1 (London, 1967), 51, 62–4, 194.

[2] T. Gardner, L. H. Wells and J. F. Schofield, 'The recent archaeology of Gokomere, Southern Rhodesia' *Transactions of the Royal Society of South Africa*, 1940, **28**, 219; K. R. Robinson, 'Further excavations in the Iron Age deposit at the tunnel site, Gokomere Hill, Southern Rhodesia', *South African Archaeological Bulletin*, 1963, **18**, 72, 155–71.

recent date overlay up to 0.9 m of occupation midden, which contained stamped pottery as well as other cultural remains. The area surrounding the entrance of the rock-shelter was formerly occupied by a large stock enclosure and houses, the remains of which outcrop from the soil. A radiocarbon date around the sixth century came from the lower levels of the same occupation. Another dated occurrence of Gokomere ware comes from the Acropolis at Zimbabwe, where the first Iron Age occupation is stratified in an ochreous earth resting on bedrock in the Western Enclosure. A single radiocarbon date from the end of the occupation, which was probably a short one, has been given as around the fourth century.[1] This level contains potsherds similar to those at the Tunnel site. A third important site in the Gokomere group is at Mabveni in the Chibi Reserve, some 50 km south-west of Zimbabwe. Here signs of Iron Age occupation extend over several acres. A number of trial trenches revealed a shallow occupation level with trace of pole and mud structures.[2] Two radiocarbon samples gave readings between the second and the sixth centuries. Another site, at Malapati on the Nuanetsi river in the Limpopo drainage system, yielded a later Gokomere occupation, dated to around the ninth century. A shallow midden contained characteristic Gokomere potsherds, which also have some features in common with some Early Iron Age sites in the Transvaal.[3]

Gokomere ware is best defined with reference to the Chibi and Gokomere sites, because the other collections are too small to be representative. Shouldered pots are the most common form of vessel, and their walls tend to be thick. Rim-bands are common, while raised horizontal bands of oblique stamping decorate the necks of many vessels. A few carinated vessels are found, and hemispherical bowls, both deep and shallow, are frequent. There are some neckless pots, but not many. Throughout the whole range of vessels, decoration is dominated by stamping. Incised decoration is rare. There are some evident typological links with the Dambwa group of southern Zambia, especially in the treatment of necks and rim-bands (fig. 55). The rest of the material culture of the Gokomere people is only slightly known, but copper ornaments, both strip and beads, were found both at Mabveni and at the Tunnel site. Economic evidence in the form of

[1] R. Summers, K. R. Robinson and A. Whitty, 'Zimbabwe Excavations, 1958', *Occasional Papers of the National Museum of Southern Rhodesia*, 1961, **23A**, 182–3.

[2] K. R. Robinson, 'An Early Iron Age site from the Chibi district, Southern Rhodesia', *South African Archaeological Bulletin*, 1961, **17**, 75–102.

[3] K. R. Robinson, 'The archaeology', in *Report of the Schoolboys' Exploration Society expedition to Buffalo Bend*, 1961, 3–8.

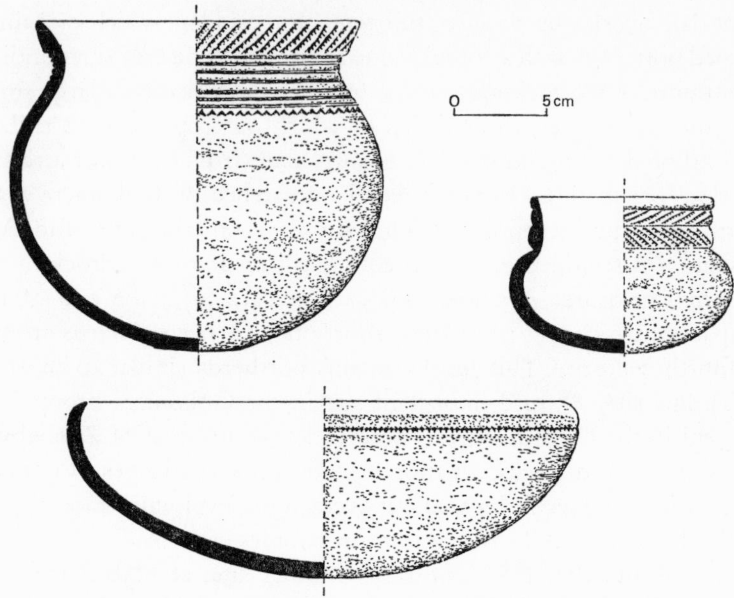

55 Gokomere pottery from central Rhodesia.
(After P. S. Garlake, *Great Zimbabwe*, 1973, fig. 21.)

animal bones has never been studied in detail, but the bones of game animals and those of domestic sheep and goats have been found at several sites, and it is probable that cattle began to be kept at some time during the Early Iron Age.

The eastern part of Rhodesia has yielded many traces of Early Iron Age settlements, most of them in the Inyanga highlands. Radiocarbon dates from the settlements range between the fourth and the eleventh centuries, parallel to those of the Gokomere and Zambian Early Iron Age sites.[1] There are many similarities between Gokomere wares and the vessels from the eastern sites, although the Inyanga vessels are sometimes better made. What must be expected is an enlargement of the area of the eastern, Ziwa-type, sites when more is known of the Early Iron Age archaeology of southern Mozambique.

Later Iron Age culture in Rhodesia during the first millennium is reflected primarily in the development of local variations on the Gokomere cultural theme, especially in the centre and the west. But, as in Malawi and in eastern and central Zambia, around the eleventh century new ceramic traditions appeared. The well-known Leopard's Kopje

[1] R. Summers, *Inyanga* (Cambridge, 1958), 138; Summers, 'Iron Age industries of southern Africa', in Bishop and Clark, eds., *Background to evolution*, 687–700.

tradition of western Rhodesia was associated with a material culture that owed little or nothing to Gokomere influence. The sites were mostly within the shelter of rocky hills, and the inhabitants made much more use than their predecessors of rough stone walling. Their pottery (fig. 56) shows little trace of Gokomere influence, and undecorated beakers, clay figurines of women and also of domestic animals, usually cattle, are common. The human figurines have exaggerated buttocks

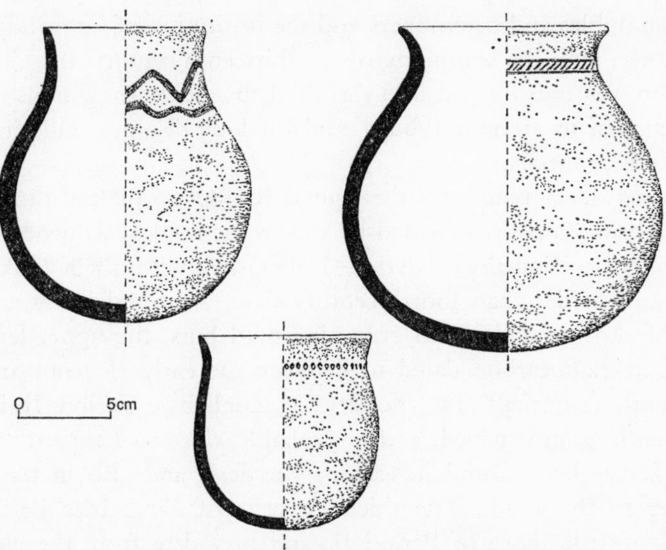

56 Early Leopard's Kopje pottery from the Leopard's Kopje site, Rhodesia. (After Garlake, *Great Zimbabwe*, fig. 22.)

and show signs of cicatrization. The sites are widely distributed in the south-west of the country, where more than one settlement has been dated to the eleventh century.[1] A variant of the Leopard's Kopje tradition occurs at the well-known Bambandyanalo site in the Limpopo valley, whose middle levels have also been dated to the middle of the eleventh century. The Leopard's Kopje tradition is intrusive, strongly cattle-oriented, and probably represents a new migration into western Rhodesia.[2] Other later Iron Age traditions are found in northern and

[1] K. R. Robinson, 'The Leopard's Kopje culture, its position in the Iron Age in Southern Rhodesia', *South African Archaeological Bulletin*, 1966, **21**, 5–51; Robinson, *Khami ruins* (Cambridge, 1959), 38; Robinson, 'The Leopard's Kopje culture: a preliminary report on recent work', *Arnoldia*, 1965, **1**, 25; T. N. Huffman, 'Early Iron Age', and Huffman, 'The linguistic affinities of the Iron Age in Rhodesia', *Arnoldia*, 1974, **7**, 7.

[2] B. M. Fagan, 'The Greefswald sequence: Bambandyanalo and Mapungubwe', *Journal of African History*, 1964, **5**, 3, 337–61.

central Rhodesia that are broadly contemporary with that of Leopard's Kopje. These people, like their Leopard's Kopje neighbours, were subsistence farmers with a loosely stratified social organization, but no signs of a centralized political authority. The Harari and Musengezi traditions were the work of peasant farmers centred in the northern Mashonaland region, who continued to live at the subsistence level until recent times. But a more southerly tradition, the Gumanje, developed into a complex culture that involved both a social distinction between nobles and commoners and the institution of a royal dynasty. Ultimately, after the beginning of the thirteenth century, the Gumanje tradition was transformed into the Zimbabwe culture, famous for the excellence of its stone buildings, and for long-distance trade in ivory and precious metals.[1]

Cultural development on the central Rhodesian plateau during the first millennium is documented by the archaeological sequence on the Acropolis at Zimbabwe. Period I deposits, with their Gokomere pottery of earlier than fourth-century date, are overlain by a sterile layer of earthy midden and crumbled mud huts, the upper levels of which are radiocarbon dated to between the early eleventh and late fourteenth centuries.[2] The pottery of Zimbabwe Period II is predominantly gourd-shaped, and is probably close to Leopard's Kopje ware. It has been found in eastern Rhodesia and also in the Chibi Reserve to the south. The thick deposits of Zimbabwe Period III directly overlie those of Period II, and may date from the eleventh century to as late as the fifteenth century (pls. 20, 21). At this stage substantial houses were built, and the construction of stone walls began, the architecture of which may have had its origin in the Leopard's Kopje village walls. The quality of the pottery improves, but still has continuity with that of Period II, with undecorated and necked vessels predominating (fig. 57). Spindle-whorls appear for the first time, and imported objects are more common. Period III deposits are few, but some small sites are found in south-eastern Rhodesia; there is an important settlement site at Mapungubwe on the southern side of the Limpopo valley, and another large site has recently been reported at Manekweni, in Mozambique some 110 km north-west of Maputo (Lourenzo Marques).[3] The occupants of Mapungubwe made fine

[1] Huffman, 'Linguistic affinities'.

[2] P. S. Garlake, 'Rhodesian ruins – a preliminary assessment of their styles and chronology', *Journal of African History*, 1970, 11, 4, 501. The best summary of the Zimbabwe evidence is the same author's *Great Zimbabwe* (London, 1973).

[3] P. S. Garlake, 'An investigation of Manekweni, Mozambique', *Azania*, 1976, 11, 25–48.

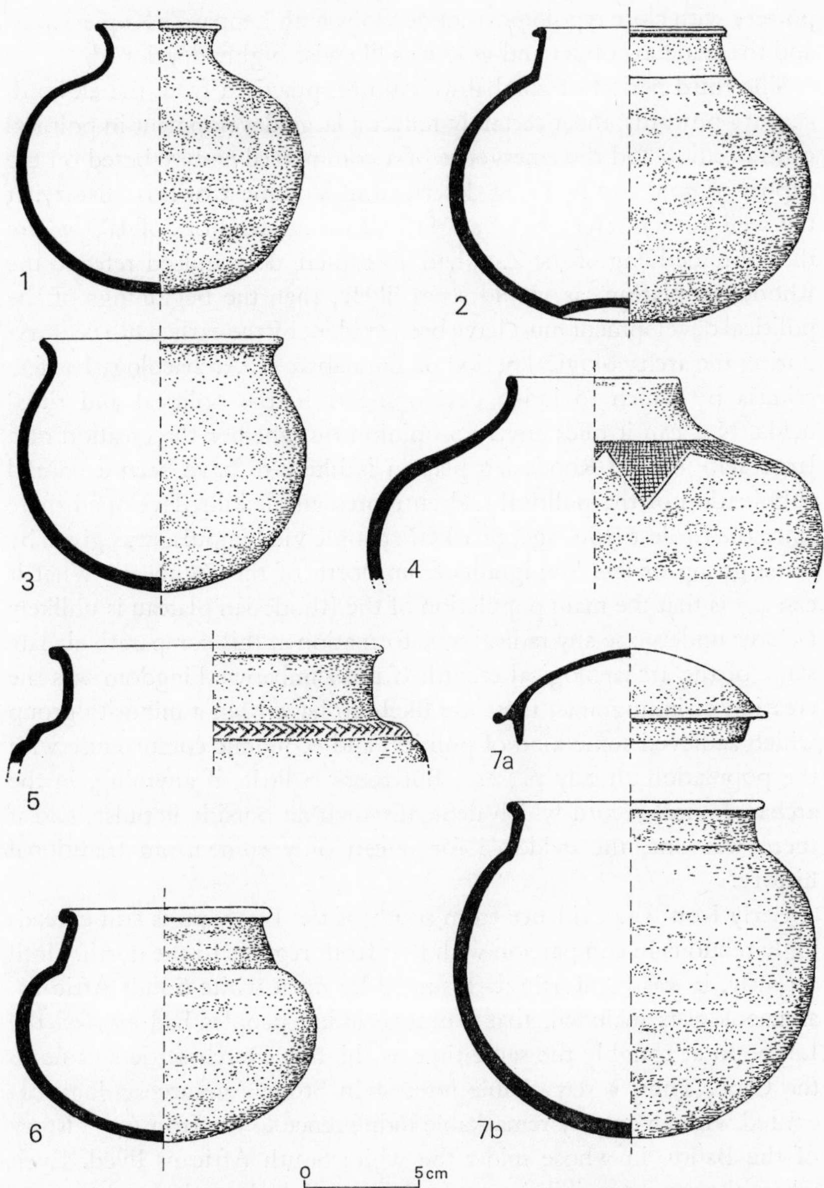

57 Pottery types from Periods II to IV at Zimbabwe.
Nos. 1 and 3 are assigned by Robinson to his Zimbabwe Period II; no. 2 to Period III; no. 4 to 'Zimbabwe Period III influenced by IV'; no. 6 to Period IV. Nos. 5, 7a and 7b, excavated from related ruins, would also be considered typical Period IV forms.
(After Garlake, *Great Zimbabwe*, fig. 19.)

pottery with close typological connections with Leopard's Kopje wares, and the trade in copper and gold was likewise highly developed.

The third period of Zimbabwe culture, practised from the eleventh century onwards, must certainly reflect a large development in political centralization and the emergence of a commercial empire based on the export of gold and ivory, as described in Volume 3 of this History. If the well-known reference of al-Mas'ūdī to 'the land of Sofala',[1] where the supreme King of the Zanj had his capital, does indeed refer to the Rhodesian plateau, as would seem likely, then the beginnings of the political development must have been evident by the early tenth century, during the archaeological period of Zimbabwe II. Archaeology has few criteria by which to judge developments in the political and ritual fields. Nor can it offer any firm opinion on whether the creation of a large state on the Rhodesian plateau is likely to have been a natural culmination of the political and entrepreneurial skills developed there since the earliest Iron Age, or whether some vital impulse was given by some group of late immigrants from north of the Zambezi.[2] What it can say is that the main population of the Rhodesian plateau is unlikely to have undergone any radical transformation at this comparatively late stage of the archaeological record. If the Zimbabwe kingdom was the creation of immigrants, these are likely to have been a minority group which achieved some kind of political and economic compromise with the population already present. But there is little, if anything, in the archaeological record which demands such an outside impulse, and if there was one, the evidence for it can only come from traditional history.

Early Iron Age evidence from south of the Limpopo is still exceedingly tenuous in comparison with that from regions to the north. Until recently, it was comfortingly assumed by most white South Africans, archaeologists included, that Bantu-speaking peoples had crossed the Limpopo at roughly the same time as the first Dutch settlers came to the Cape. Thus, a remarkable interest in Stone Age archaeology coexisted with an equally remarkable indifference to the Iron Age history of the Bantu, in whose midst the white South Africans lived. Even when the new possibilities opened by radiocarbon dating began to be used by archaeologists in tropical Africa, scholars in South Africa were slow to follow suit. Our present comparative ignorance is there-

[1] Freeman-Grenville, *East African coast*, 15.

[2] T. N. Huffman, 'The rise and fall of Zimbabwe', *Journal of African History*, 1972, 13, 3, 353–66.

fore to be attributed more to the lack of research than to any basic absence of data. Fortunately, this situation seems at last to be changing.

A small number of highly significant Early Iron Age sites have recently come to light in the Transvaal and Swaziland that provide abundant evidence for the early settlement of South Africa by farmers and iron-workers.[1] The Silverleaves site near Tzaneen yielded incised pots with grooved rims, which have been compared by the excavator with the Nkope pottery of Malawi. Two radiocarbon dates in the third and fourth centuries AD provide the earliest evidence for Iron Age occupation south of the Limpopo. Another site near Letaba in the north-eastern Transvaal is assigned to the same cultural tradition and is radiocarbon dated to around the seventh century. Revil Mason associates the Silverleaves tradition with the Castle Cavern site in the Ngwenya area of Swaziland, dated by two radiocarbon samples to the early fifth century.[2] This site is an artificial cave, excavated by early miners in search of haematite ore, who left it piled with haematite rubble and occupation debris to a depth of 1.5 m. Pottery described as 'Channelled', smelted iron and numerous iron-mining tools were found in the deposits from which the radiocarbon samples were obtained. An extensive Early Iron Age settlement at Broederstroom near Brits yielded thousands of Early Iron Age potsherds with few known affinities, thirteen collapsed huts, two furnace accumulations and bones of domestic cattle, associated with a date around the fifth century. This ware, too, has been compared with pottery from Nkope, and even with that from Kwale. If substantiated, this would indicate that the earliest Iron Age culture reached South Africa through Mozambique rather than Rhodesia.

None of these newly discovered settlements contains pottery that bears any close resemblance to the Gokomere tradition so widely distributed in Rhodesia. But the Matokoma (Happy Rest) site about 30 km west of Louis Trichardt on the southern side of the Zoutpansberg range, which was investigated before the invention of radiocarbon dating, yielded a large collection of Gokomere-type wares.[3] The pottery forms and decoration bear a close resemblance to those from Malapati and Gokomere in Rhodesia, which have been dated to the sixth century

[1] R. J. Mason, M. Klapwijk and T. M. Evers, 'Early Iron Age settlement of southern Africa', *South African Journal of Science*, 1973, **69**, 324–6.

[2] R. A. Dart and P. Beaumont, 'Ratification and retrocession of earlier Swaziland iron ore mining radiocarbon datings', *South African Journal of Science*, 1968, **64**, 6.

[3] J. B. de Vaal, ''N Soutpansbergse Zimbabwe: 'n voorlopige ondersoek van 'n bouval op die Plaas Solvent', *South African Journal of Science*, 1943, **40**, 303–18.

and the ninth or tenth centuries respectively. The Matokoma site is still undated, and has not yet been systematically excavated, but the pottery typology from the surface collections would argue a sixth- to ninth-century date. Thus, it would seem likely that the southward expansion of the Gokomere tradition from Rhodesia into South Africa occurred later than the spread of a more easterly Iron Age tradition through the coastal region of southern Mozambique.

As we have seen, there is no doubt that the Leopard's Kopje tradition extended to the southern side of the Limpopo valley at Bambandyanalo, where the beakers and other clay vessels, and also the imported glass beads, are typical of this period of the culture in south-western Rhodesia. It is true that iron objects and implements of tillage are rare at Bambandyanalo, although grindstones and hoe-butts have been found on the surface of the site. It is true that the bones of domestic animals are common, and that conspicuous layers of cattle dung in the middle of the mound testify to the existence of a central cattle enclosure. But these features are typical both of Leopard's Kopje sites in Rhodesia and of the Kalomo mound sites in Zambia, in which agriculture was certainly practised along with pastoral pursuits. There is thus no support for Gardner's view that the inhabitants of Bambandyanalo were Khoi herders. In fact, the Bambandyanalo site is larger and much more permanent than modern Khoi settlements, which are, and were in the seventeenth century, temporary villages with a negligible midden accumulation. Gardner was undoubtedly much influenced in his interpretation by the fact that seventy-four skeletons found in the central part of the settlement were pronounced by one of the leading physical anthropologists of the day to be of a non-negroid physical type. But more recent research has shown that the alleged non-negroid osteological features of the Bambandyanalo skeletons are found in sites throughout southern Central Africa, while the thorough researches by de Villiers on the skulls of South African Negroes have provided much more detailed criteria for the range of variation within the negroid type in South Africa, which show that the Bambandyanalo skeletons fall well within the range of the negroid physical type.[1]

A special problem is presented by two recent excavations in the

[1] L. Fouché, *Mapungubwe* (Cambridge, 1937); G. Gardner, *Mapungubwe II* (Pretoria, 1963); Fagan, 'The Greefswald sequence'; A. Galloway, *The skeletal remains of Bambandyanalo* (Johannesburg, 1959); P. V. Tobias, 'Skeletal remains from Inyanga', in Summers, *Inyanga*; H. de Villiers, *The skull of the South African Negro* (Johannesburg, 1968); G. P. Rightmire, 'Iron Age skulls from southern Africa reassessed by multiple discrimination analysis', *American Journal of Physical Anthropology*, 1970, 33, 2, 147–68.

Transvaal, which, while yielding dates that should belong to the Early Iron Age, have revealed pottery bearing no relation to the stamped and grooved pottery traditions of the Early Iron Age of Rhodesia, Zambia and Malawi. Early copper-mining sites at Phalaborwa in the north-eastern Transvaal have been investigated by Van der Merwe and others. Radiocarbon datings from mining shafts and occupation sites range from about the eighth century AD to recent times, with a cluster of dates in the eleventh and twelfth centuries. Although the pottery has not been published in detail, it is stated to have a close relationship to the modern Sotho pottery of the area.[1] Again, at Melville Koppies on the Witwatersrand near Johannesburg, a series of iron-smelting furnaces has been investigated by Revil Mason, and one of them has been radiocarbon dated to around the eleventh century. This furnace is correlated with the so-called Uitkomst culture of the Transvaal, which is linked with stone cattle enclosures and villages of known Sotho manufacture. Most of these structures date to the latter half of the second millennium, but the Uitkomst type-site, a cave with a series of iron-smelting furnaces, gave a seventeenth-century date for the uppermost of several ovens associated with Uitkomst wares almost certainly of Sotho manufacture.[2]

It would certainly be a mistake, at the present very early stage of Iron Age research in South Africa, to attempt to draw more than hypothetical conclusions from such a thin scatter of evidence. Nevertheless, it would seem very likely that the first Iron Age penetration of the area occurred through the coastal plain of southern Mozambique, and, if so, the ethnic affinities of the pioneers is most likely to have been with the ancestors of the modern Tsonga. These, alone among the south-eastern Bantu, combine cereal agriculture with fishing in an environment which is little suited to cattle-keeping, whereas their Nguni and Sotho neighbours prize cattle above all their other possessions, dislike boats, and observe a positive taboo against eating fish. Tsonga peoples today occupy the coast of Mozambique from the Sabi river to Nkosi Bay, and it is known that formerly they spread far into Natal.[3] It seems likely that in Mozambique between the Zambezi and the Sabi, as also in the coastal areas of Natal, people of a similar origin and culture to the Tsonga were later overlaid and absorbed by very different Shona and Nguni populations moving down to the coastal plain from the interior

[1] M. Stuiver and N. J. van der Merwe, 'Radiocarbon chronology of the Iron Age in sub-Saharan Africa', *Current Anthropology*, 1968, 9, 54–8.

[2] R. Mason, *The prehistory of the Transvaal* (Johannesburg, 1962).

[3] Wilson and Thompson, eds., *Oxford history of South Africa*, I, 176–9.

plateau. While there was undoubtedly some penetration of Early Iron Age people across the middle Limpopo from Rhodesia into South Africa, as witnessed by the Matokoma site with its Gokomere pottery, the main expansion of pastorally oriented Bantu peoples from the Rhodesian plateau to those of the Transvaal and the Orange Free State seems to have occurred in later Iron Age times. It is beyond doubt that representatives of the Leopard's Kopje tradition had spread their influence as far south as the central Transvaal by the end of the first millennium. While it is not yet possible to distinguish in the archaeological record between the ancestors of the Nguni and the Sotho-Tswana, it is clear that these must have been the main groups involved.

It remains for the present an unsolved problem how, when and where some groups of Khoi hunters learned the elements of a pastoral economy without losing their linguistic and cultural identity in the process. It may be that we have here to distinguish between the herding of sheep and goats on the one hand, and the breeding and milking of cattle on the other. On the whole it would seem that Khoi are the most likely population to have kept domestic sheep in cave sites in the Cape Province during the latest period of the Stone Age. If, as we have suggested (p. 376), Khoi peoples were once spread all the way from the Cape to southern Angola and from there eastwards to central Tanzania, it is possible that some of them could have acquired these animals by contact with the Southern Cushitic-speaking practitioners of the Stone Bowl culture, although this must remain a purely speculative hypothesis so long as evidence is lacking of a pastoral phase of Late Stone Age culture in any of the regions between central Tanzania and the Cape. However this may be, it would seem unlikely that Khoi acquired cattle until after the central stream of Early Iron Age culture had brought these animals within reach of the main block of later Khoi territory to the west and south of the upper Zambezi. Presumably cattle-raising by Khoi developed from very small beginnings somewhere around the northern fringes of the Kalahari desert with the capture or purchase of cattle by a Khoi band inhabiting an area too arid to be attractive to a Bantu population of mixed farmers. Once specialized pastoralism developed as an adjunct to hunting and gathering, it could well have expanded faster in the region to the west of the Kalahari than mixed farming did in the region to the east. Too much store, therefore, need not be set by the fact that the Nguni and Sotho-Tswana words for 'cow', 'milk' and 'fat-tailed sheep' appear to be derived from

Khoi roots.[1] If more northerly Bantu languages showed the same feature, it might indeed point to the conclusion that the Khoi had acquired cattle before the main eastward and southward expansion of the Bantu peoples. As it is, the fact that the Khoi bordered with both the Sotho-Tswana and the Nguni probably means simply that these two Bantu groups adopted the terminology of the neighbouring pastoral specialists with whom they traded, fought and intermarried.

PROBLEMS OF WESTERN CENTRAL AFRICA

The archaeological evidence surveyed so far suggests that the Iron Age entered Bantu Africa across the western half of its northern frontier. It may have travelled by the river system through the forest, reaching Kinshasa and the southern savanna by about the third century BC, but the main penetration seems to have followed the north-eastern margins of the Congo forest towards the well-watered highlands on either side of the Western Rift. From there, as we have seen, easterly variants of the Early Iron Age culture spread across Tanzania to the Indian Ocean, southwards through Malawi to Rhodesia and probably also through Mozambique to South Africa, affecting all these areas between about the second and the fifth century AD. It is much harder, with the evidence at present available, to follow the development of the main central stream of Early Iron Age culture, which, apart from its brief movement around the northern shores of Lake Victoria to Urewe, seems to have expanded mainly southwards, and mainly to the west of the great lakes. Over the whole of southern Zaïre the Iron Age archaeological record is deplorably thin. A collection of pottery sherds from the Ile des Mimosas in the Congo river near Kinshasa has been radiocarbon dated to about the fifth century AD.[2] Several complete pots described as 'Dimple-based' were found during mining operations at Tshikapa in the Kasai province,[3] and a single 'Dimple-based' sherd has been found in a site dating from the eleventh to the fourteenth century at Katoto in Katanga.[4] Otherwise, the only professionally excavated Iron Age site in southern Zaïre belonging definitely to the first millennium AD is the

[1] Wilson and Thompson, *Oxford history*, I, 104.

[2] B. M. Fagan, 'Radiocarbon dates for sub-Saharan Africa', *Journal of African History*, 1965, **6**, 113.

[3] J. Nenquin, 'Dimple-based pots from Kasai, Belgian Congo', *Man*, 1959, **59**, no. 242.

[4] J. Hiernaux, E. Maquet and J. de Buyst, 'Le cimetière préhistorique de Katoto', *Actes du VIe Congrès Panafricain de préhistoire, Dakar* 1967 (Chambéry, 1972), 148–58.

great cemetery at Sanga, investigated by Hiernaux and Nenquin in 1957 and 1958.[1]

Here, where the upper Congo, or Lualaba, flows through a chain of small lakes some 300 km north of the modern copper-mining town of Jadotville, was found a huge burial-ground, stretching along the shores of Lake Kisale. Of many thousands of graves, Hiernaux and Nenquin excavated some sixty, and found skeletons richly accompanied with pottery vessels, iron and copper ornaments, weapons, and a few long-distance imports such as glass beads and seashells. Two radiocarbon dates for skeletons buried with 'Kisalian' pottery gave readings between about the eighth and about the tenth century. Kisalian pots have rounded bases, contracted shoulders and flaring necks with inturned rims. The shoulders are decorated with half-moon motifs, and the inverted rims are often grooved, incised or comb-stamped (fig. 58). While there is no very close resemblance to any other known pottery group, it is clear both from the vessel forms, from the bevelled rims and grooved decoration, that Kisalian ware is descended from the generalized Early Iron Age tradition of East and Central Africa. Within this, it must be seen as a developed form of an Early Iron Age pottery tradition of Katanga, the earlier history of which is at present quite unknown.

The significance of the material culture revealed at Sanga lies in its wealth in copper and iron, and in the comparatively very advanced techniques, such as wire-drawing and welding, by which these metals were being worked (fig. 59). This degree of wealth, and especially these skills, existing right at the heart of the sub-continent where contact with the outside world was clearly minimal, would seem to imply that the great mineral deposits of the Katanga had already by the eighth and ninth centuries been known and exploited for a long time. Even though the accidents of scientific investigation have so far left the earlier evidence concealed, the Sanga site alone makes it entirely reasonable to suppose that the Katanga was an important centre of metallurgical progress within sub-equatorial Africa as a whole. We have seen that, from about the fifth century onwards, a series of sub-cultures in Zambia to the west of the Luangwa seem to have stemmed from this region. And the question must seriously be asked whether the Later Iron Age cultures represented by the Luangwa tradition in Zambia and the Leopard's Kopje and neighbouring traditions in Rhodesia did not spread into southern Africa from, or through, the

[1] J. Nenquin, *Excavations at Sanga*, 1957 (Tervuren, 1963); and Nenquin, 'Notes on some early pottery cultures in northern Katanga', *Journal of African History*, 1963, 4, 9–32.

Plate 11 A newcomer: the camel. [ch. 5]
(Photo: Documentation française, Paris.)

Plate 12 Neolithic village of Loude, near Akreijit, Mauretania. Such villages in the same good state of preservation are to be found by the score along the Tichit-Walata escarpment. [ch. 5]
(Photo: P. Munson.)

Plate 13 Neolithic pottery found in the middle of the Tenere, at Guelb Berliet, hundreds of kilometres from the modern southern limit of the desert. [ch. 5]
(Photo: Montengerand; Missions Berliet-Tenéré.)

Plate 14 Bowl-horned bull near Lake Chad.
These animals belong to the *Bos africanus* family (Hamitic Longhorn) related to the Egyptian Apis oxen. [ch. 5]
(Photo: M. Dupire; courtesy Institut fondamental d'Afrique Noire [IFAN], Dakar.)

Plate 15 Graham Connah's excavation of Daima tell, north-west Nigeria, with a stratigraphy ten metres deep, running from about 500 BC to about AD 1000. [ch. 5]
(Photo: Dr G. E. Connah.)

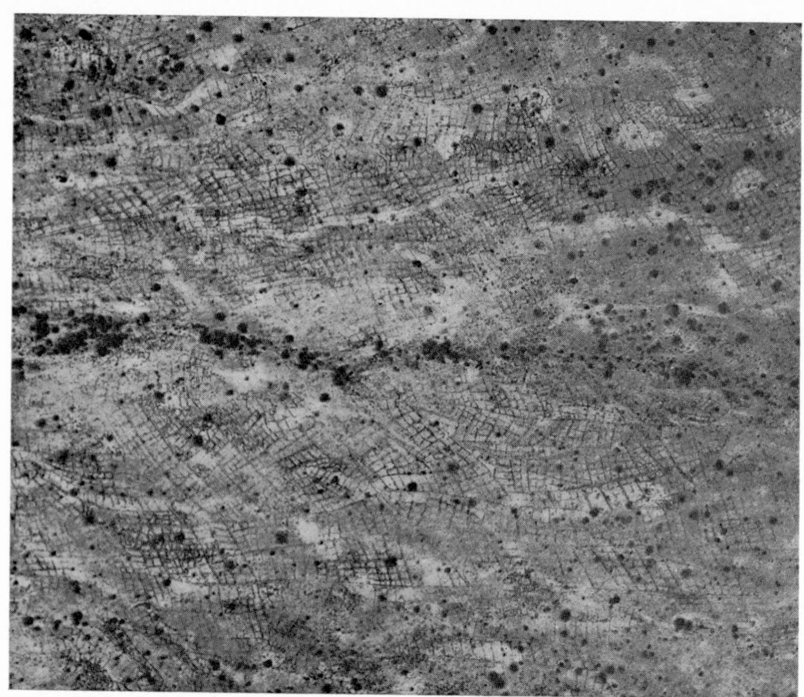

Plate 16 Engaruka, Tanzania: part of the southern system of stone-lined enclosures. [ch. 6]
(Photo: H. Sassoon.)

Plate 17 Engaruka, Tanzania: partly paved interior of a small hut enclosure. [ch. 6]
(Photo: H. Sassoon.)

Plate 18 Kapwirimbwe, Zambia: general view of excavations in Cutting III, seen from the south-east, showing postholes dug into the natural sub-soil. [ch. 6]
(Photo: D. W. Phillipson; courtesy National Monuments Commission, Zambia.)

Plate 19 Excavations on Isamu Pati mound, Zambia. [ch. 6]
(Photo: B. M. Fagan, *Southern Africa in the Iron Age*, 1966, pl. 13; courtesy Thames and Hudson.)

Plate 20 The Acropolis at Zimbabwe, viewed from the west. The key stratigraphic sequence was obtained from the Western Enclosure in the foreground. [ch. 6]
(Photo: David Attenborough.)

Plate 21 The Great Enclosure at Zimbabwe. [ch. 6]
(Photo: courtesy Department of Information, Salisbury, Rhodesia.)

Plate 22 Djemila: general view and the Antonine baths. [ch. 7]
(Photo: W. H. C. Frend.)

Plate 23 Djemila: Temple to the Augustii, AD 229. [ch. 7]
(Photo: W. H. C. Frend.)

Plate 24 Baptismal font from Optatus Church (Donatist) at Timgad, *c.* AD 385. [ch. 7]
(Photo courtesy Office Algérién d'Action Economique et Touristique [OFALAC].)

Plate 25 Timgad: Christian cemetery from the church, looking north. [ch. 7]
(Photo: W. H. C. Frend.)

Plate 26 Rural church, Henchir Guesses (central Algeria), showing relics in place below the altar enclosure. [ch. 7] (Photo: W. H. C. Frend.)

Plate 27 Fourth-century Christian stone carving at Ain Zirara. [ch. 7] (Photo: W. H. C. Frend.)

Plate 28 Djemila: baptismal font, with baptistery behind, probably early fifth century AD. [ch. 7]
(Photo courtesy OFALAC.)

Plate 29 Bir Djedd: rustic church in central Numidia, fourth–fifth century AD. [ch. 7]
(Photo: W. H. C. Frend.)

Plate 30 Mechta Azrou: rustic church in central Numidia, fourth–fifth century AD. Martyrs' relics are beneath the slab in altar enclosure. [ch. 7] (Photo: M. Martin.)

Plate 31 Mechta Azrou: choir and apse. [ch. 7] (Photo: M. Martin.)

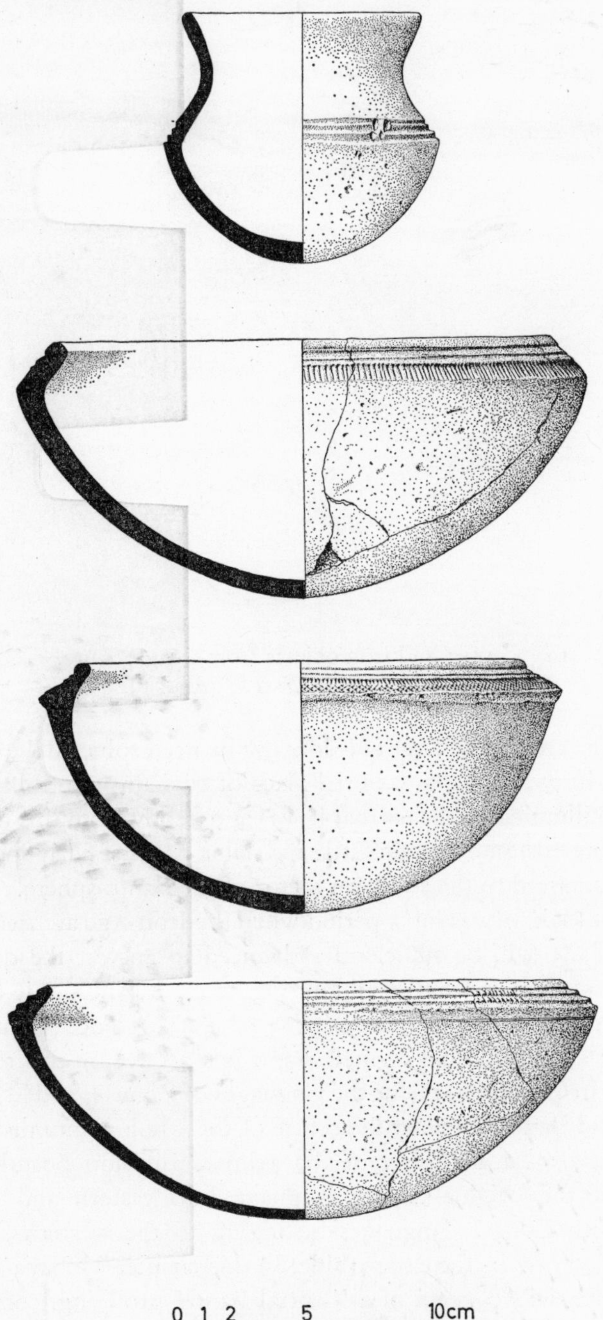

58 Kisalian pottery from Sanga, Zaïre. (After J. Nenquin, *Excavations at Sanga*, 1957, pl. 58.)

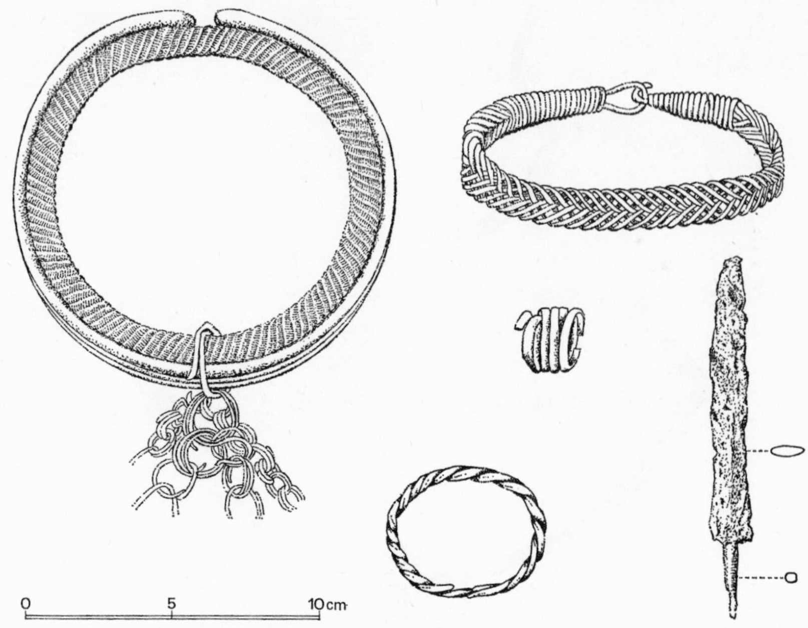

59 Copper and iron objects from Sanga, Zaïre. (After Nenquin, *Excavations at Sanga*, pl. 60.)

same general area. The Sanga site does not by itself solve all the relevant problems. In particular, as a burial-place of riverain fisherfolk, it does nothing to illuminate the fact that it was apparently from this direction that both the earliest domestic cattle and, later, the first fairly specialized pastoralists passed to the southern sector of the Bantu sphere.

We must look forward to a period when the Iron Age archaeology of southern Zaïre will be sufficiently advanced to answer the questions which press upon it from neighbouring areas. Meantime, it must be borne in mind that the reassessment of the evidence from Bantu linguistic classification has opened a new perspective on this region in particular. In Guthrie's scheme the languages of Zones L and M, headed by Luba and Bemba, were at the centre of the whole Bantu dispersion. They were also at the heart of the primary division postulated by Guthrie of the original Bantu language into eastern and western dialects, with Zone L languages belonging to the western side and those of Zone M to the eastern side. In this chapter we have thus far accepted Henrici's concept of a 'Central Bantu' grouping, comprising the languages of Zones D–S, and stemming from a parent language somewhere on the margin of Zone C. It is not yet clear how Guthrie's western and eastern dialects should be accommodated in the new scheme. It is obvious from his 'Catalogue of Common Bantu'[1] that the A–B languages have special lexical affinities with those of Zones H, K and R. At the same time there are many common roots, absent from Zones A and B, which have a distribution extending from Zones C or D into Zones L, K and R as well as into eastern zones. It would thus seem that influences emanating from Zones A and B intermingle with those from Zones C and D in Zones K, L and R. In this criss-crossing, the western influences are likely to have been the sub-stratum, dating to Late Stone Age times, while the central influences may date only from the Iron Age. As we have seen (p. 352), there is evidence of a dense Late Stone Age occupation in the region to the south-west of the Congo forest, in the borderlands of Zaïre and northern Angola. On the other hand, the evidence of exceptional wealth and technical achievement within an Early Iron Age context is in the region to the south-east of the forest, in Kivu and Katanga.

It is obviously a question of the greatest interest to determine which aspects of Early Iron Age culture were capable of passing through the great forest, and which of necessity had to circumvent it. Here, it is certainly remarkable that the common word-roots connected with cereal agriculture and most of those connected with cattle-raising are absent from the forest languages, although many of them occur to the south of the forest in both the eastern and the western halves of the Bantu sphere. It is this, more than anything else, which suggests that, when we have more archaeological evidence from southern Zaïre and Angola, much of it will prove to be connected with the central rather than the western stream of Iron Age influence. Of the possible Early Iron Age sites so far investigated in northern Angola, one, at Furi mine, dated to around the second century AD, contained indeterminate potsherds and charcoal in association with Late Stone Age artefacts, which could represent the projection of a western tradition. Another, at Dundo airfield, dated to around the eighth century, had pottery comparable to Early Iron Age wares from eastern and central Africa.[2] At Feti la Choya, near the headwaters of the Kunene, a site fortified with stone walls and traditionally associated with the ancestors of the largely pastoral Ovimbundu people, yielded from a large midden dates of around the eighth and around the thirteenth century.[3] This site is thus contemporary with the 'Kalomo' culture of Zambia and, when

[1] Guthrie, *Comparative Bantu*, III and IV.

[2] Clark, *Further palaeo-anthropological studies*, 192.

[3] Fagan, 'Radiocarbon dates', 113.

fully studied, should help to illuminate the transition from Early Iron Age to later Iron Age cultures in Central Africa.

The region of sub-equatorial Africa for which there is as yet literally no dated archaeological evidence for the Early Iron Age is the north-western quadrant, which is dominated geographically by the great forest. As we have seen, this is the region comprising Guthrie's A–C zones, where linguistic differentiation is greatest, and where some fairly widespread occupation by Bantu communities must be presumed to have existed from Late Stone Age times onwards. Surface finds of ground stone axes and hoes provide some evidence of Stone Age food production, while the evidence from 'general' Bantu roots is consistent with an economy based on fishing and vegeculture. The probability is that the knowledge of iron-working spread through the forest at approximately the same period as it encompassed its fringes, and that, here as elsewhere, the food-producing economy was strengthened by its presence. Forest clearance was no doubt facilitated by iron tools, and even if sources of iron were comparatively sparse in forest areas, the improved boat-building made possible with iron tools probably extended the range of river-borne trade with iron-producing regions to the north and the south. At the same time it has to be remembered that cereal food-crops and cattle, which were such important concomitants of the Iron Age in most of sub-equatorial Africa, would have had a much more limited significance in the forest region. It is noteworthy that in modern times the staple food-plants of the forest have been those of South American origin – maize, cassava and sweet potato. There is ample evidence that, before the introduction of these crops in the sixteenth and seventeenth centuries, the food-plants of greatest importance in the forest region were those of South-East Asian origin – banana, yam and cocoyam. These plants are still the staples in some parts of the region, and they have survived as subsidiary crops nearly everywhere else. The indigenous African food-plants – millets and sorghums, beans and cowpeas – have survived mainly as 'agricultural fossils', grown for use in religious rituals.[1]

It is likely, therefore, that the introduction of the South-East Asian food-plants was the most significant event of Early Iron Age times in the forest region. This must presumably have been a process which started on the east coast of Africa with the oceanic voyages of Indonesian traders and migrants. It cannot have spread among the indigenous inhabitants of eastern Africa until these were food-producers, and the

[1] J. Vansina, *Kingdoms of the savanna* (Madison, 1966), 21.

indications are that in this region food production did not precede the Iron Age. By the early centuries AD, however, the coastal Bantu peoples would have been in a position to assimilate the new food-plants, and to transmit them to those inland peoples living in the moister environments best suited to their use. While many routes were no doubt followed, the easiest was probably one passing inland at the latitude of Lake Malawi and spreading up the valley of the Western Rift. Such a route is, indeed, indicated by the distribution of the *-tooke* word-root for 'banana'.[1] From here westwards the diffusion could have been on a broad front, passing both to the north and the south of the forest, as well as through it. It is probable that at every stage the impact of new methods of food production was felt more strongly in the progressive clearance of the forest fringes than in the centre of the region, where Early Iron Age food-producers, no less than their Late Stone Age predecessors, would have formed sparsely distributed communities, largely confined to river lines and patches of natural savanna.

Some useful light may be thrown upon an earlier situation by considering the areas where the advance of food production has been most recent, and where pygmy peoples representative of the earlier hunting and gathering economy still survive in recognizable groups. Significantly these areas are all in the northern half of the forested region – in southern Cameroun, northern Gabon and the Congo Republic, and again in the Ituri region of Zaïre, to the east of the great bend of the Congo. Within the Congo bend, primary forest has long been reduced into areas insufficient to maintain a separate and specialized hunting economy, and the former pygmy population has intermarried and integrated with the food-producers to such an extent that, although the pygmy physical type is widely discernible in the population at large, pygmy culture has ceased to exist. The indication is that, in recent centuries at least, the inroads of food production have been stronger upon the southern margin of the forest than in the north. Very likely, this was a process which started with the spread of South-East Asian food-plants from the south-east, and continued with the more recent spread of South American crops from the hinterland of Angola.

For the north-eastern part of the forest region, Turnbull has presented an apparently convincing picture of an area only recently penetrated by any kind of food production.[2] He finds that the Ituri today is shared by some forty thousand pygmies, living in small bands as

[1] Guthrie, *Comparative Bantu*, IV, 117.
[2] C. Turnbull, *Wayward servants* (London, 1965), 19–23.

hunter-gatherers, and by an approximately equal number of food-producing villagers, drawn from eight or nine different ethnic and linguistic groups, most of which have their main population bases outside the forest to the east or the north. According to the traditions of both hunters and villagers, the penetration of the food-producers has occurred entirely within the last three or four centuries, reaching its climax in the last century, when it became necessary for hunting bands to forge permanent alliances with one or other of the competing groups of food-producers, agreeing to serve them as hunters, scouts and spies, in exchange for plantation food and drink, metal goods and pottery, on all of which they gradually became dependent. The villagers on their side underwent a cultural adaptation at least as profound as that of the hunters, abandoning their cattle and cereal crops, and taking to a highly specialized kind of forest cultivation, growing bananas and cassava as staples, together with some dry rice, beans, ground-nuts and oil-palms. For protein they fished the rivers. For meat they depended on the hunters. Their main daily preoccupation was with forest clearance, for the sour soils usually ceased to yield crops after about three years, and the village settlements were constantly moving up and down the lines of rivers, streams and forest tracks, so that the primary forest became seamed with once planted areas which had reverted to secondary growth.

The non-pygmy, food-producing villagers of the Ituri include not only Bantu-speakers like the Bali, the Bira and the Budu, but speakers of Central Sudanic languages like the Momvu and the Lese, and of the eastern Niger-Kordofanian languages like the Zande. The essential point seems to be that the penetration of this particularly difficult area did not begin until some representatives of all these varied peoples had turned themselves into specialized cultivators of the South-East Asian and perhaps also the South American food-plants. This consideration emphasizes the importance of the forest fringes, and of the corridors of more viable territory separating the major enclaves of primary forest. So far as the Ituri is concerned, there can be no doubt of the great significance of the narrow corridor of more or less open country between the eastern limits of the forest and the Western Rift. All the food-producing peoples of the eastern forest – the Rega, the Bembe, the Bira and the Budu – claim their origins in this corridor,[1] and the fact that their languages belong to the north-eastern Zone D rather than the north-western Zone C supports this claim. It was probably through the

[1] A. Moeller, *Les Grandes Lignes des migrations des Bantous de la Province Orientale du Congo Belge* (Brussels, 1936), 34ff.

agency of these peoples, and of their relations in the corridor itself – especially the Nande, the Amba and the Konjo – that the South-East Asian plants were transmitted around the northern fringes of the forest to the Central Sudanic peoples and the eastern Niger-Kordofanians.

One reason for the late penetration of the Ituri by food-producers is very likely that it is a watershed region, difficult of access by canoe. Rivers there are in plenty, but they are in their rushing, tumbling infancy, and navigation, even by small craft, is constantly broken by rapids and waterfalls. The same consideration applies to the other great area of primary forest, which forms the watershed between the Gabon, Equatorial Guinea and southern Cameroun coastlands, and the tributary valleys running southwards to the Ubangi and the Congo. Here, too, pygmy hunter-gatherers survive to the present day, though not in such numbers as in the Ituri. However, the evidence is strong that they formed the main population of the whole area prior to its food-producing colonization by the Fang peoples during the nineteenth century. Between the watershed and the Atlantic coast there lies a comparatively thin belt of lowland forest, intersected by many rivers, which is the home of many small Bantu-speaking peoples speaking the languages of Zones A and B, some of whom claim to have come from the north, others from the south, while some have no traditions of origin in any other region.[1] East of the watershed, however, across the whole 1100 km stretch between the Sangha valley and Kisangani, and between the upper Ubangi in the north and the Equator in the south, there is a region seamed with easily navigable waterways, bearing evidence of long occupation by food-producing communities, and redolent with traditions of great population movements from the north towards the south.

These are the peoples who speak the languages of Zone C, and it is particularly significant that in this region, alone among those which border the north of the Bantu sphere, there is convincing evidence that Bantu languages were once spoken well to the north of the present Bantu line. In his studies of the Zande and the Nzakara, carried out in the first decade of this century, de Calonne Beaufaict reported the existence of submerged groups of Bantu-speaking Ngbinda living all over the eastern part of the Central African Republic, between Yakoma on the Uele and the upper tributaries of the Bahr al-Ghazal.[2] More

[1] H. Deschamps, *Traditions orales et archives au Gabon*, (Paris, 1962), 21–34.
[2] A. de Calonne Beaufaict, *Azande* (Brussels, 1921).

recently, Professor A. N. Tucker has confirmed that Ngbinda is indeed a Bantu language, and he has also discovered the existence of a still more northerly language, Buguru, which is the only Bantu language spoken within the frontiers of the Sudan Republic.[1] In these submerged remnants we may have a pointer to the location of the Bantu who first came into contact with Iron Age food production sometime during the second half of the first millennium BC. What is certain is that in more recent times a large, formerly Bantu-speaking area extending far to the north of the forest has been overrun by Zande, Nzakara and other peoples speaking languages of the eastern branch of Niger-Kordofanian. These include the Banda, Gbaka and Ngbandi, who have pressed southwards from the upper Chari, across the great bend of the Ubangi and on towards the Congo. To the west again, the Vute and Mbum have displaced the Bantu-speaking Bulu, Beti and Fang.[2] Though there was a stabilization of the linguistic frontier approximately at the northern margin of the forest, there can be no doubt that the southward drift of population continued far beyond this line. In particular, the Mongo, living within the great bend of the Congo, show many signs of strong northerly influence. Though it is known from traditional history that the latest phases of these southerly movements by peoples speaking eastern Niger-Kordofanian languages were still in progress as late as the eighteenth century, the earlier phases are still chronologically uncharted. On the whole it sould seem likely that they represent a westerly counterpart of the long, slow drift of peoples speaking Central Sudanic, Nilotic and Paranilotic languages into the eastern half of the Bantu sphere, which has continued through most of the present millennium, if not for longer. In all probability these movements should be seen as the ultimate repercussions upon the equatorial belt of Africa of the desiccation of the Saharan borderlands much further to the north.

CONCLUSIONS

In conclusion, one might perhaps speculate that at the beginning of our period, around the middle of the first millennium BC, Bantu peoples speaking languages ancestral to those of Zones C and D were living astride the northern margins of the Congo forest. Those within the forest were already specialized to a riverside existence of fishing and

[1] Personal communication from Professor A. N. Tucker.

[2] P. Alexandre, 'Proto-histoire du groupe Beti-Bulu-Fang', *Cahiers d'etudes africaines*, 1965, 5, 503–60.

forest vegeculture, and had perhaps already established a bridgehead in the forest margins to the south. Those living north of the forest were perhaps already participating in a kind of Stone Age food production based on cereal agriculture and stock-raising. With the coming of the Iron Age from the regions still further to the north, it was the latter mode of food production which gained the greatest advantage, though the geographical opportunities for its expansion lay more to the south-east than to the south-west. Hence the dramatic expansion of the eastern Bantu food-producers over against the hunting and gathering peoples of eastern and southern Africa. In the moister conditions of the forest region, the Iron Age, though still advantageous, had not the same potential for explosive expansion, so that the Bantu forest culture was finally overtaken by the Bantu savanna culture moving round it to the east and the south.

At all events, we may be fairly confident that by the end of the first millennium AD Bantu-speaking food-producers of more or less negroid physical type had long established themselves throughout most of the area occupied today by their descendants. It would seem that everywhere the basis of the Bantu ascendancy was their comparative efficiency as iron-using farmers with the ability to adapt their methods of food production to a wide range of environments. Over most of the area occupied by speakers of the D–S languages, the economy was based on cereal agriculture and stock-raising, but in the moister areas in and surrounding the Congo forest an older planting and fishing economy survived. Although by modern standards the population of Bantu Africa at the end of the first millennium AD must still have been exceedingly sparse, there is no doubt that it would have represented a revolutionary increase over the population of Late Stone Age times. It must have been the comparatively rapid rate of population growth among the food-producers which was mainly responsible for the absorption of the earlier hunting and gathering populations, and for the emergence of the many and varied Bantu peoples which have occupied the scene during the past thousand years.

Although individual communities were no doubt small by modern standards and much more widely scattered over the face of the land, there is plenty of evidence that, even during the Early Iron Age, communities were extensively linked by trade. Iron Age food-producers required a much wider range of raw materials than their Stone Age predecessors. For example, whereas the hunter-gatherer could obtain all the salt he needed from the game which he consumed, the cultivator with his predominantly carbohydrate diet required regular supplies of salt, which could be obtained only by boiling certain species of river grasses or else, in cake form, evaporated by boiling from a limited number of saline deposits. Such deposits became the natural centres of local trading systems, extending in some cases over a couple of hundred kilometres. Uvinza in western Tanzania is an example of a salt-producing site which is known both from its pottery and from radiocarbon dates to have been operating since the Early Iron Age.[1] Again, deposits of iron ore, and still more of copper and gold, are by no means ubiquitous, and both ore and manufactured metal objects must have been widely traded from Early Iron Age times onwards. Among early centres of the iron trade it would seem certain, for example, that the haematite outcrops of Swaziland, exploited, as we have seen, since the fifth century, were mined for widespread distribution. The trade in copper is much more easily attested than that in iron – for example, by the presence of copper ornaments at Dambwa and other Early Iron Age sites in southern Zambia, far from the copper outcrops of the Kafue Hook to the north or the Gwaai river valley to the south. Perhaps it is significant that the makers of the Sanga cemetery lived in an area rich in copper and salt, where the conditions for the development of local and interregional trade were excellent. Long-distance trade-routes crossing the Katanga were still in the ninth century a thing of the future, but the foundations of the elaborate trading networks attested in the oral traditions of later centuries must surely have been laid during the first millennium.[2]

A scatter of exotic objects, such as glass beads and seashells, has come from Early Iron Age sites in the southern half of Bantu Africa. The early middens at Mabveni in Mashonaland yielded a few glass beads, which belong within the general range of those found in the bedrock layer at Zimbabwe. A seashell and beads came from the Early Iron Age level at the Tunnel rock-shelter at Gokomere, while cowrie shells have been excavated from a fourth century horizon at the Kalundu mound in the Kalomo district of Zambia, and from a fifth-century context at Gundu mound, 100 km north-east of Kalundu. These scattered finds do not indicate the operation of regular long-distance caravans from the

[1] B. M. Fagan, 'Early trade and raw materials in south central Africa', in R. Gray and D. Birmingham, eds., *Pre-colonial African trade* (London, 1970), 24–38; B. M. Fagan and J. E. Yellan, 'Ivuna: ancient salt-working in southern Tanzania', *Azania*, 1968, **3**, 1–44; J. E. G. Sutton and A. D. Roberts, 'Uvinza and its salt industry', ibid. 45–86.

[2] B. M. Fagan, 'Early trade and raw materials in south central Africa', *Journal of African History*, 1969, **10**, 1–15.

east coast to the far interior, but rather the effects of tentative and indirect trading contacts between coastal markets and the ultimate sources of raw materials far from the Indian Ocean. But by the end of the first millennium, at least in southern Bantu Africa, the situation may well have been different. We have the reference by al-Masʿūdī to a flourishing export trade in ivory from the land of Zanj, and the context suggests that this was centred in the country behind Sofala.[1] And from the Rhodesian plateau we have the archaeological evidence of the commercial prosperity and political centralization, manifest at least from the eleventh century in the Period III remains at Zimbabwe. Here, as at Sanga, we may have the first tantalizing glimpses of the elaborate chieftainships and political structures of later centuries. It is significant that these occur in the areas most esteemed by the food-producing Bantu and, later, by the outside world.

[1] Freeman-Grenville, *East African coast*, 15.

CHAPTER 7

THE CHRISTIAN PERIOD IN MEDITERRANEAN AFRICA, *c.* AD 200 to 700

INTRODUCTION

For more than three centuries, from the reign of Constantine (AD 306–37) to the Arab invasions of the 630s, Mediterranean Africa was the scene of a prosperous and brilliant Christian civilization. Never before or since has North Africa exercised so great an influence on contemporary events and thought. The Christian leaders, Augustine of Hippo (AD 354–430) and Cyril of Alexandria (died AD 444), moulded the teaching of the Latin and Greek Churches respectively in a way that has survived for centuries. Augustine's theology of grace was accepted by Protestants and Roman Catholics alike during the Reformation era, Cyril's theology of the Incarnation remained standard orthodox teaching to modern times, and these examples illustrate the extent to which Mediterranean Africa faced towards Europe rather than towards the remainder of Africa for long periods in its history.

The transition from Graeco-Roman to Christian North Africa resulted in profound changes at every level of society. At the beginning of the third century AD, Mediterranean Africa was dominated by its cities, the final brilliant product of the military and economic power of Rome, and the lives of its peoples were watched over by the 'immortal gods of Rome', associated with the territorial and tribal gods and goddesses the origin of whose worship was lost in the mists of time. For the ordinary provincial the emperor was the intermediary between the world of gods and their own, a distant but kindly providence to whom recourse could be had against the extortions of his servants.[1] On the emperor's welfare depended also that of his subjects; there was a sense of identification between ruler and ruled. There are North African inscriptions calling on the gods to protect the emperor.[2] A

[1] For instance, the farmers on the imperial estate of the Saltus Burunitanus (Souk el-Khmis) petition the 'divine providence' of the Emperor Commodus in AD 183 for protection against injuries inflicted on them by his bailiffs; *Corpus Inscriptionum Latinarum* [*CIL*], **8**, 10570, col. 3, lines 1–2.

[2] For instance, *CIL*, **8**, 895, 'Mars Augustus protector domini nostri' from Villa Magna in honour of Gordian III, and compare ibid. 6353, 'Saturnus et Iuppiter omnipotens Augustus conservator sacer Augustorum' (Mastar, a Christian centre in the fourth century).

century later the official religion of the Graeco-Roman world was Christianity. Wealth previously lavished on public buildings or public entertainment was being bequeathed to the clergy or the monasteries. The bishop had replaced the mayor (*curator*) as the chief inhabitant of the town, and many of the functions of civil government were falling to his responsibility. The countryside was also witnessing changes. Over great areas in North Africa, tribal life had already given way to settled life, and the villagers were finding that their olive-oil was becoming a staple product throughout the western Mediterranean. In contrast to their counterparts on the northern shores of the Mediterranean, they retained an element of prosperity throughout the whole of this period. In the seventh century, the Arab invaders found themselves moving through a continuous forest of olive trees extending westwards from Tripolitania to the Chott el-Hodna. In Egypt, the monastery, often a large agricultural unit, dominated the scene as landlord, provider and refuge for the Coptic peasantry. Christianity permeated every level of society. While it was not the only thing that was happening in Mediterranean Africa in these centuries, it was by far the most important.

This chapter outlines the history of this civilization from its beginnings to its collapse before the Arabs, partial in Egypt but complete in North Africa. Inevitably Christianity itself must take the centre of the stage. The survey thus falls into two parts. The Church in North Africa west of the Gulf of Syrtis (Sidra) was separated from that in Egypt and Cyrenaica by geography, language and theological tradition. The North Africans were Latin-speaking, their theology was cast in a puritan mould, they were sectarian and inward-looking, emphasizing the work of the Holy Spirit to maintain the integrity of the Church pure from the taint of the outside world and the state, and they were concerned with issues connected with membership of this body of the saved, especially with predestination and grace. The Church in Egypt and Cyrenaica was, on the other hand, Greek-speaking and outward-looking, responsible for missions to Nubia, Ethiopia and south India, and while not denying the importance of ecclesiastical discipline, directed its energies towards arriving at an understanding of the mystery of human salvation through the Incarnation. The issues that moved it were doctrinal, and these owed much to the influence of the philosophical school of Alexandrian Jewry, above all to Philo (died *c*. AD 40). Its theology tended to regard God and his relation to creation in terms of God and His Word or Reason incarnate in Jesus Christ, a binitarian approach to theology, whereas the North Africans, lacking a similar Jewish philosophical tradition, emphasized instead the biblical religion of Father, Son and Holy Spirit. Despite many efforts to reach mutual understanding, especially at the Council of Chalcedon in 451, the differences in interpretation between the two halves of Christendom were fundamental, and their persistence contributed to the ultimate weakness of the Christian position in the southern Mediterranean when threatened by the apparently all-conquering message of Islam.

THE EARLY YEARS OF THE CHURCH IN EGYPT AND CYRENAICA

The origins of the Church in Egypt and Cyrenaica are almost as obscure as those of the Church in North Africa. By the time Eusebius wrote his *Ecclesiastical history* in AD 324 there was a firmly held Church tradition which named Peter's disciple Mark as the founder of the Christian community there.[1] Apollos, who 'knew only the baptism of John' (Acts 18:25), was an Alexandrian, but nothing is known of any mission by him in his native city after he had received 'more perfect instruction' from Paul. As at Carthage, the only tangible point of departure is provided by the Jews, and perhaps the apocryphal *Acta Marci*, telling how Mark came from Rome and evangelized in the Jewish quarter of Alexandria, preserves a folk memory of how Christianity started there. There had been Jews in Egypt for the previous four centuries. There was a temple modelled on that at Jerusalem, at Leontopolis, and a vigorous literary tradition that had been responsible for the production of the Septuagint. By the first half of the first century AD, the Jews dominated two of the five quarters into which Alexandria was divided, and were scattered in considerable numbers (Philo thought one million all told) between Cyrenaica and Egypt's border with Nubia. They were self-conscious communities, largely unreconciled with their Greek and Egyptian neighbours, and on two occasions, in AD 73 and 115, rose against them. In Alexandria itself, the Jewish *politeuma* had its own treasury and court of justice. There the smouldering hostility between Jew and Greek led to a *pogrom* of Jews in AD 38 followed by two famous embassies by the Jews, first to Caligula and then to his successor Claudius. Claudius firmly delimited the privileges of the Alexandrian Jews.

[1] See F. C. Burkitt, 'The Christian Church in the East', in S. A. Cook, F. E. Adcock, M. P. Charlesworth and N. H. Baynes, eds., *Cambridge ancient history*, XII (Cambridge, 1939), 476.

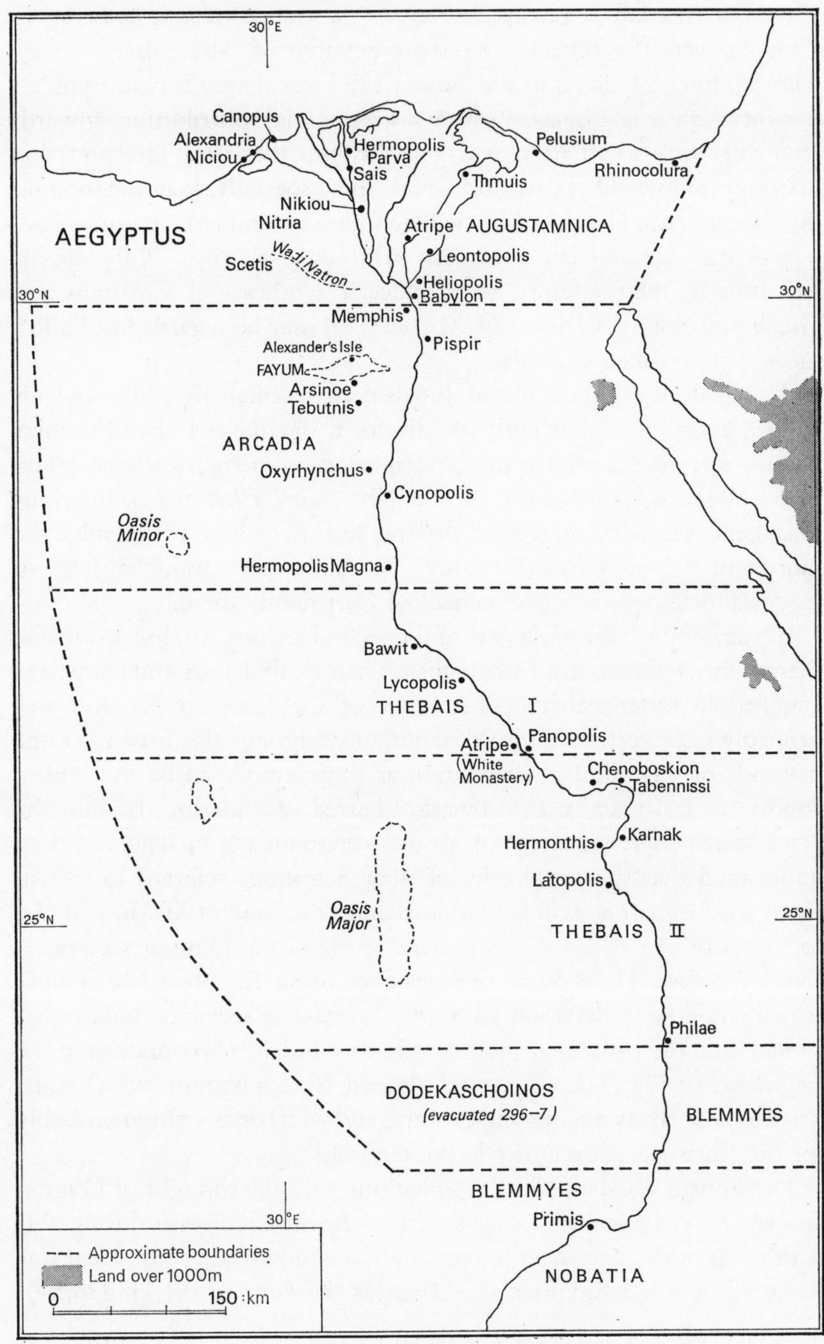

60 Egypt in late Roman times.

Philo, who left a record in *Legatio ad Gaium* of the embassy to Caligula, was the outstanding representative of Alexandrian Jewry. Though intensely loyal to the *Torah* he did not share his countrymen's hostility towards Graeco-Roman society. His contribution towards reconciliation was an attempt largely through allegorical interpretation of Scripture to weld Jewish and Greek and, especially, Platonic thought into one system. He lacked immediate followers and two centuries later it was the Alexandrian Christians who were to copy Philo almost verbatim in their attempt to produce a synthesis of Christian and Greek philosophy. Clement (fl. AD 180–200) may be regarded as Philo's most distinguished disciple.

Alongside the philosophical Judaism represented by Philo and his school, there was a strongly ascetic form of Judaism that Eusebius describes, represented by the Therapeutae, who had settlements on Lake Mareotis, south-west of the city (*Hist. Eccl.* II.17). Eusebius mistakenly regarded these as Christians, so closely did they resemble the monks of the early fourth century. In this respect also, the Jews of Egypt anticipated the development of Christianity there.

It was not until the early part of the second century AD, however, that there is firm evidence for Christianity. Then we find Jews and Christians engaged in bitter debate. The writer of the *Letter of Barnabas* was probably a convert from the Alexandrian synagogue. He used the same methods of scriptural interpretation as those employed by the rabbis, combined, however, with a fanatical hatred of Judaism. To him the Jews were 'wretched men' of absurd ceremonial law, who failed to understand that the prophecies of their Scriptures referred to Christ. Even so, *Barnabas* concluded by describing the 'way of life' in contrast to 'the way of darkness' in the same terms as the Q'mran sectaries a century before. He showed the existence of an Egyptian Christianity which could be understood within the context of sectarian Judaism. A similar animosity directed against orthodox Judaism is contained in the fragments of the *Unknown Gospel* gleaned from a papyrus which must date to the early or mid second century, and which was written probably for the Christian community in Alexandria.[1]

The Fourth Gospel, with its affiliations with the thought of Q'mran and strong criticism of 'the Jews', was also in circulation during this period. Another papyrus discovery indicates how the ascetic ideal was regarded by some Egyptian Christians as the door to the kingdom of

[1] Published by H. I. Bell and T. C. Skeat, eds., *Fragments of an unknown gospel* (London, 1935).

Heaven. The *Gospel of Thomas*, in origin probably an Aramaic gospel and compiled not later than the end of the first century AD, had its readers at Oxyrhynchus and elsewhere in the Nile Valley.[1] The existence of a Jewish-Christian strain in the Christianity of the second century is attested further by the fragments of the *Gospel according to the Egyptians* and the *Gospel according to the Hebrews* preserved by Clement.

These early beginnings of Christianity may have been caught up in the disastrous rising of the Jews in AD 115–17, which started in Cyrenaica and spread far down the Nile Valley. Christianity next emerges *c.* 135, when the surviving Jewish background was that of philosophy and theosophy. The Gnostic movements, which dominated the Christian scene at Alexandria between *c.* 135 and *c.* 180, associated with its great teachers Basilides, Valentinus and Heracleon, owed much to this legacy; they passed it on to their orthodox successors in what became the Alexandrian theological tradition.

The important place which Gnosticism held in Egyptian Christianity is demonstrated by the discovery of a complete library of forty-eight Gnostic books in a fourth–fifth century AD site at Nag-Hammadi, north of Luxor.[2] These documents reveal the Egyptian Gnostics as theosophical dualists concerned to understand the ultimate secrets of the universe and of man's place within it. Their interest in the psychology of dreams, as indicating the fearsome loneliness of individual man, reminds one of some aspects of existentialism. The framework, however, in which they elaborated their systems still owed much to Jewish attitudes, with its scenes set in the Temple or the Mount of Olives.

What made Gnosticism a formidable movement was its application of the concepts of current Middle Platonic philosophy to interpret the message of the Jewish Scriptures. The dualism of the Q'mran sectaries was combined with the allegorizing of Philo, with the result that by the middle of the second century AD the Alexandrian Gnostics had won an intellectual dominance of Christian thought in the Mediterranean, and in Alexandria this seems to have led to a widespread interest in Christianity among educated Greeks.

The price, however, was too high for the Church to pay. The Gnostic scheme of salvation allowed no place for the ministry of Jesus and very

1 Fragments of the Gospel containing Logia were first found at Oxyrhynchus in 1895 (see B. P. Grenfell and A. S. Hunt, eds., *Oxyrhynchus Papyri, Λογια Ιηαου* ['Logia Jesu'] [London, 1897]). The entire text was recovered in the Gnostic library of Nag-Hammadi. For its Aramaic background, see H. W. Montefiore in *New Testament Studies*, 1961, 5, 220–48.

2 The publication of these important documents has hung fire. The best summary in English is W. Foerster, *Gnosis*, vol. 2 (Oxford, 1975).

little for the New Testament. Christ was deprived of human personality, as surely as he was in the more extreme interpretations of Egyptian Monophysitism three centuries later. Its categorization of humanity into the illumined, the redeemable (the Psychics) and the vast mass of the remainder (Hylics) cut at the root of any thought of man 'made in the image of God' and equipped with free will. It was a Christianity without ethical impulse; Nirvana replaced heaven and hell. By *c.* AD 180 there were the beginnings of a successful orthodox reaction in Alexandria, as exemplified by the emergence of a catechetical school attached to the bishopric, and the first firm record of a bishop of Alexandria and of the Church there governed by the bishop and twelve presbyters. In 189 the presbyters elected Demetrius as bishop and he was destined to preside over the Church for the next forty-three years.

The Church which produced the catechetical school, led first by a converted Stoic Pantaenus (*c.* AD 180) and then by Clement, was becoming a well-organized and comparatively wealthy community. To many of its adherents it represented itself as a mystery with its own 'Secret Gospel of Mark' open only to baptized initiates. In this it stood near to its Gnostic rivals. But it was already a missionary church directing its message largely at the educated Greek-speaking community in Alexandria. Clement (*c.* AD 150–*c.* 215) was an Athenian immigrant to Egypt, but he interpreted exactly the outlook of the Alexandrian Christians. His convictions and his method of presenting Christianity were the exact opposite of those of his contemporary Tertullian in Carthage. His theology forbade the rejection of philosophy and the separation of the Christian from the remainder of society. If God's Word was the source of all being, then it was also the source of mankind and of his approaches to God as reflected in his philosophies. These might miss the finer chords of the 'true music of Amphion' contained in the Gospels. Mosaic writings preceded by far the Greek philosophers. Plato had plagiarized the Jewish prophets, but together Judaism and Greek philosophy prepared their adherents for the final truth of Christianity. 'There is but one river of truth,' Clement wrote, 'but many streams pour into it. The law is for the Jew what philosophy is for the Greek, a schoolmaster to bring them to God.'[1] Clement was addressing himself to an intellectual and upper-class community, people who would appreciate the ideal of the 'true Gnostic', a spiritual élite differentiated only from the disciples of the Gnostic teachers, Platonizing philosophers, by their acceptance of the ethic and institution

[1] Clement, *Stromateis*, 1.5.28.

of the Church. Even his view of Christ 'wholly without passion' and enjoying 'no emotional movement' differed little from that taught by his Gnostic contemporaries.[1] His ethic, too, recorded in his sermon *On the rich man's salvation*, unlike Tertullian's, did not reject wealth: it could be sanctified by its generous use. Asceticism and philosophical study of the truth of Scripture rather than martyrdom were the means of the Christian's salvation. Reason had an equal place with faith in the Christian's scale of values. All this was far from the hard school of Christianity that had developed in Carthage. Indeed by AD 200 the two great centres of Mediterranean Christianity were preaching diametrically opposed gospels.

Clement's career ended in AD 203, when he fled from Alexandria as the result of the same wave of persecution that caused the deaths of Perpetua and Felicitas in Carthage. His place as head of the catechetical school was taken by a young man of eighteen, whose father had been executed as a Christian. Origen has been regarded as the greatest figure in the Christian Church between Paul and Augustine. His name ('born of Horus') suggests Egyptian parentage, as does the fact of his removal from Alexandria in 215 when Caracalla cleared the city of native Egyptians. He had always been something of a child prodigy, with a passion both for Scripture and secular learning. Emotionally he felt himself on the side of the Church against the Gnostics and for martyrdom as against avoiding persecution. He was an enthusiast in all he did, including the one fatal error in his life when he accepted Matthew 19:12 literally, and hence precluded himself from a normal ecclesiatical career. His ordination as presbyter by the bishops of Jerusalem and Caesarea in AD 229 during an overland journey from Alexandria to Greece estranged him from Bishop Demetrius. He was forced to live the last twenty-two years of his life an exile in Caesarea, where he died in 253 or 254 after suffering cruel treatment in the Decian persecution.

Origen's importance lies in his ability to integrate Scripture and Greek philosophy in a single theological system and place the results in the service of the Greek-speaking Church for all time. He was first and foremost a teacher and a man of the Bible. There was scarcely a single book of Scripture on which he did not write an extensive commentary, elaborating his theology as he moved from verse to verse. Comparatively early in his career, he embarked on a vast work of scriptural exegesis. Arguing that one could not interpret rightly the revelation of the Divine Word through Scripture without an accurate text, he set to work

[1] Ibid. VI.8.69.

to collate the Septuagint with the Hebrew Bible and three current Jewish-Christian versions. This great work, known as the Hexapla through its arrangement in six parallel columns (Hebrew, Hebrew transliterated into Greek, the LXX, and the versions of Aquila, Symmachus and Theodotion), provided him with the foundation for his true purpose of instructing and interpreting.

While still a young man, Origen had come under the influence of the founder of the Neo-Platonist school in Alexandria, Ammonius Saccas. From him he learnt the value of Greek philosophy, and he applied this knowledge with enthusiasm to the whole range of his scriptural exegesis. Through the language and text of Scripture always emerges the Platonist concept of God and the Stoic maxim for man, 'know thyself'. And when the individual had come to know himself, he would be able to advance towards spiritual perfection in Christ. Man's ultimate objective in Origen's eyes – like in those of Clement – was to become 'like God', and in this progress wisdom and knowledge were the highest Christian attributes. The method was asceticism. Small wonder that the monks of Nitria in the next century regarded Origen as one of their most revered authorities.

Middle Platonism affected his approach to Scripture and his approach to a theology of the Trinity. Always a fighter, he recognized Gnosticism and Monarchian theories as enemies of the Church which either merged Father and Son in a composite pantheistic figure, or represented the Son as simply the highest of the prophets. Gnosticism had been his target in the two most important of his earlier works, *On first principles* (*Peri Archon*) and the *Commentary on John*. Here he pointed to the inadequacy of the Gnostic ethic based on predestination, and stressed instead the supreme value of human free will and man's ability through moral reform to gain for himself the means of salvation. In his attempt, however, to find an answer to the Docetic view of Christ held by the Gnostics (i.e. that he was not truly man), and to the pantheism of other misbelievers (e.g. the Monarchians who tended to conflate God and Christ into a single undifferentiated Being), he was led to postulate a clear distinction between God the Father and His Word, the Son. God alone was unbegotten. The Son was also God, eternally with the Father, and therefore eternally generated, but the essential difference between non-generation and generation remained. 'Do we then say two Gods?' Origen asked a startled bishop suspected of Monarchianism. 'The power' might be one, but the distinction between God (ὁ Θεός) and the Divine Word (Θεός) had to be recognized. Origen's solution came as near as possible to a satisfactory apprehension of the Divine on the assumption of the Platonic view of God. But however it was presented, it always entailed a subordination of Son to Father, a lack of connection with the Jesus of history, and found little place for the Holy Spirit. In all this Origen prepared the way for the Arian and Christological controversies in which Alexandria and Egyptian Christianity would be deeply concerned in the next centuries.

Origen marks a watershed in the relations between pagan and Christian in Egypt. The Christian philosopher could now speak to his pagan contemporary on level terms. In AD 214 Origen was consulted by the governor of the province of Arabia – not summoned to renounce his faith; in *c.* 232 he was convoked to the imperial court at Antioch to discuss religious matters with the Empress Julia Mammaea. He was regarded highly by the Emperor Philip and his wife Otacilia Severa (AD 244–9), both favourable to Christianity. When he started his career, Christianity had been hardly more than a sect. Now it had become one of the major religions of the Graeco-Roman world. In his *Commentary on Matthew* written *c.* 248, Origen had foreseen the possibility of a world-wide persecution against the Christians. He was not far wrong. In AD 248 there was a vicious *pogrom* in Alexandria. Next year, in 249, the unsuccessful Philip gave way to Decius, and Egypt experienced the same persecution by inquisition that befell North Africa. Commissions supervising the performance of sacrifices were set up in towns and villages, and in the Fayum no less than forty-three *libelli* dating between 26 June and 12 July AD 250 have survived to show what happened. One typical example may be quoted:

To the commission chosen to superintend the sacrifices at the village of Alexander's Isle. From Aurelius Diogenes, son of Satabous, of the village of Alexander's Isle, aged 72 years, with a scar on the right eyebrow. I have always sacrificed to the gods, and now in your presence in accordance with the edict I have made sacrifice, and poured a libation, and partaken of the sacred victims. I request you to certify this below. Farewell. I, Aurelius Diogenes, have presented this petition.

2d Hand. I, Aurelius Syrus, saw you and your son sacrificing.

3d Hand. . . . onos . . .

1st Hand. The year one of the Emperor Caesar Gaius Messius Quintus Trajanus Decius Pius Felix Augustus, Epeiph 2 [26 June AD 250].[1]

[1] See J. P. Knipfing, 'The *Libelli* of the Decian persecution', *Harvard Theological Review*, 1923, 16, 345–90. The elaborate imperial title which occupied five lines of the papyrus is paralleled on other municipal documents of this period where formal proof of identification was required, e.g. *Papyrus Oxyrhynchus* [*P. Oxy.*], 2892 (application for a Corn Dole, AD 269).

As in North Africa, Egyptian Christianity is revealed at this time as largely an urban movement. There were few incidents in the countryside and in Alexandria resistance was soon broken. Origen's pupil, Dionysius, who was bishop AD 247–64, wrote to his colleague in Antioch that, on the arrival of the emperor's edict,

all cowered with fear. And of many of the more eminent persons, some came forward immediately through fear, others in public positions were compelled to do so by their business, and others were dragged by those around them. Called by name, they approached the impure and unholy sacrifices, some pale and trembling, as if they were not for sacrificing but rather to be themselves the sacrifices and victims to the idols, so that the large crowd that stood around heaped mockery upon them, and it was evident that they were by nature cowards in everything, cowards both to die and to sacrifice. But others ran eagerly towards the altars, affirming by their forwardness that they had not been Christians even formerly; concerning whom the Lord very truly predicted that they shall hardly be saved. Of the rest, some followed one or other of these, others fled; some were captured, and of these some went as far as bonds and imprisonment, and certain, when they had been shut up for many days, then forswore themselves even before coming into court, while others, who remained firm for a certain time under tortures, subsequently gave in.[1]

Throughout Mediterranean North Africa, the Decian persecution was the most serious moment for Christianity. At this stage the Christians formed well-established but also easily identifiable communities under leaders who were known and influential but not necessarily liked. Few seem to have been prepared to make a final break with the Graeco-Roman civilization that surrounded them. Only when this civilization became increasingly impoverished and oppressive, and Christianity began also to reflect the ideals of the rural population, were the traditional religions of the empire in danger. Meantime Alexandria, like Carthage, recovered relatively quickly from the persecution. When in AD 257 Dionysius had again to face a judicial inquisition, in this case directed specifically at the leaders of the Church, he had a well-organized community once more behind him. Refusing to undertake not to hold services or gather at the Christian cemeteries, Dionysius was exiled by the Deputy Prefect, Aemilian, to Kufra Oasis, but there he took the opportunity to promote successful missionary work among the inhabitants. More fortunate than Cyprian, he was not recalled to be executed, and in the confusion and civil war that followed the downfall of Valerian in 260, he played an influential part in attempting to

[1] Eusebius, *Historia Ecclesiastica*, VI.41.11 (trans. by J. E. L. Oulton).

conciliate the factions that had divided Alexandria like 'a new Red Sea'. When plague broke out, his clergy, like their North African brethren, remained at their posts.

Much of Dionysius's final years as bishop were spent in theological debate. First, he took up the challenge presented by the Sabellians in Cyrenaica, who failed to make any substantial distinction between God the father and God the Son, and then used his influence against Paul of Samosata, Bishop of Antioch, at the opposite extreme of the theological spectrum, who believed that Jesus was essentially man though wholly inspired by the Spirit. In both events he represented effectively the views of his master Origen. Even so, the questions that had been raised remained to be answered by his successors.

Under Dionysius, Alexandria had become the undisputed centre of the Church in Egypt. Already Demetrius had appointed suffragan bishops directly responsible to him, and we find Dionysius disciplining one of these, Nepos of Arsinoe, for maintaining millenarist views of Scripture, an indication perhaps of the survival of the biblical and prophetic tendency in Egyptian Christianity outside Alexandria. In addition, Dionysius introduced a system whereby the date of Easter was announced to all congregations each year in a circular letter from Alexandria. These Festal Letters provided him and his successors with the means of maintaining contact and control of the Christian congregations throughout Egypt and of pronouncing on ecclesiastical and doctrinal themes.

From the death of Dionysius in AD 264 to the outbreak of the Great Persecution forty years later, few facts are known about the Church in Alexandria. Profound changes, however, were beginning to take place in Egyptian society. In 199–200, Septimius Severus had visited Alexandria and perhaps the antiquities of the Nile Valley also, and he had given to Alexandria a city council (*Boulé*) of the provincial municipal type. Elsewhere in Egypt the districts (nomes) had been reorganized, and for the first time in their history their chief city was treated like a cantonal capital in other provinces of the empire. By AD 206–7, Oxyrhynchus had been organized into six quarters with their 'tribes' (*phylai*) modelled on those of the city of Rome, whose residents qualified for a monthly corn ration as part of their citizen rights.[1] In AD 212 (or 214), Severus's son, Caracalla, had published in Egypt the *Constitutio Antoniniana*, which extended Roman citizenship to all free

[1] See J. R. Rea, ed., *P. Oxy.*, XL (London, 1972), 7, publishing the Corn Dole archive from Oxyrhynchus (*P. Oxy.*, 2892–2940), dating AD 268–72.

men in the empire except for the comparatively small class of *dedicitii*.[1] Though an underlying reason for these reforms may have been to oblige the wealthier inhabitants to undertake the burdens of municipal office and hence to contribute more taxes, they were also a recognition of a blurring of distinctions between the various communities in Egypt and a sign of the province's relative prosperity. In Egypt, as in Roman Africa, two centuries of *pax Romana* had led to the emergence of a predominant town-oriented civilization, represented by a class of medium landowners and merchants who were not unwilling to undertake the administrative services of their district so long as these were honorific enough. In addition, Greek education was being extended progressively into the countryside. Writing a reasonably literate letter and compiling accounts were not the perquisite of a few. Literacy was assumed: illiteracy was specially recorded on official documents. Under the Severi, Egypt shared for once in the general well-being of the empire.

This situation, however, was not destined to last. By the time of the Decian persecution there is an impressive accumulation of evidence showing that the prosperity of the Severian age had become a distant memory. The Egyptian economy was always balanced on a knife-edge. The impossibility of extending the areas under cultivation because of the lack of rainfall and the existence of rock-strewn desert, the fickleness of the annual level of the Nile flood, and the insoluble problem of irrigating land beyond a short distance from the river have plagued Egypt from time immemorial. Now, in addition, the same increases in taxation required to meet mounting external threats that crippled the North African cities also demoralized those in Egypt. The system of liturgies, whereby holders of land found themselves compulsorily qualified to undertake particular administrative office, had always been burdensome. Now it became doubly oppressive. No one wanted to undertake even potentially lucrative offices, such as that of public banker, let alone the more menial positions. No one knew how the old and newly imposed burdens were to be met and, if they were not, arrest, confiscation and beating hung over the heads of the unfortunate

[1] *Papyrus Giessen*, 1.40; for the dating, AD 214, see F. Millar, 'The date of the *Constitutio Antoniniana*', *Journal of Egyptian Archaeology*, 1962, **48**, 124–31. It is not known who the *dedicitii* really were. It is suggested, however, that they included some of the barbarians settled by the emperors within the empire's frontiers. In Egypt, many of the native population did not receive citizenship after Caracalla. See M. I. Rostovtzeff, *The social and economic history of the Roman Empire*, 2nd edn, revised by P. M. Fraser, 2 vols. (Oxford, 1957), 720.

citizens.[1] From the cities, decline spread to the surrounding villages. There is a certain pathos in the plea by the villagers in the nome of Arsinoe to the prefect of Egypt, Appius Sabinus, to be freed from obligations to the town under the terms of an edict of Septimius Severus. The case was brought to the unsympathetic Prefect's court in AD 250.

Serenus [Counsel for the senate of Arsinoe]: 'To the law of Severus, I will say, Severus ordained the law in Egypt while the cities were still prosperous.' *The Prefect*: 'The argument from prosperity, or rather the decline from prosperity, is equal both for the villages and the cities.'[2]

The ignorance of elementary economics was blissful, and the villagers' additional plea that the imposition was a new one which 'the sacred Fortune of Decius Augustus will relieve' was brushed aside. Little wonder that many threw up their holdings in despair. A little later one finds these among the questions put to oracles: 'Am I to become a beggar?', 'Shall I take to flight?', 'Is my flight to end?'[3] Flight into the neighbouring desert had been the age-old refuge from oppression in Egypt. By AD 270 this was becoming associated with the religious aspirations of an increasing number of the Egyptian peasants, which were beginning to be reflected in Christianity and its rival, Manichaeism.

Antony's decision to leave his 300-*aroura* holding and adopt an ascetic Christian life was a milestone in the religious history of Egypt. Apart from a few biblical papyri, Christianity has left no trace even on popular Graeco-Egyptian literature during the first three centuries. Combined, however, with the declining prosperity of town and countryside in the mid third century AD, went a growing weakness of Egyptian religion. This was above all rooted in tradition extending back far beyond pharaonic times. Yet as the third century progresses, the lack of its hold on the hearts of the people becomes obvious. The old priestly language of the hieroglyphics was dead. The last emperor recorded in hieroglyphs was Decius in AD 250. While villagers still observed the traditional sacrifices to the gods, they did so, if we are to believe the writer of the *Life* of Pachomius, with decreasing conviction.[4] Worse was that, in an era of growing misery and stress, temples continued to be used as the

1 *P. Oxy.*, 1642; compare similar incidents in the period of Diocletian related in *P. Oxy.*, 1415 and 1405, where an entire property was ceded to the imperial fisc to avoid acceptance of an office (probably mid third century).

2 See T. C. Skeat and E. P. Wegener, 'Trial before the Prefect of Egypt, Appius Sabinus, AD 250', *Journal of Egyptian Archaeology*, 1935, **21**, 235–7.

3 *P. Oxy.*, XII.1477 (late third or early fourth century AD).

4 *Vita Pachomii*, 3 (= *Patrologia cursus completus, series latina* [*PL*], 73, cols. 231–2).

centres where taxes were paid. The old Egyptian gods were thus associated not only with the synthetic Graeco-Egyptian cult of Sarapis, a reminder of the era of Egyptian subjection to Macedonian conquerors, but with the increasingly rapacious demands of the Roman overlords. One of the attractions of Antony's community of ascetics was that the 'imprecations of the tax-collectors' were no longer heard.[1]

Antony, the son of a Coptic farmer in Upper Egypt, combined a streak of individualism with a strictly biblical idea of Christianity and a consciousness of a distinct Coptic heritage which the new religion could express. Though he had avoided formal schooling, he had absorbed the lessons of the New Testament so that, when his parents died, he literally 'took no thought for the morrow'. He sold his parental farm, placed his sister in an already existing *parthenaion* (convent for women) and established himself as an ascetic not far from his own village. Thence he moved via ancient tombs to an abandoned fort in the mountains east of the Nile where he stayed for about the twenty years AD 285–305. For the Jews, pagans and Christians, the wilderness was traditionally where demons were to be encountered; Antony recalls how his cell was 'filled with the forms of lions, bulls, bears, leopards, serpents and scorpions',[2] and to these hallucinations was added bodily illness. He was, however, beginning to attract disciples, and at the outbreak of the Great Persecution in AD 303 the 'desert was becoming full of monks'.

In Egypt, as in North Africa, Diocletian's effort to crush Christianity came too late, but the conflict between pagan and Christian lasted nearly a decade and left a deep and permanent impression on Egyptian folk memory. The years leading up to the Great Persecution had witnessed major administrative and fiscal reforms, the revolt of Achilleus in AD 297, the onset of raids by the Blemmyes across the southern frontier, and the massive increase in official control over the daily lives of the inhabitants. Diocletian divided Egypt into three separate provinces and appointed in each a military commander (*dux*), with three or four times as many troops under him as the modest garrison which the prefect had previously commanded. The increase was probably justified on account of the attacks of the Blemmyes, but the rise in the total garrison and the administrative staffs of the provinces meant heavier burdens for the inhabitants. It is in this period that private letters and receipts speak of

[1] 'Life of St Antony', ch. 44. The text is to be found in J. P. Migne, *Patrologia cursus completus, series Graeca* [*PG*], **26**, 835–976. See K. Heussi, *Der Ursprung des Mönchtums* (Tübingen, 1936), 78–108.

[2] Ibid. ch. 9.

supplies in kind (*annona*) being requisitioned for 'the honourable soldiers'. Taxation based on notional assessments of property (*iugatio*) and manpower (*capitatio*) became intolerably heavy, and nomination for municipal office, which involved responsibility for the collection of the quota, was regarded as something to be avoided at all costs and even as a means of paying off old scores against an enemy. A papyrus dated to AD 296 shows also how omnipresent was the hand of the bureaucracy. A smallholder who failed to supply two oxen requistioned to build a water conduit had to submit an officially verified statement to the effect that one of her beasts had a damaged foot. The owner came from a family of some consequence; what happened to less influential people is not hard to imagine. The unsuccessful revolt of Achilleus seems to have been the outcome.

More important was the psychological effect of these conditions. It is difficult not to see some element of cause and effect in the massive desertion of the traditional gods and the adoption of Christianity by the Copts in the years immediately before the Great Persecution. The historian Eusebius of Caesarea was a contemporary, and he tells how the persecution found Egypt a prey to religious ferment. Once the prime example of the land of idols, its people were now turning in droves to Christ. Eusebius himself witnessed the last violent spasm of persecution in the Thebaid under the Emperor Maximin in AD 311, and described how, despite every form of death and torture inflicted by the authorities on the Christians, churches were replacing altars in the villages of Egypt. The Bible too had been translated into Coptic.

The beginning of the Great Persecution gave little hint of what was to come. One Christian of Oxyrhynchus got a friend to sacrifice in a court case for him. It was a rather unexpected but minor nuisance. The first reaction of Peter, Bishop of Alexandria, had been flight, while in the nomes congregations tried to carry on as usual. In AD 304–5 pressure was gradually increased as churches were dismantled and the laity were being forced to sacrifice. Peter was by now in prison, finding himself at odds with one of his senior bishops, Meletius, Bishop of Lycopolis in the Thebaid, on how the lapsed should be treated at the end of the persecution. So far, the situation had been no worse than under Decius, with some Christians standing firm but many others content either to conform or to use some transparent subterfuge to circumvent the emperor's edict. In the eleven-month pause that followed Diocletian's abdication on 1 May 305, Peter drew up a series of comparatively mild canons with the aim of restoring the lapsed to communion as smoothly as possible. These were published at Easter 306. Meletius and his followers rejected them and entered on a schism.

The Emperor Maximin, who ruled Egypt first as Caesar under Galerius, and then as Augustus, restarted the persecution during AD 306. The officials he appointed as Prefect of Egypt, such as Sossius Culcianus (305–7) and Hierocles, were convinced pagans. For six years persecution continued, though for some reason Antony and his followers were not molested. Eusebius gives a vivid account of the final stages of what in the Thebaid had by now become a civil war:

> And we ourselves also beheld, when we were at these places, many all at once in a single day, some of whom suffered decapitation, others the punishment of fire; so that the murderous axe was dulled and, worn out, was broken in pieces, while the executioners themselves grew utterly weary and took it in turns to succeed one another. It was then that we observed a most marvellous eagerness and a truly divine power and zeal in those who had placed their faith in the Christ of God. Thus, as soon as sentence was given against the first, some from one quarter and others from another would leap up to the tribunal before the judge and confess themselves Christians; paying no heed when faced with terrors and the varied forms of tortures, but undismayedly and boldly speaking of the piety towards the God of the universe, and with joy and laughter and gladness receiving the final sentence of death; so that they sang and sent up hymns and thanksgiving to the God of the universe even to the very last breath.[1]

It was not only the rural Christians who suffered. On 25 November 311, Bishop Peter was executed in Alexandria. This terrible time was never forgotten. In Christian Egypt, the Era of Diocletian became known to this day as the Era of the Martyrs.

Events in the West, culminating in Constantine's victory over Maxentius at the Milvian Bridge on 28 October AD 312, brought relief. Next year Maximin was defeated by Constantine's colleague Licinius, who took over the government of the East and was favourable to Christianity. The aftermath of the ten years of persecution proved at first to be an almost exact parallel to the situation in North Africa. The schism between the followers of Peter and Meletius hardened. Meletius won conspicuous support among the Copts in the Thebaid and a significant amount in the Delta and in Alexandria. There one of his adherents was a learned cleric named Arius. He made his peace with Peter's successor, Achillas, was ordained presbyter, and in a few years rose to be priest in a rich Alexandrian suburb. To Meletius, however, he was a traitor. Seven

[1] Eusebius, *Hist. Eccl.*, VIII.9.4–5 (trans. by J. E. L. Oulton).

years later, in AD 318/19, his followers brought him down on a charge of heresy.

As we have seen, Origen's theology had its weaknesses. To regard Christ as the link between God and creation may have been intellectually satisfying, but it inevitably raised the question whether Christ belonged to the created order or not, and, if he did so, did he not himself need redemption? This might be an academic question so long as Christian theology remained a matter of debate among Greek-speaking intellectuals schooled in Platonism, but it was a different matter when it became a popular religion among ignorant but fanatical Egyptians, who saw in Christianity release from the threat of demons represented not least by the old gods of Egypt. Christ must be truly God in order to guarantee salvation. The Meletians represented the popular point of view, and Arius laid himself open to attack by claiming that not only was Christ as Divine Word subordinate to God, but that He also 'grew in stature' and was subject to temptation. He was therefore neither fully divine nor fully human. Arius found himself condemned by a council of Egyptian bishops and exiled *c.* AD 320. For the next four years the conflict simmered. Arius had powerful friends, including the historian Eusebius and another Eusebius, bishop of the capital, Nicomedia; Bishop Alexander of Alexandria was pressed to restore him. Meantime, Licinius, realizing perhaps that conflict with Constantine was inevitable, had turned against Christianity. There was a period of sporadic harassment of Christians in the East, ended only in September 324 when Constantine gained a decisive victory at Chrysopolis on the east side of the Bosphorus and became ruler of the entire Roman world. At once he set about attempting to heal the religious disorders in Egypt caused by Arius's doctrines and the Meletian schism. Early in 325 he summoned at Nicaea an ecumenical council representing the Church in all his dominions. It was designed to settle not only these disputes, but all other outstanding questions that divided the Christian world.

FROM NICAEA TO CHALCEDON

The Council that opened on 20 May AD 325, and sat for a month, was the most significant assembly in the early Church. It had been summoned by the emperor himself, a symbol of the part the civil power was to play in the affairs of the Church in the eastern Roman provinces, and not least in Egypt. After a month of confused debate, Arius and his followers were condemned. The formula through which the relationship of the Father and the Son was expressed – 'of the same substance' (*homoousios*) – satisfied the aspirations of those who believed that salvation could not be guaranteed except through One who was truly God, but was at heart unacceptable to the majority of the Greek-speaking bishops in the eastern Roman world. These insisted that the distinction between God and Christ must somehow be maintained, if the Church was not to accept a statement of faith which could be interpreted no differently from Jewish monotheism. If the popular view found its spokesman in Bishop Alexander's deacon Athanasius, the eastern bishops also had a measure of right on their side. In addition, the ecclesiastical canons which were agreed by the council put into formal terms the special status of the three leading sees of Christendom – Rome, Alexandria and Antioch. Their right of supervision over the suffragan bishops in the territories under their control was conceded. Alexandria became the head of a vast diocese extending from the borders of Libya to the Nubian frontier. Of Constantinople, still Byzantium, a medium-sized town under the jurisdiction of the metropolitan of Thrace at Heraclea, there was no mention.

In the history of the Church of Egypt one other incident at the Council was as important as the condemnation of Arius. Constantine went out of his way to greet and embrace the confessor Paphnutius, a Copt and an ascetic bishop who had been cruelly maimed during the persecution. This act symbolized that the empire had taken an entirely new direction, and that the bitter memories of the past could be directed against Constantine's pagan predecessors alone. It was a shrewd move, too, for it indicated the support the emperor was prepared to give to the ascetics. Monasticism had already found a response among the Egyptian people as no other movement was to do. About AD 320, Amoun, a close friend of Antony, established the first of a number of vast settlements in the mountains of Nitria, south-west of the Delta. About the same time, a discharged soldier named Pakhom (Pachomius) was founding the first organized monastic communities at Tabennissi in Upper Egypt. With the eye of genius, Constantine accepted the ascetics for the power they were. In so doing he turned to the service of the empire what could have been a force as disruptive to it as the North African Circumcellions. There was to be no popular revolt in Egypt, even at the time of the Persian and Arab invasions.

The Meletians had received a fair deal at the Council. By now the Bishop of Lycopolis could claim that he had one bishop in every three towns in the Thebaid, and one in every six or seven in the Delta, while we learn from papyrus sources of a highly organized Meletian monastic movement. His Church of the Martyrs had not won an outright victory, but it could not be ignored. An arrangement was made that Meletius was to submit to the Bishop of Alexandria once more, retaining his title of bishop but without function, while his bishops were to act as coadjutors to those of Alexander's communion and be eligible for election in their stead as their sees fell vacant. Egypt had had no tradition of schism as had existed in North Africa, and the arrangement was workable provided there was good will. Before this was tested adequately, however, Alexander died (April 328), and in his stead after six weeks of intrigue the deacon Athanasius was elected on 8 June 328.

The bishops had chosen Athanasius as 'an upright man, pious, a Christian and an ascetic'. The last-named quality was vital. Alexandria itself was the object of dislike and envy in the rest of Egypt; no Alexandrian bishop who was not an ascetic could hope to keep the Church in Egypt united. Athanasius soon showed the Meletians and everyone else how he intended unity to be retained. Whatever engagements his predecessor had entered into were thrust aside. The Meletian leaders were treated brutally as Athanasius sought to undermine their hold among the Copts. His outstanding success came in AD 329, when he visited Pachomius's monastery and at a stroke won over his movement to his side. The Pachomian monks were from now on among his devoted supporters. His unceasing activity in the first years of his episcopate determined the future course of his reign. One of the few Greek churchmen who had a working knowledge of Coptic, his visitations throughout his vast diocese gained him authority and respect among the masses of the new Christians among the peasants, but he was opposed bitterly by the remaining Meletian leaders. These found support from Athanasius's theological opponents.

In the decade following Nicaea, the eastern bishops who opposed the *Homoousios* formula had progressively gained the upper hand. In AD 327, a second Council of Nicaea had restored Arius to communion, but not to his office of presbyter, and in the next few years the main supporters of the formulas of the creed of Nicaea had been dismissed from their sees. Constantine, without abrogating the creed he had helped to evolve, had accepted the attitudes of the eastern bishops who dominated his court. By 332 the latter were becoming aware of Athanasius's mistreatment of the Meletians. Constantine himself was anxious to see Christendom finally united by the restoration of Arius to his former position. On both these issues Athanasius was adamant. In 334 he outwitted an inquiry meeting at Caesarea in Palestine to investigate allegations that he had murdered a Meletian bishop named Arsenius. Arsenius had merely been kidnapped and manhandled and was produced alive at the meeting. Next year, however, the coalition of his opponents proved too strong. A commission visited Egypt, and reported to a major council assembled at Tyre that Athanasius had used violence against the Meletians and that his election as bishop was void. The findings were accepted. In September 335, Athanasius was condemned to deprivation of his see. A dramatic appeal to the emperor failed. Athanasius was exiled to Trier, where he remained until Constantine's death. Meanwhile Arius had died (perhaps by poisoning) in 336, on the very day before he was to be restored solemnly to the presbyterate.

Constantine's acceptance of Christianity had meant more than that Christianity was to be the religion of the Roman empire. He had used his adopted faith as part of a vigorous diplomatic offensive among the client kingdoms on the eastern borders of the empire and as a lever against the Persians. His subjects had been quick to follow his example. Whereas the expansion of Christianity in North Africa was blocked by the Sahara desert, Alexandria was the terminus for the whole of Rome's seaborne trade with Arabia and further east. Along this trade-route merchants began to spread the Christian faith, especially to the Himyarites in southern Arabia and the Ethiopians through their port at Adulis (Massawa). The story of Frumentius's success in Ethiopia illustrates the energy with which Christianity was being propagated along the trade-routes frequented by Roman merchants at this period. (See chapter 4.)

Athanasius's consecration of Frumentius ensured Alexandria's permanent interest in missions beyond the southern frontier of the empire. In future the *abuna*, or metropolitan, of Ethiopia would be seeking consecration at the hands of the patriarch of Alexandria. From the sixth to the end of the fourteenth century at least, his colleagues in the Nubian Christian kingdoms would be doing likewise.[1] Much though Constantine II might protest to the King of Aksum in AD 357 that the religious unity of mankind was determined by the religion of the emperor, Athanasius's appointment of Frumentius was accepted, and he won thereby a permanent place for the see of Alexandria in African Christianity. Of equal importance in the history of the Church

[1] For the discovery of the body of Bishop Timotheos at Qasr Ibrim and his title-deed of consecration showing that he had been consecrated Bishop of Pachoras (Faras) and Tilbye (Ibrim) by the Patriarch Gabriel IV (1372–80) at Old Cairo, see J. M. Plumley, *The scrolls of Bishop Timotheos found at Q'asr Ibrim*, Egypt Exploration Society monograph (London, 1975).

in Egypt was Athanasius's binding friendship with the monastic leaders, through which an alliance was forged between the Alexandrian bishopric and the new force of monasticism. At first sight there would seem to be no logical connection between the biblical religion of the Coptic monks and the Greek philosophical Christianity of the bishops of Alexandria. Had the Meletians produced a leader of Athanasius's calibre, the alliance would have been severely tested. As it was, the Meletian threat faded, though the sect survived in Upper Egypt until the arrival of the Arabs. Antony and Pachomius remained Athanasius's firm allies, and Antony's bequest of his sheepskin cloak to the bishop sealed what became a permanent relationship. When in 346 Athanasius returned from exile, the tumultuous welcome he received alike from the Alexandrian magistrate and the Coptic monks showed that henceforth the bishop of Alexandria would be Egypt's new Pharaoh.

In the succeeding decade Athanasius consolidated his position. His theology was gradually refined and made just flexible enough to attract the adherence of some of his Origenist opponents. His third exile in AD 356 only increased his popularity. When Julian entered on the scene as emperor at the end of 361, he found Athanasius an insuperable stumbling block to the success of his pagan reaction. In 362 Athanasius held one of the most significant of many theological synods at Alexandria. Many Origenist bishops and the leaders of the main parties in the see of Antioch accepted his leadership and the Nicene formula. The day was won for *Homoousios*. From now on until he died in May 373, Athanasius's position was unchallengable throughout the whole of Christendom from Aksum to the shores of Britain. Alexandria was the leader of Christianity in the East.

With the accession of Theodosius I as emperor in January AD 379, a change took place in the fortunes of Alexandria. Theodosius was a westerner and strongly Nicene, and he was determined to unite the empire under Nicene orthodoxy as understood by Rome and Alexandria. But new factors in the form of the greatly enhanced importance of the see of the capital city and the new-found orthodoxy of Antioch were beginning to come into the reckoning. The Second Ecumenical Council, which Theodosius convoked at Constantinople in 381 to set the seal on the Nicene orthodoxy, was presided over first by Meletius, Bishop of Antioch, to whom Athanasius had refused communion, and, on Meletius's death during the session, by Gregory Nazianzen, who had been brought to the capital to establish himself as orthodox bishop there. The Egyptians were affronted, and attempted in vain to impose their own nominee as bishop of Constantinople. Their interference in the affairs of Constantinople was resented and censured implicitly in the second Canon. While the patriarchal rights of Alexandria were safeguarded by the Council, rather incidentally the third Canon declared 'however [*mentoi*], the Bishop of Constantinople has the primacy of honour after the Bishop of Rome, because Constantinople is new Rome'. For Theodosius and his advisers, this arrangement seemed impeccable. The capital of the empire was now Constantine's city and it naturally acquired the religious and secular prerogatives of the former capital. Rome was one, and the only difference between Old and New Rome was a difference of precedence; but New Rome was superior to all other sees. For Alexandria, however, as for Rome itself, this was a gross affront. It undermined the authority of the Council of Nicaea, for at that time Constantinople, i.e. Byzantium, was a bishopric under the jurisdiction of the metropolitan of Thrace, and it had no claim to apostolic foundation. To wipe out the effect of this decision became the main objective of the bishops of Alexandria for the next seventy years. In this aim they were seconded by the Popes of Rome.

Inevitably in Greek-speaking eastern Christendom, the issue would be fought out largely within the framework of metaphysical debate. Acceptance of the credal statements of Nicaea did not end doctrinal differences among the major eastern sees, and Alexandria, Antioch and Constantinople represented different standpoints. If Christ was acknowledged as 'of one substance with the Father' and therefore divine, how was he also to be 'of one substance with man', and capable of sharing human experiences in order to redeem man? While Athanasius had been battling with his opponents over Trinitarian orthodoxy, this issue had fallen into the background. At the Council of Alexandria in AD 362, however, it had been raised by rival delegations from Antioch. Athanasius again rose to the occasion. He condemned those who believed that the Divine Word had been present in Christ in the same manner as it had in the prophets (i.e. as Paul of Samosata was believed to have taught), but he did not show how Christ as redeemer was also consubstantial with man, contenting himself with a bare assertion of His 'full humanity'. His great prestige preserved him from awkward questions. Within a few years, one of his disciples, Apollinarius, Bishop of Laodicea in Syria (*c.* 310–90), attempted to answer these for him. Apollinarius maintained that the rational soul, or the governing element in each human being, had been replaced in Christ by the divine Word. There was no distinction in Scripture he argued, between the Word and his flesh (compare John 1:14). Christ was one nature (*physis*), one individuality (*hypostasis*) and one person (*prosopon*) at once wholly God and wholly man. The phrase, 'the one incarnate nature of the Word', evolved by Apollinarius in the 370s, was to become the watchword of the Alexandrian bishops of the fifth century and thence of the Monophysite Christians in the Nile Valley and Ethiopia.

The shift of the theological debate from Trinitarian to Christological issues confronted Athanasius's successors with the same problem of reconciling the broad masses of Egyptian Christians with their own sophisticated reasoning as had confronted Athanasius himself. Theophilus (AD 398–412) and Cyril (412–44) were able to surmount these crises largely because they could refer doubters to the prestige and success of Athanasius. In addition, the great majority of Egyptian Christians identified themselves with the see of Alexandria and were prepared to give articulate support to its leaders. The ambitions of these now extended to vindicating their superiority over Constantinople and Antioch and to asserting a position approaching equality with Rome.

In Egypt itself the key factor was the attitude of the monks, who could provide the massive and terrifying popular support to the Alexandrian bishops which made their cause well-nigh invincible in the first half of the fifth century. By AD 400 monasticism had exploded into a vast popular movement. Writing from Palestine, Jerome affirmed that nearly 50,000 Pachomian monks attended the annual assembly of their order at Tabennissi. At Oxyrhynchus, the whole town, according to Rufinus (*c.* 390), who visited the area, had been taken over by the monks. There were he said some 10,000 around the city. Many Pachomian monasteries had become self-sufficient economic units. Palladius's description of Panopolis enumerates the trades to be found among 300 monks there. There were fifteen tailors, seven smiths, four carpenters, fifteen fullers, twelve camel-drivers, 'and every type of craft, and with their surplus output they provide for the needs of the women's convent and the prisons'.[1] The monasteries were by now vast welfare centres affording protection against the storms of economic calamity and the perils of barbarian raiders from the desert. Their inhabitants, because of the aura of sanctity that attached to their vocation, were effectively beyond the reach of the tax-collector and even the law.

How had this situation arisen? Documentary evidence from papyri

[1] Palladius, *Historia Lausiaca*, XXXII.9 (ed. by C. Butler, Cambridge, 1898). For monks engaged in milling and irrigation at Shenute's White Monastery in the fifth century, see Besa, *Life of Shenute*, chs. 17 and 24 (ed. by H. Wiesman, *Corpus Scriptorum Christianorum Orientalum*, Scriptores Coptici, II.4, Paris, 1931).

for economic conditions in rural Egypt is relatively abundant. It shows a relentless decline in the position of the rural proprietor, who had provided an age-long stability to Egyptian society in face of economic pressure and external threats. In the reign of Constantine, peasant proprietors were still very numerous and the bulk of the soil of Egypt was held by them. At Hermopolis, south of Oxyrhynchus, it seems that only about one-sixth of the total of 400,000 *arourae* (an *aroura* was about $\frac{1}{3}$ hectare) in the city territory was held by urban landowners and the remainder by villagers.[1] At Theadelphia in AD 332, the total taxable area of the village was 500 *arourae*, and of these only two holdings of 30 *arourae* each were held by urban landowners. The remainder was held by 23 villagers whose holdings were even less extensive.[2] On this reckoning even Antony's holding of 300 *arourae* must be accounted very considerable. Throughout the century there was a steady shift towards larger units as more and more of the former public land was assigned to those who were prepared to farm it. With the emergence of a class of larger landowners went the tendency of villagers to put themselves under the protection of these as a safeguard against extortionate tax-gatherers or the oppressive official demands for labour services. Those who were unlucky were faced with the alternatives of flight, ruin or peonage. By the end of the century Egypt had become the classic land of patronage, as an increasing number of villagers chose to become labourers (*coloni*) on some larger estate where an owner would provide them with protection and the means of eking out their existence. Only the more powerful could escape the effects of the periodical assessments (*indictiones*). The law of 415, *De Patrociniis vicorum*, shows how high officials and officers were joining in the racket.[3] Orders that the 'very name of patronage should become extinct', and that patrons who had acquired clients since 397, the date of the last prohibition, were to stand trial before the Augustal prefect, fell on deaf ears. Even in this apparently complete ban on patronage, the Church of Alexandria was allowed to retain its client villages so long as the villagers paid all their taxes and performed all due services. Thus the growth of monastic settlements, which to all intents and purposes were communities of villagers enjoying some freedom from official exploitation, was to be expected. By

[1] See A. H. M. Jones, 'Census records of the later Roman Empire', *Journal of Roman Studies*, 1963, **43**, 59–60, 63–4.

[2] One of the twelve peasants listed owned $58\frac{3}{4}$ *arourae*, but six had holdings ranging from $12\frac{7}{8}$ to $1\frac{1}{4}$ *arourae*. For the Theadelphia register, see *Papyrus Princeton*, 134, analysed by Jones in 'Census records', 63–4, and in Jones, *The later Roman Empire*, II (Oxford, 1964), 773.

[3] *Codex Theodosianus*, XI, 24.6.

AD 400 or even earlier, rural Egypt had become almost entirely Christian, the pagan population being confined mainly to members of the Hellenized urban aristocracies for whom the monks had little love. The Christian Church formed a vast privileged corporation, powered by the clergy of Alexandria, whose sources of wealth included a stake in sea and river trading enterprises which extended to include the provisioning of Constantinople. From bishop to the humblest Coptic monk, all had an interest in the continued prosperity of the Church of Alexandria, even if the price was unquestioning obedience to its bishop.

The monasteries, however, still needed careful handling. In 401, Theophilus of Alexandria found himself embroiled with John Chrysostom, Bishop of Constantinople, because some monks of Nitria in the desert south-west of Alexandria had laid a complaint against him at the capital. Theophilus eventually manoeuvred himself into the position of accuser and, cheered on by Egyptian sailors in the port of Constantinople, he humiliated John at the Synod of the Oak in 403. The incident showed, however, that the support of the monks must be won and not assumed.

The first clash between Alexandria and Constantinople resulted in John Chrysostom's exile in AD 404 and his death three years later. Theophilus could not, however, influence the choice of a new bishop of Constantinople. For nearly a quarter of a century an equilibrium was maintained between Alexandria and Constantinople. Then, following a disputed election of a patriarch of Constantinople, the Emperor Theodosius II summoned Nestorius, a presbyter in the Church of Antioch, to the capital, and had him consecrated bishop in April 428. Nestorius was a bad choice. He was headstrong and impulsive, garrulous and limited in his intellectual training, and he represented to an extreme degree the theological tradition opposed to that of Alexandria. Concerning Christ, the Antiochenes tended to emphasize the humanity of the Saviour and to affirm the reality of the human nature existing within Christ alongside the Godhead. To them Christ existed 'in two natures'. Either being ignorant, or not caring about Alexandrian theology, Nestorius began to preach his views uncompromisingly, in particular to reject the term *Theotokos* ('God-bearing') as applied to the Virgin Mary. He said this was inappropriate because what the Virgin bore was the manhood and not the Godhead of Christ. Meantime, in Alexandria Theophilus had been succeeded by his nephew Cyril (412–44), a violent individual if a deep-thinking theologian, who for years had been working out the theology of the unity of the Godhead and humanity of the Incarnate Christ. Christ was indeed 'of two natures', Godhead and manhood, but the Incarnation resulted in the Word being 'made flesh' (John 1:14) in a complete union of essential natures and not, as the Antiochenes asserted, joined to the nature of a human being; hence in Cyril's view the term *Theotokos* was the proper one to apply to Mary, and the formula 'in two natures' was unacceptable.

Cyril was as ruthless and dedicated to the ambitions of his see as his uncle Theophilus had been, and he also realized the need of consolidating Egyptian monastic opinion on his side. The monks doubted the biblical justification for the term *Theotokos*. When early in 429 he found himself set on a collision course with Nestorius, Cyril sent the monks a full and shrewd account of his theological position and, without being able to point to a single scriptural proof text, assured them that Athanasius would have approved. If Christ was merely 'an instrument of God' as Nestorius claimed, how could he overthrow death and ensure their own victory over the demons?[1] The medicine worked. With a mixture of sincere attachment to a theological position, energy, guile and aggression, Cyril was able to obtain the summons by the emperor of a Council at Ephesus in June 431, at which he was in the position to act both as papal plenipotentiary and accuser and judge of Nestorius. By the evening of 22 June, the latter had been deposed as 'the new Judas', and the crowds in Ephesus were dancing their acclaim of Cyril and his vindication of Mary as *Theotokos*.

Alexandria had triumphed once more over Constantinople. Cyril was now 'archbishop' and 'patriarch', but his triumph was not complete. In the later stages of his controversy with Nestorius, he had required the latter to assent to twelve propositions, which came to be known as the Twelve Anathemas. These Anathemas revealed that Cyril came near to accepting the Christological theses of Apollinarius, by insisting on a union of essence (a *hypostatic* union) between the Word and the manhood of Christ, and so confusing the body of Christ and the Divine Word that dwelt in it. These Anathemas were not accepted by the Council of Ephesus, but they remained in the forefront of popular Egyptian Christology. In 433 Cyril was obliged by the emperor to make his peace with the Antiochenes, and in the Formula of Reunion to accept an affirmation of the 'two natures' of Christ without seeking to define their relationship further.

Under Cyril, the see of Alexandria reached the height of its power. It was enormously wealthy; even after dispensing massive bribes to

[1] Cyril, *Ep.* 1 (*PG* 77, col. 36).

members of the imperial Court, Cyril still bequeathed a private fortune amounting to 635 kgs of gold; he had complete authority over the bishops throughout a great area extending from Cyrenaica to the First Cataract; and the monks were his loyal supporters. Above all, Alexandria appeared to have the alliance of the Roman see, though sooner or later the clash between their respective claims in ecclesiastical jurisdiction and theology would have put a heavy strain on their relations. By failing to leave well alone, Cyril's successor, Dioscorus (444–51), wrecked this achievement and forced Alexandria into an ecclesiastical and theological isolation whence it was never entirely to emerge.

Dioscorus aimed at asserting the full range of Cyril's theology as the orthodoxy of Christendom against the Antiochenes, and at humbling for all time his rival at Constantinople. In carrying out these aims he had considerable advantages. Popular Christianity in the East instinctively accepted Cyril's theology, and the Emperor Theodosius II, profiting from his experiences with Nestorius, had put his authority behind it. Dioscorus also had the support of a considerable body of monastic opinion in Syria and in the capital, whose chief representative, the archimandrite Eutyches, presided over a monastery of 300 monks. On the other hand, his opponents, Domnus, Patriarch of Antioch, and Flavian, the patriarch of the capital, were weak men whose personal situations were insecure. Leo at Rome was powerful, but distant from the scene of action.

Once again Alexandria appeared to triumph, when Flavian had Eutyches deposed by a Council in Constantinople (November AD 448). Eutyches, supported by the court, appealed to the major sees of Christendom and, in March 449, the emperor summoned a judicial assembly of about 130 bishops to meet at Ephesus in August under Dioscorus's presidency. There, amid scenes of violence and disorder, Flavian, Domnus and their supporters were deposed and Eutyches restored to office. The theology of Cyril, stated uncompromisingly in the Twelve Anathemas, became the creed of Christendom. Christ must be acknowledged as One Incarnate Nature. A long papal statement, written to Flavian in June 449, known as the *Tome* of Leo, which affirmed the two natures of Christ, was ignored. Alexandria was hailed as 'city of the orthodox' and Dioscorus as 'oecumenical patriarch'. For a brief moment the leadership of Christendom was in his hands.

Until Theodosius II died on 28 July 450, as the result of a hunting accident, Dioscorus was supreme. There were, however, three serious weaknesses in his position. First, it relied heavily on the favour of the

Byzantine court, and Theodosius II was replaced by the pro-western Marcian (450–7), who married the Augusta, Pulcheria, who had been consistently hostile to Dioscorus. Secondly, he had mortally offended Pope Leo, and thus at a stroke he destroyed the long-standing alliance between Rome and Alexandria. Thirdly, if he was a faithful representative of Cyril's theology, he had a profound dislike for Cyril's relatives. His treatment of one of these aroused deep hostility in Alexandria, and denied him much-needed support when he faced his opponents at the Council of Chalcedon in October 451.

Marcian and Pulcheria had at once set about undoing Dioscorus's work. A new general Council, with the object of confirming the faith, was summoned to meet at Chalcedon on the Bosphorus opposite Constantinople in October 451. Over 500 bishops participated. Dioscorus was cornered. He was deposed from his bishopric, not indeed as a heretic, but because of his defiance of Pope Leo and his misdeeds towards some of his clergy. Eutyches was also condemned again, and the faith of Christendom defined in a manner acceptable to the papal legates, that Christ was to be acknowledged 'in two natures inseparably united', each sharing the characteristics of the other. 'Cyril and Leo taught alike', cried the assembled bishops in their joy at the downfall of 'Pharaoh'. The story of the relations between the major centres of Christianity in the Mediterranean in the next two centuries would demonstrate that they did not.

Alexandria had been humbled. It is often believed that its stubborn adherence to the One-nature or 'Monophysite' Christology from then on was the reflection of Egyptian nationalist sentiment directed against the ecclesiastical and civil domination of Constantinople. This is only partly true. More than any other province, Egypt had developed a sense of unity. The vast majority of its people, apart from the inhabitants of Alexandria itself, depended on the Nile. The Coptic language, also, gave the Egyptian Christian a strong sense of self-identity, which was reflected in the attitude of some of the monks towards outsiders. Even so, there was little trace of national pride among the Christians at this time. If such pride existed, it was expressed by Greek-speaking pagans, people such as Horappolon (*c.* 480), who researched learnedly into the Egyptian past and perhaps into the meaning of the hieroglyphs. Many Egyptian Christians wanted to do nothing better than forget their heritage, even to the point of changing their names from Egyptian ones to those derived from Old Testament prophets. A frequent contrast among monks and holy men was between 'Egyptians' (i.e. worldly minded and idolatrous-hearted individuals) and 'those from Jerusalem' – the true Christians.[1]

The monks contributed most towards providing the Coptic Christian peasant with a self-conscious sense of identity during the fifth century. There was always tension between them and the remnants of the old Hellenized pagan aristocracy. Throughout the first half of the fifth century AD, the monks were led by a remarkable man who possessed something of the charisma of a prophet but combined with practical hard-headedness. This was Shenute, abbot of the great Pachomian White Monastery at Atripe, with over 2,000 monks and 1,800 nuns, from *c.* 385 to his death in 451. A Copt, impatient of the shortcomings of his fellow monks and laymen, he none the less reserved the venom of his highly coloured sermons for the Greek-speaking local aristocracy in the neighbouring town of Panopolis. In his *Life*, attributed to his disciple Besa, he is recorded as on one occasion having the holdings of landowners on an island in the Nile sunk beneath the waters on the grounds that they were charging their tenants extortionate rents. Fanatically loyal to the cause of Cyril against Nestorius and his allies, Shenute's eloquence and concern for the downtrodden and needy fired the imagination of the Copts. His monasticism gave them a new status, a place in Christian society and an assurance of personal salvation. He stands in the succession of Antony and Pachomius, and was responsible more than any other figure for uniting Cyril's theology with a popular movement among the Coptic peasantry which it was always to retain. It was not a movement, however, directed against 'the God-loving emperors' at Constantinople. Until all hope had vanished that the empire would accept the Alexandrian theology as the norm of orthodoxy, the Copt was loyal to the Byzantine state.

The news of Dioscorus's downfall in 451 and of the acceptance of the Definition of Chalcedon was received with angry shock in Alexandria. There were riots, and only the rapid despatch of troops from Constantinople restored the situation. However, the Church was divided. At Chalcedon itself, four out of the seventeen Egyptian bishops who had accompanied Dioscorus had acquiesced in their master's deposition and signed the Definition. Before returning, they had consecrated Proterius, Dioscorus's trusted presbyter, as patriarch. Proterius eventually won the support of fifteen bishops, a section of the Pachomian

1 Thus Zacharias Scholasticus's description of the Egyptian monk, Isaiah, 'cum corpore Aegyptius et animae autem nobilitate Hierosolymitanus'; 'Vitae virorum apud Monophysitarum celeberrimorun', ed. and trans. by E. W. Brooks, *Corp. Script. Christ. Orient.*, Scriptores Syri, III.25 (Paris, 1907). Compare Palladius, *Hist. Lausiaca*, XXI (Butler edn p. 66).

monks, and influential minorities in some of the Egyptian towns, including Oxyrhynchus. However, the majority of the monks and the Alexandrian populace were against him. Even Dioscorus's death in exile at Gangra in September 454 made little difference to his position. In August 455, the Emperor Marcian himself wrote to the Prefect of Egypt complaining that Alexandria and Egypt alike were a prey to the heresies of Eutyches and Apollinarius.

The revolution was not long delayed. Marcian died on 26 January AD 457. By mid February this was known in Alexandria. At once a committee of dissident monks was formed. On 16 March, one of Cyril's presbyters, Timothy 'the Cat', who had been removed from office by Proterius, was consecrated bishop. While the new emperor, Leo I, wavered, the mob acted. On Maundy Thursday, 18 March, Proterius was lynched. The immediate upshot was a schism within the Egyptian Church, for the Proterian succession was maintained through another Timothy, 'Wobble-cap', but no attempt was made by Timothy the Cat to form a Church out of communion with the Church in Constantinople The horror caused by the events in Alexandria, however, made his recognition as legitimate Patriarch impossible. Following a 'plebiscite' of the entire eastern episcopate in 458, Leo decreed that Timothy was unworthy of his office and ordered him into exile, where he was destined to remain, first at Gangra, then in the Crimean town of Cherson, until a new round of events in Constantinople provided him with a chance to assert his claims once more.

These events were the death of Leo in January 474, after a reign of seventeen years, and, after the brief reign of Leo II, the accession of the Isaurian warrior-chief Zeno (November 474). This was followed, however, by the latter's expulsion as the result of a revolution in favour of the dowager-empress's brother, Basiliscus (9 January 475). Basiliscus committed himself strongly to the Alexandrian cause. Timothy the Cat was recalled from exile. Timothy represented the first generation of Egyptian Monophysitism. His aim was to secure the emperor's rejection of Chalcedon and the restoration of the *status quo ante* the death of Theodosius II. He was prepared to condemn Eutyches along with Pope Leo's *Tome* and the Council of Chalcedon. Basiliscus was ready to accept most of this; an imperial encyclical of August 475 informed all bishops under his jurisdiction that the faith consisted of the creed of Nicaea confirmed by the doctrine of the Council of Constantinople (381) and both Councils of Ephesus (431 and 449), and that the *Tome* of Leo and the 'innovations' of Chalcedon were to be rejected. The Alexandrian triumph was checked by Acacius, Patriarch of Constantinople, who saw through Timothy's ambitions and the danger they presented to his own see. In August 476, however, Zeno was restored by a counter-revolution, and Timothy was again under threat of exile when he died in July 477.

Alexandria had shown that its chosen leader was a power to be reckoned with. Zeno and Acacius accepted the inevitable and on 28 July 482, in a letter addressed to Timothy's successor, Peter Mongus (477–90), and to 'the bishops, monks and laymen of Alexandria, Egypt and Cyrenaica', set out the terms of a compromise. The letter, known to history as the *Henotikon* ('Edict of Unity'), went as near as possible to meet the Alexandrian requirements without actually denouncing the Council of Chalcedon. Orthodoxy was affirmed as the creed of Nicaea, confirmed at Constantinople and Ephesus I, but Cyril's Twelve Anathemas were accepted as canonical. Christ, affirmed to be consubstantial with both God and man, 'incarnate from the Holy Spirit and Mary the Virgin *Theotokos*, was one and not two'. Nestorius and Eutyches were condemned. The emperor invited all churches to reunite in agreement. The *Henotikon* was a masterpiece of drafting, allowing each side to accept just as much as it wanted from the text, and it had partial success. Peter Mongus was under constant pressure from a formidable body of dissident monks to accept nothing less than the denunciation of both the *Tome* and Chalcedon. To retain his position he was obliged to do this, but he was none the less able to maintain communion with Constantinople. No successor was appointed to continue the Chalcedonian line of bishops in Alexandria. In the capital, however, Acacius found himself embroiled with the papacy, who regarded the restoration of communion with Peter Mongus as outrageous. In 484 Acacius was excommunicated by Pope Felix III, and the Acacian schism dividing Rome from Constantinople and the other eastern patriarchates lasted for the next thirty-five years.

In this period, covered by the reigns of Zeno (died AD 491) and Anastasius (491–518), the Egyptians were not unduly perturbed by the schism with Rome. They remained in communion with Constantinople on their own terms. The Chalcedonian Church shrank almost to nothing. Peter Mongus died in 490 and his successors, Athanasius II and John I and II, left little mark on history, for little happened to threaten their security. By this time power in the countryside was shared between the great landowners and the monasteries. The authorities had lost their battle over patronage. Huge estates had been amassed.

The municipal administration had been replaced by the more local and less powerful pagarchies. Members of the family of Flavius Apion, who was the Emperor Anastasius's quartermaster-general in the Persian campaign of 502–5, owned about two-fifths of the acreage of the combined city territories of Oxyrhynchus and Cynopolis (112,000 out of 280,000 *arourae*), and they were not the only great landowners who had replaced the peasant proprietors and urban landowners of former days. An army of agents, hierarchically graded like members of an official bureaucracy, farmed their estates. They maintained their own police and postal service and a private army of retainers (*bucellarii*). Their cultivators paid their rents and worked in gangs under foremen; all resemblance of personal freedom had been lost.

Some of the larger monasteries organized themselves in the same way. They also acted as agricultural corporations, had their *coloni* and retainers, and they found patrons valuable. One such was the Count John, who seems to have looked after the interests of the Pachomian monastery of Stratonikis. These houses often possessed very large properties. The vast estates of Shenute's White Monastery may have been exceptional, but many had become corporations owning villages whose inhabitants leased from the monastery their equipment for ploughing and for irrigating vineyards, and whose work was supervised by monastic officials. In the Delta, the Metanoia monastery, which seems to have been the Mother-house of the Pachomians in northern Egypt, had its own fleet of boats administered by monastic stewards. We hear of these receiving a grant of grain from the revenues of the village of Aphrodite, perhaps a benefaction from the Emperor Zeno. In Egypt, the era of Zeno and Anastasius seems to have been something of a golden age for the great landowner whether lay or monastic. For the latter, wealth accumulated at an enormous rate through benefactions. Money was left to them for 'the redemption of captives' or simply for the good of the soul. In addition, centres of pilgrimage such as the shrine of St Menas near Alexandria, also endowed by Zeno, became a sort of Lourdes of the Byzantine world. Water from its holy spring was exported in special pilgrim flasks stamped with the saint's name. Little wonder that in 505 the newly elected Patriarch John II of Nikiou could offer the emperor Anastasius 900 kgs of gold in return for his complete rejection of the Council of Chalcedon. The offer was refused, but, for all its imperfections, the *Henotikon* of Zeno had brought religious peace to the Byzantine empire and particularly to Egypt.

In these years, Egyptian Monophysitism became a missionary movement, concentrating on the trade-routes leading from Alexandria down the Red Sea towards the Horn of Africa. About AD 502 missionaries known as the Nine Saints arrived in Ethiopia, whose Church already had close links with Alexandria. To judge from their names, they included Syrians as well as Egyptians. They set about restoring and extending monastic Christianity of the coenobitic Pachomian type, establishing the great monastery of Debre Damo on a hill overlooking the capital, Aksum. A start, if no more, was made at translating the Scriptures into Ge'ez, the language of northern Ethiopia. These missionaries gave a great impetus to the spread of Christianity though the Ethiopian highlands, and also to its zealous acceptance by the reigning house. In 523–4, the King of Ethiopia took an army across the Red Sea into the kingdom of the Himyarites to avenge the persecution of the Christians there.

By the end of the reign of Anastasius, the Monophysite tradition interpreted by Dioscorus's successors had become part of the Egyptian heritage, to be guarded jealously against all outside interference. An instance of this occurred in 516, when the Patriarch John II died and Peter Mongus's nephew, Dioscorus II, was consecrated in his place. Rightly or wrongly, the populace of Alexandria suspected the hand of the imperial officials in this election, and though Dioscorus had an impeccable Monophysite background and the Emperor Anastasius favoured the same outlook, there was strong opposition. In the ensuing riot in Alexandria, the Augustal Prefect of Egypt, Theodosius, was set upon and killed 'because', as the chronicler Theophanes said, 'he praised the emperor'.[1] The Alexandrians thought there was no city like their own, and their chauvinism, allied with the unbreakable loyalty of the Copts to the symbol of Cyril and its representatives, had combined to convert Monophysitism into a national creed. The aim of its leaders, however, remained that it should become accepted as the religion of Constantinople and the empire as a whole.

This hope was shattered in the religious revolution that followed the death of Anastasius in July 518. The new ruler, Justin I (518–27), was a native of one of the few remaining Latin-speaking provinces of the empire and a westerner in outlook. From the start of his reign he saw his duty as the restoration of communion between Constantinople and Rome, and he was willing to pay a high price for this. A clean sweep was made of the Monophysite leaders who in the latter years of Anastasius's

[1] Theophanes, *Chronicon*, A. M. 6009 (ed. by J. Claasen, Bonn, 1839–41, I, 251).

reign had come to occupy key positions in the eastern episcopate. Some, like Severus, Patriarch of Antioch, and his colleague and, later, adversary, Julian of Halicarnassus in the province of Caria in Asia Minor, found refuge in Alexandria. There they found also that 'all Egypt was ready to do battle for the Monophysite belief',[1] and Justin was wise enough not to put that resolve to the test.

Justin was succeeded on 1 August 527 by his nephew, Justinian, who had been at his elbow as unofficial co-adjutor for the previous seven years. His basic aim was to reunite the empire as it had been in the days of Constantine and Theodosius. This involved the overthrow of the Germanic kingdoms in Italy, Africa and even Spain, and a strict alliance with the Pope. How these aims could be reconciled with the need to maintain the loyalty of the Syrian and Egyptian Monophysites was to be the test of Justinian's statesmanship. He failed because it was an aim impossible to fulfil.

At Alexandria, Dioscorus II had died in October 517. His successor, Timothy III (517–35), was left undisturbed by both Justin and Justinian. His rule, however, was not uneventful, and witnessed the emergence of two separate issues which were to leave their mark on Byzantine Christianity in Africa. Both arose from the fact that with the presence there of Severus as an exile, Alexandria became the centre of a standing Monophysite council which the ex-patriarch of Antioch formed in his effort to keep contact with his vast diocese. The main administrative problem confronting him was the diminishing number of clergy faithful to his cause. By 530 the persecution initiated by Justin after the formal ending of the Acacian Schism in 519 had been continuing for a decade, and the Monophysites faced a crisis. With great reluctance Severus and his friends authorized John, Bishop of Tella in eastern Syria, to ordain likely candidates as priests and deacons. As he went from place to place through provinces of the Oriental diocese he found the response overwhelming. It was 'like a river bursting its banks', so great was the flood of ordinands.[2] Within a few months a new priesthood owing nothing to the Chalcedonian hierarchy had come into being. It had taken seventy years after Chalcedon for the foundations of a separate Monophysite Church to be laid, but now that this had been done, it would only be a matter of time before the Churches in Africa under the lead of Alexandria developed their own hierarchies independent of Constantinople.

[1] Severus, *Select letters*, v.II (ed. by E. W. Brooks, London, 1902–4, 328).

[2] Thus John of Ephesus, *Lives of the eastern saints* (ed. by E. W. Brooks, *Patrologia Orientalis* [*PO*], 18, 518).

The second question was doctrinal. The Monophysite doctrine in the hands of Timothy the Cat and Severus was simply a development of Cyril's theology, including the Twelve Anathemas. Christ was consubstantial with the Father as God, and with man, but His humanity was joined to the Deity in one person and one nature. Any suggestion of 'two natures', however united, was condemned. But Severus maintained that through voluntary self-emptying (*Kenosis*), Christ had become completely man, subject to all man's experiences, sin excepted. He had hungered and thirsted for man's sake, and he had also tasted death. On this last point, however, Severus was challenged by his colleague in exile, Julian of Halicarnassus, who maintained that Christ's body could not be corruptible, because if it were, it would have been liable to sin as well. It was useless for mankind to worship that which could be corrupted. The argument spread beyond the scope of exchanging increasingly angry letters and treatises. The latent pro-Eutychist wing of the Egyptian monks saw Julian's doctrine as the answer to their difficulties. Very soon Julianist missionaries were taking his teaching to wherever Monophysitism was strong, particularly to Armenia and Ethiopia.

Timothy's death in February AD 535 provided what proved to be the last chance for the Monophysites to follow their previous policy and make their creed that of the empire. First, however, in Alexandria there were scenes that recalled the riots that accompanied Dioscorus II's election in 516. The Empress Theodora, strongly Monophysite in her leanings, secured the consecration of the deacon Theodosius with the support of the senior imperial officials in Egypt. The popular reaction was immediate. An opposition candidate, the archdeacon Gaianus, who was a strong supporter of Julianism, was consecrated as a rival bishop. Apart from the monks, support came from 'some of the clergy, the landowners of the city, the guilds, the soldiers, the nobles and the whole province', we are told by a contemporary but North African historian, Liberatus of Carthage.[1] Once again, a cross-section of Egyptian society had supported the candidate to the patriarchate who was not the government's choice. Once again, force had to be used to oust the dissident (May 535).

Theodosius, however, survived his inauspicious start and was destined at the end of thirty years' rule to be one of the most influential figures in Monophysitism. Within a few months of the removal of his rival a strange situation had arisen in the capital. The Patriarch Anthimus

[1] *Breviarum causae Nestorianorum et Eutychianorum*, xx, in *PL*, **68**, col. 1037a.

(535–6) had come to the conclusion that the One Nature Christology was truer than the Chalcedonian Definition, and had entered into communion with Severus and Theodosius. For a short time early in 536, Constantinople had a pro-Monophysite patriarch and communion had been restored with Alexandria on this basis.

Theodora's effort, however, to turn the empire Monophysite failed. The empire was committed to a western-oriented policy which had been emphasized by the conquest of Vandal Africa and the occupation of Sicily and Dalmatia. This time Justinian determined to establish Chalcedon once more in Egypt. As usual his policy was well considered and his timing was impeccable. The choice also of Paul, the *Hegemon* (abbot) of the Pachomian monastery of Canopus, who happened to be in the capital in connection with a law suit, was a shrewd one, for Canopus had been the centre of Egyptian opposition to Dioscorus. After an interval of more than fifty years the Chalcedonian cause was to be rekindled from there. In the autumn of 537 Paul was consecrated with as much show as possible. The ceremony, however, was performed not in Alexandria, but in Constantinople by the Patriarch Menas (who had displaced Anthimus), with the Roman legate, Pelagius, and representatives of the churches of Antioch and Jerusalem present. The Patriarch Theodosius, meantime, had been summoned to the capital and interned. Paul was given military authority to enforce Chalcedon on the Egyptians. The effect of these actions was to split Christianity in Egypt into two camps, each ultimately organized under its own hierarchy, but from the start the Chalcedonians looked to Constantinople. Though they gradually extended their hold among the official classes and Greeks, and were strong throughout Cyrenaica and in large centres such as Arsinoe and Rhinoclura on the Palestinian frontier, they never gained a real foothold in the Nile Valley. The vast majority of the monasteries remained loyal to the Monophysite tradition. The difference between the two communities was accentuated by the fact that, after Paul, the Chalcedonian patriarchs were invariably foreigners, which emphasized, as nothing had previously, the official character of the Chalcedonian Church. By the beginning of the seventh century, the Coptic or Monophysite patriarch was being contrasted with the Greek or Chalcedonian patriarch. A Coptic-Monophysite national Church had become a fact.

THE CONSOLIDATION OF THE COPTIC CHURCH IN EGYPT AND NORTH-EAST AFRICA

Justinian's imposition of a Chalcedonian patriarch in Alexandria was followed closely, perhaps in AD 539, by far-reaching administrative reforms. The position of *praefectus Augustalis* as chief civil official in the whole diocese of Egypt was abolished. In his place were five provincial heads of government, independent of each other, but combining military and civil responsibilities. All these had the title of *Dux*, and two of them, namely the governors of Alexandria and the Thebaid, carried that of *Augustalis* in addition. The concentration of power in the hands of a very few individuals had some effect on the history of Christianity in the Nile Valley. In 542 Theodora had only to secure the aid of the *Dux Thebaidis* to ensure the success of her Monophysite-oriented mission to the Nubians, and in 631 Heraclius placed Egypt under the supreme command of the Patriarch Cyrus by combining the office of patriarch with that of *Augustalis*.

In 540 Paul was implicated in a charge of murder and deposed, his place being taken as Chalcedonian patriarch by a Palestinian monk named Zoilus, who was the choice of the powerful Patriarch of Antioch, Ephraim. The Monophysite cause, however, was about to win a major success which contributed to its permanent survival in Africa. South of the Egyptian frontier the three Nubian kingdoms, successors to the Meroitic empire, Nobatia, Makuria and ʻAlwa extended down the Nile Valley beyond Khartoum and perhaps as far as Ethiopia. Though Christianity had made some headway among the poor of the capital of the Nobatian kingdom, Faras (Pachoras), in the fifth century, and in scattered areas elsewhere (see chapter 9), the majority of the Nubians were pagan. Since 451 they had been permitted by treaty to celebrate the annual feast of Isis on the island of Philae on their frontier with the empire. In 539 Justinian abrogated this agreement and sent his general, Narses, to close the temple. The Nubians may not have been resisted strongly, for not long after (the exact date is obscure) we find the Nubian King Silko supported by Narses in a victorious campaign against the Blemmyes on the east bank of the Nile. Silko ascribed his victory to 'god' while obliging the Blemmyes to swear by their 'idols' to keep the peace.[1] It looks as though Silko had strong leanings towards Christianity, and when in 542 a Christian mission under the presbyter

[1] For Silko, *Corpus Inscriptionum Graecarum* [*CIG*], III.5072. See J. B. Bury, *History of the later Roman Empire*, II (London, 1923), 330.

Julian arrived at Faras the ground had been prepared. This was a Monophysite mission sponsored by the Empress Theodora, who cleverly anticipated a rival party sent by her husband. So thoroughly did Julian preach Monophysitism that when Justinian's mission eventually arrived, its leader was told that, while the emperor's gifts and alliance were welcome, his 'wicked religion' was not.[1] Thus Monophysitism became the religion of Nobatia. In 580 the southern kingdom of 'Alwa was converted by Bishop Longinus, who had been consecrated by the exiled Monophysite patriarch, Theodosius. Sometime before 700, when it was united with Nobatia, Makuria, which had become Chalcedonian between 566 and 570, also turned to Monophysitism. Theodora's initiative had ensured that her faith became the faith of the Nile Valley from Alexandria to Aksum, and it remained so for the next 800 years.

The death of Justinian in 565, however, found two churches firmly ensconced in Egypt. The Chalcedonians were ably led by the Patriarch Apollinaris (551–70), who managed to knit together much of the support that had once been given to Proterius. Outwardly Alexandria looked like a Chalcedonian city. The great churches in the Greek parts of the city were in Chalcedonian hands, while the Coptic-Monophysite centres were in or near the traditional Egyptian suburb of Rakotis. The Chalcedonians included the rich men of the province both in Egypt and Cyrenaica, some Pachomian monks, and scattered communities in the Delta, some of whom remained faithful to Chalcedon until long after the Arab conquest. It was a cohesive and wealthy Greek-speaking Church destined to share the fortunes of the Byzantines in Egypt. At this stage, its Monophysite rival was at a low ebb. Its leadership was reduced to a dispirited group of four or five bishops, of whom the long-lived Theodore of Philae, bishop from 524–77, was the only man of stature. They were divided among themselves between Severans or Theodosians, Julianists, and the descendants of dissenters of earlier periods, and for a decade they were to bicker over the election of a new patriarch. With the possible exception of Pisentios, Bishop of Coptos, *c.* 600, they produced no intellectual figures or theologians. Their strength lay almost exclusively in the silent support of the monasteries and the mass of Coptic peasants.

Egypt had become a land of monasteries. Apart from great monastic estates, there were smaller private foundations and the cells of hermits. Altogether, these were very numerous. In the Wadi Habib they are

[1] John of Ephesus, *Hist. Eccl.*, IV.6–7 (ed. by E. W. Brooks, *Corp. Script. Christ. Orient.*, Scriptores Syri, Louvain, 1935–6).

described as 'growing up like the plants of the field'. Near Alexandria there were said to be 'six hundred flourishing monasteries all inhabited by the orthodox' (i.e. Monophysites), administered by the Coptic patriarch.[1] These houses owned their own lands, which were farmed by peasants who also accepted Monophysitism and who were paid in kind for their services. As we have noted, they were regularly enriched by frequent gifts. Monks and clergy alike were men of the people, the clergy ordained mainly to perform the liturgy, and in many ordinary ways acting as local leaders.

The Egyptians suffered to a full extent the disasters that followed the overthrow of the Emperor Maurice in AD 602. Within a few years Alexandria and the Delta were the scene of violent civil war between the partisans of Maurice's supplanter, Phocas, and his rival, Heraclius. For a few years popular hopes were fixed on John the Almsgiver, the remarkable Chalcedonian Patriarch whom Heraclius appointed in 611. John was the son of a former governor of Cyprus, and had been a layman before his sudden translation to a position of ecclesiastical power in Alexandria. He worked with zeal for the Chalcedonian cause, but in his eight years of rule he established a well-deserved reputation for shrewd but open-handed charity. Homes for the poor, hospitals and charitable institutions were established through Church funds, and a vast sum of 100,000 solidi and craftsmen were sent to Jerusalem in 617 to rebuild the city devastated by the Persians and Jews. It was little wonder that John came to be accepted as a saint by Chalcedonian and Monophysite alike.

Two years later, in 619, the Persians invaded Egypt in force. Byzantine resistance collapsed surprisingly; and the invaders captured Alexandria in 620 and occupied the whole country from Cyrenaica to the Nubian frontier. The reaction of the Copts is instructive. The Persians were treated as enemies and received no support. Far down the Nile Valley at Coptos, Bishop Pisentios fled at their approach. 'Because of our sins', he lamented, 'God has delivered us to the nations without mercy.' Even so, there was no popular rising against the conqueror, only a fatalistic acceptance of events. The way was being prepared for the popular attitude towards the Arabs twenty years later.

Heraclius's victory over the Persians, culminating in the recapture of Jerusalem and the restoration of the True Cross in 630, was followed by the final and, as it proved, disastrous attempt to restore unity between the Monophysites and Chalcedonians. The 'Monergist' compromise

[1] *History of the patriarchs*, 1, ch. 14 (ed. by B. T. Evetts, *PO*, 1, 473).

worked out by Heraclius with his advisers, the Patriarch of Constantinople, Sergius, and Cyrus, Metropolitan of Lazica, a Black Sea principality, had much to be said for it. The attribution of one impulse of action (*energeia*) in the incarnate Christ represented a real effort to think beyond the terms of Chalcedonian orthodoxy. Indeed, the Alexandrians themselves were quick to grasp that 'one energy' must be equated to 'one nature', and hence Chalcedon had been renounced in all but name.

Unfortunately, the name proved to be the sticking-point. The man selected by Heraclius to try to persuade the Egyptians to accept the compromise did not possess a personality suitable for his task. This was Cyrus, appointed in 631 to the dual offices of patriarch and civil governor, a reminder, if one were needed, that Byzantine rule involved the integration of Church and state. Cyrus was a man of great energy and courage, but he was harsh and merciless to his opponents. Moreover he was a foreigner, a 'Caucasian', in the eyes of the Copts the supplanter of their own patriarch, Benjamin. They were right not to trust him, for Cyrus's correspondence shows that he was ready also to proclaim the orthodoxy of the *Tome* of Leo. After some initial success, he failed to convince the great majority of the monks that acceptance of Monergism was possible without the emperor denouncing Chalcedon.

When persuasion failed, Cyrus turned to force. In the six years 635–41, whatever loyalty had survived towards Heraclius in Egypt ebbed away. A 'sullen gloom', as A. J. Butler described it, settled on the land.[1] When eventually the Arabs attacked, in December 639, there was utter confusion. Some Egyptians fought for their lives and possessions against the invaders; others stood aside or harrassed the Byzantine forces. In the cities, the circus factions flew at each other's throats. There was strife between Monophysite and Chalcedonian. Only Cyrus's capitulation at Alexandria in September 641 ended the chaos. The Arabs were accepted and some highly placed Egyptians even aided the Arab invasion of Cyrenaica in the following year.

By this time Egypt was in many ways ceasing to belong to the Byzantine world. Coptic art, strongly independent in its choice and treatment of motifs, whether pagan or Christian, had developed alongside the surviving Graeco-Egyptian tradition. Egyptian place names were reverting from Greek to Coptic. In Alexandria itself Coptic was increasingly heard. Egypt was becoming more and more part of an Oriental and African world. The success of the Arabs set the seal on the new direction of her history.

[1] A. J. Butler, *The Arab conquest of Egypt* (Oxford, 1902), 191.

The Muslim conquest had found the Church in the patriarchate in Alexandria a strong body, steeled by misfortune and united under the Coptic Patriarch Benjamin. For a generation all went well. No tears were shed for the Byzantines by seventh-century writers in Egypt. Their defeat had been a just reward for their sins. Thus John, Bishop of Nikiou in the Delta, wrote, *c.* 680, 'the expulsion [of the Romans] and the victory of the Muslims was due to the wickedness of the Emperor Heraclius and the persecution of the orthodox through the Patriarch Cyrus. This was the cause of the ruin of the Roman and the subjugation of Egypt by the Moslem.'[1] By every token, the Coptic Church should have continued to flourish and, as in Norman England, the military caste of the invaders should have been slowly absorbed into the native population to form a new Egyptian nation. That nothing of the sort happened, but that through the eighth and succeeding centuries AD the Coptic Church gradually lost its grip on the population until it was reduced to a small minority in a Muslim population, is a phenomenon which has not yet been adequately explained. (However, see also chapter 8, pp. 545–9.) In the event, only Ethiopia was to preserve the Christian heritage in Africa until modern times.

THE EARLY YEARS OF THE CHURCH IN NORTH-WEST AFRICA

The Church in Roman Africa breaks suddenly on to the stage of history with the trial of twelve Christians before the Proconsul of Africa, Vigellius Saturninus, at Carthage in July AD 180. Before this, practically nothing is known about Christianity there. Unlike Alexandria, Carthage claimed no Apostolic origin. Contact with Christianity in Rome is attested by Tertullian,[2] but similarities of organization, particularly the strongly monarchical episcopate and liturgical practices, point also to influences from Syria. This may perhaps be explained partly by the position of the Jews in North Africa. These have left their traces in synagogues and cemeteries in many North African towns from Carthage to as far west as Volubilis in Morocco, and they seem to have maintained links with their co-religionists in the eastern Mediterranean and beyond. Carthaginian rabbis are cited in the Babylonian Talmud, and alone among the western Jewish communities the Jews at Carthage and Volubilis used Hebrew as well as Greek and Latin on their funerary inscriptions. In the early part of the third century AD Christians in

[1] John of Nikiou, *Chronicle*, ch. 123.4.

[2] *De Praescriptione*, 36.

Carthage were known by the Jews as 'Nazarenes' and not as 'Christians', suggesting that they were regarded as schismatics rather than as adherents of a different religion, and they may have derived some background influences from North African Jewry, e.g. from the Hebrew Bible. As elsewhere in the Mediterranean world, individuals under Jewish influence contributed probably to the Church's early converts, and the Jews of Carthage were among its earliest and fiercest persecutors.[1] Down to the last two decades of the second century, however, Christian influence in North Africa was minimal. The age, as we know from Apuleius, was not irreligious, but the thorough excavation of North African town-sites by French archaeologists since the beginning of the present century has revealed no single identifiable Christian monument datable earlier than the middle of the third century. In this, the contrast with the situation on the eastern frontier of the Roman empire at Dura Europos, where the fine Christian house-church was established by AD 232, is striking. The Christians who were brought before Vigellius Saturninus on 17 July 180 must have seemed a rare if irritating phenomenon.

By good fortune what appears to be a transcript of the brief proceedings against Speratus and his friends has survived.[2] It illustrates the chasm that separated the pagan North Africa, which was approaching the climax of its achievement, from the Christianity that was to supplant it.

Speratus said: 'We have done no wrong, we have never turned our hands to wickedness; we have cursed no one, but return thanks when abused; and therefore we are loyal to our emperor.'
Saturninus the proconsul said: 'We too are religious, and our religion is simple, and we swear by the genius of our lord the emperor, and we make offerings for his safety which you ought to do to.'
. . .
Speratus said: 'I do not recognise the empire of this world; I serve instead the God "whom no man has seen or can see with mortal eyes" [I Tim. 6:16]; I have not committed theft; but if I buy anything I pay the tax on it; for I recognise my lord, the king of kings and emperor of mankind.'

After further argument, the martyrs refused an offer of a thirty-day respite for reflection. They declared themselves Christians and on condemnation to death cried '*Deo Gratias*. Today as martyrs we shall be in heaven.' These few lines tell us much about the spirit of North African

[1] Tertullian, *Apol.* 7.3. 'Tot hostes eius quot extranei et quidem proprie ex aemulatione Iudaei, ex concussione milites, ex natura ipsi etiam domestici nostri.'

[2] Ed. by R. Harris, *Cambridge texts and studies* (Cambridge, 1891) I, ii, 106.

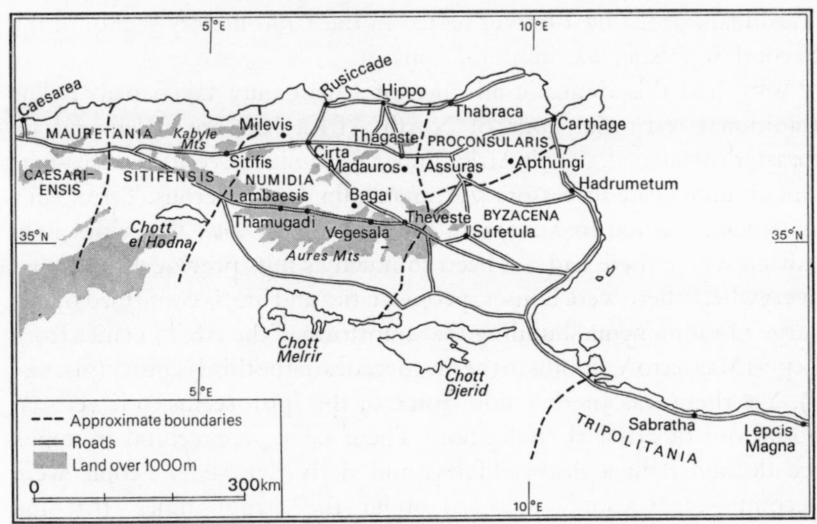

61 North Africa: fourth-century AD provinces and area.

Christianity. The accused reject utterly the proconsul's invitation to swear by the emperor's genius. They refuse any recognition of 'the empire of this world'. They hope instead for immediate reward in heaven as martyrs, and their ideals are inspired by their understanding of the Bible. The 'books and letters of Paul, a just man', they carried with them. There was an African Bible in existence available to wide sectors of the provincial community. The conflict with the Roman government and religious tradition left little room for compromise.

The persecution, however, was not renewed. In the next decade two proconsuls are stated to have protected the Christians, but their situation was precarious, usually depending on the attitude of individual governors or city magistrates. Christians, however, increased considerably in numbers in Carthage and in some other towns in Proconsular Africa (modern Tunisia). In his earliest works, dated to AD 197, the Christian writer Tertullian (*c.* 160–*c.* 240) taunts his pagan adversaries with the ever-growing multitudes of Christians. 'Day by day', he says, 'you groan over the increasing numbers of Christians. Your constant cry is, that the state is beset by us, that the Christians are in your fields, your camps, your blocks of tenements [*insulas*]. You grieve over it as a calamity, that every age, in short, every rank is passing over from you to us.'[1] Fifteen years later, he repeated this claim in a tract addressed to the Proconsul Scapula. Christians 'were made, not born', and

[1] *Ad Nationes*, 1.14.

Tertullian, probably a lawyer reared in the Latin literary school of the Second Sophistic, was himself a convert.

Why had this dramatic advance of Christianity taken place? The traditional territorial gods of North Africa had not failed and no disaster threatened. North Africa under Septimius Severus (AD 193–211) and his immediate successors was outstandingly prosperous. Tertullian's statement, written in AD 213 in his tract *On the soul*, that cities now existed where there had not been so much as huts previously, and that everywhere there were houses, people, cities and life, is confirmed by the surge of monumental building that transformed the African cities from Lepcis Magna to Volubilis in the first decades of the third century (pls. 22–3). Yet there was another side. Some of the spirit seems to have been going out of classical civilization. These same architectural triumphs are decorated in a heavy, lifeless and derivative style. People were becoming increasingly sceptical about the 'happy times' that the emperors claimed to bring. Christians such as Hippolytus and Tertullian said the age was not of gold but of iron, the last and worst of the demonic imperial ages.[1] Pagans also, such as the retired civil servant, Dio Cassius, deplored the luxury and cruelty of the times. The constancy of Christians 'ever ready for death'[2] contrasted with the evident futility of public displays associated with the pagan cults. 'We have seen Jove's brother too, hauling out the corpses of the gladiators, hammer in hand', wrote Tertullian,[3] and he and many others turned away in disgust to Christianity. In addition, deeply felt provincial and cultural distinctions were becoming blurred and flattened under the impact of uniform romanization. This process had extended to religion. During the second century, Baal and his consort Tanit, the North African deities, were being tamed, deprived of their once traditional human sacrifice, given the Roman names of Saturn and Caelestis, decked out in Roman dress, set in Roman-style temples, and associated with other Roman gods. Christianity, with its reputation for conspiratorial activity and opposition to pagan Roman society, gained converts. In North Africa it was the religion of protest.

By the first decade of the third century AD it was foreshadowing many of its later characteristics. It was puritanical in outlook and sectarian in attitude. Christians kept to themselves, united 'by a common apprehension of religion and bond of hope'.[4] They took pride in being a

[1] Hippolytus, *In Danielem*, II.12 (ed. by N. Bonwetsch, 68) and Tertullian, *De Cultu Feminarum*, II.13.6 (*Corpus Scriptorum Ecclesiasticorum Latinorum* [*CSEL*], 70, 95).

[2] Tertullian, *Apol.* 50 and *De Spectaculis*, I.

[3] *Apol.* 15, 3–6.

[4] Ibid. 39.1.

close-knit 'sect' or 'school', living in vivid expectation of the Last Day 'when this old world and all its generations would be consumed in one fire', and all their enemies with it, especially the Jews and the pagan magistrates.[1] Above all, their personal hope lay in the crown of martyrdom.

An example of this is provided by an account of the martyrdom in Carthage of Perpetua and Felicitas, victims perhaps of a rescript by Septimius Severus in AD 202 forbidding conversion to Judaism or Christianity.[2] A version of Perpetua's diary edited by local Christians not long afterwards has survived.[3] Vibia Perpetua came from a wealthy family, and was still an unbaptized catechumen when she was arrested together with her friend, the slave-girl Felicitas. They were tried before the procurator and done to death in the amphitheatre at Carthage on 7 March 203. Their ideals were set down in accounts of their dreams and visions while they were in prison, and may reflect the teaching of the Church in Carthage at this time. This teaching was evidently strongly apocalyptic. The Book of Daniel, the *Similitudes* of Enoch, the Book of Revelation, the works of the Roman prophet Hermas, and perhaps the lurid Apocalypse of Peter all seem to have played a part in the confessors' instruction. Baptism merely opened the way for 'the suffering of the flesh'. Contempt for the pagan world, defiance of the Roman authorities, and exaltation at the prospect of martyrdom reveal themselves as the predominant features of North African Christianity.

These ideas found permanent expression in the work of one of the most skilful and intransigent of Christian propagandists of all time, Quintus Septimius Florens Tertullianus. Tertullian typifies the sense of angry frustration and revolt against the ideals of the *pax Romana* that underlay much of the movement towards Christianity. Without political disloyalty, he saw the world around him as God's enemy and his own. 'What has Athens to do with Jerusalem?', he demanded as he turned his back on his literary education, which had provided him with an encyclopaedic knowledge of Roman history and religion. 'Idolatry' included a vast range of harmless-seeming occupations from which he would ban his fellow Christians. He was a man who saw everything in black and white, to whom compromise was merely diabolical weakness.

[1] Tertullian, *De Spectaculis*, 30.

[2] I have argued for the reality of the Severan persecution in Frend, 'Open questions concerning the Christians and the Roman Empire in the age of the Severi', *Journal of Theological Studies* N.S., 1974, **25**, 2, 333–52.

[3] Text in H. Musurillo, *The acts of the Christian martyrs* (Oxford, 1972), 106–31. See W. H. C. Frend, *The Donatist Church*, 2nd edn (Oxford, 1971), 116–18, and T. D. Barnes, *Tertullian, a historical and literary study* (Oxford, 1971), 71–80.

His earliest targets were the glorification of the role of the Christian confessor and the inconsistencies in the treatment of the Christians by the Roman authorities. In AD 197, in an imaginary lawyer's plea before the magistrates of Carthage (the *Apologeticum*), he ridiculed the official policy towards the Christians that had been in force since Trajan's time. By this, Christianity was regarded as illegal and adherence was punishable by death, but Christians who recanted and acknowledged the Roman gods were to be freed without further ado. Tertullian poured scorn on a system which encouraged the guilty to win freedom simply by denying his guilt. He also ridiculed current popular suspicions of Christianity with a comment which has passed into history:

If the Tiber reaches the walls, if the Nile does not rise to the fields, if the sky does not move or the earth does, if there is famine, if there is plague, the cry is at once 'The Christians to the lion.' What, all Christians to one lion![1]

Tertullian was a prolific writer, attacking heretics – such as the followers of Marcion – and slackers within the Christian fold. He was a moral zealot, anxious to impose in the name of Christian integrity a code of behaviour and taboo little different from that of the Pharisees. It is not surprising that he quarrelled with more moderate Christians and with the presbyterate of Rome, who apparently maintained close contact with their counterparts in Carthage. He joined the rigorous sect of the Montanists, latter-day saints, originally from Phrygia in Asia Minor but whose teaching, based on the validity of their prophecies and imminence of the Last Day, had spread to Africa, Gaul and Rome. Tertullian's later works subscribed fully to their views. Under his influence, we find the Church in Carthage involved in a dispute with the Roman Church over the nature of the Christian community. With Christians increasing in numbers on both sides of the Mediterranean, was it possible to maintain attitudes acceptable to a small, self-contained sect? The Bishop of Rome, Callistus (AD 217–22), thought not. The issue centred on the Church's power to pardon those who offended against one of the three traditional categories of deadly sin in Judaism and Christianity, namely adultery, apostacy and bloodshed. Callistus, whose career before he became bishop had been varied and not always creditable, decided that the tares within the Christian body must grow up with the wheat, and in particular he was prepared to extend the peace of the Church to adulterers, even among his own clergy. Tertullian took up the challenge. His work *On chastity* (*De Pudicitia*) written *c*. AD 220,

[1] *Apol.* 40.

gives classic expression to the theology of the gathered Church ranged against institutional religion. The Church, he claimed, was the dwelling-place of the Holy Spirit, and it was therefore intolerable that it should contain notoriously sinful members. 'One does not communicate with the works of darkness', he asserted, in words which were to echo down the history of North African Christianity.[1] The Church was the representative of the martyrs and community of men of the Spirit. Peter and Paul had been examples of the discipline of the Spirit in Rome, and Peter's keys were reserved for those who followed in their way. Only if Callistus could demonstrate his apostolic gifts could he claim apostolic powers.

Tertullian had set his seal on the Church in North Africa. Puritanism, the cult of martyrs, expectation of the end of the world, the judgement on those outside the Church, and an ambivalent attitude towards the Roman see were always to be represented in one form or another among its members. But the opposition was strong also. There were the mystically inclined who accepted Christianity as a means of plumbing the secrets of the universe, an élite who found refuge in the esoteric beliefs and dualist ethic of Gnosticism and later in Manichaeism, and there were the many who became Christians without intending any radical break from the predominant pagan society. Why not go to watch the shows in the arena; after all God himself looked down upon them?

The mid third century AD was not a period to reconcile the views of these opposing camps. The murder of the Emperor Alexander Severus by his troops at Mainz on the Rhine frontier in March AD 235 ushered in a period of instability and confusion which profoundly affected the urban civilization of the Mediterranean. Civil wars were added to the continuous wars fought on the imperial frontiers against the Persians and the barbarians. Taxes were increased and the value of the traditional coinage fell rapidly. The urban populations were ruined. The towns of the empire never recovered their previous role. North Africa was itself the scene of a brief but destructive civil war between the army and a considerable proportion of the romanized landowners and town-dwellers in Proconsular Africa. In AD 238 the latter had supported the revolt of the Gordians, who were African senatorial landowners, in a bid to overthrow the Emperor Maximinus. The Third Legion, the only Roman legion in North Africa, stood by Maximinus and initially the revolt failed. Before Maximinus was removed by events in Italy, bloody reprisals had been taken against his opponents. Between AD 244

[1] *De Pudicitia*, 21.

and 284 there is evidence for a dramatic decline in public buildings and donations by the one-time wealthy. Only some half-dozen inscriptions have been found recording public building or dedications. The costly superstructure of urban life – the paved streets, baths, market-places, temples, libraries, aqueducts and public latrines – lacked funds for its upkeep. Signs of decay began to show themselves, there was disease and a growing lack of confidence in the future. Many thought that the end of the world was coming.[1] It was a climate of opinion in which the uncompromising demands of African Christianity found a receptive audience.

The North African countryside was not affected so seriously. A century of peace and freedom from tribal war, coupled with the intelligent encouragement by the authorities of intensive olive culture, had led to a large increase in population. In AD 240 the historian Herodian remarked on the proverbial fertility of the Libyans. Though he was speaking about the revolt of the Gordians, which was centred in Proconsular Africa, a series of inscriptions found in western Numidia and Mauretania Sitifensis show that throughout the whole of the first half of the third century the native fortified settlements (*castella*) were spilling out over their former boundaries, and some were wealthy enough to acquire the status of towns.[2] For them the main threat lay in razzias from the unassimilated African tribes inhabiting the Kabyle mountains, and between AD 253 and 262 these developed into full-scale warfare. The ten-year revolt of the Bavari of the Kabyles indicated that the empire was threatened from within as well as by the Saharan tribes from without. In addition, taxes on produce, notably the *annona* and forced labour obligations, became heavier. The great increase of milestones dating to the period between the Gordians and Constantine (AD 238–337) indicates strict demarcation of responsibility as between different villages for the upkeep of a highway and its services rather than sudden governmental concern for wayfarers.[3]

In the generation after Tertullian's final works, Christianity had gained further ground. Its organization was by now strongly episcopal, and in *c.* AD 245 no less than ninety bishops had met in the military

[1] As the Carthaginian magistrate, Demetrianus, against whom Cyprian wrote the *Ad Demetrianum* in AD 251 (ed. by W. Hartel, *CSEL*, III, 1, Vienna, 1868).

[2] J. Carcopino, 'Les castella de la plaine de Sétif', *Revue Africaine*, 1918, **62**, 1ff.

[3] For an example of the establishment of a military highway between AD 217–38 in the far west of the North African provinces, see P. Salama, 'La voie romaine de la vallée de la Tafna', *Bulletin d'Archéologie Algérienne*, 1966–7, **2**, 183–217. For the use of milestones in Asia Minor as points of demarcation for forced labour, see Frend, 'A third-century inscription relating to angareia in Phrygia', *Journal of Roman Studies*, 1956, **46**, 46–56.

capital, Lambaesis in southern Numidia, to try and depose a colleague for heresy and misconduct. The first identifiable Christian cemeteries (*areae*) at Hadrumetum (Sousse) and Sbikhra (in southern Tunisia) may date to this period.[1] The Church was making an impact on provincial society, and in AD 248 the clergy and Christian people of Carthage elected a wealthy convert, Thascius Caecilius Cyprianus, as their bishop. He was to govern the Church in Africa for ten years, and the collection of his surviving correspondence, amounting to eighty-one letters and some fifteen treatises, throws a wealth of light on the Church in North Africa at a critical moment of its history.

The strains within the empire were soon to confront the Church with a supreme test of survival. Faced with a serious invasion of Goths across the Danube frontier, the army had acclaimed its general Decius as emperor in AD 249. Decius believed that part of the rot had been caused by the pro-Christian attitude of his predecessors, and that the salvation of the state could be guaranteed only by unequivocal service to the traditional gods of Rome and a return to the virtues of the past. In January AD 250, Fabian, Bishop of Rome, was executed, and soon Cyprian himself was in hiding. Sometime in June or early July 250, commissions composed of the senior citizens of each town supervised the sacrifices to the gods which the emperor had ordered to take place. The temples were besieged by willing crowds, Christians mingling with their pagan neighbours. The Church had been caught at a disadvantage. It was swollen with nominal adherents. Some of its bishops were combining ecclesiastical office with duties as bailiffs to landowners. For them the zeal of the previous generation seemed remote. The Church also was at this time almost entirely an urban organization, whose leaders would be well known though not necessarily well liked. They were unprepared for the crisis. All who sacrificed, Christian and pagan alike, received a certificate (*libellus*). There was little resistance. For a short time it seemed that the Church in North Africa had collapsed.

The few who had stood out restored the Church's fortunes. These confessors were mainly humble folk in the towns – 'little instructed in holy Scripture', as one was described – but they knew their rights. Their confession had made them 'friends of the Lord' and they could sit in judgement with Him. Meantime they would spend the merit they had acquired as they wished. Thousands who had lapsed were repenting of their folly and were clamouring to be allowed to return to the Church.

[1] Christian cemeteries are mentioned by Tertullian, *Ad Scapulam*, 3. The coin series connected with the Christian cemetery at Sbikhra extends back to Gordian III (AD 238–44).

The confessors were soon giving out recommendations for indulgence wholesale. Cyprian himself was told by them to preserve his 'peace with the holy martyrs'.[1] The evident abuse of these proceedings gave Cyprian his chance to restore his authority. By Easter AD 251 he was back in Carthage, and soon afterwards he summoned a council at which a scale of penances was decided for various degrees of lapse. Responsibility was laid on the bishops for their readmission of the fallen.

This was a major triumph for Cyprian. Henceforth the power of the bishop in the North African Church was never challenged. Moreover, within a very short time, the Church in North Africa had regained its former strength. In a situation of growing insecurity, its close-knit organization and the evident wealth that even permitted the payment of monthly stipends to its clergy, began to make a serious impression on the minds of the provincials. Decius had fallen in battle against the Goths in June AD 251. His successor, Gallus (AD 251–2), tried to reactivate the persecution. The Jews of Carthage made common cause with the pagans against the Church. For a moment Cyprian's life was in danger, but the storm passed. In the next year the provinces were struck by plagues followed by the revolt of the Kabyle tribes. In face of the one, the Christian ministers stood firm and died at their posts; in face of the other, a large sum was collected for the ransom of prisoners. In retrospect these years may well have marked the turn of the tide in favour of Christianity in North Africa. The Church alone had proved itself able to confront the perils of the time and survive. Meantime Cyprian had been able to place his own stamp of orthodoxy on the Church in North Africa. This was based on a series of rigid deductions from monotheism. If there was one God, there was also one Church, one bishop in each community. The Church consisted of bishop and people united in each other. There could be no other altar, no other priesthood, no other Church than this. The worst crime was disobedience to the priesthood, and the worst situation for a man to be in was that of schism. There was no salvation outside the Church, in whom the bishop was intermediary between God and His people and the chosen vehicle of the Holy Spirit. These essentially Old Testament, indeed Judaistic, ideas were associated with a rigorous view of the purity of the Church itself, 'the lily among thorns' and pure bride of Christ. Thanks to Tertullian and Cyprian, the Church in Africa had already developed an unshakable theology that embraced Mono-

[1] Cyprian, *Letter*, 23.

theism, the Church and the duties of the individual in a single rigid system.

Cyprian's disputes with the Roman see over the right to readmit to clerical status bishops who had lapsed during the persecution, and on the validity of sacraments, especially Baptism, given outside the Church (e.g. by schismatics and heretics), belong more to the general history of the Church than to the history of Africa. In both these issues, however, Cyprian adopted an uncompromising attitude. Sacraments given by a cleric outside the Church were positively harmful to their recipients. It was necessary for a congregation to separate from a cleric who was in a state of sin and in whom the Holy Spirit no longer operated. Those baptized by heretics and converted to the Catholic Church must be baptized anew. There was no salvation outside the Church, and the Church was the pure 'bride of Christ', whose integrity must be preserved above all else.

These ideas, passionately held by Cyprian, commanded general support in North Africa and were upheld in Church councils summoned during AD 255 and 256. However, schism with Rome seemed likely when in the summer of 257 the Christians were again faced by persecution. In the new crisis, the disputes were allowed to fall into abeyance. Issues had been raised, however, of great importance for the future of the North African Church. In terms of the lives of clergy, the persecution under Valerian between AD 257 and 260 was far more costly than the Great Persecution forty years later. This time Cyprian acted with courage and statesmanship. His letters to fellow bishops in Numidia who had been condemned to the mines reflect an assurance of the ultimate victory of Christianity. He himself was first sentenced to exile and, after nearly a year in his villa at Curubis on the Gulf of Hammamet, was summoned before the proconsul to answer for his beliefs. The examination was short and to the point. Cyprian refused to sacrifice to the gods, and was condemned to death as a man of 'irreligious life' who had drawn together a number of men 'bound by an unlawful association'. On 14 September 258 the sentence of beheading was carried out in Carthage.[1]

To contemporaries, the martyrdom of Cyprian gave divine sanction to his opinions. By his uncompromising assertion of the superiority of the bishop's office and the purity of the Church through its sacraments administered by a personally blameless clergy, he set the Church in

[1] The text of the trial is in *Acta Proconsularia* (ed. by W. Hartel, III.3, pp. CX–CXIV). English trans. in J. Stevenson (ed.), *A new Eusebius* (London, 1957), 260–2.

North Africa on a course which ran contrary to most of the remainder of the Christian world and not least the Church in Rome. The next generation was to show how far the traditional rigorism of the Church of the Martyrs could survive in conditions in which Christianity was rapidly becoming the religion of the empire itself.

There are no collections of letters to illuminate the story of the next forty years. Though it is likely that the poet Commodian wrote his verses at this time, depicting Christianity in apocalyptic terms and looking forward to a reversal of the fortunes of rich and poor, his date is too uncertain to allow of any theory being built upon them. The major development, however, in the period between the death of Cyprian and the outbreak of the Great Persecution was the spread of Christianity into wide areas of the Numidian and Mauretanian countryside to become the predominant religion in these provinces. The list of bishops who attended Cyprian's council in AD 256 already shows the Church represented in parts of southern Numidia. The next list, reflecting the situation of the time of the Great Persecution, gives the names of a number of new sees in the same area, and during the interval the primate of Numidia had become sufficiently powerful to win the right of consecrating the bishop of Carthage.[1] Among the population, too, one can detect the swing towards Christianity. In AD 259, during the persecution under Valerian, fugitive Christians near Cirta were reported and handed over to the authorities. By the time of the Great Persecution, the same area had become Christian to the point of fanaticism. There seems also to have been a decline in the worship of the African national deities, particularly of Saturn, whose last-dated dedication in Numidia and Mauretania is AD 272.[2] Though in western Tunisia a fine dedication in his honour dated by the consular dates to 323 has been discovered, it does not seem to have remained the religion of the people.[3] Even local gods, like Bacax, worshipped in his grotto, in the mountains north of Aquae Thibilitanae (Hammam Meskoutine),

[1] The list of eighty-seven bishops who attended Cyprian's council at Carthage is printed in Hartel's edition of Cyprian's works, III.1, pp. 435ff. New sees in Numidia are known from the names of bishops who attended the consecration of Silvanus as Bishop of Cirta in AD 305. The right of the Numidians to participate in the consecration of the Bishop of Carthage is attested by Optatus of Milevis, *De Schismate Donatistarum*, I.18 (ed. by C. Ziwsa, *CSEL*, XXVI), and Augustine, *Psalmus contra partem Donati*, lines 44–6.

[2] *CIL*, **8**, 20435 (Sillègue in Mauretania Sitifensis). See M. Leglay, *Saturne africaine: histoire* (Paris, 1966), 96. Most of these Numidian and Mauretanian sites which have produced substantial evidence for Saturn-worship were Donatist bishoprics in the fourth century.

[3] See A. Beschaouch, 'Une Stèle consacrée à Saturne le 8 Novembre 323', *Bulletin Archéologique du Comité des Travaux Historiques*, N.S., 1968, **4** (Paris, 1969), 253–68. Leglay also found evidence for the continued popularity of the cult of Saturn in Tunisia at least down to the time of Constantine.

seem to have become neglected towards the end of the third century. The last dedication to Bacax is in AD 283.[1]

It is impossible to say just why this vast, silent revolution took place. The failure of the traditional gods to assure prosperity; the obvious brotherly concern of the Christians, coupled with their fortitude in adversity; the social content of the biblical message – these may have played the same part in North Africa as they did in Asia Minor during the fourth century. We cannot be sure. Certainly the move towards Christianity was influencing all classes, including writers such as Arnobius and Lactantius, as well as young idealists in Carthage and villagers on the Numidian high plateau. Great changes were taking place in provincial society. The reforms of Diocletian and his colleagues from AD 285 onwards were designed to restore efficiency to the administration, prosperity to the cities, discipline to the people and worship to the gods. In Africa the first aim resulted in the radical alterations in the provincial boundaries which have been described in chapter 3. The net result of these changes was to increase the number of provinces and the bureaucrats who administered them. These in turn had to be sustained by the provincials. Additional burdens on the latter resulted from the massive restoration of the cities that accompanied these changes. In many towns, such as Djemila (Mauretania Sitifensis), Lambaesis, Macomades and Ad Maiores (all in Numidia), aqueducts and other public buildings 'long ago collapsed' were restored, and similar zeal was shown in restoring temples to the gods of the Roman state. A contemporary African, albeit a convert to Christianity, commented bitterly on the cost of these enterprises to the provincial. It may be that the association of the restoration of Roman gods with the costly restoration of the Roman towns and the spawning of a greedy bureaucracy had some influence in turning him against the religion of the empire.

The real wealth of North Africa had now become concentrated in the villages on the high plateau of Numidia and Mauretania Sitifensis. It was there also that a new form of the traditional North African interpretation of Christianity was fast taking root. By the end of the third century AD, these areas, consisting of a high table-land sandwiched between the coastal Atlas to the north and the Aures mountains in the south, had produced a distinctive rural economy. There were towns,

[1] *CIL*, 8, 5504–19 and 18828–57 for the series of inscriptions commemorating the annual sacrifices to Bacax in the grotto of Jebel Thaya by the magistrates of the town of Aquae Thibilitanae (Hammam Meskoutine).

especially in the narrow strip of land immediately north of the Aures, where rainfall was comparatively abundant and the garrisons of the Third Legion attracted the civil population to settle around them. Broadly speaking, however, the Mauretanian and Numidian high plains were peopled by villagers. The work of Stéphane Gsell in mapping the Romano-Berber village sites before they were destroyed by advancing modern urbanization cannot be praised too highly.[1] The detailed work of André Berthier and his colleagues immediately before the Second World War showed a density of one Romano-Berber settlement in the typical Commune Mixte of Ain Mlila to about every 4 km, and some were comparatively large agglomerations.[2] The inhabitants were Berbers, with probably much the same knowledge of Punic and Latin as their descendants possessed of Arabic and French. They were *coloni* on great imperial and private estates, enjoying, however, the status secured for them under the *Lex Mancia* in the second century. The basis of their livelihood was flourishing harvests of olives and barley. These villagers were now deserting the age-old worship of Saturn for Christ. Their literal acceptance of the biblical word brought a powerful reinforcement to the puritan elements among the older established Christian communities. In AD 295 the case of the young recruit Maximilian from a village near Thebeste (Tebessa), who preferred martyrdom to service in the army despite the presence of Christian officers in its ranks, was a portent.[3]

In contrast, in many of the towns, particularly in Carthage, the long peace and the development of a standardized administrative hierarchy in the Church centred on the diaconate, had blunted the edge of much of the idealism of Cyprian's time. Confessors were no longer to be volunteers, bones of alleged martyrs were to receive no veneration before recognition by the Church authorities. The archdeacon (*archidiaconus*) was emerging as the most powerful cleric in the diocese, overshadowing the presbyters. Here too was a potential source of friction. Church and state appeared to be working happily together. Young Christians who sighed for braver times found no encouragement in Carthage.

This was the situation when Diocletian at last threw down the gage

[1] S. Gsell, *Atlas archéologique de l'Algérie* (Algiers, 1911).

[2] A. Berthier *et al.*, *Les Vestiges du Christianisme antique dans la Numidie centrale* (Algiers, 1942), 23–4, and the present writer's description of Romano-Berber rural sites he has observed, in *Donatist Church*, 44–5.

[3] Passio Maximiliani; see R. Knopf and G. Krueger, eds., *Ausgewählte Märtyrerakten*, 86–7, and the discussion by P. Monceaux, *Histoire littéraire de l'Afrique chrétienne*, 7 vols. (Paris, 1901–23), III, 114–21.

to the Christians in February AD 303. By early May the first edict had arrived, requiring the surrender of the Scriptures and the destruction of church buildings, and this was reinforced by a demand that the Christian clergy should sacrifice to the gods. But there was to be no bloodshed, and laity, if they did not provoke the authorities, were to be left in peace. Once again, as under Decius and Valerian, the authorities achieved great initial success. At Cirta, Bishop Paulus was summoned before the *curator* (mayor) of the city on 19 May and the following conversation took place:

The Mayor to Paul the Bishop: 'Bring out the writings of the law and anything else you have here, according to the order, so that you may obey the command.'
The Bishop: 'The readers have the Scriptures, but we will give what we have here.'
The Mayor: 'Point out the readers or send for them.'
The Bishop: 'You all know them.'
The Mayor: 'We do not know them.'
The Bishop: 'The municipal office knows them, that is, the clerks Edusius and Junius.'
The Mayor: 'Leaving over the matter of the readers, whom the office will point out, produce what you have.'[1]

The bishop complied and allowed church plate and other property including a large amount of men's and women's clothing to be brought out. It was heaped in front of the clergy and was duly inventoried. One of those who took part in the scene was Silvanus, a sub-deacon, who later became the Donatist bishop. He was not allowed to forget this incident.

Similar scenes took place in the Proconsular Province. Action by the authorities was often swift. The first that ordinary people saw of the persecution was burning churches and clergy and church officials being required to hand over Scriptures. It was not until the late autumn that resistance began to gather from congregations indignant at the pusillanimous behaviour of their clergy. In the small town of Abitina in the upper valley of the Medjerda, a group of forty-seven Christians led by the presbyter Saturninus were arrested while holding a service. Their bishop had apostatized, but their enthusiasm had been maintained by the presence among them of young idealists from Carthage. Their subsequent fortunes affected the future of North African Christianity. At their trial before the Proconsul Anulinus in Carthage in February

1 *Gesta apud Zenophilum* (ed. by C. Ziwsa, *CSEL*, XXVI), 186–8. (English trans. in Stevenson, *New Eusebius*, 287–9.)

AD 304, they maintained their faith, and were returned to prison. Thereupon they seem to have held a sort of council at which they made a solemn declaration that no one who resorted to the communion of *traditores* would participate with them in the joys of Paradise. Thus after half a century, confessors claimed once again the right of binding and loosing on earth. The challenge apparently was taken up by the leading cleric in the church at Carthage, the archdeacon Caecilian. He was said to have forbidden visitors and supplies from reaching the confessors in prison. Whether they starved or not is not known, but Caecilian was no Cyprian. He became associated with collaboration with the authorities and hostilities to the martyrs.

By the spring of AD 304, Diocletian had been stricken with a serious, lingering illness. Effective government was in the hands of his Caesar, Galerius, and, following the precedent of Decius, he ordered that everyone should now sacrifice to the gods. Doubts have been raised whether this Fourth Edict was ever enforced in North Africa. In particular, the inscription from Castellum Elephantum (Rouffach) which names 'martyrs of Milevis' who suffered in the 'days of the thurification under the *praeses* Florus',[1] is suspect, for Florus had ceased to be governor of a united Numidia by the time Diocletian celebrated his *Vicennalia* on 20 November 303, five months before the Fourth Edict was promulgated. However, it was only the Fourth Edict that forced laymen to sacrifice, and a significant number of African martyrs, including a group of thirty-four commemorated on a mosaic in a church at Ammaedara (Haidra in Tunisia), were laymen.[2] Certainly, the church historian Eusebius believed that Africa suffered only a little less than Egypt during the Great Persecution, and this would have been impossible to credit in the light of the scanty evidence for martyrdoms in AD 303. The Numidian Church Council held in March 305 to elect a successor to Bishop Paulus shows that it was comparatively easy for bishops to escape the order to sacrifice or surrender the Scriptures. All in all, it would seem wise to accept the evidence of the *Acta Crispinae* to the effect that the year 304 witnessed a massive effort to enforce sacrifices by the Christian laity and that many, particularly in Numidia, resisted

[1] *CIL*, **8**, 6700 = 19353. For the view that the Fourth Edict of persecution was not enforced in the west, see G. E. M. de Ste Croix, 'Aspects of the Great Persecution', *Harvard Theological Review*, 1954, **47**, 84ff., and, on Florus, see L. Leschi, 'Le Centenarium d'Aqua Viva', *Revue Africaine*, 1943, **87**, 5–22.

[2] Published in *Bulletin Archéologique du Comité des Travaux Historiques*, 1934, **69**, with a comment by H. Delehaye in *Analecta Bollandiana*, 1936, **54**, 313–16. For inscriptions commemorating Numidian martyrs of the period AD 303–4, see also Monceaux, *Histoire littéraire*, III, 177–8, and Berthier *et al.*, *Les Vestiges du Christianisme*, 210ff.

and were martyred. Sixty years afterwards popular folklore associated these acts incorrectly with the previous phase of the persecution for which Florus was responsible.

THE DONATISTS

By March AD 305, two months before Diocletian and Maximian abdicated, the persecution had ended in Africa. It did not bring peace to the Church. At Cirta the mob had already taken matters into their own hands. For Bishop Paulus's successor they had chosen the sub-deacon Silvanus, and they shut the citizens among the Christians in the cemetery of the martyrs while the election was carried through. When twelve Numidian bishops assembled on 5 March to consecrate Silvanus, four of their number were guilty of having been *traditores* and one was a murderer as well. None the less Silvanus, despite his record during the persecution, was duly consecrated.

For most of the next seven years North Africa was governed by officials appointed by the usurper Maxentius (AD 306–12). Church property was restored and churches were open again. The administration was just tolerant enough to allow hostility between confessors and *traditores* to fester without interference, and the inherent suspicions between Carthage and Numidia to come to the surface. In 311, however, the Bishop of Carthage died. As misfortune would have it, Caecilian was chosen as his successor, and his consecration was hurried through before the Numidian primate could arrive and exercise his right to participate in the event.

The Numidians were not to be outdone, and Caecilian's record in the Great Persecution had not been forgotten. Finding that Caecilian's title was disputed by the people at large, the Numidian primate, Secundus of Tigisis, appointed an *interventor* (temporary administrator of the see) and only after his murder did he proceed to the election of a new bishop (summer? AD 312). The choice fell on Majorinus, the chaplain to the household of a Spanish *grande dame* named Lucilla, whom Caecilian had offended mortally by forbidding her to kiss the bone of an unauthenticated martyr before she received Communion. The North African Church was rent in schism.

Such was the situation that confronted Constantine on the morrow of his victory over Maxentius at the Milvian Bridge on 28 October AD 312. North Africa was essential to him for the supply of Rome with food through the winter. The provinces had surrendered without a blow.

The all-important question was whose support to win, not least among the powerful community of North African Christians. Constantine unhesitatingly made the wrong choice, upholding Caecilian from the outset, subsidizing him from the imperial treasury, and threatening his enemies. On 15 April 313 the latter appealed to the emperor to appoint Gallic justices to decide the issues between Caecilian and themselves. Gaul had been little affected by the persecution, and the appeal to the emperor may be interpreted as an appeal to the senior magistrate of the empire to appoint judges in a matter of litigation (much as the Antiochene clergy had approached Aurelian in AD 272, to remove Paul of Samosata from his see and his palace). It was not an admission of the emperor's right to intervene in religious questions.

Constantine accepted the plea and asked the Bishop of Rome, Miltiades, himself an African, to try the case. Before the latter could convoke his assessors, Majorinus had disappeared from the scene. The opponents of Caecilian chose a far abler man in his place, Donatus of Casae Nigrae on the Saharan border of Numidia, who quickly won the unchallenged support of both the Carthaginian and Numidian elements in the opposition to Caecilian. He was to be a thorn in the Roman government's flesh for forty years.

Miltiades's hearing took place in the Lateran Palace at Rome between 2 October and 5 October AD 313. The verdict was given in favour of Caecilian, and Donatus was condemned as a disturber of ecclesiastical discipline. This could have been the end of the matter, but in Africa public opinion was running strongly in favour of Donatus. Rumours suggested that Caecilian had been consecrated by a *traditor* in the person of Felix, Bishop of Apthungi. There were suspicions, too, that Miltiades had not been impartial and had to cover up his own failure in the Persecution. Another appeal was made to Constantine, and the latter reluctantly convoked a Council of bishops from the whole Prefecture of the Gauls (Britain, Gaul and Spain) to meet at Arles on 1 August AD 314. Meantime there was to be an on-the-spot inquiry into the case of Felix of Apthungi. The Council, as might be expected, went against the Donatists, and also decided that the African custom of rebaptizing reconciled heretics must be abandoned (Canon 9). Another aspect of Cyprian's work was thus being threatened by outsiders. The Donatists refused to submit. Their case was aided by legal delays which prevented Felix from being cleared until February 315, and also by the outbreak of war between Constantine and Licinius (314–15). Both Caecilian and Donatus were kept in Italy at the emperor's pleasure. By the summer of

315, Constantine had decided to rehear the case himself; he even planned to go to Africa to lay down there and then 'how the supreme deity should be worshipped'. Only after Donatus had escaped detention and Caecilian had followed him back to North Africa did Constantine give his final verdict, in favour of Caecilian, on 10 November 316.

By this time however, Donatus's hold on Africa was almost complete. It was not disturbed either by Constantine's effort to coerce his supporters between AD 317–21, nor by a scandal in Numidia in 320 which demonstrated that many of Donatus's best-known supporters were themselves *traditores*. Caecilian was among the few western bishops who attended the Council of Nicaea in 325, and he then disappears from history without trace. Within the next decade or so, as Jerome admits, 'nearly all North Africa' accepted the Church of Donatus.[1]

The reasons for Donatus's success lie in the complex of the psychological and social factors which play so large a part in mankind's religious history. Though none of his writings has survived, his opponents testify to him as a formidable and dedicated leader, combining the qualities of orator and administrator. He was regarded by his supporters as a prophet who had direct access to the secrets of the Lord. Men swore by 'his white hairs' as under Islam they were to swear 'by the beard of the prophet'. In Carthage he carried to extreme lengths the Old Testament concepts of the North African sacerdotal episcopate. Like some Jewish High Priest, he celebrated the mysteries alone, allowing no one to participate with him; and he claimed sovereign authority for himself. He was known by contemporaries simply as 'Donatus of Carthage'. Yet, like Cyprian, he could also give way in the cause of the unity of his Church. When, *c.* AD 336, bishops in Mauretania again challenged the re-baptism rule on behalf of those who had been baptized by clergy who had at that stage been in communion with Caecilian, he summoned a council of 270 bishops and accepted the consensus that this should be remitted. Like Cyprian, he accepted that the supreme voice of the Church rested in the unanimity of its bishops assembled in council. The other factor in his favour was his complete identification with the theology of Cyprian and with the whole rigorist tradition of the African Church. No tares were accepted in the Lord's field, namely the Church. There was to be no interference in its affairs by the state, whether the emperor was Christian or not. His question to the imperial commissioners sent to him in 346 by the Emperor Constans,

[1] Jerome, *De Viris Illustribus* 93: 'paene totam Africam (Donatus) decepit', writing *c.* AD 392.

'What has the emperor to do with the Church?', has won its place in the folklore of western Christendom.[1]

Donatus's energy reflects the further advance of Christianity in all parts of Roman North Africa. The first half of the fourth century AD witnessed the earliest recognizably Christian inscriptions and buildings.[2] Many of the towns, however, retained a strong pagan influence, especially among the local ruling citizens. There are more inscriptions in honour of the Emperor Julian the Apostate (361–3) than to any of his longer-lived colleagues. The well-known *Album* of Timgad, dating to about 363, lists all the members of the city council (*curia*) together with their offices and the names of the imperial officials stationed in the town. It provides a document of the greatest interest regarding the social structure, administration and religious composition of the upper classes in a relatively ancient (Timgad was founded as a colony of veterans in *c.* AD 100) and prosperous city in Numidia. Out of 158 offices mentioned, there were 11 *clerici* – almost certainly Christian clergy. Of the remainder, most of the *sacerdotales* and *flamines* (priests) must have been pagans, and those who were not would have to attend sacrifices on public occasions. We know, however, from other evidence that Timgad was one of the most important Donatist strongholds, and outside the city boundaries was growing up a large Christian quarter dominated by a vast cathedral, while away to the south of the town was a Christian cemetery which eventually contained no less than 15,000 graves (pls. 24–5). In North Africa as elsewhere in the empire, Christianity came up from below, through the artisan class, and only later did it penetrate the city aristocracies. Though the cities still had an intellectual life based on the Latin classics, these aristocracies were now very different from the wealthy corporations that a century earlier had established their splendours. Despite the considerable efforts by some individual governors, notably Publilius Ceionius Albinus, governor of Numidia 364–7, to re-equip them with market-places and water supplies, the inscriptions record increasingly their ruined and broken-down appearance. A few big houses of 'patrons', some ornate churches and baptisteries, ill-repaired public buildings and streets and a Christian quarter surrounding a large church outside the original walls, composed of

[1] Optatus, *De Schismate Donatistarum*, III.3.

[2] The earliest dated church in North Africa is oddly enough from the military settlement of Altava in the far west of Mauretania Caesariensis, a '*basilica*' dating to AD 309 (a clear piece of evidence that Maxentius's policy was not anti-Christian). See J. Marcillet-Jaubert, *Les Inscriptions d'Altava* (Paris, 1968), no. 19. Another early dated church also comes from the same province – Castellum Tingitanum (AD 324); *CIL*, **8**, 9708.

rather squalid buildings: such must have been the picture of many North African cities towards the end of the fourth century AD.[1]

The villages, especially those in Numidia and Mauretania, presented a different picture (pls. 26–31). The tenant farmers, donkey-drivers and small tradesmen that made up a typical village population with its twice-monthly market day, would be Christians to a man. Small Romano-Berber settlements, such as Mechta Azrou or Oued R'zel on the Algerian high plateau, had a dozen churches between them, all built on the same general plan, simple basilica-type buildings with baked mud and stone walls and beaten earth floors, centred on an alleged martyr's tomb, and sometimes with adjacent storage rooms for grain and olive-oil. In the 340s AD, these villages became the scene of a movement which combined religious with social protest and in some respects foreshadowed similar explosions of agrarian discontent in the European Middle Ages. The Circumcellions emerged as religious fanatics seeking martyrdom and openly threatening the social order, and they continued to be active until the arrival of the Vandals in Africa in 429. A great deal of research has been devoted to them.[2]

Scholars tend to emphasize either the religious or the economic roles of the Circumcellions. Were they an *ordo* composed of free labourers who circulated the great landed estates in Numidia and Mauretania, offering their services at times of intensive labour demand such as the olive harvest? Were the *cellae* around which they dwelt 'for the sake of their food', granaries or martyrs' chapels? What was their relationship to the Donatist Church? All contemporary authorities were agreed on a number of points. The Circumcellions were peasants (*agrestes*) whose main radius of action was 'upper Numidia and Mauretania'.[3] They dominated some of the hill-fort settlements in Augustine's diocese of Hippo, and they were Donatists. They regarded themselves as having a specifically religious calling. Their leaders were known as 'captains of the saints'.[4] The women who were included among their bands were described even by Augustine as *sanctimoniales*; they perambulated the shrines of martyrs, and the discovery in several rustic churches of silos

[1] A good example is provided by Cuicul (Djemila) where five big courtyard-type town houses dating to the last part of the fourth century AD were discovered. See Y. Allais, *Djemila* (Paris, 1938), 45.

[2] Particularly by H. J. Diesner, in essays collected under the heading *Kirche und Staat im spätrömischen Reich* (Berlin, 1963); by E. Tengström, *Donatisten und Katholiken* (Göteborg, 1964), 24–78; by S. Calderone, in *La Parola del Passato*, 1967, CXIII, 94–109; and by Frend, *Donatist Church*, 171–4, and in *Journal of Theological Studies*, N.S., 1969, **20**, 542–9.

[3] Praedestinatus, *De Haeresibus*, 69: 'in partibus Numidiae superioris et Mauretaniae'.

[4] Optatus, *De Schismate Donatistarum*, III.4: 'Fasir et Axido duces sanctorum'.

and storage jars suggests that their *cellae* were in fact shrines. At the same time, they were revolutionaries. Both Optatus of Milevis and Augustine detail outrages against the rich and the landowners. 'No one could feel secure in their estates. The debtors' bond lost its force. In those days no creditor had the liberty of exacting payment of a debt.'[1] Rich men would find themselves bundled out of their carriages and forced to change places with their slaves. However, even these activities fulfilled a religious purpose. The object was to provoke martyrdom. Magistrates would be accosted and given the alternatives either of ordering the execution of the Circumcellions or of being murdered themselves. At the foot of the cliffs around Nif en-Nisr near Ain Mlila on the Numidian high plateau, a series of roughly cut inscriptions on individual rocks and boulders, bearing the name of an individual and the date of his *reditum* ('rendering' his soul to God), provide mute evidence of the extent to which fanaticism would take them. The Circumcellions were not political separatists and they used the Latin of the Donatist Church as their idiom, but they represented in an extreme state the apocalyptic hopes of rural North African Christianity, and its complete rejection of the official christianization of the empire. The struggle against the world, the domain of the Devil, continued. For three quarters of a century the Circumcellion war cry 'Deo Laudes' was more dreaded than the lion's roar.

The Circumcellions were the immediate cause of Donatus's exile in AD 347. In the previous year, perhaps expecting the same favour from Constans as Athanasius had received from Constantius, Donatus had petitioned Constans for recognition as undisputed Bishop of Carthage. The emperor sent out a commission of inquiry under two officials, Paul and Macarius. In Numidia, however, they ran into trouble and had to fight a pitched battle against Circumcellion insurgents near Bagai, where the bishop had turned his church into a fortress. When the commissioners returned to Carthage, the Donatists were proscribed, and Donatus was sent into exile in Gaul, where he died in AD 355. There followed fourteen years of Catholic ascendancy. Before this was suddenly and completely ended at the accession of Julian in 361, the Catholics had been able to establish themselves as an alternative Church. Some towns, notably Thagaste (Souk Ahras), came over to them and did not return to the Donatist allegiance.[2] In Optatus of Milevis

[1] Ibid., and compare Augustine's description of Circumcellion activities over seventy years later in *Letter*, 185.4.15.

[2] This fact had a great effect on North African history, for Augustine was born at

(*fl.* 365–85), they produced a notable historian, who was able also to argue their case on doctrinal grounds as well as to provide invaluable evidence for the origins and development of the schism.

Julian's policy of unrestricted toleration for all Christian sects, in the hope that the Church would collapse in factional strife, came near to success in North Africa. The Donatists returned in strength, and in a few months of 362 the Catholics were swept from the scene amid every form of ignominy. In plundered Catholic churches, the Eucharist was thrown to the dogs, and in some towns Catholics were boycotted. Moreover, Donatus had chosen his successor wisely. Parmenian, though a Gaul or Spaniard, soon adapted himself to Africa. In his thirty years' tenure of office, the Donatists came quietly to dominate the ecclesiastical scene. The Church led by Parmenian was in every way a continuation of the African Church of a century before. Its characteristics were the integrity manifested by its priesthood and members, the mystical union of the saints guided by the Holy Spirit, a sense of predestination, and the glorification of martyrdom. As the writer of the *Acts of Saturninus*, a fourth-century Donatist tract, wrote: 'The virtues of the people are multiplied in the presence of the Spirit. The glory of the Spirit is to conquer in the martyrs and triumph in the confessor.'[1] The remainder of western Christendom rejected the Donatists. This made no difference to their position in Africa, and it was unaffected even by their implication in the revolt of the Kabyle chieftain, Firmus, during 373–5. With more than 300 bishops, the almost complete support of the rural populations, and the adherence of many educated laity in the towns, the Church of Donatus seemed impregnable. But the death of Parmenian in 391 and the arrival of Augustine on the African scene were to bring about profound changes.

AUGUSTINE AND THE CATHOLIC REVIVAL

Augustine was the greatest figure in North African Christianity, though his legacy was to be European rather than African. He was born at Thagaste, in November AD 354, during the period of the Catholic revival, a fact which determined the course of his life. His father, Patritius, was a pagan city councillor, but his mother, Monnica, was a strong-minded native Catholic Christian. In the history of Christianity

Thagaste in AD 354 during the Catholic ascendancy. For his comment on the religious situation there, see *Letter*, 93.5.17.

[1] *Acta Saturnini*, 20 (*PL*, VIII, col. 703).

in North Africa, Augustine's importance lies in the fact that it was very largely through his genius that those elements which were opposed to the predominant rigorist party in the Church, namely the Gnostics and Catholics, and which had hitherto remained in the background, now came into their own. In the twenty years from 410 to 429 that separate the fall of Rome to Alaric and the Vandal invasion of North Africa, the Catholics gained the upper hand. Donatist Christianity was mercilessly driven underground, and when it re-emerged in strength at the end of the sixth century AD, it was too late to arrest the general decline of Christianity that had already set in.

Augustine's brilliance was comparatively slow to show itself. At school he disliked Greek, and he moved through a normal career of grammar school at Madaura to the university at Carthage. Already, however, he was becoming interested in Latin philosophy, one of his main legacies from his pagan father. He studied Cicero's *Hortensius* with enthusiasm. His other interest was psychological – the problem of evil – and at first his mind was directed towards the Gnostic dualist solution, at this period represented by the sect of the Manichees. With the Manichees, too, acceptance of their tenets did not involve rejection of the pagan classics as was demanded by the Donatists. Augustine became a Hearer in the sect *c.* 373, but apparently never ceased to regard himself as a Christian. From that time Augustine prospered. He received a prize for rhetoric at the hands of the Proconsul Vindicianus in *c.* 379, and wider horizons than those provided by provincial Africa opened up. Meanwhile he was becoming disillusioned with the Manichees. He found their leader, Faustus of Milevis, ignorant and provincial, and, dissatisfied with Africa and the sect, he moved first to Rome (*c.* 382) and then, some two years later, to an appointment as public speaker at the court of Valentinian II at Milan. The provincial graduate had made good.

Augustine was three years at Milan, and there he came under the influence first of Neo-Platonism and then of the eloquent Christian expounder of the Neo-Platonist works, Bishop Ambrose. From the one he was able to free himself of the last encumbrances of Manichaeism by grasping that evil could better be understood as deprivation of good than as a positive force in itself. From Ambrose, he learnt how Neo-Platonist mysticism and idealism could be made compatible with Catholic Christianity. Still Milan held him, though by the summer of 385 he was enrolled among the catechumens of the Church. His real choice was more serious and more personal. For fifteen years he had a mistress and she had born him a son; now he had to take a crucial decision. To pursue his career, to 'aspire to honour and money', there must also be marriage. His mother, Monnica, had joined him in Milan. The mistress was sent home, but the Italian heiress who was selected for him proved a disaster. All Augustine's concern for evil, sex and sin returned. The story of Victorinus, the Neo-Platonist philosopher of a generation before, who had conquered his pride to become a Christian, pointed the way to him. The tale of how monks converted two friends of a colleague to abstinence finally made up his mind. There followed the scene in the garden in Milan in August 386, his baptism in Ambrose's cathedral the following Easter, and eventually his return to Africa in 388 after the death of Monnica.

Augustine had been converted to the full implication of Christianity while in Italy. He had embraced what he accepted as a reasonable faith which placed the self-denial of asceticism among its highest goals. It was also a world-wide faith, the faith of a world empire as well as of Milan and Carthage. The casualty on the way to these conclusions had been the rustic, Judaistic Christianity of his mother. Now he had returned to Africa. For the Donatists he could have no sympathy, for however restricted its true members might be in the sight of God, the Church could not be confined to one province. After nearly a century, the Donatists had failed to win acceptance in the West as a whole. Then, if the Church was universal, so also must its sacraments be. Christ was their fount; the personal character of the minister counted for nothing. Hence the Donatist insistence on rebaptizing their converts was erroneous. So too, was their intransigent insistence that the state must always stand condemned as the counterpart of Babylon. An individual's adherence to Babylon or Jerusalem depended only on his personal will, or the direction of his love – as Augustine insisted. Then, the Donatist version of the origins of their dispute with the Catholics was manifestly false. Caecilian had been truly vindicated. Their own party contained *traditores*. They were the schismatics, and schism, denoting lack of charity, was the worst of sins.

The times favoured the re-emergence of the African Catholics. Parmenian's long government was followed by a disputed succession. Many Donatists, particularly those in the more romanized areas of Proconsular Africa and Byzacena, favoured a return to the lineage of Donatus, and supported a kinsman named Maximian. The Numidians opposed their choice. They doubted Maximian's vigour. In a series of manoeuvres in AD 392–4, they first repulsed a Maximianist attempt to unseat their own candidate, Primian, for the see of Carthage; at a vast council of no less than 310 bishops held at Bagai in southern Numidia in 394, they condemned the Maximianists in unmeasured terms; and then within a short time they readmitted all who accepted Primian as true bishop of Carthage. Meantime, Augustine had become presbyter in 391, and then co-adjutor to the Bishop of Hippo, and finally in 396, himself Bishop of Hippo, a medium-sized port on the coast. Donatist quarrels were grist to his mill. He opened his account by writing to several Donatist bishops, trying to persuade them of the error of their Church. But he was not successful. The Donatists were still in the position to assert that theirs was the true Catholic Church in Africa, and their arguments were upheld in a series of cases heard before imperial officials between 394 and 397 which involved claims by the victorious Primianist party against the Maximianists. In the latter year, however, they weakened their position in the eyes of the imperial government by espousing the cause of the rebel, Gildo. Gildo was the brother of Firmus, who had rebelled without success a generation before, but in the interval he had built up a vast personal patrimony and had received the title of count from the emperor. What he intended to do had he proved victorious is unknown. Separatism does not seem likely. In 398 he was defeated, captured and executed, and one of the principal Donatist leaders, Optatus, Bishop of Thamugadi (Timgad) shared his fate.

Augustine saw his chance and from that moment never relaxed his efforts to destroy the Donatists. He was ably helped by his friends, Aurelius, Bishop of Carthage, and Alypius, Bishop of his native Thagaste, who could watch the situation in Numidia. His first object was to have the Donatists made liable to the current severe anti-heretical legislation. By 399 he had succeeded, and in a treatise 'Against the Letter of Parmenian' written that year, he pointed to an important legal decision that deprived a Donatist bishop of a legacy on the grounds that no heretic could benefit under a will. He felt matters were moving rapidly, 'valde velociter'. In 403 a Donatist rejection of a conference demanded by Augustine was followed by Circumcellion attacks on Catholic clergy and property. Prompted by Augustine, the Catholics appealed to the emperor, and were rewarded by a series of severe laws in 405 aimed at suppressing the Donatists and enforcing unity on Catholic terms. From then on, Augustine supported the forceful suppression of Donatism. He had always had the use of the civil power in the back of his mind (in marked contrast to his insistence that the

Manichees, who had been proscribed by law for a century, should be convinced by argument and dealt with gently). From 405 onwards, Augustine began to use the quotation from Luke 14:23 – 'Compel them to come in' – with fateful consequences for the religious history of western Europe.[1]

The persecution continued until 411. By that time the Donatists were ready at least to justify their position before the imperial authorities. The conference that took place under the aegis of the Tribune and Imperial Notary, Marcellinus, in May and June 411, was the last great occasion in the history of the Church of North Africa. Each side made strenuous efforts to assemble the largest support possible. In the end the Catholics mustered 286 bishops to their opponents' 284. The debate lasted for three days, and ranged both over the history of the dispute and its doctrinal issues. Each participant had to stand up and identify himself, and from the list of bishops present, it is evident that the Donatists were in a majority in the country areas and in Numidia and Mauretania, while the Catholics prevailed among the more romanized areas of Proconsular Africa and Byzacena. Like recent nationalist movements, the Donatists represented the mass of peasantry, whose leaders were however drawn from the middle classes and often possessed legal training. The Catholics predominated among the possessing classes and the new aristocracy dependent on imperial patronage, the *honorati*, and were supported by the imperial government. The issue was hardly in doubt. The final day belonged to Augustine, who skilfully concentrated the argument on the historical origins of the dispute, where the Donatists were on weak ground. Marcellinus, who was a friend of Augustine, decided that the Catholics were the true Church in Africa. On 26 June he ordered the confiscation of Donatist churches and property and forbade the Donatists to hold services. On 30 January 412, the Emperor Honorius proscribed Donatism throughout the empire. The Donatist clergy were offered the alternatives of exile or submission.

The Catholic victory was followed by fifteen years of prosperity. While the remainder of the West was under constant threat of Germanic invasion and conquest, the African Catholics emerged as the most influential single force in western Christendom. From the moment the heretic Pelagius's associate, Celestius, applied for ordination at Carthage in 411, the Africans had realized the danger to their predestinarian theology contained in Pelagius's ideas. Almost single-handed, Augustine campaigned against these, and with the support of well-organized

[1] Augustine, *Letter*, 93.2.5.

Church councils was able to bring such pressure on the papacy that Pope Zosimus was obliged in 418 to withdraw his qualified acceptance of Pelagius and condemned his doctrines outright. In a series of disciplinary cases between 417 and 422, the African Church asserted its right to independence in its internal affairs against interference by the papacy. In these years, the Catholic councils almost attained the splendour of the Donatist gatherings of a generation past. While the churches in Europe were in disarray, the African Catholics led by Augustine and Aurelius were establishing themselves as a powerful regional Church. This influence was accompanied by a great expansion in the Church's material prosperity. The Donatists complained of their rivals' wealth, and in these years the Catholics demonstrated the fact. At Cuicul (Djemila) in Mauretania, a Christian quarter complete with baptistery, churches and an episcopal palace was built, perhaps by Bishop Cresconius, who after 411 was bishop of a reunited Catholic and ex-Donatist community.[1] The town of Hippo boasted of no less than seven churches and a Christian quarter with buildings surrounding a large church and cemetery similar in style to that at Djemila. At Tipasa the vast seven-aisled basilica paved throughout with mosaic floors dates approximately to this period.[2] All over North Africa and especially in the towns, the late fourth and early fifth century AD marks the high-water mark of Christian architectural and artistic achievement. The African Catholics so long in the shadows had entered on a splendid heritage.

THE VANDAL INVASION AND THE ECLIPSE OF CHRISTIANITY IN NORTH-WEST AFRICA

In fact, their victory was pyrrhic. Donatism was not crushed. The Donatist leaders managed to hold councils, carry out ordinations, retain many of their churches, and defy the imperial authorities. There were unresolved social tensions. The Circumcellions may have been driven underground, but jealousy of the great landed proprietors remained. 'They alone live' was the murmur recorded by Augustine.[3] Meantime,

[1] See E. Albertini, in *Bulletin Archéologique du Comité des Travaux Historiques*, 1922, 26–32, for the view that the Christian quarter may date to the late fourth rather than the fifth century; and that Cresconius's mosaic may have nothing to do with the discomfiture of the Donatists, see P. A. Février, *Le développement urbain en Afrique du Nord* (Paris, 1964), 18.

[2] Tipasa on the coast west of Algiers was a traditional Catholic centre which had defended itself successfully against Firmus in AD 373. On the great basilica built in honour of St Salsa, see S. Gsell, in *Mélanges de l'École Française à Rome*, 1894, 14, 290ff.

[3] Augustine, *Sermo*, 345.1: 'Isti soli vivunt'. For evidence for the aristocratic nature of Augustine's congregation at Hippo, see Frend, *Donatist Church*, 327–8.

as Augustine was ageing, a new enemy was beginning to threaten the position of Christianity as a whole. Christianity had been extraordinarily successful in the towns and settled areas of North Africa, but had never made an impact on the tribes inhabiting the plateaux on the edge of the Sahara, nor, it appears, on the hill-tribes of the Aures and Kabyles, who were kept quiet by treaty relationships backed by internal *limes* fortifications. Neither the Donatists nor the Catholics seem ever to have undertaken missions comparable to those of the Syrian Monophysites to the Arab tribes on the edges of the settled areas along the Syrian frontier. This was unwise, for, as Augustine had written once to a Roman senator, 'not only along the frontiers, but throughout all the provinces [of Africa] we owe our peace to the sworn oaths of the barbarians'.[1] The African tribesmen seem simply to have fallen outside the perspective of the romanized town- and country-dwellers. The price of this error was to be high.

The progressive weakening of Roman military power in Africa had now given these tribesmen their opportunity to raid and plunder unrestrained by any concern for Christians. In 426 Augustine wrote to the military commander, Count Boniface, of the 'hordes of African barbarians, plundering and destroying without resistance'.[2] Two years later the situation had become intolerable. Quodvultdeus, Aurelius's archdeacon and successor at Carthage, referred to the burning of churches, and to the massacre of clergy and layfolk by the barbarians. The arrival of the Vandals in 429 completed the disaster which the African invaders had begun. Gaiseric is reported to have brought 80,000 Vandals with him, together with an undefined number of adventurers from the Goths and Alans. It was a great gamble, hazarding the very existence of his tribe, but it succeeded. By AD 435 Augustine was dead, Hippo had fallen, a relieving army had been heavily defeated and, according to Augustine's biographer, Possidius of Calama, only 'three churches' – Hippo, Cirta and Carthage – survived the orgy of pillage and devastation that accompanied Gaiseric's army. In 439 Carthage itself fell, and the wealthiest portion of North Africa lay at the mercy of the Vandals.

Possidius exaggerated, but it is none the less true that with the defeat of Boniface and the Roman forces, Roman rule collapsed. The Catholics could organize no resistance. The basis of their success had been too narrow. They failed to solve the social tensions in the provinces that had sustained Donatism.[3] The story of Christianity in North Africa is from

[1] Augustine, *Letter*, 47.2. [2] Ibid. 220.7.

[3] Possidius admits, *Vita Augustini*, 23, that 'the clergy were hated because of their

now on one of continuous decline. The havoc caused by the razzias of the African tribesmen forbids full credence to be given to the statement written *c.* 487 by Victor of Vita (probably a Carthaginian cleric) that the Vandals entered on a rich and peaceful province. Divisions, combined with failure to attempt to convert and civilize the nomadic tribes beyond the *limes*, contributed powerfully to the ultimate extinction of Christianity in North Africa. An immense amount of damage, however, was caused by Gaiseric's army during three years of fighting, 429–32, and this was followed by a long period of intermittent persecution directed at the Catholics. Of the Donatists one hears little. They existed – some of their leaders were driven into exile in southern Gaul – and they regarded Gaiseric's rule in the same terms of diabolical inspiration as they had regarded that of the emperors, but, beyond the *Liber Genealogus* drawn up in successive editions between 427 and 463, they have left few written memorials for the Vandal period. Gaiseric was the one barbarian ruler who was actively hostile towards the western empire and the western Church, and he was determined to assert the predominance of the Arian Christianity of his people. Both Possidus of Calama and Victor of Vita (writing *c.* 487) give similar accounts. Victor in particular records how 'Gaiseric raged in particular against the churches and basilicas of the saints and the cemeteries of the martyrs and the monasteries' throughout a major part of his long reign.[1]

Gaiseric had invaded North Africa to find land for his people and a kingdom for himself. The 'Catholic Church' and 'the nobility' had become almost synonymous. As the great landowners, they were the obvious targets for dispossession, and they were also in the process of carving out the *sortes Vandalorum* (the allocation of land for the conquerors). Moreover, to judge from the final rescripts of the Emperor Valentinian III to the African provinces, these measures could not have been unpopular with the North Africans themselves.[2] By the treaty of 442 with Valentinian III, which ceded the provinces of Proconsular Africa, Byzacena, Tripolitania and the eastern part of Numidia to the Vandals, that land-hunger had been satisfied. Indeed the Vandals never colonized Byzacena to any degree, and their influence diminished

possessions'. We hear of bishops acting as bailiffs on great estates as some of their number had in Cyprian's time (Council of Carthage 397, Canon 15).

[1] Possidius, *Vita Augustini*, 28; Victor Vitensis, *Historia persecutionis*, 1.4; compare also 1.6 and 1.9–11 for similar statements. Victor was a cleric on the staff of the Bishop of Carthage and seems to have had access to the archives of that see.

[2] See *Novel*, 12, 'De Pecunia Afris credita et Fidei jussoribus eorum', dated 19 October 443, where extortion by the rich against the poor provincials is described vividly. The rapacity of creditors 'exceeded that of the enemy', it was claimed.

rapidly the further west into Numidia one proceeded. Of all the Germanic kingdoms that established themselves in the western empire during the fifth century, the legacy of the Vandals was the least. Much of what is known of the policies of their rulers in North Africa comes from hostile clerical chroniclers, and concerns their struggle to repress the former Catholic aristocracy. Both Gaiseric and his son and successor Huneric (477–84) aimed at maintaining the Arian interpretation of Christianity as their Vandal religion. In common with other Germanic tribes during the fourth century, they had accepted Arianism from missionaries from the Danube provinces of the empire, and it now served to distinguish them from the great majority of their North African subjects. Perhaps to emphasize the relative positions of the two peoples, Gaiseric kept the see of Carthage vacant between 440 and 454, when he finally allowed the Catholics to consecrate Deogratias as bishop. In 457, however, the latter was exiled, and no new consecration was made until the time of Zeno's treaty with the Vandal kingdom in 481. In the same spirit of harassment, Gaiseric is alleged by Victor to have forbidden Catholic episcopal vacancies to be filled in the provinces of Zeugitana and Proconsular Africa. The Vandals were determined to keep themselves separated from the Catholic Africans.[1] Thus in Proconsular Africa, where the Vandals were most thickly settled, the number of Catholic bishops declined from 164, apparently the full establishment in the archive of the Church in Carthage, to 3. While Victor may have been reporting a particular moment of acute crisis, there is little doubt that Gaiseric's acts inflicted a succession of blows on the Catholic party from which it never completely recovered.

Gaiseric died in January 477. Under his three successors, Huneric (477–84), Gunthamund (484–96) and Thrasamund (496–523), the Catholics continued to suffer sporadic but sometimes violent persecution. In May 483, Huneric summoned the Catholic bishops from all over the Vandal empire, including Sardinia and the Balearic Islands, for a conference to be held on 1 February 484 between Catholic and Arian representatives. A curious list (the *Notitia provinciarum et civitatum Africae*) purports to record the bishops to whom summonses were sent. It contains no less than 466 names, including 54 from Proconsular Africa, but a disproportionate number of 120 from Mauretania Caesariensis, which lay effectively outside the Vandal dominions. The *Notitia*

[1] The policy is quite evident from the opening words of Huneric's decree of 20 May 483, preserved in Victor, *Historia*, II. 39: 'Non semel sed saepius constat esse prohibitum ut in sortibus Vandalorum sacerdotes vestri conventus minime celebrarent.' Vandal clergy even went to outlying Vandal settlements such as Tipasa; see Victor, *Historia*, III.29.

presents a problem which has not been solved completely, but if it is not entirely valueless it suggests that in the previous decade or so the Catholics had recovered some lost ground.[1] Perhaps the Vandals were not too concerned about the situation outside the area they had reserved for their own settlement (the *sortes Vandalorum*). In Carthage itself the Catholics could claim 500 clergy! Huneric's reaction to the fruitless gathering, however, was to impose on the Catholics the same anti-heretical laws that in their time they had imposed on the Donatists. They were given the choice of conversion to Arianism or exile, and many bishops were exiled under harsh conditions. In 502, prominent Catholic bishops were deported from Africa, some to Vandal-held Sardinia. Like the measures taken against the Donatists after the conference of 411, these actions failed to achieve their aim. The *Life* of Fulgentius of Ruspe (465–527), who became Bishop of Ruspe in 499 and was among the exiles, throws some light on the reasons.

The Vandal population was small in comparison with that of the Romano-Africans, and included too few individuals able to administer their territories. Outside the *sortes Vandalorum*, administration had to be left to the local aristocracy, who were nearly always Catholics. Fulgentius himself had been a senior official (*procurator*) in Byzacena as a young man before he became attracted towards monasticism. Monasteries, we learn from his *Life*, were being founded by wealthy Catholic laymen on good agricultural land, and provided continuity and cohesion among the Catholic communities when their bishops were exiled. The Catholics, moreover, maintained an intellectual ascendancy over their Arian rivals. Apart from Thrasamund himself, whom Fulgentius treated as an equal, no serious defender of the Arian position arose. Fulgentius, sure of his theology derived from the tradition of Augustine, and enjoying the support of the papacy, wrote with authority even in the long periods of exile he spent in Sardinia. There is some evidence that individual Vandals were influenced by the religion of the conquered provincials. Victor records some cases of Vandal 'confessors'. An inscription from Thibiuca records the dedication by a certain Hegerit 'to God and St Felix' in the church there. Felix was the local martyr, a victim of the Great Persecution.[2] Despite all that their

[1] See C. Courtois, *Victor de Vita et son oeuvre* (Algiers, 1954), 91–100, on the successive phases of the compilation of the *Notitia*.

[2] Recorded by J. Cintas and G. L. Fenille, 'Eglise et Baptistère de Thibiuca', *Karthago*, 1953, **2**, 205. Compare the discovery of Vandal burials in the Catholic (or Donatist) churches at Ammaedara (Haidra) and Mactar in Tunisia. Listed by C. Courtois, *Les Vandales et l'Afrique* (Algiers and Paris, 1955), 386–7, nos. 160, 164, 169 (Cherchell) and 170 (Tipasa).

rulers could do, by the first decade of the sixth century AD the Vandals were beginning to be absorbed into the mass of the Afro-Latin population. In this respect the religious and social history of North Africa resembles that of Burgundy, Spain and Italy at this period.

There was a further point of resemblance between North Africa and the barbarian successor states in the western Roman empire, namely the astonishing vigour of the Latin language. One would expect this among ecclesiastics, but Vandal Africa produced poets such as Luxorius and Dracontius, and even humble versifiers who found scope for reminiscences of Virgil on their tombs. The Vandal challenge awoke in the North African provincials a sense of cultural identity expressed through the Latin language and silent adherence to the Roman empire represented by the emperor at Constantinople.[1] If ever North-West Africa looked like becoming a Romance-speaking area, it was during the fifth and early sixth centuries AD.

Significant changes were, however, taking place in the social and economic life of North-West Africa which were to prevent Catholicism from regaining the power it possessed on the eve of the Vandal invasion, and Latin from becoming the basis of a Mediterranean African language. Outside the immediate neighbourhood of Carthage and the Tunisian coastlands, the African towns on which Church organization had been based were declining irrevocably. Lepcis Magna was becoming choked with encroaching sand. Timgad and Bagai were abandoned in face of the ever-increasing depredations of the Aures mountaineers; silt and rubbish lay a metre deep over the forums of Sbeitla and Dougga. Only one civil building, the baths at Tunes (Tunis), can be dated beyond dispute to the century of Vandal rule. Urban life as it had been understood even in the fourth century had come to an end.[2]

The countryside by contrast remained relatively prosperous. The *Tablettes Albertini*, discovered in what today is wilderness 100 km south of Theveste, indicate that the rural population were still *coloni* cultivating their land under the terms of the Lex Mancia as they had two centuries before. The only indication that this evidence dates to the Vandal period is the mention of the reigning monarch, Gunthamund. Otherwise it

1 An appeal for intervention by the Emperor Zeno on behalf of the African Catholics was the main reason for Victor of Vita's writing his history of the persecution of the African Catholics; Victor, *Historia*, III.65 and 68.

2 The writer's personal observation at both Sbeitla and Dougga and also Thuburbo Maius. Much more could have been learnt about the decline of North African urban life had proper record been made of the layers of silt dividing the Roman from Byzantine occupation in these and other centres. For the Byzantines rebuilding cities *a fundamentis*, see *CIL*, **8**, 4677/16869 (Madauros) and 1863/16507 (Theveste).

reflects landed society unchanged from the late Roman period. There was a great estate owned by Flavius Geminius Catullinus in which new vineyards were being planted, and the level of well-being among the cultivators was relatively high. To judge from inscriptions in Donatist Churches, churches continued to be built and repaired. Ain Ghorab, Ain Ateuch and Henchir Tarlist are examples from Numidia. Towards the end of the sixth century, the Latin poet Corippus looked back to Vandal times as a golden age in rural Byzacena.

The new factor in the situation was the emergence of Berber Africa, whether in the form of the tribal kingdoms in the Kabyles, the Aures and the mountains south-west of Tunis, or in the confederation of camel-riding nomads encroaching from the desert to the south and south-east of the Vandal domain. The tribes had always existed, sometimes restive, scarcely touched by nominal treaty relationships with the Roman authorities. Now they came into their own. After the death of Gaiseric, the Vandals gradually lost control, first of the Aures massif, then of the whole area west of Ain Beida, including Timgad, and finally of Tripolitania and most of Byzacena. The kingdoms established by the mountain chieftains in western Numidia and Mauretania resemble, in their retention of Latin and Roman titles, the petty Celtic kingdoms that grew out of the wreckage of Roman Britain. At the turn of the sixth century AD, these kingdoms, though fiercely independent of the Vandals, still used Latin as an official language and the Roman system of provincial dating, and retained Christianity, but the purely native African element was also coming to the surface again after four centuries of Roman rule. The group of royal tombs known as the Djedar in Mauretania 200 km east of Altava, which are dated later than 480, were built in the style of the pre-Roman Medracen, the tomb of the Numidian kings, though in one case the Christian faith of its owner is also affirmed, with the inscription *Spes in Deo* cut on the lintel.[1] Farther west in the region of the Oued Chelif, far beyond the Vandal frontier, there is surprising evidence for the continuation of Roman and Christian influence. The old military settlements of Pomaria, Altava and Albulae have produced no less than fifty Christian inscriptions written in good Latin by dedicants with Latin names but who lived between 450 and 655, another indication that the emergent Berber kingdoms fully deserve the title of sub-Roman.[2] It would be interesting to know

[1] Described by Marcel Christophe, *Le tombeau de la Chrétienne* (Paris, 1951), and see Courtois, *Les Vandales*, 335.

[2] Courtois, *Les Vandales*, 336–8. The same is true of the area of Volubilis in Morocco, where Latin-Christian inscriptions dating to the seventh century have been found. See R.

whether the ordinary language spoken was Romance, or Berber and African. With the nomads, however, it was a different story. The confederation known as the Louata, who were beginning to migrate westwards along the old Roman frontier from Cyrenaica, cared nothing for the civilization and religion of the town-folk and farmers in their way. They were worshippers of Baal-Hammon, as their ancestors had been centuries before. The Vandals were no match for them. By the end of Thrasamund's reign, the royal army had been heavily defeated and the Louata were firmly ensconced under their king, Antalas, on the plains of southern Byzacena. This was a decisive moment in the history of North-West Africa.

The rise of the independent Berber kingdoms in the second half of the Vandal occupation dashed any hope of a restoration of the status quo in the wake of declining Vandal Africa. Over a large part of the territory, the Berbers would remain independent. Thrasamund had been succeeded in AD 523 by Hilderic, the son of Huneric and the Byzantine princess Eudocia. His sympathies were strongly Catholic: exiled bishops were restored to their sees, and the Church sprang into life. In Byzacena particularly, new church councils were assembled at Junca and Sufes. In 525 Boniface held a two-day gathering at Carthage of more than 200 bishops from all over Vandal Africa. Though Hilderic was deposed in a conspiracy in 530, his successor Gelimer (530–4) could not reverse the tide before Belisarius landed in 533 to destroy the Vandal kingdom and with it the Germanic Arian religion in North Africa. Within a year, a century of Vandal rule had collapsed and perished, leaving hardly a trace. The Catholics hailed the Byzantine victory with enthusiasm. As in 412 religious unity could be restored on their terms. In more than one church in Byzacena the priest in charge was commemorated as a *presbyter unitatis*.

Justinian had sanctioned Belisarius's expedition ostensibly to bring relief to the North African Catholics. This was accomplished by the publication of the edict of 1 August 535 which restored Catholicism in toto to the position of unchallenged authority. The inheritance on which the Byzantines entered was an impoverished one. Beyond Proconsular Africa and the coastal area of Byzacena, the former provinces had to be reconquered from the mountaineers and nomads. In the next twenty years, the Byzantine armies were generally speaking successful against the one, but failed to check the inroads of the other. By 550 Byzantine

Thouvenot, 'Les origines chrétiennes en Mauretanie Tingitane', *Revue des Études Anciennes*, 1969, 71, 375–7.

authority had been extended to cover Tripolitania (with a great fortress far to the south of Lepcis at Zuila), most of Byzacena to the line of the Tunisian Chotts, and westwards to the boundary of Mauretania Sitifensis, with outposts along the coast still further west. Beyond were the Berber kingdoms. But within this area, the mountains were held by hostile tribes, kept in submission only by chains of massive fortresses erected at vast expense. Former Roman cities such as Theveste, Ammaedara, Mactar, Dougga and Thuburbo Maius were pillaged of their monuments to provide the massive blocks of masonry for the fortresses that sealed off the town centres from their once flourishing suburbs. New and heavy taxes were imposed and a draconian land survey was carried out to ensure that the provincials paid for their own defence and administration. There was little security beyond the fortress walls. The nomad raiders, with their camels and herds and barbaric gods, form a permanent part of the scene in Byzantine Africa. No part of the country was safe from them. North Africa was taking a long step back to the tribalism and subsistence agriculture of the pre-Roman era.

Efforts were made to restore both the cities and the churches within them. Lepcis Magna was rebuilt on the emperor's orders; a great church was built within the wall of the civil basilica of Septimius Severus. In Byzacena, Sbeitla and Thelepte became Christian centres again, with fine churches and baptisteries. Within the Byzantine fortresses there were churches and chapels, though little – perhaps too little – evidence has been found to establish the character of urban life in this period. At Carthage itself the port was developed and new baths erected in honour of the Empress Theodora. There was administrative activity and some intellectual fervour. Within fifteen years of the official restoration of Catholicism, the North Africans had already resumed their role as active critics of imperial intervention in Church affairs. The Carthaginian deacon, Liberatus, and Facundus, Bishop of Hermiane in Byzacena, were among the few effective critics of Justinian's policy aimed at condemning the Three Chapters. The tradition of support for decision by councils reinforced a conviction in favour of the Two-Nature Christology championed by Rome and the West for centuries. The Definition of Chalcedon was upheld against every effort to undermine its authority from whatever quarter. In 550 the Africans, in the same spirit of independence from pope and emperor that they had shown in the decade before the Vandal invasion, excommunicated Pope Vigilius because of his wavering.

Their opponents denounced this attitude as 'Donatist', but this was only literary invective. The falsity of the charge, however, should not blind the historian to the Donatist character of the stirrings in the reconquered Numidian countryside. During the last half of the sixth century, the papacy acquired considerable estates in this area. From the correspondence between Pope Gregory (590–604) and his agent Bishop Columbus (probably of Nicivibus – N'gaous in south-west Numidia), one hears of a development which can only be interpreted as the re-emergence of Donatism. In the first year of his episcopate, Gregory wrote to the Exarch of Byzantine Africa requesting him to deal with heretics, and in 591 these heretics are identified as Donatists who were bribing Catholic clergy in some of the south Numidian towns to gain their acquiescence in the election of Donatist clergy. For the next six years, the danger of the 'execrable wickedness of the Donatists creeping up into importance' in Numidia was a recurring theme of Gregory's letters to North Africa.[1]

It has indeed been argued that Gregory had mistaken the danger, and that what he was witnessing was the emergence of serious provincial independence through the local Catholic clergy.[2] Gregory, however, was advised by an experienced agent, and jealous though the Numidian Catholics were of their privileges, no amount of obduracy would have brought down on their heads Gregory's demand addressed to Pantaleo, the Praefectus Praetorio and senior imperial officer in the west, that they should be punished as Donatist heretics. Byzantine churches that have been excavated in southern Numidia, with their dedications to non-canonical martyrs, their reliquaries and their inscriptions relating to persecution, show continuity in rite and outlook with the churches of two centuries before. Southern Numidia had lain outside Vandal control except for occasional punitive expeditions against the Aures mountaineers. The return of the Byzantines meant the return of exploitation by absentee landlords and grasping officials, factors to encourage the resurgence of Donatism. So far as the religious life of the people was concerned, only the importation of some specifically Eastern saints into the Numidian martyrology distinguished their chapels from those of two centuries before.

[1] Gregory, *Letters*, I.72; compare I.82, II.33 and 46, and III.32. It is doubtful whether Catholics, however independent they may have felt themselves to be with regard to the papacy, would imitate Donatist custom and rebaptize converted opponents.

[2] For instance, by R. A. Markus, 'Religious dissent in North Africa in the Byzantine period', in C. J. Cuming, ed., *Studies in church history*, III (Leiden, 1966), 149; and compare his 'Donatism, the last phase', in ibid. I (Leiden, 1964), 118–26.

The early years of the seventh century AD saw the North African provinces again play an important part in the affairs of the Byzantine empire. In 608, the Exarch Heraclius used Carthage as the starting-point for his successful revolution against the tyrannical Emperor Phocas. So long as Heraclius ruled, the links between North Africa and Constantinople remained close. The exarchate was held by officials of high standing, such as the Patrician Peter (died 637). At Carthage and in the coastal towns, the Catholic episcopate remained vigorous enough to denounce the Monothelite doctrines of Heraclius and his successor Constans II at a council held in 645. The celebrated Maximus the Confessor lived in Carthage between 640 and 646, and there debated triumphantly with Pyrrhus, the Monothelite leader, before the Exarch Gregory.

This activity could not, however, disguise the decline of Christianity as a cultural and religious influence in the province as a whole. Churches in the seventh century were shoddy in comparison with those built in the previous century. Even the church dedicated by the Exarch Gregory at Timgad in 645 can barely be distinguished from the small native structures that surrounded it. In Numidia the churches were now not essentially different from the rectangular native *gourbis* in which the inhabitants dwelt. The last dated Christian inscription in Numidia, from a chapel at the foot of the Jebel Teioualt and recording the solemn deposition of relics by five bishops, was written in execrable Latin that has taken nearly forty years of scholarly effort to decipher. Only in the far west in the former province of Mauretania Caesariensis, as already mentioned, did something of the one-time vigour of Christian civilization survive. On the eve of the Arab invasion, there could be no greater contrast between the situation in the Maghrib and that in Egypt.

The last phase of Mediterranean North-West Africa in the Christian period is wrapped in legends preserved by the Arab chroniclers. By 642, however, the Arabs had occupied Cyrenaica and five years later they invaded the Maghrib. On the plains near Sbeitla, by then apparently the second most important city in the province, Gregory was completely defeated. Though another generation was to elapse before Byzantine authority in Byzacena and Numidia was to cease, the civilization that had been built up over the previous seven centuries was now in irredeemable decline. Geography turned to the disadvantage of urban and settled life. The plains of Byzacena and Numidia became open to incursions from the Arab armies and the equally formidable Berber nomadic tribes. With the murder of the Emperor Constans II in Sicily in 668, the last effort to restore Byzantine power in the western Mediterranean and North Africa came to an end. The succession of battles fought between the Berbers and Arab invaders in the last thirty years of the seventh century took place on desert tracks and near water supplies vital for the survival of nomad armies. The towns and villages of Romano-African civilization no longer counted. Carthage itself had become an isolated outpost when it fell finally to Ḥasan b. al-Nuʿmān in 698. Nor was the battle one between Christians and Islam. No Christian leader emerged as heir to the Byzantines. The famous Berber queen, the Kāhina, who fought the final valiant struggle against the Arabs between 690 and 698, may even have been a Jewess. What had happened to the organization of the Church during this period is unknown, for on their final defeat at Bir el-Kahena in 698 many of the Berber tribes accepted Islam rather than pay tribute to the Arabs.[1] Then, to quote the Arab historian Ibn ʿAbd al-Ḥakam:

> The Lawāta later [i.e. after the defeat of the Byzantines] split up and spread over this part of the Maghrib [Tripolitania and Tunisia] until they reached Sousse. The Hawarra established themselves at Lebda and the Nefusa in the territory of Sabratha. The Rum [i.e. Byzantines] who were occupying these lands were forced to leave, but the Afāriq who were subject to the Rum remained, paying a tribute which they were accustomed to render to all who occupied their country.[2]

That is to say, the Byzantines left: the Berber farming population remained behind until they too were slowly driven into the mountains by the nomads. Christianity and Latin civilization gradually died out amid the ruin of the olive plantations and villages of its adherents. By AD 700 the Christian period in North-West Africa had for all practical purposes ended.

[1] A similar phenomenon was observed among the Fezzan tribes a century later. See the discussion of a ninth-century text by R. Brunschvig, 'Un texte arabe du IXe siècle intéressant le Fezzan', *Revue Africaine*, 1945, **89**, 21–5.

[2] Ibn ʿAbd al-Ḥakam, *Futūḥ Ifriqiya wa'l Andalus*; ed. and trans. into French by A. Gateau (Algiers, 1942), 31. Also see Frend, 'North Africa and Europe in the Early Middle Ages', *Transactions of the Royal Historical Society*, 1955, 5, 5, 61–81.

CHAPTER 8

THE ARAB CONQUEST AND THE RISE OF ISLAM IN NORTH AFRICA

PROBLEMS OF SOURCES

The Arab conquests, which created a great new empire and led to the establishment of Islam as one of the great religions of the world, are one of the traditional landmarks of history. For European historians they are a part of that perennial problem, the transition from the ancient to the medieval world. Conventionally it was the conquests themselves in the seventh century AD which were decisive; or, with greater refinement, it has been suggested that the landmark should be placed in the eighth, when the caliphate was transferred from Damascus to Baghdad. The most celebrated opinion of the last fifty years is that of Pirenne, who argued that the Arab conquest of the eastern and southern Mediterranean cut off western Europe from the long-distance trade on which its economy had depended, and drove it back into rudimentary self-sufficiency. The criticism to which this theory has been subjected, however, illustrates the elementary point that the introduction of a new language into the sources, whatever it may be said to represent, has created a separate discipline to rank with the study of medieval Latin and Byzantine Greek among the successors to the Classics. At the same time the primarily European concern of Pirenne's hypothesis indicates the major interest of historians and the disparity of these disciplines in terms of the attention each has hitherto received. In this way the problems of Mediterranean history have been complicated rather than clarified; there has been neither a global treatment nor an adequate specialization. It is therefore ironic that the Arab conquests and the appearance of Islam in Africa should have been judged by those historians concerned with the more recent discipline of African history to represent the arrival on the continent of a unifying factor not only in terms of culture, but more basically in terms of source materials. The same strictures apply. The question of continuity and discontinuity is obscured by the problems of a new language and its literature.

How complicated these problems are, and how intimately they concern the underlying problems of the society, begins to appear from the fact that the earliest extant works in Arabic date from the end of the eighth century AD, and that the written tradition to which they belong cannot be considered to be much earlier than the middle of that century. They belong to a growing religious or semi-religious literature which rapidly attained great size and variety. To compensate for this late development, this literature is preoccupied with the historical origins and growth of the Muslim community, purporting to give, inter alia, a detailed and faithful account of sayings and doings which were carefully remembered until they were at last written down. It has therefore yielded a coherent story of the appearance of the new religion among the Arabs, and of the subsequent Arab conquests, which has been generally accepted as basically correct. The gist of this story is that the religion we know was in existence at the death of the Prophet Muḥammad in AD 632, and was the inspiration of the conquests which followed. But the possibility of the false tradition has been a professional preoccupation of Muslim scholars ever since these traditions were circulated in writing, and it is generally conceded that despite their care, many are spurious. From the existence of such traditions, the late Joseph Schacht went on to reopen the question of the origin of the *sharīʿa*, the Islamic Law which is central to Muslim belief and practice, showing first the debt to behaviour, external influence and law-making over the first hundred years after the conquests, and, secondly, the manner in which the rules and regulations of the Muslim community were arranged and authorized over the next hundred years by systematic ascription to the Prophet. This is quite other than an attempt to isolate a residual original from subsequent accretions; it is a demonstration of the way in which a whole corpus of narrative was established because of the care of Muslim scholars to obtain a single divine authority for arguments, beliefs and practices coming from different times and different places. Each item in the corpus is accordingly suspect, and those which have been declared false often represent simply the failure of a doctrine to gain acceptance.

A similar opinion has been entertained about the *Sīra*, the traditional biography of Muḥammad – that its details have been worked out in accordance with the interests and ideas of a later age about the life that a prophet should have led. In particular, the question is beginning to arise about the Koran, the Book of God which was revealed to Muḥammad, that far from being an established possession of the Muslim community from the beginning, it took its present form along with the Law in the course of scholarly argument which culminated in the ninth century in the consecration of the text as a heavenly original.[1] Whatever the lengths to which such arguments are taken, they reveal that the Arabic literature of the ninth century turned to a very large extent upon a vision of the past established in accordance with the criteria of a subsequent period. The preoccupation with the historical origins and development of the Muslim community, the painstaking record of what had been said and done, are seen as devices without any necessary relationship to anything which may have happened. The multitude of specific statements about the past, which were the units of knowledge and the data of argument, turn out to be formal requirements whose necessity was only established towards the end of the eighth century as a means of giving precise expression to contemporary opinion. In no sphere was the apparently historical statement so highly developed as in the case of the Law, but, required for religious purposes, it became central to Arabic learning and literature at large. Robert Brunschvig, for example, has convincingly shown that the work of the earliest extant Muslim historian of Egypt and North Africa, the ninth-century Egyptian writer Ibn ʿAbd al-Ḥakam, is to a considerable extent a collection of specifically legal traditions and, furthermore, of historical anecdotes employed in the same way to justify religious and political opinions.[2]

Thus the narrowly historical interest of the material derives in the last rather than the first place from a literature whose development is intrinsic to that of Islam itself. The problem for the historian is twofold. On the one hand it is of a kind familiar to students of Judaism and Christianity: to use the literature as evidence for the formation rather than the elaboration of the new religion. On the other, it is to perceive what happened before the process of formation was complete and the vision of the past took shape. It is fortunate for the historian of Africa that the question of Arabian origins lies strictly outside his competence. Yet the work of Brunschvig shows that the problem is still real. Whatever the ultimate conclusions, it is now unwise for the African historian to rely without hesitation upon the traditional story. In practice this means that it is necessary to dissociate the appearance of Islam, as the religion we know, from the Arab conquests. The presence of a religious element in those conquests is certain, but it is hard to see what form it took within the general Judaeo-Christian tradition. It may have been

[1] For specific references, see the bibliography for this chapter.

[2] R. Brunschvig, 'Ibn Abdal'hakam et la conquête de l'Afrique du Nord par les Arabes: étude critique', *Annales de l'Institut des Études Orientales* (Algiers), 1942–7, 6, 108–55.

apocalyptic; it probably laid stress upon meeting, prayer and preaching; and doubtless it acted as a bond for the community. But rather than go further, it is preferable to concentrate on this community of conquerors, its composition and growth.

Here at last it is a question of isolating a residual historical truth from statements which, whatever their origin, have been placed on an equal footing for the purpose of religion. Legal traditions were late in appearing, and drew partly upon less formal material, of which there is a glimpse in Ibn ʿAbd al-Ḥakam. Under the name of *khabar* (pl. *akhbār*), 'information', such material dealt for example with the doings of individuals and families under the empire. Despite exaggeration, falsification and legend, it might be thought to represent the historical consciousness of a community before this was shaped by formal criteria. It should have transmitted to the extant sources a quantity of reliable information. The difficulty is to decide whether the standards of acceptance and rejection at work in each successive phase in the development of the written tradition were such as to subvert the greater part, if not the whole. Here the African historian is more positively fortunate. Writing some years before Schacht, Dennett justified a fundamental confidence in the Arabic sources for the administration and taxation of the empire in the seventh and eighth century, by pointing to the great variety of conflicting statements which they contain. This, he considered, refuted the claim of Caetani that the story they offered was a stereotype, and suggested that they faithfully recorded the variety of practice in the various provinces.[1] While Caetani may have been wrong to give the impression of uniformity, it is clear from Schacht that each statement has in fact been shaped by jurisprudence. Many traditions, notably those relating to the two caliphs ʿUmar I and ʿUmar II, must be regarded as false, while the remainder, which make a fundamental distinction between land taken at the conquest *ʿanwatan*, 'by force', and land taken *ʿahdan*, 'by compact', do not so much record what actually happened as translate it into legal terms. That the translation stayed close to the original, however, can be shown not only from the fact that the accounts vary from province to province. In Egypt they are substantially borne out by the papyrus documents which have survived from the whole of this period from the seventh to the ninth century AD, at first almost all in Greek, changing in the course of the eighth century to Arabic.

[1] D. C. Dennett, *Conversion and the poll-tax in early Islam* (Cambridge, Mass., 1950), 3–13, esp. 11, with reference to L. Caetani, *Annali dell' Islam*, 10 vols. (Milan, from 1905).

The Egyptian papyri form an invaluable record; they also demonstrate that the written tradition, when it made its appearance in Egypt from the middle of the eighth century onwards, was indebted to an archive going back to the establishment of a regular administration under Arab control. The importance of such an archive can be gauged from the unsatisfactory nature of the story of the conquest of the lands further west, where no regular administration was established before the beginning of the eighth century at Kairouan (more properly Qayrawān) in modern Tunisia, and Cordoba in Spain. Even then, no documents other than coins survive, and the matter is complicated by the fact that the earliest writers on the subject are Egyptian or Oriental. The local historical tradition did not begin to appear in writing before the tenth century AD, and by the time the extant works in this tradition were compiled between the twelfth and fourteenth centuries, information about the very early period has become suspiciously orderly, fitted into a well-developed scheme of history in which the place of Islam and its adherents is both central and secure. Nevertheless, the fact of an archive in the western capitals may be assumed from the beginning of regular administration after the year 700, and this lends a little substance to the account of Ibn ʿAbd al-Ḥakam until he begins to rely from about 725 onwards on the contemporary witness of the first writers in the Egyptian tradition.

The value of these first writers is still very problematic, and it is fortunate that the literature can be supplemented from the end of the seventh century onwards by the archaeological investigation of art and architecture. The principal remains have been examined and described in detail by Cresswell from a base in Egypt and the Middle East, and by Georges Marçais and his successors from a base in Tunisia. Their work is at present being greatly extended by the systematic excavation, not only of Muslim sites, but even more important of sites which show a continuity from the late classical period onwards. One obvious and natural conclusion is that the peoples concerned did not disappear, but slowly changed. It goes to the heart of the question of Islamic origins, which is commonly put in terms of the failure of Christianity to survive south of the Mediterranean except as the religion of a minority in Egypt. For the moment it is more important that the tradition of the Coptic Church of Egypt offers the only substantial alternative to the Muslim version of the conquest and subsequent history of the country. This tradition is by no means independent. The cardinal figure in its composition, the tenth century Sāwīrūs (Severus) b. Muqaffaʿ, Bishop of Ashmunayn in Upper Egypt, had the record of the Patriarchate of Alexandria down to his own day assembled and translated from Greek and Coptic into Arabic. Severus was especially concerned to refute the work of a rival, Eutychius, known as Saʿid b. Baṭrīq, the head of the small Orthodox Church in the country. Eutychius composed a history from the time of Adam which naturally opposed the claim of the Coptic or Monophysite, the Yaʿqūbī or Jacobite Church, to be the true church of the Apostle St Mark in Egypt. He too wrote in Arabic, and found the Muslim scheme sufficiently convenient to arrange his later material by the reigns of the caliphs.

The content of both Severus and Eutychius is in consequence very similar to the Muslim material, even when it presents an opposite point of view. Accounts of different origins have been consolidated in a tale of Christian virtue in which heretics are abominable, but docility towards the Muslim regime conforms to the disposition of the world in the eyes of the Muslim historians. The varying value of the information is concealed, although the bias of particular authors is detectable. Severus and his team of translators were governed to some extent by what they could find in the monastery of St Macarius. It is possible that from time to time Muslim versions have been appropriated for a Christian purpose. The selectivity of the *History of the Coptic patriarchs* nevertheless appears from a comparison with a previous work in the same tradition. This survives only in an Ethiopic translation of an Arabic version of passages originally in Greek and Coptic, but for this reason must be considered a composition like that of Severus's, a ninth- or tenth-century edition of the work of the original author, John Bishop of Nikiou in Lower Egypt at the end of the seventh century. Thus edited, John's *Chronicle* is interesting, since its scheme, an account of Egypt in the context of a universal history culminating in a Muslim dominion, is precisely that of Ibn ʿAbd al-Ḥakam, with the difference that the appearance of Christianity is naturally the cardinal event, and the present regime is one of 'pagan impostors' from whom the faithful have been preserved as before from 'perfidious heretics'. Notwithstanding, it contains what are certainly the earliest accounts of the Arab conquests.

THE ARAB OCCUPATION OF EGYPT

Severus deals with the Arab conquest of Egypt, but is brief to the point of ignoring almost everything except the reappearance of the

Coptic Patriarch Benjamin I after years of hiding from Byzantine persecution directed by 'al-Muqawqas'. Eutychius says more, but merely to identify 'al-Muqawqas', whom he calls the financial superintendent, as a 'Jacobite', an heretical Copt, who betrayed the country to the Arabs out of hatred of 'Rome'. It was the *Chronicle* of John of Nikiou which was largely used by Butler to settle the identity of 'al-Muqawqas', and establish a convincing account. The mysterious 'Muqawqas' was Cyrus, Bishop of Phasis in Colchis, appointed by the Emperor Heraclius not only as an Orthodox or 'Melkite' Patriarch of Alexandria in the last of many attempts by Constantinople to recover the Church in Egypt from the Monophysite heresy, but also as the governor of the country. When the Arabs invaded the country from Palestine under ʿAmr b. al-ʿĀṣ in December 639, it was Cyrus who first defended and then negotiated the surrender of the fortress of Babylon at the head of the Delta during the years 640 and 641. After a brief dismissal, he returned to Egypt to negotiate the surrender of Alexandria, the Byzantine capital, in 642. As Butler saw it, the problem was to account for the motives of a man who could so capitulate, even though Alexandria in 641 had proved impregnable. Did he hope to remain as governor under the Arabs, dying before his plans could mature?

The question of Cyrus's treachery, however, depends on a view of the situation in Egypt as a three-cornered contest between the Monophysite Copts, the Orthodox Greeks, and the Muslim Arabs. Cyrus, the Orthodox Greek, is then an evil genius who weakens the Byzantine regime by persecution of its heretical subjects, only to turn traitor to his religion and his king. This theme of religions and races is certainly that of the later sources, both Muslim and Christian. It is not so clearly that of John of Nikiou. The confusion of his narrative was remarked by Butler, who considered that in this section of the work many sentences and pages had been displaced at some stage preceding the Ethiopic translation. In some cases this appears to be true; in particular, the absence of the passage dealing with some thirty years from the accession of the Emperor Heraclius in 610, resuming only with the Arabs, or 'Ishmaelites', already in the country, makes it hard to understand what follows. There are however two notable inconsistencies. Cyrus is on the one hand a tyrant and on the other a tragic figure acting in the best interests of the community. ʿAmr, the Arab leader, appears as both a cruel oppressor and a benevolent ruler. It may be suggested that the principal confusion of the narrative arises from a conflation of two alternative accounts whose attributions have been lost in the course of translation. What then emerges is the sketch of a situation which does not lend itself to simple categories.

Granted the presence of alternative versions, it is quite likely that two apparently dissimilar events are in fact the same. There is however a strong theme of collaboration with the Arabs on the part of both governors and governed. Sometimes this seems directed against the imperial government and its church, as in the initial account of fighting in the Fayum, and the mention of two worthies, Kalājī and Sābendīs, who had defected. Elsewhere, renegades take up arms against their fellows, and specifically, it would seem, against the Jacobites. These reports may be compared with those which illustrate a second theme, the enmity between the various sectors of the population, between the inhabitants of Lower Egypt and those at the head of the Delta, between the factions of the Blue and Green at Alexandria, and between Melkites and Jacobites. Both themes shade off into that of ʿAmr's oppression, with which is linked the complicity of high officials. The prefect George builds a bridge to ʿAmr's command. The prefect Menas and his two henchmen, who hate the Egyptians, are employed by ʿAmr to exact forced labour by terror. John, prefect of Alexandria, on the other hand, collaborates to protect his charges. Cyrus himself, at the head of a party favouring accommodation, against a background of metropolitan Byzantine politics and in the face of popular opposition, acts in what he believes to be the best interests of the Egyptians. The brutal persecutor has another side, which is not that of a traitor.

Certainly there is no clear-cut polarity. The invaders themselves appear as only one among many conflicting parties. Their principal successes, the negotiation of the surrender of Babylon in 640/1, and that of Alexandria in 641/2, take place against a background of confused warfare in the Delta over two or three years. The campaign took the form of an advance up the right branch of the Nile to Babylon, then down the left branch to Alexandria. But not only did ʿAmr depend to an unspecified extent upon local recruits and local allies; the opposition had its moments also. Kalājī and Sābendīs are won back to the loyalists. The Arabs are defeated at Samanud. Those of Lower Egypt who oppose collaboration attack those in favour, and make themselves feared. ʿAmr's foray into the eastern Delta is unsuccessful. As to his men, the Arabs or 'Ishmaelites' were the nucleus, but all may not have been foreigners. As in Syria and Iraq, there may have been Arabs of a kind already in or on the borders of the Nile Valley. In the first century BC,

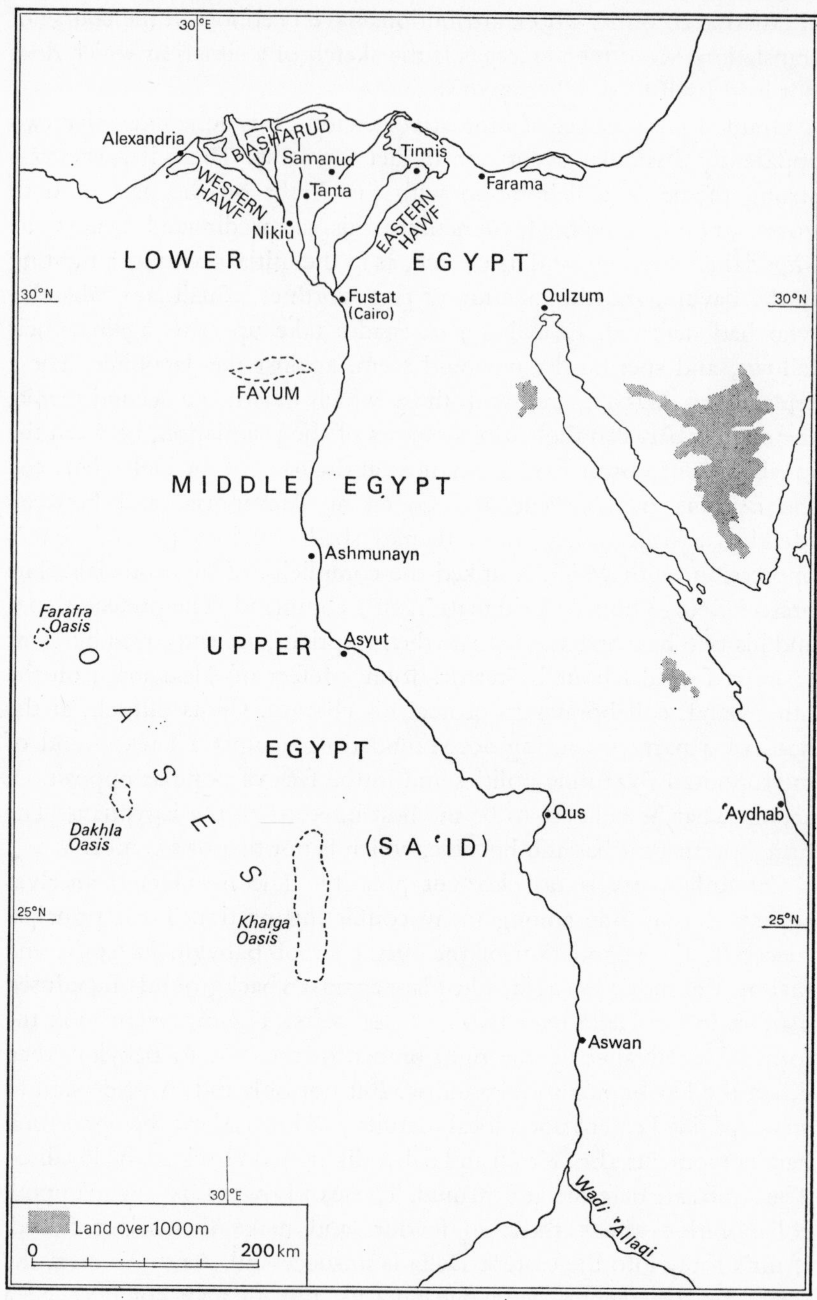

62 Egypt, from the seventh to the ninth centuries.

Strabo had called the east bank of the river 'Arabia',[1] and told how camel merchants brought goods from the Red Sea to Koptos in Upper Egypt.[2] ʿAmr himself is said, however apocryphally, to have become familiar with the country as a merchant in the days before he joined the Prophet. At the same time it is possible that with the Ishmaelites had come recruits of miscellaneous origin, whose numbers increased as local men came forward.

The matter was resolved when the Byzantines withdrew on the instructions of Constantinople,[3] and the Coptic Duke Sanutius (Shenute) took what may have been a personal decision to place the Egyptian fleet at the disposal of ʿAmr in return for favour shown to the Jacobite Church.[4] The Byzantines returned in 645 to recapture Alexandria, but were driven out in the following year. Meanwhile the fleet assisted in the conquest of Cyrenaica, and the Patriarch Benjamin came out of hiding to be reinstated as the rightful successor of St Mark. His Church was made official, and came into full possession of ecclesiastical property in Egypt, which it held on the basis of the Roman law of *piae causae*. Titles to this effect were probably the subject of privileges granted from the beginning by the new regime,[5] along with tax exemptions. In return it may be supposed that the Coptic Church helped to ensure that the Arabs took over the country and its administration quickly and smoothly. The initial levies of food and clothing were abandoned. The Coptic population was classified as *dhimmī*, 'protected', in token of which a poll-tax was imposed on adult males. The basic taxes remained the same, notably the taxes in kind, which were levied in accordance with a periodic assessment of what the land would bear, and the labour services required for public works. The distinction in the sources between land taken *ʿanwatan*, 'by force', and land taken *ʿahdan*, 'by compact', reflects the distinction between domain land, confiscated from the Byzantine state and the Byzantine nobility, and land under the district administration, the pagarchy. On domain land, taxes were levied directly from individual occupants; elsewhere they were levied for the most part through a village quota.

[1] *The geography of Strabo*, ed. and trans. by H. L. Jones (London and Cambridge, Mass., revised reprint, 1935), VIII, 71, 85, 135.

[2] Ibid. 119–21.

[3] Cf. G. Ostrogorsky, *History of the Byzantine state*, trans. by J. Hussey (Oxford, 1956), 101–3.

[4] Cf. R. G. Goodchild, 'Byzantines, Berbers and Arabs in 7th century Libya', *Antiquity*, 1967, **41**, 115–24.

[5] For examples from the eleventh and twelfth centuries AD, cf. S. M. Stern, *Fāṭimid decrees* (London, 1964).

The new dispensation was a movement away from the power of the landlord towards control by a central government. Whereas in the sixth century the great estates of the Byzantine aristocracy had been *autopracts*, self-governing territories which had provided their owners with the wealth and influence to dominate the state officials in the localities,[1] the flight of the proprietors opened the way to stronger direction from above. The authority of the pagarchs, the district governors, was increased; at the same time they were required to make regular visits to the capital. It was a movement, however, which stayed well within the old bounds of government in Egypt. These were fundamentally determined by the economy. Egypt's dependence upon the Nile is a commonplace, but the problems of agriculture have varied from the narrow valley of Upper Egypt, the Ṣaʿīd, to the marshy coast of the Delta. The old system of basin irrigation – the controlled flooding of the countryside – was straightforward in the southern part of the valley, required the building of canals in the more northerly section and in the southern part of the Delta, and was scarcely practicable nearer to the sea. To build and maintain the dykes, canals, wells and ditches which were needed throughout the year, and especially to organize the collective effort required to manage the flood, local initiative at a village or at most a district level was necessary but sufficient. Until the introduction in the nineteenth and twentieth centuries of a system of dams and barrages requiring unified control of the river below Aswan, there was no basic economic need for a central government, an 'hydraulic despotism' whose management was essential to production. While the state may have been able to provide a measure of co-ordination, it was never able to overcome the problem of recurrent famine; its economic policy was more designed to feed the capital and maintain the level of exports, and its other activities might be responsible for long periods of depression. Revenue was the overriding consideration, and the principal purpose of centralization. In practice, the state rarely possessed an administration of sufficient competence to supervise the entire country, and it tended to delegate its authority to men on the spot.

The Romans had relied extensively on tax-farmers to organize production and guarantee the yield. The Byzantine aristocracy had carried the process a step further in the direction of the autonomous

[1] Cf. briefly H. I. Bell, 'Egypt and the Byzantine empire', in *The legacy of Egypt*, 1st edn, ed. by S. R. K. Glanville (Oxford, 1942), 332–47; C. Préaux, 'Graeco-Roman Egypt', in ibid., 2nd edn, ed. by J. R. Harris (Oxford, 1971), esp. 347–52.

local magnate. With the coming of the Arabs, the balance was not so much redressed as refined. The departure of the Byzantines meant that native Egyptians, who already provided the administration with the bulk of its personnel, came to hold all but the highest 'ministerial' posts. The pagarchs were drawn from a class of property owners who appear in the papyri from Aphrodito in Upper Egypt under the name of *proteuontes*. These formed a separate group, along with the city and the villages, as one of the three constituents of the pagarchy, the unit of administration. Partly no doubt because of the disappearance of the Greeks, by the end of the seventh century AD some of them seem to have been very rich indeed. The pagarchs themselves, in their official capacity, enjoyed considerable discretion despite the supervision to which they were subjected. As might be expected, they were closely connected with the Church, which seems to have been able to depend upon the Faithful to make good any losses caused by the occasional exactions of the Arabs. Christians in fact understood each other's problems very well, and the charity extended to both rich and poor may well have amounted to a conspiracy to live their lives under the Arabs with the least possible interference. Their behaviour, which amounted to a substantial degree of independence, could perhaps have been summed up in Severus's theme, valid at the time of composition in the tenth century, of patient acceptance of whatever the Lord might send by way of infidel rule.

The Arabs themselves made their capital at Babylon, the fortress commanding the junction of the Nile Valley and the Delta. Outside the castle they made a camp which became a *miṣr* (pl. *amṣār*), a 'garrison city', called Fusṭāṭ (Latin *fossa*, Greek *phossaton*, 'trenches'; Arabic 'tent') or, simply, Miṣr, an old name for Egypt which happened to be the same as the common noun, of Syriac origin, for a foundation of this kind. It was centred on what became the Mosque of ʿAmr, the house of the commander and place of assembly. Beginning as a tented camp, it rapidly acquired more permanent buildings, and like Roman legionary foundations such as Chester or York, and Lambaesis in Roman Africa, it developed a civilian character. This should not obscure the original military nature of the settlement, or of its first inhabitants. They were called by one or more of a cluster of terms hinging on the notion of trust, submission, agreement and protection. From *amn* or *amān*, 'safety', 'peace', comes *īmān*, 'entering safety', 'faith', and *mu'min*, 'faithful'. From *salm* or *salām*, 'peace', comes *islām*, 'acceptance of peace', 'submission', and *muslim*, 'one who submits'. With these went *bayʿa*, 'homage'; *dhimma*, 'protection'; *'ahd*, 'agreement'; and *ṣulḥ*, 'peace'. All these terms have acquired a specifically, sometimes exclusively, religious meaning, stemming ultimately from the strong biblical notion of covenant. But whatever their religious connotation may have been in the seventh century, all of them translated the relevant Latin terms of Roman law, especially as this was being modified in practice by the late classical and early medieval trend towards personal allegiance. It was at least as much a question of fidelity and obedience to human masters. *Mu'min*, the term contained in the principal title of the new monarch, *Amīr al-Mu'minīn* ('Commander of the Faithful'), seems to have been originally reserved for the first adherents to the cause, the Arabs. *Muslim* may have been interchangeable with *dhimmī*, the term eventually applied to Christian, Jewish and Zoroastrian subjects, and designated non-Arabs of inferior status before becoming the chief word for a believer.

In Egypt itself, the papyri distinguish between the *moagaritai* and *mauloi*, that is, *muhājirūn* and *mawālī*. *Muhājirūn* is a term connected with the name of 'Hagarenes', sons of Hagar or Ishmaelites, by which the Arabs were known. Specifically, however, it meant 'emigrants', those who had made a *hijra* ('hegira') or exodus. The term was subsequently restricted to those who had made the Hijra – that is, to those who had accompanied Muḥammad in his flight from Mecca to Medina in AD 622, which was taken as the beginning of the Muslim era. But in this context it referred to those Arabs who had 'emigrated' out of the wilderness into the armies of the *amṣār*, the garrison cities, for the sake of the cause. It was thus a term like *mu'minūn*, distinguishing Arabs who had committed themselves in this way from those who had not. Originally this *hijra* must have been encouraged as well as desired, and the *muhājirūn* must have been all the Arabs who came to Egypt, where they formed a nomadic horde based on Fusṭāṭ, but migrating up and down the eastern side of the Delta. From the end of the seventh century, however, the *muhājirūn* were enrolled in tribal regiments on a register, *dīwān* (pl. *dawāwīn*), which was used to limit the size of the force. *Hijra* then became a kind of enlistment which could be denied to most of the beduin, the 'people of the countryside'.[1]

The history of the *muhājirūn* is echoed and corroborated by that of the *mawālī* (sing. *mawlā*), 'clients'. *Walā'*, the client-patron relationship,

[1] For *hijra* in this sense cf. H. A. R. Gibb, 'The fiscal Rescript of 'Umar II', *Arabica*, 1955, 2, 1, 1–16. The Rescript purports to be a general directive of the early eighth century, but may well have been composed in Egypt in the ninth, with reference at this point to the final exclusion of the Arabs from the *dīwān* in 834.

which included the relationship of a freedman to his former owner, may have been known in Arabia before the conquests, although not under this name, which originally meant 'friendship'. As defined after the conquests, however, it corresponded to a relationship of very long standing in the Mediterranean world, where it was governed by Roman law. In the early community of the Faithful it was associated with *islām*, 'submission', in the procedure of *muwālāt*, which entailed the creation of *walā'* between the new *muslim* and the one who received his 'submission'.[1] By 800 the procedure was defunct, but the early association of *islām* with *walā'* may be compared with the association of *hijra* with membership of the community in the case of the Arabs, as a means of entry into the *amṣār* by those of largely non-Arab origin. These became *muslimūn*, 'Muslims', as they were affiliated to a patron and took his tribal name. To judge from the *Chronicle* of John, this recruitment at first was voluntary, as individuals joined the invaders. Later it became more regular, as the Arabs endeavoured to maintain their strength over a wider and wider area, and more selective; the Qibṭ or Copts, the native Egyptians, were excluded, and more reliance was placed upon slaves who were freed by this initiation. Like the *muhājirūn*, the *mawālī* were organized into tribal regiments; one ʿAbd al-Raḥmān was rewarded with the command of his fellow *mawālī*, clients of the Arab tribe Tujīb, for his valour in killing the rival caliph, Ibn al-Zubayr, at Mecca in 692. But others were employed in garrison duties, specifically to guard the mouths of the Nile. In 673 Wardān, *mawlā* of ʿAmr b. al-ʿĀṣ, was killed in a Byzantine raid on Burullus. About 720 a body of *mawālī* perished during a similar raid on Tinnis, while in 750 the *mawlā* in command of the *mawālī* at Alexandria was killed in revolt against Marwān II. In this capacity the *mawālī* were associated with the native Christians who were called up for military duties as one of the liturgies or labour services they were required to provide. These were called *machimoi*, 'fighters', rendered into Arabic as *maqāmiṣa*,[2] and were especially responsible for manning the fleet.

By no means all *mawālī*, however, were government troops, or even *muslimūn* in any religious sense. The client, like the slave, was a familiar figure. It was natural that the Arabs, the new rulers, should acquire both as personal attendants. Many would have been the slaves or clients of lesser men. With little standing and no public function,

[1] J. Schacht, *The origins of Muhammadan jurisprudence* (Oxford, 1950; corrected reprint, 1953), 161, 173.

[2] M. A. Shaban, *Islamic history*, AD 600–750 (Cambridge, 1971), 157–8.

they would have been the nucleus of a civilian population in the garrison cities. No doubt the majority counted themselves as *muslimūn* out of loyalty to their owners and patrons, but some may have remained, for example, Christian. So with the slaves and clients of the great. About 700 the *ghulām* or slave Talīd was appointed governor of Barce (Barca) by his master ʿAbd al-ʿAzīz, the governor of Egypt. People complained that he was a slave, and therefore he was freed to become a *mawlā*; the question of religion does not come into the issue. Talīd is more important as an example of the way in which the household retinues of the leaders of the community were growing in size and importance. Slaves ranged from domestics to young men of trust, *ghilmān* (sing. *ghulām*), or *fityān* (sing. *fatā*), 'pages', who escorted their master and grew up to provide him with loyal aides. Emancipated like the *ghilmān* of Muḥammad b. Yazīd, who brought him news in prison of the death of his successor as governor of the Maghrib, they became his *mawālī* along with many others. Some might form a whole personal regiment following their patron into battle; they moved into and out of the regular army. During the warfare of the 740s, for example, Ḥafṣ b. al-Walīd constituted a following called the Ḥafṣiya out of the *mawālī* and the *maqāmiṣa*, and ʿAmr b. al-Waḍḍāḥ led a troop of the Waḍḍāḥiya into Egypt, while Zabbān b. ʿAbd al-ʿAzīz led the *mawālī* of the family to the defeat of the rebel Thābit. Many of these had probably commended themselves to their patron in accordance with the common practice of the ancient and early medieval world. Some may have been Arabs, even men of good birth, who like members of the native aristocracy accepted *walā'* for the sake of advancement. To judge from practice further west, Peter, governor of Upper Egypt, and his brother Theodore, who were obliged to become *muslim* by al-Aṣbagh, son of the governor ʿAbd al-ʿAzīz, about 704/5, are likely to have become his personal clients. All might aspire to power, wealth and ennoblement as they assisted their lord in his career, for the retinue and the clientele was the key to success, the means to occupy positions of importance with men of trust.

In this way the aristocracy itself grew in size. Its nucleus consisted of the leading Arab families, who owed their supremacy to the conquests and to the government of a growing empire. The rise of this aristocracy was summed up in the career of the Banū Umayya. The empire had been created by ʿUmar, 634–44, under whom Syria, Iraq and Egypt were won. The Byzantine empire survived, but the Persian empire was destroyed, and the Arabs went on to annex Iran. Egypt, which had been conquered by ʿAmr b. al-ʿĀṣ, was given to ʿAbd Allah b. Saʿd b. Abī Sarḥ, a relative of ʿUmar's successor ʿUthmān. ʿUthmān is said to have favoured his family, the Banū Umayya, provoking a rebellion in which he was murdered in 656. His successor ʿAlī was challenged by Muʿāwiya, the Umayyad governor of Syria, who in 661 became the first ruler of the Umayyad Dynasty. After a period of civil war from 683 to 693, the hegemony of the family was restored by ʿAbd al-Malik, 685–705, who appointed his brother ʿAbd al-ʿAzīz governor of Egypt for an unparalleled period of twenty years. The sons of ʿAbd al-ʿAzīz remained wealthy and powerful while his successors in office came and went. His rule in Egypt, like the reign of his brother at Damascus, was the beginning of a change in the character of government away from that of the *miṣr*, the garrison city, to that of the royal court. While the central buildings at Fusṭāṭ were reconstructed as the Mosque of ʿAmr for mainly religious purposes, ʿAbd al-ʿAzīz built for himself a new palace, the Dār al-Mudhahhab, the 'Golden Hall'. He went on to build outside the city at Helwan a residence which became a summer capital where the district governors were each required to build a house, and the patriarch himself built a church, since he too was required to make regular visits from Alexandria. ʿAbd al-ʿAzīz may have hoped to succeed his brother as Amīr al-Mu'minīn, but he died in the same year, 705.

THE ADVANCE INTO THE MAGHRIB

The necessary background to these developments in Egypt was provided by the lands to the west and south. Cyrenaica had been conquered by 645; as in the case of Egypt, the Byzantine capital of Apollonia or Sozusa on the coast was abandoned in favour of Barce, an inland site on the first terrace of the Jebel Akhdar, opposite the last Byzantine stronghold of Tokra. In 652 ʿAbd Allah b. Saʿd b. Abī Sarḥ is credited with an expedition as far as the Nubian capital of Dongola, and the conclusion of a treaty called the *baqṭ* providing basically for the exchange of corn for slaves. *Baqṭ* has been derived from an ancient Egyptian *bakh*, meaning 'barter',[1] but this may depend too much upon the element of exchange in the ninth-century Arabic accounts. It is more likely to be Latin *pactum*, Greek *pakton*, suggesting that a long-standing relationship going back to Roman times was endorsed and continued by the Arabs. Over the next twenty years or so, raids against

[1] Cf. *Encyclopaedia of Islam*, 2nd edn (Leiden and London, 1954—), under *bak̩t*. For a text of this *baqt*, see ch. 9, pp. 566–7.

Tripoli and Byzantine Africa are attributed to Muʿāwiya b. Ḥudayj, and it may be about this time that the Arabs first entered the Fezzan.

Cyrenaica, Nubia and the Fezzan all have similar tales told about them in the ninth-century sources. In these accounts, the people of Barce submitted willingly to ʿAmr, who made peace with them; thereafter they paid their tribute by themselves, without the need for a tax-collector. The Berber people called the Lawāta, however, rebelled, and as a punishment it was specified that they might sell their children to pay what they owed. In the case of the Fezzan, the inhabitants submitted to ʿAmr and made an agreement which they then broke. This agreement was restored by ʿUqba b. Nāfiʿ on his way west in 666/7, on condition that 360 'heads' were sent every year as tribute. In the case of Nubia, the *baqṭ*, the agreement concluded by ʿAbd Allah, included the same stipulation of 360 'heads' a year because once again the Nubians had broken an initial agreement with ʿAmr. To this number, a further forty were said to have been added as a present, while the Arabs undertook to supply commodities such as grain in exchange.

All three stories are fictions; with their common theme, they are the product of Muslim jurisprudence, which by the ninth century had concluded that it was illegal to enslave peoples who had entered into a pact of any kind with the Muslims. This was a logical deduction from a view of the world in which the peoples were arranged in order below the Muslims at the top of the scale, down through Christians, Jews and Persians to unbelievers. A second scale described the actual relations of the Muslim community with other peoples as these had been established at the time of the conquests, ranging from domination through various less comprehensive states of peace to actual or potential war. This went with yet a third, which turned on the opposition of Islam and slavery as two extremes of the human condition; no Muslim could become a slave (even though a slave might become a Muslim), nor might any of those who were protected by Islam as partners to any kind of agreement. Slavery could only arise by birth, or by the capture of someone in a state of war, a non-Muslim to whom Islam was under no obligation. These scales had been derived from Roman law.[1] Applied to Egypt, they may have reflected the relations of Byzantium with the neighbouring lands. The three accounts have to be seen as an attempt to justify an infringement of the scheme, the taking of slaves from peoples who should have been exempt. The anomaly is explained as a justifiable punishment.

[1] For the element of Roman law, cf. P. Crone, 'The Mawālī in the Umayyad period', unpublished Ph.D. thesis (University of London, 1973).

The slave-trade in question was probably very old, but was greatly promoted by the Arab conquests. Large numbers of captives were taken in wars and raids, and their allocation as part of the booty was a major preoccupation. From what happened still further west, it is clear that human tributes were then required, partly to meet the demand for female slaves, but also to keep up the numbers of *mawālī*. The recruitment of the Qibṭ, the native Copts, was prohibited either by voluntary enlistment or through enslavement; the regime preferred to keep them as tax-paying subjects for fiscal purposes. When in 744 *islām* was briefly encouraged by the exemption of the new *muslim* from the poll-tax, this was an opportunity to become a soldier. It was clearly exceptional. *Mawālī* may have been sent as reinforcements from the east. Some were probably obtained by the slave-trade from Nubia. The majority, however, were drawn by this means from the Barbar, the Berbers of the Libyan area and beyond, whose conquest proved indispensable as well as profitable.

Around the Gulf of Syrtis (Sidra) the desert reaches the sea, forming a natural frontier between Barce and Tripoli. Tripoli was a part of Byzantine Africa, with its capital at Carthage, covering this stretch of the Libyan coast, Tunisia and eastern Algeria. Once again, the initial conquest of Tripoli is attributed to ʿAmr. About 647/8 ʿAbd Allah is said to have advanced into the heart of the Byzantine province to slay the exarch Gregory, in revolt against Constantinople, in an epic encounter at Sufetula (Sbeitla) in Tunisia. Subsequent expeditions are associated with Muʿāwiya b. Ḥudayj. It is perhaps acceptable to date the first attempt at occupation to about 670 with the establishment of a *miṣr* or *qayrawān* (a 'caravan' or halt) on the edge of the steppe about 130 km south of Carthage, from which the Byzantines exercised an uncertain authority. The purpose may have been to capture the port as part of the Arab attack upon Constantinople which occupied the decade. The site chosen by the founder, ʿUqba b. Nāfiʿ, was at the foot of the Tunisian Dorsal, the range which runs from the Aures mountains in the south-west towards Cape Bon in the north-east, and separates the lower and drier lands around the Gulf of Gabes from the higher and wetter country of the Medjerda valley and the Constantinois. The new city of Kairouan (i.e. Qayrawān) would, however, have been abandoned in the 680s during the civil wars which unsettled the Umayyads at this time, when the invaders seem to have fallen back on Tripoli and Barce. The successful attempt at conquest came in the 690s after ʿAbd al-Malik had restored the authority of the dynasty in the east. Carthage was then

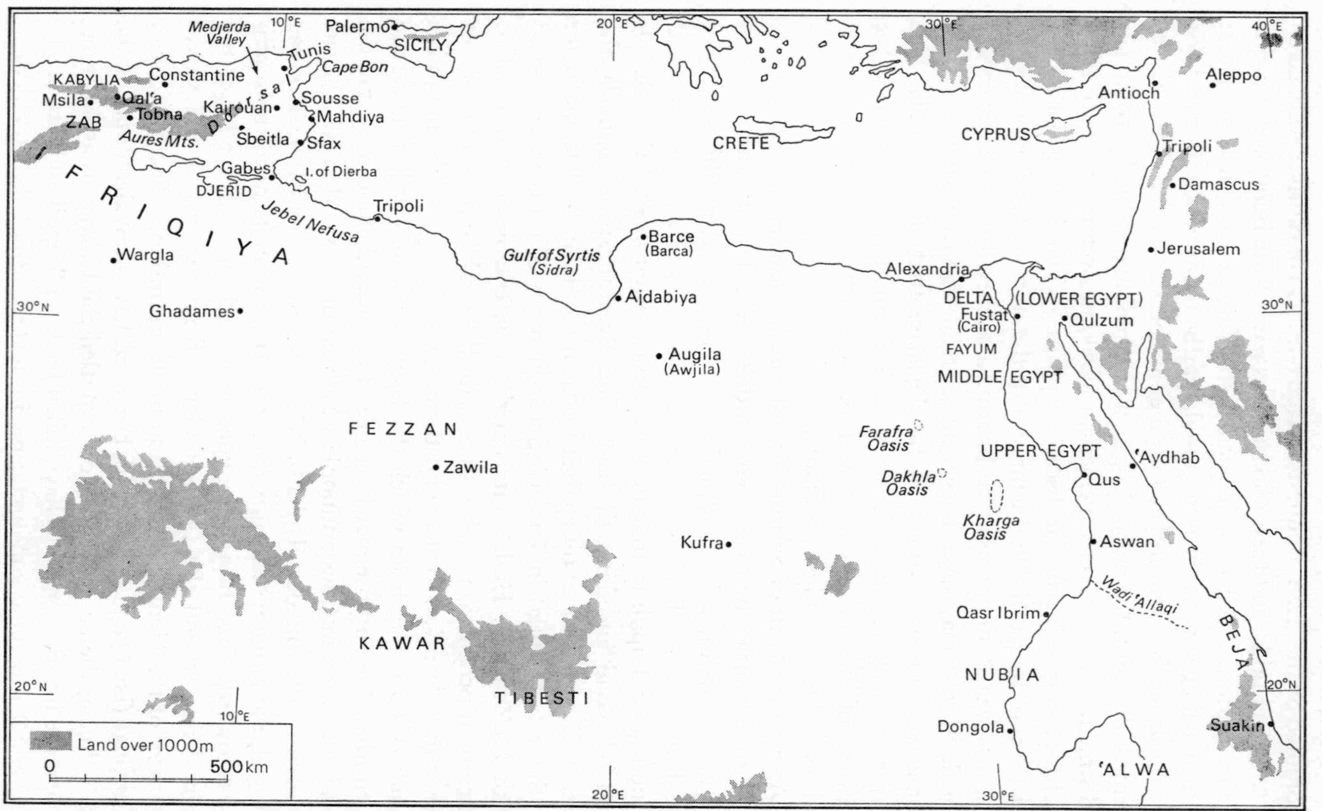

63 Egypt, Nubia and Ifrīqiya, from the seventh to the ninth centuries.

taken, destroyed and rebuilt as Tunis. By 705 Ḥasan b. al-Nuʿmān had converted the former Byzantine territory into a new province with the same name, Ifrīqiya.

The result testifies to the Byzantine achievement. Although the power of Carthage had been doubtful for fifty years, the area it had once controlled survived as an administrative unit. How it came to do so is obscure, but the explanation is probably to be found in the opposition which the Arabs encountered from native princes who saw themselves as the true heirs of Rome. The names we have are Kasīla (Kusayla), who would seem to have killed ʿUqba b. Nāfiʿ about 683 and to have ruled the country from Kairouan, and the Kāhina, 'the Prophetess', who ten years later would seem to have repelled the Arabs yet again before her final defeat and death. The one would have been for the time a *muslim* ally, the other perhaps a Jewish queen. In one account, however, Kasīla becomes the son of the Kāhina, whose Arabic title may be simply a deformation of a proper name Kahyā (Dahyā).[1] The argument for her Judaism is weak, and if Kāhina is indeed a deformation, 'she' may have been a man. The earliest extant Maghribī source, the *Riyāḍ al-Nufūs* of al-Mālikī in the eleventh century, would suggest that the Kāhina was a Christian. All sources make a connection between the two personages and the Rūm, the Byzantines, and it is likely that, whoever they were, they helped maintain the Byzantine tradition until the Arabs were strong enough to win the succession for themselves.

This conclusion is supported by the archaeological evidence, which points to a continuity of occupation of urban sites from the late Roman, Christian period into the early Muslim period. At Belalis Major in north-western Tunisia there was first a forum, then a Christian church built and rebuilt some distance away while the forum was given over to housing. An Arabic coin of the early eighth century has been found in the base of the rectangular fort which was erected on the site of this church probably towards the end of the century.[2] At the beginning of their effective occupation, the Arabs seem to have encountered a population whose ways were those of the Byzantine world. Beyond this, however, the deficiences of the literary sources make this population difficult to perceive.

The term Ifrīqī (pl. Afāriq or Afāriqa), 'African', evidently derived

[1] Cf. H. Z. Hirschberg, 'The Berber heroine known as the Kāhina' (in Hebrew), *Tarbiz*, 1957, **26**, 4, 370–83.

[2] A preliminary account of the excavation by A. Mahjoubi is in the *Actes* of the Premier Congrès d'Histoire et de Civilisation du Maghreb, Tunis, Dec. 1974.

from the toponym Ifrīqiya, 'Africa', which the Arabs took from the Latin, is used by Ibn ʿAbd al-Ḥakam for the inhabitants of the country, as Qibṭ, 'Copt', is at first a word for the native Egyptian. The plural form Afāriq, Afāriqa, then evolves, like Qibṭ, as the name of a community. Ibn ʿAbd al-Ḥakam specifies that after his victory over the Kāhina, Ḥasan b. al-Nuʿmān organized the government of Ifrīqiya, imposing regular taxes upon the *ʿajam* and such of the Barbar as were, like the *ʿajam*, Christian. As in Egypt, religion is the criterion, although the terms are racial and linguistic. Barbar is the expression for most of the inhabitants of the lands west of Egypt; *ʿajam*, the other term used, means non-Arab in the sense of non-Arabic-speaking. A little later in the ninth century, al-Yaʿqūbī makes the same distinction.[1] Elsewhere, however, he uses *ʿajam* more generally to embrace the Barbar, the Afāriq and the Rūm.[2] The Rūm should properly be Greeks, lingering on perhaps after the conquest; the Barbar remain as before. The Afāriq, on the other hand, have clearly become something less than the inhabitants of Ifrīqiya. In the tenth century, al-Muqaddasī lists alongside Arabic and Berber a language resembling 'the Rūmī', most plausibly Latin, which was used for inscriptions down to the eleventh century. From this, following Georges Marçais, it may be conjectured that the Afāriq were specifically the Latins of the Byzantine period, surviving as a church. Beside them, the Jews were probably represented by numerous self-contained communities.

The Barbar present a different problem. According to Ibn ʿAbd al-Ḥakam they were a race; their language was recognized by Ibn al-Kalbī in Iraq about 800. They are divided by Ibn ʿAbd al-Ḥakam into two groups, the Barānis and the Butr, when dealing with the period 675–725; thereafter, when events fall within the lifetime of ʿUthmān b. Ṣāliḥ, his principal source, these terms are replaced by names of individual peoples. When they reappear, notably in the work of the fourteenth-century Ibn Khaldūn, it is in genealogical guise as the descendents of the eponymous Barnis and al-Abtar, sons of a founding-father Barr. The genealogies appear to be an invention, the product perhaps of a literary genre which sought to establish the claim to fame of each nation within Islam. They need not testify to any profound ethnographic distinction, despite the attempt of E.-F. Gautier to identify the two groups as sedentaries and nomads in perpetual com-

[1] al-Yaʿqūbī, *Kitāb al-Buldān*, ed. by M. de Goeje (Leiden, 1892), 347; French trans. by G. Wiet, *Le Livre des pays* (Cairo, 1937), 208.

[2] Ibid. 350/trans. 212.

petition with each other.[1] William Marçais suggested a reference to dress, *barānis* being the plural of *burnus*, 'burnous', *abtar* meaning 'cut short'.[2] All that appears from Ibn ʿAbd al-Ḥakam is firstly a religious distinction; the Barbar who were Christian like the *ʿajam* were mostly *Barānis*. Al-Kindī in fact uses the term in an Egyptian context to refer to Christians; when Arabic was introduced in place of Greek for the *dawāwīn*, 'the registers', ʿAbd Allah b. ʿAbd al-ʿAzīz dismissed one Ashnās from the Dīwān, 'the Ministry', and forbade anyone of the *barānis* (to belong? to join? to serve?). Ashnās or Anītās is referred to previously as a man in charge of money. It may be relevant that *burnus* is the Arabic for the garment of a Coptic priest. More to the point, the term Barānis when first used in Ifrīqiya would seem to have been of foreign origin.

It is all the less clear. For the fourteenth century Ibn ʿIdhārī, Kasīla is al-Burnusī, while the Kāhina is of the Butr, Christian or otherwise. The Butr have a different claim to fame as the people, according to Ibn ʿAbd al-Ḥakam, upon whom the Arabs relied to the exclusion of the Barānis for their military recruits. While this may once again reflect the Christian character of the Barānis, it means that the Butr appear in the first instance as *mawālī*. They lead straight back to the business of the human tribute from the lands to the west of Egypt. According to Ibn ʿIdhārī, the Barbar supplied troops in return for *amān*, 'safe conduct', extended to *ṭāʿa*, 'obedience', and finally *islām*, 'submission'. Subsequently some at least are described as *rahāʾin*, 'hostages'.

Ibn ʿIdhārī is late, and his terminology may be suspect, but this element of formal agreement in return for the provision of human beings is so close to the theme of the stories of Nubia, Cyrenaica and the Fezzan, that these accounts may be considered to be, at some considerable remove, tales of the same kind. Recruitment to an Ifrīqiyan force would simply mean the extension of the process further west with the foundation of the new *miṣr* of Kairouan. *Mawālī* of local origin are first mentioned in the withdrawal to Tripoli about 684. Then come the specific references to the Butr in the service of Ḥasan b. al-Nuʿmān, expanded by the mention of *mawālī* in the service of the aristocracy. Of these the most famous is Ṭāriq b. Ziyād, the conqueror of Spain, *mawlā* of Ḥasan's successor Mūsā b. Nuṣayr. Among these *mawālī* were members of the native nobility who associated themselves in this way with the new rulers. In Ibn ʿAbd al-Ḥakam's story, the two

[1] E.-F. Gautier, *Le Passé de l'Afrique du Nord: les siècles obscurs* (Paris, 1952), 215–80.
[2] Ibid. 241.

sons of the Kāhina submit to Ḥasan and are rewarded with high command. Indeed, the whole purpose of her prophetic power is to foretell a great future for them with the victorious Arabs. The tale may well be a fragment from the legend of some notable *mawlā*, perhaps that of Ṭāriq himself. Although nothing more is heard of the sons of the Kāhina, the force of Butr placed under the command of the elder becomes a force of 12,000 to which were allocated Arab teachers of the Koran, and ends up – wrongly, in the opinion of Ibn ʿAbd al-Ḥakam – under the command of Ṭāriq at Tangier. A little later, in a second cluster of stories, the Butr are the Barbar who are the *mawālī* of the dead Mūsā b. Nuṣayr. In 720 they kill the new governor, Yazīd b. Abī Muslim, when he proposes to turn them into his *ḥaras*, or guard.

The scheme of the new province thus appears somewhat different from that of Egypt. Apart from the Christian Afāriq, liable like the Qibṭ of Egypt to regular taxation in return for *dhimma*, 'protection', *islām* seems to have been employed as an instrument of government. Of Ḥasan b. al-Nuʿmān, Ibn ʿIdhārī says that he returned to Kairouan *baʿda mā ḥasuna islām al-Barbar*, 'after the *islām* of the Barbar had been made good'. By this may be understood a situation in which Berber peoples and their leaders had elected, or had been compelled, to acknowledge Arab overlordship. This meant the supply of recruits to the armies; more generally, it meant the fealty of the peoples from whom the recruits were drawn. Their leaders entered the clienteles of Arab leaders; they probably supplied contingents as well as recruits for Arab expeditions. A wide periphery of 'allies' came into being, of peoples who had made their *islām*, their 'submission', in little more than a political sense, just as many of them had become Christian as part of an alliance with Byzantium. They were in contrast to the *kuffār*, the 'unbelievers' beyond the Muslim pale, the peoples on the horizon of the conquest as it advanced along a line through Barce and Tripoli to Kairouan, then on towards the Maghrib al-Aqṣā, 'the furthest west'.

The conquest continued to be led by the Egyptian aristocracy. Although, after its creation by Ḥasan b. al-Nuʿmān, Ifrīqiya became independent of the governor of Egypt, Mūsā b. Nuṣayr, who was appointed Ḥasan's successor in 705, was *mawlā* to the great ʿAbd al-ʿAzīz, and his family, like that of ʿUqba b. Nāfiʿ, flourished in both countries. With their slaves and clients, they were well placed to be the agents of further expansion. With the dynasty secure, the new caliph Walīd (705–15) undertook the conquest of Khurasan in the far north-east. The capture of Carthage had opened the western Mediterranean to

Arab piracy. From Kairouan Mūsā envisaged the conquest of the lands beyond the Byzantine frontier, the old Roman Mauretanias and Visigothic Spain. The execution was rapid, complete within ten years, a brevity in contrast to the time taken to occupy Ifrīqiya. Gautier thought this was because the nomads, whom he identified with the Butr, had passed from hostility to alliance. It is necessary rather to think of an Ifrīqiyan army, with an increasing Berber component, which advanced along and garrisoned a route through Tlemcen to Ṭinja (Tangier). At Tangier, where he was installed by Mūsā in 710, the *mawlā* commander Ṭāriq b. Ziyād was close to Ṣibta (Septem, Ceuta), ruled by a count known to the Arabs as Julian, whose predecessors had been Byzantine governors. Ṣibta was a focal point for a region on either side of the Straits of Gibraltar, and it was with help from the count that Ṭāriq crossed into Spain in 711 to inflict a total defeat upon Roderic, the Visigothic king. Rapidly exploited by Ṭāriq and by Mūsā, this victory brought most of Spain within a vast dominion ruled from Kairouan. The governor of Ifrīqiya had become the governor of the Maghrib, 'the West', a comprehensive term which only later came to refer more narrowly to the Atlas region.

THE FALL OF THE UMAYYADS

Mūsā celebrated his triumph with his return to Damascus with unheard-of booty in 715. It was a high point of Umayyad history, just before the failure of the great siege of Constantinople in 717–18 which should have been the climax. Thereafter the vast empire became perplexed with administrative problems. The magnificence of ʿAbd al-ʿAzīz in Egypt had been deliberate. In Damascus his brother ʿAbd al-Malik had proclaimed the royal character of his authority by usurping the privileges of the Byzantine emperor. A new gold coinage had been struck, Arabic had been introduced into official documents, and mosques built to rival the finest churches. At the same time, administrative difficulties made their appearance. In the empire at large, these are associated with the name of al-Ḥajjāj, the governor of Iraq. In Egypt they were first marked by the imposition of a poll-tax on Coptic monks by al-Aṣbagh, son of ʿAbd al-ʿAzīz, in 693–4. The next thirty years saw the taking of censuses, the insistence on passports and other more drastic marks of identity, and brutal attempts to recover fugitive peasants. These measures reflect a persistent flight of the peasant from the village where he was registered to escape the burdens of tax. This flight was not new.

Apart from peasants who passed themselves off as monks, obliging the authorities to penalize the Church, others migrated from district to district with the connivance of the pagarchs, who allowed them to settle without inscribing them on the tax-lists. Valuable labour was thus gained to bring more land under cultivation without any increase in the tax quota. The regime was trying to remedy what was clearly, from its point of view, an abuse.

The attempts, sporadic and ineffectual as they seem to have been for many years, were a sign of increased efficiency on the part of the government. The introduction and growing use of Arabic as a language of administration was accompanied, for example, by the development of the *dawāwīn* (registers) for the army; it may have had as a corollary the *islām* of certain high Coptic officials and the dismissal of others such as Ashīnās who remained Christian. Such zeal is unlikely to have been without cause. More revenue may have been required to meet new expenses, not least a heavy building programme. But as time went on, the government was probably struggling to prevent a fall.

In his *Beiträge*, and again in his *Islamstudien*,[1] Becker argued that this was because so many of the Copts had converted to Islam for the sake of the lighter tax, the *ʿushr* or tithe, due from the Muslim. To maintain its income, the state was obliged to increase the fiscal burden on those who were left. A vicious circle was created, which was hardly broken when a distinction was made between the *jizya*, the poll-tax from which the convert was exempt, and the *kharāj*, the land-tax for which he continued to be liable. It was Dennett's aim to refute this thesis, not least because there was very little conversion before 750. What had happened was that magnates like ʿAbd al-ʿAzīz and his sons had begun to acquire great estates, carved in the first instance out of the state domain created by the confiscation of Byzantine property at the time of the conquest. Such estates, around Alexandria and to the north and south of Fusṭāṭ, certainly paid less tax, if indeed they paid any at all. As the government looked for compensation to tighter controls over the rest of the country, it is likely that the pagarchs were prevented from harbouring fugitives to the same extent as before, and an era of comparative neglect and comparative ease came to an end. The flight of the peasantry, on the other hand, was if anything accelerated by the new severity, and aimed increasingly at the new estates, whose owners could afford to be generous. The troubles of the early

[1] C. H. Becker, *Beiträge zur Geschichte Ägyptens*, 2 vols. (Strasburg, 1902–3), II; Becker, *Islamstudien*, 2 vols. (Leipzig, 1924), I.

eighth century should probably be seen as symptoms of the classical syndrome of Roman Egypt as the country began to revert towards the conditions of the Byzantine period.

In 725 the reform of the administration culminated in the appointment of ʿUbayd Allah b. al-Ḥabḥāb as *ʿāmil* or financial controller of Egypt, an official henceforth independent of the *wālī* or governor, answering directly to Damascus for the revenue of the country. His arrival was greeted by a peasant revolt in the northern part of the Delta. This was a distinct region where basin irrigation was not practicable, and each peasant tended to have his own plot instead of an annual allotment of the flooded area. There were no estates. Conditions of tenure would have made flight within the region difficult; presumably the peasant would have found it equally hard to leave the region altogether to engage in the different kind of cultivation further south. Revolt, of which that of 725/6 was the first of a series, became one of the few remedies. On this occasion it was crushed, and under ʿUbayd Allah the government had the situation generally in hand.

But difficulties with the Copts became political when they extended to the Faithful. Arabs excluded from the army were settled in the eastern Ḥawf, the border of the desert to the east of the Delta, on terms which they disliked. They appear in al-Kindī in opposition to the *ahl al-dīwān*, 'the men of the register'. Their resentment was shared by the civilian population of Fusṭāṭ, where the community had grown out of a camp-following side by side with the Copts of Babylon. These Muslims may have felt poor and underprivileged; in 728/9 the favour shown to the Coptic Church provoked a riot which came close to rebellion. Within the professional army, jealousy was occasioned by the growing reliance of the Umayyads on Syrian Arabs. This was only an aspect of a general division into rival factions, the Qaysites and the Yemenis, the North and South Arabians, which ran throughout the empire. As they affected the aristocracy and eventually the dynasty itself, these factions made for sedition. More fundamentally, the right of the Umayyads to hold power was called in question.

The Umayyads relied upon the religion of the community, which they called *dīn* or *Dīn Allah*, 'the religion of God', to support their imperial claims. The Dome of the Rock at Jerusalem, and the Great Mosque of Damascus, demonstrated the superiority of an Arabic faith and its champions. The Dome of the Rock was solemnized with inscriptions in Arabic of verses to be found in the Koran. The Great Mosque of Damascus was yet a more pointed example. Influenced by the architecture of Constantinople, it is in the form of a three-aisled church employed for worship, not along the length of the building towards the short wall in the east, but across its width towards the long wall in the south, so that the transept has become the nave. Meanwhile, as Commanders of the Faithful, the Umayyads legislated by decree after the Roman fashion, borrowing heavily from Roman law. A special official, the *qāḍī* or judge, was appointed on behalf of the ruler to deal with cases involving members of the community. The beginning of a written Arabic literature in the first half of the eighth century, however, marked the growth of a tradition of scholarship centred on the *Dīn Allah*. In this scholarship it was coming to be affirmed that the law of the community was the custom of the community, and that this custom was not the product of continuous legislation, but had been established by Muḥammad, the founder, being handed down from generation to generation. In this sense it was coming to be equated with the religion of the community, religion in the form of a rule to be obeyed by all who believed. The right of the prince to take charge of this rule depended very much upon his acceptance as caliph (*khalīfa*, pl. *khulafā'*), the deputy and successor of Muḥammad. Acceptance of the Umayyads had never been unqualified. Now their right was challenged once again by those who saw themselves as the true heirs of the Prophet. Under Hishām (724–43) the empire as a whole remained quiet. In the Maghrib, however, the reign ended in revolt.

The west was now divided into three, the old Byzantine province of Ifrīqiya, the old Roman Mauretanias ruled from Tlemcen and Tangier, and the old Visigothic kingdom under the name of Andalus, ruled from Cordoba in the valley of the Guadalquivir, all under the governor in Kairouan. Government, however, was still largely a matter of conquest by land and sea branching out from the main line of advance from Egypt into Spain. From Ifrīqiya raids were made upon Sicily and Sardinia, from Andalus across the Pyrenees into France, and from Tlemcen down into the Sus, the border of the desert reached through the gap between the Moroccan Atlas and the Algerian plateau.[1] Here the raid of Ḥabīb b. Abī ʿUbayda, the grandson of ʿUqba b. Nāfiʿ and the senior commander of the armies in North Africa, which is said to have reached 'the land of the Blacks', is dated to about 736. It was for

[1] This Sus, the Sūs al-Aqṣā or 'far Sus', is to be understood as the whole of the pre-Saharan region in the west, in contrast to a Sūs al-Adnā or 'hither Sus' formed by the same region in the east (cf. Sūsa, Sousse in modern Tunisia), rather than as the subsequent Sūs al-Aqṣā, the valley of the river Sous in southern Morocco, in contrast to a Sūs al-Adnā formed, according to Ibn Abī Zarʿ, in the fourteenth century AD, by the valley of the Sebou in the north.

such expeditions that the aristocracy, the armies and the allies were organized, going annually against the 'unsubmitted' not only on the far horizon but also in the mountains nearer at hand. Captives, with women perhaps in the majority, were taken in large numbers, and sent back as tribute to the east. The power of Kairouan, however, was probably limited to appointments and summary dismissals. In 734 ʿUbayd Allah b. al-Ḥabḥāb, the *ʿāmil* of Egypt, was transferred to the Maghrib as *wālī* or governor, no doubt to use his talent for administration to bring the whole vast province into line with the rest of the empire. ʿUbayd Allah appointed his son Ismāʿīl to Tlemcen and Tangier, and it was probably the unaccustomed strength of this family regime which brought an unstable situation to a head.

According to the *History of the patriarchs*, echoed by Ibn ʿIdhārī, the Barbar of Ifrīqiya revolted against ʿUbayd Allah because he had taken the daughters of their nobles to send as presents to the caliph, and destroyed sheep to obtain Persian lambskins. The rebels, it would seem, were *muslim* allies, and it might be conjectured that they rose in defiance of an attempt to hold them to their original obligation to provide a human tribute after a period when slaves had been taken only from *kuffār*, the unbelievers who were the target of the annual raids. In his main narrative, Ibn ʿIdhārī follows Ibn ʿAbd al-Ḥakam, and concentrates in the first place upon al-Murādī, the representative of ʿUbayd Allah and Ismāʿīl at Tangier, whose crime is the *takhmīs al-Barbar*. In other words, according to the author of the *Bayān*, he considered the Barbar as *fay'*, booty, and liable therefore to the *khums*, the fifth of the booty accruing by law to the state, a treatment previously meted out only to those who had not accepted *islām*.

While the story makes clear that it was a question of the *muslim* Barbar, Ibn ʿIdhārī's gloss is not necessarily correct; the term *takhmīs* is more specific. Speaking of the murder of the governor Yazīd b. Abī Muslim by his Berber guard about 720, Ibn ʿAbd al-Ḥakam says that the men killed him because he had made them into *akhmās* ('fifths'). Here the meaning of *akhmās* is most probably 'tribal regiments'.[1] It is likely that this episode is not unconnected with the events of 739. The stories are very similar. In both, the governor 'makes fifths'; in both, the action is unpopular, and leads to his assassination, Yazīd in 720, al-Murādī in 739. That the action was indeed the same in both cases might be inferred from the fact that two late authors, Ibn al-Athīr in

[1] Cf. H. Djaït, 'La Wilāya d'Ifrīqiya au IIe–VIIIe siècle: étude institutionnelle', pt 1, *Studia Islamica*, 1967, **27**, 113–14.

the thirteenth century and Ibn Khaldūn in the fourteenth, give oppressive taxation as the reason for both murders, and it could be argued that this is because the two references to fifth-making had been read alike in the sense of Ibn ʿIdhārī. More striking is the fact that in the second version of the story of Yazīd supplied by Ibn ʿAbd al-Ḥakam, the Barbar in question are already the *mawālī* of the late Mūsā b. Nuṣayr, and in the story of al-Murādī, one of the rebels is given as ʿAbd al-Aʿlā b. Ḥudayj al-Ifrīqī, Rūmī (Greek) in origin, and *mawlā* of Ibn Nuṣayr. It is possible that the two stories are the same, and that we have to deal with the scattered reflections of a single event which took place at the later date.

However this may be, it would seem that the grievances of the allies were capped by those of the *mawālī*. These were not necessarily Berber, or opposed to recruitment as such. It was their personal loyalties and professional jealousies which made them susceptible to the preaching of revolutionaries. The rebels are called *khawārij* (sing. *khārijī*), literally rebels, 'those who go out'. In this way, however, they are identified with a movement going back to the seventh century. This was Kharijism. Kharijites are mentioned by al-Kindī in Egypt in 683, at the beginning of the civil war in which they were violently hostile to the Umayyads, especially in Iraq. By the eighth century they were connected not only with this tradition of dissidence, but with an argument over the status of the sinner, whom they held to have 'gone out' of the community, and to be worthy of death. Applied to the *imām* or leader of the community, such a belief was a prescription for revolt. The Kharijites, however, also known as the Mubayyiḍūn, 'the Whites', had become divided into groups, Azraqī, 'Blue', Ṣufrī, 'Yellow', and Ibāḍī, 'White' again, supposedly called after founders with these names – al-Azraq, al-Aṣfar and Ibn Ibāḍ. These groups had had various careers in Iraq, militant like the Azraqīs or quiescent like the Ibadites. During the reign of Hishām they entered a new phase as arguments over doctrine developed in conjunction with political strains on the regime. Their agitators spread out from Iraq. At a time when politics centred on personalities, their desire for a new order turned on the demand for a new ruler with the favour of God. In the Maghrib they found a situation to exploit. At Tripoli the Kharijites were Ibāḍī; further west, those initially responsible for the revolt were Sufrites.

The revolt broke out at Tangier in 739–40 under one Maysara, who proclaimed himself caliph. Maysara is called al-Midgharī or al-Maṭgharī, which would make him a Berber from the region. He is also called

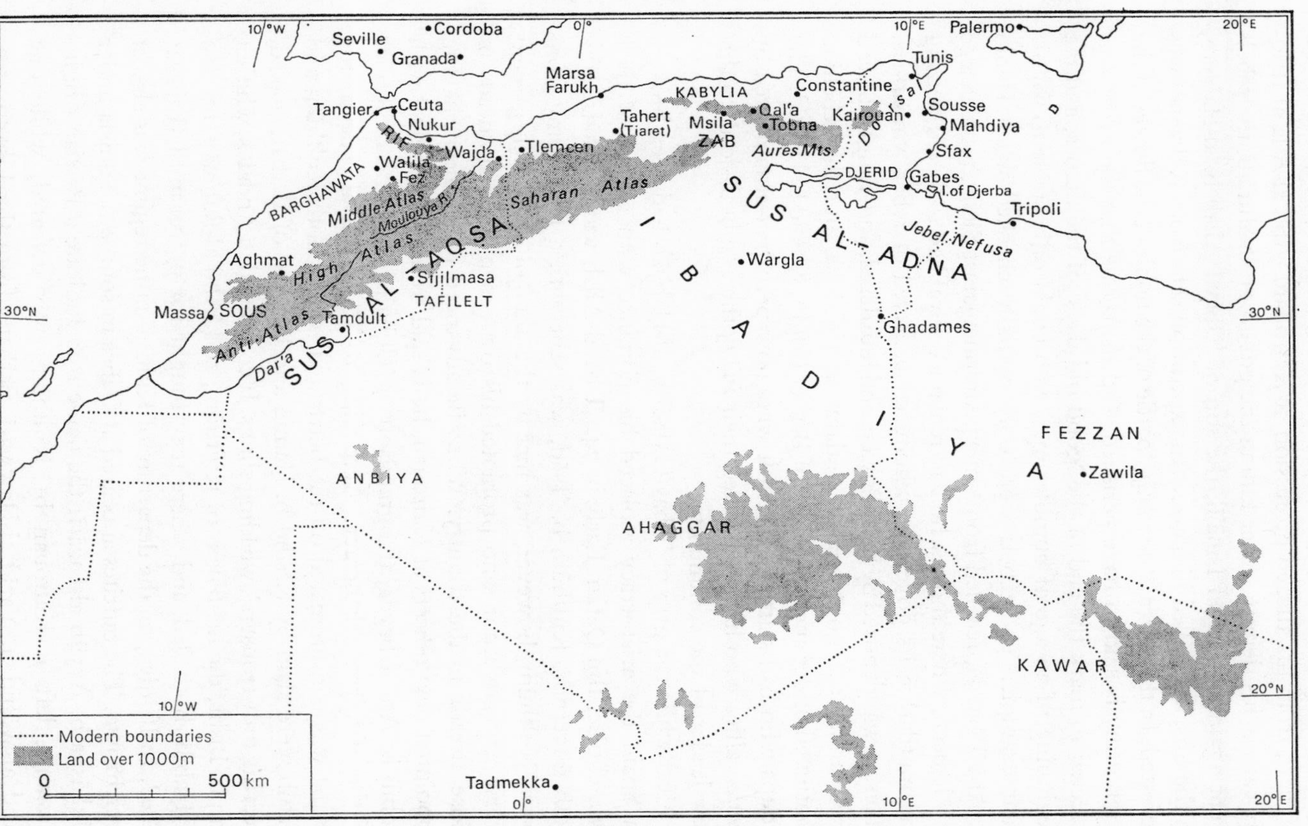

64 The Maghrib in the eighth and ninth centuries.

al-faqīr, the poor or holy, *al-ḥaqīr*, 'the vile', and *al-saqqā'*, 'the water-carrier', from his alleged profession at Kairouan. ʿAbd al-Aʿlā al-Ifrīqī appears as his deputy. After killing the governor al-Murādī, the rebels went against his chief Ismāʿīl, the son of ʿUbayd Allah b. al-Ḥabḥāb, in the Sus, and killed him also. An expedition sent from Kairouan was defeated. In this *ghazwat al-ashrāf*, 'battle of the nobles', the flower of the Arab army is said to have perished, and it may be that the event was selected to mark the end of the 'good old days' of the heroes, and the beginning of an age of humbler men who could only strive to follow their example. The rebels were only partially checked when Ḥabīb b. Abī ʿUbayda, recalled from an expedition against Sicily, took charge at Tlemcen, where those who had remained loyal had gathered, seizing and mutilating its governor, whom he suspected of rebel sympathies. Maysara was deposed by his followers and murdered, and Tangier placed itself under the governor of Andalus at Cordoba, but the rebellion continued under another leader of Berber origin, Khālid b. Ḥamīd. The troops who had started the revolt were now perhaps outnumbered by *muslim* allies who had transferred their *islām*, their 'submission', to this new leader of the community.

Meanwhile the grip of ʿUbayd Allah b. al-Ḥabḥāb had been broken. In Spain the aristocracy replaced his nominee with a man of their own choice, Ibn Qaṭan. Early in 741 ʿUbayd Allah was recalled, and a fresh governor, Kulthūm b. ʿIyāḍ, was sent with a fresh army from Syria. Kulthūm, however, was met by the antagonism which greeted every new governor who promoted his own men over the heads of those already in the country. When he advanced to Tlemcen, having appointed new officers at Kairouan, he is said to have quarrelled with Ḥabīb b. Abī ʿUbayda, the grandson of ʿUqba b. Nāfiʿ and the leader of the Ifrīqiyan aristocracy. According to Ibn ʿAbd al-Ḥakam, the drama was consummated on the battlefield, where both Kulthūm and Ḥabīb were slain by Khālid b. Ḥamīd and his host of Barbar, 'naked, wearing only trousers', wielding slings. It continued in Andalus, whither Balj b. Bishr, the lieutenant of Kulthūm, and ʿAbd al-Raḥmān, the son of Ḥabīb, both fled, and where they fought for power until Balj was killed. In Ifrīqiya, on the departure of Kulthūm, the regime was almost overthrown. The Sufrites appeared at Gabes in southern Tunisia under ʿUkkāsha b. Ayyūb al-Fazārī; the name may indicate a Persian origin. Maslama, left at Kairouan by Kulthūm, was defeated, while one ʿAbd al-Wāḥid b. Yazīd al-Hawwārī, perhaps from the Libyan area, proclaimed himself caliph at Tunis.

In the event the rebellion enjoyed only a limited success. Kairouan was saved with great difficulty in 742 by Ḥanẓala b. Ṣafwān, the governor of Egypt. The Sufrites were forced back among the Berber peoples of the Djerid, the oasis area of southern Tunisia. But when in 744 the Caliph Walīd II was murdered, Ḥanẓala was driven back to Egypt by ʿAbd al-Raḥmān b. Ḥabīb, great-grandson of ʿUqba b. Nāfiʿ, who returned triumphant from Andalus. Events in the Maghrib thus joined up with events in the empire at large. The murder of Walīd II was the signal for the *fitna*, the civil war which came to mark the end of the 'good old days'. The antagonisms within the community of the Faithful came to a head in six years of strife which occupied the reign of the Caliph Marwān II. Egypt was effectively held for the dynasty by the sons of ʿAbd al-ʿAzīz, but revolts in Palestine, Syria and Iraq kept the Umayyads from dealing either with the Maghrib or with the situation in Khurasan, where revolutionary agitation produced a still more formidable challenge. The Kharijites were not alone in the world. In the argument over the status of the sinner were others, the Murji'ites, those who left the decision to God, and the Muʿtazilites, who held that the sinner was separated. The doctrine of Murji'a, or 'postponement', was widespread in learned opinion which was potentially critical of the regime. Muʿtazila, or Iʿtizāl, 'separation', was, like Kharijism, an ambiguous term with an equally ambiguous history; it might mean 'dissidence'. The Muʿtazilites supported another group which claimed the caliphate.

This group upheld the right of descendants of the Prophet to succeed him as Commanders of the Faithful. The most obvious descendants were the offspring of Ḥasan and Ḥusayn, the sons of ʿAlī, the fourth caliph, by Fāṭima, the daughter of Muḥammad. Their supporters were called the Shīʿa, 'the Party (of ʿAlī)', and there was a long history of Shiʿite revolts on behalf of pretenders from the family. Starting about 720, the appeal of these ʿAlids was exploited by a conspiracy which developed to place a member of the house of the Prophet, as yet unnamed, upon the throne. Beginning in Iraq, the conspiracy extended itself over a period of thirty years to Khurasan, where after the outbreak of the *fitna* in 744 it came into the open under the command of its local agent, Abū Muslim. By 748 the province was won, and the army of the Musawwidūn, 'the Blacks', advanced upon Iraq. In 750 Marwān II was defeated, pursued into Egypt and killed. The *dawla* or 'revolution' became the *dawla*, the state, of a new dynasty, descended, as it transpired, not from ʿAlī but from ʿAbbās, the uncle of the Prophet.

Shiʿites may have felt deceived, but the ʿAbbasids put forward a sweeping claim to have been sent by God to restore the true faith of the early community before the Umayyads usurped control. Justice had returned to earth. The messianic message is conveyed by the *History of the patriarchs*, written at this point by a contemporary witness, John the Deacon, secretary to the Patriarch Michael I. The problem of being safely on the winning side had led to a number of premature revolts, and John's account shows that the Church was hard put to survive the transfer of power. In his apology, Abū Muslim comes under the sign of the Cross as a man sent from God to deliver His people, Muslim and Christian alike, from the tyrant. The Copts of the coastal marshes rebel, and, while the patriarch denounces their action, he refuses to pay an extortionate levy. He is therefore accused and grossly maltreated until God gives victory to the invaders. Thereafter there is misunderstanding; evil-minded officials cause the new governor to restore the exorbitant taxes of the old regime, while Christians are encouraged to abandon their religion. In the end, however, a happy relationship is formed. The ʿAbbasid *dawla* is seen as what it claimed to be, a turning-point.

STATESMEN AND SCHOLARS

In the Maghrib, on the other hand, AD 750 was no such critical year. The ʿAbbasid revolution is a mere interpolation in the text of the *Bayān*, which becomes the principal source after the ending of Ibn ʿAbd Al-Ḥakam's narrative about the year 746/7. After the departure of Ḥanẓala b. Ṣafwān, ʿAbd al-Raḥmān had gone on to defeat the Ibāḍī Kharijites who had gained control of Tripoli. Confirmed in his usurpation by Marwān II, he ruled Ifrīqiya as far as Tlemcen. If he recognized the new caliphs, it was not to submit and obey. In Andalus this rejection of the new order was taken still further with the arrival in 755 of the fugitive Umayyad ʿAbd al-Raḥmān al-Dākhil, 'the immigrant', who established a completely independent regime. It was a victory for the old aristocracy and the tribal regiments whose quarrels had brought about the *fitna* on the death of Walīd II. As for the Kharijites, the success of the ʿAbbasids in the east had set the seal on their failure to generate an insurrection of more than local significance in the west, but they were no less active. The factors at work in 739 continued to operate in a struggle for Kairouan. When in 755 ʿAbd al-Raḥmān b. Ḥabīb was murdered by his brothers, one of these, ʿAbd al-Wārith, allied with the Arab troops in the capital and with the Ṣufrī Warfajjūma people in the Djerid, against ʿAbd al-Raḥmān's son Ḥabīb. While Ḥabīb relied upon his father's followers, the coalition was founded on an appeal to a common *islām* in the name of the ʿAbbasid *dawla*. The common front was supposedly broken after its victory over Ḥabīb, when the Warfajjūma committed an atrocious massacre and installed their own leader, ʿAbd al-Malik. Fourteen months later, however, it was still in existence when in 758 ʿAbd al-Malik was himself overthrown by Abū 'l-Khaṭṭāb, the *imām* of the Ibadites of the Jebel Nefusa in Tripolitania. Abū 'l-Khaṭṭāb, who had already recaptured Tripoli, was according to tradition one of three men sent from Iraq at the invitation of the Libyans. Now he installed his colleague ʿAbd al-Raḥmān b. Rustam at Kairouan, and the Kharijite ambition to gain control of Ifrīqiya was briefly realized.

Briefly, because from 759 the ʿAbbasids set out to recover the province for the empire. In 761 Abū 'l-Khaṭṭāb was killed on the borders of Cyrenaica by the governor of Egypt, Ibn al-Ashʿath, and the road to Kairouan was open. While ʿAbd al-Raḥmān b. Rustam fled westwards to establish a new capital at Tahert (Tāhart or Tīhart), the old Roman Tiaret on the high plains of western Algeria some 250 km east of Tlemcen, the victors pursued the Ibadites as far as Zawila in the Fezzan. If there is anything historical about the stories of the Libyans who broke their first agreement and had to be reconquered, it is probably this. Any thought that the ʿAbbasid *dawla* was an opportunity for reconciliation was mistaken. Kairouan was fortified. But in 765 the new ʿAbbasid governor, Ibn al-Ashʿath, was driven back to Egypt by a revolt of the army. The situation which had brought about the downfall of his Umayyad predecessors had not changed; rather, the source of the malaise was becoming clear. What was resented by the troops and their commanders was the formation by each new governor – ʿUbayd Allah, Kulthūm, ʿAbd al-Raḥmān, Ḥabīb, Ibn al-Ashʿath – of a *jund*, an army within an army which enjoyed special privileges in return for special loyalty. This resentment made other grievances dangerous. The erstwhile allies were opposed to regimes which repeatedly tried to subject them. The Kharijite leadership, although it had been purged from the army and relegated to the fringe of the province, continued in consequence to attract support for an alternative government. According to Ibn al-Athīr, the revolt which caused Ibn al-Ashʿath to retire was the outcome of a previous rebellion by an officer who had fallen back on the support of Ibn Rustam at Tahert.

Nevertheless it proved to be a losing battle, not only against the superior forces of the east, but against the whole tendency of government at the time. The kind of proconsular regime which went back to the days of Mūsā b. Nuṣayr and beyond, based upon the power of patronage, was becoming more systematic with the years; a new and typical institution was in the making. The reorganization of the army was a necessary preliminary. This was begun by Ibn al-Ashʿath when he fortified Kairouan. It was continued by his successors, al-Aghlab and ʿUmar b. Ḥafṣ Hazarmārd, even as they fought unsuccessfully against the troops on the one hand, the Kharijites on the other. A new command was created in the Zab, the high plains of eastern Algeria, based upon Tobna (Ṭubna), the old Roman Thubunae. After al-Aghlab was killed at Kairouan in a revolt of the army in 767, ʿUmar was able to defeat an attack from the west by Ibn Rustam in alliance with Abū Qurra, the new Ṣufrī ruler of Tlemcen. Although he fell in his turn at the siege of Kairouan by the Ibadites of Tripoli under their leader Abū Ḥātim in 771, Tobna proved a refuge for his men. The arrival of Yazīd b. Ḥātim al-Muhallabī with yet another army from the east was decisive. The Ibadites were expelled. The reorganization of the army was completed. Yazīd set up three commands, one at Tobna, one at Kairouan and one at Tripoli, building a series of castles in the Byzantine manner instead of the open camps of the conquests. The army, from now on known collectively as the *jund*, was thus split up into local garrisons under local commanders. Yazīd himself controlled the centre, and was a monarch who amassed estates and a personal following large enough to ensure that his family inherited his power and position at his death in 787.

The trouble with the *jund* was only temporarily at an end, but the attempt of the Kharijites to install themselves at Kairouan was finally defeated. Troops continued to flee to Tahert, but they were refugees rather than revolutionaries. Tahert itself was exceptional. From being the seat of a government in exile, it became the capital of a monarchy in the hands of Ibn Rustam, who died between 784 and 790, and his descendants. Their power was nevertheless limited to the region of the city and the port of Marsā Farūkh, which gave them access to the Mediterranean. Only their prestige extended to the main bodies of Ibadites in the Djerid and the Jebel Nefusa. These recognized the ruler of Tahert as the *imām* or leader of their community, and might contribute to his treasury, but could not be described as subjects. They were becoming identical with the Berber peoples of the region, an ethnic group for whom the preachings of the revolutionaries were turning into the articles of a distinct and separate faith. The government of this population was by family custom and family connection joined with the authority of the shaykhs, the 'elders' of the sect. An *imām difāʿ*, 'defence leader', might be chosen if necessary. Regulating themselves with the minimum of interference from Kairouan, the people concerned were abandoning the conflicts of the past to take advantage of the new opportunities which had been created. The movement of soldiers, slaves and tribute to and fro along the North African coast from Egypt to Spain had revived the market economy after the lapse into subsistence of the late Roman and Byzantine period. A hundred years after their brutal induction into the Arab empire, the inhabitants of the northern Sahara were not merely trading amongst themselves in livestock, crops and manufactures over a distance of 1,500 km from Tahert in the north-west to Zawila in the Fezzan in the south-east. The routes which bound together their scattered communities were often old. They had allowed the political and religious influence of Byzantium to enter the desert, and the Arabs to extract their human tribute. Now they extended on into Spain, Ifrīqiya and Egypt, supplying a demand for slaves and to a lesser extent for gold. These were drawn from regions further and further to the south.

The western Maghrib lies beyond the scope of this history, indeed, almost beyond the scope of any history at all. After his victory over Kulthūm in 742, Khālid b. Ḥamīd is not heard of again. The few indications that survive suggest that this was still an affair of the peoples affected by the conquest along the route through Tlemcen to Tangier, and down into 'the Sus'. It was in this Sus, the border of the desert reached by the gap between the Moroccan Atlas and the Algerian plateau, that Sijilmasa was reputedly founded in 757 by a band of Sufrites who amalgamated with immigrant nomads of the Miknāsa people to the north to build a city ruled by the dynasty of the Banū Midrar in the oasis region of the Tafilelt. In 765 the Sufrite Abū Qurra established himself as caliph at Tlemcen. Along the Mediterranean coast of Morocco appeared the principality of Nukūr, which shared the historical connection of Tangier with Spain. More mysterious are the references to the Muʿtazilites, encountered in the east before the ʿAbbasid revolution, but previously unknown in the Maghrib. In the ninth century, al-Yaʿqūbī speaks of the otherwise unknown city of Ayzaraj to the west of Tahert, whose Muʿtazilite inmates engage in learned dispute with their Ibadite neighbours. More to the point, it is said to have been a Muʿtazilite, ʿAbd al-Ḥamīd or Abū Layla Isḥāq b.

Muḥammad b. ʿAbd al-Ḥamīd, who was the leader of the Awraba of Walila, Volubilis, the capital of the old Roman Mauretania Tingitana, and still from its archaeology the second city of the region after Tangier. At Walila in 788 he received Idrīs b. ʿAbd Allah, in flight from the east. Idrīs claimed descent from Ḥasan, the elder of the two sons of ʿAlī and Fāṭima, and had shared in both of the revolts of his branch of the family in Arabia in 761–3 and 786, when he and his brothers had tried without success to wrest the caliphate from those whom they regarded as usurpers. Shiʿite propaganda may have prepared the way for his arrival in the west. Aided by Isḥāq, Idrīs took Tlemcen from Abū Qurra in 789/90, and in the same year founded as his capital the city of Fez. Any threat to the ʿAbbasids was removed when he was apparently poisoned by an ʿAbbasid emissary in 795, but his state survived in trust for his posthumous son. In spite of the lack of information, it is possible to suggest that in the region first conquered by Mūsā b. Nuṣayr, among the peoples he had conscripted, Kharijism had been largely superseded.

Events in the west thus called in question the ʿAbbasid claim to be the true government of the entire community of the Faithful. The empire had begun to break up, and the *dawla* was an important step along the way. For the ʿAbbasids this was the supreme paradox; yet they could only assist its development. The territorial limitation of their power was a symptom of something much more fundamental, the appearance of government as an institution no longer identical either with the community or with its religion. The reorganization of Ifrīqiya by Yazīd b. Ḥātim al-Muhallabī was a reflection of still more systematic measures in the east. The shift of government from the *miṣr* to the palace of the ruler, in evidence in Egypt under ʿAbd al-ʿAzīz, had continued. In Syria the later Umayyads built country seats, such as Quṣayr ʿAmra and Qaṣr al-Ḥayr, from which they directed the empire. These grew in size and strength until they culminated in the immense unfinished Mshatta, 'the Winter Palace'. In 762 the ʿAbbasid ruler al-Manṣūr founded an entirely new capital city in Iraq near the site of the old imperial Persian capital of Ctesiphon, which the Arabs had destroyed at the conquest. Madīnat al-Salām, Baghdad, was a circular fortress, over 2 km across, walled and moated. An inner fortification surrounded the palace itself and the great mosque, while the outer ring was divided into wards to accommodate the army and the principal servants of the regime. The civilian city grew up outside. While Madīnat al-Salām resembled a *miṣr* in being a single self-contained settlement for the purpose of government, it was not designed for an army and its commander so much as for a sovereign who had become an absolute monarch. Both the administration and the professional army had become an extension of his household, quartered in an extension of his residence. Everything centred on the court with its elaborate ceremony and staff, which in its turn revolved around the person of the caliph.

The great fortress was the symbol as well as the instrument of a 'new model' government which can conveniently be called *sulṭa*, 'power', 'government', or *sulṭān*, '(man of) power'. It was a technical achievement which completed the work of the Umayyads in the administration of the empire. The monarch was secluded by the diligence of the *ḥājib*, the chamberlain. Responsibility for the conduct of affairs devolved upon the vizier (*wazīr*), an official of Persian origin who supervised the various ministries, *dawāwīn* (sing. *dīwān*). These were reformed and enlarged with salaried staff after the fashion of the old Persian empire. The change to Arabic as the language of administration was completed. The nucleus of the army was made up of the men of Khurasan. The preference shown for these soldiers from the home of the revolution continued the trend towards troops of a single origin, ethnic or regional, which had been apparent in the reliance placed by the Umayyads on the Syrian Arabs. It showed an appreciation of the fighting ability, esprit de corps and loyalty to a leader of units of this kind. The trend by no means overcame the growing reliance upon armies of retainers; rather, it gave these armies a more formal character. At Madīnat al-Salām, in the palace household of the ʿAbbasid emperor, they became part of the structure of the state.

In the central provinces, the new government proved an effective method of control. The Umayyad distinction between the *wālī* or governor and the *ʿāmil* or financial superintendent was maintained, while a new officer, the *ṣāḥib al-barīd*, 'the master of the post office', represented a new ministry of posts and communications, reporting among other things on the loyalty and efficiency of his colleagues. Egypt was firmly held in this way. For a few years the government was located in the *muʿaskar*, 'the camp', called al-ʿAskar, 'the Army', which was set up to the north of Fusṭāṭ as the headquarters of the first ʿAbbasid governors and their troops. In 763, however, the administration returned to the city, occupying for a while the fortress of Babylon in the south-west corner. The estates of the Banū ʿAbd al-ʿAzīz were confiscated and redistributed; the regime rewarded its supporters with land. Sporadic revolts of the peasants of the northern Delta continued to occur, notably in 767–9. On the other hand, the government was able to deal with revolts in the army in support of Shiʿite pretenders, as in 761 in connection with the first revolt of the Ḥasanids in Arabia. The attempt of the Umayyad pretender Diḥya to revive the family interest in Upper Egypt in 785 came to nothing.

By contrast, in Ifrīqiya the government of the caliphs was a model to be copied. Yazīd b. Ḥātim al-Muhallabī ruled more in imitation of his master. In 787 his son inherited his office because, it is said, his *mawālī* would obey no one else. When the army of Ifrīqiya, the *jund*, revolted once again in opposition to this family regime, and in 794 drove the last of the Muhallabids from the country, it was not to reverse the process of formation of an independent state. Instead of fresh troops, in 795 the Caliph Hārūn al-Rashīd sent one of his chief lieutenants, Harthama b. Aʿyān, to impose a settlement. The reorganization of the province by Yazīd was carried a step further. To isolate the trouble-makers at Kairouan and Tunis, while maintaining the defence of the empire against attack from the west, Harthama appointed the most influential leader of the army in the Zab to an almost independent command. This was Ibrāhīm b. al-Aghlab, the son of the governor killed in 767, whose first task may have been to procure the murder of Idrīs at Fez. In 797 the scheme was complete when the Zab was constituted a separate province with Ibrāhīm as governor. But following the return of Harthama to the east, in 799 Ibrāhīm himself was called upon to intervene at Kairouan. In 800 he was recognized by Baghdad as the ruler of a reunited Ifrīqiya with plenipotentiary powers.

The *jund* in its citadels throughout the country was evidently unreliable. To meet and overcome the inevitable rebellion of its leaders, Ibrāhīm began the construction in 801 of a palace fortress 3 km to the south of Kairouan loyally named al-ʿAbbasiya, 'the ʿAbbāsid'. To it the government was transferred when the building was finished in 810. Reproducing the concept of the ʿAbbasid capital, it completed the transformation of the *wālī* or governor into a *sulṭān*, a monarch after a new fashion. Its principal occupants were members of the *ḥasham*, the retinue of the ruler, expanded and formally developed. Among those closest to the person of the prince were the *fityān* (sing. *fatā*) or *ghilmān* (sing. *ghulām*), the corps of 'young men' or 'pages' who began life as boys in the service of their master, and went on to provide his military escort and his staff of senior officers. They were purchased as slaves, like the *mawālī* of the *ḥaras* or guard. This was increased by Ibrāhīm to a force said to number 5,000. Al-Balādhurī, who gives this information later in the ninth century, uses the term *ʿabīd* (sing. *ʿabd*) in its basic sense to mean the slaves bought by Ibrāhīm for this purpose; subsequent writers who refer to the episode use *ʿabīd* to mean the troops themselves. This was a general usage from the tenth century onwards. It is often taken to mean that the troops in question were Negro, but this is incorrect. When applied to soldiers it always has the sense of troops of slave origin, though technically freed. The colour is irrelevant, as when the fifteenth-century Egyptian writer al-Maqrīzī, using the synonymous *mamālīk* (sing. *mamlūk*), speaks of [*al-*] *ʿabīd al-mamālīk al-Atrāk*, 'the Turkish slave troops or mamluks'.[1] Essentially they were *mawālī*, normally of a single ethnic group. Those of Ibrāhīm b. al-Aghlab were probably *ṣaqāliba* (sing. *ṣiqlabī*), 'Slavs', Europeans, who figure at about the same time in the comparable army of the Umayyad ruler at Cordoba. Not till the end of the ninth century does the use of the term *sūdān* (sing. *aswad*), 'blacks', indicate that the slave troops recruited by Ibrāhīm II were undoubtedly Negro. It is just possible that some recruits were furnished by the Afāriq, the native Christian population.

This transformation of government under the ʿAbbasids went with the development of Islam as a religion. The revolutionary fervour of the middle of the eighth century arose against a background of prayer and preaching in the place of worship. It was connected with the beginning of doctrinal argument over membership of the community which invoked the will of God rather than the will of man; and it focused on the demand for a leader who enjoyed the divine blessing. The ʿAbbasid *dawla* stood for a theological achievement, of which the Round City of Madīnat al-Salām was a visible symbol. The name means 'City of Peace', the peace of God which was the ideal state of heaven and earth, the product of perfect faith. This peace had been brought into the world with the community, which was charged with its establishment on earth. At a very basic level, therefore, it was *islām*, submission to the representatives of God. Conversely, *islām*, 'acceptance of peace', was more than an undertaking between human beings. It was an act of faith in God as well as men. This was the sense which developed, so that Islam became the principal designation of the *dīn Allah*, and Muslim the chief word for a believer. By 800 any original association of *islām* with *walā'* was dead. It was a simple and direct relationship to God.

[1] al-Maqrīzī, *Kitāb al-Mawāʿiẓ wa 'l-Iʿtibār fī dhikr al-khiṭaṭ wa 'l-āthār* [*Khiṭaṭ*], ed. by G. Wiet (Cairo, 1911), II, 46.

As to the form of this relationship, the 'Abbasids made an important contribution when they claimed to have restored the community to the perfection it must have enjoyed in the days of its founder. The Umayyads were accused of establishing a secular kingdom at variance with the custom of the Rāshidūn, the first four 'orthodox' caliphs. An historical explanation was thus provided for the notion of a return to lost standards, while approval was given to the basic concept of an ideal past which served as a sanction for the present. This was in keeping with the new learning which was taking shape in the growing body of writing at the hands of the men of letters. Whoever they were, and the majority were of non-Arab origin, living in Iraq, expressing in Arabic things which a generation earlier they might have written in other languages on behalf of Christianity and Judaism, they were concerned with the elaboration and justification of the newer faith. At the heart of the matter was the question of authenticity. Christianity was guaranteed by the Church, which traced itself back to its divine foundation through the apostolic succession, the consecration of bishop by bishop in an unbroken line from the twelve Apostles. Judaism was guaranteed by scholars who were competent to expound the holy Law by what might be called the rabbinical succession of teachers and pupils. Muslims had relied upon the succession of caliphs to keep the faith. But the need to spell out that faith in terms acceptable in the world at large led not to the pronouncement of their authority, but away from it. The Jewish model was preferred.

The Babylonian Talmud had been compiled in the course of the fourth and fifth centuries AD. It reduced to writing the mass of learning and teaching which had grown up beside the Torah or Pentateuch, the first of the three divisions of the Hebrew Bible. Together with the Torah, the Talmud formed the textual base of a sacred Law, specifications for correct behaviour in every sphere of life, ordained by God. These specifications were authorized by the written material, but depended upon its correct interpretation by the scholars, the *amoraim*, who were competent to decide without reference to a Jewish priesthood or a Jewish state, both of which had ceased to exist. It was a Law of this kind, which systematically elaborated the seminal notions of divine revelation, inspired prophecy and Holy Scripture, towards which Islam was working. The starting-point was current practice, the laws and customs of the community which had grown up in various ways for various purposes, some to determine the rituals of worship, others to regulate the behaviour of the Faithful towards each other and towards their leaders. In the course of the eighth century, these customs and laws were converted into something else – the requirements of God for conduct towards Himself. The conversion took place locally, on the basis of local practices which varied from place to place. The assumption, however, was everywhere the same, that the ways of the community were the ways of the Prophet; that what had been done by the Prophet and his companions had been done by divine inspiration; and that in consequence the ways of the community consisted of a series of divine commandments. The problem was to show just what had been revealed in this way by God to man.

Although it was essential to the argument that the community must be right in what it did, this did not mean uncritical acceptance. The present was compared with the past, to decide what should be done by what had been done. Reference was made to what Schacht calls the 'good old days', a time which had ended with the outbreak of the *fitna* in 744, but was steadily pushed back to the days of the Prophet in keeping with the ʿAbbāsid view of the golden age of the Rāshidūn. In fact, the description of what the *sunna*, the practice of the community, had been and should be depended very much upon the opinion of respected individuals. This dependence is apparent in the first extant work of *fiqh* or jurisprudence, the *Muwaṭṭa'* of Mālik b. Anas of Medina, who died in 796. The *Muwaṭṭa'* consists of the discussion of topics by quotation of conflicting statements followed by the judgement of the master as recorded by the pupils who compiled the work. It shows indeed how far the process had gone. The description was what mattered, while the operation was in the hands of a recognizable body of students and teachers who came to be called the *fuqahā'* (sing. *faqīh*), 'jurisprudents', who were counted among the *ʿulamā'* (sing. *ʿālim* or *ʿalīm*), 'the wise'. The *Muwaṭṭa'* reveals the formality of their procedure, and the way in which their argument continued from generation to generation. The significance of what they were doing is apparent in the administration of justice. Under the Umayyads, the *qāḍī* or judge had been appointed to act on behalf of the caliph and his governors in all cases concerning members of the community. He was an important official whose decisions helped to make the law; in Ifrīqiya he was a justiciar who ruled in the absence of the *wālī*, as in 755 when the *qāḍī* Abū Kurayb is said to have taken charge at Kairouan when Ḥabīb b. ʿAbd al-Raḥmān went against the Warfajjūma. Under the ʿAbbasids, the *qāḍī* was incorporated into the more elaborate system of administration which was typical of the regime. A department appeared under a

Chief Qāḍī, the *qāḍī 'l-quḍāt* or 'judge of judges'. Nevertheless, although the growth of the Muslim community made justice increasingly complex, the higher degree of organization which was required was achieved, not through the *qāḍī* as in former days, but at his expense. The caliph reserved to himself the right to try *maẓālim*, 'complaints' or appeals, at his discretion. Criminal cases were dealt with separately. This was because the law for which the *qāḍī* was responsible was ceasing to be a set of regulations largely made by men for practical purposes. Instead it was turning into a moral law composed of detailed obligations and prohibitions, recommendations and condemnations, procedures and punishments, a religion in the sense of a binding rule prescribed by God. This rule met the civil needs of society only by accident. It was necessary for the ruler to limit its strict application in the courts to ensure the continuation of effective government.

Meanwhile the appearance of the scholars was accompanied by that of other kinds of holy man. They grew up alongside the prayer leaders and preachers in the mosques, which remained the focus of their activities. As they moved from exhortation to exposition, simpler persons preached a simpler message of right and wrong. A passion for holiness produced ascetics of a kind familiar in Christian Egypt and North Africa under the Roman empire as hermits and monks, men of frequently violent zeal. Their devotion was specifically related to the military organization of the early community. The expression *murābiṭan* occurs from the seventh century onwards in al-Kindī and Ibn ʿAbd al-Ḥakam with the meaning 'in or as a garrison'. In the second half of the eighth century, the reform of the Ifrīqiyan army by Yazīd b. Ḥātim al-Muhallabī included the building of coastal forts for defence against Byzantine raids from Sicily. These were called *rubuṭ* or *ribāṭāt* (sing. *ribāṭ*), 'ribats' or places of guard. That of Sousse was a small square castle built round a courtyard. With its prayer-hall on the second floor, it served as a mosque as well as a place of refuge for the small town. It was defended by archers, probably *mawālī*, but at the same time *mujāhidūn*, fighters in the *jihād*, the 'holy war' against the infidel, who were ruled by a strict religious as well as military discipline. These *murābiṭūn*, 'men of the ribat', may have had their counterparts in Egypt. Their dedication was part of a general enthusiasm. It was indignation at the flogging to death of the holy Buhlūl b. Rāshid, because he denounced the sending of weapons, iron and copper to the Byzantines in Sicily, which contributed to the rising which brought Ibrāhīm b. al-Aghlab to power.

THE NINTH CENTURY AD

Matters of religion thus combined with matters of politics. As in 739, events in Ifrīqiya proved significant of a more general discontent. The Egyptian army had rebelled over pay in 789, the Arabs of the eastern Ḥawf in 794. These were put down by Harthama on his way west in 795, and members of the dynasty were appointed as governors over the province. But in 802 the Arabs rose again, and their rebellion spread into Syria and down into Arabia. Taxes were refused, and in 807 the routes to Mecca and Medina were cut. Persian troops were sent from Iraq, and the Arab chiefs seized and deported. In 809, however, the army at Fusṭāṭ rioted again over pay. Such troubles may indicate a government continually short of revenue. They were not peculiar to Egypt. In the same year, 809, the Caliph Hārūn al-Rashīd died on his way to deal with the situation in Iran. His death meant a struggle for power between his two sons, Amīn and Ma'mūn, which developed into civil war throughout the empire. At Fusṭāṭ the army divided into the *ahl Miṣr*, the men of Egypt, and the Persian newcomers. The men of Egypt, with the Arabs of the Ḥawf, declared for Amīn, while Harthama b. Aʿyān set the steward of his Egyptian estates to raise the country for Ma'mūn with the wealth at his disposal.

Amīn was defeated and killed by Ma'mūn in 813, but the fighting continued. Egypt was split between two military leaders, both Persian officers, Sarī b. al-Ḥakam and Ibn al-Wazīr al-Jarawī. Sarī and the Persians held Fusṭāṭ, claiming to rule on behalf of Ma'mūn; Ibn al-Wazīr, however, had allied himself with the Arabs of the eastern Ḥawf, and established himself at Tinnis in the north-east. The frontier was the division between the northern and southern Delta, a line between two economies which neither Sarī nor his opponent could cross. In 816 a third party appeared. Two years before, at Cordoba in Spain, the populace had rioted under the leadership of the men of religion, provoking the Umayyad ruler to destroy a 'suburb' and exile the inhabitants. Some sailed for Egypt, presumably with seamen from the coast, a band of militants in search of a home. At Alexandria they found the Ṣūfīya, zealots at odds with the governor who helped them to capture the city.[1] Thereupon they made themselves the masters, and set up their own republic. Ma'mūn in Iraq was too pre-occupied to

[1] The Ṣūfīya are called a *ṭā'ifa* ('group'), led for a time by one Abū ʿAbd al-Raḥmān al-Ṣūfī: al-Kindī, *Governors and judges of Egypt*, ed. by R. Guest (Leiden and London, 1912), 162, 440; cf. also A. Mez, *The renaissance of Islam*, trans. by S. K. Bakhsh and D. S. Margoliouth (Patna, 1937), 281–2.

intervene. Sarī and Ibn al-Wazīr were both effectively independent, and when in 820 they were each succeeded by their various sons, the division of the country was enhanced.

In Ifrīqiya in 810, Ibrāhīm b. al-Aghlab defeated the first rebellion of the *jund* since his accession. The populace of Kairouan rose with the military, obliging the *amīr* finally to take up residence in his new fortress city. In 812 he died, and it was not until the reign of his second son, Ziyādat Allah I, that his work was seriously tested. The rising of an officer of the guard in 822 was followed by revolts of the *jund* in 823 and 824. That of 824, led by Manṣūr al-Tunbudhī, was at Tunis, the second city of Ifrīqiya and the chief centre of opposition since the eighth century. Having taken the place of Carthage, it was a natural capital for the northern districts, where the leaders of the *jund* in their castles were coming to form a powerful aristocracy. The attempt of Ziyādat Allah to recapture the city was repulsed, and although the attack of Manṣūr upon ʿAbbāsiya was defeated, in 825 the Aghlabid *amīr* was routed at Sbiba to the west of Kairouan. His authority was then restricted to the metropolis, the east coast or Sahel, and the south as far as Tripoli, while the remainder was held by the rebel lords. Like Egypt, the country was divided into its natural zones, as previously in the wars against Byzantine Carthage, when Kairouan had been founded as a frontier city.

From 826, however, central government recovered its power in both Ifrīqiya and Egypt. Ziyādat Allah defeated a rebel attempt to invade the Djerid in the south, while ʿAbd Allah b. Ṭāhir, appointed viceroy of the western provinces by Ma'mūn, entered Egypt. The factions submitted, and unity was restored. In 827 the Andalusians were obliged to evacuate Alexandria. They sailed for Crete, which they took from the Byzantines and colonized as pirates. In the same year Ziyādat Allah felt strong enough to launch a more ceremonious invasion of the other Byzantine island of Sicily in support of a rebel governor, Euphemius. The expedition, under the auspicious leadership of the great *qāḍī*, Asad b. al-Furāt, appealed to all sections of the Muslim community, and seems to have distracted attention from the rebellion, which over the next few years petered out. In Egypt, on the other hand, the climax was yet to come. In 828 ʿAbd Allah b. Ṭāhir was succeeded as viceroy of the west by the heir apparent, Muʿtaṣim, the son of Ma'mūn. The attempt of his nominees to restore regular taxation led to risings of both Copts and Arabs in the northern Delta and the Eastern Ḥawf, the lands once ruled by Ibn al-Wazīr, in 829, 830 and 831. These required the presence of Muʿtaṣim and his Turkish general Afshīn; then in 832 the presence of Maʾmūn himself. The region was only pacified with the decimation of the people of the Basharūd, the Copts of the coastal marshes, after they had refused to listen to the appeal of the patriarch. In 834 the Arabs of the Ḥawf, who had probably reasserted their claim to be treated as regular soldiers during the civil war, were finally struck off the register, and their pay, *ʿaṭāʾ*, stopped. A brief revolt under a son of Ibn al-Wazīr was put down.

In Ifrīqiya, the Aghlabid ruler emerged from his trial of strength with the *jund* as the undisputed head of a central government, a *sulṭān*. He was wealthy, with estates, *ḍiyāʿ* (sing. *ḍayʿa*), around Kairouan and in the Sahel. To the south in the barren region of the Qammūda, water works were built to a Syrian pattern, most probably to pasture his herds of horses, an important military asset.[1] Sousse, Sfax and Gabes, the cities of the Sahel, were held by his governors, as were Tripoli and Tobna, the capital of the Zab. Elsewhere in the west and north, however, the lords of the *jund* formed an hereditary military aristocracy which the *sulṭān* could only dominate with the superior force of the *ḥasham*, the royal retinue. Their strongholds and their men-at-arms reproduced on a smaller scale the model of ʿAbbāsiya, just as ʿAbbāsiya reproduced Baghdad. They took the devolution of power still further. The system was irregular and incomplete, omitting wide areas and many peoples even within the Ifrīqiyan compass. In the mountains and the deserts were largely self-governing communities, amongst them the Ibadite populations, ruled – if they were ruled at all – by military expeditions. By the middle of the ninth century the picture seems static. A period of calm from 850 onwards is perhaps to be understood as a time when the Aghlabids, engaged in Sicily and southern Italy, let sleeping dogs lie.

Egypt fared differently. Devolution there was, but of a different kind. The establishment of the Aghlabids in Ifrīqiya was indeed prophetic; the appointment by Maʾmūn of viceroys over the western and the eastern provinces is evidence of the growing strain upon government from Baghdad. Under this scheme, however, Egypt was downgraded, with governors appointed by the new overlord, ʿAbd Allah, followed by Muʿtaṣim. When Muʿtaṣim became caliph in 834, the

1 The works were to water livestock: cf. M. Solignac, 'Recherches sur les installations hydrauliques de Kairouan et des Steppes Tunisiennes du VIIe au XIe siècle', *Annales de l'Institut des Études Orientales* (Algiers), 1952, **10**, 5–273; 1953, **11**, 61–170. A hundred years later, the Kalbid rulers of Sicily kept large herds of horses: cf. M. Amari, *Storia dei Musulmani di Sicilia*, 2nd edn, ed. by C. Nallino (Catania, 1933–5), **2**, 441–2.

affairs of the province were finally settled. He was a warrior who had created a large 'slave' army of Turks from central Asia. In 836 he transferred this army to a new capital city at Samarra further up the Tigris. The task of appointing the governor of Egypt was then given to a Turkish officer at Samarra, first Ashīnās and then Ītākh. These became absentee landlords, enjoying much of the country's wealth. The estates and the tax-farms reached their greatest extent as the fiscal burden increased, land went out of production and was let on favourable terms to concessionaries who tried to induce the peasants to return. While there is no need to think with Becker in terms of a catastrophe, it was probably a period of depression, when the area under cultivation was on the whole reduced, and the population may have fallen. The chief beneficiaries in the country were probably the Coptic managers, the tax-collectors and tax-farmers, the bailiffs and the stewards.

The weakness of the government at Fusṭāṭ heightened the effect. There was no question of army leaders continuing to divide the province, but the exclusion of the Arabs from the register was probably an indication of a reduction in the size of the force at the governor's disposal. The restoration of law and order culminated in 836 when official contact was made with Christian Nubia, the *baqṭ* was renegotiated to a Muslim formula, and a son of the Nubian king made his way to Iraq (see further chapter 9, pp. 577–8). But in the 840s the Nubians and the Beja peoples of the deserts bordering the Red Sea invaded Upper Egypt, and were only pushed back by Arab tribesmen wandering south into the region of Aswan. While, according to al-Yaʿqūbī, a stretch of the valley in Upper Egypt was evacuated, a prey to nomads and brigands, these Arabs made Aswan their 'capital'. Together with immigrants from across the Red Sea, they colonized the hilly region of the Wadi Allaqi to the south-east, mining for gold with the labour of black slaves. From the Wadi Allaqi they entered into relations, not with the more familiar Nubian kingdom at Dongola, but with the second Christian state of ʿAlwa on the Nile in the region of Khartoum, which was reached directly across the desert. Further to the north, says al-Yaʿqūbī, gold and ivory entered Egypt from the Red Sea through ʿAydhab, the successor to the old Greek port of Berenice, which gave access to the Nile at Qus. These various activities were carried on by people largely beyond the reach of the authorities at Fusṭāṭ.

By 850, therefore, Egypt was reduced in size as well as status. Nevertheless it continued to share in the concerns of the wider community. In 814 there came to Fusṭāṭ with a governor appointed by Ma'mūn the great jurist al-Shāfi'ī, who remained there until his death in 821, composing his major work, the *Risāla*. The *Risāla* dealt directly with the problem which underlay the *Muwaṭṭa'*, the problem of proof. Those who relied upon the opinion of the wise to guarantee the Law had been obliged to concede that this opinion should if possible be grounded in scripture. There was, however, no agreement about what this scripture was to be. It was in these years, for example, that the *kitāb Allah*, 'the Book of God', the Koran, if it did not assume its final form at least became the object of controversy: whether it was not a source of Law at all; whether it was the sole source; or whether it was, like the Torah, the focal point of the corpus. Still more important was the question of the *ḥawādīth* (sing. *ḥadīth*), 'traditions' of the sayings and doings of the Prophet and his companions which were being written down in the form: 'B told A that C told B that D told C . . . that Y told X that he had seen or heard one of these founders do or say such and such.' This recitation of the *isnād*, the chain of transmission from teller to teller, was the pedigree by which the authenticity of the story was judged. At first the *ḥawādīth* were not admitted for legal purposes against the opinion of the wise, but since they purported to give an account of the *sunna*, the practice of the community, at the very beginning of its history, acceptance of their authenticity meant that they could not be ignored.

It was the achievement of al-Shāfi'ī to resolve this argument with an arrangement of the *uṣūl*, the 'roots' or sources of the Law, in order of importance. The Koran was given pride of place as the Word of God revealed to Muḥammad. Its relatively short text was to be supplemented in the second place by *ḥadīth*, the record of the Sunna or Practice of the Prophet. Should that record still leave anything obscure, then the *sunna*, or the practice of the existing community, which was deemed to transmit the Sunna of the Prophet by continuous usage, might be invoked under the name of *ijmā'*, 'consensus'. In the last resort, a jurist might rely upon *qiyās*, his own reasoning by analogy. The scheme, resembling that of Talmudic Judaism, was successful because its logic was incontrovertible. The Word of God Himself had to come first. The recognition of *ḥadīth* as a scriptural record of a divine revelation at the root of the legal practice of the community then placed the sacred character of its Law finally beyond doubt. The individual *ḥawādīth* were the proof. Their use completed the transformation of the laws and customs of the Umayyads into a unique dispensation. Expressed as traditions handed down from teller to teller, beliefs and practices of any date from the seventh to the beginning of the ninth century were formally ascribed to Muḥammad and so to God.

Al-Shāfiʿī established the principle without bringing the argument over the Law to an end. Different traditions gave scriptural force to different opinions. The majority of the *fuqahā'* held that the traditions which defined the Sunna of the Prophet defined their own *sunna*, which had remained faithful to the great original by the grace of God; thus they alone could give a correct interpretation. These Sunnites were opposed to the Shiʿites, who gave especial weight to traditions about ʿAlī, and saw in his descendants the recipients of divine guidance to compare with the inspiration which more orthodox jurists claimed for their scholarship. Such guidance was likewise claimed by the ʿAbbasids as caliphs from the house of the Prophet. The question of who should decide in matters of doctrine became acute over the Koran. About 800 the Muʿtazilites emerged as a school of philosophy and theology. They were not a school of Law, but took up a position on the Law when they insisted on the priority of the Koran to the exclusion of *ḥadīth*. They were thus in opposition to the majority of the *ʿulamā'*. The Muʿtazilites, however, became fashionable at court at a time when Ma'mūn was seeking the political support of the Shīʿa, and turning away from the *ahl al-Sunna* or 'people of the Practice'. It was a serious matter when Ma'mūn endorsed the Muʿtazilite doctrine that the Koran had been created by God against the view that it was, like God, eternal. When in 833 he promulgated this so-called *khalq* doctrine, or doctrine of creation, as the law of the empire, it was seen as an attack upon the Sunnites and the authority upon which they relied. The decree was enforced by a *miḥna*, an 'inquisition', to compel jurists and *qāḍīs* to subscribe on pain of disgrace, imprisonment and even death.

The *miḥna* was a drastic if unsuccessful attempt by the caliph to arbitrate in matters of faith. It was introduced into Egypt in 833, and renewed under the caliph Wāthiq in 842. It produced a crop of martyrs before the decree was rescinded at the accession of Mutawakkil in 849. The hand of the ʿAbbasids continued to be heavy – witness the disgrace of the Banū ʿAbd al-Ḥakam, the family of jurists to which the historian Ibn ʿAbd al-Ḥakam belonged, on a charge of peculation in the 850s. The failure of the *khalq* decree was nevertheless a victory for the scholars. This appears from the tale of events in Ifrīqiya, which may have been modelled on the story of Iraq. The Qāḍī of Ifrīqiya had kept his original importance as chief justice of the realm. Standing also for the Law, he enjoyed immense prestige as a leader of the community quite apart from the *amīr* who appointed him. The post was held by some eminent men. Asad b. al-Furāt not only led the expedition to Sicily in 827. As a jurist he improved upon the *Muwaṭṭa'* of Mālik b. Anas with a treatise called the *Asadiya*, an exposition of the Law obtained by the device of systematically questioning an older master. After his death in camp in 828, he was succeeded as the outstanding jurist of Kairouan by Saḥnūn, the author of the *Mudawwana*. This was the definitive successor to the *Asadiya*, using the same technique of the *su'āl* or *mas'ala*, the question, to elicit replies more formally in accordance with the *uṣūl* described by al-Shāfiʿī. The place of Asad as Qāḍī of Ifrīqiya, however, was taken by the Muʿtazilite Ibn Abī 'l-Jawād, who remained in office under Ziyādat Allah I, his brother Abū ʿIqāl (838–41), and Abū ʿIqāl's son Muḥammad I. Saḥnūn was patronized by a family of *wazīrs*, ʿAlī b. Ḥumayd and his sons. But in 846/7 this family was overthrown in a coup by Muḥammad's brother, and Saḥnūn was tried for his life by the Qāḍī in the matter of the 'created Qur'ān'. The situation was only redressed when Muḥammad disgraced his brother, and Saḥnūn himself was made Qāḍī and had his predecessor flogged so that he died.

This savage justice stood for the triumph of the Sunna over its opponents. It did so because it was the particular victory of the Mālikī school. The schools of opinion in the eighth century had been regional, comprising the scholars of Arabia or Iraq. The emphasis upon the transmission of doctrine from master to pupil, made increasingly precise by the technique of question and answer, meant a growing concentration upon personalities, and the selection by each school of an intellectual ancestor. Thus the school of Mecca and Medina, taking Mālik b. Anas for a founder, became the Mālikī school, while that of Iraq became the Ḥanafī school after his near contemporary Abū Ḥanīfa. In the ninth century in Egypt, a third school formed from the disciples of al-Shāfiʿī, while a fourth derived from Ibn Ḥanbal, who fell victim to the *miḥna* at Baghdad in the 840s. The ancestry, especially in the case of the earlier figures, was not precise; the authority of the founder was invoked for the labours of subsequent scholars as a guarantee of continuity between past and present. It ensured that their understanding of the Law which had been revealed to Muḥammad was correct. In this way the *Mudawwana* of Saḥnūn, for example, which stated the views of the wise in the ninth century, became of necessity a true interpretation of the way of God, even though it differed on certain points from the equally authoritative compendia of the other schools.

Thus the Law, the *sharīʿa* or *sharʿ*, terms with the connotation of 'enactment', 'fountain' and 'way', assumed its final form. On the one hand it was a single scheme, a divine product which it was humanly impossible to know and to follow in its perfection. On the other, it was the extent of human knowledge of this ideal, based on divine revelation, preserved by custom and tradition with petty discrepancies which marked the imperfection of human understanding, and eventually spelt out in the writings of the ninth century. This codification in accordance with the divergent doctrines of each school was decisive. From the tenth century onwards, the concern of the scholar was no longer with the *uṣūl*, the 'roots' and their meaning, but with the *furūʿ*, the 'branches', the ramifications from the trunk. As far as other opinions were concerned, the 'people of the Sunna' agreed to differ on points which were admittedly trivial but at the same time fundamental, part of the divine dispensation. The schools divided accordingly into four *madhāhib* (sing. *madhhab*), 'roads along which to go'. Differences between these *madhāhib* and the Shiʿite and Kharijite schools which stood outside this Sunnite tradition were considered to be more substantial. These unorthodox schools, however, had all evolved along the same lines in the same milieu to produce the same kind of doctrine in the same form. The majority of Shiʿites, for example, who had come to settle on the line of Ḥusayn as the line of the true *imāms*, referred back to the sixth such *imām*, Jaʿfar, who died in 765. Called significantly al-Ṣādiq, 'the Authentic', he stood in the same kind of relation to their tradition as his contemporary Abū Ḥanīfa to the Sunnite school of Iraq. The differences which distinguished them from the orthodox majority were still no more than differences in detail.

These divisions were reflected in society at large. The Muslim community was dividing into confessions as it became politically divided into states and regions. The Maghrib was particularly varied, with Ibadites and Sufrites, Shiʿites and Sunnites, side by side. Sunnī Islam was centred upon Ifrīqiya, where Kairouan was the religious capital of the Muslim west. A minority of jurists were Hanafite, but the majority, following Saḥnūn, were Malikite. Malikites likewise predominated in the Delta, but in Upper Egypt Shafiʿites were numerous. The effect of these divisions varied. On the whole Sunnites lived together, worshipped together, and might intermarry. Shiʿites and Kharijites were more segregated. In the tenth century, in the Sus in south-west Morocco, Ibn Ḥawqal reported that Sunnites and Shiʿites used the same mosque on alternate days.[1] At the same time in Ifrīqiya, Sunnites were not prepared to allow Ibadites to have their own mosque in an Ifrīqiyan city, or to take Sunnite wives.[2] Faction-fighting, however, took place in Baghdad between Malikites and Shafiʿites as well as between Malikites and Shiʿites.[3] Communalism was maintained by the needs of justice; in principle, different *madhāhib* meant different judgements by different persons. In practice, the state made little allowance, although the Aghlabids for example made a habit of appointing a Hanafite to assist or even replace the Malikite who held the post of Chief Qāḍī, not for the sake of the Law so much as their own political convenience. Instead, the members of a school might submit their cases privately to a jurist of their choice. In this way it was in fact possible for them to order their lives without recourse to the machinery of the Muslim state.

Such behaviour came naturally to a persecuted minority, such as the Ibadites in the major Ifriqiyan cities; it was already typical of the Jews, who had devised their Law to meet the needs of a people without a state of their own. It is therefore not surprising that it became more generally characteristic of a religion which resembled Talmudic Judaism so closely. The orthodox majority became accustomed to settling its affairs 'out of court'. Irrespective of the school, Islamic jurisprudence was well fitted to control by advice and consent. It did so by an extension of the technique of question and answer from theoretical to actual cases. The problem posed by the petitioner, the answer came not as a judgement binding upon the parties, such as a court might give, but as a considered opinion of what the Law required, just like the solutions propounded as examples in the books of *fiqh*. This opinion was the *fatwā* (pl. *fatāwī*, *fatāwā*); he who gave it, a *muftī*. It provided the basis for agreement, or for action. The giving of these formal consultations became a common practice. A *fatwā* might be requested for the sake of politeness, as a compliment to a great scholar by one able to afford an appropriate present.[4] In any case it would be preserved by the recipient on the one hand, the disciples on the other, to pass eventually into collections adding to the store of works of reference. As a contribution to the life of the community, it made

[1] Ibn Ḥawqal, *Kitāb ṣūrat al-arḍ*, ed. by J. H. Kramers (Leiden, 1938–9), 91–2; trans. by J. H. Kramers and G. Wiet, *Configuration de la Terre* (Beirut and Paris, 1964), 90.

[2] H. R. Idris, *La Berbérie orientale sous les Zīrīdes, Xe–XIIe siècles* (Paris, 1962), 744–5.

[3] Mez, *Renaissance*, 215.

[4] Idris, *Berbérie orientale*, 176–7.

possible an alternative system of government in which the *sulṭān*, the (man of) power, the state, had no necessary part to play.

In theory perhaps this was not so; it is commonly said that in Islam, as opposed to Christendom, church and state are one, since the holy Law is administered by the ruler.[1] Even so, the ruler stands in the same relation to the Law as the emperor to the Pope in the eyes of an Innocent III. Moreover, the Law was in the hands of its professional guardians, the *'ulamā'* or men of knowledge, a clerical body whose authority, at least in Sunnite Islam, was beyond the ruler's reach. Meanwhile the state departed so regularly from the *sharī'a* that in many ways it was a law to itself. The theory is discovered to be a compromise; the ruler acted under a dispensation called the *siyāsa shar'īya*, 'legitimate expediency' in political matters, which allowed him to do as he thought fit in the execution of his duty. Thus the practice of restricting the jurisdiction of the *qāḍī* and his court to ritual matters and family affairs was formally permitted. Beyond that, any illegality might be ignored on the grounds that any ruler was better than none. The refusal of the *'ulamā'* to countenance rebellion was not merely subservience, nor even simple prudence; it was a more fundamental abstention. Refraining from such decisions, they preserved their legal rectitude, their ritual purity, the condition which fitted them to offer their considered opinions, the fruits of their wisdom, to the world. The special nature of this position was celebrated. When, says the eleventh-century poet, Ibn Rashīq, of the glories of Kairouan,

> the number of its pulpits was the flower of the land ... how many were in it of nobles and gentles ... a school which gathered all accomplishments, and squandered its treasure to its lord and to its people; *imāms* who brought together the sciences of religion, setting right the uses of *ḥadīth* and problems of the Qur'ān; doctors who if you asked them rolled away the clouds with jurisprudence and eloquent elucidation ... you shall see the giants among kings in their presence bend their necks, lowering their chins; in their dread they cannot say a word, simply make signs with their hands and eyes; such men fear God and all mortals fear them, as dogs the lion in the hunt; awe of them makes you forget the loftiness of kings and the grandeur of sultans; their lightest thoughts weigh as mountains, and their excellence, like the sun, is not hidden anywhere.[2]

[1] Cf. e.g. E. I. J. Rosenthal, *Political thought in medieval Islam* (Cambridge, 1958), 23–4; the author avoids the contrast between *sulṭān* and *'ālim* by discussing the relationship of the caliph to the simple *amīr*.

[2] *Qaṣīda* quoted by Ibn Nājī, *Ma'ālim al-imān* (Tunis, AH 1320), 15–18, lines 1–18; cf. M. Brett, 'Fitnat al-Qayrawān', unpublished Ph.D. thesis (University of London, 1970), 485–6.

To sages such as these, the faithful might safely look for guidance in their everyday affairs, whoever ruled the land.

The eulogy of Ibn Rashīq expressed a legend which had gained strength in the tenth century, when Ifrīqiya was ruled by the Shiʿite Fatimid Dynasty, and the starkness of the separation of the men of wisdom from the men of power was brought home to the Sunnites as previously to the Ibadites. A more normal relationship is apparent in the history of the *qāḍī* and his office in Ifrīqiya. The *qāḍī* was in an ambiguous position, on the one hand an officer of state, on the other a minister of the Law. As an officer of the ʿAbbasids in the east, his powers were limited and his post shunned by the scholars, who were unwilling to convert an imperfect opinion into an imperfect but irrevocable judgement. As a minister, he nevertheless enjoyed immense prestige as a leader of the community quite apart from the ruler who appointed him. Thus in the tenth century al-Kindī could produce two lists to describe the history of Muslim Egypt, one of the *wulāt*, the governors, the other of the *quḍāt*, the judges. As an officer of the Aghlabids in the west, the power of the Qāḍī of Ifrīqiya was enhanced by his prestige; throughout the ninth century he continued to supervise the general administration of justice, although his judgements over this wide field were probably equitable rather than strictly doctrinal. His grandeur is expressed by the tale of Ibn Ghānim, who refused to rise in the presence of Ibrāhīm b. al-Aghlab. His peril, however, is apparent in the story of Ibn al-Farūk, who in 787 was forced to accept the office on pain of death, and in that of Saḥnūn himself, who upon his appointment is said to have declared that he was 'slaughtered without a knife'.[1] These stories anticipate a long decline from the time of Asad b. al-Furāt to the twelfth century, when the state had begun to appoint and pay a *muftī* to advise the *qāḍī* on his judgements in a more restricted area. As in the east, the position of the *qāḍī* had suffered from the growing separation of powers and authorities. At the same time, the appointment of a *muftī* from the ranks of the *fuqahā'* shows how far government by command and compulsion, and government by adjudication and agreement, had become not alternative but complementary. The *sulṭān* found the mediation of the *ʿālim* convenient, and sometimes necessary. In 875 the Aghlabid Ibrāhīm II was able to set aside his nephew's claim to the throne with the aid of a *ḥīla*, a 'device', a dispensation from his oath of loyalty declared licit by the jurists of Kairouan.

[1] Quoted by N. J. Coulson, *A history of Islamic Law* (Edinburgh, 1964), 126.

ISLAMIZATION AND ARABIZATION

The principal symbol of the religion of Islam and its community was the mosque or *masjid*, the 'place of worship', in the form of the *jāmiʿ* or 'congregational' mosque, a place of assembly and meeting, the seat perhaps of the *qāḍī* and his court, the location of the scholars with their circles of students, but most especially the place where the Faithful gathered on a Friday for the chief public prayer. Then, if ever, 'church and state' were one as the *khuṭba* or 'sermon' was pronounced in the presence of the ruler or his representative, either in his name or in that of the sovereign from whom he claimed his power. Repeated week after week, the pronouncement became a necessary mark of the true prince. It was worth the effort to ensure that the edifice which provided the scene was of a size and splendour to match the occasion. In the ninth century, all the great mosques of Egypt and North Africa which dated from the early days of the conquest were enlarged to their present size, while new ones were founded. In the Maghrib the original N-S-E-W orientation, which may have been determined by the layout of the *miṣr* as a Roman square, and certainly antedates the time when it was felt necessary to pray and to build in the direction of Mecca, was retained; it was only changed for mosques built after the tenth century. The nave and transept form of the prayer hall in the Great Mosque of Damascus was modified by the Iraqi design of a flat roof supported by row upon row of columns to give a more extensive covered area on one side of a colonnaded court. This feature of the mosque of al-Aqṣā, built at Jerusalem in 780, was copied in 787 by ʿAbd al-Raḥmān I at Cordoba. In 827 ʿAbd Allah b. Ṭāhir ordered the mosque of ʿAmr at Fusṭāṭ to be doubled in size. In 836 at Kairouan, the mosque of ʿUqba, rebuilt by Yazīd b. Ḥātim, was demolished by Ziyādat Allah I, and the present edifice with its large square minaret was begun. In 850/1 the great mosque of Sousse replaced the prayer hall of the *ribāṭ* with a new and separate building. Meanwhile a fresh lead was taken by Iraq with the erection of the great mosque of Samarra as part of the palace city complex founded by Muʿtaṣim. When Abū Ibrāhīm Aḥmad completed the great mosque of Kairouan in 862/3, it was with material imported from Iraq or in the Samarran style. In 864 it was by the command of the Caliph Mustaʿīn that the great mosque of Tunis, the Zaytūna, was rebuilt in its present form.

The progressive construction and enlargement of these great buildings, however, was not simply a product of the new monarchy and its taste for grandeur. It seems that building went forward roughly in proportion to the growth of the Muslim city.[1] As the elements of ancient culture were refashioned into 'the renaissance that was Islam', to read the title of a well-known work in the sense in which it was intended,[2] society as a whole was transformed. The community which had begun as a predominantly military body had turned into a cross-section of the population. How this happened is obscured rather than illuminated by the growing clarity of the faith. The history of recruitment had ended with the exclusion of the tribes from the *dīwān* and the formation of armies of *ʿabīd*. Islam on the other hand looked back to the conquests as the accomplishment of the divine purpose, and saw in the profession of faith an upward progress in the divine scheme. As a subject requiring further description and explanation, the continuous increase in the number of Muslims was largely ignored. Such indeed was the strength of this point of view that in many cases where new believers might be suspected, their *islām* has been attributed to the time of the Futūḥ, or considered to be a faith happily improved after a period of ignorance and neglect. Rather more revealing are the discussions of the related matters of language and race. Admiration of the Arabs as the people of the Prophet, and of Arabic as the language of God Himself in the Koran, went back to the situation in the seventh century, but did not wholly match the Muslim concept. The discrepancies were used to justify attitudes of historical, social and cultural superiority. In Iraq, Arabs and Persians satirized each other in the so-called *Shuʿūbiya*, 'the Nationalisms', a kind of polemic which became a theme of the new literature. In the Maghrib, the Berbers were attacked and defended in sayings attributed to Muḥammad. The ascetic Buhlūl b. Rāshid is said to have celebrated the proof that his ancestry was wholly Arab with a feast. By contrast, the Rustamids of Tahert prided themselves upon descent from the royal house of ancient Persia, while their Berber followers claimed to be the elect of God, fighting for the faith rather than – like the Arabs – for material reward.

The invariable use of Arabic for such literary boasting illustrates a change which was not necessarily religious. In Andalus, the *muwalladūn*, 'those brought up as Arabs', had adopted both Islam and Arabic; the *mustaʿribūn* (Mozarabs), 'those claiming to be Arabs', were Christians who had adopted only Arabic. The situation was evidently the same in Egypt, where in the tenth century Severus b. Muqaffaʿ explained that he

[1] A. Lézine, 'Notes d'archéologie ifriqiyenne', *Revue des Études Islamiques*, 1967, **35**, 69–70.
[2] See Margoliouth, 'Introductory note', in Mez, *Renaissance*.

was obliged to have his material translated, with great difficulty, out of Greek and Coptic, since the knowledge of these original tongues had almost disappeared. In Ifrīqiya the use of Latin is attested in inscriptions down to the eleventh century at Kairouan, as well as in papal letters of Leo IX and Gregory VII, but may have been severely restricted. The Jews certainly kept their Hebrew for religious purposes, but for others they came to write Arabic in Hebrew characters. The reasons for the increasing use of Arabic have little to do with its status as the language of Islam. They are more probably related to its official use in Egypt and North Africa as the language of administration and affairs. The situation for illiterates may well have been different. Here the classical languages may have lingered despite what Severus says;[1] in the twelfth century, Idrīsī has a report of Latin spoken in the Djerid.[2] There can be no doubt about the persistence of the languages of the Berber speakers, whatever their religion, since these languages have survived to the present not only in the more remote regions of the Maghrib, but also, with particular tenacity, among the remaining Ibadite communities. The spread of Arabic among this section of the population is much harder to perceive and to explain, involving as it has done the development of vernaculars apart from the written standard.

Nevertheless, the adoption of Arabic by non-Muslims emphasizes their refusal to accept the religion with which it was so closely associated even after the prohibitions upon membership of the community had become a thing of the past, and the profession of faith was largely open. It is apparent that differences of creed continued to serve some purpose. In Egypt their utility seems to go back to the end of the seventh century, when pressure was put upon the higher officials of the administration to abandon their Christianity. At the beginning of the eighth century there was an attempt, connected with the name of Ashīnās, to exclude Christians from 'the ministry'. It is perhaps possible to see the beginning of a compromise in the structural reform of the administration which separated the *amīr* from the *'āmil*, the governor from the intendant of finance. Although the evidence does not accumulate until a later period, it is likely that this separation of powers extended to the pagarchy which the Arabs had first taken over and strengthened. It survived the breakdown during the civil war, helping to produce within the administration an important distinction between the chancery and the treasury, the

[1] Cf. *Encyclopaedia of Islam*, 1st edn (Leiden and London, 1913–38), under Ḳibṭ.

[2] al-Idrīsī, *Kitāb nuzhat al-mushtāq fī ikhtirāq al-āfāq*, ed. and trans. by R. Dozy and M. J. de Goeje, *Description de l'Afrique du Nord et de l'Espagne* (Leiden, 1866), 121 trans. 141.

secretariat and the fiscal regime. It was with the latter that the Christian official was progressively identified, making it his particular preserve. An alternative career was provided by the Church, which continued to be well endowed. The *proteuontes* of the Greek papyri may have turned to tax-farming, a traditional form of investment, as well as to estate management on behalf of aristocratic landowners. The wealthier among them were probably tempted to abandon their Christianity, joining the ranks of the *aʿyān*, the notables of the Muslim period. But the loss of such people to the Coptic community was perhaps a measure of the opportunities available at a lower level to those Christians with the necessary skill and talent in clerical work, administration and handicraft. It is likely that such specialized activites ensured that the towns of Egypt, with exceptions like Fusṭāṭ, where an original population had been outnumbered by Muslim immigrants, were still mainly Christian.

The peasants, on the other hand, derived no such advantage from their faith. Although they were slow to change, it is possible to see in their situation in the ninth century the conditions which prepared the way for their complete islamization. The suppression of the revolt of the Basharūd in 832, which ended the series of peasant rebellions which began in 725, was taken by the fifteenth-century al-Maqrīzī as the beginning of a Muslim majority in the country. Glossing the account of al-Kindī, he says that from that date

> God abased the Qibṭ in all the land of Egypt; their strength waned so that they were incapable of resistance to the *sulṭān*. The Muslims prevailed in, or took possession of, the villages (*ghalaba al-muslimūn ʿalā ʾl-quran*), and the Qibṭ turned to plot against Islam and its people, notably by having a hand in the collection of taxes.[1]

From this Becker concluded that the Arabs had settled as agriculturalists on the land, while the Qibṭ had accepted Islam at least in appearance, thereby mingling with the Muslims to the extent of taking Muslim wives.[2] There is no warrant for this conclusion in the Arabic, which looks too much like an attempt to account historically for the unpopular Christian official. If the date will not stand, however, the hypothesis is plausible. The relevant factor is not the occurrence or suppression of rebellion, which took place mainly in the northern Delta, but the flight from the villages which elsewhere accompanied the growth of the estates. A large measure of resettlement was evidently involved. New men found new masters, all the more because the fugitive continued to

[1] al-Maqrīzī, *Khiṭaṭ*, I, 334–5.

[2] Becker, *Beiträge*, II, 120–1, 135.

be a wanted man in need of protection.[1] This fitted well with contemporary practice, in which followings of slaves and clients were the rule; it must have been encouraged by the state itself when the tax-farmer was commissioned to attract labour onto uncultivated land with the offer of favourable terms. It was consonant with a return to conditions resembling those of the Byzantine period.

In the ninth century religion was not necessarily involved. A peasant, leaving home, may have professed a new faith in God when he accepted a new bond to man. On the other hand, the tax-lists from the Arabic papyri of the ninth century contain for the most part Christian names. Even when they are Arab, the bearers may not have been Muslim. In the tenth century, Ibn Ḥawqal considered that the Qibṭ were the people of Egypt.[2] On the other hand, the Christian peasant, who had once been forbidden to become a client member of the Muslim community lest the land go out of production, now found himself on the same footing as Muslims in a similar condition of dependence. Whereas the Muslims of the towns, growing in number by natural increase and by immigration, may have emphasized their Islam as a measure of their difference from the Christians of the Coptic quarters, in and around the old fortress of Babylon for example, those of the countryside may have been less exclusive. The appearance of a rural Muslim population began with the stationing of Arab beduin on either side of the Delta. By the ninth century, these had either been settled as cultivators, or obliged to perform duties such as the transport of grain to Qulzum on the Red Sea, unless they had wandered south. Meanwhile the acquisition of estates by the Muslim aristocracy had brought their followers onto the irrigated land. The lord's men and the tribesmen seem to have come together. A papyrus which lists peasants with Arab names speaks also of 'ten beduin of my lord'. It is reasonable to think that many such beduin, as in more recent times, came to settle individually as cultivators, especially at a time when peasant labour was scarce and valuable. In these circumstances, in which Muslims and Christians encountered each other in the countryside on the same terms, it is possible that Islam, and in this particular instance vernacular Arabic, spread in the rural population by demographic extension from generation to generation. For Becker, the Copts accepted Islam to the extent of taking Muslim wives; but given what must be assumed to be a fundamentally static population fluctuating between a maximum of seven million and a

[1] Becker, 'Papyrusstudien', *Zeitschrift für Assyriologie*, 1909, **22**, 137–54.

[2] Ibn Ḥawqal, *Ṣūrat al-arḍ*, 161 trans. 159.

minimum of two or three,[1] the taking of Christian wives by Muslims, Coptic wives by Arabs, could simply have enlarged the number of Muslims and the number of native Arabic speakers in each succeeding generation, until rural Egypt had been in effect repopulated.

Such an account, of colonization rather than conversion, leaves out of consideration the undoubted passion of Islam. This may have owed something to the native Christian tradition of monks and hermits. Dhū 'l-Nūn al-Miṣrī, 'the Egyptian', who died in 860, is said to have studied the hieroglyphs in his search for wisdom. He is one of the traditional founders of Sufism, the widespread devotionalism apparently called after *ṣūf*, 'wool', the material of the garment worn by the pious contemplative. The Ṣūfīya who aided the Andalusians at Alexandria in 816, however, were more fanatical. Standing upon the obligation to command the good and prohibit the bad, they were critical of, or actively opposed to, the state in much the same way as the *murābiṭūn* of Ifrīqiya. In 869, one Ibn al-Ṣūfī may have claimed divine inspiration for an attack upon the ungodly; the town of Asna was sacked, its people massacred, and the commander who had been sent against the insurgents mutilated and crucified. The likelihood that such behaviour stemmed from the specifically Islamic activity of the holy war need not conflict with the notion of an origin in some earlier enthusiasm. This, indeed, would make the Muslim practice more comprehensible. Here as elsewhere, it is probable that Islam was conforming to a type. But although religious agitation may have been symptomatic, it was inconclusive. Only in the Maghrib did fervour find an outlet.

The Afāriq were comparable to the Qibṭ. The dearth of evidence, however, is in itself a sign that their situation was more precarious. Unlike the metropolitan Jacobite Church, their church was merely a province of Rome. Comparing unfavourably with the Church in Spain, it failed to produce any manifestation of note either within the western or, more important, within the Arabic tradition. By the twelfth century their Christianity was extinct. This feebleness can be partly explained by the presence of a second native population. The first attempt to rule the Barbar had ended in the creation of a separate Muslim community. The outcome followed from the methods used, which had procured for the conquerors adherents rather than subjects. Similar methods continued to produce similar results. The Barbar were inducted into a new society in the course of wars, raids, expeditions and alliances. The Muslim

[1] Cf. Préaux, 'Graeco-Roman Egypt', 350; F. Mengin, *Histoire de l'Égypte sous le gouvernement de Mohammed-Aly* (Paris, 1823), II, 616.

order of the ninth century was superimposed upon naturally mobile peoples, and brought their wanderings for cultivation and pasture within the scope of a commercial as well as a political economy. What began with slaves and fleeces sent to Damascus developed into trade. Seasonal movements and seasonal campaigns went with seasonal markets and seasonal caravans. The network took in the traffic of the Sahara, extending westwards to Spain, eastwards to Egypt, and northwards across the central Mediterranean. The appearance of merchant families among the Ibadite populations is evidence of the growth of the market, and some indication of its capacity to reward those who made it their business.

The pattern was complicated. Berber girls were valued in the east, while Berber soldiers appeared in the armies of Egypt and Iraq (see chapter 10). Europeans and Negroes were imported, some for re-export. Refugees came and went. Rebels from the Ifriqiyan *jund* fled to Tahert, Fez and Andalus, while some of the fugitives from Cordoba in 814 were received by the Aghlabids. Many came from the east to trade, or to sell their services as soldiers and statesmen, artists, craftsmen and technicians. Syrians seem to have built the reservoirs to the south of Kairouan which opened up a barren district, most probably to horses, herded perhaps by nomads in the *sulṭān*'s employ.[1] The use of black slaves as labourers in the Djerid may have enlarged the irrigated area;[2] further north, colonies of Negroes appeared on marshy land near the coast. Meanwhile immigration into the cities turned Sousse, for example, from a *ribāṭ* to a major port. Around the cities cultivation spread in various ways. It was probably always possible to make a freehold in the waste for the family or clan. Lordships, on the other hand, led to sharecropping on terms which ranged from *munāṣafa*, division of the produce into equal halves, to what was later called *khammāsa*, retention of a fifth by the tenant. Proprietors might be rich or poor, the occupants anyone from the man who took the land to be worked for him by another, to the serf or slave. Such tenancies applied to all kinds of land with all kinds of husbandry – from irrigated to dry, from trees to standing crops to animals – and may have offered considerable inducements to the cultivator. Pastoral nomads may have been encouraged by the market for livestock, leather and wool. While

[1] The anecdote cited by Idris, *Berbérie orientale*, 749, of an Ibadite shaykh who herded horses in Cap Bon (?), may reflect such an arrangement.

[2] In the Djerid in 826, the rebel ʿĀmir b. Nāfiʿ raised a thousand *sūdān* armed with axes and spades: Ibn ʿIdhārī, *Kitāb al-Bayān al-mughrib fī akhbār al-Andalus wa'l-Maghrib*, ed. by G. S. Colin and E. Lévi-Provençal, I (Leiden, 1948), 101.

the mountain peoples kept to themselves, it is likely that individuals continually left the hills for the new civilization.

While Arabic was slow to spread beyond the cities, the growth of the new Ifrīqiya was actively religious. As the Arabian cities of Mecca and Medina became established as *the* Holy Places of Islam, the *ḥajj* or pilgrimage grew into a regular routine. This characteristic act of medieval piety was an added motive for travel which gave purpose and direction to the wanderings of the merchant in search of a market, the student in search of a teacher, or the man in search of the world. A pilgrimage was not yet perhaps the goal of life, but it added to the traffic and the business of the routes, even if those who set out for the east from Andalus, for example, seem often to have got no further than Kairouan. The pilgrim may have been easily diverted to pious ends which seemed more urgent. Among these was the holy war. The odyssey of the refugees from Cordoba, their welcome by the Ṣūfīya at Alexandria, and their subsequent conquest of Crete, showed how easily the zealous took up arms. When in 827 the Aghlabids resumed the offensive in the central Mediterranean, the armada which sailed for Sicily was composed of contingents from many sectors of the population, the Arabs, the *jund*, the Barbar, and yet more of the Andalusians who had fled from Spain. *Muṭṭawiʿūn*, 'volunteers', in the general as well as the specific sense of irregulars who followed the host for material as well as spiritual reward, they were not simply raiders but also settlers who, for the first time for a hundred years, established a new Muslim community *ex nihilo* in a new country.

Their achievement is a measure of the Islam of Ifrīqiya. It was not the work of the original army, which had been transformed out of existence. The impetus had to be recreated under different conditions. These were the conditions of society under the Aghlabids. The energies which went into the pursuit of power, plunder, profit, employment and land across the Mediterranean were those of North Africa, powerfully concentrated by a militant fervour. They were promoted as well as revealed by the Sicilian venture, which showed clearly the opportunities open to the Faithful, and was an added inducement to move in upon their society, economy and culture. Some indication of the success of Islam in these circumstances is provided, paradoxically, by the transformation of the *murābiṭūn*, the men of the ribats who had been the inspiration of the Sicilian venture, from devout soldiers into monk-like devotees. The change can be seen at Sousse, where in 821 there was a significant addition to the function of the *ribāṭ* as a fortress and a mosque, with the building of a round tower as a look-out post as well as a minaret. From the time of the invasion of Sicily in 827, however, the town grew rapidly, and in 850/1 the fact was recognized with the building of the great mosque by the side of the *ribāṭ*. In 859 the old building then lost its military importance with the building of the town walls and the erection of the citadel on the hill above the port. It simply continued as a kind of monastery for its inhabitants, ascetics who had lost any military character apart from the discipline they observed.

As this happened, the term *ribāṭ* ceased to have any necessary application to a garrison or fortress, although it continued to be used in this sense. It became a name for any house of such holy men, and eventually acquired a spiritual sense as a synonym for *jihād* or *islām*. The name *murābiṭ* evolved like that of *ṣufī* in the east with a more general meaning of 'holy man', *faqīr* (pl. *fuqarā'*), literally 'poor man'. Saints of this kind were familiar from their prototypes, beggars, monks, hermits and priests, Christian and pagan, and it is likely that their appearance in these roles was in itself a sign of the growing acceptance of their faith. From the cities they moved into the countryside, where they might enjoy exceptional authority for the blessing they brought and the curse they could bestow. Away from the main towns, this authority became an important part of village and tribal life, restraining the quarrelsome and restricting the perpetual feuds. In the ninth century, the principal examples of such authority were provided by the Ibadite shaykhs of the south, persuading, advising, exhorting and commanding their followers in the name of God. Many grew rich and powerful, gathering their disciples around them in settlements of which they were chiefs. Other holy men were less reputable. Their wanderings brought them nevertheless into contact with the people who did not leave home, but may have become Muslim by degrees, simply by acknowledging the existence of the man of God in their midst and making use of his powers and skills. To the west of Ifrīqiya such persons may have settled in the Tell, the mountainous belt between the plateau and the sea, claiming descent from Ḥasan, son of ʿAlī, to pass as natural saints in secluded valleys to the north of the main route to Tlemcen.[1]

The notion of hereditary holiness, developing out of the feeling for the family of the Prophet which had played so important a part in the history of the community, brought these characters into the lineage structure of the population. As one of the basic ways in which their Islam spread to the people, the phenomenon is a special case of the

[1] Cf. M. Talbi, *L'Émirat aghlabide, 184–296/800–909: histoire politique* (Paris, 1966), 567–9.

demographic process of change which, applying to Egypt, can be considered as one of the ways in which this process occurred in the Nile Valley. In the Maghrib it was one among many factors which operated outside the Aghlabid dominions either separately or in conjunction with each other. Immigration was of fundamental importance in the creation of the main cities. After its foundation by Ibn Rustam, Tahert was populated by a continuous stream of arrivals from the east, mainly from Ifrīqiya, but some from as far away as Iraq; the cosmopolitan mixture was described by the traveller Ibn al-Ṣaghīr towards the end of the ninth century. Fez, refounded in 809 by Idrīs II, attracted yet another band of exiles from Cordoba who settled on the right bank of the stream, called after them the ʿAdwat al-Andalusiyyīn, about 818. These were followed in 826 by refugees from the rebellion against Ziyādat Allah I at Kairouan, who settled on the left bank, the ʿAdwat al-Qarawiyyīn or Qayrawānī Bank. These and other towns, like Nukūr in the Rif,[1] dominated their respective regions, drawing people into their vicinity and compelling recognition by the hill-men of the rugged countryside.

This domination was still to a large extent the product of military occupation and conquest. The Rustamid monarchs controlled the route to the sea at Marsā Farūkh. The twenty years of the reign of Idrīs II at Fez, from the time he came into his kingdom until his death in 829, saw the creation of a family dominion in northern Morocco; the region of Tlemcen was ruled by his cousins, the sons of his uncle Sulaymān, whom his father Idrīs b. ʿAbd Allah had set there in place of Abū Qurra. Southwards the Idrisids crossed the Middle Atlas to the upper valley of the Moulouya river. Leaving the Banū Midrār at Sijilmasa in the Tafilelt on their left, they turned south-westwards along the Saharan slopes of the High Atlas towards the Atlantic. Princes of the line built castles at Tāmdult in the valley of the upper Darʿa, and perhaps also at Igli in the valley of the Sous. In this region the military and political motives were confused with the commercial. The upper Darʿa was rich in silver and copper; the Sous could produce crops such as cotton. The Idrisids were preceded and accompanied by wanderers and merchants from as far away as Libya, coming through Tahert and Sijilmasa to model this 'far Sus' upon the society and the economy of the Djerid, the Jebel Nefusa and the Fezzan. As yet there was no

[1] al-Bakrī, *Kitāb al-masālik wa'l-mamālik*, ed. and trans. by M. G. de Slane, *Description de l'Afrique septentrionale*, 2nd edn (Algiers, 1911–13; reprinted Paris, 1965), 90ff., trans. 180ff.

question of a direct trade across the desert with the western Sudan.[1] But from al-Yaʿqūbī's vague references to gold and a 'land of Ghast', it is apparent that the old route across the western Sahara, the so-called 'ṭrīq Lamtūnī', followed by the veiled Berber nomads of the desert, was being drawn into the system in much the same way as the easterly routes from Ifrīqiya to the Niger bend and the central Sudan. Meanwhile it would seem that ships went by sea from the port of Massa in the Sous northwards to the Mediterranean.

Although this progressive colonization lacked the unity of the conquest of Sicily, it served to create a Muslim society out of a native population of mountaineers and desert tribesmen. By the ninth century, the *islām* exacted by the first conquerors had become the Islam demanded by Idrīs II when he named his new city of Fez al-ʿAliya, 'the city of ʿAlī', in defiance of the Aghlabid city of al-ʿAbbāsiya. It is the Idrisids who may perhaps be credited with the Shiʿite community which according to Ibn Ḥawqal shared a mosque with a Sunnite community in the Sous. More striking is Massa on the coast, which is described as a *ribāṭ* with a large community of holy men. Ibn Ḥawqal in the tenth century considered the religion of these people *ḥashwī*, 'crudely anthropomorphic', but as a Shiʿite himself he was prejudiced.[2] It was probably from the area of the Darʿa and the Sous that Muslims first entered inner Morocco, the lands within the curve of the Atlas between the mountains and the Atlantic, coming over the high passes to the south. Aghmat near Marrakesh was the first place of importance. Behind it in the valley of the Oued Nfiss, the Wadi Niffīs, on the northern side of the High Atlas, appeared a notable colony of holy men, while the town itself became a merchant city of some importance.

The entry of Islam from the north was for a long time peculiar. If Idrīs II did in fact conquer as far as the Oued Nfiss,[3] it was an isolated episode, and is perhaps no more than a variant of the legendary theme of conquest by ʿUqba b. Nāfiʿ.[4] In this south-westerly direction, it is likely that the Idrisids confined themselves within the limits of Roman Mauretania, as Mūsā b. Nuṣayr had done. After the death of Idrīs II in

[1] Cf. M. Brett, 'Ifrīqiya as a market for Saharan trade from the tenth to the twelfth century AD', *Journal of African History*, 1969, **10**, 3, 358–9 and note 74.

[2] Ibn Ḥawqal, *ṣūrat al-arḍ*, 91–2 trans. 90.

[3] Ibn ʿIdhārī, *Bayān*, I, 211.

[4] Cf. E. Lévi-Provençal, 'Un nouveau récit de la conquête de l'Afrique du Nord par les Arabes', *Arabica Occidentalia*, 1954, I, 17–43, introducing and translating the work of the fourteenth-century Moroccan author Ibn ʿAbd al-Ḥalīm. The narrative, judged by Lévi-Provençal to be based upon an early and accurate tradition, seems to me quite the reverse; its straightforward character as an account of the conquest of the Maṣmūda people of the High Atlas is much more likely to be the product of rationalization than a proof of authenticity.

829, and especially after the death of Yaḥyā II in 859, their dominion was divided among the many princes of the family. Meanwhile in the middle of the ninth century there appeared an eccentric movement among the Barghawāṭa people of the Tamesna, the coastal plain to the south of Casablanca. The prophet Yūnus traced his inspiration to his grandfather Ṣāliḥ and his great-grandfather Tārif, who was said to have succeeded Maysara as the leader of the Kharijites in the west; for this reason the movement is usually ascribed to the events of 739. But according to al-Bakrī, the principal source, Yūnus is also said to have come from Andalus, and his doctrine, that Ṣāliḥ had been sent by God to provide His people with a Berber Qur'ān before he left to come again as the Mahdi, 'the rightly-guided one', after seven successors had sat on the throne, is much too reminiscent of Shiʿite ideas of the ninth and even the tenth century, when the information was supplied to the authorities at Cordoba by a Barghawāṭa delegation. The descendants of Yūnus, rulers equipped with *ḥasham* and *jund*, made annual raids upon their neighbours, especially upon the infidels to the south, for booty and tribute. They seem to illustrate that power of the holy man to arouse enthusiasm for a war of conquest which was apparent in Ifrīqiya in the invasion of Sicily. In this case, however, unhindered by any existing *sulṭān*, the preacher and his followers created their own state. On the far western frontier of Islam, they pointed to the possibility of a new Muslim revolution.

Their contribution, indeed, may have been specific. The conflict engendered in the broad lands between the Oum er-Rbia and the Oued Tensift, between the Barghawāṭa to the north and the peoples, merchants and holy men who came over the High Atlas to Aghmat and the Oued Nfiss to the south, was perhaps the ultimate origin of the similar, more famous movement of the Almoravids of the eleventh century, created by the zeal of Ibn Yāsīn among different peoples far away in the Sahara. Islam, whose North African institutions bound the Maghrib together in a broad, if patchy commonwealth, was in the process of passing far beyond the horizon of the first conquest.

CHAPTER 9

CHRISTIAN NUBIA*

INTRODUCTION

With the coming of Christianity during the period following the fourth century AD, the history of Nubia enters a new stage. The ending of the Meroitic state described in chapter 4 did not result in any substantial cultural changes. Though fashions in material objects changed slowly – these changes being shown most clearly in the pottery – the general life of the country, the styles of buildings and the nature of the agricultural village life remained substantially the same. The evidence for this is now considerable and, as a result of the extensive archaeological work undertaken in face of the threat of inundation from the High Dam at Aswan, there is a very great deal of material from which the life of the time can be reconstructed.

It should be borne in mind that this great increase in knowledge is confined to the area between the First and Second Cataracts and that, in spite of some new investigations, little more is known about areas further south than was known forty or fifty years ago, and, for the period under consideration, many important regions still lack more than the most superficial investigation.

In the northern regions, and – it can be assumed – further south also, life went on after the end of centralized Meroitic rule in much the same way. The basis of life was the cultivation of the river banks by the use of the *saqia* wheel, and the villages of late Meroitic times continued to be inhabited in the fifth and sixth centuries much as they had been from the time of the repopulation of Lower Nubia early in the Christian era. Material objects changed their styles under the mysterious dictates of fashion, largely influenced from the north, but the general continuity and stability of Nile Valley life continued without major upheavals. Even if there were incursions by Nobatae or Blemmyes, and even if rulers, such as those buried at Ballana, may have been of foreign origin, the basic population and way of life continued unchanged.

What did alter was the religion, and with the coming of Christianity

* The time scope of this chapter has been extended beyond the closing date of the volume so as to encompass the whole period of Christianity in Nubia up to its demise about the fourteenth century. [Ed.]

changes were set in train which, giving a somewhat different flavour to the culture, persisted for many hundreds of years. In spite of continuities in material culture, the coming of the new religion marked a change which distinguished it from earlier and later periods so that Sudanese history of this time, often defined as that of 'Christian Nubia' or 'Medieval Nubia', can be studied and described on its own, even though the general pattern of life remained the same, as it has done in some areas until recent times.

The beginnings of Christianity in Nubia and the changes it produced are not very clearly understood. The conventional date for the first christianization of *c.* AD 540 is too precise, and, although it may represent the date at which a ruling group adopted the new religion, there is now some evidence for the small-scale penetration of Christianity for some time before this. Christianity had become an important element in the life of Egypt by the second century AD, and as a focus for national aspirations, the Coptic Church, which, in defence of its own theological position, Monophysitism (the doctrine of the single nature of Christ, declared heretical at the Council of Chalcedon in 451), had broken away from the main tendency of the Orthodox, or Melkite, Church of Byzantium. By becoming identified with Egyptian nationalism and as hostile to Byzantine rule, the Church in Egypt maintained an independent and determined position with its own patriarch and ordained priesthood, a position which has lasted to the present day.

The strong influence of Christianity in Egypt is likely to have been felt in Nubia and, though the First Cataract marked a political, religious and linguistic frontier as it had done since pharaonic times, it was not impassable. In earlier times Egyptians, Greeks and even Romans had travelled through the Dodekaschoenus (see chapter 4) and some had reached as far south as Meroe. Objects with Christian emblems have been found in graves of the fourth and fifth centuries and, though in no way conclusive proof of the religion of their owners, they show that such emblems were current and suggest that Christians had to some extent moved into the area.

As a result of this christianization (which will be examined in detail below), the fact of the existence of a Christian Church and a Christian ruler became the dominant feature of Nubian history and culture for about 800 years – from the first formal missionary activity in the mid sixth century until the taking of power by a Muslim ruler in the mid fourteenth. Christian buildings, Christian symbols and Christian belief formed the characteristic culture of the period.

The history of this Christian period is known in somewhat greater detail than that of earlier periods in the Sudan. There are written sources of a variety of kinds, and a very generalized story of the main political events can be told. The main sources have been known for many years, and many of them were published and translated by Quatremère in the early nineteenth century.[1] They are in the main writings in Arabic by Muslim historians and geographers, though there are also a few by Christian writers. Indigenous writings, almost exclusively theological in nature, add little to our historical knowledge, and the evidence derived from the archaeological activities of the 1960s, though providing much valuable information on the material side of Nubian life, has, with few exceptions, added nothing to our knowledge of historical events. The exception is the information derived from the Polish excavation at Faras from 1961 to 1964, which, in addition to providing material of the greatest importance for the study of Nubian art and architecture, has also provided additional information for the chronology of Nubian kings and for the history of the bishopric of Faras. More recent discoveries at Qasr Ibrim (still largely unpublished) are adding further details.

The writers who have provided information for the history of Nubia in the Middle Ages have been listed and their information summarized in convenient form by Vantini,[2] and also by Yūsuf Fadl Hasan (who is rather better for the Arabic sources).[3] Of these writers, the most important for historical purposes are John the Deacon (*c.* 770), who in his 'Life of the Patriarch Michael', which was used by Severus (Sāwīrūs b. al-Muqaffaʿ) for his lives of the patriarchs, gives details of a number of eighth-century kings; al-Balādhurī (*c.* 890), who describes the early Arab attacks, drawing on other writers, as is often the case with medieval Arab compilers; al-Tabarī (839–923), who describes conflicts between Arabs and the Beja, the inhabitants of the territory to the east of the Nile as far as the Red Sea; Abū Ṣāliḥ, the Armenian; Ibn Khaldūn (1332–1406); and al-Maqrīzī (1364–1442). There are a number of references to Nubia in the works of other medieval Arab writers, but they add little more to our knowledge. What is known of Nubian history rests almost entirely on the testimony of those writers listed above and, from lack of additional information and, in most cases, of

[1] E. M. Quatremère, *Mémoires géographiques et historiques sur l'Égypte et sur quelques contrées voisines* (Paris, 1811).

[2] G. Vantini, *The excavations at Faras – a contribution to the history of Christian Nubia* (Bologna, 1970), 41–119.

[3] Yūsuf Fadl Hasan, *The Arabs and the Sudan* (Khartoum, 1973), 182–202.

Plate 32 The 'Palace' at Old Dongola. [ch. 9]
(Photo: P. L. Shinnie.)

Plate 33 The church at Adendan. [ch. 9]
(Photo: P. L. Shinnie.)

Plate 34 The church at Adendan: the interior. [ch. 9]
(Photo: P. L. Shinnie.)

Plate 35 The church at Mograka. [ch. 9]
(Photo: P. L. Shinnie.)

Plate 36 St Anna (first half of eighth century AD). [ch. 9]
(Photo courtesy The John Hillelson Agency Ltd, London.)

Plate 37 Queen Mother Martha, protected by the hand of the Virgin Mary (end of eleventh century; detail). [ch. 9] (Photo courtesy the John Hillelson Agency Ltd.)

Plate 38 Nativity scene (late tenth–early eleventh century). [ch. 9]
(Photo courtesy the John Hillelson Agency Ltd.)

modern editions of the writers, the standard history of Nubia by Monneret de Villard stands as the main authority,[1] and, as already indicated, there is little new to add. Any outline of the historical facts, deriving from the accounts by Arab writers, which contain contradictory and sometimes obviously wrong information, must lean very heavily on Monneret de Villard. But some of his hypotheses can now be discarded, and a much fuller account of Nubian cultural achievements can be given.

THE BEGINNINGS OF CHRISTIANITY IN NUBIA

Although the accepted date for the first Christian missionary activity in Nubia is AD 543 there is, as already mentioned, some evidence for an earlier entry of Christianity. It has been suggested that the inscription of Silko shows him to have been Christian, but a reference to 'god' does not seem to be sufficient evidence to deduce that he meant the Christian God, any more than the presence of objects bearing Christian symbols in X-Group graves gives certain evidence of the religion of those buried in them. It is worth noting that, though on the island site of Meinarti pottery lamps have been found with designs of crosses on them from the period 500–50, there was no church there until after 600.

It has been argued that there is evidence for Christians residing at Faras as early as 400,[2] and the Polish expedition found what they claim with some probability were the remains of a mud brick church on a stone foundation below the ruins of a pagan palace. This building is considered by the excavators to date from about the middle of the fifth century, and thus to antedate the arrival of the first official Christian mission by about one hundred years. The remains of the church, which was on a very slightly different alignment from the great cathedral which was later built above it, are very fragmentary, and most of the plan as published is hypothetical. But the apse is clear enough, and, however surprising, the presence of a church at this early date may be accepted. The walls of the church as found stood to a uniform height of about 75 cm, and this gives the impression that the church was not overthrown, but that it was deliberately reduced to a regular height. It was then filled with rubble consisting of broken brick, Nile mud, and sherds of pottery of the earliest Christian style and some of X-Group times. All this suggests that an attempt was made to construct

[1] U. Monneret de Villard, *Storia della Nubia Cristiana* (Rome, 1938), note 6.

[2] K. Michalowski, *Faras – Die Kathedrale aus dem Wüstensand* (Zurich, 1967), 48–9.

a platform on which to build what has been interpreted as a palace of an X-Group ruler (*c.* 500). It contained no objects to suggest Christianity, but a number of finds show late Meroitic and X-Group styles. If the archaeological evidence has been understood aright, this suggests that a premature Christian community existed at Faras before 500, built its church, and was then either suppressed or became too weak to maintain a church any longer. The palace, thought to be that of the local ruler, the viceroy of late Meroitic times, or an independent X-Group leader, perhaps one of those buried at nearby Ballana, was destroyed early in the seventh century, and it has been suggested that this was due to attack by the Sassanians who occupied Egypt for a few years from 616.[1] Although there is no direct evidence that the Sassanians entered Nubia, it is known that they reached the First Cataract, and they could well have gone further.

The formal introduction of Christianity and the conversion of the rulers, apparently soon followed by that of the greater part of the population, came in the middle of the sixth century with the arrival in 543 of missionaries from Byzantium. By this date, the important centre of Isis-worship in the temple at Philae had been terminated by imperial decree, and the influence of pagan cults at the gateway to Nubia much weakened. Not only the written sources, but also the archaeological evidence for a change from pagan to Christian burial customs, show that the last half of the sixth century saw a rapid adoption of Christianity not only by the rulers but also by the mass of the people.

An inscription in the Temple of Dendur probably gives the name of the Nubian king at the time of the mission. This inscription, in Coptic, describes the turning of the pagan temple into a church on 22 January in either the year 559 or 574, by the writer, the priest Abraham. It gives the name of the reigning king, Eirpanome, and says that Abraham received the cross – whose setting up in the temple the inscription describes – from Bishop Theodoros of Philae. This was presumably the same as the Bishop Theodoros associated with Julian in the first Monophysite mission to Nubia. The Dendur text is also interesting as providing names and titles of officials of the kingdom, of whom the most important was Joseph, the exarch (presumably governor) of Talmis. Another inscription of about the same time, describing the foundation of a fort at Ikhmindi, gives the name of another king, Tokiltoeton, and again Joseph, exarch of Talmis, is mentioned. The dating is not sufficiently without ambiguity to make it clear which

[1] K. Michalowski, *Faras – Centre artistique de la Nubie Chrétienne* (Leiden, 1966), 9.

king came first, nor is there any evidence for a relationship between them.

There are accounts of two separate Christian missions, one of orthodox (Melkite) beliefs, said to have been encouraged by the emperor Justinian, and the other Monophysite (Jacobite), sent under the patronage of his wife, Theodora, well known to have been a supporter of the Monophysite tendency. The most fully documented is the Monophysite mission, known from the partisan account by John of Ephesus.[1] The story, written in Syriac, has been told a number of times,[2] but may be briefly summarized here.

Encouraged by Theodora, Julian, a Monophysite, proceeded to Nubia in 543, whilst the rival Melkite mission was detained, by Theodora's intrigues, in Upper Egypt, where the empress persuaded or ordered the governor of the Thebaid to prevent their passage. Egypt at this time, though still under Byzantine rule, was predominantly Monophysite in allegiance, and attempts to circumvent imperial orders would have been welcome to the nationalist population of Egypt. Arriving in Nubia, Julian seems to have been well received, and his preaching was welcomed. On his return, two years later, to Byzantium, his work was continued by Theodoros, the Bishop of Philae. If the account is right, the latter spent some six years away from his see, and then, after a period when no named missionary is known to us, Longinus, also from Byzantium, arrived in Nubia *c.* 569, and remained, presumably at Faras, until 575, when he returned to Egypt. In 578 he returned once more to Nubia, and two years later went much further south, at the invitation of the king of 'Alwa (Soba) to take the Christian message to that country. The details of the journey are interesting, since John of Ephesus describes how the hostility of the state of Makuria forced Longinus to abandon the river route and strike out far to the east, where, by the help of the Blemmyes, he was enabled to avoid the attempts of the Makurian king to stop him. Thus he arrived safely at 'Alwa, where it is said the king was baptized after a few days, shortly to be followed by his people. Longinus was not the first Christian to arrive in 'Alwa, since he found there members of the heretical sect of Halicarnassus, who would have come from Ethiopia.

This account, with its suggestion that the Monophysite missionaries were everywhere successful, needs to be viewed with some scepticism,

1 *Ecclesiastical history of John of Ephesus*, trans. by R. Payne-Smith (Oxford, 1860).

2 L. P. Kirwan, 'A contemporary account of the conversion of the Sudan to Christianity', *Sudan Notes and Records*, 1937, **20**, 289–99.

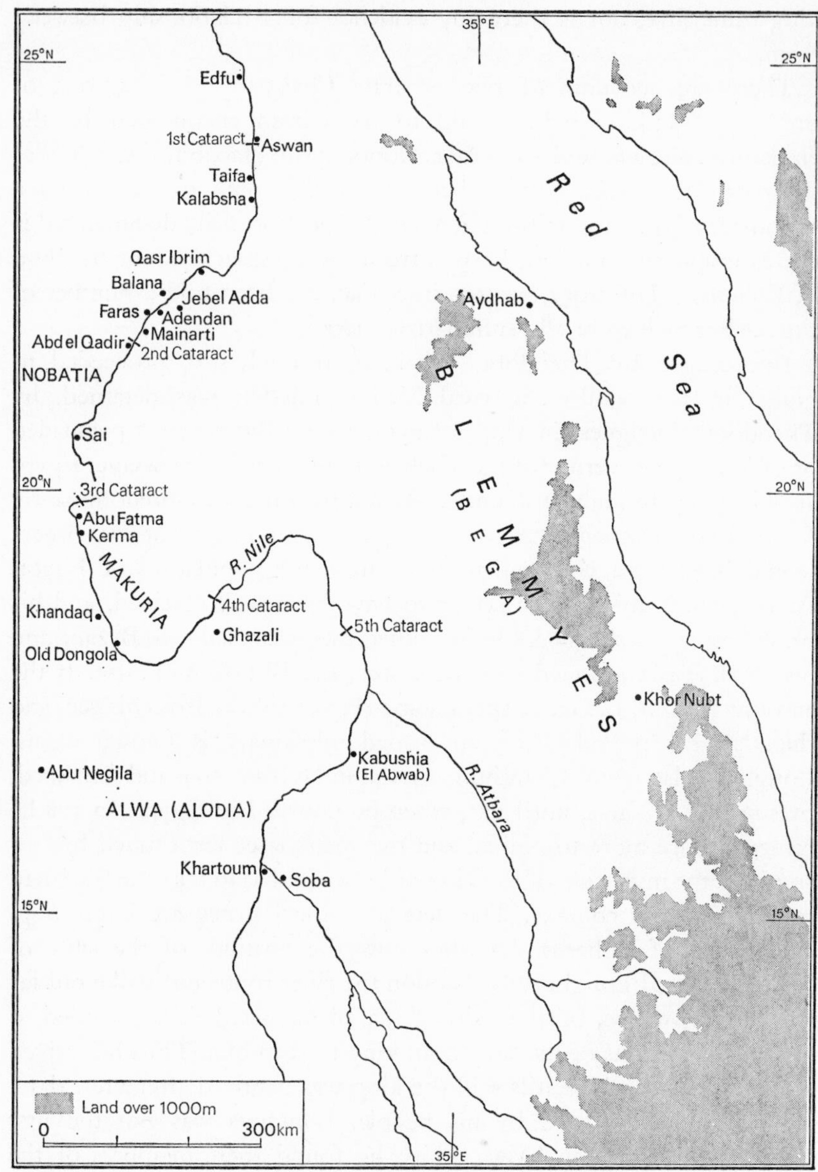

65 Medieval Nubia.

and an account by a supporter of the rival Melkite tendency gives a rather different description. This tells that Makuria, already noted as hostile to Longinus, had been converted to Melkite beliefs in about 570. It is likely that both these highly partisan accounts give only details which reflect well on their own party, but together they give some picture of the Nubia of the time. It should be noted that the inscription of Eirpanome certainly suggests that the region over which he ruled was Monophysite.

These two differing accounts of the early christianization provide information concerning the existence of three separate kingdoms: Nobatia, the most northerly, presumably the kingdom of the rulers buried at Ballana, with their capital at Faras, and connected with the Nobatae; Makuria (Arabic: Maqurra), somewhere further south, but which it seems reasonable to assume was based on Old Dongola, subsequently to become the capital of a single northern Nubian state; and further south still, ʻAlwa (Latin: Alodia), perhaps the real heir of Meroe, with its capital at Soba on the Blue Nile.

We know little more of these kingdoms at this time other than their names and their alleged religious persuasions. It seems clear enough that the confusion following the collapse of a centralized Meroitic administration was now largely over, and that the three states, perhaps all Nubian-speaking, were exercising some form of control over their respective areas. It is unlikely that the usually accepted neat division of dominant theological allegiance is as simple as it seems, and it is more reasonable to suppose that even if the royal houses fitted into the pattern of a Monophysite Nobatia and ʻAlwa, and a Melkite Makuria, the reality was more complex.

The Nubian cultivators are unlikely to have been deeply concerned with the fine theological differences which had caused such fierce controversy in Eastern Christendom ever since the Council of Chalcedon. Their rulers may have chosen their allegiance for political reasons, or perhaps just by the chance of which missionary reached them first. It seems probable, in view of proximity to Egypt, that the Monophysite Church would tend to predominate, and the history of the see of Faras appears to bear this out. But even at Faras, as later history shows, there were periods when bishops of Melkite allegiance were appointed. The real situation is far from clear. The study of tombstones, both in Coptic and in Greek, shows that the prayers of the orthodox Melkite Church were in common use; the evidence of the iconography from the Faras paintings is inconclusive; and it does not seem that there were clear-cut liturgical and artistic differences. As in Egypt, both groups had supporters, but, though there was not the same nationalist feeling to support the Monophysite Church as there was in Egypt, and though there remained for centuries a strong Byzantine Greek influence in Nubia, the bulk of the evidence suggests that for most of its history Christian Nubia was predominantly Monophysite (Coptic).

Whatever the case, there is no question but that Christianity was rapidly accepted by the Nubians. The literary evidence indicates this and it is strongly supported by the archaeological evidence. This evidence, largely from cemeteries, suggests that there was a quite sudden change from the burial custom of X-Group times, when the burials were accompanied by a considerable number of grave-goods, to the Christian style, where the body was usually put in the grave without any objects. There is also the evidence from the ruined churches. The first ones were built soon after 600, while the Rivergate church at Faras, originally a pagan building, was turned into a church by the middle of the sixth century, and can be presumed to be the first church to be used officially for Christian worship by a ruler.

THE FIRST ARAB ATTACKS

During the later years of Byzantine rule in Egypt and prior to the Arab conquest, there was the short period (619–26) of Sassanian Persian occupation. Whether or not the Sassanians went further (it seems unlikely), they certainly came to the First Cataract, and hints of Sassanian influence in later Nubian art may be attributed to this early-seventh-century contact.

Soon after the invasion and successful occupation (639–41) of Egypt by the Arabs under the leadership of ʿAmr b. al-ʿĀṣ, they attacked Nubia, and as early as 641, ʿUqba b. Nāfiʿ led a cavalry army south of the First Cataract. Al-Balādhurī gives the following account:

> When the Muslims conquered Egypt, ʿAmr b. al-ʿĀṣ sent to the villages which surround it cavalry to overcome them and sent ʿUqba b. Nāfiʿ, who was a brother of al-ʿĀṣ, to his mother. The cavalry entered the land of Nubia like the summer campaigns against the Greeks. The Muslims found that the Nubians fought strongly, and they met showers of arrows until the majority were wounded and returned with many wounded and blinded eyes. So the Nubians were called 'the pupil smiters'.

This description of the Nubians as skilful archers shows the continuance of a military technique first recognized by the Pharaonic Egyptians, who called the people to their south 'The Nine Bows', and perpetuated by the Meroites, from whose time there are many representations of the lion-headed war-god Apedemek holding a bow in his hand, as well as finds of bows and arrows in the tombs. No weapons have been found from Christian times, but the documentary evidence makes it clear enough that skill in archery remained a Nubian speciality. Al-Balādhurī goes on to say, quoting from one of his sources:

I went personally to Nubia twice during the rule of ʿUmar b. al-Khattab, and I saw one of them [ie, the Nubians] saying to a Muslim, 'Where would you like me to place my arrow in you', and when the Muslim replied, 'In such a place', he would not miss. They were many in shooting arrows and their arrows did not fall to the ground. One day they came out against us and formed a line; we wanted to use swords, but we were not able to, and they shot at us and put out eyes to the number of one hundred and fifty.[1]

The informant goes on to say that, since there was little booty to be got, and Nubian military ability was considerable, it was thought better to make peace, but that ʿAmr b. al-ʿĀṣ was unwilling to stop campaigning and that it was only when he was succeeded by ʿAbd Allah b. Saʿd, in 645, that peace was made. Verisimilitude is added to the story of the Nubian skill in archery by the giving of the name of one of those who lost an eye in battle.

The accounts of the military activities and the treaty that brought them to an end are rather confused, but it seems that warfare broke out again in 651. Perhaps this was as al-Maqrīzī describes it, because the Nubians under King Qalidurut had broken the first peace treaty. ʿAbd Allah then led a force of 5,000 into Nubia and attacked Old Dongola, the capital of Makuria and, perhaps by this date, of Nobatia also. The town was attacked and damage done to the cathedral by the use of catapults. It was probably as a result of this campaign that the more permanent peace, which lasted for several centuries, was made. The treaty which concluded the military activities has been much discussed, since it was of an unusual type.[2] The Nubians did not sue for peace, and although the nature of the treaty is not exactly of one between equals, there was an element of reciprocity about it. A number of Arabic writers mention the treaty and its unusual provisions, and though details vary in the different versions, by using Maqrīzī's account, which is the fullest, some description of it can be given. Although normally now known as the *baqṭ*, this term seems originally to have been used only for the handing over of the slaves which were the Nubian contribution to the exchange. The Arab writers discuss at some length the nature of the treaty, whose unusual features caused problems to Muslim jurists. The main problem

[1] This and the previous quotation from al-Balādhurī are the present writer's translations.

[2] P. Forand, 'Early Muslim relations with Nubia', *Der Islam*, 1971, **48**, 111–21; and for a discussion of the meaning and significance of *baqṭ*, see ch. 8, p. 505.

was how to define a treaty of this kind, which was made with a country that was neither integrated into the world of Islam, *Dār al-Islām*, nor was *Dār al-harb*, the area which could be freely attacked by Muslims, and for which there was some obligation to attempt forcibly to include it in the realm of Islam. The text as given by al-Maqrīzī is as follows:

Covenant from the amir ʿAbd Allah b. Saʿd Abī Sarḥ to the king [*ʿaẓim*] of the Nubians and to all of the people of his kingdom; a covenant binding upon great and small among the Nubians from the frontier of the land of Aswan to the border of the land of ʿAlwa. ʿAbd Allah b. Saʿd b. Abī Sarḥ has established it for them as a guarantee and a truce to be effective among them and the Muslims of Upper Egypt who live adjacent to them, as well as other Muslims and *dhimmīs*. Verily, you are communities of Nubia enjoying the guarantee of Allah and that of His Messenger Muḥammad, the Prophet; with the condition that we shall not wage war against you, nor declare war against you, nor raid you, as long as you abide by the stipulations which are in effect between us and you. [Namely,] that you may enter our territories passing through but not taking up residence in them, and we may enter yours passing through but not taking up residence in them. You are to look after the safety of any Muslim or ally [of the Muslims] who lodges in your territories or travels in them until he departs from you.

You are to return every slave of the Muslims who runs off to you, sending him back to the land of Islam. You are to return any Muslim engaged in hostilities against the other Muslims, who seeks refuge with you. You are to send him forth from your territories to the land of Islam, neither inclining to [help] him nor preventing him from [returning].

You are to look after the mosque which the Muslims have built in the courtyard of your capital, and you are not to prevent anyone from worshipping in it, nor interfere with any Muslim who goes to it and remains in its sanctuary, until he departs from it. And you are to sweep it, keep it lighted and honor it.

Each year you are to deliver 360 slaves which you will pay to the *imām* of the Muslims from the finest slaves of your country, in whom there is no defect. [They are to be] both male and female. Among them [is to be] no decrepit old man or woman or any child who has not reached puberty. You are to deliver them to the *wali* of Aswan.

It shall not be incumbent upon any Muslim to defend [you] against any enemy who attacks you or to prevent him on your behalf from doing so, from the frontier of the land of ʿAlwa to the land of Aswan.

If you do harbour a slave belonging to a Muslim, or kill a Muslim or ally, or if you expose to destruction the mosque which the Muslims have built in the courtyard of your capital, or if you withold any of the 360 slaves, this truce and guarantee which we and you have equally set down will be void, 'so that God will judge between us' – 'and He is the Best of Judges.' [Qur. x, 109.]

Incumbent upon us hereby is [observance of] the pact of God and His agreement and His good faith, and the good faith of His Messenger Muḥammad. And incumbent on you toward us is the utmost observance of the good faith of the Messiah and that of the Disciples and of any of the people of your religion and community whom you reverence. God be the Witness of that between us.

ʿUmar b. Shurahbil wrote [this] in Ramaḍān in the year thirty-one [March–April, AD 651].[1]

This text is probably not the original version, which, deposited amongst the archives in Fusṭāṭ (Cairo), was said to have been destroyed by fire, but a compilation from a number of sources all of them dating from long after the time when the treaty was made. This version leaves out the important fact, noted by al-Balādhurī, that the giving was not only one way, and makes no reference to the food supplies, cloth and wine which were to be given in exchange by the Muslims. The place at which the exchange took place has not been identified – it was called al-Qaṣr, 'the castle', and was described as being a short way south of Aswan and near to the Island of Philae. As the natural, and frequently political, frontier between Egypt and Nubia, this would be entirely appropriate.

The results of this treaty were of considerable importance for Nubia. The relief from the danger of Arab invasion and the resultant peaceful conditions which lasted, with a few war-like interludes, for about five hundred years, allowed the development of a distinctive Nubian culture, which, on the edge of the Muslim world, was an unusual feature. Nubia benefited from cultural and commercial contact with Egypt, and though there was a steady, small influx of Muslims, presumably merchants, into northern Nubia over the centuries, this was not sufficient to affect native Nubian culture with its strong Byzantine and Coptic flavour. The years from 700 to 1100 show the growth and flourishing of literate civilization with a well-developed art, a stable administration and distinctive cultural traditions. Trade with Egypt during the seventh and eighth centuries is illustrated by the large number of wine amphorae, probably the products of Coptic monasteries, and perhaps traded by Copts rather than Muslims.

Apart from the mutual agreement of non-agression implied by the *baqṭ*, the other factor that strengthened Nubia, both politically and culturally, was the combination of the two states of Nobatia and Makuria into one. The precise date at which this happened is not certain, but it was in the latter part of the seventh or early eighth

[1] al-Maqrīzī, *Kitāb al-Mawāʿiẓ wa 'l-Iʿtibār fī dhikr al-khiṭaṭ wa 'l-āthār* [*Khiṭaṭ*], ed. by G. Wiet (Cairo, 1911), I, 323. (Eng. trans. by Forand, in 'Early Muslim relations', 114–15).

centuries, perhaps between AD 690 and 710, in which latter year King Merkurios of Nubia put up an inscription at Taifa, far to the north of the earlier frontier of Makuria, recording the establishment of a church. So it is reasonably assumed that by this date Makuria had either absorbed Nobatia or that there had been a mutual agreement between the two states. The process by which two separate entities became one is not known, but the frontiers and political relationships were probably rather fluid, and we are liable to get a false impression of relations between states if they are thought of in terms of modern nations with their rigidly defined boundaries. Nobatia and Makuria had an identical material culture, spoke the same language and had been under a unified Meroitic government. It is surprising that Nobatia, with considerable traditions of a measure of self-government, should be the one to lose its separate identity, but there seems no doubt that from *c.* 700 on Old Dongola became the residence of the king. Nobatia, however, retained an element of separateness, and as there had been a Meroitic viceroy or governor of the area, so through much of the Middle Ages, Nobatia, often known to the Egyptians as Maris (from the Coptic word used for the southern regions), had a governor, the *eparch*, whose powers are not known, but whose distinctive dress and horned head-gear are illustrated in several church frescoes.

Merkurios was described as the 'new Constantine' by the Egyptian Christian chronicler John the Deacon in his 'Life of the Patriarch [of Alexandria] Michael', which was written *c.* 768–70. This suggests that he played some significant part in the development of Christianity in Nubia, and one view is that his reign marked a decisive victory of the Monophysite trend. If the traditional view of a rigid division between Monophysite Nobatia and Melkite Makuria were true, this would imply the curious situation of the theology of the area taken over triumphing over that of the new ruling group. The obvious paradox of this is probably an indication that the situation is not fully understood, and that, as already suggested, the lines were not so rigidly drawn between the different groups as they were in Egypt.

The beginning of the reign of Merkurios can now be fixed, since a foundation stone of his eleventh year, dated to 707, is known from Faras. This puts his accession at 697, and is further evidence for his control of Faras; this inscription also gives the name of the eparch of Nubia, Markos, and of the fifth Bishop of Faras, Paulos – which would imply that the see was founded early in the seventh century.

Another obscurity in dating these events is that in the Arabic accounts of the mid-seventh-century invasion there is no mention of two kingdoms, Dongola is the only capital city referred to, and it is the aim of the invaders to reach it. This may mean that Nobatia had ceased to exist as an independent kingdom even earlier than usually supposed.

THE FLOWERING OF CHRISTIAN NUBIA, *c.* 750–1050

From the time of Merkurios, there is evidence for the full political and cultural development of Christian Nubia. There is some historical data to be gained from Arab writers, while the archaeological material is rich and much is now known of the material culture. At this time Nubia was at the height of its prosperity, with marked cultural and material advances. Reasons for this were in part political and in part economic. One important underlying factor may have been the comparatively stable Nile flood, at a level adequate for agriculture, but not so high as to cause damage to settlements.

Merkurios, who died presumably during the period 710–*c.* 730, was succeeded – on the evidence of the 'Life of the Patriarch Michael' – by a number of kings who may have been his relatives. His son Zakaria is said to have been more concerned with religion than with temporal power. But our authority implies that he remained the power behind the throne whilst various dynastic struggles took place: King Simon was succeeded by Abraham, who was then exiled, and then followed by Markos, who in his turn was followed by Kiriakos. Of Kiriakos we have more details. It is said that in about 745 he intervened in Egyptian affairs to demand the release of Khael, Patriarch of Alexandria (743–67), who had been imprisoned during a period of persecution of the Copts by the governor of Egypt on the orders of the Caliph Marwān II. Failure of an embassy sent to demand the patriarch's release was followed by a Nubian invasion of Egypt, said to have reached Fusṭāṭ. However, Meinardus has recently thrown doubt on the reality of this military exploit, suggesting that the story is an invention by the author of the 'Life of the Patriarch Michael' arising from conflation of known Nubian invasions of Upper Egypt and the liberation of the patriarch. It also coincides with a period of Coptic uprising in the Delta.[1]

At some time during the eighth or early ninth centuries, there was a marked decrease in the amount of Egyptian pottery, particularly amphorae, imported into Nubia. It is possible that the end of the

[1] Otto F. A. Meinardus, 'The Christian kingdom of Nubia', *Nubie–Cahiers d'Histoire Égyptienne*, 1967, 10, 147.

Umayyad caliphate of Damascus in 750 may have been the political cause of this; that by creating disruption in the Islamic world, it led to a decrease in contact between Egypt and Nubia. Certainly the coming to power of the ʿAbbasids in Baghdad led to increased persecution of the Copts, which may well have exacerbated Nubian feelings. It is also possible that restrictions were placed on the Coptic monasteries of Upper Egypt, which had been the suppliers not only of the amphorae but also of the wine which they contained.

Whatever the real reasons for at least a temporary breakdown of contacts with Egypt, the results can be seen in a development of more localized pottery styles. The now well known 'Classic' Christian wares with their elaborate painted decorations, often zoomorphic, begin to appear in the latter half of the eighth century. The origins of the style are far from clear; the Nubian patterns and shapes are not easily to be confused with pottery from other areas, but there are hints of Persian and Byzantine influence. They are certainly, in spite of some coincidence of design, different from those on the pottery produced by Coptic potters in Egypt, and they never made use of glaze, which had now become common in most Islamic countries. It is also noteworthy that in the Faras cathedral there is the development of what is called the 'Violet' style of fresco painting, in which strong Byzantine elements appear. So strong is this influence, and so different from Coptic painting of the time, that work by visiting Byzantine artists has been suggested. It is perhaps relevant to note that the years 760–70 mark the height of the Iconoclastic movement in Byzantium, and it is known that artists and monks emigrated in some numbers to Italy and elsewhere, and it is therefore possible that some even reached Nubia (although passing through Islamic and Coptic Egypt would have presented difficulties).

Churches of this time show architectural changes, with the development of a typically Nubian version of the basilican style, of which the main new features were the enclosing of rooms at the western end in place of the narthex found in earlier churches, and – a unique Nubian feature – an ambulatory at the east end passing behind the tribune and joining the two small rooms (*diakonikon* on the south and *prothesis* on the north, in the vocabulary of the Orthodox Church) which lay on either side of the *haikal*, or sanctuary.

Villages were larger and some, such as Debeira, Ermenna and Mainarti, can perhaps be classified as small towns. The domestic architecture shows some changes and the characteristic Nubian brick vault appears as a roofing device. The population increased, and towns

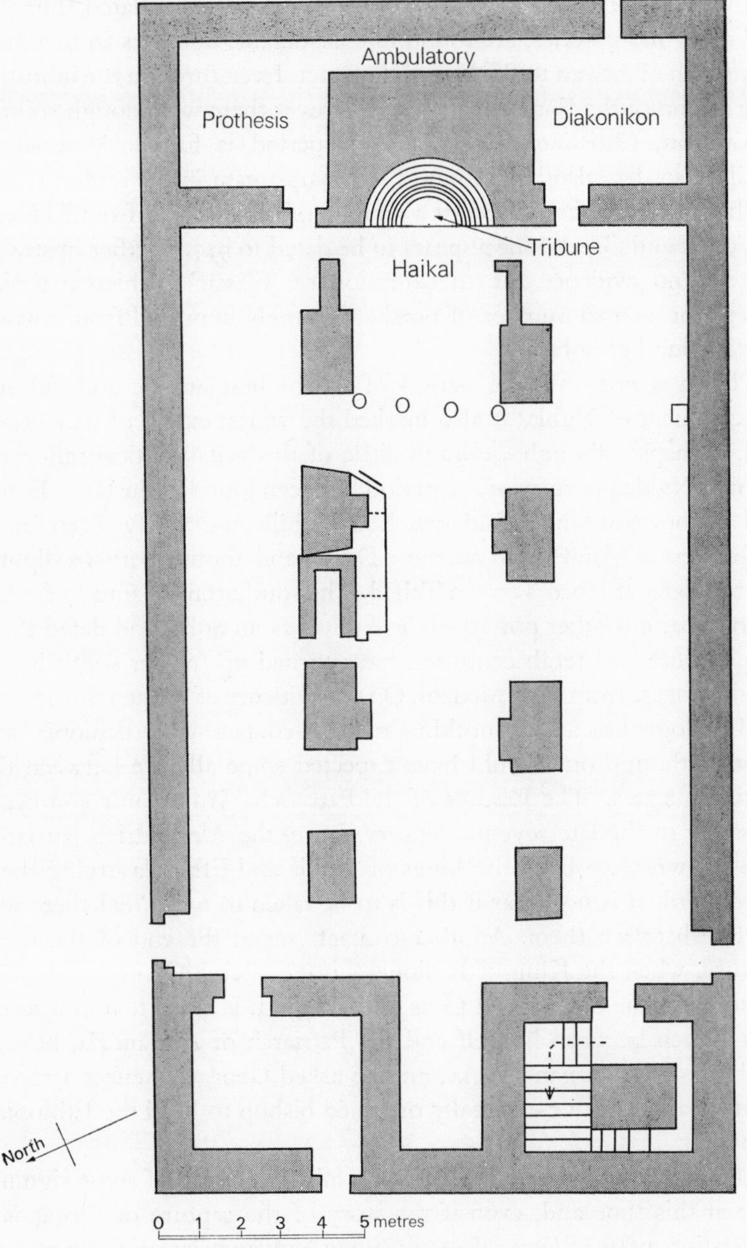

66 Plan of the church at Ghazali.
(After Shinnie and H. N. Chittick, *Ghazali – a monastery in the northern Sudan*, 1961, p. 12.)

and villages, nearly all with their churches, as well as isolated churches and a few monasteries, are found in considerable numbers from a little way south of Aswan to the Fourth Cataract. Even through the inhospitable region of the Fourth Cataract, wherever there was enough soil for cultivation, Christian pottery of this period is found. Material of similar date has also been found further upstream in the region of the Fifth Cataract, where, amongst a number of grave stones from El Koro in Coptic and Greek, one appears to be dated to 917. Further upstream there is no evidence for an extension of 'Classic' Nubian material, except for a small number of potsherds, surely imported from further north, found at Soba.

This was not only the period of the highest artistic and cultural development of Nubia; it also marked the widest extent of its cultural and, perhaps – though we know little of this – its political influence. Typical Nubian pottery of the period has been found at Fusṭāṭ in Egypt and at Khor Nubt in the Sudanese Red Sea hills; it may have been found in the west at 'Ain Fara in northern Darfur and, though perhaps slightly later in date, at Koro Toro in Tchad. The southernmost find so far has been Soba, but other pottery styles known from Soba, and dated there to the ninth and tenth centuries, have turned up further south in the Gezira not far from Wad Medani. On the evidence of written documents (archaeology has as yet nothing to say) contact with Ethiopia was slender, though one would have expected some alliance between the Christian states. 'The History of the Patriarchs' is our only source. It says that in the late seventh century, Isaac, the Alexandrian patriarch (686–9), wrote to both the kings of Nubia and Ethiopia urging them to concord. It is not clear if this is to be taken to mean that there was warfare between them. Another contact was at the end of the tenth century, when the King of Ethiopia wrote to King George of Nubia, presumably the one known to us as George II. He said that as a result of a breach between himself and the Patriarch of Alexandria, he was unable to resist pagan attacks, and he asked George to effect a reconciliation and send a canonically ordained bishop to head the Ethiopian Church.

There is no doubt that Nubia was a military power of some significance at this time and, even if the story of the capture of Fusṭāṭ is a fabrication, parts of Upper Egypt were in Nubian occupation on several occasions. In 962 the Nubians went as far as Akhmim, and southern Upper Egypt was certainly at times influenced by Nubian culture. Edfu seems to have been for a while a centre of Nubian culture, and it is likely that the Nubian language was spoken for some distance north of the First Cataract, which is normally thought of as the language frontier.

Military activity was also carried on against the Beja of the Red Sea hills and against Arab infiltrators interested in the gold deposits there. By the middle of the ninth century, the Muslims had penetrated Nubia sufficiently to have established a mosque at Sinkat, and treaties were made in 831 and 855/6 defining Muslim rights, protecting mosques and extracting from the Beja a promise not to interfere with Muslim gold-miners. This activity reflects increasing Arab penetration of Nubia, witnessed also by the appearance of a number of Arabic tombstones in Nubia, at Mainarti and Debeira East, as well as by inscriptions on the walls of Nubian buildings at Debeira West. In addition, by the tenth century there was an Arab settlement, presumably of gold-seekers, at Khor Nubt, where a number of gravestones in Arabic have been found. Nubian influence still remained strong in the area as late as 1272, when King David of Nubia captured the important trading port of ʿAydhāb.

This Nubian military activity is known only from Arabic written sources and there is no indication of weapons or armies in archaeological discoveries. If archaeology were the only available source, Nubian society would have to be described as a peaceful, agricultural one, largely obsessed by religion. A very large number of the artefacts known bear Christian symbols. There can, however, be no doubt that, from the days of the 'pupil smiters' to the capture of ʿAydhāb, the military strength of the kingdom of Dongola was considerable.

This period also marked the appearance of documents written in the indigenous language, Nubian, in the form known as Old Nubian. Whatever the origins of the Nubian language (and a large area of the northern Sudan spoke a group of closely related languages of which Nubian was one), prior to the coming of Arabic as a serious and ultimately largely successful rival from the thirteenth century onwards, there is no doubt that the main language of the christianized people of the Sudanese Nile was Nubian. After the last documents in Meroitic in the early fifth century, there is a period of more than three hundred years in which no documents in an indigenous language are known. All writings – and they are not many – are in Greek (as the inscription of Silko) or Coptic (as in the case of Eirpanome). From the eighth century, documents in Old Nubian are known, the earliest dated one being a graffito of a prayer in the temple of Rameses II at Wadi es

Sebu', which is dated to the year of the Era of the Martyrs 511, the equivalent of AD 795. (Dating by the Era of the Martyrs, which refers to the persecutions by Diocletian in the year 284, is the most usual method of dating in the Nubian documents, though others were also in use.) From this time on a number of documents are known, and the number has been substantially increased by finds in the 1960s and 1970s, many of them still unpublished.

The Nubian documents, in a language ancestral to the modern Mahass dialect of river Nubian, were written in the Coptic form of the Greek alphabet with the addition of three signs for sounds in Old Nubian which did not occur in Coptic. It has been argued that these three signs are derived from Meroitic ones. If this is so, the appearance of virtual illiteracy between the time of the last known Meroitic writing and the first Old Nubian documents may be illusory, and it is possible that there was an overlap of the two languages and the two writing systems.

The presently known documents are largely religious in nature, but two written on leather deal with legal matters concerning land tenure or ownership of slaves. The large number of letters found at Qasr Ibrim will, when published, add substantially to the corpus of lay writings. None of the documents at present published adds much historical information, though some royal names are given. Two of these are of kings otherwise unknown: Eilte, recorded in one of the leather documents of private transactions; and Arron, whose name is contained in a graffito from the Abu Negila hills of northern Kordofan, which is unusual in being the only written example of Old Nubian found away from the river Nile.

Although as yet of no great directly historical value, the corpus of Nubian writing is in itself of interest from both a linguistic and a cultural point of view. It is evidence that writing, although perhaps restricted to a small group, was spread throughout Nubia, and was used not only for formal documents but also in many casual graffiti. An elaborate document, such as that known as 'The Miracle of St Menas' (British Museum Oriental MS. 6805), written in a good, clear hand with an attractive head-piece and a drawing of the saint, indicates the high level of Nubian culture.

The most spectacular witness to the cultural development is to be seen in the cathedral discovered and excavated by a Polish expedition from 1961 to 1964 at Faras. At this site, already known from earlier work to have been a major centre of Nubian civil and religious administration, excavation discovered a large cathedral in a very good state of preservation, though roofless, and containing a large number of painted frescoes of saints, bishops and religious scenes. The cathedral was originally built in the seventh century on the site of a large building, perhaps a palace, which had been erected on top of the mud church, already described, the first Christian building on the site. The first cathedral, with a nave and two aisles, was built at some time in the seventh century; it was then renewed in 707, on the evidence of two foundation stones, one in Greek, one in Coptic, by Paulos, the fifth Bishop of Faras. Both foundation stones mention King Merkurios, and are further evidence that he was a patron of ecclesiastical building. The rebuilding of 707 was on a considerable scale, and the new cathedral was larger and more magnificent than its predecessor and consisted of a nave and four aisles. It is from this period that the splendid series of frescoes begins. Although only traces of the very earliest were found, beginning from about 750 a series of paintings covered the walls. From a study of them and from the fortunate fact that in a number of cases later paintings overlaid earlier ones, the development and chronology of the main artistic periods can be determined to be between *c.* 750 and the eleventh century. In addition to religious scenes, such as a magnificent painting of the nativity with several unique Nubian elements in it (pl. 38), there are also paintings of saints, bishops and a few royalties, including one particularly interesting one of 'Martha, the queen mother', which shows Martha being protected by the Virgin Mary, who holds the child Jesus in her arms (pl. 37). This painting, to be dated to the end of the eleventh century, is not only of importance as reflecting the role of the queen mother, with its significance for the inheritance system of Nubian royalty, but also gives a splendid example of royal robes, and by the representation of the queen mother's face in darker colour than that of the Virgin, shows that the Nubian artist was genuinely intending to represent one of his own people. The same dark tone is also used in representations of all those, kings and bishops, who might be assumed to be Nubians.

The Faras cathedral and surrounding buildings have also produced much other material of historical value. Foundation stones of Kings Merkurios and Zakaria III give important new chronological information; the latter, dated to 930, gives it as the tenth year of Zakaria, thus providing a date for the death of the long-lived George I in 920; other kings are represented by paintings, as are several eparchs of Nubia. Probably the most remarkable discovery of all is a list of bishops with their lengths of reign, found painted on the wall of a chapel in the south-east corner of the cathedral. This list of twenty-seven bishops gives not only the names but the years of their episcopates, and the month and day, but not the year, of the death of several of them. From the fortunate discovery of tombstones with the exact year of death of some of the bishops, who can be identified from the list, it has been possible to restore the chronology for many of them, though damage to the inscription and difficulties of reading still leave gaps. The first fifteen names are all in the same hand, and for these bishops the day and month of death are not given. From the time of Bishop Andreas (902) various hands are found, so it is certain that the list was compiled from an earlier one, containing only partial information, either on the death of the previous bishop, Kyros, or on the accession of Andreas, but in any case in 902. It is not possible, because of gaps in the list, to date the founding of the see of Faras, but we know that Paul, the fifth bishop, held the episcopate in 707, the year in which he reconstructed the cathedral. On the basis of the average of eighteen years for each bishop whose dates are known, the first canonically recognized bishop would thus have been about the year 625. The establishment of the chronology of the bishops has also been of importance in dating the artistic styles of the paintings. In several cases bishops whose dates are known are portrayed, since it seems to have been the normal custom for a bishop to arrange for his portrait to be painted as one of his first actions after his consecration. Bishop Kyros, the last bishop in the original list, is the first Bishop of Faras to be given the title of metropolitan. This shows that at that time Faras, as well as Dongola, was a metropolitan see, and the painting of Kyros which shows him wearing as part of his ecclesiastical vestments the shawl known as *shamla* is good evidence for the Monophysite allegiance of the Church, since Melkite bishops did not wear it.

There is an enormous amount of information to be obtained from the large number of paintings, not only for the chronology of artistic styles, but also for details of ecclesiastical practice and iconography, and ecclesiastical and royal dress. There are also a number of graffiti, still largely unpublished, in the three languages current in Nubia: Old Nubian, Coptic and Greek. Many of these are just short prayers, or appeals to God for help for a named person, but there are also some longer ones. They provide much valuable information for the linguistic situation in Nubian society. This seems to have been a multi-lingual one; though there is little doubt that Old Nubian was the language of the majority, it was not used for writing so much as the others, which were perhaps considered more suitable for religious and official purposes.[1]

It seems that at some time between 926 and 930 the cathedral was damaged by a fire which destroyed the roof, and twenty-five years later it was reconstructed in a different style. The original wooden roof was replaced by a barrel-vaulted mud brick one; the granite columns in the nave were replaced by brick piers; the large west door was bricked up, leaving the main access from the south; and some bishops' burials were placed outside the west wall in front of the blocked doorway. During the period of disuse of the cathedral, a new church was built to the south, and a foundation inscription shows the year to have been 930. This inscription refers to a queen mother Miriam, and also contains the first dated reference to an eparch of Nobatia. The final damage to the cathedral took place sometime around 1170, when the central dome and the nave vault collapsed or were deliberately destroyed. This destruction may be connected with military events of the time which are described below. No attempt was subsequently made to rebuild the roof of the nave, but the fallen brick was removed and screening walls built to close off the side aisles so that they could be independently used.

To return to the historical narative, the next event of which there is an account is that of a visit to the ʿAbbasid Caliph Muʿtaṣim, then resident in Baghdad, by George, son of King Zakaria of Nubia, in 836. The occasion for this visit was to answer a complaint by the caliph that the Nubian part of the *baqṭ* had not been paid. The Nubian embassy was successful in having the *baqṭ* payment reduced from annual to triennial, and in the conclusion of a new treaty. The effect of this journey, and the making of the treaty by George, presumably the one who subsequently became the King George I, was to make Nubia widely known in the Near East, and it was the occasion for rejoicing by the Christian minorities of the region. These were still considerable in number, but the presence of a prince from a Christian country and his meetings with both the patriarchs of Alexandria and Baghdad caused much excitement. The story of the journey is known from several sources – there are confusions in the versions known, and one has George going only as far as Cairo at the request of Ibrahim, brother of the Caliph Ma'mūn (813–33). According to this version, the treaty was made in Cairo,

1 P. L. Shinnie, 'Multilingualism in medieval Nubia', in Abdelgadir Mahmoud Abdulla, ed., *Studies in ancient languages of the Sudan* (Khartoum, 1974), 41–7.

George receiving special consideration from Ibrahim by being presented with houses in Giza and Fusṭāṭ, and the Patriarch of Alexandria, Joseph (831–50), was allowed to accompany him for part of his return to Nubia.

The matter is further complicated by the account of another journey by George to Baghdad, this time in 852/853, where, in company with the King of the Beja, ʿAlī Bābā, the two are described as prisoners. It is not certain whether George really made the two contrasted journeys, or whether there is confusion on the part of the writers. The reference to ʿAlī Bābā, King of the Beja, is an indication of further Arab interest in the Red Sea hills area, which remained an important source of gold and, therefore, a magnet for Arab adventurers. The Beja themselves had been carrying out many raids against towns in southern Egypt, including Kom Ombo, Esna and Edfu. Mutawwakil, who became caliph in 849, sent Muḥammad al-Qummi in command of a punitive expedition against them in 852, and it was as a result of this campaign that ʿAlī Bābā was captured. At about the same time an independent Arab leader, al-ʿUmarī, not only tried to establish rights over gold-producing areas of the Eastern Desert and Red Sea hills, but also raided the Nile Valley and carried out sporadic warfare against the Nubians.

The account of this warfare gives us names of further Nubian kings and tells us something of their relationships and feuds. George I had a long reign from about 860 to 920 (as is shown by his portrait at Faras, done in old age), and he appointed his nephew, Niuty, who as the king's sister's son would have been his natural heir, to lead an army against al-ʿUmarī. But Niuty rebelled against his uncle, perhaps in an attempt to gain the throne before his time, and successfully opposed a son of George, who was forced to take refuge in ʿAlwa. Another of George's sons, Zakaria, then made a change of policy, and at first allying himself with the Muslims, used them against Niuty. Although initially defeated, and according to the picturesque detail provided by the writer al-Maqrīzī, our main source for this story, escaping on horseback across the Nile accompanied only by two slaves, ultimately the Nubian-Muslim alliance overcame Niuty, who was killed by a trick. Zakaria then turned on al-ʿUmarī and successfully won over some of his Arab supporters, who were given a grant of land near to a place which may be identified with Adendan near to Faras. This land-grant is the first indication of the holding of land in any quantity by Muslims in Nubia, and marks an important stage in the penetration of Arabic-speaking Muslims into Nubia. The later events are confused; al-ʿUmarī seems to have continued a warlike career in the intervals of gold-mining, and was embroiled not only with the Nubians, but also with the Beja, the indigenous inhabitants of much of the gold-producing areas, as well as with elements of his own Arab supporters. He was also in conflict with Aḥmad b. Ṭūlūn (868–84), the new ruler of Egypt, and in spite of initial military success was ultimately murdered, probably by agents of Ibn Ṭūlūn.

The tenth century shows a continuation of a high level of Nubian power and culture during the period which Adams has called 'Classic Nubian'. There is some evidence that there was a series of high Niles, but not such as to cause serious damage to settlements. Greater prosperity is witnessed by the development of church architecture and decoration, by an increased import of Egyptian pottery, and probably also by easy access and free movement by Arab merchants, who, on the evidence of tombstones, were now settling in the region downstream of the Second Cataract. There was continued military activity against Egypt, which after the end of the 'Abbasid caliphate in 868 was under the rule of the Tulunids and Ikshidids. In 956 the Nubians attacked Aswan and plundered it, but subsequently suffered a serious defeat and surrendered the important fortified position of Qasr Ibrim. By 962 they were attacking again and went at least as far as Akhmim in Middle Egypt; a graffito at Aswan refers to a three-year occupation by the Nubians of the towns of Esna and Armant.

There seems to have been an uneasy balance of power, for the evidence is often contradictory. Within a few years of the Nubian occupation of Upper Egypt, Jawhar, al-Muʿizz's general, is writing to the Nubian King George II (of whom, like his namesake, there is a painting in the Faras cathedral), returning to the old theme of non-payment of the *baqṭ*, and also attempting a conversion of the Nubians to Islam. This letter was taken by ʿAbd Allāh Aḥmad b. Sulaym al-Aswani (usually known as al-Aswani, 'the man from Aswan'), who wrote an account of Nubia which became the main source for al-Maqrīzī's description.

By 969, during the reign in Nubia of George II, the coming to power of the Fatimids in Egypt, whose rule continued until their overthrow by the Ayyubids in 1171, led to two centuries of comparative peace and good relations. The unusual situation of the Fatimids as Shiʿa rulers in an area of Islam which was predominantly Sunni may have led the rulers of Egypt to emphasize some form of alliance with Nubia as a counter-weight to hostile Sunnis. It appears that the King of Nubia was accepted as at least a semi-official protector of the Coptic Patriarch of Alexandria, and thus in some sense responsible for the whole Christian population of Egypt.

Nubia continued prosperous during the latter part of the tenth and eleventh centuries, though there is not a great deal of detail known. Abū Ṣāliḥ mentions King Raphael in 1002 as having built in red brick 'in the style of Baghdad' at Old Dongola, and says that King Solomon was buried in the monastery of St George at Khandaq, a building still unidentified. The Church continued to play an important part in the life of the country. The Faras cathedral remained in being with a wealth of paintings, and there was also the large church, also probably a cathedral, recently found at Old Dongola. There were a number of monasteries, though the only ones known by excavation are at Wizz and at Ghazali, where a dated gravestone is of 999. The persecution of the Christians in Egypt by al-Ḥākim al-Manṣūr (996–1021) led many, including monks, to flee to Nubia, and the predominance of Coptic inscriptions at Ghazali may be due to this.

The information from Faras, again the main Nubian source, apart from providing the names and dates of bishops, also suggests some variation in the allegiance of the Church. It has been argued that the three bishops who ruled the see from 997 to 1056 – Ioannes III, Marianos and Merkurios – were Melkite (orthodox), though Petros (1058–62) was Monophysite. But during this time Christodoulos, Patriarch of Alexandria, visited Nubia, surely good evidence for a close relationship between the head of the Coptic Church and his province of Nubia. The situation is far from clear, and at least one scholar doubts the evidence for a return to orthodox worship.[1]

The nature of the liturgy, largely unknown, of prayers on gravestones, both Coptic and Greek, and the varying languages in use, are not conclusive evidence, and even the appearance of a typical orthodox prayer on the Greek gravestones is not in itself necessarily proof of control by the Melkite Church. In 1097, however, in the time of Bishop Chael III, it is reasonably certain that the Melkite rite was reintroduced, and it is noticeable that from this time there are no inscriptions in Coptic. The middle of the century shows a considerable increase in the use of Old Nubian for the writing of graffiti. The use of Greek also revived from 900–26 in the time of Bishops Kolluthos and Stephanos.

[1] M. Krause, 'Zur Kirchen und Theologiegeschichte Nubiens', in E. Dinkler, ed., *Kunst und Geschichte Nubiens in Christlicher Zeit* (Recklinghausen, 1970), 71–86.

Such information as we have – and it is virtually all from Arab writers, some of whom are unsympathetic and most of whom are ignorant of Nubia at first hand – shows the King of Nubia, living at Old Dongola, perhaps in the building formerly regarded as a church but now suggested to have been the palace (pl. 32), as having absolute power in secular matters, and probably with considerable powers over the Church, though not having the right to appoint bishops, whom it seems were still appointed from Alexandria.

We do not know precisely how the claim to the throne was established, nor do we know when, and if, the throne passed to different families through the long years of Christianity in Nubia. There was a tradition that the royal family was of Arabian origin, though it is difficult to see how this could be. The king had the title of *Kabil* (or *Kamil* – the reading is uncertain) and he was a priest as well as king, and had the right to celebrate the mass unless he had been responsible for killing a man. His vestments are known from paintings at Faras, and for regalia he had a throne, a parasol, a crown and a gold bracelet. In spite of this appearance of elaborate regalia, the ambassador of Tūrān-Shāh describes how, when his mission came to Dongola about the year 1175, the king rode out in extremely simple garb to meet it, and on a horse without trappings.

By some accounts succession was from father to son, but this may be a misunderstanding on the part of Arab writers who would have had difficulty in conceiving of any other system. There is certainly evidence, most of it rather late, that a quite different succession system, suspected also for Kushite times, was used. In this system, the son of the king's sister succeeded, and this was perhaps the reason for the importance of the lady known in Meroitic times as Candake (*Kandace*), if she was the king's mother. In the Nubian period, the 'king's mother' is twice depicted on the walls of the Faras cathedral. There are traces of this system still among modern Nubians, and some Arab descriptions make it quite clear that this was happening, on some occasions, at least, in the Nubian royal family. The conflict between Zakaria and Niuty, both of whom claimed the succession to George, can be explained by the existence of this succession system, and we know that Niuty based his claim on his being the son of a sister of King George. The nature of Zakaria's claim, since he was a son of George, has suggested to some that there were both patrilineal and matrilineal systems in conflict. But Kronenberg has shown that the existence of a system of matrilineal parallel cousin-marriage provides an explanation, and that Zakaria's claim was not based on his being the son of the king, but on being the son of George's sister's daughter, that is the sister of Niuty, whom Zakaria properly addressed as his uncle, that is to say the brother of his mother.[1] It was proposed in the aftermath of Niuty's death that al-ʿUmarī should marry his widow, who was herself sister to Zakaria – such a marriage would have ensured the succession to the son of al-ʿUmarī. It is worth noting that Abū Ṣāliḥ refers to Baḥrīya, a son of the king's sister, as being the first Nubian to be converted to Christianity.

Details of administration and the organization of the royal court are scanty, but we can assume the dominance of the king and also that he had some part in the control of the Church. There were a number of high officials of the court, of whom the eparch of Nubia, 'The Lord of the Horses' – and not apparently 'Lord of the Mountain', as the title had previously been read[2] – must be presumed to be the main one, though he was based at Faras with his own court and administration and did not reside with the king at Dongola. Later he appears to have moved his residence to the more easily defended town of Qasr Ibrim. The actual function of this powerful viceroy is not known in detail, but he remained as a vestige of the once independent kingdom of Nobatia. He was appointed by the king, though perhaps the title and office became hereditary in later times. He wore a distinctive dress and regalia, of which the most striking part was a two-horned head-dress. His duties included not only control of the northern and most vulnerable province; he was also charged with most of the dealings with Egypt and with foreign merchants and travellers. He also controlled access by foreigners to areas south of the Second Cataract, since by the tenth century it seems that settlement by foreigners in the area between the First and Second Cataracts was permitted and had become increasingly common – as the presence of Arabic tombstones throughout the region attests.

Of the other officials, all of lesser importance than the eparch, we know virtually nothing more than their titles. The early inscription of Eirpanome already contains some titles; one Papnute is called the *stepharis*, though the meaning of the title is obscure, and Epephanios has a title which perhaps is to be read 'Keeper of the Seal'. Later we find Byzantine titles in use: the *domestikos*, *protodomestikos*, *meizon*, *protomeizoteros* and others. These all closely follow Byzantine usage and seem to be concerned largely with the details of running the court,

[1] A. Kronenberg, 'Parallel cousin marriage in mediaeval and modern Nubia–Part I', *Kush*, 1965, **13**, 256–60.

[2] J. M. Plumley, 'Qasr Ibrim, 1969', *Journal of Egyptian Archaeology*, 1970, **56**, 14.

which may have included general administrative responsibility for the country as a whole.

The organization of the Church can be assumed to have depended on the bishoprics, at times metropolitan, of Faras and Dongola. A list of these bishoprics is known, and the following places can be identified as bishops' sees: Kalabsha, Qurta, Qasr Ibrim, Faras, Sai and Dongola and, finally, one unidentified one, Suenkur, which is likely to have lain upstream of Dongola.

LATE CHRISTIAN TIMES, *c.* 1160–1400

The replacement in the years 1169–71 of Fatimid rule by that of the Ayyubid Ṣalāḥ al-Dīn (Saladin), who, originally vizier to the last Fatimid ruler, al-ʿĀḍid, had progressively taken over the control of Egypt, marked a change in the fortunes of Nubia. The Fatimids, with their attention to the arts and their heretical but rather liberal attitudes, had maintained for two hundred years a state of reasonable peace with Nubia, and had recruited what are described as 'black' troops, either Nubians, or people from further south whose journeys to Egypt would have been facilitated by the Nubians. In the year 1171, the Nubians attacked Aswan, perhaps in an attempt to give aid to their Fatimid allies, and during the next year advanced into Upper Egypt. This threat called forth a strong response from Ṣalāḥ al-Dīn, who sent his brother, Tūrān-Shāh, in command of an army which drove the Nubians back. On 2 January 1173, he captured the strongpoint of Qasr Ibrim, took many prisoners, turned the Church of St Mary into a mosque, and killed 700 pigs that were found there. Archaeology has provided considerable evidence, from an analysis of animal bones, that the Nubians kept and ate pigs in considerable quantity, and the detail adds authenticity to the story. The cross on top of the church was burnt, and the muezzin gave the call to prayer from the top of the church dome. The greater fanaticism of the new invaders is clearly shown in these activities, as also by the taking prisoner and torturing of the bishop. The place was pillaged, stocks of cotton removed and a garrison of Muslim cavalry installed there under the command of Ibrāhīm al-Kurdi. The troops made a number of incursions further south, in one of which Ibrāhīm was drowned near to Adendan, just across the river from Faras. Perhaps as a result of this, the garrison of Qasr Ibrim was withdrawn in 1175, and Christian reoccupation and restoration of the church took place.

Shortly after this, Tūrān-Shāh sent an embassy to Dongola to report on the land, perhaps with a view to deciding on whether an invasion would be profitable. It was the leader of this embassy who reported on the apparent poverty of the king already mentioned, and his description of the country as producing nothing more than a little grain and a few palm trees persuaded the Muslim leader that further military adventures would not be profitable. There seems to have been no further interference in Nubia on the part of the Ayyubids, and for the next hundred years no information is available on conditions or events in the country.

The seizure of power in Egypt by the Mamluks led to a decisive change in Egyptian relations with Nubia. The Mamluks were more aggressive than their predecessors, and reacted strongly to any disturbances along their southern frontier. An attack on Aswan in 1272 by King David of Nubia, who had already been in trouble with Sultan Baybars of Egypt for non-payment of the *baqṭ*, and had captured ʿAydhāb in the same year, resulted in a military victory by the Mamluks in which a number of leading Nubian personalities, including the Lord of the Horses, were captured, taken to Egypt and executed. It initiated, not only continuing military activity by the Mamluks, but also a long period of interference by them in the internal affairs of Nubia.

Taking advantage of dynastic feuds and supporting those elements who were already seeing the advantage of Muslim help in achieving their ends, the Mamluks became deeply involved in the situation in Nubia, thus helping to prepare the way for the eventual collapse of the Nubian kingdom and the decline of Christianity and its ultimate replacement by Islam. As Adams has ably shown, the archaeological evidence shows considerable changes in Nubian life and these must, in part, be due to the political and military pressures of the time.[1] The most obvious is the reduction in number, but the increase in size, of the towns and villages which in earlier centuries were so numerous throughout Nubia downstream of the Second Cataract. This, in the area lying closest to Egypt, is the most sensitive indicator of changes in Nubian life. The impression given not only by the concentration of population into fewer, and better-defended, localities, but also by the increase of late Christian communities in the remote area of the 'Belly of the Rocks', an obvious refuge area, is that people were looking for safe and defensible

[1] W. Y. Adams, 'Post-pharaonic Nubia in the light of archaeology, III', *Journal of Egyptian Archaeology*, 1966, **52**, 147–62.

places in which to live, and this coincides closely with what the few written records say about the increasingly disturbed conditions.

The historical account is full of military and political events and intrigues. The story starts with the arrival in 1275 of Shekanda, nephew of David, at the court of Baybars, to gain support for his claim to the throne against David II, who had now succeeded. If our view of the Nubian succession system is right, Shekanda would have had the legal claim, and we do not know how David II had gained the kingship. Baybars supported Shekanda and sent a force into Nubia which, after capturing the town of Daw (modern Jebel Adda), and an island, perhaps Mainarti, advanced further into Nubia. David fled, and the eparch changed sides and supported Shekanda, who became king. The Mamluks made heavy claims on Shekanda for the help they had given him, and the northern part of Nubia, that governed by the 'Lord of the Horses', was made directly subject to Egypt. In addition the *baqṭ* payments were enforced once more, and to them was added the requirement to hand over each year what must now properly be considered as tribute – three elephants, three giraffes and many camels and bullocks. The humiliation of Nubia was further strengthened by the destruction of a church at Dongola which King David had built with the labour of Muslims captured at Aswan and ʿAydhāb, and by the removal to Egypt of objects of gold and silver contained in it.

David had fled south to al-Abwab, presumably part of the kingdom of ʿAlwa, and was surrendered by the king of that place (who was tributary to ʿAlwa, unless the Arab writer misunderstood and meant the king of ʿAlwa itself) to the Mamluks in 1277. In 1286 the King of al-Abwab, Ador, perhaps the same ruler, complained about Shekanda to Sultan Qalāʾūn (1279–90). As a result of intrigues of which we know nothing, Shekanda was deposed and replaced by Shemamun, who skilfully managed to retain the rule of Nubia, in spite of various Mamluk raids, until nearly the end of the thirteenth century. In the early years of the fourteenth century, the king for a short time was Amy. But he was murdered in about 1310, to be succeeded by Kudanbes, who was the last Christian king that we know to have ruled from Dongola. During this time Muslim influence was very much increased, and an inscription in the palace building at Old Dongola claims that the upper part was turned into a mosque in 1317. It is likely that some part of the Nubian population had now become Muslim. The Banū Kanz, and their leader who bore the title of Kanz al-Dawla, who lived in the northern part of Lower Nubia, seem to have become Muslim and partly arabized, though still speaking the Kanzi dialect of Nubian as they do to this day. They seem to have played a considerable part, as allies of the Mamluks, in the attacks on the king of Old Dongola. By 1323 Kanz al-Dawla had become king, although relations between the new ruler and his former allies became strained, and the confused account suggests that the Mamluks had second thoughts about the reliability of Kanz al-Dawla as their agent in Nubia. For a time at least, they supported Kudanbes in an attempt to regain power, but by 1323 they had either lost interest or again changed their policy, and Kudanbes, who was waiting at Aswan for Mamluk military aid, found that none was forthcoming.

Although it has been known that, in spite of the growth of Muslim influence in Nubia, Christianity did not disappear suddenly in the first half of the fourteenth century, it is only recently that firm information about the later manifestations of Nubian culture and Christian religion have come to light.

The period from the reign of Kanz al-Dawla on, known largely from the writings of al-Maqrīzī (1364–1442), was one of an increasingly chaotic situation, with raids and counter-raids caused to a considerable extent by the coming into Nubia of Arab tribes, originally from Arabia, who had been forced or persuaded out of Upper Egypt by the Mamluks. Kings continued to rule in Nubia, though they may in the main have been Muslims, as the name of one, Nāṣir, who came to Cairo in 1397, suggests. After 1365, the destruction of Old Dongola seems to have led the ruler to move his residence to Daw (usually identified with Jebel Adda, much further north), and here apparently was based the last remnant of the kingdom of Dongola. Although the islamized Banū Kanz controlled, in their boisterous way, the northernmost part of Nubia, the kingdom of Dotawo, which is reasonably identified with Daw (Lower Do), remained Christian and Nubian-speaking and writing. This is indicated by a few documents in Old Nubian which refer to Dotawo and give the names of kings (Eltei, Siti, Koudlaniel). A leather document, which deals with a private sale of unknown commodites, also gives the name of King Eltei; the names of officials and of witnesses to the transaction are all Nubian, several of them having the characteristic Nubian name ending of *-kuda*. The existence of kings of Dotawo has been known for many years, but it was only in recent times that new discoveries have given more precise information and shown that the kingdom lasted into the fifteenth century. One document found at Jebel Adda dates to 1484 and gives not only the name of a king, Joel, but also that of a bishop – good evidence for the persistence of Christianity. Evidence that Qasr Ibrim had remained the seat of a bishopric into the fourteenth century at least was the discovery there of the burial of a bishop who had been consecrated in 1372. Dotawo may have preserved some kind of independence even until the coming of the Ottomans under Ozdemir Bey in the mid sixteenth century.[1]

The information derived from this scanty literary tradition as well as from the archaeological evidence for very late Christian communities in more remote areas upstream of the Second Cataract, strongly suggests that Nubian cultural traditions and Christianity did not end suddenly in the middle of the fourteenth century as has been assumed, but that they continued, though perhaps harrassed, well into the fifteenth century. Certain scraps of information, though not of a very reliable kind, suggest that some Christian communities persisted very much later. There are almost no written sources for the fifteenth, sixteenth and seventeenth centuries in Nubia, but from the latter part of the seventeenth century the Franciscans made attempts to carry out missionary activities in Ethiopia, some of them travelling there along the Nile. From them came stories of the existence of Christian communities. Perhaps these represent wishful thinking, but even as late as 1742 we have a letter from a Father Giocomo Rzimarz, resident in Cairo, who reported that his Nubian servant had told him of a group of Christians on the island of Tanqussi, which is upstream from Old Dongola. In 1540, Alvares, a Portuguese missionary in Ethiopia, had reported that he had met a group of Nubian Christians come to the emperor of that country to request his help in obtaining priests. The very latest and somewhat bizarre account, of at least one Christian in what must have been otherwise an exclusively Muslim land, is contained in the account by R. S. Ensor of his visit to Old Dongola in 1870 and of his meeting there with an Ethiopian priest. There are also some slight indications of Christian influence from Nubia having penetrated to the western Sudan. The Franciscans showed considerable interest in testing the truth of the stories; they were sufficiently convinced for two brothers to have set out from Tripoli in 1710 to investigate, but the expedition failed with their death.

Events in the kingdom of 'Alwa are even more obscure than in the north. The good grazing areas within its boundaries made it more

[1] P. M. Holt, 'Sultan Selim and the Sudan', *Journal of African History*, 1967, **8**, 19–23.

attractive to the groups of Juhayna and Quraysh Arabs, who were moving south, than were the barren desert lands of the north. Details are not known of the penetration of Arabs, who brought their language and religion with them. But we can suppose that it was not the sudden attack of a large number of fierce warriors, as often suggested, but rather the gradual penetration of small groups moving with their families and animals and simple household goods. In time they formed groups which began to have political aspirations, and when a leader, ʿAbdullāh Jammāʿ – perhaps a mythical figure, since his name means ' ʿAbdullāh the gatherer', a suitable name for an eponymous founder who had coalesced disparate groups – formed a unified 'tribe', the ʿAbdullāb, they were able to face the rulers of ʿAlwa with adequate force.

It has usually been assumed that Soba, the capital of ʿAlwa, was captured shortly after 1504 by ʿUmāra Dūnqas, ruler of the Funj, a people who appeared on the upper part of the Blue Nile, and established their capital at Sennar. Traditions, which may be part of a consciously invented political myth, claim that the Funj allied with the ʿAbdullāb and brought the kingdom of ʿAlwa to an end. But a recent study throws doubt on this, and suggests that the ʿAbdullāb had already conquered ʿAlwa before the arrival of the Funj in the area, perhaps as early as the fourteenth century, and that the Funj in their turn established control over the ʿAbdullāb.[1] Whatever the exact details of the end of Christian ʿAlwa, there is no doubt of the complete acceptance by the inhabitants of ʿAlwa of the culture, religion and language of the conquerors. The area today is the most arabized of all parts of the Sudan. All trace of Nubian, if indeed it was the language of ʿAlwa, has gone, except for a few place names, whereas in the north it has survived, and it was in the region of the Blue Nile that from the seventeenth century onwards the teachings of Islam were more strongly propagated by a group of learned men, many from other lands, than in any other part of the Sudan.

[1] P. M. Holt, 'A Sudanese historical legend: the Funj conquest of Suba', *Bulletin of the School of Oriental and African Studies*, 1960, **23**, 1–17.

CHAPTER 10

THE FATIMID REVOLUTION (861–973) AND ITS AFTERMATH IN NORTH AFRICA*

THE END OF THE NINTH CENTURY AD

In AD 861 the ʿAbbasid Caliph Mutawakkil was murdered by the Turkish guard in the imperial capital of Samarra on the Tigris at the instigation of the heir to the throne, his son Muntaṣir. As heir to the throne, Muntaṣir had held the province of Egypt under the system in force since the accession of Muʿtaṣim in 834. Under this system, the *wālī* or governor had been appointed not by the caliph, but by some high officer or prince at court to whom the province was assigned. In 856 Muntaṣir had appointed one Yazīd b. ʿAbd Allah from the Turks who were the *corps d'élite* of the army in Iraq, the first Turk to hold the position in Egypt. Yazīd remained in office for about ten years, but his power was limited by the separation of Alexandria and Barce (Barca) in Cyrenaica from the government at the Egyptian capital of Fusṭāṭ, as well as by the independent appointment of the *ʿāmil*, the financial superintendent, who was responsible for the collection of revenue and the remittance of an annual *māl*, literally 'wealth', to the treasury at Samarra. Thus divided, the government of Egypt was comparatively weak, and the far south had been abandoned to Arab tribes around Aswan. Revenue accruing to the state seems also to have fallen. Much of the land was in the possession of men like Muntaṣir, aristocrats who may not even have lived in the country. Much of the remainder was progressively alienated to tax-farmers charged with the task of attracting peasants back on to land which had gone out of cultivation. The Copts who formed the bulk of the population seem to have fled from the harsh fiscal regime of the state in search of new masters. The Muslim population, including the beduin tribes and the army, was susceptible to agitation on behalf of Shiʿite pretenders. Even before the death of Mutawakkil, Yazīd was hunting out *rawāfiḍ*, 'Shiʿite heretics', and sending them to Iraq.

* Events in Egypt after AD 973 are covered in Vol. 3, ch. 2. For maps, see pp. 498, 508 and 519 of ch. 8 of this volume. [Ed.]

There may have been an attempt at reform or greater efficiency. In 861, the year of Mutawakkil's murder, Ibn Mudabbir was transferred from Syria to Egypt as *'āmil*. Ibn Mudabbir has a bad reputation; for al-Maqrīzī in the fifteenth century, he was one of those 'cunning devils of scribes' who had always oppressed the people with unjust taxes despite the efforts of a few enlightened rulers to bring the fiscal system into line with the Islamic Law.[1] He it was who had made the mining of natron into a state monopoly, and introduced the taxes known as *mukūs*. He was thus a prime example of that indifference to the true welfare of the country which had characterized the government since the Muslim conquest, and caused its revenue to fall from twenty million dinars under the Romans to something of the order of three or four million.[2] Al-Maqrīzī seems to be developing the argument of the late-ninth-century traveller al-Ya'qūbī, who asserted that the revenue had fallen from fourteen million dinars under 'Amr b. al-'Āṣ to no more than three million as the result of the conversion of the population to Islam.[3] These statements apparently justify the opinion of Becker that in the course of the Middle Ages Egypt experienced a long decline from classical prosperity (see chapter 8, pp. 514–15, 535–6). But both are unreliable, if only because the initial figure is far too high. So far as Ibn Mudabbir is concerned, the view of al-Maqrīzī might suggest that he was a person of some prominence in the Egyptian tradition, with some claim to be considered an architect of the medieval fiscal system.

If Ibn Mudabbir's achievements were more than legendary, however, they are obscured by political events. In the decade following the murder of Mutawakkil, four caliphs came and went, made and unmade by the Turkish guard. It was the occasion for more widespread instability, not least at the popular level. Dissaffection – social, political and religious – had been endemic in the empire since the seventh century, partly because of the exclusive nature of successive regimes. Over the years it had been increasingly focused by an historic cause, the claim of the descendants of the fourth caliph, 'Alī, to the imamate, the leadership of the Muslim community held by the caliph in his capacity as the deputy of Muḥammad. About 862, one such descendant, Abū Ḥadarī, who had gathered a following of some kind, was arrested by Yazīd and dispatched to Iraq, and an order was received from Samarra

[1] al-Maqrīzī, *Kitāb al-Mawā'iẓ wa 'l-I'tibār fī dhikr al-khiṭaṭ wa 'l-āthār* [*Khiṭaṭ*], ed. by G. Wiet (Cairo, 1911), II, 81.

[2] Ibid. II, 69.

[3] al-Ya'qūbī, *Kitāb al-Buldān*, ed. by M. J. de Goeje (Leiden, 1892), 339; French trans. by G. Wiet, *Le Livre des pays* (Cairo, 1937), 197–8.

prohibiting any ʿAlawī or member of the family of ʿAlī from owning an estate, riding a horse, travelling outside Fusṭāṭ, or possessing more than one slave. The specifications reveal how a rebellion might be organized by an ambitious nobleman. In 864 six more ʿAlawīs were deported. But the rebellion which broke out in 866 presents the familiar spectacle of a revolt of the Arab tribes and the army, which proclaimed an ʿAlawī only after its first success.

The revolt was begun by one Jābir b. al-Walīd among the Arabs of the western Ḥawf, the border of the desert in the region of Alexandria, from whom it extended to the Christians (*ṣulbiyya*) and the *mawālī*. These were troops. Of the leaders mentioned by al-Kindī alongside Jābir of the Banū Mudlij, one is Jurbaj al-Naṣrānī *al-Ḥāris*, 'the Christian, the guardsman', one of the very worst of the Nazarenes. A Christian militia, almost certainly of foreign, most probably Byzantine, origin, is indicated. The *mawālī* would also be soldiers, but from a different part of the world. A second leader is ʿAbd Allah al-Marīsī, 'the southern Egyptian', a term used by the contemporary al-Yaʿqūbī for the Copts of Upper Egypt. But from the time of al-Masʿūdī in the tenth century, the term was used for the Nubian population of the valley beyond Aswan.[1] It is likely that the Muslim ʿAbd Allah of al-Kindī's tenth-century reference is to be compared with the last leader to be mentioned, Abū Harmala al-Nūbī, 'the Nubian', 'a terrible man'. Together they would represent a body of 'Sudanese' soldiery, quite in keeping with the practice of the time, which throughout the Muslim world was to form units of particular ethnic origins often out of imported slaves. The revolt quickly spread across the northern Delta, where the rebels attempted to levy taxes in a manner which recalls the independence of this distinct region earlier in the century during the great civil war on the death of the Caliph Hārūn al-Rashīd. The Turkish garrison at Fusṭāṭ was defeated, an ʿAlawite, one Ibn al-Arquṭ, was proclaimed, Yazīd was recalled, and the rebellion put down only with the arrival of fresh Turkish troops from Iraq. These, the ʿ*abīd* or 'slave troops' par excellence of the Muslim world (see chapter 8, pp. 528–9), were the critical factor in the composition of the army. The caliph depended upon them, but their privileges provoked the jealousy of other units.

The rebellion was suppressed in 867. Meanwhile responsibility for the government of Egypt had fallen to one Bāyakbak, a high Turkish officer at Samarra, who in 868 appointed another Turkish officer,

[1] al-Masʿūdī, *Les Prairies d'or* (*Murūj al-dhahab*), text and trans. by C. Barbier de Meynard and P. de Courteille (Paris, 1864), III, 32.

Aḥmad b. Ṭūlūn, to Fusṭāṭ. The circumstances are obscured by retrospective accounts. On his arrival, it is said, he was greeted by the two officials whose power acted as a check upon the *wālī* – namely Shukayr, the *ṣāḥib al-barīd*, the 'postmaster', and Ibn Mudabbir, the *ʿāmil*, the latter with a gift of 10,000 dinars or gold coins, and an escort of 100 *ghilmān* or 'pages'. Ibn Ṭūlūn is said, in memorable fashion, to have refused the gold and to have taken the escort instead. This prompted a report to Samarra that he was not interested in money, only soldiers, and was evidently seeking independence. A letter to this effect, written by Ibn Mudabbir, was returned from Samarra to Ibn Ṭūlūn, who imprisoned the *ʿāmil* several times, only to be obliged on each occasion to allow him to return to his duties. The story is symbolic, an epitome for the reality. Ibn Ṭūlūn's immediate task was to deal with a revival of the revolt of Jābir in the west under a second ʿAlawite pretender. When the rebel had been killed in the south in 869, yet a third pretender appeared in Upper Egypt with the significant name of Ibn al-Ṣūfī. Whatever his claim to ʿAlawite descent, his name and his actions seem to show him as a zealot in the popular tradition of the preacher and the holy man, claiming divine inspiration for an attack on the ungodly. The town of Asna was sacked, and its people, who may have been mainly Christian, massacred; the commander sent against Ibn al-Ṣūfī by Ibn Ṭūlūn was mutilated and crucified. Early in 870 Ibn al-Ṣūfī was defeated at Akhmim, and driven out to the Wāḥāt, the oases of Kharga and Dakhla. But already events in Egypt were overshadowed by events in Iraq.

Bāyakbak was murdered, to be succeeded so far as Egypt was concerned by Yārjūkh, the father-in-law of Ibn Ṭūlūn, whose appointment was naturally confirmed. However, while Ibn al-Ṣūfī was expelled from Egypt, in 869 a similar pretender in Iraq began the revolt of the Zanj. The Zanj were mainly black slaves, mostly from the eastern side of Africa, who worked on the salt flats at the mouth of the Euphrates. Within a year their movement controlled the southern part of the country, and the government itself was in danger. Perhaps in consequence, early in 870 the governor of Palestine revolted, seizing Damascus, and confiscating the annual 'wealth' of Egypt on its way to Samarra. Ibn Ṭūlūn went out against him with 'the blacks' and others, possibly 'Greeks'. The force retired, but its composition is strongly reminiscent of the rebels of 866/7, and suggests that the new governor had begun to build up his forces with troops who could be recruited directly into Egypt. Later in the year work began just to the north of

Fusṭāṭ upon a site chosen for a palace city, to be called al-Qaṭā'i', 'the Wards' or 'Quarters'. It was a major move from the position of a simple *wālī* or governor towards that of a *sulṭān* or monarch after the fashion of the caliph himself. In 871 the authority of Ibn Ṭūlūn was formally increased when Alexandria and Barce were added to his command; it was perhaps the year when the *'āmil* Ibn Mudabbir was withdrawn, and Ibn Ṭūlūn was appointed to the *kharāj*, the collection of revenue. The accumulation of power was complete in 872 when Yārjūkh died at Samarra and was only nominally replaced by Muwaffad, the young son of the caliph. Under the strain of the Zanj war, the system inaugurated by Ma'mūn and Mu'taṣim some fifty years earlier had broken down, and, after a long period of relative insignificance, Egypt was at last following Ifrīqiya, under the Aghlabid dynasty, towards independence.

It was a lesser rather than a greater Egypt. The region of Aswan was under the control of one al-'Umarī,[1] who in 872 defeated the pretender Ibn al-Ṣūfī when he launched an attack from the western oases, and drove him across the Red Sea to Mecca. Al-'Umarī had a hand in the gold-mines of the Wadi Allaqi as well as in the traffic of the Nile Valley between Egypt and Nubia. He may have acted as an agent, helping to supply Ibn Ṭūlūn with the *sūdān*, the 'blacks' he required for his growing regiments of *'abīd*. Many if not most of these *sūdān*, however, may have come not from Nubia but from the central Sudan via Zawila in the Fezzan, the most probable source of slaves for the equally novel black army of Ibn Ṭūlūn's energetic Ifriqiyan contemporary, the Aghlabid Ibrāhīm II. Their recruitment is the first sign of the wealth now being concentrated in the hands of the ruler of Egypt instead of sent as tribute or rent to Iraq.[2] This was evidently sufficient to maintain the much larger army, as well as to complete the building of al-Qaṭā'i'; the laying out of the *maydān*, the open space to the east; the construction of a *bīmāristān* or hospital; and finally the erection of the great Mosque of Ibn Ṭūlūn, begun in 876, it is said, because the people complained that the presence of the troops in attendance on their master at the Friday prayer in the old Mosque of 'Amr made the building too

[1] For the career of this al-'Umarī, see also ch. 9, pp. 578–82., and also vol. 3, p. 72.

[2] Cf. al-Maqrīzī, *Khiṭaṭ*, II, 62–3: the revenue rose from 800,000 dinars a year to 4,300,000, giving Ibn Ṭūlūn the distinction of being, along with the Umayyad *'āmil* 'Ubayd Allah b. al-Ḥabḥāb, one of the only two administrators who raised the revenue to any extent after its initial fall below 3,000,000 dinars a year. The statement serves Maqrīzī's polemical purpose, and is not to be taken literally; but a considerable increase in revenue at the disposal of the *sulṭān* is plausible on the assumption that Ibn Ṭūlūn had come to enjoy the rents of the great estates as well as the product of taxation. Al-Maqrīzī refers to such a combination of income in connection with the Ikhshidids, ibid. II, 65.

crowded. The expenditure was probably beneficial. The demand for gold attested by the state monopoly imposed upon the robbing of ancient tombs, as well as the mining activity noted by al-Yaʿqūbī in the Wadi Allaqi, may reflect an increase in cash payments. More generally the expenditure almost certainly increased the import of a wide range of commodities, including slaves, against the export of Egyptian grain and cloth.

While Egypt was coming to independence at the hands of one of the new Turkish nobles of the empire, against a background of popular revolt, Ifrīqiya illustrated an apparently different path to power. In 875 the *fuqahā'* of Kairouan are said to have recognized the virtues of Ibrāhīm, the elder brother of the *amīr* who had just died, and to have devised a *ḥīla*, a dispensation, to enable him to ascend the throne instead of the infant nephew to whom he had sworn allegiance. This would have been a fitting climax to a period of some twenty-five years since the appointment of the great jurist Saḥnūn as Qāḍī of Ifrīqiya, when the Aghlabid rulers had lived by the Law, and the country had been in consequence peaceful and prosperous.[1] This golden age, however, must be seen for what it is, a legend which forms the opening section of a dramatic narrative constructed on a regular pattern. The view of early Muslim history as the restoration of the practice of the Prophet after an interval in which it had been threatened by the unfaithfulness of the rulers, was a vision of moral excellence leading through moral failure to moral regeneration which was available to historians of subsequent periods. The latter part of the reign of Muḥammad I, and those of the pious prince Abū Ibrāhīm Aḥmad (856–63), who provided the city of Kairouan with a reservoir and completed the Great Mosque, Ziyādat Allah II (863–4), and Muḥammad II (864–75) provide a comparable starting-point for a similar story.

Abū Ibrāhīm Aḥmad may well have been pious. The dynasty had pursued an actively Muslim policy in Sicily, where the jihad was still carried on in annual expeditions. It is clear that the *ʿulamā'* were influential in the main towns, and that it was politic to win their approval by the appointment of a *qāḍī* from their ranks. In virtue of his office, the Qāḍī of Ifrīqiya was a statesman and a politician. At the same time, the *amīr* was able to manage a difficult person such as Saḥnūn by appointing a more pliant colleague to handle the bulk of the work. This colleague might belong to a different *madhhab*. Even without

[1] For this picture, cf. M. Talbi, *L'Émirat Aghlabide, 184–296/800–909: histoire politique* (Paris, 1966), 250–6, 258–60, 265–73.

doctrinal differences, however, the Muslim community was split up. Justice was largely local. Power was extensively delegated. The lords of the *jund* in the north and west were semi-independent. Tribal peoples governed themselves, often beyond the reach of the *sulṭān* and his representatives on their forays. In consequence, the affairs of the capital were fundamentally parochial. When in the middle of the ninth century they dominate the story, so that the other cities, still less the outlying districts, are scarcely mentioned, it says something for the regime. The twenty-five years of peace might be construed as twenty-five years of comparative neglect. The only recorded activity to east and west is a punitive expedition against the Berbers of Tripolitania in 859, and another under Muḥammad II which came to grief against the peoples of the Aures mountains and the Zab. In these circumstances, the accession of Ibrāhīm II looks more simply like a well-laid plot.

Despite the common theme of a world in Muslim hands, particularism is the impression left by contemporary writers, to whom the future was naturally unknown. The accounts of the Arab conquests, written down in the Futūḥ, the 'conquests' literature, told a tale of Islam as the climax of world history while its achievements on the ground were being plotted. Writers like Ibn ʿAbd al-Ḥakam in Egypt went on to describe the conquered localities in the beginning of the Khiṭaṭ, the 'places' literature. From the second half of the ninth century such descriptions were contained in general geographical accounts of the countries, towns and itineraries of the *Dār al-Islām*. From the traveller al-Yaʿqūbī comes much of our knowledge of the diversity and the political fragmentation of the Maghrib at this time. The fragmentation, on the other hand, was the counterpart of economic unification. The Ibadites of Tahert (Tiaret), the Djerid and the Jebel Nefusa were developing the routes across the Sahara through Zawila to the central Sudan and through Ghadames and Wargla to the Niger bend; their trade extended into Egypt, Ifrīqiya and Spain. If the trans-Saharan connections of Sijilmasa in the Tafilelt, Tāmdult in the valley of the Darʿa and Igli in the valley of the Sous are less certain (see chapter 8, pp. 553–4), this region to the south of the High Atlas was important in its own right as a producer of silver and copper;[1] the developing of mining, for silver, copper, iron and lead, in Ifrīqiya as well as in Morocco, was indeed one of the revolutionary features of the early Muslim period.[2] From Massa,

[1] Cf. B. Rosenberger, 'Tāmdult: cité minière et caravanière', *Hespéris Tamuda*, 1970, 11, 104–39.

[2] Cf. M. Lombard, *Les Métaux dans l'ancien monde du Ve au XIe siècle* (Paris and the Hague, 1974), 159–62, 180–95, 235–6.

the *ribāṭ* which was the port of the Sous, it would seem that ships sailed to the Mediterranean, where they contributed to the international traffic of the Old World. Of this al-Yaʿqūbī and his contemporary Ibn Khurdādhbih provide a glimpse, including merchants ranging as far as China. The market economy as a whole was growing, with corn, fruit, olive-oil, vegetables, cotton, flax and animals produced for sale sometimes over distances of hundreds of kilometres. Cloth was commercially the most important manufacture, but only one of a vast range of arts and crafts. Many of these went into building, which came into its own in mosques, palaces, fortifications and reservoirs.

Egypt derived a characteristic benefit from the continuation of the Zanj war as it diverted the trade of the Indian Ocean from the Persian Gulf to the Red Sea. The war had a crippling effect on the revenues of the caliphate, and according to tradition it was a question of money – the size of the much-reduced tribute paid by Ibn Ṭūlūn to Samarra and its recipient, the caliph Muʿtamid or his powerful brother Muwaffaq – which in 877 led to open conflict. While Muʿtamid bestowed upon Ibn Ṭūlūn the *thughūr*, 'the marches' (the region of Cilicia with its capital at Tarsus which formed the military frontier between Syria and the Byzantine empire), Muwaffaq, the effective head of government, attempted to depose him, entrusting to one Mūsā b. Bughā the task of installing Amājūr, the governor of Damascus, at Fusṭāṭ. But Mūsā remained throughout the year at Raqqa on the Euphrates, until his troops deserted and both he and Amājūr died. In 878 Ibn Ṭūlūn marched through Syria to Cilicia, meeting little resistance. He retired to Egypt at the news of the revolt of his son ʿAbbās, whom he had left as regent at Fusṭāṭ. ʿAbbās fled with his men to Tripoli, where they were beaten by the Aghlabids, then back to Barce, where he eventually surrendered to his father in 881. Syria however remained loyal until in 882 the *ghulām* Lu'lu', a slave of Ibn Ṭūlūn's personal guard sent to Damascus at the head of an army, deserted to Muwaffaq. Ibn Ṭūlūn himself advanced into Syria, where it is said the Caliph Muʿtamid himself tried to reach him in an attempt to escape from his brother the *wazīr*. At Damascus, Ibn Ṭūlūn summoned the *fuqahā'* of Egypt and Syria to declare that Muwaffaq had forfeited his claim to obedience and ought to be deposed.

In this way the master of Egypt found himself not very differently placed from the ruler of Ifrīqiya, seeking the approval of the Law for his actions. The approval was given, although not apparently by the virtuous Qāḍī of Egypt, Bakkār b. Qutayba, who was imprisoned for his refusal. For this, it is said, Ibn Ṭūlūn died penitent, returning from Cilicia to expire at Fusṭāṭ early in 884. In the sources he enjoys a good reputation, but here too hindsight has been at work. The sins of the father have been visited on his second son, his successor Khumārawayh, whose wicked indulgence has become the explanation of, and the justification for, the ultimate extinction of the upstart dynasty. Muwaffaq had put down the Zanj in 883, but was unable to dislodge the young man either from Egypt or from Syria. In 886 he recognized his independence for thirty years in return for a modest tribute. After the death of Muwaffaq in 891 and that of Muʿtamid in 892, the pact was sealed by the fabulous marriage of Khumārawayh to the daughter of the new caliph, Muʿtaḍid. Where his father had built a mosque, however, Khumārawayh built a sumptuous palace adorned with life-size statues of the royal family, paintings and reliefs, and equipped with a bed floating in a pool of mercury brought, presumably by sea, from Spain. When in 896 he was murdered at Damascus by members of his household, a voice was heard at the funeral quoting from the Koran: 'seize him and cast him into the Fire'.[1] The end of the Tulunids was at hand, though not for any real fault. The unpopularity of Jaysh, the elder son of Khumārawayh, led to his murder by an uncle. Characteristically, however, the army preferred the direct line, and installed a second son, Hārūn. The regime was sustained by virtue of this loyalty, although the caliph was able to exploit the crisis and revise the pact made with Khumārawayh. In 899 he regained control of Cilicia, and raised the tribute of Egypt to 450,000 dinars a year.

As in Egypt, so in Ifrīqiya. Ibrāhīm II turned from a virtuous prince into a monster. He has the character of an Ivan the Terrible, as a friend of the people driven by the plots of the aristocracy to abhorrent cruelty. On the one hand he dispenses justice; on the other hand he slays. In 878 it is the *mawālī* of his predecessor whom he exterminates, presumably *ṣaqāliba* or troops of European origin whom he replaces with *sūdān*, 'blacks', in the new palace city of Raqqāda which he builds to the south of Kairouan. In 893 it is the turn of his *fityān*, the 'pages' or *ghilmān* in training, to be his bodyguard and men of trust, followed by the Arabs of the *jund* at Balazma to the west. His own family is not safe. The revolt of Tunis and the leaders of the north confines him briefly to his new stronghold, but this is stamped out in 894. In 896 he goes through the Jebel Nefusa to Tripoli, where his cousin and potential rival, Muḥammad, is put to death. He advances to the Egyptian frontier at

[1] Cf. P. K. Hitti, *History of the Arabs*, 7th edn (London and New York, 1960), 454–5.

Ajdābiya, where he orders the heads of fifteen victims to be cooked and brought to table. It may be that he suffered from melancholia;[1] it may be, again, that insanity drove him to weaken though not to destroy the civil and military aristocracy which dominated the society and the politics of the country. However savage the means, on the other hand, the intention was probably deliberate, to rectify the weakness of the central government by increasing the size of the army. To the west was the spectacle of Andalus, where in the second half of the century the country fell into the power of local lords like those of Ifrīqiya, and the Umayyads barely survived. To the east was the example of Ibn Ṭūlūn, whose son had attacked Tripoli in 880. Heavier contributions to pay for the troops may have provoked the opposition which made them necessary. The great revolt of 893/4, comparable in character, scale and effect to that of al-Ṭunbudhī in 824/5, doubtless confirmed Ibrāhīm in his judgement, while the final justification may have been the support given by the ʿAbbasid Caliph Muʿtaḍid to Ibrāhīm's cousin Muḥammad at Tripoli.

It is certainly the history of the east which explains the form of the story. As the ʿAbbasids, now back in Baghdad, prepared for the reconquest of Egypt, they seem to have envisaged some assertion of their suzerainty over Ifrīqiya. Early in 902 an embassy came from Iraq to Ibrāhīm. Later in the year the *amīr* handed over the government of Ifrīqiya to his son ʿAbd Allah II and embarked for the war in Sicily. For twenty years after the fall of Syracuse in 878, the Muslim effort in the island had flagged. It was renewed when ʿAbd Allah led a preliminary expedition in 900/1. Ibrāhīm commanded a strong force, and proceeded to complete the conquest with the storming of the Byzantine capital of Taormina. In the autumn he died at the siege of Cosenza on the mainland. It was an edifying end. Ostensibly he had laid down his life in battle against the infidel, having first laid down the power he had so grossly abused at the behest of his rightful lord. Whatever the truth, it was an auspicious beginning to the restoration of justice to the world, the completion of which was to be the return of Egypt to the lawful authority of the caliph. It is therefore ironic that the fall of Egypt was precipitated by a second revolutionary movement in the Fertile Crescent, and that in Ifrīqiya it was not the ʿAbbasids who reaped the honour of the affair. Instead, the vices of Ibrāhīm went to justify the triumph of an enemy, whose campaign, building to a head, entirely overthrew the Aghlabids.[2]

[1] For the list of atrocities and this diagnosis, cf. Talbi, *L'Émirat Aghlabide*, 304–18.

[2] The origin of the tradition hostile to Khumārawayh and his successors is clear from the

In the aftermath of the Zanj war in Iraq, the long tradition of rebellion in the name of ʿAlī and his descendants was concentrated by the Ismāʿīlī sect. The majority of Shiʿites, those who followed the family, had come to consider that the headship of the house descended in the direct line of Ḥusayn, ʿAlī's second son. As they came to accept the authority of Jaʿfar al-Ṣādiq, the great-grandson of Ḥusayn, for their legal doctrine, however, so they converted into an article of faith their support for the claim of these *imāms* to be the true rulers of the Muslim community. The conversion was complete when the direct line came to a mysterious end in 878, and the twelfth and last head of the house became a figure destined to reappear at the end of the world. A minority, on the other hand, preferred to consider Ismāʿīl, the son of Jaʿfar al-Ṣādiq, the sixth *imām*, whom his father was said to have excluded from the succession, as the seventh and last *imām*. He too had disappeared, but his return, by contrast, was imminent. The doctrine of the Ismaʿilites, therefore, was revolutionary in the way that the Messianism of the ʿAbbasid *dawla* had once been. They employed the technique of the secret society to prepare the way for the Mahdi, 'the rightly-guided one', the precursor of the Qā'im, 'the bringer of the Resurrection', the *imām* himself. About 890, one Ḥamdān Qarmaṭ set up in Iraq a *Dār al-Hijra*, a 'place of emigration', to compare not so much with the

ʿAbbasid poetry which celebrated the end of the regime (see p. 601, n. 2). In the same way in Ifrīqiya, the victorious Fatimids were responsible for the tale of the Aghlabids which has come down to us through the lost chronicle of the eleventh-century Zirid historian al-Raqīq; cf. Talbi, *L'Émirat Aghlabide*, 308–9. In the case of Ibrāhīm II, who died before the Fatimid campaign came into the open, there is evidence of a previous story distorted to deny that there was any virtue in his expedition to Sicily (cf. Ibn ʿIdhārī, *Kitāb al-Bayān al-mughrib fī akhbār al-Andalus wa'l-Maghrib*, ed. by G. S. Colin and E. Lévi-Provençal, I [Leiden, 1948], 131–2, 133; French trans. by E. Fagnan, *Histoire de l'Afrique du Nord et de l'Espagne intitulée Al-Bayano 'l-Moghrib* [Algiers, 1901], 176, 178; Talbi, *L'Émirat Aghlabide*, 320); the 'year of justice', when Ibrāhīm remitted the taxes before his departure, was called by the people the 'year of injustice'. The original tale of pious preparation whose existence is revealed by this anecdote may have stood alone. That it was meant in fact to stand in contrast to the story of Ibrāhīm's wickedness as evidence of his penitence may appear from the statement in the *Bayān*, I, 131, that the remission of taxes was an act of expiation prompted by the inexorable progress of the *dāʿī* among the Kutāma. The original of *this* statement, which forms part of the Fatimid gloss, is perhaps to be found in the assertion by two fourteenth-century authors, al-Nuwayrī and Ibn Khaldūn, that Ibrāhīm was deposed for his sins by the ʿAbbasid caliph (cf. Talbi, *L'Émirat Aghlabide*, 318). This detail, found only in these two late sources, nevertheless agrees with the kind of construction put upon the history of the Tulunids by Baghdad. It may indicate an attempt to make capital out of events in the west as part of the campaign to recover Egypt. Given the obscurity of the activities of the Fatimid agent Abū ʿAbd Allah in the Maghrib at this time (see pp. 600–1), there is no need to think, with Talbi (*L'Émirat Aghlabide*, 319–20), in terms of an actual attempt to deal with a threat of revolution which only later became apparent. It seems more likely that the story of Ibrāhīm, the 'penitent tyrant', was in origin a fiction of the previous phase of politics in the ʿAbbasid empire.

old *amṣār* as with Medina, the place to which the Prophet had 'emigrated' to establish Islam. This became the centre of a new community, a society of initiates known as the Qarmaṭiya, the Carmathians, whose scattered cells worked in hiding against the ʿAbbasid regime. At the same time, the coming of the Mahdi in the person of one Saʿīd b. Ḥusayn was being preached clandestinely by his *duʿāt* (sing. *dāʿī*), literally 'the callers', from his headquarters in Syria. These achieved their first overt success in the Yemen, but from there the *dāʿī* Abū ʿAbd Allah went to Ifrīqiya about 893.

Abū ʿAbd Allah established himself among the Kutāma Berbers of the Little Kabyle mountains in the north-west of Ifrīqiya, an area dominated by the lords of the *jund* in their citadels, notably those at Mila and Setif. On the model of Muḥammad at Mecca and Medina, he is said first to have settled down as a teacher at the village of Ikjān, and then to have made a *hijra*, an emigration leading his followers to the village of Tāzrūt. This story of the re-enactment of the beginning of Islam in accordance with the accepted version, however, is suspect, coming as it does from an Ismaʿilite source concerned to present the triumph of the Ismaʿilite *daʿwa*, or 'calling', as the triumph of the true faith in accordance with the Scriptures.[1] It is likely that the *dāʿī* was in the tradition of the popular preacher, demanding the destruction of a great abomination before the coming of the Lord. What was of fundamental importance was that his appeal was directed in the first instance, not to the world at large, nor yet to the Ifriqiyan rebels of 893/4, but to a particular people on the fringe of the Muslim world. Abū ʿAbd Allah's purpose was served by the situation of the Kutāma, largely independent but intermittently aggrieved, able and willing to band together in a new *islām* for a new conquest. What made the appeal effective was doubtless the technique of secrecy, watching and waiting for the appointed hour, which gave time to win support and build an army. The reluctant were coerced, a horde of horsemen prepared, and the moment set for 903, the year 290 of the *Hijra*, when the Mahdi was due to reveal himself.

As the year approached, the crisis developed. The Carmathians set up a robber-state at Hofuf in eastern Arabia, from where they began to raid across the desert. In the absence of Ibrāhīm II in Sicily, Abū ʿAbd Allah attacked Mila in 902. Repulsed, he returned to the attack in 903, while the Carmathians invaded Syria. The Mahdi did not appear;

[1] al-Qāḍī Abū Ḥanīfa al-Nuʿmān (al-Qadī 'l-Nuʿmān), *Iftitāḥ al-Daʿwa wa ibtidā' al-Dawla*, ed. by W. al-Qāḍī (Beirut, 1970).

instead, Saʿīd b. Ḥusayn went covertly from Syria to the Maghrib, where he eventually reached Sijilmasa.[1] But at Damascus the Tulunid governor, the Turk Ṭughj b. Juff, was surprised and routed, and the Iraqi army of the new caliph, Muktafī, was required to expel the intruders. In 904 the ʿAbbasid troops came back as invaders. The Tulunid commanders were driven into Egypt. The preparations of Hārūn were interrupted when he was murdered by his uncle Shaybān. For the dynasty it was a fatal blow. Condemning the deed, army leaders like Ṭughj b. Juff sent an invitation to the ʿAbbasid commander Muḥammad b. Sulaymān. In 905 the ʿAbbasid army entered the country, and Shaybān surrendered. It was fitting that after the impiety of Khumārawayh and the alleged drunkenness of Hārūn, the last of the Tulunids should have been an assassin. Justice was done and seen to be done when al-Qaṭā'iʿ, the home of such wickedness, was burnt; only the mosque of Ibn Ṭūlūn, and perhaps his hospital, were spared. The ʿAbbasid poets rejoiced.[2] Those of Egypt, on the other hand, lamented, and their nostalgia may have been rather more than a conventional response to the fall of the mighty. All of the *quwwād*, the commanders, and all of the *mawālī* of the accursed dynasty were deported to Iraq. But while Ṭughj b. Juff, for example, was appointed governor of Qinnaṣrīn in Palestine, some of the officers en route to Baghdad escaped at Aleppo. Under one Ibn al-Khalīj, they made their way back to defeat the new ʿAbbasid prefect and drive him from Fusṭāṭ. Acclaiming a son of Khumārawayh as the rightful representative of the caliph in Egypt, Ibn al-Khalīj was hailed as a deliverer until his capture and execution in 906. Both his name, 'son of the canal', and his fame are significant. The Tulunids had created an army upon whose loyalty and vested interest their survival had depended. When that loyalty was shaken, and Turks like Ṭughj b. Juff saw their future with a different master, the fallen rulers were retrospectively identified with the cause of the men of Egypt, half military, half popular, which went back beyond Ibn Ṭūlūn through the rebellion of Ibn al-Arquṭ to the beginning of the ninth century.

[1] He is said to have done so disguised as a merchant, evading the clutches of the ʿAbbasids and the Aghlabids, until he was imprisoned at Sijilmasa at the request of Ziyādat Allah III; the story is hard to verify, but all sources agree that the Mahdī was eventually brought from Sijilmasa by Abū ʿAbd Allah.

[2] al-Kindī, *Governors and judges of Egypt*, ed. by Rhuvon Guest (Leiden and London, 1912), 248ff.

THE ESTABLISHMENT OF THE FATIMIDS

In Ifrīqiya meanwhile, the Aghlabid *amīr* ʿAbd Allah II was murdered by his son Ziyādat Allah III in 903. This still more unnatural crime did not have the immediate results of the killing of Hārūn. In the eyes of the chroniclers, however, the martyrdom of Ibrāhīm II had been in vain. The new ruler joined in celebrating the ʿAbbasid cause, protesting his loyalty to Baghdad and his determination to defend the caliph against the Ismaʿilite foe. By his action the dynasty was nevertheless damned. Setif fell to Abū ʿAbd Allah in 904, and the *dāʿī* began the conquest of the Zab. The open country passed under his control with his victory at Kayūna in 905, the province itself with the fall of the principal citadels in 906 and 907. In 909 the last Aghlabid army, blocking the way to Kairouan, was dispersed at Laribus. Ziyādat Allah fled to the east, and the Mahdi was brought from Sijilmasa (see chapter 11, p. 647) to enter the palace city of Raqqāda in January 910. History as written by the ʿAbbasids had been appropriated by their enemies. Saʿīd b. Ḥusayn styled himself ʿUbayd Allah to become the first of the Fatimid dynasty, called after the mother of the Imams, Fāṭima, the daughter of the Prophet. The ancestry was spiritual rather than physical, a matter of reincarnation. Like the ʿAbbasid claim to belong to the house of the Prophet, it was a chosen support for a challenge for the rightful headship of the Muslim world. With Ziyādat Allah, the self-proclaimed champion of Baghdad, out of the way, the confrontation of the Ismaʿili *daʿwa* with the ʿAbbasid *dawla* became direct. Starting from a base in the west, the Fatimids set out to overthrow their rivals as the ʿAbbasids themselves had once overthrown the Umayyads from a base in the east.

In other respects, however, the situation was radically different from that of 750. Then, the Muslim world had been politically united. Now, it was divided among a number of separate states, of which the ʿAbbasid empire, despite its recovery of Syria and Egypt, was only one. As a government of the *Dār al-Islām*, the ʿAbbasid caliphate was a fiction. It served at best to lend support to other rulers who acknowledged their allegiance, and at worst it was ignored. The Fatimids slipped easily into the system. Their *daʿwa*, or 'calling', the preaching of their doctrine, went from strength to strength, but it was increasingly based upon the power of their *sulṭān*, their Ifriqiyan regime. The history of their first ten to fifteen years is the history of the way in which they found themselves to be engaged, not upon further revolution, but upon a war between two states for which the prize was Egypt. So far as the

ʿAbbasids were concerned, it was the period when, partly because of the need to defend Syria and Egypt, the contrast between their historic aspirations and the political reality was finally made clear. From the accession of Muqtadir in 908, the caliph was increasingly a *roi fainéant* on whose behalf the government was controlled by the commander of the army. For the next twenty-five years this was the eunuch Mu'nis b. Muẓaffar, whose rise was directly proportionate to the growth of the Fatimid threat. Whereas the ʿAbbasids had attacked an energetic Umayyad monarch whose position had been undermined by civil war, the Fatimids were confronted by a nominal emperor upheld by the effective master of an efficient army.

There had been nothing inevitable about the fall of the Aghlabids in Ifrīqiya. The attack of Abū ʿAbd Allah had coincided with a succession crisis, converting a moment of weakness into a moment of peril which proved fatal on the battlefield. Despite its previous history and its ultimate aims, the new regime did no more than continue the drive towards a strong central government which had begun with Ibrāhīm II, and which Ziyādat Allah, who had disposed of other relatives besides his father, likewise pursued. It was in this way, by a ruthless purge of his supporters, that the Mahdi solved the problem of his own succession, disciplining the forces which the revolution had released. In 911 the *dāʿī* Abū ʿAbd Allah was assassinated. Over the next two years ʿUbayd Allah and his son Abū 'l-Qāṣim had to contend with a revolt among the Kutāma in the Zab in support of a rival Mahdi, as well as more conventional hostility from the peoples of Tahert, Tripoli and Sicily. But the Kutāma were converted into a regular army, a navy was formed, and in 914 the Kutāma general Ḥabāsa invaded Egypt. The invasion illustrated the strengths and weaknesses of the two sides. The force at the disposal of Takīn, the Turkish governor of Egypt, was weak, while the appearance of a new and notably successful ʿAlawite champion provided a focus for the opposition manifested in Ibn al-Khalīj's adventure of 906. Barce, guarding the west, was a long way from the Nile and hard to hold; the attempt of Takīn to strengthen its government as a precaution simply provoked the Ifriqiyan expedition. After Barce, Alexandria was taken with the aid of the Fatimid fleet. Yet Alexandria, as the ninth century had shown, stood apart from the rest of the country, and the invaders' lines of communication were already very long. The further advance of 160 kilometres into the heart of Egypt proved too far. In January 915, heavily reinforced from Syria, Takīn routed the attack upon Fusṭāṭ at Giza on the opposite bank of the

Nile. The Fatimid army retired as Mu'nis b. Muẓaffar himself arrived from Iraq. Baghdad had shown its ability to concentrate a superior force in the time available.

The Iraqi troops, however, were unpopular, and were quickly withdrawn. All the old antipathies were resurrected as Egypt was caught between the power in the east and the power in the west. Those who had been in correspondence with the Fatimids were imprisoned; many had their hands and feet cut off by the new governor, Dhakā. But the tension was apparent when Sunnite slogans were painted on the wall of the mosque of ʿAmr. The populace was divided, and when those in favour demonstrated with the support of the prefect of police, they were attacked by troops; the slogans were found to have been effaced. The Berber tribes to the west of Alexandria revolted. In 919, faced by a second Fatimid invasion under Abū 'l-Qāṣim, the son of ʿUbayd Allah, the regime almost collapsed. Yet the pattern of events was the same. Although Alexandria was captured, and the Fatimid army maintained itself in the country for two years, in the end the Ifriqiyan fleet was destroyed by ships brought from Cilicia, Alexandria was recaptured, and Abū 'l-Qāṣim and his men driven back across the desert with great loss by Mu'nis, who once again arrived from Iraq. Mu'nis was rewarded with the title al-Manṣūr, 'the victorious', his mastery of Baghdad assured. Egypt was briefly disturbed by a revolt of the army over pay, but when the veteran Takīn was reappointed in 924, the province remained quiet until his death in 933.

The Fatimids had turned their attention to the west, even though, in 921, the Mahdi had taken up residence in a city built to promote the eastern enterprise. This was al-Mahdiya, 'the city of the Mahdi', situated to the south of Sousse on a well-selected site, a sharp promontory 180 metres across at the neck, which was barred by a wall with an immense iron gate. It was a palace fortress, a capital and a naval base with a harbour cut in the solid rock. It was also a symbol. The courtyard of the great mosque was entered not from either side, but through a grand gateway opposite the entrance to the prayer hall. By this novel means the Mahdi made a ceremonious approach to God. A new formula, 'Come to the better work', was added to the call to prayer throughout his dominions. As the earthly representative of the heavenly Imam, he naturally assumed the position of caliph, Amīr al-Mu'minīn, 'Commander of the Faithful'. The Law was to be administered in accordance with the opinion of Jaʿfar al-Ṣādiq, the sixth Imam. But although the Ismaʿili creed thus became the official standard, there was no mass conversion. The Isma'ilis came to be organized under a Chief *Dā'ī*, or *Dā'ī 'l-Du'āt*. The higher ranks were initiated into a secret though by no means eccentric doctrine; the lower grades were a laity. Together they formed a sect whose members within the country were for the most part the personnel of the regime. After some initial persecution, which contributed to the legends of the school of Kairouan, Sunnite Muslims were merely obliged to bear the affront of heresy in high places. They did so in the belief that any government was better than none, an extension in practice of the *siyāsa shar'iya*, the permission granted to a ruler to exercise his discretion in affairs of state. On this basis they might with a good conscience render unto Caesar the things that were Caesar's, and unto God the things that were God's.

Just as politically, therefore, the Fatimid *da'wa* was one among other Muslim states, so in religion it was one among other groups and denominations. While it professed to be ecumenical, in keeping with the claim of its leader to be the legitimate ruler of Islam, it was in fact polemical, turning to a sacred history to confound its opponents with chapter and verse. The arguments adduced were brought to bear by Fatimid diplomacy to attack an enemy or to secure an ally. To the west of Ifrīqiya, the ideological opposition of Umayyads, Idrisids, Rustamids and Aghlabids had fallen into abeyance. It was reformed and revived by the Fatimids. In 909, the victorious Abū 'Abd Allah drove the dynasty of the Banū Midrār out of Sijilmasa when he went to fetch the Mahdi from the city. While he bided his time in the Tafilelt, Sa'īd b. Ḥusayn may already have attracted a following from the Miknāsa, the people of the Banū Midrār. Together with the Banū Ifrān (Yafrān) and the Maghrāwa, the Miknāsa belonged to the Zanāta, a group of what may have been largely pastoral peoples centred on the critical area to the east, west and south of Tlemcen. These had been prominent among the Ṣufri Khawārij, the followers of Khālid b. Ḥamīd, 'al-Zanātī', and Abū Qurra, 'al-Ifrānī', the Ṣufrī Caliph of Tlemcen, as well as Abū 'l-Qāṣim, 'al-Miknāsī', the founder of Sijilmasa, in the eighth century. They had since been variously submitted to the Idrisids and the Rustamids, but in accordance with the pattern of the ninth century had gone on to produce their own chiefs, such as the lord who had taken the place of an Idrisid at Ṣabra near Tlemcen. Although the tribesmen were still no doubt the naked horde which had overwhelmed Kulthūm in 741, these leaders were more professional warriors, horsemen who may have learned their trade in Spain. The arrival of the Fatimids set them to fight.

In 911, Tahert was finally conquered. Its Ibāḍī community fled into exile at Sedrāta near Wargla in the Sahara, while the remainder shifted back to the original Roman site of Tiaret a few kilometres away. Tiaret was given to the Miknāsa chief Maṣāla b. Ḥabūs, and a Miknāsī *dāʿī* was appointed. Maṣāla was at once opposed by the Banū Midrār, who returned to Sijilmasa after Abū ʿAbd Allah and the Mahdi had gone, and by Muḥammad b. Khazar of the Maghrāwa from the district of Oran. About 917–21 he was nevertheless strong enough to raid Nukūr on the coast of the Rif, to defeat the Idrisid Yaḥyā IV of Fez, and to appoint another chief of the Miknāsa, Mūsā b. Abī ʾl-ʿĀfiya, as overlord of this western region. In 921 Maṣāla installed a more compliant member of the dynasty in Sijilmasa, and in 922/3 deposed Yaḥyā at Fez. The prospect of a powerful Fatimid vassal at Tiaret, however, was destroyed in 924 by the death of Maṣāla at the hands of his Maghrāwa rival, Ibn Khazar. The balance was partly redressed by Abū ʾl-Qāṣim. In 925 the heir apparent strengthened the Zab with the foundation of a new fortified capital at Msila under ʿAlī b. Ḥamdūn; in 927 and 928 he attacked the Maghrāwa, advancing as far as Tiaret. But in 927 the Umayyad *amīr* of Cordoba, ʿAbd al-Raḥmān III, occupied Melilla across the Straits. In the following year, after a long period of disintegration which the Fatimids had tried to exploit, he completed the reunification of Muslim Spain. In 929 he replied to the Ismaʿilite challenge by taking for himself the title of caliph, basing a military regime upon the jihad, holy war against the Christian infidel and the Fatimid impostor. Ceuta was garrisoned in 931, while Mūsā b. Abī ʾl-ʿĀfiya went over to his side. Expeditions from Ifrīqiya in 933 and 935 failed to end his influence. The power of Mūsā was broken, but in his place the Idrisids returned as clients of Cordoba. The main results of the expedition of the Fatimid general Maysūr in 935 were further to the east. A loyal governor was placed in Tiaret, while a chief of the Talkāta people of the mountains round Algiers, Zīrī b. Manād, was encouraged to build a citadel at Ashīr overlooking the plateau to the south. Hope of a Zanāta ally in the region of Tlemcen gave way to reliance upon a less distant people to uphold the Fatimid interest in the west.

The new policy is attributable to a new caliph. Abū ʾl-Qāṣim succeeded his father ʿUbayd Allah, the Mahdi, in 934, taking the significant title of al-Qāʾim, 'the bringer of the Resurrection'. It would seem that he, rather than his father, was regarded as the finally awaited one, the revealed Imam. Over the last ten years of his reign, ʿUbayd Allah is reputed to have deferred to his son as to one greater than himself. As caliph, al-Qā'im may have been the first to employ as a sign of his supreme authority the jewelled umbrella which became one of the distinctive emblems of the dynasty.[1] On the other hand, al-Qā'im did not set out to startle or to shock the Muslim world by the extravagance of his powers. Under him first rose to prominence the man always known for his authority on the Law of the sect as al-Qāḍī 'l Nuʿmān. In the many writings of this chief scholar and propagandist there is none of the philosophical speculation current in Shiʿite writing in Iraq, or of the antinomianism of which the Ismaʿilis were accused. The exposition of the Qāḍī was firmly grounded in Muslim scholarship, and designed to show that, like the Christian Messiah, the Fatimid Imam had come to fulfil rather than to abrogate the Law. As such it is probable that the primary intention was not to win converts, but to make out a good case. The arrival of the *Qā'im*, in fact, only served to confirm the character of the *daʿwa* as this had developed since its establishment in Ifrīqiya. And if from this point of view the advent of the millennium was muted, so was it also in politics. In 934 the new ruler sent out a fleet which sacked Genoa, but the expedition of Maysūr to the west in the following year served in the event to cover a withdrawal. The absence of these troops in Morocco may account for the failure to intervene effectively in Egypt in 936, but the episode reveals an unreadiness to exploit a situation that had been developing in the east since 933.

The crisis which supervened in Egypt on the death of Takīn in that year was part of the collapse of the regime of Mu'nis b. Muẓaffar in Iraq. In 932 Mu'nis had deposed and killed the Caliph Muqtadir, but in 933 he was himself overthrown and executed. The immediate cause was that recurrent weakness, an inability to pay the troops. Those who mutinied in Egypt expelled the son of Takīn, and attacked and killed the *ʿāmil* for his tightfistedness. It was the occasion for a return to old rivalries. For the first time, in the chronicler al-Kindī, we find the use of the term Mashāriqa (sing. Mashriqī), 'Easterners', applied to the mainly Turkish forces who stood out for Ibn Takīn against a new governor, Ibn Kayghalagh. Those who supported Ibn Kayghalagh, on the other hand, are called Maghāriba (sing. Maghribī), 'Westerners'. Towards the end of the century the use of this term was justified by the presence of a large force of Kutāma Berbers from the Maghrib, 'the West'. There had been Berbers in the Egyptian army from a very early date; if they do not appear in the accounts of Ibn Ṭūlūn, it is note-

[1] Ibn ʿIdhārī, *Bayān*, I, 208 trans. 300–1: the statement that he did *not* employ the umbrella may represent a copyist's error.

worthy that among the generals of Hārūn b. Khumārawayh was one al-Barbarī. Egypt was indeed the obvious source of supply for the Berber soldiers in the service of Mu'nis in Iraq who killed the Caliph Muqtadir. But in Egypt it may be that the term Maghāriba was not yet so precise, merely an opposite of 'Easterner' which embraced troops of several origins.

Initially the Maghāriba were victorious. At the accession of a new caliph in Baghdad in 934, Ibn Takīn reappeared in Egypt, claiming appointment in succession to Ibn Kayghalagh, but he was defeated in battle and exiled to Upper Egypt. A final attempt to restore some order to the empire, however, led to the installation at Damascus of one Faḍl b. Jaʿfar, charged with the supervision of Syria and Egypt, and in particular with the collection of revenue, which since the recovery of Egypt from the Tulunids had once again been a separate office. Ibn Kayghalagh was dismissed, and Muḥammad b. Ṭughj b. Juff, the son of the old Tulunid general, was nominated in his place. Ibn Kayghalagh and the Maghāriba prepared to resist, but Ibn Kayghalagh stood down at the approach of Muḥammad b. Ṭughj in 935, supported by the Cilician fleet. Abandoned, the Maghāriba succeeded in capturing the fleet as it sailed on the inland waterways. Under their captain Ḥabashī b. Aḥmad, they raided Fusṭāṭ, then escaped via Alexandria and Barce to Ifrīqiya. In response to their appeal, Abū 'l-Qāṣim, al-Qā'im, sent an expedition in 936 which captured Alexandria, but was quickly driven out. It was not to be compared to the great invasions of 914 and 919. The Fatimids were not prepared to take advantage of the general instability in the east.

In Iraq the struggle for power continued as the army commanders succeeded each other and the caliphs were deposed and blinded, while the Carmathians snatched the Black Stone from the Kaʿba at Mecca, Mosul in northern Iraq fell to the Hamdanid dynasty, and western Persia was overrun by the Buwayhids or Buyids, the Shiʿite leaders of a people from the mountains of the Caspian who in 934 made their capital at Shiraz in the south. In Syria, Faḍl b. Jaʿfar was at the centre of a complicated marriage alliance between himself, Muḥammad b. Ṭughj, and Ibn Rāyiq, the *amīr al-umarā'* (commander-in-chief) at Baghdad. In 939 the arrangement brought Ibn Ṭughj the honorific Persian title of al-Ikhshīd, i.e. Servant (of the caliph). At the end of the year, driven from Baghdad by a rival, Ibn Rāyiq himself occupied Syria, but his death in 941 left the country to Muḥammad. The power of the Ikhshīd was formally extended in 943, when his authority over

Egypt and Syria was recognized by the caliph, and he received on the one hand the lordship of Cilicia, and on the other the government of the Holy Places of Mecca and Medina. These were mixed blessings, for Cilicia was coming under Byzantine attack, and Mecca and Medina were vulnerable to attack by the Carmathians from across the peninsula. In 944 Ibn Ṭughj suffered an actual reverse when Aleppo and the north of Syria was lost to the Hamdanids from Mosul. But, like Ibn Ṭūlūn, he had successfully created his own Egyptian dominion. In 945 the redistribution of power in the Fertile Crescent was complete when the Buwayhids took Baghdad itself. Although Shiʿites, they refused to recognize the Fatimid claim to the caliphate, preferring to install themselves as protectors of the ʿAbbasids. In this way the old line survived, but as an anomaly, its members holding an office stripped of all but the name. When Ibn Ṭughj died in 946, the ʿAbbasid empire had at last disappeared, its government finally dispersed among more competent successors.

As the soldiers reached a solution to the problem of power which had proved in the end impossible to achieve through the old *dawla*, the incidence of popular rebellion declined. The Fatimids and the Carmathians had turned their successful movements into states. In Egypt, one Ibn al-Sarrāj, an ʿAlawite rebel who 'went out' in Upper Egypt in 942 and quickly fled to the west, did indeed continue the tradition. But the activities of the Maghāriba had shown not merely that the Qā'im, of whom great things were to be expected, was unready to act, but that agitation was largely confined to the army. If dissatisfaction and zeal remained, spontaneity had been eclipsed by professionalism. It was ironical therefore that in Ifrīqiya matters were very different. Not only did the Qā'im not go abroad to seize the power he claimed; his reign came to an end in the midst of a revolution inspired by the fervour his father had aroused. This fervour had always been dangerous. Following the assassination of Abū ʿAbd Allah, ʿUbayd Allah had been faced with a rival Mahdi among the Kutāma. In addition to the Barghawāṭa and their prophet in the far west, a prophet called Hā Mīm, after one of the suras or chapters of the Koran, had appeared in the Moroccan Rif in the 920s. In 934, on the death of ʿUbayd Allah, a rival *Qā'im*, Ibn Ṭālūt, rebelled among the Berbers of Tripoli. The weapon turned decisively against the dynasty in the hand of Abū Yazīd, the Ṣāḥib al-Ḥimār, 'the Man on a Donkey'. He was born, it is said, in the Sudan to a merchant of the Djerid by a black slave bought at Tadmekka, hence his further appellation, al-Ḥabashī 'l-Aswad, 'black Ethiop'. Likewise he is said to have spent a long career as scholar and teacher at Tahert and in the Djerid, becoming the head of the Nukkārī branch of the Ibāḍīs, those who believed that an unjust ruler should be deposed. Much of this is perhaps once again an 'imitation of Muḥammad', in this case distorted by hostile reports. What seems clear is that he spent many unaccounted-for years among the Hawwāra people of the Aures mountains between Tunisia and the Zab, whence he emerged in 943.

Because in the end he failed, Abū Yazīd has a bad reputation in Ismāʿīlī, Sunni and Ibāḍī accounts alike, as the 'enemy of God', the great destroyer, one of the legendary scourges of the land. Because of this reputation, it is difficult to perceive the reasons for his initial success. The fact that the regime gave offence to the pious is not a sufficient explanation. Fatimid taxes were deemed illegal – that is, not according to the Law. This however was true of any Muslim government, whose revenues like its administration were based on other things besides the *sharīʿa*. There is no evidence that such taxes were an excessive burden on the economy, although they were collected strictly, and doubtless gave cause for material as well as moral complaint. Probably more important was a harsh policy towards the tribes among whom the rebellion began. Before Abū Yazīd made any appeal to the people at large as the defender of true religion against the heretic, the populace against the tyrant, or self-interest against the state, he should be credited with achieving the kind of military following built up among the tribes of the Aures which Abū ʿAbd Allah had created among the Kutāma. Like the Mahdi, he came as a deliverer. Once begun, his campaign attracted the wider following which seems to have joined in every major rebellion, and it proved Abū 'l-Qāṣim al-Qā'im as vulnerable as any Aghlabid faced with a general rising. Ignoring the forces centred on Msila to the west, Abū Yazīd went east from the Aures towards Kairouan, riding, it is said, on the donkey which gave him his soubriquet and his apocalyptic allure. Taking the city while his opponents were disconcerted by a revolt at Tunis, he received the approval of the *ʿulamā'*, and exchanged his previous austerity for what the sources condemn as luxury, but which were probably the trappings of sovereignty. Coins were struck in his name. From Kairouan, Abū Yazīd went on to defeat and kill Maysūr, the Fatimid commander-in-chief, advancing with legendary atrocity to the siege of Mahdiya. Begun in January 945, the siege lasted eight months, during which time the power of the Qā'im extended no further than the great iron doors of his fortress city.

Mahdiya, however, proved impregnable. When Abū Yazīd eventually retired, the Fatimid forces broke out of the city, while those of the Zab under ʿAlī b. Ḥamdūn and Zīrī b. Manād took the rebel in the rear. When the Qā'im died in May 946, the final battle was at hand. Kairouan barricaded itself against Abū Yazīd on his return from an attempt upon Sousse. The historic capital of the country was occupied instead by Ismāʿīl, the new Imam, who fought off the rebel's assault until the battle was won. Abū Yazīd fled to the west, while the Andalusian fleet sent to his aid by ʿAbd al-Raḥmān III, in the expectation of his victory, turned back. The announced revolution came to nothing. During the winter of 946–7, the would-be sovereign was pursued by Ismāʿīl and his lieutenants, Jaʿfar, son of ʿAlī b. Ḥamdūn, who had died in the fighting, and Zīrī b. Manād. In August 947 Abū Yazīd was killed near Msila. His skin, stuffed with straw, made a fearful trophy.[1] Tiaret which had defected, was recovered. Ismāʿīl returned to take the title of al-Manṣūr, 'the Victorious', and to build at Kairouan a new palace fortress under the name of Ṣabra, 'Fortitude', known as al-Manṣūriya, 'the city of Manṣūr'. Situated to the south-south-east of the city, it took the place of Raqqāda a kilometre or two away, which became a park and a parade ground. To it, from Mahdiya, was transferred the seat of government. The dynasty took on a new lease of life. The last resistance of the Aures was overcome, while the defence of the west was assured by Zīrī b. Manād at Ashīr, which was enlarged and strengthened. Zīrī's son Buluggīn occupied Miliana at the head of the Chelif, on the edge of the territory of the Maghrāwa leader Muḥammad b. Khazar. Jaʿfar retained his father's seat at Msila as governor of the Zab. With Abū Yazīd safely accounted for as the great Enemy who should come against the Imam before the final triumph, al-Manṣūr was free to attend to the ultimate victory. A symbolic act introduced the new era. In 951 the Carmathians were persuaded to return to Mecca the Black Stone they had removed from the Kaʿba twenty years before. In 953, however, al-Manṣūr died. It was left to his son, al-Muʿizz li-Dīn Allah, 'he who is mighty by the religion of God', to pursue the great enterprise to a fresh conclusion.

CIRCUMSTANCES LEADING UP TO THE CONQUEST OF EGYPT

Circumstances had changed yet again. By the middle of the tenth century AD, the troubles which had afflicted both Islam and Christendom

[1] For Abū Yazīd, cf. *Encyclopaedia of Islam*, 2nd edn (Leiden and London, 1954—), under ʿAbū Yazīd'.

over the past hundred years had resulted in a new political order. The world about the Mediterranean was dominated by a series of states which owed their success to victory at home and abroad. ʿAbd al-Raḥmān III had refounded the Umayyad dominion of Andalus. In the Christian West, Germany and Italy had been formed into a new empire by Otto the Great. Legislating against the estates of the aristocracy in favour of the property of smallholders, Romanus I had recreated the Byzantine empire as a formidable power. The Buwayhids had taken control of Iraq. In Egypt and Syria the survival of the Ikhshidid Dynasty was assured after the death of its founder by his *ghulām*, 'page', the black eunuch Abū 'l-Misk Kāfūr, on behalf of his young son Unūjūr. The name is a pun, Misk meaning 'musk', which is black, and Kāfūr meaning 'camphor', which is white. Coming to Fusṭāṭ as a slave either from Abyssinia or more probably from Nubia, he became the virtual ruler of the country in succession to his patron. For a man from south of the Sahara, his achievement was unique, surpassing that of *sūdān* who rose from the ranks of *ʿabīd* and *fityān* to stop, like the Fatimid commander Ṣandal, at the rank of general. His achievement was so great, however, because in other respects it was typical of a form of palace government in which the queen mother was a central figure, while the chief eunuch, the master of the household, became an officer whose responsibilities might amount to those of head of government, relegating the vizier (*wazīr*), the head of the administration, to a subordinate position. In Fatimid Ifrīqiya at this time, the post was held by the eunuch Jawdhar. There, as in Egypt, it carried the title of *Ustādh*, 'Tutor', since it involved the education of the royal children. It was this duty which, with the connivance of the queen mother, gave Kāfūr his authority on the death of Muḥammad b. Ṭughj, since he took power as guardian of the young prince. That power he retained, despite at least one attempt by Unūjūr to break free.

Relations with the Buwayhids of Baghdad were good, and the fiction of ʿAbbasid suzerainty was upheld by the recital of the *khuṭba*, the address at the Friday prayer, in the name of the reigning caliph. The attempt of the Hamdanid ruler of Aleppo, Sayf al-Dawla, to seize Damascus on the death of Ibn Ṭughj was defeated, although Cilicia was lost; having thus acquired control over the Byzantine frontier, Sayf al-Dawla turned away to put his energies into annual campaigns against the empire in the north. Control of Egypt was established in 947 with the defeat of the rebellion of Ghalbūn, the governor of Upper Egypt. As for many years past, the far south was beyond effective control;

nevertheless, when after a raid on the oases of Kharga in 950, the Nubians invaded Upper Egypt in 956, the Egyptians retaliated with the sack of Qasr Ibrim, the Nubian fortress on the Nile some 210 km south of Aswan. In 954 the Byzantine fleet descended on Farama on the coast of the Delta. For the moment, however, such incidents were isolated. Kāfūr controlled the country by patronage, farming the taxes for revenue and, it is said, keeping his protégé on a very modest allowance; it is likely that 'the palace' in general, however, was well provided with estates. As far as the administration was concerned, it was probably a formative period, when the 'men of the pen' as distinct from the 'men of the sword' were established in offices, notably the *Dīwān al-Rasā'il* or *Dīwān al-Inshā'*, the chancery, which continued to develop over the next two hundred years. These offices bred their own traditions, presented by a long series of authors who expounded the history of the country as well as the history and practice of the administration from a clerical point of view. In these traditions a much less shadowy founding figure than Ibn Mudabbir is the Jewish convert Ya'qūb b. Killīs, who was discovered by Kāfūr, and went on to dominate the administration for twenty years thereafter. Whatever his achievements, he may be taken to represent the continuity between the administration of the Ikhshidids and their successors.

Despite such professional memories, however, too little is known about the government of the Ikhshidids, partly because the period is still very early for information to survive, partly because al-Kindī died at Fusṭāṭ in 961 before he could complete the *Kitāb al-Wulāt*, the 'History of the Governors', which is the essential narrative of the period since the conquest. His work closes with the death of Muḥammad b. Ṭughj, and the continuation of the story down to the death of Kāfūr is not only slight, but tails off rapidly. This dearth of information is not made good elsewhere, but is in fact characteristic. The author responsible was a younger contemporary, Ibn Zūlāq, who died in 997, and added the postscript to al-Kindī while himself composing a work which displayed the same bias, a long notice of Muḥammad b. Ṭughj, followed by something much briefer and more anecdotal on his successors. It is probably to be explained by the fact that for Ibn Zūlāq, and hence for those who followed him, the later Ikhshidids lived like the Tulunids in the shadow of the future. In their case, they were not so much blamed or lamented as ignored, while Kāfūr, their mentor, was placed in a limbo of stories appropriate to his origins and career. It was a treatment which came to be reserved for chief ministers, ensuring for them a place of honour in the records of the 'men of the pen', while very often disguising the circumstances of their political career. As far as the history of Egypt was concerned, a period of some twenty years was effectively sterilized, a period during which the future was prepared elsewhere.

The Fatimid threat was not immediately apparent. The return of the Black Stone by the Carmathians in 951 was a symbolic act which asserted the claim of the Fatimids to be the true protectors of the Holy Places, and hence the true rulers of Islam. It was directed therefore at the ʿAbbasids, but more specifically at the Ikhshidids, on whom the guardianship had been bestowed. In its own way it recognized the changes which had taken place over the past forty years: while the ʿAbbasid caliph had become a figurehead, Egypt had become a fully independent power. More than ever before, it stood in the way of Fatimid ambitions in the east, but equally it called for circumspection. As the Qāḍī al-Nuʿmān approached the height of his skill and influence, his writings developed the Fatimid case at a high intellectual level. While the propaganda mounted, however, and the missionaries worked in secret throughout the Middle East, the Fatimid forces were engaged in the west. The efforts of the Ifriqiyan navy had been directed against the western extremity of the Byzantine empire, in southern Italy. From the time of Ibrāhīm II, Sicily had been ruled from North Africa only with difficulty. Troubles which began in 936 were not put down until 941, and recommenced during the rebellion of Abū Yazīd. In 947 Ḥasan al-Kalbī recovered the island for Manṣūr, taking his place alongside Zīrī b. Manād and Jaʿfar b. ʿAlī as a lieutenant with sufficient independence to transmit his office to his son. He and his descendants resumed the raids of the Aghlabids upon the Italian mainland with considerable success. Meanwhile Muʿizz, like his grandfather al-Qā'im, turned his attention to Morocco. On the death of Manṣūr, the governor of Tiaret, Yaʿlā al-Ifrānī, changed his allegiance to Cordoba, prompting his rival, the Maghrāwa leader Muḥammad b. Khazar, to make his peace with the Fatimids. The old rulers of Sijilmasa, the Banū Midrār, were once again independent, although the influence of the Umayyads can be seen in the reigning prince's abandonment of Ṣufrī Kharijism in favour of Malikite orthodoxy. Northern Morocco, where the Idrisids still survived, was dominated by ʿAbd al-Raḥmān III through Ceuta and Tangier. In 955/6, however, the Fatimid fleet raided the Spanish port of Almeria, and in 958/9 the Fatimid general Jawhar overran the whole of the region at stake, capturing Tiaret, Sijilmasa and Fez.

With the west temporarily secure, Muʿizz could turn at last to the east. In doing so he enjoyed an inestimable advantage, the affluence which came from economic prosperity.[1] The description of the Ismāʿīlī traveller Ibn Ḥawqal, who visited the Maghrib in 947–51 and again in 971, may well have been biased. It is nevertheless compatible with the description by his Andalusian contemporary, Ibn al-Warrāq, preserved by the eleventh-century author al-Bakrī, writing in Spain in 1068. Through its officials, who bought their posts and retained anything which they collected in addition to what was due, the Fatimid regime levied taxes on persons and property, agriculture, pasture and commerce. Abuses were clearly possible, and Ibn Ḥawqal's statement that twice as much could have been collected with little more severity seems ingenuous. On the other hand, it is equally clear that Ifrīqiya could afford to pay. Since the Arab conquests, geography and history had combined to recreate a market economy in the country after the return towards subsistence in late classical times. The *sūq*, the market, might take the form of an open space on neutral ground between two peoples, or it might become the focus of a new settlement. It was reproduced more substantially in the towns, which drew in foodstuffs and primary products in return for manufactures and luxuries. By such means local demands were met, while articles might travel across the country or enter from outside. The network supported the regular trade of the caravans, which tended to move along particular routes at particular times, acquiring the name of *mawāṣim* (sing. *mawṣim*), 'seasons' (whence 'monsoon'). Traffic of this kind, duplicated by shipping at sea, brought goods over long distances, the specialities of each region to be exchanged for those of another. Ifrīqiya was at the centre of such a system, attracting the trade of the Mediterranean, North Africa and the Sahara. Over the years, supply and demand had built up to a high level.

The *sūq*, the actual market, was of great importance. In the countryside it was governed by custom as a time and place of truce; in the towns it was regulated by an overseer, the *muḥtasib*. There it became much more elaborate, a place where things were made as well as bought and sold. Particular commodities acquired particular importance. Grain, for example, the most basic of all, was traded in the first instance to make up for temporary shortages. Thus it tended to move from the better grain-growing areas to more pastoral regions and to peoples

[1] Examples of the period from the tenth to the twelfth century illustrating this reconstruction of the way in which the market economy worked will be found in H. R. Idris, *La Berbérie orientale sous les Zīrīdes, Xe–XIIe siècles* (Paris, 1962), 603–86; S. D. F. Goitein, *A Mediterranean society*, 2 vols. (Berkeley and Los Angeles, 1967—, in progress).

whose cultivation was more erratic. In the case of cities, the demand for grain was a constant, often leading to long-distance trade. Kairouan was regularly supplied from the region of Beja in the area of higher rainfall to the north-west, while the cities of the Sahel imported grain from Sicily. In return they exported olives and oil from the coastal districts they controlled. The oasis cities of the Djerid exported dates from their extensive palm groves. The pressing of olive-oil, however, was an elementary industry, and this aspect became more pronounced when it was a question of animals and animal products. All cities imported animals for meat; the butchers, who performed a religious function when they slaughtered a beast by cutting its throat as the Law required, were members of a wealthy and important profession. At the same time they supplied the hides and skins for a large tanning industry, while the wool and hair went to make cloth. It was the cloth industry which had become the distinguishing feature of Ifriqiyan production for export, from regions such as the Jebel Nefusa as well as from the towns. The cloth was mainly woollen, but there was cotton and linen, and even silk was woven and embroidered. Such fabrics, of varying fineness, enabled Ifrīqiya to sustain its position as a focus of trade in the Mediterranean and in the Sahara, where cloth was not only a commodity but a form of currency. In return, slaves continued to come northwards into and across the desert.

In the *sūq*, goods might be bought from the producer or the maker. Even in local commerce, however, the professional trader was a prominent figure, often working as an agent, *simsār* (pl. *samāsira*), entrusted with the sale of goods in return for a commission, as well as buying and selling on his own account. Such middlemen handled individual items from jewellery to slaves, or bulk commodities like a crop produced by a number of small-holders or gathered by a landlord as rent from his tenants. In trade over a distance, they acted in similar fashion, owning part of the stock themselves while undertaking to sell goods entrusted to them, or to employ money given them for the purpose. *Qirāḍ* was a general name for such an undertaking, but there were different kinds of contract, probably resembling those found at a later date in the trade of Ifrīqiya with Italy. The merchant, *tājir* (pl. *tujjār*), was responsible for transport; on land, pack-animals would be bought and sold for each journey, but at sea the merchant might be the owner, sometimes the captain, of the ship. To assist him he relied heavily on his family, which might extend to the clan, the community or the confession, as with the Jews and the Ibāḍīs. Sometimes whole peoples were involved, as with the tribes who obtained some share in the traffic passing through their country, perhaps by demanding payment, perhaps by supplying transport, or perhaps by monopolizing the trade. In such cases political leadership and organization were involved, as at Zawila in the Fezzan, where the family of the Banū Khaṭṭāb became rulers at the beginning of the tenth century.

In Ifrīqiya, the *sulṭān*, the government, although not ostensibly a commercial institution, was in fact closely concerned, and exercised a powerful influence. This came only initially, and partially, from the taxation of trade. It arose more fundamentally from what the state had at its disposal. When many taxes were paid in kind, the state came into possession of much of the country's surplus, quite apart from what was derived from the monarch's estates, largely leased to cultivators under various sharecropping agreements. Produce thus accumulated was used for payment, or offered for sale. In either case, it came onto the market. Governors, tax-collectors and troops, who took or received much of their reward in kind, were important suppliers of commodities, such as grain, to the public. So was the ruler himself. The business was handled by merchants, who naturally profited; the *tājir al-sulṭān*, the 'sultan's merchant', who acted for the government, was a great man. Such merchants extended their activities on behalf of their patrons to foreign trade, employing the capital entrusted to them in ventures on a grand scale; the Fatimid raid upon Almeria in 955/6, for example, is said to have been in revenge for the capture at sea of a Fatimid vessel sailing from Sicily to Ifrīqiya by a much larger ship belonging to ʿAbd al-Raḥmān III, bound for the east with merchandise. The interest of the state, hardly distinguishable from that of its officers, became almost equally indistinguishable from that of trade. This was all the more true since the state and its aristocracy were at the same time great consumers, their wealth affecting demand as well as supply. The more expensive goods and services, jewellery, perfumes, spices, silks, armour, weapons, horses, skilled slaves, and all the arts and crafts which went into palatial building, decorating and furnishing, were most obviously concerned – not forgetting parchment, paper and books. In this way what began with taxes and rents, augmented by sales and investments, was eventually distributed. The income, and consequently the demand, of the *ʿāmma*, the populace, was reduced on the one hand but increased on the other.

It is not possible to say what proportion of a gross national product was represented by this income and expenditure, but if they are regarded as typical of a fairly broad upper class, the proportion which they represented may have been fairly high. That the balance between what was taken and what was put back was favourable, and led to a measure of economic growth which persisted through the inevitable years of bad harvests and disasters both natural and man-made, might appear from the condition of the towns, which continued to flourish after their great expansion in the eighth and ninth centuries. Tunis in particular probably continued to grow; the expansion of Mahdiya may have taken place at the expense of Kairouan, and the new port certainly seems to have declined with the moving of the capital back to the older city. Another indicator, however, is provided by the history of the Saharan trade-routes in the tenth century, and especially by the trade in gold. Although Abū Yazīd was ostensibly a Kharijite, he was not representative of the Ibadite community, which repudiated the man and his movement. With Muʿizz, the relations of the Ibadite peoples of the Djerid and the Jebel Nefusa were as good as could be expected from this turbulent region. This resulted from the general attempt of the caliph to procure allies, but also reflected the prosperity of the trade into and out of Ifrīqiya with which these peoples were concerned. A sign of this prosperity is provided by the ruins of Sedrata in the desert near Wargla, where the Ibāḍīs of Tahert took refuge after their expulsion in 911. The remains of the mosque and of some substantial residences show considerable decoration influenced by the art of the Muslim east.[1] Most important of all, however, is the appearance at this time of a direct connection across the western Sahara between Sijilmasa and the settlement of Awdaghust on the southern edge of the desert.

The connection between the two centres, which for al-Yaʿqūbī was a mere rumour of 'the land of Ghusṭ', was obvious to Ibn Ḥawqal, who visited Sijilmasa and was impressed by the value of trans-Saharan business.[2] His report appears to be confirmed by the excavation of the site of Tegdaoust in southern Mauritania, which has yielded articles of the Fatimid period in Ifrīqiya.[3] From al-Bakrī, it would seem that half of the merchants at Awdaghust were Ifriqiyan, either from Kairouan or

[1] Cf. M. van Berchem, 'Deux campagnes de fouilles sur la site de l'ancienne cité musulmane de Sedrata', *Actes des Congrès Nationaux des Sociétés Savantes* (Section d'Archéologie, Congrès 79, Algiers, 1954; Paris, 1957).

[2] Cf. N. Levtzion, 'Ibn Ḥawqal, the cheque, and Awdaghost', *Journal of African History*, 1968, **9**, 2, 223–33; M. Brett, 'Ifrīqiya as a market for Saharan trade from the tenth to the twelfth century AD', *Journal of African History*, 1969, **10**, 3, 347–64, esp. 358–9.

[3] Cf. D. S. Robert, 'Les Fouilles de Tegdaoust', *Journal of African History*, 1970, **11**, 4, 471–93.

from the Ibadite region, who had abandoned the long route via Wargla to the Niger bend in favour of the shorter though more arduous crossing to the west; the remainder were Zanāta, presumably from Sijilmasa itself. Their trade, at least in part, was centred on gold. This came as *tibr*, dust, which was used in Awdaghust for currency, al-Bakrī noting that they had no silver for this purpose as in North Africa and Spain.[1] For export it was refined and made into twisted wire. Although gold had previously reached the Maghrib by the older routes from the western Sudan, this sudden boom, comparable to the gold-rush in the Wadi Allaqi a hundred years before, indicated a new demand for a new use. Gold had always been valued as treasure to be hoarded in works of art and craft, from gold vessels and jewellery to garments embroidered with gold thread and illuminated manuscripts. Its use as currency, however, was restricted. Copper was used for the lowest denomination of the coinage, the *fals* or *fils* (pl. *fulūs*), from Latin *follis*, the copper coin of Byzantium. Above the *fals* was the silver *dirham*, from Greek *drachma*, derived however from the coinage of the old Persian empire. The *dirham* was valued at about a tenth of the gold *dīnār*, from Latin *denarius*, the equivalent of the Byzantine *solidus*. In fact it is likely, as al-Bakrī's reference to Awdaghust suggests, that normally only the copper and the silver coins were used as money, the dinar being on the whole a money of account, a means of expressing a value rather than an actual sum. A principal purpose of the dinar as a coin was to be a mark of sovereignty on the part of the ruler in whose name it was struck. Throughout the ninth century, it would seem that gold was sufficiently plentiful in Iraq to be used as a currency, but in the crisis of the 920s and 930s the gold disappeared, and the Buwayhids returned to a silver standard. In Egypt, Ibn Ṭūlūn and his son may have been able to increase the circulation of gold. By the middle of the tenth century, however, it was the turn of Ifrīqiya. The Fatimid caliph required gold not only for treasure, but for war. His demand, making itself felt on the market, led to the opening up of the route through Sijilmasa in a way which owed little to the fleeting Fatimid control of the city. Under Muʿizz, this substantial addition to the range of the Ifriqiyan economy yielded a supply large enough to be employed for political ends.

As Jawhar departed for the Maghrib al-Aqṣā in 958, the Byzantine

[1] al-Bakrī, *Kitāb al-masālik wa'l mamālik*, ed. by M. G. de Slane (Algiers, 1911); French trans. by M. G. de Slane, *Description de l'Afrique septentrionale*, 2nd edn (Algiers, 1911–13; reprinted Paris, 1965), 158, trans. 300.

generals Nicephorus Phocas and John Tzimisces at long last turned successfully upon the aggressive Sayf al-Dawla in Aleppo with the taking of two cities in northern Syria and Iraq. As Jawhar returned to Kairouan in 960, Nicephorus Phocas launched the invasion of Crete, occupied by Muslim pirates since 827. In 961 the reconquest of the island was complete. In reply, Sayf al-Dawla, as champion of Islam, preached jihad against the Christian enemy. This led to no more than riots against the Copts in Egypt, where Unūjūr had died in 960 to be succeeded by his brother ʿAlī, still under the tutelage of Kāfūr. In 962 Nicephorus advanced into Syria to capture Aleppo itself, although Sayf al-Dawla held out in the citadel. In Egypt the Nile was low, and Berber tribes coming from the west into the region of Alexandria unsettled the Arabs of the western Ḥawf. These Arabs, now amalgamated into the tribes of the Banū Qurra, began to raid into the Delta. When Nicephorus Phocas became emperor in 963, these difficulties increased; the Carmathians from across the Arabian peninsula attacked Ikhshidid Syria, while the Nubians advanced into Upper Egypt as far as Akhmim. With the Nile flood again low, 964 saw the destruction of an expedition sent against the Berbers around Alexandria; a second expedition against the beduin of Transjordan had achieved little. The Carmathians continued their attacks in conjunction with the tribes, and the combination of such raiders east and west began to be a serious nuisance. In 965 Nicephorus Phocas completed the conquest of Cilicia, and the fleet which he sent to occupy Cyprus destroyed what was probably the whole of the Egyptian navy as it cruised off the island. Standing at the peak of his career, in 966 Kāfūr was recognized by the ʿAbbasid caliph as the legitimate ruler of Egypt in succession to ʿAlī, but the Byzantine emperor was at the gates of Antioch, the beduin plundered the pilgrimage from Damascus to Mecca of wealth belonging to Syrian refugees fleeing to the Holy Places, and the Nile continued low.

The Byzantine initiative was essentially independent; the series of low Niles was unfortunate; but the attacks of the Carmathians and the nomads were concerted. A grand design was shaping, in which Fatimid diplomacy, backed by Fatimid preaching and by Fatimid bribes, envisaged the isolation of the Ikhshidid regime, and its steady erosion. At the court of Muʿizz, the influence of the venerable Qāḍī 'l-Nuʿmān was at its height. His works, submitted to the caliph for correction or confirmation by this supreme representative of God on earth, set out in full the doctrines and the claims of the Fatimids. The propaganda of the *daʿwa* was relayed to the Faithful as far away as India by the missionary apparatus of the sect. The Byzantine victories could be exploited. The Carmathians were willing to co-operate to their own advantage. The tribes were not simply marauders from outside. On the borders of Egypt they lived alongside the government, habitually demanding concessions which were as often denied. Aswan was under the control of Arab groups. To the west of the Nile in the oases of Dakhla and Farafra, the Banū 'l-ʿAbdūn were a Lawāta Berber family ruling over a Coptic agricultural population. Beside them, according to Ibn Ḥawqal, dwelt the Arab tribes of the Banū Hilāl, who made their summer quarters in the oases at the time of the harvest. Already it is likely that they represented an amalgam of peoples, as the underlying process of fission and fusion broke down existing groups, while others formed upon dominant lineages, leading to a steady transformation of the inhabitants of the eastern Sahara from Berber into Arab. In the north, the Banū Qurra continued a long tradition of revolt. Against the perpetual drift of individual families into the peasant population of the valley, long after their ancestors had been excluded from the regular army, the prospect of something more rewarding than the simple nomadic way of life helped to keep the bands together on the fringe of the military and political system. In the 960s, such peoples provided the Fatimids with the material for a widespread coalition.

Alliances were made with the Ibāḍī shaykhs of Tripolitania. Beginning in 966, as Jawhar set out again for the west on a leisurely tax-collecting tour, preparations were made for a stately march upon Egypt. The wells along the route were inspected, and as far as the frontier town of Ajdābiya the building of fortified pavilions was undertaken to provide the commander of the army, or the caliph himself, with accommodation at each stage of the journey. In 967, as the veteran Sayf al-Dawla died at Aleppo, the Fatimids made peace with the Byzantines in Sicily. The Christian empire resigned itself to the loss of the island, while both sides were free to pursue their converging ambitions in the Levant. Kāfūr, in his capacity as guardian of the Holy Places, negotiated the return by the Carmathians of some of the plunder captured by the beduin the previous year. At the beginning of 968 he received from Baghdad robes of office and the honorific title of *Ustādh*, which he had borne in Egypt since the days of Muḥammad b. Ṭughj, but three months later he died, to be succeeded by the child Aḥmad, son of ʿAlī, whose claims he had previously set aside. Real power fell to Jaʿfar b. Faḍl b. al-Furāt, the vizier who had been for so long subordinate to the chief eunuch, while the regent Ḥasan b. ʿUbayd Allah, a cousin of ʿAlī, took charge of Syria and Palestine. It was a fragile arrangement. Ya'qūb b. Killīs, the Jewish convert whom Kāfūr had promoted in the administration at the expense of Ja'far, fled to the Fatimid caliph Mu'izz. In October the Carmathians overran Syria, driving out Ḥasan, who returned to Egypt to imprison the vizier. Meanwhile Nicephoras Phocas laid siege to Antioch.

Jawhar returned to Ifrīqiya with the tribute of the west to find a great army assembled. In January 969 Ja'far b. Faḍl was released and reinstated, and Ḥasan returned to Syria, buying off the Carmathians with an indemnity and the promise of an annual tribute. But in February Jawhar set out from Kairouan, and by May he was at Alexandria. The Ikhshidid regime, impoverished by years of famine, given up for lost by those who regarded a Fatimid victory as inevitable, was divided, with a majority in favour of surrender. Ja'far sent to negotiate the entry of Jawhar into the capital. It was delayed only by a brief resistance from the Ikhshidid guard. In July Jawhar took possession of Fusṭāṭ, and immediately traced out the site of a new palace city to be a capital worthy of his master. This was beyond the area of al-Qaṭā'i', the city of Aḥmad b. Ṭūlūn, still further to the north-east of Fusṭāṭ where the Ikhshidids had had their residence on the bank of the Khalīj, the large canal which had once connected the Nile at Babylon with the Red Sea. The new city of al-Qāhira, Cairo, 'the Victorious', was a massively walled rectangle about a kilometre in length, centred on two principal palaces, with the Mosque of al-Azhar in the south-eastern quadrant. It was a monument to a great achievement. Virtually without a blow, without any revolutionary violence, simply with the promise of government in accordance with the Law, the Fatimids stepped into the place of the Ikhshidids. Their victory was a masterpiece of the art of succession, of capturing support for a winning cause. Ironically, it was a measure of the Ikhshidid achievement in creating a political system in which such a smooth transfer of power from one dynasty to another could occur.

Preparations went on methodically for the climax, the arrival of the Fatimid caliph himself, which waited only for the completion of the building. Undeterred by the news from Syria, where the coalition had fallen apart, and Fatimids and Carmathians were fighting each other for possession of Damascus, undeterred too by trouble in the west, Mu'izz settled his Ifriqiyan estate, and in August 972 set out with his household, his treasure and the coffins of his ancestors on a long, slow, triumphal procession along the coast. In May 973 he arrived at Barce, where he took ship for Alexandria and Fusṭāṭ. In June he entered his new city of al-Qāhira. It was intended for what it became, a permanent home. The possibly apocryphal detail of a palace especially built to house the ʿAbbasid rival when Baghdad at last should fall illustrates the fact that the dynasty had no intention of moving a second time. The fighting in Syria was undoubtedly an effective hindrance to any advance upon Iraq, but that was not central to the design. At the summit of their career, the Fatimids did not reopen the question of the Islamic empire as a single state. So far as government was concerned, the Ikhshidid inheritance was sufficient. Through it, the Fatimids came to their full stature. As they settled in Egypt, their achievement was to complete the new political order of the tenth century.

THE ZIRID SUCCESSION

Nothing illustrates this better than the arrival of Muʿizz at Cairo as the pattern of his new empire was already taking shape. When, after the fall of Egypt, real fighting broke out in Syria, the Fatimids were not so successful. Within a few years they were trying to maintain a frontier north of Damascus against incursions from Iraq and expeditions by the Byzantines, who had taken Antioch in October 969. In the west, Muʿizz had dealt with a revolt in the Aures mountains which only briefly disturbed his good relations with the Ibadite shaykhs. But the prospect of his departure had led to a war over the succession. By the end of 970, Muʿizz was turning away from his first choice as lieutenant of Ifrīqiya, Jaʿfar b. ʿAlī, the governor of the Zab at Msila, who was suspected of relations with Cordoba, and was looking instead to Zīrī b. Manād and his son Buluggīn at Ashīr. Early in 971 Buluggīn defeated and killed the Maghrāwa chief Muḥammad b. al-Khayr near Tlemcen. But Jaʿfar abandoned Msila with his treasure and his guards, and joined with Muḥammad's son to defeat and kill Zīrī at Tiaret. While Jaʿfar took Zīrī's head to present to the Umayyad Ḥakam II, who had succeeded his father, the great ʿAbd al-Raḥmān III, at Cordoba in 961, Buluggīn restored the situation with a second victory over the Zanāta at Sijilmasa, to be rewarded with the government of Jaʿfar's territories in addition to his father's. In 972 he accompanied his sovereign on the first stages of his journey to the east, then remained behind apparently as viceroy over all except Sicily and Tripoli. As a mark of this exceptional favour he was renamed and restyled Sayf al-Dawla ('Sword of State') Abū 'l-Futūḥ ('Man of Victories') Yūsuf.

It was characteristic of Buluggīn that despite this elevation, he at once returned to fight in the west. Although he held the Maghrib for the caliph, confirmed in this position by Muʿizz's son and successor ʿAzīz in 975, and was further endowed with Tripoli in 979, he remained essentially the lord of the west with his capital at Ashīr. His visits to Kairouan were few, and from 974 the capital and the whole of the Tunisian region were entrusted to ʿAbd Allah b. Muḥammad al-Kātib, 'the Secretary', an aristocratic product of the Fatimid chancery, one of the great departments of state. The whole machinery of central government was thus in the hands of a deputy, and it was he who was apparently the recipient of the caliph's demands upon the province. In 976 ʿAbd Allah assembled a fleet, perhaps in support of ʿAzīz's first expedition to Syria, and went on to make a special levy which in the event ʿAzīz ordered to be repaid. After the final departure of Buluggīn for the west in 979, the *sijillāt*, the official letters of the caliph in Egypt, were sent to the viceroy as far away as Fez, and returned from there to Kairouan long after their date of composition[1] – but these documents were probably official newsletters of the progress of the cause of the Imam in the east rather than instructions. ʿAbd Allah divided his time between Mahdiya and Ṣabra/Manṣūriya, where he amassed a treasure, and where in 983 he assembled a force of *ʿabīd sūdān*, black slave soldiers, several thousands strong, by demanding their price from the officials of the administration and his own followers. The master of Kairouan clearly commanded the obedience of appointed subordinates, many from his own entourage and all probably members of the Ismaʿilite sect, who had taken the place of the Aghlabids and the *jund* in the period since 909.[2] Ten years after the departure of Muʿizz, the Zirids were in danger of returning to their old position as lords of the frontier at Ashīr. Kairouan, which continued to be the capital, seemed likely by contrast to produce a new dynasty.

In allowing such a situation to develop, Buluggīn acted partly from necessity. The departure of Muʿizz provoked the rebellion of Tiaret and Tlemcen, which he was obliged to suppress. The flight of Jaʿfar into Spain, however, had more serious consequences. After favouring the Idrisids, Ḥakam II now drove them from Fez, sending Jaʿfar and his brother Yaḥyā to recruit a following in the Maghrib al-Aqṣā. This policy was continued after his death in 976 by Ibn Abī ʿĀmir, called

[1] Ibn ʿIdhārī, *Bayān*, I, 237 trans. 347.

[2] Partly by assimilation; ʿAbd Allah b. Muḥammad al-Kātib is said to have been of the Aghlabid family; Idris, *La Berbérie orientale*, 48–9.

Almanzor (al-Manṣūr), the great minister who became regent of Andalus. Although Ja'far returned to Spain, Yaḥyā established himself at Basra on the Atlantic coast, the Zanāta between Fez and Tlemcen rallied to the Umayyads, and in 978 the Maghrāwa chief Khazrūn b. Fulful evicted the last of the Banū Midrār from Sijilmasa. In 979 Buluggīn replied with an expedition which captured Fez, and in 980 pursued the Zanāta from Sijilmasa as far as the Umayyad base of Ceuta. Ceuta was as impregnable as ever, but Basra was taken, and from 981 to 983 the Barghawāṭa to the south were attacked, their ruler killed, and prisoners sent back to Kairouan. As Buluggīn returned in 983, however, the Banū Khazrūn re-entered Sijilmasa. In 984 Buluggīn died as he marched against them, and in 985 the army sent by his son was routed by a second Maghrāwa leader, Zīrī b. 'Aṭīya. Fifty years after the foundation of Ashīr to guard against such a threat, the west had reverted to the power of the Umayyads and their Zanāta allies. As a precaution, Manṣūr, the son and successor of Buluggīn, brought his main army to Ashīr but remained there, giving no aid to Ḥasan, the last Idrisid of Fez, who had appealed to 'Azīz in Egypt, and been sent by him to recover his kingdom.

At Ashīr, Manṣūr was joined by 'Abd Allah al-Kātib, who had left his son Yūsuf in his place at Kairouan and Mahdiya. In their absence, Yūsuf aided the Fatimid *dā'ī* Abū 'l-Fahm, sent from Egypt, on his way into the Kutāma country, where he set up his standard in 986. When Manṣūr returned to Kairouan in 987, he found himself taking the oath of allegiance to Cairo at the hands of 'Abd Allah, who had also been appointed *dā'ī* or missionary representative of the Imam in his highest and most spiritual capacity. The story as we have it has been deformed by subsequent chroniclers of the Zirid dynasty, who tell how at his accession Manṣūr first deposed and then reinstated 'Abd Allah, announcing that he himself held his power by hereditary right from his ancestors of the ancient Arab people of Himyar in the Yemen. The tale of 'Abd Allah then becomes one of rebellion against a legitimate monarch, with the connivance of Cairo. It should perhaps have dealt with the attempt of the Fatimid sovereign to impose a new settlement upon Ifrīqiya at the death of Buluggīn, preferring 'Abd Allah to Manṣūr as the principal representative of the caliph in the Maghrib, and distinguishing the Kutāma with a special envoy to mark their status as the source of recruits for a major branch of the Fatimid army in the east. On the other hand, to judge by the good relations subsequently enjoyed by Manṣūr with 'Aziz, the Fatimids may have had little to do with a domestic affair. But however we are to understand the sequel, the assassination of ʿAbd Allah and his son by Manṣūr, the hunting down in 988 of Abū ʾl-Fahm, whose corpse was reputedly eaten by the ʿ*abīd*, the revolt of the Kutāma under a pretender called Abū ʾl-Faraj in 889–90, and their eventual subjection to regular government, the outcome seems clear. Manṣūr reunified the country at the cost of moving his residence in 991 from Ashīr to Ṣabra and Kairouan. His brother Yaṭṭūfat took his place at Ashīr, while the Zab was entrusted to Saʿīd b. Khazrūn, brother of the ruler of Sijilmasa, who had preferred to seek his fortune with the Zirids, and was installed at Tobna (Ṭubna) from about 988. As far as Cairo was concerned, the episode helped to establish the character of the empire as an area within which the Fatimids attached very great importance to the formal acknowledgement of their supremacy, but over which they exercised no administrative control outside Egypt, Syria, and to some extent the Hejaz.

The relationship of the Zirids to their suzerain is indicated by the honorific title bestowed upon Manṣūr, ʿUddat al-ʿAzīz, 'the Instrument of ʿAzīz' – in the loftiest sense. Their *ṭāʿa*, 'obedience', hardly interfered with their power. It was, on the other hand, a solemn obligation by which they were known, not to be repudiated without risk to the loyalty of inferiors on which they themselves relied. The position of the Zirid *sulṭān* was by no means certain. The move to Ṣabra was an attempt to seat the monarchy more firmly, but it was not a final solution. In the west it meant a retreat. In 988, Zīrī b. ʿAṭīya became head of the Maghrāwa, and was recognized by Cordoba as its representative in northern Morocco. He was at once involved in a long struggle with Yaddū b. Yaʿlā of the Banū Ifrān, the rival Zanāta people, for the possession of Fez. This was complicated by the intervention of Abū ʾl-Bahār, a brother of Buluggīn who fled from his nephew Manṣūr, taking with him the governor of Tiaret. By 994, however, Zīrī b. ʿAṭīya was completely victorious, founding as his capital the city of Wajda (Oujda) to the west of Tlemcen. The excursion of Abū ʾl-Bahār was more cause for alarm in Ifrīqiya. The Zirids were beginning to divide over the sultanate – whether the succession was to be monopolized by the eldest son or to pass to one of the more senior members of the family. It was a division between a monarchy based on the size and strength of the *ḥasham*, the household army of clients and slaves, and an aristocracy which shared power by age and aptitude among the princes of the line. When Manṣūr died in 996, six months before his Fatimid suzerain ʿAzīz, the accession of his son Bādīs, a boy of eleven, was ensured by the *ʿabīd*, the most probably Negro regiments who were the nucleus of the army. Their solidarity against their rivals, the cavalry of the nobility, meant that the attempt of the uncles to impose a regent was defeated, and that the young *sulṭān* ruled in person from the beginning.[1] Yaṭṭūfat and Ḥammād, the brothers of Manṣūr, contented themselves with Tiaret and Ashīr. The rift in the family opened after Almanzor's son at Cordoba was appointed viceroy at Fez in 998. In 999, Zīrī b. ʿAṭīya returned to the attack upon Tiaret, defeating both Yaṭṭūfat and Ḥammād. As they fell back upon Ashīr, the six brothers of Buluggīn, the oldest generation of the Zirids, came out against their juniors.

Led by Abū 'l-Bahār, they allied on the one hand with Zīrī b. ʿAṭīya, and on the other with Fulful, son of Saʿīd b. Khazrūn, who had succeeded his father as governor of the Zab. The rebellion of Fulful kept Bādīs from advancing to the aid of Ḥammād, who remained on the defensive further to the west. The following year trouble broke out in the east when the Zirid governor of Tripoli fled to Egypt, and the new Fatimid Caliph Ḥākim seized the occasion to send the governor of Barce to take his place. In 1001, however, Zīrī b. ʿAṭīya died, leaving Ḥammād free to put down the revolt of his uncles, one of whom fled into Spain to become the lord of Granada. Bādīs drove Fulful from the Zab, while the governor of Barce was killed at Tripoli by Zirid troops. The victory in the west was the opportunity for a fresh settlement, a compromise. From 1005 Ḥammād, like his father Buluggīn before him, was entrusted with the whole of the central Maghrib under Zirid control. In 1008 he abandoned the westerly fortress of Ashīr for a new capital in the mountains to the north-east of Msila. Called the Qalʿa – the castle – of the Banū Ḥammād, the city he founded was more strategically placed to command the Zab and the Kabyle mountains which were now the heart of his domain. It was populated by communities deported from Msila and from the old ʿAlawī settlement of Sūq Ḥamza (Bouïra), the seat of a ruler who was the greatest of many such lords each with his castle and his men. The pattern was repeated by his enemies in the west. With the approval of Cordoba, the son of Ibn ʿAṭīya took possession of Fez as the Umayyad viceroy of all except Sijilmasa, where the Banū Khazrūn owed a separate allegiance. The Banū Yaʿlā were installed at Tlemcen. This was the position when,

[1] Cf. Brett, 'Ifrīqiya as a market', 354–5 and note 34; Brett, 'The military interest of the battle of Ḥaydarān', in V. J. Parry and M. E. Yapp, eds., *War, technology and society in the Middle East* (London, New York and Toronto, 1975), 78–88.

following the death of Almanzor in 1002, the second son of the great minister was murdered in 1009, and the Umayyad dominion fell apart. While Andalus was parcelled out among the so-called *mulūk al-ṭawā'if*, 'the kinglets', their counterparts in the Maghrib ruled from the borders of Tunisia to the Atlantic. There is little point in thinking of the intermittent conflict which continued between the Hammadids and their neighbours to the west as a struggle between two nations, 'Ṣanhāja' as opposed to 'Zanāta', still less between two ways of life, the sedentary as opposed to the nomadic.[1] It was the legacy of an imperial rivalry which had abolished the Rustamids and the Idrisids, the Kharijites and the old Shi'ites in that part of the world, and raised up a new generation of warriors to settle the quarrel in their own way.

Bādīs the *sulṭān*, monarch of Ifrīqiya with its central government, its regular income, its men of property and its loyal professional army which, when deployed, was the master of any battlefield, was prepared to acquiesce. Eastwards it was a different matter. Fleeing from the Zab, Fulful b. Sa'īd was welcomed at Tripoli after the governor of Barce had been killed. In 1002 he was joined by none other than Yaḥyā b. 'Alī b. Ḥamdūn, brother of Ja'far, the old rival of Buluggīn, who had been briefly installed at Basra in northern Morocco. He was sent now from Egypt by the Fatimid Caliph Ḥākim with an army drawn from the Banū Qurra, the Arabs of the western Delta, and an appointment as governor of Tripoli and Barce. Ḥākim's purpose is obscure; Yaḥyā's appointment was not necessarily an attempt to change the status quo in the way that 'Azīz may have hoped to alter the succession on the death of Buluggīn. It was perhaps the simple opportunism of a medieval ruler, for whom loyalty and treachery went hand in hand as the supreme instrument, however crude. In this case Yaḥyā retired when he was deserted by the Banū Qurra at the siege of Gabes in 1003, and Fulful was left in sole command. His independence at Tripoli was the first sign of something more profound, the end of the harmony created by Mu'izz li-Dīn Allah along the route to Egypt, which had been maintained for many years by the equitable division of Libya between the Zirids in the west and their suzerains in the east. At Alexandria, the Banū Qurra revolted, and were massacred. About 1005 they joined the Berber Lawāta in support of the first major pretender to rise against the Fatimids since Abū Yazīd. This was Walīd b. Hishām – an Umayyad name to indicate his claim to Umayyad descent – called 'Abū Rikwa', 'the man with a goatskin water-bottle', to mark his character as a vengeful

[1] E.-F. Gautier, *Le Passé de l'Afrique du Nord: les siècles obscurs* (Paris, 1952), 387–408.

preacher in the Fatimid tradition. Capturing Barce, he caused panic in Egypt when the Kutāma refused to fight against him. It was not until troops were brought from Syria that the rebel was driven to take refuge in Nubia, whence he was returned and put to death in 1007.

The Banū Qurra, however, remained restless. The revolt of Abū Rikwa was followed by a series of low Niles. In 1009 Ḥākim added to his difficulties with the famous destruction of the Church of the Holy Sepulchre at Jerusalem, followed by a purge of the administration which drove the victims to conspire with the Arabs of Palestine. In 1010 Fulful b. Saʿīd died at Tripoli, and Bādīs himself marched upon the city to install one of his principal lieutenants, Muḥammad b. al-Ḥasan; the surviving chiefs of the Zanāta band were appointed governors in the Djerid. But in 1012, as Jerusalem was captured by the Arabs of Palestine, Mukhtār b. al-Qāṣim of the Banū Qurra seized Barce. The Zanāta chiefs rebelled in the Djerid, while a pretender – who may have been the son of Abū Rikwa – appeared among the Kutāma in their Ifriqiyan homeland. Cairo and Kairouan combined to defend their hegemony. Ḥākim, who had tried to place a Fatimid governor in Tripoli, now gave Barce to Bādīs. The expedient failed. Mukhtār b. al-Qāṣim recovered the city, and signalled the fact by waylaying the gifts sent by Bādīs to Cairo in 1014/15. Barce remained in his possession.

Ifrīqiya, on the other hand, was overtaken by a crisis complicated by the controversy which marked the final phase of Ḥākim's reign, when prominence was given to the crucial but alarming doctrine that the Fatimid Imam was the incarnation of the Divine Spirit. In 1015 Bādīs ordered Ḥammād to relinquish the province of Constantine and the Kutāma country to Bādīs's son and heir, the infant Muʿizz. Ḥammād rebelled along with his brothers, and attacked Beja in the Medjerda valley inland from Tunis. He may have declared for Baghdad, and certainly the capture of Tunis is associated with a massacre of Ismaʿilites at Tunis. Ḥammād was driven back to the Qalʿa by the weight of the *sulṭān*'s army, which he was unable to face in the field, and was saved only by the death of Bādīs during the siege in 1016. The army, notably the *ʿabīd*, procured the succession for Bādīs's son, the boy Muʿizz who had been left at Mahdiya. While the generals prepared for a second campaign in 1017, however, the Ismāʿīlīs were attacked and massacred in Kairouan and in cities as far away as Tripoli at the instigation of the Malikite *ʿulamā*'. The story is obscured by the dynastic tradition which would give the credit for the massacres to Muʿizz, but it should be seen in the light of the claims put forward on Ḥākim's behalf, which at about the same time, or a year or two later, led to similar scenes in the Egyptian capital, when much of old Fusṭāṭ was burnt. At Kairouan, the riots could not be controlled, and the government was obliged to take its revenge in subsequent reprisals by the army.

Despite the riots, the reign of Muʿizz began well in the charge of a great lady, Umm Mallāl, the sister of Bādīs, who entrusted the education of the young prince to the secretary of the chancellery, Ibn Abī 'l-Rijāl, a native of Tiaret, known in the Latin West as Abenragel, the author of a treatise on astronomy. In 1017 Ḥammād was in fact soundly defeated, and the opportunity was taken to restore harmony. His independence was recognized, and the compact sealed by the marriage, in 1024, of his son ʿAbd Allah to the sister of Muʿizz, Umm al-ʿUlū. Only in the Djerid did the Zanāta remain troublesome, led by Khalīfa b. Warrū, the nephew of Fulful. Their moment came with the destitution of Muḥammad b. al-Ḥasan, who had been summoned from Tripoli on the death of Bādīs to take command of the central government for the royal family. In 1022 he was executed, like ʿAbd Allah al-Kātib before him, on a charge of treason, of conspiring to obtain for himself the investiture of Cairo. At his fall, the brother whom he had left at Tripoli rebelled and invited Khalīfa b. Warrū to enter the city. Khalīfa was eventually confirmed in its possession. With Mukhtār b. al-Qāṣim al-ʿArabī at Barce, supported by the Banū Qurra in possession of the Buḥayra to the west of Alexandria, there were now two virtually independent principalities which controlled the route from Ifrīqiya to Egypt. At least part of the explanation is the search for some permanent prize by captains created by the wars of the tenth century: immigrants into the Libyan area in the case of the Zanāta lords of the Banū Khazrūn; drawn from the beduin population in the case of the Arabs. The prizes in question were the two main cities along this stretch of coast, and part of the reward was a share in the profits of the trade which passed through them by land and sea.

The trade and the profits, however, were no longer as great as they had been in the previous generation. The removal of the Fatimids to Egypt had meant good business along the way from Kairouan, a boom in trade between the old and the new capital of the Fatimid empire, which no doubt helped to keep the peace for several decades as the peoples of Libya shared a common prosperity. By the beginning of the eleventh century, however, the attraction of Cairo meant that merchants were abandoning Kairouan, and that the volume of trade was falling.

From about this time there appeared at the Egyptian capital a community of immigrant Ifriqiyan Jews who consigned their papers to the cellar of their synagogue, the so-called Geniza (storehouse), lest they destroy the name of God which may have been written upon them, and thus ensured their survival. The arrival of these Jews at Cairo speaks for itself, but so does their curious archive, in which letters refer to the poor prospects for trade in Ifrīqiya about 1020, as well as to the obstacles created by the new rulers of Barce, who intercepted ships and caravans, levied tolls, and sold expropriated goods – undoubtedly with the connivance of the Fatimid authorities – in the Nile Valley. Dealings with Syria and Iraq, and the Red Sea trade to the Indies, seem more successful. The Jewish merchants traded for preference by sea, but their evidence is probably valid also for trade by land, as well as for trade conducted by Muslims.[1] It is likely that the trade of Libya was falling back to a more normal level, together with that of Ifrīqiya, from which the imperial government had departed. After the unusual prosperity of the period since 950, the adjustment was doubtless painful, and the political consequences considerable. It is probable that along the Libyan coast more and more people, from the *sulṭān* of Ifrīqiya through the upstart *amīrs* of Tripoli and Barce to the Caliph of Egypt, were trying to lay hands upon and participate in a diminishing commerce.

Ifrīqiya itself was affected. When Bādīs in 1015 forced shopkeepers to move from the main city to the *sūq* of Ṣabra, where rents were high (and presumably paid to the government), he may have been trying to protect his revenues against a fall in business. It is very likely that an economic grievance was at work in the riots against the Ismāʿīlīs. In the provincial cities the underlying resentment was directed at Kairouan, and at the system which gave so much importance to the metropolis. Wherever they took place, attacks upon the Ismāʿīlīs were attacks upon the regime and not far removed from a general attack upon the right of the Zirids to hold their power from the Fatimids, and to rule Ifrīqiya as they did. The criticism was not necessarily violent. The high society of the capital and the country was very close-knit, involving men of letters and learning as well as of wealth and power, who shared the same patrons, the same clients, the same education in the schools of Kairouan, and the same courtly venue in and around the palaces of the *sulṭān*. The general opinion was growing within this coterie

[1] Cf. Goitein, *A Mediterranean society*, I, 30–2, 327–8, *et passim*; Goitein, *Studies in Islamic history and institutions* (Leiden, 1966), 308–28.

of predominantly Sunni conviction that the Fatimid connection was an embarrassment which might usefully be broken off. It is said that Ibn Abī 'l-Rijāl had provided his royal pupil with an education which brought him up as an orthodox Muslim with the intention of repudiating the suzerainty of Cairo. This is certainly too strong; nevertheless by the 1030s Muʿizz seems to have been consulting the leading jurists of Kairouan about the propriety of his position, and receiving the answer that it was inconsistent. If a formal break with Cairo was not a complete answer to the problems of the Zirid regime, it is likely that already Muʿizz had begun to see it as a hinge upon which a solution might turn.

Since the mysterious disappearance of Ḥākim outside Cairo in 1021, the Fatimid government had been in the hands of viziers acting on behalf of the palace. Three-quarters of a century earlier, the Byzantines had made peace with the Caliph Muʿizz li-Din Allah, conceding defeat in Sicily. In 1038, as part of a general treaty, the Fatimids recognized Byzantine ambitions in the island. Civil war had broken out between members of the Kalbid dynasty. Ifriqiyan piracy and seafaring had revived, and in 1036 the Zirids had intervened on the island in an attempt to impose a Zirid ruler. The attempt failed when the east of the island was invaded by the Byzantine general, George Maniaces, who remained until his death in 1043. Frustrated in what appeared to be a promising venture, Muʿizz was faced with a worsening situation to the south. In 1026 Cairo had confirmed Khalīfa b. Warrū in power at Tripoli with an undertaking to secure the caravan routes. But although presents were exchanged by Khalīfa and Muʿizz, it may be that the dynasty of the Banū Khazrūn had a hand in the raids which brought the Zanāta of the Djerid close to the Ifriqiyan capital. There was fighting also between Zirid forces and the Ibadite peoples of the region, giving Muʿizz a bad name in Ibadite tradition. The erstwhile concord had turned to growing enmity. It only remained for the killing of Khalīfa's successor, Saʿīd b. Khazrūn, at Tripoli in 1038, to signal the arrival of yet more immigrants into the troubled area, in this case the Zughba, one of the tribes of the Banū Hilāl, now moving westward from their tenth-century location by al-Wāḥāt, the oases of Egypt.[1]

The killing of Saʿīd by the Zughba did not prevent the succession of his brother Muntaṣir and the continuation of the dynasty. The new ruler took the opportunity to expel from the city the jurist Ibn al-

[1] See M. Brett, 'The Zughba at Tripoli, 429H (1037–8 AD)', *Society for Libyan Studies, sixth annual report*, 1974–5, 41–7.

Munammar, who twenty years previously had directed the massacre of the Ismāʿīlīs at Tripoli, and had remained a political figure. It may have been Ibn al-Munammar who had already brought about a breach with Cairo, attested by a dinar of 1033/4 struck at Tripoli with a Sunni inscription. He was expelled because he had opened the gates to a cousin who was promptly ousted by Muntaṣir, but the episode is significant of the tension which continued to exist between rulers and the more fanatical men of religion. The lesson was not lost on Muʿizz, that the profession of orthodox Islam might give him the authority he required to deal with such men, preachers capable of arousing the mob against a Shiʿite government. The tribes of the Banū Hilāl were another matter. As immigrants into the area, they had turned away from the pastoral routine described by Ibn Ḥawqal to something more war-like. They were a threat but also a promise. As warriors, they were probably employed by the descendants of Khazrūn at Tripoli in much the same way, perhaps, as their relatives the Banū Qurra were associated with the ruler of Barce. Further west, Muʿizz was increasingly obliged by the hostility of the Ibadite peoples of the Djerid and the Jebel Nefusa to provide for the safety of the route along the coastal plain from Tripoli to Gabes. In 1045/6 he defeated the Lawāta of the Jebel Nefusa, and it may have been then that he set the Hilālī tribes of Riyāḥ and Zughba in this narrow strip between the hills and the sea. Their employment as aliens, who were hostile to the original inhabitants, to secure this vital line was a critical decision by Muʿizz. It was an essential part of a much grander design upon the Libyan coast.

THE ABANDONMENT OF KAIROUAN[1]

In 1048 Muʿizz took the decisive step of denouncing the Fatimids and recognizing the ʿAbbasid caliph in Baghdad. It was a time when the Buwayhids were weakening at the approach of the Seljūq Turks from the north-east, and the ʿAbbasid caliph was encouraged to seek diplomatic recognition from the princes of the Muslim world. For his part, Muʿizz acted deliberately to place himself at the head of a nation of true believers, in a position to deal with his opponents and to go forward to the creation of a new empire. The change of allegiance was systematically

1 This section is based upon my unpublished Ph.D. thesis, M. Brett, 'Fitnat al-Qayrawān' (University of London, 1970); cf. also Brett, 'Ifrīqiya as a market', 'The Zughba at Tripoli', 'The military interest of the battle of Ḥaydarān'; and Brett, 'Sijill al-Mustanṣir', paper presented to the Premier Congrès d'Histoire et de Civilisation du Maghreb, Tunis, Dec. 1974, to be published in the *Actes du Congrès*.

celebrated in standard fashion. The *khuṭba*, the address at the Friday prayer, was in the name of Baghdad; a new gold coinage was issued; and the titles used in diplomatic correspondence were altered. The Fatimid colour white was changed for the ʿAbbasid colour black; perhaps by a deliberate play upon these symbols, Muʿizz was hailed as the one who had turned night into day. He laid particular claim to the genealogy by which he was descended from the old Arab kings of Himyar in the Yemen. These, it was said, had been forced to emigrate with their people from the city of Ma'rib by the breaking of the great dam which had irrigated their land in the days before Islam, and had therefore come to North Africa long before the upstart Fatimids were heard of. Presents were made to Muntaṣir b. Khazrūn at Tripoli, who may have come in person to offer his allegiance. In 1051–2, Jabbāra b. Mukhtār al-ʿArabī at Barce burnt the insignia of the Fatimids, cursed them from the pulpits and announced his obedience to Muʿizz in the name of Baghdad. Cairo could make no effective reply. Al-Yāzūrī, who became vizier and head of the Egyptian government on behalf of the young caliph Mustanṣir on 1 June 1050, had no other weapon than vituperation. His only satisfaction was the flight of the *qāḍī* of Ṣabra to Egypt, and the interception of an ambassador bearing insignia from Baghdad to Kairouan in 1051. The ambassador was publicly humiliated. He had been apprehended in the first instance by the Byzantines, who handed him over partly, it would seem, because of Zirid piracy in southern Italy. It is not unlikely that Muʿizz hoped that Sicily would at last fall into his hands.

Yet Muʿizz was not entirely happy, as the way in which he asserted his new authority makes clear. The issue of a new coinage, although it was metallically sound, caused a panic hoarding. In 1049/50 the administration was purged of the nominees of a great military officer, ʿAbbād, who had probably been head of government. In the following year, the *sulṭān* expelled from Kairouan the popular preacher Ibn ʿAbd al-Ṣamad, to have him assassinated, most probably by the Hilālī Arabs, on his way from Gabes to Tripoli; there were many who accused Muʿizz of the murder. More important, by 1051 there was trouble with the Riyāḥ and Zughba. These Hilālī tribes were dissatisfied with their agreement with the *sulṭān*, perhaps because it confined them to a fairly barren region. When negotiation finally failed, they advanced beyond the strategically situated fortress city of Gabes to enter the somewhat more fertile lands to the north. Thus challenged, in the spring of 1052 Muʿizz himself prepared to lead what was probably an annual expedition to the south to collect the taxes and impose the peace. As a test of their loyalty, the Riyāḥ and Zughba may have been summoned to attend the muster, drawing them towards Kairouan. Instead of submitting, however, they surprised the *sulṭān* and his army on the march in rough country perhaps 50 km from the capital. When the Arabs charged on horses, which Muʿizz may well have given them to improve their fighting power, the cavalry of the Zirid aristocracy fled, leaving the *ʿabīd* to take the weight of the attack. Muʿizz was saved by the discipline of these infantrymen, and retreated under their escort to Ṣabra, but his camp was plundered of all it contained by way of treasure and equipment and pack-animals. Kairouan was besieged. While Muʿizz concentrated the remnant of his army in Ṣabra, and supervised the hasty erection of walls and barricades around the main city, the Arabs roamed the countryside, plundering and taking prisoners.

All was not lost. For a year after this, the battle of Ḥaydarān, Muʿizz was engaged in bargaining with the tribes, who seem to have demanded *iqṭāʿāt*, concessions of land where they could live as masters, no more perhaps than they had enjoyed when they first entered the service of the *sulṭān*, but in more favourable districts. After a period of two hundred and fifty years, during which time the rulers of Ifrīqiya had thought it prudent to keep Kairouan defenceless, the city was provided with an enceinte. The rest of the country waited on events. Then the Riyāḥ and the Zughba quarrelled over the booty they had taken at Ḥaydarān, and appealed to the vizier al-Yāzūrī in Egypt, who saw a great opportunity. In 1053–4 he sent an ambassador, Amīn al-Dawla Ḥasan b. ʿAlī b. Mulhim, as far as Gabes. Ibn Mulhim adjudicated the dispute, urged the tribes under the leadership of Mu'nis b. Yaḥyā to return to the siege of Kairouan, and proclaimed the return of Fatimid suzerainty. Muʿizz was abandoned by important members of the Zirid dynasty and the Zirid aristocracy, who came to Gabes to offer their submission. One was appointed governor of the city. If the claim of Cairo that the whole of Ifrīqiya had returned to obedience was exaggerated, it was perhaps no coincidence that during the same year Sousse revolted. As the Egyptian envoy returned in triumph with his share of the loot of Ḥaydarān, Muʿizz prepared to leave Kairouan for Mahdiya. His son Tamīm was installed there as governor, and the transfer of treasure began. With the writing on the wall, the population of the old metropolis began to emigrate, and the poets to lament. The theme of descent from the legendary kings of Himyar took on a fresh meaning. Kairouan was compared to the old city of Ma'rib, which had likewise been abandoned by its inhabitants. In 1057 Muʿizz departed. In 1058 he acknowledged once again his allegiance to the Fatimids, and in 1062 he died.

It was the end of an era. Ifrīqiya, the Byzantine province which the Arabs had inherited, had dissolved into its component parts. The central government was not defeated so much as deserted. Kairouan, the old metropolis, shrank to a fraction of its former size. Tunis, Sfax, Gabes, and Gafsa in the Djerid were all independent. The Zirids were confined to Mahdiya and Sousse; only after many years did Tamīm, Muʿizz's son and successor, manage to extend his authority in the Sahel. It only remained to offer an explanation. Already before the emigration of Muʿizz to Mahdiya, the legend of Ma'rib had given the answer. Like the land of Himyar, Ifrīqiya had been devastated by a flood, not of water but of men, the Banū Hilāl. The Arab tribes were a convenient scapegoat. When Muʿizz returned to the Fatimid fold, the metaphor attained the status of myth. In that year, 1058, the Fatimid vizier al-Yāzūrī, who had directed the Egyptian intervention in the affairs of Ifrīqiya, and had boasted extravagantly of his responsibility for the downfall of the Zirid *sulṭān*, was disgraced and put to death. As the two dynasties were reconciled in accordance with the fiction of the divine harmony which prevailed throughout the dominions of the Fatimid Imam, it was possible to say of the fallen minister that he had been the insignificant cause of a great natural disaster, comparable to the breaking of the Ma'rib dam, an act of God for which no one, least of all the two sovereigns, could really be held to blame. With this judgement upon them, the Banū Hilāl, who had helped to extend into Ifrīqiya proper the political fragmentation into smaller, independent principalities which had begun in the Libyan area at the beginning of the eleventh century, passed into history as the great destroyers – Ibn Khaldūn's swarm of locusts who had devastated the land and left it permanently waste.

CHAPTER 11

THE SAHARA AND THE SUDAN FROM THE ARAB CONQUEST OF THE MAGHRIB TO THE RISE OF THE ALMORAVIDS*

THE TRADE OF THE SAHARA

The Saharan trade and the introduction of Islam were the two principal external factors in the history of West Africa before 1500. Through trade and Islam, Africa south of the Sahara became irreversibly linked to the wider world. In this process the second half of the first millennium AD, or the centuries following the Arab conquest of North Africa, may be viewed as the formative period. The Arab invasion set in motion a transformation of North Africa and its society which extended into the Sahara and eventually reached the Sudan.

Oral traditions in the Sahara and the Sudan seek direct association with ʿUqba b. Nāfiʿ, the general who led the Arab troops to the Maghrib al-Aqṣā, i.e. to the 'Farthest Maghrib' or 'Farthest West', the territory now known as Morocco, to reach the Sea of Darkness (the Atlantic) in the west, and the Sea of Sand (the Sahara) in the south. According to some traditions, ʿUqba continued his raids as far as the frontiers of the Sudan. Fulani traditions describe ʿUqba as the leader of their migration from the (north-) east. The arabized Kunta, a Saharan tribe of saints and scholars, trace their pedigree back to ʿUqba, claiming that he himself had conquered Biru (i.e. Walata) and Takrur. The fourteenth-century Ibn Abī Zarʿ says that the Banū Wārith, a Ṣanhāja tribe in the neighbourhood of Adrar, were converted to Islam by ʿUqba b. Nāfiʿ.

This traditional evidence about the Saharan exploits of ʿUqba b. Nāfiʿ is perhaps an echo of a much earlier tradition, recorded by Ibn ʿAbd al-Ḥakam (died 871). Shortly after his appointment to the supreme command of the Arab troops in Tripoli, in 663, ʿUqba b. Nāfiʿ led 400 horsemen and 400 camel-riders south of Tripoli, through Wadan and Djerma (the then capital of the Fezzan) into the Sahara, past 'the

* The first draft of this chapter was written at St John's College, Cambridge. The author is grateful to the Master and Fellows of the College for electing him to an Overseas Fellowship in 1972–3.

site of the present Zawila to the oases of Kawar.[1] The latter is described elsewhere as 'a region of the land of the Sūdān to the south of Fazzān'.[2]

Although Ibn ʿAbd al-Ḥakam's account of the conquest of the Maghrib has elements of fable and tendentious traditions,[3] there is no reason to doubt that ʿUqba did penetrate deep into the Libyan desert. Ibn ʿAbd al-Ḥakam recorded another southward raid, which was led by ʿUqba's grandson, Ḥabīb b. Abī ʿUbayda b. ʿUqba. About 734 – that is, not long after the Arabs had established their rule over the Maghrib al-Aqṣā – he raided the Sus and the land of the *Sūdān*. It is significant that the two raids on record, at both ends of the Sahara, were carried along lines which later became two of the principal routes of the Saharan trade.

ʿUqba b. Nāfiʿ, it is said, imposed a tribute of slaves upon the rulers of Wadan, Djerma and Kawar. These Libyan chiefs, like the Garamantes of the fifth century BC reported by Herodotus, raided their black neighbours to the south for slaves. From antiquity until the middle of the nineteenth century, slaves were the staple commodity on the Chad–Tripoli route. By the middle of the eighth century, Zawila in the Fezzan had emerged as the principal centre for the slave-trade, as described by al-Yaʿqūbī (in the second half of the ninth century) and al-Iṣṭakhrī (in the middle of the tenth century). The latter says that most of the black slaves who were sold in Muslim countries were imported through Zawila. Although many slaves, both male and female, were sent to Egypt and to other parts of the Muslim East, some remained in Ifrīqiya as domestics and labourers. There is evidence for black communities in Ifrīqiya as early as the ninth and tenth centuries.[4]

The recruitment of black slaves assumed political significance as successive dynasties in Ifrīqiya created corps of black slaves known as *ʿabīd*. About the same time that their overlords, the ʿAbbasid caliphs of Bagdad, purchased Turks in the steppes to form the corps of *mamlūks*, the Aghlabid emirs turned to their immediate reservoir of slaves south

[1] Ibn ʿAbd al-Ḥakam, *Kitāb futūḥ Miṣr waʾl-Maghrib wa-akhbārihā*, ed. by C. C. Torrey (New Haven, 1922), 195–6, Quotations from the Arabic sources are from the forthcoming volume *Medieval Arabic sources on West Africa*, trans. and annotated by J. F. P. Hopkins and N. Levtzion. Since footnote references here must be limited, readers are referred to the detailed references to the sources given in N. Levtzion, *Ancient Ghana and Mali* (London, 1973).

[2] Yāqūt, *Kitāb muʿjam al-buldān*, ed. by F. Wüstenfeld (Leipzig, 1866), IV, 315.

[3] R. Brunschvig, 'Ibn Abdal'hakam et la conquête de l'Afrique du Nord par les Arabes: étude critique', *Annales de l'Institut des Études Orientales* (Algiers), 1942–7, **6**, 121–2; H. T. Norris, *Saharan myth and saga* (London, 1972), 33.

[4] T. Lewicki, *Études ibāḍites nord-africaines* (Warsaw, 1955), 92–6.

of the Sahara. Ibrāhīm b. al-Aghlab (800–12), founder of the Aghlabid dynasty, had bought 5,000 black slaves, whom he manumitted (following the *mamlūk* system of the east), and settled close to the capital. He used the *ʿabīd* to check the influence of the Arab troops (the *jund*). The Fatimids also had a corps of *ʿabīd*. Their successors, the Zirid emirs, had the *ʿabīd* as their personal guard. The *ʿabīd*, who owed exclusive allegiance to their emir, became involved in the struggle for power within the dynasty. In 983/4, a governor of Ifrīqiya, who sought to increase his power at the expense of his emir, acquired many thousands of *ʿabīd*. The emir al-Muʿizz (1016–51) is said to have bought 30,000 *ʿabīd*. He also received slaves as part of a gift from a Sudanese king. The *ʿabīd* maintained their prominence until the defeat of the Zirid army by the Hilāli at the battle of Ḥaydarān in 1052. A special agent of the emir, *hāshid al-Sūdān*, was responsible for the recruitment of the *ʿabīd*.

The journey across the Sahara with slaves must have been extremely difficult and exhausting. This is fully borne out in an anecdote about an Ibāḍī from Wargla in the eleventh century: 'He was exhausted with his slave men and women. This woman had grown thin, this one was hungry, this one was sick, this one had run away, this one was afflicted by the guinea worm. When they encamped they had much to occupy him.'[1]

The same trader, known as *al-Nakhkhās* ('the Drover'), combined the northbound trade in slaves with the southbound trade in horses. In this trade system, horses – like fire-arms in the later Atlantic trade – were paid for in slaves. Horses, like fire-arms, added to the intensity of slave-raiding. Kanem, which emerged as the dominant state in the Chad basin, was in fact a slave-raiding empire. It developed therefore along a pattern different from that of Ghana and its successors in the western Sudan, where gold was the raison d'être of the trade system.

Whereas ʿUqba b. Nāfiʿ had collected tribute in slaves in the Libyan desert, seventy years later his grandson brought back from the western Sahara 'as much gold as he wanted'. The raid of Ḥabīb b. Abī ʿUbayda b. ʿUqba in the 730s seems to have been an official expedition, sent by the Umayyad governor of Ifrīqiya, to explore the Sahara after the pacification of the provinces of Sus, Darʿa and Tafilelt. The amount of gold which is believed to have been brought back demonstrated beyond

[1] T. Lewicki, 'Quelques extraits inédits relatifs aux voyages des commerçants et des missionnaires ibāḍites nord-africains au pays du Soudan occidental et central au moyen âge', *Folia Orientalia*, 1960, 2, 11.

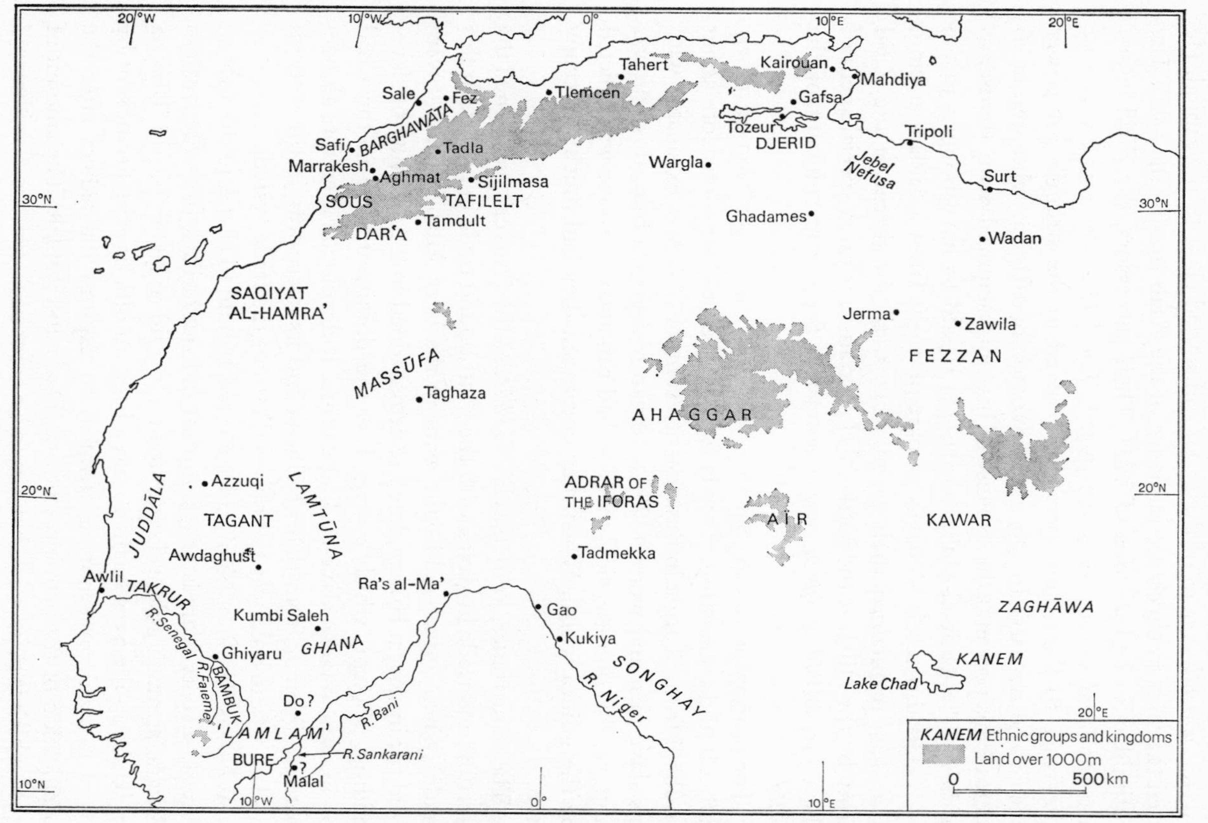

67 The Maghrib and the western and central Sahara and Sudan.

doubt the prospects of trade with the lands south of the Sahara. As governor of the Maghrib in 747–55, ʿAbd al-Raḥmān, son of the above-mentioned Ḥabīb b. Abī ʿUbayda, ordered the digging of wells along routes leading from southern Morocco to the Sudan. The last of these wells was about sixteen days' travel from the Wadi Darʿa.

The Umayyad government sought to encourage the flow of gold from the Sudan. But direct imperial involvement in the organization of the gold-trade was short-lived. In 750, when the Umayyad caliphate was overthrown, the Maghrib was in the throes of a Berber revolt under the banners of different sects of the Khārijiyya. In 761/2, Kairouan, as well as parts of Tripoli and Ifrīqiya, was recaptured by the ʿAbbasid governor of Egypt. But the separatism of the Kharijites survived in the pre-Saharan steppes and in the oases, which by that time had assumed strategic importance as the termini of a growing trans-Saharan trade.

The Ibadites (Ibāḍiyya) were the largest of the various sects of the Kharijites (Khārijiyya) in the Maghrib, and the one which lasted longer than others. During the first half of the eighth century, the activities of the Ibadites in North Africa were directed from their headquarters in southern Iraq, at Basra. There, the Ibāḍī community counted among its members wealthy merchants with widespread commercial relations. Wealth and commercial interests contributed to the moderation of the Ibadites. On their travels, the Ibāḍī merchants acted also as missionaries. Their commercial ethos was inherited by the Ibadite communities in the Maghrib, which combined economic enterprise and missionary zeal with religious moderation and tolerance.

In the ninth century, Basra declined and Ibadites in the eastern parts of the ʿAbbasid caliphate came under increasing pressure. Ibadite merchants migrated to North Africa, where they could establish their homes in flourishing Ibāḍī communities. In the ninth and tenth centuries, the presence of merchants from Basra, Kufa and Khurasan was recorded in Tahert, Zawila and Sijilmasa. They brought with them capital and experience which they successfully employed to dominate the trans-Saharan trade.

From its foundation by ʿAbd al-Raḥman b. Rustam in 776/7 or 778/9 until its fall to the Fatimids in 909, the imamate of Tahert was the religious and political centre for Berber tribes of the Ibāḍiyya from Tlemcen in the west to Tripoli in the east. On the basis of his Ibadite sources, T. Lewicki assumed that the *imāms* of Tahert exercised political authority over the whole southern belt of Ifrīqiya and over most of the province of Tripoli. Only in 839 did the Aghlabid emirs of Kairouan conquer the regions of Gafsa and Djered and cut the Ibadite domains into two. On the other hand, M. Talbi, who studied this same period from the viewpoint of the Aghlabid emirate, is convinced that provinces like Surt, Tripoli, Nafzawa, Gabes, Quastiliya and Gafsa were subject to Kairouan.[1] It appears that the authority of the *imāms* of Tahert was not always and everywhere strictly political. As a politico-religious system, the imamate had the allegiance of Ibadites even where they lived under the political domination of the Aghlabids. The latter consented to allow the Ibadites to pay the *ṣadaqa*, the religious tax, to their *imām* in order to prevent open revolt inside their territories and so as to win the goodwill of the Ibāḍīs who controlled the trade-routes from the Sudan to Kairouan.

The prosperity of Tahert attracted Ibadites from eastern Muslim lands as well as from other parts of the Maghrib; it also attracted non-Ibāḍī Muslims and Jews. They 'made their permanent home among them . . . because of the opulence in the town, the laudable conduct of its *imām*, his justice towards his subjects and the security of life and property . . . The roads to the land of the Sūdān and to all the countries of the East and West were brought into use for trade and all kinds of goods.'[2]

The rulers of Tahert sought the advice of tribal notables, merchants and religious leaders, and their internal and external policy reflected religious, political and commercial interests. Non-Ibāḍīs were free to practise their religions in Tahert and, in spite of religious differences, the *imāms* of Tahert maintained cordial relations with the Aghlabids (who were Sunnites) and with the rulers of Sijilmasa (who belonged to the Ṣufriyya sect of the Khārijiyya). The route from Tahert to Ghana passed through Sijilmasa, while another route, via Wargla, linked Tahert with Gao.

There is also some evidence for diplomatic relations between Tahert and the kingdoms of the Sudan. During the reign of the second *imām*, ʿAbd al-Wahhāb (784/5–823/4), his son al-Aflaḥ expressed his intention to go to Gao. He had to give up this idea under the pressure of his father. But al-Aflaḥ's interest in the Sudan continued when he himself became the *imām* (823/4–871/2). Towards the end of his reign he sent

[1] T. Lewicki, 'The Ibādites in Arabia and Africa', *Journal of World History*, 1971, 13, 103–5; M. Talbi, *L'Émirat Aghlabide, 184–296/800–909: histoire politique* (Paris, 1966), 355–9.

[2] Ibn Ṣaghīr, 'Chronique d'Ibn Ṣaghīr sur les imāms rostémides de Tahert', ed. by A. de C. Motylinski, in *Actes du 14e Congrès international des Orientalistes* (Algiers, 1905), pt 3, 13.

one of the notables of Tahert 'in a deputation to the king of the *Sūdān* with a gift'.[1]

The reigns of ʿAbd al-Wahhāb and his son al-Aflaḥ marked the peak of Tahert's power and prosperity. In the second half of the ninth century, Tahert declined, and the authority of its *imāms* over the Ibadite Berbers was challenged in a series of political splits and religious schisms, with the emergence of several local sub-sects. The *imām* of Tahert was unable to offer serious resistance to the Fatimid attack in 909, and sought refuge at Wargla.

That was the end of the Ibāḍī imamate, but Ibadite communities flourished until the twelfth century. From their centres in Tripoli, Ghadames, Djered, Quastiliya and Wargla, the Ibadites maintained their prominent role in the trade with the Sudan over all the important routes of the Sahara. Deep in the desert, and in direct contact with the lands of the *Sūdān* (i.e. the Black peoples), Ibadites settled in three important commercial towns: Zawila, Tadmekka and Awdaghust.

Zawila, which had not been in existence in the 660s when ʿUqba raided the Fezzan and Kawar, developed in the eighth century with the growth of Muslim trade on the Chad–Tripoli route. It was from Tripoli, which had been one of the earliest Ibadite centres, that members of this sect secured control of Zawila. In 761–2, after he had conquered Kairouan, the ʿAbbasid general Ibn al-Ashaʿth attacked Zawila and exterminated the Ibadites there. Zawila, however, remained an important centre of the Ibāḍiyya. Writing in 891, al-Yaʿqūbī reported that all the people of Zawila were Ibāḍīs. In 918/19, a chief of the Hawwāra tribe, ʿAbd Allāh b. Khaṭṭāb, conquered Zawila and established there a dynasty which survived until the end of the twelfth century. Like most of the Hawwāra in the tenth century, the Banū Khaṭṭāb were Ibadites.

The Ibadites of Zawila played a leading role in the slave-trade, and it appears that some of the blacks who settled in North Africa at that period were themselves Ibāḍīs. Ibadite sources refer to a community in Jebel Nefusa known as *Ijnāw(un)*, which could be read as *Ignaun*, the plural of *agnaw*, meaning 'blacks'. This community produced some eminent Ibāḍī shaykhs, among them Abū ʿUbayda ʿAbd al-Ḥamīd al-Janāwnī. In 811/12, the latter was appointed by the *imām* of Tahert as his representative (*ʿāmil*) in Jebel Nefusa. It is said that he could speak Arabic, Berber and the language of Kanem (*al-lugha al-kānimiyya*).[2] This might be an indication of the origin of this group.

Zawila was an outpost of Islam in the direction of Kanem. At that

[1] *Chronique d'Ibn Ṣaghīr*, 31.   [2] Lewicki, *Études ibāḍites*, 92–6.

time, the nearest Muslim town to Gao was Tadmekka, in Adrar of the Iforas. Ibāḍī merchants from southern Tunisia traded with Tadmekka, and some even settled there and attained great wealth. One of those merchants was Kīdād, from Tozeur, who bought a slave-girl at Tadmekka *c.* 883. Abū Yazīd, who grew up to lead the Kharijite revolt against the Fatimids in North Africa in 943–7, was her son. It appears that Abū Yazīd was born in the far south, because his father – worried about a birth-mark on his tongue – is said to have taken the baby to a diviner in Gao.[1]

From their strongholds in Tripoli and in Ifrīqiya, the Ibadites extended their commercial and religious influence along the routes leading to Lake Chad through Zawila, and to Gao, east of the Niger bend, via Tadmekka. But the Ibadites went even farther to participate in the remunerative gold-trade with Ghana. Ibāḍīs from Jebel Nefusa and from Wargla travelled to Ghana. One of them, a shaykh, continued towards the sources of the gold, and reached 'Ghiyāra, whose people he found to be naked. He kept his home there until he died.'[2]

The southern commercial centre of the Berbers opposite Ghana was Awdaghust, on the route from Sijilmasa and Wadi Darʿa. In that town of the western Sahara, 'most of the inhabitants were natives of Ifrīqiya, members [of such tribes as] Barqajāna, Nafūsa, Lawāta, Zanāta and Nafzāwa'.[3] All those tribes belonged, according to the sources analyzed by T. Lewicki, to the Ibāḍiyya. Also the name of 'one of the merchants of Awdaghust', Abū Rustam al-Nafūsī, suggests that he was an Ibāḍī. The presence of merchants from Ifrīqiya in Awdaghust, as part of the spreading network of the Ibāḍiyya, introduced Zanāta elements into a trade system which should have been exclusively in the hands of the Ṣanhāja of the south-western Sahara. Evidence about the presence of Ibāḍīs in Awdaghust goes back only to the tenth century. But the involvement of members of the Sufrites, another Kharijite sect, in the trade of the western Sahara began with the foundation of Sijilmasa, in the oases of Tafilelt, by a group of Miknāsa Berbers in 757/8.

Faithful to the egalitarian doctrines of the Khārijiyya (who esteem piety more than noble descent, saying that even a black slave may be elected caliph), 'they made ʿIsā b. Yazīd al-Aswad ('the Black') their leader'.[4] In southern Morocco, as in Jebel Nefusa, blacks from the

[1] Ibn Ḥammād, *Akhbār mulūk Banī ʿUbayd wa-sītatuhum*, ed. by M. Vonderheyden (Algiers and Paris, 1927), 18.

[2] Lewicki, 'Quelques extraits', 20.

[3] al-Bakrī, *Kitāb al-masālik wa'l-mamālik*, ed. by M. G. de Slane (Algiers, 1911), 158.

[4] al-Bakrī, *Masālik*, 149.

Sudan were prominent among the Kharijites. They could well have contributed to the southward orientation of the emerging Kharijite centres. About this time, in the 750s, al-Mushtarī b. al-Aswad ('the Black'), who was in all probability both a black and a Kharijite, led successive raids from the Sūs al-Aqṣā to the land of the Anbiya, Ṣanhāja of the western Sahara, raids which reached perhaps as far as the Senegal river.[1]

Not more than three years after his election, the first Ṣufrī chief of Sijilmasa, the black 'Isā, was deposed and executed. The new chief, Abu'l-Qāsim Samghū b. Wāsūl al-Miknāsī, was the founder of a dynasty which ruled over Sijilimasa for almost two centuries. In 814/15, during the reign of his son al-Yasaʿ, a wall was built around the town, which must have grown fast in the preceding decades. A few years later, Sijilmasa became the home of Andalusian refugees who had left Cordoba after the Rabaḍ revolt of 818. The Andalusians, who contributed also to the urban development of Fez, were attracted by the commercial prospects of Sijilmasa. The settlement of Jews in Sijilmasa was also associated with the growth of its trade. The ruling dynasty of Sijilmasa became known as Banū Midrār after their most powerful ruler, Midrār, known also as al-Muntaṣir b. al-Yasaʿ b. Abū'l-Qāsim, who reigned for over fifty years (823/4–876/7). Midrār expanded his authority over the town of Darʿa, which had a silver-mine in its vicinity. Darʿa, as we shall see later, was important also as the point of departure for the trans-Saharan caravans.

In 891 al-Yaʿqūbī described a route 'from Sijilmāsa towards the south, making for the land of the Sūdān . . . a distance of fifty stages in the desert'. This route reached across the territory of the Ṣanhāja to the town of Ghust.[2] This is undoubtedly the earliest record of the town of Awdaghust as the southern terminus, and of Sijilmasa as the northern terminus, of a trans-Saharan route.

Al-Yaʿqūbī's knowledge of the Maghrib, the Sahara and the early kingdoms of the Sudan is exceptionally good compared with that of other eastern Arab geographers. Their geographical notions were generally vague, a mixture of hearsay evidence and legends. Nevertheless they all associate Sijilmasa with the trade in gold. Al-Masʿūdī (died 956)

[1] Ibn al-Faqīh, *Mukhtaṣar kitāb al-buldān*, ed. by M. G. de Goeje (Leiden, 1885), 64. This was related by al-Mushtarī himself to Abu'l-Khaṭṭāb, the first Ibāḍī *imām* of the Maghrib. The latter came to the Maghrib about 757/8 and was killed in 761. The name al-Mushtarī seems to have been a Kharijite name, related to *shurāt*, by which name the Kharijites call themselves.

[2] al-Yaʿqūbī, *Kitāb al-buldān*, ed. by M. J. de Goeje (Leiden, 1892), 360.

refers to 'the story of the Land of Gold, which is opposite Sijilmasa'. From Sijilmasa, 'merchants carry goods to the shore of a great river' where they exchange them for gold.[1] Al-Masʿūdī refers to this trade in terms of the impersonal barter known as 'the silent trade', which is often reported in accounts of trade with little-known peoples in remote countries. According to Herodotus, such a trade had been conducted by the Carthaginians on the Atlantic coast. Al-Iṣṭakhrī, writing *c.* 951, believed that Sijilmasa ('a medium-sized town') was close to the mine of gold, which he located 'between Sijilmāsa, the Land of the Sūdān and the Land of Zawīla'.[2]

In 951 Ibn Ḥawqal visited Sijilmasa, and his account throws full light on the commercial role of the town:

> There is at Sijilmāsa an uninterrupted trade with the Land of the Sūdān and other countries, abundant profits and the constant coming and going of caravans.

Ibn Ḥawqal was impressed by the broad-mindedness and enterprise of the inhabitants of Sijilmasa:

> They are well-bred in their actions and perfect in morals and deeds. In their manners they do not share the pettiness of other people of the Maghrib in their dealings and customs, but act with great frankness. They are known for their ready charity and show manly concern for one another ... They put aside all feuds and quarrels ... out of nobility, forgiveness and natural generosity ... which they have acquired in their numerous travels, long periods of absence from home and separation from their country.

At Sijilmasa Ibn Ḥawqal saw a document which related to a debt of 42,000 dinars owed to a merchant of Sijilmasa by one of the merchants of Awdaghust, who was himself from Sijilmasa. Ibn Ḥawqal himself could not conceal his excitement:

> I have never seen or heard anything comparable to this story in the East. When I told it to people in ʿIrāq, Fārs and Khurasān, it was considered remarkable.

This unique reference is evidence not only of the volume of the trade between Sijilmasa and Awdaghust, but also of the sophistication of its commercial system, which must have been elaborated over a long period (perhaps a century and a half). Ibn Ḥawqal estimated the annual revenue of the *amīr* of Sijilmasa at about 400,000 dinars, which was

[1] al-Masʿūdī, *Kitāb murūj al-dhahab wa-maʿādin al-jawhar*, ed. by C. Barbier de Meynard and P. de Courteille (Paris, 1864–77), IV, 92–3.

[2] al-Iṣṭakhrī, *Kitāb al-masālik wa'l-mamālik*, ed. by M. J. de Goeje (Leiden, 1870), 39.

about half 'the total income of the Maghrib from end to end, of about 800,000 dinars'. This revenue came from

taxes on caravans setting out for the Land of the Sūdān . . . from what was bought and sold there, such as camels, sheep, cattle and other merchandise going out and coming in from Ifrīqiya, Fez, Spain, Sūs and Aghmāt, along with other sums due from the mint.[1]

In 910 the Fatimids began to intervene in Sijilmasa with the arrival of the *dāʿī* Abū ʿAbd Allāh to rescue his lord the *mahdī*, ʿUbayd Allāh, who had been imprisoned in Sijilmasa, possibly at the instigation of the Aghlabid ruler. For the next fifty years, the Fatimids maintained their supremacy over Sijilmasa, although the actual government of the town remained in the hands of members of the Midrārid dynasty. Almost imperceptibly the latter relinquished their Ṣufri tenets to become Sunnis. Sijilmasa, and the rest of the Maghrib al-Aqṣā, became the principal battleground for the religious and imperial rivalry between the Fatimids of Ifrīqiya and the Umayyads of Spain, or rather between their allies, the Ṣanhāja and Zanāta respectively.

The creation of the Fatimid caliphate put an end to even the theoretical unity of the Muslim world under the ʿAbbasid caliphate, and in 929 the Umayyad ʿAbd al-Raḥman III assumed the caliphal title, thus asserting his equality of status with his Fatimid rival. A year earlier, in 928, ʿAbd al-Raḥman had ordered the minting of his own dinars. This was considered to be the prerogative of the caliph, and a symbol of complete independence, but he also acted in this way in order to prevent the circulation of Fatimid dinars in his dominions. For the minting of their dinars, the Umayyads depended almost exclusively on the gold of the Sudan. The Fatimids needed gold to finance their extensive propaganda network and to prepare for the conquest of Egypt. These competing demands for gold not only intensified the rivalry between the two empires, but also, it would seem, engendered an increase in the supply of gold and in the volume of the Saharan trade. In the second half of the tenth century, Sijilmasa changed hands and rulers more than once. But whatever losses it suffered in warfare were repaired by the benefits of the trade.

The interest of the Fatimids in Sijilmasa decreased considerably after they had moved their capital to Egypt in 972, not only because of the distance, but also because they diversified the sources of their gold, which they could now also obtain from Nubia and perhaps even from

[1] Ibn Ḥawqal, *Kitāb ṣūrat al-arḍ*, ed. by J. H. Kramers (Leiden, 1938–9), 99–100.

East Africa. The Umayyads, on the other hand, were more determined than ever in the second half of the tenth century to secure their supremacy over Sijilmasa. They supported their Zanāta allies to ward off the pressure of the Zirids, the viceroys of the Fatimids. By the end of the tenth century, two Zanāta dynasties had established their rule over the principal commercial centres of Morocco, namely Sijilmasa, Aghmat and Fez.

For the middle of the eleventh century we have the detailed, and generally reliable, account of al-Bakrī. Sijilmasa had by then emerged as the centre of a busy network of trade-routes, which linked it with Aghmat, Fez, Tlemcen, Tahert and Kairouan. Yet all the routes leading north and east were in fact feeders and outlets for the trade with the Sudan, which was the raison d'être of the system.

The earliest routes from the Maghrib al-Aqṣā to the Sudan crossed the Sahara not far from the Atlantic Coast. Whereas further to the east, human life was dependent on scattered oases, in this coastal zone the influence of the ocean and its currents served to temper the harsh conditions of the Sahara desert. The Ṣanhāja nomads could thus pasture their herds almost throughout the westernmost Sahara, and as a result they provided a virtually unbroken link between Morocco and the Senegal.

A coastal route of two months' travelling distance between Awlil, north of the Senegal, and Nūl, south of Morocco, offered the easiest crossing of the Sahara, with an adequate supply of sweet water. This route, however, was of little commercial importance. More important were two, almost parallel, inland routes which are described in detail by al-Bakrī. One route, from Tāmdult to Awdaghust, passed through the Adrar mountains, the desert of Waran and Tagant. The second route, a little to the east, led from Wadi Darʿa directly to Ghana. This was a more difficult route, and the caravans had to cross 'the Great Desert' (*al-Majāba al-Kubrā*) for eight days without water. More difficult still was a third route, which traders took from Sijilmasa to Tātantāl, a mine where salt was dug out in slabs and where there were a castle and houses built of rock-salt. The description and location (twenty days' march from Sijilmasa) of this mine suggest that this was the same as the salt deposits known later as Taghaza. In the middle of the fourteenth century, Ibn Baṭṭūṭa joined a caravan which took this route, and described the difficulties and dangers encountered by travellers. The route from Sijilmasa to the Sudan via Taghaza became the busiest of all routes, in spite of its hardships, because Taghaza was the principal source of salt for the Sudan until the middle of the sixteenth century. Earlier, when caravans departed from Tāmdult or Wadi Darʿa on the western routes, Sijilmasa offered an easy access to those two termini from Kairouan, Tahert, Tlemcen and even from Fez, avoiding the high passes of the Atlas.[1]

The oases of Tafilelt, stretching along the Ziz river, formed the agricultural hinterland of Sijilmasa. Wheat, dates, grapes and raisins were produced there, and marketed as provisions for the caravans or exported to the Sudan, where the demand for such food increased with the growth of Maghribi communities in the towns of the Sahel.

The more important Arabic sources from the ninth to the eleventh centuries – al-Yaʿqūbī, Ibn Ḥawqal and al-Bakrī – indicate the importance of Awdaghust as a commercial centre in the southern Sahara:

> The people of Awdaghust enjoy extensive benefits and great wealth. The market there is at all times full of people, so that owing to the great crowd and the noise of voices it is almost impossible for a man to hear the words of one sitting beside him ... There are handsome buildings and fine houses.[2]

At the outlet of the Rkiz valley in southern Mauritania (17°26′ N 10°25′ W), excavations on the site of Tegdaoust have revealed several layers of a medieval town, which flourished from the eighth or ninth to the thirteenth or fourteenth centuries, with houses built of stone in a Mediterranean style. Among the objects unearthed were imported glassware and enamelled ceramics as well as oil lamps. Glass ornaments were similar to those discovered in Raqqāda, the ninth-century residential town of the Aghlabids in Ifrīqiya. Small gold weights made of glass, and five gold bars and trinkets (the first ever unearthed in a medieval site in West Africa) clearly point to trade in gold. Tegdaoust was undoubtedly an important commercial town, with a large Muslim population and close connections with the Maghrib. It is unlikely that there was at this time and in this region a town of this description other than the Awdaghust of the Arabic sources.[3]

An interesting, perhaps even intriguing, pattern of commercial centres developed in the tenth and eleventh centuries in the southern Sahara and the Sahel. Awdaghust, a Muslim and Berber town, flourished at a distance of fifteen days' travel north-west of the capital of Ghana. The latter, in its turn, was composed of two towns, a Muslim

[1] See maps in C. Vanacker, 'Géographie économique de l'Afrique du Nord selon les auteurs arabes du 9e au milieu du 12e siècle', *Annales: Economies, Sociétés, Civilisations*, 1973, **28**.

[2] al-Bakrī, *Masālik*, 158.

[3] D. S. Robert, 'Les Fouilles de Tegdaoust', *Journal of African History*, 1970, **11**, 4, 471–93.

town and a royal town. Farther to the east, on the site of Es-Souk in Adrar of the Iforas, Tadmekka, a Muslim and Berber town, flourished at a distance of nine days' travel north of Gao, the Songhay capital. Gao, in its turn, was divided into two towns, a Muslim town and a royal town.

This pattern may reflect a stage in the development of trading relations between the North Africans and the people of the Sudan. Both parties seem to have been rather cautious in exposing themselves to the full impact and consequences of unrestricted commercial and social relations. From the North African end, we have an injunction by the authoritative jurist of Kairouan, Ibn Abī Zayd (died 996): 'Trade to the territory of the enemy and to the Land of the Sūdān is reprehensible.'[1] It appears as if the North African traders preferred to have their southern entrepôts in the domains of the Berbers, which they considered as being within *Dār al-Islām*.

In the following centuries, with the spread of Islam in the kingdoms of the Sudan, the cultural and religious boundary which had existed between the peoples of the Sahara and the Sahel lost its significance. Walata, and later Timbuktu, had a mixed population of Berbers and Sudanese. Ethnic distinctions increasingly gave way to a social dichotomy, that between the urban and rural societies of the western Sudan.

The principal routes of the Sahara were generally in a north–south direction, linking the Sahel with Morocco, the Niger bend with the central Maghrib, and Lake Chad with Tripoli. The dynamics of this trade system, however, also induced a more complex pattern with diverse ramifications. Merchants from Ifrīqiya were prominent in Awdaghust; Tadmekka traded with Ghana, and Ghadames with Gao. There were also important routes from west to east. Thus along the northern fringes of the Sahara, Sijilmasa was linked by a route to Kairouan.

Significantly one of the earliest routes recorded in the Arabic sources was one leading from Ghana in a north-easterly direction through Gao, Aïr and Tibesti and over the oases of Kharga and Dakhla (al-Waḥāt) to Egypt. It seems that by the time Ibn al-Faqīh described this route, in 902 or 903, caravans had stopped using it. Ibn Ḥawqal says that Aḥmad b. Ṭulūn, the ruler of Egypt in 868–84, ordered traders not to take this route because many caravans had been lost in sandstorms or at the hands of brigands. By the middle of the tenth century,

[1] Ibn Abī Zayd al-Qayrawānī, *al-Risāla*, ed. by L. Bercher (Algiers, 1952), 318. I owe this reference to J. O. Hunwick.

according to al-Iṣṭakhrī, 'the Oases' (al-Waḥāt) had been deserted. There were, however, signs that those places had been populated and prosperous in the past. Al-Idrīsī mentions two towns between the Oases and the Sudan which had prospered before they were covered by sands and their water resources dried up.

THE ṢANHĀJA AND THE ALMORAVIDS

During the eighth and ninth centuries, the people of the western Sahara were known to the Arabs as Anbiya. The earliest reference to them dates from the middle of the eighth century, when the black Kharijite al-Mushtarī b. al-Aswad reported his raids from al-Sūs al-Aqṣā, 'the Farthest Sus', to 'the land of the Anbiya'.[1] In the first half of the ninth century, al-Fazārī described the vast (2,500 by 600 *farsakhs*) 'province of Anbiya', extending between the provinces of Sijilmasa and Ghana.[2] The name Anbiya appears for the last time in Ibn al-Faqīh's text, written in 902/3. The derivation of this name and its meaning are both uncertain. Shortly before this name disappeared from our sources, al-Yaʿqūbī (writing in 891) had presented a more detailed account of the Anbiya and indicated their association with the Ṣanhāja:

> He who travels from Sijilmāsa towards the south, making for the land of the Sūdān . . . goes in a desert a distance of fifty stages. In the desert he will be met by a people called Anbiya of the Ṣanhāja. They have no permanent dwelling, and it is their custom to veil their faces with their turbans. They do not wear [sewn] clothes but wrap themselves in lengths of cloth. They subsist on camels, for they have no crops or wheat.[3]

Al-Yaʿqūbī's description of the Anbiya's way of life is repeated, sometimes even verbally, by later geographers in their accounts of the Ṣanhāja, a name which replaced Anbiya in the tenth century. In the middle of the tenth century, according to Ibn Ḥawqal, there were two powerful rulers in the desert, namely the king of the Massūfa and the king of 'the Ṣanhāja of Awdaghust':

[1] Ibn al-Faqīh, *Mukhtaṣar*, 64. (See also p. 645, n. 1, where the dating of al-Mushtarī's evidence to the eighth century is explained.)

[2] Quoted in al-Masʿūdī, *Murūj*, IV, 39. It has been generally accepted that this work of al-Fazārī was written towards the end of the eighth century, and it has therefore been considered to be the earliest reference to Ghana. Yet, on the basis of a recent study by M. Hadj Sadok (in the 'Introduction' to his edition of al-Zuhrī, *Kitāb al-Jaʿrāfiyya*, *Bulletin d'Études Orientales*, 1968, **21**, 26–31), it is clear that the al-Fazārī quoted by al-Masʿūdī was not Abū Isḥāq Ibrāhīm b. al-Ḥabīb, who lived at the time of the caliphs al-Manṣūr (754–75) and Hārūn al-Rashīd (786–809), but his son Abū 'Abd Allāh Muḥammad b. Ibrāhīm, a contemporary of the Caliph al-Ma'mūn (813–33). Al-Fazārī's reference to Ghana is probably not earlier than that of al-Khwārizmī.

[3] al-Yaʿqūbī, *Buldān*, 360.

Banū Massūfa are a great tribe who live far inland [between Awdaghust and Sijilmasa] around inadequate waterpoints ... They have a king who rules them and administers their affairs. The Ṣanhāja and other people of those regions respect him, because they control the route ... They levy dues from every camel and load belonging to those who pass through their territory to trade and from those returning from the land of the Sūdān with gold.

The Massūfa king gained power through the control of the principal trade-routes, and his people served as guides to the caravans. The Massūfa were responsible also for the development of the salt-mine of Taghaza (al-Bakrī's 'Tatantal'), where they employed their slaves in quarrying the salt bars. Another centre of power developed among the 'Ṣanhāja of Awdaghust' who 'live apart deep in the deserts'. Ibn Ḥawqal's informant met their chief, Ti-n-Bārūtān b. Usfayshar, who was considered to be 'king of all the Ṣanhāja':

Ti-n-Bārūtān told him that he had been ruling over them for twenty years, and that each year people came to visit him whom he had never known before, nor heard of, nor set eyes on. He said that there were about 300,000 tents, including shelters and hovels, and that the kingship over this tribe had always been in his family.[1]

This contemporary account, recorded from an eyewitness, may be collated with al-Bakrī's information. Although al-Bakrī wrote in 1067/8, much of his information about Awdaghust is borrowed from Muḥammad b. Yūsuf al-Warrāq (died 973–4), who had written about a century earlier, and was therefore also a contemporary of that Ṣanhāja king. In this version he is called Ti-n-Yarūtān b. Wīsanū b. Nizār and is considered 'ruler of Awdaghust'. He ruled during the 960s.

This Ṣanhāja chief ruled over Awdaghust, but it is unlikely that he made this town his capital. The Ṣanhāja were attached to their nomadic way of life, and their chief would not have settled in a cosmopolitan urban centre like Awdaghust, where the majority of the inhabitants were Zanāta and Arabs. He must have ruled over Awdaghust from his nomad camp, as did the fifteenth-century Tuareg chief Akillu who exercised authority over Timbuktu. The Ṣanhāja presumably were not involved directly in the commercial transactions of the trans-Saharan trade, which was then in the hands of Zanāta and Arab, predominantly Ibadite, traders. The Ṣanhāja derived income and power by the control of the routes and the commercial centres, collecting dues and presents as protectors and fees as guides.

As chief of the southern Ṣanhāja near the Sahel, Ti-n-B/Yarūtān interacted with his Sudanese neighbours. According to Ibn Ḥawqal,

[1] Ibn Ḥawqal, *Ṣurat al-arḍ*, 100–1.

this King of Awdaghust maintained relations with the ruler of Ghana and exchanged gifts with the ruler of Kūgha. Both rulers, he adds, 'stand in pressing need of the kings of Awdaghust, because of the salt which comes to them from the lands of Islam. They cannot do without this salt.'[1]

Whereas Ibn Ḥawqal is concerned with the commercial and diplomatic relations between the Berber ruler of Awdaghust and the Sudanese rulers of Ghana and Kūgha, al-Warrāq, as reported by al-Bakrī, says that the authority of this Berber chief 'was recognized by more than twenty kings of the Sūdān, every one of whom paid him tribute'. Ti-n-B/Yarūtān also intervened in a dispute between the chiefs of Māsin and Awghām, both provinces of Ghana. 'He came to the aid of the chief of Māsin with 50,000 camelry, and they invaded, pillaging and burning, the country of Awghām, whose soldiers were taken unawares.' The king of Awghām was killed, and many of the women of Awghām committed suicide.[2]

In the middle of the tenth century the Ṣanhāja seem to have exerted political and military pressure on the Sudanese kingdom of Ghana. But within less than a century the people of Awdaghust are said to have 'accepted the authority of the king of Ghana'.[3] This might be interpreted as an indication that the balance of power had been redressed in favour of the Sudanese kingdom.

Al-Bakrī, whose information about the Sahara and the Sahel is updated to the middle of the eleventh century, does not explain in what circumstances Awdaghust had come under the authority of Ghana only a few decades earlier. According to al-Bakrī, there was no connection between Ti-n-Yarūtān, ruler of Awdaghust in the 960s, and Muḥammad Tārashnā (or Tarsina), the Lamtūna chief who was killed 'in a place called Qanqāra in the land of the Sūdān' in the first half of the eleventh century. Three centuries later, however, Ibn Abī Zarʿ (who wrote in 1326) presented an apparently coherent tradition, which covers the period from the eighth to the eleventh centuries. Ibn Abī Zarʿ's chronicle, as elaborated by Ibn Khaldūn, has been accepted by modern historians as a principal source for the political history of the Ṣanhāja of the western Sahara. Nevertheless, a critical study of these accounts by Ibn Abī Zarʿ and Ibn Khaldūn reveals that we are dealing not with coherent historical traditions, but with a 'scissors-and-paste' manipulation of al-Bakrī's text and other unknown sources.[4]

[1] Ibid. 101. [2] al-Bakrī, *Masālik*, 158. [3] Ibid. 168.

[4] This is demonstrated in the notes to al-Bakrī, Ibn ʿIdhārī, Ibn Abī Zarʿ and Ibn Khaldūn in the forthcoming *Medieval Arabic sources*.

Following the overthrow of the first line of chiefs (in the description of which one may detect clear elements of al-Bakrī's account of Ti-n-Yarūtān), Ibn Abī Zarʿ postulated 120 years of disunity and confusion. The Ṣanhāja could not agree on one ruler, 'until there arose among them the emir Abū ʿAbd Allāh Muḥammad b. Tīfāt, known as Tārashnā al-Lamtūnī. They agreed upon him and made him their leader.'[1] Was Awdaghust lost to the Ṣanhāja during that period of disunity and confusion? If we accept Ibn Abī Zarʿ's perception of the political organization of the Ṣanhāja as a confederation of tribes which went through a cyclical process of cohesion and disintegration, this was perhaps the case. When the emir Abū ʿAbd Allāh b. Tīfāt (alias Muḥammad Tārashnā) of the Lamtūna died he was succeeded as ruler of the Ṣanhāja by his in-law (*ṣihr*), Yaḥyā b. Ibrāhim of the Juddāla.

The Ṣanhāja confederation, according to Ibn Abī Zarʿ, brought together the Lamtūna and Juddāla tribes. The alliance between the two tribes was cemented by intermarriage of the two chiefly families, and the chieftaincy rotated between them. The evidence for such a procedure is doubtful. Al-Bakrī, from whom Ibn Abī Zarʿ learned the names of the two chiefs, had not indicated any relationship between Tārashnā of the Lamtūna and Yaḥyā of the Juddāla, as each of them had been mentioned in the context of his own tribe. It is quite likely that in his attempt to present a coherent chronicle, Ibn Abī Zarʿ invented the marital relationship to link together the two chiefs mentioned by al-Bakrī. In doing so, Ibn Abī Zarʿ may have had in mind other cases of intermarriage between the two tribes. The mother of Abū Bakr b. ʿUmar the Lamtūna is said to have been of the Juddāla.

The fourteenth-century historians (Ibn Abī Zarʿ and Ibn Khaldūn) sought to establish a political connection between the Lamtūna and the Juddāla as a background to the emergence of the Almoravid movement, in which both tribes were involved. But this writer's own interpretation would suggest that the Almoravids did not reconstruct a tribal confederation which had existed in the past, but introduced a new element into the segmentary politics of the Sahara. This politico-religious movement, under the combined leadership of the spiritual authority and the tribal *amīr*, mobilized the resources of the Ṣanhāja, and made them rulers of the Maghrib and Spain.

Muslim traders from the Maghrib – Berbers and Arabs – carried

[1] Ibn Abī Zarʿ, *al-Anīs al-muṭrib bi-rawḍ al-qirṭās fī akhbār mulūk al-Maghrib wa-ta'rīkh madīnat* Fās, ed. by C. J. Tornberg (Uppsala, 1843–66), 76. It is quoted also in Ibn Khaldūn, *Kitāb ta'rīkh al-duwal al-Islāmiya bi'l-Maghrib min Kitāb al-ʿIbar*, ed. by M. G. de Slane (Paris, 1847), I, 236.

Islam into the Sahara. Under their influence the veiled Ṣanhāja of the desert entered upon the long process of islamization. Towards the end of the ninth century, according to al-Yaʿqūbī, the king of Ghust (Awdaghust) 'did not follow any religious practice nor possess any revealed law'.[1] He was therefore considered to be an infidel. Although Ibn Ḥawqal and al-Bakrī say nothing about the religion of Ti-n-B/Yarūtān in the middle of the tenth century, it is likely that he was already a Muslim, and the whole of the Sahara was considered as *Dār al-Islām*. This is confirmed by al-Muhallabī, who wrote in 985.

The earliest Ṣanhāja chief who is positively described as Muslim was 'Muḥammad known as Tārashnā, a pious man of virtue, who performed the Pilgrimage to Mecca and participated in the Holy War. He was killed in the place called Qanqāra in the land of the Sūdān.'[2] It is likely that the jihad he led was against the black people of the Sahara and the Sahel. A century and a half earlier, the infidel king of Ghust had already raided the land of the *Sūdān*. It seems as though raids on the *Sūdān* turned into a jihad after the Ṣanhāja chiefs had adopted Islam.

Muḥammad Tārashnā is praised not only for taking part in the jihad, but also for performing the Pilgrimage to Mecca. At least two other Ṣanhāja chiefs in the first half of the eleventh century went to Mecca, namely ʿUmar, father of Yaḥyā and Abū Bakr, the future leaders of the Almoravids,[3] and the Juddāla chief Yaḥyā b. Ibrāhīm. Students of West African history are aware of the significance of the Pilgrimage to Mecca, and of the journey through the Maghrib and Egypt, in stimulating reform movements. The pilgrims discovered the contrast between the diluted forms of Islam as practised by their own people and Islam as taught in the main centres of Islamic learning.

This is indeed what happened to Yaḥyā b. Ibrāhīm, the Juddāla chief, who set out for the Pilgrimage to Mecca in 1035/6:[4]

During his return journey Yaḥyā b. Ibrāhīm met the jurist Abū ʿImrān al-Fāsī [in Kairouan]. The jurist asked him about his native country, its customs, and which religious doctrines were professed there, but found him wholly ignorant, though avid to learn, full of good intentions and firm of faith. So he spoke thus: 'What prevents you from studying the religous law properly, and from ordering good and prohibiting evil?' Yaḥyā replied: 'Only those teachers come to us who possess neither piety nor knowledge of the Sunna.' Then he asked Abū ʿImrān to send with him one of his disciples, a man of

[1] al-Yaʿqūbī, *Buldān*, 360. [2] al-Bakrī, *Masālik*, 164.

[3] al-Bakri (*Masālik*, 167) refers to their brother as Yannū b. ʿUmar al-Hājj.

[4] This date is given by Ibn Abī Zarʿ (*Rawḍ*, 76). The dates given in the various sources are compared and evaluated in the notes to the forthcoming *Medieval Arabic sources*.

whose learning and piety he was sure, who could teach them and uphold the precepts of the *sharīʿa*.[1]

As Abū ʿImrān could not find anyone among his disciples in Kairouan who would be willing to go with Yaḥyā, he sent the latter with a letter to one of his former disciples, Waggāg b. Zalwī in the Sūs al-Aqṣā. Waggāg chose from among his companions a man called ʿAbd Allāh b. Yāsīn, who accompanied Yaḥyā b. Ibrāhīm to the camps of the Juddāla.

ʿAbd Allāh b. Yāsīn saw the reprehensible actions which were evident and widespread among the Ṣanhāja. He encountered men who married six, seven or ten wives, or whatever number they desired... He found that most of them did not pray nor know aught of Islam except the declaration of faith (*shahāda*), and were entirely overcome by ignorance... Then he began to teach them religion and to explain the law and the Sunna to them, to command them to do good and to forbid them to do evil.[2]

Before we follow the changing fortunes of Ibn Yāsīn's reform, the setback he suffered at an early stage in his mission among the Juddāla, his retreat (*hijra*), and the subsequent emergence of the Almoravid movement, we should attempt to understand the religious message of Ibn Yāsīn and its origins. This exploration passes through Waggāg's school in southern Morocco and back to Kairouan, so retracing Ibn Yāsīn's spiritual descent from Abū ʿImrān al-Fāsī and the religious milieu in the capital of Ifrīqiya.

After it had served as a base for the military operations of the Arabs during the conquest of the Maghrib, Kairouan became the centre for the propagation of Islam among the Berbers. As Berber groups in the countryside responded to the teachings of Kharijite and Shiʿite sects, Kairouan remained the stronghold of the Sunna, of Islamic orthodoxy. From the ninth century onwards, this spirit of Islamic militancy was sustained by a body of *fuqahā'* of the Mālikī school of law. By the time that the first disciples of Mālik b. Anas (died 795) came to Ifrīqiya at the beginning of the ninth century, *fuqahā'* of the Ḥanafī school had already secured positions of influence and were favoured by the Aghlabid emirs. The Malikites turned to win the sympathy of the commoners, and gradually gained influence among the people, who admired their strict adherence to the Koran and the Sunna, their piety and devotion. A spirit of self-sacrifice and popular support helped the Malikites to

[1] al-Bakrī, *Masālik*, 164.

[2] Ibn Abī Zarʿ, *Rawḍ*, 78. Cf. H. T. Norris, 'New evidence on the life of ʿAbdullāh b. Yāsīn and the origins of the Almoravid movement', *Journal of African History*, 1971, **12**, 265 n. 40. Norris exposes the stereotypic nature of this account of a sinful society in arguing that the Ṣanhāja society is fundamentally monogamous.

overcome the worst of all ordeals, that of the Fatimid domination in the tenth century.

Biographical accounts are full of stories about *fuqahā'* who refused to accept the Fatimid doctrines or to pray in mosques where the *khuṭba* was pronounced in the name of ʿAlī and the Fatimid caliph. The resistance of the Malikites became more significant because of the compliance of the Hanafites, who collaborated with the Fatimid rulers. The Malikites kept alive the glow of popular recalcitrance, and openly supported the anti-Fatimid revolt of Abū Yazīd the Kharijite. After the Fatimid caliphs transferred their capital to Egypt, the Malikite *fuqahā* encouraged the Zirid viceroys to break off relations with their overlords, and instigated the massacre of the Shiʿites. Among the leading *fuqahā'* who exerted pressure on the Zirid emir al-Muʿizz b. Badīs to remove the last vestiges of the Fatimids' sovereignty was Abū ʿImrān al-Fāsī. It was at the beginning of AH 430 (end of AD 1038 or beginning of 1039), when the rupture with the Fatimids was about to reach its conclusive stage and the militancy of the Malikites was at its height, that the Juddāla chief Yaḥyā b. Ibrāhīm visited Kairouan, and met Abū ʿImrān. The timing of this visit must be significant for the understanding of the origins of the Almoravid movement.

The *fuqahā'* of Kairouan were supported in their successive struggles by the *murābiṭūn*, the people of the *ribāṭs*. As has been seen in chapter 8, these had first been established as military posts along the coast of Ifrīqiya against attacks by the Byzantine fleet. But after the Muslim fleet had asserted its supremacy in the Mediterranean, the *ribāṭs* lost their military vocation, and became centres for religious and ascetic devotion and for the propagation of the faith. Militancy, however, remained a salient feature of those *ribāṭs*, with the notion of a perpetual jihad, both temporal and spiritual. In Kairouan and in the *ribāṭs* the Malikites combined the study of Islamic jurisprudence (*fiqh*) with the practice of asceticism (*zuhd*). Though ascetics, they did not withdraw entirely from worldly matters; they were in constant communication with the ordinary people. They became guardians of the commoners' interests, challenged the rulers on such issues, and emerged as popular leaders. In the fusion of *fiqh* and *zuhd*, legalism and asceticism, Ibn Yāsīn and the Almoravids were true heirs to those Malikites of Ifrīqiya.

In the tenth and eleventh centuries, Kairouan was an important centre of Islamic learning, and almost all the important *fuqahā'* of the Maghrib studied there for some time. Abū ʿImrān, a native of Fez, had studied in Kairouan and then settled there to be one of the leading *fuqahā'* of his time. Students from all over the Maghrib came to study with him, and among them Waggāg b. Zalwī.

Waggāg b. Zalwi al-Lamṭī from the people of the Farthest Sūs travelled to Kairouan, where he studied under Abū ʿImrān al-Fāsī. He then returned to the Sūs, and established a house, which he named Dār al-Murābiṭīn for students of science and for reciters of the Koran. The Maṣmūda used to visit him to be blessed by his invocations, and to seek his prayers for rain whenever they were afflicted by drought.[1]

Waggāg's *Dār al-Murābiṭīn* may be viewed as an extension of the Malikite tradition of Kairouan. For the purpose of our study, Waggāg represents the link between his master Abū ʿImrān and his disciple ʿAbd Allāh b. Yāsīn. Likewise, Waggāg's country, southern Morocco, mediated between Ifrīqiya and the Sahara.

From the eighth to the eleventh centuries, the Maghrib al-Aqṣā was a refuge for a number of heretical sects. Most important of those were the Barghawāṭa, who held sway over the Atlantic plains of Morocco between Sale and Safi for three centuries. Their prophet Ṣāliḥ gave them a new Koran in the Berber language, altered the Muslim liturgy, and developed syncretic doctrines in which Berber cultural values were mixed with Islamic elements borrowed from different sects. The jihad against the Barghawāṭa was considered a religious obligation. The *ribāṭ* of Sale defended 'the Land of Islam' (*Bilād al-Islām*) against the Barghawāṭa. On his way back from Spain, ʿAbd Allāh b. Yāsīn passed through the land of the Barghawāṭa, and was impressed by the power of those heretics. Years later, at the head of the Almoravids, Ibn Yāsīn resolved to crush their power and eradicate their heresy. He was killed in this jihad. South of the Barghawāṭa, in Sus, in the Atlas and in Darʿa, were groups of Kharijites and Shiʿites. In describing one of those Shiʿite groups and their abominable heresy, al-Bakrī adds that it is against them that the Prophet said: 'In the Maghrib there is a mountain called Daran. On the Day of Resurrection it will hurry along with its inhabitants down to hell like the bride who is taken to her groom.'[2] According to Ibn Abī Zarʿ, those Rawāfid were exterminated by Ibn Yāsīn.

Apart from the *ribāṭ* of Sale, facing the Barghawāṭa, two other *ribāṭs* are mentioned along the Atlantic coast. These *ribaṭs* were strongholds of Islamic orthodoxy confronting the hinterland, which was a nest of heresy. Scholars from southern Morocco who had gone to Kairouan

[1] al-Tādilī, *Kitāb al-tashawwuf ilā rijāl al-taṣawwuf*, ed. by A. Faure (Rabat, 1958), 66.

[2] al-Bakrī, *Masālik*, 160–1; see also Ibn Ḥawqal, *Ṣūrat al-arḍ*, 91–2, 102.

to study brought back the militant spirit of the Malikites of Ifrīqiya, and found a fertile ground in their own country to carry that same tradition. One of the centres where this tradition – of militancy, piety and asceticism – was cultivated was Waggāg's *Dār al-Murābiṭīn*:

In his *ribāṭ* he is devoted to the service of Allāh, reads science, and summons people to pursue the Good. He has many disciples who study religious sciences under him.[1]

From this *ribāṭ*, ʿAbd Allāh b. Yāsīn set out to the Sahara with that same spirit of militancy against negligence and heresy.

Al-Bakrī, and later Arab authors who followed his account, stress religious laxity and negligence as the principal weakness of Islam in the southern Sahara – which Ibn Yāsīn was determined to reform. Islam, very likely, did lie rather lightly on the Saharan nomads. But it appears that in the first half of the eleventh century the Ibāḍiyya also had significant influence over the nomads of the Sahara, and was particularly strong in the commercial towns of the southern Sahara, like Awdaghust and Tadmekka. This is perhaps what one may read into the text of the twelfth-century geographer al-Zuhrī. In referring to the nomads of the Sahara (whom he calls *al-murābiṭūn*), he says:

These people accepted Islam when the people of Wārqlān [Wargla] did so in the time of [the Umayyad] Hishām b. ʿAbd al-Mālik [724–43]. But they adopted a school which took them outside the Holy Law. They returned to orthodox Islam when the people of Ghana, Tadmekka and Zāfūn adopted Islam.[2]

Al-Zuhrī implies in this passage that the nomads of the Sahara had been followers of an unorthodox school of Islam since the eighth century. According to the evidence discussed earlier in this chapter, they must have been Ibāḍīs. They returned to the Sunna when the people of Ghana adopted Islam. This was, according to al-Zuhrī, in 1076/7, under the impact of the Almoravids. One result of the Almoravids' exploits in the Sahara was, therefore, the eradication of the influence of the Ibāḍiyya and its traces. Paulo de Moraes Farias has already suggested that the Almoravids' practice of killing all dogs might have been an anti-Ibāḍī measure because, it seems, the custom of eating dogs prevailed (as a survival of pre-Islamic times) in Kharijite centres, such as Sijilmasa, Gafsa and Qastiliya.[3] There is, therefore,

[1] Ibn Abī Zarʿ, *Rawḍ*, 77. [2] al-Zuhrī, *Kitāb al-Jaʿrāfiyya*, 126.

[3] P. F. de Moraes Farias, 'The Almoravids: some questions concerning the character of the movement during its period of closest contact with the Western Sudan', *Bulletin de l'IFAN*, 1967, **29**, 809–10.

enough evidence to conclude that Ibn Yāsīn carried into the Sahara the struggle against heresy which was one of the features of Malikite militancy in Ifrīqiya and in southern Morocco.

The Juddāla chief Yaḥyā b. Ibrāhīm complained to Abū ʿImrān al-Fāsī about the absence of qualified teachers in the Sahara. It appears, however, that the Juddāla had had their own *fuqahā'* before the arrival of Ibn Yāsīn. Most prominent among them was Jawhar b. Sakkum, 'a man learned in law', who – according to one version, that of al-Bakrī, led the Juddāla opposition against Ibn Yāsīn, as 'it seems that they found some contradictions in his judgements'.[1] H. T. Norris suggests that Jawhar rose to protect the interests of the Juddāla élite.[2] But perhaps it was the clash between a local *faqīh*, who defended the established pattern of Islam, and a reformer from the outside. Confrontations of this kind are known from the nineteenth century.

Ibn Yāsīn began his mission with the teaching of the Koran, the *hadīth* and the Muslim Law. He imposed the stipulated punishment (*ḥudūd*) in the strict application of the *sharīʿa*. In this Ibn Yāsīn followed the Malikite tradition of Kairouan, where Mālik's own disciple Saḥnūn (776–856) is said to have carried out the *ḥudūd* in the Great Mosque.[3] Other rulings of Ibn Yāsīn, such as the observance of the public prayer or the killing of all dogs, may be viewed as an enforcement of the *Muwaṭṭa'*, the work of Mālik b. Anas. Ibn Yāsīn carried out reforms during the progress of the Almoravids' conquest, and changed what was not in conformity with the precepts of Islam. He abolished illegal taxes, and levied the legally prescribed tax (*ṣadaqa* or *ʿushr*) only. He established the public treasury (*bayt al-māl*), and carefully distributed the booty according to the Law.

But Ibn Yasīn proceeded beyond the strict application of the letter of the Law. He preached repentance, which involved also purification from past transgressions. Those who joined his movement experienced a new conversion (*islāman jadidan*). This was a process of reclamation, purification and reconversion, which he considered a preparatory stage for the military exploits. He himself 'led a monastic and ascetic life (*tarahhaba wa-nasaka*)... He refrained from eating meat and drinking milk, because he considered all their property impure.'[4] Piety and puritanism, zeal and militancy led Ibn Yāsīn to extremism. For al-Bakrī, who lived in the sophisticated and cultivated milieu of Cordoba, Ibn

[1] al-Bakrī, *Masālik*, 165. [2] Norris, 'New evidence on Ibn Yāsīn', 259.

[3] al-Qāḍī ʿIyāḍ, *Tartīb al-madārik wa-taqrīb al-masālik li-maʿrifat aʿlām madhhab Mālik*, ed. by Aḥmad Bakīr Maḥmūd (Beirut, 1967), IV, 601.

[4] Ibn Khaldūn, *Ta'rīkh al-duwal*, I, 230; al-Bakrī, *Masālik*, 165.

Yāsīn's rulings were considered eccentric, verging on sheer ignorance. Norris rightly points out that al-Bakrī's account of Ibn Yāsīn shows 'the whole man, "warts and all", as a jurist, miracle-worker, fanatic and ascetic, a connoisseur of feminine beauty, a military leader of some accomplishment'.[1] It is a near-contemporary account of a controversial personality. The fourteenth-century Ibn Abī Zarʿ, on the other hand, described Ibn Yāsīn in the hagiographical style, having words of praise only for his intelligence, nobility, piety and erudition.

Ibn Yāsīn's extremism brought about his expulsion from among the Juddāla. According to al-Bakrī, followed by Ibn ʿIdhārī, Ibn Yāsīn had the full support of his master Waggāg during this crisis. It is significant, however, that al-Nuwayrī (died 1332) says that Waggāg disapproved of Ibn Yāsīn's extremism and reproached him for excessive bloodshed. Ibn Yāsīn replied to his master in a letter which is worth quoting:

> As for your rebuke of what I did and your regret for sending me out, you have sent me to an ignorant nation [describing in detail their vices] . . . I have advised them what is prescribed to them, the words of the Law, and the stipulated punishment . . . I have not exceeded Allah's commandments.[2]

In his religious message, Ibn Yāsīn followed the militant tradition of the Malikite school as it had developed in Kairouan and had been carried on in Waggāg's *Dār al-Murābiṭīn* in the Sus. The excessive rigidity, however, seems to have been the result of a combination of Ibn Yāsīn's personal temperament and what he considered to be the deplorable conditions of Islam among the Ṣanhāja.

ʿAbd Allāh b. Yāsīn resolved to enforce a rigorous observance of the *sharīʿa* in a society notorious for its ignorance of Islam and its laxity. The distance separating the ideal norms exhorted by Ibn Yāsīn from the debased practices of the Ṣanhāja could not have been bridged over without a crisis. In rejecting Ibn Yāsīn's reform, the Juddāla were led by a *faqīh*, one of their former religious leaders, and by two tribal elders. They resented his religious teaching and feared its political implications. Ibn Yāsīn was compelled to retreat from among the Juddāla. The withdrawal of the reformer from the resisting society could be compared with the *hijra* of the Prophet Muḥammad. Away from the sinful society, the reformer created a new community guided solely by his teachings, and uninhibited by former religious values and socio-political traditions. It was only after the *hijra* that Ibn Yāsīn consolidated his

[1] Norris, 'New evidence on Ibn Yāsīn', 265.

[2] al-Nuwayrī, *Nihāyat al-ʿArab* (Granada, 1919), XXII, 176.

position as the supreme authority, and only then did the Almoravid movement emerge out of the secular tribal society.

Ibn Yāsīn came out of his retreat at the head of a devoted body of *murābiṭūn*, inspired by his teachings and ready to spread them among their fellow tribesmen by persuasion or through jihad. The larger tribes, the Juddāla and the Lamtūna, seem to have been coerced into the movement. Other tribes of the Sahara offered their submission and became incorporated into the movement. A new politico-religious system brought unity to the Ṣanhāja tribes of the Sahara, and released a great potency and energy. This was soon diverted to the expansion of the Almoravids northwards to Morocco and southwards to the Sudan.

The foregoing is an analytical abstract of the origins of the Almoravid movement, which attempts to take into consideration at least six versions of this account in the Arabic sources. A more detailed study of the elements of the various accounts would involve lengthy discussions and digressions, which might obscure the essentials of the process.

Ibn Yāsīn had begun his mission among the Juddāla, but at a certain stage – perhaps after their rebellion which forced his retreat – Ibn Yāsīn found his most ardent supporters among members of the chiefly family of the Lamtūna. Yaḥyā b. ʿUmar of the Lamtūna became the *amīr*, the military commander of the movement. ʿAbd Allāh b. Yāsīn attended to their religious and judicial affairs and administered their public treasury (*bayt al-māl*). He was, however, 'the real *amīr* because it was he who ordered and prohibited, who gave and took away'.[1] Ibn Yāsīn's authority over the *amīr* is well illustrated in an anecdote which tells how Yaḥyā b. ʿUmar had submitted himself to a flogging before he was even told of his sin. This pattern of dual leadership continued as long as Ibn Yāsīn was alive.

Ever since the appointment of Yaḥyā b. ʿUmar, the Almoravid movement, despite the supratribal character that Ibn Yāsīn had aspired to give it, became more narrowly identified with the Lamtūna, who held the prominent political positions. The Juddāla, who had reluctantly been coerced to rejoin the movement, waited for an opportunity to secede. This they did when the main force of the Almoravids was engaged in military operations in Sijilmasa and Awdaghust. Yaḥyā b. ʿUmar was killed in battle against the rebellious Juddāla. 'From that time', al-Bakrī says, 'the Almoravids made no more attempts against the Juddāla.'[2]

After the Almoravids had conquered southern Morocco, disturb-

[1] Ibn Abī Zarʿ, *Rawḍ*, 80. [2] al-Bakrī, *Masālik*, 168.

ances in the desert occurred again. The conflict was between Juddāla and Lamtūna, according to one version, or between the Massūfa and the Lamtūna, according to another source.[1] Although the Juddāla and the Massūfa might have resented the dominant role of the Lamtūna, members of those two tribes participated in the exploits of the Almoravids in the Maghrib, and held positions of leadership.

The *hijra* and the transformation of a tribal society into a politico-religious community suggest parallels between Ibn Yāsīn and the Prophet Muhammad. The comparison may be extended farther to the military expansion outside the desert after the unification of the tribal nomads. The economic and demographic factors which some modern scholars have considered in explaining the expansion of the Arabs into the Fertile Crescent appear also in the interpretation of the Almoravids' conquest of the Maghrib. Both the medieval historian Ibn al-Athīr (died 1233) and the modern historian Terrasse speak of the over-population in the Sahara which the limited resources of the desert could not have supported.[2] The weakness of this explanation is that it does not account for this unique case of a northbound migration of Saharan Berbers at a time when they were still advancing southwards at the expense of black sedentaries.

An economic factor of greater significance was the desire of the Ṣanhāja to reassert their control of the trans-Saharan trade. This is clearly indicated by the fact that they had first moved north to take possession of Darʿa and Sijilmasa, and then moved back southwards across the Sahara to capture Awdaghust. Some decades earlier Awdaghust had come under the authority of the king of Ghana, whereas the northern termini, Sijilmasa and Darʿa, were being ruled by Zanāta chiefs.

Two Zanāta dynasties established principalities in Morocco in the last quarter of the tenth century as vassals of the Umayyads of Spain. The Banū Ifran had their capitals at Sale and Tadla, whereas the Maghrāwa ruled at Fez, Sijilmasa and Aghmat. In the second quarter of the eleventh century, these Zanāta rulers were engaged in internal feuds. In Morocco, as in Spain, the last decades before the Almoravids' conquest were those of 'party kings' (*mulūk al-ṭawāʾif*).[3] Ibn Abī Zarʿ,

[1] Ibn ʿIdhārī al-Marrākushī, *Kitāb al-Bayān al-mughrib fī akhbār al-Andalus wa'l-Maghrib*, ed. by A. H. Miranda, *Hespéris-Tamuda*, 1961, **2**, 55; Ibn Khaldūn, *Ta'rīkh al-duwal*, I, 239. The two sources give different dates to this event; 462/1071, and 453/1061, respectively.

[2] Ibn al-Athīr, *Kitāb al-Kāmil fi'l-ta'rīkh*, ed. by C. J. Tornberg (Leiden, 1851–76), IX, 425–6; H. Terrasse, *Histoire du Maroc* (Casablanca, 1949–50), I, 217–18.

[3] This comparison is made by Ibn ʿIdhārī, *al-Bayān*, 48.

the chronicler of Fez, described the deterioration of political and economic conditions under the Zanāta regime during this period. He says that they oppressed their subjects, shed their blood and violated their women, and that commodities became in short supply and prices went up. As food became scarce, chiefs of the Banū Ifran and the Maghrāwa used to break into homes to seize food and to deprive traders of their goods. In such circumstances, people greeted the arrival of the Almoravids as a salvation, especially as the Almoravids immediately abolished all the illegal taxes.[1]

Maghrāwa rule over Wadi Darʿa affected the free movement of the northern Ṣanhāja tribes, such as the Lamṭa and the Jazūla. Waggāg b. Zalwī al-Lamṭī and ʿAbd Allāh b. Yāsīn al-Jazūlī were members of these tribes. Beyond the grievances of their own tribesmen, the Malikite *fuqahā'*, in the tradition of Kairouan, defended the cause of the people against oppression by the rulers.

Relations between Waggāg and Ibn Yāsīn continued after the latter's departure to the Sahara. Waggāg encouraged Ibn Yāsīn to carry on his mission after he had been rejected by the Juddāla. It is related that after his victory over the Saharan tribes, Ibn Yāsīn sent presents to the scholars (*ṭalaba*) and judges (*quḍāt*) of the land of the Maṣmūda. It was very likely to his former colleagues in the circle of Waggāg that these presents were sent.

In AH 447 [AD 1055] the learned and pious men of Sijilmāsa and Darʿa wrote to the *faqīh* ʿAbd Allāh b. Yāsīn and to the *amīr* Yaḥyā b. ʿUmar and the Almoravid shaykhs urging them to come to their country to purify it of the evil practices, injustice, and tyranny which were rife there. They told him of the oppression, contempt and tyranny suffered by men of science and religion and the rest of the Muslims at the hands of the *amīr* Masʿūd b. Wānūdīn al-Zanātī al-Maghrāwī.[2]

Ibn Khaldūn, who says that Waggāg lived at Sijilmasa, states that it was Waggāg who wrote the letter calling on the Almoravids to overthrow the emirs of Sijilmasa. In the fourteenth century, historians in Morocco believed that the Almoravids' drive northwards and their conquest of Sijilmasa and the Sūs al-Aqṣā were in response to the call of the *fuqahā'* there. Waggāg must have played an important role, as the anonymous author of *Mafākhir al-Barbar* wrote in 1312/13: 'These two, namely Waggāg and ʿAbd Allāh b. Yāsīn, were the reason for the

[1] Ibn Abī Zarʿ, *Rawḍ*, 71–2; see also Ibn al-Athīr, *al-Kāmil*, IX, 428.
[2] Ibn Abī Zarʿ, *Rawḍ*, 81.

aggression of the *mulathammūn*, known as *murābiṭūn*, out of the desert by the order of Abū ʿImrān al-Fāsī.'[1]

This fourteenth-century historical interpretation ought to be considered by modern historians, as it brings into focus quite a few elements which have been analysed in this chapter. The Almoravid movement should be viewed as an offshoot of the Malikite school in Kairouan, which, after its initial success in the Sahara, rebounded to impose rigorous Malikism in the Maghrib and Spain. The potential force of the Ṣanhāja of the desert was recruited by the inspiration of a militant Islamic ideology to fight for the cause of Malikism and Ṣanhāja supremacy.

GHANA

The Almoravids, and in particular their leader, Abū Bakr b. ʿUmar, are credited by oral traditions in Mauritania with the final dispossession of the Blacks from their strongholds in the Sahara. In fact, the Almoravids' exploits marked a decisive stage in a long process in which black sedentaries retreated south to the Sahel as the Berber nomads advanced.

Archaeological and traditional evidence indicates that over two thousand years ago black sedentaries lived as far north as 20° N. One tradition suggests that Blacks even reached as far as the region of Saqiyat al-Hamra':

> One whom I found to be trustworthy told me that a man used to travel with his cow from the Sāqiya 'l-Ḥamrā' to Kayhīdi [St Louis]. He did not pass the night in a solitary waste, nor was his cow thirsty. This was due to the great number of Negroes [there].[2]

The withdrawal of the black sedentaries, which had been initiated by the desiccation of the Sahara, was accelerated from the third or the fourth centuries onwards by the camel-riding Ṣanhāja. By the ninth century, when Arabic sources provide the earliest contemporary evidence, the Ṣanhāja had spread all over the Sahara and had made contact with the Sudanese of the Sahel. There were, however, black groups in the interior of the Sahara. Al-Bakrī reported black highway robbers north of Awdaghust, beyond a country inhabited by the Ṣanhāja. The Lamtūna chief Muḥammad Tarashnā was killed in war against the black people of Gangara, perhaps in Adrar. Abū Bakr b.

[1] *Mafākhir al-Barbar*, ed. by E. Lévi-Provençal in *Textes Arabes Marocaines* (Rabat, 1934), 69.

[2] 'The ancient history of the Mauritanian Adrār and the sons of Shams al-Dīn', by ʿAbd al-Wadūd b. Aḥmad Mawhid al-Shamasdī (died 1944/5), in Norris, *Saharan myth*, 132.

ʿUmar, the Almoravid leader, is said to have been killed in war against the Blacks in Tagant, where his grave is shown about 55 km south of Tijikja. These geographical indications suggest that most of the wars of the Ṣanhāja leaders, as reported by the Arab sources (al-Yaʿqūbī, al-Bakrī, Ibn Abī Zarʿ), could have been against black groups in the Sahara itself, and not necessarily against the land of the *Sūdān* in the Sahel.

The intricate pattern of relations between the tenth-century Ṣanhāja ruler of Awdaghust and the kingdom of Ghana has already been referred to. Whereas Ibn Ḥawqal mentioned the exchange of gifts between the two rulers and their mutual commercial interests, al-Bakrī (relying on al-Warrāq) provides evidence concerning the military intervention of the Ṣanhāja chief in a province of Ghana. Furthermore, the passing of Awdaghust under the authority of the King of Ghana suggests that the northern frontier of the Sudanese kingdom with its Berber neighbours was not static. It is likely that it moved in either direction in accordance with the balance of power.

The pressure of the nomads on the black sedentaries of the Sahel increased during periods of severe drought, when the nomads moved south in search of water and pasture. This must have had a devastating effect on agriculture in the Sahel, where there was minimal rainfall and a long dry season. As a result the desert expanded at the expense of the Sahel, and cultivated country became a nomad domain. One example of this process is the region of Kumbi-Saleh, which has been presumed to be the site of Ghana's capital. Today nomads here roam over a land of low grass, thorny scrub and scattered acacia trees. But the ruins of the town and traces of villages prove that the country had formerly been settled. Al-Bakrī described wells around the capital of Ghana, 'from which the people drink, and with which they grow vegetables'.[1] With the retreat of the sedentary population, the wells were neglected and became filled with sand, the nomads' herds destroyed the vegetation and erosion completed the deterioration of the barren land.

The Soninke, the people of ancient Ghana, are the northernmost Sudanic people. Before the arrival of the Berbers, their ancestors had occupied the Sahara, as is suggested by the survival of black groups in Walata, Nema, Tichit, and as far as Shinqit, who speak Azer, which is a Soninke dialect. The Soninke were among the earliest peoples of the Sudan to adopt food production and metallurgy, and to experience the consequent social, economic and political developments. They also had

[1] al-Bakrī, *Masālik*, 175.

the longest contact with the nomads of the Sahara, and were exposed to the nomads' pressure and to the impact of the trans-Saharan trade. Both external influences stimulated socio-political reorganization on a larger scale, so as to repulse any aggression from the nomads and to gain control over the trade system.

The name Sahel for the northern belt of the western Sudan is derived from the Arabic *sāḥil*, meaning 'shore'. It is the shore of the desert, the sea of sand. Towns which developed in the Sahel played the role of ports, where caravans unloaded imported goods – principally salt – and loaded the products of the Sudan, principally gold. The gold came from the interior, and a system of trade-routes developed between the termini of the Saharan routes and the goldfields of Bambouk, at the confluence of the Senegal and Faleme rivers. The kingdom of Ghana emerged in the second half of the first millennium – when the Saharan trade gained momentum – and extended its authority over that part of the Sudan which became integrated into the developing trade system.

Along the Saharan trade-routes scattered pieces of information reached the Arabs north of the Sahara, and thence went on to Baghdad, the caliphal capital, and to other eastern centres where the science of Muslim geography began. The name of Ghana first appears in the Arabic sources in the 830s, in the works of al-Fazārī and al-Khwārizmī. But nothing was then known about that kingdom beyond its association with gold. In 872, al-Ya'qūbī provided the earliest evidence, vague as it was, about political organization in the Sudan. He mentions the three principal kingdoms known at that period – Ghana, Gao, and Kanem – and says that the rulers of these kingdoms had other kings under their authority.[1] Al-Ya'qūbi seems to have recognized a basic principle in the pattern of political organization in West Africa, where the so-called empires – those names which appear prominently in our sources – were in fact superstructures imposed over smaller chiefdoms.

During the following two centuries, between al-Ya'qūbī (872) and al-Bakrī (1067/8), Arab geographers added only little to our knowledge of Ghana. Al-Bakrī's account is invaluable not only because of the amplified description and its apparent reliability, but also because we owe to him a panoramic view of the western Sudan, focused on Ghana, shortly before this region experienced far-reaching changes as a result of the intervention of the Almoravids. Al-Bakrī's description of the twin towns in the capital of Ghana is among the most widely quoted texts of African history:

[1] al-Ya'qūbī, *Kitāb al-Ta'rīkh*, ed. by H. T. Houtsma (Leiden, 1863–6), 219–20.

The city of Ghana consists of two towns situated on a plain. One of these towns, which is inhabited by Muslims, is large and possesses twelve mosques, in one of which they assemble for the Friday prayer. There are salaried *imāms* and muezzins, as well as jurists and scholars. In the environs are wells with sweet water, from which they drink and with which they grow vegetables.

The king's town is six miles [about 10 km] distant from this one and bears the name of al-Ghāba. Between these two towns there are continuous habitations. The houses of the inhabitants are of stone and acacia wood. The king has a palace and a number of domed dwellings all surrounded with an enclosure like a city wall.

In the king's town, and not far from his court of justice, is a mosque where pray such Muslims as pay him formal visits.

Around the king's town are domed buildings and groves and thickets where the sorcerers of these people, men in charge of the religious cult, live. In them are their idols and the tombs of their kings. These woods are guarded and none may enter them and know what is there.[1]

The Muslim town, which comprised also the commercial quarters of Ghana, seems to have been larger and more spacious than the royal town. The relations between the two towns were perhaps comparable to the relations between such twin towns in modern Ghana as Salaga and Kpembe or Gambaga and Nalerigu – that is, a commercial-Muslim-cosmopolitan town which is politically dependent on a royal-traditional inward-looking village. Each town had its own places of worship; twelve mosques in the Muslim town, and the sacred grove contiguous to the royal town (the name of which, *al-Ghāba*, 'forest', may have been derived from that grove).

The pattern of separate towns for the Muslims and the chiefs, which al-Bakrī described in the eleventh century in Ghana and in Gao, continued until the modern period. But this residential segregation did not prevent close communications between the two parties. Although the king of Ghana adhered to his ancestral religion, he was a friend to the Muslims. Because of their literacy and their association with the foreign traders, he appointed Muslims to senior positions in the administration: 'The king's interpreters, the official in charge of his treasury, and the majority of his ministers were Muslims.' It was for these officials and for Muslim visitors that the king built a mosque near his palace. Out of respect for the Muslims' way of life, the king exempted them from greeting him in the traditional way of his subjects, who 'fall on their knees and sprinkle dust on their heads'. Instead the Muslims 'greet him only by clapping their hands'.

[1] al-Bakrī, *Masālik*, 175.

Significantly, al-Bakrī refers to religious rather than ethnic or racial distinctions. That he does not speak about white and black, Berbers and Sudanese, but about Muslims and 'people who profess the same religion as the king', might suggest that there were Muslims among the Soninke subjects of the king. These would very likely be the Sudanese traders who plied between the goldfields of Bambouk and the capital of Ghana. On the other hand, there was in Ghana a group of people of white complexion (said to have been descendants of troops sent by the Umayyads to Ghana), who 'follow the religion of the people of Ghana'.[1]

Al-Bakrī's informants left Ghana after the old king Basī had been succeeded by his sister's son Tunka Manīn, in 1063; according to this information, royal succession in Ghana was matrilineal. This, however, is far from certain, because the Soninke are patrilineal, and were such in all probability nine hundred years ago. It has been suggested that perhaps the royal family of Ghana came under the influence of the Ṣanhāja of the southern Sahara, who do follow a matrilineal mode of succession.[2]

Visitors to Ghana must have been impressed by the trappings and the pomp of the king's audience, which is described by al-Bakrī in some detail. The king, adorned like a woman, with a high cap decorated with gold and wrapped in a turban of fine cloth, sat in a domed pavilion. Behind him were ten pages holding shields and swords, and to his right sons of (vassal) kings of his country. In front of him, the governor of the town and the ministers sat on the ground. The door was guarded by dogs of excellent pedigree. The spectator must have been dazzled by the glittering gold which decorated shields, swords, garments and even the dogs' collars.

Such a court was in all probability the principal consumer of luxury goods imported from the Maghrib. But lesser chiefs soon imitated their sovereign and, along with the foreign traders resident in the capital, created an ever-expanding market for imports. The Saharan trade, which started with the importation of such a basic commodity as salt, increased in volume and became more diversified and sophisticated.

International trade added to the power of the monarch because it guaranteed a source of income beyond the economic resources of the country, and independent of the lower echelons of the political system. Al-Bakrī gives some idea of the tolls levied by the king of Ghana:

[1] Ibid. 179.

[2] For a more detailed discussion, see N. Levtzion, 'Was royal succession in Ghana matrilineal?', *International Journal of African Historical Studies*, 1972, 5, 91–3.

On every donkey-load of salt the King of Ghana levys one golden *dinār* when it is brought into his country and two *dinārs* when it is sent out. From a load of copper the king's due is five *mithqāls* and from a load of other goods ten *mithqāls*.[1]

The other goods must have been luxurious imports of great value, to justify the high rate of duty levied. Copper and other goods were consumed in Ghana and were therefore taxed only once. But part of the salt was carried further south from Ghana, and was taxed a second time when it left and at twice as high a rate. Transportation is a decisive element in the cost of salt, which is a bulky commodity, and its value could have doubled when carried from the northern to the southern frontiers of Ghana.

There is no record of a tax on exported gold. The king of Ghana had a share in the production of gold through a regulation that 'rare nuggets, weighing between an ounce and a pound (*roṭl*), found in the mines were reserved for the king and only gold dust was left for the people'. Perhaps the king exploited popular superstition about the mysterious quality of gold nuggets, which only the supernatural power attached to the king could overcome. 'The King of Ghana', says al-Idrīsī, 'had in his palace a brick of gold weighing thirty pounds (*roṭls*) made of one piece.' The king of Mali also boasted of a huge stone of gold.[2]

Al-Bakrī says nothing about the slave-trade in Ghana, but according to al-Idrīsī's account, almost a century later, the people of Ghana, Takrur and Silla – who represented the developed nations of the northern belt of the western Sudan – raided the country of the Lamlam – the stateless people in the interior. They brought back slaves and sold them to merchants from the Maghrib.

In the middle of the eleventh century, Ghana was by far the largest and most powerful kingdom in the western Sudan. It is difficult to draw its frontiers accurately or to determine the extent of its authority over outlying provinces. Al-Bakrī's information, however, offers a few valuable indications. The northern frontier of Ghana seems to have been conditioned by the balance of power between the Ṣanhāja nomads and the Soninke kingdom. Shortly before the rise of the Almoravids, Ghana reached its farthest point to the north with the conquest of Awdaghust. To the west, there were several small chiefdoms of the Sahel in a buffer

[1] al-Bakrī, *Masālik*, 176.

[2] al-Idrīsī, *Kitāb nuzhat al-mushtāq fī ikhtirāq al-āfāq*, ed. by R. Dozy and M. J. de Goeje Leiden, 1866), 7; Ibn Khaldūn, *Ta'rīkh al-duwal*, I, 266–7.

zone separating Ghana from Silla and Takrur. The last province of Ghana to the east was Safanqu, three days' travel from Ghana, north of Ra's al-Mā' on the Niger. The Songhay kingdom, with its capital at Gao, did not extend at that period west of the Niger bend.[1]

To the north, west and east, Ghana interacted with peoples and kingdoms who had reached a similar level of political development. It was towards the south that the Soninke of Ghana could expand through conquest, migration or trade. Archaeological and traditional evidence suggests that Soninke migrants, who might have been associated with Ghana, settled in the Niger valley, and as far as Dia and Jenne. Farther to the west the southern frontier of Ghana touched the gold-bearing region of Bambouk beyond the upper Senegal river. It is not clear what sort of authority the king of Ghana had over the goldfields, but these must have been within the sphere of influence of Ghana, through whose territory most of the gold was exported northwards.

Al-Bakrī says that the best gold of Ghana came from the town of Ghiyārū, eighteen days' travel from the capital of Ghana. Ghiyārū was a trading-post on the right bank of the upper Senegal not far from the modern town of Kayes. West of Ghiyārū was Yarasnī, another important commercial centre, where an isolated Muslim community flourished, and from which Sudanese merchants carried the gold to other countries. Al-Bakrī does not mention Muslim communities along the route from Ghana to Ghiyārū and Yarasnī, but says that 'when Muslims enter their country, the people treat them with respect and step out of their way'.[2]

Beyond the upper Senegal, in the country of the Malinke, al-Bakrī noted the emergence of two chiefdoms, Do (or Daw) and Malal, which marked the beginning of greater political cohesion among the Malinke people. It was perhaps about this time that trade-routes were extended beyond the upper Senegal towards new sources of gold in Bure on the upper Niger. It is certainly significant that not long after the emergence of these early chiefdoms of the Malinke, their rulers came under the influence of Islam. Indeed, one of the most instructive accounts of a process of islamization in West Africa is that given by al-Bakrī in relation to Malal, one of the two Malinke chiefdoms:

The King of Malal is known as al-Muslimānī. He is thus called because his country became afflicted with drought for year after year; the inhabitants prayed for rain, sacrificing cattle till they had exterminated almost all of them, but the drought and the misery only increased. The king had as his guest a

[1] *Ta'rīkh al-Fattāsh*, ed. and trans. by O. Houdas and M. Delafosse (Paris, 1913), App. II, trans. 334.

[2] al-Bakrī, *Masālik*, 177.

Muslim who used to read the Koran and was acquainted with the *sunna*. To this man the king complained of the calamities that assailed him and his people. The man said: 'O King, if you believed in God (who is exalted) and testified that He is One, and testify as to the Prophetic mission of Muḥammad (God bless him and give him peace) and if you accepted all the religious laws of Islam, I would pray for your deliverance from your plight and that God's mercy would envelop all the people of your country and that your enemies and adversaries might envy you on this account.' Thus he continued to press the king until the latter accepted Islam and became a sincere Muslim. The man made him recite some easy passages from the Koran and taught him religious obligations and practices which no one may be excused from knowing.

Then the Muslim made him wait till the eve of the following Friday, when he ordered him to purify himself by a complete ablution, and clothed him in a cotton garment which he had. The two of them came out towards a mound of earth, and there the Muslim stood praying while the king, standing at his right side, imitated him. Thus they prayed for a part of the night, the Muslim reciting invocations and the king saying 'Amen'.

The dawn had just started to break when God caused abundant rain to descend upon them. So the king ordered the idols to be broken and expelled the sorcerers from his country. He and his descendants after him as well as his nobles were sincerely attached to Islam, while the common people remained polytheists. Since then their rulers have been given the title of al-Muslimānī.[1]

The Muslim converted the chief of Malal after he had given proof of the omnipotence of Allah. Praying to Him saved the kingdom after all the rituals of the traditional religion had been used in vain. It was the magical aspects of Islam that aided Muslims to win over the chiefs in competition with the local priests. Only the chief, his family and the nobility were converted, whereas the commoners remained attached to their old religion. The role of the chiefs as early recipients of Islamic influence is a salient feature in the process of islamization in other parts of West Africa. That the king of Malal was taught only those religious obligations which no one might be excused from knowing might indicate the superficial islamization of the chief, whose ties with the traditional religion were not totally severed.

In the thirteenth century, Malal and Do, together with other chiefdoms of the Malinke, were incorporated into the empire of Mali. Although Ghana and Mali were the kingdoms of two separate ethnic groups, the Soninke and the Malinke respectively, they succeeded each other in the hegemony over the Sahel and the termini of the Saharan trade. This perception of political continuity features in the indigenous

[1] Ibid. 178.

historiography of the western Sudan, as is exemplified in the seventeenth-century *Ta'rīkh al-Fattāsh*: 'The kingdom of Mali rose to power only after the fall of the kingdom of the Kaya-Magha, ruler of the whole western region.'[1] The kingdom of the Kaya-Magha is the name given by the two *Ta'rīkhs* of Timbuktu to the ancient Soninke kingdom. Both recorded versions of a similar tradition, saying that the dynasty of Kaya-Magha began long before the coming of the Prophet Muḥammad, and that the kings were originally white (one version says Ṣanhāja) and their subjects Soninke. Both versions imply that eventually power was taken over by the Soninke.

Another set of historical traditions, recorded during the present century, gives different versions of the ancient kingdom of the Soninke, which is here called Wagadu.[2] Dinga, the ancestor of the Soninke, came from the east, and settled in the Sahel, not far from Nioro. One of his sons, Dyabe, established a kingdom with its capital at Kumbi, between Goumbou and Nema. The guardian of this place was the black snake Bida, who gave permission to Dyabe to settle there on condition that a beautiful young virgin would be presented to him every year. In return Bida promised abundant rain and much gold. The kingdom of Wagadu, as it became known, prospered under the rule of Dyabe Sisse and his descendants until the day when the suitor of the virgin chosen to be presented to Bida killed the snake. The dying snake pronounced a dreadful curse which caused the desiccation of the land and the cessation of the flow of gold. Deprived of rain and gold, Wagadu was ruined, the country became desert and its Soninke people dispersed.

Peoples and clans of Soninke origin are now scattered all over the western Sudan as far as the Volta basin, the upper Niger and the Gambia river. Some left the Sahel because of the pressure of the nomads who took possession of the cultivated lands. Others migrated south as traders, and played a leading role in the extension of the trade system. For all these Soninke clans in their dispersion, the legend of Wagadu is the starting point of their own stories of origin, and it explains their status in terms of the role their ancestors had played in the ancient kingdom of the Soninke.

The traditions about Wagadu recorded in recent times, those about Kaya-Magha which were committed to writing in the seventeenth

[1] *Ta'rīkh al-Fattāsh*, 41–2/trans. 75–9; see also al-Sa'dī, *Ta'rīkh al-Sūdān*, ed. and trans. by O. Houdas (Paris, 1900), 9/trans. 18.

[2] The different versions of the legend of Wagadu were collated by C. Monteil in 'La Légende du Ouagadougou et l'origine des Soninkés', *Mélanges ethnologiques* (Dakar, 1953), 369–82.

century, and the contemporary evidence of the Arab geographers about Ghana refer, perhaps, to the same ancient Soninke kingdom. The different versions represent the changing perspectives of a kingdom which had passed away as early as the thirteenth century, viewed from different points of time and place. There are however a few common elements in all the accounts, such as the association of the Soninke kingdom with gold. Al-Saʿdī, the author of the *Ta'rīkh al-Sūdān*, identified the capital of Kaya-Magha with the Ghana of the Arabs, whereas both *Ta'rīkh al-Fattāsh* and the legends of Wagadu refer to Kumbi as the capital of the Soninke kingdom. These references to Kumbi, as well as general geographical indications in all the sources and the local traditions, led archaeologists to the site of Kumbi-Saleh, between Goumbou and Nema (15°46′ N, 8° W).

After preliminary surveys in 1914 and 1939, the site was excavated by Thomassey, Mauny and Szumowski in 1949–51. They found remains of a large town which covered about 3 sq. km. The upper section of the town was built of stone with spacious, often two-storey, buildings. These houses probably belonged to rich merchants, who used the ground floor for storing goods. Isolated stone buildings were also found in the lower section of the town, but other houses there were of lesser quality. The houses were built close together with rather narrow streets, which indicates that the town was quite densely inhabited. Mauny estimated its population at about fifteen to twenty thousand. A great east-west avenue, 12 m wide, opens up at its western end to form a large square, 30 m across, which could have been the market-place. Outside the town were two extensive cemeteries. Objects found on the site were both of local production, such as iron lances, knives, nails and farming tools, and imported goods, such as Mediterranean pottery. There were stones with Arabic inscriptions of verses from the Koran and others with decorative paintings. Glass weights were discovered which were of such a small size that it is likely that they were used for weighing gold. Such findings support the architectural evidence that a rich Muslim community lived at Kumbi-Saleh.

Such a large town, which was an important commercial centre, in this part of the Sahel may, at least tentatively, be identified with the capital of Ghana. The radiocarbon dates indicate that the town flourished at the beginning of the first millennium (see chapter 5, p. 340). Perhaps the site of Kumbi-Saleh was that of the Muslim town of Ghana, described by al-Bakrī. It has been pointed out above that the royal town of Ghana could have been no more than a large

Soninke village with little or no stone buildings. This has not been found, but if it were, no spectacular discoveries might be expected.

TAKRUR

From the fourteenth century onwards, the whole of the western Sudan became known in the Arabic sources as Takrur. In the eleventh century, al-Bakrī used the name to refer to a Sudanic kingdom on the 'Nile' (i.e. the lower Senegal) not far from the Atlantic. This kingdom flourished in the region now known as Futa Toro, and the name of its present people, the Tukolor (French: Toucouleur), is a corrupted form (through Wolof and French) of the Arabic *Takārīr*, or 'the people of Takrur'. The eleventh-century Takārīr, like the modern Tukolor, were among the most thoroughly islamized peoples of the western Sudan. Compared with the qualified acceptance of Islam by the rulers of Malal and Gao, whose subjects maintained their old religions, the king of Takrur zealously embraced Islam and imposed the new religion in all its vigour upon his people:

> The people of Takrur are black, who were previously, like all the other Sūdān, idolators and worshipped *dakākīr* (*dakkūr* is their word for an idol) until Wār Jābī b. Rabīs became their ruler. He embraced Islam, introduced among them the Muslim religious law and compelled them to observe it, thus opening their eyes to the truth. Wār Jābī died in 432/1040–1 and the people of Takrur are Muslims today.
>
> From the town of Takrur you go to Silā. This place too consists of two towns situated on both banks of the Nīl. Its inhabitants are Muslims who were converted to Islam by Wār-Jābī, may God have mercy upon him . . . The King of Silā is at war with the infidels.[1]

Here is one of the very few cases prior to the eighteenth and nineteenth centuries of a militant Islamic state, where the ruler compelled his subjects to observe the *sharī'a* and endeavoured to convert another king (that of Silā), who seems to have been under Takrur's influence. Wār-Jābī imparted his militancy to the King of Silā, who carried on a jihad against the infidels.

It appears as if Islam in Senegal maintained its uniqueness, compared with other regions of the western Sudan, from the eleventh century to modern times. Today the influence of the marabouts in Senegal far exceeds their role elsewhere in West Africa. In a way, maraboutism in

[1] al-Bakrī, *Masālik*, 172.

Senegal is a Sudanic extension of Moorish maraboutism in the south-western Sahara. This might be explained, among other reasons, by the fact that in the western Sahara there were continuous human contacts across the desert from southern Morocco to the Senegal river.

Wār Jābī died in 1040/1, that is about the time ʿAbd Allāh b. Yāsīn came to the desert. His conversion must therefore have been before the rise of the Almoravid movement. There had perhaps been zealous preachers among the Ṣanhāja before the arrival of Ibn Yāsīn. The Lamtūna chief Muḥammad Tārashnā is described as 'a pious man of virtue, who performed the pilgrimage to Mecca and led the jihad'. Yaḥyā b. Ibrāhīm of the Juddāla and his predecessors were also probably committed to Islam. It seems likely that it was as a result of contacts with the Juddāla that a militant preacher converted Wār Jābī. The Blacks of Takrur seem to have accepted this Islamic teaching with greater commitment than their Ṣanhāja neighbours. Indeed, when ʿAbd Allāh b. Yāsīn was expelled from among the Juddāla 'he wanted to leave them and go to the land of the Sūdān who had adopted Islam'.[1]

Ibn Yāsīn contracted an alliance with Takrur, the king of which, Labī son of Wār-Jābī, was with Yaḥyā b. ʿUmar in the battle against the rebellious Juddāla in 1056. As allies of the victorious Almoravids, Takrur probably extended its influence up the Senegal river; this may be inferred from the twelfth-century account of al-Idrīsī. Takrur thus came to challenge the exclusive control of the trade with Bambouk which Ghana had enjoyed in the middle of the eleventh century.

The oral traditions of Futa Toro, as recorded in Arabic by Siré Abbas Soh, offer a different view of the history of the region of Takrur. According to these traditions, the first dynasty of Futa Toro was that of the Dyaʿogo, who are said to have been of white origin, and who therefore could have been Berber nomads who had infiltrated into the lower Senegal valley. Perhaps the interaction and the intermarriage between these pastoralists and the sedentary Tukolor (*Takārīr*, i.e. 'people of Takrur') gave rise to the Fulani, the ubiquitous herdsmen of modern West Africa, who speak the language of the Tukolor.

We do not know for how long the Dyaʿogo had reigned before they were overthrown by a black dynasty, known to the traditionalists as the Manna. Was al-Bakrī's Wār Jābī a member of this dynasty? Perhaps, if any conflation of the oral traditions with the contemporary evidence is to make sense. Contact with pastoralists, the process of state-building, and the spread of Islam brought about the differentiation of the

[1] Ibn Abī Zarʿ, *Rawḍ*, 78.

Tukolor from their southern neighbours, the Wolof. Among the latter, state-building began in the thirteenth century and the conversion to Islam was a slower process.

GAO AND THE SONGHAY

Songhay, the last of the great empires of the western Sudan, was in its origins a contemporary of Ghana. Under the name of Kawkaw (which could cover the name of both the ancient capital Kukiya and of the later one, Gao), the kingdom of Songhay was mentioned together with Ghana by al-Khwarizmī in the first half of the ninth century. By then Kawkaw must have become a kingdom of some importance for its name to have reached the caliph's court in Baghdad. There had been commercial relations between Gao and Tahert in the central Maghrib since the end of the eighth century. Towards the end of the reign of the second *imām* of Tahert, ʿAbd al-Waḥhāb (784/5–823/4), the *imām*'s son al-Aflaḥ, is said to have prepared for the journey to Jawjaw (another way of writing Kawkaw in Arabic script), but had to give it up by order of his father.

In 872 al-Yaʿqūbī considered the kingdom of Kawkaw to be

> the greatest of all the realms of the Sūdān, the most important and powerful . . . There are a number of kingdoms whose rulers pay allegiance to the king of Kawkaw and acknowledge his sovereignty, although they are kings in their own lands.[1]

About a century later, the Egyptian geographer al-Muhallabī described, for the first time, a Sudanic town divided by the 'Nile' (i.e. the Niger). Kawkaw was composed of two towns. On the eastern bank of the river (towards the desert) was the town called Sarnāh (perhaps the present site known as Sané), 'where there are markets and trading houses and to which there is continuous traffic from all parts'. There was another town on the west bank, 'where [the king] and his men and those who have his confidence live'.[2]

According to the historical traditions of the Songhay, their ancient capital was at Kukiya, just north of the Falls of Labezanga (the present frontier between the republics of Mali and Niger). But with the introduction of the Songhay into the trans-Saharan trade, the new town of Gao developed north of Kukiya as the terminus of the Saharan tracks. Some time after the establishment of the commercial quarter of Gao on

[1] al-Yaʿqūbi, *Ta'rīkh*, 220. [2] Quoted in Yāqūt, *Muʿjam*, IV, 329.

the eastern bank of the river, the Songhay rulers also moved north, and established a royal town on the opposite bank, in order to secure control over the trade and to reap its benefits. This process took place between the second half of the eighth century, when the trade with Tahert had begun, and the middle of the tenth century.

Commercial relations and social interaction with the Muslim residents of Kawkaw brought the ruler and the local people under the influence of Islam. There is some ambiguity in al-Muhallabī's account that 'their king makes a show of Islam before his subjects (*yuẓāhiru raʿyatahu bi'l-islām*) and most of them make a show before him (*yuẓāhiru bihi*)'. There was a mosque in the royal town where the king prayed, and a communal prayer-ground between the two towns. Al-Muhallabī's implication that the ruler of Gao was not an unqualified Muslim may be somewhat clearer when we refer to al-Bakrī's more detailed account, which relates to the middle of the eleventh century. Al-Bakrī confirms the division of Kawkaw into two towns, 'one being the residence of the king and the other inhabited by the Muslims'. However he suggests something more complex than a straightforward religious dichotomy because, although the people of Kawkaw 'worship idols as do the other Sūdān . . . their king is a Muslim, for they entrust the kingship only to Muslims'. On his accession to the throne, the king was given 'a signet ring, a sword, and a copy of the Koran which, they assert, were sent to them by the Commander of the Faithful [the caliph]'. Although the kingship became closely associated with Islam, it was not relieved of its traditional pre-Islamic heritage:

> When their king sits down [to partake of a meal] a drum is beaten . . . and nobody in the town goes about his business until he has finished his repast, the remnants of which are thrown into the Nile. At this [the courtiers] shout out boisterously so that the people know that the king has finished his meal.[1]

Customs which are designed to screen the king's meals are known from other West African societies, and will shortly be mentioned also in the case of ancient Kanem. These customs are perhaps connected with divine kingship. In order to maintain his position among the subjects, taboos which guard his person and office had to be observed. Hence the mixing of Islamic and traditional elements, which is so typical of islamized kingdoms in the western Sudan.

The external Arabic sources shed light on a Sudanic kingdom when

[1] al-Bakrī, *Masālik*, 183.

it had become linked to the Saharan trade and thus had been exposed to Islamic influence. The earlier stages in the development of such a kingdom are dealt with in the historical traditions. One set of traditions, which has been transmitted orally until the present century, begins with the mythological ancestor of the Sorko, the fishermen of the Niger, called Faran Maka Bote. He led the Sorko from the present frontiers of Dahomey and Nigeria up the Niger river to the region of Bentia, north of Tillabery, where they found hippopotamuses in abundance. The Niger played an important role throughout the history of Songhay, because the Sorko fishermen were the dominant element among the heterogenous Songhay people. The complementary elements were the Gow hunters and the Do farmers, who seem to have accepted the leadership of the mobile and warlike Sorko, masters of the Niger.

Another set of traditions, recorded by the Muslim chroniclers of Timbuktu in the seventeenth century, could be interpreted as referring to another stage in the political development of Songhay. According to these traditions, the people of Songhay had worshipped a monstrous fish, and were subject to its stringent laws, until it was killed by a stranger ('who came from the Yemen'). According to one version, he was aided by a blacksmith and a drummer. He became King of the Songhay and was the founder of the earliest known dynasty, that of the Dya.[1] The myth of the dragon-killer who becomes king is known from various parts of West Africa. This myth is often interpreted as a change in the basis of authority, from that of the priest who was acting for the fish or 'the spirit of the river' to that of a ruler who soon gained a monopoly over the use of coercive power, employing political rather than religious sanctions. The traditions, as they are recorded in Muslim chronicles, suggest that this political process could have been influenced by contact with the Berbers of the Sahara.

Although it might be possible to arrange different cultural elements of Songhay along a sequence of political development, it is significant that what we considered to be the oldest components are dominant in current oral traditions. The old has not been rejected by a newly acquired culture, but has survived in an uneasy symbiosis. When Gao became the new capital of Songhay, Kukiya retained its position as the ancestral capital, where kings were ceremonially invested, and where they often sought rest from the busy cosmopolitan capital. Later on, after Islam seems to have triumphed over the traditional religion, the latter proved its vitality in a cultural resurgence.

1 al-Saʿdī, *Taʾrīkh al-Sūdān* 4–5/trans. 6–9; *Taʾrīkh al-Fattāsh*, App. II, trans. 329–31.

THE ZAGHĀWA AND KANEM

'Zaghāwa' is the earliest ethnic name from the Sahara and the Sudan to be recorded in the Arabic sources. Wahb b. Munabbih, who died in AD 728 or 732, counted the Zaghāwa among the races of the *Sūdān* together with the Nūba, Zanj, Ḥabasha, Copts and Berbers.[1] The Zaghāwa, who now live in Wadai and Darfur, are part of the Teda-Tubu group, black nomads of the eastern Sahara. Indeed, it appears that Wahb b. Munabbih used Zaghāwa as a generic name for the whole Teda-Tubu group.

More than a century later, writing between 836 and 847, the geographer al-Khwārizmī mentioned the Zaghāwa together with the two oldest states of the Sudan, Ghana and Gao. That Zaghāwa was considered also as a kingdom was confirmed by al-Ya'qūbī in 872. He describes 'the kingdom of the Zaghāwa who live in a place called Kānim'.[2] Kanem, which is mentioned here for the first time, consisted of several vassal kingdoms, as also did Ghana and Gao according to the same account of al-Ya'qūbī. In the tenth century the kingdom was still known to the author of *Akhbār al-Zamān* and to al-Muhallabī as 'the kingdom of the Zaghāwa'.[3] Mānān, one of the two towns of the Zaghāwa mentioned by al-Muhallabī, was described by the thirteenth-century geographer Ibn Sa'īd as the capital of the kings of Kanem before their conversion to Islam. From the time of al-Bakrī in the eleventh century, the kingdom became known as Kanem. Before that, as it is evident from al-Ya'qūbī, Kanem was simply a geographical term. Indeed, it is generally accepted that the name Kanem is derived from the word for 'south' (*anem*) in the Teda and Kanuri languages.[4]

The desiccation of the Sahara caused a southward movement of population into the more humid lands of the Chad basin. Such a north-to-south migration is reflected in the oral traditions of peoples in the region, and is supported by linguistic evidence. Kanembu, the language spoken north-east of Lake Chad, is derived from the group of Teda-Daza languages, to which the Zaghāwa language also belongs. It was during the first millennium that people speaking those languages

[1] Quoted in Ibn Qutayba, *Kitāb al-Ma'ārif*, ed. by F. Wüstenfeld (Göttingen, 1850), 14.

[2] al-Ya'qūbī, *Ta'rīkh*, 219.

[3] *Akhbār al-Zamān*, ed. by 'Abd al-Ḥamīd Aḥmad Ḥanafī (Cairo, 1938), 66; al-Muhallabī, quoted in Yāqūt, *Mu'jam*, II, 932.

[4] Abdullahi Smith, 'The early states of the central Sudan', in J. F. A. Ajayi and M. Crowder, eds., *History of West Africa*, I, (London, 1971), 163n.; H. R. Palmer, *The Bornu, Sahara and Sudan* (London, 1936), 162.

migrated to Kanem and contributed to the formation of the Kanuri people.

In the ninth century the Zaghāwa of Kanem still lived as nomads. 'Their dwellings', al-Ya'qūbī says, 'are huts made of reeds and they have no towns.' But a century later al-Muhallabī said that the Zaghāwa had two towns and that their king had a palace though, like their houses, it was probably still made of reeds. These glimpses of the 'kingdom of the Zaghāwa' through two sources separated by a century suggest that the Zaghāwa nomads who had moved into the more humid lands of the Lake Chad basin went through a process of sedentarization.

As a ruler of nomad origin, the wealth of the king of the Zaghāwa 'consists of livestock, such as sheep, cattle, camels and horses'. But the tribal headman turned into a powerful monarch, who 'has unlimited authority over his subjects. He enslaves among them anyone he wants.' It was probably in this process, and as a result of the contact with the Sudanic population of Kanem, that the authority of the king became buttressed by what look like traits of divine kingship:

> They exalt their king and worship him instead of God. They imagine that he does not eat any food. There are persons who have charge of this food secretly, and bring it to his house. It is not known where it is brought from. If it happens that one of his subjects meets the camels carrying his provisions, he is killed instantly on the spot. He drinks his beverage in the presence of his select companions. . . . Their religion is the worship of their kings, for they believe that they bring life and death, sickness and health.[1]

The nomads had a military superiority over the settled population of Kanem, largely because of their cavalry. The settled people who became integrated into the political system expressed their allegiance to the *mai* in terms of their own politico-religious institutions. Traits of 'divine kingship' prevail among Sudanic peoples, such as the Jukun, who probably had a common civilization with predynastic societies of the Chad basin. 'Divine kingship', as described by al-Muhallabī in the tenth century – and other elements of the socio-political organization of the kingdoms – was contributed by the Sudanic subjects of the Saifawa.

At this time, towards the end of the tenth century, there is as yet no reference to the introduction of Islam to Kanem. In the middle of the eleventh century al-Bakrī had little to say about the Kanemis who 'live beyond the desert of Zawīla . . . They are heathen Sūdān . . . and scarcely anyone reaches them.'[2] Even a century later, in the middle of the twelfth century, al-Idrīsī described Manān, the pre-Islamic capital of

[1] Quoted in Yāqūt, *Mu'jam*, II, 932. [2] al-Bakrī, *Masālik*, 11.

Kanem, as 'a small town without industry of any sort and little commerce'.[1] Indeed, in these early accounts there is no record of extensive trade with the Lake Chad region beyond the slave-trade which was based on Zawila. Only in the account of Ibn Saʿīd (died 1286) does Kanem emerge as a powerful Muslim kingdom, which expanded northwards towards the Fezzan.

According to Ibn Saʿīd, the first Muslim King of Kanem was 'the fourth grandfather' (*al-jadd al-rābiʿ*) of the king who reigned in his time; this would take us back five generations before the middle of the thirteenth century, i.e. to *c.* 1100. 'He was converted to Islam by Muslim scholars and then Islam spread through the rest of the land of Kānim.'[2] The conversion of the first king of Kanem is recorded also in a *maḥram*, 'a letter of immunity', which is believed to have been granted by Mai (i.e. King) Humai (who reigned towards the end of the eleventh century, according to traditional evidence) to his Muslim tutor Muḥammad b. Mānī. According to this document, Muḥammad b. Mānī had read parts of the Koran with three of Mai Humai's predecessors, who rewarded him generously. But it was only Mai Humai who officially embraced Islam.

According to our interpretation of the *maḥram*, the conversion of the king was the outcome of a long process in which Muslim men of religion had sown the seeds of Islam. It is significant that both Ibn Saʿīd and the *maḥram* say that soon after the conversion of the king, Islam spread throughout the land of Kanem. In other contemporary kingdoms (like Gao and Malal) only the kings embraced Islam, while the common people retained their ancestral religions. It was therefore only at both ends of the Sudan – in Takrur in the west and in Kanem in the east – that the people followed their rulers in accepting Islam. Islam gained an almost universal adherence in Kanem and Takrur perhaps because of the closer contacts of those two kingdoms with their northern neighbours, the nomads of the desert. By the time of Ibn Saʿīd in the thirteenth century, the kings of Kanem had already claimed to be 'of the posterity of Sayf b. Dhī Yazan'.

In a recent study of the early history of Kanem, based on the collation of external Arabic sources and a local dynastic chronicle (*Dīwān al-Salāṭīn*), Dierk Lange postulates a change of dynasties in Kanem, perhaps in the second half of the eleventh century.[3] A dynasty which claimed

[1] al-Idrīsī, *Nuzhat*, 12.

[2] Ibn Saʿīd, *Kitāb basṭ al-arḍ fi'l ṭūl wa'l-ʿarḍ*, ed. by J. V. Gines (Tetuan, 1958), 28.

[3] D. Lange, *Le Dīwān des sultans du* [*Kanem-*] *Bornū: chronologie et histoire d'un royaume africain*

descent from Sayf b. Dhī Yazan replaced the earlier Zaghāwa dynasty, which had led a group of nomads known to Kanuri traditions as the Magumi in the foundation of the kingdom that al-Yaʿqūbī and al-Muhallabī described. Islamic influence had already been evident during the reign of the last two rulers of the first dynasty, but it was with the accession of Humai, the first ruler of the new Saifawa dynasty, that Islam gained ground in Kanem. If the new dynasty had come from a more strongly islamized milieu, it might help explain the subsequent pervasive influence of Islam in Kanem.

Dīwān al-Ṣalāṭīn says about the fifth ruler in the supposedly new dynasty that he was called Salmama because he was black, whereas none of the sultans before him had been born black; they were all red like the Arabs.[1] We have here, as in the case of the early states of the western Sudan, a tradition with a clear Islamic bias which claims that the rulers of the state had originally been white. Accounts which may be interpreted as indicating a change of dynasties are opposed by what may be considered as the official tradition which insists on the continuity of one dynasty from the pre-Islamic origins of Kanem, in the eighth or ninth centuries, into the Islamic period.

Both Arabic and traditional sources bear evidence to a process of a fusion of different segments of society in Kanem and the development of a common culture by the former nomad and settled communities. It was perhaps after this process had begun that the kingdom became known to contemporary Arabs by the name of the country 'Kānim', instead of, as before, by the generic name of the nomads, 'the Zaghāwa'. Some of the nomads became assimilated into the composite population of Kanem. Those who retained their nomadic way of life had moved away. Certain sections of the Zaghāwa who now live in Wadai and Darfur claim to have come from Bornu.

The middle of the eleventh century has been chosen to mark the end of the period covered in this volume. This is certainly an appropriate date at which to end this chapter. In North Africa, invasions of nomads from two ends of the Maghrib – Banū Hilāl from the east and the Almoravids from the south – were of great significance in the shaping

(Wiesbaden, 1977), 95–129. For other records and analysis of the Kanuri traditional lore, see Palmer, *The Bornu*; Palmer, ed. and trans. *Sudanese memoirs* (Lagos, 1928; reprinted London, 1967); Y. Urvoy, *Histoire de l'empire du Bornou* (Dakar, 1949). One of the best studies of the history of Kanem is A. Smith's 'Early states of the Central Sudan', but see his p. 168 n. 26, where he almost completely rejects the evidence of the Arabic sources.

1 Lange, *Le Dīwān*, 36–7 trans. 70–1.

of the ethnic, cultural, religious and political makeup of the Maghrib. The Banū Hilāl accelerated the pace of arabization in North Africa, while the Almoravids contributed to the homogeneity of Islam in North Africa, by securing the victory of the Mālikī school over heterodoxy. Under the Almoravids, Morocco emerged as one distinct political entity.

The Almoravids left their impact also in the Sudan, where their intervention brought about the islamization of Ghana and eradicated traces of Ibāḍī influence. By the middle of the eleventh century the basis for the political, religious and economic development of the western Sudan had already been laid. The process of state-building, the growth of trade and the diffusion of Islam continued until the eighteenth and nineteenth centuries along patterns which may already be discerned at this early period.

Our knowledge about the stage of development reached by the peoples of the western Sudan in the middle of the eleventh century would have been poorer without al-Bakrī's description of the region. Indeed, because of the scarcity of contemporary sources for the early history of West Africa, this rich and credible account may almost be said to mark the beginning of the period from which the history of West Africa may be reconstructed from written sources.

BIBLIOGRAPHICAL ESSAYS

1. THE LEGACY OF PREHISTORY

The initial and main impetus for the study of African prehistory, which began in the latter part of the last century, has come from two directions: on the one hand from French geologists, palaeontologists and archaeologists working in the Maghrib and later in the Sahara, who applied the western European terminology; and, on the other hand, from investigators in South Africa who introduced their own terminology (Goodwin and Lowe, 1929) because of the morphological differences between the artefact assemblages from Africa and Europe and the lack of reliable means of dating and making correlations over such great distances. Over the past twenty years, the significant contributions of the radiometric and palaeo-magnetic chronologies have provided a new dimension to palaeo-anthropological and archaeological studies in Africa. This dating evidence is set out in detail in Bishop and Miller (1972), and this and later Quaternary chronology is summarized in J. D. Clark (1975). Although work began later in East Africa (L. S. B. Leakey, 1931), the very rich finds from the Rift Valley are now the main source of knowledge of early hominid anatomy and behaviour. Today there are few parts of the continent where prehistoric investigations have not been carried out, although, as yet, systematic studies in some regions, such as the West African Sahel, Ethiopia and Mozambique have only recently begun.

A general review of Quaternary studies in Africa, designed to develop greater precision in the interrelated fields of stratigraphic geology, palaeontology, palaeo-anthropology, physical anthropology and archaeology, and to suggest revisions, in particular in matters of archaeological method and terminology, was undertaken in 1967 (Bishop and Clark), and various regional terminologies in current use south of the Sahara have followed from these recommendations. Prehistoric cultural distributions in relation to climatic and palaeo-environmental factors are set out in the *Atlas of African prehistory* (J. D. Clark, 1967). Triennial reviews (eight to date, beginning in 1966 and covering the period from 1950) of palaeo-ecological, archaeological and related studies throughout the continent are edited by Van Zinderen

Bakker (*Palaeo-ecology of Africa*, Cape Town), and fluctuations in late Quaternary closed lake basins, indicative of climatic change, are reviewed by Butzer, Isaac, Richardson and Washbourn-Kamau (1972) and by Street and Grove (1976).

Some idea of the extent to which archaeological knowledge has developed can be obtained from the general syntheses of African prehistory (L. S. B. Leakey, 1936; Alimen, 1957; J. D. Clark, 1959, 1970). During the last five years many new and important discoveries have been reported, especially with regard to fossils and sites of early man. Three works in particular provide the latest information on the Plio-Pleistocene hominids and the cultural manifestations up to the end of the Middle Pleistocene (Isaac and McCown, 1976; Coppens, Howell, Isaac and Leakey, 1976; and Butzer and Isaac, 1975).

For the various geographic regions of the continent there are a number of monographs providing detailed and/or specialized information. For northern Africa, Balout (1955, 1958) and Vaufrey (1955, 1969) are concerned with the Maghrib and the more northern and western parts of the Sahara; McBurney (1960) covers the whole of northern Africa from the Maghrib to the Nile. The latest detailed review is that by Camps (1974), while Wendorf and Marks (1975) contains a number of important overviews and specialist reports on recent research in North Africa and discussions on how this relates to the culture sequence in the Levant. Monographs on individual sites and locality sequences that are crucial for North African prehistory are McBurney (1967), Wendorf (1968), Caton Thompson (1952) and J. Chavaillon (1964). There is a voluminous literature on the Palaeolithic and Neolithic of North Africa and the Sahara, mostly in French. Some of the more important items have been listed in the footnotes to this chapter, and others will be found in the bibliographies to the appropriate chapters in Volume 1 of this *History*.

In West Africa, archaeologists have been mostly concerned with the post-Pleistocene period, but regional overviews are given by Davies (1964, 1967) and, for Nigeria, by Soper (1965). Sites with pre-Neolithic, Later Stone Age assemblages are described by Shaw (1944, 1972b), Willett (1963), and Fagg, Eyo, Rosenfeld and Fagg (1972).

In the Horn of Africa (Ethiopia and Somalia) the cultural sequence as it was known twenty-five years ago can be found in J. D. Clark (1954, reprinted 1972), written, however, prior to the introduction of radiocarbon dating. Since then, besides the team investigation of Plio-Pleistocene hominid localities in the lower Omo valley and in the

Ethiopian Rift, the most important works are on Acheulian and Developed Oldowan living sites at Melka Kunture (Chavaillon and Chavaillon, 1971); on localities in the Plain of Gadeb and at the south end of the Afar Rift (Clark and Williams, forthcoming; Clark and Kurashina, forthcoming); and at Middle and Later Stone Age open air and cave settlements in the Lake Zwai basin (Wendorf and Schild, 1974).

For East Africa, a regional synthesis is provided by S. Cole (1963), but many new discoveries have since been made and must be looked for in monographs and journal articles; a general review for the earlier Pleistocene is Isaac (1969). A key locality for knowledge of the earlier Pleistocene cultural sequence is the Olduvai Gorge (M. D. Leakey, 1971), and monographs on other primary context sites are those of Isaac (forthcoming, and 1967), Howell, Cole and Kleindienst (1962) and G. H. Cole (1967a). Earlier descriptions of the Lake Victoria sequence (O'Brien, 1939; Van Riet Lowe, 1952; L. S. B. Leakey and Owen, 1945) are still valuable. Most of what is known about the Middle and Later Stone Ages in East Africa is summarized in S. Cole (1963) and, although currently work is being carried out at Lukenya Hill, Apis Rock and sites in the Nakuru-Naivasha basins, this is mostly unpublished. For the Middle Stone Age see Anthony (1972); for a re-excavation of Magosi and discussion on the 'Magosian' see G. H. Cole (1967b); and, for the Later Stone Age, Isaac, Merrick and Nelson (1972). An important sequence from central Tanzania covering more than 20,000 years is described by Inskeep (1962); for some of the more important East African Later Stone Age sites see Robbins (1974), Posnansky and Nelson (1968), Nelson and Posnansky (1970) and Soper and Golden (1969). For Ruanda-Burundi, Nenquin (1967) describes a series of excavations and analyses showing the close association between these elevated volcanic uplands and the low-lying Congo basin.

Pioneer studies in the Congo basin were carried out by Colette (1931) in Zaïre, and by Janmart (1947) in north-eastern Angola. The terminology used has gone through several vicissitudes, summarized in Breuil, Cabu and Van Riet Lowe (1944), Mortelmans (1962), and J. D. Clark (1971b). The geographical and cultural successions in various parts of the basin are set out in de Ploey (1965) and van Moorsel (1968) for lower Zaïre; L. S. B. Leakey (1949) and J. D. Clark (1963, 1968) for north-east Angola; and de Heinzelin (1952) for north-east Zaïre. The best-known Acheulian assemblage from the southern Congo is that described by Cahen (1975). Another important monograph, on the early Holocene, lakeside site of Ishango on Lake Edward, is by de Heinzelin (1957).

In Zambia, early work, particularly on the succession in the upper Zambezi valley, is described by J. D. Clark (1950a), but this should now be read in conjunction with later studies of various specific localities. The longest and most complete sequence with successive stages from the Acheulian to the Iron Age is that at Kalambo Falls (J. D. Clark, 1969, 1974). The nature of the Middle Stone Age assemblages where quartz was the raw material are shown in reports on the Mumbwa Caves (Dart and del Grande, 1931; J. D. Clark, 1942), on Twin Rivers Kopje (J. D. Clark, 1971a), on Kalemba (D. W. Phillipson, 1973) and on the upper Zambezi (L. Phillipson, 1968). The Later Stone Age assemblages have been described in a number of journal articles and monographs, a well-dated introduction being D. W. Phillipson's report on Kalemba (1973). Gwisho Springs, a particularly important locality, since vegetable and faunal remains as well as burials are preserved there, has been described by Gabel (1965) and Fagan and Van Noten (1971). Inskeep (1959) has described a Later Stone Age camping-site west of Livingstone, and a special study of use-wear patterns has been made on an artefact assemblage from the Copperbelt (Phillipson and Phillipson, 1970). In northern Zambia, the Nachikufan Industrial Complex, first described by J. D. Clark (1950b) has been analysed by Miller (1972), who has also reviewed the dating (1971). In Malawi, the cultural sequence at the north end of the lake is described in Clark, Haynes and Mawby (1970), and that at sites on the northern part of the plateau by Robinson and Sandelowsky (1968). An annotated list of all sites recorded in Malawi up to 1973 is also available (Cole-King, 1973).

A bibliography of Rhodesian archaeology has been compiled by C. K. Cooke (1974), and pioneer studies were carried out by Jones (1926, 1949). Armstrong's report (1931) on excavations at Bambata Cave presented the first well-stratified cultural sequence beginning early in the Middle Palaeolithic. The Acheulian is attested from old *dambo* deposits on the watershed at Lochard and elsewhere (Bond, 1963), and several important caves, rock-shelters and open sites, excavated by C. K. Cooke (1957, 1963, 1971), Cooke and Robinson (1954) and others, have provided detailed information on cultural successions and regional variability. The revised terminology in use in Rhodesia is set out in various papers (e.g. C. K. Cooke, Summers and Robinson, 1966; C. K. Cooke, 1966, 1969).

The greatest volume of literature pertains to South Africa, and very important site and locality studies are found in the *Bulletin* of the South African Archaeological Society and the *South African Journal of Science*. Besides the pioneer work of Goodwin and Lowe (1929) referred to above, there must also be mentioned that of Burkitt (1928) and the regional study of Söhnge, Visser and Lowe (1937), now in need of revision. A broad overview of southern African prehistory up to the 1950s is provided by J. D. Clark (1959). The latest comprehensive study of the Stone Age in southern Africa is that of Sampson (1974), which also contains a full bibliography to which reference should be made. Mason's monograph (1962a) is still the main source for the archaeology of the Transvaal.

On the Australopithecines, the literature is voluminous, beginning with Dart (1925) on *A. africanus*. Dart published more than fifty papers on his fossil discoveries at Makapan, of which may be cited those on the tool-making habits of the man-apes (Dart, 1957, 1960). Broom, working at the Krugersdorp group of sites, was equally productive, and his 1950 book gives much of the history of his discoveries. Some of the earliest comparative studies of the South African Australopithecines were made by Le Gros Clark (1947, 1955) and, later, again by J. T. Robinson (1972). Mason (1962b) and M. D. Leakey (1970) provide studies of some of the stone artefacts associated with *A. robustus* and *Homo* species at the South African sites.

The southern African Acheulian sites were reviewed by Howell and Clark (1963) and, since then, important descriptions have appeared on the Acheulian at Montagu Cave (Keller, 1973), Amanzi Springs (H. J. Deacon, 1970) and the Cave of Hearths (Mason, 1967). H. J. Deacon (1975) reviews current concepts of the Acheulian in South Africa. Discoveries, development of concepts and the dating of the Middle Stone Age are covered in Sampson (1974), which, as has been mentioned, provides a bibliography. The first quantitative study of a stone industry from South Africa is that of Mason (1957) on the Middle Stone Age Pietersburg Industry from the Transvaal. Interest has recently focused on the diet of Middle Stone Age man, and the work of Klein in particular (1972, 1974, 1975a, 1975b) sets out the evidence for the use of marine resources and the extinction of the megafauna.

Later Stone Age sites are very numerous in South Africa, and for a general overview of current knowledge reference should again be made to Sampson (1974); other reviews are given by Inskeep (1967, 1969). The definitive report on the cultural sequence in the Wilton Rock Shelter is now available (J. Deacon, 1972), and a review of cultural variability within the different biotic zones in southern Africa has been carried out by H. J. Deacon (1972). Excavations by Parkington and Poggenpoel (1971) provide evidence for seasonal movement of populations during later prehistoric times. Recently, also, Carter and Vogel (1974) have shown that seasonal human occupation of Lesotho rock-shelters dates back to the Middle Stone Age.

On mammalian faunas and their relevance for the dating of archaeological assemblages, reference should be made to H. B. S. Cooke (1963, 1967, 1968), H. B. S. Cooke and Maglio (1972) and Jaeger (1975). For early hominid fossils, apart from the Australopithecines, to which reference has already been made, the reader is referred to Howell (1960), Tobias (1968), Pilbeam (1975) and Rightmire (1975a, 1976). The evidence on early Holocene populations in the Sahara is presented by Chamla (1968), and the factors and circumstances leading to the differentiation of the present African races are set out in Hiernaux (1974).

Much information relative to the behaviour of man in the Later Stone Age is available in the rock-art – engravings and paintings – especially that of the Sahara and Nile Valley, Tanzania, Rhodesia and South Africa. Again a voluminous literature exists, but general descriptions can be found in Lhote (1958), Lajoux (1962), and Camps (1974) for the Sahara; in Summers (1959) for Zambia, Malawi and Rhodesia; in Fosbrooke *et al.* (1950) for Tanzania, and in Willcox (1963) and Rudner and Rudner (1970) for South Africa.

The development of food production is more generally associated with the so-called 'neolithic' occurrences in northern and West Africa and in the East African Rift. For the Sahara, a good summary is found in Camps (1974), while the several authors in de Wet, Harlan and Stemler (1976) discuss both the plant and cultural evidence for domestication. Arkell (1953) has described the earliest settlement in the Sudan with domestic stock and its antecedent, riverside, hunting–fishing community (1949). Evidence for domestication in Ethiopia is summarized in J. D. Clark (1976). Information on the East African 'Stone Bowl' cultures, for which the earliest pastoralists in the eastern Rift were responsible, will be found in Leakey and Leakey (1950), Sutton (1973), and Odner (1972).

The above summary provides some introduction to further reading and overviews of various aspects of African palaeo-anthropological studies. The bibliographical essays and footnotes in Volume 1 are the sources suggested for more detailed appreciations, as well as journals such as *Azania* (British Institute in Eastern Africa, Nairobi); *ASEQUA* (Bulletin de Liaison of the Association Sénégalaise pour l'Étude du Quaternaire de l'Ouest africain); *Libyca*; *The West African Journal of Archaeology* (Ibadan, Nigeria); the *South African Archaeological Bulletin* (Cape Town); and the *South African Journal of Science* (Johannesburg).

2. NORTH AFRICA, c. 800 TO 323 BC

The period from the eighth to the fourth centuries BC is covered in Volumes 3 to 6 of the *Cambridge Ancient History*: this deals fully with events in Egypt, but is much less helpful for the history of Cyrenaica and Carthage during this period. It is by now, of course, considerably out of date, especially as regards archaeological evidence.

There are no contemporary records of the establishment of the Phoenician and Greek settlements in northern Africa. The history of Phoenician and Greek colonization has to be reconstructed on the basis of archaeological evidence and traditions recorded later by Greek historians. The literature of the Phoenicians themselves is lost, and Phoenician traditions survive only in so far as they are reported by Greek writers. A very useful general survey of early Greek colonization, with emphasis on the archaeological evidence, is given by Boardman (1973). For the Phoenicians and their colonizing activities, the best general account, again emphasizing the archaeological evidence, is that by Harden (1971). The account by Moscati (1968) is also useful, but the more recent work by Herm (1975) is slighter and much less valuable. For the chronology of Phoenician settlement in the western Mediterranean, one can still usefully consult Carpenter (1958).

The part of northern Africa whose history is best documented in this period is, of course, Egypt. Indigenous sources, represented by monumental inscriptions and papyrus documents, are relatively numerous. For the XXVIth Dynasty (663–525 BC) the main indigenous sources can be found in Volume 4 of Breasted (1906–7), while those for the first period of Persian rule (525–404 BC) are brought together by Posener (1936). The papyrus documents relating to the Jewish colony at Elephantine can be found in Cowley (1923). Supplementary contemporary documentation is provided by the records of the other major Near Eastern empires with which Egypt was in contact, such as Assyria, Babylon and Persia: for the period of the XXVIth Dynasty, the relevant Babylonian documents can be found in Wiseman (1961). In addition, there are the Greek sources. Little of the Greek material is contemporary, the major sources being later accounts based on traditions or upon earlier written sources no longer extant. For the XXVIth Dynasty and the early Persian period, the main Greek source is Herodotus: an evaluation of his evidence for the period of the XXVIth dynasty is offered by De Meulenaere (1951). For the revolt of Inaros in the mid fifth century BC, the main authority is Thucydides; for events in the fourth century, the principal source is Diodorus Siculus; while Alexander's conquest of Egypt in the late fourth century is recounted by Arrian. For Greek settlement in Egypt, archaeological evidence is also crucial: the relevant archaeological evidence is usefully summarized by Boardman (1973). The history of Egypt during the whole period 663 to 323 BC is treated briefly in the general histories of Egypt by Gardiner (1961) and Drioton and Vandier (1962). Fuller accounts can be found in Elgood (1951), and especially in Kienitz (1953) and Gyles (1959). For relations between Egypt and its southern neighbour, the kingdom of Kush, see also Arkell (1961). Greek involvement in Egypt during the seventh and sixth centuries BC is discussed by Austin (1970). For the policy of ʿAhmose (569–525 BC) towards the Greeks in Egypt, the article by Cook (1937) is also useful, while the evidence suggesting that the Greeks were responsible for the introduction of iron-working into Egypt is discussed by Williams (1969).

The history of the Greek settlements in Cyrenaica rests upon a combination of Greek literary sources, archaeological evidence and local monumental inscriptions. For the seventh and sixth centuries BC the principal literary source is Herodotus, whose account was based upon oral traditions. For the fifth and fourth centuries, evidence on Cyrenaica in Greek literature is exiguous, though some useful material can be found in Diodorus Siculus. The archaeological evidence for the establishment of the Greek settlements in Cyrenaica is extensive, and can be found summarized in Boardman (1966, 1973). Local inscriptions in this period are not numerous, but there are some of considerable importance: an inscription which purports to record the circumstances of the foundation of Cyrene is discussed by Graham (1960), while an inscription of the late fourth century BC which is important for internal political and social developments is discussed by Kwapong (1969). For the Greek occupation of Cyrenaica, and for the history of Cyrene under the Battiad dynasty (*c.* 639 to *c.* 439 BC), there is a very useful general account by Chamoux (1953), though this needs updating in the light of the archaeological evidence reported by Boardman. For the relations of Cyrene with the Persian empire, see also Mitchell (1966). The history of Cyrenaica after the fall of the Battiad dynasty has not attracted comparable treatment – a reflection of the fragmentary character of the sources for this later period. For a discussion of the oracle of Zeus Ammon and its significance in the Greek world, see Parke (1967).

For the history of Carthage and its empire, we are primarily dependent upon the evidence of Greek and Roman writers, since the literature of the Carthaginians themselves is lost. The principal source for early Carthaginian history is Diodorus Siculus; additional material of importance is to be found in Justin, Polybius, Livy, Appian and Strabo. This foreign material varies greatly in quality, illuminates primarily the relations of the Carthaginians with the Greeks and Romans, and becomes reasonably detailed and reliable only from the late fifth century BC. For the history of Phoenician and Carthaginian colonization in northern Africa, archaeological evidence is also important, though very uneven: the evidence is most accessibly summarized in Harden (1971). Carthaginian epigraphic material is not voluminous, and contributes little. The history of Carthage is treated at great length in Volumes 1 to 4 of Gsell (1913–29). More succinct and more up-to-date accounts can be found in Warmington (1969), which is probably the most useful, Charles-Picard (1964, 1968) and Hubac (1952). For the fifth-century BC crisis in Carthaginian history, which led to the emergence of Carthage as an African as well as a Mediterranean power, see also Hands (1969). For the character of Carthaginian civilization, there is a useful general compilation by Charles-Picard (1958); for Carthaginian religion, see also Charles-Picard (1954) and, for the specific problem of the origins of the goddess Tanit, Giustolisi (1970). A useful summary of Carthaginian administrative practice in North Africa, as far as it can be reconstructed, is given by Ilevbare (1974); for Carthaginian activities in Morocco and Tripolitania see also, respectively, Cintas (1954) and Merighi (1940); and for Carthaginian involvement in the trans-Saharan trade, see Carpenter (1956) and Law (1967). For Carthaginian maritime enterprise down the Atlantic coast of Africa, the main sources are Herodotus, the *Periplus* of Hanno, and the *Periplus* of Pseudo-Skylax: the texts of Hanno and Pseudo-Skylax are to be found in Müller (1855–61). Hanno's *Periplus* purports to be a Greek translation of a Phoenician original, but Germain (1957) regards it as a Greek forgery. The problems of Hanno's voyage have been extensively discussed by modern scholars: among the more useful contributions are, in addition to that of Germain, those of Cary and Warmington (1963), Carcopino (1943), Harden (1948), Rousseau (1949), Mauny (1955a, 1955b) and Charles-Picard (1958).

For the history of the 'Libyans', the indigenous peoples of northern Africa west of Egypt, in this period there is little evidence. The Libyans themselves were illiterate, and Greek literature is not generous with information about them. The main Greek source for the Libyans in this period is Herodotus. The earlier account of Hekataios is unfortunately lost: extant fragments of it are collected in Jacoby (1923—). Useful material can also be derived from later writers such as Strabo and Pliny. Archaeological evidence for the ancient Libyans, apart from rock-art, is exiguous, but some information can be gleaned from the general surveys of North African prehistory by Wulsin (1941) and McBurney (1960); for the use of copper in north-western Africa in this period, see also Camps (1960). The problem of the language of the ancient Libyans is dealt with by Bynon (1970). There is as yet no general account of the culture of the ancient Libyans, but an exhaustively detailed description of the eastern Libyan peoples is offered by Bates (1914), and a brief but useful account of the Garamantes of the Fezzan by Daniels (1970).

3. NORTH AFRICA, 323 BC TO AD 305

The period from the late fourth century BC to the early fourth century AD is covered in Volumes 7 to 12 of the *Cambridge Ancient History*. For the Hellenistic period, this deals adequately with Egypt and Carthage, but is more cursory in its treatment of the history of Cyrenaica and the indigenous kingdoms of the Maghrib. For the Roman period, its coverage is more even. It requires, of course, substantial updating in the light of the literature of the last forty years.

The history of Egypt and Cyrenaica during the Hellenistic period (late fourth to first centuries BC) needs to be seen in the context of the history of the Greek world as a whole. Useful introductions to the history and civilization of the Hellenistic world are Tarn and Griffith (1952) and Rostovtzeff (1941). The history of Egypt in this period is lavishly, if unevenly, documented, not only by narrative histories such as those of Diodorus Siculus and Polybius, but also by monumental inscriptions and the voluminous papyrus documents. A useful introduction to the character of the papyrus documentation of this period can be found in Bell (1948). Evidence for the history of Cyrenaica is much more fragmentary, comprising only occasional references in the literary histories and a few inscriptions. The best general account of Egypt under the dynasty of the Ptolemies (323–30 BC) is still Bevan (1927); a much briefer treatment is offered by Bell (1948). The wealth of documentation, especially from the papyri, has been the basis for several substantial studies of particular aspects of the Egyptian state and Egyptian society in the Ptolemaic period: the economic activities of the Ptolemaic state are discussed by Préaux (1939); the military organization by Lesquier (1911); the legal system by Taubenschlag (1955); religion by Bell (1957); relations between Greek and Jewish settlers and the indigenous Egyptians by Davis (1951); artistic developments by Noshy (1937); and the culture of the capital city, Alexandria, by Fraser (1972) and Marlowe (1971). For relations between Egypt and the kingdom of Kush, see also Arkell (1961) and Shinnie (1967).

The history of Carthage during the third and second centuries BC, down to its destruction by the Romans in 146 BC, is based entirely on Greek and Roman sources: the principal sources are Polybius and Livy, with additional material of importance supplied by Appian and Justin. This period in Carthaginian history is adequately treated in the general histories of Carthage by Warmington (1969) and Charles-Picard (1968). There is also a detailed, but pedestrian, account of the wars between Rome and Carthage by Dorey and Dudley (1971), and a readable, but uncritical, biography of Hannibal, the principal hero of Carthaginian resistance to Rome, by De Beer (1969).

The history of the indigenous kingdoms of Numidia and Mauretania is also based primarily on Greek and Roman sources. For the period down to the death of the Numidian King Micipsa (118 BC), the principal sources are Polybius and Livy, supplemented by Appian; for the reign of Jugurtha (118–105 BC), there is the account of Sallust; for later times fragmentary documentation can be derived from the works of Appian, Cassius Dio, Caesar, Tacitus and others. The writings of Juba II, King of Mauretania (25 BC to AD 23), are unfortunately lost: surviving fragments are collected in Jacoby (1923—). Local inscriptions and coins supply a limited amount of supplementary information: for the numismatic evidence, see Mazard (1955). The history of the Numidian and Mauretanian kingdoms is treated in great detail in Volumes 5 to 8 of Gsell (1913–29). A more up-to-date account, whose scope is much more comprehensive than its title suggests, is provided by Camps (1960). The reign of the Numidian King Masinissa (206–148 BC) is also discussed, mainly with reference to his relations with Carthage and Rome, by Walsh (1965); the war of Jugurtha against Rome is treated by

Holroyd (1928); and some useful material on the later history of the Mauretanian kingdom can be found in Carcopino (1943).

The history of northern Africa during the period of Roman rule needs to be related to the history of the Roman empire as a whole. The classic study by Mommsen (1886), Volume 2 of which contains chapters dealing with Egypt and North Africa, is still worth reading. For the economic history of the empire, there is the massive study by Frank (1933–40), of which Volume 2 deals with Egypt and Volume 4 with North Africa. Other useful general studies of the Roman empire are Rostovtzeff (1957-63) and Millar *et al.* (1967). It is also illuminating to read the contemporary geographical compilations of Strabo and Pliny, both of which deal at some length with northern Africa.

The history of Egypt in this period continues to be relatively generously documented, principally by local epigraphic and papyrus records. General accounts of the history of Egypt as a Roman province are offered by Bell (1948) and Johnson (1951). Studies of particular topics include Wallace (1938) on taxation; Lesquier (1918) on military organization; Jouguet (1968) on the autonomous municipalities; Bell (1957) on religion; and Lindsay (1963, 1965) on various aspects of 'every-day' life. The tensions and disturbances surrounding the Jewish community in Alexandria have been studied in detail by many scholars, for example by Stuart Jones (1926), Bell (1931), Davis (1951), and Smallwood (1969); a sample of local anti-Semitic literature, preserved in papyrus, is given by Musurillo (1952). For the relations of Egypt with Kush in this period, Arkell (1961) and Shinnie (1967) need to be supplemented with Jameson (1968). For Greek commercial enterprise along the East African coast in this period, the principal source is the *Periplus* of Pseudo-Arrian, the text of which is in Müller (1855–61); a discussion can be found in Cary and Warmington (1963). The economic decline of Egypt under the Romans is examined by Milne (1927), and some third-century AD attempts at reform by Bell (1947) and Parsons (1967).

The history of Cyrenaica under the Romans is less fully documented. The main source of information is local epigraphic material: one important group of inscriptions is studied by De Visscher (1940). The basic history of Cyrenaica as a Roman province is Romanelli (1953). For the Jewish rebellion of AD 115, this can be supplemented with information from Smallwood (1969); while the efforts of the Emperor Hadrian to restore the cities of Cyrenaica after this catastrophe are discussed by Fraser (1950).

The history of North-West Africa during the Roman period is based primarily on local epigraphic and archaeological evidence. The best general history is Romanelli (1959). The general studies by Albertini (1949) and Charles-Picard (1959) are less substantial, but also of value. The recent general study in English by Raven (1969) is readable and well illustrated, but otherwise undistinguished. Useful studies of particular provinces are Merighi (1940) on Tripolitania and Broughton (1929) on Africa Proconsularis; while there is some interesting material on Roman Mauretania in Carcopino (1943). The military organization of the Roman provinces in North-West Africa is studied by Cagnat (1913); for the organization of frontier defence in the hinterland of Tripolitania see also Goodchild and Ward-Perkins (1949) and Goodchild (1950, 1954); and for the organization of the frontier further west, see Baradez (1949). A useful survey of Roman administrative practice is given by Ilevbare (1974); while Roman colonization and municipal organization are studied by Teutsch (1962), and more briefly and more accessibly by Thompson (1969). The religion of Roman Africa is discussed by Charles-Picard (1954), and its literary culture by Bouchier (1913). A biography of Septimius Severus, the most distinguished of the Roman emperors of North African origin, is provided by Birley (1971). The controversial problem of the survival of Punic culture and language under Roman rule has been treated by Frend (1942), Courtois (1950), Gautier (1952) and Millar (1968); the equally controversial history of the introduction of the camel by Gautier (1952), Brogan (1954) and Bovill (1956). For Roman involvement in the trans-Saharan trade, see Aurigemma (1940) and Law (1967).

The history of the North African elephant during the Hellenistic and Roman periods, including its use in war by Egypt, Carthage and Numidia and its ultimate extinction, is documented by Scullard (1974). The question of Greek and Roman perceptions of black Africans during the same period is the subject of Snowden (1970).

4. THE NILOTIC SUDAN AND ETHIOPIA

A virtually complete bibliography up to 1963 is given in Gadallah (1963). Meroitic studies are still very heavily dependent on the basic excavation reports and descriptions of standing monuments and few attempts have been made to produce a synthetic statement. In the absence of readable Meroitic texts, all writers must rely on archaeological evidence, except for the period when historical inscriptions in the Egyptian language were still being written. Basic publications of these texts are listed by Gadallah (1963) and useful commentaries are embodied in the mainly historical surveys by Haycock (1965a, 1968, 1972). Of special importance are some of the inscriptions from Kawa published by Macadam (1955).

Shinnie (1967) is the only over-all survey of history and material culture so far published, but in view of the ever-increasing research is now somewhat out of date, and by using largely material from the northern fringes of the Meroitic state to illustrate the culture as a whole gives a distorted view. Arkell (1955, reprinted 1973) gives the history as known in the mid 1950s within the general historical framework of the ancient Sudan, but some of the book, in particular suggestions as to widespread Meroitic influence in Africa, is highly imaginative. Adams, *Nubia: corridor to Africa* (1977) gives the most up-to-date account. Much of it is based on the author's own fieldwork.

Of excavation reports the most important are the volumes I, II, IV and V of *Royal Cemeteries of Kush* by Dunham (1950, 1955, 1957, 1963). These give details of the excavation of the royal and other burials by Reisner from 1916 to 1923 and were published many years after his death. Although extremely useful as catalogues of tomb contents and descriptions of the architecture of the tombs, the books are difficult to use and suffer from some lack of detail and rather summary drawings, and have no commentary. In spite of this they provide essential raw material for Meroitic history, chronology and material culture. A volume on the tomb chapel reliefs was published as Chapman (1952) and is Volume III of the series. Garstang (1911) is a brief and inadequate account of the first season of his 1909–14 campaign at Meroe, but there is nothing else. Subsequent seasons were even more summarily published as Garstang (1911, 1912, 1913, and 1914). Griffith's work at Sanam Abu Dom is published as Griffith (1922, 1923), and at Faras as Griffith (1924, 1925). These reports, often no more than a list of grave contents, are selective. Details of the contents of all the graves are available in typescript in the Griffith Institute, Oxford.

On the linguistic side, Griffith in Randall MacIver and Woolley (1909) and in Griffith (1911) describes his successful attempts to determine the phonetic values of the Meroitic writing. The most up-to-date statement on the linguistic situation is Trigger in Hintze (1973), which gives references to all other major contributions in this difficult field. Hintze in *Meroitica III – Beiträge zur meroitischen Grammatik*, now in press, takes the analytical study of the language much farther.

Meroitica I – Sudan im Altertum (1973), which publishes papers given at the first international congress of Meroitic studies held in Berlin in 1972, provides the most up-to-date views on such topics as chronology, language, ceramics, methods of field investigations and others. A further conference was held in Paris in 1973 and the report is now in the press. A refreshingly iconoclastic view of the Meroitic civilization in Lower Nubia was given by Adams (1964, 1965), and the ideas expressed there have been repeated in further detail and with some modifications by the same author in a number of papers – his latest views and detailed bibliographical references will be found in *Nubia: corridor to Africa*, referred to above.

The descriptions of early travellers are useful in showing the state of the major monuments before more settled conditions and increase in population caused greater destruction in the nineteenth and twentieth centuries than in the previous thousand years or more. Of these travellers Linant de Bellefonds, *Journal d'un voyage à Méroé dans les années 1821 et 1822* (1958) and F. Caillaud, *Voyage à Méroé, au Fleuve Blanc, au-delà de Fazoql* (1826, reprinted 1972) are the earliest. A number of other nineteenth-century travellers made less substantial, but useful, contributions, and in 1843–4 the Royal Prussian Expedition led by C. R. Lepsius made a detailed study of monuments and collected many inscriptions published as *Denkmäler aus Aegypten und Aethiopien* (1849–59, reprinted, in a reduced format, 1973).

Of recent years there have been a number of articles published either dealing with small specific points or again and again going over the scanty material. The journal *Kush*, the official journal of the Sudan Antiquities Service, has now reached Volume xv (though there is a ten-year gap between volumes xiv and xv); the results of recent fieldwork are published there. The *Meroitic News Letter/Bulletin d'Informations Méroïtiques* is published at irregular intervals alternately from Paris and Montreal. Number 14 appeared in February 1974. It acts as an exchange of views between people working on the subject and carries short accounts of recent research.

5. TRANS-SAHARAN CONTACTS AND WEST AFRICA

The question of contacts across the Sahara during Neolithic times has been raised by many writers; the most recent are J. D. Clark, *The prehistory of Africa* (1970), Camps, *Les Civilisations préhistoriques de l'Afrique du Nord et du Sahara* (1974) and Hugot, *Le Sahara avant le désert*

(1974), all of whom deal with the problems involved in the desiccation of the Sahara and the beginnings of agriculture and of animal husbandry. Théodore Monod had shown the way in numerous writings; see especially his chapter, 'The late Tertiary and Pleistocene in the Sahara', in Howell and Bourlière, eds., *African ecology and human evolution* (1963), 117–229, a book which includes other useful chapters on related problems. Saharan climatology has been treated by many geographers, meteorologists and prehistorians, such as Balout (1955), Capot-Rey (1953), Butzer (1958–9) and Dubief (1963).

Lhote, in numerous papers, has made a special study of the activities of chariots in the Sahara following its desiccation and during the period of the ancient civilizations in North Africa. In collaboration with Mauny, he established the lines of the two main trans-Saharan 'chariot tracks'; for a general discussion of this question, see Mauny's *Les Siècles obscurs de l'Afrique noire* (1970), 60–5.

For the classical references to the presence of the camel in Africa, see Zeuner, *A history of domesticated animals* (1963), 349–58. Gsell (1913) overemphasized the camel's importance; Courtois, in his *Les Vandales et l'Afrique* (1955), favoured a lesser distribution in early times. The real diffusion dates from the time of the arrival of the Arabs in the northern Sahara; Ibn 'Abd al-Ḥakam and al-Bakrī give several typical examples for the period from the seventh to the ninth centuries.

As for the possibility of maritime contact with West Africa, there has been a debate between those in favour of continuous voyaging along the west coast from Phoenician times onwards, for example Cary and Warmington, *The ancient explorers* (1963), 61–8, relying principally on Hanno's *Periplus*, and those such as Tauxier ('Les deux rédactions du Périple d'Hannon', 1882), Germain ('Qu'est-ce que le Périple d'Hannon?' 1957) and Mauny (*Les Siècles obscurs*, 78–112), who believe that the *Periplus* is a fake, and that the sailors of ancient times did not navigate along the Saharan coasts because the contrary trade winds would not permit their ships, with square sails and lacking rudders, to make the return journey northwards.

Many authors have written about food production at the end of the Neolithic. In addition to Monod, already cited, mention should be made of J. D. Clark, 'The problem of neolithic culture in sub-Saharan Africa', in Bishop and Clark, eds., *Background to evolution in Africa* (1967), 601–27, and 189 ff. of his *Prehistory of Africa* (1970); and the contributions by Portères, J. D. Clark, Baker and others in a special number of the *Journal of African History* (1962, **3**, 2) and of Davies,

Hugot and Seddon on 'The origins of African agriculture' (1968). The hypothesis advanced by Murdock in his *Africa: its peoples and their culture history* (1959), 229–33, that there was a cradle of agriculture on the upper Niger, has been criticized by Baker (1962), Fage ('Anthropology, botany and the study of African history', 1961) and others. Botanical evidence has been provided by Patrick Munson's work on the neolithic villages of the Tichit-Walata escarpment (unpublished, but see Mauny, *Les Siècles obscurs*, 51–3), while for evidence on animal husbandry see Zeuner (1963) and the references there given.

The transition from the Late Stone Age to the Iron Age in West Africa was marked in Mauritania by a Copper Age, related to a similar one in the Maghrib; this has been studied by Lambert, 'Les industries sur cuivre dans l'ouest saharien' (1971). On the question of the cradle of iron-working and its diffusion, there is a controversy between Cheikh Anta Diop, 'La Métallurgie du fer sous l'Ancien Empire égyptien' (1973), and his wife L.-M. Diop, 'Métallurgie traditionelle de l'Âge du Fer en Afrique' (1968), on the one hand, and Leclant, 'Le Fer dans l'Égypte ancienne, le Soudan et l'Afrique' (1956), and Mauny (e.g. *Les Siècles obscurs*, 66–76) on the other. The first two favour an Egyptian cradle, while the others prefer an origin in the Near East with a late diffusion to Egypt and Africa. The argument may in some measure be resolved when the iron slag-heaps of Meroe have been dated, though this seems to be a matter of some difficulty; however Trigger, 'The myth of Meroe and the African Iron Age' (1969), invites scepticism of the concept of Meroe as an 'African Birmingham'.

For the peoples of West Africa during the period, see Briggs, *The living races of the Sahara desert* (1958) and Chamla, *Les Populations anciennes du Sahara* (1968). But mention should also be made of the current work by N. Petit-Maire on coastal neolithic kitchen middens in western Mauritania.

For bibliographies, reference may be made to Blaudin de Thé, *Essai de bibliographie du Sahara français* (1960), Mauny, 'Bibliographie de la préhistoire et de la protohistoire de l'Ouest africain' (1967, 1970) and Brasseur, *Bibliographie générale du Mali* (1964).

6. THE EMERGENCE OF BANTU AFRICA

Although the emergence of Bantu Africa is today rightly discussed mainly on the basis of archaeological evidence, it is important to remember that the problem was originally posed by ethnographers and linguists. In southern Africa the Bantu were early delineated as comparatively recent invaders, and attention was focused upon the remnant populations of Khoi and San, which appeared to have had a longer history in the region. As comparative studies on the interrelationship of the Bantu languages developed during the later nineteenth century, it was quickly realized by scholars like Meinhof and Johnston that the ancestral Bantu language had been spoken by people living in a forested environment, and must therefore have originated in the north-western quadrant of the Bantu sphere. In fact, Johnston in 1913 read a paper to the Royal Anthropological Institute, based mainly on linguistic and ethnographic evidence, which presented a picture of the Bantu dispersion not so very different from that given here. Towards the end of his life Johnston became increasingly interested in the Bantu-like languages spread out across West Africa, which strengthened the hypothesis of a north-westerly origin. This trend was carried further by Westermann in the 1920s and 1930s, before being reduced into its current simplicity by Greenberg in the 1950s. The hypothesis of a West African origin of the Bantu was likewise accepted by leading ethnographers such as Frobenius, Ankermann, Herskovits and, most recently, Murdock.

During all this time archaeology remained a negligible influence in recent African prehistory. Although a few Early Iron Age sites, such as the Tunnel shelter at Gokomere and the Urewe sites in western Kenya, were discovered in the 1930s and 1940s, it was not until the 1950s that the development of radiocarbon analysis provided the crucial tool for the dating of simple, unstratified sites, and so gave the incentive for a significant attack on the archaeology of the Iron Age. In archaeology, therefore, the main developments in research have taken place during the last twenty years, and they have been the work of a handful of scholars. In Rwanda and Burundi, Kivu and Katanga, the pioneers were Hiernaux, Maquet and Nenquin. In East Africa they were Soper, Posnansky and Sutton. In Zambia they were Clark, Fagan, Phillipson and Vogel. In Malawi and Rhodesia they were Summers, Robinson, Garlake and Huffman. In South Africa they were Schofield, Mason, Inskeep, Maggs and Van der Merwe. Vast areas of Bantu Africa, including Cameroun, Gabon, the Congo Republic, the Central African Republic, most of Zaïre, most of Angola, Namibia or South-West Africa, and Mozambique are still virtually unexplored. Inevitably, therefore, most generalizations have still to be regarded as tentative, and it must be realized that research is still in a stage when a single major new discovery can radically alter the perspective in which a picture of this whole period of 1,500 years has to be presented. Nevertheless, during these twenty years a fairly convincing picture has emerged of the spread of an Early Iron Age culture, comprising some kinds of cereal agriculture, some kinds of herding, and a basically common tradition of pottery manufacture, which spread over the whole of eastern, central and southern Africa between about the third century BC and about the fifth century AD. While no correlation can be absolutely proved, it is difficult to avoid the conclusion that the relatively rapid supersession of hunting and gathering cultures by a single, basic food-producing culture must have been connected with the spread of the Bantu languages over the same area.

The main practical difficulty in handling the primary literature of Iron Age archaeology is that radiocarbon dates frequently appear many years after the excavation reports to which they refer. Hence the great importance of the complete record of radiocarbon dates for the food-producing period in sub-Saharan Africa maintained by the *Journal of African History* since 1962. The first six contributions were by Fagan and consisted of annotated lists arranged by country; since 1970 they have been replaced by survey articles, among which the Bantu region has been treated by Phillipson (1970), Sutton (1972) and Soper (1974). The same journal has also made a practice of commissioning articles of a synthetic and interpretative nature concerning the Iron Age, of which those particularly relating to Bantu Africa include those by Wrigley (1960), Guthrie (1962), Summers (1962), J. D. Clark (1962), Nenquin (1963), Fagan (1963, 1964) and Oliver (1966). All these were reprinted in Fage and Oliver, eds., *Papers in African prehistory* (1970), and they have since been followed by Posnansky (1968), Phillipson (1968), Hiernaux (1968), Garlake (1970) and Greenberg (1972). To a large extent these articles constitute the recent secondary literature of the Bantu problem, to which may be added Shinnie, *The African Iron Age* (1971), a collection of regional surveys with contributions on Bantu Africa by Sutton, Nenquin, Fagan and Inskeep. Another series of shorter regional surveys is to be found in the Iron Age sections of Bishop and Clark, eds., *Background to evolution in Africa* (1967). Among general works, the only recent one to attempt an integrated survey covering the whole of Bantu Africa is Oliver and Fagan (1975), but Phillipson (1977) is a valuable synthesis for much of the area.

It is to be remarked that the major comparative study of the Bantu languages by Malcolm Guthrie, which was in preparation from the

1940s, is still a very recent publication (1967–71) and its possible uses as a source for the prehistory of the area are as yet relatively unexplored. It has been widely judged that Guthrie seriously misinterpreted the historical conclusions to be drawn from his own work, but his collection of basic data stands, not only as a monument, but as a mine awaiting much further exploitation than it has yet received.

7. THE CHRISTIAN PERIOD IN MEDITERRANEAN AFRICA

The Christian period in Mediterranean Africa was an era of civilization wholly different from that which preceded and followed it. It produced great theologians and men of action, such as Athanasius and Augustine, passionate debates concerning both Christian belief and the nature of Christian society, and movements within the Church, such as monasticism, which have affected Christendom profoundly. A bibliography attempting to cover the ideas, personalities and social movements of the period would be huge and unwieldy. It will not be attempted here. A student of the period would be advised to consult the list of sources at the end of Jones, *The later Roman Empire* (1964), Volume II, pp. 1464–76; Altaner and Stuiber, *Patrologie (Leben, Schriften und Lehre der Kirchenväter)*, 7th edn (1964), under 'Athanasius', 'Augustinus', 'Cyrillus von Alexandrien' etc; and the bibliographies contained in Frend, *The Donatist Church*, 2nd edn (1971), and *The rise of the Monophysite movement* (1972). This essay restricts itself to the primary sources used in this chapter, and a brief bibliography of selected secondary works.

Egypt and Cyrenaica

Papyri provide the basis for a study of the social background to the rise of Christianity in Egypt and also shed light on the outlook of Egyptian Christians. The volumes of the Oxyrhynchus papyri published by the Egypt Exploration Society (1898—) are a primary source of information. The increasing difficulties of the middle classes in Egypt during the third century are shown graphically in a series of papyri (*PO* 1412–19) recording sessions of the senate of Oxyrhynchus in the second half of the third century; *PO* 2601 and 2673 provide some details of how the Great Persecution was carried out. Papyrus *libelli* of the persecution of Decius in 250 have been published by Knipfing, 'The *Libelli* of the Decian persecution' (1923), and there have been additions to the collection since. Christian texts circulating in Egypt have been published by Grenfell and Hunt, eds., *Oxyrhynchus papyri* ['Logia Jesu'] (1897), and

'New sayings of Jesus', and 'Fragment of a lost gospel' (1904). These 'sayings' turned out to be fragments of the *Gospel of Thomas*, a complete copy of which was found in the library of Gnostic documents from Nag-Hammadi. (An English translation of some complete Gnostic works from this collection is by Foerster, *A selection of Gnostic texts* (1974).) *Fragments of an unknown gospel*, dating to the first decades of the second century with phraseology suggestive of both Luke and John, were published by Bell and Skeat on behalf of the Trustees of the British Museum in 1935. In 1941 the clearance of rubbish from caves at Tura south of Cairo revealed a small papyrus library of patristic works, written probably in the sixth century, but including Origen's *Contra Celsum*, Bks I–VI, a hitherto unknown *Dialogue with Heracleides*, and gospel commentaries by Didymus the Blind (*c*. 390). The editio princeps of the *Dialogue* is that of Scherer, under the title *Entretien d'Origène avec Héraclide et les évêques, ses collègues, sur le Père, le Fils et l'Ame* (1949). Finally, successive volumes of the Bodmer collection of papyri, *Papyrus Bodmer*, contain important early Christian works circulating in Egypt, such as the Acts of Phileas and Philoromus; see *Papyrus Bodmer*, XX, ed. by Martin (1964).

Tools of study would be dominated by Opitz's magisterial *Athanasius' Werke* (1934—), and *Untersuchungen zur Überlieferung der Schriften der Athanasius* (1935), but for Opitz's death on the Russian front in 1941, which prevented their completion. As it is, a great deal of work on Athanasius, Didymus the Blind, and Cyril remains to be done. For the post-Chalcedonian period, the valuable series of studies published in the *Journal of Theological Studies* (1970—) by Ebeid and Wickham on Syriac manuscript sources relating to the works of Timothy the Cat and the Monophysite patriarchs of Alexandria are steadily widening the scope of knowledge on the complex problem of Christianity in Byzantine Egypt.

The major secondary sources are: Bell, *Jews and Greeks in Egypt* (1924), the second part of which is particularly valuable for relations between Athanasius and the Meletians, and *Egypt from Alexander the Great to the Arab conquest* (1948); Frend, *The rise of the Monophysite movement* (1972); Hardy, *The large estates of Byzantine Egypt* (1931), and *Christian Egypt, church and people* (1952), useful for the Meletians and later development of monasticism; Maspero, *Papyrus grecs de l'époque byzantine*, 3 vols. (1910–16); Leipoldt, 'Schenute von Atripe und die Entstehung des national-aegyptischen Christentums' (1904); and Woodward, *Christianity and nationalism in the later Roman Empire* (1916), rather dated, but a classic statement of the non-theological influences on heresy and schism. On Egyptian monasticism, see Lietzmann, *Geschichte der alten Kirche* (1944), IV, Chapter 4, and the excellent chapter by de Labriolle in Palanque, Bardy and de Labriolle, *De la paix Constantinienne à la mort de Théodose* (Vol. 3 of Fliche and Martin, *Histoire de l'église* (1947)), which includes a bibliography. For Chalcedon and post-Chalcedon in Egypt, see the essays in A. Grillmeier and H. Bacht's monumental *Das Konzil von Chalkedon*, Vols. I and II (1951–3).

North-West Africa

The primary source of equivalent importance to the Oxyrhynchus papyri for the study of the Christian period in North-West Africa is the volumes of the *Corpus Inscriptionum Latinarum*, esp. VIII, *Africa*, ed. by Wilmanns (1881–1916), supplemented by Gsell and Pflaum, *Inscriptions latines d'Algérie* (1923–57), and Cagnat and Merlin, *Inscriptions latines d'Afrique* (1923). These, together with the North African inscriptions published in the *Année épigraphique* (Paris, 1888 onwards), form an almost inexhaustible supply of basic material on many aspects of life and thought throughout the Roman, Vandal and Byzantine occupations. Monographs on individual sites include Monceaux, *Timgad chrétien* (1911); Allais, *Djemila* (1938); Marec, *Hippone* (1950); Leschi, *Tipasa* (1950); and Berthier, *Tiddis* (1954); all of these had large Christian quarters as well as the Roman city.

For the study of Donatism, an understanding of the historical geography of Roman North Africa is essential. Gsell's great work, *Atlas archéologique de l'Algérie*, published in 1911 when the population was still relatively small and ancient sites less subject to disturbance than at present, remains the starting-point for research. Some of the results of this work have been incorporated by Lancel in Vols. I and IV of his study of North African Donatism and Catholicism, based on the record of the disputation at Carthage between the two communities in June 411 (see *Sources chrétiennes*, vol. 195, under the title, 'Actes de la conférence de Carthage'). The text of the proceedings have been preserved in Migne, *PL*, XI, 1223–1420, together with texts of imperial laws against the Donatists.

Between 1935 and 1940, many rural sites in Numidia were surveyed, and some were partially excavated by André Berthier, director of the '7e Circonscription archéologique' centred on Constantine. Though paucity of datable material often prevented an adequate distinction between sites occupied in the later Roman and those occupied in the Byzantine period, Berthier's *Les Vestiges du Christianisme antique dans la Numidie centrale* (1942), written in collaboration with Logeart and Martin, remains the basic work of Christian archaeology in rural Numidia.

On the literary side, the works of Tertullian, Cyprian, Optatus of Milevis, Augustine, and the sixth-century writers Liberatus of Carthage and Facundus of Hermiana are all available in standard collections of Patristic texts. The *Acta* of the North African martyrs can best be studied in Musurillo's *The acts of the Christian martyrs* (1972).

Donatist *Acta martyrum* are preserved in *PL* VIII, cols. 698–784. Dominating the whole field of North African Christian history down to 411 is Monceaux's seven-volume *Histoire littéraire de l'Afrique chrétienne* (1901–23). This is a great work, a landmark in the scholarly study of Christian North Africa and of permanent value to all who research into its problems. Barnes, *Tertullian, a historical and literary study* (1971), despite its controversial tone, is a useful contribution towards understanding Tertullian's pagan background. Saumagne's *Cyprien, évêque de Carthage, 'Pape' d'Afrique* (1975) is a challenging and individual interpretation of Cyprian's career, and this may be said also of Tengström's interpretation of Donatism in *Donatisten und Katholiken* (1964). Brown's *Augustine of Hippo, a biography* (1967), and *Religion and society in the age of St Augustine* (1972), have become classic studies of Augustine and his age. The social history of the fourth century is treated by Diesner, *Der Untergang der römischen Herrschaft in Nordafrika* (1964).

The literature on Vandal Africa is dominated by C. Courtois, *Les Vandales et l'Afrique* (1955), and the study of the Vandal period tablets relating to property rates near Theveste by Courtois, Leschi, Perrat and Saumagne, *Tablettes Albertini, actes privées de l'époque vandale* (1952).

No great work has been written to succeed Diehl's classic *L'Afrique byzantine* (1896) for Africa during the Byzantine reconquest; the partial study of Markus, 'Donatism, the last phase' (1964), and Février and Duval's 'Inscription martyrologique sur plomb de la région de Telergma (AD 637)' (1969), are useful. The transition from Byzantine to Arab Africa is chronicled by Ibn ʿAbd al-Ḥakam, *Futūh Ifriqiya wa'l Andalus* [*The conquest of Africa and Andalusia*], ed. and trans. into French by A. Gateau (1942). Gautier's *Le Passé de l'Afrique du Nord* (1937) and Frend's 'North Africa and Europe in the early Middle Ages' (1955) may be helpful.

The major secondary works are as follows: Berthier, Logeart and Martin, *Les Vestiges du Christianisme antique dans la Numidie centrale* (1942); Brisson, *Autonomisme et Christianisme dans l'Afrique romaine de*

Septime Sévère à l'invasion vandale (1958); Brown, *Augustine of Hippo, a biography* (1967); Buonaiuti, *Il Cristianesimo nell, Africa Romana* (1928); Diesner, *Der Untergang der römischen Herrschaft in Nordafrika* (1964); Frend, *The Donatist Church*, 2nd edn (1971); Tengström, *Donatisten und Katholiken* (1964); Warmington, *The North African provinces from Diocletian to the Vandal conquest* (1954); and Frend, *Religion popular and unpopular in the early Christian centuries* (1976) – the writer's articles on Athanasius, the Circumcellions, early Nubian Christianity etc.

8. THE ARAB CONQUEST AND THE RISE OF ISLAM IN NORTH AFRICA

The principal source is the Arabic literature of the Middle Ages, represented for this purpose by a series of regional and confessional, but closely interconnected, traditions. These developed through successive works of synthesis, many of which are now lost, to culminate in the major collections of the period from the thirteenth to the sixteenth century AD.

As far as Egypt is concerned, the central work in the Muslim tradition is that of the tenth-century al-Kindī, *Governors and judges of Egypt*, ed. by Guest (1912), supplemented by the ninth-century work of Ibn ʿAbd al-Ḥakam, *The history of the conquest of Egypt, North Africa and Spain*, ed. by Torrey (1922), and the very much later work of the fifteenth-century al-Maqrīzī, *Al-Mawāʿiẓ wa 'l-Iʿtibār fī dhikr al-khiṭaṭ wa 'l āthār*, usually called *Khiṭaṭ*, ed. by Wiet (1911); the introductions by Guest and Torrey give useful accounts of the growth of the tradition. An important source from outside Egypt is the ninth-century Iraqi writer al-Balādhurī, *Kitāb futūḥ al-Buldān* (various editions from that of de Goeje (1863–6) onwards) whose work, dealing with the whole subject of the Arab conquests east and west, overlaps that of Ibn ʿAbd al-Ḥakam but, unlike the Egyptian author, does not deal with the pre-Islamic period. Additional information is provided by the geographical writer al-Yaʿqūbī, *Kitāb al-Buldān*, ed. by de Goeje (1892); French trans. by Wiet, *Le Livre des pays* (1937).

The Christian sources are initially the compilation attributable in whole or in part to John, Bishop of Nikiou at the end of the seventh century, surviving only in an Ethiopic version, the *Chronique de Jean, Évêque de Nikiou*, ed. and trans. by Zotenberg (1883). The main work is the *History of the Coptic patriarchs of Alexandria*, as compiled for this period by the tenth-century Sāwīrūs (Severus) b. Muqaffaʿ, ed. and trans. by Evetts (in *Patrologia Orientalis*, I, 2; I, 4; V, I; X, 5, paged by volume but also consecutively; 4 parts, to AD 849 only (1901ff.)). This is to be compared with the Orthodox history of Eutychius, known as Saʿīd b. Baṭrīq, also in the tenth century, *Eutychii Patriarchae Alexandrini Annales*, ed. by Cheikho (1906, 1909).

Relevant papyri are summarized in Karabacek *et al.*, *Papyrus Erzherzog Rainer: Führer durch die Ausstellung* (1894). The special collection of papyri from Aphrodito in Upper Egypt is published in *Aphrodito Papyri*, ed. by Bell (1917).

For Libya and the Maghrib, the basic account for the period down to 744 is that of Ibn ʿAbd al-Ḥakam; the relevant portion is published in a revised edition with French translation by A. Gateau, *Conquête de l'Afrique du Nord et de l'Espagne*, 2nd edn (1948), again supplemented by al-Balādhurī. Local traditions do not appear in writing before the tenth century. They are contained on the one hand in the biographical Ṭabaqāt literature represented by the eleventh-century al-Mālikī, *Riyāḍ al-nufūs fī ṭabaqāt ʿulamāʾ al-Qayrawān wa Ifrīqiya*, Volume I, ed. by Monès (1951). The annalistic and more generally historical literature, on the other hand, is best represented by the fourteenth-century Moroccan Ibn ʿIdhārī, *Kitāb al-Bayān al-mughrib fī akhbār al-Andalus wa 'l-Maghrib*, ed. by Colin and Lévi-Provençal, Vol. I (1948); French trans. by Fagnan, *Histoire de l'Afrique du Nord et de l'Espagne intitulée Al-Bayano 'l-Mogrib* (1901). The relevant portions of the great work of the thirteenth-century Oriental historian Ibn al-Athīr, *Al-Kāmil fī 'l-ta'rīkh* (various editions, from that of Tornberg, 1851–76, and 1301–2/1884–5), French trans. by Fagnan, *Annales du Maghreb et de l'Espagne* (1898), are somewhat more remote from the lost originals. The work of Ibn Khaldūn, *Kitāb al-ʿIbar* (various complete editions, from that of Būlāq, 1284/1867–8), French trans. of Volumes VI and VII by de Slane, *Histoire des Berbères*; 2nd edn, by Casanova and Pérès (1925–56), is of only marginal importance for this period.

Geographical accounts, with much historical information, are those of al-Yaʿqūbī in the ninth century, Ibn Ḥawqal, *Ṣūrat al-arḍ* (ed. by Kramers [1938–9], French trans. by Kramers and Wiet [1964]), in the tenth, and the great eleventh-century al-Bakrī, *Description de l'Afrique septentrionale*, ed. and trans. by de Slane, 2nd edn (1911–13, reprinted 1965). To these may be added, for Tahert, the ninth-century witness of Ibn al-Ṣaghīr, *Akhbār al-a'imma al-rustumiyyīn*, ed. by Motylinski, 'Chronique d'Ibn Ṣaghīr sur les imāms rostémides de Tahert' (1908), pp. 3–132. The principal representative of the Ibadite tradition is the sixteenth-century al-Shammākhī, *Kitāb al-siyar*, lithograph edn (1301/1883–4). For this period it is supplemented by Lewicki, 'Quelques extraits inédits relatifs aux voyages des commerçants et des missionnaires ibāḍites nord-africains au pays du Soudan occidental et central au moyen âge' (1960).

The essential work of reference is the *Encyclopaedia of Islam*, 1st edn (1913–38), and 2nd edn (1954—, in progress), which has so far reached the letter K. *The shorter encyclopaedia of Islam*, ed. by Gibb and Kramers (1961), is a useful extract of the articles in the first edition dealing with religion and the law, with bibliographies brought up to date. For Judaism, see *The Jewish encyclopaedia* (1916).

The view taken of the development of Islam in the present chapter ultimately depends upon Schacht, *The origins of Muhammadan jurisprudence* (1950, revised reprint, 1953). For *ḥadīth* cf. also Horowitz, 'Alter und Ursprung des Isnads' (1918, 1921). The composition of the Sīra, the traditional biography of the Prophet, is approached for example by Andrae, *Die Person Muhammads in Lehre und Glaube seine Gemeinde* (1918). The Sīra raises the question of the Koran (cf. e.g. Burton, '"Those are the high-flying cranes"' (1970)); this is considered by Wansborough, *Quranic Studies: sources and methods of scriptural interpretation* (1977). The relevance of Schacht to historiography appears from Brunschvig, 'Ibn Abdal'hakam et la conquête de l'Afrique du Nord par les Arabes' (1942–7), in which, prior to the publication of Schacht's *Origins*, he showed the extent to which Ibn ʿAbd al-Ḥakam's account was modelled upon points of law.

Schacht's conclusions are usefully resumed in his later work, *An introduction to Islamic Law* (1964); *A history of Islamic Law* by Coulson (1964), covers the same ground. More general works are Goldziher, *Muhammadanische Studien* (1888–9), trans. by Barber and Stern, *Muslim studies* (1967–71); Becker, *Islamstudien* (1924), Volume 1; von Grünebaum, *Mediaeval Islam*, 2nd edn (1953); the same author's *Islam: essays in the nature and growth of a cultural tradition*, 2nd edn (1961); Levy, *The social structure of Islam* (1957). The work of Mez, *The renaissance of Islam*, trans. by Bakhsh and Margoliouth (1937), is especially valuable for its detailed information. Among general histories, Becker, 'The expansion of the Saracens', in the *Cambridge mediaeval history*, II (1912), is still readable; more recent is the *Cambridge history of Islam*, ed. by Lewis, Holt and Lambton (1972). See also, e.g., Shaban, *Islamic history*, AD 600–750 (1971).

8. THE ARAB CONQUEST IN NORTH AFRICA

The essential study of the Arab conquest of Egypt is Butler, *The Arab conquest of Egypt and the last thirty years of the Roman dominion* (1902). There has been no general history in English of the country in the medieval period since Lane-Poole, *A history of Egypt in the Middle Ages*, 4th edn (1921). In French there is Wiet, *L'Égypte Arabe* (*Histoire de la Nation Égyptienne*, ed. by Hanotaux, IV (1937)); in German the various studies by Becker, notably in *Islamstudien*, I, and *Beiträge zur Geschichte Ägyptens* (1902–3). For irrigation techniques, see Willcocks and Craig, *Egyptian irrigation*, 3rd edn (1913); for the geography of the Delta, Guest, 'The Delta in the Middle Ages' (1912). Besides the work of Becker, the administration of Egypt in the early period is dealt with by Bell, 'The Aphrodito Papyri' (1908), and the same author's 'The administration of Egypt under the Umayyad Khalifs' (1928). The important work of Dennett, *Conversion and the poll-tax in early Islam* (1950), revises Becker's theory of Muslim taxation and its consequences. Useful information is contained in Shaban, *Islamic history* (1971).

There is no suitable history of Libya in English. The conquest of Cyrenaica is examined by Goodchild, 'Byzantines, Berbers and Arabs in 7th-century Libya' (1967); that of Libya as a whole by Brunschvig, 'Ibn Abdal'hakam et la conquête' (1942–7). The basic general history of the Maghrib is Julien, *Histoire de l'Afrique du Nord*, 2nd edn, Volume I, revised by Courtois, *Des origines à la conquête arabe* (1951), which deals briefly with the survival of Christianity after the Arab conquest; Volume II, revised by Le Tourneau, *De la conquête arabe à 1830* (1952), has been translated by Petrie and edited by Stewart, *History of North Africa from the Arab conquest to* 1830 (1970); both the French and the English editions have extensive bibliographies. A more detailed treatment of the early period is Marçais, *La Berbérie musulmane et l'Orient au moyen âge* (1946); it is dealt with discursively by Gautier, *Le Passé de l'Afrique du Nord: les siècles obscurs*, 2nd edn (1952). Regional histories are the *Histoire de la Tunisie*, Volume I, *L'Antiquité*, by Mahjoubi, Slim and Belkhodja (1973); Volume II, *Le moyen âge*, by Dachraoui, Djaït, M'rabet and Talbi (1974); Terrasse, *Histoire du Maroc des origines à l'établissement du Protectorat français* (1949–50); Brignon, Amin *et al.*, *Histoire du Maroc* (1967); and Gsell, Marçais and Yver, *Histoire de l'Algérie* (1927). The essential work is Talbi, *L'Émirat Aghlabide, 184–296/800–909: histoire politique* (1966), reviewed by Wansbrough in an important article, 'On recomposing the Islamic history of North Africa' (1969). Government is dealt with by Hopkins, *Mediaeval Muslim government in Barbary* (1958), and in more detail by

Djaït, 'La Wilāya d'Ifrīqiya au IIe–VIIIe siècle: étude institutionnelle' (1967, 1968). The Ibadites have been studied in numerous articles by T. Lewicki; cf. *Encyclopaedia of Islam*, 2nd edn, under 'Ibāḍiyya', for a general description and complete list of references; also Brett, 'Ifrīqiya as a market for Saharan trade, from the tenth to the twelfth century AD' (1969). For the Jews, see Hirschberg, 'The problem of the Judaized Berbers' (1963), and *A history of the Jews in North Africa*, 2nd, revised edn, trans. from the Hebrew (1974). The colonization of the Darʿa is described by Rosenberger, 'Tāmdult: cité minière et caravanière' (1970).

The basic work on architecture is Cresswell, *Early Muslim architecture*, 2nd edn (1970); an abridgement of the first edition of 1932–40 is provided by *A short account of early Muslim architecture* (1958). For the Maghrib see also Marçais, *Architecture musulmane d'Occident* (1954), and Lézine, *Architecture d'Ifrīqiya* (1966).

9. CHRISTIAN NUBIA

The main literary sources for the history of Nubia during the Middle Ages are in Arabic and are not easily available. The most important of the Arabic writers were Abū Ṣāliḥ the Armenian (*fl.* 1200) (1893), and al-Maqrīzī (1314–1442) (1911–27). Neither of these had first-hand knowledge of Nubia, but al-Maqrīzī incorporated valuable material from an otherwise lost work by ʿAbd Allāh Aḥmad b. Sulaym al-Aswānī (*fl.* latter part of tenth century). This work is of special value because al-Aswānī travelled to Dongola as an emissary of the Fatimid ruler, Gawhar. Quatremère (1811) translates many of the relevant Arabic documents into French. Vantini (1970) provides a useful summary, with brief extracts, of all the ancient literary sources, as well as an erratic bibliography, full of mistakes. An English translation of the Arabic writers, without original texts, by the same author is due soon. Documents in the Old Nubian language, until recently very few in number and almost exclusively religious in content, are now being found in some quantity at Qasr Ibrim (Plumley, 1975), and when fully published will add to historical knowledge.

The only book length history of the area and period is by Monneret de Villard (1938). Although written long before the recent archaeological activity, only points of detail need to be changed, and it remains an essential work. Adams, *Nubia: corridor to Africa* (1977), gives a rather different version, though still based on the literary material used by Monneret, since it also incorporates much of the evidence from recent excavations; the historical story remains much the same but the account of the material culture is now fuller, and greater attention is paid to ecological and economic factors. Arkell (1961), for long the standard history of the ancient Sudan, has one chapter on the period 600–1500, and the title of the chapter 'The coming of Islam' shows the main theme. It seriously underrates the Nubian culture.

Apart from Arabic sources, the only other major ancient work is the *Ecclesiastical history* written in Syriac by John of Ephesus in the sixth century. This work describes the first missionary activity in Nubia, and provides, apart from rather dubious archaeological evidence, the only information for the beginning of Christianity. An English translation was published by Payne-Smith (1860) and a Latin one by Brooks (1935–6). Since John was a strong supporter of the Monophysite cause, his account is biased and must be used with caution. For a simple, straightforward and brief account of history and culture, Shinnie (1954) is useful as a beginning, though it is now out of date on the archaeological side. Shinnie (1965) draws attention to some of the new material.

The first archaeological investigations were concerned almost exclusively with the study of churches, many of which remained standing until the waters of Lake Nubia removed them. The first studies, both of high quality, are Mileham (1910) and Somers Clarke (1912); these writers visited all the sites they described, and, being architects, made useful and accurate plans. Monneret de Villard (1935–57) is a much fuller description of standing sites, but in many cases the author did not visit them and compiled his descriptions from other sources – the plans are rather rough.

During the period between the wars, there was no excavation and little first-hand investigation of archaeological sites, other than the work by Monneret de Villard (1935–7) already mentioned. There was some general writing and Crowfoot (1927), although short and unassuming, remains one of the best and most perceptive appraisals of the culture.

When the excavation started after the Second World War, the first publications were Shinnie (1955) and Shinnie and Chittick (1961). Both of these were pioneering attempts, and suffer from lack of comparative material and vagueness in the chronology. Since 1961 there have been many excavations and the literature is profuse. Many new studies and excavation reports have appeared in recent years – the most important perhaps being the very large number of publications on Faras and its paintings. Michalowski (1962, 1965) gives an account of the excavation and some of the finds; Michalowski (1967) gives a good general account, placing Faras in its historical and artistic setting; Michalowski (1974) is a detailed catalogue of the paintings from the cathedral now in Warsaw. Michalowski's colleagues and students have produced a very large number of papers and several books. Amongst these may be noted in particular Jakobielski (1972), which gives an historical account of the bishopric of Faras based on the inscriptions and the famous painted list of bishops, all of which the author has studied at first hand, and Kubinska (1975), which studies the Greek inscriptions and graffiti. Other volumes in the Faras series are forthcoming.

Of other excavations full reports are still awaited in most cases, but attention should be drawn to Weeks (1967), which is not only a model of what an excavation report should be, but also contains an interesting chapter on general historical and economic questions. Preliminary reports on excavations in the Sudan are published in *Kush*, but the last volume published (in 1974) is dated 1967/68; however by that date most of the rescue excavations had been completed. Reports on excavations in Egypt are more scattered, but the annual surveys in the journal *Orientalia* by Leclant give brief descriptions of work carried out and excellent bibliographies. Adams in particular has dealt with specific aspects of the archaeology. His work on the pottery (Adams, 1962) has been of particular value in providing a chronological framework. The article referred to is considerably modified by Adams (1967–8) and other still unpublished works. Lister (1967) is also a valuable study of pottery, by one who is herself a potter and has a good understanding of the processes involved in making pots. Changing styles of church plan and architecture are studied, and a chronology proposed, by Adams (1965a). Other topics, except for church paintings, have not yet been the subject of special studies.

For the Old Nubian language and publication of those texts known at the date of publication, Griffith (1913) is fundamental. Zyhlarz (1928, reprinted 1966) provides a much more detailed study of the grammar, but is less clear and needs to be used with care; old Nubian grammar needs much further study, and a new work is promised by Hintze.

The Society for Nubian Studies organized conferences at Warsaw in 1972 and Chantilly in 1975, following a first conference, before the founding of the society, at Essen in 1969. The publication of the papers read at these conferences – Essen (Dinkler, 1970), Warsaw (Michalowski, 1975) – gives the most up-to-date information on many topics. Papers from the Chantilly conference are expected to be published in 1977.

10. THE FATIMID REVOLUTION IN NORTH AFRICA

The references are essentially those for chapter 8, 'The Arab conquest and the expansion of Islam in North Africa'. Useful articles will be found in the *Encyclopaedia of Islam*, 1st and 2nd edns, under, e.g., Abū Yazīd, Aḥmad b. Ṭūlūn, Fāṭimids, Ḳarmaṭiya, Muḥammad b. Tughj. The fullest source for the Ikhshidids is Ibn Sa'īd, *Kitāb al-mughrib fī ḥulā 'l-Maghrib*, Bk IV, ed. and trans. into German by K. L. Tallqvist (1899), which is derived from the work of the contemporary Ibn Zūlāq; Tallqvist's edition includes the relevant section of al-Kindī's work, with a translation, for comparison. A certain amount of information on the administration in this early period is to be found in Rabie, *The financial system of Egypt*, AH 564–741/AD 1169–1341 (1972).

The history of the Fatimids in the Maghrib has not yet become the subject of a monograph. The sources for the Fatimid and Zirid period down to 1062 for the most part go back to the lost chronicles of al-Raqīq and his continuator Ibn Sharaf, variously represented in the *Bayān* of Ibn 'Idhārī, the *Kitāb al-Kāmil* of Ibn al-Athīr, and the *Kitāb al-'Ibar* of Ibn Khaldūn (for details see bibliographical essay for chapter 8). To these may be added the geographers, al-Ya'qūbī, *Kitāb al-Buldān*, *Bibliotheca geographorum arabicorum*, ed. by de Goeje, VII (1892); Ibn Ḥawqal, *Ṣurat al-arḍ*, ed. by Kramers (1938–9), French trans. by Kramers and Wiet, *Configuration de la terre* (1964); and al-Bakrī, *Description de l'Afrique septentrionale*, ed. and trans. by de Slane (1911–13, reprinted 1965). The principal secondary work following upon Talbi, *L'Émirat Aghlabide* (1966), is Idris, *La Berbérie orientale sous les Zīrīdes*, 2 vols. (1962). For the economic history of the subject, cf. Brett, 'Ifrīqiya as a market for Saharan trade, from the tenth to the twelfth century AD' (1969). The account of the eleventh century is based essentially upon Brett's unpublished Ph.D. thesis, 'Fitnat al-Qayrawān' (1970); cf. Brett, 'The Zughba at Tripoli, 429H (1037–8 AD)' (1974–5); 'The military interest of the battle of Ḥaydarān', in Parry and Yapp (1975); 'Sijill al-Mustanṣir' (1974). The account of the Geniza material is contained in Goitein, *A Mediterranean society*, I (1967).

II. THE SAHARA AND THE SUDAN

Works by Arab geographers and historians are the principal sources for the history of the Sahara and the Sudan, at least until the fifteenth century. In the ninth and tenth centuries most of the geographers lived in Baghdad and in the Iranian provinces of the ʿAbbasid caliphate. Their information about Africa south of the Sahara was limited to the recording of names of the principal kingdoms of the Sudan (Ghana, Gao and Kanem/Zaghāwa), to some vague accounts of the gold trade, and to a few allusions to the trade-routes of the Sahara. Their texts should be carefully and critically read, with a special warning against anachronisms, which are the result of unacknowledged borrowings of later authors from their predecessors.

Among the authors whose accounts indicate the development of the Arabs' knowledge of the Sudan, one can mention al-Khwārizmī and al-Fazārī (first half of the ninth century), al-Yaʿqūbī (the latter part of the ninth century), Ibn al-Faqīh (*fl.* 903), Ibn Ḥawqal (who visited Sijilmasa in 951), al-Muhallabī (an Egyptian of the second half of the tenth century), and al-Bakrī (who wrote in 1067/8).

The contribution of al-Bakrī is by far the most detailed and accurate. He is the first in the line of geographers and historians from the Muslim West (Spain and the Maghrib), who had access to information about the Sahara and the Sudan from traders and other travellers. Al-Bakrī's account, written towards the end of the period covered in this chapter, is indispensable for the study of the early states of Takrur, Ghana and Gao as well as for the understanding of the complex Saharan trade system. Ibn Saʿid of the twelfth century has some valuable information about the earlier period, mainly in connection with Kanem. Ibadite sources, from the eighth to the twelfth centuries, provide important evidence about the role of traders of that sect in developing communication with the western Sudan. The Ibadite texts have been edited, translated and analysed by T. Lewicki (1960).

Most of the Arabic sources of this period form part of the classical literature of Arab geography. The texts were edited and translated (mainly into French) by distinguished orientalists from the second half of the nineteenth century onwards. A selection of Arabic texts on Africa south of the Sahara, with a Russian translation, has been published by Koubbel and Mateev (1965) in two volumes, covering the period between the seventh and twelfth centuries. Cuoq has recently (1975) published a French translation of the Arabic sources on West

Africa. An annotated English translation of over fifty texts, by Hopkins and Levtzion, is now in press.

The Arabic sources on Africa were first studied by Cooley (1841), and were used by all those who were concerned with the early history of Africa. The development of African historiography during the last two decades has called for a reinterpretation and a revaluation of those sources. This task has been undertaken by Lewicki (1969, 1974), Levtzion (1968, 1972, 1973), Norris (1972), Farias (1974) and others.

Whereas the Arabic sources offer a series of snapshots of the past of Africa, the real dynamics of its history, seen from the viewpoint of the Africans, may be discerned from oral traditions. Such traditions relating to the earlier states of the western Sudan were recorded as early as the seventeenth century in the chronicles of Timbuktu, namely *Ta'rīkh al-Sūdān* and *Ta'rīkh al-Fattāsh*. Monteil (1953) and Bathily (1975) have studied the traditions of Wagadu about the ancient kingdom of the Soninke. Traditions of Futa Toro have been presented by Soh (1913). Saharan traditions and myths have been dealt with by, among others, Basset (1909) and Norris (1972). Rouch (1953) has analysed the traditions of the Songhay. Urvoy (1949), Palmer (1936), Smith (1976) and Lange (1977), have used oral traditions as well as external and local Arabic sources for the study of Kanem.

The elusive nature of oral traditions and the scarcity of contemporary sources leave many gaps in the history of the early states of the Sudan. Archaeology is one discipline which has not yet exerted itself, and ought to be given more resources in an attempt to fill some of the gaps. Mauny (1961) provides an excellent survey of the results of archaeological findings. Mauny and Thomassey excavated Kumbi Saleh, the probable site of the capital of Ghana (see Thomassey and Mauny, 1951, 1956). Robert and Devisse have led a series of expeditions to Tegdaoust, which is tentatively identified as the site of Awdaghust (see Robert and Devisse, 1970). Colin Flight, of the University of Birmingham, is currently engaged in the study of several sites in the complex of Gao.

The rise of the Almoravid movement is central to the history of the period in all the three zones covered in this chapter, namely the Sahara, the Maghrib and the central Sudan. Its spiritual origins go back to Kairouan, and the religious history of the Maghrib between the ninth and the eleventh centuries provides the background to the movement. For this the works of Bel (1938), Idris (1955, 1957, 1962), Faure (1957) and Monès (1962) should be consulted. The principal Arabic sources on the Almoravids are al-Bakrī (who wrote in 1067/8, and presented a contemporaneous account of the earliest phase in the emergence of the movement), al-Qāḍī ʿIyāḍ (1088–1149, a militant Mālikī devoted to the Almoravid Dynasty), al-Zuhrī (of the mid twelfth century), Ibn al-Athīr (died 1233), Ibn ʿIdhārī (who wrote in 1306, and whose valuable account of the Almoravids has only relatively recently [1959] been published by Miranda), Ibn Abī Zarʿ, and Ibn Khaldūn (of the fourteenth century, whose accounts are best known to historians but ought to be carefully used). Among modern studies on the Almoravids are those of Lévi-Provençal (1957), Miranda (1959), Semonin (1964), Farias (1967), Norris (1971, 1972) and Levtzion (1973, pp. 29–42).

The trans-Saharan trade and its implications for the economic history of the Maghrib and the Sudan have been dealt with by many scholars. For detailed studies one may refer to Lombard (1947), Brett (1969), Devisse (1970) and Vanacker (1973). For more general syntheses, see Mauny (1961), Bovill (1968) and Levtzion (1973).

State-building in the Sudan is a principal theme in the history of that period. It has been the subject of several interpretative essays, such as Fage (1964) and Koubbel (1972). The latter, a Soviet scholar, presents a Marxist interpretation of the process. Interesting insights into this process at a period considered to be 'the dawn of African history' sometimes appear in general works on African history.

BIBLIOGRAPHY

GENERAL

The following bibliographical and reference works are of value to the study of the period covered by this volume as a whole. Space permits only a very selective list, which does not purport to be comprehensive.

The most complete guide to the literature of African studies available is P. Duignan's *Guide to research and reference works on sub-Saharan Africa*, Stanford, 1971. This most valuable work should be consulted for further information.

General bibliographies

Altaner, B. and Stuiber, A. *Patrologie (Leben, Schriften und Lehre der Kirchenväter)*, 7th edn. Freiburg, 1964. [Bibliography.]

Blaudin de Thé, Cdt. *Essai de bibliographie du Sahara français et des régions avoisinantes*. Paris. 1960.

Brasseur, Paule. *Bibliographie générale du Mali*. Dakar, 1964.

Cooke, C. K. 'A bibliography of Rhodesian archaeology from 1874', *Arnoldia*, 1974, **6**, 38, 1–56.

Frend, W. H. C. *The Donatist Church*, 2nd edn. Oxford, 1971. [Bibliography.]

Frend, W. H. C. *The rise of the Monophysite movement*. Cambridge, 1972. [Bibliography.]

Gadallah, E. 'Meroitic problems and a comprehensive Meroitic bibliography', *Kush*, 1963, **11**, 196–216.

Jones, A. H. M. *The later Roman Empire*. Oxford and Norman, Oklahoma, 1964. [Bibliography, Vol. II, 1464–76.]

Julien, C-A. *Histoire de l'Afrique du Nord*. Paris, 1951 and 1952, 2 vols. English trans. by J. Petrie, ed. by C. C. Stewart. London, 1970. [Bibliography by C. C. Stewart.]

Levtzion, N. *Ancient Ghana and Mali*. London, 1973. [Bibliography.]

Mauny, R. 'Bibliographie de la préhistoire et de la protohistoire de l'Ouest africain', *Bulletin de l'IFAN* (sér. B), 1967, **29**, 879–917; 1970, **32**, 333–40.

General works

Ajayi, J. F. A. and Crowder, M. eds. *History of West Africa*, Vol. I, 2nd edn. London, 1976.

Arkell, A. J. *A history of the Sudan to* AD 1821. London, 1955; 2nd edn, 1961; reprinted 1973.

Baumann, H., Thurnwald, R. and Westermann, D. *Völkerkunde Afrikas*. Essen, 1940. French trans., *Les peuples et les civilisations de l'Afrique*. Paris, 1948.

Cambridge ancient history, Vols. III–VI, Cambridge, 1925–7; Vols VII–XII, Cambridge, 1928–39.

Cambridge history of Islam, ed. by B. Lewis, P. M. Holt and A. K. S. Lambton. Cambridge, 1972. 2 vols.

Cambridge medieval history, Vol. II. Cambridge, 1913.

Cary, M. and Warmington, E. H. *The ancient explorers*, revised edn. London, 1963.

Douglas, M. and Kaberry, P. eds. *Man in Africa*. London, 1969.

Encyclopaedia of Islam. Leiden and London, 1913–38; 2nd edn [letters A–K] in progress from 1954.

Gautier, E.-F. *Le Passé de l'Afrique du Nord: les siècles obscurs*, 2nd edn. Paris, 1952.

Gibb, H. A. R. and Kramers, J. H. eds. *The shorter encyclopaedia of Islam*. Leiden and London, 1961.

Gray, R. and Birmingham, D. eds. *Precolonial African trade*. London, 1970.

Gsell, S. *Histoire ancienne de l'Afrique du Nord*. Paris, 1913–29. 8 vols.

Hiernaux, J. *The people of Africa*. London, 1974.

The Jewish encyclopaedia. New York, 1916.

Julien, C.-A. *Histoire de l'Afrique du Nord*, Vol. I, *Des origines à la conquête arabe*, 2nd edn (revised by C. Courtois). Paris, 1951. Vol. II, *De la conquête arabe à 1830* (revised by R. Le Tourneau), Paris, 1952. English trans. by J. Petrie, ed. by C. C. Stewart, *History of North Africa from the Arab conquest to* 1830. London, 1970.

Kamal, Y. *Monumenta cartographica Africae et Aegypti*. Cairo and Leiden, 1926–51. 5 vols.

La Roncière, C. de. *La Découverte de l'Afrique au moyen âge*. Cairo, 1924–7. 3 vols.

Mauny, R. *Tableau géographique de l'ouest africain au moyen âge. Mémoires de l'IFAN* (Dakar), 1961, no. 61; reprinted Amsterdam, 1967.

Mauny, R. *Les siècles obscurs de l'Afrique noire: histoire et archéologie*. Paris, 1970.

Murdock, G. P. *Africa, its peoples and their culture history*. New York, 1959.

Oliver, Roland and Mathew, Gervase, eds. *History of East Africa*, Vol. I. Oxford, 1963.

Schacht, Joseph. *An introduction to Islamic Law*. Oxford, 1964.

Seligman, C. G. *The races of Africa*. London, 1930.

Thompson, L. A. ed. *African societies in southern Africa*. London, 1969.

Thompson, L. A. and Ferguson, J. eds. *Africa in classical antiquity*. Ibadan, 1969.

Vansina, Jan, Mauny, R. and Thomas, L. V. eds. *The historian in tropical Africa*. Oxford, 1964.

Wilson, M. and Thompson, L. M. eds. *Oxford history of South Africa*, Vol. I. Oxford and London, 1969.

Chronology and radiocarbon dating

Balout, L. *Préhistoire de l'Afrique du Nord: essai de chronologie*. Paris, 1955.

Boardman, J. 'Evidence for the dating of Greek settlements in Cyrenaica', *Annual of the British School at Athens*, 1966, **61**, 149–56.

Butzer, K. W., Isaac, G. L., Richardson, J. L. and Washbourn-Kamau, C. K. 'Radiocarbon dating of East African lake levels', *Science*, 1972, **175**, 1069–76.

Campo, M. van. 'Pollen analyses in the Sahara', in Wendorf and Marks, eds., *Problems in prehistory* (*see under* 'General' section, Prehistory), 45–64.

Carter, P. L. and Vogel, J. C. 'The dating of industrial assemblages from stratified sites in eastern Lesotho', *Man*, N.S., 1974, **9**, 557–70.

Dart, R. A. and Beaumont, P. 'Ratification and retrocession of earlier Swaziland iron ore mining radiocarbon datings', *South African Journal of Science*, 1968, **64**, 6.

Diop, C. A. *Le Laboratoire de Radiocarbone de l'IFAN*. Dakar, 1968.

Fagan, B. M. 'Radiocarbon dates for sub-Saharan Africa', *Journal of African History*: 1961, **2**, 137–9; 1963, **4**, 127–8; 1965, **6**, 107–16; 1966, **7**, 495–506; 1967, **8**, 513–27; 1969, **10**, 149–69.

Flight, Colin. 'A survey of recent results in the radiocarbon chronology of northern and western Africa', *Journal of African History*, 1973, **14**, 4, 531–54.

Phillipson, D. W. 'Notes on the later prehistoric radiocarbon chronology of eastern and southern Africa', *Journal of African History*, 1970, **11**, 1, 1–16.

Phillipson, D. W. 'The chronology of the Iron Age in Bantu Africa', *Journal of African History*, 1975, **16**, 321–42.

Shaw, Thurstan. 'On radiocarbon chronology of the Iron Age in sub-Saharan Africa', *Current Anthropology*, 1969, **10**, 2–3, 226–31.

Soper, R. C. 'New radiocarbon dates for eastern and southern Africa', *Journal of African History*, 1974, **15**, 2, 175–92.

Stuiver, M. and Van der Merwe, N. J. 'Radiocarbon chronology of the Iron Age in sub-Saharan Africa', *Current Anthropology*, 1968, **9**, 54–8.

Sutton, J. E. G. 'New radiocarbon dates for eastern and southern Africa', *Journal of African History*, 1972, **13**, 1–24.

Wendorf, F. and others. 'Dates for the Middle Stone Age of East Africa', *Science*, 1974, **187**, 740–2.

Wenig, S. 'Bemerkungen zur Chronologie des Reiches von Meroe', *Mitteilungen des Instituts für Orientforschung der deutschen Akademie der Wissenschaften zu Berlin*, 1967, **13**, 10–44.

Crops, agriculture and domestication

Allen, W. *The African husbandman*. Edinburgh, 1965.

Clark, J. D. 'The domestication process in sub-Saharan Africa with special reference to Ethiopia', *IXe Congrès de l'Union Internationale des Sciences Préhistoriques et Protohistoriques* (*Nice, Sept. 1976*). Preprint volume, Colloque xx, *Origines de l'élevage et de la domestication*, 56–115 [forthcoming].

Dalziel, J. M. *The useful plants of west tropical Africa*. London, 1937.

Davies, Oliver, Hugot, H. J. and Seddon, D. 'The origins of African agriculture', *Current Anthropology*, 1968, **9**, 5, 478–509.

Harlan, J. R. *Crops and man*. Madison, 1975.

Harlan, J. R., de Wet, J. M. J. and Stemler, A. B. L. eds. *Origins of plant domestication in Africa*. The Hague and Paris, 1976.

Hutchinson, Sir James, ed. *Essays in crop plant evolution*. London, 1965.

Portères, R. 'Berceaux agricoles primaires sur le continent africain', *Journal of African History*, 1962, **3**, 2, 195–210.

Portères, R. 'Le Millet coracan, ou finger millet (*Eleusine coracana gaertner*)', in Harlan and others, eds., *Origins* . . . (*see above*).

Shaw, Thurstan. 'Early agriculture in Africa', *Journal of the Historical Society of Nigeria*, 1972, **6**, 143–91.

Snowden, J. D. *The cultivated races of sorghum*. London, 1936.

Ucko, P. J. and Dimbleby, G. W. eds. *The domestication and exploitation of plants and animals*. London, 1969.

Zeuner, F. E. *A history of domesticated animals*. London, 1963.

Languages

Abdelgadir Mahmoud Abdulla, ed. *Studies in ancient languages of the Sudan*. Khartoum, 1974.

Dalby, D. ed. *Language and history in Africa*. London, 1970.

Greenberg, Joseph H. *Studies in African linguistic classification*. New Haven, 1955.

Greenberg, Joseph H. *The languages of Africa*. The Hague, 1963. Rev. edn Bloomington, 1966. Also printed in *International Journal of American Linguistics*, 1963, **29**, 1, Pt 1.

Greenberg, Joseph H. 'Linguistic evidence regarding Bantu origins', *Journal of African History*, 1972, **13**, 2, 187–216.

Guthrie, Malcolm. 'Languages and history', *Journal of African History*, 1964, **5**, 1, 135–6.

Guthrie, Malcolm. *Comparative Bantu*: *an introduction to the comparative linguistics and prehistory of the Bantu languages*. Farnborough, 1967–71. 4 vols.

Heine, B. 'Zur genetische Gliederung der Bantu-Sprachen', *Afrika und Ubersee*, 1972–3, **56**, 164–85.

Henrici, Alick. 'Numerical classification of Bantu languages', *African Language Studies*, 1973, **14**.

Shinnie, P. L. 'Multilingualism in medieval Nubia', in Abdelgadir Mahmoud Abdulla, ed., *Studies* . . . (*see above*), 41–7.

Studies in ancient languages of the Sudan. *See above under* Abdelgadir Mahmoud Abdulla.

Westermann, D. 'Die westlichen Sudansprachen und ihre Beziehungen zum Bantu', *Mitteilungen des Seminars für orientalische Sprachen*, 1927, **30**.

Patrologia, inscriptions and papyri

Cagnat, R. and Merlin, A. *Inscriptions latines d'Afrique*. Paris, 1923.

Corpus Inscriptionum Graecarum [*CIG*]. Berlin, 1825–77.

Corpus Inscriptionum Latinarum [*CIL*]. Berlin, 1881–1916. [Vol. VIII concerns Africa.]

Corpus Scriptorum Christianorum Orientalium [*Corp. Script. Christ. Orient.*]. Paris, Louvain, etc. *Scriptores Arabici, Scriptores Coptici, Scriptores Syri.*

Corpus Scriptorum Ecclesiasticorum Latinorum [*CSEL*]. Vienna.

Cowley, A. E. ed. *Aramaic papyri of the fifth century BC.* Oxford, 1923.

Gsell, S. and Pflaum, H. G. *Inscriptions latines d'Algérie.* Paris, 1923–57.

Knopf, R. and Krueger, G. *Ausgewählte Märtyrakten.* 1901– .

Maspero, J. *Papyrus grecs de l'époque byzantine.* Paris, 1910–16. 3 vols.

Papyrus Bodmer [*P. Bodmer*], Vol. xx, ed. by V. Martin. Geneva, 1964.

Papyrus Oxyrhynchus [*P. Oxy.*]. Egypt Exploration Society (London), from 1898.

Patrologia cursus completus, series Graeca [*PG*], ed. by J.-P. Migne. Paris, 1857–66.

Patrologia cursus completus, series Latina [*PL*], ed. by J.-P. Migne. Paris, 1844–64.

Patrologia Orientalis [*PO*], ed. by B. T. A. Evetts. Paris, from 1901.

Prehistory and human evolution

Alimen, H. *The prehistory of Africa.* London, 1957.

Bishop, W. W. and Clark, J. D. eds. *Background to evolution in Africa.* Chicago, 1967.

Bishop, W. W. and Miller, J. A. eds. *Calibration of hominoid evolution.* Edinburgh, 1972.

Brooks, C. E. P. *Climate through the ages.* London, 1949.

Butzer, K. W. and Isaac, G. L. eds. *After the Australopithecines: stratigraphy, ecology and culture change in the Middle Pleistocene.* The Hague, 1975.

Campbell, B. G. *Human evolution*, 2nd edn. Chicago, 1972.

Clark, J. D. *The prehistory of Africa.* London and New York, 1970.

Clark, J. D. ed. *Atlas of African prehistory.* Chicago, 1967.

Clark, W. E. Le Gros. *The fossil evidence for human evolution.* Chicago, 1955.

Coppens, Y., Howell, F. C., Isaac, G. L. and Leakey, R. E. F. eds. *Earliest man and environments in the Lake Rudolf basin. Prehistoric archeology and ecology*, **2**. Chicago, 1976.

Davies, Oliver. *West Africa before the Europeans.* London, 1967.

Fage, J. D. and Oliver, Roland eds. *Papers in African prehistory.* Cambridge, 1970.

Hawkes, J. and Woolley, Sir Leonard. *Prehistory and the beginnings of civilization*, Vol. 1 of UNESCO *History of mankind.* UNESCO and London, 1963.

Howell, F. C. and Bourlière, F. eds. *African ecology and human evolution.* Chicago, 1963.

Hugot, H. J. ed. *Actes du VIe congrès panafricain de préhistoire et de l'étude du Quaternaire (Dakar, 1967).* Chambéry, 1972.

Isaac, G. L. and McCown, E. R. eds. *Human origins: Louis Leakey and the East African evidence.* Menlo Park, Calif., 1976.

Kurth, G. ed. *Evolution and hominisation*, 2nd edn. Stuttgart, 1968.

Mortelmans, G. and Nenquin, J. eds. *Actes du IVe congrès panafricain de préhistoire.* Tervuren, 1962.

Oakley, K. P. *Man the toolmaker*, 6th edn. Chicago, 1976.

Oliver, Roland and Fagan, B. M. *Africa in the Iron Age*. Cambridge, 1975.
Phillipson, D. W., *The later prehistory of eastern and southern Africa*. London, 1977.
Pilbeam, D. *The ascent of man: an introduction to human evolution*. New York, 1972.
Shinnie, P. L. ed. *The African Iron Age*. Oxford, 1971.
Tuttle, R. L. H. ed. *Palaeoanthropology: morphology and ecology*. The Hague, 1975.
Washburn, S. L. and Moore, R. *Ape into man: a study of human evolution*. Boston, 1974.
Wendorf, F. and Marks, A. E. eds. *Problems in prehistory: North Africa and the Levant*. Dallas, 1975.
Van Zinderen Bakker, E. M. ed. *Palaeoecology of Africa*. Cape Town, from 1966.

Arabic texts: collections

Cuoq, J. Med. *Recueil des sources arabes concernant l'Afrique occidentale du 8e au 16e siècle (Bilād al-Sūdān)*, trans. with notes by J. Cuoq. Paris, 1975.
Hopkins, J. F. P. and Levtzion, N. eds. *Mediaeval Arabic sources on West Africa*, trans. and annotated by J. F. P. Hopkins and N. Levtzion. Cambridge [forthcoming].
Kamal, Y. *Monumenta cartographica Africae et Aegypti*. 13 fascicules, Cairo/Leiden, 1926–51.
Koubbel, L. E. and Mateev, V. V. eds. *Arabskie istochniki VII–XII vekov po etnografii i istorii Afriki yuzhnee Sakhary*. Moscow–Leningrad, 1965. 2 vols.
Lévi-Provençal, E. ed. *Textes Arabes Marocains*. Rabat, 1934.
Lewicki, T. *Arabic external sources for the history of Africa south of the Sahara*. London, 1969.

Arabic writers

Akhbār al-Zamān, ed. by ʿAbd al-Ḥamīd Aḥmad Ḥanafī. Cairo, 1938.
al-Bakrī. *Kitāb al-masālik wa'l mamālik*, ed. by M. G. de Slane. Algiers, 1911. French trans. by M. G. de Slane, *Description de l'Afrique septentrionale*. Algiers, 1911–13; reprinted Paris, 1965. *See also* V. Monteil, 'Routier de l'Afrique blanche et noir de nord-ouest: al-Bakrī (Cordova, 1068)', *Bulletin de l'IFAN*, 1968, **30** (sér. B), 39–116.
al-Balādhurī. *Kitāb futūḥ al-Buldān*, ed. by M. J. de Goeje. Leiden, 1863–6.
Ibn ʿAbd al-Ḥakam. *Kitāb futūḥ Miṣr wa'l-Maghrib wa-akhbārihā*, ed. by C. C. Torrey. English trans., *The history of the conquest of Egypt, North Africa and Spain*. New Haven, 1922. Revised edn. and French trans. of the part dealing with the Maghrib by A. Gateau, *Conquête de l'Afrique du Nord et de l'Espagne*. Algiers, 1942; 2nd edn, 1948.
Ibn ʿAbd al-Ḥalīm, in E. Lévi-Provençal, 'Un Nouveau Récit de la conquête de l'Afrique du Nord par les Arabes', *Arabica Occidentalia*, 1954, **1**, 17–43.
Ibn Abī Zayd al-Qayrawānī. *al-Risāla*, ed. by L. Brecher. Algiers, 1952.
Ibn Abī Zarʿ. *al-Anīs al-muʿrib bi-rawḍ al-qirṭās fī akhbār mulūk al-Maghrib wa-ta'rīkh madīnat Fās*, ed. by C. J. Tornberg. Uppsala, 1843–66.
Ibn al-Athīr. *Kitāb al-Kāmil fi 'l-ta'rīkh*, ed. by C. J. Tornberg. Leiden, 1851–76 and Cairo, 1884–5. French trans. by E. Fagnan, 'Débuts de la

dynastie almoravide', *Revue Africaine*, 1900, **44**, 175–9. Also in *Annales du Maghreb et de l'Espagne*. Algiers, 1898.

Ibn Baṭṭūṭa. *Tuḥfat al-nuẓẓār fī gharā'ib al-amṣār wa-'ajā'ib al-asfār* [*Voyages*], ed. and trans. by C. Defrémery and R. B. Sanguinetti. Paris, 1922.

Ibn al-Faqīh. *Mukhtaṣar kitāb al-buldān*, ed. by M. J. de Goeje. Leiden, 1885.

Ibn Ḥammād. *Akhbār mulūk Banī 'Ubayd wa-sīratuhum*, ed. by M. Vanderheyden. Algiers and Paris, 1927.

Ibn Ḥawqal. *Kitāb ṣūrat al-arḍ*, ed. by J. H. Kramers. Leiden 1938–9. French trans. by J. H. Kramers and Gaston Wiet, *Configuration de la terre*. Beirut and Paris, 1964.

Ibn 'Idhārī al-Marrākushī. *Kitāb al-Bayān al-mughrib fī akhbār al-Andalus wa 'l-Maghrib*, ed. by G. S. Colin and E. Lévi-Provençal. Leiden, 1948–51. French trans. by E. Fagnan, *Histoire de l'Afrique du Nord et de l'Espagne intitulée Al-Bayano 'l-Moghrib*. Algiers, 1901.

Ibn 'Idhārī al-Marrākushī. 'Un fragmento inedito de Ibn Idhari sobre los Almorāvides', *Hespéris-Tamuda*, 1961, **2**, 43–111.

Ibn Khaldūn. *Kitāb ta'rīkh al-duwal al-Islāmiya bi'l-Maghrib min Kitāb al-'Ibar*, ed. and French trans. by M. G. de Slane [*Histoire des Berbères et des dynasties musulmanes de l'Afrique septentrionale*]. Paris, 1847. 2nd edn, ed. by H. Casanova and H. Pérès, Paris, 1925–56.

Ibn Khurdādhbih. *Kitāb al-masālik wa'l-mamālik*, ed. by M. J. de Goeje. Leiden, 1889.

Ibn Nājī. *Ma'ālim al-imān*. Tunis, AH 1320.

Ibn Qutayba. *Kitāb al-Ma'ārif*, ed. by F. Wüstenfeld. Göttingen, 1850.

Ibn Ṣaghīr. *Akhbār al-a'imma al-rustumiyyīn* ['Chronique d'Ibn Ṣaghīr sur les imāms rostémides de Tahert'], ed. by A. de C. Motylinski. *Actes du 14e Congrès international des Orientalistes, Algiers, 1905*. Paris, 1908, 3–132.

Ibn Sa'īd. *Kitāb al-mughrib fī ḥulā 'l-Maghrib*, Book IV, ed. and trans. into German by K. L. Tallqvist, *Geschichte der Ikšîden und Fusṭâṭensische Biographien*. Leiden, 1899.

Ibn Sa'īd. *Kitāb basṭ al-arḍ fi'l ṭūl wa'l-'arḍ*, ed. by J. V. Gines. Tetuan, 1958.

al-Idrīsī. *Kitāb nuzhat al-mushtāq fī ikhtirāq al-āfāq*, ed. and trans. by R. Dozy and M. J. de Goeje [*Description de l'Afrique du Nord et de l'Espagne*]. Leiden, 1866.

al-Iṣṭakhrī. *Kitāb al-masālik wa'l-mamālik*, ed. by M. J. de Goeje. Leiden, 1870.

al-Khwārizmī. *Ṣūrat al-arḍ*, ed. by H. von Mžik. Vienna, 1926.

Mafākhir al-Barbar, in Lévi-Provençal, ed., *Textes Arabes* . . . (*see under* Arabic texts).

al-Malikī. *Riyāḍ al-nufūs fī ṭabaqāt 'ulamā' al-Qayrawān wa Ifrīqiya*, ed. by H. Monès. Cairo, 1951.

al-Maqrīzī. *Kitāb al-Mawā'iẓ wa 'l-I'tibār fī dhikr al-khiṭaṭ wa 'l-āthār* [*Khiṭaṭ*], ed. by Gaston Wiet. Cairo, 1911–27. 4 vols.

al-Mas'ūdī. *Kitāb murūj al-dhahab wa-ma'ādin al-jawhar*, ed. and trans. by C. Barbier de Meynard and Pavet de Courteille [*Les Prairies d'or*]. Paris 1864–77. Revised edn trans. by C. Pellat. Paris, 1965.

al-Nuwayrī. *Nihāyat al-'Arab*. Granada, 1919.

al-Qāḍī ʿIyād. *Tartīb al-madārik wa-taqrīb al-masālik li-maʿrifat aʿlām madhhab Mālik*, ed. by Aḥmad Bakīr Maḥmūd. Beirut, 1967.

al-Qāḍī ʾl-Nuʿmān [Abū Ḥanīfa al-Nuʿmān]. *Iftitāḥ al-Daʿwa wa ibtidāʾ al-Dawla*, ed. by W. al-Qāḍī. Beirut, 1970.

al-Saʿdī. *Taʾrīkh al-Sūdān*, ed. and trans. by O. Houdas. Paris, 1900.

Saʿīd b. Baṭrīq [Eutychius]. *Eutychii Patriarchae Alexandrini Annales*, ed. by L. Cheikho (*Corp. Script. Christ. Orient.*, *Scriptores Arabici*, 3rd series, Vols. VI, VII). Beirut, Paris and Leipzig, 1906, 1909.

al-Shammākhī. *Kitāb al-siyar* [lithograph edn]. Cairo, 1883–4.

al-Tādilī. *Kitāb al-tashawwuf ilā rijāl al-taṣawwuf*, ed. by A. Faure. Rabat, 1958.

Taʾrīkh al-Fattāsh, ed. and trans. by O. Houdas and M. Delafosse. Paris, 1913.

al-Yaʿqūbī. *Kitāb al-Buldān*, *Bibliotheca geographicorum arabicorum*, VII, ed. by M. J. de Goeje. Leiden, 1892. French trans. by Gaston Wiet, *Le Livre des pays*. Cairo, 1937; Institut Français d'Archéologie Orientale.

al-Yaʿqūbī. *Kitāb al-Taʾrīkh*, ed. by H. T. Houtsma. Leiden, 1863–6.

Yāqūt. *Kitāb muʿjam al-buldān*, ed. by F. Wüstenfeld. Leipzig, 1866.

al-Zuhrī. *Kitāb al-Jaʿrāfiyya*, ed. by M. Hadj Sadok, *Bulletin d'Études Orientales*, 1968, **21**, 1–312. Also (as al-Zouhri) in Y. Kamal, *Monumenta cartographica . . .* (*see under* General works), Vol. III.

1. THE LEGACY OF PREHISTORY

Alimen, H. *The prehistory of Africa*. London, 1957.

Alimen, M. H. 'Les "Isthmes" Hispano-Marocain et Siculo-Tunisien aux temps acheuléens', *L'Anthropologie*, 1975, **79**, 399–436.

Andrews, P. and Walker, A. 'The primate and other fauna from Fort Ternan, Kenya', in Isaac and McCown, eds., *Human origins . . .* (*see under* 'General' section, Prehistory), 279–303.

Anthony, B. 'The Stillbay question', in Hugot, ed., *VIe congrès panafricain . . .* (*see under* 'General' section, Prehistory), 80–2.

Arkell, A. J. *Early Khartoum*. Oxford, 1949.

Arkell, A. J. *Shaheinab*. Oxford, 1953.

Arkell, A. J. *The prehistory of the Nile Valley*. Leiden–Cologne, 1975; *Handbuch der Orientalistik*, I (2,A).

Armstrong, A. L. 'Rhodesian archaeological expedition, 1929: excavation in Bambata Cave and researches on prehistoric sites in Southern Rhodesia', *Journal of the Royal Anthropological Society of London*, 1931, **120**, 715–21.

Balout, L. *Préhistoire de l'Afrique du Nord: essai de chronologie*. Paris, 1955.

Balout, L. *Algérie préhistorique*. Paris, 1958.

Bishop, W. W. 'Pliocene problems relating to human evolution', in Isaac and McCown, eds., *Human origins . . .* (*see under* 'General' section, Prehistory), 139–53.

Bishop, W. W. and Clark, J. D. eds. *Background to evolution . . . See under* 'General' section, Prehistory.

Bishop, W. W. and Miller, J. A. eds. *Calibration of hominoid evolution. See under* 'General' section, Prehistory.

Bond, G. 'Pleistocene environments in southern Africa', in Howell and

Bourlière, eds., *African ecology* ... (*see under* 'General' section, Prehistory), 308–34.

Bonnefille, R. 'Associations polliniques actuelles et quaternaires en Ethiopie (vallées de l'Awash et de l'Omo)'. Doctoral thesis, University of Paris, 1972.

Bonnefille, R. 'Palynological evidence for an important change in the vegetation of the Omo basin between 2.5 and 2 million years', in Coppens and others, eds, *Earliest man* ... (*see under* 'General' section, Prehistory), 421–31.

Bordes, F. 'Considérations sur la typologie et les techniques dans le Paléolithique', *Quartar*, 1967, **18**, 25–55.

Brain, C. K. *The Transvaal ape-man-bearing cave deposits*. Pretoria, 1958; *Transvaal Museum Memoirs*, **11**, 1–131.

Breuil, H., Cabu, F. and Van Riet Lowe, C. 'Le Paléolithique au Congo Belge d'après les recherches du docteur Cabu', *Transactions, Royal Society of South Africa*, 1944, **30**, 2, 143–74.

Brooks, C. E. P. *Climate through the ages*. London, 1949.

Broom, R. *Finding the Missing Link*. London, 1950.

Burkitt, M. C. *South Africa's past in stone and paint*. London, 1928.

Butzer, K. W. and Isaac, G. L. eds. *After the Australopithecines* ... *See under* 'General' section, Prehistory.

Butzer, K. W. and others. 'Radiocarbon dating ... lake levels'. *See under* 'General' section, Chronology.

Cahen, Daniel. *Le site archéologique de la Kamoa* [Shaba, Zaïre]. Tervuren, Kon. Museum voor Midden-Afrika, 1975, **84**.

Campbell, B. G. *Human evolution*, 2nd edn. Chicago, 1972.

Campo, M. Van. 'Pollen analyses in the Sahara', in Wendorf and Marks, eds., *Problems in prehistory* ... (*see under* 'General' section, Prehistory), 45–64.

Camps, G. *Les civilisations préhistoriques de l'Afrique du Nord et du Sahara*. Paris, 1974.

Carter, P. L. and Vogel, J. C. 'The dating of industrial assemblages ...' *See under* 'General' section, Chronology.

Caton-Thompson, G. *Kharga Oasis in prehistory*. London, 1952.

Chamla, M.-C. *Les populations anciennes du Sahara et des régions limitrophes*. Paris, 1968; Centre de Recherches Anthropologiques, Préhistoriques et Ethnographiques (Algiers), Mémoire **9**.

Chavaillon, J. *Les formations quaternaires du Sahara nord-occidental*. Paris, Centre National de la Recherche Scientifique, 1964.

Chavaillon, J. and N. 'Présence éventuelle d'un abri oldowayen dans le gisement de Melka-Kontouré (Éthiopie)', *Comptes rendus, Académie des sciences de Paris*, 1971, **D-273**, 623–5.

Clark, J. D. 'Further excavations (1939) at Mumbwa Caves, Northern Rhodesia', *Transactions of the Royal Society of South Africa*, 1942, **29**, 133–201.

Clark, J. D. *The Stone Age cultures of northern Rhodesia*. Cape Town, 1950 [1950a].

Clark, J. D. 'The newly-discovered Nachikufu culture of Northern Rhodesia and the possible origin of certain elements of the South African Smithfield culture', *South African Archaeological Bulletin*, 1950, **5**, 19, 2–15 [1950b].

Clark, J. D. *The prehistoric cultures of the Horn of Africa*. Cambridge, 1954; reprinted New York, 1972.

Clark, J. D. *The prehistory of southern Africa*. Harmondsworth, 1959.

Clark, J. D. *Prehistoric cultures of north-east Angola and their significance in tropical Africa*. Lisbon, Companhia de Diamantes de Angola, 1963. 2 vols.

Clark, J. D. *Further palaeo-anthropological studies in northern Lunda*. Lisbon, Companhia de Diamantes de Angola, 1968.

Clark, J. D. *Kalambo Falls prehistoric site*. Cambridge, 1969 and 1974. 2 vols.

Clark, J. D. *The prehistory of Africa*. London and New York, 1970.

Clark, J. D. 'Human behavioural differences in southern Africa during the late Pleistocene', *American Anthropologist*, 1971, **73**, 1211–36 [1971a].

Clark, J. D. 'Problems of archaeological nomenclature and definition in the Congo basin', *South African Archaeological Bulletin*, 1971, **26**, 67–78 [1971b].

Clark, J. D., 'The British expedition to the Air mountains', *Geographical Journal*, 1971, **137** (4), 455–7.

Clark, J. D. 'Africa in prehistory: peripheral or paramount?', *Man*, N.S., 1975, **10**, 175–98.

Clark, J. D. 'A comparison of the Late Acheulian Industries of Africa and the Middle East', in Butzer and Isaac, eds., *After the Australopithecines ...* (*see under* 'General' section, Prehistory), 605–59.

Clark, J. D. 'The domestication process ...' *See under* 'General' section, Crops.

Clark, J. D. ed. *Atlas of African prehistory*. Chicago, 1967.

Clark, J. D., Haynes, C. V. and Mawby, J. E. 'Interim report on palaeo-anthropological investigations in the Lake Malawi Rift', *Quaternaria*, 1970, **13**, 305–53.

Clark, J. D. and Kurashina, H. 'New Plio-Pleistocene archaeological occurrences from the Plain of Gabed, upper Webi Shebele basin, Ethiopia, and a statistical comparison of the Gadeb sites with other Early Stone Age assemblages', *Union Internationale des Sciences Préhistoriques et Protohistoriques*, IXe Congrès, Nice, Sept. 1976, *Colloque V*, *The earliest stone industries of Africa* [preprint vol.].

Clark, J. D., Williams, M. A. J. and Smith, A. B. 'The geomorphology and archaeology of Adrar Bous, central Sahara: a preliminary report', *Quaternaria*, 1975, **17** [1973], 245–97.

Clark, J. D. and Williams, M. A. J. 'Recent archaeological research in south-eastern Ethiopia (1974–5): some preliminary results', *Annales d'Éthiopie*, Addis Ababa [forthcoming].

Clark, J. D., Williams, M. A. J. and Williamson, K. R. *Further excavations (1974) in the Porc Epic Cave, Dire Dawa, Ethiopia* [forthcoming].

Clark, W. E. Le Gros. 'Observations on the anatomy of the fossil Australopithecinae', *Journal of Anatomy*, 1947, **81**, 300–33.

Clark, W. E. Le Gros. *The fossil evidence ... See under* 'General' section, Prehistory. [Le Gros deals with the Australopithecines in his ch. 4.]

Cole, G. H. 'The later Acheulian and Sangoan of southern Africa', in Bishop and Clark, eds., *Background to evolution ...* (*see under* 'General' section, Prehistory), 481–528 [1967a].

Cole, G. H. 'A reinvestigation of Magosi and the Magosian', *Quaternaria*, 1967, **9**, 153–68 [1967b].

Cole, S. *Prehistory of East Africa*. London, 1963.

Cole-King, P. A. *Kukumba Mbiri mu Malawi: a summary of archaeological research to March* 1973. Zomba, Malawi, 1973; Department of Antiquities Publication, **15**.

Colette, J. R. F. 'Essai biométrique sur la station préhistorique de Kalina (Congo belge)', *Comptes rendus, XVe Congrès International d'Anthropologie et d'Archéologie Préhistorique*. Paris, 1931, 278–85.

Conroy, G. C. and Pilbeam, D. '*Ramapithecus*: a review of its hominid status', in Tuttle, ed., *Palaeoanthropology* . . . (*see under* 'General' section, Prehistory).

Cooke, C. K. 'The Waterworks site at Khami, Southern Rhodesia: Stone Age and proto-historic', *Occasional Papers, National Museum, Southern Rhodesia*, 1957, **3**, 1–60.

Cooke, C. K. 'Report on excavations at Pomongwe and Tshangula caves, Matopo Hills, Southern Rhodesia', *South African Archaeological Bulletin*, 1963, **18**, 63–151.

Cooke, C. K. 'Re-appraisal of the industry hitherto named Proto-Stillbay', *Arnoldia*, 1966, **2**, 7–14.

Cooke, C. K. 'A re-examination of the "Middle Stone Age" industries of Rhodesia', *Arnoldia*, 1969, **4**, 7, 1–21.

Cooke, C. K. 'Excavation at Zombepata Cave, Sipolilo District, Mashonaland, Rhodesia', *South African Archaeological Bulletin*, 1971, **26**, 104–27.

Cooke, C. K. 'Bibliography . . .' *See under* General bibliographies.

Cooke, C. K. and Robinson, K. R. 'Excavations at Amadzimba Cave, located in the Matopos Hills, Southern Rhodesia', *Occasional Papers, National Museum, Southern Rhodesia*, 1954, **2**, 699–728.

Cooke, C. K., Summers, R. and Robinson, K. R. 'Rhodesian prehistory re-examined; Part I, the Stone Age', *Arnoldia*, 1966, **2**, 1–7.

Cooke, H. B. S. 'Pleistocene mammal faunas of Africa with particular reference to southern Africa', in Howell and Bourlière, eds., *African ecology* . . . (*see under* 'General' section, Prehistory), 65–116.

Cooke, H. B. S. 'The Pleistocene sequence in South Africa and problems of correlation', in Bishop and Clark, eds., *Background to evolution* . . . (*see under* 'General' section, Prehistory), 175–84.

Cooke, H. B. S. 'Evolution of mammals in southern continents: II, The fossil mammal fauna of Africa', *Quarterly Review of Biology*, 1968, **43**, 234–64.

Cooke, H. B. S. and Maglio, V. J. 'Plio-Pleistocene stratigraphy in relation to Proboscidean and Suid evolution', in Bishop and Miller, eds., *Calibration of hominoid evolution* (*see under* 'General' section, Prehistory), 303–29.

Coppens, Y. and others, eds. *Earliest man* . . . *See under* 'General' section, Prehistory.

Curtis, G. H., Drake, T., Cerling, T. E. and B. L. and Hempel, J. H. 'Age of KBS tuff in Koobi Fora Formation, East Rudolf, Kenya', *Nature*, 1975, **258**, 395–8.

Dart, R. A. '*Australopithecus africanus*, the man-ape of South Africa', *Nature*, 1925, **115**, 195–9.

Dart, R. A. *The osteodontokeratic culture of Australopithecus prometheus*. Pretoria, 1957; Transvaal Museum Memoir, **10**.

Dart, R. A. 'The bone-tool manufacturing ability of *Australopithecus prometheus*', *American Anthropologist*, 1960, **62**, 134–43.

Dart, R. A. and del Grande, N. 'The ancient iron-smelting cavern at Mumbwa', *Transactions, Royal Society of South Africa*, 1931, **29**, 379–427.

Davies, Oliver. *The Quaternary in the coastlands of Guinea*. Glasgow, 1964.

Davies, Oliver. *West Africa before the Europeans*. *See under* 'General' section, Prehistory.

Day, M. H. 'Omo human skeletal remains', *Nature*, 1969, **222**, 1135–8.

Deacon, H. J. 'The Acheulian occupation at Amanzi Springs, Uitenhage District, Cape Province', *Annals of the Cape Provincial Museum* (Cape Town), 1970, Natural History, **8**, 89–189.

Deacon, H. J. 'A review of the post-Pleistocene in South Africa', *South African Archaeological Society, Goodwin Series*, 1972, **1**, 26–45.

Deacon, H. J. 'Demography, subsistence and culture during the Acheulian in southern Africa', in Butzer and Isaac, eds., *After the Australopithecines . . .* (*see under* 'General' section, Prehistory), 543–70.

Deacon, J. 'Wilton: an assessment after fifty years', *South African Archaeological Bulletin*, 1972, **27**, 10–48.

Debénath, A. 'Découverte de restes humains probablement atériens à Dar es Soltan (Maroc)', *Comptes Rendus de l'Académie des Sciences* (Paris), 1975, **281**, 875–6.

F.A.O. [Food and Agricultural Organization]. *Food composition tables for use in Africa*. Maryland and Rome, 1968.

Fagan, B. M. and Noten, F. van. *The hunter-gatherers of Gwisho*. Tervuren, 1971.

Fagg, B., Eyo, E., Rosenfeld, A. and Fagg, A. 'Four papers on the Rop rockshelter, Nigeria', *West African Journal of Archaeology*, 1972, **2**, 1–38.

Ferembach, D. 'Les restes humains atériens de Temara (Campagne 1975)', *Bull. et Mem. de la Soc. d'Anthrop. de Paris*, 3, Series XIII, 1976, 175–80.

Ferembach, D. 'Les restes humains de la Grotte de Dar-es-Soltane 2 (Maroc), Campagne 1975', *Bull. et Mem. de la Soc. d'Anthrop. de Paris*, 1976, **3**, Series XIII, 183–93.

Ferring, C. R. 'The Aterian in North African prehistory', in Wendorf and Marks, eds., *Problems in prehistory . . .* (*see under* 'General' section, Prehistory), 113–26.

Flannery, K. V. 'Origins and ecological effects of early domestication in Iran and the Near East', in Ucko and Dimbleby, eds., *Domestication and exploitation . . .* (*see under* 'General' section, Crops), 50–79.

Fosbrooke, H. A. and others. 'Tanganyika rock paintings: a guide and record', *Tanganyika Notes and Records*, 1950, **29**, 1–61.

Gabel, C. *Stone Age hunters of the Kafue*. Boston, 1965.

Goodwin, A. J. H. and Van Riet Lowe, C. *The Stone Age cultures of South Africa*. Cape Town, 1929; *Annals of the South African Museum*, **27**.

Gurdler, R. W. and Styles, P. 'Two stage Red Sea floor spreading', *Nature*, 1974, **247**, 7–11.

Harlan, J. R. *Crops and man*. *See under* 'General' section, Crops.

Harlan, J. R. and others, eds. *Origins of plant domestication . . . See under* 'General' section, Crops.

Hay, R. L. *Geology of the Olduvai Gorge*. Berkeley, 1976.

Heinzelin de Braucourt, J. de. *Sols, paléosols, et désertifications anciennes dans le secteur nord-oriental du bassin du Congo*. Brussels, Institut National pour l'Étude Agronomique du Congo belge, 1952.

Heinzelin de Braucourt, J. de. *Les fouilles d'Ishango*. Brussels, Institut des Parcs Nationaux du Congo belge, 1957.

Hiernaux, J. *The people of Africa*. London, 1974.

Howell, F. C. 'European and North-West African Middle Pleistocene hominids', *Current Anthropology*, 1960, **1**, 195–232.

Howell, F. C. and Clark, J. D. 'Acheulian hunter-gatherers of sub-Saharan Africa', in Howell and Bourlière, eds., *African ecology . . .* (*see under* 'General' section, Prehistory), 458–533.

Howell, F. C., Cole, G. H. and Kleindienst, M. R. 'Isimila, an Acheulian occupation site in the Iringa Highlands, Southern Highlands Province, Tanganyika', in Mortlemans and Nenquin, eds., *IVe congrès panafricain . . .* (*see under* 'General' section, Prehistory), 43–80.

Howell, F. C. and Coppens, Y. 'An overview of Hominidae from the Omo succession, Ethiopia', in Coppens and others, eds., *Earliest man . . .* (*see under* 'General' section, Prehistory), 522–32.

Hsü, K. J., Ryan, W. B. F. and Cita, M. B. 'Late Miocene desiccation of the Mediterranean', *Nature*, 1973, **242**, 240–4.

Inskeep, R. R. 'A Late Stone Age camping site in the Upper Zambezi valley', *South African Archaeological Bulletin*, 1959, **14**, 91–6.

Inskeep, R. R. 'The age of the Kondoa rock paintings in the light of recent excavations at Kisese II rock shelter', in Mortelmans and Nenquin, eds., *IVe congrès panafricain . . .* (*see under* 'General' section, Prehistory), 249–56.

Inskeep, R. R. 'The Late Stone Age in southern Africa', in Bishop and Clark, eds., *Background to evolution . . .* (*see under* 'General' section, Prehistory), 557–82.

Inskeep, R. R. 'The archaeological background', in Wilson and Thompson, eds., *Oxford history of South Africa* (*see under* General works), 1–39.

Isaac, G. L. 'The stratigraphy of the Peninj Group – Early Middle Pleistocene formations west of Lake Natron, Tanzania', in Bishop and Clark, eds., *Background to evolution . . .* (*see under* 'General' section, Prehistory), 229–57.

Isaac, G. L. 'Studies of early culture in East Africa', *World Archaeology*, 1969, **1**, 1–28.

Isaac, G. L. 'The diet of early man: aspects of archaeological evidence from Lower and Middle Pleistocene sites in Africa', *World Archaeology*, 1971, **2**, 278–98.

Isaac, G. L. 'Stratigraphy and cultural patterns in East Africa during the middle ranges of Pleistocene time', in Butzer and Isaac, eds., *After the Australopithecines . . .* (*see under* 'General' section, Prehistory), 495–542.

Isaac, G. L. 'East Africa as a source of fossil evidence for human evolution', in Isaac and McCown, eds., *Human origins . . .* (*see under* 'General' section, Prehistory), 121–37 [1976a].

Isaac, G. L. 'The activities of Early African Hominids: a review of archaeological evidence from the time span two and a half to one million years ago', in Isaac and McCown, eds., *Human origins . . .* (*see under* 'General' section, Prehistory), 483–514 [1976b].

Isaac, G. L. *Olorgesailie. Prehistoric archaeology and ecology*, **4**. Chicago, 1977.

Isaac, G. L. and McCown, E. R. eds. *Human origins . . . See under* 'General' section, Prehistory.

Isaac, G. L., Merrick, H. V. and Nelson, C. M. 'Stratigraphic and archaeological studies in the Lake Nakuru basin', in Van Zinderen Bakker, ed., *Palaeoecology . . .* (*see under* 'General' section, Prehistory), 1972, **6**, 225–32.

Jaeger, J. J. 'The mammalian faunas and hominid fossils of the Middle Pleistocene of the Maghreb', in Butzer and Isaac, eds., *After the Australopithecines . . .* (*see under* 'General' section, Prehaistory), 399–418.

Janmart, J. *Stations préhistoriques de l'Angola du nord-est: analyse géologique, climatologique et préhistorique d'un sondage fait en bordure de la rivière Luembe* (*Angola du nord-est*). Lisbon, Companhia de Diamantes de Angola, 1947.

Johanson, D. C. and Taieb, M. 'Plio-Pleistocene hominid discoveries in Hadar, Ethiopia', *Nature*, 1976, **260**, 293–7.

Jones, N. *The Stone Age in Rhodesia*. Oxford, 1926.

Jones, N. *The prehistory of southern Rhodesia: an account of progress of the research from 1900–1946*. Cambridge, 1949.

Keller, C. M. *Montagu Cave in prehistory: a descriptive analysis*. Berkeley, 1973; *Anthropological Records*, **28**.

Kennett, J. P., Houtz, R. E. and others, eds. *Initial reports of the Deep Sea Drilling Project*, **39**. Washington, 1975.

Klein, R. G. 'Preliminary report on the July through September 1970 excavation at Nelson Bay cave, Plettenberg Bay (Cape Province, South Africa)', in Van Zinderen Bakker, ed., *Palaeoecology . . .* (*see under* 'General' section, Prehistory), 1972, **6**, 177–210.

Klein, R. G. 'Environment and subsistence of prehistoric man in the southern Cape Province, South Africa', *World Archaeology*, 1974, **5**, 249–84.

Klein, R. G. 'Middle Stone Age man–animal relationships in southern Africa: evidence from Die Kelders and Klasies River Mouth', *Science*, 1975, **190**, 265–7 [1975a].

Klein, R. G. 'Ecology of Stone Age Man at the southern tip of Africa', *Archaeology*, 1975, **28**, 238–47 [1975b].

Kretzoi, M. 'New ramapithecines and *Pliopithecus* from Lower Pliocene of Rudabanya in north-eastern Hungary', *Nature*, 1975, **257**, 578–81.

Lajoux, J.-D. *Merveilles du Tassili n'Ajjer*. Paris, 1962.

Leakey, L. S. B. *The Stone Age cultures of Kenya Colony*. Cambridge, 1931.

Leakey, L. S. B. *Stone Age Africa*. London, 1936.

Leakey, L. S. B. *Tentative study of the Pleistocene climatic changes and Stone Age sequence in north-eastern Angola*. Lisbon, Companhia de Diamantes de Angola, 1949.

Leakey, L. S. B. and Owen, Archdeacon. *A contribution to the study of the Tumbian culture in East Africa*. Nairobi, 1945; Coryndon Memorial Museum Occasional Papers, **1**.

Leakey, M. D. 'Stone artifacts from Swartkrans', *Nature*, 1970, **225**, 1221–5.

Leakey, M. D. *Olduvai Gorge*, Vol. III, *Excavations in Beds I and II, 1960–1963*. Cambridge, 1971.

Leakey, M. D. 'Cultural patterns in the Olduvai Sequence', in Butzer and Isaac, eds., *After the Australopithecines* ... (*see under* 'General' section, Prehistory), 477–93.

Leakey, M. D. and L. S. B. *Excavations at the Njoro River Cave*. Oxford, 1950.

Leakey, M. D., R. L. Hay, G. H. Curtis, R. E. Drake and M. K. Jackes, 'Fossil hominids from the Laetolil Beds', *Nature*, 1976, **262**, 460–6.

Leakey, R. E. F. 'Further evidence of Lower Pleistocene hominids from East Rudolf, North Kenya, 1973', *Nature*, 1974, **248**, 653–6.

Leakey, R. E. F. 'New hominid fossils from the Koobi Fora Formation in northern Kenya', *Nature*, 1976, **261**, 574–6.

Leakey, R. E. F. and Walker, A. C. '*Australopithecus*, *Homo erectus* and the single species hypothesis', *Nature*, 1976, **261**, 572–4.

Lhote, H. *A la découverte des fresques du Tassili*. Paris, 1958.

Livingstone, D. 'Late Quaternary climatic change in Africa', *Annual Review of Ecology and Systematics*, 1975, **6**, 249–80.

Lowe, C. Van Riet. *The Pleistocene geology and prehistory of Uganda*, Vol. II, *Prehistory*. Uganda Geological Survey, 1952, Memoir **6**.

Lumley, H. de. 'Cultural evolution in France in its palaeoecological setting', in Butzer and Isaac, eds., *After the Australopithecines* ... (*see under* 'General' section, Prehistory), 745–808.

McBurney, C. B. M. *The Stone Age of northern Africa*. Harmondsworth, 1960.

McBurney, C. B. M. *The Haua Fteah (Cyrenaica) and the Stone Age of the south-east Mediterranean*. Cambridge, 1967.

McBurney, C. B. M. and Hey, R. W. *Prehistory and Pleistocene geology in Cyrenaican Libya*. Cambridge, 1955.

Maggs, T. M. O'C. 'Some observations on the size of human groups during the Late Stone Age', in M. Schoonraad, ed., *Rock paintings of southern Africa, South African Journal of Science* (Johannesburg), Special Publication **2**, 1971, 49–53.

Mann, A. E. *Some palaeodemographic aspects of the South African Australopithecines*. Philadelphia, 1975; Pennsylvania University Publications in Anthropology, **1**, *The palaeodemography of Australopithecus*.

Marks, A. E. 'The current status of Upper Palaeolithic studies from the Maghrib to the north-west Levant', in Wendorf and Marks, eds., *Problems in prehistory* ... (*see under* 'General' section, Prehistory), 439–58.

Mason, R. J. 'The Transvaal Middle Stone Age and statistical analysis', *South African Archaeological Bulletin*, 1957, **12**, 119–43.

Mason, R. J. *Prehistory of the Transvaal*. Johannesburg, 1962 [1962a].

Mason, R. J. 'Australopithecines and artifacts at Sterkfontein: part II, the Sterkfontein artifacts and their maker', *South African Archaeological Bulletin*, 1962, **17**, 109–26 [1962b].

Mason, R. J. 'Analytical procedures in the Earlier and Middle Stone Age cultures in southern Africa', in Bishop and Clark, eds., *Background to evolution* ... (*see under* 'General' section, Prehistory), 737–64.

Miller, S. F. 'The age of Nachikufan industries in Zambia', *South African Archaeological Bulletin*, 1971, **26**, 143–6.

Miller, S. F. 'The archaeological sequence of the Zambian Later Stone Age', in Hugot, ed., *VIe congrès panafricain ... (Dakar, 1967)* (*see under* 'General' section, Prehistory), 567–72.

Moorsel, H. van. *Atlas de préhistoire de la plaine de Kinshasa*. Kinshasa, 1968.

Mortelmans, G. 'Vue d'ensemble sur la préhistoire du Congo occidental', in Mortelmans and Nenquin, eds., *IVe congrès panafricain ...* (*see under* 'General' section, Prehistory), 129–264.

Nelson, C. M. and Posnansky, M. 'The stone tools from the re-excavation of Nsongezi rock shelter', *Azania*, 1970, **5**, 119–206.

Nenquin, J. *Contributions to the study of the prehistoric cultures of Rwanda and Burundi*. Tervuren, 1967; *Sciences humaines*, **59**.

Oakley, K. P. *Man the tool-maker*, 6th edn. Chicago, 1976.

O'Brien, T. P. *The prehistory of the Uganda Protectorate*. London, 1939.

Odner, K. 'Excavations at Narosura, a Stone Bowl site in the southern Kenya Highlands', *Azania*, 1972, **7**, 25–92.

Oxnard, C. E. 'The place of the Australopithecines in human evolution: grounds for doubt?', *Nature*, 1975, **258**, 389–95.

Parkington, J. E. and Poggenpoel, C. 'Excavations at De Hangen, 1968', *South African Archaeological Bulletin*, 1971, **26**, 1–36.

Phillipson, D. W. 'The prehistoric succession in eastern Zambia: a preliminary report', *Azania*, 1973, **8**, 3–24.

Phillipson, L. 'Middle Stone Age material from sites near Katima Mulilo on the upper Zambezi', *South African Archaeological Bulletin*, 1968, **23**, 90–101.

Phillipson, L. and D. W. 'Patterns of edge damage on the Late Stone Age Industry from Chiwemupula, Zambia', *Zambia Museums Journal*, 1970, **1**, 40–75.

Pilbeam, D. *The ascent of man ... See under* 'General' section, Prehistory.

Pilbeam, D. 'Middle Pleistocene hominids', in Butzer and Isaac, eds., *After the Australopithecines ...* (*see under* 'General' section, Prehistory), 809–56.

Ploey, J. de. 'Position géomorphologique, genèse et chronologie de certains dépôts superficiels au Congo occidental', *Quaternaria*, 1965, **7**, 131–54.

Portères, R. 'Le millet coracan ...' *See under* 'General' section, Crops.

Posnansky, M. and Nelson, C. M. 'Rock paintings and excavations at Nyero, Uganda', *Azania*, 1968, **3**, 147–66.

Rightmire, G. P. 'New studies of post-Pleistocene human skeletal remains from the Rift Valley, Kenya', *American Journal of Physical Anthropology*, 1975, **42**, 351–69 [1975a].

Rightmire, G. P. 'Problems in the study of Later Pleistocene man in Africa', *American Anthropologist*, 1975, **77**, 28–52 [1975b].

Rightmire, G. P. 'Relationships of Middle and Upper Pleistocene hominids from sub-Saharan Africa', *Nature*, 1976, **260**, 238–40.

Robbins, L. H. *The Lothagam Site*. East Lansing, Michigan State University Museum, 1974.

Robinson, J. T. *Early hominid posture and locomotion*. Chicago, 1972.

Robinson, K. R. and Sandelowsky, B. 'The Iron Age of northern Malawi: recent work', *Azania*, 1968, **3**, 107–46.

Roche, J. and Texier, J.-P. 'Découvertes de restes humains dans un niveau atérien supérieur de la Grotte des Contrebandiers à Temara (Maroc)', *Comptes Rendus de l'Académie des Sciences* (Paris), 1976, **282**, 45–7.

Rudner, J. and I. *The hunter and his art: a survey of rock art in southern Africa*. Cape Town, 1970.

Sampson, C. G. *The Stone Age archaeology of southern Africa*. New York and London, 1974.

Sarich, V. M. 'A molecular approach to the question of human origins', in P. C. Dolhinow and V. M. Sarich, eds., *Background for man*. New York, 1972, 60–91.

Servant, M. 'Séquences continentales et variations climatiques: évolution du bassin du Tchad au Cénozoique supérieur'. Doctoral thesis, University of Paris, 1973.

Shackleton, N. and Kennett, J. P. 'Late Cenozoic oxygen and carbon isotopic changes at DSDP Site 284: implications for glacial history of the northern hemisphere and Antarctica', in Kennett and Houtz, eds., *Initial reports . . . (see above)*.

Shaw, Thurstan. 'Report on excavations carried out in the cave known as "Bosumpra" at Abetifi, Kwahu, Gold Coast Colony', *Proceedings of the Prehistoric Society*, 1944, **10**, 1–67.

Shaw, Thurstan. 'Finds at the Iwo Eleru rock shelter, Western Nigeria', in Hugot, ed., *VIe congrès panafricain . . . (Dakar, 1967)* (*see under* 'General' section, Prehistory), 190–2 [1972a].

Shaw, Thurstan. 'Early agriculture . . .' *See under* 'General' section, Crops.

Söhnge, P. G., Visser, D. J. L. and Lowe, C. Van Riet. *The geology and archaeology of the Vaal River Basin*. Pretoria, 1937; *Geological Survey Memoir*, **35**, Pts 1 and 2.

Soper, R. C. 'The Stone Age in northern Nigeria', *Journal of the Historical Society of Nigeria*, 1965, **3**, 175–94.

Soper, R. C. and Golden, B. 'An archaeological survey of Mwanza region, Tanzania', *Azania*, 1969, **4**, 15–79.

Street, F. A. and Grove, A. T. 'Environmental and climatic implications of late Quaternary lake-level fluctuations in Africa', *Nature*, 1976, **261**, 385–90.

Summers, R. ed. *Prehistoric rock art of the Federation of Rhodesia and Nyasaland*. London, 1959.

Sutton, J. E. G. *The archaeology of the western highlands of Kenya*. London, 1973.

Taieb, M., Johanson, D. C., Coppens, Y. and Aronson, J. L. 'Geological and palaeontological background of Hadar hominid sites, Afar, Ethiopia', *Nature*, 1976, **260**, 289–93.

Tixier, J. *Typologie de l'Épipaléolithique du Maghreb*. Paris, 1963; Centre de Recherches Anthropologiques, Préhistoriques et Ethnographiques (Algiers), **2**.

Tobias, P. V. 'Middle and early Upper Pleistocene members of the genus *Homo* in Africa', in Kurth, ed., *Evolution and hominisation* (*see under* 'General' section, Prehistory), 176–94.

Tobias, P. V. 'African hominids: dating and phylogeny', in Isaac and McCown, eds., *Human origins* . . . (*see under* 'General' section, Prehistory), 377–422.

Tuttle, R. L. H. ed. *Palaeoanthropology: morphology and ecology*. The Hague, 1975.

Van Zinderen Bakker, E. M. 'Upper Pleistocene and Holocene stratigraphy and ecology on the basis of vegetation changes in sub-Saharan Africa', in Bishop and Clark, eds., *Background to evolution* . . . (*see under* 'General' section, Prehistory), 125–47.

Van Zinderen Bakker, E. M. ed. *Palaeoecology of Africa*. Cape Town, from 1966.

Vaufrey, R. *Préhistoire de l'Afrique*, I, *Le Maghreb*. Paris, 1955; Institut des Hautes Études de Tunis, Vol. IV.

Vaufrey, R. *Préhistoire de l'Afrique*, II, *Au nord et à l'est de la grand forêt*. Tunis, 1969; Publications de l'Université de Tunis, Vol. IV.

Vrba, E. S. 'Chronological and ecological implications of the fossil Bovidae at Sterkfontein Australopithecine site', *Nature*, 1974, **250**, 19–23.

Washburn, S. L. 'Behaviour and the origin of man', *Proceedings of the Royal Anthropological Institute for 1967*, 1968, 21–7.

Washburn, S. L. and Moore, R. *Ape into man* . . . *See under* 'General' section, Prehistory.

Wendorf, F. ed. *The prehistory of Nubia*. Dallas, 1968. 2 vols.

Wendorf, F. and Marks, A. E. eds. *Problems in prehistory* . . . *See under* 'General' section, Prehistory.

Wendorf, F. and Schild, R. *A Middle Stone Age sequence from the Central Rift Valley, Ethiopia*. Warsaw, Polska Akademia Nauk, Institut Historii Kultury Materialnej, 1974.

Wendorf, F. and Schild, R. 'The Palaeolithic of the Lower Nile Valley', in Wendorf and Marks, eds., *Problems in prehistory* . . . (*see under* 'General' section, Prehistory), 127–69.

Wendorf, F. and others. 'Dates for the Middle Stone Age . . .' *See under* 'General' section, Chronology.

Wendt, W. E. *Die ältesten datierten Kunstwerke Afrikas,* special issue, *Felskunst* (Stuttgart), Bild der Wissenschaft, 1975, 44–50.

White, T. 'A method of calculating the dietary percentage of various food animals butchered by aboriginal peoples', *American Antiquity,* 1953, **18**, 396–8.

Willcox, A. R. *The rock art of South Africa*, Johannesburg, 1963.

Willett, F. 'The microlithic industry from Old Oyo, Western Nigeria', in Mortelmans and Nenquin, eds., *IVe congrès panafricain* . . . (*see under* 'General' section, Prehistory), 261–72.

Wolpoff, M. H. 'Competitive exclusion among Lower Pleistocene hominids: the single species hypothesis', *Man*, 1971, **6**, 4, 601–14.

2. NORTH AFRICA, *c.* 800 TO 323 BC

Appian. *Roman history,* ed. and with an English trans. by H. White. London, 1912–13. 4 vols.

Aristotle. *Politics,* ed. by W. D. Ross. Oxford, 1957.

Arkell, A. J. *A history of the Sudan to 1821*, 2nd edn. London, 1961.

Arrian. *The Anabasis of Alexander*, ed. and with an English trans. by E. I. Robson. London, 1929–33. 2 vols.

Athenaios. *Deipnosophistai,* ed. and with an English trans. by C. B. Gulick. London, 1927–41. 7 vols.

Austin, M. M. *Greece and Egypt in the Archaic age. Proceedings of the Cambridge Philological Society,* Supplement 2, 1970.

Bates, O. *The eastern Libyans*. London 1914.

Boardman, J. 'Evidence for the dating...' *See under* 'General' section, Chronology.

Boardman, J. *The Greeks overseas: the archaeology of their early colonies and trade*, 2nd edn. London, 1973.

Breasted, J. H. *Ancient records of Egypt: historical documents from the earliest times to the Persian conquest*. Chicago, 1906–7. 5 vols.

Bynon, J. 'The contribution of linguistics to history in the field of Berber studies', in D. Dalby, ed., *Language and history in Africa*. London, 1970.

Cambridge ancient history. Vols. III–VI. *See under* General works.

Camps, G. 'Les traces d'un âge du bronze en Afrique du Nord', *Revue Africaine,* 1960, **104**, 31–55.

Carcopino, J. *Le Maroc antique*. Paris, 1943.

Carpenter, Rhys. 'A trans-Saharan caravan route in Herodotus', *American Journal of Archaeology*, 1956, **60**, 231–42.

Carpenter, Rhys. 'Phoenicians in the West', *American Journal of Archaeology*, 1958, **62**, 35–53.

Cary, M. and Warmington, E. H. *The ancient explorers,* revised edn. London, 1963.

Chamoux, C. *Cyrène sous la monarchie des Battiades*. Paris, 1953.

Charles-Picard, G. *Les Religions de l'Afrique antique*. Paris, 1954.

Charles-Picard, G. *Carthage,* trans. by M. and L. Kochan. London, 1964.

Charles-Picard, G. and C. *Daily life in Carthage at the time of Hannibal,* trans. by A. Hamilton. London, 1958.

Charles-Picard, G. and C. *The life and death of Carthage: a survey of Punic culture from its birth to the final tragedy,* trans. by D. Colon. London, 1968.

Cintas, Pierre. *Contribution à l'étude de l'expansion Carthaginoise au Maroc*. Paris, 1954; Publications de l'Institut des Hautes-Études Marocaines, **56**.

Cook, R. M. 'Amasis and the Greeks in Egypt', *Journal of Hellenic Studies,* 1937, **57**, 227–37.

Cowley, A. E. ed. *Aramaic papyri of the fifth century B.C.* Oxford, 1923.

Daniels, C. *The Garamantes of southern Libya*. Madison, 1970.

Dio Chrysostom. *Discourses,* ed. and with an English trans. by J. W. Cohoon and H. L. Crosby. London, 1932 and 1951. 2 vols.

Diodorus Siculus. *Library of history,* ed. and with English trans. by C. H. Oldfather, C. B. Welles, R. M. Greer and F. F. Walton. London, 1933–67. 12 vols.

Drioton, E. and Vandier, J. *L'Égypte,* Vol. II of *Les Peuples de l'Orient,* 4th edn. Paris, 1962.

Elgood, P. G. *The later dynasties of Egypt*. Oxford, 1951.

Farias, P. 'Silent trade: myth and historical evidence', *History in Africa,* 1974, **1**, 9–24.

Gardiner, A. *Egypt of the Pharaohs: an introduction*. Oxford, 1961.

Germain, G. 'Qu'est-ce que le Périple d'Hannon? Document, amplification littéraire, ou faux intégral?', *Hespéris,* 1957, **44**, 205–48.

Giustolisi, V. *Le Origine della Dea Tanit e dei suoi simboli*. Parlemo, 1970.

Graham, A. J. 'The authenticity of the 'ΟΡΚΙΟΝ ΤΩΝ ΟΙΚΙΣΤΗΡΩΝ of Cyrene', *Journal of Hellenic Studies,* 1960, **80**, 94–111.

Gsell, S. *Histoire ancienne . . . See under* General works.

Gyles, M. F. *Pharaonic policies and administration, 663–323 BC*. Chapel Hill, 1959; James Sprunt Studies in History and Political Science, **41**.

Hands, A. R. 'The consolidation of Carthaginian power in the fifth century BC', in Thompson and Ferguson, eds., *Africa in classical antiquity* (*see under* General works), 81–98.

Hanno. *Periplus,* in Müller, ed., *Geographici . . .* (*see below*).

Harden, D. 'The Phoenicians on the West Coast of Africa', *Antiquity,* 1948, **22**, 141–50.

Harden, D. *The Phoenicians,* 2nd edn. London, 1971.

Herm, G. *The Phoenicians: the purple empire of the ancient world,* trans. by C. Hiller. London, 1975.

Herodotus. *Histories,* ed. by C. Hude. Oxford, 1908. 2 vols.

Hubac, P. *Carthage*. Paris, 1952.

Ilevbare, J. A. 'The impact of the Carthaginians and the Romans on the administrative system of the Maghrib', *Journal of the Historical Society of Nigeria,* Pt I, 1974, **7**, 2, 187–97.

Jacoby, F. *Die Fragmente der griechischen Historiker*. Berlin, from 1923. Several vols.

Julien, C.-A. *Histoire . . . See under* General works.

Justin. *Epitoma historiarum Philippicarum Pompeii Trogi,* ed. by O. Seel. Stuttgart, 1972.

Kienitz, F. K. *Die politische Geschichte Ägyptens vom 7 bis 4 Jahrhundert vor der Zeitwende*. Berlin, 1953.

Kwapong, A. A. 'Citizenship and democracy in fourth-century Cyrene', in Thompson and Ferguson, eds., *Africa in classical antiquity* (*see under* General works), 99–109.

Law, R. C. C. 'The Garamantes and trans-Saharan enterprise in classical times', *Journal of African History,* 1967, **8**, 2, 181–200.

Livy. *Ab urbe condita,* ed. and with an English trans. by B. O. Foster, F. G. Moore, E. T. Sage and A. C. Schlesinger. London, 1919–59. 14 vols.

McBurney, C. B. M. *The Stone Age of northern Africa. See under* ch. 1.

Mauny, R. 'Cerné, l'île de Herné (Rio de Oro), et la question des navigations antiques sur la côte ouest-africaine', *Comptes rendus de la IVe conférence internationale des Africanistes de l'Ouest, Santa Isabel, 1951*. Madrid, 1955, II, 73–80 [1955a].

Mauny, R. 'La navigation sur les côtes du Sahara pendant l'antiquité', *Revue des Études Anciennes,* 1955, **57**, 92–101 [1955b].

Merighi, A. *La Tripolitania Antica dalle origini alla invasione degli Arabi.* Verbania, 1940. 2 vols.

Meulenaere, H. de. *Herodotos over de 26st Dynastie*. Louvain, 1951.

Mitchell, B. M. 'Cyrene and Persia', *Journal of Hellenic Studies,* 1966, **86**, 99–113.

Moscati, S. *The world of the Phoenicians,* trans. by A. Hamilton. London, 1968.

Müller, K. ed. *Geographici Graeci Minores*. Paris, 1855–61. 2 vols.

Olmstead, A. T. *History of the Persian Empire*. Chicago, 1948.

Palaiphatos. *περὶ ἀπίστων*, ed. by N. Festa. *Mythographi Graeci* III, fasc. 2. Leipzig, 1902.

Parke, H. W. *Oracles of Zeus*. Oxford, 1967.

Pindar. *Odes,* ed. by C. M. Bowra, 2nd edn. Oxford, 1947.

Pliny, *Naturalis historia,* ed. and with an English trans. by H. Rackham, W. H. S. Jones and D. E. Eichholz. London 1938–63. 10 vols.

Polybius. *Histories,* ed. and with an English trans. by W. R. Paton. London, 1922–7. 6 vols.

Posener, G. *La première domination perse en Égypte*: *recueil d'inscriptions hiéroglyphiques*. Cairo, 1936; Bibliothèque d'Études de l'Institut Français d'Archéologie Orientale, Vol. XI.

Pseudo-Skylax. *Periplus,* in Müller, ed., *Geographici . . . (see above)*.

Rousseau, M. 'Hannon au Maroc', *Revue Africaine,* 1949, **93**, 161–232.

Strabo. *Geography,* ed. and with an English trans. by H. L. Jones. London, 1917–32; revised reprint, London and Cambridge, Mass., 1935. 8 vols.

Thompson, L. A. and Ferguson, J. eds. *Africa in classical antiquity*. *See under* General works.

Thucydides. *Histories,* ed. by H. S. Jones, 2nd edn (revised by J. E. Powell). Oxford, 1942. 2 vols.

Warmington, E. H. *Carthage,* 2nd edn. London, 1969.

Williams, D. 'African iron and the classical world', in Thompson and Ferguson, eds., *Africa in classical antiquity* (*see under* General works), 62–80.

Wiseman, D. J. *Chronicles of the Chaldean Kings (626–556 BC) in the British Museum*. London, 1961.

Wulsin, F. R. *The prehistoric archaeology of north-west Africa*. Cambridge, Mass., 1941; Papers of the Peabody Museum of African Archeology and Ethnology, Harvard University, XIX, 1.

3. NORTH AFRICA, 323 BC TO AD 305

Albertini, E. *L'Afrique romaine*. Algiers, 1949.

Appian. *Roman history. See under* ch. 2.

Apuleius. *The golden ass*, ed. and with an English trans. by S. Gaselee. London, 1915.

Arkell, A. J. *History of the Sudan . . . See under* General works.

Aurigemma, S. 'L'Elefante di Leptis Magna e il commercio dell'avorio e delle "Libycae ferae" negli Emporia Tripolitani', *Africa Italiana,* 1940, **7**, 67–86.

Baradez, J. *Vue-Aérienne de l'organisation romaine dans le sud-Algérien*: *Fossatum Africae*. Paris, 1949.

Bates, O. *The eastern Libyans*. London, 1914.
Bell, H. I. 'Anti-Semitism at Alexandria', *Journal of Roman Studies,* 1931, **21**, 1–18.
Bell, H. I. 'The *Constitutio Antoniana* and the Egyptian poll-tax', *Journal of Roman Studies,* 1947, **37**, 17–23.
Bell, H. I. *Egypt from Alexander the Great to the Arab conquest: a study in the diffusion and decay of Hellenism*. Oxford, 1948.
Bell, H. I. *Cults and creeds in Graeco-Roman Egypt*. Liverpool, 1957.
Bevan, E. R. *The house of Ptolemy: a history of Egypt under the Ptolemaic dynasty*. London, 1927.
Birley, A. *Septimius Severus, the African emperor*. London, 1971.
Bouchier, E. S. *Life and letters in Roman Africa*. Oxford, 1913.
Bovill, E. W. 'The camel and the Garamantes', *Antiquity,* 1956, **30**, 19–21.
Brogan, O. 'The camel in Roman Tripolitania', *Papers of the British School at Rome,* 1954, **22**, 126–31.
Broughton, T. R. S. *The romanization of Africa Proconsularis*. Baltimore, 1929.
Caesar. *Commentarii,* ed. by R. du Pontet. Oxford, 1908. 2 vols.
Cagnat, R. *L'Armée romaine d'Afrique et l'occupation militaire de l'Afrique sous les Empereurs,* 2nd edn. Paris, 1913.
Cambridge ancient history, Vols. VII–XII. *See under* General works.
Camps, G. 'Massinissa, ou les débuts de l'histoire', *Libyca,* 1960, **8**.
Carcopino, J. *Le Maroc antique*. Paris, 1943.
Cary, M. and Warmington, E. H. *The ancient explorers*. *See under* ch. 2.
Cassius Dio. *Roman history,* ed. and with an English trans. by E. Cary. London, 1914–27. 9 vols.
Charles-Picard, G. *Les Religions* . . . *See under* ch. 2.
Charles-Picard, G. *La Civilisation de l'Afrique romaine*. Paris, 1959.
Charles-Picard, G. *Life and death of Carthage* . . . *See under* ch. 2.
Courtois, C. 'Saint Augustin et le problème de la survivance du Punique', *Revue Africaine,* 1950, **94**, 259–82.
Davis, S. *Race relations in Ancient Egypt: Greek, Egyptian, Hebrew, Roman*. London, 1951.
De Beer, G. *Hannibal: the struggle for power in the Mediterranean*. London, 1969.
Diodorus Siculus. *Library of history*. *See under* ch. 2.
Dorey, T. A. and Dudley, D. R. *Rome against Carthage*. London, 1971.
Frank, T. 'Rome and Carthage: the first Punic War', in *Cambridge ancient history* VII (*see under* General works).
Frank, T. ed. *An economic survey of Ancient Rome*. Baltimore, 1933–40. 5 vols.
Fraser, P. M. 'Hadrian and Cyrene', *Journal of Roman Studies,* 1950, **40**, 77–90.
Fraser, P. M. *Ptolemaic Alexandria*. Oxford, 1972. 3 vols.
Frend, W. H. C. 'Note on the Berber background in the life of Augustine', *Journal of Theological Studies,* 1942, **43**, 188–91.
Gautier, E.-F. *Le Passé* . . . *See under* General works.
Goodchild, R. G. 'The *Limes Tripolitanus*', Pt II, *Journal of Roman Studies,* 1950, **40**, 30–8.
Goodchild, R. G. 'Oasis forts of *Legio III Augusta* on the routes to the Fezzan', *Papers of the British School at Rome,* 1954, **22**, 56–68.

Goodchild, R. G. and Ward-Perkins, J. B. 'The *Limes Tripolitanus* in the light of recent discoveries', *Journal of Roman Studies*, 1949, **39**, 81–95.
Gsell, S. *Histoire ancienne . . . See under* General works.
Holroyd, M. 'The Jugurthine war', *Journal of Roman Studies*, 1928, **18**, 1–20.
Ilevbare, J. A. 'Impact of Carthaginians and Romans . . .' (*see under* ch. 2), Pt II, 1974, **7**, 3, 385–402.
Jacoby, F. *Die Fragmente . . . See under* ch. 2.
Jameson, S. 'Chronology of the campaigns of Aelius Gallus and C. Petronius', *Journal of Roman Studies*, 1968, **58**, 71–84.
Johnson, A. C. *Egypt and the Roman Empire*. Ann Arbor, 1951.
Josephus. *Works*, ed. by H. Thackeray, R. Marcus, A. Wikgren and L. H. Feldman. London, from 1926. 9 vols.
Jouguet, P. *La vie municipale dans l'Égypte romaine*. Paris, 1968.
Julien, C.-A. *Histoire . . . See under* General works.
Justin. *Epitoma . . . See under* ch. 2.
Law, R. C. C. 'The Garamantes . . .' *See under* ch. 2.
Lesquier, J. *Les institutions militaires de l'Égypte sous les Lagides*. Paris, 1911.
Lesquier, J. *L'armée romaine d'Égypte d'Auguste à Dioclétien*. Cairo, 1918; Mémoires de l'Institut Français d'Archéologie Orientale, **41**.
Lindsay, J. *Daily life in Roman Egypt*. London, 1963.
Lindsay, J. *Leisure and pleasure in Roman Egypt*. London, 1965.
Livy. *Ab urbe condita. See under* ch. 2.
Manetho. *History of Egypt*, ed. and with an English trans. by W. G. Waddell. London, 1940.
Marlowe, J. *The golden age of Alexandria: from its foundation by Alexander the Great in* 331 *BC to its capture by the Arabs in AD 642*. London, 1971.
Mazard, J. *Corpus Nummorum Numidiae Mauretaniaeque*. Paris, 1955.
Merighi, A. *La Tripolitania Antica . . . See under* ch. 2.
Millar, F. 'Local cultures in the Roman Empire: Libyan, Punic and Latin in Roman Africa', *Journal of Roman Studies*, 1968, **58**, 126–34.
Millar, F. and others. *The Roman Empire and its neighbours*. London, 1967.
Milne, J. G. 'The ruin of Egypt by Roman mismanagement', *Journal of Roman Studies*, 1927, **17**, 1–13.
Mommsen, T. *The provinces of the Roman Empire from Caesar to Diocletian*, trans. by W. P. Dickson. London, 1886. 2 vols.
Müller, K. ed. *Geographici . . . See under* ch. 2.
Musurillo, H. A. ed. *The acts of the pagan martyrs: Acta Alexandrinorum*. Oxford, 1952.
Noshy, I. *The arts in Ptolemaic Egypt: a study of Greek and Egyptian influences in Ptolemaic architecture and sculpture*. London, 1937.
Parsons, P. J. 'Phillipus Arabs and Egypt', *Journal of Roman Studies*, 1967, **57**, 134–41.
Pliny. *Naturalis historia. See under* ch. 2.
Plutarch, *Lives*, ed. and with an English trans. by B. Perrin. London, 1914–26. 11 vols.
Polybius. *Histories. See under* ch. 2.
Préaux, C. *L'économie royale des Lagides*. Brussels, 1939.

Pseudo-Arrian. *Periplus*, in Müller, ed., *Geographici* . . . (*see under* ch. 2).
Raven, S. *Rome in Africa*. London, 1969.
Romanelli, P. *La Cirenaica Romana (96 a.C – 642 d.C)*. Verbania, 1953.
Romanelli, P. *Storia delle Province Romane dell'Africa*. Rome, 1959.
Rostovtzeff, M. I. *Social and economic history of the Hellenistic world*. Oxford, 1941. 3 vols.
Rostovtzeff, M. I. *The social and economic history of the Roman Empire*, 2nd edn (revised by P. M. Fraser). Oxford, 1957. 2 vols.
Sallust. *Works*, ed. and with an English trans. by J. C. Rolfe. London, 1921.
Scullard, H. H. *The elephant in the Greek and Roman world*. London, 1974.
Shinnie, P. L. *Meroe, a civilisation of the Sudan*. London, 1967.
Smallwood, E. M. 'The Jews in Egypt and Cyrenaica during the Ptolemaic and Roman periods', in Thompson and Ferguson, eds., *Africa in classical antiquity* (*see under* General works), 110–31.
Snowden, F. *Blacks in antiquity: Ethiopians in the Greco-Roman experience*. Cambridge, Mass., 1970.
Strabo. *Geography*. *See under* ch. 2.
Stuart Jones, H. 'Claudius and the Jewish Question at Alexandria', *Journal of Roman Studies*, 1926, **16**, 17–35.
Tacitus. *Annales*, ed. by C. D. Fisher. Oxford, 1906.
Tacitus. *Historiae*, ed. by C. D. Fisher. Oxford, 1911.
Tarn, W. and Griffith, G. T. *Hellenistic civilisation*, 3rd edn. London, 1952.
Taubenschlag, R. *The law of Greco-Roman Egypt in the light of the papyri, 332 BC–AD 640*. Warsaw, 1955.
Tertullian. *Quae supersunt omnia*, ed. by J.-P. Migne [*Patrologia Latina* series]. Paris, 1845 and 1879, 2 vols.
Teutsch, L. *Das Städtewesen in Nordafrika in der Zeit von C. Graccus bis zum Tode des Kaisers Augustus*. Berlin, 1962.
Thompson, L. A. 'Settler and native in the urban centres of Roman Africa', in Thompson and Ferguson, eds., *Africa in classical antiquity* (*see under* General works), 132–81.
Thompson, L. A. and Ferguson, J. eds. *Africa in classical antiquity*. *See under* General works.
Visscher, F. de. *Les Édits d'Auguste découverts à Cyrène*. Louvain, 1940.
Wallace, H. le R. *Taxation in Egypt from Augustus to Diocletian*. Princeton, 1938.
Walsh, P. G. 'Masinissa', *Journal of Roman Studies*, 1965, **55**, 149–60.
Warmington, E. H. *Carthage*. *See under* ch. 2.

4. THE NILOTIC SUDAN AND ETHIOPIA

Adams, W. Y. 'Post pharaonic Nubia in the light of Archaeology', *Journal of Egyptian Archaeology*, Pt I, 1964, **50**, 102–20; Pt II, 1965, **51**, 160–78.
Adams, W. Y. *Nubia: corridor to Africa*. London, 1977.
Addison, F. *Jebel Moya* [The Wellcome excavations in the Sudan; Vol. I, text, Vol. II, plates]. London, 1949.
Anfray, F. 'Aspects de l'archéologie éthiopienne', *Journal of African History*, 1968, **9**, 345–66.

4. THE NILOTIC SUDAN AND ETHIOPIA

Anfray, F. 'L'Archéologie d'Axoum en 1972', *Paideuma*, 1972, **18**, 60–78.

Arkell, A. J. *History of the Sudan ... See under* General works.

Bellefonds, Linant de. *Journal d'un voyage à Méroé dans les années 1821 et 1822.* Khartoum, 1958.

Buxton, D. *The Abyssinians.* London, 1970.

Caillaud, F. *Voyage à Méroé, au Fleuve Blanc, au delà de Fazoqli.* Paris, 1826; reprinted 1972.

Chapman, S. E. *Decorated chapels of the Meroitic pyramids at Meroe and Barkal* [with text by Dows Dunham], Vol. III of *Royal cemeteries of Kush.* Cambridge, Mass., 1952.

Crawford, O. G. S. and Addison, F. *Abu Geili, Saqadi and Dar el Mek* [The Wellcome Excavations in the Sudan, Vol. III]. London, 1951.

Crowfoot, J. W. 'Some Red Sea ports in the Anglo-Egyptian Sudan', *Geographical Journal*, 1911, **37**, 523–50.

Denkmäler aus Aegypten und Aethiopien. Berlin, 1849–59; reprinted [smaller] Geneva, 1973.

Dombrowski, J. *Excavations in Ethiopia: Lalibela and Natchabiet Caves, Begemder Province.* Doctoral thesis, Boston University, 1971.

Doresse, J. *L'Empire du Prêtre-Jean.* Paris, 1957. 2 vols.

Dunham, D. *El Kurru*, Vol. I of *Royal cemeteries of Kush.* Cambridge, Mass., 1950.

Dunham, D. *Nuri,* Vol. II of *Royal cemeteries of Kush.* Cambridge, Mass., 1955.

Dunham, D. *Royal tombs at Meroe and Barkal*, Vol. IV of *Royal cemeteries of Kush.* Cambridge, Mass., 1957.

Dunham, D. *The West and South Cemeteries at Meroe*, Vol. V of *Royal Cemeteries of Kush.* Cambridge, Mass., 1963.

Gadallah, E. 'Meroitic problems ...' *See under* General bibliographies.

Garstang, J. *Meroe – the city of the Ethiopians.* Oxford, 1911.

Garstang, J. 'Interim report on the excavations at Meroe', *Liverpool Annals of Archaeology and Anthropology*: 2nd report, 1911, **4**, 45–71; 3rd report, 1912, **5**, 73–83; 4th report, 1913, **6**, 1–21; 5th report, 1914, **7**, 1–24.

Green, D. L. and Armelagos, G. *The Wadi Halfa Mesolithic population.* Research Report no. 11, Dept of Anthropology, University of Massachusetts (Amherst), 1972.

Greenberg, Joseph L. *Languages of Africa. See under* 'General' section, Languages.

Griffith, F. L., in D. Randall MacIver and C. L. Woolley, *Areika* (*see below*).

Griffith, F. L. *Karanog, the Meroitic inscriptions of Shabul and Karanog.* Philadelphia, 1911.

Griffith, F. L. 'Oxford excavations in Nubia', *Liverpool Annals of Archaeology and Anthropology*: 1922, **9**, 37–124; 1923, **10**, 73–171; 1924, **11**, 115–25 and 141–80; 1925, **12**, 57–172.

Haycock, B. G. 'The kingship of Kush in the Sudan', *Comparative Studies in Society and History*, 1965, **7**, 461–80 [1965a].

Haycock, B. G. 'Towards a date for King Ergamanes', *Kush*, 1965, **13**, 264–6 [1965b].

Haycock, B. G. 'Towards a better understanding of the kingdom of Cush (Napata-Meroe)', *Sudan Notes and Records*, 1968, **49**, 1–16.

Haycock, B. G. 'Landmarks in Cushite history', *Journal of Egyptian Archaeology*, 1972, **58**, 225–44.

Hintze, F. *Die Sprachliche Stellung des Meroitischen*. Berlin, 1955.

Hintze, F. *Studien der Meroitischen Chronologie und zu den Opfertafeln aus den Pyramiden von Meroe*. Berlin, 1959.

Hintze, F. 'Preliminary report on the excavations at Musawwarat es Sufra, 1960–1', *Kush*, 1962, **10**, 177–8.

Hintze, F. *Die Inschriften des Löwentempels von Musawwarat es Sufra*. Berlin, 1962.

Hintze, F. 'The Latin inscription from Musawwarat es Sufra', *Kush*, 1964, **12**, 296–8.

Hintze, F. *Musawwarat es Sufra: I. 2, Der Löwentempel*. Berlin, 1971.

Hintze, F. ed. *Meroitica I – Sudan im Altertum*. Berlin, 1973.

Hintze, F. *Meroitica III – Beiträge zur meroitischen Grammatik* [forthcoming].

Hofman, I. *Studien zum meroitischen Königtum*. Brussels, 1971.

Jacquet-Gordon, H., Bonnet, C. and Jacquet, J. 'Pnubs and the Temple of Tabo on Argo Island', *Journal of Egyptian Archaeology*, 1969, **55**, 103–11.

Kirwan, L. P. 'Rome beyond the southern Egyptian frontier', *Geographical Journal*, 1957, **123**, 13–19.

Kirwan, L. P. 'The decline and fall of Meroe', *Kush*, 1960, **8**, 163–73.

Kirwan, L. P. 'The *Christian Topography* and the kingdom of Axum', *Geographical Journal*, 1972, **138**, 166–77.

Kraus, T. 'Der Kiosk von Naqa', *Archäologische Anzeiger*, 1964, 834–68.

Macadam, M. F. L. *The Temples of Kawa*, Vol. I, *The inscriptions*. London, 1949. Vol. II, *History and archaeology of the site*. London, 1955.

Meroitica I. See above under Hintze, ed. *Meroitica III. See above under* Hintze [forthcoming].

Millett, N. B. 'Meroitic Nubia'. Doctoral thesis, Yale University, 1968.

Nielson, O. V. *Human remains*. Scandinavian Joint Expedition to Sudanese Nubia, Stockholm, 1970, **9**.

Préaux, C. 'Les communications de l'Éthiopie avec l'Égypte Hellénistique', *Chronique d'Égypte*, 1952, 257–81.

Priese, K. H. 'Nichtägyptische Namen und Worter in den ägyptischen Inschriften der Königer von Kusch I', *Mitteilungen des Instituts für Orientforschung der deutschen Akademie der Wissenschaften zu Berlin*, 1968, **14**, 165–91.

Randall MacIver, D. and Woolley, C. L. *Areika*. Oxford, 1909.

Reisner, G. A. 'The Meroitic kindom of Ethiopia', *Journal of Egyptian Archaeology*, 1923, **9**, 34–77 and 157–60.

Sauneron, S. and Yoyotte, J. 'La campagne nubienne de Psammetique II et sa signification historique', *Bulletin de l'Institut d'Archéologie Orientale*, 1952, **50**, 157–207.

Sayce, A. H. 'A Greek inscription of a king (?) of Axum found at Meroe', *Proceedings of the Society for Biblical Archaeology*, 1909, **31**, 189–203.

Sayce, A. H., in J. Garstang, *Meroe . . .* (*see above*).

Shinnie, P. L. 'A late Latin inscription', *Kush*, 1961, **9**, 284–6.

Shinnie, P. L. *Meroe . . . See under* ch. 3.

Shinnie, P. L. 'Multilingualism in mediaeval Nubia', in Abdelgadir Mahmoud Abdulla, ed., *Studies . . .* (*see under* 'General' section, Languages).

Trigger, B. G. *History and settlement in Lower Nubia*. New Haven, 1965.

Trigger, B. 'The languages of the northern Sudan: an historical perspective', *Journal of African History*, 1966, **7**, 19–25.

Trigger, B. G. 'The myth of Meroe and the African Iron Age', *African Historical Studies*, 1969, **2**, 1, 23–50.

Trigger, B. G. in Hintze, ed., *Meroitica I* (*see above*).

Vercoutter, J. 'Un Palais des "Candaces" contemporain d'Auguste', *Syria*, 1962, **39**, 263–99.

Wainwright, G. A. 'Some ancient records of Kordofan', *Sudan Notes and Records*, 1947, **28**, 11–24.

Wenig, S. 'Bemerkungen zur Chronologie des Reiches von Meroe', *Mitteilungen des Instituts für Orientforschung der Deutschen Akademie der Wissenschaften zu Berlin*, 1967, **13**, 1–44.

Zyhlarz, E. 'Das Meroitische Sprachproblem', *Anthropos*, 1930, **25**, 409–63.

5. TRANS-SAHARAN CONTACTS AND WEST AFRICA

Arkell, A. J. 'Gold Coast copies of Vth–VIIIth-century bronze lamps', *Antiquity*, March 1950, 38–40.

Arkell, A. J. *A history of the Sudan . . . See under* General works.

Armstrong, R. G. 'The use of linguistic and ethnographic data in the study of Idoma and Yoruba history', in Vansina and others, eds., *The Historian in tropical Africa* (*see under* General works), 127–44.

Bailloud, G. 'Dans les tiroirs du Tchad', *Le Nouvel Observateur* (Paris), 1965, **14**, 1.

Bailloud, G. 'L'Évolution des styles céramiques en Ennedi', *Actes du première colloque international d'archéologie africaine* (Fort-Lamy, 1966), 1969, 31–45.

Baker, H. G. 'Comments on the thesis that there was a centre of plant domestication near the headwaters of the river Niger', *Journal of African History*, 1962, **3**, 2, 229–33.

al-Bakrī [El-Bekri]. *See under* 'General' section, Arabic writers.

Balout, L. *Préhistoire de l'Afrique du Nord . . . See under* 'General' section, Chronology.

Balout, L., in Bishop and Clark, eds., *Background to evolution . . .* (*see under* 'General' section, Prehistory).

Baumann, H. and Westermann, D. *Les Peuples et les civilisations de l'Afrique*. Paris, 1948. [Translation of Baumann, R. Thurnwald and Westermann, *Völkerkunde Afrikas*, Essen, 1940.]

Bishop, W. W. and Clark, J. D. *Background to evolution . . . See under* 'General' section, Prehistory.

Blaudin de Thé, Cdt. *Essai de bibliographie . . . See under* General bibliographies.

Bouveignes, O. de. 'Note sur quelques monnaies trouvées au Congo belge', *Brousse* (Leopoldville), 1966, **1–2**, 20–6.

Bovill, E. W. *The golden trade of the Moors*, 2nd edn. Oxford, 1968.

Brasseur, P. *Bibliographie ... du Mali. See under* General bibliographies.

Breuil, H., Abbé. *Les roches peintes du Tassili n-Ajjer*. Paris, 1964.

Briggs, L. C. *The living races of the Sahara desert*. Cambridge, Mass., 1958.

Butzer, K. W. *Studien zum vor- und Frühgeschichtlich Landschaftwandel der Sahara*. Wiesbaden, 1958–9.

Camps, G. 'Les Traces d'un âge du bronze ...' *See under* ch. 2.

Camps, G. *Amekni, Néolithique ancien du Hoggar*. Centre de Recherches Anthropologiques, Préhistoriques et Ethnographiques (Algiers), 1969, Mémoire **10**, 230.

Camps, G. *Les Civilisations préhistoriques ... See under* ch. 1.

Capot-Rey, R. *Le Sahara français*. Paris, 1953.

Cary, M. and Warmington, E. H. *Ancient explorers. See under* General works.

Caton-Thompson, G. 'The camel in dynastic Egypt', *Man*, 1934, **34**, 21.

Chamla, M.-C. *Les Populations anciennes ... See under* ch. 1.

Chapelle, J. *Nomades noirs du Sahara*. Paris, 1957.

Chevalier, A. 'Le Sahara, centre d'origine des plantes cultivées', in 'La Vie dans les régions désertiques nord-tropicales de l'ancien monde', *Mémoire de la Société de Biogéographie de Paris*, 1938, **6**, 307–22.

Childe, V. G. *New light on the most ancient East*. London, 1954.

Clark, J. D. *The prehistory of Africa*. London and New York, 1970.

Clark, J. D. 'The British expedition to the Air mountains'. *See under* ch. 1.

Coppens, Y. 'L'Époque haddadienne: une page de la protohistoire du Tchad', Publicações da Faculdade de Letras (Lisbon), *In Memoriam do Abade H. Breuil*, 1965, **1**, 207–16.

Coppens, Y. 'Les Cultures protohistoriques et historiques du Djourab', *Actes du première colloque international d'archéologie africaine* (Fort-Lamy, 1966), 1969, 129–46.

Courtin, J. 'Le Néolithique de Borkou', *Actes du premier colloque international d'archéologie africaine* (Fort-Lamy, 1966), 1969, 147–59.

Courtois, C. *Les Vandales et l'Afrique*. Algiers and Paris, 1955.

Dalby, D. ed. *Language and history ... See under* 'General' section, Languages.

Dalziel, J. M. *The useful plants ... See under* 'General' section, Crops.

Davies, Oliver. 'The Iron Age in sub-Saharan Africa', *Current Anthropology*, 1966, **7**, 4, 470–1.

Davies, Oliver. *West Africa before the Europeans. See under* 'General' section, Prehistory.

Davies, Oliver, Hugot, H. J. and Seddon, D. 'Origins of African agriculture'. *See under* 'General' section, Crops.

Desanges, J. 'Le Triomphe de Cornelius Balbus (19 BC)', *Revue Africaine (Algiers)*, 1957, **101**, 5–43.

Desanges, J. 'Catalogue des tribus africaines de l'antiquité classique à l'ouest du Nil', *Publications de la Section d'Histoire de la Faculté des Lettres de Dakar*, 1962, **4**, 297f.

Desanges, J. 'Note sur la datation de l'expédition de Julius Maternus au pays d'Agyisymba', *Latomus, Revue d'Études Latines*, 1964, **23**, 4, 713–15.

Diop, C. A. *Le Laboratoire de Radiocarbone de l'IFAN*. Dakar, 1968.

Diop, C. A. 'La métallurgie du fer sous l'ancien empire égyptien', *Bulletin de l'IFAN*, 1973, **35**, 3 (sér. B), 532–47.

Diop, L.-M. 'Métallurgie traditionnelle de l'âge du fer en Afrique', *Bulletin de l'IFAN*, 1968, **30**, 1 (sér. B), 10–38.

Doggett, H. 'The development of the cultivated sorghums', in Hutchinson, ed., *Crop plant evolution* (*see under* 'General' section, Crops).

Dubief, J. *Le Climat du Sahara*. Algiers, 1959 and 1963. 2 vols.

Ducos, P. 'The Oriental Institute excavation at Mureybit, Syria: preliminary report of the 1965 campaign; Part IV, Les restes d'équidés', *Journal of Near Eastern Studies*, 1970, **29**.

Du Puigaudeau, O. *La route du l'ouest* (*Maroc-Mauritanie*). Paris, 1945.

Fage, J. D. 'Anthropology, botany and the study of Africa' [review of Murdock, *Africa*], *Journal of African History*, 1961, **2**, 2, 299–309.

Fernandes, V. *Description de la côte occidentale d'Afrique*, Vol. I ed. by P. de Cenival and T. Monod, Paris, 1938; Vol. II ed. by T. Monod, A. Texeira da Mota and R. Mauny, Bissau, 1951.

Flight, Colin. 'Kintampo, 1967', *West African Archaeological Newsletter*, 1968, **8**, 15–19.

Frisk, H. ed. *Periplus of the Erythraean Sea*. Göteborg, 1927.

Gast, M. *Alimentation des populations de l'Ahaggar, étude ethnographique*. Algiers, 1968; Centre de Recherches Anthropologiques, Préhistoriques et Ethnographiques, Mémoire **8**.

Gautier, E. F. *Le Passé . . . See under* General works.

Germain, G. 'Qu'est-ce que le Périple d'Hannon?' *See under* ch. 2.

Gsell, S. *Histoire ancienne . . . See under* General works.

Gsell, S. 'La Tripolitaine et le Sahara au IIIe siècle de notre ère', *Mémoires de l'Académie d'Inscriptions et Belles Lettres* (Paris), 1926, **43**, 149–66.

Guthrie, Malcolm. 'Some developments in the prehistory of the Bantu languages', *Journal of African History*, 1962, **2**, 2, 275–82.

Guthrie, Malcolm. *Comparative Bantu . . . See under* 'General' section, Languages.

Harlan, J. R. and others, eds. *Origins of plant domestication in Africa. See under* 'General' section, Crops.

Hawkes, J. and Woolley, Sir L. *Prehistory . . . See under* 'General' section, Prehistory.

Howell, F. C. and Bourlière, F. eds. *African ecology . . . See under* 'General' section, Prehistory.

Huard, P. 'Contribution à l'étude du cheval, du fer, et du chameau au Sahara occidental', *Bulletin de l'IFAN*, 1960, **22** (sér. B), 134–78.

Huard, P. 'Nouvelle contribution à l'étude du fer au Sahara et au Tchad', *Bulletin de l'IFAN*, 1964, **26** (sér. B), 297–396.

Huard, P. 'Introduction et diffusion du fer au Tchad', *Journal of African History*, 1966, **7**, 3, 377–404.

Huard, P. 'Contribution à l'étude des premiers travaux agraires au Sahara tchadien', *Bulletin de la Société Préhistorique Française, Études et Travaux*, 1970, **67**, 2, 539–58.

Hugot, H. J. ed. *Missions Berliet Tenéré-Tchad, Documents Scientifiques*. Paris, 1962.

Hugot, H. J. *Le Sahara avant le désert*. Paris, 1974.

Hutchinson, Sir James, ed. *Crop plant evolution . . . See under* 'General' section, Crops.

Ibn ʿAbd al-Ḥakam. *See under* 'General' section, Arabic writers.

Jeffreys, M. D. W. 'Maize and the Mande myth', *Current Anthropology*, 1971, **12**, 3, 291–320.

Kalous, M. 'A contribution to the problem of Akori beads', *Journal of African History*, 1966, **7**, 1, 61–6.

Kalous, M. 'Akori beads', *Bässler Archiv.*, 1968, **16**, 1, 89–97.

Kamal, Y. *Monumenta cartographica . . . See under* General works.

Lambert, N. 'Les industries sur cuivre dans l'ouest saharien', *West African Journal of Archaeology*, 1971, **1**, 9–21.

La Roncière, C. de. *La Découverte . . . See under* General works.

Lebeuf, J.-P. *Carte archéologique des abords du lac Tchad*. Paris, Centre National des Recherches Scientifiques, 1969, 2 vols.

Leclant, J. 'Témoignage des sources antiques sur les pistes menant à l'Oasis d'Ammon', *Bulletin de l'Institut Français d'Archéologie Orientale*, 1950, **49**, 193–253.

Leclant, J. 'Le Fer dans l'Égypte ancienne, le Soudan et l'Afrique', *Annales de l'Est*, 1956, Mémoire **16**, 83–91.

Lewicki, T. *West African food in the Middle Ages according to the Arabic sources*. Cambridge, 1974.

Lhote, H. 'Le cheval et le chameau dans les peintures et gravures rupestres du Sahara', *Bulletin de l'IFAN*, 1953, **15**, 3 (sér. B), 1138–1228.

Lhote, H. *Les Touaregs du Hoggar*, 2nd edn. Paris, 1955.

Lhote, H. 'Découverte de chars de guerre en Aïr', *Notes Africaines* (*Dakar*), 1970, **127**, 83–5.

Lucas, A. and Harris, J. R. *Ancient Egyptian materials and industries*, 4th edn. London, 1962.

McBurney, C. B. M. *The Haua Fteah . . . See under* ch. 1.

Malhomme, J. 'Les gravures préhistoriques du Grand Atlas de Marrakech', *7e congrès, Association Française pour l'Avancement des Sciences* (Tunis, 1951), 1953, 149–53.

Malhomme, J. 'Représentations de haches du bronze (Grand Atlas)', *Bulletin de la Société Préhistorique du Maroc*, 1953, 105–9.

Mauny, R. 'L'Ouest africain chez Ptolémée (vers+141 AD)', *IIe Conferencia Internacional des Africanistas Ocidentais* (*Bissau*, 1947), Vol. 1. Lisbon, 1950. 241–93.

Mauny, R. 'Notes historiques autour des principales plantes cultivées d'Afrique Occidentale', *Bulletin de l'IFAN*, 1953, **16**, 684–730.

Mauny, R. 'Catalogue des restes osseux humains préhistoriques trouvés dans l'Ouest africain', *Bulletin de l'IFAN*, 1961, **23** (sér. B), 3–4, 388–410.

Mauny, R. *Tableau géographique . . . See under* General works.

Mauny, R. 'Le Périple de la mer Erythrée et le problème du commerce romain en Afrique au sud du limes', *Journal de la Société des Africanistes*, 1968, **38**, 1, 19–34.

Mauny, R. *Les Siècles obscurs de l'Afrique noire, histoire et archéologie*. Paris, 1970.

Mauny, R. 'Les peintures rupestres de l'abri d'Aguantour el-Abiod à Tegdaoust', in Robert and others, eds., *Tegdaoust I . . .* (*see below*).

Mauny, R. 'Bibliographie de la préhistoire . . .' *See under* General bibliographies.

Monod, T. *Majabat al-Koubra, contribution à l'étude de l'empty quarter ouest saharien*, *Mémoires de l'IFAN*, **52**, 1958, 407ff.

Monod, T. 'The late Tertiary and the Pleistocene in the Sahara', in Howell and Bourlière, eds., *African ecology . . .* (*see under* 'General' section, Prehistory).

Monod, T. and others, eds. *Description de la côte . . . See above under* Fernandes.

Morgan, W. B. 'The forest and agriculture in West Africa', *Journal of African History*, 1962, **3**, 2, 235–9.

Munson, P. J. 'The Tichitt tradition: a late prehistoric occupation of the southwestern Sahara'. Doctoral thesis, University of Illinois.

Munson, P. J. 'Corrections and additional comments concerning the "Tichitt tradition"', *West African Archaeological Newsletter*, 1970, **10**, 47.

Munson, P. J. 'Archaeological data on the origins of cultivation in the southwestern Sahara and their implications for West Africa', in Harlan and others, eds., *Origins of African plant domestication* (*see under* 'General' section, Crops).

Murdock, G. P. *Africa . . . See under* General works.

Portères, R. 'Berceaux agricoles . . .' *See under* 'General' section, Crops.

Posener, G. ed. *Dictionnaire de la civilisation égyptienne*. Paris, 1959.

Reygasse, M. *Monuments funéraires préislamiques d'Afrique du Nord*. Paris, 1950.

Richir, C. 'Constructions et vestiges protohistoriques du massif du Rkiz. Essai de paléoethnoécologie'. Doctoral thesis, Paris I University, 1974.

Roberts, D. & S. and Devisse, J. eds. *Tegdaoust I: recherches sur Aoudaghost*. Paris, 1970.

Robinson, A. L. 'The camel in antiquity', *Sudan Notes and Records*, 1936, 47–69.

Rosenberger, B. 'Les vieilles exploitations minières et les anciens centres métallurgiques du Maroc'. *Revue de Géographie du Maroc*, 1970, **17–18**, 71–102.

Roset, J. P. 'Art rupestre en Aïr', *Archeologia* (Paris), 1971, **39**, 24–31.

Schofield, J. F. 'L'âge des peintures rupestres du sud de l'Afrique', *L'Anthropologie* (Paris), 1949, 20–32.

Seddon, D. in Roland Portères, H. J. Hugot and D. Seddon, 'Origins of African agriculture', *Current Anthropology*, 1968, **9**, 5, 489.

Shaw, Thurstan. 'On radiocarbon chronology . . .' *See under* 'General' section, Chronology.

Shinnie, P. L. *Meroe . . . See under* ch. 3.

Snowden, J. D. . . . *sorghum*. *See under* 'General' section, Crops.

Souville, G. 'Recherches sur l'existence d'un âge du bronze au Maroc', *Atti del VI Congresso internazionale delle Scienze Preistoriche e Protohistoriche*, Vol. II. Rome, 1965, 419–29.

Spruytte, J. 'Le cheval et le char de l'Égypte ancienne', *Plaisirs Équestres*, 1971, **51**, 171–6.

Tauxier, H. 'Les deux rédactions du Périple d'Hannon', *Revue Africaine* (Algiers), 1882, 15–37.

Trigger, B. G. 'The myth of Meroe . . .' *See under* ch. 4.

Vansina, Jan, Mauny, R. and Thomas, L. V. eds. *The historian . . . See under* General works.

Vaufrey, R. 'Le Néolithique para-Toumbien: une civilisation agricole primitive du Soudan', *Revue Scientifique*, 1967, No. 3267, 205–32.

Wainwright, G. A. 'Iron in the Napatan and Meroitic ages', *Sudan Notes and Records*, 1945, **26**, 5–36.

Williams, D. *Icon and image*. London, 1974.

Yoyette, J., in Posener, ed., *Dictionnaire . . .* (*see above*).

Zeuner, F. E. *A history of domesticated animals*. London, 1963.

al-Zuhrī. *See under* 'General' section, Arabic writers.

6. THE EMERGENCE OF BANTU AFRICA

Adams, W. Y. 'A re-appraisal of Nubian culture history', *Orientalia*, 1970, **39**, 2, 269–77.

Adams, W. Y. 'The Nubian campaign: retrospect and prospect', in *Mélanges K. Michalowski*. Warsaw, 1967, 13–30.

Alexandre, P. 'Proto-histoire du groupe beti-bulu-fang', *Cahiers d'études africaines*, 1965, **5**, 503–60.

Allchin, F. R. 'Early cultivated plants in India and Pakistan', in Ucko and Dimbleby, eds., *Domestication . . .* (*see under* 'General' section, Crops), 323–9.

Allen, W. *African husbandman*. *See under* 'General' section, Crops.

Anfray, F. '. . . archéologie éthiopienne'. *See under* ch. 4.

Baumann, H., Thurnwald, R. and Westermann, D. *Völkerkunde Afrikas*. *See under* General works.

Bishop, W. W. and Clark, J. D. eds. *Background to evolution . . . See under* 'General' section, Prehistory.

Calonne Beaufaict, A. de. *Azande*. Brussels, 1921.

Clark, J. D. 'A note on the pre-Bantu inhabitants of Rhodesia and Nyasaland', *South African Journal of Science*, 1950, **47**, 80–5.

Clark, J. D. *Stone Age cultures . . . See under* ch. 1.

Clark, J. D. *Atlas . . . See under* 'General' section, Prehistory.

Clark, J. D. 'The problem of neolithic culture in sub-Saharan Africa', in Bishop and Clark, eds., *Background to evolution . . .* (*see under* 'General' section, Prehistory), 601–27.

Clark, J. D. *Further . . . studies . . . northern Lunda*. *See under* ch. 1.

Clark, J. D. *Prehistory of Africa*. *See under* 'General' section, Prehistory.

Clark, J. D. *Kalambo Falls . . . See under* ch. 1.

Clark, J. D. and Fagan, B. M. 'Charcoals, sands and channel-decorated pottery from northern Rhodesia', *American Anthropologist*, 1965, **67**, 354–71.

Cohen, D. *The historical tradition of Busoga, Mukama and Kintu*. Oxford, 1972.

Cohen, M. 'A reassessment of the Stone Bowl culture of the Rift Valley, Kenya', *Azania*, 1970, **5**, 27–38.

Crazzolara, J. P. *The Lwoo*. Verona, 1950–4. 3 vols.

Dart, R. A. and Beaumont, P. 'Ratification and retrocession...' *See under* 'General' section, Chronology.

Davidson, B. *Africa: history of a continent*. London, 1966.

Davies, Oliver. *West Africa before the Europeans*. *See under* 'General' section, Prehistory.

Deschamps, H. *Traditions orales et archives au Gabon*. Paris, 1962.

De Vaal, J. B. ''N Soutpansbergse Zimbabwe: 'n voorlopige ondersoek van 'n bouval op die Plaas Solvent', *South African Journal of Science*, 1943, **40**, 303–18.

De Villiers, H. *The skull of the South African Negro*. Johannesburg, 1968.

Douglas, M. 'Is matriliny doomed in Africa?', in Douglas and Kaberry, eds., *Man in Africa* (*see under* General works).

East, R. *Akiga's story*. London, 1965.

Ehret, C. *Southern Nilotic history*. Evanston, 1971.

Ehret, C. 'Patterns of Bantu and Central Sudanic settlement in Central and southern Africa', *Trans-African Journal of History*, 1974, **4**, 1–27.

Fagan, B. M. 'Radiocarbon dates...' *See under* 'General' section, Chronology.

Fagan, B. M. 'The Iron Age sequence in the Southern Province of Zambia', *Journal of African History*, 1963, **4**, 2, 157–78.

Fagan, B. M. 'The Greefswald sequence: Bambandyanalo and Mapungubwe', *Journal of African History*, 1964, **5**, 3, 337–61.

Fagan, B. M. *Southern Africa in the Iron Age*. London, 1966.

Fagan, B. M. *Iron Age cultures of Zambia*, Vol. I. London, 1967.

Fagan, B. M. 'Early trade and raw materials in south central Africa', *Journal of African History*, 1969, **10**, 11–15.

Fagan, B. M. 'Early trade and raw materials in south central Africa', in Gray and Birmingham, eds., *Precolonial African trade* (*see under* General works).

Fagan, B. M. 'The later Iron Age in South Africa', in Thompson, ed., *African societies*... (*see under* General works), 50–69.

Fagan, B. M. in Shinnie, ed., *African Iron Age* (*see under* 'General' section, Prehistory).

Fagan, B. M. 'The Iron Age pottery', in Clark, *Kalambo Falls*... (*see under* ch. 1), 8–56.

Fagan, B. M., Phillipson, D. W. and Daniels, S. G. H. *Iron Age cultures in Zambia*, Vol. II. London, 1969.

Fagan, B. M. and Yellen, J. E. 'Ivuna; ancient salt-working in southern Tanzania', *Azania*, 1968, **3**, 1–44.

Fage, J. D. and Oliver, Roland, eds. *Papers in African prehistory*. *See under* 'General' section, Prehistory.

Flight, Colin. 'Kintampo, 1967'. *See under* ch. 5.

Flight, Colin 'Radiocarbon chronology...' *See under* 'General' section, Chronology.

Fouché, L. *Mapungubwe*. Cambridge, 1937.

Freeman-Grenville, G. S. P. *The East African coast*. Oxford, 1962.

Freeman-Grenville, G. S. P. *The medieval history of the Tanganyika coast*. London, 1962.

Galloway, A. *The skeletal remains of Bambandyanalo*. Johannesburg, 1959.

Gardner, G. A. *Mapungubwe II*. Pretoria, 1963.

Gardner, T. Wells, L. H. and Schofield, J. F. 'The recent archaeology of Gokomere, Southern Rhodesia', *Transactions of the Royal Society of South Africa*, 1940, **28**, 219–53.

Garlake, P. S. 'Rhodesian ruins – a preliminary assessment of their styles and chronology', *Journal of African History*, 1970, **11**, 4, 495–514.

Garlake, P. S. 'The value of imported ceramics in the dating and interpretation of the Rhodesian Iron Age', *Journal of African History*, 1968, **9**, 13–34.

Garlake, P. S. *Great Zimbabwe*. London, 1973.

Greenberg, Joseph H. '... linguistic classification', *See under* 'General' section, Languages.

Greenberg, Joseph H. *Languages of Africa*. *See under* 'General' section, Languages.

Greenberg, Joseph H. 'Linguistic evidence regarding Bantu origins', *Journal of African History*, 1972, **13**, 2, 189–216.

Grindley, J. R., Speed, E. and Maggs, T. M. O'C. 'The age of the Bonteberg Shelter deposits, Cape Province', *South African Archaeological Bulletin*, 1970, **25**, 97, 24.

Guthrie, Malcolm. 'Some developments in the prehistory of the Bantu languages', *Journal of African History*, 1962, **3**, 261.

Guthrie, Malcolm. 'Languages and history'. *See under* 'General' section, Languages.

Guthrie, Malcolm. *Comparative Bantu* ... *See under* 'General' section, Languages.

Heine, B. 'Zur genetischen Gliederung der Bantu-Sprachen', *Afrika und Übersee*, 1972–3, **56**, 164–85.

Henrici, Alick. 'Numerical classification ...' *See under* 'General' section, Languages.

Hiernaux, J. 'Note sur une ancienne population de Ruanda-Urundi: les Renga', *Zaire*, 1956, **4**, 351–60.

Hiernaux, J. *La diversité humaine en Afrique subsaharienne: recherches biologiques*. Brussels, 1968.

Hiernaux, J. 'Bantu expansion: the evidence from physical anthropology confronted with linguistic and archaeological evidence', *Journal of African History*, 1968, **9**, 505–15.

Hiernaux, J. 'Le début de l'âge des métaux dans la région des Grands Lacs africains', in Mortelmans and Nenquin, eds., *Actes IVe congrès panafricain* ... (*see under* 'General' section, Prehistory), **3**, 381–9.

Hiernaux, J. and Maquet, E. 'Cultures préhistoriques de l'âge des métaux au Ruanda-Urundi et au Kivu', *Académie Royale des Sciences Coloniales, Bulletin des Séances*, Pt I, 1957, 1126–49; Pt II, 1959.

Hiernaux, J., Maquet, E. and de Buyst, J. 'Le cimetière préhistorique de Katoto', in Hugot, ed., *Actes du VIe congrès panafricain* ... (*see under* 'General' section, Prehistory).

Huffman, T. N. 'The Early Iron Age and the spread of the Bantu', *South African Archaeological Bulletin*, 1970, **25**, 3–21.

Huffman, T. N. 'The rise and fall of Zimbabwe', *Journal of African History*, 1972, **13**, 3, 353–66.

Huffman, T. N. 'Test excavations at Makuru, Zambia', *Arnoldia*, 1973, **39**, 5.

Huffman, T. N. 'The linguistic affinities of the Iron Age in Rhodesia', *Arnoldia*, 1974, **7**, 7.

Inskeep, R. R. 'The archaeological background', in Wilson and Thompson, eds., *Oxford history of South Africa* (*see under* General works), 1–39.

Inskeep, R. R. 'South Africa', in Shinnie, ed., *African Iron Age* (*see under* 'General' section, Prehistory), 245–74.

Jackson, G., Gartlan, J. S. and Posnansky, M. 'Rock gongs and associated rock paintings from Lolui Island, Lake Victoria, Uganda', *Man*, 1965, **65**, 38–9.

Jaffey, A. J. E. 'A reappraisal of the history of the Rhodesian Iron Age up to the fifteenth century', *Journal of African History*, 1966, **7**, 189–96.

Johnston, H. H. 'A survey of the ethnography of Africa: and the former racial and tribal migrations of that continent', *Journal of the Royal Anthropological Institute*, 1913, **43**, 391–425.

Junod, H. A. *The life of a South African tribe*. London, 1927.

Kendall, R. L. and Livingstone, D. A. 'Paleoecological studies on the East African plateau', in H. J. Hugot (ed.), *Actes du VIe Congrès Panafricain du Préhistoire*, Chambéry, 1972, 386.

Kirkman, J. *Men and monuments on the East African coast*. London, 1964.

Leakey, L. S. B. *Stone Age cultures of Kenya Colony*. *See under* ch. 1.

Leakey, M. D. 'Notes on the ground and polished axes of East Africa', *Journal of the East Africa and Uganda Natural History Society*, 1943, 182–95.

Leakey, M. D. and L. S. B. . . . *Njoro River Cave*. *See under* ch. 1.

Leakey, M. D., Owen, W. E. and Leakey, L. S. B. 'Dimple-based pottery from central Kavirondo, Kenya Colony', *Occasional Papers of the Coryndon Museum* (Nairobi), 1948, **2**.

Lewis, H. S. 'The origins of the Galla and Somali', *Journal of African History*, 1966, **7**, 38–9.

Mason, R. J. *The prehistory of the Transvaal*. Johannesburg, 1962.

Mason, R. J., Klapwijk, M. and Evers, T. M. 'Early Iron Age settlement of southern Africa', *South African Journal of Science*, 1973, **69**, 324–6.

Mauny, R. *Tableau géographique* . . . *See under* General works.

Mills, E. A. C. and Filmer, N. T. 'Chondwe Iron Age site, Ndola, Zambia', *Azania*, 1972, **7**, 129–46.

Moeller, A. *Les grandes lignes des migrations des Bantous de la Province Orientale du Congo Belge*. Brussels, 1936.

Murdock, G. P. *Africa* . . . *See under* General works.

Nenquin, J. 'Dimple-based pots from Kasai, Belgian Congo', *Man*, 1959, **59**, No. 242.

Nenquin, J. *Excavations at Sanga*, 1957. Tervuren, 1963.

Nenquin, J. 'Notes on some early pottery cultures in northern Katanga', *Journal of African History*, 1963, **4**, 9–32; also in Fage and Oliver, eds., *Papers in African prehistory* (*see under* 'General' section, Prehistory), 223–38.

Nenquin, J. . . . *prehistoric cultures of Rwanda and Burundi. See under* ch. 1.

Nenquin, J. 'Notes on the protohistoric pottery cultures in the Congo–Rwanda–Burundi region', in Bishop and Clark, eds., *Background to evolution* . . . (*see under* 'General' section, Prehistory), 651–8.

Nenquin, J. 'The Congo, Rwanda and Burundi', in Shinnie, ed., *African Iron Age* (*see under* 'General' section, Prehistory), 183–214.

Oliver, Roland, 'Discernible developments in the interior, *c.* 1500–1540', in Oliver and Mathew, eds., . . . *East Africa*, 1 (*see under* General works).

Oliver, Roland, 'The problem of the Bantu expansion', *Journal of African History*, 1966, **7**, 361–76; also in Fage and Oliver, eds., *Papers in African prehistory* (*see under* 'General' section, Prehistory), 141–52.

Oliver, Roland and Fagan, B. M. *Africa in the Iron Age. See under* 'General' section, Prehistory.

Periplus of the Erythrean Sea, ed. by W. H. Schoff. New York and London, 1912. *See also under* ch. 5 [Frisk, ed.]; trans. in Freeman-Grenville, *East African coast* (*see above*).

Phillipson, D. W. 'The Early Iron Age in Zambia – regional variants and some tentative conclusions', *Journal of African History*, 1968, **9**, 191–211.

Phillipson, D. W. 'Early iron-using peoples of Southern Africa', in Thompson, ed., *African societies* . . . (*see under* General works), 24–49.

Phillipson, D. W. '. . . radiocarbon chronology . . .' *See under* 'General' section, Chronology.

Phillipson, D. W. 'Early Iron Age sites on the Zambian Copperbelt', *Azania*, 1972, **7**, 93–128.

Phillipson, D. W. 'Prehistoric succession . . .' *See under* ch. 1.

Phillipson, D. W., 'Iron Age history and archaeology in Zambia', *Journal of African History*, 1974, **15**, 1, 1–26.

Phillipson, D. W. 'Chronology . . . in Bantu Africa'. *See under* 'General' section, Chronology.

Posnansky, M. 'Pottery types from archaeological sites in East Africa', *Journal of African History*, 1961, **2**, 177–98.

Posnansky, M. 'The Early Iron Age in East Africa', in Bishop and Clark, eds., *Background to evolution* . . . (*see under* 'General' section, Prehistory), 630–4.

Posnansky, M. 'Bantu genesis – archaeological reflections', *Journal of African History*, 1968, **9**, 1–5.

Rightmire, G. P. 'Iron Age skulls from southern Africa reassessed by multiple discrimination analysis', *American Journal of Physical Anthropology*, 1970, **33**, 2, 147–68.

Robinson, K. R. *Khami ruins*. Cambridge, 1959.

Robinson, K. R. 'An early Iron Age site from the Chibi district, southern Rhodesia', *South African Archaeological Bulletin*, 1961, **17**, 75–102.

Robinson, K. R. 'The archaeology', in *Report of the Schoolboys' Exploration Society expedition to Buffalo Bend* [n.p.], 1961, 3–8.

Robinson, K. R. 'Further excavations in the Iron Age deposit at the tunnel site, Gokomere Hill, southern Rhodesia', *South African Archaeological Bulletin*, 1963, **18**, 155–71.

Robinson, K. R. 'The Leopard's Kopje culture: a preliminary report on recent work', *Arnoldia*, 1965, **1**, 25.

Robinson, K. R. 'The Leopard's Kopje culture, its position in the Iron Age in Southern Rhodesia', *South African Archaeological Bulletin*, 1966, **21**, 5–51.

Robinson, K. R. 'A preliminary report on the recent archaeology of Ngonde, northern Malawi', *Journal of African History*, 1966, **7**, 169–88.

Robinson, K. R. 'The Iron Age of the southern lake area of Malawi', *Department of Antiquities, Zomba, Publication* 8, 1970, 117–18.

Sassoon, H. 'Engaruka: excavations during 1964', *Azania*, 1966, **1**, 79–100.

Sassoon, H. 'New views on Engaruka, northern Tanzania: excavations carried out for the Tanzania Government in 1964 and 1966', *Journal of African History*, 1967, **8**, 201–18.

Sautter, G. *De l'Atlantique au fleuve Congo*. Paris, 1966.

Schmidt, P. [Notes in] *Tanzania Zamani*, 1970, **7**, 4–6 and 1971, **8**, 6–7.

Schmidt, P. *Historical archaeology in an African culture* [forthcoming].

Schoff, W. H. ed. *The Periplus of the Erythrean Sea. See under Periplus* (above).

Seligman, C. G. *Races of Africa. See under* General works.

Shaw, Thurstan. 'Early agriculture . . .' *See under* 'General' section, Crops.

Shinnie, P. L. ed. *African Iron Age. See under* 'General' section, Prehistory.

Siiriaien, A. 'The Iron Age site at Gatung'ang'a, central Kenya', *Azania*, 1971, **6**, 199–232.

Simoons, F. J. 'Some questions on the economic prehistory of Ethiopia', *Journal of African History*, 1965, **6**, 1, 1–14.

Smolla, G. 'Prähistorische Keramik aus Ostafrika', *Tribus*, 1957, **6**, 35–64.

Soper, R. C. 'Kwale: an Early Iron Age site in south-eastern Kenya', *Azania*, 1967, **2**, 1–18.

Soper, R. C. 'Iron Age sites in north-eastern Tanzania', *Azania*, 1967, **2**, 19–36.

Soper, R. C. 'A general review of the Early Iron Age of the southern half of Africa', *Azania*, 1971, **6**, 5–38.

Soper, R. C. 'Early Iron Age pottery types from East Africa: comparative analyses', *Azania*, 1971, **6**, 39–52.

Soper, R. C. 'Iron Age sites in Chobi sector, Murchison Falls, National Park, Uganda', *Azania*, 1971, **6**, 53–88.

Soper, R. C. 'Resemblances between East African Early Iron Age pottery and recent vessels from the north-eastern Congo', *Azania*, 1971, **6**, 233–41.

Soper, R. C. 'Early Iron Age pottery types from East Africa', in Hugot, ed., *Actes du VIe congrès panafrican . . .* (*see under* 'General' section, Prehistory), 36–41.

Soper, R. C. 'Radiocarbon dates . . .' *See under* 'General' section, Chronology.

Stuiver, M. and Van der Merve, N. J. 'Radiocarbon chronology . . .' *See under* 'General' section, Chronology.

Summers, R. *Inyanga*. Cambridge, 1958.

Summers, R. 'The Rhodesian Iron Age', *Journal of African History*, 1962, **3**, 1–13. Also in Fage and Oliver, eds., *Papers in African prehistory* (*see under* 'General' section, Prehistory), 157–72.

Summers, R. 'Iron Age industries of southern Africa', in Bishop and Clark, eds., *Background to evolution . . .* (*see under* 'General' section, Prehistory), 687–700.

Summers, R., Robinson, K. R. and Whitty, A. 'Zimbabwe excavations, 1958', *Occasional Papers of the National Museum of Southern Rhodesia*, 1961, **23A**.

Sutton, J. E. G. 'The interior of East Africa', in Shinnie, ed., *African Iron Age* (*see under* 'General' section, Prehistory), 142–82.

Sutton, J. E. G. 'Radiocarbon dates . . .' *See under* 'General' section, Chronology.

Sutton, J. E. G. *The archaeology of the western highlands of Kenya*. Nairobi, 1973.

Sutton, J. E. G. and Roberts, A. D. 'Uvinza and its salt industry', *Azania*, 1968, **3**, 45–86.

Thompson, L. A. ed. *African societies . . . See under* General works.

Tobias, P. V. 'Skeletal remains from Inyanga', in Summers, *Inyanga* (*see above*).

Turnbull, C. *Wayward servants*. London, 1965.

Tweedie, A. 'Towards a history of the Bemba from oral tradition', in E. Stokes and R. Brown, eds., *The Zambesian past*. Manchester, 1966, 197–225.

Van der Kerken, G. *L'Ethnie Mongo*. Brussels, 1944. 3 vols.

Van Noten, F. L. *Les Tombes du roi Cyirima Rujugiza et de la reine-mère Nyirayulu Kanjogera: description archéologique*. Tervuren, Musée Royal de l'Afrique Centrale, 1972.

Vansina, Jan. *Kingdoms of the savanna*. Madison, 1966.

Vogel, J. O. 'Iron Age research project of the Livingstone Museum', *Archaeology*, June 1968, 216–18.

Vogel, J. O. 'The Kalamo culture of southern Zambia', *Zambia Museums Journal*, 1971, 77–8.

Vogel, J. O. *Kamangoza*. Zambia, 1971.

Vogel, J. O. *Kumadzulo*. Nairobi, 1972.

Vogel, J. O. 'Some Early Iron Age sites in Southern and Western Zambia', *Azania*, 1973, **8**, 25–54.

Westermann, D. 'Die westlichen Sudansprachen . . .' *See under* 'General' section, Languages.

Wilson, M. 'The Nguni people' and 'The Sotho, Venda and Tongo', in Wilson and Thompson, eds., *Oxford history of South Africa*, 1 (*see under* General works), 75–130, 131–86.

Wilson, M. and Thompson, Leonard, eds., *Oxford history of South Africa*, 1. *See under* General works.

Wrigley, C. 'Speculations on the economic prehistory of Africa', *Journal of African History*, 1960, **1**, 189–204. Also in Fage and Oliver, eds., *Papers in African prehistory* (*see under* 'General' section, Prehistory), 59–74.

7. THE CHRISTIAN PERIOD IN MEDITERRANEAN AFRICA

The following abbreviations have been used in this section (for details, see under 'General' section, Patrologia, inscriptions and papyri).

CIG *Corpus Inscriptionum Graecarum*
CIL *Corpus Inscriptionum Latinarum*

Corp. Script. Christ. Orient. *Corpus Scriptorum Christianorum Orientalium*
CSEL *Corpus Scriptorum Ecclesiasticorum Latinorum*
PG *Patrologia cursus completus, series Graeca*
PL *Patrologia cursus completus, series Latina*
PO *Patrologia Orientalis*
P. Oxy. *Papyrus Oxyrhynchus*

Texts, inscriptions etc. not otherwise listed will be found in one of these collections.

Acta Proconsularia, ed. by W. Hartel.

Acta Saturnini, in *PL*, **8**.

Albertini, E., in *Bulletin Archéologique du Comité des Travaux Historiques*, 1922, 26–32.

Albertini, E., in *Comptes Rendus de l'Académie des Inscriptions et Belles Lettres*, 1939, 100.

Allais, Y. *Djemila*. Paris, 1938.

Altaner, B. and Stuiber, A. *Patrologie (Leben, Schriften und Lehre der Kirchenväter)*, 7th edn. Freiburg, 1966.

Barnes, T. D. *Tertullian, a historical and literary study*. Oxford, 1971.

Bell, H. I. *Jews and Greeks in Egypt*. Oxford, 1924.

Bell, H. I. *Egypt from Alexander . . . See under* ch. 3.

Bell, H. I. and Skeat, T. C. eds. *Fragments of an unknown gospel*. London, 1935.

Berthier, A. *Tiddis*. Algiers. 1954.

Berthier, A., Logeart, F. and Martin, M. *Les Véstiges du Christianisme antique dans la Numidie centrale*. Algiers, 1942.

Besa. *Life of Shenute*, ed. by H. Wiesman. *Corp. Script. Christ. Orient., Scriptores Coptici*, II. Paris, 1931.

Beschouach, A. 'Une stèle consacrée à Saturne le 8 Novembre 323', *Bulletin Archéologique du Comité des Travaux Historiques*, N.S., 1968, **4** (Paris 1969), 253–68.

Breviarum causae Nestorianorum et Eutychianorum, xx; in *PL*, **68**.

Brisson, J. P. *Autonomisme et Christianisme dans l'Afrique romaine de Septime Sévère à l'invasion vandale*. Paris, 1958.

Brooks, E. W. ed. and trans. *Vitae virorum apud Monophysitarum celeberrimorun. Corp. Script. Christ. Orient., Scriptores Syri*, III, 25. Paris, 1907.

Brown, P. R. L. *Augustine of Hippo, a biography*. London, 1967.

Brown, P. R. L. *Religion and society in the age of St Augustine*. London, 1972.

Brunschvig, Robert, 'Un texte arabe du IXe siècle intéressant le Fezzan', *Revue Africaine*, 1945, **89**, 21–5.

Buonaiuti, E. *Il Christianesimo nell' Africa romana*. Bari, 1928.

Burkitt, F. C. 'The Christian Church in the East', in *Cambridge ancient history*, Vol. XII. Cambridge, 1939, 476ff.

Bury, J. B. *History of the later Roman Empire*, Vol. II. London, 1923.

Butler, A. J. *The Arab conquest of Egypt and the last thirty years of the Roman dominion*. Oxford, 1902.

Cagnat, R. and Merlin, A. *Inscriptions... See under* 'General' section, Patrologia.

Calderone, S., in *La Parola del Passato*, 1967, **113**, 94–109.

Carcopino, J. 'Les Castella de la plaine de Setif', *Revue Africaine*, 1918, **62**, 1ff.

Christophe, Marcel. *Le Tombeau de la Chrétienne*. Paris, 1951.

Cintas, J. and Fenille, G. L. 'Église et Baptistère de Thibiuca', *Karthago*, 1953, **2**.

Courtois, C. *Victor de Vita et son oeuvre*. Algiers, 1954.

Courtois, C. *Les Vandales... See under* ch. 5.

Courtois, C., Leschi, L., Perrat, C. and Saumagne, C. *Tablettes Albertini, actes privés de l'époque vandale*. Algiers and Paris, 1952.

Cross, F. L. ed. *The Jung codex*. Oxford, 1955.

Cyprian. *Ad Demetrianum, Letters, Works*, ed. by W. Hartel. *CSEL*, III, I. Vienna, 1868.

Danielou, J. *Origène*. Paris, 1955.

Delehaye, H. 'Contributions récentes à l'hagiographie de Rome et de l'Afrique', *Analecta Bollandinaa*, 1936, **54**, 313–16.

Diehl, E. *L'Afrique byzantine*. Paris, 1896.

Diesner, H. J. *Kirche und Staat im spätrömischen Reich*. Berlin, 1963.

Diesner, H. J. *Der Untergang der römischen Herrschaft in Nordafrika*. Weimar, 1964.

Diesner, H. J. *Fulgentius von Ruspe als Theolog und Kirchenpolitiker*. Berlin, 1966.

Ebeid, R. Y. and Wickham, L. R. 'A collection of unpublished Syriac letters of Timothy Achirus', *Journal of Theological Studies*, N.S., 1970, **21**, 321–69.

Ebeid, R. Y. and Wickham, L. R. 'An unknown letter of Cyril of Alexandria in Syriac', *Journal of Theological Studies*, N.S., 1971, **22**, 420–34.

Ebeid, R. Y. and Wickham, L. R. 'A note on the Syriac version of Athanasius' *Ad Epictetum* in Ms BM Add. 14557', *Journal of Theological Studies*, N.S., 1972, **23**, 144–54.

Eusebius. *Historia Ecclesiastica*, trans. by J. E. L. Oulton. *See also below under* Stevenson, ed., *A new Eusebius*.

Février, P. A. *Le développement urbain en Afrique du Nord*. Cahiers archaéologiques, 14, Paris, 1964.

Février, P. A. and Duval, Y. 'Inscription martyrologique sur plomb de la région de Telergma (AD 637)', *Mélanges de l'école française à Rome*, 1961, **81**, 257–320.

Foerster, W. *A selection of Gnostic texts*, Vol. II. Oxford, 1974.

Frend, W. H. C. 'North Africa and Europe in the early Middle Ages', *Transactions of the Royal Historical Society*, 1955, **5**, 5, 61–81.

Frend, W. H. C., 'Circumcellions and Monks', *Journal of Theological Studies*, N.S., 1969, **20**, 2, 542–49.

Frend, W. H. C. *The Donatist Church*, 2nd edn. Oxford, 1971.

Frend, W. H. C. *The rise of the Monophysite movement*. Cambridge, 1972.

Frend, W. H. C. 'Open questions concerning the Christians and the Roman Empire in the age of the Severi', *Journal of Theological Studies*, N.S., 1974, **25**, 2, 333–52.

Frend, W. H. C. *Religion popular and unpopular in the early Christian centuries.* London, 1976.

Gautier, E.-F. *Le Passé . . . See under* General works.

Gesta apud Zenophilum, ed. by C. Ziwsa. *CSEL*, xxvi. English trans. in Stevenson, ed., *A new Eusebius* (*see below*).

Grenfell, B. P. and Hunt, A. S. eds. *Oxyrhynchus papyri, ΛΟΓΙΑ ΙΗCΟΥ* ['Logia Jesu']. London, 1897. 'New sayings of Jesus' and 'Fragment of a lost gospel'. London, 1904.

Grillmeier, A. and Bacht, H. *Das Konzil von Chalkedon.* Würzburg, 1951–3. 2 vols.

Gsell, S., in *Mélanges de l'école française de Rome*, 1894, **14**, 290ff.

Gsell, S. *Atlas archéologique de l'Algérie.* Algiers, 1911.

Gsell, S. and Pflaum, H. G. *Inscriptions latines de l'Algérie.* Paris, 1923–57.

Hardy, E. R. *The large estates of Byzantine Egypt.* New York, 1931.

Hardy, E. R. *Christian Egypt, church and people.* New York and Oxford, 1952.

Harris, J. R. ed. *The Acts of the Scillilan Martyrs*, Vol. I, no. 2 of *Cambridge texts and studies.* Cambridge, 1891.

Heussi, K. *Der Ursprung des Mönchtums.* Tübingen, 1936.

Ibn ʿAbd al-Ḥakam. *See under* 'General' section, Arabic writers.

John of Ephesus. *Historia ecclesiastica,* ed. by E. W. Brooks. *Corp. Script. Christ. Orient. Scriptores Syri.* Louvain, 1935–6.

John of Ephesus. *Lives of the eastern saints*, ed. by E. W. Brooks. *PO*, **18**.

John of Nikiou. *Chronique de Jean, Évêque de Nikiou*, ed. and trans. by A. Zotenberg. Paris, 1883.

Jones, A. H. M. 'Census records of the later Roman Empire', *Journal of Roman Studies*, 1963, **53**, 49–64.

Jones, A. H. M. *The later Roman Empire.* Oxford and Norman, Okla., 1964.

Knipfing, J. P. 'The *Libelli* of the Decian persecution', *Harvard Theological Review*, 1923, **16**, 345–90.

Knopf, R. and Krueger, G. *Ausgewählte . . . See under* 'General' section. Patrologia.

Labriolle, P. de. 'Les débuts du monachisme', in J. R. Palanque, G. Bardy et P. de Labriolle, *De la paix Constantinienne à la mort de Théodose*, Vol. III of A. Fliche and V. Martin, *Histoire de l'église.* Paris, 1947.

Lancel, Serge, ed. 'Actes de la conférence de Carthage', *Sources chrétiennes* (Paris), 1972, **195**.

Leglay, M. 'La vie intellectuelle d'une cité africaine aux confins de l'Aurès', *Collection Latomus*, 1960, **45**.

Leglay, M. *Saturne africaine: histoire.* Paris, 1966.

Leipoldt, J. 'Schenute von Atripe und die Entstehung des national-aegyptischen Christentums', in *Texte und Untersuchungen*, Vol. xxv. Leipzig. 1904.

Leschi, L. 'Le Centenarium d'Aqua Viva', *Revue Africaine*, 1943, **87**, 5–22.

Leschi, L. *Tipasa.* Algiers, 1950.

Lietzmann, H. *Geschichte der alten Kirche.* Berlin, 4 vols., 1937–44.

Marcillet-Jaubert, J. *Les Inscriptions d'Altava.* Paris, 1968.

Marec, E. *Hippone.* Algiers, 1950.

Markus, R. A. 'Donatism, the last phase', in C. J. Cuming, ed., *Studies in church history*, Vol. I. Leiden, 1964, 118–26.

Markus, R. A. 'Religious dissent in North Africa in the Byzantine period', in C. J. Cuming, ed., *Studies in church history*, Vol. III. Leiden, 1966, 140–9.

Maspero, J. *Papyrus grecs de l'époque byzantine*. Paris, 1910–16. 3 vols.

Michalowski, K. *Faras: die Kathedrale aus dem Wüstensand*. Zurich, 1967.

Migne, J.-P. ed. *PG*, *PL*.

Millar, F. 'The date of the *Constitutio Antoniniana*', *Journal of Egyptian Archaeology*, 1962, **48**, 124–31.

Monceaux, P. *Histoire littéraire de l'Afrique chrétienne*. Paris, 1901–23. 7 vols.

Monceaux, P. *Timgad chrétien*. Paris, 1911.

Montefiore, H. W., in *New Testament Studies*, 1961, **5**, 220–48.

Musurillo, H. *The acts of the Christian martyrs*. Oxford, 1972.

Opitz, H. G. *Athanasius' Werke*. Berlin, from 1934.

Opitz, H. G. *Untersuchungen zur Überlieferung des Schriften der Athanasius*. Berlin, 1935.

Optatus of Milevis. *De Schismate Donatistarum*, ed. by C. Ziwsa. *CSEL*, XXVI.

Origen. *Dialogue with Heracleides*, ed. by J. Scherer as *Entretien d'Origène avec Héraclide et les évêques, ses collègues, sur le Père, le Fils et l'Âme*. Cairo, 1949.

Palladius. *Historia Lausiaca*, ed. by C. Butler. Cambridge, 1898.

Papyrus Bodmer. See under 'General' section, Patrologia.

Papyrus Oxyrhynchus. See under 'General' section, Patrologia.

Passio Maximiliani, ed. by R. Knopf and G. Krueger, in *Ausgewählte* . . . (*see under* 'General' section, Patrologia).

Plumley, J. M. *The scrolls of Bishop Timotheos found at Q'asr Ibrim*. London, Egypt Exploration Society Monograph, 1975.

Rea, J. R. ed. *P. Oxy.*, Vol. XL. London, 1972.

Rostovtzeff, M. I. *Social and economic history* . . . *See under* ch. 3.

Severus. *Select letters*, ed. by E. W. Brooks. London 1902–4.

Ste Croix, G. E. M. de. 'Aspects of the Great Persecution', *Harvard Theological Review*, 1954, **47**, 84ff.

Salama, P. 'La voie romaine de la vallée de la Tafna', *Bulletin d'Archéologie Algérienne*, 1966–7, **2**, 183–217.

Saumagne, C. *Cyprien, Évêque de Carthage, 'Pape' d'Afrique*. Paris, Centre National de la Recherche Scientifique, 1975.

Simon, M. 'Le Judaisme berbère dans l'Afrique ancienne', *Revue de l'histoire et philosophie religieuse*, 1946, **26**, 1ff and 105ff; reprinted in *Recherches d'histoire judéo-chrétienne, Études juives*, 1962, **8**.

Skeat, T. C. and Wegener, E. P. 'Trial before the Prefect of Egypt, Appius Sabinus, AD 250', *Journal of Egyptian Archaeology*, 1935, **21**, 229–47.

Stevenson, J. ed. *A new Eusebius*. London, 1957.

Tengström, E. *Donatisten und Katholiken; soziale wirtschaftliche und politische Aspekte einer nordafrikanischen Kirchenspaltung*. Göteborg, 1964.

Tertullian, in *PL*, Paris, 1845 and 1879, and *CSEL*, Vienna, 1868– .

Theophanes. *Chronicon*, ed. by J. Claasen. Bonn, 1839–41.

Thouvenot, R. 'Les origines chrétiennes en Mauretanie Tingitane', *Revue des études anciennes*, 1969, **71**, 354–78.

Victor Vitensis. *Historia persecutionis africanae ecclesiae*, ed. by M. Petschenig. *CSEL*, VII. Vienna, 1881.

Vita Pachomii, in *PL*, **73**.
Warmington, B. H. *The North African provinces from Diocletian to the Vandal conquest*. Cambridge, 1954.
Woodward, E. L. *Christianity and nationalism in the later* Roman *Empire*. London, 1916.
Zulueta, F. de. *De Patrociniis Vicorum*, Vol. I of *Oxford Studies in social and legal history*, ed. by P. Vinogradoff. Oxford, 1909.

8. THE ARAB CONQUEST AND THE RISE OF ISLAM IN NORTH AFRICA

Note: Items marked * are relevant to ch. 10 also.

*Amari, M. *Storia dei Musulmani di Sicilia*, 2nd edn. Catania, 1933–5.
Andrae, T. *Die Person Muhammads in Lehre und Glaube seine Gemeinde*. Stockholm, 1918.
Aphrodito Papyri. *See below under* H. I. Bell, ed.
*al-Bakri. *See under* 'General' section, Arabic writers.
al-Balādhurī. *See under* 'General' section, Arabic writers.
Becker, C. H. *Beiträge zur Geschichte Ägyptens*. Strasburg, 1902–3. 2 vols.
Becker, C. H. 'The expansion of the Saracens', in *Cambridge medieval history*, Vol. II (*see under* General works), 329–90.
Becker, C. H. *Islamstudien*. Leipzig, 1924. 2 vols. [Vol. I is relevant.]
Becker, C. H. 'Papyrusstudien', *Zeitschrift für Assyriologie*, 1909, **22**, 137–54.
Bell, H. I. 'The Aphrodito Papyri', *Journal of Hellenic Studies*, 1908, **28**, 97–120.
Bell, H. I. 'The administration of Egypt under the Umayyad Khalifs', *Byzantinische Zeitschrift*, 1928, **28**.
Bell, H. I. 'Egypt and the Byzantine empire', in S. R. K. Glanville, ed., *The legacy of Egypt*, 1st edn. Oxford, 1942, 332–47.
Bell, H. I. ed. *Aphrodito Papyri*, (Vol. IV of *Greek Papyri in the British Museum*), London, 1917.
*Brett, Michael. 'Ifrīqiya as a market for Saharan trade, from the tenth to the twelfth century AD', *Journal of African History*, 1969, **10**, 3, 347–64.
*Brett, Michael. 'Fitnat al-Qayrawān'. Doctoral thesis, University of London, 1970.
*Brignon, J., Amin, A. and others. *Histoire du Maroc*. Casablanca, 1967.
Brunschvig, Robert. 'Ibn Abdal' hakam et la conquête de l'Afrique du Nord par les Arabes: étude critique', *Annales de l'Institut des Études Orientales* (Algiers), 1942–7, **6**, 108–55.
Burton, J. '"Those are the high-flying cranes"', *Journal of Semitic Studies*, 1970, **15**, 246–65.
Butler, A. J. *Arab conquest of Egypt . . . See under* ch. 7.
Caetani, L. *Annali dell' Islam*. Milan, from 1905. 10 vols.
Cambridge medieval history. *See under* General works.
Coulson, N. J. *A history of Islamic Law*. Edinburgh, 1964.
Cresswell, K. A. C. *A short account of early Muslim architecture*. London, 1958.
Cresswell, K. A. C. *Early Muslim architecture*, 2nd edn. Oxford, 1970.
Crone, P. 'The Mawālī in the Umayyad period'. Doctoral thesis, University of London, 1973.

*Dachraoui, F., Djaït, H., M'rabet, M. and Talbi, M. *Le moyen âge*, Vol. II of *Histoire de la Tunisie* (*see below*).

Dennett, Daniel C. *Conversion and the poll-tax in early Islam*. Cambridge, Mass., 1950.

Djaït, H. 'La Wilāya d'Ifrīqiya au IIe–VIIIe siècle: étude institutionnelle', *Studia Islamica*, Pt. 1, 1967, **27**, 77–121; Pt. 2, 1968, **28**, 79–105.

**Encyclopaedia of Islam*. *See under* General works.

Eutychius [Saʿīd b. Baṭrīq]. *See under* 'General' section, Arabic writers.

Evetts, B. T. A. ed. and trans. *Patrologia Orientalis*. Paris, from 1901. 4 pts.

Gautier, E.-F. *Le Passé . . . See under* General works.

Gibb, H. A. R. 'The fiscal rescript of ʿUmar II', *Arabica*, 1955, **2**, 1, 1–16.

*Gibb, H. A. R. and Kramers, J. H. eds. *Shorter encyclopaedia of Islam*. *See under* General works.

Goldziher, Ignaz. *Muhammadanische Studien*. Halle, 1888–9. 2 vols. English trans. by C. R. Barber and S. M. Stern, *Muslim studies*. London, 1967–71.

Goodchild, R. G. 'Byzantines, Berbers and Arabs in 7th-century Libya', *Antiquity*, 1967, **41**, 115–24.

Grünebaum, G. E. von. *Islam: essays in the nature and growth of a cultural tradition*, 2nd edn. London, 1961.

Grünebaum, G. E. von. *Mediaeval Islam*, 2nd edn. Chicago, 1953.

*Gsell, S., Marçais, G. and Yver, G. *Histoire de l'Algérie*. Paris, 1927.

*Guest, Rhuvon. 'The Delta in the Middle Ages', *Journal of the Royal Asiatic Society*, 1912, 941–80.

Hirschberg, H. Z. 'The Berber heroine known as the Kāhina' [in Hebrew], *Tarbiz*, 1957, **26**, 4, 37–83.

*Hirschberg, H. Z. 'The problem of the Judaized Berbers', *Journal of African History*, 1963, **4**, 313–39.

*Hirschberg, H. Z. *A history of the Jews in North Africa*, 2nd, revised edn. [trans. from the Hebrew]. Vol. I, Leiden, 1974.

**Histoire de la Tunisie*, Vol. I, *L'Antiquité*, by A. Mahjoubi, H. Slim and K. Belkhodja; Vol. II, *Le Moyen Âge*, by F. Dachraoui, H. Djaït, M. M'rabet and M. Talbi. Tunis, 1973–4.

*Hopkins, J. F. P. *Mediaeval Muslim government in Barbary*. London, 1958.

Horowitz, J. 'Alter und Ursprung des Isnads', *Der Islam*, 1918, **8**, 39–47; 1921, **11**, 264–5.

Ibn ʿAbd al-Ḥakam. *See under* 'General' section, Arabic writers.

Ibn ʿAbd al-Ḥalim. *See under* 'General' section, Arabic writers.

*Ibn al-Athīr. *See under* 'General' section, Arabic writers.

*Ibn Ḥawqal. *See under* 'General' section, Arabic writers.

*Ibn ʿIdhārī. *See under* 'General' section, Arabic writers.

*Ibn Khaldūn. *See under* 'General' section, Arabic writers.

*Ibn Nājī. *See under* 'General' section, Arabic writers.

Ibn al-Ṣaghīr. *See under* 'General' section, Arabic writers.

Idris, H. R. *La Berbérie orientale sous les Zīrides, Xe–XIIe siècles*. Paris, 1962.

*al-Idrīsī. *See under* 'General' section, Arabic writers.

The Jewish encyclopaedia. *See under* General works.

John of Nikiou. *See under* ch. 7.

*Julien, C.-A. *History of North Africa . . . See under* General works.

Karabacek, J. and others. *Papyrus Erzherzog Rainer: Führer durch die Ausstellung.* Vienna, 1894.

*al-Kindi. *Governors and judges of Egypt*, ed. by R. Guest. Leiden and London, 1912.

*Lane-Poole, S. *A history of Egypt in the Middle Ages*, 4th edn. London, 1921.

Lévi-Provençal, E. 'Un Nouveau Récit de la conquête de l'Afrique du Nord par les Arabes', *Arabica Occidentalia*, 1954, **1**, 17–43.

*Levy, R. *The social structure of Islam.* Cambridge, 1957.

Lewicki, T. 'Quelques extraits inédits relatifs aux voyages des commerçants et des missionnaires ibāḍites nord-africains au pays du Soudan occidental et central au moyen âge', *Folia Orientalia*, 1960, **2**, 1–27.

*Lewis, B., Holt, P. M. and Lambton, A. K. S. eds. *Cambridge history of Islam. See under* General works.

Lézine, A. *Architecture d'Ifrīqiya.* Paris, 1966.

*Lézine, A. 'Notes d'archéologie ifriqiyenne', *Revue des Études Islamiques*, 1967, **35**, 53–101.

*Mahjoubi, A, Slim, H. and Belkhodja, K. *L'Antiquité*, Vol. 1 of *Histoire de la Tunisie* (*see above*).

*al-Mālikī. *See under* 'General' section, Arabic writers.

*al-Maqrīzī. *See under* 'General' section, Arabic writers.

*Marçais, G. *La Berbérie musulmane et l'Orient au moyen âge.* Paris, 1946.

Marçais, G. *Architecture musulmane d'Occident.* Paris, 1954.

Mengin, F. *Histoire de l'Égypte sous le gouvernement de Mohammed-Aly.* Paris, 1823.

*Mez, A. *The renaissance of Islam*, trans. by S. K. Bakhsh and D. S. Margoliouth. Patna, 1937.

*Ostrogorsky, G. *History of the Byzantine state*, trans. by J. Hussey. Oxford, 1956.

Préaux, C. 'Graeco-Roman Egypt', in *The legacy of Egypt*, 2nd edn, ed. by J. R. Harris. Oxford, 1971, 323–54.

Rosenberger, B. 'Tāmdult: cité minière et caravanière', *Hésperis-Tamuda*, 1970, **11**, 104–39.

Rosenthal, E. I. J. *Political thought in medieval Islam.* Cambridge, 1958.

Sāwīrūs [Severus] b. Muqaffaʿ. *History of the Coptic patriarchs of Alexandria*, compiled to the tenth century AD by Sāwīrūs (Severus) b. Muqaffaʿ, ed. and trans. by B. T. A. Evetts [4 pts, to 849 only]. In *Patrologia Orientalis* (*see under* 'General' section, Patrologia), 1, 2; 1, 4, v, 1; x, 5.

Schacht, Joseph. *The origins of Muhammadan jurisprudence.* Oxford, 1950; revised reprint, 1953.

Schacht, Joseph. *Introduction to Islamic Law. See under* General works.

Shaban, M. A. *Islamic history,* AD 600–750. Cambridge, 1971.

*al-Shammākhī. *See under* 'General' section, Arabic writers.

Shorter encyclopaedia of Islam. See under Gibb and Kramers, eds., General works.

*Solignac, M. 'Recherches sur les installations hydrauliques de Kairouan et des Steppes Tunisiennes du VIIe au XIe siècle', *Annales de l'Institut des Études Orientales* (Algiers), 1952, **10**, 5–273; 1953, **11**, 61–170.

*Stern, S. M. *Fāṭimid decrees*. London, 1964.

Strabo. *Geography*. *See under* ch. 2.

*Talbi, M. *L'Émirat Aghlabide, 184–296/800–909: histoire politique*. Paris, 1966.

*Terrasse, H. *Histoire du Maroc des origines à l'établissement du Protectorat français*. Casablanca, 1949–50.

*Wansbrough, John. 'On recomposing the Islamic history of North Africa', *Journal of the Royal Asiatic Society*, 1969, 161–70.

Wansbrough, John. *Quranic Studies: sources and methods of scriptural interpretation*, London Oriental Series, XXXI. Oxford, 1977.

*Wiet, Gaston. *L'Égypte Arabe*, Vol. IV of *Histoire de la Nation Égyptienne*, ed. by G. Hanotaux. Paris, 1937.

Willcocks and Craig. *Egyptian irrigation*, 3rd edn. London, 1913.

*al-Yaʿqūbī. *See under* 'General' section, Arabic writers.

9. CHRISTIAN NUBIA

Abu Saleh al-Armani. *Churches and monasteries of Egypt*. trans. by B. T. A. Evetts. Oxford, 1893.

Adams, W. Y. 'The Christian potteries at Faras', *Kush*, 1961, **9**, 30–43.

Adams, W. Y. 'An introductory classification of Christian Nubian pottery', *Kush*, 1962, **10**, 245–88.

Adams, W. Y. 'Sudan Antiquities Service excavations in Nubia', *Kush*, 1964, **12**, 216–48.

Adams, W. Y. 'Architectural evolution of the Nubian church', *Journal of the American Research Center in Egypt*, 1965, **4**, 87–139 [1965a].

Adams, W. Y. 'Sudan Antiquities Service excavations at Meinarti, 1963–4', *Kush*, 1965, **13**, 148–76 [1965b].

Adams, W. Y. 'Post-pharaonic Nubia in the light of archaeology', *Journal of Egyptian Archaeology*, Pt. II, 1965, **51**, 160–78; Pt. III, 1966, **52**, 147–62.

Adams, W. Y. 'Progress report on Nubian pottery', *Kush*, 1967–8, **15**, 1–56.

Adams, W. Y. 'Settlement pattern in microcosm: the changing aspect of a Nubian village during twelve centuries', in K. Chang, ed., *Settlement archaeology*. Palo Alto, 1968, 174–207.

Adams, W. Y. 'The evolution of Christian Nubian pottery', in Dinkler, ed., *Kunst und Geschichte Nubiens . . .* (*see below*), 111–28.

Adams, W. Y. 'The University of Kentucky excavation at Kulubnarti. 1969', in Dinkler, ed., *Kunst und Geschichte Nubiens . . .* (*see below*), 141–54.

Adams, W. Y. *Nubia: corridor . . . See under* ch. 4.

Arkell, A. J. *History of the Sudan . . . See under* General works.

Brooks, E. W. *Ioannis Ephesin; Historiae Ecclesize*, Pars Tertia. Louvain, 1936.

Clarke, Somers. *See* Somers Clarke.

Crawford, O. G. S. *Castles and churches in the Middle Nile region*. Khartoum, 1953; Sudan Antiquities Service, Occasional Paper, **2**.

Crowfoot, J. W. 'Christian Nubia', *Journal of Egyptian Archaeology*, 1927, **13**, 141–50.

Dinkler, E. ed. *Kunst und Geschichte Nubiens in Christlicher Zeit*. Recklinghausen, 1970.

Ecclesiastical history of John of Ephesus, trans. by R. Payne-Smith. Oxford, 1860.

Farand, P. 'Early Muslim relations with Nubia', *Der Islam*, 1971, **48**, 111–21.

Griffith, F. L. *The Nubian texts of the Christian period*. Berlin, 1913.

Hintze, F. . . . *Meroitischen Grammatik*. *See under* ch. 4.

Holt, P. M. 'A Sudanese historical legend: the Funj conquest of Suba', *Bulletin of the School of Oriental and African Studies*, 1960, **23**, 1–17.

Holt, P. M. 'Sultan Selim and the Sudan', *Journal of African History*, 1967, **8**, 19–23.

Jakobielski, Stephan. *A history of the Bishopric of Pachoras*, *Faras*, Vol. III. Warsaw, 1972.

John of Ephesus. *Historia ecclesiastica*, ed. by E. W. Brooks. *See under* ch. 7.

Kirwan, L. P. 'Notes on the topography of the Christian Nubian kingdoms', *Journal of Egyptian Archaeology*, 1935, **21**, 57–62.

Kirwan, L. P. 'A contemporary account of the conversion of the Sudan to Christianity', *Sudan Notes and Records*, 1937, **20**, 289–99.

Krause, M. 'Zur Kirchen und Theologiegeschichte Nubiens', in Dinkler, ed., *Kunst und Geschichte Nubiens . . .* (*see above*), 71–86.

Kronenberg, A. 'Parallel cousin marriage in mediaeval and modern Nubia – Part I', *Kush*, 1965, **13**, 256–60.

Kubinska, J. *The Greek inscriptions*, *Faras*, Vol. III. Warsaw, 1975.

Lister, F. C. *Ceramic studies of the historic periods in Ancient Nubia*. University of Utah Anthropological Papers No. 86, Nubian series no. 2. Salt Lake City, 1967.

al-Maqrīzī. *See under* 'General' section, Arabic writers.

Meinardus, Otto F. A. 'The Christian kingdom of Nubia', *Nubie – Cahiers d'Histoire Égyptienne*, 1967, **10**, 133–64.

Michalowski, K. *Faras – fouilles Polonaises*: *1961*, Warsaw, 1962; *1961–2*, Warsaw, 1965.

Michalowski, K. *Faras – centre artistique de la Nubie Chrétienne*. Leiden, 1966.

Michalowski, K. *Faras – die Kathedrale aus dem Wüstensand*. Zurich, 1967.

Michalowski, K. *Faras – wall paintings in the collection of the National Museum in Warsaw*. Warsaw, 1974.

Michalowski, K. ed. *Nubia – récentes recherches*. Warsaw, 1975.

Mileham, G. S. *Churches in Lower Nubia*. Eckley B. Coxe, Jn. Expedition to Nubia, Vol. II. Philadelphia, 1910.

Monneret de Villard, Ugo. *La Nubia médiévale*. *Mission Archéologique de Nubie, 1929–34*. Cairo, 1935–57. 4 vols.

Monneret de Villard, Ugo. *Storia della Nubia Cristiana*. Rome, 1938.

Oates, J. F. 'A Christian inscription in Greek from Armenna in Nubia', *Journal of Egyptian Archaeology*, 1963, **49**, 161–71.

Plumley, J. M. 'Qasr Ibrim, 1969', *Journal of Egyptian Archaeology*, 1970, **56**, 14.

Plumley, J. M. 'The Christian period at Qasr Ibrim: some notes on the MSS finds', in Michalowski, ed., *Nubia . . .* (*see above*), 101–7.

Plumley, J. M. and Adams, W. Y. 'Qasr Ibrim, 1972', *Journal of Egyptian Archaeology*, 1974, **60**, 212–38.

Quatremère, E. M. *Mémoires géographiques et historiques sur l'Égypte et sur quelques contrées voisines*. Paris, 1811.

Shinnie, P. L. *Mediaeval Nubia*. Museum Pamphlet No. 2, Sudan Antiquities Service. Khartoum, 1954.

Shinnie, P. L. *Excavations at Soba*. Sudan Antiquities Service, Occasional Paper 3. Khartoum, 1955; reprinted 1961.

Shinnie, P. L. 'Multilingualism . . .' *See under* 'General' section, Languages.

Shinnie, P. L. and M. 'New light on mediaeval Nubia', *Journal of African History*, 1965, **6**, 263–73.

Shinnie, P. L. and Chittick, H. N. *Ghazali – a monastery in the northern Sudan*. Sudan Antiquities Service, Occasional Paper 5. Khartoum, 1961.

Somers Clarke. *Christian antiquities in the Nile Valley*. Oxford, 1912.

Trigger, B. G. 'The cultural ecology of Christian Nubia', in Dinkler, ed., *Kunst und Geschichte Nubiens* . . . (*see above*), 347–79.

Vantini, G. *The excavations at Faras – a contribution to the history of Christian Nubia*. Bologna, 1970.

Vantini, G. 'Le Roi Kirki de Nubie à Baghdad: un ou deux voyages?', in Dinkler, ed., *Kunst und Geschichte Nubiens* . . . (*see above*), 41–8.

Weeks, Kent R. *The classic Christian townsite at Arminna West*. Publications of the Pennsylvania-Yale expedition to Nubia, 3. New Haven and Philadelphia, 1967.

Yūsuf Fadl Hasan. *The Arabs and the Sudan*. Khartoum, 1973.

Zyhlarz, Ernst. *Grundzüge der Nubischen Grammatik im christlichen Frühmittelalter*. Leipzig, 1928; reprinted 1966.

10. THE FATIMID REVOLUTION IN NORTH AFRICA

Note: Reference should also be made to items marked * in the bibliography to chapter 8.

Berchem, M. van. 'Deux campagnes de fouilles sur la site de l'ancienne cité musulmane de Sedrata', *Actes des Congrès Nationaux des Sociétés Savantes* (Section d'Archéologie, Congrès 79, Algiers, 1954). Paris, 1957.

Brett, Michael. 'The Zughba at Tripoli, 429H (AD 1037–8)', *Society for Libyan Studies, Sixth Annual Report*, 1974–5, 41–7.

Brett, Michael. 'The military interest of the battle of Ḥaydarān', in Parry and Yapp, eds., *War, technology and society* . . . (*see below*), 78–88.

Brett, Michael. 'Sijill al-Mustanṣir', paper presented to the Premier Congrès d'Histoire et de Civilisation du Maghreb (Tunis, December 1974); in *Actes du Congrès, 1974*.

Gautier, E.-F. *See under* General works.

Goitein, S. D. F. *Studies in Islamic history and institutions*. Leiden, 1966.

Goitein, S. D. F. *A Mediterranean society*. Berkeley and Los Angeles, 1967 [in progress]. 2 vols.

Hitti, P. K. *History of the Arabs*, 7th edn. London and New York, 1960.

Ibn Saʿīd. *See under* 'General' section, Arabic writers.

Levtzion, N. 'Ibn Ḥawqal, the cheque, and Awdaghost', *Journal of African History*, 1968, **9**, 2, 223–33.

Lombard, M. *Les métaux dans l'ancien monde du Ve au XIe siècle*. Paris and The Hague, 1974.

al-Masʿūdī. *See under* 'General' section, Arabic writers.

Parry, V. J. and Yapp, M. eds. *War, technology and society in the Middle East.* London, New York and Toronto, 1975.

al-Qāḍī 'l-Nuʿmān. *See under* 'General' section, Arabic writers.

Rabie, H. *The financial system of Egypt,* AH *564–741* AD *1169–1341.* London Oriental Series, **25**. London, New York and Toronto, 1972.

Robert, D. S. 'Les Fouilles de Tegdaoust', *Journal of African History,* 1970, **11**, 4, 471–93.

II. THE SAHARA AND THE SUDAN

Ajayi, J. F. A. and Crowder, M. *History of West Africa. See under* General works.

Akhbār al-Zamān. See under 'General' section, Arabic writers.

al-Bakrī. *See under* 'General' section, Arabic writers.

Basset, R. 'Recherches historiques sur les Maures', in *Mission au Senegal.* Paris, 1909.

Bathily, A. 'A discussion of the traditions of Wagadu with some reference to ancient Ghana', *Bulletin de l'IFAN*, 1975, **37**, 1–94.

Bekri, C. 'Le Kharijisme berbère: quelques aspects du royaume rustamide', *Annales de l'Institut d'Études Orientales de la Faculté des Lettres d'Alger* (Algiers), 1958, **16**, 55–106.

Bel, A. *La Religion musulmane en Berbérie.* Paris, 1938.

Bovill, E. W. *The golden trade . . . See under* ch. 5.

Brett, Michael. 'Ifriqiya as a market . . .' *See under* ch. 8.

Brunschvig, Robert. 'Ibn ʿAbd al-Ḥakam . . .' *See under* ch. 8.

Canard, M. 'L'impérialisme des Fatimides et leur propagande', *Annales de l'Institut d'Études Orientales* (Algiers), 1942–7, **6**, 156–93.

el-Chennafi, M. 'Sur les traces d'Awdaghust: les Tagdawest et leur ancienne cité', in Robert and Devisse, *Tegdaoust I* (*see below*), 97–107.

Cooley, W. D. *The Negroland of the Arabs.* London, 1841.

Cuoq, J. M. ed. *Recueil des sources . . . See under* 'General' section, Arabic texts.

Daveau, S. 'Itinéraire de Tamadalt à Awdaghust selon al-Bakrī', in Robert and Devisse, *Tegdaoust I* (*see below*), 33–8.

Delafosse, M. *Haut-Sénégal-Niger* (*Soudan français*). Paris, 1912.

Delafosse, M. 'Traditions musulmanes relatives à l'origine des Peuls', *Revue du Monde Musulman*, 1912, **20**.

Delafosse, M. 'Le Ghana et le Mali et l'emplacement de leurs capitales', *Bulletin du Comité d'Études Historiques et Scientifiques de l'AOF*, 1924, **7**, 479–542.

Devisse, J. 'La Question d'Awdaghust', in Robert and Devisse, *Tegdaoust I* (*see below*), 109–56.

Fage, J. D. 'Ancient Ghana, a review of the evidence', *Transactions of the Historical Society of Ghana*, 1957, **3**, 77–98.

Fage, J. D. 'Some thoughts on state formation in the western Sudan before the seventeenth century' in J. Butler, ed., *Boston University papers in African history*, I. Boston, 1964, 17–34.

Farias, P. F. de Moraes. 'The Almoravids: some questions concerning the character of the movement during its period of closest contact with the western Sudan', *Bulletin de l'IFAN*, 1967, **29**, 794–878.

Farias, P. F. de Moraes. 'Silent trade: myth and historical evidence', *History in Africa*, 1974, **1**, 9–24.

Faure, A. 'Le *taṣawwuf* et l'école ascetique marocaine des 11e–13e siècles', *Mélanges Louis Massignon* (Damascus), 1957, **2**, 119–31.

Gautier, E. F. *Le passé de l'Afrique du Nord: les siècles obscurs du Maghreb*. Paris, 1927.

Hama, Boubou. *Histoire des Songhay*. Paris, 1968.

Hazard, H. W. *The numismatic history of late mediaeval North Africa*. New York, 1952.

Hirschberg, H. Z. '... Judaized Berbers'. *See under* ch. 8.

Hopkins, J. F. P. and Levtzion, N. eds. *Mediaeval Arabic sources ... See under* 'General' section, Arabic texts.

Ibn ʿAbd al-Ḥakam. *See under* 'General' section, Arabic writers.

Ibn Abī Zarʿ. *See under* 'General' section, Arabic writers.

Ibn Abī Zayd al-Qayrawānī. *See under* 'General' section, Arabic writers.

Ibn al-Athīr. *See under* 'General' section, Arabic writers.

Ibn Baṭṭūṭa. *See under* 'General' section, Arabic writers.

Ibn al-Faqīh. *See under* 'General' section, Arabic writers.

Ibn Ḥammād. *See under* 'General' section, Arabic writers.

Ibn Ḥawqal. *See under* 'General' section, Arabic writers.

Ibn ʿIdhārī al-Marrākushī. *See under* 'General' section, Arabic writers.

Ibn Khaldūn. *See under* 'General' section, Arabic writers.

Ibn Khurdādhbīh. *See under* 'General' section, Arabic writers.

Ibn Qutayba. *See under* 'General' section, Arabic writers.

Ibn Ṣaghīr. *See under* 'General' section Arabic writers.

Ibn Saʿīd. *See under* 'General' section, Arabic writers.

Idris, H. R. 'Deux maitres de l'école juridique Kairouanaise sous les Zirides', *Annales de l'Institut d'Études Orientales* (Algiers), 1955, **13**, 30–60.

Idris, H. R. 'Contribution à l'histoire de la vie religieuse en Ifrīqiya zīride', *Mélanges Louis Massignon* (*Damascus*), 1957, **2**, 327–59.

Idris, H. R. *La Berbérie ... sous les Zīrīdes*. *See under* ch. 8.

al-Idrīsī. *See under* 'General' section, Arabic writers.

al-Iṣṭakhrī. *See under* 'General' section, Arabic writers.

al-Qāḍī ʿIyād. *See under* 'General' section, Arabic writers.

Julien, C.-A. *History of North Africa ... See under* General works.

al-Khwārizmī. *See under* 'General' section, Arabic writers.

Koubbel, L. E. 'On the history of social relations in the West Sudan in the 8th to the 16th centuries', *Africa in Soviet Studies* (Moscow), 1968, 109–28.

Koubbel, L. E. 'Le problème de l'apparition des structures étatiques au Soudan occidental', *Congrès International des Africanistes* (Paris, 1972), 37–46.

Koubbel, L. E. and Mateev, V. V. *Arabskie istochniki ... See under* 'General' section, Arabic texts.

La Chapelle, F. de. 'Esquisse d'une histoire du Sahara occidental', *Hespéris*, 1930, **2**, 35–95.

Lange, D. *Le Dīwān des sultans du* [*Kānem-*] *Bornū: chronologie et histoire d'un royaume africain*. Wiesbaden, 1977.

Laroui, A. *L'Histoire du Maghrib: un essai de synthèse*. Paris, 1970.

Lessard, J. M. 'Sijilmassa – la ville et ses relations commerciales au XIe siècle d'après El-Bekri', *Hésperis-Tamuda*, 1970, **11**, 5–36.

Le Tourneau, R. *Fès avant le protectorat*. Casablanca, 1949.

Le Tourneau, R. 'La révolte d'Abu Yazid au 10e siècle', *Cashiers de Tunisie*, 1953, **1**, 103–25.

Lévi-Provençal, ed. *Textes Arabes Marocaines*. Rabat, 1934.

Lévi-Provençal, E. 'La Fondation de Marrakech (462/1070)', *Mélanges de l'histoire et d'archaéologie de l'Occident musulman*, II: *Hommage a G. Marçais*. Algiers, 1957, 117–20.

Levtzion, N. 'Ibn Ḥawqal, the cheque . . .' *See under* ch. 10.

Levtzion, N. 'Was royal succession in Ghana matrilineal?', *International Journal of African Historical Studies*, 1972, **5**, 91–3.

Levtzion, N. *Ancient Ghana and Mali*. London, 1973.

Lewicki, T. *Études ibāḍites nord-africaines*. Warsaw, 1955.

Lewicki, T. 'La répartition géographique de groupements ibāḍites dans l'Afrique du Nord au moyen âge', *Rocznik Orientalistyczny*, 1957, **21**, 304–43.

Lewicki, T. 'À propos d'une liste de tribus berbères d'Ibn Ḥawqal', *Folia Orientalia*, 1955, **1**, 203–55.

Lewicki, T. 'Quelques extraits . . . aux voyages des commerçants . . . ibāḍites'. *See under* ch. 8.

Lewicki, T. 'Pages d'histoire du commerce trans-Saharien: les commerçants et les missionnaires Ibāḍites au Soudan central et occidental aux 7e–12e siècles', *Pzeglad Orientalistyczny*, 1961, 3–18.

Lewicki, T. 'L'État nord-africain de Tahert et ses relations avec le Soudan occidental à la fin du 6e et au 9e siècle', *Cahiers d'études africains*, 1962, **2**, 513–35.

Lewicki, T. 'L'Afrique noire dans le *Kitāb al-Masālik wa'l -mamālik* d'Abū 'Ubayd al-Bakrī (11e siècle)', *Africana Bulletin*, 1965, **2**, 9–14.

Lewicki, T. *Arabic external sources . . . See under* 'General' section, Arabic texts.

Lewicki, T. 'The Ibāḍites in Arabia and Africa', *Journal of World History*, 1971, **13**, 51–130.

Lewicki, T. *West African food . . . See under* ch. 5.

Lombard, M. 'Les bases monétaires d'une suprématie économique: l'or musulman du 7e au 11e siècle', *Annales*: *Économies, Sociétés, Civilisations*, 1947, **2**, 143–60.

Mafākhir al-Barbar, in Lévi-Provençal, ed., *Textes Arabes* . . . (*see under* 'General' section. Arabic texts).

Maḥmud, H. A. *Qiyām dawlat al-Murābiṭīn*. Cairo, 1957.

Marty, P. *Études sur l'Islam et les tribus du Soudan*. Paris, 1920.

al-Mas'ūdī. *See under* 'General' section, Arabic writers.

Mauny, R. 'The question of Ghana', *Africa*, 1954, **27**, 200–13.

Mauny, R. *Tableau géographique . . . See under* General works.

Mauny, R. *Les Siècles obscurs . . . See under* General works.

Miranda, A. H. 'La salida de los Almorávides del Desierto y el Reinado de Yusuf b. Tāshfīn', *Hespéris*, 1959, **46**, 155–82.

Monès, H. 'Le Malékisme et l'échec des Fatimides en Ifrīqiya', *Études d'Orientalisme dédiées à la mémoire de Levi-Provençal* (Paris), 1962, **1**, 197–220.

Monteil, C. 'Les "Ghana" des géographes arabes et des européens', *Hespéris*, 1951, **38**, 441–52.

Monteil, C. 'La Légende du Ouagadou et l'origine des Soninkés', *Mélanges ethnologiques* (Dakar), 1953, 369–82.

al-Nakar, U. 'Takrūr: the history of a name', *Journal of African History*, 1969, **10**, 365–74.

Norris, H. T. 'New evidence on the life of ʿAbdullāh b. Yāsīn and the origins of the Almoravid movement', *Journal of African History*, 1971, **12**, 255–68.

Norris, H. T. *Saharan myth and saga*. London, 1972.

al-Nuwayrī. *See under* 'General' section, Arabic writers.

Palmer, H. R. *The Bornu, Sahara and Sudan*. London, 1936.

Palmer, H. R. ed. and trans. *Sudanese memoirs*: *being mainly translations of a number of Arabic manuscripts relating to the central and western Sudan*. Lagos, 1928; reprinted London, 1967.

Robert, D. S. 'Les Fouilles de Tegdaoust'. *See under* ch. 10.

Robert, D. & S. and Devisse, J. eds. *Tegdaoust I*. *See under* ch. 5.

Rouch, J. *Contribution à l'histoire des Songhay*. Dakar, 1953.

al-Saʿdī. *See under* 'General' section, Arabic writers.

Sauvaget, J. 'Les épitaphes royales de Gao', *Bulletin de l'IFAN*, 1950, **12**, 418–40.

Semonin, P. 'The Almoravid movement in the Western Sudan: a review of the evidence', *Transactions of the Historical Society of Ghana*, 1964, **7**, 42–59.

Smith, Abdullahi. 'The early states of the central Sudan', in Ajayi and Crowder, eds., *History of West Africa* (*see under* General works).

Soh, Siré Abbas. *Chroniques des Fouta Sénégalais*, trans. by M. Delafosse. Paris, 1913.

al-Tādilī. *See under* 'General' section, Arabic writers.

Talbi, M. *L'Émirat Aghlabide* . . . *See under* ch. 8.

Taʾrīkh al-Fattāsh. *See under* 'General' section, Arabic writers.

Terrasse, H. *Histoire du Maroc* . . . *See under* ch. 8.

Thomassey, P. 'Note sur la géographie et l'habitat de la région de Koumbi Saleh', *Bulletin de l'IFAN*, 1951, **13**, 476–86.

Thomassey, P. and Mauny, R. 'Campagne de fouilles à Koumbi Saleh', *Bulletin de l'IFAN*, 1951, **13**, 438–62; 1956, **18**, 117–40.

Trimingham, J. S. *A history of Islam in West Africa*. London, 1962.

Urvoy, Y. *Histoire de l'empire du Bornou*. Dakar, 1949.

Vanacker, C. 'Géographie économique de l'Afrique du Nord selon les auteurs arabes du 9e au milieu du 12e siècle', *Annales*: *Économies, Sociétés, Civilisations*, 1973, **28**, 659–80.

al-Yaʿqūbī. *al-Buldān*. *See under* 'General' section, Arabic writers.

al-Yaʿqūbī. *al-Taʾrīkh*. *See under* 'General' section, Arabic writers.

Yāqūt. *See under* 'General' section, Arabic writers.

al-Zuhrī. *See under* 'General' section, Arabic writers.

INDEX

Page numbers in italic indicate substantive references